Small Business Management 18e

LAUNCHING & GROWING ENTREPRENEURIAL VENTURES

Justin G. Longenecker
Baylor University

J. William Petty
Baylor University

Leslie E. Palich
Baylor University

Frank Hoy
Worcester Polytechnic Insitute

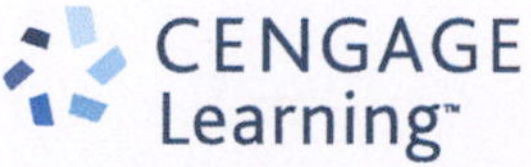

Australia • Brazil • Mexico • Singapore • United Kingdom • United States

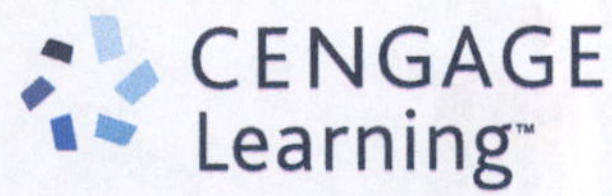

Small Business Management: Launching & Growing Entrepreneurial Ventures, 18e

Justin G. Longenecker
J. William Petty
Leslie E. Palich
Frank Hoy

Vice President, General Manager, Social Science & Qualitative Business: Erin Joyner

Product Director: Jason Fremder

Content Developer: John Sarantakis

Product Assistant: Jamie Mack

Marketing Director: Kristen Hurd

Marketing Manager: Emily Horowitz

Marketing Coordinator: Christopher Walz

Senior Content Project Manager: Kim Kusnerak

Manufacturing Planner: Ron Montgomery

Production Service: SPi Global

Senior Art Director: Linda May

Cover/Internal Designer: Joe Devine/Red Hangar Design

Cover Image: © Joe Devine

Intellectual Property Analyst: Diane Garrity

Project Manager: Sarah Shainwald

Design Elements: Hand writing on iPad: ©Ximagination/iStockphoto.com; Rocket ship: ©07_av/iStockphoto.com; Glass doors with handles: ©Marlon Lopez MMG1 Design/Shutterstock.com; Come in Open sign: ©FooTToo/Shutterstock.com; Open Looking Ahead/Closed Looking Back signs: ©robertlamphoto/Shutterstock.com; iPad: ©Ilja Generalov/Shutterstock.com; Compass on map: ©OlegDoroshin/Shutterstock.com; Glowing globe over hand: ©solarseven/Shutterstock.com; Seedling growing: ©Kletr/Shutterstock.com

Library of Congress Control Number: 2015947525

ISBN: 978-1-305-40574-5

Cengage Learning
20 Channel Center Street
Boston, MA 02210
USA

Cengage Learning is a leading provider of customized learning solutions with employees residing in nearly 40 different countries and sales in more than 125 countries around the world. Find your local representative at **www.cengage.com**.

Cengage Learning products are represented in Canada by Nelson Education, Ltd.

To learn more about Cengage Learning Solutions, visit **www.cengage.com**

Purchase any of our products at your local college store or at our preferred online store **www.cengagebrain.com**

Printed at CLDPC, USA, 02-19

Brief Contents

Contents

Part 1
Entrepreneurship: A World of Opportunity

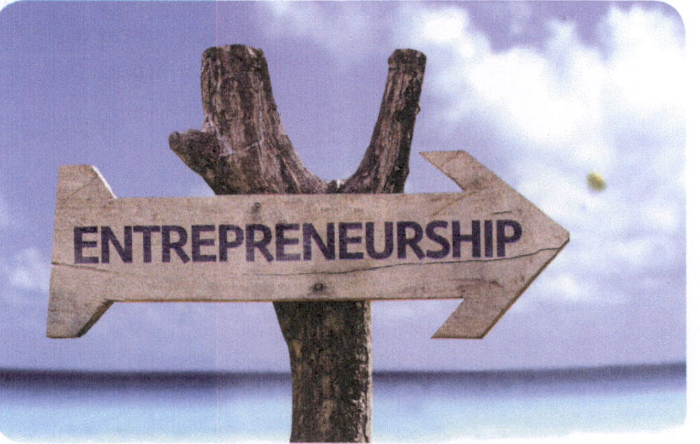

© GUSTAVO FRAZAO/SHUTTERSTOCK.COM

Part 2
Starting from Scratch or Joining an Existing Business

© GUSTAVO FRAZAO/SHUTTERSTOCK.COM

Part 3
Developing the New Venture Business Plan

Part 4
Focusing on the Customer: Marketing Growth Strategies

© MONKEY BUSINESS IMAGES/SHUTTERSTOCK.COM

Preface

> *I didn't realize how hard it was to run a small business.*
>
> **—*Andrew Mason, former CEO of Groupon***
>
> Andrew Mason, the founder of Groupon, is featured in the case for Chapter 19. Even though Mason created the company, he was eventually fired by the board. He clearly had a creative idea but discovered too late that building and running a successful business require more than having a good idea—this concept, along with many others, will be explored in more depth throughout this latest edition of *Small Business Management: Launching and Growing Entrepreneurial Ventures.*

Welcome to the 18th edition of *Small Business Management: Launching and Growing Entrepreneurial Ventures*, which continues to be the leading textbook in the field of small business management. As the authors, we attribute its success to our decision to approach each new edition as though we were writing the book for the very first time. By doing so, we are certain that you will be provided with the best and most recent advice on running your business.

We completely agree with the age-old saying that you can't judge a book by its cover. But you can learn a lot about a textbook and its success simply by knowing how many students have chosen to keep it rather than sell it at the end of a semester. *Small Business Management* has become a part of many students' permanent library. As one student explained, "*Small Business Management* is one of the few books from my college days that I have kept for future reference."

Why do so many consider the book to be a "keeper"? We believe that they find in its pages practical ways of thinking and acting that help them achieve their dreams of starting and building successful enterprises. For example, readers have described how the chapters on finance helped them to understand financial statements and to make better decisions based on that information. Others have said that the business plan chapter, with the real-life examples it presents, provides an excellent guide for writing their own plans. Readers have also described how the chapters on managing the business have kept them from making the kinds of mistakes that Andrew Mason and others have made.

Small Business Management lays out, step by step, the knowledge and insights needed to lead and manage a small business. Our aim is to provide instruction and guidance that will greatly improve your odds for success as you take your own entrepreneurial journey. In this edition, we present the best information available today about launching and growing small businesses. Furthermore, we offer examples throughout the text to demonstrate that there is not a single path to success. The goal is to help you to find one that will work best for you.

It is our hope that the information presented in this book—and in the ancillaries that accompany it—will support the varied goals of those seeking independent business careers, either directly or indirectly. Most of all, we encourage you to continue learning every day, building on the foundation provided by this text. This advice is supported by the words of Richard Branson, founder and chairman of the Virgin Group, which comprises more than 400 companies: "My biggest motivation? Just to keep challenging myself. Everyday I'm learning something new."

Throughout the text, we emphasize the importance of building relationships along the way. Managing a business is a team sport. As the owner, you are the key to making the basket, reaching the goal line, crossing home plate (or whatever analogy you want to use)—but you cannot do it alone. Even if you are the company's only employee, working alone in your own apartment or basement or in your parents' garage, you still have relationships with and depend on others, including your family, a banker, suppliers, and customers. And you must be effective in your relationships with other people. The bottom line: You cannot accomplish anything of any real significance by yourself!

Follow Your Dreams

As you will see, *Small Business Management* focuses on teaching you the essential concepts and building skills that you will need to grow and manage a business successfully. It also considers a much broader concern—the pursuit of entrepreneurial dreams. Entrepreneurs build businesses to fulfill dreams—for themselves, their families, their employees, and their communities. Your journey will always be about more than the money. Entrepreneurs are individuals whose business lives have an impact on a wide range of people. For most entrepreneurs, what they do matters.

Many students enroll in colleges and universities to gain qualifications that will help them to get a job. In fact, most colleges spend the bulk of the curriculum teaching students how to work for someone else. But the best way to achieve your goals, no matter what your major is, may be through owning a business of your own. If so, why not make it something special—something that solves a problem that makes life better for others, that builds wealth while at the same time providing a way for you to give back to your community and to nonprofit organizations that you believe in.

There are definite advantages to initially working for someone else. It may allow you to learn an industry, build relationships, and develop important skills for the future. But many individuals choose to start their own company early in life:

- Michael Dell started assembling computer parts and selling personal computers when he was a premed student at the University of Texas.
- Fred DeLuca opened a submarine sandwich shop when he was 17 years old to earn money to pay his tuition at the University of Bridgeport. Today, his legacy, SUBWAY, has more locations worldwide than any other franchise organization.
- Jeremy Hitchcock started Dyn, a global leader in software as a service (SaaS), when he was a management information systems major at Worcester Polytechnic Institute. (Chapter 16, "Pricing and Credit Decisions," and the case for the chapter present more information about this company.)

This list could go on for pages. We all know entrepreneurs and small business owners who will not be the next Bill Gates, but who will build or already own small businesses that create value and make a difference in the community. These small companies are the heart and soul of our economy. We challenge you to give serious thought to joining them—and if you do, *dream big*. Follow a dream that you really care about, and enjoy a life that you truly want to live! *Our best wishes to you for a challenging and successful learning experience!*

MindTap

MindTap is an online, highly personalized learning experience built upon Cengage Learning content. MindTap combines student learning tools—readings, multimedia, activities, and assessments—in a singular Learning Path that guides students through the course. Instructors personalize the experience by customizing authoritative Cengage Learning content and learning tools, including the ability to add their own content to the Learning Path via apps that integrate the MindTap framework seamlessly with Learning Management Systems. For the 18th edition of *Small Business Management*, MindTap has been expanded and vastly improved to include the following:

Lead, Choose, Learn. This engaging exercise places students firmly in the driver's seat of a business's future. Given a scenario, students decide how to proceed and then see how that decision impacts the business and future decisions. Students travel different paths and the scenarios change based on each student's decisions. The unique and practical learning model provides students with the valuable opportunity to practice managerial analysis and crucial decision-making skills.

Experiential Exercises. Leveraging third party technology, YouSeeU is an innovative experience that provides students a critical platform for self, peer or instructor review—whether it be in the form of a sales pitch or the polishing of a presentation. Live or recorded video exercises, which include both individual and group work projects, allow for collaboration and engagement similar to what students will experience in the business world.

Video Cases. New documentary-style videos highlight such entrepreneurs and small businesses as Theo Chocolate, Camp Bow Wow, and Honest Tea. Candid interviews provide insight into marketing, financial forecasting, and product development, among many other topics, appropriately marrying chapter concepts with real-world examples.

Whiteboard Videos. We're excited to offer for the first time "whiteboard" videos. These fun and relevant stories capture key terms, important topics, and overarching themes. By creating a narrative independent from any particular company, we've constructed a more flexible and yet more tailored experience. The result is crucial lessons for future entrepreneurs to digest and apply.

What's New?

A primary purpose of *Small Business Management* is to present current, relevant content in unique and interesting ways, drawing on an abundance of real-world examples to keep the reader completely engaged. Thus, the 18th edition of *Small Business Management* offers plenty of updates, including the following:

- A host of misconceptions about becoming a small business owner can cause you to give up your entrepreneurial dream. We have revised Chapter 1, "The Entrepreneurial Life," to help you better understand your motivations for starting a business and to avoid distorted concepts about what is required for you to be an effective business owner. Getting off on the right foot is critical to your success.
- Social entrepreneurship has become a major topic in entrepreneurial circles, both in practice and on college campuses. Recognizing this trend, Chapter 2 introduces some of the important concepts and principles involved in the launch

of a socially oriented enterprise. We have also included examples of socially minded entrepreneurs, such as Alicia Polak at Khaya Cookie Company, Father Greg Boyle at Homeboy Industries, and Nick Frey at Boo Bicycles.

- Prioritizing a small business owner's responsibilities to major stakeholders can be difficult. With that in mind, Chapter 2, "Integrity, Ethics, and Social Entrepreneurship," presents a framework (adapted from the writings of ethics and morality scholar Archie Carroll) for managing stakeholder considerations as a unified whole, which will help owners to determine how to balance stakeholder interests.
- We are thrilled to continue offering *LivePlan* from Business Plan Pro, the unquestioned leader in business planning software. *LivePlan* has interactive features that guide you through the writing process in ways not previously available.
- Chapter 8 covers the organizational plan for a startup or small business, and it has been further developed to provide direction for alternative paths that small business owners may choose to take. For example, though an increasing number of startups are being launched by entrepreneurial teams, we expanded the section on operating as a solo entrepreneur for those who choose this option. We also provide a more complete description of legal forms of organization that can be adopted, including the B Corporation, so that the reader will be able to pick the organizational form most suitable for his or her needs and interests.
- The number of small businesses being launched on the Internet continues to grow. Chapter 9, "The Location Plan," includes an expanded section on effective models of e-commerce and emerging options that can lead to new business opportunities for online entrepreneurs.
- In a previous edition, we improved the presentation of financial statements (Chapter 10, "Understanding a Firm's Financial Statements") and the preparation of financial forecasts for small businesses (Chapter 11, "Forecasting Financial Requirements"). Our goal was to make the material more logical for the reader to follow. We have continued to build on this approach in the 18th edition in order to make the material even easier to grasp.
- Updated information on raising capital to grow a business, including best practices for raising money on the Internet (crowdfunding), is provided in Chapter 12, "A Firm's Sources of Financing." But stay tuned: Regulations concerning such topics are constantly evolving, and entrepreneurs must be aware of the fast-changing landscape of publicly raised capital.
- Because of the importance of establishing and improving relationships with customers, and the development of new and more sophisticated tools to make this more manageable, we continue to expand and update the sections on creating and using customer data in Chapter 14, "Building Customer Relationships." These sections now offer more practical instruction on CRM methods that make sense for small businesses, regardless of the level of sophistication, and provide insights on available software packages that may be most suitable for a small business. The section on call centers has also been significantly revised and expanded using information and cost figures from up-to-date research and analysis provided by the consulting firm McKinsey & Co.
- Challenges related to product development continue to be among the most difficult that confront small firms, and Chapter 15 has been revised to reflect

this. For this reason, the 18th edition includes, for example, more cutting-edge approaches in a significantly reworked section on the development of the physical product. We have also provided more information regarding the rules applying to brand name selection, specifically addressing the circumstances resulting from doing business online.

- Small business owners are discovering that social media can offer cost-effective ways of getting their message out. They are also learning that more and more customers rely on social media to make buying decisions. With this in mind, Chapter 17, "Promotional Planning," has been rewritten to place greater emphasis on social media marketing strategies.
- Legal regulations of human resource management practices continue to become more complicated. For this reason, Chapter 20, "Managing Human Resources," has been revised to provide helpful hiring information, including updated descriptions of relevant employment laws, further insights into interview questioning, and other issues related to compliance in hiring practices.
- The world of health care and insurance provided by small businesses is undergoing major changes. Chapter 23, "Managing Risk in the Small Business," has been revised to help entrepreneurs adjust to these changes.
- Updated Living the Dream features in each chapter capture entrepreneurs in action as they face the challenges of small business and entrepreneurship. The authors' personal conversations and correspondence with many of the entrepreneurs profiled add depth to these features and ensure accuracy.
- In addition to the cases appearing in the book, many others, old and new, are available on the instructor resource website (www.cengage.com).

Achieving Your Best

Small Business Management is organized to help students and future entrepreneurs achieve success in whatever field they choose. The wide spectrum of content, applications, cases, graphics, stories, and other details offered in *Small Business Management* has assisted many small business entrepreneurs in making their dreams come true. With a focus on learning, our features emphasize activities that capture student interest and guarantee practical knowledge, including the following:

- **In the Spotlight.** The chapter-opening "In the Spotlight" feature profiles an amazing collection of entrepreneurs, whose unique insights into how to start, run, and grow a business will help readers identify and explore the full range of issues facing today's business owners.
- **Unique Support for Building a Business Plan.** The material in Part 3, "Developing the New Venture Business Plan," is integral to learning how to develop workable plans. Closely aligned with the approaches to planning that we present in the textbook, additional business plan templates can be found on the instructor resource website.
- **Integrated Learning System.** Our integrated learning system uses each chapter's learning objectives to give structure and coherence to the text content, study aids, and instructor's ancillaries, all of which are keyed to these objectives. The numbered objectives are introduced in the "Looking Ahead" section, and each is concisely addressed in the "Looking Back" section at the end of each chapter. The integrated learning system also simplifies lecture

and test preparation. The lecture notes in the *Instructor's Manual* are grouped by learning objective and identify the PowerPoint® slides that relate to each objective. Questions in the *Test Bank* are grouped by objective as well. A correlation table at the beginning of each *Test Bank* chapter permits selection of questions that cover all objectives or that emphasize objectives considered most important by individual instructors.

- **You Make the Call.** "You Make the Call" sections at the end of each chapter are very popular with both students and instructors because they present realistic business situations that require the examination of key operating decisions. By having students take on the role of a small business owner, these exercises give them a leg up in addressing issues facing small businesses.
- **Living the Dream.** Practical examples from the world of small business and entrepreneurship carry both instructional and inspirational value. "Living the Dream" boxes appear at critical junctures throughout the chapters, refueling and refreshing chapter concepts with documented experiences of practicing entrepreneurs.
- **STARTUPS.** The "STARTUP" feature highlights useful entrepreneurial tools, actions, and resources for new businesses, as well as ways to transform the ventures. These boxes are interspersed throughout the chapters in appropriate settings.

Updated and Enhanced Supplements

All resources and ancillaries that accompany *Small Business Management*, 18th edition, have been created to support a variety of teaching methods, learning styles, and classroom situations.

- ***Instructor's Manual.*** Lecture notes in the *Instructor's Manual* are grouped by learning objective and tied to PowerPoint® slides that relate to each objective. The manual also contains sources of audio/video and other instructional materials, answers to the "Discussion Questions," comments on "You Make the Call" situations, and teaching notes for the cases.
- ***Test Bank.*** Questions in the *Test Bank* are grouped by learning objectives and include true/false, multiple-choice, and discussion questions. Metadata tags are attached to each question.
- ***Cognero® Testing Software.*** Cengage Learning Testing Powered by Cognero® is a flexible, online system that allows you to import, edit, and manipulate content from the text's *Test Bank* or elsewhere, including your own favorite test questions; create multiple test versions in an instant; and deliver tests from your LMS, your classroom, or wherever you want.
- ***PowerPoint® for Instructors.*** A complete PowerPoint® package is available to aid in lecture presentation. The PowerPoint® slides are available on the password-protected instructor resource website.
- ***"Startup Stories" Videos.*** Available through MindTap, videos created for this text let you in on some very big ideas at work in a variety of innovative small businesses. Some of the small businesses covered include TWO MEN AND A TRUCK, River Pools & Spas, and Graeter's Ice Cream, among many others. Use these videos to bring the real world into your classroom, and let your students learn from the experts.

- ***LivePlan®***. Students learn how to use the award-winning, best-selling professional software *LivePlan* to create a business plan. This online resource provides all the essentials to create winning business plans, including step-by-step instructions for preparing each section of a plan. Ready-to-customize samples, advice, a detailed marketing analysis with links to demographic and marketing tools, and helpful financial tools make it easy to create a solid plan. Video and written tutorials from Palo Alto Software founder Tim Berry ensure that students fully understand how to maximize *LivePlan*'s dynamic tools.

Special Thanks and Acknowledgments

There are numerous individuals to whom we owe a debt of gratitude for their assistance in making this project a reality. In particular, we thank our friends—and we mean *good friends*—at Cengage Learning. We are especially indebted to Jason Fremder, John Sarantakis, Emily Horowitz, and word master Jeanne Yost. Without them, this book would exist only in our heads! They are amazing when it comes to coordination and motivation, keeping us on track and moving forward. Besides all that, they let us have a little fun along the way. They are just wonderful people, and they take seriously their roles in making certain that *Small Business Management* continues its tradition of excellence.

We also want to offer words of appreciation and acknowledgment to Wes Bailey, who was a contributing author of Chapter 23, "Managing Risk in the Small Business." Mr.Bailey is president of Bailey Insurance and Risk Management, Inc., in Waco, Texas, and is well recognized as a leader in the industry. His assistance with the authorship of this chapter should assure readers that they are receiving timely and relevant information about risk management. And we thank Bradley Norris, a colleague and senior lecturer at Baylor University, for his suggestions regarding Chapter 21, "Managing Operations." Finally, we thank Brian Lovin at Baylor University for assisting us with our research and for his contribution to the writing of some of the cases.

Finally, we offer heartfelt appreciation for the understanding and patient support of our wives—Donna, Dianna, and Patricia—during this process. Their faithful encouragement made the arduous task of bringing our best to this edition all the more manageable.

For their insightful comments and thoughtful suggestions, which helped to shape this edition, we are grateful to the following reviewers:

J. David Allen
Baylor University
Dr. Jeffrey Alstete
Iona College
David Ambrosini
Cabrillo College
Mark Andreasen
Northwest College
Kimberly Asonevich
Mount Aloysius College
Chandler Atkins
Adirondack Community College

Barrett Baebler
Webster University
Lee Baldwin
University of Mary Hardin-Baylor
Francis B. Ballard
Florida Community College
Andrea Balsamo
Consumnes River College
Hilton Barrett
Elizabeth City State University
Melissa Baucus
University of Louisville

Bill Bauer
Carroll University
Verona K. Beguin
Black Hills State University
Narendra C. Bhandari
Pace University
Greg Bier
Stephens College
Karl Binns
University of Maryland Eastern Shore
Karen Bishop
University of Louisville

Ross Blankenship
State Fair Community College

John Boos
Ohio Wesleyan University

Marvin Borgelt
University of Mary Hardin-Baylor

Steven Bradley
Austin Community College

Don B. Bradley III
University of Central Arkansas

Margaret Britt
Eastern Nazarene College

Mark Brosthoff
Indiana University

Penelope Stohn Brouwer
Mount Ida College

Rochelle R. Brunson
Alvin Community College

Kevin Chen
County College of Morris

Felipe Chia
Harrisburg Area Community College

Mike Cicero
Highline Community College

Edward G. Cole
St. Mary's University

Michael D. Cook
Hocking College

Roy A. Cook
Fort Lewis College

George R. Corbett
St. Thomas Aquinas College

Brad Cox
Midlands Technical College

Karen Cranford
Catawba College

George W. Crawford
Clayton College & State University

Bruce Davis
Weber State University

Helen Davis
Jefferson Community College

Terri Davis
Howard College

Bill Demory
Central Arizona College

Michael Deneen
Baker College

Sharon Dexler
Southeast Community College

Warren Dorau
Nicolet College

Max E. Douglas
Indiana State University

Bonnie Ann Dowd
Palomar College

Michael Drafke
College of Dupage

Franklin J. Elliot
Dine College

Franceen Fallett
Ventura College

R. Brian Fink
Danville Area Community College

Dennette Foy
Edison College

David W. Frantz
Purdue University

Janice S. Gates
Western Illinois University

Armand Gilinsky, Jr.
Sonoma State University

Darryl Goodman
Trident Technical College

William Grace
Missouri Valley College

William W. Graff
Maharishi University of Management

Jack Griggs
Texas Heritage Bank

Mark Hagenbuch
University of North Carolina, Greensboro

Carol Harvey
Assumption College

James R. Hindman
Northeastern University

Betty Hoge
Limestone College

Eddie Hufft
Alcorn State University

Sherrie Human
Xavier University

Ralph Jagodka
Mt. San Antonio College

Larry K. Johansen
Park University

Michael Judge
Hudson Valley Community College

Mary Beth Klinger
College of Southern Maryland

Charles W. Kulmann
Columbia College of Missouri

Rosemary Lafragola
University of Texas at El Paso

William Laing
Anderson College

Ann Langlois
Palm Beach Atlantic University

Rob K. Larson
Mayville State University

David E. Laurel
South Texas Community College

Alecia N. Lawrence
Williamsburg Technical College

Les Ledger
Central Texas College

Michael G. Levas
Carroll University

Richard M. Lewis
Lansing Community College

Thomas W. Lloyd
Westmoreland County Community College

Elaine Madden
Anne Arundel Community College

Kristina Mazurak
Albertson College

James J. Mazza
Middlesex Community College

Lisa McConnell
Oklahoma State University

Richard McEuen
Crowley's Ridge College

Angela Mitchell
Wilmington College

Frank Mitchell
Limestone College

Douglas Moesel
University of Missouri-Columbia

Michael K. Mulford
Des Moines Area Community College

Bernice M. Murphy
University of Maine at Machias

Eugene Muscat
University of San Francisco

John J. Nader
Grand Valley State University

Marc Newman
Hocking College

Charles "Randy" Nichols
Sullivan University

Robert D. Nixon
University of Louisville
Marcella M. Norwood
University of Houston
Mark Nygren
Brigham Young University-Idaho
Donalus A. Okhomina, Sr.
Jackson State University
Rosa L. Okpara
Albany State University
Timothy O'Leary
Mount Wachusett Community College
Pamela Onedeck
University of Pittsburgh at Greensburg
Dick Petitte
SUNY Brockport & Monroe Community College
Claire Phillips
North Harris College
Dean Pielstick
Northern Arizona University
Mark S. Poulos
St. Edward's University
Julia Truitt Poynter
Transylvania University
Fred Pragasam
University of North Florida
Thomas Pressly
Penn State-Shenango
Mary Ellen Rosetti
Hudson Valley Community College
June N. Roux
Delaware Technical and Community College
Jaclyn Rundle
Central College
John K. Sands
Western Washington University
Craig Sarine
Lee University
Duane Schecter
Muskegon Community College
Joseph A. Schubert
Delaware Technical and Community College
Matthew Semadeni
Texas A&M University
Marjorie Shapiro
Myers University
Sherry L. Shuler
American River College
Cindy Simerly
Lakeland Community College
James Sisk
Gaston College
Victoria L. Sitter
Milligan College
Bernard Skown
Stevens Institute of Technology
Kristin L. H. Slyter
Valley City State University
William E. Smith
Ferris State University
Bill Snider
Cuesta College
Roger Stanford
Chippewa Valley Technical College
George Starbuck
McMurry University
Phil Stetz
Stephen F. Austin State University
Johnny Stites
J&S Construction
Peter L. Stone
Spartanburg Technical College
John Streibich
Monroe Community College
Ram Subramanian
Montclair State University
James Swenson
Minnesota State University Moorhead
Ruth Tarver
West Hills Community College
Paul B. Thacker
Macomb Community College
Darrell Thompson
Mountain View College
Melodie M. Toby
Kean University
Charles N. Toftoy
George Washington University
Charles Torti
Schreiner University
Gerald R. Turner
Limestone College
Barry L. Van Hook
Arizona State University
Brian Wahl
North Shore Community College
Mike Wakefield
University of Southern California
Charles F. Warren
Salem State College
Bill Waxman
Edison Community College
Janet Wayne
Baker College
Charles Wellen
Fitchburg State College
Nat B. White, Jr.
South Piedmont Community College
Jim Whitlock
Brenau University
Ira Wilsker
Lamar Institute of Technology
Patricia A. Worsham
Cal Poly Pomona

To the Instructor

As a final word of appreciation, we express our sincere thanks to the many instructors who use our text in both academic and professional settings. Based on years of teaching and listening to other teachers and students, *Small Business Management* has been designed to meet the needs of its readers. And we continue to listen and make changes in the text. Please write or call us to offer suggestions to help us make the book even better for future readers. Our contact information is Bill Petty (254-710-2260, bill_petty@baylor.edu), Les Palich (254-710-6194, les_palich@baylor.edu), and Frank Hoy (508-831-4998, fhoy@wpi.edu). We would love to hear from you.

About the Authors

JUSTIN G. LONGENECKER

Justin G. Longenecker's authorship of *Small Business Management* began with the first edition of this book. He authored a number of books and numerous articles in such journals as *Journal of Small Business Management, Academy of Management Review, Business Horizons,* and *Journal of Business Ethics*. He was active in several professional organizations and served as president of the International Council for Small Business. Dr. Longenecker grew up in a family business. After attending Central Christian College of Kansas for two years, he went on to earn his B.A. in political science from Seattle Pacific University, his M.B.A. from Ohio State University, and his Ph.D. from the University of Washington. He taught at Baylor University, where he was Emeritus Chavanne Professor of Christian Ethics in Business until his death in 2005.

J. WILLIAM PETTY

J. William "Bill" Petty is Professor of Finance and the W. W. Caruth Chairholder in Entrepreneurship at Baylor University and the first executive director of the Baylor Angel Network. He holds a Ph.D. and an M.B.A. from the University of Texas at Austin and a B.S. from Abilene Christian University. He has taught at Virginia Tech University and Texas Tech University and served as dean of the business school at Abilene Christian University. He has taught entrepreneurship and small business courses in China, the Ukraine, Kazakhstan, Indonesia, Thailand, and Russia. Dr. Petty has been designated a Master Teacher at Baylor and was named the National Entrepreneurship Teacher of the Year in 2008 by the Acton Foundation for Excellence in Entrepreneurship. His research interests include acquisitions of privately held companies, shareholder value-based management, the financing of small and entrepreneurial firms, angel financing, and exit strategies for privately held firms. He has served as co-editor for the *Journal of Financial Research* and as editor of the *Journal of Entrepreneurial Finance*. He has published articles in a number of finance journals and is the co-author of a leading corporate finance textbook, *Foundations of Finance*. He is a co-author of *Value-Based Management in an Era of Corporate Social Responsibility* (Oxford University Press, 2010). Dr. Petty has worked as a consultant for oil and gas firms and consumer product companies. He also served as a subject-matter expert on a best-practices study by the American Productivity and Quality Center on the topic of shareholder value-based management. He was a member of a research team sponsored by the Australian Department of Industry to study the feasibility of establishing a public equity market for small and medium-size enterprises in Australia. Finally, he serves as the audit chair for a publicly traded energy firm.

LESLIE E. PALICH

Leslie E. "Les" Palich is Professor of Management and Entrepreneurship and the W. A. Mays Professor of Entrepreneurship at Baylor University, where he teaches courses in small business management, international entrepreneurship, strategic management, and international management to graduate and undergraduate students. He is also the associate director of the Entrepreneurship Studies program at Baylor. Dr. Palich holds a Ph.D. and an M.B.A. from Arizona State University and a B.A. from Manhattan Christian College. His research has been published in the *Academy of Management Review, Strategic Management Journal, Entrepreneurship Theory & Practice, Journal of Business Venturing, Journal of International Business Studies, Journal of Management, Journal of Organizational Behavior, Journal of Small Business Management,* and several other periodicals. He has taught entrepreneurship and strategic management in a host of overseas settings, including Austria, Costa Rica, the Czech Republic, Germany, Italy, Switzerland, Cuba, France, the Netherlands, the United Kingdom, and the Dominican Republic. His interest in entrepreneurial opportunity and small business management dates back to his grade school years, when he set up a produce sales business to experiment with small business ownership. That early experience became a springboard for a number of other enterprises. Since that time, he has owned and operated domestic ventures in agribusiness, automobile sales, real estate development, and educational services, as well as an international import business. Dr. Palich currently owns and operates Lead Generation X, an Internet marketing firm that employs cutting-edge promotional methods to serve its clients and their customers.

FRANK HOY

Frank Hoy is the Paul R. Beswick Professor of Innovation and Entrepreneurship in the School of Business at Worcester Polytechnic Institute. Dr. Hoy, who was previously director of the Centers for Entrepreneurial Development, Advancement, Research and Support at the University of Texas at El Paso (UTEP), also serves as director of the Collaborative for Entrepreneurship & Innovation (CEI) in WPI's nationally ranked entrepreneurship program in the School of Business. He joined the WPI faculty in August 2009. He holds a B.B.A. from the University of Texas at El Paso, an M.B.A. from the University of North Texas, and a Ph.D. in management from Texas A&M University. He spent 10 years as a faculty member in the Department of Management at the University of Georgia, where he founded and directed the Center for Business and Economic Studies, coordinated the entrepreneurship curriculum, and served as state director of the Georgia Small Business Development Center. In 1991, he returned to El Paso, Texas, to join UTEP as a professor of management and entrepreneurship and dean of the College of Business Administration. Dr. Hoy is a past president of the United States Association for Small Business and Entrepreneurship and past chair of the Entrepreneurship Division of the Academy of Management. He is president of the Family Enterprise Research Conference and a member of the global board of directors of STEP, the Successful Transgenerational Entrepreneurship Practices project. His research has appeared in the *Academy of Management Journal, Academy of Management Review, Journal of Business Venturing,* and *Family Business Review,* and he is a past editor of *Entrepreneurship Theory and Practice.*

ENTREPRENEURSHIP

© GUSTAVO FRAZAO/SHUTTERSTOCK.COM

CHAPTER 1

The Entrepreneurial Life

The story of Table Occasions is one of classic entrepreneurship. Chia Stewart and Claudia Narvaez have engaged in a decade-long process of making their dream happen, by first creating a strategy, a company, and a brand, and then adapting and growing as opportunities present themselves and life's curve balls come their way.

Stewart and Narvaez launched their table-decorating business in 2006 and helped it blossom into a center for event-planning activity for their community. What started with rentals of higher-end party tables, chairs, and linens has transformed into a one-stop shop for all event needs—from rentals, to planning and coordination, to execution. The result of this new "industry" that has set a high standard for party-throwing in El Paso, Texas, has been that other new, related businesses—such as creative bakeries and custom stationary shops—have cropped up or expanded all around town to take part in the new economic activity.

The friendship that started in middle school transformed into something much

© BILL PETTY

In the SPOTLIGHT
Table Occasions, Inc.
www.tableoccasions.com

OPEN
LOOKING AHEAD

After studying this chapter, you should be able to . . .

1-1. Explain the importance of small business and entrepreneurship in our society.

1-2. Distinguish between the terms *small business* and *entrepreneurial opportunity*.

1-3. Explain the basic characteristics of entrepreneurs, and describe different kinds of entrepreneurship.

1-4. Discuss the importance of understanding your motivations and perceptions related to owning a small business.

1-5. Describe five potential competitive advantages of small entrepreneurial companies over large firms.

1-6. Explain the concept of an entrepreneurial legacy and its challenges.

different in the business partnership that Stewart and Narvaez formed. Together, they saw an opportunity for a business where each partner could bring to the table something different and exciting, creating one complete and new concept.

When Table Occasions started its operations, events were not a big deal in the community—at least not from an artistic perspective. But Stewart and Narvaez saw an unexploited niche that they could develop. They made event decorating a "must" in social and professional circles, to the point that skimping on decorations is now seen as showing a lack of dedication to the cause. This has solidified their customer base and redefined decorating expenses as "essential," which is why the recent recession did not weaken their sales and revenues.

The services and products that Table Occasions offers are truly transformative, reflecting the party thrower's personality, with unique tablecloths, flowers, cakes, catering, entertainment, lighting, and more. As Stewart says, "We use products that, when coordinated with a wide range of event concepts, help the planners pull off the perfect memorable and successful event—without overwhelming themselves in the process. Almost every event in town is now a virtual wonderland of visual treats for event-goers to enjoy and remember. It has truly made events magical."

Their well-recognized success has inspired others to start competitive businesses in town. But Table Occasions continues to lead the pack due to its commitment to quality, community service, creativity, professionalism, and personal attention to every event. As a matter of fact, Stewart and Narvaez still engage in hard labor when it is needed to get a job done right. They know that the buck stops with them, and they always make sure that every host is proud of every event.

And now the duo is starting to make plans for the next stage of their entrepreneurial venture: franchising Table Occasions. New locations, new partnerships, and new strategies are being explored in order to make calculated risks and investments in franchises that can take advantage of the economies of scale that Table Occasions can now offer through the infrastructure developed in El Paso. The risks may be large, but the partners' passion and willingness to invest their time and money in building an effective team, leading the industry in creativity and trendsetting, providing high-quality services and products, and being the first to grasp new opportunities will lead them to success.

Much like a marriage, Stewart and Narvaez have struggled personally and professionally through changes, in good times and bad times. But together, they manage complex situations, support each other, and reap the rewards of a successful company. The hardest part of their work does not come from the physical labor but from having to juggle their work and personal lives. Both are working mothers (with one divorce thrown into the mix), and weekends away, early mornings, late nights, last-minute changes, and weather emergencies pull them away from their families. Its hard work . . . so hard it hurts! However, Stewart and Narvaez have learned to rely on the different strengths that each brings to the company, to support each other's visions, and to always act with the utmost integrity toward one another. "Without trust in each other, we would not have been able to come this far" claims Stewart. "Business is all about people, and we have to surround ourselves with people we can depend on, and who depend on us."

Source: Interview with Chia Stewart, founder and CEO, Table Occasions, Inc., December 28, 2014.

Having worked for over four decades with both entrepreneurs and students who aspire to own companies, we have designed this book to prepare you for owning your own small business—one that may even grow over time to become a large firm. In addition, we will be drawing on the extensive experience of entrepreneurs who offer their advice and counsel on important issues. Understand that this book is not just about learning facts; rather, we want to prepare you to act on your dreams. We want your study of small business management to change your life!

We believe that owning a business is one of the most noble of all professions—*especially if done well*. No other life's work does more to help you learn and develop as a person, contribute to the success of a team, create value for customers, and make a significant difference in the community. While owning a business is generally about producing a product or service and selling it for a profit, you will find that the deepest rewards from owning your own business come from helping your employees grow, both professionally and personally, and offering goods or services that improve the lives of your customers. After all, what happens at work carries over into your personal life.[1] But you should understand that the road can be rough, with some big potholes along the way. We believe that the words of Theodore Roosevelt over a century ago, when he described "the man in the arena," apply perfectly to these entrepreneurs:

> *It is not the critic who counts; not the man who points out how the strong man stumbles, or where the doer of deeds could have done them better. The credit belongs to the man who is actually in the arena, whose face is marred by dust and sweat and blood; who strives valiantly; who errs, who comes short again and again, because there is not effort without error and shortcoming; but who does actually strive to do the deeds; who knows great enthusiasms, the great devotions, who spends himself in a worthy cause; who at the best knows in the end the triumph of high achievement, and who at the worst, if he fails, at least fails while daring greatly, so that his place shall never be with those cold and timid souls who neither know victory nor defeat.*[2]

The primary purpose of this chapter is to offer words of encouragement for anyone wanting to be a small business owner. We will begin the chapter by providing an overview of small business and entrepreneurship, along with stories of entrepreneurs who started and grew businesses. Then we will quickly get you started thinking about your motivations and perceptions related to owning a small business. Next, we will explain the ways small firms can be competitive, even against industry giants. Finally, we want you to think about building an entrepreneurial legacy that you can leave to those who follow in your footsteps.

So, if you, like many others who come from many different walks of life, want to have your own business, then read on. You are about to embark on a course of study that will prove invaluable in reaching your goal. Entrepreneurship can provide an exciting life and offer substantial personal rewards. We passionately contend that there is no finer calling.

1-1 SMALL SIZE, GREAT SIGNIFICANCE

Explain the importance of small business and entrepreneurship in our society.

If you have a serious interest in starting and operating your own business—now or in the future—you are not alone. You may be part of what Paul Reynolds, a leading researcher in the entrepreneurship field, calls a major social phenomenon.[3] Isabell M. Welpe, a business professor at Technische Universität München, captures the significance of entrepreneurship for an individual and society at large in these words:

> *Entrepreneurship is a necessity in our society. It is a philosophy based on individual initiative and on the insight that entrepreneurship is more than just getting a job. Entrepreneurship achieves self-fulfillment, gains respect and enables real innovation by looking at the next necessary steps toward a better world.*[4]

The significance of small business can also be observed in its contribution to the economy. Within the United States, it is estimated that 12 million people are involved in some form of entrepreneurial venture, and that as many as half of all adults will be engaged in self-employment at some point during their working careers.[5] The following facts provide an understanding of the important role of small businesses in the United States:[6]

- There are 27.8 million small businesses in the United States with fewer than 500 employees, a common definition of a small business.
- Small companies account for 99.7 of all businesses—and 90 percent have fewer than 20 employees!

- Fifty-five million people work in small businesses, representing 49 percent of all employees and 42 percent of all salaries paid to employees.
- Small enterprises hire 43 percent of all high-tech employees (scientists, engineers, computer programmers, and others).
- Many small companies have been going global, representing 97 percent of all exporters.
- Business owners are well educated, with 50 percent having a college degree, an increase of 32 percent from 2000 to 2010.
- About one-fourth of the 23.5 million military veterans in the United States are interested in starting or buying their own business.

Given this information, it's clear that individuals who start and lead small businesses make a significant contribution to the economy and the quality of our lives. On the other hand, we know that a lot of people talk about owning a business but never make it happen. Also, the number of young persons who own private businesses in the United States is at a 24-year low. According to *The Wall Street Journal*, only 3.6 percent of households headed by young adults (less than 30 years of age) owned private businesses in 2013—compared to 10.6 percent in 1989. This trend potentially has negative implications for future economic growth.

It is difficult to pinpoint the reasons for the decline in young people choosing to own a small business. Possible reasons include the difficulty in raising capital during the Great Recession and, possibly, a lower tolerance for risk by young people. Ruth Simon and Caelainn Barr write:

> *The decline also reflects a generation struggling to find a spot in the workforce. Younger workers have had trouble gaining the skills and experience that can be helpful in starting a business. Some doubt their ability.*[7]

On the other hand, the Kauffman Foundation estimates that 70 percent of young people still dream of owning their own business sometime in the future.[8] Thus, it seems fair to say that while young people today are generally less inclined to start a business, they have in no way given up hope of eventually owning their own business. So, it makes us, as the authors of this text, all the more committed to help young people be better prepared to start a small business. Our hope is that your study of *Small Business Management* will give you the confidence and skills that you need to be successful in owning your own business. And that is not only important for you, but for those you could serve as well.

Distinguish between the terms *small business* and *entrepreneurial opportunity*.

1-2 SMALL BUSINESS AND ENTREPRENEURIAL OPPORTUNITY: IS THERE A DIFFERENCE?

Let's take a more detailed look at the terms *small business* and *entrepreneurial opportunity* to gain a better understanding of what they represent. Both are at the heart of all that you will study in this book.

1-2a What Is a Small Business?

What does it mean when we talk about "small business?" A neighborhood restaurant or bakery is clearly a small business, and Toyota is obviously not. But among small businesses, there is great degree of diversity in size, in growth potential, in organizational structure, and often in culture.

Many efforts have been made to define the term *small business*, using such criteria as number of employees, sales volume, and value of assets. But there is no generally accepted or universally agreed-on definition. Size standards are basically arbitrary, adopted to serve a particular purpose. For example, the U.S. Small Business Administration defines a small business as having fewer than 500 employees.[9] But in specific cases, the government may define a small business differently—such as one with fewer than 10 employees—in order to exempt a very small business from certain regulations, if compliance would prove to be too costly, given its small size.

In addition to size, small businesses differ drastically in their growth potential. Those few businesses with phenomenal prospects for growth are called **high-potential ventures**, or **gazelles**. Even within this group, there is variation in styles of operation and approaches to growth. Very few begin as high-tech startups—the kind that made Silicon Valley famous. In contrast to such high-potential ventures, **attractive small firms** offer substantial financial rewards for their owners. Income from these entrepreneurial ventures may grow into the millions or even tens of millions of dollars. They represent a major segment of small businesses—solid, healthy firms that can provide rewarding careers and create financial wealth for the owners.

The least profitable types of small businesses—including many small service companies, such as pool-cleaning businesses, dry cleaners, beauty shops, and appliance repair shops—provide modest returns to their owners. These are called **microbusinesses**, and their distinguishing feature is their limited ability to generate significant profits. Entrepreneurs who devote personal effort to such ventures receive a profit that essentially compensates them for their time. Many companies of this type are also called **lifestyle businesses** because they permit an owner to follow a desired lifestyle, even though they provide only modest financial returns. Employing fewer than 10 employees, lifestyle businesses make up the largest sector of the U.S. economy. Such enterprises usually do not attract investors and are financed with owner savings or money provided by friends and family.

Lifestyle businesses are not only important to the U.S. economy, but they have also become vital for many individuals in developing countries in Asia, South America, and Africa. In these countries, starting and running a small business can easily double or triple a family's income and make a significant difference in the quality of family members' lives. To help these individuals, some organizations are providing **microloans**, sometimes for only a few dollars, to allow them to buy inventory or do whatever else needs to be done to get started in business.

So, understanding a small business is dependent on our definition of *small* and the firm's growth potential. For our studies, we will mostly be directing our attention to **small businesses** that meet the following criteria, at least in spirit:

1. Compared to the largest firms in the industry, the business is small; in most instances, the business has fewer than 100 employees.
2. Except for its marketing function, the business's operations are geographically localized.
3. No more than a few individuals provide the equity financing for the business. Equity financing (discussed in Chapter 12) is the money invested in the business by the owners and possibly by a few other individuals.
4. The business may begin with a single individual, but it has the potential to become more than a "one-person show" and may eventually grow to be a mid-sized company or even a large firm.
5. The business must have growth potential, whether or not the owner chooses to capture that growth.

high-potential venture (gazelle)
A small firm that has great prospects for growth.

attractive small firm
A small firm that provides substantial profits to its owner.

microbusiness
A small firm that provides minimal profits to its owner.

lifestyle business
A microbusiness that permits the owner to follow a desired pattern of living.

microloans
Very small loans, often provided to entrepreneurs in developing countries.

small business
A business with growth potential that is small compared to large companies in an industry, has geographically localized operations, is financed by only a few individuals, and has a small management team.

Obviously, some small businesses will fail to meet all of these standards, but they are still of great interest to us. For example, a small executive search firm—a firm that helps corporate clients recruit high-level managers—may operate in many sections of the country and thereby fail to meet the second criterion. Nevertheless, the discussion of management concepts in this book is aimed primarily at the type of firm that fits the general pattern outlined by these criteria.

1-2b What Is an Entrepreneurial Opportunity?

At its core, the entrepreneurial process begins with identifying an attractive opportunity, which is more than merely having a good idea. Such opportunities make the enterprise economically attractive for the owners while offering customers a product or service that is so appealing that they are willing to let go of their hard-earned money to buy it. In other words, an entrepreneur must find a way to create value for customers. An **entrepreneurial opportunity**, then, is an *economically attractive and timely opportunity* that creates value both for prospective customers and for the firm's owners. (In Chapter 3, you'll learn how to identify good opportunities.)

So an **entrepreneur** is a person who relentlessly pursues an opportunity, in either a new or an existing enterprise, to create value while assuming both the risk and the reward for her or his efforts. Entrepreneurs generally think differently about resources than do employee-managers. While managers in large corporations so often think like administrators or bureaucrats—wanting larger budgets or more employees—entrepreneurs work to do more with less. They may try to use other people's resources, which is called **bootstrapping**. For example, an entrepreneur might resort to bartering or, in the early days of a business, work to create income from other sources to fund the business. Let's look at three ventures started by some present-day entrepreneurs who have successfully created value for customers and themselves alike.

entrepreneurial opportunity
An economically attractive and timely opportunity that creates value for interested buyers or end users.

entrepreneur
A person who relentlessly pursues an opportunity, in either a new or an existing business, to create value while assuming both the risk and the reward for his or her efforts.

bootstrapping
Doing more with less in terms of resources invested in a business, and, where possible, controlling the resources without owning them.

KELLY'S DELIGHT (HEWITT, TX)[10]

After graduating from college, Patrick Linstrom knew he needed to do something to help pay off his student loans. He had an idea for a product that he wanted to sell that was not quite available yet: all-natural liquid cane sugar. With just a concept in mind, Linstrom set off on his journey to enter this untapped market. "It is vital to learn as much as you can about the overall business, before investing your time and money into such a venture." Linstrom says. After researching the liquid sugar market for over eight months, he was ready to make a product. By maxing out all of his credit cards and taking out a personal loan, Linstrom was able to pay for the initial production of his product. With an actual product in hand, he began selling his liquid sugar to local businesses.

© KELLYSDELIGHT

Despite positive feedback from local customers, lack of a good distribution strategy hurt the startup. Linstrom knew he needed to expand if he wanted his company to experience significant profits. He decided to update his strategy to reach more customers by changing the small packet design for his product into a 16-ounce bottle. With a better-designed product, Linstrom was set on getting his liquid cane sugar on the shelves of H-E-B, a major grocery chain in Texas. "I probably called H-E-B 100 times before I was able to meet someone. I think I finally got to the right buyer who thought this was a good product," says Linstrom. His first meeting proved successful, and H-E-B decided to test Kelly's Delight in 125 stores. "We owe our business to H-E-B," Linstrom says. "They were the first retailer that took a chance on us, and it has made a world of difference."

In the meantime, Linstrom knew he needed to continue expanding his retail store footprint. Through a mutual friend, Linstrom was able to meet with Tom McClintock, a vice president of Coca-Cola. McClintock loved the product idea and quit his job at Coca-Cola to join Linstrom's team at Kelly's Delight. After teaming up with McClintock, Linstrom never looked back.

As of 2014, Kelly's Delight was selling in over 7,000 retailers across the country, including such stores as Walmart, Target, H-E-B, and many other locations. Competitors have entered the market, but Linstrom continues to maintain competitive prices by keeping his manufacturing costs minimal and his management team lean. He believes that he is still far from reaching his goals and plans to enter the Asian market soon.

Liquid sugar may seem like a simple concept, but executing a final product at a price consumers are willing to pay is the hard part. Linstrom says, "Sometimes you have to fake it before you make it. You have to believe you can accomplish what you set out to do, and take the risk that is necessary to accomplish your goals. From my experience, I would say that a successful business takes inspiration, preparation, and opportunity. Many people have inspiration but have not taken the time to prepare. So when the opportunity is presented to them, they are not able to capitalize on their risk. [They] should always be preparing and know that opportunity will strike if they just stay persistent."

BLANK LABEL (BOSTON, MA)[11]

When Fan Bi was working his first professional job in London in 2006, he was introduced to the business world's dress code. Bi loved custom tailoring but understood that this luxury came at a price. He discovered the vast difference in experience between shopping by size for pre-made clothes and shopping by style of fabric for customizable clothes.

"I used to buy dress shirts off the rack," Bi says. "But this idea of going to a fabric market, being measured, being able to choose different fabrics . . . I thought, 'Wow, you know, this is a really different experience.'" Then, during a vacation to Shanghai in the summer of 2008, where custom tailoring was provided at a far more competitive price, he asked the question "Can custom be affordable?"

Bi came up with the idea for affordable custom shirts during his study abroad program at Babson College. The faculty at Babson helped Bi hone his idea and recruit campus sales reps. One of these sales reps was Danny Wong, a student at nearby Bentley University. Unfortunately, the idea was met with a lack of interest from the college students. Also, the business was not scalable and lacked a clear supply chain. So Bi partnered with Wong to bring the business online, where overhead expenses were lower and the potential market was large. At the beginning of 2010, they launched the Blank Label website.

"We wanted to be the destination where people can come and design their own apparel," Bi says. Online visitors were able to design a custom shirt by selecting fabric, color combination, and style of cuff, collar, placket, pocket, button, monogram, and even custom label—all for less than $100.

Since going online in 2010, the pair has seen their customer demographic shift toward business professionals who purchase six to ten dress shirts per year. They went from generating $345,000 in sales during their first year of business to over $1.1 million in 2011. By June 2012, Blank Label had sold 30,000 dress shirts.

The web-savvy founders managed almost the entire process remotely. "Thanks to the Internet," Bi says, "you can work with the best people in the world, not just the best people in your neighborhood." But Bi and Wong weren't content just being shirt makers. Wong wanted Blank Label to emerge as a hub for everything "co-created."

In 2013, Blank Label opened its first pattern room in downtown Boston. The reason behind this decision was consumers' preference to touch and feel products before making a purchase. This was especially true when it came to buying ties, chinos, jackets, and suits. "We thought that maybe we should experiment, and that has paid off in spades," Bi observes.

The store quickly began generating revenues of about $100,000 a month, increasing 10 to 15 percent month over month. Its physical store sales were expected to account for 70 percent of its total by the end of the year. Also, the number of employees went from 4 to 22, with Bi raising $500,000 from investors to fund the company's growth. With the initial success, Bi and Wong decided to open a second store in Boston's Downtown Crossing area, with plans to open six more stores along the East Coast.

HUGHES GROUP LLC (TACOMA, WASH.)[12]

Even if it were true that the entrepreneurial spirit is born and not made, it would still remain that this characteristic comes with no birthright of success. It's a hard truth that Patrick L. Hughes, Sr., founder and CEO of Hughes Group LLC, stumbled many times before his company was named the National Minority Small Business of the Year.

"My mother said I was a true entrepreneur from the time I was a child. When the other kids wanted to play cowboys and Indians, I always wanted to run the general store or saloon. I loved capitalism without even knowing what capitalism was," said Hughes, who got his first taste of the full-time business world after retiring from the Army in 2003. "But when I finally went into business for myself, I sure made a lot of mistakes early on."

His Tacoma, Washington–based logistics company provides products and services to federal and commercial markets. "We are a minority-owned and service disabled veteran–owned company," said Hughes, noting that the company has 213 employees in 11 locations across the nation, and saw just over $8 million in revenue in 2011 and was expecting $8.5 million to $9 million in 2012 revenue.

Like many business success stories, the tale of Hughes Group is one that started small—as a carpet-cleaning business in Hughes's garage while he was a logistics officer in the Army—and grew over time. But Hughes says the difference between where his company is today and the hundreds of other startups specializing in logistics is that he never considered for an instant that his small business should stay small.

"If there's anything I see small businesses doing wrong, it's thinking they've got to stay in a niche," said Hughes. "Diversity is the lifeblood of a small business; become an expert in your area, and then branch out from there. In other words learn how to do other different, but related, skills."

Today, Hughes Group has expanded to a full-bore logistics company that offers a facility maintenance and supply division, as well as a division with management, assessment, development, and support services. Hughes Group has clients in both the government and the commercial arena.

Though Hughes Group wasn't officially founded until 2004, Hughes spent his last years in the military planning what life would look like post-service. He had accumulated nearly 30 years of logistics experience but lacked the know-how to run a business. Luckily, his first big job was close to home: Hughes landed a contract with the military, which parlayed into a series of other logistics contracts.

First, he needed funding. "When I was first reading about the 8(a) Business Development Program offered by the Small Business Administration (SBA), I took my application into the local SBA office. They scratched it up and circled it in red where

I did it wrong," said Hughes, laughing. He eventually qualified for an initial $300,000 line of credit—enough to get Hughes Group off the ground. He had the loan; now he needed business smarts.

"What you don't realize at the start is when you make a dollar, you do not have a dollar to spend," Hughes said. "I think this is where many 8(a) businesses fail; you may get 15 cents off that $1 you made because you already spent it before you got it. There's always overhead, taxes, and so on." Over the next few years, Hughes's increasing business skill allowed him to take out another loan backed by the SBA and the Grow America Fund along with the city to buy a 15,000-square-foot building.

Now, in addition to running his company from the headquarters, Hughes uses some of the office space to help foster other startups operating in the government market space, especially those run by disadvantaged owners such as veterans, minorities, and women. "One of the greatest things you can have in business is a network," Hughes says. "We're essentially offering a network for these disadvantaged businesses to accelerate into the government contracting arena." Though the fee for the space rental is nominal, Hughes sees its value as being greater to the local business community. "I learned from the mistakes I made early on, and I am sure I will make some more over the years. But I want to pass the knowledge on to others," Hughes said.

1-3 ENTREPRENEURIAL QUALITIES: BIG EGO NOT REQUIRED

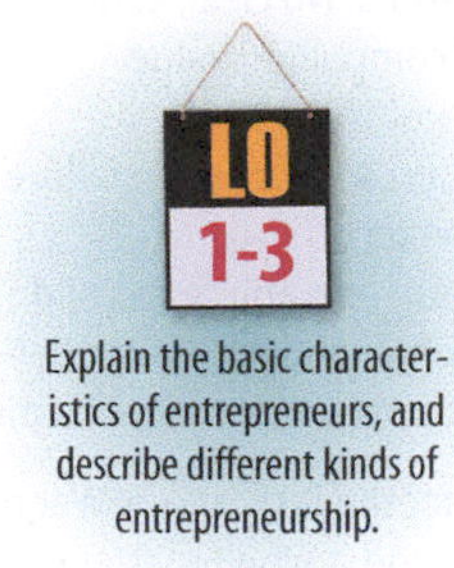

Explain the basic characteristics of entrepreneurs, and describe different kinds of entrepreneurship.

People often ask, "Are entrepreneurs born or made?" That question has long been debated with little agreement. However, Stephen Spinelli and Robert Adams have nicely summarized research on entrepreneurial characteristics. The entrepreneurs they describe as having and exhibiting "desirable and acquirable attitudes and behaviors" fall under the following six descriptors:[13]

1. *Commitment and determination*—Tenacious, decisive, and persistent in problem solving.
2. *Leadership abilities*—Self-starters and team builders who focus on honesty in their business relationships.
3. *Opportunity obsession*—Aware of market and customer needs.
4. *Tolerance of risk, ambiguity, and uncertainty*—Risk takers, risk minimizers, and uncertainty tolerators.
5. *Creativity, self-reliance, and adaptability*—Open-minded, flexible, uncomfortable with the status quo, and quick to learn.
6. *Motivation to excel*—Goal-oriented and aware of personal strengths and weaknesses.

On the other side of the coin, some attitudes and behaviors should be avoided at all costs. An almost certain way to fail as an entrepreneur, as many have learned by experience, is to do the following:

1. Overestimate what you can do.
2. Lack an understanding of the market.
3. Hire mediocre people.
4. Fail to be a team player, which is usually the result of taking oneself too seriously.

5. Be a domineering manager.
6. Fail to share ownership in the business in an equitable way.

Three Harvard Business School professors had similar conclusions based on a survey of company founders, asking them what they got wrong when starting their companies.[14] For one thing, the founders acknowledged not listening to prospective customers as they were designing their product or service. Instead, they basically "built" what they thought customers would want without ever really asking. A majority of the founders also admitted that their passion and egos caused them to react negatively to criticism and to discount ideas from others for improving their products or services. We frequently hear that an entrepreneur must have passion, which is true—but *unchecked passion can be destructive*.

To some extent, the foregoing traits and behaviors describe a leader who lacks some measure of humility. Contrary to popular belief, humility is a quality that serves leaders well.

Five Reasons Businesses Fail[15]

Eric T. Wagner, a contributor to *Forbes Magazine* and long-time entrepreneur gives five reasons for business failure that he has observed over years of experience:

Reason 1: Not in touch with customers through deep dialogue.
Reason 2: No real differentiation of product or service in the market.
Reason 3: No clear, concise, and compelling value propositions.
Reason 4: Leadership failure at the top.
Reason 5: Inability to build a profitable business model with proven revenue streams.

Fail for the last reason, Wagner says, and it won't matter if you avoid the other causes for failure. You will fail.

1-3a Founders and Second-Stage Entrepreneurs

We typically think of "pure" entrepreneurs as being **founders** of new businesses that bring new or improved products or services to market. However, at some point after a new firm is established, it may be purchased or taken over by a second-generation family member or another individual who was managing the company. These "second-stage" entrepreneurs do not necessarily differ greatly from founding entrepreneurs in the way they manage their businesses. Sometimes, these well-established small firms grow rapidly, and their orientation will be more akin to that of a founder than to that of a manager. Nevertheless, it is helpful to distinguish between entrepreneurs who start or substantially change companies and those who direct the continuing operations of established businesses. Ryan Gibson, a young entrepreneur and partner in Rydell Holdings in Waco, Texas, says he has come to understand that his passion and aptitude are for starting new companies, which he has successfully done on several occasions. However, when the business is up and running, he turns the operations over to his team. He knows that one of his strengths is not running a business on a day-to-day basis. Again, it comes back to understanding yourself—your motivations and personality—if you want your journey to be a good one in the long run.

1-3b Franchisees

Franchisees comprise yet another category of entrepreneurs. According to the International Franchise Association, 44 percent of businesses in the United States are franchises. **Franchisees** differ from other business owners in the degree of their independence. Because of the guidance and constraints provided by contractual arrangements with franchising organizations, franchisees function as limited entrepreneurs.

The franchisee is authorized to market the company's products or services and expects the franchisor to provide support in operating the business. Such support will almost always include operating systems, training, financing, advertising, and other services. In addition to paying an annual franchising fee, the franchisee must also pay a portion of its profits to the franchisor. (Chapter 4 presents more information about franchisees.)

founder
An entrepreneur who brings a new firm into existence.

franchisee
An entrepreneur whose power is limited by a contractual relationship with a franchising organization.

Living the Dream

ENTREPRENEURIAL EXPERIENCES

Advice from Experienced Entrepreneurs

There is no way around it, starting and building a successful business is just hard. It can be exhilarating, but it can also be frightening—a time of taking risks like you have never known. Consider the words of the following three successful entrepreneurs, words that carried them through the good times and bad times alike.

© BILL PETTY

April Anthony, Founder and CEO, Encompass Home Health & Hospice

Pursue Your Calling: My entry into home health care came accidentally. I wasn't looking for a career, I was simply looking for a short-term job on my way to becoming a stay-at-home mom. However, much to my surprise, when I entered the home health care industry, I not only found a job. What I really found was my life's calling and my passion. When you find your passion, everything changes.

I became so convinced about WHY we had to deliver exceptional care to our elderly patients that I was determined to figure out HOW to do it better than anyone else. When you find your calling, the hurdles that you face as an entrepreneur no longer seem so daunting. Instead, your commitment to overcome them becomes almost obsessive.

After 23 years, I can honestly say that I love my work today as much as I ever have because it isn't really work—it is my calling, my passion, and my inspiration.

© BILL PETTY

Johnny Stites, CEO, J&S Construction

Think First about Making a Difference in Others' Lives, and Emulate Successful People: I sold books for Southwestern Publishing Company, door to door, in the summers between my college semesters. I learned when I focused on making money or how many sales I had made, I did not enjoy my job nearly as much as when I focused on helping people. I also did not make as much money.

I carried that into my construction career of 43 years. During that time, I realized again my time was much more enjoyable when I focused first on those I sought to help. I observed that my construction crews were far more fulfilled in their jobs when I started emphasizing and measuring the clients' reaction to our construction teams. It magnified the "self-worth" of construction workers, one of the lowest self-esteem industries on earth. When they began to focus on the needs of our clients, instead of their own issues at work, they enjoyed their day better and actually did a more professional job.

I often say, "If you do what successful people do, you will be successful." That works best when you correctly define what success looks like. I was not that smart, but I emulated the actions and practices of some wise and honest leaders, and that assured my successful life and career.

(continues)

Living the Dream

ENTREPRENEURIAL EXPERIENCES

"Don't Think. Do": So said a stranger to Jeff Curran, founder and CEO of Curran Catalog, a high-end home furnishings company in Seattle, more than 20 years ago. The two men were sitting next to each other on a cross-country flight, and Curran, then 25, had just broken into the catalog business. They got to talking, and Curran spilled his idea for a startup while his neighbor interjected with "devil's-advocate" questions. When the plane landed, the stranger spoke those insightful words. Those words inspired Curran to pour $15,000 of his own cash into launching his company, which has grown into a profitable brand.

"After that plane flight, I pick up [a financial] magazine at my parents' house, and this guy was on the cover," remembers Curran, now 47. The man was mutual-fund maven Mario Gabelli.

Curran still lives by Gabelli's advice. Earlier this year, after learning about profit margins in the high-end car-accessories business, Curran Catalog launched a new product line: designer flooring for collector and European automobiles. "There is such a thing as overthinking a big decision," Curran says. "Sometimes, you just have to get it done."

Sources: As written by April Anthony and Johnny Stites, and adapted from Matt Villano, "That's My Motto," *Entrepreneur*, May 2013, p. 88.

1-3c Entrepreneurial Teams

Our discussion thus far has focused on entrepreneurs who function as individuals, each with his or her own firm. And this is frequently the case. However, entrepreneurial teams can be beneficial, if not essential, particularly in ventures of any substantial size. An **entrepreneurial team** consists of two or more individuals who combine their efforts to function in the capacity of entrepreneurs. In this way, the talents, skills, and resources of two or more entrepreneurs can be concentrated on one endeavor. This very important form of entrepreneurship is discussed at greater length in Chapter 8.

1-3d Social Entrepreneurs

entrepreneurial team
Two or more people who work together as entrepreneurs on one endeavor.

Historically, if someone dreamed of owning a business, the primary objective was to pursue an opportunity that would create personal (mostly financial) benefits for the founder. Also significant, but much less emphasized, was the aim of improving society through economic means—for example, by providing a useful product or service that would make life better for customers, creating jobs for employees who can then take care of their families, and paying taxes to help support the community. But if that same individual had a keen interest in addressing a social need or solving an environmental problem, he or she would most likely have had to launch a not-for-profit organization or to sign on with a governmental agency. Today, fortunately, the choices are no longer mutually exclusive.

An increasing number of small businesses are being launched with the explicit and fundamental purpose of addressing a major social challenge or human need—sometimes in the community where the business is located but also in underdeveloped countries where living conditions are badly in need of improvement. According to the *Global Entrepreneurship Monitor's* "Report on Social Entrepreneurship,"[16] the drive to pursue this form of activity is greater in the United States than in any other country. But it may not surprise you to know that the same study found that the impulse to become a social entrepreneur is strongest for Americans who are between the ages of 25 and 45. Reflecting this trend, an increasing number of universities across the United States are offering courses and even entire degree programs in social entrepreneurship. The wildfire apparently has already been lit.

Small business owners have countless paths they can take when it comes to making a difference in the lives of others, from giving to local schools to participating in mentoring programs for at-risk youth to allowing employees to spend a portion of their on-the-clock hours serving the community organizations they believe in most. But **social entrepreneurship** entails more than shifting resources to serve others. It involves focusing on a social purpose and making it an integral part of the company itself. Social entrepreneurs find ways to weave their social purpose into the very fabric of the ventures they launch.[17]

The topic of social entrepreneurship will be examined in greater depth in Chapter 2. If the idea of pursuing this kind of venture strikes a chord in you, we think it would be wise for you to explore this alternative more exhaustively.

1-3e Women Entrepreneurs

In 2012, there were nearly 9 million privately held women-owned firms in the United States, with an estimated $1.4 trillion in revenues.[18] Between 1997 and 2013, when the number of businesses in the United States increased by 41 percent, the number of women-owned firms increased by 59 percent—a rate almost 1.5 times the national average. Also, publicly traded corporations and privately held majority-owned women corporations were the only businesses that provided a net increase in employment during this time period. Finally, women-owned businesses perform extraordinarily well in the fields of healthcare and educational services.[19]

While women's ownership of private firms has certainly increased in recent years, the entrepreneurial world still holds a lot of potential for women, as their businesses comprise only (1) 30 percent of all U.S. firms, (2) 16 percent of all companies with employees, and (3) 3.8 percent of all revenues.[20] Moreover, women represent fewer than 10 percent of founders of high-growth businesses. Based on these facts, Alicia Robb and Dane Stangler drew the following conclusion:

> *[Given] the long-term pessimism about growth in the United States, and the rising share of women among educated workers, it seems clear that the future of American entrepreneurship and growth is in the hands of women. We need to figure out what will help the country take advantage of this opportunity.*[21]

In the 2014 study, these researchers also identified women's primary motivations for starting their own businesses. Their reasons are not materially different from those of men. Specifically, they:

- Liked the small business culture.
- Had long wanted to own their own business.

social entrepreneurship
Entrepreneurial activity whose goal is to find innovative solutions to social needs, problems, and opportunities.

- Had a business idea and wanted to capitalize on it.
- Did not find working for someone else particularly appealing.
- Wanted to build personal wealth.

The researchers further identified two primary challenges that women entrepreneurs face: (1) a lack of available mentors and advisors, and (2) a financing gap (nearly 80 percent of the women surveyed had to rely on personal savings as their primary funding source).

Regarding the latter challenge, a recent survey of *Inc.* 500/5000 firms identified a difference in financing strategies between women and men who founded high-growth firms. First, men were more than three times as likely as women to access equity financing through private investors. Second, men were more likely than women to use networks of close friends and business acquaintances. However, women and men business owners were similar in their use of bank financing as a source of capital. The net result of the financing gap for women: Men start firms with nearly twice the capital that women do.[22]

Although a woman who wants to own a business may experience challenges not encountered by a man, it's important to understand that women are very competitive business owners. In a study sponsored by the Kauffman Foundation, Alicia Robb and John Watson found no difference in firm performance between companies owned by women and those owned by men. There were no differences between the two groups in failure rates, in profitability, and in the returns earned relative to the risk assumed. The findings indicate that women are just as effective as men when it comes to running profitable, wealth-creating businesses. Based on their findings, the authors offer encouragement to women who aspire to start a business:

> *Women who are contemplating starting a new venture [should] not be discouraged from doing so by a false belief that new ventures initiated by women are less likely to succeed than those initiated by men.*[23]

1-3f Be a Small Business Owner Who Thinks and Acts Like an Entrepreneur

While they are not precisely the same, we will use the terms *small business owner* and *entrepreneur* interchangeably. After all, a business owner is fundamentally different from a salaried employee. The business owner takes risks not assumed by employees and is rewarded or punished financially based on the results he or she can achieve. But we recognize that many small business owners fail to think or act entrepreneurially—identifying and capturing new opportunities to grow the business are not objectives they care to pursue. The choice to grow or not to grow begins with the owner's personal preferences, which ideally should be aligned with his or her life objectives.

What type of opportunity do you want to pursue? In answering this question, you should be intentional. Don't let your business endeavors develop by chance. Consider seeking opportunities that have growth potential and that challenge you to grow personally. You may start small, but we would encourage you to dream big. Think and act entrepreneurially. The late Ewing Marion Kauffman, the founder of Marion Laboratories, offered this encouragement to entrepreneurs and small business owners:

> *You should not choose to be a common company. It is your right to build an uncommon company if you can—to seek the opportunity to compete, to desire to take the calculated risks, to dream, to build—yes, even to fail or succeed.*[24]

Living the Dream

ENTREPRENEURIAL EXPERIENCES

Honoring Women Entrepreneurs

In 2014, the International Council for Small Business honored 10 international women leaders who are making inroads and achieving success in their respective countries. Following is the story of one of these women: Amy George.

Amy George is the CEO and co-founder of the U.S. lifestyle products company, BlueAvocado, which has sought to create simple solutions to combat waste in our everyday lives. In particular, her company focuses on rising landfills and has successfully led its customers in avoiding the use of over 152 million disposables, while simultaneously providing financing for 700 micro-entrepreneurs. George has also steered the company through four years of consecutive year-over-year revenue growth, while sparking retailer relationships with companies such as Whole Foods, The Container Store, Amazon, Target, and Bed Bath & Beyond. The BlueAvocado model utilizes the power of business to drive environmental, social, and economic value through its innovative approach to household goods.

© ROSS HAILEY/MCT/NEWSCOM

Amy George, Blue Avocado.

In addition to her role at BlueAvocado, George has partnered with multinational companies to implement real-time sustainability software, helped microfinance organizations to reach new investors with online tools, and launched a downtown farmers market with the Austin Sustainable Food Center. With a background in entrepreneurship and environmental management, she is truly following her dream with BlueAvocado as she also balances her life as a mother to two young boys.

George co-founded BlueAvocado in 2007 with the simple goal of making it affordable for everyday consumers to reduce their environmental footprint through waste reduction. At the time, San Francisco was one of the first U.S. cities to pass a ban on the use of plastic bags, following in the footsteps of countries such as Australia and Hong Kong. George and her colleagues believed that the rest of the country would soon follow and that an opportunity existed to assist both retailers and consumers in their efforts to be more environmentally conscious. From reusable bags to snack packs, BlueAvocado offers a resourceful and reusable shopping system that people find practical and kind to the environment, food, and the shopper.

George plans to use her spare time expanding the work of Nobel Prize–winning economist Elinor Ostrom, who emphasized the model of B corporations to uplift those who embrace the preservation of natural resources. She also has future plans to launch more businesses that will focus on resource preservation and poverty alleviation.

Source: Adapted from International Council of Small Businesses, "Women Entrepreneurial Leader Profiles," November 19, 2014, http://www.icsb.org/2014/11/19/icsb-women-entrepreneur-leader-profiles, accessed December 20, 2014.

Finally, while we have suggested that an entrepreneur is fundamentally different from a salaried employee, that distinction is not as clear today as it once was. To a large extent, even salaried employees need to think more like an entrepreneur. In fact, we would go so far as to say that in today's world *we are all entrepreneurs.* Make peace with this reality, and your life will be better for it. And we think that you will have more fun along the way.

Living the Dream

ENTREPRENEURIAL EXPERIENCES

My First Step

Jeff Sandefer, a highly successful entrepreneur, leading educator, and the founder of the Acton MBA in Entrepreneurship, tells a fun story and offers some words of encouragement to anyone wanting to be an entrepreneur.

My first step toward an entrepreneurial calling began with my burning desire for air conditioning.

As a teenager, my father wisely insisted that I work summers as a laborer in the oil fields, under an unrelenting West Texas sun. I hated what seemed like meaningless manual labor, the bullying, and the boasting conversations about sex, drugs, and alcohol. But most of all I hated the relentless heat, which started at dawn and made even the wind feel like a blast furnace.

To me, heaven was the inside of an air-conditioned pickup truck, the spot reserved for a foreman, a spot no one was going to give to a teenage boy.

But as I went on with my sweaty work, longing to sit in that position of air-conditioned power, I began to notice things. First, I noticed that all the heavy equipment lying around wasn't needed for the light painting and clean-up work that occupied most of our time, but was nonetheless charged to customers. Then I noticed that my fellow laborers, paid by the hour, had little incentive to do anything other than shirk work and wait for quitting time to come.

So I formed a plan to get into air conditioning. I partnered with my best friend, and we convinced our high school football coaches to go to work for us. They contributed the use of their pickup trucks to haul painting equipment, and we agreed to pay them by the job, not the hour. They, in turn, hired their football players to work for them and paid them the same way. My job became finding customers and overseeing the work. My partner handled the operations.

The hourly workers painted a large metal storage tank in three days. Our crews arrived at dawn, painted until dark, and could finish three tanks a day—a ninefold-productivity gain.

I was seventeen that summer, and my best friend and I made $100,000. More importantly, I got to spend most of my time in air conditioning.

You should know that Sandefer ultimately sold an energy investment firm that had several billion dollars in assets.

Source: Jeff Sandefer and Robert Sirico, *A Field Guide for the Hero's Journey* (Grand Rapids, MI: Acton Institute, 2012), p. 2.

Discuss the importance of understanding your motivations and perceptions related to owning a small business.

1-4 YOUR MOTIVATIONS FOR OWNING A BUSINESS

Before you choose to enter the small business game, you need to think carefully about the person you want to be and how owning a business will help make you that person. In other words, you do not begin with the business; *you begin with you*. Jeff Sandefer, puts it this way: "[W]hen you embark upon a heroic journey—a life filled with meaning and purpose—the first step is to heed the admonition inscribed over the entrance to the Oracle of Delphi in ancient Greece: 'Know Thyself.' Search out who you are, and then you will be equipped to discover your heroic calling."[25]

As we have already said, being an entrepreneur is extremely challenging. There will be times when you will be discouraged, maybe even terrified. Some days, you will wish you had opted for the security (or at least the perception of security) of a regular job in an established company.

Understanding clearly why you want to own a small business and what motivates you is vital to eventually achieving fulfillment through your business. Founders who know what their core values are and what is important to them are more likely to create businesses that they find rewarding. According to Noam Wasserman, an associate professor at Harvard Business School,

> *One of the key things about entrepreneurs is that they have far more potential to make decisions with both head and heart. . . . When you're taking the world on your shoulders, you have to ask yourself, why am I doing this? If you only listen to your head, the decisions you make at every fork in the road can drive you further from your personal promised land.*[26]

You may decide to own a small business because of the influence of family members or friends who have their own businesses. Researchers at Case Western Reserve University's Weatherhead School of Management have found a strong connection between entrepreneurship and genetics. Also, the U.S. Census Bureau reports that half of all small business owners worked in their family's business before founding their own ventures.[27] In other words, they had the opportunity to observe the "entrepreneurial life" up close. Starting a business may also provide an escape from an undesirable job situation. Some individuals become entrepreneurs after being laid off by an employer. Unemployed personnel with experience in professional, managerial, technical, and even relatively unskilled positions often contemplate the possibility of venturing out on their own. Those who started or acquired small businesses as a result of financial hardship or other severely negative conditions have appropriately been called **reluctant entrepreneurs**.

Individuals may also flee the bureaucratic environment of a corporation that seems stifling or oppressive to them. In a survey of 721 office workers, 42 percent had considered quitting their jobs over bureaucratic hassles.[28] Entrepreneurship often provides an attractive alternative for such individuals, who are sometimes called **corporate refugees**.

Michelle Lawton left the corporate world to do her own thing. She had done well as an executive with such firms as Procter & Gamble, Pepperidge Farm, Lavazza Coffee, and Rémy Cointreau. She had also been compensated very well, at least until you consider the long hours she worked. She finally decided she had endured enough of the corporate world. "I was at a point in my life where I was looking for a real shift," Lawton says. She wanted to do something that she was really passionate about and that would allow her to pave her own way moving forward. As her own boss in food and beverage branding, Lawton was able to do things she never could do before, such as lunchtime yoga and Pilates classes. "It's something I can't quantify," explains Lawton. "I've never been healthier. What I'm not gaining in financial rewards, I've gained in personal well-being. It sounds like a cliché, but it's a trade-off."[29]

Being influenced by friends and family or simply wanting to make a change in your current situation is not a sufficient reason to start your own business. You need to understand the specific motivations that will keep you going on the tough days.[30] Chris DeLeenheer, founder of Sunzer Consulting Group in Bangalore, India, and more recently a partner in Rydell Holdings (a group that invests in entrepreneurial companies), describes his early days when starting his first business and what got him through the tough times:

> *In starting my company, it was really challenging. We knew no one, had no reputation in the region, and low initial start-up capital. At times there were long*

reluctant entrepreneur
A person who becomes an entrepreneur as a result of some severe hardship.

corporate refugee
A person who becomes an entrepreneur to escape an undesirable job situation.

days with what felt like little return, but the journey has been a rich experience. Three things kept me going: a drive to win, determination not to give up, and the discipline to work on the right stuff.[31]

The point is, it's vitally important that you understand your personal motivations before you get into the small business game.

1-4a Types of Entrepreneurial Motivations

A recent Harris poll inquiring into the reasons entrepreneurs give for owning a company includes the following: (1) to improve financial well-being (73%), (2) to be the boss (41%), and (3) to follow a passion (22%).[32] We believe that there are four fundamental reasons, which incorporate those listed in the Harris poll: personal fulfillment, personal satisfaction, independence, and financial rewards. These motivations, along with specific examples of each, are shown in Exhibit 1.1 and discussed in the following sections.

PERSONAL FULFILLMENT

Owning a business should provide significant personal fulfillment. If it doesn't, then you should look elsewhere. All other motivations will not be enough in the really tough times—and those times are sure to come. Apple co-founder Steve Jobs said it well: "[T]he only way to do great work is to love what you do. If you haven't found it yet, keep looking. Don't settle. As with all matters of the heart, you'll know when you find it."[33] If you want to get started on the right foot, we suggest that the core reason for becoming an entrepreneur and owning your own business should be *to make the world a better place*. L. John Doerr, one of the most famous venture capitalists of all time, inspired the phrase "make meaning," suggesting that the most impactful and

EXHIBIT 1.1 Entrepreneurial Motivations

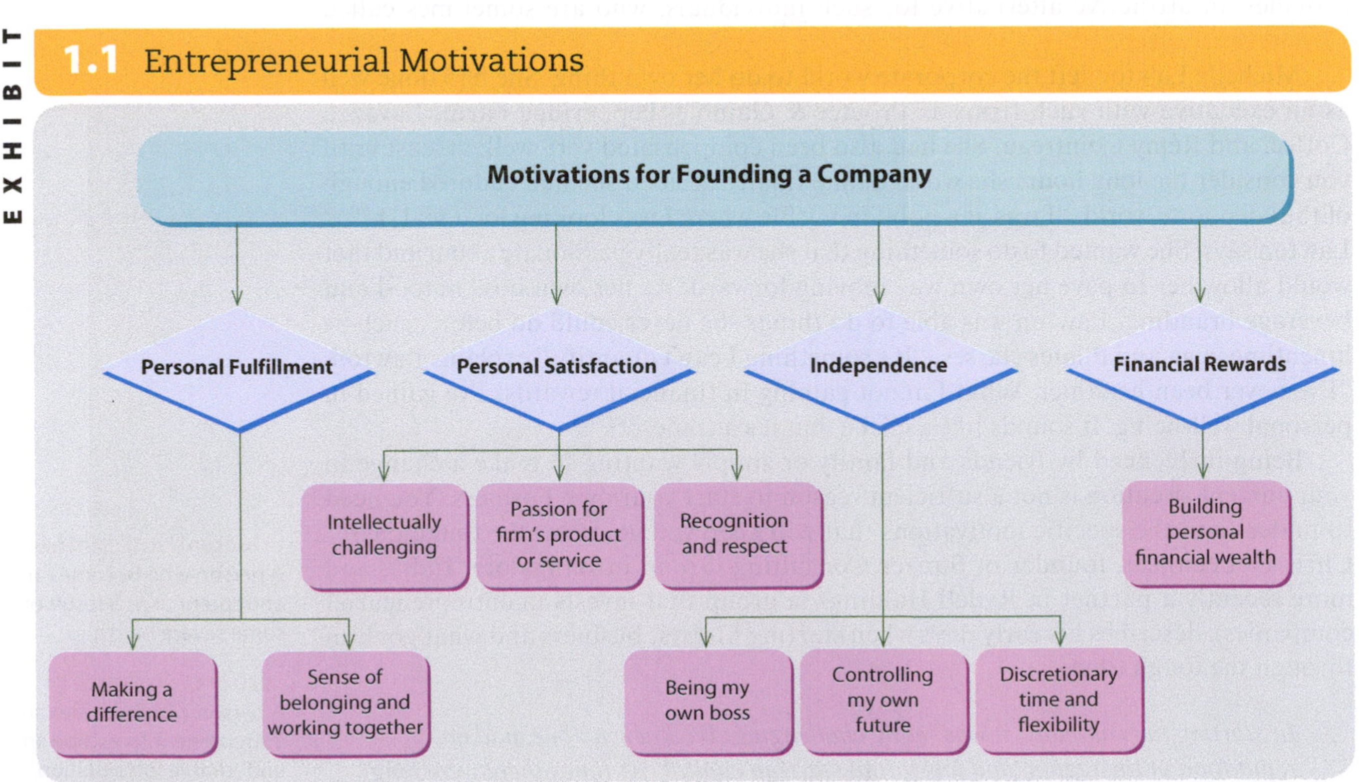

sustainable businesses are built on such a foundation.[34] Your first goal should be to create a product or service that improves life for others. Only when your company is about something more significant than yourself, will you have a sense that what you are doing is meaningful and well worth the effort.

Entrepreneurs are some of the most giving people we know. In fact, the names on many university buildings are those of entrepreneurs who have given back to their alma maters. Bill Waugh, the founder of Casa Bonita, a very successful chain of Mexican food restaurants that includes Taco Bueno, sought to make a difference by providing his company's resources to not-for-profit organizations. He said, "My company is my base for helping others."

Small business owners usually don't—and shouldn't—expect anything in return for their community stewardship. It should be about others, not yourself. Good may come from what you do, and you will most likely reap benefits, but that should not be your reason for giving to the community. In a Gallup Poll of over 100,000 working adults, researchers examined the relationship between work and happiness for different occupational groups. They developed an overall index of contentment based on six criteria: emotional health, physical health, job satisfaction, healthy behaviors, access to basic needs, and self-reports on overall life quality. Business owners were found to outrank all other occupational groups in terms of overall contentment.[35]

Compare these results with a more recent Gallup poll asking employees if they were excited about their jobs. The researchers found that 52 percent of all full-time workers are not involved in, enthusiastic about, or committed to their work. Another 18 percent were "actively disengaged," suggesting that they could even be undermining their company's mission and goals. That leaves only 30 percent of workers who feel excited about their jobs. (It's important to note that the cost of employee disengagement to the economy is estimated to be about $500 billion per year!) Finally, the survey results found that employees at companies with 10 or fewer employees reported higher engagement levels than those in larger groups.[36] This finding certainly suggests that small business owners can better personalize morale-boosting efforts in more intimate groups. Richard Duncan, president of Rich Duncan Construction in Salem, Oregon, offers a possible explanation for the Gallup findings:

> *Small businesses can encourage their employees to feel that they are a part of the team that not only cares for them as individuals, but also rewards them for their efforts. A small-business owner can also offer a better opportunity for employees to feel that the top decision maker has an open-door policy and readily welcomes the employee's input on business matters.*[37]

We can reasonably surmise that personal fulfillment is not limited to the entrepreneur but extends to the employees of small companies as well. Working as a team provides a sense of belonging for both owner-managers and employees. They come to understand that they can do nothing of significance alone. It can be a win-win for everyone if done well.

PERSONAL SATISFACTION

Closely related to personal fulfillment is the personal satisfaction that business owners frequently experience from their businesses. For one thing, entrepreneurs feel rewarded in working with a particular product or providing a service and being good at it. They find great satisfaction in being the best at what they do. Rick Davis, founder and CEO of Davaco, a Dallas-based company, says, "There is nothing else I would rather do. I love the challenges, working with others to see our dreams come true, and making a difference in the community. It is fun."[38]

Entrepreneurs are also energized by enjoyable associations within their businesses. There is a reward that comes from helping their people develop. Jack Griggs, CEO of Southwestern Bancorp, Inc., and chairman of the board of Texas Heritage Bank, believes that one of his primary roles is to help his employees become better at what they do. He takes great pride in the number of his employees who have gone on to great careers, even if not at one of his banks. Also, because they share similar experiences, business owners enjoy friendships with other business owners, and they learn from one another. Finally, if they are visible within the community, small business owners can garner the respect of those who live there. So for many entrepreneurs, the personal satisfaction received from business is no small matter in their lives.

Understand also that the satisfaction of owning a business is not limited to the young. An increasing number of baby boomers are starting businesses, even in their 50s or even 60s. For example, Mary Liz Curtin and her husband started Leon & Lulu, a destination lifestyle store in Detroit, Michigan. She realizes that the risk of losing their investment could be more devastating at their age and should be considered carefully. But she cannot imagine doing anything else:

> *In the nine years since we opened, we have purchased a second building to expand our selling space from 15,000 to 23,000 square feet as well as an offsite warehouse when we could have been sailing with the seniors, playing bridge or getting discounts at the movies. We have no plans to retire and are lucky to be healthy enough to keep up the hectic pace.*[39]

INDEPENDENCE

Many people have a strong desire to make their own decisions, take risks, and reap the rewards. They find it important to be free to make their own choices in their work. In other words, the more control they have over their work, the happier they are.

Business owners also have discretion about when they want to engage in nonbusiness activities. They have the freedom to decide when to work, when to be with family, and when to be engaged in community activities in ways that employees frequently cannot be.

Aimee Marnell likes this aspect of small-business ownership. She and her husband, John, were in the same industry for several years and finally got tired of being directly under management. So they started Carlot-Solutions in Austin, Texas. Marnell explains:

> *We didn't have a lot of savings, but we had knowledge about cars, so we started an auto repair business. We made connections quickly and had more work than we could handle or were prepared for.*[40]

When asked what she enjoys most about having her own business, she replies, "I love the freedom to make choices. Whether I succeed or fail, I believe in what I do."[41]

Of course, independence does not guarantee an easy life. Most entrepreneurs work very hard and for long hours. They must remember that the customer is, ultimately, the boss. But they do have the satisfaction of making their own decisions within the constraints required to build a successful business.

FINANCIAL REWARDS

As a general rule, when businesses are profitable, everyone benefits. Jobs are created, taxes are paid, and charities receive donations. Furthermore, like any other job or career, starting a business is a way to earn money and make ends meet. Of course, some entrepreneurs earn *lots* of money. In *The Millionaire Next Door*, Thomas Stanley and William Danko note that self-employed people are four times more likely to be millionaires than are those who work for others.[42]

How much money should an entrepreneur expect to get in return for starting and running a business? Making a profit is certainly necessary for a firm's survival. Many entrepreneurs work night and day (literally, in some cases) just to generate enough profits to survive; others receive a modest income for their time and investment. From an economic perspective, however, the financial return of a business should compensate its owner not only for his or her investment of personal time (in the form of a salary equivalent) but also for any personal money invested in the business (in the form of cash distributed to the owner and the increased value of the business) and for the risk he or she is taking.

A significant number of entrepreneurs are, no doubt, highly motivated by the prospect of making money. While some entrepreneurs do become rich quickly, the majority do not. Therefore, a more reasonable goal would be to "get rich slowly." Wealth will most likely come, provided the business is economically viable and the owner has the patience and determination to make it happen. When it comes to making money, keep in mind the adage "Money is not a problem, but money without wisdom is a problem."

Develop Good Mentors in Business and Life

Seek out **mentors**—personal mentors *and* business mentors—as soon as you can. You cannot start too early (preferably when you are still in school). They will be *very* helpful when you are starting a business. Most entrepreneurs also find mentors along the way, individuals who can offer guidance based on their experience in a given field. Mentors can show you how to avoid mistakes. They want you to succeed, and they support your efforts. Mentors will also encourage you on those days when you want to throw in the towel.

While we can suggest possible motivations, only you can know why owning your own business is appealing *and* rewarding. Undoubtedly, there will not be just one motivation, but multiple ones—even one or more that we have not discussed. Whatever the reasons, it is wise to identify what truly motivates you to be an entrepreneur. It will help you understand what is important to you and give you guidance when making decisions. Clayton Christensen, a professor at the Harvard Business School, offers wise advice:

> *It is impossible to have a meaningful conversation about happiness without understanding what makes you tick. When we find ourselves stuck in unhappy careers—and even unhappy lives—it is often the result of a fundamental misunderstanding of what really motivates us.*[43]

To conclude, we advise you to do a bit of self-reflection to come to understand your own reason(s) for wanting to own a business. Only then can you align your own personal mission with the first steps you take in becoming an entrepreneur.

1-4b Understanding Your Paradigm

Knowing your motivations is important to anyone interested in starting a business. But that is not enough. You also need to understand if your perceptions of what it takes to be successful in business are accurate. In *The 7 Habits of Highly Effective People*, Stephen Covey teaches that to make important changes in our lives, we need to change from the *inside-out*. He says that having a positive attitude or working harder is not enough. Instead, we have to change how we fundamentally see a situation, or what he calls a **paradigm shift**.[44] So the question for someone wanting to start a business is, "What do you believe it will take for you to create a successful business?" Your answer to this question will depend largely on your past experiences, which have a significant influence on your paradigm (the framework for how you see the situation).

In his book, *The E-Myth Revisited: Why Most Businesses Don't Work and What to Do About It*, Michael Gerber describes three paradigms, or what he calls *personalities*, that come into play when a person is starting a business: the technician personality, the

mentor
A knowledgeable person who can offer guidance based on experience in a given field.

paradigm shift
A change in how we fundamentally see a situation.

manager personality, and the entrepreneur personality.[45] He contends that everyone exhibits these personalities to some varying degree, and successful business owners need a balance of all three. Let's briefly look at the three personalities, which are shown graphically in Exhibit 1.2. As you read about these personalities, consider how you would describe yourself.

THE TECHNICIAN PERSONALITY

If you start an auto repair business because you love working on cars or a pie shop because your friends say you make the best pies they have ever eaten, you most likely have what Gerber calls a technician personality. The **technician personality** is usually a steady worker, experienced at *doing* what he or she knows best. The technician dislikes managing, wanting instead to be left alone to get the job done. He or she lives in the moment, without thinking of the future. To the technician, starting a business may be both a dream-come-true and a nightmare at the same time. The thought of no longer being managed and having total control over what gets done is exciting, but the need to be organized and think strategically is daunting.

A technician's approach to business decision making can be characterized in the following ways:

- Paternalistic (he or she guides the businesses much as he or she might guide family members).
- Reluctant to delegate authority.
- Defining marketing strategy in terms of the traditional components of price, quality, and company reputation.

EXHIBIT 1.2 Understanding Your Business Paradigm

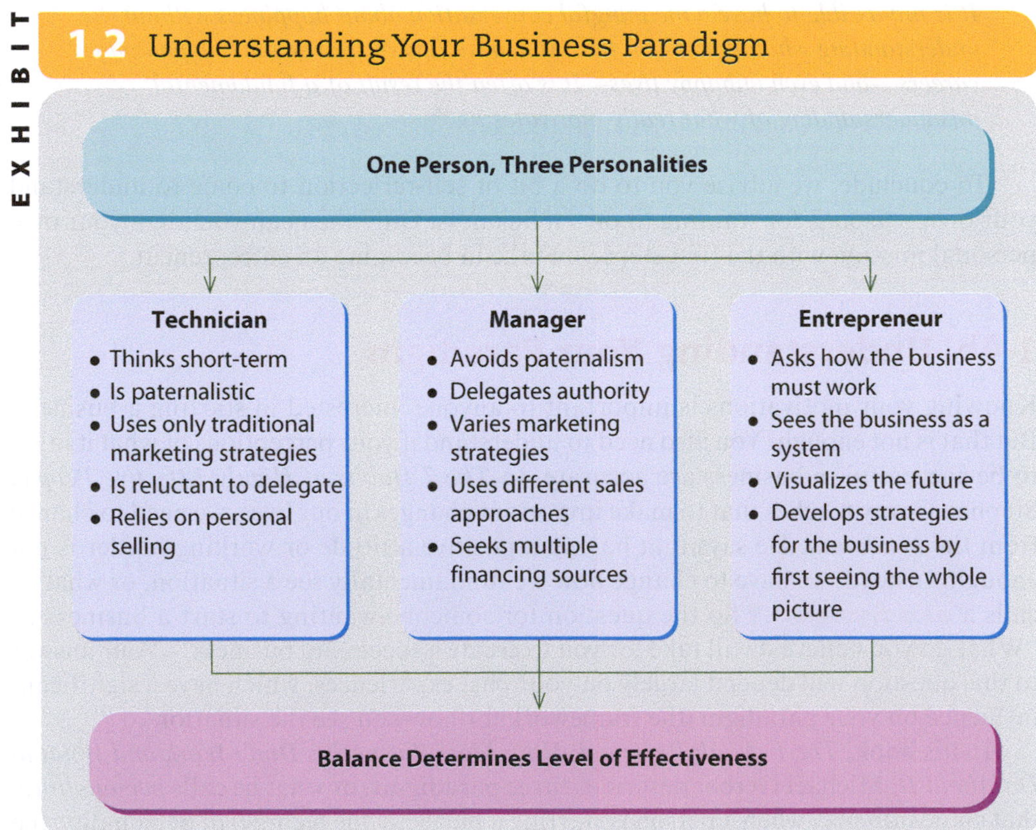

technician personality A personality that focuses on an already developed technical skill, wants to be left alone to get the job done, and is primarily concerned about the present.

- Focusing on sales efforts that are primarily personal.
- Short-term thinking, with little planning for future growth or change.

The technician is prone to making a fatal assumption. According to Gerber, the technician thinks that "if you understand the technical work of a business, you understand the business that does that technical work.... But the technical work of a business and a business that does that technical work are two totally different things!"[46]

THE MANAGER PERSONALITY

An individual with a **manager personality** is pragmatic, assuming responsibility for the planning, order, and predictability of the business. In Gerber's words, "The manager is the part of us that goes to Sears and buys stacking plastic boxes, takes them back to the garage, and systematically stores all the various mixed nuts, bolts, and screws in their own carefully identified drawer."[47] A manager personality tends to do the following:

- Avoid paternalism.
- Delegate authority as necessary for growth.
- Employ diverse marketing strategies.
- Use different types of sales efforts.
- Obtain original financing from more than two sources.

In contrast to a technician, a manager's job is to prepare the business for growth by educating herself or himself sufficiently, in order to ensure that the company's foundation and structure can carry the additional weight. The manager's boundary is defined by how many technicians she or he can supervise effectively or how many subordinates she or he can organize into a productive effort. A small building contractor and developer who adopts a relatively sophisticated approach to management, including detailed accounting and budgeting, precise bidding, and thorough market research has a manager personality.

THE ENTREPRENEUR PERSONALITY

The **entrepreneur personality** takes an idea and turns it into an opportunity. This personality does not look at the work that a business does. Instead, the entrepreneur examines how the business does what it is intended to do. In this way, the entrepreneur is able to see the big picture and develop strategies that will help the venture flourish. According to Gerber, this personality needs to be harnessed effectively, or it will wreak havoc by trying to pull the business in many directions at the same time.

The entrepreneurial personality tends to do the following:

- Ask the question, "How must the business work?"
- See the business as a system for producing outside results for the customer, and in so doing, producing profits.
- Start with a picture of a well-defined future and then attempt to change the present to match the vision.
- Develop strategies for the business by first seeing the whole picture.

The entrepreneur looks at the business as the product. In this way, the business is tailored to meet the needs of the customer and not the needs of the business owner (as is the case with a technician-founded business).

manager personality
A personality that is pragmatic and likes order and planning operations.

entrepreneur personality
A personality that focuses on the business as a whole and providing results for the customer.

We all have a bit of each of these personalities. However, for most of us, one personality dominates the others to the detriment of the business *and, possibly, the owner's personal life as well.* Thus, Gerber offers the following counsel:

> *Without all three of these personalities being given the opportunity, the freedom, the nourishment they each need to grow, your business cannot help but mirror your own lopsidedness. . . . And if they were equally balanced, we would be describing an incredibly competent individual. The entrepreneur would be free to forge ahead into new areas of interest; the manager would be solidifying the base of operations; and the technician would be doing his technical work. Each would derive satisfaction for the work he does best, serving the whole in the most productive way.*[48]

So, if you don't understand who you are as a business owner, you may think that the business is the problem, when in reality you are the problem. You need to know your motivations for wanting to be a business owner and how your past experiences affect how you see the business. By first understanding yourself, you can potentially avoid a lot of disappointment and long-lasting problems.

Living the Dream

ENTREPRENEURIAL EXPERIENCES

LeiLei Secor: NFIB Young Entrepreneur of the Year

Market research helped LeiLei Secor of Hagaman, New York, launch an online jewelry shop that's on its way to earning her six figures.

At age 9, Secor started making braided friendship bracelets. In her teen years, she branched out into beaded and macramé jewelry. When, as a high school junior, she needed a summer job, she thought, "Why can't I sell my jewelry online?"

In July 2012, Secor opened a shop on Etsy.com, which allows artists to sell their products. Her shop, Designed by LeiLei, specializes in handmade wire rings and earrings. Just two years after the business launched, her profits were close to six figures, which will help finance her college education.

Armed with self-taught techniques (Secor learned the art of wire jewelry-making on YouTube) and a desire to set herself apart in an exceptionally competitive arena (a million vendors sold goods on Etsy in 2013), she researched photography, marketing, and search engine optimization by comparing successful and unsuccessful Etsy shops and noting their different tactics. She uses a high-quality DSLR camera and natural light to achieve simple, elegant photography. Fans post the photos to sites such as Pinterest and Wanelo, generating a viral marketing buzz. As a result, Secor has sold more than 8,000 items, most priced around $10.

"LeiLei's business has a clear marketing plan, incredible growth, a viral interest from potential customers, and lots of additional upside potential," says nominator and NFIB member Thomas Ulbrich, assistant dean and executive director of the University at Buffalo School of Management Center for Entrepreneurial Leadership, and founder of Mow More Supplies in Lancaster, New York.

Secor's jewelry-making and shipping supplies accompanied her to her dorm room at the University of Virginia, where she is studying business. She plans to invest around 12 hours a week in making jewelry and fulfilling orders. After graduation, she hopes to work in finance or start another business.

"My Etsy shop has taught me not to shy away from any opportunity," Secor says. "It has made me fall in love with the entrepreneurial spirit."

Source: Adapted from Kristen Lund, "Meet the Young Entrepreneurs Who Will Run Tomorrow's Top Businesses," http://www.nfib.com/article/meet-the-young-entrepreneurs-who-might-run-tomorrows-top-businesses-mybiz-so2014-66444, accessed September 15, 2014, pp. 12.

1-5 THE ENTREPRENEUR'S COMPETITIVE EDGE

LO 1-5 Describe five potential competitive advantages of small entrepreneurial companies over large firms.

How is it that small and entrepreneurial firms can hold their own and often gain an edge over successful, more powerful businesses? The answer lies in the ability of new and smaller firms to exploit opportunities. If a business can make its product or service cheaper, faster, and better, then it can be competitive. Small companies—if well managed—are just as able as larger firms to develop strategies that offer a competitive advantage.

In this section, we will take a look at some ways in which new firms can gain a competitive advantage. In Chapter 3, we'll elaborate on strategies for exploiting these potential advantages and capturing the business opportunities they make possible.

1-5a Integrity and Responsibility

The beginning point of any competitive advantage begins with a commitment to integrity. In order to maintain a strong competitive advantage, it is essential that a business owner add a solid reputation for honesty and dependability to good customer service and excellent product quality. In fact, the quickest way to lose a competitive advantage is to act without regard for others—or worse, to act dishonestly. We all respond positively to evidence of integrity because we all have, at times, been taken advantage of when buying a product or service.

Consistently operating with integrity can set a small business apart as being trustworthy at a time when stories of corporate greed and corruption abound. Above all else, the core values of the entrepreneur, as reflected in what she or he says and does, determine the culture within a business. Others will do business with a company only when they feel that they can trust that company. Trust is the foundation of all relationships, including business relationships. Chapter 2 discusses the critical importance of integrity and its role in entrepreneurship.

1-5b Customer Focus

Business opportunities exist for those who can produce products and services desired by customers. Small companies are particularly adept at competing when they commit to a strong customer focus. Good customer service can be provided by a business of any size. However, in many instances, small businesses have a greater potential than larger firms to achieve this goal. If properly managed, small entrepreneurial companies have the advantage of being able to serve customers directly and effectively, avoiding the layers of bureaucracy and corporate policies that tend to stifle employee initiative. In many cases, customers are personally acquainted with the entrepreneur and other key people in the small business.

Jerry Kwok, the CEO of Spectrum Label Corporation in Hayward, California, provides an example of an entrepreneur who has a strong customer focus. His firm manufactures the labels used on packages in the food, pharmaceutical, and nutritional products industries, among others. He has used data and forecasting to manage inventory and make his business a vital link in the supply chain for his clients. In his words:

> *For us to stay competitive, we have to be able to provide a product that is not just a commodity—one that can't be outsourced where customers can deal with long lead times. We're in printing, but the customers we support typically have a very short lead time or no lead time. We are delivering labels in a day or two.*[49]

Not all small enterprises manage to excel in customer service. But many do make it happen. Having a small number of customers and having a close relationship with them makes customer service a powerful tool for entrepreneurial businesses. We will provide further discussion of this subject in Chapter 14.

1-5c Quality Performance

There is no reason that a small business needs to take a back seat to larger firms when it comes to achieving quality in operations. We frequently talk to owners of small businesses whose operations not only equal the quality performance of larger firms but, in fact, also surpass the performance of the giants.

No finer example of quality performance can be found than MFI International Manufacturing in El Paso, Texas, owned by Lance and Cecilia Levine. A visitor to MFI can feel the Levines' passion for quality. As small business owners, they can insist on high levels of quality without experiencing the frustration of a large-company CEO who may have to push a quality philosophy through many layers of bureaucracy. The Levines are convinced that a small business owner should have no fears about being able to compete when it comes to quality. It just needs to be part of the business culture.

In general, quality is mostly independent of firm size. But if there is an advantage, it most often goes to the smaller business. As a small business owner, you should not accept anything less than the highest-quality performance. An uncompromising commitment to quality will move you a long way on the road to having a competitive advantage relative to other firms in your industry.

1-5d Innovation

How the world has changed! When Bill Clinton was president of the United States, hardly anyone—with the exception of a small number of people in the government and academia—had e-mail. Today, billions of people send hundreds of millions of messages, share 20 million photos, and exchange at least $15 trillion in goods and services *every minute.*[50] Innovation, both in products or services and in competitive strategies, is within the reach of the small business in ways that were not thought possible a few years ago. The SBA's Office of Advocacy has a history of funding research that documents the role, nature, and importance of innovation and technological breakthrough by small firms. Office of Advocacy research shows that small businesses outperform their larger counterparts in producing more patents per employee (a measure of innovation). Small firm patents also outperform those of larger firms along a number of measures, including growth, citation, and originality. Small "patenting firms" produce 16.5 times more patents per employee than large firms do, and these patents are twice as likely as those from large firms to be among the 1 percent most cited by others in their patent applications.[51] Most of the radical inventions of the last century, such as the computer and the pacemaker, came from small companies, not large ones. And this will not change.

Research departments of big businesses tend to focus on improving existing products. Creative ideas may be side tracked because they are not related to existing product lines or because they are unusual. But preoccupation with an existing product can obscure the value of a new idea. In his book, *The Innovator's Dilemma,* Clayton Christensen documents how large established companies have missed major transformations in a number of industries—computers (mainframes to PCs), telephones (landline to mobile), photography (film to digital), stock markets (floor trading to online trading), and many others.[52] For this reason, more than a few large companies acquire or at least engage in a joint venture with small technological businesses. Some large companies and their plans for joining with smaller firms are shown in Exhibit 1.3.

When discussing the role of entrepreneurs in innovation, Amar Bhide, a noted business researcher at Columbia University, describes how entrepreneurs excel at developing others' ideas. Bhide advises us not to equate innovation with technological breakthroughs and scientists in white coats, because few small businesses can afford the luxury of spending large amounts of money on research and development. Instead, he contends that entrepreneurs are better able to take inventions or innovations developed elsewhere and put them into use, which requires marketing, sales, and organization.[53] In Bhide's opinion, these latter activities are just as innovative as creating something in a science lab. The mere fact that a small business is not "high tech" should not be taken to mean that it is not innovative; it may be just the opposite.

Access to technology has also helped smaller firms compete. It has clearly leveled the playing field with larger companies. Sophisticated technology platforms, once

EXHIBIT **1.3** Gaining Access to Innovation

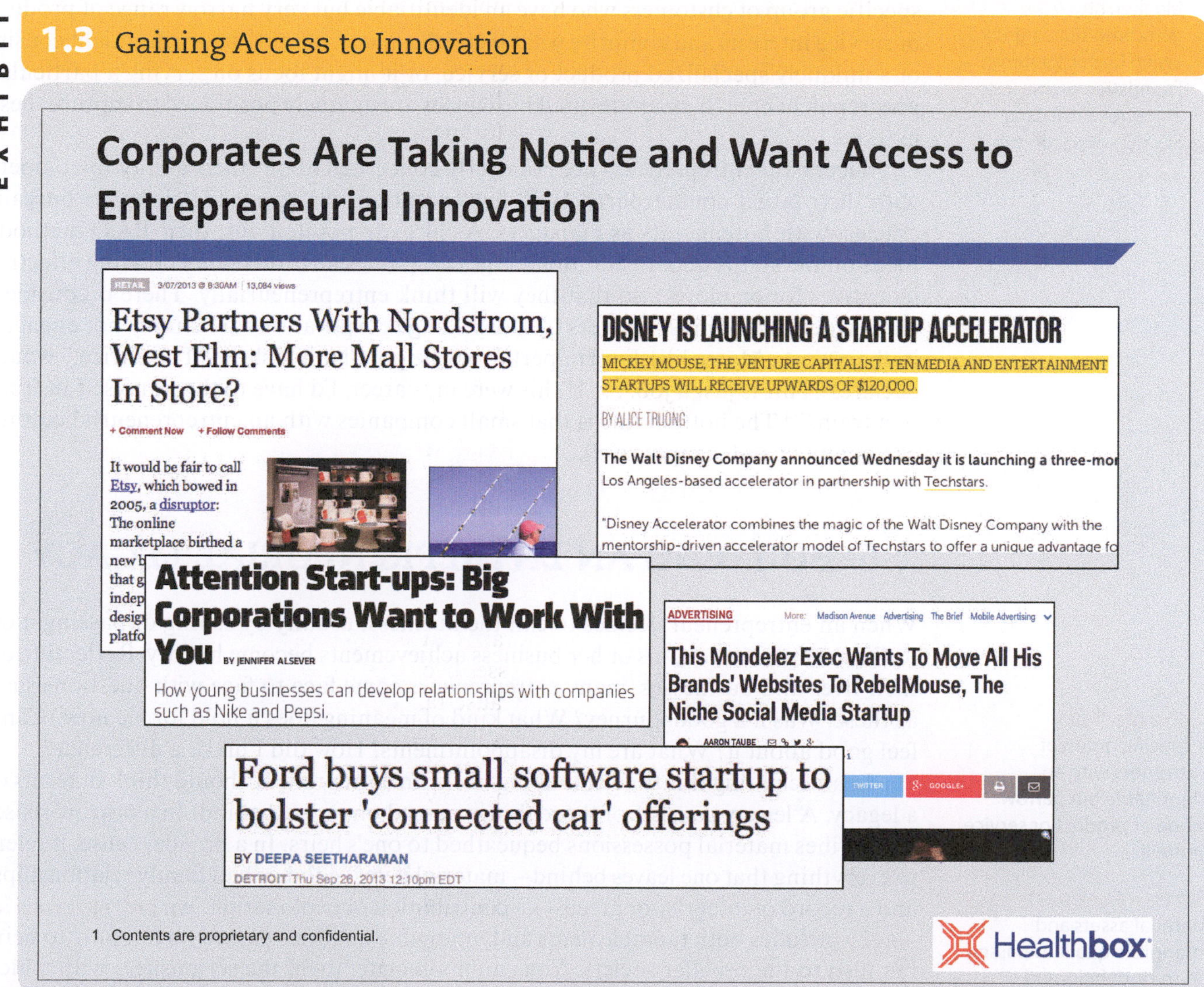

Source: From speech delivered by Nina Nashif, CEO of Healthbox, to the United States Association of Small Businesses and Entrepreneurs (USASBE), Tampa, Florida, January 24, 2015.

Websites for Small Business Owners

Every small business owner should take advantage of the following websites:

- U.S. Small Business Administration: www.sba.gov
- National Federation of Independent Business: www.nfib.com
- Global Entrepreneurship Monitor: http://gemconsortium.org/docs
- Ewing Marion Kauffman Foundation: www.entrepreneurship.org
- SCORE: www.score.org

accessible only to large businesses, are now available at prices small companies can afford. In fact, the Web is full of free tools to help entrepreneurs start, run, and grow their businesses.

As an example of using existing technology to innovate, consider the current practice among many small businesses to take advantage of "location-based social networking." Restaurants, retailers, and other types of small businesses are signing up for services provided by such companies as Facebook and Foursquare that allow consumers equipped with smartphones to "check-in" and broadcast their current store location to their entire social network. This type of viral marketing is an inexpensive and easy way for small businesses to get their names out in the marketplace in real time and to engage other consumers who might be perusing their social networks. While these small businesses did not create this technology, they are clearly being innovative in using it.

1-5e Niche Markets

Almost all small businesses try to shield themselves from competition by targeting a specific group of customers who have an identifiable but very narrow range of product or service interests and comprise what is called a **niche market**. The niche might consist of a uniquely specialized product or service, or it might focus on serving a particular geographical area. Numerous small businesses are uniquely positioned to capture these markets.

Successful entrepreneurs are not overly concerned about their ability to compete with their larger counterparts. With few exceptions, large corporations are bureaucracies, with bureaucrats as managers. As already pointed out, their R&D methods focus on the status quo. In addition, large companies have difficulty creating effective incentives for employees so that they will think entrepreneurially. There is considerable evidence that most workers in today's huge corporations are simply not engaged in their work. Many, like Jim Halpert from the popular TV show "The Office," would declare, "This is just a job. . . . If this were my career, I'd have to throw myself in front of a train."[54] The bottom line is that small companies with an entrepreneurial culture can compete and compete well.

1-6 BUILDING AN ENTREPRENEURIAL LEGACY

When an entrepreneur decides to exit the business, usually by selling or passing it on to the next generation, his or her business achievements become history. Reflecting on their lives and businesses, many entrepreneurs come face to face with questions such as these: Was it a good journey? What kind of meaning does it hold for me now? Can I feel good about it? What are my disappointments? How did I make a difference?

In anticipating this time of looking back, an entrepreneur should think in terms of a legacy. A legacy consists of those things passed on or left behind. In a narrow sense, it describes material possessions bequeathed to one's heirs. In a broader sense, it refers to everything that one leaves behind—material items, good or bad family relationships, and a record of integrity or greed—of contribution or exploitation. An **entrepreneurial legacy** includes both tangible items and intangible qualities passed on not only to heirs but also to the broader society. You can appreciate, then, the seriousness with which the entrepreneur needs to consider the kind of legacy he or she is building.

niche market
A specific group of customers with an identifiable but narrow range of product or service interests.

entrepreneurial legacy
Material assets and intangible qualities passed on to both heirs and society.

It is easy for entrepreneurs to get caught up in activities, working harder and harder to keep up with the busy pace of life. Ultimately, such entrepreneurs may find their business accomplishments overshadowed by the neglect or sacrifice of something more important to them. It's possible to score points in the wrong game or win battles in the wrong war.

Ed Bonneau revolutionized the distribution of sunglasses in the United States and eventually dominated that market with his highly successful business. While growing the firm, Bonneau purchased Pennsylvania Optical (with its patents and contracts with Walmart and Kmart) and industry giant Foster Grant (with its patents and manufacturing divisions). Then, Bonneau sold the business and walked away from it all. From a business standpoint, his was a huge entrepreneurial success story. However, in a comment on how he'd like to be remembered, Bonneau downplayed his financial wealth:

> *I would hope that they knew something else besides that I once ran the biggest sunglass company in the world. That's not the number one thing that I'd want to be known for. It's okay, but I'd much rather have that final assessment made by my kids and have them say, "He was a terrific dad." I never wanted to sacrifice my family or my church for my business.*[55]

And Bonneau's advice to younger entrepreneurs follows a similar theme:

> *Take your faith and your family with you when you go into business, and keep that balance in your life. Because when you get to be 60 years old and you look back over your life, if all you have is the biggest sunglass company in the world and a pot full of money in the bank . . . it won't be enough. Your life is going to be hollow, and you can't go back and redo it.*[56]

When he was an MBA student, Ty Findley talked about his father, Steven Findley, who founded and was CEO of Titan Dynamics. Ty explains, "His legacy as an entrepreneur was not limited to building a company. He also wanted to make a difference through his family and community involvement. Dad managed to balance operating his business with raising and supporting a family of eight children." Steven Findley adds, "It means a lot to know that my children have always felt loved by their father, and that they are growing into individuals who will hopefully have a positive impact on the world."[57]

In entrepreneurial terms, what constitutes a worthy legacy? One issue is the nature of the endeavor itself. For most entrepreneurs looking back on their careers, *fulfillment* requires that their businesses have been constructive or positive in their impact. The late Bernard Rapaport, a highly successful, principled, and generous entrepreneur, stressed the importance of the means a person takes to achieve a given end. "Whatever it is you want to achieve," he said, "*how* you achieve it is more important than if you achieve it." Reflecting on his life and legacy at the age of 93, he said, "What do I want to do? I want to save the world."[58] Such idealism can guide an entrepreneur into many endeavors that are useful to our economic system and even society, either during their business life or afterward.

It is the authors' deepest hope that your journey in owning your own business and being an entrepreneur—if you should choose to take that step—will be a richly rewarding experience, not only financially but also in the other important facets of your life. Above all, we hope that your legacy will bring both satisfaction *and* fulfillment for you and the important people in your life.

Learning to Think about Resources

In a small business, there is no more important issue than efficiently managing resources. Thus, learning how to think about resources—information technology, money, people, facilities, and even bartering—may mean the difference between success and failure. To help you develop this skill set, we recommend Nancy Lublin's *Zilch: The Power of Zero in Business* (New York, NY: Penguin, 2010). The book is based on Lublin's experiences as the leader of an organization that helps teenagers effect social change and her interviews with individuals she calls the "rock stars" of not-for-profit organizations.

Living the Dream

ENTREPRENEURIAL EXPERIENCES

Watch Out for This Myth

In the early years of a business, it often feels as though there is never enough time to do everything that needs to be done. So, you just work harder *and* longer. Wayne Rivers, a writer for *The Wall Street Journal* and co-founder of the Family Business Institute, remembers hearing the following advice from a speaker at a conference he attended: "One of the key ingredients is to work harder and longer than any of your employees. If they don't see you working hard, they won't work hard either, and they won't respect you." According to Rivers,

This is a powerful and pervasive myth. The idea that a 100-hour workweek is the only way to earn respect and be productive is simply ridiculous!

He wisely explains that what is of primary importance is not the time you put into the business, but rather the results that you produce through people. The true test of success according to Rivers is focusing less on yourself and more on developing talent in your organization.

Vivek Wadhwa offers similar advice, after learning the hard way. Wadhwa, a successful entrepreneur, had taken his company public and revived another but then had a heart attack at the age of 45. He urges entrepreneurs to have regular medical checkups, exercise faithfully, and learn to relax:

You may not believe in anything called a work-life balance, but your body certainly does.

Rivers and Wadhwa offer sound advice for anyone daring to be an entrepreneur.

© G-STOCKSTUDIO/SHUTTERSTOCK.COM

Sources: Wayne Rivers, "Entrepreneurs: Stop Working So Hard!" *The Wall Street Journal*, http://www.wsj.com/articles/whats-the-worst-business-advice-these-entrepreneurs-ever-heard-1409749444?autologin=y, accessed December 29, 2014; and "Entrepreneurs Anonymous," *The Economist*, September 3, 2014, http://www.economist.com/node/21618816/print, accessed January 3, 2015.

1-7 WHERE TO FROM HERE?

An airplane pilot not only controls the plane during take-off but also flies it and lands it. Similarly, entrepreneurs not only launch firms but also "fly" them; that is, they manage their firm's subsequent operation. In this book, you will find a discussion of the entire entrepreneurial process. It begins in the remainder of Part 1 (Chapter 2) with an examination of the fundamental values of the entrepreneur. Parts 2 and 3 look at a firm's basic strategy, the various types of entrepreneurial ventures, and the initial planning that is required for business startups. Parts 4 through 6 deal with the marketing and management of a growing business, including its human resources, operations, and finances.

1-1. Explain the importance of small business and entrepreneurship in our society.

- Entrepreneurs who start and lead small businesses make a significant contribution to the economy and to quality of life.
- There are 27.8 million small businesses in the United States with fewer than 500 employees, which account for 99.7 percent of all businesses—and 90 percent with fewer than 20 employees!
- Fifty-five million people work at small businesses, representing 49 percent of all employees and 42 percent of all salaries paid to employees.
- Small enterprises hire 43 percent of all high-tech employees (scientists, engineers, computer programmers, and others).
- Many small companies have been going global, representing 97 percent of all exporters.
- About one-fourth of the 23.5 million military veterans in the United States are interested in starting or buying their own business.

1-2. Distinguish between the terms *small business* and *entrepreneurial opportunity*.

- Definitions of *small business* are arbitrary, but we focus on firms that are small (fewer than 100 employees) compared to the largest firms in the industry, have mostly localized operations, are financed by a small number of individuals, and have growth potential.
- An *entrepreneurial opportunity* is an economically attractive and timely opportunity that creates value both for prospective customers and for the firm's owners. Entrepreneurs relentlessly pursue an opportunity, in either a new or an existing enterprise, to create value while assuming both the risk and the reward for their efforts. They generally think differently about resources than do employee-managers. They even try to use other people's resources, which is called bootstrapping.

1-3. Explain the basic characteristics of entrepreneurs, and describe the different kinds of entrepreneurship.

- Research suggests that there are desirable and undesirable qualities of entrepreneurs.
- Desirable characteristics include commitment and determination, a focus on honesty in business relationships, awareness of market and customer needs, tolerance of risk and uncertainty, creativity, self-reliance, adaptability, and a motivation to excel.
- Undesirable characteristics include overestimating one's ability, lacking an understanding of the market, taking oneself too seriously, having a domineering management style, and failing to share business ownership in an equitable way.
- "Pure" entrepreneurs are often considered to be the founders of new businesses that bring new or improved products or services to market.
- Second-generation, or "second-stage," owner-managers are similar in orientation to founders.
- Franchisees differ from other business owners in the degree of their independence.
- An entrepreneurial team consists of two or more individuals who combine their efforts to function in the capacity of entrepreneurs.
- Social entrepreneurs engage in activities with the goal of improving society.
- Women entrepreneurs are competitive business owners who are doing extraordinarily well in the fields of health care and educational services.

1-4. Discuss the importance of understanding your motivations and perceptions related to owning a small business.

- Understanding clearly why you want to own a small business and what motivates you are vital to eventually achieving fulfillment through your business.
- Friends and family who own or have owned businesses can be influential in your decision to start a business.
- Entrepreneurship often provides an attractive alternative for individuals fleeing from undesirable job situations.
- One of the primary reasons for becoming an entrepreneur is gaining personal fulfillment through making the world a better place. Other reasons include achieving personal satisfaction, independence, and financial rewards.
- Three personalities come into play when you are starting a business: the technician personality, the manager personality, and the entrepreneur personality.

- The technician personality dislikes managing, wanting instead to be left alone to get the job done, and lives in the moment, without thinking of the future.
- An individual with a manager personality is pragmatic, assuming responsibility for the planning, order, and predictability of the business.
- The entrepreneur personality is able to see the big picture and develop strategies that will help the business become successful.

1-5. Describe five potential competitive advantages of small entrepreneurial companies over large firms.

- *Integrity and responsibility*: Independent business owners can build an internal culture based on integrity and responsibility that is reflected in relationships both inside and outside the firm, thereby strengthening the firm's position in a competitive environment.
- *Customer focus*: Small business owners have an opportunity to know their customers well and to focus on meeting their needs.
- *Quality performance*: By emphasizing quality in products and services, small firms can build a competitive advantage.
- *Innovation*: Many small firms have demonstrated a superior talent for finding innovative products and developing better ways of doing business.
- *Niche markets*: Small firms that find a distinct market segment of some type can gain an advantage in the marketplace.

1-6. Explain the concept of an entrepreneurial legacy and its challenges.

- Building a legacy is an ongoing process that begins with the launch of the firm and continues throughout its operating life.
- An entrepreneur's legacy includes not only money and material possessions but also nonmaterial things such as personal relationships and values.
- Part of the legacy is the company's contribution to the community.
- A worthy legacy includes a good balance of values and principles important to the entrepreneur.

Key Terms

attractive small firm p. 5
bootstrapping p. 6
corporate refugee p. 17
entrepreneur p. 6
entrepreneur personality p. 23
entrepreneurial legacy p. 28
entrepreneurial opportunity p. 6
entrepreneurial team p. 12
founder p. 10
franchisee p. 10
high-potential venture (gazelle) p. 5
lifestyle business p. 5
manager personality p. 23
mentor p. 21
microbusiness p. 5
microloans p. 5
niche market p. 28
paradigm shift p. 21
reluctant entrepreneur p. 17
small business p. 5
social entrepreneurship p. 13
technician personality p. 22

You Make the Call

Situation 1

In the following statement, a business owner attempts to explain and justify his preference for slow growth in his business.

> *I limit my growth pace and make every effort to service my present customers in the manner they deserve. I have some peer pressure to do otherwise by following the advice of experts—that is, to take on partners and debt to facilitate rapid growth in sales and market share. When tempted by such thoughts, I think about what I might gain. Perhaps I could make more money, but I would also expect a lot more problems. Also, I think it might interfere somewhat with my family relationships, which are very important to me.*

Question 1 Should this venture be regarded as entrepreneurial? Is the owner a true entrepreneur?
Question 2 Do you agree with the philosophy expressed here? Is the owner really doing what is best for his family?
Question 3 What kinds of problems is this owner trying to avoid?

Situation 2

Bear Bills, Inc., was started in 2008 by three Baylor University alumni in their early twenties as a solution to a problem every college student faces—paying utilities. The company's name originated from the university's mascot, the Baylor Bears. The business helps students pay their utility bills without all the hassles of having to collect from each roommate and getting a check to the utility company. Bear Bills pays the bills each month and splits the amount based on each student's prorated portion. The utility companies like the arrangement and are willing to give Bear Bills a commission for increasing their market share. The apartment houses where the students live like the deal because the utilities remain in the renters' names and the management receives a referral fee from Bear Bills. Of course, the students sign up because they do not have to bug a roommate to pay their share of the bill. And Bear Bills makes money.

The first year, Bear Bills signed up over 2,000 college students at the university. The second year, it incorporated as Simple Bills, Inc., and went to other college campuses, doubling its customer base to over 4,000.

At this point, the concept is proven, but the owners have a decision to make. They can raise money from investors and grow the company faster to capture market share, but that will mean they will have to give up some of their ownership in the company. Alternatively, they can continue to bootstrap the business to conserve ownership percentage but then cannot grow it as rapidly. In other words, they would limit the growth of the business to what can be financed from the cash flows currently being generated from operations.

Question 1 What do you like and not like about the Simple Bills concept?
Question 2 Would you recommend raising funds from outside investors and growing faster or continuing to bootstrap the operations to conserve ownership? Why?
Question 3 What strategy would you suggest for growing the business, assuming new investors are brought in?
Question 4 If you choose to raise funds, whom might you seek as investors?

Situation 3

Bracken Arnhart, the founder and CEO of WSR Tool Services, Inc., has immersed himself for the past 10 years in growing his business and has been unquestionably successful in doing so. When he started the company, there were only three employees. Today, he has over 100 employees, and he has achieved more than he even had hoped for in terms of financial rewards.

To realize the goals he set out for the business, Arnhart knows it has been at some cost to his personal and family life. He explains that he always tries to be at home when his children get up in the morning and is there to help tuck them into bed at night. The rest of the time, he is focused on the business. In discussing his work-life balance, he says,

> *Living a balanced life is generally more accepted by society than sacrificing much of one's time to pursue one thing in particular. However, I would argue that to truly do something great, one must give an inordinate amount of time and hard work to see it come to pass.*
>
> *There are the people that are just not ok with the fact that there are only 24 hours in a day. However, unable to alter this fact of life, they are bent on wringing the most out of those 24 hours, and doing it eight days a week, 53 weeks out of the year, only slowing down when they die (and even then, still going at about half-pace). They welcome angels such as caffeine, and curse crutches such as food and sleep. I would probably fall into this category.*
>
> *I would say that I have exchanged work-life balance for building a business. I am told that I'm pretty hard to get ahold of, and even when I do have "free time," my mind is still fully engaged with my business. I am passionate about what I am doing and wouldn't want to be doing anything else. I'll admit that I may miss meals, social events, and really anything that could distract me from my goal, and I am generally ok with it.*
>
> *I believe that this is perfectly acceptable for entrepreneurs, possibly even necessary. Work-life balance is a great debate between entrepreneurs, small business owners, and even those attempting to climb the corporate ladder faster than most. Many are of the opinion that living a balanced life is essential for personal "success," whatever that may look like. However, I strongly believe that tipping the scales toward building a business is the only way to go.*

Question 1 Is work-life balance for everyone?
Question 2 Is work-life balance simply a preference, or is it a necessity when growing a business?
Question 3 As an entrepreneur, would there be areas in your life that you would place at a higher priority than growing a business? Explain.

Case 1

DashLocker (P. 646)

In 2010, Robert Hennessy left his job and started his own company, a high-tech laundry service in Manhattan's Upper East Side. What inspired the career change? Hennessy simply saw a need in the market and felt a call to respond. What initially began as a simple coin-operated laundromat grew into a business currently known as DashLocker, a round-the-clock dry cleaning and wash-and-fold service. The case introduces the student to issues faced in deciding whether to start a new business, including such matters as a founder's motivations, the nature of the opportunity, and what is involved in getting started.

Alternative Cases for Chapter 1

Video Case 1, KlipTech, website only
Case 3, The Kollection, p. 649
Case 5, Iaccarino & Son, p. 654
Case 8, Couchsurfing International, p. 658
Case 19, Andrew Mason, p. 685

Endnotes

1. Clayton Christensen, a Harvard Business School professor, develops this theme in his e-book *How Will You Measure Your Life?* (New York: HarperCollins, 2012). Christensen says that there is no more noble profession than *being in business*. We believe that what he says is even more true of owning your *own business*. Reading his book will be well worth your time.
2. Theodore Roosevelt, excerpt from a speech, "Citizenship in a Republic," delivered at the Sorbonne in Paris, France, April 23, 1910.
3. Paul D. Reynolds and Richard T. Curtin, "Business Creation in the United States: Panel Study of Entrepreneurial Dynamics II, Initial Assessment," *Foundations and Trends in Entrepreneurship*, Vol. 4, No. 3 (2008), p. 158.
4. Isabell M. Welpe, "Fostering an Entrepreneurial Culture," *Amway Global Entrepreneurship Report 2013*, http://assets1.bywebtrain.com/501483/2013_amway_global_entrepreneurship_report_1.pdf?r=1280, accessed December 10, 2014.
5. *Ibid.*, p. 175.
6. U.S. Government Printing Office, "The Small Business Economy 2012," https://www.sba.gov/sites/default/files/advocacy/Small_Business_Economy_2012.pdf, accessed August 24, 2014; U. S. Government Printing Office, "SBA Office of Office of Advocacy FAQ," http://www.sba.gov/sites/default/files/FAQ_March_2014_0.pdf, accessed November 30, 2014; "Entrepreneurial Attitudes and Perceptions," *Global Entrepreneurship Monitor 2013 Report*, http://www.gemconsortium.org/docs/download/3106, accessed November 20, 2014; United States Census Bureau, "News Release on U.S. Businesses," http://www.census.gov/newsroom/releases/archives/business_ownership/cb11-110.html, accessed November 19, 2014; and Tracy Stapp, "The 10 Most Popular Franchises for Military Veterans," http://www.entrepreneur.com/article/219846, accessed October 30, 2014.
7. Ruth Simon and Caelainn Barr, "Endangered Species: Young U.S. Entrepreneurs—New Data Underscore Financial Challenges and Low Tolerance for Risk among Young Americans," *The Wall Street Journal*, January 2, 2015.
8. Angel Capital Association, "Celebrating Entrepreneurs and Angels—Key to Our Economy," November 19, 2014, http://www.angelcapitalassociation.org/blog/celebrating-entrepreneurs-angels, accessed January 20, 2015.
9. The SBA's definition of a small business varies depending on the industry, but the criterion of 500 employees is the starting point.
10. Interview with Patrick Linstrom, founder and CEO, Kelly's Delight, January 15, 2015.
11. Interview with Fan Bi, May 21, 2012; "What Is Blank Label?" http://www.blanklabel.com/story.aspx, accessed May 10, 2012; K. Dziadul, "New Co-Creation Concept Drives Business Model for Blank Label," http://bostinnovation.com/2010/09/09/new-co-creation-concept-drives-business-model-for-blank-label, accessed January 29, 2014; J. Holland, "Two College Entrepreneurs Dress for Success," *Entrepreneur*, March 2011; Kyle Alspach, "Startup Updates—Blank Label, LevelUp," *Boston Business Journal*, June 2012, http://www.bizjournals.com/boston/blog/start-ups/2012/06/blank-label-levelup-cambridge.html, accessed September 8, 2013; Krystina Gustafson, "Custom Men's Wear Shop on Expansion Track," CNBC, June 29, 2014, http://www.cnbc.com/id/101789406#, accessed November 6, 2014; and Dennis Keohane, "Online Style Meets Downtown Class," betaboston, August 11, 2014, http://betaboston.com/gallery/2014/08/11/blank-label-offers-an-offline-twist-to-its-online-shopping-experience-in-boston-gallery, accessed November 6, 2014.
12. Adapted from Bethany Overland, "Ready for Takeoff after 30-Year Army Career," *The Business Journals*, http://www.bizjournals.com/bizjournals/beginners/2013/hughes-group-ready-for-takeoff.html?page=all, accessed November 16, 2014; and interview with Patrick Hughes, February 14, 2015.
13. Stephen Spinelli and Robert Adams, *New Venture Creation: Entrepreneurship for the 21st Century*, 9th ed. (New York, NY: McGraw-Hill/Irwin, 2012), pp. 37–43.
14. Vincent Onyemah, Martha Rivera Pesquera, and Abdul Ali, "What Entrepreneurs Get Wrong," *Harvard Business Review*, May 2013.
15. Excerpts from "Five Reasons 8 Out of 10 Companies Fail," September 12, 2013, http://www.forbes.com/sites/ericwagner/2013/09/12/five-reasons-8-out-of-10-businesses-fail, accessed December 1, 2014.
16. Sirji Terjesen, *Global Entrepreneurship Monitor*, "Report on Social Entrepreneurship, Executive Summary," 2011, http://www.gemconsortium.org/docs/download/376, accessed November 30, 2014.
17. See Christian Seelos and Johanna Mair, "Social Entrepreneurship: Creating New Business Models to Serve the Poor," *Business Horizons*, 2005, pp. 241–246 , http://2008.sofimun.org/SOFIMUN2008-CM-UNECOSOC-Topic-A-extra_info-2.pdf, accessed December 4, 2014.

18. U.S. Census Data, 2012.

19. "The 2013 State of Women-Owned Businesses Report: A Summary of Important Trends," commissioned by American Express OPEN, March 13, 2013, https://c401345.ssl.cf1.rackcdn.com/wp-content/uploads/2013/03/13ADV-WBI-E-StateOfWomenReport_FINAL.pdf, accessed November 15, 2014.

20. Alicia Robb and Dane Stangler, "Sources of Economic Hope: Women's Entrepreneurship," Ewing Marion Kauffman Foundation, November 2014, p. 5.

21. *Ibid*, p. 5.

22. Susan Coleman and Alicia Robb, forthcoming.

23. Alicia M. Robb and John Watson, "Gender Differences in Firm Performance: Evidence from New Ventures in the United States," Journal of Business Venturing, Vol. 27, No. 5 (September 2012), pp. 544–558.

24. Personal conversation with Ewing Marion Kauffman, October 2005.

25. Jeff Sandefer and Robert Sirico, *A Field Guide for the Hero's Journey* (Grand Rapids, MI: Acton Institute, 2012), p. 11.

26. Quoted in Leigh Buchanan, "What Drives Entrepreneurs?" *Inc.*, February 28, 2012, http://www.inc.com/magazine/201203/motivation-matrix.html, accessed October 1, 2012.

27. Quoted in Lena Basha, "The Entrepreneurial Gene," *MyBusiness*, December/January 2007, p. 15.

28. Ram Charan, "Stop Whining, Start Thinking," *Bloomberg Businessweek*, August 24, 2008, p. 58.

29. Elizabeth Alterma, "Employees Bid Goodbye to Corporate America," *USA Today*, August 20, 2011, http://www.usatoday.com/money/workplace/story/2011/08/Employees-bid-goodbye-to-corporate-America/50059194/1, accessed May 14, 2012; and http://joyfulplate.com/index.html, accessed October 15, 2014.

30. Very limited academic research has been conducted into the motivations of entrepreneurs. See Alan Carsrud and Malin Brannback, "Entrepreneurial Motivations: What Do We Still Need to Know?" *Journal of Small Business Management*, Vol. 49, No. 1 (2011), pp. 9–26.

31. Personal conversation with Chris DeLeenheer, partner in Rydell Holdings, September 5, 2014.

32. Michelle Di Gangi, "Small Business Survey Reveals 'No Regrets' Surprise," Harris Poll sponsored by the Bank of the West, September 9, 2014, http://blog.bankofthewest.com/small-business-survey-reveals-regrets-surprise, accessed February 23, 2015.

33. "Jobs: 'Find What You Love,'" *The Wall Street Journal*, October 6, 2011, http://www.wsj.com/articles/SB10001424052970203388804576613572842080228, accessed January 14, 2015.

34. For a discussion of "making meaning," see Guy Kawasaki, *The Art of the Start* (The Woodlands, TX: Portfolio, 2004), pp. 4–6.

35. Sue Shellenbarger, "Plumbing for Joy? Be Your Own Boss," *The Wall Street Journal*, September 15, 2009, http://www.wsj.com/articles/SB10001424052970203917304574414853397450872, accessed February 24, 2015.

36. Melissa Korn, "Employed, but Not Engaged on the Job," *The Wall Street Journal*, June 13, 2013, http://www.wsj.com/articles/SB10001424127887323495604578539712058327862, accessed October 15, 2014.

37. Richard Duncan, "One Major Benefit of Working a Small-Business Job," *The Wall Street Journal*, November 12, 2014, http://blogs.wsj.com/experts/2014/11/06/one-major-benefit-of-working-a-small-business-job, accessed December 21, 2014.

38. Personal conversation with Rick Davis, founder of Davaco, Inc., April 6, 2014.

39. Mary Liz Curtin, "How I Launched My Dream Business after Age 50," *The Wall Street Journal*, November 3, 2014, http://blogs.wsj.com/experts/2014/11/03/how-i-launched-my-dream-business-after-age-50, accessed December 14, 2014.

40. Bridget Gamble, "MyLife with Aimee Marnell," National Federation of Independent Business, http://www.nfib.com/article/mylife-with-aimee-marnell-62770, accessed February 4, 2015.

41. *Ibid.*

42. Thomas J. Stanley and William D. Danko, *The Millionaire Next Door* (New York, NY: Simon & Schuster, 1996), p. 227.

43. Clayton Christensen, *The Innovator's Dilemma* (New York, NY: Harper Business, 1997).

44. Stephen R. Covey, *The 7 Habits of Highly Effective People* (New York: Free Press, 2004), pp. 95–144.

45. Michael Gerber, *The E-Myth Revisited: Why Most Small Businesses Don't Work and What to Do About It* (New York, NY: HarperCollins, 1995), p. 19.

46. *Ibid.* p. 13.

47. *Ibid.* p. 25.

48. *Ibid.* p. 31.

49. Michelle Di Gangi, "Made Here: Adding an Inventory Service to the Product Mix," Bank of the West, http://blog.bankofthewest.com/made-adding-inventory-service-product-mix-2, accessed February 23, 2015.

50. Pew Research Center, 2005–2014.

51. For a number of studies by the Small Business Administration regarding the role of small firms in innovation, see "Innovation in Small Business: Drivers of Change and Value," 2009, http://www.sba.gov/advo/research/rs342tot.pdf; "An Analysis of Small Business Patents by Industry and Firm Size," 2008, http://www.sba.gov/advo/research/rstot335.pdf; "Innovation and Small Business Performance: Examining the Relationship Between Technological Innovation and the Within-Industry Distributions of Fast Growth Firms," 2006, http://www.sba.gov/advo/research/rs272tot.pdf; "Small Firms: Why Market-Driven Innovation Can't Get Along without Them," 2005, http://www.sba.gov/advo/research/sbe_05_ch08.pdf; "Small Firms and Technology: Acquisitions, Inventor Movement, and Technology Transfer," 2004, http://www.sba.gov/advo/research/rs233tot.pdf; "Small Serial Innovators: The Small Firm Contribution to Technical Change," 2003, http://www.sba.gov/advo/research/rs225tot.pdf; and "Influence of R&D Expenditures on New Firm Formation and Economic Growth," 2002, http://www.sba.gov/advo/research/rs222tot.pdf.

52. Christensen, *The Innovator's Dilemma, op. cit.*

53. Amar Bhide, *The Venturesome Economy* (Princeton, NJ: Princeton University Press, 2008).

54. Alan Murray, "The End of Management," *The Wall Street Journal*, August 21, 2010, p. W3.

55. Comments by Ed Bonneau to an entrepreneurship class, November 20, 2014.

56. *Ibid.*

57. Based on Ty Findley's interview of his dad, Steve Findley, October 15, 2013.

58. Personal conversation with Bernard Rapaport, 2009.

CHAPTER 2

Integrity, Ethics, and Social Entrepreneurship

© ISTOCKPHOTO.COM/ISTOCK

After studying this chapter, you should be able to. . .

2-1. Define *integrity*, and understand its importance to small businesses.

2-2. Explain how integrity applies to various stakeholder groups.

2-3. Identify some common challenges and benefits of maintaining integrity in small businesses.

2-4. Suggest practical approaches for building a business with integrity.

2-5. Define *social entrepreneurship*, and describe its influence on small companies and startup opportunities.

OPEN LOOKING AHEAD

In the SPOTLIGHT
The Home Grown Farm
www.thehgf.com

The Home Grown Farm got its start when Pam Tull and her adult children, Brandon, Toby, and Melanie—all graduates of Baylor University—decided to expand a small hobby farm in Gholson, Texas, into a larger business that could provide more nutritional food options for those seeking a healthier lifestyle. But their intentions are even broader. For example, they also want to make consumers more aware of how their food is grown, prove that family farming can still succeed (and even flourish), and provide another path to supporting local economies.

The Tulls' efforts have already been paying off, and in very important ways. One customer started buying produce from the Home Grown Farm when her four-year-old daughter developed asthma problems; she found that adding more "real" food to her daughter's diet provided significant relief from her symptoms. As a bonus, the customer was pleasantly surprised when the overall health of her entire family started to improve. "I would rather spend my money on good food than on health care," she now declares. Others offer rave reviews regarding the taste of the produce. "The tomatoes are absolutely scrumptious," says one faithful Home Grown Farm shopper. Another adds, "They grow the most gorgeous carrots. And they are so fresh. I had forgotten that carrots could taste like that."

Perhaps the Home Grown Farm works so well because it is truly a team effort. Pam came up with the idea of starting the business, is considered the "chief researcher"

for the farm, and helps with all aspects of planning for the venture. Toby was able to draw upon his management information systems degree and previous work experience as an IT specialist to help the farm reach a wider market. As he puts it, "We knew that what we were doing on the farm was the right thing, and we wanted to be able to expand." But he also realized that doing so would require better distribution and an improved customer experience, challenges for which his particular skills were well adapted. "We live in a world of consumers who are used to being able to get what they need 24/7, and it can be difficult for a farm to bend to those demands," he observes. "I knew technology would be the way to create a bridge to that customer experience."

Brandon's focus has been on the food: "There was no way we were going to compromise on the integrity of our product. My job is to produce the best-quality, most natural, best-tasting food for our customers." By improving the ordering and delivery systems and integrating them more closely with the farm's growing operations, the brothers were able to come up with a revamped approach that gives customers more of what they want at a price that most households can readily afford.

In all aspects of the business, customer needs take priority. "Farming is a field as old as humans," Toby observes. "Everyone is doing it as it's always been done, but what if it were customer-driven? People lead busy lives. We have to give them a choice." Rethinking the venture from this point of view, Toby designed the Home Grown Farm website so that those who sign up for the service can order exactly what they want each week. For example, if a customer goes on vacation or does not like the produce that is available that week, the credits can be rolled over to subsequent weeks. And to make delivery more convenient, customers can choose from a number of produce pick-up locations, and they are free to choose a different location from week to week.

Purchasers are guaranteed the freshest produce possible, and the process that the Tulls use has been tweaked so that the time from harvest to delivery is cut to an absolute minimum. "Vegetables begin to lose nutritional value the minute they are harvested," Toby says. "It's crucial to decrease the amount of time between when the produce leaves the field until the time it reaches the customer's plate." This emphasis fits nicely with the Tulls' mission to provide a customer-centered source of healthy, chemical- and pesticide-free food to those who want to improve the way they eat.

This focus on the consumer may be more unique in farming than most people realize. "I always thought of farmers as 'salt of the earth' people, but I have had a rude awakening," reports Toby. "Some farmers buy from someone else and sell the produce as organic when it isn't. I insist on transparency in what we do. [Customers] are invited to visit our farm and see where their food is grown."

Since January of 2013, purchases have been handled entirely online. Buyers are invited to sign up at various levels of participation (from $225 to $375 for a 15-week growing season), and the dollar amount selected can be spent in the online store, according to the customer's needs. Orders may be placed as late as 5 p.m. on the day before scheduled delivery, and text-message reminders are sent out to alert customers that their produce is available. Personal deliveries can be arranged for a small, additional fee.

More recently, the Home Grown Farm has developed partnerships with other farmers in the area to provide their customers with a broader range of produce options. But remaining true to their customer focus, the Tull family insists that their partners operate according to the same lofty principles. To provide assurances, they created their own set of standards (even more demanding than those required for organic certification) and extend "home grown certification" only to those farms that meet them. "It's impossible for one farmer to grow all things well," said Toby. "So we find other farms and certify them to our standards. We get a bigger variety, and we can support other farms with our technology."

"Right now, we have very few certified partners," said Brandon. "We have high standards in our growing practices and personal integrity, and we demand the same from everyone we work with. That means we're very picky about who we do business with. If we can't run a business without honesty and integrity, then we don't want a business."

© ELIZABETH O. WELLER/SHUTTERSTOCK.COM

Sources: Janet Jones, "Healthy, Fresh Options: Area Families Enjoying Produce, Added Benefits with Home Grown Farm," *Waco Tribune-Herald*, May 28, 2015, http://www.wacotrib.com/waco_today_magazine/healthy-fresh-options-area-families-enjoying-produce-added-benefits-with/article_1fcd93cc-a270-59a2-827c-816a110bdb1c.html?mode=jqm, accessed July 1, 2015; Franci Rogers, "Technology with a Social Cause," *Baylor Business Review*, Fall 2013, pp. 37–44; and The Home Grown Farm," http://www.thehgf.com, accessed July 1, 2015.

The Home Grown Farm is a unique small business. The Tull family is very interested in financial performance, but they also pay careful attention to the crucial relationships that help the business operate smoothly, especially those involving their customers and partners.

This emphasis on the people part of the puzzle has served the Home Grown Farm very well. But the company's emphasis on the environment and the production of healthy, organic food is also important and has played a key role in generating positive results. Consistent with its founding principles, the Tulls have given serious consideration to the needs and interests of those who impact or are impacted by the firm's operations. They see this as a matter of integrity—of being true to the character of the enterprise and those who run it—and it's paying off in many ways.

But what is integrity? That's a very important question. In this chapter, we define and discuss this fundamental concept, recognizing integrity as the foundation for ethical behavior in small businesses. We also provide frameworks to guide you toward principled management.

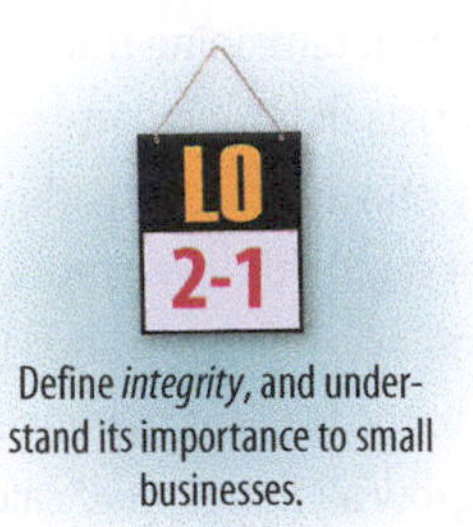

Define *integrity*, and understand its importance to small businesses.

2-1 WHAT IS INTEGRITY?

The seeds of business misdeeds are sown when individuals compromise their personal *integrity*—that is, when they do not behave in a way that is consistent with the noble values, beliefs, and principles they claim to hold. According to Karl Eller—the highly successful entrepreneur who turned the business of outdoor advertising into the revenue powerhouse that it is today—a person has integrity if his or her character remains whole, regardless of the circumstances:

> *[A person of integrity] doesn't fold in a crunch; doesn't lie, cheat, flatter; doesn't fake credentials or keep two sets of books. He doesn't blame others for his mistakes or steal credit for their work. She never goes back on a deal: her handshake matches the tightest contract drawn up by the fanciest law firm in town.*[1]

In other words, **integrity** refers to a general sense of honesty and reliability that is expressed in a strong commitment to doing the right thing, regardless of the circumstances.

Some acts, such as cheating on taxes, clearly violate this standard, while others are less obvious but may be just as inappropriate. For example, one entrepreneur who owned a flooring sales business often sold sheets of linoleum at first-quality prices, even though they were graded as "seconds" by the factory. To hide his deception, he developed an ink roller that changed the factory stamp from "SECONDS" to read "SECONDS TO NONE!" Those who caught the inaccuracy probably figured it was a typo and gave it no more thought, but unsuspecting customers were paying for first-quality flooring, only to receive imperfect goods. By any measure, this shady business practice reveals a lack of integrity on the part of the entrepreneur.

As discussed in Chapter 1, a successful entrepreneur seeks financially rewarding opportunities while creating value, first and foremost, for prospective customers and the firm's owners. This perspective makes clear that relationships are critical and integrity is essential to success. Financial gain is important, but it should not be the only goal. In fact, "doing anything for money" can quickly lead to distortions in business behavior. There are numerous motivations for misconduct in companies, but acts such as price fixing, overcharging customers, using pirated software, and a host of others are driven primarily by financial motives. Acting with integrity requires that an individual first consider the welfare of others.

integrity
A general sense of honesty and reliability that is expressed in a strong commitment to doing the right thing, regardless of the circumstances.

Fortunately, many small business owners strive to live up to the highest standards of honesty, fairness, and respect in their business relationships. Although unethical practices receive extensive attention in the news, most entrepreneurs and other business leaders are people of principle, whose integrity regulates their quest for profits.

2-2 INTEGRITY AND THE INTERESTS OF MAJOR STAKEHOLDERS

Explain how integrity applies to various stakeholder groups.

It is probably evident by now that the notion of integrity is closely tied to ethical issues, which involve questions of right and wrong.[2] Such questions go far beyond what is legal or illegal. Entrepreneurs often must make decisions regarding what is respectful and fair, and these decisions are becoming more important over time.

An honest assessment of the marketplace recognizes that ethical problems sometimes crop up there. A recent Ethics Resource Center survey indicated that employees witness various forms of misconduct in their workplaces, with the most frequently observed offenses involving abusive behavior and lying to employees. (See Exhibit 2.1 for the percentages of workers who observed these and other forms of unethical behavior.) These are significant failures. And because a wide range of individuals may be involved and/or affected, it can be challenging for a small business owner to determine how to best address the underlying issues or resolve lingering problems related to such misbehavior.

When it comes to ethical behavior, small business owners guided by integrity must consider the interests of a number of different groups when making decisions. These groups include owners (or stockholders), customers, employees, the community, and the government, among others. Individuals in these groups are sometimes referred to as stakeholders, indicating that they have a "stake" in the operation of the business. Though definitions vary, **stakeholders** are typically described as those individuals or groups who either can affect the performance of the company or are affected by it.

stakeholders Individuals or groups who either can affect or are affected by the performance of the company.

EXHIBIT 2.1 Most Frequently Observed Forms of Workplace Misconduct

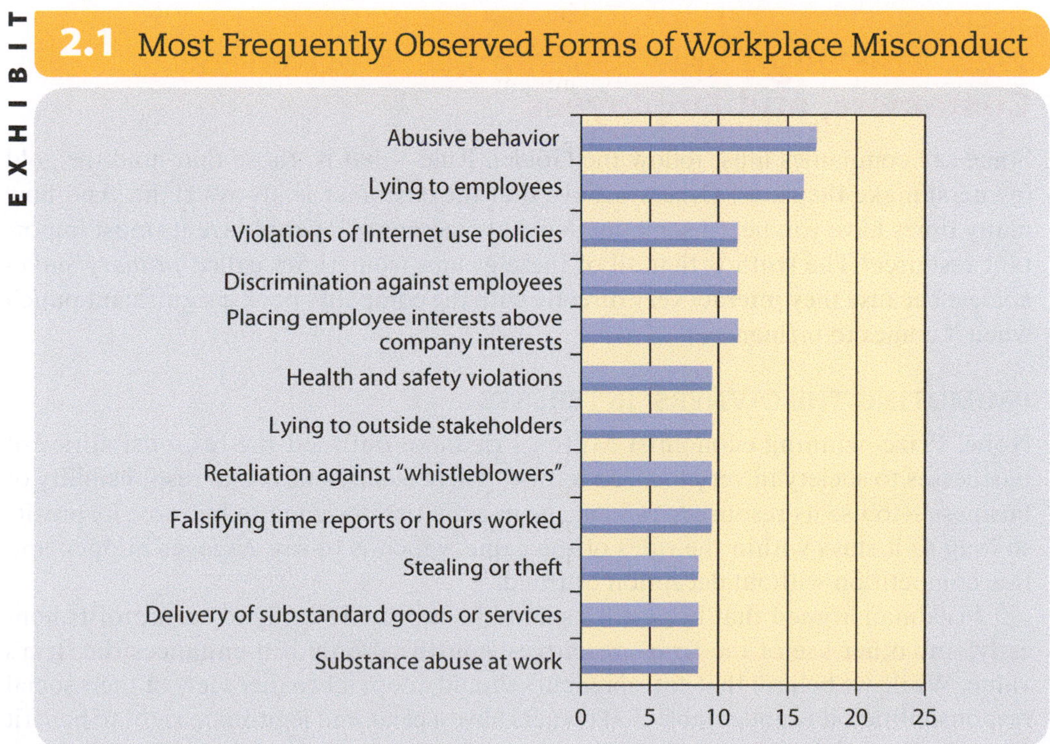

Source: Adapted from Ethics Resource Center, "National Business Ethics Survey of the U.S. Workforce," 2014, pp. 41–42.

EXHIBIT 2.2 Four Types of Responsibilities for Small Businesses

Type of Responsibility	Societal Expectation	General Focus
Economic	Required	Be profitable.
Legal	Required	Obey all laws, adhere to all regulations.
Ethical	Expected	Avoid questionable practices.
Discretionary	Desired/Expected	Be a good corporate citizen, and give back.

Source: Based on Carroll/ Buchholtz, Business and Society: Ethics, Sustainability, and Stakeholder Management, 9e. © 2014 Cengage Learning, p. 35.

Because the interests of various stakeholder groups sometimes conflict, decisions can be very difficult to make. And because there may not be one completely right or wrong position to take, managing the process can be complicated.[3]

As suggested by business ethics and morality scholar Archie Carroll, some of a company's responsibilities cannot be negotiated away (see Exhibit 2.2). For example, a firm must remain profitable to stay in business, and it must also obey the law if it wishes to keep its doors open. Societal expectations regarding a venture's ethical performance may leave a small business owner with a bit more latitude, but it is very limited. Ignoring such expectations, while legal in a strict sense, is likely to tarnish the firm's reputation and can lead to serious repercussions, including negative publicity, consumer protests, or even lawsuits—and these can easily affect financial outcomes. Finally, discretionary responsibilities, such as providing support to the community, offer greater flexibility. But even here, failing to respond is likely to have negative consequences. The concerns of important stakeholders are fundamental to the management of the business. If neglected, any one group can use its influence to negatively affect the performance of the company. Therefore, stakeholder interests should be carefully considered and wisely balanced.[4]

2-2a The "Big Three" Stakeholders—Owners, Customers, and Employees

Some say companies must follow the Golden Rule—that is, those that hold the gold (owners) make the rules! Others believe that the customer is always right. And how many times have you heard someone say that a company's people are its most important resource? The truth is that all of these groups (sometimes called *primary stakeholders* because they interact very directly with the company) pack a significant punch when it comes to influence.

PROMOTING THE OWNERS' INTERESTS

Nobel Prize–winning economist Milton Friedman outlined the responsibilities of businesses to society in very focused terms: "There is only one social responsibility of business—to use its resources and engage in activities designed to increase its profits so long as it stays within the rules of the game, which is to say, engages in open and free competition without deception or fraud."[5]

Friedman argued that businesses should be expected simply to earn profits honestly; any other use of the firm's resources is justified only if it enhances the firm's value. While we believe that entrepreneurs should adopt a broader view of their social responsibilities, it is undeniable that owners have a clear and legitimate right to benefit from the financial performance of the company.

Many businesses, even small ones, have more than one owner. When this is the case, high standards of integrity require an honest attempt to promote the interests of all the owners, which include a commitment to financial performance and protection of the firm's reputation. Though entrepreneurs should be able to make their own decisions about personal matters, they have an obligation to make choices that protect the financial investment of other owners in the company.

In many small businesses, a number of people own a small part of the enterprise but have no direct involvement in its operation. When this is the case, questions concerning proper conduct can arise in a number of areas. For example, entrepreneurs sometimes face ethical issues when reporting financial information. They must decide the extent to which they will be honest and candid. Because a firm has considerable discretion when revealing performance results, financial reports can sometimes be misleading without technically being illegal. But providing misleading financial information could easily persuade the other owners to make poor decisions regarding their investment in the company. The same could also be said for some who do not have ownership—outsiders such as bankers and suppliers who depend on a firm's financial reports to be accurate. It is always best to make honest disclosures that do not mislead in order to protect critical relationships and the reputation of the firm.

CARING ABOUT CUSTOMERS

Customers are obviously one of the most important stakeholder groups that a company must please. The fact that they are central to the purpose of any business has implications for integrity. Owners who take customers seriously and care about them as individuals are apt to have more of them—and those they do have are likely to return often.

It is easy to fall into the habit of seeing every client as merely a dollar sign, but this narrow view can lead to a wide range of questionable practices. For example, entrepreneurs are often tempted to take advantage of customers by being less than honest with them. And marketing decisions can be particularly complicated when it comes to ethical issues. Advertising content must sell the product or service but also tell the truth. Salespeople often must walk a fine line between persuasion and deception. In some businesses, a sales representative might obtain contracts more easily by offering improper incentives to buyers or by joining with competitors to rig bids. This is clearly illegal and eventually may result in damage to the company's reputation, which will affect relationships with existing and potential customers.

Companies with integrity recognize the importance of treating their customers with care, but it should be clear by now that this also just makes good sense. At its core, the formula for business success is actually quite simple: When a company delivers an excellent product with excellent service, customer satisfaction and healthy sales are likely to follow.

VALUING EMPLOYEES

A firm's level of integrity is also expressed by the value it places on employees. Through management decisions, an owner affects employees' personal and family lives. Issues of fairness, honesty, and impartiality are inherent in decisions and practices regarding hiring, promotions, salary increases, dismissals, layoffs, and work assignments. Employees are also concerned about privacy, safety, and health issues, and these should not be ignored.

In communicating with employees, an owner may be truthful and fair, vague and misleading, or totally dishonest. Some entrepreneurs treat outsiders with great courtesy but display demeaning behavior toward subordinates. Showing proper appreciation for subordinates as human beings and as valuable members of the team is an essential ingredient of managerial integrity. It is also wise, since employees are a firm's most important resource.

Many entrepreneurs recognize the importance of looking after the needs of their employees, creating a positive work environment, and rewarding them generously for their contributions. According to recent research, when employees feel that they are valued and socially connected at work, they tend to be highly engaged and much more productive.[6] To complete the picture, employees who are loyal to the business naturally devote themselves to their work, which leads to high-quality service, very loyal customers, and ultimately, increased profits.[7] So, the owners' interests are well taken care of, and everyone is happy in the end. This really is no mystery—it all works beautifully when you see how the pieces fit together.

But, unfortunately, there are many ways that companies can stray from the integrity track. For example, some small business owners give little thought to the standards of conduct that guide everyday behavior, thinking that an occasional shortcut won't hurt anything. However, lapses in integrity are easily passed down from superiors to subordinates, replicating like a life-threatening virus that spreads throughout the organization. As this influence expands, employees of small firms are likely to face pressure from various sources to act in ways that conflict with their own sense of what is right and wrong. For example, a salesperson may be pushed to compromise personal ethical standards in order to make a sale. Or an office employee may feel forced by her or his boss to act unethically, perhaps by destroying documents or misrepresenting production data. Such situations are guaranteed to spawn an organizational culture that erodes integrity.

Getting Assistance from the SBA

Finding it difficult to get a grasp of your small firm's legal responsibilities? Just go to www.sba.gov, and choose the "Starting and Managing" option to locate helpful government services from federal, state, and local agencies.

Sometimes, employees engage in unethical behavior at their employer's expense. They may fail in their ethical obligation to do "an honest day's work." Loafing on the job and taking unjustified sick leave are examples of such failure. Some employees even feign injury and draw fraudulent workers' compensation checks, thereby inflating a company's insurance costs.

According to FBI estimates, employees who steal supplies, merchandise, tools, or equipment from work may cost employers as much as $150 billion each year,[8] and this figure does not include losses from embezzlement (that is, when an employee steals money from the firm). These problems are serious, with some experts estimating that one-third of all new businesses fail because of employee theft of one kind or another.[9]

2-2b Social Responsibility and Small Business

As we discussed in Chapter 1, an ethical business not only treats customers and employees honestly but also acts as a good citizen in its community. These broader obligations of citizenship are called **social responsibilities**.

Some regard social responsibility as the price of freedom to operate independently in a free economy. They believe that the public has certain expectations regarding business behavior, not all of which are required by law. Accordingly, they regard some expenditures on social responsibilities as proper, even when they are costly.

Companies have increasingly accepted responsibility to the communities where they do business. Their contribution starts with creating jobs and adding to local tax revenues, but many entrepreneurs feel a duty to give back even more to the community in return for the local support they enjoy—and they usually benefit from increased goodwill as a result. It is important to recognize that opinions differ as to the extent to which businesses are obligated to engage in socially desirable activities, and the response of small businesses to that obligation also varies.

social responsibilities
A company's ethical obligations to the community.

Contributions to the community can take many different forms. Ryan Allis and Aaron Houghton met when they were still students at the University of North Carolina. Using their experience in Web marketing, Web design, and software development, they started a new company to sell an innovative Web-based, e-mail list management tool that Houghton had developed. They called their new venture iContact, and the market loved their product. Because the venture was profitable from its second year in business, Allis and Houghton chose to support charitable enterprises very early on. They established a social responsibility policy called the "4-1s" program: iContact gives 1 percent of its employees' work time, 1 percent of its payroll, 1 percent of its product, and 1 percent of its equity to worthy nonprofit organizations. In a single year, the company gave away 475 days of employee time to 63 organizations, contributed $109,000 in cash donations, and allowed 700 nonprofits to use its product free of charge.[10] The company was acquired in 2012 by the cloud-based marketing and PR software firm Vocus, but the very impactful 4-1s program was continued at the iContact unit.[11]

Entrepreneurs should think carefully about their community commitments, because building a business on a foundation of "doing good" may add to a small company's financial burden. This is often more than offset by increased loyalty from customers and employees who buy into the mission, which leads to improved productivity and morale. It also sets a company apart from competitors that offer similar products or services but make no charitable contributions. Perhaps most important, this commitment is often rewarded by customers in two ways—repeat sales and a willingness to pay a little more for what they get. These are strong incentives to give serious consideration to a firm's dedication to the community.[12]

© ZUMA PRESS, INC/ALAMY

Muna Haji, center, joined volunteers from Habitat for Humanity and Women Build as they held up the first wall of what became her new home, Monday, June 11, 2012. Haji's home was the first to kick off Women Build 2012.

But how do small business owners compare with big-business CEOs in their view of social responsibility? The evidence is limited, but research suggests that entrepreneurs who head small, growth-oriented companies may be more narrowly focused on profits and therefore less socially sensitive than CEOs of large corporations. With simple survival as the most pressing priority, many small firms see social responsibility as a luxury they simply cannot afford. Small business philanthropy often takes place anyway, but in the form of personal contributions by business owners.

Entrepreneurs must reconcile their social obligations with the need to earn profits. Earning a profit is absolutely essential, and meeting the expectations of society can be expensive. For example, small firms must sometimes make expensive changes to conserve energy or engage in recycling. It is evident that acting in the public interest often requires spending money, which reduces profits. There are limits to what particular businesses can afford.

Fortunately, many types of socially responsible actions can be consistent with a firm's long-term profit objective.[13] A National Federation of Independent Business study found that 91 percent of small businesses made contributions to their communities through volunteering, in-kind assistance, and/or direct cash donations. The same study reported 74 percent of all small business owners volunteered for community and charitable activities, and the average commitment was just over 12 hours per month (which translates to 18 working days per year).[14] Overall, the evidence on performance impact is far from certain, but it suggests that taking social responsibilities seriously may very well be good for business.

2-2c Integrity and Governmental Regulations

Government at all levels serves a purpose, though there is much debate as to whether it has too much power or too little. It intervenes directly in the economy when it establishes laws to ensure healthy competition. But its reach extends to other business matters as well—workplace safety, equal employment opportunities, fair pay, clean air, and safe products, to name a few. Entrepreneurs must comply with governmental laws and regulations if they are to maintain integrity—and avoid spending time behind bars.

One glaring example of unethical behavior by small firm management is fraudulent reporting of income and expenses for income tax purposes. This conduct includes *skimming* (that is, concealing some income), as well as improperly claiming personal expenses to be business-related. We do not mean to imply that all or even most small companies engage in such practices. However, tax evasion does occur, and the practice is common enough to be recognized as a general problem.

Avoid Drowning in a Sea of Regulatory Paperwork

Starting a business may require you to complete, notarize, and file a dozen or more documents. But a new company called License123.com offers a very inexpensive service that will help you locate, fill out, and file all required license and permit forms. Given the serious hassles it can eliminate, it's quite a bargain!

Tax avoidance can be flagrant and very intentional, but entrepreneurs often come up short on their tax commitments because of casual accounting systems, single-minded focus on their product or service, or both. One student entrepreneur confesses that he had a close brush with the law because he and his friends were creating clothing in his dorm room and selling it on campus, but the company did not legally exist, and he was not keeping track of sales and expenses because he didn't take seriously the obligations and advantages of maintaining good records. But after a close encounter with Internal Revenue Service (IRS) agents, this young entrepreneur learned that accurate recordkeeping and legal formalities are necessary to ethical practice and, just as important, to peace of mind.[15]

When the topic of tax avoidance comes up, most people think of income taxes, but employee payroll tax—local, state, and federal obligations such as Social Security, Medicare, and unemployment—and other taxes must also be withheld. These often present the biggest tax burden on small businesses because they are owed regardless of whether the company makes a profit. And because tax authorities like the IRS do not always push hard enough to collect these taxes, small businesses can easily fall behind.[16] In any case, it should be clear that paying all forms of required taxes is a nonnegotiable feature of integrity, especially for a small business owner who would like to stay in business.

2-3 THE CHALLENGES AND BENEFITS OF ACTING WITH INTEGRITY

Identify some common challenges and benefits of maintaining integrity in small businesses.

Small companies face unique challenges to integrity, especially at such critical stages as getting started and establishing a name, launching online operations, and expanding internationally. Small companies are often vulnerable because of their size and their desire to succeed. But the benefits of integrity are real and can offer small businesses a distinct advantage in the marketplace. Therefore, we will discuss how the payoff from managing with integrity can make a small business, and how the lack of it can break one.

2-3a Small Companies and the Legitimacy Lie

Walking the straight and narrow may be more difficult and costly on Main Street than it is on Wall Street. That is, small, privately held firms that are not part of the corporate world epitomized by Wall Street may face greater pressures to act unethically than do large businesses. Indeed, because small firms usually do not have the deep pockets and superior resources of their larger competitors, their owners may find it easier to rationalize, say, inappropriate gift giving or bribery as a way of offsetting what seem to be unfair limitations in order to establish a level playing field in the marketplace. It's easy to cave in to the pressure when your back is against the wall.

Because startups do not have a history and a reputation to lean on when trying to sell customers on their new product or service or to impress other important stakeholders, entrepreneurs often are uniquely tempted to resort to telling what some researchers call *legitimacy lies*.[17] That is, they sometimes misrepresent the facts or create false impressions to mislead others intentionally and earn their confidence. How do you feel about the following situations (which actually took place)?

- An entrepreneur launched his own fundraising business in South Carolina with only a few local projects to work on. Profits were slim, but that didn't stop him from telling everyone that business was great. Consistent with this false storyline, he set up a toll-free number and launched a website to create an image of greater scale.[18]
- A small business owner who had just started a trucking company in Michigan sometimes used the phone in "creative ways" to shade customer impressions about the business. For example, "she pretended to transfer customers to different lines and used phony voices to make the company seem bigger."[19]
- Partners in an auto sales startup rented a large lot for their business but could afford only four cars for inventory—a turn-off for would-be buyers. So the partners offered free parking in their lot to any employee of the big firm next door who would allow them to put a false price tag on her or his car during the day as if it were for sale. Many accepted, and soon the lot was full every morning and mostly empty by late afternoon. Passersby figured the company must be doing a booming business, and predictably, actual sales soon followed.[20]

When small business owners create false impressions to make their companies look good, are they being dishonest or simply resourceful? Pretending to be something they are not can lead small business owners into what is, at best, a gray area. The drive and ingenuity of these entrepreneurs is certainly impressive, but their behavior raises questions about ethical standards. Such moves may save companies, but how would customers feel if they knew they were being manipulated in this way?

Telling legitimacy lies threatens the reputation of the business and the trust that goes along with it. If (when) the truth is revealed, future sales or support could very well be compromised. It would be better—and much more honest—to understand the factors that move customers to have confidence in a purchase and to provide truthful information. Research has shown that customers are less likely to decide to purchase if they have significant questions about the product or service that the new venture is offering, about those who represent and/or run the business, and about the organization itself.[21] (We call these features *PRO factors*—*P*roducts, *R*epresentatives, and the *O*rganization—to emphasize that they can promote firm performance when customers are satisfied with them.) The concerns of prospective customers include the following:

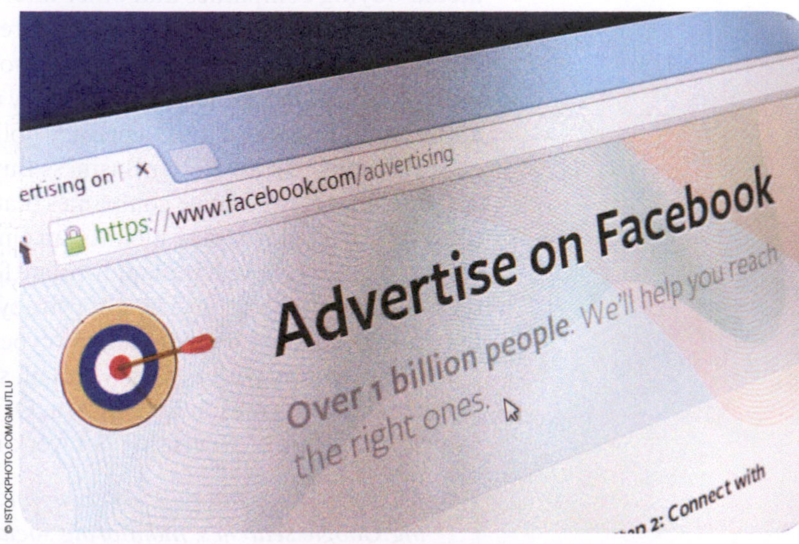

© ISTOCKPHOTO.COM/GMUTLU

- Will the *product* (or *service*) serve my needs better than alternatives, and will it be a hassle to change from the brand I currently buy? (Research indicates that product/service knowledge is the most important of the three factors when customers make purchase decisions.[22])

- Do the company's *representatives* know what they are talking about, and will they (can they) live up to their assurances?
- Will the *organization* still be around to stand behind its product or service if I have a problem with it six months from now?

These are all reasonable concerns, and it is important that the new venture find a way to address them. For example, advertising can help to get product or service information out to prospective customers. But because this can be expensive, many new ventures choose to lean on a well-crafted publicity program, social media tools, or other promotional strategies instead (more on these in Chapter 17).

Often, a small firm's legitimacy is staked on the reputation of its owner, but it is important to highlight and honestly bolster the credibility of anyone who represents the venture. It is best to make the credentials (educational background, expertise, industry experience, etc.) of key employees known, as well as to encourage those employees to participate in trade, business, and community organizations where they can build important relationships and associations. The business itself can establish legitimacy by setting up a high-quality website, insisting on professional behavior from all customer-contact employees, forming strategic alliances with well-respected partner firms, and taking other, similar measures. The point is that a new venture or small company may be at a legitimacy disadvantage when compared to established competitors, but there are ways to close the gap. And while the focus is primarily on the reactions of customers, many of these principles clearly apply to relationships with investors, suppliers, and other important stakeholders as well.

2-3b Integrity and the Internet

Legitimacy and trust are important to all small businesses, but those using the Internet face a host of ethical issues that are unique to the online marketplace. One issue of great concern to Internet users is personal privacy. In fact, a poll by an online media company found that more than 80 percent of Web users worry about how well their personal information is being protected.[23]

Businesses and consumers often disagree about how private the identity of visitors to websites should be. For example, businesses can use cookies (digital "ID tags") to collect data on consumers' buying habits related to a particular Internet address. In this way, a business can create a detailed profile of customers, which it may then sell to media buying companies and other interested groups. While the collection of personal information may allow a business to create a more personalized shopping experience and offer convenience to the buyer, it also opens the door to potential misuse of data. To minimize customer concerns, a company must be honest and transparent with customers about its practices and draft a privacy policy that conforms to the guidelines provided by organizations like the Better Business Bureau or through consultation with an attorney.

But it is not just online companies that have to worry about privacy issues. The extent to which an employer may monitor an employee's Internet activity is also hotly debated. Many workers believe it is inappropriate for employers to monitor their e-mail, a practice they consider to be an invasion of privacy. Employers, on the other hand, are concerned that employees may be engaging in "cyberslacking" at the office—that is, wasting company time dealing with personal e-mail, shopping online, and surfing the Internet. And it appears there is reason for concern. Of 3,200 people surveyed recently by Salary.com, 64 percent admitted to visiting nonwork-related websites every day while on the job.

> *Most people spend time checking their personal email, visiting news sites, performing Google searches, monitoring social media, and shopping online. It probably*

comes as no surprise that Facebook topped the list [of visited sites]. The social media behemoth, with nearly 850 million users worldwide, was visited by 41 percent of respondents. That was followed closely by LinkedIn at 37 percent, Yahoo at 31 percent, Google+ at 28 percent, and Amazon.com with 25 percent.[24]

Many employers are convinced such activity hinders workplace productivity and thus are taking steps to do something about it. An increasing number of small businesses are installing software to monitor Internet use, and one study found that 38 percent of firms go so far as hiring staff to read or otherwise analyze employees' e-mail.[25] Beyond productivity concerns, companies are very worried these days about leaks of sensitive information and system exposure to risky viruses and malware. But these must be balanced against respect for employee privacy.

In the past, the courts tended to give firms great freedom to monitor personal e-mail accounts accessed from company networks, but that is quickly changing. In a number of cases, the courts have ruled that a firm does not have a legal right to monitor personal e-mail at work unless it has explicitly informed employees that it may do so.[26] Most small companies choose not to monitor workers' Internet use, but those that do should be sure to develop a carefully worded and legally sound policy first, and then ensure that all employees are aware of it.[27] Taking such measures is very practical—it helps head off costly legal challenges—and it also communicates the firm's respect for its employees and its sound commitment to high standards of integrity.

Widespread use of the Internet has also focused attention on the issue of protecting **intellectual property**. Traditionally, protection has been granted to original intellectual creations—inventions, literary works, and artistic products such as music—in the form of patents, copyrights, trademarks, design rights, and trade secrets. The law allows originators of such intellectual property to require compensation for its use. However, the Internet has made it easy for millions of users to copy intellectual property free of charge.

The problem of intellectual property rights violations was highlighted recently when accusations were leveled against eBay, claiming that the auction powerhouse was in part responsible for rapidly increasing sales of counterfeit goods. At one point, the French company LVMH, a world leader in prestige products, sampled eBay's online listings and found that 90 percent of the 300,000 Dior and 150,000 Louis Vuitton handbags offered for sale were fake.[28] And when MarkMonitor, a brand protection firm, investigated illicit use of one major luxury brand's products, it found 15,000 websites that were selling "knockoff" versions of its offerings.[29] Regardless of the legal liabilities, it is clear that the sale of counterfeit goods is a violation of the law and a breach of integrity. The practice cannot be defended.

Protection of intellectual property is a political as well as an ethical issue. Recent congressional hearings, lawsuits, and proposed legislation suggest that additions or changes to current laws are likely, and international enforcement continues to be a major problem.

2-3c Integrity and Doing Business Abroad

Sooner or later, small business owners operating abroad will confront challenging ethical questions, and they could relate to just about any part of the company's operations. For example, should your firm agree to provide consulting services to a foreign government if it refuses to support basic human rights or represses its citizens politically? Since China's environmental protections are relatively weak, would it be acceptable to use toxic chemicals in production processes there, as long as the local authorities approve of it? If giving a gift to a business partner in Bolivia fits with local custom but is considered a bribe by U.S. standards, is there any harm in following such a practice? Such quandaries are bound to come up time and again when doing business abroad.

intellectual property
Original intellectual creations, including inventions, literary creations, and works of art, that are protected by patents, copyrights, trademarks, design rights, and trade secrets.

Living the Dream

ENTREPRENEURSHIP + INTEGRITY

Online Stalkers May Be Closer Than You Think!

Small businesses are much more likely to achieve success if they are good at overseeing the work of their employees and can manage them toward productivity and high performance. But this can be difficult to pull off, especially when the work takes place offsite and far from the watchful eyes of supervisors. When this is the case, what should a small company do to ensure that workers are actually completing their assigned duties?

Accurid Pest Solutions, a Franklin, Virginia–based pest control business had to grapple with this very question. Dennis Gray, the company's general manager, suspected that some of his drivers were spending way too much time in the field, given their work assignments. To check on them, he quietly installed GPS tracking software on the company smartphones issued to 5 of the 18 employees. Gray noted that by following their movements on his computer, he quickly determined that two of the tracked drivers were doing "something other than work" while out on assignment. When he revealed what he had been doing, the two men confessed to their misdeeds, and both were let go.

Newly developed tracking technology is now highly cost-effective and reliable, which allows owners to manage employees at a distance. According to a 2012 study by the research firm Aberdeen Group, more than 37 percent of companies use mobile devices or vehicle-installed equipment to track the real-time locations of workers sent out on service calls. Taking this step has allowed them to improve accountability, while reducing incidents of employee theft, harassment, and other unwanted conduct. Software from a company called MIX Telematics actually goes one step further, offering software that can even be used to decelerate a truck, for example, if the driver allows it to get too close to another rig. "Big Brother" business is not only watching; it is also reaching over and taking the wheel!

Legally speaking, the tracking technology used by companies remains largely unregulated. The federal government

© ALPHASPIRIT/SHUTTERSTOCK.COM

does not restrict such employer use of GPS, though some states, such as Delaware and Connecticut, require that workers be informed if their electronic communications are being monitored. Employees should therefore assume that their mobile phone usage, e-mail exchanges, and other online activities are being monitored, unless they absolutely know otherwise.

Many employers are open about their use of tracking or anti-theft software, and that can lead to better employee performance and higher pay. One study found that the use of NCR's theft-monitoring software in 392 restaurants across 39 states led to an impressive 22 percent reduction in server theft, along with a 7 percent increase in revenues. Results such as these are impressive, offering a financial boost that far outweighs the cost of the monitoring software. Given these findings, and anticipating that the technology will only continue to get better over time, the trend toward use of surveillance systems is sure to increase—assuming no new legal restrictions. But no matter which way it goes, this is certainly something to keep your eye on.

Sources: "Accurid Pest Solutions," http://www.accuridpest.com, accessed October 24, 2014; Spencer E. Ante and Lauren Weber, "Memo to Workers: The Boss Is Watching," *The Wall Street Journal*, October 23, 2013, p. B1; and Steve Lohr, "Unblinking Eyes Track Employees," *The New York Times*, June 22, 2014, p. A1.

So what are entrepreneurs to do? Frequently, they simply apply U.S. standards to the situation. But this approach is sometimes criticized for resulting in **ethical imperialism**, an arrogant attempt to impose American values on other societies. Some guidance is provided by restrictions specified in the Foreign Corrupt Practices Act, which makes it illegal for U.S. businesses to use bribery in their dealings anywhere in the world. Regardless of local practices, American firms must comply with these laws, even though "gray areas" exist in which there are no definite answers.

Another viewpoint, sometimes called **ethical relativism**, is troublesome because it implies that anything goes if the local culture accepts it. To define its ethical landscape and work out its position on difficult issues, a small business must consider the nuances of its particular international environments. Training is also needed to ensure that each employee understands the firm's commitment to integrity, and consulting an attorney in the United States with appropriate expertise is highly recommended.

Also, bear in mind that one-time practices may set a pattern for future behavior. Some business owners have observed that offering a bribe to make a business deal possible often creates expectations for more of the same in the future. Owners who refuse to pay these "fees" say that they may have to deal with frustrating inconveniences in the short term (for example, shipped products being held up by customs), but it is likely to discourage such demands in the future. This is one of the ways in which integrity in business may offer unanticipated rewards.

2-3d The Integrity Edge

When it comes to establishing the legitimacy of a startup, taking operations online, expanding internationally, and so many other features of managing a small business, it is not always easy to stay on the high road of proper conduct. Indeed, the price of integrity is high, but the potential payoff is incalculable. The entrepreneur who makes honorable decisions, even when it comes to the smallest of details, can take satisfaction in knowing that she or he did what was right, even if things do not turn out as planned.

But integrity yields other important benefits as well. In his book *Integrity Is All You've Got*, Karl Eller observes that through his long career as a successful entrepreneur, he has seen one constant: the crucial role of integrity to achievement in business. As he puts it, "Those who have [integrity] usually succeed; those who don't have it usually fail."[30] Entrepreneurs with integrity are aware of the importance of the bottom line, but this is not their singular focus. Nonetheless, extraordinary financial performance often follows their efforts.

A growing body of research supports the simple notion that ethical business practices are good for business. Citing specific studies, the advocacy group Business for Social Responsibility (BSR) contends that there are numerous long-term benefits of adopting ethical and responsible business practices. These benefits include the following:[31]

- Improved financial performance
- Enhanced brand image and reputation
- Increased sales and customer loyalty
- Improved productivity and quality
- Better recruitment and reduced employee turnover
- Fewer regulatory inspections and less paperwork
- Improved access to capital

This is consistent with research conducted by the Institute of Business Ethics, which found that firms operating with a "clear commitment to ethical conduct" consistently outperform companies that do not. These findings prompted Philippa Foster Back,

ethical imperialism
The belief that the ethical standards of one's own country can be applied universally.

ethical relativism
The belief that ethical standards are subject to local interpretation.

director of the institute, to declare, "Not only is ethical behavior in the business world the right and principled thing to do, but it has been proven that ethical behavior pays off in financial returns."[32]

Perhaps the greatest benefit of integrity in business is the *trust* it generates. Trust results only when there's a match between the stated values of a company and its behavior in the marketplace. When a small business owner considers the needs of others and follows through on her or his promises, stakeholders notice. Customers buy more of what a firm sells when they realize that the company is doing its best to make sure that its products are of high quality and its customer service is excellent. Employees are much more likely to "go the extra mile" for a small company when it is clear that the company considers them to be more than simply replaceable parts in an impersonal machine.

And members of the community also respond positively when they are convinced that a firm is living up to its commitments to protect the environment and pay its fair share of taxes. Community support can keep the company going, even if it falls on hard times. It all comes down to trust.

2-4 BUILDING A BUSINESS WITH INTEGRITY

Suggest practical approaches for building a business with integrity.

The goal of a small business owner with integrity should be to operate honorably in all areas of practice, which sets the entrepreneur on a path toward crafting the worthy legacy that was discussed in Chapter 1. Those at the top must provide the leadership, culture, and training that support appropriate ethical perspectives and proper behavior.

2-4a The Foundations of Integrity

The business practices that a firm's leaders and employees view as right or wrong reflect their **underlying values**. An individual's beliefs affect what that person does on the job and how she or he acts toward customers and others. Business behavior, then, reflects the level of a person's commitment to honesty, respect, truthfulness, and so forth—in other words, to integrity in all of its dimensions. Such values are often evident in the business enterprise's mission statement.

Values that serve as a foundation for integrity in business are based on personal views of the role of humankind in the universe and, naturally, are part of basic philosophical and/or religious convictions.[33] In the United States, Judeo-Christian ideals have traditionally served as the general body of beliefs underlying business behavior, although there are plenty of examples of honorable behavior based on principles derived from other religions. Since religious and/or philosophical principles are reflected in the business practices of firms of all sizes, a leader's personal commitment to certain basic values is an important determinant of his or her firm's commitment to business integrity. A long-time observer of high-tech startups commented on the significance of an entrepreneur's personal standards to investment decisions:

> *I can tell you, even with the smallest high-technology companies, the product had to be good, the market had to be good, the people had to be good. But the one thing that was checked out most extensively by venture capitalists was the integrity of the management team. And if integrity wasn't there, it didn't matter how good the product was, how good the market was—they weren't funded.*[34]

underlying values
Beliefs that provide a foundation for ethical behavior in an individual or a firm.

It seems apparent that a deep commitment to basic values affects behavior in the marketplace and gives rise to business practices that are widely appreciated and admired. Without a strong commitment to integrity on the part of small business leadership, ethical standards can easily be compromised.

2-4b Leading with Integrity

In a small organization, the influence of a leader is more pronounced than it is in a large corporation where leadership can become diffused. This fact is recognized by J. C. Huizenga, the founder and chairman of National Heritage Academies, which is one of the fastest-growing education providers in the United States:

> *The executive of a small company must often face moral challenges more directly, because he or she has more direct contact with customers, suppliers, and employees than an executive in a large corporation who may have a management team to deliberate with. The consequences of his or her choices often affect the business more significantly because of the size of the issue relative to the size of the company.*[35]

© DOCSTOCKMEDIA/SHUTTERSTOCK.COM

In effect, the founder or head of a small business can say, "My personal integrity is on the line, and I want you to do it this way." Such statements are easily understood. And a leader becomes even more effective when she or he backs up such statements with appropriate behavior. In fact, a leader's behavior has much greater influence on employees than her or his stated philosophy does. Everyone watches how the leader behaves, and this conduct establishes the culture of the company, underscoring what is allowed or encouraged and what is prohibited.

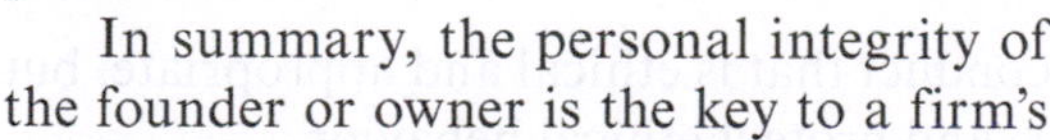

In summary, the personal integrity of the founder or owner is the key to a firm's ethical performance. The dominant role of this one person (or the leadership team) serves to shape the ethical performance of the small company, for good or for ill.

2-4c An Ethical Organizational Culture

Integrity in a business requires a supportive organizational culture. Ideally, every manager and employee should instinctively resolve every ethical issue by simply doing what is right. An ethical culture requires an environment in which employees at every level are confident that the firm is fully committed to honorable conduct. To a considerable degree, strong leadership helps build this understanding. As a small business grows, however, personal interactions between the owner and employees occur less often, creating the need to articulate and reinforce principles of integrity in ways that supplement the personal example of the entrepreneur. A good place to start is to establish an ethics policy for the company.

In their highly influential book *The Power of Ethical Management*, Kenneth Blanchard and Norman Vincent Peale offer insights to guide the development of an ethics policy. They suggest that the policy be based on the following five fundamental principles:[36]

- ***Purpose.*** The vision for the company and your core values will guide business conduct.
- ***Pride.*** When employees take pride in their work and their company, they are much more likely to be ethical in their dealings.
- ***Patience.*** If you push too hard for short-term results, sooner or later acting unethically will seem to be the only way to achieve the outcomes you seek.
- ***Persistence.*** Stand by your word, which is the foundation of trust. If you are not committed to an ethical framework, your integrity is at risk, as is the reputation of the company.
- ***Perspective.*** Stop from time to time to reflect on where your business is going, why it is going that way, and how you plan to get there. This will allow you to be more confident that you are on the right track now and will continue to be in the future.

To define ethical behavior in the company more specifically, the owner-manager of a small firm should formulate a **code of ethics** similar to that of most large corporations. A survey of MBA students employed by small and medium-size companies revealed that codes of ethics shape and improve conduct in their organizations in a number of ways:[37]

- By defining behavioral expectations
- By communicating that those expectations apply to employees at all levels in the business
- By helping employees convey the company's standards of conduct to suppliers and customers
- By serving as a tool for handling peer pressure
- By providing a formal channel for communicating with superiors without fear of reprisal

In other words, a code of ethics identifies conduct that is ethical and appropriate, but it is also a practical tool that can encourage and protect ethical behavior.

A well-written code expresses the principles to be followed by employees of the firm and gives examples of these principles in action. A code of ethics might, for example, prohibit acceptance of gifts or favors from suppliers but point out standard business courtesies, such as a lunch or a couple of movie tickets, that might be accepted without violating the policy. If a code of ethics is to be effective, employees must be aware of its nature and convinced of its importance. At the very least, each employee should read and sign it. As a company grows larger, employees will need training to ensure that the code is well understood and taken seriously.

Entrepreneurs further reinforce ethical culture in the business when they hire and promote ethical people, recognize and correct behavior that is unethical, and lead by example in business dealings, while encouraging all employees to do the same. With training and consistent management, employees can develop the level of understanding needed to act in the spirit of the code when faced with situations not covered by specific rules. A code of ethics, however, will be effective only to the degree that the entrepreneur's behavior is consistent with her or his own stated principles. Employees can easily spot hypocrisy, and double standards quickly dull the ethical sensibilities of the organization.

code of ethics
Official standards of employee behavior formulated by a business owner.

2-4d Better Business Bureaus

Sometimes, the business conduct of small companies is shaped by external forces. Because unethical operations reflect adversely on honest members of the business community, privately owned companies in many cities have joined together to form Better Business Bureaus (BBBs). The purpose of such organizations is to promote ethical conduct on the part of all businesses in a region, and they do so in the following ways:

- By providing consumers with free information to help them make informed decisions when dealing with a company
- By creating an incentive for businesses to adhere to proper business practices and earnestly address customer complaints
- By resolving questions or disputes concerning purchases through mediation or arbitration.

As a result, unethical business practices often decline in a community served by a Better Business Bureau.

Though BBBs report relevant information to law enforcement agencies, they are not government entities, and they cannot collect money or impose penalties on companies that engage in unethical business practices. However, a BBB can provide information on a company's operating track record, which will affect the firm's reputation and, in turn, its success in the marketplace. This creates an incentive for companies to adopt fair and proper business practices and address customer complaints appropriately in order to avoid losing business.

Managing Your Online Reputation

Tools like Google Alerts, Viralheat, and Trackur can help you track online customer comments, and for some of these, there is no charge. If you feel that you need more assistance in getting your online reputation straightened out, companies like Reputation.com, Big Blue Robot, and Metal Rabbit Media can help, but their services are pricey. If the price seems too steep, consider using BrandYourself.com's easy-to-use tutorial that will lead you through the reputation management process for free.

2-4e The Ethical Decision-Making Process

Ethical decision making often is not a very clear-cut process. In fact, even after much thought and soul searching, the appropriate course of action still may not be apparent in some business situations. The Ethics Resource Center offers a decision-making process that may help with challenging dilemmas. We have adapted this simple six-step process to help small business owners see the issues more clearly and make better, more ethical decisions.[38]

STEP 1: DEFINE THE PROBLEM

How you define the problem is important because this will guide where you look for solutions. For example, if you have a customer who is often late in paying invoices, is this a problem because he doesn't manage his books well, is he trying to conserve his working capital by forcing you to carry this debt for him for as long as possible, or are his own customers consistently slow in paying him for the goods he sells them? If your customer is careless with his books or is just trying to stretch out his accounts payable, a penalty for the delay may correct the problem. However, penalizing that customer is not likely to solve the problem if the delays are actually the result of his cash-strapped customers' struggling to find a way to pay him. In fact, penalizing him in this case may only make matters worse. Looking for the root of the problem is the best place to start in your search for a solution to a challenging ethical problem.

STEP 2: IDENTIFY ALTERNATIVE SOLUTIONS TO THE PROBLEM

It is tempting to go with an "obvious" solution or one that has been used in the past, but often this is not the best answer—even if it is ethical. Be open-minded, and consider creative alternatives. Often, an innovative solution is available that is consistent with your personal ethics, protects the interests of other affected parties, and offers superior outcomes. Seeking advice from trusted friends and advisors who have faced similar situations can spur your thinking and lead to options that you might otherwise overlook.

STEP 3: EVALUATE THE IDENTIFIED ALTERNATIVES

Rotary Club International, a worldwide organization of business and professional leaders, has set a high standard for business conduct. It calls on its members to ask the following four questions when they prepare to make a decision about the things they think, say, or do:[39]

1. Is it the *truth?*
2. Is it *fair* to all concerned?
3. Will it build *goodwill* and better *friendships*?
4. Will it be *beneficial* to all concerned?

Taking a similar approach, you might ask yourself, "How would I feel if my decision were reported in the daily newspaper?" Or, the question can be even more personal: "How well could I explain this decision to my mother or children?" The answer could help to steer you away from unethical behavior.

Perhaps the most widely recommended principle for ethical behavior is simply to follow the Golden Rule: "Treat others as you would want to be treated." This simple rule is embraced, in one form or another, by most of the world's religions and philosophies,[40] and its influence is very far reaching. For example, the philosopher Immanuel Kant introduced the so-called categorical imperative, a sophisticated way of asking, "How would it be if everyone decided to do what you intend to do?"[41] Raising such questions can be a very practical way for an entrepreneur to evaluate ethical decisions and guard her or his integrity.

© ESA HILTULA/ALAMY

No matter what approach you take, evaluating alternatives requires time and patience. In addition, personal perceptions and biases are likely to cloud the way you see solutions. Therefore, it is important to separate what you *think* is the case from what you *know* to be true. It often helps to write down your thoughts about alternatives so that you can keep track of your concerns as well as important facts and details. You might list the ethical pros and cons of each alternative or identify the impact of each option on every person or company that will be affected. Another possibility is to rank all potential options based on their overall merits and then narrow the list to the two or three best solutions to consider further. This will allow you to organize your thoughts and make a better selection.

STEP 4: MAKE THE DECISION

The next step is to choose the "best" ethical response, based on your evaluation of all possible alternatives. On the surface, this sounds easy enough, but unfortunately no single option will completely solve the problem in most cases. In fact, you may not even be able to identify an obvious winner. No matter how you go about making the decision, keep your vision and core values firmly in mind—this is essential to making solid decisions that do not compromise your ethical standards.

STEP 5: IMPLEMENT THE DECISION

Entrepreneurs sometimes put off responding to ethical challenges because any response will be bad news for someone involved. But avoiding action on the decision may allow a small problem to grow into a major crisis, and it may cause you to spend more time thinking about the problem when other important matters deserve your attention.

STEP 6: EVALUATE THE DECISION

The goal of making a decision is to resolve an ethical dilemma. So, has the situation improved, gotten worse, or stayed about the same? Has the solution created ethical issues of its own? Has information come to light indicating that your decision was not the most ethical course of action? Everyone makes mistakes. You may very well need to reopen the matter to make things right. But remember, if your decision was based on the best of intentions and information available at the time, you can wade back into the waters of ethical turmoil with a clear conscience, and there is no substitute for that.

2-5 SOCIAL ENTREPRENEURSHIP: A CONTINUING TREND

Define *social entrepreneurship*, and describe its influence on small companies and startup opportunities.

The social issues affecting businesses are numerous and diverse. Businesses are expected—at different times and by various groups—to help solve social problems related to education, crime, poverty, and the environment. In fact, these expectations converge in a form of venturing called **social entrepreneurship**, which continues to gain momentum. Though the term has been defined in different ways, Harvard researchers suggest that *social entrepreneurship* refers to "entrepreneurial activity with an embedded social purpose."[42] It has been described more poetically as "[having] a vision of a greater good and working to make it real."[43] In other words, a social entrepreneur is one who comes up with innovative solutions to society's most pressing needs, problems, and opportunities and then makes them happen.

2-5a Social Entrepreneurship and the Triple Bottom Line

Becoming a social entrepreneur usually does not mean that a business owner is no longer concerned with making money—financial gain is just one of an expanded set of goals. In fact, the outcomes of interest are sometimes referred to as the "triple bottom line" because they focus on people, profits, and the planet. Clearly, no enterprise can exist for long without making a profit. But social entrepreneurs believe that ventures should also be concerned with people and the environment. To get a feel for the wide range of enterprises that fall under the social entrepreneurship umbrella, consider the following cases:

- Alicia Polak moved to South Africa and started the Khaya Cookie Company to create jobs in the poor towns outside Capetown. After growing the company into a sizeable and successful enterprise, she sold it back to local South Africans in the true spirit of empowerment.[44]
- Homeboy Industries grew out of a jobs program launched by Father Greg Boyle to offer an alternative to gang violence. Today, it touches the lives of thousands of previously incarcerated men and women a year, many of whom re-enter the workforce through its many small businesses, which include the Homeboy Bakery, Homegirl Café & Catering, Homeboy Farmers Markets, and a handful of other enterprises.[45]

social entrepreneurship Entrepreneurial activity that provides innovative solutions for social issues.

- For years, Bart Weetjens has been training rats in the African nation of Tanzania to sniff out the deadly unexploded land mines that litter the countryside in so many war-torn nations. It turns out that rats are better than dogs for this work—lighter, cheaper to keep, and less prone to tropical diseases—and they clear areas so that children can run and play without fear of stepping on a mine. "They save human lives," says Weetjens, who calls the rodents "heroes."[46]

These entrepreneurs clearly do not fit the money-obsessed stereotype that some associate with business owners. They are hoping to do more than make a profit, but they are doing well financially, too. And this is not surprising. According to Nielsen's 2013 "Consumers Who Care" study, 50 percent of global consumers said they would pay more for the goods and services of companies that give back to society.[47]

2-5b Small Business and the Natural Environment

At one time, there was little concern for the impact that businesses had on the environment, but that is rapidly changing. For instance, releasing industrial waste into streams, contaminants into the air, and noise into neighborhoods is no longer acceptable. In fact, escalating concern for the environment has spawned a shift toward **sustainable small business**. This trend recognizes that a company must be profitable to stay in business, but it also promotes the use of eco-friendly practices (careful use of resources, energy conservation, recycling, etc.) through all facets of a company's operations. In short, a sustainable enterprise must respond to customer needs while showing reasonable concern for the environment. This is consistent with the concept of integrity outlined in this chapter.

SUSTAINABILITY MATTERS

The interests of small business owners and environmentalists are not necessarily in conflict. Some business leaders, including many in small companies, consistently work and act for the cause of **environmentalism**, and in many cases, this emphasis makes sound financial sense. For example, companies can actually save money by buying or leasing LEED-certified buildings. (This designation stands for "Leadership in Energy and Environmental Design." It is a stamp of approval granted only to those facilities that have been built to strict standards established by the U.S. Green Building Council to promote energy and water conservation, reduce CO_2 emissions, and improve indoor air quality.) Though more expensive to construct, such buildings can decrease energy costs from operations by as much as 20 percent, and healthier workplace environments improve employee productivity, reduce illness and absences, improve recruitment, and raise retention—all of which can create a net savings for the company. One analyst estimates that a 2 percent initial investment in eco-friendly design can generate a tenfold savings in operating costs.[48]

We need to emphasize, however, that the sustainability news for small business is not all good. For example, some firms are adversely affected by new laws passed to protect the environment. Businesses such as fast lube and oil change centers, medical waste disposal operations, self-service car washes, and asbestos removal services have been especially hard hit by expanding environmental regulations. The costs can be punishing. In fact, many companies in these industries and others have closed because of the financial burden of environmental controls. While small companies that enjoy favorable market conditions can often pass higher environmental costs on to their

sustainable small business
A profitable company that responds to customers' needs while showing reasonable concern for the environment.

environmentalism
The effort to protect and preserve the environment.

customers, these costs can easily sink a small, struggling firm with older equipment that may need to be upgraded and limited resources.

Regardless of the financial impact, it is critical to follow the environmental regulations that apply to your business. To ignore this responsibility is to violate the law. GreenBiz.com cautions businesses to comply with regulations at all levels—federal, state, and local—but its overall message is actually very upbeat: "There are dozens of ways companies of all sizes can reduce their environmental footprints, save money, earn consumer trust and stakeholder confidence, comply with government regulations, be ready to snag new market opportunities, and boost efficiency and productivity."[49]

Win-win solutions are possible. For example, firms whose products leave minimal environmental impact are generally preferred by customers over competitors whose products pollute. And some entrepreneurs are able to build their small businesses on planet-saving products and services, such as repair shops that service pollution-control equipment on automobiles. Furthermore, compliance with environmental regulations may actually lead to unexpected benefits, such as a reduction in paperwork for companies that can show they are in line with regulations.

In any case, resources are available to help you avoid the potentially disastrous consequences of noncompliance. The Small Business Administration is prepared to lead you through the sometimes-choppy waters of environmental law, and the U.S. Environmental Protection Agency (EPA) offers the Small Business Gateway, an Internet portal that will connect you to information, technical assistance, and solutions to challenges related to the environment. The EPA also provides online access to "Managing Your Hazardous Waste: A Guide for Small Businesses," which helps make compliance much easier to manage.[50]

GREEN OPPORTUNITIES FOR SMALL BUSINESS

Although they add to the cost of doing business for some small companies, environmental concerns open up great opportunities for others. In fact, many startups have come to life precisely because of the "greening" of business and the potential opportunities that this has created.

The level of interest in ventures that can be labeled "green," "clean," or "sustainable" continues to rise, and this trend has led to the launching of many innovative eco-focused startups. However, according to Joel Makower, chairman and executive director of GreenBiz Group and author of *Strategies for the Green Economy*, "Green succeeds only to the extent that it means better—it's cheaper to buy, it operates better, it lasts longer, it's cooler for my image. People want to do the right thing, but they don't want to go out of their way to do it. They love 'change' when it's a noun; they hate it when it's a verb."[51]

Some green businesses are based on sophisticated technologies that are well beyond the reach of the typical small business. However, many opportunities in this category are very accessible to small companies and startups. Perhaps a recent green startup story will inspire you to think about new venture possibilities that could be right for you: You may know that bamboo is one of the world's fastest-growing plants, but it will probably surprise you to learn that a number of new ventures have sprouted up to make bicycles out of the sturdy stuff. As owner of Boo Bicycles, Nick Frey builds and sells high-performance bikes with bamboo frames, and business is good. His prices range from \$3,000 for a basic frame to \$10,000 for a tricked-out racer—he even sold a frame as art to a Spanish gallery![52] But beyond aesthetics, the company's website points out that its custom bikes "can be raced successfully at the highest levels but are designed to provide a lively, forgiving ride, which increases stability and traction on descents and reduces fatigue."[53] The product definitely turns heads—and opens wallets, too.

Living the Dream

ENTREPRENEURSHIP + INTEGRITY

Green Ventures That Don't Go into the Red

For Reilly Starr and Katie Sue Nicklos, founders of Naked Sports Gear, the decision to run their startup as a green venture is just one factor that makes their company unique. In Starr's words, "For us, not going green was not an option. It just wasn't ever on the table." These entrepreneurs have combined their passion for distinctive women's athletic apparel—made from tan-through, moisture-wicking material—with a strong and abiding commitment to sustainable business practices. In fact, the duo's conviction runs so deep that they are willing to pay as much as three times more for fabric and labor than they would by offshoring production to China.

In their eyes, the added expense is a small price to pay for being able to walk down the street to visit their vendors and keep a close eye on the manufacturing process to ensure that working conditions are appropriate and quality is high. And their approach seems to be working. Since opening in May of 2012, the growth in sales of Naked Sports Gear apparel has been 300 percent a year, as the company offers its merchandise through a number of websites, including Amazon, OpenSky, and AHAlife. Both Starr and Nicklos attribute their success to their customers' desire for locally produced merchandise with an ethical focus. In fact, research has consistently shown that consumers are very motivated to buy from companies they perceive as valuing sustainable and socially responsible business practices. When two products are similar in price and quality, most consumers will choose the brand supporting a greater social purpose.

On the other hand, businesses must also continually monitor their spending on green initiatives and weigh this against the impact it has on the bottom line. Although consumers are generally concerned about sustainability, studies have also shown that most are unwilling to pay more for a green product. So taking this path may require some creativity and careful planning—but it can be done.

Consider Chaz Berman, a serial entrepreneur and CEO of Grower's Secret. His small company offers a line of 32 all-natural fertilizers that compete for shelf space against powerhouse brands like Scotts and Miracle-Gro. But Berman has managed to mesh a social-cause focus with bottom-line cost savings. One way that he does this is by offsetting the 15 percent higher cost of recycled packaging by locating the company's core operations where they make the most sense (for example, processing is located in Oakland, California, with sales and marketing in San Francisco and accounting operations in Honolulu). The subsequent reduction in office space allows Grower's Secret to save about 10 percent on rent and utilities. Taking such measures has led to a successful mix of care for the environment and smart financial management. "This is a way for companies to save expenses, differentiate themselves in the market, and hopefully make more money," observes Berman. It seems to be working that way for Grower's Secret.

Sources: "Grower's Secret: Innovative Organic Solutions," http://www.growerssecret.com, accessed October 27, 2014; Michelle Goodman, "Are You Green Enough?" *Entrepreneur*, Vol. 43, No. 12 (2013), pp. 45–49 ; Julia Love, "Grower's Secret Takes Root with Organic Growth," *San Francisco Business Times*, http://www.bizjournals.com/sanfrancisco/print-edition/2012/10/19/growers-secret-takes-root-with.html?page=all, accessed October 27, 2014; and "Naked Sports Gear: About Us," https://www.nakedsportsgear.com/about-us, accessed October 27, 2014.

Interest in the sustainability trend can take many different forms. For a growing number of small business owners, the ultimate goal is to save the planet; others recognize that sustainable business practices can hold down costs, attract customers, and generate value for shareholders. The movement will provide huge opportunities for companies with determination and creativity, as long as they can execute the plan. This is prime territory for small entrepreneurial companies, given their flexibility and innovative thinking. Entrepreneurs may be able to do well financially *and* do good, by guarding the environment and their integrity at the same time.

2-1. **Define *integrity*, and understand its importance to small businesses.**

- Integrity refers to a general sense of honesty and reliability that is expressed in a strong commitment to doing the right thing, regardless of the circumstances. "Doing anything for money" can quickly lead to distortions in business behavior.
- Many small business owners strive to achieve the highest standards of honesty, fairness, and respect in their business relationships.

2-2. **Explain how integrity applies to various stakeholder groups.**

- Closely tied to integrity are ethical issues, which go beyond what is legal or illegal to include more general questions of right and wrong.
- When they make business decisions, entrepreneurs must consider the interests of all stakeholder groups, in particular those of the owners, customers, employees, the community, and the government, among others.
- A company's owners have a clear and legitimate right to benefit from the financial performance of the business.
- Those companies that take customers seriously and serve them well are likely to have more of them.
- Showing proper appreciation for employees as human beings and as valuable members of the team is an essential ingredient of managerial integrity.
- Most people consider an ethical small business to be one that acts as a good citizen in its community.
- Research suggests that most small business owners exercise great integrity, but some are apt to cut corners when it comes to social responsibilities if profits will be affected.
- Entrepreneurs must obey governmental laws and follow applicable regulations if they want to maintain their integrity and avoid jail time.

2-3. **Identify some common challenges and benefits of maintaining integrity in small businesses.**

- Small firms' limited resources and desire to succeed make them especially vulnerable to allowing or engaging in unethical practices.
- Startups and small companies sometimes resort to telling legitimacy lies, but they can win customers and attract other important stakeholders by paying close attention to the PRO factors (those related to the firm's products, its representatives, and the organization itself).
- Use of the Internet has highlighted ethical issues such as invasion of privacy and threats to intellectual property rights.
- Cultural differences may complicate ethical decision making for small firms operating abroad. The concept of ethical relativism is troublesome because it implies that ethical standards are subject to local interpretation.
- Research supports the notion that ethical business practices are good for business. When customers and employees trust a small company to act with integrity, their support can help keep the company going.

2-4. **Suggest practical approaches for building a business with integrity.**

- The underlying values and the behavior of business leaders are powerful forces that affect ethical performance.
- An organizational culture that supports integrity is key to achieving appropriate behavior among a firm's employees. Small firms should develop codes of ethics to provide guidance for their employees.
- Many small companies join Better Business Bureaus to promote ethical conduct throughout the business community.
- Following an ethical decision-making process can help entrepreneurs protect their integrity and that of their business.

2-5. **Define *social entrepreneurship*, and describe its influence on small companies and startup opportunities.**

- Researchers have defined social entrepreneurship as "entrepreneurial activity with an embedded social purpose."
- Social entrepreneurship continues to gain momentum and leads to innovative solutions to society's most pressing needs, problems, and opportunities.
- Social entrepreneurs focus on an expanded set of priorities—a triple bottom line, which takes into account a venture's impact on people, profits, and the planet.

- A *sustainable small business* is a profitable company that responds to customer needs while showing reasonable concern for the natural environment.
- Environmental regulations adversely affect some small firms, such as dry cleaners.
- Win-win outcomes are possible in many cases—the cost of eco-friendly business practices can often be more than offset by operational savings, increased customer interest, and reduced paperwork, for example.
- The SBA, the EPA, and other public and private resources stand ready to help small businesses comply with environmental regulations.
- Small companies are sometimes launched precisely to take advantage of opportunities created by environmental concerns. Creating environmentally friendly products and services requires creativity and flexibility, areas in which small businesses tend to excel.

Key Terms

code of ethics p. 52
environmentalism p. 56
ethical imperialism p. 49
ethical relativism p. 49
integrity p. 38
intellectual property p. 47
social entrepreneurship p. 55
social responsibilities p. 42
stakeholders p. 39
sustainable small business p. 56
underlying values p. 50

You Make the Call

Situation 1

Sally started her consulting business a year ago and has been doing very well. About a month ago, she decided she needed to hire someone to help her since she was getting busier and busier. After interviewing several candidates, she decided to hire the most-qualified one of the group, Mary. She called Mary on Monday to tell her she had gotten the job. They both agreed that Mary would start the following Monday and that she could come in and fill out all the hiring paperwork at that time.

On Tuesday of the same week, a friend of Sally's called her to say that she had found the perfect person for Sally. Sally explained that she had already hired someone, but the friend insisted, "Just meet this girl. Who knows, maybe you might want to hire her in the future!" Rather reluctantly, Sally consented. "Alright, if she can come in tomorrow, I'll meet with her, but that's all."

"Oh, I'm so glad. I just know you're going to like her!" Sally's friend exclaimed. And Sally did like her. She liked her a lot. Sally had met with Julie on Wednesday morning. She was everything that Sally had been looking for and more. In terms of experience, Julie far surpassed any of the candidates Sally had previously interviewed, including Mary. On top of that, she was willing to bring in clients of her own, which would only increase business. All in all, Sally knew this was a win-win situation. But what about Mary? She had already given her word to Mary that she could start work on Monday.

Source: http://www.sba.gov/smallbusinessplanner/manage/lead/SERV_BETHICS.html, accessed September 30, 2010.

Question 1 What decision on Sally's part would contribute most to the success of her business?
Question 2 What ethical reasoning would support hiring Mary?
Question 3 What ethical reasoning would support hiring Julie?

Situation 2

Darryl Wilson owns Darryl's Deals on Wheels, a small used-car dealership in Humble, Texas. Wilson started the company three years ago, but he is still struggling to get a solid footing in the industry. The slow economy isn't helping—no one seems to have money to buy cars right now—and there is plenty of competition. The business provides the main source of income for his family, which includes his wife and two teenage daughters. Wilson has to make this business work to keep food on the table and to pay the typical expenses involved in raising a family.

Finding customers is essential to success in the car sales business, but so is holding down costs. This means Wilson has to find "rolling stock" that is in demand and inexpensive, but that is not easy to do because all the other dealers in his area are in the same boat. They, too, are trying to snap up the best deals, and this is driving up the cost of inventory. So, controlling costs means looking at other features of the business, and Wilson thinks he has found something that just may help. The state of Texas requires dealers to report the purchase of all vehicles they acquire for resale, which means the dealer will have to pay a 2.5 percent inventory tax (based on the purchase price) when it sells the car later. But when Wilson buys a car from a private seller, he can usually convince him or her to sign over the title without designating a specific buyer. This allows Wilson to fill in that part of the title and the transfer form with the name of the person who buys the car from him, when that time comes. In the end, the state has no evidence of Wilson's involvement in the transaction, which allows him to avoid paying administrative fees and the inventory tax—a savings of about $250 on a typical sale. The state doesn't catch on, and his customers never seem to notice because they have to pay administrative fees and sales tax anyway when they buy the car and transfer the title into their own names.

So far, Wilson has not run into any problems with this practice. In his mind, this is nothing more than "heads-up business." Furthermore, his profits are so slim right now that playing by the book would probably mean that he would have to go out of business. Even the state would lose money then, because a company that is out of business pays no income taxes and Wilson would have to start collecting unemployment.

Question 1 What are the advantages and possible drawbacks to Wilson's title-transfer scheme?

Question 2 Which stakeholders are affected by this approach, either positively or negatively? How great are their gains/losses?

Question 3 Wilson finds it hard to identify a downside to his approach. What risks might he be overlooking?

Question 4 What would you do if you were in Wilson's shoes? If his competitors are following the same practice (and some of them surely are), would that make any difference to you?

Situation 3

Ben London owns and operates Fantastic Footage, a film-editing company in Los Angeles that does contract work mostly for production companies in Hollywood. Not long ago, a local landscaping business completed nearly $5,500 worth of work around London's offices. While the initial bid now seems a little high for the amount of work that was actually done, there is no question that the work completed was of high quality, and London finally feels comfortable inviting potential clients to meet him at his office to discuss possible deals. However, because of an apparent oversight, the landscaping contractor never submitted a bill. It's been more than 15 months since the completion of the project, and London has come to conclude that the contractor somehow lost track of the project. He is thinking about calling the company to ask for a final invoice so that he can settle up, but business has been really slow over the last year or so, and it hasn't been easy to pay all of the bills as it is. Forking over $5,500 for the landscaping would not be impossible, but it would be pretty challenging to scrape up that kind of money right now. So, he is trying to figure out what he should do.

Question 1 In your opinion, whose responsibility is it to initiate the payment of this debt?

Question 2 What if London is unable to come up with the money to pay the bill when (if) it is finally submitted? What should he do then?

Question 3 What options are available to London in this case? Assess these options using each of the following tests: (1) the Rotary Club's four-questions test, (2) the "newspaper report" test, (3) the "explain it to my mother" test, and (4) the Golden Rule. Do you arrive at the same conclusion when applying each of these? If not, which one should London use to decide what he should do?

Video Case 2

PortionPac® Chemical Corporation (P. 647)

PortionPac manufactures highly concentrated, premeasured cleaning products that reduce resources used and provide sustainable, cost-effective, and environmentally friendly solutions. This case discusses PortionPac's progressive leadership, user-centric educational services, and innovative products and packaging, highlighting its integrity and ethical behavior toward various stakeholder groups, including customers, employees, and the community.

Alternative Cases for Chapter 2

Case 3, The Kollection, p. 649
Case 5, Iaccarino & Son, p. 654
Case 8, Couchsurfing International, p. 658
Case 18, Auntie Anne's Pretzel in China, p. 682

Endnotes

1. Karl Eller, *Integrity Is All You've Got: And Seven Other Lessons of an Entrepreneurial Life* (New York, NY: McGraw-Hill, 2005), p. 89.
2. The terms *integrity* and *ethics* are often used interchangeably, but while closely related conceptually, they are not precisely equivalent. In our view, ethics most often refers to standards of conduct derived from an *externally* created system of rules or guidelines, such as those established by a professional board or industry association. In contrast, integrity is based on an *internal* system of principles that guide behavior, making compliance a matter of choice rather than obligation. However, both can powerfully shape the thoughts and conduct of conscientious individuals.
3. R. Edward Freeman promoted the stakeholder view in his book, *Strategic Management: A Stakeholder Approach* (Boston, MA: Pitman, 1984), but he recognizes that this framework can make decision making difficult. There usually are no hard-and-fast rules to guide the balancing of stakeholder interests in a given situation. Though others would take issue with Freeman's conclusions, he nonetheless argues that the survival of the firm can be jeopardized if these interests are not kept in balance.
4. See Archie B. Carroll and Ann K. Buchholtz, *Business and Society: Ethics, Sustainability, and Stakeholder Management* (Mason, OH: Cengage Learning, 2015) for a more complete discussion.
5. Milton Friedman, *Capitalism and Freedom* (Chicago, IL: University of Chicago Press, 1963), p. 133.
6. April Joyner, "Happiness Begins at the Office," *Inc.*, Vol. 32, No. 4 (2010), p. 8.
7. This is consistent with the findings of an extensive meta-analysis detailing a strong linkage between employee job satisfaction and customer satisfaction. See Steven P. Brown and Sun K. Lam, "A Meta-Analysis of Relationships Linking Employee Satisfaction to Customer Responses," *Journal of Marketing*, Vol. 84, No. 3 (2008), pp. 243–255.
8. "Employee Theft: Legal Aspects—Estimates of Cost," http://law.jrank.org/pages/1084/Employee-Theft-Legal-Aspects-Estimates-cost.html, accessed September 26, 2014.
9. "Employee Theft," http://www.criminal-law-lawyer-source.com/terms/employee-theft.html, accessed September 24, 2014.
10. "Email and Social Media Marketing You Can Feel Good About," http://www.icontact.com/about/social-responsibility, accessed September 26, 2014; and Joel Holland, "Save the World, Make a Million," *Entrepreneur*, April 2010, http://www.entrepreneur.com/article/205556, accessed September 26, 2014.
11. Ryan Allis, "iContact and Vocus Combine Forces," http://blog.icontact.com/blog/company-announcement, accessed September 26, 2014.
12. Raymund Flandez, "Small Companies Put Charity into Their Business Plan," *The Wall Street Journal*, November 20, 2007, p. B3.
13. The popular business press provides numerous examples to support this position, but we recognize that the evidence from academic studies on the subject is mixed. For an excellent review of this research, see Michael L. Barnett, "Stakeholder Influence Capacity and the Variability of Financial Returns to Corporate Social Responsibility," *Academy of Management Review*, Vol. 32, No. 3 (2007), pp. 794–816.
14. William J. Dennis, Jr. (ed.), "Contributions to Community," http://www.411sbfacts.com/sbpoll.php?POLLID=0025, accessed September 26, 2014.
15. Eric Knopf, "One Step at a Time," in Michael McMyne and Nicole Amare (eds.), *Beyond the Lemonade Stand: 14 Undergraduate Entrepreneurs Tell Their Stories of Ethics in Business* (St. Louis, MO: St. Louis University, 2004), pp. 47–48.
16. Martin Vaughn, "IRS Too Easy on Payroll Taxes, Study Finds," *The Wall Street Journal*, July 29, 2008, p. A8.
17. For an interesting discussion and useful analysis of legitimacy lies, see Matthew W. Rutherford, Paul F. Buller, and J. Michael Stebbins, "Ethical Considerations of the Legitimacy Lie," *Entrepreneurship Theory and Practice*, Vol. 33, No. 4 (2009), pp. 949–964.
18. Paulette Thomas, "Virtual Business Plans Require Human Touch," *The Wall Street Journal*, August 2, 2005, p. B2.
19. Nadine Heintz, "For Rolling Up Her Sleeves," *Inc.*, Vol. 26, No. 4 (2004), pp. 128–129.
20. Miroslav Pivoda, Frank Hoy, Kiril Todorov, and Viktor Vojtko, "Entrepreneurial Tricks and Ethics Surveyed in Different Countries," *International Journal of E-Entrepreneurship and Innovation*, Vol. 2, No. 3 (2011), pp. 46–65.
21. For an in-depth look at the theoretical framework and empirical tests involved in the study mentioned here, see Dean A. Shepherd and Andrew Zacharakis, "A New Venture's Cognitive Legitimacy: An Assessment by Customers," *Journal of Small Business Management*, Vol. 41, No. 2 (2003), pp. 148–167.
22. *Ibid.*
23. Survey results reported in Karen R. Harned, "Why Website Privacy Policies Matter," *MyBusiness*, September/October 2010, p. 39.
24. Aaron Gouveia, "Wasting Time at Work 2012," http://www.salary.com/wasting-time-at-work-2012, accessed September 30, 2014.
25. Dionne Searcey, "Some Courts Raise Bar on Reading Employee Email," *The Wall Street Journal*, November 19, 2009, p. A17.
26. *Ibid.*
27. For excellent guidance regarding the legal issues related to the regulation of Internet use at work, see William P. Smith and Filiz Tabak, "Monitoring Employee E-Mails: Is There Any Room for Privacy?" *Academy of Management Perspectives*, Vol. 23, No. 4 (2009), pp. 33–48.
28. "Handbagged," *The Economist*, Vol. 387, No. 8585 (2008), p. 76.
29. Jayne O'Donnell, "Counterfeits Are a Growing—and Dangerous—Problem," *USA Today*, June 7, 2012, p. 8A.
30. Eller, *op. cit.*, p. 90.
31. This research is cited in Stephen K. Henn, *Business Ethics: A Case Study Approach* (Hoboken, NJ: John Wiley, 2009), pp. 11–12.
32. For more on this, see Robert Moment, "The 7 Principles of Business Integrity," http://www.successfuloffice.com/the-seven-principles-of-business-integrity.htm, accessed September 26, 2014.
33. Justin G. Longenecker, Joseph A. McKinney, and Carlos W. Moore, "Religious Intensity, Evangelical Christianity, and Business Ethics: An Empirical Study," *Journal of Business Ethics*, Vol. 55, No. 2 (2004), pp. 373–386 . This study provides evidence to support this position. The results show that religious values play a part in ethical decision making, though general religious categorizations (such as Catholic, Protestant, Jewish) do not seem to have similar impact.
34. Nicholas G. Moore, "Ethics: The Way to Do Business," https://www.bentley.edu/centers/sites/www.bentley.edu.centers/files/moore-monograph.pdf, accessed September 26, 2014.

35. Excerpt from J. C. Huizenga, "Virtuous Business and Educational Practice," *Religion & Liberty*, Vol. 12, No. 5, http://www.acton.org/pub/religion-liberty/volume-12-number-5/virtuous-business-and-educational-practice, accessed September 26, 2014.

36. Kenneth H. Blanchard and Norman Vincent Peale, *The Power of Ethical Management* (New York, NY: HarperCollins, 1989).

37. J. Michael Alford, "Finding Competitive Advantage in Managing Workplace Ethics," paper presented at the 2005 meeting of the United States Association for Small Business and Entrepreneurship, Indian Wells, CA, January 13–16, 2005.

38. Ethics Resource Center, "The PLUS Decision Making Model," http://www.ethics.org/resource/plus-decision-making-model, accessed September 26, 2014.

39. Rotary International "Guiding Principles," https://www.rotary.org/en/guiding-principles, accessed October 27, 2014.

40. Brian K. Burton and Michael Goldsby, "The Golden Rule and Business Ethics: An Examination," *Journal of Business Ethics*, Vol. 56, No. 3 (2005), pp. 371–383. This article offers an extended discussion of the history, meaning, and problems of the Golden Rule. The authors document the appearance of this general principle in the writings of several major world religions and philosophers, and provide examples of companies that have used the Golden Rule explicitly as a guide for decision making (e.g., Charles Schwab and Lincoln Electric Co.). The influence of the Golden Rule is so pervasive that Burton and Goldsby conclude that it "seems to be one of the few candidates for a universally acceptable moral principle."

41. Kant actually offered a critique of the Golden Rule, but only as a footnote to his discussion of the categorical imperative. In his opinion, the categorical imperative is a superior concept for a number of reasons, all of which are related to his expanded view of the imperative. See Immanuel Kant, *Grounding for the Metaphysics of Morals, with a Supposed Right to Lie Because of Philanthropic Concerns*, 3rd ed., trans. J. W. Ellington (Indianapolis, IN: Hackett Publishing, 1993).

42. James Austin, Howard Stevenson, and Jane Wei-Skillern, "Social and Commercial Entrepreneurship: Same, Different, or Both?" *Entrepreneurship Theory & Practice*, Vol. 30, No. 1 (2006), pp. 1–22.

43. University of Minnesota, "Doing Good: Improving Your Community with Social Entrepreneurship," http://www.takingcharge.csh.umn.edu/tips-change/doing-good-improving-your-community-social-entrepreneurship, accessed September 29, 2014.

44. *Impact Hub*, "Let's Talk African Entrepreneurship," December 11, 2013, http://bayarea.impacthub.net/event/lets-talk-african-entrepreneurship, accessed September 29, 2014.

45. "Homeboy Industries," http://www.homeboyindustries.org, accessed September 29, 2014.

46. "Tanzania—Hero Rats," http://www.pbs.org/frontlineworld/stories/tanzania605/video_index.html, accessed September 29, 2014.

47. Sujan Patel, "Social Entrepreneurship Has Unexpected Benefits for the Bottom Line," *Entrepreneur*, August 27, 2014, http://www.entrepreneur.com/article/236326, accessed September 29, 2014.

48. Rese Fox, "An Inconvenient Value," http://www.harriscompanyrec.com/blog/2011/01/post_361.html, accessed September 29, 2014.

49. GreenBiz.com, "Greening Your Business: A Primer for Smaller Companies," http://us.smetoolkit.org/us/en/content/en/2773/Greening-Your-Business-A-Primer-for-Smaller-Companies, accessed September 29, 2014.

50. Environmental Protection Agency, "Managing Your Hazardous Waste: A Guide for Small Businesses," http://www.epa.gov/epawaste/hazard/generation/sqg/handbook/k01005.pdf, accessed September 26, 2014.

51. Jason Daley, "Green Fallout," *Entrepreneur*, Vol. 38, No. 8 (2010), pp. 72–75.

52. Malia Wollan, "Bamboo Bikes Appeal to Earth-Conscious Bikers," *Waco Tribune-Herald*, August 15, 2010, p. A3.

53. "Boo Bicycles—Design," http://boobicycles.com/about/design, accessed September 29, 2014.

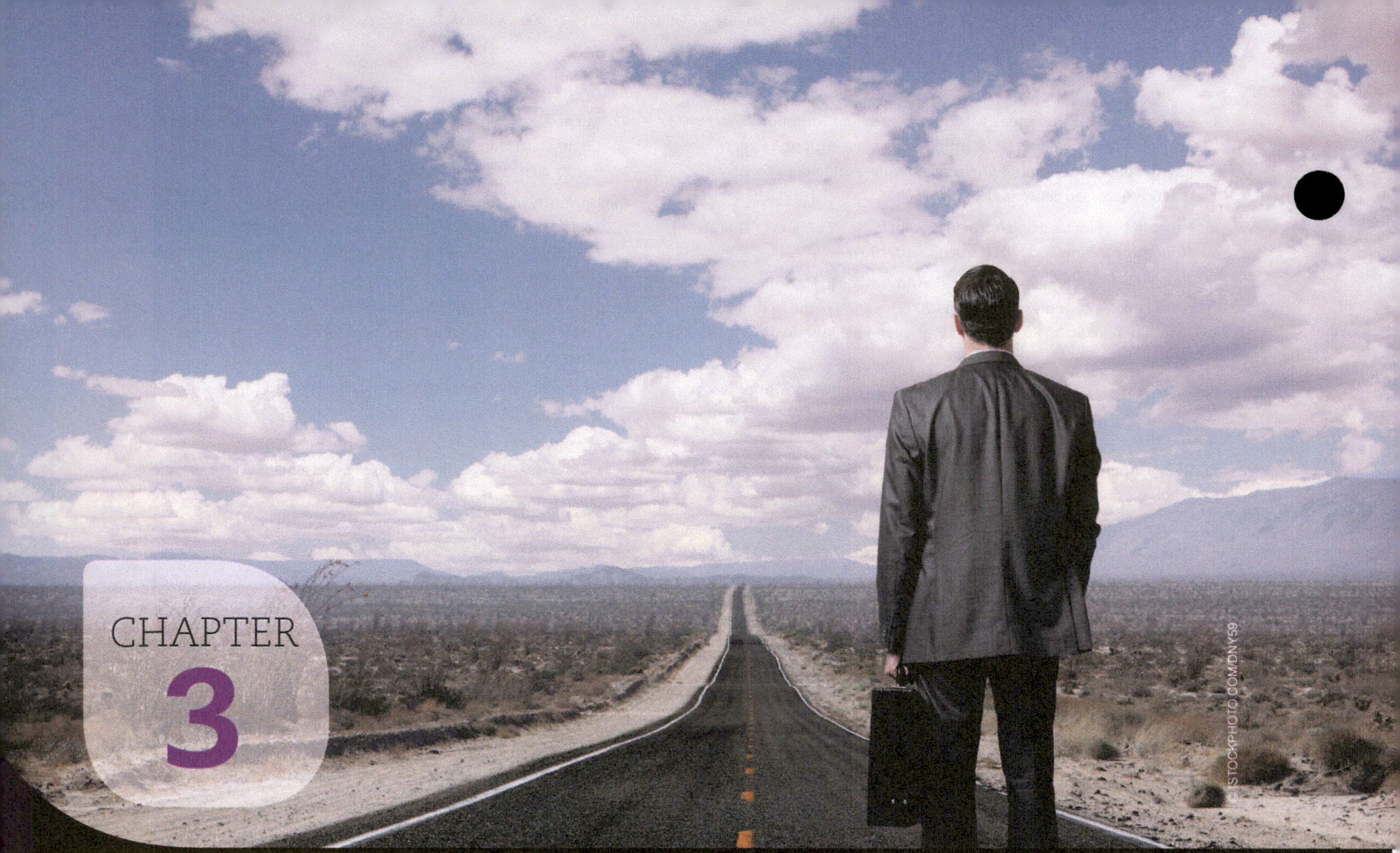

CHAPTER 3

Starting a Small Business

After studying this chapter, you should be able to . . .

3-1. Distinguish among the different types and sources of startup ideas.

3-2. Use innovative thinking to generate ideas for high-potential startups.

3-3. Describe external and internal analyses that can shape the selection of venture opportunities.

3-4. Explain broad-based strategy options and focus strategies.

3-5. Screen business ideas to identify those with the greatest potential.

3-6. Assess the feasibility of a startup idea.

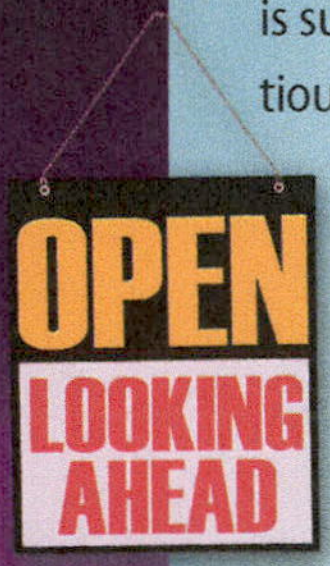

OPEN
LOOKING AHEAD

The Centers for Disease Control and Prevention estimate that 100,000 people die from hospital-acquired infections in the United States every year. And the solution is surprisingly simple: The spread of infectious disease can be curbed through careful hand washing, using antibacterial soap or gel. But studies have shown that hospital staff only follow prescribed hand-washing practices at work about 50 percent of the time. To Yuri Malina and Mert Iseri, who met while they were students at Northwestern University, this was more than a problem—it was also a very attractive and potentially life-saving business opportunity. To address this issue, the pair created SwipeSense, a portable hygiene dispenser that is equipped with a monitoring system

In the SPOTLIGHT
SwipeSense
www.swipesense.com

that allows health-care administrators to track the relationship between hand hygiene and infection outbreaks.

Malina and Iseri first noticed the problem as they observed shifts at an intensive-care unit and saw medical staff often wiping their hands on their scrubs instead of washing them. To address the problem, these friends developed a portable, non-intrusive device that healthcare workers could use to disinfect their hands. They experimented with a variety of designs and even posed as interns during a focus group session with nurses to get honest feedback on early prototypes. After testing 70 versions of their product, the team settled on the current design, which resembles an Apple computer mouse. When paired with wall-mounted sanitation stations and proximity sensors, the portable dispenser collects data and sends them to a cloud-based platform, which then tracks changes in hygiene compliance, frequency of room visits, and other trends.

No company can offer a product or service for free and stay in business, no matter how important the problem it solves. So Malina and Iseri developed a pricing model that bills hospitals based on their size and capacity, charging these facilities $50 per bed, 80 cents for cartridge refills, and an annual fee of $99 per user. Given that hospital-acquired infections cost the health-care system between $4.5 billion and $11 billion each year, SwipeSense's solution is very cost effective. However, emerging competitors are giving the startup a real run for the money. It's very difficult to reach profitability when industry heavyweights like GE Healthcare start offering their own hygiene-tracking systems with features similar to those of SwipeSense.

But Malina and Iseri refuse to give up, choosing instead to tackle these obstacles head-on. For example, they have expanded their trial base from two medical facilities to ten and have relocated production from the United States to China to help reduce costs and increase profit margins. Despite competitive challenges, these founders remain optimistic about the future. "At some point, we're going to figure out how to get people to wash their hands," Iseri has declared.

SwipeSense is only the first of several ventures that these very motivated entrepreneurs have in the works to address important issues. "If you're young and smart and American, you don't have to go to Africa to help people," said Malina. "There are plenty of problems to solve in your own neighborhood." But, first, you need to be able to recognize good business opportunities when you see them.

Sources: Tom Corrigan, "SwipeSense: Forgot to Wash?" *The Wall Street Journal*, October 7, 2014; Brigid Sweeney, "How SwipeSense Could Save Your Life," *Chicago Business.com*, October 13, 2013, http://www.chicagobusiness.com/article/20131011/ISSUE01/131019976/how-swipesense-could-save-your-life, accessed November 13, 2014; and "SwipeSense: Hand Hygiene Just Got a Whole Lot Easier," https://www.swipesense.com/#about_us, accessed November 13, 2014.

Just as you can count on the sun to rise in the morning, you can bet that entrepreneurs are going to keep coming up with innovative ways of doing things. The new businesses they create often change the way we live. But to get the ball rolling in the right direction, an entrepreneur must be able to recognize high-potential startup ideas that others have overlooked. This is precisely what Yuri Malina and Mert Iseri were able to do when they came up with the concept for SwipeSense, which is profiled in this chapter's opening Spotlight feature. We should emphasize that identifying imaginative new products or services that may lead to promising business ventures is so central to the entrepreneurial process that it has its own name—**opportunity recognition**.

What sets entrepreneurs apart from everyone else is their ability to see the potential that others overlook and then take the bold steps necessary to get businesses up and running. In some cases, the identification of a new business opportunity may be the result of an active search for possibilities or insights derived from personal or work experiences. In other cases, the search for opportunities may be a less deliberate and more automatic process.[1] Economist Israel Kirzner proposed that entrepreneurs have a unique capability, which he called **entrepreneurial alertness**. According to this view, entrepreneurs are not actually the source of innovative ideas. Rather, they are simply "alert to the opportunities that exist *already* and are waiting to be noticed."[2] When these opportunities align with an entrepreneur's knowledge, experience, and aspirations, they are even more likely to be spotted.

A discussion of the finer points of entrepreneurial alertness is beyond the scope of this book, but it is important to understand that being watchful for conditions that might lead to new business opportunities can really pay off.[3] Try it for yourself to see if new possibilities for a business become apparent: Over the next week or so, take note of trends, changes, and situations that might support a new business. You will probably be surprised at how many potential opportunities you can identify. If you continue this rather deliberate search, over time you may find that it becomes a habit.[4]

opportunity recognition
Identification of potential new products or services that may lead to promising businesses.

entrepreneurial alertness
Readiness to act on existing, but unnoticed, business opportunities.

Perhaps you already have a business idea in mind that you would like to pursue. With good planning and the right strategy, you may soon be on your way to success as an entrepreneur. On the other hand, you may have a passionate desire to start your own company but are not sure that you have locked onto the right business idea to get you there. Or maybe you have an *idea* in mind but are not sure if it is a good *business opportunity*. No matter which group you fall into, we will help to get you started on the right foot, with the right idea and the right strategy.

In this chapter, we focus mostly on opportunity recognition and strategy options as these apply to **startups**—that is, businesses that did not exist before entrepreneurs created them. However, the chapters that follow will go beyond a discussion of startups and consider business opportunities that already exist, such as purchasing a franchise or buying an existing business (Chapter 4) or joining a family business (Chapter 5). These can all be high-potential options. As you read this chapter, keep in mind that many of the insights and strategies described here also apply to ongoing small businesses, not just to startups.

3-1 DEVELOPING STARTUP IDEAS

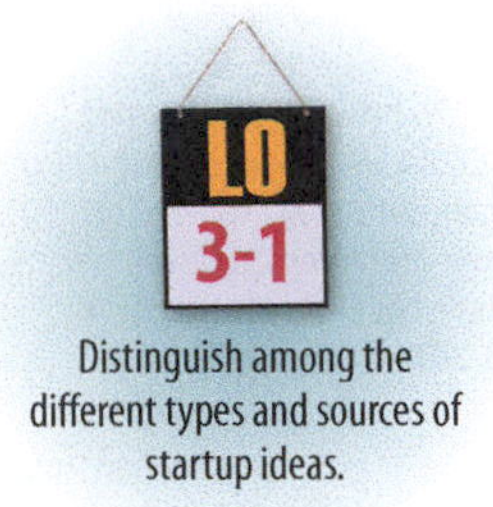

Distinguish among the different types and sources of startup ideas.

As outlined in Chapter 1, you may choose to become an entrepreneur for any of a number of different reasons. But several motivations may lead you to consider starting an enterprise from scratch rather than pursuing other alternatives. For example, you may have a personal desire to develop the commercial market for a recently invented or newly developed product or service, or you may be hoping to tap into high-potential resources that are uniquely available to you—an ideal location, advanced information technologies, a powerful network of connections, and so on. Some entrepreneurs get "startup fever" because they want the challenge of succeeding (or failing) on their own, or they hope to avoid undesirable features of existing companies, such as unpleasant work cultures or smothering legal commitments. There are almost as many reasons as there are aspiring entrepreneurs!

So how do you get started? It all begins with a promising business idea. But new venture concepts are not all equal, and they can come from many different sources. By recognizing the nature and origin of startup ideas, an entrepreneur can broaden the range of new ideas available for his or her consideration.

3-1a Types of Startup Ideas

Exhibit 3.1 shows the three basic types of ideas from which most startups are launched: ideas to enter new markets, ideas based on new technologies, and ideas that offer new benefits. Each of these has its own unique features.

Numerous startups develop from **new market ideas**—that is, those concerned with providing customers with a product or service that does not exist in a particular market but does exist somewhere else. Randall Rothenberg, an author and former director of intellectual capital at the consulting firm Booz Allen Hamilton, says that this type of startup idea may have the greatest potential: "There's ample evidence that some of the biggest businesses are built by taking existing ideas and applying them in a new context."[5] Because it has so much potential, taking this angle on new venture ideas should be given careful consideration.

Other startups are based on **new technology ideas**, which involve new or relatively new knowledge breakthroughs. This type of business can be high risk because there is usually no definitive model of success to follow, but it can also offer tremendous promise. You should pay especially close attention to the fundamental features of a well-conceived new venture of this type. For starters, the technology involved needs to be

startups
New business ventures created "from scratch."

new market ideas
Startup ideas centered around providing customers with an existing product or service not available in their market.

new technology ideas
Startup ideas involving new or relatively new technology, centered around providing customers with a new product or service.

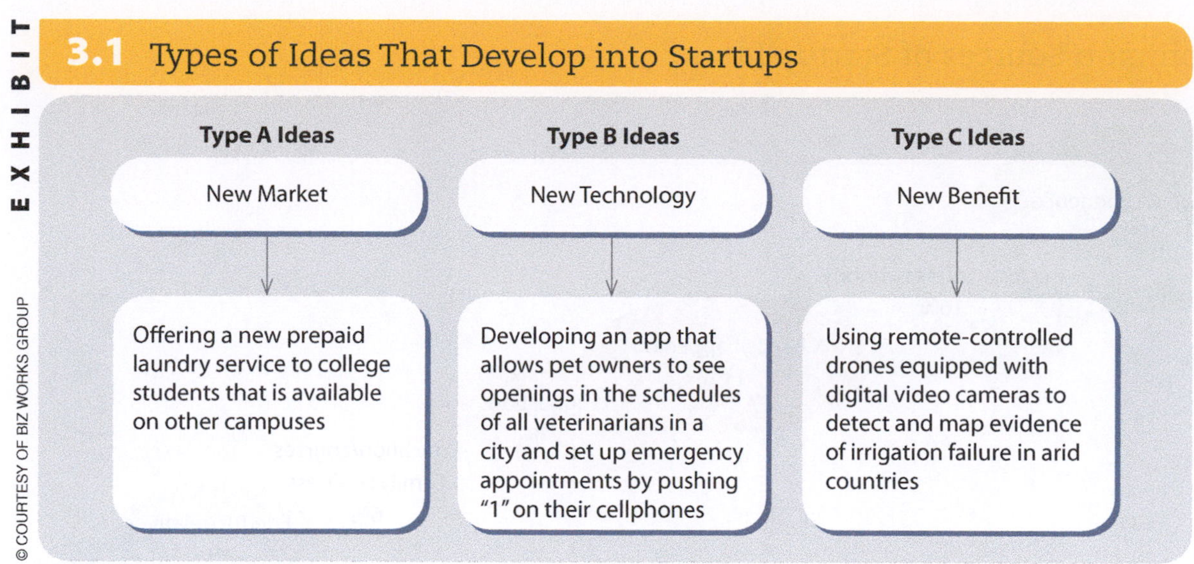

unique, better than others currently available, feasible to implement, and focused on a market need that is deep enough to generate sufficient sales. Also, the founders should have the knowledge, skills, resources, and connections necessary to build a profitable company around the new technology.

EXHIBIT
3.1 Types of Ideas That Develop into Startups
Type A Ideas
New Market
Offering a new prepaid laundry service to college students that is available on other campuses
Type B Ideas
New Technology
Developing an app that allows pet owners to see openings in the schedules of all veterinarians in a city and set up emergency appointments by pushing "1" on their cellphones
Type C Ideas
New Benefit
Using remote-controlled drones equipped with digital video cameras to detect and map evidence of irrigation failure in arid countries
© COURTESY OF BIZ WORKS GROUP

Because of the complexities involved with new technology businesses, it often becomes necessary for entrepreneurs to **pivot** at some point after startup. This refers to fundamentally refocusing the startup as it unfolds or completely recreating it if the initial concept turns out to be seriously flawed. According to Kevin Systrom, co-founder of Instagram, the idea behind the pivot is to "try out new ideas, shed them quickly if they don't catch on, and move on to the next new thing."[6] In other words, if the initial idea turns out to be unsound, it is best to fail fast and fail cheap. While pivoting is sometimes helpful for other types of startups, it is common and frequently necessary (often more than once) for those based on new technologies.

New benefit ideas—those based on offering customers benefits from new or improved products or services or better ways of performing old functions—account for a significant number of startups. Consider Nicky Bronner, who founded Unreal Brands, Inc., in 2012 when he was only 15 years old. To satisfy his sweet tooth without wrecking his health, he set out to "unjunk" snacks by creating and selling his own version of M&Ms, Snickers, Reese's, and other popular candies that are still as tasty but made of far more wholesome ingredients. Today, Bronner's products can be found on the shelves of 20,000 stores, including those of Target, CVS, Staples, and 7-Eleven, which proves that focusing on new benefits can sometimes lead to really sweet business ideas.[7]

3-1b Common Sources of Startup Ideas

Several studies have identified sources of ideas for small business startups. Exhibit 3.2 shows the results of one such study by the National Federation of Independent Business (NFIB), which found that prior work experience accounted for 45 percent of new ideas. However, there are other important sources. As indicated in the exhibit, the NFIB study found that personal interests and hobbies represented 16 percent of the total, and chance happenings accounted for 11 percent.

Ideas for a startup can come from anywhere, but for now we will focus on three possible sources: personal/work experience, hobbies and personal interests, and accidental discovery.

pivot
To refocus or recreate a startup if the initial concept turns out to be flawed.

new benefit ideas
Startup ideas centered around providing customers with new or improved products or services or better ways of performing old functions.

EXHIBIT 3.2 Common Sources of Startup Ideas

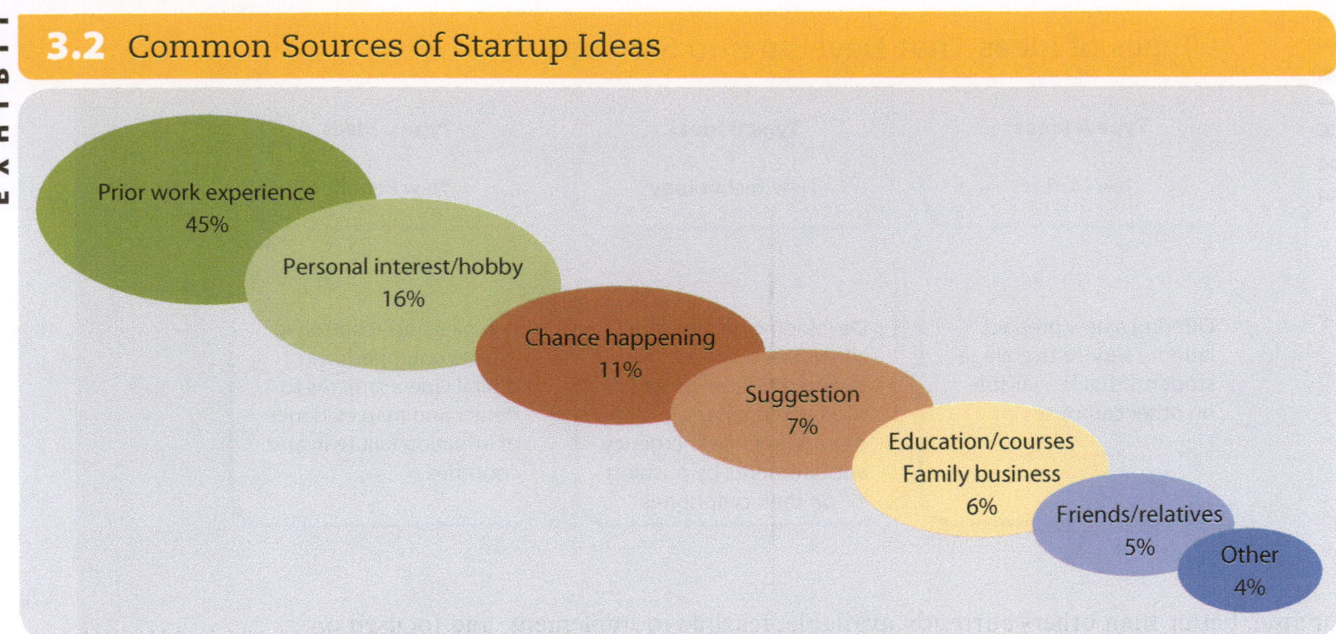

Source: Data developed and provided by the National Federation of Independent Business and sponsored by the American Express Travel Related Services Company, Inc.

PERSONAL/WORK EXPERIENCE

One of the primary sources of startup ideas is personal experience. Often, knowledge gleaned from a present or former job allows a person to see possibilities for modifying an existing product, improving a service, becoming a supplier that meets an employer's needs better than current vendors, or duplicating a business concept in a different location. Perhaps your personal contacts (your network) include suppliers that are interested in working with you or customers whose needs are not currently being met. Startup concepts may even result from trying personal circumstances or misfortunes, especially when the entrepreneur can use work experience or technical skills to address the challenge at hand. Regardless of the situation, these insights may lead you to an opportunity with tremendous potential.[8]

That's how it worked for Adrienne Kallweit, whose attempts to find a suitable babysitter for her young child proved to be more challenging than she had expected. From this experience—which reflects a very real need for so many young couples who need safe and reliable child care—Kallweit decided to launch SeekingSitters, which provides "an on-demand babysitter referral service." Apparently, Kallweit's experience was a great predictor of opportunity, because the company has been expanding rapidly since it was launched.[9]

HOBBIES AND PERSONAL INTERESTS

Sometimes, hobbies grow beyond being leisure activities to become businesses, and they can add surprising energy to the startup process. For instance, people who love skiing might start a ski equipment rental operation as a way to make income from an activity that they enjoy. Or, think about Mark Zuckerberg when he started Facebook. He didn't intend for the venture to grow into the massive company that it is today; rather, he just "liked having it be this hobby and getting people around [him] excited." But in time, he recognized the business potential of the concept, and you know now that his instincts turned out to be right on the money! While we don't expect all or even most small businesses to grow into life-changing technology giants, Facebook's story proves that fun side projects can sometimes grow into significant new companies with serious profit potential.[10]

ACCIDENTAL DISCOVERY

Another source of new startup ideas—accidental discovery—involves something called **serendipity**, a facility for making desirable discoveries by accident. Awareness obviously plays a role here, but anyone may stumble across a useful idea in the course of day-to-day living. That is exactly what happened to Simone Gonzales, a struggling artist in Los Angeles, when the 26-year-old came across some interesting fabric and decided to see what she could do with it. "After playing with the thick, mummy-like elastic bands and shaping them into a simple tube skirt—no zipper, hem, or serious tailoring required—Gonzales realized she may be onto something."[11] She decided to make a few skirts from it, which she sold at a friend's boutique. From that small start, Gonzales got enough traction to launch her company, Pleasure Doing Business. Within a few years, things really started to take off, showing that promising business ideas sometimes just happen—even when you're not really looking for them.[12]

Spotting Trends

You can spot trends by listening to customers, staying in tune with industry changes, and using such marketing tools as in-person focus groups, social media groups, and chat rooms. Consulting websites like Trendhunter.com and JWTIntelligence.com can also help you spot emerging developments and meaningful patterns.

OTHER IDEA LEADS

If the sources of startup ideas just discussed do not reveal a specific entrepreneurial opportunity that is right for you, examine the following methods, which have been useful to many entrepreneurs:

- Tap personal contacts with potential customers and suppliers, professors, patent attorneys, former or current employees or co-workers, venture capitalists, and chambers of commerce.
- Visit trade shows, production facilities, universities and research institutes, and successful entrepreneurs (in other markets) who are doing what you want to do.
- Observe trends, such as those related to material limitations and energy shortages, emerging technologies, recreational practices, fads, pollution problems, personal security needs, and social movements.
- Pay close attention to all forms of change, including shifts in specific industries and markets, demographic swings, and emerging discoveries or scientific breakthroughs.
- Read trade publications, bankruptcy announcements, and profiles on entrepreneurs and various business opportunities in *Inc.*, *FastCompany*, and other, similar periodicals.
- Search the Internet, where you can find an unlimited supply of information on the startup process and even specific opportunities. For example, *Entrepreneur* magazine (entrepreneur.com) offers such online tools as the Business Idea Center, which profiles business ideas that can be browsed by industry, interest, profession, startup costs, and other criteria.

serendipity
A facility for making desirable discoveries by accident.

3-2 USING INNOVATIVE THINKING TO GENERATE BUSINESS IDEAS

Use innovative thinking to generate ideas for high-potential startups.

If you haven't come up with a startup idea from the common sources just identified, you may need to dig deeper. Commit to a lifestyle of creative thinking so that everyday thoughts work in your favor to generate business ideas.[13] Although the following suggestions are designed to help guide your search for that one great idea for a startup, they can also help keep an existing business fresh, alive, and moving forward.

Borrow Heavily from Existing Product and Service Ideas or Other Industries "Good artists borrow; great artists steal," said Pablo Picasso or T.S. Eliot or Salvador Dalí—no one seems to know for sure. This principle launched Apple Computer on the road to greatness when one of its co-founders, Steve Jobs, identified technologies that Xerox had developed but was not using. It can work for you, too, within the limits of the law and ethical conduct. Think deeply about how you might put ideas and practices that you come across to work in launching a startup or accelerating the growth of an existing business. Research shows that this is a powerful starting place for innovation.

Combine Two Businesses to Create a Market Opening Putting two businesses together can sometimes lead to unique products, services, or experiences that customers can't get elsewhere. Examples include theaters that combine dinner and a movie, and bookstores that add a coffee shop. Andy Levine's company, Sixthman, organizes "floating music festivals" that allow hardcore fans of artists such as KISS, Lynyrd Skynyrd, and Florida Georgia Line to go on cruises with their musical heroes and spend some time hanging out together. These one-of-a-kind vacations have been a tremendous hit, with customers indicating that there is a 60 percent chance that they will be repeating the experience.[14]

At some point, it may make sense to start (or buy) more than one business without merging the operations, a strategy known as *diversification*. Consider Motor City Denim Company, a family firm that is now run by Mark D'Andreta. The Detroit-based enterprise started as a tailor shop but shifted its focus to making protective covers for robotic machines on auto assembly lines. When the recession hit in 2008 and demand for cars slackened, automakers slashed their orders for the company's product. To make ends meet, D'Andreta started producing handbags, jeans, and other apparel items on some of his machines. The strategy worked, allowing the firm to stage a bit of a comeback. "To survive," D'Andreta says, "you have to be flexible."[15]

Begin with a Problem in Mind High-potential business ideas often address problems that people have or a "pain" that a new venture idea could relieve. Think about a significant problem or hassle that people have to deal with, dissect it, chart it out on a sheet of paper, and roll it over and over in your mind while considering possible solutions. Lots of smart business ideas are likely to come to mind. If the pain you are trying to address is your own, the results can be especially good, since you are an expert on the problem and will feel passionate about finding a solution. This notion is validated by Richard Branson, uber-entrepreneur and founder of the Virgin Group empire. "All startups should be thinking, 'What frustrates me, and how can I make it better?'" he says. "It might be a small thing or it might be a big thing, but that's the best way for [entrepreneurs] to think. If they think like that, they're likely to build a very successful business."[16]

Recognize a Hot Trend, and Ride the Wave Fads can lead to serious, though sometimes short-lived, money-making opportunities (for an example, Google Pet Rocks), but *trends* provide a much stronger foundation for businesses because they are connected to a larger change in society. Even more powerful is the product or service that builds on three or four trends as they come together. For example, the outrageous success of Apple's iPad is the result of multiple merging trends: consumer desires for increased mobility, instant gratification, and no hassles all tied together with the product's slick design and "coolness" factor.

Living the Dream

ENTREPRENEURIAL EXPERIENCES

Shifting into High Gear through Diversification: Want a Latte to Go with That Bike?

Many bicycle-shop owners across America are radically transforming their stores and business models to boost customer satisfaction and increase sales. In addition to the products and services you would expect to find, these shops are now offering food, drinks, entertainment, and even fitness classes to their customers. This increased focus on experience and broader consumer appeal marks a sharp break from the old way of doing business. In the words of Carolyn Szczepanski, spokeswoman for the League of American Bicyclists, "There's a stereotype about what a bike shop is like—it's dirty, it's mostly men, it's an intimidating place to be, let alone hang out." But results of a 2013 survey conducted by the National Bicycle Dealers Association (NBDA) suggest that this stereotype might be changing. Sampling 4,000 establishments, the survey found that 12 percent have coffee bars, 11 percent provide spinning classes, nearly 5 percent serve beer—1 percent even offer massages, yoga, or full-service dining experiences.

The transformation may be a response to lackluster market growth. Bicycle sales have been stable since 2005, hovering around the $6 billion mark. However, local bike shops have fallen in number and increased in square footage during this same period. The rising popularity of urban bike-sharing programs, combined with increasing used-bike sales, have forced several smaller retailers out of business. For many stores, diversification is the key to survival.

CamRock Café and Sport is an example of an outfit that has shifted into high gear using this strategy. Customers turn to this shop in Cambridge, Wisconsin, when they need to rent a mountain bike, have a flat fixed, or pick up cycling accessories. But many also stop in to enjoy a gourmet espresso, grab a salad and crêpe in the café, take part in a spin class, or even catch a string-quartet or steel-drum concert on Saturday. Customers have become very loyal to the shop, shrugging off somewhat-higher repair charges because the overall experience is so good. It appears that CamRock has managed to ditch the bicycle-shop stereotype; indeed, locals now call it the "general store for cool stuff."

© ISTOCKPHOTO.COM/THOMAS_EYEDESIGN

Other bicycle retailers have cultivated similar images and now enjoy the benefits of a committed clientele. NBX Bikes of Narragansett, Rhode Island, started attracting people "who had never ridden a bike" with its yoga classes. Shenandoah Bicycle Company in Harrisonburg, Virginia, saw a similar influx, perhaps after word spread about its acai bowl selection. Velo Cult Bike Shop in Portland, Oregon, even hosted a wedding ceremony in the store!

Diversification has enabled many local bike shops to redefine themselves in the face of stable, but stagnant, market growth. According to the NBDA, the average bike shop today earns just 3.5 percent of its revenue from sales outside of bikes, parts, and services. But operators like CamRock and Velo Cult have pumped up this percentage and, in the process, have redefined what a bike-shop business can be. Because the model seems to work so well, many competitors have started to follow suit, leading analysts to predict that by 2018 the number of hybrid stores in the United States may increase fivefold. With such aggressive growth, it may only be a matter of time before the bike-shop business is changed forever.

Sources: "CamRock Café and Sport," http://www.camrocksport.com, accessed November 14, 2014; National Bicycle Dealers Association, "A Look at the Bicycle Industry's Vital Statistics," http://nbda.com/articles/industry-overview-2013-pg34.htm, accessed November 14, 2014; "Shenandoah Bicycle Co.," http://www.shenandoahbicycle.com, accessed November 14, 2014; "The NBX Story," http://nbxbikes.com/about/the-nbx-story-pg586.htm, accessed November 14, 2014; "Velo Cult: About," http://velocult.com/about, accessed November 14, 2014; and Jen Wieczner, "Coming Soon to a Bike Shop Near You: Lattes, Craft Beer—and Wedding Cake," *The Wall Street Journal*, August 29, 2013, p. D3.

Also look for countertrends. For example, in this age of digital addiction, some hotels, resorts, and travel companies have started offering "unplugged" or "digital detox" packages to guests if they surrender their digital devices at check-in. These offers appeal to guests who need an excuse to take a *complete* break from their work.[17] To identify a countertrend, make it a habit to ask those who resist a trend (such as the coffee drinker who refuses to go to Starbucks) what products or services would appeal to them and then see what possibilities come to mind. Set aside your preconceived notions of what "ought to be" and get into the minds of those who resist the flow. If you use the trend as your starting point, you will know better where to look for the countertrend, and that's where you can get ahead of the game.

Explore Ways to Improve the Function of an Existing Product or Service Almost all suitcases have wheels these days, but that wasn't always the case. The innovation was perfected by Robert Plath, who created the Rollaboard design in 1987. The product was so popular that Plath decided to quit his job as a commercial pilot to start Travelpro International, now a major luggage company.[18] Luggage without wheels is still functional, but adding this feature opened the door to new sales and a new venture.

Think of Possible Ways to Streamline a Customer's Activities Many people are busy, so they look to firms that can bear some of life's burdens for them. That's what keeps businesses like grocery-delivery services going. Take some time to ponder the day-to-day experiences of people in the market segment you would like to serve. What activities would they gladly offload?

Consider Adapting a Product or Service to Meet Customer Needs in a Different Way Many new ventures get their start by borrowing a product or service that was already working well somewhere else and adapting it to a different need or situation. For example, eBay's online auction model has been adapted with great success by many startups, such as Etsy.com (to sell handmade goods, vintage products, and art supplies) and DesignerSocial.com (to sell pre-owned luxury products). Or, consider Michelle Marciniak and Susan Walvius's launch of a company called Sheex, which uses the moisture-wicking performance fabrics found in workout clothes to manufacture super-comfortable bedsheets.[19] The possibilities are endless.

© COURTESY OF AUTHENTIC HAVEN BRAND

Imagine How the Market for a Product or Service Could Be Creatively Expanded Annie Haven's family ranch in Southern California had few takers for the "fertilizer" that its cattle produced, so she decided to package the growth-stimulating stuff in three- by five-inch pouches (a box of nine bags sells for $27.95) and sell it to gardening enthusiasts. Customers simply steep each bag in one to five gallons of water and use that "tea" to water their plants. Haven has definitely found a way to create a new business by expanding the market for her product, and she is earning a tidy profit, with sales growing at a very healthy clip.[20]

Offer Products through a Subscription Service In recent years, countless item-of-the-month and quarterly offer startups have sprung up around the idea of shipping a different set of niche item to subscribers on a set schedule. The products being sold this way range from pet toys to healthy snacks to "glam grunge" cosmetics. These companies combat the "choice fatigue" that many buyers feel when they get frustrated trying to choose from the dizzying array of products available for sale. Subscription services solve this problem by eliminating the selection process altogether, sending out packages of carefully curated items to members for fees that can run anywhere from $10 a month (beauty and grooming products at BirchBox.com) to $559 per quarter (luxury items at Svbscription.com). This type of business is not without its challenges—dealing with packaging and shipping crunches, for instance, and offering selections that are fresh and interesting enough to bring customers back for more. But many entrepreneurs are managing to keep their subscribers happy and are earning handsome returns for their efforts.[21]

Cash In on the Sharing Economy You may know about high-profile startups like Airbnb and Uber that give consumers low-cost access to apartment and home rentals and car rides, respectively. But the sharing economy apparently is far from tapped out. As evidence, one recent analysis found that nearly one-tenth of ventures launched by early-stage entrepreneurs in the Boston area were designed to help consumers or businesses connect with products or services that were not being fully used. The concept makes sense. But unfortunately there are plenty of potholes on the road to shared-economy riches, and plenty of startups have fallen into them, including BlackJet (the "Uber for jet travel") and carpooling startup Ridejoy, among many others.[22] But success stories like Rent the Runway and Bag Borrow or Steal show that making products like high-end designer dresses and luxury handbags available to average consumers on an as-needed, rental basis can provide a platform for success.[23]

Study a Product or Service to See If You Can Make It "Green" A great surge of effort and investment has been flowing toward ventures that focus on protecting the environment. Examples of recent green startups include a company that strips trouble-making minerals and chemicals from pool water so that it can be reused (Calsaway Pool Services), an upscale paper-saving electronic invitation service for weddings and other formal events (Greenvelope), and "upcyclers" that transform refuse items into high-quality products (LooptWorks).[24] Given the success that many of these companies are having, it clearly can pay to think "green."

Keep an Eye on New Technologies New technologies often open up potential opportunities for startups, but only those who take note of the possibilities can reap the rewards. Read widely, consult industry experts and government offices that promote new technologies, drop by the technology transfer office of a nearby university, or visit with faculty who work at the cutting edge of their fields. Regardless of where you look, be sure to research innovations that have potential commercial value, particularly for new ventures.

These options represent only a few of the many possibilities. We encourage you to seek and size up new venture ideas in whatever circumstances you find yourself. By considering a number of internal and external factors, you should be able to fit together the pieces of the opportunity puzzle.

Living the Dream

ENTREPRENEURIAL EXPERIENCES

A Green Startup Mushrooms into a Huge Success

Nikhil Arora and Alejandro Velez earned the nickname the "Mushroom Guys" after developing a do-it-yourself mushroom-growing kit and building a business around the product. The initial idea came to the pair while they were attending the University of California at Berkley, where they became inspired by a vision of turning agricultural waste streams into fresh, local food. They used this inspiration to launch a business that has grown from a fraternity-house kitchen experiment into a company that is on track to generate $5.4 million a year in sales.

During a class at UC Berkley, Arora and Velez learned that mushrooms could grow in discarded coffee grounds. Intrigued, the two students approached their instructor, individually, and ended up meeting one another and becoming friends. Working together, the duo got started by filling paint cans with scavenged coffee grounds and donated mushroom spores. Their first nine crops failed to grow, but the tenth attempt was successful. The partners took this crop to Chez Panisse, a local gourmet restaurant, and offered celebrity chef Alice Waters a sample. Impressed, Waters started placing orders for the mushrooms. With this initial order in hand, the team managed to secure financial backing through various grant programs and used these funds to expand their concept and create DIY kits that would allow anyone to grow the mushrooms at home.

But offering mushroom kits was just the beginning. Arora and Velez continued to research urban-farming techniques and came up with a system that converts fish waste into fertilizer for plants, which in turn clean the water for the fish. Developing the idea led to the invention of AquaFarm, a product designed to shrink the process so that it could be used in the kitchen or the classroom. To finance development, their company, Back to the Roots, initiated a Kickstarter campaign, which raised over $240,000 in less than three weeks. Today, the product is available from mainstream retailers like Whole Foods and Nordstrom's, as well as via direct order through sites like ThinkGeek and UncommonGoods, which offer unique products.

Despite all of their financial success, the entrepreneurs remain focused on their core values, which emphasize a commitment to green innovation. Customers have bought into the company's vision, which is evident in the phenomenal growth of the venture. And the company's relocation to expanded facilities will almost certainly fuel its growth well into the future. At this rate, the business is sure to be sustainable—in every way imaginable.

Sources: "Back to the Roots: Our Story," https://www.backtotheroots.com/about-us, accessed November 14, 2014; Ben Paynter, "From Mushrooms to Aquaponics: How Back to the Roots Is Taking Over Home Growing," *FastCompany*, July 18, 2013, http://www.fastcoexist.com/1682610/from-mushrooms-to-aquaponics-how-back-to-the-roots-is-taking-over-home-growing, accessed November 17, 2014; and Amy Westervelt, "How a Good Idea Mushroomed," *The Wall Street Journal*, September 30, 2013, p. R3.

Describe external and internal analyses that can shape the selection of venture opportunities.

3-3 USING INTERNAL AND EXTERNAL ANALYSES TO ASSESS NEW BUSINESS IDEAS

Two general approaches can help to identify business ideas—outside-in and inside-out analyses. In other words, entrepreneurs can look for needs in the marketplace and then determine how to use their own capabilities to pursue those opportunities (outside-in), or they can first evaluate their capabilities and then identify new products or services they might be able to offer to the market (inside-out).[25] It is important to understand the finer points of the two methods because they can reveal business ideas that may otherwise be overlooked.

3-3a Outside-In Analysis

Entrepreneurs are usually more successful when they study a business context in order to identify potential startup opportunities and determine which are most likely to accomplish their goals. This outside-in analysis should consider the general environment, or big picture, and the industry setting in which the venture might do business. It should also factor in the competitive environment that is likely to have an impact. The **general environment** is made up of very broad factors that influence most businesses in a society, while the **industry environment** is defined more narrowly as the context for factors that directly impact a given firm and all of its competitors. The **competitive environment** is even more specific, focusing on the strength, position, and likely moves and countermoves of competitors in an industry.

THE GENERAL ENVIRONMENT

The general environment encompasses a number of important trends, as shown in Exhibit 3.3. *Economic trends* include changes in the rate of inflation, interest rates, and even currency exchange rates, all of which promote or discourage business growth. *Sociocultural trends* refer to societal currents that may affect consumer demand, opening up new markets and forcing others into decline. *Political/legal trends* include changes in tax law and government regulations (e.g., safety rules) that may pose a threat to existing companies or devastate an inventive business concept. *Global trends* reflect international developments that create new opportunities to expand markets, outsource, invest abroad, and so on. As people and markets around the world become increasingly connected, the impact of the global segment on small business opportunities will increase.

Developments that grow out of *technological trends* spawn—or wipe out—many new ventures. And given the rapid rate of change in this segment of the general environment, it is very important that small business owners stay current on these trends and understand the impact that they may have. Some recent technological developments to keep an eye on include the following:

- The creation of high-quality, affordable, virtual-reality hardware that could radically transform entertainment and communications.
- The Internet of Things, which connects and combines the limited computing power embedded in devices in the home and office to make advanced automation possible

EXHIBIT 3.3 Trends in the General Environment

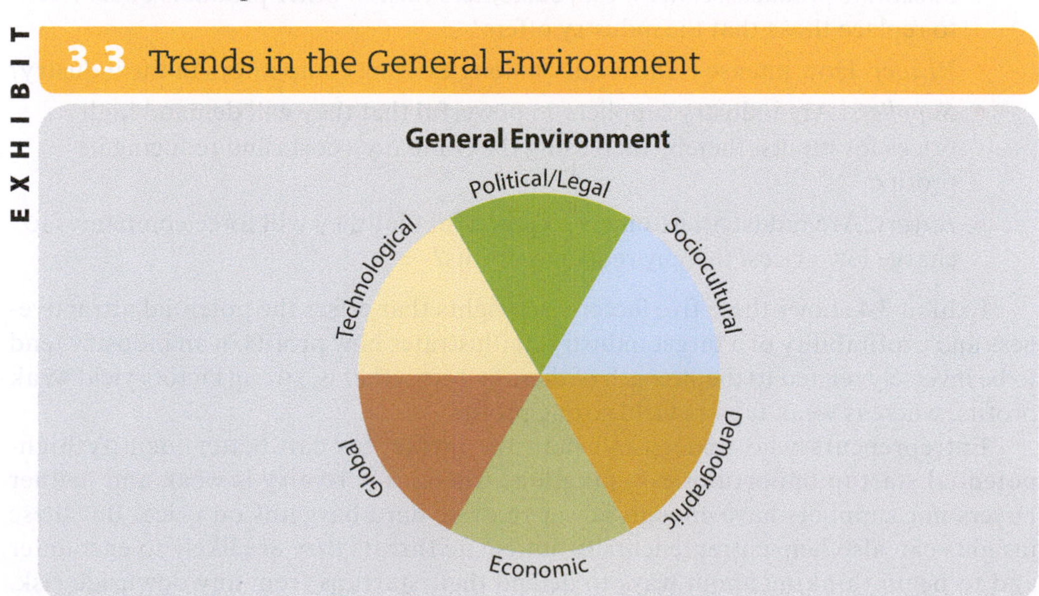

general environment
The broad environment, encompassing factors that influence most businesses in a society.

industry environment
The environment that includes factors that directly impact a given firm and all of its competitors.

competitive environment
The environment that focuses on the strength, position, and likely moves and countermoves of competitors in an industry.

Reading Economic Trends
Need a better read on economic trends in order to make better business decisions? VISA's "Small Business Spend Insights Report" is a free report on the economic confidence of small business owners based on VISA spending data and responses to a quarterly survey. See current and archived reports at http://usa.visa.com/small-business/resources-and-tools/index.jsp#/detail/22470 for data and analysis. (You will need to enter "Spend Insights" in the search box to access archived reports.)

- The fast-falling price of 3-D printing, which makes the creation of just about any suitable product possible, as well as fast, inexpensive, and completely customizable
- The exponential growth and availability of data collected online, or big data, that make high-powered analytics and decision making faster and less expensive

Finally, *demographic trends* also play an important role in shaping opportunities for startups. These trends include population size, age structure, ethnic mix, and wage distribution. For example, a focus on aging baby boomers (the 78 million Americans born between 1946 and 1964) may really pay off, given their $2 trillion in annual spending power and willful self-indulgence. And there is no limit to the products and services that can be targeted to this age group. Cell phones with larger keys that can easily be seen in dim lighting and magazines that focus on health issues in the retirement years are business ideas that have emerged with this demographic trend in mind.

Some people believe that evaluation of the general environment is appropriate only for large firms that have corporate staffs to manage the process, but small businesses can also benefit from such analysis. For example, today one-third of Americans are considered obese (not including those who are considered overweight) and that number is projected to increase to around 50 percent by the year 2030, if current trends persist.[26] Entrepreneurs have realized that a multitude of business opportunities can be launched based on this rising tide, from weight-loss services to products that help obese people live more comfortably with their condition. Among the many businesses launched by those reading the trend are startups offering airline seatbelt extenders, high-capacity bathroom scales, and oversized furniture.

THE INDUSTRY ENVIRONMENT

An entrepreneur will be even more directly affected by the startup's industry than by the general environment. The impact can be substantial, with studies reporting that industry influences can explain anywhere from 8 to 30 percent of firm profitability.[27] To outline these dynamics, Michael Porter lists five factors that determine the nature and degree of competition in an industry:[28]

- *New competitors.* How easy is it for new competitors to enter the industry?
- *Substitute products/services.* Can customers turn to other products or services to replace those that the industry offers?
- *Rivalry.* How intense is the rivalry among existing competitors in the industry?
- *Suppliers.* Are industry suppliers so powerful that they will demand high prices for inputs, thereby increasing the company's costs and reducing its profits?
- *Buyers.* Are industry customers so powerful that they will force companies to charge low prices, thereby reducing profits?

Exhibit 3.4 shows these five factors as weights that offset the potential attractiveness and profitability of a target industry. It illustrates how profits in an industry tend to be inversely related to the strength of these factors—that is, strong factors yield weak profits, whereas weak factors yield strong profits.

Entrepreneurs who understand industry influences can better identify high-potential startup opportunities—situations where, say, rivalry is weak and neither buyers nor suppliers have enough power to drive hard bargains on price. But these insights can also help entrepreneurs to anticipate threats they are likely to encounter and to begin thinking about ways to defend their startups from any downside risk.

EXHIBIT 3.4 Major Factors Offsetting Market Attractiveness

Entrepreneurs who recognize and understand Porter's five industry factors can position their ventures in a way that makes the most of what the industry offers.

THE COMPETITIVE ENVIRONMENT

Within any given industry, it is important to determine the strength, position, and likely responses of rival businesses to newcomers. In fact, experts insist that such analyses are a critical input for the assessment of any business idea. William A. Sahlman of Harvard Business School contends that every aspiring entrepreneur should answer several questions about the competitors he or she is likely to encounter in the marketplace:[29]

- Who would be the new venture's current competitors?
- What unique resources do they control?
- What are their strengths and weaknesses?
- How will they respond to the new venture's decision to enter the industry?
- How can the new venture respond?
- Who else might see and exploit the same opportunity?
- Are there ways to co-opt potential or actual competitors by forming alliances?

This analysis helps an entrepreneur to evaluate the nature and extent of existing competition and to fine-tune future plans. It can also help to identify high-potential business opportunities based on the competitive situation.

Entrepreneurs should take one more step when analyzing the competition: They should identify the thinking that shapes their rivals' moves, which often is based on the assumption that businesses must operate in a certain way because they always have.

But this clearly is not the case. For example, it wasn't all that long ago that teenagers had to do their bargain shopping at the mall, realtors had to use cameras to take pictures of investment properties for out-of-state buyers, and customers had to use cash or a credit cards to pay for purchases. Today, these can all be done by cell phone, and forward-thinking businesses can gain an advantage by changing their models to reflect these new realities. In other words, innovative entrepreneurs often can overtake established rivals by using their commitment to time-honored approaches against them. This is what happened to Blockbuster when its old way of doing business left it vulnerable to a startup (Netflix) that challenged conventional wisdom and adopted an inventive set of "rules for the game" (offering videos online or through the mail) to which Blockbuster was not able to adapt. Blockbuster had to file for bankruptcy in 2010 and continues to struggle for survival.

Save Money with Social Media

Want to learn more about what people are saying about your industry, but on a shoestring? Join industry groups on sites like LinkedIn and Facebook, and follow influential industry blogs. Such efforts will help you to get a sense of the major players and to identify hot-button issues.

3-3b Inside-Out Analysis

Identifying opportunities in the external environment is definitely worth the effort, but business concepts make sense only if they fit well with the resources, capabilities, and competencies that an entrepreneur can bring to the world of business. The search for a startup opportunity can actually *begin* with an inside-out analysis, one that catalogs the startup's sources of potential strengths (including those that can reasonably be obtained or created) and the unique competencies that can be formed from them. These can provide a platform from which the fruit of new business opportunities can be reached and harvested.

BUILDING ON INTERNAL RESOURCES AND CAPABILITIES

Entrepreneurs who want to start or build a business based on inside-out analysis will first need to have a solid grasp of the resources and capabilities that are available to them and can be used to make this happen. The term **resources** refers to those inputs that an entrepreneur can use to start and/or operate a business, such as cash for investment, knowledge of critical technologies, access to essential equipment, and capable business partners, to name just a few. A startup or small business can have both tangible and intangible resources. **Tangible resources** are visible and easy to measure. An office building, manufacturing equipment, and cash reserves are all examples of tangible resources. But these are very different from **intangible resources**, which are invisible and difficult to assess. Intangible assets can include intellectual property rights such as patents and copyrights, an established brand, a favorable reputation, and an entrepreneur's personal network of contacts and relationships.

Though the terms are often used interchangeably, *resources* technically are not the same as *capabilities*. Whereas resources are inputs to the work of a business, **capabilities** are best viewed as the company's routines and processes that coordinate the use of these productive assets to achieve desired outcomes. Resources can do nothing on their own. Rather, entrepreneurs who figure out how to work with and integrate resources in ways that create value for customers are those most likely to create and build successful ventures.

resources
The basic inputs that an entrepreneur can use to start and/or operate a business.

tangible resources
Those organizational resources that are visible and easy to measure.

intangible resources
Those organizational resources that are invisible and difficult to assess.

capabilities
A company's routines and processes that coordinate the use of its productive assets in order to achieve desired outcomes.

core competencies
Those capabilities that distinguish a firm competitively and reflect its focus and personality.

competitive advantage
A benefit that exists when a firm has a product or service that is seen by its target market as better than that of competitors.

CORE COMPETENCIES AND COMPETITIVE ADVANTAGE

Once entrepreneurs have an accurate view of their resources and capabilities, they will be in a better position to identify core competencies that can be created and used to compete. **Core competencies** are those crucial capabilities that distinguish a company competitively and reflect its general focus and personality. In most cases, these strengths make it possible to achieve a **competitive advantage**, which gives a startup or small business the upper hand by helping it to provide products or services that customers will choose over available alternatives.

An illustration of how all of this works is provided by Starbucks, which offers a nice selection of gourmet coffees. But that is not its only edge in the marketplace. In fact, many of its competitors, large and small, also provide high-quality coffee products. So why has the company been so successful? Most observers believe that it is the premium product, combined with the special "Starbucks experience," that has allowed the coffee icon to grow from a single store in the mid-1980s to more than 21,000 retail locations in 65 countries today.[30] As one observer put it, "For many of its customers, Starbucks isn't really in the business of selling coffee. Instead, it's offering a place to hang out that happens to sell coffee."[31]

Though the success of Starbucks is undeniable, the company's growth has actually unleashed a torrent of new rivals by whetting the market's appetite for both the product and the experience. But how do small firms compete in a Starbucks-saturated market? By focusing on their own unique core competencies and the advantages they can support. Many small shops thrive in this environment by providing free refills, paying meticulous attention to product quality, emphasizing connections with the local community, or taking other steps to showcase their own unique character and individuality. In other words, they establish core competencies by using resources and capabilities in unique ways that reflect the "personality" of their own enterprises.

3-3c Integrating Internal and External Analyses

A solid foundation for competitive advantage requires a reasonable match between the strengths and weaknesses of a given business and the opportunities and threats present in its relevant environments. This integration is best revealed through a **SWOT analysis** (standing for *S*trengths, *W*eaknesses, *O*pportunities, *T*hreats), which provides a simple overview of a venture's strategic situation. Exhibit 3.5 lists a number of factors that can

SWOT analysis
An assessment that provides a concise overview of a firm's strategic situation.

EXHIBIT **3.5** Examples of SWOT Factors

	POSITIVE FACTORS	NEGATIVE FACTORS
Inside the Company	***Strengths***	***Weaknesses***
	• Important core competencies • Financial strengths • Innovative capacity • Skilled or experienced management • Well-planned strategy • Effective entry wedge • Strong network of personal contacts • Positive reputation in the marketplace • Proprietary technology	• Inadequate financial resources • Poorly planned strategy • Lack of management skills or experience • Limited innovation capacity • Negative reputation in the marketplace • Inadequate facilities • Distribution problems • Insufficient marketing skills • Production inefficiencies
Outside the Company	***Opportunities***	***Threats***
	• An untapped market potential • New product or geographic market • Favorable shift in industry dynamics • High potential for market growth • Emerging technologies • Changes allowing overseas expansion • Favorable government deregulation • Increasing market fragmentation	• New competitors • Rising demands of buyers or suppliers • Sales shifting to substitute products • Increased government regulation • Adverse shifts in the business cycle • Slowed market growth • Changing customer preferences • Adverse demographic shifts

be classified by this framework; however, these are merely representative of the countless possibilities that may exist.

In practice, a SWOT analysis provides a snapshot view of current conditions. Outside-in and inside-out approaches come together in the SWOT analysis to help identify potential business opportunities that match the entrepreneur and his or her planned venture. However, because a SWOT analysis focuses on the present, the entrepreneur needs to also consider whether the targeted opportunity will lead to other opportunities in the future (for example, through skill building or an expanded network) and whether pursuit of the opportunity is likely to lead to a competitive response by potential rivals. Obviously, the most promising opportunities are those that lead to others (which may offer value and profitability over the long run), promote the development of additional skills that equip the venture to pursue new prospects, and yet do not provoke competitors to strike back.

When potentials in the external environment (revealed through analysis of the general, industry, and competitive environments) fit with the unique resources, capabilities, and core competencies of the entrepreneur (highlighted by internal assessment) and threats outside the startup or weaknesses within it are manageable, the odds of success are greatly improved. As shown in Exhibit 3.6, this is what we call the entrepreneur's "opportunity sweet spot," an area that typically offers the greatest potential for superior business results. With this in mind, we encourage you to be observant and systematic in your search for opportunities and to think carefully about how these opportunities fit your background and skills, as well as your interests and passions. If you do so, you are much more likely to enjoy the adventure.

Clearly, conducting outside-in and inside-out analyses and integrating the results can help you identify potential business opportunities and then build a solid foundation for competitive advantage. With that foundation, an entrepreneur can begin to position the new venture concept or established company with a well-defined strategy that will be more likely to generate superior financial results.

EXHIBIT 3.6 The Entrepreneur's Opportunity "Sweet Spot"

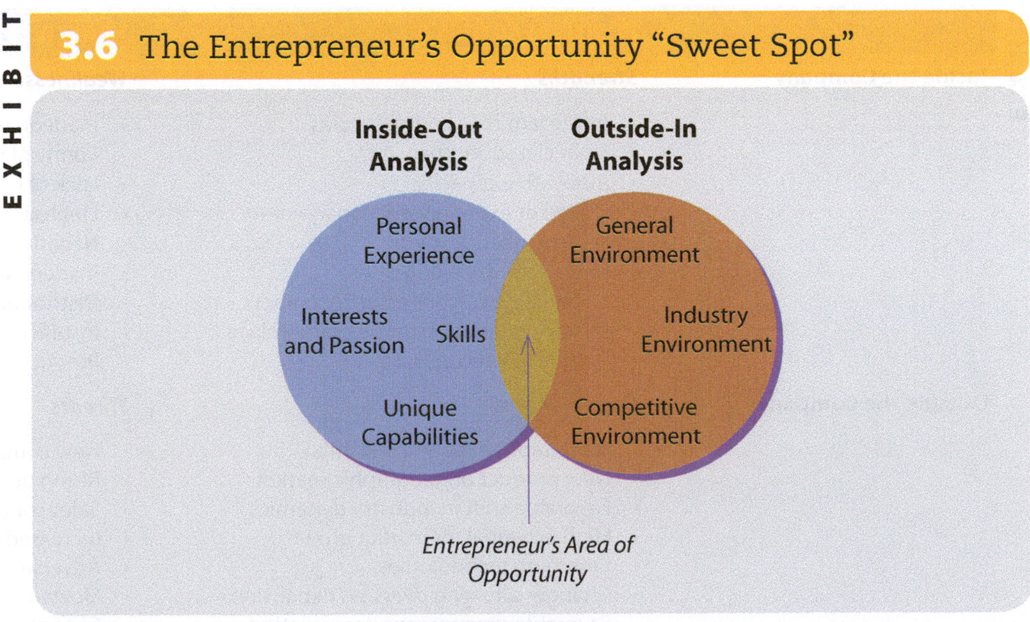

3-4 SELECTING STRATEGIES THAT CAPTURE OPPORTUNITIES

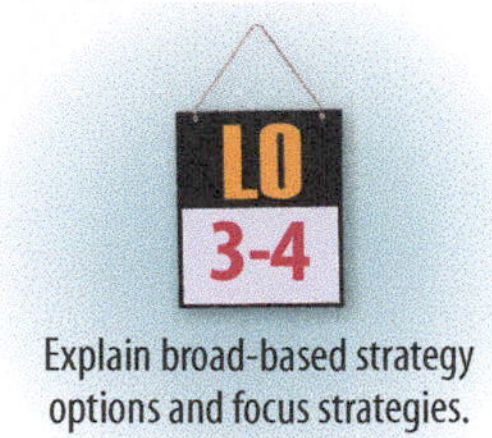

Explain broad-based strategy options and focus strategies.

A **strategy** is, in essence, a set of actions that coordinates the resources and commitments of a business to boost its performance. Choosing a strategy that makes sense for a particular entrepreneur and startup is a critical early step toward superior performance. But keeping an eye on strategy options—both broad-based and focus strategies—can also guide established companies toward success.

3-4a Broad-Based Strategy Options

Firms competing in the same industry can adopt very different strategies. Broadly speaking, companies can choose to build their strategies around an emphasis on either low cost or differentiation as they consider how to position themselves relative to their competitors.

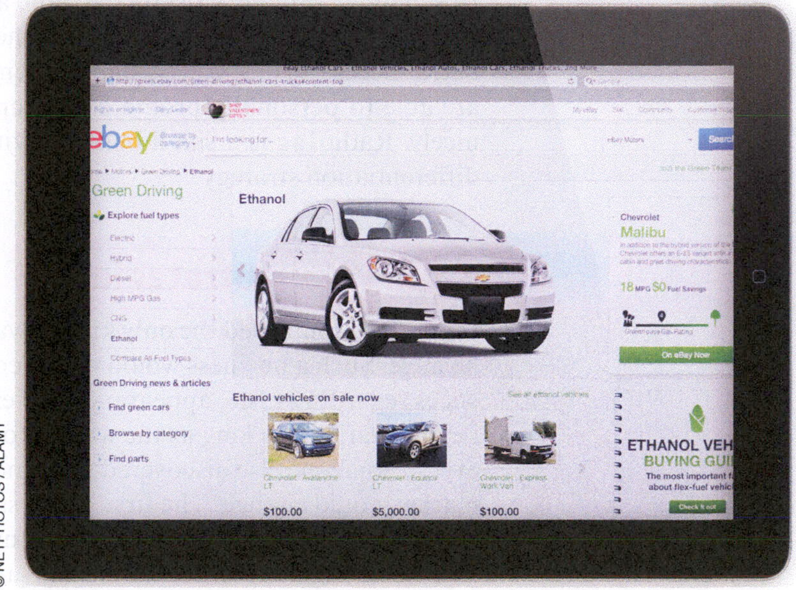

© NETPHOTOS / ALAMY

COST-BASED STRATEGY

To follow a **cost-based strategy**, a firm must hold down its costs so that it can compete by charging lower prices for its products or services and still make a profit. The sources of cost advantages are varied, ranging from low-cost labor to efficiency in operations. Many people assume that cost-based strategies will not work for small companies, and often this is true. However, cost-advantage factors are so numerous and diverse that, in some cases, small businesses may be able to use them with great success. Think about the thousands of small operators who sell used cars on eBay as a primary occupation. Although they lack the scale advantages of the large dealerships against which they compete, they operate with very little overhead by selling exclusively online and handling all features of the transactions involved in order to limit costs. It appears that motivated entrepreneurs can almost always find ways to compete on cost and undercut their much larger competitors.

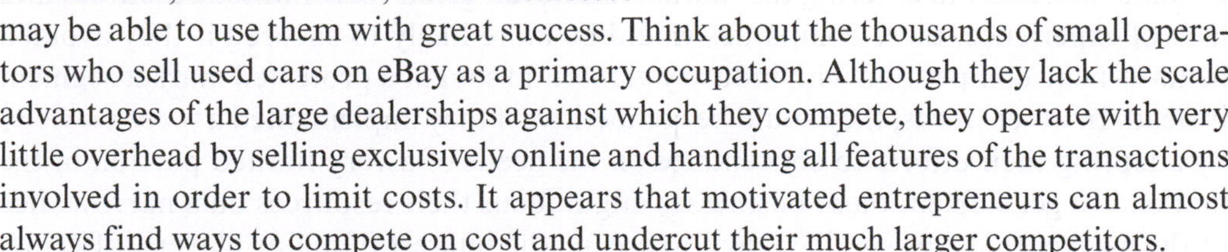

To be sure, taking the low-cost path is not without its risks, especially if doing so sparks a price war with established competitors that have deeper pockets and are inclined to take shots at upstarts that want to steal their customers. But perhaps the most enduring downside of this strategy is that it attracts customers who are always searching for the best deal. As a result, it can be a great challenge to develop customer loyalty and generate long-term success.

DIFFERENTIATION-BASED STRATEGY

The second general option for building a competitive advantage is following a **differentiation-based strategy**, an approach that emphasizes the uniqueness of a firm's product or service (in terms of some feature other than cost). A firm that can create and sustain an attractive differentiation-based strategy is likely to be a successful

strategy
A plan of action that coordinates the resources and commitments of an organization to achieve superior performance.

cost-based strategy
A plan of action that requires a firm to hold down its costs so that it can compete by charging lower prices and still make a profit.

differentiation-based strategy
A plan of action designed to provide a product or service with unique attributes that are valued by consumers.

performer in the marketplace. For the strategy to be effective, the consumer must be convinced of the uniqueness and value of the product or service, whether real or perceived. A wide variety of operational and marketing tactics, ranging from design to promotion, can lead to product or service differentiation.

After spending many years in the music industry, Brian Landau and Pete Rosenblum were bothered that hit songs didn't always generate the market response they deserved. So in 2003 they launched New York City–based RadioTag, a full-service marketing agency. Right from the start, differentiation was the foundation of their strategy. While most radio stations let the DJs do all the talking, RadioTag allows artists to introduce their own work via recordings. With this approach, Taylor Swift can describe her emotional connection to a song, or members of Maroon 5 might explain how their latest album came together. "That was really the whole point," says Rosenblum. "Put an artist on the radio and let people become more familiar with who the artist is, what the song is, and how they can buy it." It is clearly a different approach, and a successful one. Radio stations benefit from the free promotional content, artists are able to personally promote their creative works, and the company has profited nicely. RadioTag is a small business with a well-designed and competently executed differentiation strategy.[32]

3-4b Focus Strategies

If one firm controlled the only known water supply in the world, its sales volume would be huge. Such a business would not be concerned about differences in personal preferences regarding taste, appearance, or temperature. It would consider its customers to be one market. As long as the water product was wet, it would satisfy everyone. However, if someone else discovered a second water supply, the first company's view of the market would change. The first business might discover that sales were drying up and take measures to modify its strategy. In any case, the level of rivalry would likely rise as rivals struggled for position in the same industry space.

If the potential for water sales was enormous, small businesses would eventually become interested in entering the market. However, given their limited resources and lack of experience, these companies would be more likely to succeed if they avoided head-to-head competition with industry giants and sought a protected market segment instead. In other words, they could be competitive if they implemented a **focus strategy** by adapting their efforts to concentrate on the needs of a very limited portion of the market. To get started, these businesses might focus their resources on a narrow slice of the market that was small enough to escape the interest of major players (offering, say, filtered water delivered to individual homes) or even take a completely new approach to permit entry without immediate competitive response (perhaps by filling market gaps resulting from supply shortages).

Focus strategies represent a strategic approach in which entrepreneurs try to shield themselves from market forces by targeting a specific group of customers who have an identifiable but very narrow range of product or service interests (often called a *market niche*). By focusing on a specialized market, some small businesses develop unique expertise that leads to higher levels of value and service for customers, which is great for business. In fact, this advantage prompted marketing guru Philip Kotler to declare, "There are riches in niches."[33]

focus strategy
A plan of action that isolates an enterprise from competitors and other market forces by targeting a restricted market segment.

The two broad options discussed earlier—cost-based and differentiation-based strategies—can also be used when focusing on a niche market. Although few entrepreneurs adopt a cost-based focus strategy, it does happen. For example, outlets with names like Drinking Water Depot and H2O To Go have opened over the years, with most using an efficient purification system to offer high-quality drinking water to price-sensitive customers at a fraction of the price charged by competitors.

Contrast this approach with the differentiation-based focus strategy that Mark Sikes adopted for his small business, Personalized Bottle Water. Since launching the company in Little Rock, Arkansas, in 1997, he has been selling bottled water featuring custom labels for corporate clients and anyone who wants to celebrate a special occasion, including schools, funeral homes, hotels, and brides and grooms. He has plans to expand the business, but the emphasis will still be on personalization.[34] Without this focus, there is no way that Sikes would be able to compete head to head with a bottling giant like Coca-Cola Company (which owns Dasani), but flexibility and customization—foundations for differentiation—give Personalized Bottle Water a fighting chance.

Entrepreneurs can usually select and implement a focus strategy that will allow them to target a niche market within a sizeable industry, thereby avoiding direct competition with larger competitors. This can be accomplished in a number of ways, as discussed in the following section.

FOCUS STRATEGY SELECTION AND IMPLEMENTATION

By selecting a particular focus strategy, an entrepreneur decides on the basic direction of a business, which determines the venture's very nature. A firm's overall strategy is formulated, therefore, as its leader decides how the firm will relate to its environment—particularly to the customers and competitors in that environment. This can involve a delicate balancing act, one that keeps the venture out of the crosshairs of industry heavyweights and yet offers enough market promise to provide the startup with a reasonable shot at getting off the ground.

Selection of a very specialized market is, of course, not the only possible strategy for a small firm. But focus strategies are very popular because they allow a small firm to operate in the gaps that exist between larger competitors. They also leave entrepreneurs with plenty of room to maneuver as they come up with creative new venture ideas. For starters, focus strategies can be set up in the following ways:

- By restricting the target market to a single subset of customers
- By emphasizing a single product or service
- By limiting the market to a single geographical region
- By concentrating on the superiority of the product or service

If a small firm chooses to compete head to head with other companies, particularly large corporations, it must be prepared to distinguish itself in some way in order to make itself a viable competitor. If you want to succeed as a focus player, it's wise to pinpoint a profitable niche and develop great depth of competence in it so that you can *own* it. In the words of Jack Trout, one of the pioneers of the concept of market positioning, the focuser should try to be "like the service guy who repairs only Sub-Zero appliances and becomes the best at that instead of trying to go head to head with Sears in trying to repair everything. Customers will hire [him] because they know he'll have the right parts in stock, have experience with the brand's quirks and be able to complete repairs faster."[35]

Because powerful focus strategies also offer great flexibility, entrepreneurs often find ways to start a number of different specialization strategies within the same industry, with the hope of success for each of them. At the same time, however, they must consider problems stemming from overspecialization and competition, which can threaten to erode the profits of such strategies.

DRAWBACKS OF FOCUS STRATEGIES

One small business analyst expresses a word of caution about selecting a niche market:

> *Warning! A firm can be so specialized that it may not have enough customers to be viable. Do not plan to open a pen repair shop, a shoelace boutique, or a restaurant based on the concept of toast (although one based on breakfast cereal has apparently been founded).*[36]

In addition to the dangers of becoming too specialized, firms that adopt a focus strategy often have to tread a narrow path between maintaining a protected market and attracting competition. If their ventures are profitable, these entrepreneurs are likely to face an influx of new competitors that will pursue the same niche, thereby luring away customers and driving down returns for all rivals until the segment is no longer profitable. Although it can apply to any type of competitive strategy, not just focus options, this **paradox of attraction** points out that the very feature of a market that makes it attractive to one small company (that is, the lack of competition) also makes it attractive to others. Recognizing this and other common pitfalls, strategy guru Michael Porter cautions that a segmented market can erode under any of the following four conditions:[37]

- The focus strategy is imitated.
- The target segment becomes structurally unattractive because the structure erodes or because demand simply disappears.
- The target segment loses its uniqueness.
- New firms subsegment the industry.

Stated another way, it should be clear that focus strategies do not guarantee a sustainable advantage. Small firms can boost their success, however, by developing and extending their competitive strengths. Good strategic planning can help point the way through these challenging situations, as well as shape the feasibility of the venture.

3-5 SCREENING NEW BUSINESS IDEAS

Screen business ideas to identify those with the greatest potential.

With all of the approaches to business idea generation described in this chapter, your problem may not be coming up with an idea for a startup, but coming up with too many. Since you can't pursue multiple startup ideas for now, it is important to narrow your focus to the one that seems most promising. After taking that step, you should complete an in-depth feasibility analysis (discussed later in the chapter) to determine whether the idea you have selected is viable and merits the investment of time and money that will be necessary to launch it. If your new business idea still seems to be a winner, we will then lead you through the steps required to put together a suitable business plan (discussed in Chapter 6). At this point, however, you really need to decide on the business idea that you want to consider further. The business idea screening process can help you do this.

paradox of attraction
The self-contradictory idea that an attractive market opportunity is likely to draw multiple competitors, thereby diminishing its attractiveness.

It is important to understand that the quality of the final evaluation will be only as good as the information used to generate it. For that reason, running business ideas through the screen will require adequate background research and informed estimations so that the analysis and conclusions will be based on trustworthy facts and reasonable judgments. The process must be more than a dart-throwing exercise. But it also doesn't need to be time consuming; in most cases, one hour will be enough time to complete the screening for each business idea assessed.[38]

Because the business idea screening tool is designed to provide a quick assessment, it is by no means comprehensive. Rather, it only takes into account the merits of an idea relative to five very important factors:

- *Strength of the business idea:* The best business ideas will meet a definite market need, create value for end users, and offer products or services that customers favor and find easy to use. They also will have no fatal flaws (discussed later in the chapter).
- *Targeted market and customers:* Businesses are more likely to thrive if they focus on a sizeable market that is easy to identify, growing rapidly, and composed of customers with high levels of purchasing power that they are very willing to use. Further, the best customers will be easily reachable through clear channels of promotion.
- *Industry and competitive advantage:* The most favorable industries for startups have few or no competitors, are growing quickly (to allow room for new entrants), and feature high operating margins. They also present few or no barriers to keep new businesses out and would allow your startup to establish and sustain its specific competitive advantage.
- *Capability of founder(s):* In a best-case scenario, the founder(s) will have industry-related experience, skills, and networks, as well as a great passion for and a good fit with the new business.
- *Capital requirements and venture performance:* An entrepreneur will fare best when the venture needs little capital to launch, its anticipated profit potential is great, and similar enterprises perform very well. Low levels of liability and other risks are ideal, as is the ability to start the new business incrementally or test it cheaply before full launch.

The last factor deserves further explanation. If your startup budget is tight (as is so often the case), a business idea's promise is likely to be determined by your ability to launch a limited version of that idea or to test market reactions to gauge its odds for success. This may be more manageable than you realize using free or cheap tools available online or low-tech methods that can get the job done. Many entrepreneurs have tested their ideas on a budget of $100 or less. Examples of their cost-effective methods include using SurveyMonkey.com to contact potential customers and estimate the size of the market, as well as conducting market research at no cost by joining online support groups to probe the depth of interest in a planned service offering (if this is permitted and appropriate). One entrepreneur spent about $45 to test her idea. This included setting up a website for the business using a free template (one approved for commercial use) from Joomla.org, registering a domain name (at $9.95), and spending $10.95 for Web-hosting services. After installing Google Analytics (free) to track website traffic and paying for Google AdWords, she then started setting up ads to promote the site. Within a month, she had enough responses to know that her idea was a winner.[39] Testing an idea before launching a business is almost always an advantage.

© RAWPIXEL/SHUTTERSTOCK.COM

Finally, you should remember that an idea can be assessed more than once to allow for adjustments that would improve the startup's projected viability. For example, shifting to a narrower market niche might lead to a smaller venture, but it can also reduce the number and strength of competitors, increase the willingness of customers to pay for the product, lower startup costs, boost profitability, and so on.

The screening process presented here cannot provide a *perfect* estimate of the potential of a given business idea. One reason is that all items are weighted equally for the sake of simplicity, even though some may have more impact on an idea's potential than others. Nonetheless, this practical method for assessing multiple ideas will let you efficiently decide which one would be best to pursue. Then, after you have narrowed your focus to the one concept that you want to consider further, you should complete a feasibility analysis to determine its potential in more depth.

3-6 IS YOUR STARTUP IDEA FEASIBLE?

LO 3-6

Assess the feasibility of a startup idea.

We will show you in Part 3 how to create a business plan that will spell out the details of your planned enterprise and its startup considerations. But it is very important that you take an intermediate step first, one that tells you how *feasible* your business idea may be. A **feasibility analysis** is a preliminary assessment of a business idea that gauges whether or not the venture envisioned is likely to succeed. Of course, it may also indicate that the concept has merit, but only if it is modified in some important way.

Developing a solid feasibility analysis before jumping ahead to the business plan can help ensure that the planned venture will not be doomed by a **fatal flaw**—that is, a circumstance or development that, in and of itself, could render a new business unsuccessful. John Osher, serial innovator and entrepreneur, estimates that nine out of ten entrepreneurs fail because their business concept is deficient. In his words, "They want to be in business so much that they often don't do the work they need to do ahead of time, so everything they do is doomed. They can be very talented, do everything else right, and fail because they have ideas that are flawed."[40] It is important to look deeply and honestly for potential weaknesses in your own startup ideas. No matter how remarkable the business concept may seem to be, moving forward is pointless if it must use a manufacturing process that is patent protected, requires startup capital that cannot be raised, ignores market limitations, or is unsound in some other way.

© ISTOCKPHOTO.COM/RAWPIXEL LTD

feasibility analysis
A preliminary assessment of a business idea that gauges whether the venture envisioned is likely to succeed.

fatal flaw
A circumstance or development that alone could render a new business unsuccessful.

John W. Mullins is a serial entrepreneur and a professor at the prestigious London Business School. He is also the author of *The New Business Road Test*, a book that underscores the importance of identifying the fatal flaws of a business idea before it is too late:

> *If [entrepreneurs] can find the fatal flaw before they write their business plan or before it engulfs their new business, they can deal with it in many ways. They can modify their ideas—shaping the opportunity to better fit the hotly competitive world*

in which it seeks to bear fruit. If the flaw they find appears to be a fatal one, they can even abandon the idea before it's too late—before launch, in some cases, or soon enough thereafter to avoid wasting months or years in pursuit of a dream that simply won't fly.

Better yet, if, after [questioning] and probing, testing and especially experimenting for answers, the signs remain positive, they embrace their opportunity with renewed passion and conviction, armed with a new-found confidence that the evidence—not just their intuition—confirms their [insight]. Their idea really is an opportunity worth pursuing. Business plan, here we come![41]

Deciding to complete a feasibility analysis before proceeding to the business plan stage can save a lot of time, money, and heartache. Or, as Mullins points out, it may reaffirm the power of a business idea and strengthen the resolve to move forward, providing a reserve of energy and commitment that will come in handy when the going gets tough—and it definitely *will* get tough as the venture unfolds.

Keep in mind that success in entrepreneurship is generally the result of three elements that come together in such a way that the new enterprise gets the thrust it needs to launch and the sustained power to keep it going. These three elements are a market with potential, an attractive industry, and a capable individual or team with the skills and capabilities to pull it all together (see Exhibit 3.7). A feasibility analysis investigates each of these elements.

EXHIBIT **3.7** A Feasibility Analysis Framework

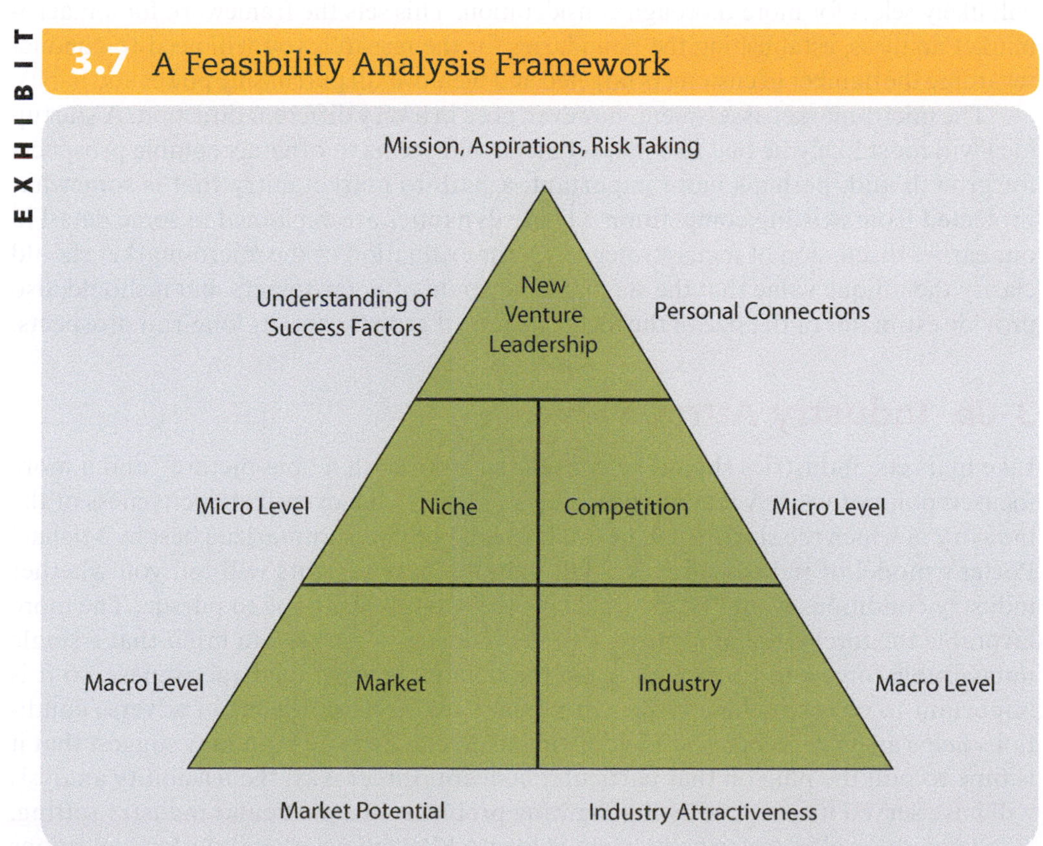

Source: Adapted from John W. Mullins, *The New Business Road Test: What Entrepreneurs and Executives Should Do before Writing a Business Plan*. (London: Financial Times Prentice Hall, 2010).

3-6a Market Potential

It is important to make clear the distinction between a market and an industry, as the two are very different. A market consists of *buyers*, current or potential customers who are interested in purchasing a particular class of products or services to satisfy wants or needs—and they must also have the ability to pay for them. An industry, on the other hand, is composed of *sellers* who compete with one another by offering identical or similar products or services for sale to the same general group of buyers.

When assessing the pool of potential buyers that a business might serve, it is important to think of that market on two levels—the broad macro-market and the fragments or niches (micro-markets) that can be identified within the broader market. Entrepreneurs with limited business aspirations may find attractive niche opportunities acceptable. However, Mullins points out that "it is also important to know which way the tides are flowing."[42] That is, a desirable niche today is likely to lose its luster over time if the broad market from which it is derived is trending toward the negative. In most cases, the health of the macro-market can be a very useful predictor of the future potential of the micro-markets within it.

An entrepreneur with lofty ambitions may be satisfied with an attractive niche only if it can serve as a point of entry into a macro-market with prospects for fast growth and ample long-term potential. The attractiveness of that niche is limited if the fundamental features of the macro-market that support it are not promising. In any case, assessments of the market should be completed on both levels, and each level will be driven by a very different set of questions.

As part of a feasibility analysis, an evaluation of the general environment will help to identify a potential-laden trend that can support promising startup ideas, one of which you will likely select for more thorough consideration. This sets the framework for a macro-market analysis, establishing the boundaries for the research you will need to conduct regarding the number of customers targeted and their overall purchasing power and habits.

The micro-market assessment, however, goes in a very different direction. A startup idea will most likely be tied to a market niche that seems to offer acceptable prospects for growth and, perhaps more important, a path to market entry that is somewhat protected from existing competition. (These dynamics are explained in some detail in our earlier discussion of focus strategies.) Your evaluation of the micro-market should clarify the unique value that the startup idea would offer customers, but it should also provide estimates of the size of the niche, its rate of growth, and its long-run prospects.

3-6b Industry Attractiveness

Like markets, industries should be considered from both a "big-picture" and a more focused point of view. A macro-level analysis assesses the overall attractiveness of the industry in which the startup will be established, perhaps summarized best by Michael Porter's model of industry forces.[43] Ultimately, these insights will tell you whether industry conditions would be favorable for the startup you hope to pursue. The more favorable the forces, the more attractive the industry—but keep in mind that a single unfavorable force can be enough to tip the balance toward unattractiveness, so it is important to consider these forces with great care. Foreknowledge of adverse conditions helps an entrepreneur make adjustments to compensate, or it may suggest that it is time to pull the plug on that particular concept. Either way, the feasibility analysis will have served its purpose by highlighting problems in a particular industry setting.

A micro-level industry assessment is focused less on whether industry conditions overall are suitable to launching a new business and more on the probability of a startup's success over the long run. This requires the aspiring entrepreneur to think carefully about the proposed venture to determine whether the advantage it has going for it can be protected from competitive pressures once rivals realize that they have a new challenger. This will be determined mostly by the startup's potential to generate adequate sales and the strength of protective barriers that will shield it from competitors' efforts to replicate its strengths.

3-6c New Venture Leadership

Finally, a new business will only be as strong as its leader, so it is important to assess whether the entrepreneur, or entrepreneurial team, is up to the task. Mullins suggests that three dimensions of capability are important here: (1) the fit of the venture with its leader's mission, aspirations, and level of comfort with the risk involved, (2) the leader's grasp of factors that are critical to the success of the enterprise and her or his ability to execute on these, and (3) the leader's connections to suppliers, customers, investors, and others in the industry who will be essential to making the venture work.

These factors will have direct and indirect effects on the venture's odds of success. For example, the intensity and consistency of an entrepreneur's mission focus, personal aspirations, and tolerance for the risks involved fuel the drive and commitment required to get a business off the ground and keep it moving forward. And the capabilities that come from a deep knowledge and understanding of the new venture, as well as a strong network of professional connections, allow a leader to sense new product and market trends before others see them coming and make wise decisions when positioning products or services in competitive spaces.[44] In the end, these qualities determine whether a leader has what it takes to break into the game of business—and whether she or he will prevail.

Conducting a feasibility analysis takes time and effort, but it serves the very important purpose of identifying flaws in a business concept that may be fatal to the proposed startup. While many of these flaws can be corrected by a course adjustment, the analysis might expose major flaws that cannot be addressed or corrected. If it does, you would be wise to abandon the concept and shift your energies to a more attractive alternative. Regardless of the final outcome, completing a feasibility analysis will let you know what needs to be done before you commit time, money, and energy to complete a full-scale business plan.

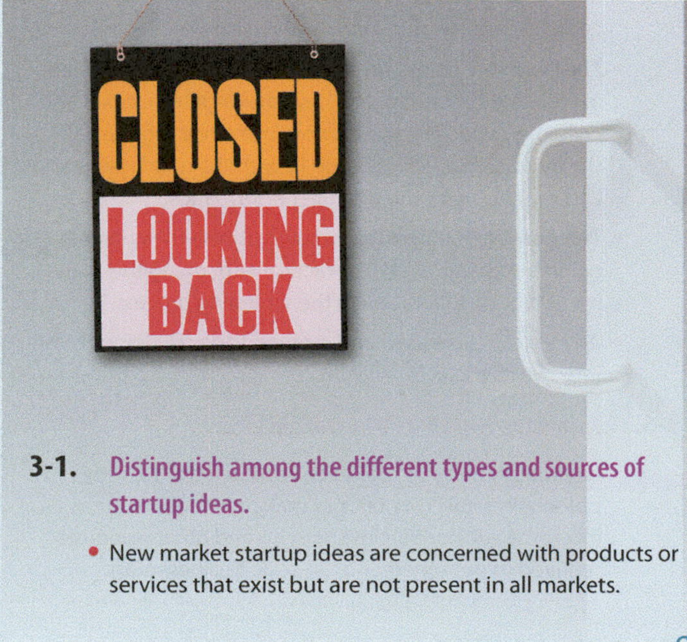

3-1. Distinguish among the different types and sources of startup ideas.

- New market startup ideas are concerned with products or services that exist but are not present in all markets.
- New technology ideas involve new or relatively new knowledge breakthroughs.
- New benefit ideas are based on new and improved products or services or better ways of performing old functions.
- Research shows that entrepreneurs claim prior work experience is the leading source of inspiration for startup ideas.
- Personal experience leads many aspiring entrepreneurs to the startup decision.
- Some entrepreneurs start their new ventures based on their hobbies and personal interests, which can add passion and energy to the enterprise.
- Accidental discoveries may also provide useful ideas for startups.
- Personal contacts, trade shows, research institutes, and trade publications are among other idea leads for startups.

3-2. **Use innovative thinking to generate ideas for high-potential startups.**

- A commitment to creative thinking can generate many ideas for new businesses and also help to keep an existing business fresh and moving forward.
- Business ideas can be spurred by borrowing ideas from existing products and services or other industries, combining businesses to create a market opening, focusing on a problem, responding to a trend, and improving the function of an existing product or service.
- Other ideas for new businesses can come from considering possible ways to make customers' lives easier, meeting customer needs in a new way, expanding the market for a product or service, offering products through a subscription service, figuring out how to cash in on the sharing economy, making a product or service "green," and tapping into new technologies.

3-3. **Describe external and internal analyses that can shape the selection of venture opportunities.**

- Outside-in analysis considers the external environment, including the general, industry, and competitive environments.
- Opportunities arise for small businesses that are alert to changes or openings in the external environment.
- Major trends in the general environment are economic, sociocultural, political/legal, global, technological, and demographic in nature.
- The major forces that determine the potential attractiveness and profitability of a target industry include the threat of new competitors, the threat of substitute products or services, the intensity of rivalry among existing competitors, and the bargaining power of suppliers and buyers.
- Inside-out analysis helps the entrepreneur to understand a startup's sources of potential strengths and the unique competencies that can be formed from them.
- Tangible resources are visible and easy to measure, whereas intangible resources are invisible and difficult to quantify.
- Capabilities refers to a firm's routines and processes that coordinate the use of its productive assets to achieve desired outcomes.
- Core competencies are those capabilities that can be leveraged to enable a firm to do more than its competitors, thereby leading to a competitive advantage.
- A SWOT analysis provides an overview of a firm's strengths and weaknesses, as well as opportunities for and threats to the organization.
- The entrepreneur's "opportunity sweet spot" is found at the point of overlap of emerging potentials in the external environment and the unique strengths and capabilities of the entrepreneur and the venture.

3-4. **Explain broad-based strategy options and focus strategies.**

- Broad-based strategy options include both cost-based and differentiation-based strategies.
- A cost-based strategy requires the firm to become a low-cost provider within the market while still making a profit.
- Product or service differentiation emphasizes the uniqueness of a firm's product or service.
- Focusing on a specific market niche is a strategy that small firms often use successfully.
- A focus strategy may involve restricting focus to a single subset of customers, emphasizing a single product or service, limiting the market to a single geographical region, or concentrating on product or service superiority.
- Entrepreneurs can exploit very different market niches within the same general industry.
- In selecting a particular focus strategy, an entrepreneur determines the basic direction of the business, and this affects the very nature of the venture.
- The benefits of a focus strategy can diminish when the firm becomes too specialized, the strategy is imitated, the target segment becomes unattractive or demand dwindles, the segment loses its uniqueness, or new firms subsegment the industry.

3-5. **Screen business ideas to identify those with the greatest potential.**

- If too many new business ideas are generated, it will be necessary to use an idea screening process to determine which idea deserves more focused attention.
- The screening of ideas can be performed quickly (usually in an hour or less) and should precede the decision to complete a feasibility analysis of the idea selected.
- The five main factors considered in the screening process include the strength of the idea, the targeted market and customers, industry and competitive advantage issues, the founder's capabilities and fit with the new business, and capital needs and venture performance.
- There are ways to test many new business ideas in part or "on the cheap," and the practicality of doing this is an important consideration in the screening process.
- An idea can be revised and screened again if doing so will improve its projected viability.

3-6. **Assess the feasibility of a startup idea.**

- A feasibility analysis should be conducted to identify potentially fatal flaws prior to making the decision to invest the substantial time, energy, and other resources required to put together a full-scale business plan.

- It's important to distinguish between a market and an industry. A market consists of all buyers of a product or service; an industry is made up of all sellers who compete for the same market.
- A feasibility analysis should assess the potential of a market on two levels—the broad macro-market and the micro-market—because the long-run potential of a market niche is determined largely by the outlook for the overall market.
- The industry should be assessed for its overall attractiveness (potential for profits) and the specific context of direct competition, which can greatly impact a startup's prospects for success.
- Entrepreneurs are likely to be successful in a startup situation to the degree that the planned venture fits with their mission, aspirations, and tolerance for risk.
- Successful entrepreneurs understand and are able to manage the factors that are critical to the operation of the enterprise, and they are able to connect with suppliers, customers, investors, and others whose involvement is crucial to the future performance of the planned venture.

Key Terms

capabilities p. 78
competitive advantage p. 78
competitive environment p. 75
core competencies p. 78
cost-based strategy p. 81
differentiation-based strategy p. 81
entrepreneurial alertness p. 65
fatal flaw p. 86
feasibility analysis p. 86
focus strategy p. 82
general environment p. 75
industry environment p. 75
intangible resources p. 78
new benefit ideas p. 67
new market ideas p. 66
new technology ideas p. 66
opportunity recognition p. 65
paradox of attraction p. 84
pivot p. 67
resources p. 78
serendipity p. 69
startups p. 66
strategy p. 81
SWOT analysis p. 79
tangible resources p. 78

You Make the Call

Situation 1

Jonathan Lugar, 17, had just finished helping his mom with a garage sale when it occurred to him that he might create a business to do the same for others and make a little money for college. The idea was to offer a service that would take the headache out of running a garage sale. Lugar would handle all advertising and sale setup, and his experience with other garage sales in the area would allow him to coach sellers on pricing so that items would actually be purchased. He figured he could charge $200 per job for sales that bring in $400 or less, but he and the seller would split sales above $400 on a 50-50 basis. Lugar believes the greatest value added from his services would be from his pricing insights, since most people rarely have a garage sale and thus have little idea about how much to ask for items. Careful pricing would make his customers happy, since they could maximize their sales and minimize the risk that they would be left with the very items they were trying to get rid of. In fact, Lugar planned to keep track of how much things sold for to fine-tune his pricing advice. He estimates that his startup costs would be minimal and would come mostly from the use of his truck and some fuel.

Question 1 How would you classify Lugar's startup idea? Is it a new market idea, a new technology idea, or a new benefit idea?
Question 2 What was the source of Lugar's startup idea?
Question 3 Would you recommend that he give this startup concept a try? Explain your reasoning.

Situation 2

Willy Whitlock loves to restore classic cars. But run-of-the-mill classics are not what he goes for—his fascination runs to rolling stock from the 1950s and 60s that are rebuilt to be fast, fun, and true works of art. And that is the focus of his restoration garage startup, Smokin' Wheels by Willy, a company name so good that it immediately gives away the essence of the business. Since the launch of his Tucson, Arizona–based company in September 2012, Whitlock has driven his new venture to $2 million in sales by offering classic beauties (at $45,000 to $150,000 each) that are "tricked out" to the specific tastes of very picky collectors and classic car enthusiasts.

Uniqueness is key to the company's strategy, but it goes further than that. Whitlock uses stunning paint work, creative pinstriping, and lots of chrome to create breathtaking cars that are guaranteed to turn heads—but painted and tricked out in each case to suit the precise tastes of the car lover who orders them. These are true works of art that balance high performance and stunning aesthetics. Whitlock's work allows clients to add time-honored classic car models to their collections, but with super-high performance drivetrains and one-of-a-kind paint applications and design details.

Question 1 Based on the frameworks introduced in this chapter, what kind of strategy is Whitlock following in his new venture?

Question 2 Identify the strengths upon which this business is built. Do you see any weaknesses that may be of concern to the company?

Question 3 Are there any particular threats that will put Smokin' Wheels by Willy at risk as time goes on? Can you see any opportunities that may allow the company to expand in the future?

Question 4 What resources and capabilities form the foundation for the business? Do you think these will be sufficient to create a *sustainable* competitive advantage for the company? Why or why not?

Situation 3

Overcoming jet lag on international trips is crucial to making good decisions when working with overseas counterparts, especially when difficult negotiations are involved. If an executive wants to be refreshed and on top of his or her game, Phillip Sanderson has a solution. Perfect Illuminations, his five-year-old company, has been offering sleep-recovery services through business-class hotels in prime cities around the world. So far, he has worked out deals with eight partner hotels in four cities: New York, Tokyo, London, and Paris. His system provides booths in which guests can bask in 30 minutes of simulated sunshine generated from electronic light boxes. Science has shown that this form of light therapy can help to restore the body's natural sleep rhythms well ahead of the recovery time that it normally takes to reset one's internal clock. The price of the service varies, depending on the city and the specific deal worked out with each partner hotel, but the client response so far has been encouraging. Now Sanderson is trying to identify other cities where he can help weary travelers reset their internal clocks.

Question 1 Will the market for Sanderson's service continue to grow in the years ahead?

Question 2 Given the company's success so far, what sources of competition should he expect?

Question 3 What steps would you recommend that Sanderson take to protect his company from the onslaught of competition that is likely to come?

Case 3

The Kollection: From Music Hobby to Startup and Beyond (P. 649)

This case describes the experiences of an entrepreneur who launched a music blog and sharing website to fill a gap in the marketplace and had to work through challenges related to strategic positioning, changes in the competitive landscape, legal/regulatory hang-ups, opportunities for diversification, and generating enough revenue to become profitable.

Alternative Cases For Chapter 3

Case 1, Dashlocker, p.646
Case 8, Couchsurfing International, p. 658
Case 13, Network Collie, p. 670

Endnotes

1. To read more about an interesting framework that integrates three forms of the search process (deliberate search, industry insight-guided search, and alertness to opportunities), see Robert A. Baron, "Opportunity Recognition as Pattern Recognition: How Entrepreneurs 'Connect the Dots' to Identify New Business Opportunities," *Academy of Management Perspectives*, Vol. 20, No. 1 (February 2006), pp. 104–119.
2. Israel M. Kirzner, *Competition and Entrepreneurship* (Chicago: University of Chicago Press, 1973), p. 74.
3. For an in-depth discussion of the alertness concept and the essence of the mindset of the entrepreneur, see Jeffery S. McMullen and Dean A. Shepherd, "Entrepreneurial Action and the Role of Uncertainty in the Theory of the Entrepreneur," *Academy of Management Review*, Vol. 31, No. 1 (2006), pp. 132–152.
4. The process of opportunity recognition is not entirely driven by thoughts; in fact, feelings and emotions can also play a very important role. For an interesting analysis of the interplay of affect and cognitive processes, see Robert A. Baron, "The Role of Affect in the Entrepreneurial Process," *Academy of Management Review*, Vol. 33, No. 2 (2008), pp. 328–340.
5. Quoted in April Y. Pennington, "Copy That: In Business, Imitation Is More Than a Form of Flattery," *Entrepreneur*, Vol. 34, No. 3 (March 2006), p. 22.
6. Quoted in Lizette Chapman, "'Pivoting' Pays Off for Tech Entrepreneurs," *The Wall Street Journal*, April 26, 2012, http://online.wsj.com/article/SB10001424052702303592404577364171598999252.html, accessed July 30, 2012.
7. "CrunchBase: Unreal Brands," http://www.crunchbase.com/organization/unreal-brands, accessed October 28, 2014; "Get Unreal: Our Story," http://getunreal.com/our-story, accessed October 28, 2014; and Sarah E. Needleman, "A Young Entrepreneur's Sweet Idea," *The Wall Street Journal*, June 14, 2012, http://online.wsj.com/article/SB10001424052702303410404577464700830700754.html, accessed October 28, 2014.
8. Personal experience can influence the *kind* of startup ideas that entrepreneurs develop, but recent evidence indicates that work experience in general, as well as experience with new ventures in particular, can improve the *quality* of concepts generated. For more on this, see Maw-Der Foo, "Member Experience, Use of External Assistance and Evaluation of Business Ideas," *Journal of Small Business Management*, Vol. 48, No. 1 (January 2010), pp. 32–43.
9. "*Inc.* 5000: SeekingSitters," http://www.inc.com/profile/seekingsitters, accessed October 28, 2014; Kevin Manahan, "A Service Born of Necessity," *Entrepreneur*, April 9, 2009, http://www.entrepreneur.com/article/201166, accessed October 28, 2014; and "SeekingSitters: Professional Babysitting Services," http://www.seekingsitters.com, accessed October 28, 2014.
10. Colleen Taylor, "Zuckerberg: Facebook Started Out as a 'Hobby' and a 'Project,' Not a Company," TechCrunch, October 20, 2012, http://techcrunch.com/2012/10/20/zuckerberg-facebook-started-out-as-a-hobby-and-a-project-not-a-company, accessed October 28, 2014.
11. Erin Weinger, "Selling Short," *Entrepreneur*, Vol. 38, No. 4 (April 2010), p. 19.
12. *Ibid.*
13. To learn more about creativity and the process of business idea generation, see Dimo Dimov, "Idea Generation from a Creativity Perspective," in Andrew Zacharakis and Stephen Spinelli, Jr. (eds.), *Entrepreneurship: The Engine of Growth* (Westport, CT: Praeger Perspectives, 2007), pp. 19–41.
14. "Industry Leader: Travel: Sixthman," *Inc.*, Vol. 33, No. 7 (September 2011), p. 200.
15. Chuck Salter, "This Is How We Do It," *Fast Company*, No. 165 (May 2012), pp. 88–89.
16. Quoted in Jason Ankeny, "The Good Sir Richard," *Entrepreneur*, Vol. 40, No. 6 (June 2012), pp. 30–38.
17. Anne Tergesen "When Guests Check In, Their iPhones Check Out," *The Wall Street Journal*, July 5, 2011, p. D1.
18. Joe Sharkey, "Reinventing the Suitcase by Adding the Wheel," *The New York Times*, October 4, 2010, http://www.nytimes.com/2010/10/05/business/05road.html?_r=0, accessed November 17, 2014.
19. Michelle Juergen, "Sleep Like a Champ," *Entrepreneur*, Vol. 40, No. 3 (March 2012), p. 74.
20. Sarah Kessler, "All Natural—From Her Ranch to Your Backyard," *Inc.*, Vol. 32, No. 4 (May 2010), p. 23; and http://www.manuretea.com/about, accessed October 31, 2014.
21. Christina Binkley, "New Ways to Give Yourself a Gift Every Month," *The Wall Street Journal*, December 19, 2013, p. D3; Nicole LaPorte, "Getting Their Fix," *FastCompany*, No. 183 (March 2014), pp. 44–46; and Charles Passy, "One Item. Hundreds of Buyers. And 30 Days to Deliver," *The Wall Street Journal*, February 3, 2014, p. R4.
22. Sarah Needleman and Angus Loten, "Startups Want to Be the Next Airbnb, Uber," *The Wall Street Journal*, May 7, 2014, p. B4.
23. Nicole Fallon, "Clothing Rental Business Makes Leasing Fashion Easy," Business News Daily, January 21, 2014, http://www.businessnewsdaily.com/544-avelle-clothing-rental-business.html, accessed August 12, 2015.
24. Jodi Helmer, "Paperless Bliss," *Entrepreneur*, Vol. 40, No. 3 (March 2012), p. 76; Jennifer Wang, "One Man's Trash," *Entrepreneur*, Vol. 39, No. 4 (April 2011), pp. 50–53; and "About Calsaway," http://www.calsaway.com/about.html, accessed October 31, 2014.
25. As a parallel to the outside-in and inside-out options, see Dimo Dimov, "From Opportunity Insight to Opportunity Intention: The Importance of Person-Situation Learning Match," *Entrepreneurship Theory and Practice*, Vol. 31, No. 4 (July 2007), p. 566. Dimov mentions two very different opportunity insight–inducing situations: In *demand-driven* situations, the entrepreneur is aware of customer needs but doesn't know of any products that could meet those needs. In *supply-driven* situations, the entrepreneur is aware of an emerging product but doesn't know of customer needs that might be satisfied by it.
26. "Obesity Trends," Harvard School of Public Health, http://www.hsph.harvard.edu/obesity-prevention-source/obesity-trends, accessed November 4, 2014.
27. Bruce R. Barringer, *Preparing Effective Business Plans: An Entrepreneurial Approach* (Upper Saddle River, NJ: Pearson Prentice Hall, 2009), p. 37.
28. Michael Porter, *Competitive Advantage* (New York: Free Press, 1985), pp. 7–29.
29. William A. Sahlman, *How to Write a Great Business Plan* (Boston: Harvard Business School Press, 2008).
30. "Starbucks Coffee International," http://www.starbucks.com/business/international-stores, accessed February 13, 2015.

31. Stephan Faris, "Grounds Zero," *Bloomberg Businessweek*, February 9, 2012, http://www.businessweek.com/magazine/grounds-zero-a-starbucksfree-italy-02092012.html#p2, accessed November 11, 2014.

32. http://getradiotag.com, accessed November 11, 2014; and Sara Wilson, "Maximizing Air Time," *Entrepreneur*, Vol. 36, No. 11 (November 2008), p. 71.

33. Philip Kotler, "Focusing and Niching: Kotler on Marketing," http://www.marsdd.com/mars-library/focusing-and-niching-kotler-on-marketing, accessed November 11, 2014.

34. "Personalized Bottle Water: Our Story," http://www.personalizedbottlewater.com/our-story.aspx, accessed November 11, 2014.

35. Gwen Moran, "Six Weeks to a Better Bottom Line," *Entrepreneur*, Vol. 38, No. 1 (January 2010), p. 49.

36. Marc J. Dollinger, *Entrepreneurship: Strategies and Resources* (Lombard, IL: Marsh Publications, 2008), p. 144.

37. Porter, *op. cit.*, p. 5.

38. Barringer, *op. cit.*, p. 36.

39. Teri Evans, "Have a Business Idea? Test It on the Cheap," October 25, 2010, http://smallbusiness.foxbusiness.com/entrepreneurs/2010/10/25/business-idea-test-cheap, accessed November 12, 2014.

40. Quoted in Mark Henricks, "What Not to Do," *Entrepreneur*, Vol. 32, No. 2 (February 2004), pp. 84–90.

41. John W. Mullins, *The New Business Road Test* (London: Financial Times Prentice Hall, 2010), pp. 3–4.

42. *Ibid*, *p. 10.*

43. Porter, *op. cit.*

44. *Ibid.*, p. 16.

© KEN WOLTER/SHUTTERSTOCK.COM; KEN WOLTER/SHUTTERSTOCK.COM; JAMES R. MARTIN/SHUTTERSTOCK.COM; JAMES R. MARTIN/SHUTTERSTOCK.COM; JOE RAVI/SHUTTERSTOCK.COM; SHUTTERSTOCK.COM

CHAPTER 4

Franchises and Buyouts

After studying this chapter, you should be able to. . .

4-1. Define *franchise*, and have an understanding of franchise terminology.

4-2. Understand the pros and cons of franchising.

4-3. Describe the process for evaluating a franchise opportunity.

4-4. List four reasons for buying an existing business, and describe the process of evaluating an existing business.

OPEN
LOOKING AHEAD

Are franchisees entrepreneurs? Many say that franchisees are people who merely buy themselves a job and operate a business under the rules of the franchisor. Some government agencies have questioned whether franchises are actually independent businesses. In 2014, the National Labor Relations Board issued a ruling that the employees of McDonald's franchises are joint employees of both the franchisor and the franchisee, suggesting that the two are co-owners.

© KEN WOLTER/SHUTTERSTOCK.COM

In the SPOTLIGHT
Castro Enterprises: The Innovative Franchisee

One McDonald's franchisee sees it differently. Richard Castro owns more than 20 McDonald's restaurants in various locations in Texas. Castro was born in Del Rio, Texas, where his father owned a small construction company and his mother worked at home as a seamstress. He worked his way through Texas State University, earning a teaching certification. A year out of college, Castro obtained an administrative assistant position with the City of Del Rio. He was rapidly promoted and eventually became city manager, serving for two years before launching his own real estate and construction company.

A friend was a McDonald's franchisee in Del Rio and encouraged Castro to look into opportunities with the company. Castro studied the option and was accepted into McDonald's training center, Hamburger University. Upon graduation, he formed Castro Enterprises and purchased a McDonald's franchise in El Paso. Castro did not see himself as buying a job, working as the manager of the restaurant. Rather, he viewed Castro Enterprises as a company that would grow beyond a single unit. His franchise proved successful, which led to building more McDonald's restaurants in El Paso and then expanding to other cities, through both startups and acquisitions.

When meeting with other franchisees in the El Paso region, Castro suggested adding a menu item—a burrito—that could appeal to Hispanic customers. The franchisor showed no interest at first but allowed the El Paso franchisees to experiment by introducing the breakfast burrito. The product caught on, leading McDonald's to offer the product at other locations and subsequently add more items with a Southwest flavor.

Castro's entrepreneurial attitude was not restricted to his business. He describes giving back to the community as part of his DNA. He has focused on education, which he sees as an equalizer that opens doors to opportunity. Castro created the HACER Scholarship Program in 1985, supporting college education for Hispanic students. The program became the model for a general scholarship fund established by the franchisor. Castro also founded CommUNITY en Acción, a philanthropic organization in El Paso, designed to bring diverse parties together to foster education, economic development, and entrepreneurship, as well as to offer cultural programs.

Is Richard Castro an entrepreneur? We think that he is—in the very best sense of the word.

Sources: Robert Gray, "Richard Castro—Owner, Castro Enterprises: King of McDonald's," *El Paso Inc.*, March 12, 2014; "2011 Faces of Diversity—Richard Castro," http://www.youtube.com/watch?v=L-CZ23wP5iA, accessed February 28, 2015; Texas State University, "Distinguished Alumni Achievement Awards 2013," http://www.liberalarts.txstate.edu/people/DAAA/DAAA2013/castro.html, accessed February 28, 2015; and Janice Yu, "Positively El Paso: Richard Castro—A Community Leader," http://www.ktsm.com/news/positively-el-paso-richard-castro-community-leader, accessed February 28, 2015.

Pick a hundred people at random, and ask them to name a franchise. It is likely that McDonald's will be mentioned more than any other company. And most of the other franchisors named will probably be fast-food businesses. But take a look at the website of the International Franchise Association (www.franchise.org), and you will find 98 industry categories listed. Franchised companies are conducting business in accounting and tax services, maid and personal services, wildlife management control, and more. These organizations play a huge role in the United States and global economies by providing products, services, and employment. Reputable franchisors offer businesses based on models that have been tested and are more likely to succeed than starting from scratch. Of course, no venture is risk-free. If you decide to go this route, you should understand what it means to be a franchisee and how to work with the franchisor.

4-1 WHAT IS A FRANCHISE?

Define *franchise*, and have an understanding of franchise terminology.

The franchise model has been around for a long time in various forms. Some say the model for modern franchising was the early Roman Catholic Church, when the pope authorized parish priests to collect tithes and remit a portion to the Vatican while retaining the remainder for parish maintenance.[1] Others trace the beginning of franchising to the Middle Ages, when a feudal lord would grant certain rights to laymen in return for a fee and their obedience in carrying out certain community activities, such as operating ferries.[2]

The Singer Sewing Machine company is credited with being the first franchisor in the United States.[3] In 1851, Albert Singer entered agreements with local retailers to give them exclusive rights to sell Singer sewing machines. His contract became the basis for those used by franchisors to this day. Some historians, however, contend that Benjamin Franklin was actually the first U.S. franchisor.[4] They cite the arrangement he made with a printer in South Carolina to reproduce *Poor Richard's Almanac* columns. (An interesting side note is that the widow of the South Carolina printer eventually took over her late husband's business, making her the first female franchisee in North America.)

4-1a Franchising Terminology

If you are considering negotiating to purchase a franchise, you will need to understand the language that is used. Two United States government agencies, the Small Business Administration (www.sba.gov) and the Federal Trade Commission (www.ftc.gov), along with the International Franchise Association (www.franchise.org), are good sources of definitions of franchising terms.

The SBA defines a **franchise** as a business model that involves a business owner who licenses trademarks and methods to an independent entrepreneur.[5] It is a legal and commercial relationship between a **franchisor** (the owner of a trademark, service mark, trade name, or advertising symbol) and a **franchisee** (an individual or group wishing to use that identification in a business). Generally, a franchisee sells goods or services supplied by the franchisor or that meet the franchisor's quality standards. The franchise itself amounts to the right to do business under the franchisor's name and to obtain the use of trademarks, support, and control.

Franchising is based on mutual trust between the franchisor and franchisee. The franchisor provides business expertise (marketing plans, management guidance, financing assistance, site location, training, etc.) that otherwise would not be available to the franchisee. The franchisee brings the entrepreneurial spirit and drive necessary to make the franchise a success.

There are two primary forms of franchising: product and trade name franchising and business format franchising.[6] In **product and trade name franchising**, a franchisor owns the right to a product or trademark and sells that right to a franchisee. Ford automobile dealers, Pepsi-Cola soft drink bottlers, and Chevron convenience stores and service stations are examples of companies engaged in this type of franchising. With **business format franchising**, the franchisor often provides a full range of services, including site selection, training, product supply, marketing plans, and even assistance in obtaining financing. Quick-service restaurants (such as Carl's Jr.), hotels and motels (such as Choice Hotels), and business services (such as Jani-King) typically engage in this type of franchising.

In order to become a franchisee, you will need to enter into a legal contract with the franchisor, spelling out your relationship and obligations to each other. This is known as a **franchise contract**. Before you sign this agreement, the franchisor must provide you with a Franchise Disclosure Document, which will be described later in this chapter. Franchisors do not grow their organizations by waiting for franchisees to come to their door. Rather, they establish organizational structures and designate employees or partners to expand the number of franchised outlets and to monitor their performance. The most frequent means for carrying out these growth strategies are through use of the following:

- A **master licensee**, which is a firm or individual having a continuing contractual relationship with a franchisor to sell its franchises. This independent company or businessperson is a type of middleman or sales agent responsible for finding new franchisees within a specified territory. Master

franchise
A business model involving a business owner who licenses trademarks and methods to an independent entrepreneur.

franchisor
The party in a franchise contract that specifies the methods to be followed and the terms to be met by the other party.

franchisee
An entrepreneur whose power is limited by a contractual relationship with a franchising organization.

product and trade name franchising
A franchise agreement granting the right to use a widely recognized product or trademark.

business format franchising
A franchise arrangement whereby the franchisee obtains an entire marketing and management system geared to entrepreneurs.

franchise contract
The legal agreement between franchisor and franchisee.

master licensee
An independent firm or individual acting as a middleman or sales agent with the responsibility of finding new franchisees within a specified territory.

licensees may provide support services such as training and warehousing, which are more traditionally provided by the franchisor. U.S.-based franchisors often use master licensing arrangements to expand into other countries, selecting successful business companies and leaders to open units of their own and subfranchise to others.

- **Multiple-unit ownership**, in which a single franchisee owns more than one unit of the franchised business.
- **Area developers**, who are individuals or firms that obtain the legal right to open several outlets in a given area.
- **Piggyback franchising**, which refers to the operation of a retail franchise within the physical facilities of another business. An example of piggyback franchising occurs when Subway operates a restaurant within a truck stop.
- **Multibrand franchising**, which involves operating several franchise organizations within a single corporate structure. Multibranding can occur at the franchisor level, such as the Moran Family of brands which includes Alto Mere, Smart View, Mr. Transmission, and Milex, all in the automotive aftermarket industry. And it can be used by franchisees, such as Sean Falk who is a franchisee for Great American Cookies, Mrs. Fields Cookies, and two other brands.
- **Co-branding**, which involves bringing two franchise brands together under one owner. You often see co-branding with service station owners who license franchises from their oil and gasoline suppliers and who also franchise quick-service restaurants, such as Subway or McDonald's.

multiple-unit ownership Ownership by a single franchisee of more than one franchise from the same company.

area developers Individuals or firms that obtain the legal right to open several franchised outlets in a given area.

piggyback franchising The operation of a retail franchise within the physical facilities of a host store.

multibrand franchising The operation of several franchise organizations within a single corporate structure.

co-branding Bringing two or more franchise brands together under one roof.

4-1b The Impact of Franchising

The International Franchise Association (IFA) sponsors studies of the impact of franchising on the U.S. economy. The mission of the IFA is to protect, enhance, and promote franchising.[7] Founded in 1960, the membership of the IFA comprises over 70 percent of all registered franchisor companies in the United States, 10,000 franchisees, and suppliers that provide products, services, and assistance to franchise systems.[8]

According to the IFA's *Franchise Business Economic Outlook: 2015*, franchised businesses actually provided more jobs than entire industries. Direct employment in 781,794 franchise establishments totaled 8,816,000 jobs. Revenues generated by these businesses amounted to $889 billion, accounting for 5.1 percent of the gross domestic product of the United States.[9] These figures underestimate the full impact of franchising on the economy, however, because franchising stimulates activity and generates growth in many nonfranchised businesses, such as suppliers and lenders. Use of the franchise model of business formation and growth is expected to increase. Not only are U.S.-based companies expanding internationally, but franchisors headquartered in other countries are also seeking to enter the U.S. market by contracting with franchisees.

Living the Dream

ENTREPRENEURIAL EXPERIENCES

Dawn Lafreeda—The Dream of Business Ownership

Dawn Lafreeda remembers being 11 years old and telling her mother, "One day I am going to own my own company and make a lot of money," and her mother replying, "Of course you are." Lafreeda's mother was single, raising three children. Working as a district manager for Denny's restaurants, she was a role model for her children.

Money was tight when Lafreeda was growing up, so at age 16 she accepted a job at Denny's as a waitress and hostess. She valued the opportunity Denny's had given her mother and became impressed with the operations of the corporation as she gained inside experience. When she was 23, she persuaded Denny's to sell her a franchise. Lafreeda was certainly not independently wealthy at that age. She reports financing her first venture with credit cards. At the time, she did not see business ownership as a major risk. Her view was that if it failed, she could start over, and she would still be in her twenties.

© LESPALENIK/SHUTTERSTOCK.COM

Eventually, Lafreeda convinced the franchisor to give her a chance in a large market and became a Denny's franchisee in San Antonio, Texas. She justified the company's commitment to her by growing her operation from a single unit to 75 restaurants in seven states by 2014. She avoided seeking external investments, plowing her profits back into growing her business.

In the beginning, Lafreeda faced obstacles based on both age and gender. She explains that she looked much younger than her actual age. People who encountered her in the restaurant assumed she was a waitress and did not take her seriously. She describes being turned down for a loan by a banker who refused to believe that she was the actual owner of the franchise.

Lafreeda learned that being a good restaurant manager is not enough for long-term survival. Economic conditions, government regulations, and other factors beyond a business owner's control can make or break the operation. She credits the franchisor with helping her through difficult situations, by first taking a chance on her when she was so young and later supporting her efforts to get financing to expand her business. And the company coached her through the Great Recession, by helping her and other franchisees cut costs and promote their restaurants.

Lafreeda explains that she sees franchising the way Southwest Airlines sees its business: Have one plane and know it very well. She knows the Denny's model very well.

Sources: Jason Daley, "How a Former Denny's Waitress Amassed an Empire of Over 75 Denny's Locations," http://www.entrepreneur.com/article/234985, accessed January 2, 2015; Jessica Elizarraras, "Rise of the Female Breadwinners: Dawn Lafreeda," http://www.sacurrent.com/sanantonio/rise-of-the-female-breadwinners-dawn-lafreeda/Content?oid=2247127, accessed January 2, 2015; "Denny's Waitress Now Owns 75 Denny's Restaurants," http://video.foxbusiness.com/v/3752331760001/dennys-waitress-now-owns-75-dennys-restaurants/#sp=show-clips&v=3752331760001, accessed January 2, 2015; and Randy Lankford, "Dawn Patrol: Denny's Largest Sole-Ownership Franchisee Enjoys Success," http://www.fsrmagazine.com/content/dawn-patrol-dennys-largest-sole-ownership-franchisee-enjoys-success, accessed January 3, 2015.

Understand the pros and cons of franchising.

4-2 THE PROS AND CONS OF FRANCHISING

"Look before you leap" is an old adage that should be heeded by entrepreneurs who are considering franchising. Weighing the purchase of a franchise against alternative paths to starting a business is an important task, and it deserves careful consideration.

4-2a The Pros

Buying a franchise can be attractive for a variety of reasons. The greatest advantage is the probability of success. Franchisors offer a business model with a proven track record. A reputable franchisor has been through the trials and errors that an entrepreneur might face when starting a business independently. One explanation for the low failure rate of franchises is how selective many franchisors are when granting them; even potential franchisees who qualify financially are sometimes rejected. Exhibit 4.1 lists some of the major advantages you can gain through franchising.

Franchised outlets also have a higher survival rate than independent ventures. Attractive franchises have names that are well known to prospective customers, such as Jiffy Lube, Century 21, and Pizza Hut. When a new franchisee comes on board, franchisors provide detailed operations manuals, so the hard work of blazing a trail has already been done. And they support their franchisees by providing training, reducing purchasing costs, designing promotional campaigns, and assisting in obtaining capital. Naturally, individual franchisors vary in the depth of support they provide.

Franchising can also be a way for existing companies to diversify. Owners of a small business who have achieved success may find themselves in mature industries with limited growth potential. Their current company may provide the resources

EXHIBIT 4.1 Advantages of the Franchise Model

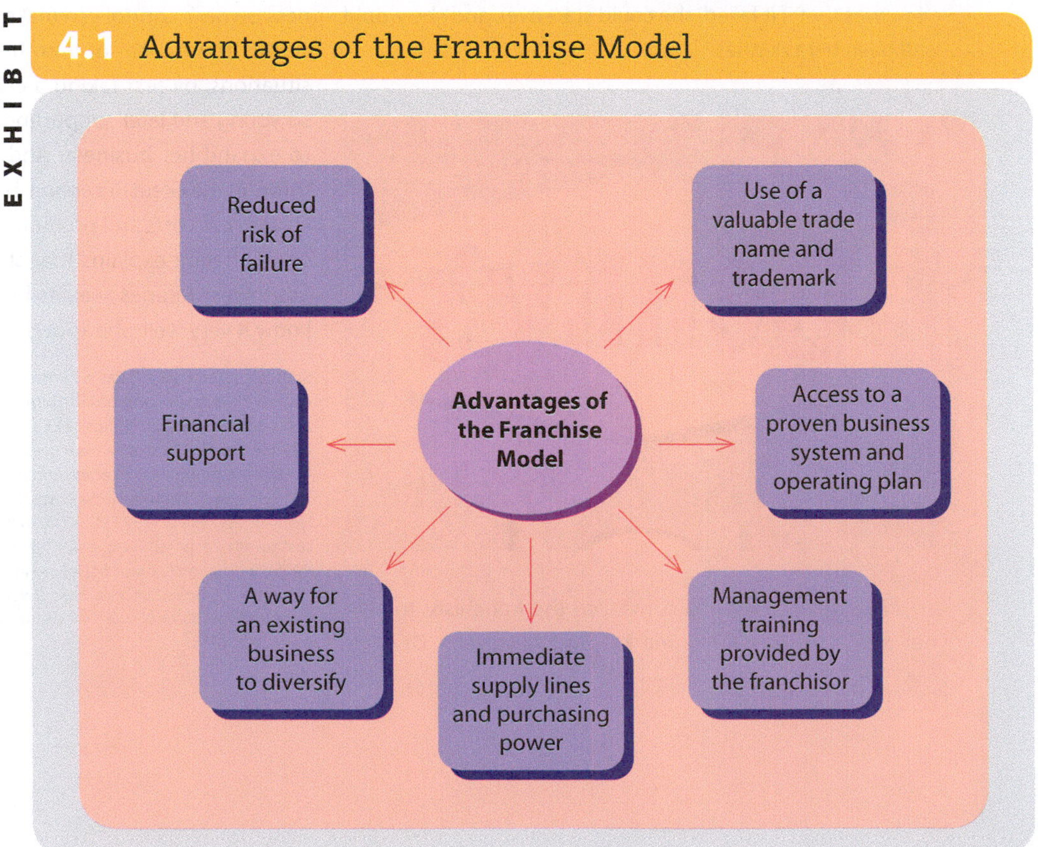

for acquiring a franchise in an industry with more opportunities. As managers of a successful enterprise, they may decide that adopting a proven model will lead to faster growth than starting from scratch.

TRADE NAMES AND TRADEMARKS

When you open your own business, it can take a long time and a lot of money to get your name established and customers in your door or to your website. When you become a franchisee, however, you expect the franchisor to have laid the groundwork. An entrepreneur who enters into a franchising agreement acquires the right to use the franchisor's trademark or brand name. Franchisors that are effective at creating market awareness and acceptance of their company and its brands serve to identify the local franchise with a widely recognized product or service. If customers have been satisfied with the products and services they have received from one unit in a chain, they are likely to do business with another store that carries that company's name.

Success for many businesses results from their intellectual property. Patents usually protect intellectual property, but a trademarked name can be just as valuable if it has become part of common public use. A trademark protects "words, names, symbols, sounds, or colors that distinguish goods and services from those manufactured or sold by others and to indicate the source of the goods. Trademarks, unlike patents, can be renewed forever as long as they are being used in commerce."[10] Think of McDonald's Golden Arches, of Big Mac, and even "You deserve a break today"![11] Trademarks and trade names make a business instantly identifiable to prospective customers and clients and can bring them right through the door. You will find more information about trademarks, patents, and copyrights and the value they add in Chapter 15.

A PROVEN BUSINESS SYSTEM AND OPERATING PLAN

In addition to a proven line of business and readily identifiable products or services, franchisors offer well-developed and thoroughly tested methods of marketing and management. The manuals and procedures supplied to franchisees enable them to function more efficiently from the start. Reputable firms that grow through franchising begin with company-owned stores, in which they develop their fundamental business model, leading to a tried-and-true method of operating the business. They document the procedures that work, compile them in an operations manual, and provide the manual to franchisees. Guidelines in the manual explain the specific steps required to operate the enterprise profitably.

An operations manual may be the single most valuable tool provided to a franchisee. Following the path laid out in the manual helps the owner avoid mistakes that often occur with a startup business, such as employing unqualified personnel and investing in the wrong equipment or inventory. The franchisee should use the manual to channel his or her energy toward the most productive activities leading to survival and profitability. And the franchisee should expect to be held accountable for following the manual. One of the most critical aspects of franchising is that customers must be able to find the same products, services, and methods of conducting business from one outlet to another. If one franchise is allowed to operate at a substandard level, it could easily destroy customers' confidence in the entire chain.

TRAINING SUPPORT

The training received from franchisors is invaluable to many small entrepreneurs because it compensates for weaknesses in their managerial skills. Training by the franchisor often begins with an initial period of a few days or weeks at a central training school and then continues at a franchise site. McDonald's is widely recognized for its off-site franchisee training at Hamburger University. Attending Hamburger University was mandatory for Richard Castro (described in this chapter's opening Spotlight feature) when he became a franchisee in 1982. Increasingly, franchisors are providing their training programs online.

Training does not have to be restricted to teaching franchisees about the company and its products. The best franchisors are constantly on the lookout to help their partners stay competitive. In the three-day training they provide to new franchisees, Cathy Deano and Renee Maloney, founders of Painting with a Twist, spend half a day illustrating how to use social media to build the business and interact with customers. Deano and Maloney continue to add more platforms for their franchisees to use.[12] Their company was ranked number 11 on *Entrepreneur* magazine's list of "New Franchise Rankings" in 2014.[13]

SUPPLY AND PURCHASING POWER

Joining a franchise network makes the entrepreneur part of a larger organization, which provides significant economies of scale. One critical benefit is efficiency in the purchasing function. A franchise network can buy in larger quantities than an individual business can, lowering per-unit costs for franchisees. Additionally, centralized purchasing activities reduce operating expenses for outlets.

Franchisees are often required to contribute to marketing expenses beyond the royalties they pay on sales. These expenses are pooled for the benefit of the entire network. The franchisor is then able to invest in more sophisticated marketing research, higher-quality advertising campaigns, and more extensive media outlets than franchisees could invest in independently. This ability leads to wider and deeper acceptance of brands and trade names, and it benefits each franchisee.

FINANCIAL SUPPORT

Companies such as GNC and Wingstop have formed alliances with banks to create preferred lending programs for franchisees. The International Franchise Association encourages franchisors to recruit minorities and veterans as franchisees by offering financial incentives. In order for a franchisor to be listed in the IFA's *VetFran Directory*, the company must agree to provide initial fee discounts, special financing terms, or other incentives. Over 600 companies are now listed in the directory.[14] Support for franchisees includes programs by AdviCoach, which offers a 15 percent discount off the standard franchise fee, and Mac Tools, which provides $10,000 of free tool inventory.[15]

Many prospective franchisees find that they can work with banks to obtain loans guaranteed by the U.S. Small Business Administration (SBA) in order to finance the franchise fee and startup costs. The SBA maintains a Franchise Registry (www.franchiseregistry.com), which speeds up loan processing for small business franchisees. The Registry also helps lenders identify new franchise systems and franchisees to which to lend.[16] This determination not only provides an assurance that the franchisor will not become dictatorial in the business relationship, but it also enables lenders to review and process loan applications more quickly for registered franchises.

Consumers' Guide for Buying a Franchise
The Federal Trade Commission (FTC), the nation's consumer protection agency, has prepared *Buying a Franchise: A Consumer Guide* to explain how to shop for a franchise opportunity, the obligations of a franchise owner, and questions to ask before you invest. You can download it at http://business.ftc.gov/documents/inv05-buying-franchise-consumer-guide.

Although many franchising systems have developed excellent support programs, you should understand that this is by no means universal. The buyer must also be aware of the disadvantages of franchising.

4-2b The Cons

The founders of the International Franchise Association were disturbed by the dishonest and unethical acts of some companies that were growing through franchising and damaging the reputation of the entire industry. These companies also sought to preempt government regulation of franchising. Firms joining the IFA are required to adhere to a code of ethics, the foundational values of which are "trust, truth, and honesty."[17] The code requires IFA members to practice mutual respect and open, frequent communication. The IFA also demands adherence to laws and offers a conflict resolution service for franchisors and franchisees. To this day, however, some franchisors engage in practices that trouble regulators, legislators, and the business community at large. These concerns, which include financial issues, franchisor competition, and management issues, have led to regulations by the Federal Trade Commission and the passage of laws in a few states.

FINANCIAL ISSUES

Major concerns have arisen regarding the true costs of becoming and remaining a franchisee. New franchisees of some franchise organizations have felt misled about their earnings opportunities. They report being told that they could expect high returns on their investments, only to discover that few, if any, franchisees achieved those results. Current and former franchisees of Quiznos, for example, sued the firm in Illinois, Pennsylvania, and Wisconsin for luring "franchisees into the system by misrepresenting contract terms and financial projections."[18] A settlement for $207 million was reached in 2010 without Quizno's admitting to any guilt. The company continued to suffer, however, declaring bankruptcy in March of 2014. Although they were able to restructure and emerge four months later, Quizno's downsized from more than 5,000 to 2,100 stores.[19]

© ISTOCKPHOTO.COM/JFMDESIGN

Other criticisms of franchisors that have come to the attention of government agencies include refusing to permit franchisees to sell their businesses in order to invest their money elsewhere and forcing franchisees to purchase products and services from subsidiaries or business associates, resulting in higher-than-market costs. Franchisees of Edible Arrangements sued the franchisor, accusing the company of unfairly altering business agreements by imposing higher costs and extending hours of operation.[20] There have also been complaints of **churning**, which refers to actions by franchisors to void the contracts of franchisees in order to sell the franchise to someone else and collect an additional fee.

FRANCHISOR COMPETITION

Franchisors have actually competed directly against their franchisees on occasion. This can occur when the franchisor opens a corporate-owned store near the franchisee's location or sells products via mail or over the Internet. A variation on this complaint is referred to as **encroachment**. A franchisor is said to encroach on a franchisee's territory when the franchisor sells another franchise location within the market area of an existing franchisee. Such actions can be virtual. For example, H&R Block was sued by a franchisee for selling Internet services within the franchisee's territory without offering any compensation.[21]

Another complaint stems from special clauses inserted into some franchise agreements. A number of franchisors impose noncompete clauses on their franchisees. From the franchisors' perspective, this makes perfect sense—after training and sharing secrets and strategies with a franchisee, they do not want the franchisee to sever the relationship and become a competitor. From the franchisees' perspective, this constitutes restraint of trade, especially if they find the franchisor to be nonresponsive to their needs or if they project that they can make more money on their own. It is only natural to think that the next business you start would evolve from your current experience. Yet the franchisor may keep you from applying those experiential skills by claiming that your new enterprise competes with the franchisor's business.

churning
Actions by franchisors to void the contracts of franchisees in order to sell the franchise to someone else and collect an additional fee.

encroachment
The franchisor's selling of another franchise location within the market area of an existing franchisee.

MANAGEMENT ISSUES

The final set of negative issues focuses on the freedom of the franchisee to run his or her own business. As a franchisee, you are not a truly independent business owner. You have a contractual arrangement with the franchisor that stipulates various conditions, and that contract may specify the products you carry, the services you offer, your hours of operation, and other aspects of how you run your company. The contract was drafted by, and most likely favors, the franchisor. Many prospective franchisees fail to recognize that many franchisors are willing to negotiate some portions of the contract. In any case, you should always have an attorney review the contract before you sign it. Some of the most common restrictions imposed on franchisees fall into the following categories:

- Limiting sales territories
- Requiring site approval for the retail outlet
- Imposing requirements regarding outlet appearance
- Limiting goods and services offered for sale
- Limiting advertising and hours of operation

A frequently heard complaint from franchisees is that when their contract expires, they are required to accept new and often costly provisions. Franchisees suspect this is an effort to extract more revenues and/or concessions from them, to force them out in order to sell the franchise to someone else, or to take their business over as a company store. Of course, the franchisor may have another explanation. During the years the contract was in force, the franchisor may have discovered ways to improve the system that were incorporated into more recent franchise contracts. Additionally, franchisors may find that some long-time franchisees have not maintained their facilities or have failed to adapt to new marketing and operating procedures. From the franchisor's point of view, these franchisees need to improve their businesses so that they will not harm the entire network.

4-2c The Costs of Being a Franchisee

If you choose to become a franchisee, you pay for the privilege. You are buying what should be a proven model, and the franchisor will charge you for the benefits being offered. Generally speaking, higher costs characterize the better-known and more successful franchises. Franchise costs have several components, all of which need to be recognized and considered. They include the initial franchise fee, investment costs, royalty payments, and advertising costs.

1. *Initial franchise fee.* The total cost of a franchise begins with an initial franchise fee, which may range from several hundred to many thousands of dollars. Liberty Tax Service estimates a total investment ranging from $57,800 to $71,900. They offer special financing to qualified veterans.[22]
2. *Investment costs.* Significant costs may be involved in renting or building an outlet and stocking it with inventory and equipment. Certain insurance premiums, legal fees, and other startup expenses must also be paid, and it is often recommended that funds be available to cover personal expenses and emergencies for at least six months.
3. *Royalty payments.* A royalty is a fee charged to the franchisee by the franchisor. It is calculated as a percentage of the gross income that the franchisee receives from customers for selling the franchised products and services. Two Men and a Truck, a moving services company, charges a 6 percent royalty. Denny's charges a royalty fee that is 5.25 percent of gross sales.[23]

4. *Advertising costs*. Many franchisors require that franchisees contribute to an advertising fund to promote the franchise. These fees are generally 1 to 2 percent of sales, sometimes even more. Franchisees pay these fees to support the franchisor in establishing the name and reputation of the business in the minds of targeted customers. Successful, well-managed franchise organizations will promote the company and its products and services more cost-efficiently than individual stores could do on their own.

If entrepreneurs could generate the same level of sales by setting up an independent business, they would save the franchise fee and some of the other costs just mentioned. However, if the franchisor provides the benefits previously described, the money that franchisees pay to start and maintain their relationship with the franchisor may well prove to be a very good investment.

4-3 EVALUATING FRANCHISE OPPORTUNITIES

Describe the process for evaluating a franchise opportunity.

Both the franchisee and the franchisor must fully assess a decision to pursue a franchising opportunity. The prospective franchisee must identify a franchising company of interest and investigate it completely. A potential franchisor who is interested in expanding her or his business must address certain questions before offering the franchise option to possible franchisees. Both parties to a franchise agreement must have knowledge of the legal issues involved.

4-3a Selecting a Franchise

With the growth of franchising over the years, the task of selecting an appropriate franchise has become easier. Personal observation frequently sparks interest, or awareness may begin with exposure to an advertisement in a newspaper or magazine or on the Internet. The headlines of these advertisements usually highlight the financial and personal rewards sought by the entrepreneur. *Inc., Entrepreneur*, and *The Wall Street Journal* are only three examples of the many publications that not only print stories about franchising, but also include franchisors' advertisements.

4-3b Investigating the Potential Franchise

The nature of the commitment required in franchising justifies careful investigation of the situation. The investment is substantial, and the business relationship generally continues over many years.

The evaluation process is a two-way effort. The franchisor wishes to investigate the franchisee, and the franchisee obviously wishes to evaluate the franchisor and the type of opportunity being offered. This requires time. You should be skeptical of a franchisor that pressures you to sign a contract without time for proper investigation. As a potential franchisee, consider asking the following questions when assessing different franchise opportunities:

- Is the franchisor dedicated to a franchise system as its primary means of product and service distribution? That is, does the company primarily distribute its goods and services through corporate-owned stores? If so, will the franchisor give as much attention to franchisees as it does to its own outlets?
- Does the franchisor produce and market quality goods and services for which there is an established consumer demand?

- Does the franchisor enjoy a favorable reputation and broad acceptance in the industry?
- Will the franchisor offer an established, well-designed marketing plan and provide substantial and complete training to franchisees?
- Does the franchisor have good relationships with its franchisees? Be sure to speak with current and past franchisees. What is/was their working relationship with the franchisor? Would they do it all over again?
- Do franchisees have a strong franchisee organization that has negotiating leverage with the franchisor?
- Does the franchisor have a history of attractive earnings by its franchisees?

There are many sources of information about franchisors to help you in your evaluation. Since many states require registration of franchises, a prospective franchisee should not overlook state offices as a source of assistance. Also, a comprehensive listing of franchisors can be found on the website of the International Franchise Association (www.franchise.org). Exhibit 4.2 displays the listing for Glass Doctor, a

EXHIBIT **4.2** Profile from International Franchise Association (2015)

Glass Doctor

Business Established:	1962
Franchising Since:	1977
Franchised Units:	212
Company Owned Units:	Not available
Total Investment:	$80,125 to $188,800

Offering Financial Assistance

In-house financing is available for the initial franchise fee.

Special Incentives

VetFran Participant
International Opportunity
Home Based Franchise

VetFran Incentive

25 % of the minimum initial franchise fee for qualified honorably discharged veterans.

Company Details

Description

Glass Doctor is North America's largest all-in-one national glass specialist for installing, replacing and repairing home, auto and business glass.

Training

You will receive **one-on-one consulting** as you move through the process of opening your Glass Doctor franchise from a dedicated start-up consultant. From grand opening to continued support, our expert consultants and professional mentors will be at your side every step of the way.

Source: Copied with permission, http://www.franchise.org/Glass-Doctor-franchise.

company offering residential, commercial, and auto glass services. In assessing published information about franchises, Mark Liston, president of Glass Doctor, cautions:

As you choose a franchisor remember—this is a marriage . . . usually for at least 10 years. This is why it is extremely important to understand the culture of the franchisor to determine if this truly will be a partnership with the franchisor and the franchisee, interdependent with each other.[24]

The better-known, more successful franchisors are likely to offer a greater chance of long-term survival and prosperity, but they are also in a position to charge premium prices for becoming part of their network. *Entrepreneur* magazine's website contains its ranking of the top 10 franchises in 2014 (see Exhibit 4.3). The rankings are based on a number of factors, with financial strength and stability, growth rate, and system size being the most important.

In recent years, franchise consultants have appeared in the marketplace to assist individuals seeking franchise opportunities. Some consulting firms, such as Francorp, conduct seminars on choosing the right franchise. Of course, care should be used in selecting a reputable consultant, and an experienced franchise attorney should evaluate all legal documents.

THE FRANCHISOR AS A SOURCE OF INFORMATION

Obviously, the franchisor being evaluated is a primary source of information. However, information provided by a franchisor must be viewed in light of its purpose—to promote the franchise. Mark Liston adds:

[You] must remember that you won't get glowing remarks from everyone. That is good. Although successful franchise organizations have an interdependency, there will be times when they simply disagree. The franchisor has to make decisions that are good for the entire network. Those decisions may not make some individual franchisees happy.[25]

EXHIBIT **4.3** *Entrepreneur*'s Top 10 Global Franchises for 2014

Name/Rank	Startup Costs
1. 7-Eleven Inc.	$37K–2M
2. Pizza Hut Inc.	$297K–2M
3. Midas Int'l. Corp.	$203K–405K
4. Subway	$117K–263K
5. McDonald's	$1M–2M
6. Baskin-Robbins	$103K–389K
7. Anytime Fitness	$79K–371K
8. KFC Corp.	$1M–3M
9. Super 8	$176K–4M
10. Hardee's	$1M–2M

Source: "Top Franchises for 2014," http://www.entrepreneur.com/franchises/topglobal/index.html, accessed January 7, 2015.

One way to obtain information about franchisors is to review their websites. Most franchisor websites will be directed toward customers, presenting information about products, services, store locations, and so on. The websites should also direct you to information for prospective franchisees. If you enter your contact information, you can expect to receive brochures and marketing materials that contain such information as startup costs and franchisees' testimonials. Your search may also lead you to websites or blogs of disgruntled franchisees, customers, and others.

If you express further interest in a franchise by completing the application form and the franchisor has tentatively qualified you as a potential franchisee, a meeting is usually arranged to discuss the Franchise Disclosure Document, which provides information about both the franchisor (finances, experience, etc.) and the franchise itself (restrictions, costs, etc.). Important considerations related to this document are examined more fully later in this chapter.

EXISTING AND PREVIOUS FRANCHISEES AS SOURCES OF INFORMATION

There may be no better source of franchise facts than existing and former franchisees. Sometimes, however, the distant location of other franchisees precludes a visit to their place of business. In that case, a telephone call or e-mail can elicit the owner's viewpoint.

4-3c Becoming a Franchisor

After a few years of running your own business, you may conclude that you want to expand and that franchising is a reasonable option for you. It is not unusual for the owners of successful businesses to be approached by individuals who ask to become franchisees. Before entering into an agreement with a potential franchisee, consider the questions discussed in the following sections.

A REPRODUCIBLE MODEL

Is your business replicable? In other words, do you have a model of doing business that someone else could adopt and use successfully in another location? A franchisee purchases an operating system as well as a product or service and a brand name. Is your system efficient, and can it be clearly explained so that others can apply it?

FINANCIAL CONSIDERATIONS

How will you finance the growth of the company? Many entrepreneurs think that franchising is a novel mechanism for financing their growing enterprises. They come up with a concept, collect franchise fees, and use those revenues to expand their operations. But franchising is not cost-free for the franchisor. There are legal documents to prepare, an operations manual to write, personnel to hire, and other tasks to be completed. Who will recruit and select franchisees? Who will train them and their managers? Who will monitor their performance to ensure that they conform to contract requirements? Responsible franchisors often find that establishing a franchise costs more than the fee covers and that they only become profitable as a result of the royalties they eventually collect from successful franchisees.

REQUIRED ASSISTANCE

What expert assistance will you need to become a franchisor? Successful entrepreneurs learn quickly that they must choose the right experts, individuals who are qualified to provide the necessary help. If you decide to franchise your business, you should have an attorney with knowledge of the franchise method. There are many consultants who specialize in franchising and can assist with drafting operations manuals, preparing disclosure documents, assisting with franchisee selection, and other aspects of the process. A good starting place for any prospective franchisor is becoming a member of the International Franchise Association.

OPERATIONS MANUAL

Earlier in this chapter, we looked at the operations manual from the franchisee's point of view. For the franchisor, this is an essential element in the value the business model offers to franchisees. What will go into your operations manual? Many companies that have grown successfully through franchising brought in consultants who specialize in making the business operating model more efficient and easier to replicate prior to writing the manual. You should be able to present an operations manual to your franchisees that spells out what steps to take in daily activities to ensure customer satisfaction while controlling expenses. The operations manual should offer detailed instructions that help franchisees avoid pitfalls and increase sales. It needs to be written from the perspective of the franchisee, who will not know the business as well as the franchisor. It is usually wise to hire a professional technical writer to put the manual together so that it communicates the process effectively. Many new franchisors have found that experts who assist in writing operations manuals also help the businesses improve the efficiencies of their operations, making startup and management easier and lowering the cost for franchisees.

GOVERNMENT REGULATIONS

Are you willing to satisfy the government's disclosure requirements? The Federal Trade Commission issued an amended **Franchise Rule** in May 2008. This rule requires that the franchisor disclose certain information to prospective franchisees. Some business owners may decide that they would rather not disclose information that they consider confidential, such as prior bankruptcies, the business experience of the principals, or litigation in which the firm is involved. In such cases, franchising may not be the appropriate method to use for growth.

LONG-TERM VALUE

Can you add value for your franchisees year after year? There are many good and successful business models that may provide the right steps for you to follow in order to avoid pitfalls in the startup process. But will your business offer value to prospective franchisees year in and year out?

A franchise agreement is in effect for a long time, typically between 10 and 15 years. What benefits will the franchisees derive from the franchisor each year? Will new products or services be introduced? Will improved marketing strategies be implemented? Will additional, updated training be offered to franchisees and their managers? Why will franchisees want to continue to make royalty payments once they have been up and running and have learned the operating procedures? If the business model does not add value for franchisees each year, franchising is not the right method for growing your company.

4-3d Legal Issues in Franchising

For a business alliance to be successful for both parties, trust is important. But a contract is essential to avoid or resolve problems that may arise.

franchise Rule
A rule that requires the franchisor to disclose certain information to prospective franchisees.

THE FRANCHISE CONTRACT

The basic features of the relationship between the franchisor and the franchisee are embodied in the franchise contract. This contract is typically a complex document of many pages. Because of its importance as the legal basis for the franchised business, the franchise contract should never be signed by the franchisee without legal counsel. In fact, reputable franchisors insist that the franchisee have legal counsel before signing the agreement. An attorney may anticipate trouble spots and note any objectionable features of the contract.

© MARLEE/SHUTTERSTOCK.COM

A prospective franchisee should also use as many other sources of help as would be practical. In particular, she or he should discuss the franchise contract in detail with a banker. The prospective franchisee should also obtain the services of a professional accounting firm to examine the franchisor's statements of projected sales, operating expenses, and net income. An accountant can help evaluate the quality of these estimates and identify any projections that may be overstated. These experts are essential to ensure that parties on both sides of the agreement comprehend their obligations. Disagreements between the parties can wind up in courts. For example, 7-Eleven Inc., which is listed in Exhibit 4.3 as the number one global franchise, has been sued on multiple occasions by franchisees who claim their contracts were terminated without proper cause.[26]

One of the most important features of the franchise contract is the provision relating to termination and transfer of the franchise. Many franchisors besides 7-Eleven have been accused of devising agreements that permit arbitrary cancellation of the franchise relationship. Of course, it is reasonable for the franchisor to have legal protection in the event that a franchisee fails to obtain an appropriate level of operation or does not maintain satisfactory quality standards. However, the prospective franchisee should be wary of contract provisions that contain overly strict or vague cancellation policies. Similarly, the rights of the franchisee to sell the business to a third party should be clearly spelled out. A franchisor who can restrict the sale of the business to a third party could potentially take back ownership of the business at an unfair price. The right of a franchisee to renew the contract after the business has been built up to a successful operating level should also be clearly stated in the contract.

FRANCHISE DISCLOSURE REQUIREMENTS

The offer and sale of a franchise are regulated by both state and federal laws. At the federal level, the minimum disclosure standards are specified by the Franchise Rule. A guide to the rule can be found on the Federal Trade Commission's website (www.ftc.gov), as can addresses of the state offices that enforce franchise disclosure laws.

A **Franchise Disclosure Document (FDD)** is a detailed statement of such information as the franchisor's finances, experience, size, and involvement in litigation. The document must inform potential franchisees of any restrictions, costs, and provisions for renewal or cancellation of the franchise. The FDD provides the accepted format for satisfying the requirements of the FTC. In May 2008, the FDD replaced the Uniform Franchise Offering Circular (UFOC) as the legal document satisfying the FTC Franchise Rule. Most franchise experts recommend that a franchisee's attorney and accountant review the document.

Franchise Disclosure Document (FDD)
A detailed statement providing information about the franchisor that satisfies the franchise disclosure requirements of the FTC.

4-4 BUYING AN EXISTING BUSINESS

List four reasons for buying an existing business, and describe the process of evaluating an existing business.

Another option for making your dream a reality is buying an existing business. You can be just as entrepreneurial buying an existing enterprise as creating one from scratch. As you look at companies available for purchase, you may discover an opportunity to turn around a company in trouble. Or perhaps you have the skills needed to make an already good business excellent. An existing firm may be the perfect platform on which to build your dream.

The decision to purchase an existing business should not be made lightly. It involves serious investment of funds, so you must give careful consideration to the advantages and disadvantages of this option.

4-4a Reasons for Buying an Existing Business

The reasons for buying an existing business can be condensed into the following four general categories:

1. To reduce some of the uncertainties and unknowns that must be faced when starting a business from the ground up
2. To acquire a business with ongoing operations and established relationships with customers and suppliers
3. To obtain an established business at a price below what it would cost to start a new business or to buy a franchise
4. To get into business more quickly than by starting from scratch

Let's examine each of these reasons in more detail.

START UP TOOLS

Advocates for Entrepreneurs

We encourage you to attend meetings and conferences, to get out and meet people, to join organizations—in other words, to network. Your network contacts may help you to discover businesses that may be for sale, see opportunities, find financing, obtain customers, and put together a venture team. Some organizations that you might find helpful include the Collegiate Entrepreneurs Organization (www.c-e-o.org), the Young Entrepreneur Council (www.yec.co), and VentureWell (www.venturewell.org).

REDUCTION OF UNCERTAINTIES

A successful business has already demonstrated its ability to attract customers, manage costs, and make a profit. Although future operations may be different, the firm's past record shows what it can do under actual market conditions. For example, just the fact that the location must be satisfactory eliminates one major uncertainty. Although traffic counts are useful in assessing the value of a potential location, the acid test comes when a business opens its doors at that location. This test has already been met in the case of an existing firm. The results are available in the form of sales and profit data. Noncompete agreements are needed, however, to discourage the seller from starting a new company that will compete directly with the one he or she is selling.

ACQUISITION OF ONGOING OPERATIONS AND RELATIONSHIPS

The buyer of an existing business typically acquires its personnel, inventories, physical facilities, established banking connections, and ongoing relationships with trade suppliers and customers. You are also acquiring the goodwill that the prior owner created. Extensive time and effort would be required to build these elements from scratch. Of course, the advantage derived from buying an established firm's assets depends on the nature of the assets. For example, a firm's skilled, experienced employees constitute a valuable asset only if they will continue to work for the new owner. The physical facilities must not be obsolete, and the firm's relationships with banks, suppliers, and customers must be healthy. In any case, new agreements will probably have to be negotiated with current vendors and leaseholders.

A BARGAIN PRICE

If the seller is more eager to sell than the buyer is to buy, an existing business may be available at what seems to be a low price. Whether it is actually a good buy, however, must be determined by the prospective new owner. Several factors could make a "bargain price" anything but a bargain. For example, the business may be losing money, the neighborhood location may be deteriorating, or the seller may intend to open a competing business nearby. On the other hand, if research indicates that the business indeed is a bargain, purchasing it is likely to turn out to be a wise investment. And it can be easier to get financing for an ongoing business than for a startup.[27]

A QUICK START

Most entrepreneurs are eager to get going in their new business and may not be comfortable waiting the months and years sometimes required to launch a business from scratch. Buying an existing business may be an excellent way to begin operations much more quickly.

4-4b Finding a Business to Buy

Sources of leads about businesses available for purchase include suppliers, distributors, trade associations, and even bankers. Realtors—particularly those who specialize in the sale of business firms and business properties—can also provide leads. In addition, **business brokers** can assist in buying and selling businesses.[28] Entrepreneurs need to be wary of potential conflicts of interest with business brokers, however. For example, if brokers are paid only if a buy-sell transaction occurs, they may be tempted to do whatever it takes to close the deal, even if doing so is detrimental to the buyer.

The Small Business Administration offers the following guidance on finding a business to buy:[29]

1. *Identify your interests.* At a minimum, eliminate businesses that hold no interest for you.
2. *Consider your talents.* You have to give this business your all, so be honest with yourself about your skills and experience.
3. *List conditions for your business.* Does location matter? How about working hours? How big do you want it to be?
4. *Quantify your investment.* How much can you afford?

4-4c Investigating and Evaluating Available Businesses

Regardless of the source of the lead, a business opportunity requires careful evaluation—what is sometimes called **due diligence**. As a preliminary step, the buyer needs to acquire background information about the business, some of which can be obtained through personal observation or discussion with the seller. Talking with other informed parties, such as suppliers, bankers, and employees of the business, is also important.

The website for the U.S. Small Business Administration provides information for performing due diligence in the purchase of a business. The list of documents that you will need to evaluate (see Exhibit 4.4) may appear long and intimidating, but this assessment is necessary.

business brokers
Specialized brokers that bring together buyers and sellers of businesses.

due diligence
The exercise of reasonable care in the evaluation of a business opportunity.

Living the Dream

ENTREPRENEURIAL EXPERIENCES

Reducing Risk or Adding Costs?

Susan Wysocki first gained experience as a chef after graduating from the Culinary Institute of America (CIA). That experience resulted in her return to CIA as a faculty member. Eventually, she felt ready to try something on her own and bought Cobbablu Café, converting it to Babycakes Café, a restaurant, bar, and catering service in Poughkeepsie, New York. She gained confidence through success as she acquired and retained customers. She was recognized as a leading business owner in the community and was selected by Metro-North and the Metropolitan Transportation Authority to open a branch café in the historic Poughkeepsie train station.

Looking at other opportunities, Wysocki decided to buy an existing business to reduce her financial risk. She negotiated the purchase of Soul Dog in Poughkeepsie, knowing that the restaurant had a customer base and assets that would enable her to start without delay. According to the U.S. Small Business Administration, by buying an existing business, an entrepreneur is likely to acquire inventory and thus have immediate cash flow.

© SOUL DOG

The seller, however, has made an investment in the company, knows that there are loyal customers, and expects a premium price to be paid for what he or she built. And Wysocki discovered there can be other, less-obvious costs. Although she tried to minimize changes initially, she eventually had to raise prices and alter the menu slightly. The existing staff at Soul Dog were accustomed to the practices of the prior owner and not comfortable with the changes. Before long, they left. And she lost customers, particularly due to the price increases. Although Wysocki did not report a problem with debt inherited from the previous owner, the SBA identifies hidden debts as a shock that some business purchasers find themselves taking on. Keeping Soul Dog going was a serious struggle for awhile.

Nevertheless, Wysocki has persevered in making changes, while attempting to retain the image the Soul Dog had established. A key step was to place emphasis on gluten-free menu items. She wants customers to know that they can get all the delicious hot dogs, chicken, and sausage they loved before, but that they will also see listed all the ingredients that go into everything on their plates. Wysocki describes Soul Dog as providing slow food in a fast-food setting. Sales are increasing, and online comments are encouraging, indicating that her purchase is becoming a winner.

Sources: Based on http://www.babycakescafe.com, accessed January 12, 2015; Karen Maserjian Shan, "Buying an Existing Business, Featuring Soul Dog in Poughkeepsie," http://www.poughkeepsiejournal.com/story/money/2014/11/09/small-business-soul-dog/18775411, accessed January 12, 2015; and "Local Restaurateur Chosen to Open Café at Poughkeepsie Train Station," http://www.mta.info/press-release/metro-north/local-restaurateur-chosen-open-caf%C3%A9-poughkeepsie-train-station, accessed January 8, 2015.

If a seller cannot supply the documents on this list, you may want to back away. Some items will not exist for every business. For example, not every company will require government certifications. Nevertheless, you should be exhaustive in your efforts to uncover relevant information that could influence the selling price or whether you should even enter into the sale. Otherwise, you may find yourself "on the hook" for unanticipated expenses that show up later.

EXHIBIT

4.4 Due Diligence for Purchasing a Business

- **Licenses and Permits:** Most businesses need licenses and permits to operate. The type of license or permit you need depends on your industry and the state in which the business is located. Use the SBA's online Find Business Licenses and Permits tool to get a listing of federal, state and local permits and licenses you will need to run your business.
- **Zoning Requirements:** Zoning requirements may affect the type of business that you are intending to operate in a particular area. Visit the SBA's online Basic Zoning Laws section for more information about zoning and to ensure your business is abiding by all laws in your area.
- **Environmental Concerns:** If you are acquiring real property along with the business, it is important to check the environmental regulations in the area. Visit the EPA's online Small Business Gateway for more information.
- **Letter of Intent:** The letter of intent should spell out the proposed price, the terms of the purchase and the conditions for the sale of the business.
- **Confidentiality Agreement:** A confidentiality agreement indicates that you will not use the information about the seller's business for any purpose other than making the decision to buy it.
- **Contracts and Leases:** If the business has a current lease for the location, be aware that you may have to work with the landlord to assume any existing lease on the business premises or to negotiate a new lease. Contracts with suppliers and clients may need to be renegotiated as well.
- **Financial Statements/Tax Returns:** Examine the financial statements from the business for at least the past three to five years. Also make sure that an audit letter from a reputable CPA firm accompanies the statements. You should not accept a simple financial review by the business itself. Also examine the business's tax returns from the past three to five years. This will help you determine the profitability of the business as well as any outstanding tax liability.
- **Important Documents:** Numerous documents should be checked during your investigation. Examples include property documents, customer lists, sales records, advertising materials, and employee and manager information.
- **Professional Help:** A qualified attorney should be enlisted to help review the legal and organizational documents of the business you are planning to purchase. Also, an accountant can help with a thorough evaluation of the financial condition of the business.

Source: Adapted from U.S. Small Business Administration, "Buying an Existing Business," http://www.sba.gov/content/researching-business-purchase, accessed January 12, 2015.

RELYING ON PROFESSIONALS

Although some aspects of due diligence require personal checking, a buyer can also seek the help of outside experts. The two most valuable sources of outside assistance are accountants and lawyers. It is also wise to seek out others who have acquired a business in order to learn from their experiences. Their perspective will be different from that of a consultant, and it will bring some balance to the counsel received. The time and money spent on securing professional help in investigating a business can pay big dividends, especially when the buyer is inexperienced. Prospective buyers should seek advice and counsel, but they must make the final decision themselves, as it is too important to entrust to someone else.

FINDING OUT WHY THE BUSINESS IS FOR SALE

The seller's *real* reasons for selling may or may not be the *stated* ones. When a business is for sale, always question the owner's reasons for selling. There is a real possibility that the firm is not doing well or that underlying problems exist that will affect its future performance. The buyer must be wary, therefore, of taking the seller's explanations at face value. Here are some of the most common reasons why owners offer their businesses for sale:

- Retirement
- Illness
- Partnership or family disputes
- Unprofitability or failure of the business
- Burnout
- Lack of capital for growth potential

A prospective buyer cannot be certain that the seller-owner will be honest in presenting all the facts about the business, especially concerning financial matters. Background checks on key personnel are essential when conducting due diligence.

EXAMINING THE FINANCIAL DATA

The first stage in evaluating the financial health of a firm is to review its financial statements and tax returns for the past three to five years or for as many years as they are available. (*If these statements are not available, think twice before buying the business.*) This review helps to determine whether the buyer and the seller are in the same ballpark on estimates and expectations. If so, the parties can move on to valuing the firm. You will find details on compiling and interpreting financial statements in Chapter 10.

As both a legal and an ethical matter, the prospective buyer may expect to sign a **nondisclosure agreement**. Under the restrictions of such an agreement, the buyer promises the seller that he or she will not reveal confidential information or violate the trust that the seller has offered in providing the information. Buyers are typically allowed to share such information with others, such as a potential lender or legal advisor, on a need-to-know basis.

The buyer should recognize that financial statements can be misleading and may require normalizing to yield a realistic picture of the business. For example, business owners sometimes understate business income in an effort to minimize their taxes. Other financial entries that may need adjustment include personal expenses and wage or salary payments. For example, costs related to the personal use of business vehicles frequently appear as a business expense, and family members may receive excessive compensation or none at all. All entries must be examined to ensure that they relate to the business and are appropriate.

The buyer should also compare the seller's balance sheet to actual assets and liabilities. Property may appreciate in value after it is recorded on the books, but physical facilities, inventory, and receivables may decline in value, so their actual worth may be less than their accounting book value.

4-4d Quantitative Factors in Valuing the Business

Once the initial investigation and evaluation have been completed, the buyer must arrive at a fair value for the firm. In valuing a firm, the buyer will rely heavily on much of the financial information acquired during due diligence (described in Exhibit 4.4). It will require more than just getting copies of the financial statements (income statements, balance sheets, and cash flow statements). The buyer will want to review supporting materials that validate the accuracy of the financial statements by scrutinizing such documents as federal tax returns, state sales tax statements, supplier invoices, and customer receipts, as well as the company's bank statements.

There are numerous techniques used for valuing a company, but they can be grouped into three basic methods: (1) asset-based valuation, (2) market-based valuation, and (3) cash flow–based valuation. Each of these methods can be used as a stand-alone measure of firm value. But, because valuation is a subjective process, most often the firm is valued using a variety of methods. Each approach generates firm values that, together, form a range rather than a specific number.[30]

4-4e Nonquantitative Factors in Valuing a Business

You should also consider a number of nonquantitative factors in evaluating an existing business. In particular, is it likely that the firm you are considering buying might be subject to change regarding any of the following?

nondisclosure agreement
An agreement in which the buyer promises the seller that he or she will not reveal confidential information or violate the seller's trust.

- *Market*. The ability of the market to support all competing business units, including the one to be purchased, should be determined. This requires doing marketing research, studying census data, and personally observing each competitor's place of business.
- *Competition*. The prospective buyer should look into the extent, intensity, and location of competing businesses. In particular, the buyer should check to see whether the business in question is gaining or losing in its race with rivals. Additionally, new competitors in the local marketplace (Walmart or Target, for example) may dramatically change an existing small firm's likelihood of success. Past performance is no guarantee of future performance.
- *Future community development*. Future developments in the community that could have an indirect impact on a business include a change in zoning ordinances already enacted but not yet in effect, a change from a two-way traffic flow to a one-way traffic flow, and the widening of a road or construction of an overpass.
- *Legal commitments*. Legal commitments may include contingent liabilities, unsettled lawsuits, delinquent tax payments, missed payrolls, overdue rent or installment payments, and mortgages of record on any of the real property acquired.
- *Union contracts*. The prospective buyer should determine what type of labor agreement, if any, is in force, as well as the quality of the firm's relationship with its employees. Private conversations with key employees and rank-and-file workers can be helpful in determining their job satisfaction and the company's likelihood of success.
- *Buildings*. The quality of the buildings housing the business should be checked, with particular attention paid to any fire hazards. In addition, the buyer should determine whether there are any restrictions on access to the buildings.
- *Product prices*. The prospective owner should compare the prices of the seller's products with those listed in manufacturers' or wholesalers' catalogs and also with the prices of competing products in the locality. This is necessary to ensure full and fair pricing of goods whose sales are reported on the seller's financial statements.

4-4f Negotiating and Closing the Deal

The purchase price of a business is determined by negotiation between buyer and seller. Although the calculated value may not be the price eventually paid for the business, it gives the buyer an estimated value to use when negotiating price. Typically, the buyer tries to purchase the firm for something less than the full estimated value; of course, the seller tries to get more than that value.

In some cases, the buyer may have the option of purchasing the assets only, rather than the business as a whole. When a business is purchased as a total entity, the buyer not only takes control of the assets but also assumes any outstanding debt, including any hidden or unknown liabilities. Even if the financial records are audited, such debts may not surface. If the buyer instead purchases only the assets, then the seller is responsible for settling any outstanding debts previously incurred. When buying the business as a whole, an indemnification clause in the sales contract may serve a similar function, protecting the buyer from liability for unreported debt.

An important part of the negotiation process is the terms of purchase. In many cases, the buyer is unable to pay the full price in cash and must seek extended terms. At this point, a lender may enter the picture and alter the purchase price. If a bank is providing a loan for buying the business, the bank may require the assets of the company to serve as collateral for the loan. Any lender must perform its own due diligence and estimate a value for the assets, and that value may be at a different level than the buyer and seller have agreed upon.

At the same time, the seller may be concerned about taxes on the profit from the sale. Terms may become more attractive to the buyer and the seller as the amount of the down payment is reduced and/or the length of the repayment period is extended. As with the purchase of real estate, the purchase of a business is closed at a specific time, and a title company or an attorney usually handles the closing. Preferably, the closing will occur under the direction of an independent third party. If the seller's attorney is the closing agent, the buyer should exercise great caution—*a buyer should never go through a closing without the aid of an experienced attorney who represents only the buyer.*

A number of important documents are completed during the closing. These include a bill of sale, tax and other government regulation forms, and agreements pertaining to future payments and related guarantees to the seller. The buyer should apply for new federal and state tax identification numbers to avoid being held responsible for past obligations associated with the old numbers. If you want a happy ending from the purchase and a clear path to your future, do not take short cuts at this stage. Meeting all legal and regulatory requirements secures your investment and your ability to successfully manage the business.

Starting a business, becoming a franchisee, and buying an existing business are all potential paths to your entrepreneurial dream. Although franchising and buying a business are usually considered to be strategies for reducing the risks associated with starting a venture, each path still requires careful research and planning. Whatever your particular circumstances, it is important to keep in mind that business owners must invest themselves, as well as their money, if they want their companies to succeed. As is so often the case in life, it is up to you to devote your time, effort, and resources if you really want to achieve your goals.

4-1. Define *franchise*, and have an understanding of franchise terminology.

- According to the U.S. Small Business Administration, a *franchise* is a business model involving a business owner (the franchisor) who licenses trademarks and methods to an independent entrepreneur (the franchisee). The franchise governs the method of conducting business between the two parties.
- The franchisor also provides the business expertise (marketing plans, management guidance, financing assistance, site location, training, etc.) that otherwise would not be available to the franchisee.
- A franchisee sells goods or services supplied by the franchisor or that meet the franchisor's quality standards.
- In product and trade name franchising, the main benefit for the franchisee is the privilege of using a widely recognized product or trademark.
- In business format franchising, entrepreneurs receive an entire marketing and management system.
- The franchise contract is a legal agreement between a franchisor and franchisee.
- A master licensee is an independent firm or individual acting as a middleman or sales agent with the responsibility of finding new franchisees within a specified territory.
- Multiple-unit ownership, in which a single franchisee owns more than one unit of a franchised business, is becoming widely used.
- Some single franchisees are area developers—individuals or firms that obtain the legal right to open several outlets in a given area.
- Piggyback franchising is the operation of a retail franchise within the physical facilities of a host store.
- Multibrand franchising involves operating several franchise organizations within a single corporate structure.
- Co-branding brings two or more franchise brands together within a single enterprise.

4-2. Understand the pros and cons of franchising.

- The primary advantage of franchising is its high probability of success.
- Other advantages of franchising include the value of trade names and trademarks, the franchisor's operations manual, training support, immediate access to supply lines and purchasing power, and financial support. It also is a way for existing businesses to diversify.
- Churning is the action by franchisors to void the contracts of franchisees in order to sell the franchise to someone else and collect an additional fee.
- Encroachment is the franchisor's selling of another franchise location within the market area of an existing franchisee.
- Disadvantages of franchising include financial issues, franchisor competition, and management issues.
- Costs associated with franchises include franchise fees, investment costs, royalty payments, and advertising costs.

4-3. Describe the process for evaluating a franchise opportunity.

- Independent third parties such as state and federal government agencies, the International Franchise Association, and business publications can be valuable sources of franchise information.
- The primary source of information about a franchise is the franchisor.
- Existing and previous franchisees are also good sources of information for evaluating a franchise.
- Before becoming a franchisor, consider the efficiency of your business model, how you will finance growth, what expert assistance you will need, the content of your operations manual, government disclosure requirements, and your ability to add long-term value for franchisees.
- A franchise contract is a complex document and should be evaluated by a franchise attorney, especially the provision relating to termination and transfer of the franchise.
- The Franchise Disclosure Document (FDD) provides the accepted format for satisfying the franchise disclosure requirements of the FTC.

4-4. List four reasons for buying an existing business, and describe the process of evaluating an existing business.

- Buying an existing firm can reduce uncertainties.
- In acquiring an existing firm, the entrepreneur can take advantage of the firm's ongoing operations and established relationships with customers and suppliers.

- An existing business may be available at a bargain price.
- Another reason for buying an existing business is that an entrepreneur may be in a hurry to start an enterprise.
- Investigating a business requires due diligence.
- A buyer should seek the help of outside experts, the two most valuable sources of outside assistance being accountants and lawyers.
- The buyer needs to investigate why the seller is offering the business for sale.
- The company's financial statements and tax returns for the past three to five years should always be examined.
- Other quantitative factors in valuing a business include state sales tax statements, supplier invoices, customer receipts, and the company's bank statements.
- Nonquantitative factors in determining the value of a business for sale include the market, competition, future community development, legal commitments, union contracts, buildings, and product prices.
- The terms of purchase are an important part of the negotiation between buyer and seller.
- Documents completed during the closing include a bill of sale, tax and other government forms, and agreements regarding future payments and related guarantees to the seller.

Key Terms

area developers p. 98
business brokers p. 112
business format franchising p. 97
churning p. 103
co-branding p. 98
due diligence p. 112
encroachment p. 103
franchise p. 97
franchise contract p. 97
Franchise Disclosure Document (FDD) p. 110
franchisee p. 97
Franchise Rule p. 109
franchisor p. 97
master licensee p. 97
multibrand franchising p. 98
multiple-unit ownership p. 98
nondisclosure agreement p. 115
piggyback franchising p. 98
product and trade name franchising p. 97

You Make the Call

Situation 1

Although he has owned the Madison, Wisconsin, franchise of 1-800-Got-Junk for seven years, John Patterson claimed he did not know whether he was making profits, breaking even, or even losing money. Still, in February of 2012, Patterson was able to buy an existing 1-800-Got-Junk franchise in the Denver, Colorado, area.

Patterson has reached his dream of recycling 100 percent of what he collects, and he is proud to report that his company has been able to prevent 75 percent of the junk collected from being deposited in landfills. Patterson tries to communicate to customers what he does with the junk they throw away, and they seem interested in knowing that their items are being recycled. And he tries to run his operation in as green a way as possible. He converted a truck using diesel to vegetable oil, and he is moving from using unleaded fuel in some trucks to running them on compressed natural gas instead.

Sources: Based on "Junk in His Trunk," *Entrepreneur*, May 2012, p. 122; and http://www.1800gotjunk.com, accessed January 27, 2015.

Question 1 Do you think that Patterson really does not know or care whether or not he is making money? Can he succeed in two locations if that is his attitude?

Question 2 What type of background do you think you would need to run a 1-800-Got-Junk franchise?

Question 3 If you were Patterson, what support would you expect to get from the franchisor?

Situation 2

Mike Treadwell's first entrepreneurial ventures involved opening a fish and chips restaurant, followed by a chicken and fish restaurant. Although he was making money, he questioned his own business competence and decided he needed to learn more by working for others. He took a job as a KFC restaurant manager, eventually becoming a training leader for KFC Corp. in Dallas, Texas. KFC gave him a chance to join one of their multi-unit franchise owners, who retired a short time later, selling his units to Treadwell.

This arrangement resulted in Treadwell being the owner of about three dozen restaurants. By 2015, Treadwell Enterprises owned not only KFC franchises, but also Taco Bell, Long John Silver's, Ruby Tuesday, and HuHot Mongolian Grill. Treadwell was operating 109 units in 10 states.

Sources: Debbie Salinsky, "Enjoying Success: Working Hard—and Enjoying It—Spells Success for Mike Treadwell," http://www.franchising.com/articles/enjoying_success_working_hard__and_enjoying_it__spells_success_for_mike_tre.html, accessed January 12, 2015; and Treadwell Enterprises, http://tefoods.com, accessed January 12, 2015.

Question 1 What risks do you think you would face if you were a successful manager in a large organization who suddenly had an offer to go into business for yourself?

Question 2 Why do you think Treadwell decided to become a multibrand franchisee instead of just staying with KFC?

Situation 3

After earning his engineering degree at a top university, Phil had numerous job offers at high salaries. He accepted a position with a well-established manufacturing company and quickly moved up the ranks. Then, he was recruited to be part of the top management team of a construction company. Life has been good, but Phil has been thinking that he'd really like to run his own business. He's established a strong reputation for both his technical and his leadership skills. He has been speaking with business brokers and with some owners that he feels might be willing to negotiate a sale, but nothing has felt right so far.

Question 1 Why do you think Phil is thinking about business ownership after the success he has achieved working in other companies? Why do you think he wants to buy instead of start a business?

Question 2 What questions do you think Phil should ask of a seller if he finds a business that he likes?

Video Case 4

Two Men and a Truck (P. 652)

Two Men and a Truck started in the early 1980s as a way for two brothers to make extra money while they were in high school. Now, over 20 years later, the company has grown to more than 200 locations worldwide and is the nation's largest franchised local moving company.

Alternative Case for Chapter 4

Case 18, Auntie Anne's Pretzels in China, p. 682

Endnotes

1. Arthur G. Sharp, "Franchising," http://www.referenceforbusiness.com/encyclopedia/For-Gol/Franchising.html, accessed February 16, 2015.
2. Roy Seaman, "History of Franchising," http://www.theukfranchisedirectory.net/page/history-of-franchising.php, accessed February 16, 2015.
3. Don Daszkowski, "The History of Franchising," http://franchises.about.com/od/franchisebasics/a/history.htm, accessed February 16, 2015.
4. Hilary Strahota, "Benjamin Franklin: Father of Franchising?" *Franchising World*, September 2007.
5. U.S. Small Business Administration, "Franchise Businesses," http://www.sba.gov/content/franchise-businesses, accessed January 27, 2015.
6. *Ibid.*
7. International Franchise Association, "About IFA," http://www.franchise.org/about-ifa, accessed January 3, 2015.
8. International Franchise Association, "Join IFA," http://www.franchise.org/join-ifa, accessed January 3, 2015.
9. International Franchise Association, "Franchise Business Economic Outlook for 2015," http://www.emarket.franchise.org/FranchiseBizOutlook2015.pdf, accessed February 28, 2015.
10. U.S. Patent and Trademark Office, "Trademark," http://www.uspto.gov/main/glossary/index.html#trademark, accessed January 3, 2015.
11. McDonald's, "Trademark Information," http://www.mcdonalds.com/us/en/terms_conditions.html, accessed January 3, 2015.

12. Jason Daley, "On the Same Page," *Entrepreneur*, June 2012, pp. 96–98; and "Painting with a Twist," http://www.paintingwithatwist.com, accessed January 6, 2015.
13. "2014 New Franchise Rankings," http://www.entrepreneur.com/franchises/rankings/topnew-115520/2014,-1.html, accessed January 6, 2015.
14. International Franchise Association, "VetFran Directory," http://www.franchise.org/veterans, accessed February 16, 2015.
15. Tracy Stapp, "Military Intelligence," *Entrepreneur*, July 2012, pp. 98–107.
16. Franchise Registry, "Making Franchise Lending Easier," http://franchiseregistry.com/index.php, accessed January 6, 2015.
17. International Franchise Association, "Mission Statement/Vision/Code of Ethics," http://www.franchise.org/mission-statementvisioncode-of-ethics, accessed February 28, 2015.
18. "Legal Briefs," *Franchise Times*, Vol. 14, No. 7 (August 2008), p. 51.
19. Ed Sealover, "Quiznos Leaves Bankruptcy Protection with New Financial Structure," http://www.bizjournals.com/denver/news/2014/07/01/quiznos-leaves-bankruptcy-protection-with-new.html?page=all, accessed January 6, 2015.
20. Elizabeth Sile, "Edible Arrangements in Legal Hot Water," http://www.inc.com/news/articles/201107/edible-arrangements-lawsuit.html, accessed January 6, 2015.
21. Jonathon Bick, "Internet-Based Franchise Encroachment Runs Rampant," *New Jersey Law Journal*, Vol. 202, No. 12, http://bicklaw.com/e-Franchiseproblems.htm, accessed January 6, 2015.
22. International Franchise Association, "Liberty Tax Service," http://www.franchise.org/Liberty-Tax-Service-franchise, accessed January 7, 2015.
23. Denny's International, "Requirements," http://dennysfranchising.com/InternationalRequirements, accessed January 7, 2015.
24. Personal communication with Mark Liston, October 27, 2010.
25. *Ibid.*
26. "Yet Another Lawsuit Brought against 7-Eleven," https://no7eleven.wordpress.com/tag/lawsuit, accessed January 7, 2015.
27. Rieva Lesonsky, "Is It Time to Sell Your Business or Buy a New One?" http://smallbiztrends.com/2012/05/sell-business-buy-a-new-one.html, accessed January 7, 2015.
28. "Business Broker," http://www.entrepreneur.com/encyclopedia/term/82270.html, accessed January 7, 2015.
29. U.S. Small Business Administration, "Buying an Existing Business," http://www.sba.gov/content/choosing-business, accessed January 7, 2015.
30. You might also read "Buying an Existing Business," at http://www.sba.gov/content/researching-business-purchase, to see the SBA's suggested approaches for valuing a business.

CHAPTER 5

The Family Business

After studying this chapter, you should be able to . . .

5-1. Define the terms *family* and *family business*.

5-2. Explain the forces that can keep a family business moving forward.

5-3. Describe the complex roles and relationships involved in a family business.

5-4. Identify management practices that enable a family business to function effectively.

5-5. Describe the process of managerial succession in a family business.

OPEN
LOOKING AHEAD

Chris Martin treasures the legacy of his great-great-great-grandfather, Christian Frederick Martin, Sr. Coming from a family of cabinet makers, C.F., Sr., studied the manufacture of guitars as an apprentice. He felt opportunities were limited in his home country of Germany, so he immigrated to the United States and set up his own company in 1833.

Chris Martin is the sixth-generation CEO of C.F. Martin & Company, Inc. He has learned many lessons from his ancestors. The founder of the firm, C.F., Sr., was willing to experiment beyond what he was taught and designed modifications to the guitars, such as an adjustable neck that could be pivoted up and down. C.F., Jr., documented how sales varied through business cycles, helping future generations grasp the influence of economic conditions. When

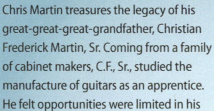

In the SPOTLIGHT
C.F. Martin & Co.
www.martinguitar.com

C.F., Jr., died unexpectedly, his 22-year-old son Frank took over the company. Frank recognized the impact of a large immigrant population from Italy and introduced mandolins as a new product line. He also vertically integrated the company by taking control of distribution channels.

C.F. III was the first college-educated family member to join the business. He credited his father, Frank, with instilling a sense of the value of education in the family. Although there were cutbacks during the Great Depression, the company continued to try new designs and introduce new products. One innovation was to change from a 12-fret to 14-fret neck, which became the industry standard, thanks to its increased flexibility. When Frank Herbert Martin succeeded his father, C.F. III, in 1970, the company engaged in acquiring other enterprises, most notably the Darco String Company, which proved to be an excellent fit with the various guitars being manufactured.

Christian Frederick Martin IV received hands-on experience growing up—first boxing strings, then helping in the office, eventually wielding a bandsaw on the shop floor and attending trade shows. He describes the time his father was approached about selling the company, and Frank Herbert asked Chris what he thought about the offer. Chris responded, "I would like to think about joining the business—I can't guarantee that I will." With that piece of information, Frank Herbert turned down the offer. Chris joined the company full-time after earning his business degree.

Chris feels he is not merely responsible for a business and its employees, but also for a set of values. He wants everyone to know that C.F. Martin & Co. adheres to high standards of musical excellence, with the goal of producing the perfect guitar. Looking ahead, he wonders if his 3-year-old daughter, Claire Frances, will be the next C.F. Martin.

© PERRY VAN MUNSTER / ALAMY

Sources: Based on http://www.martinguitar.com, accessed January 18, 2015; Adam Bluestein, "The Success Gene: Why Some Family Businesses Thrive Year after Year after Year," accessed January 18, 2015; and Dick Boak, *C.F. Martin & Co.* (Charleston, SC: Arcadia Publishing, 2014).

Stories about family businesses often make the news. We read about fights between parents and children, among siblings, between family members and nonfamily employees and investors. But we also read about the foundations that business families create, becoming philanthropists in their communities and contributing to medical research, to universities, and more. When a family puts their name on the company, their reputation accompanies it.

It is well documented that a majority of businesses in most free-market economies fit some definition of family ownership. The largest family businesses include such publicly traded companies as Walmart and For Motor Co., as well as those privately held like Cargill, Koch Industries, and Mars.[1] Although the stereotypical entrepreneur may not intentionally start a family enterprise, he or she often relies on family members to obtain the resources necessary for the startup and to pitch in when a problem arises. Family members are usually the first people to lend you money or make an investment in your company, or to step in if you get sick or if an essential employee suddenly quits. Many times, it is a family member who knows and accepts your strengths and weaknesses and is willing to work long hours, often at no pay.

But family members are not always cordial, cooperative, and compatible. They know how to make you mad, to make you feel guilty, to embarrass you. Such actions have caused the downfall of many a family enterprise, large and small. In this chapter, we investigate how family and business interact, what makes them strong, and what can destroy them. From extensive research into family firms, we introduce strategies that have helped family businesses succeed.

5-1 WHAT IS A FAMILY BUSINESS?

Define the terms *family* and *family business*.

What exactly is a family? This may seem like a silly question to ask, but definitions of *family* vary in different parts of the world. They include the classic "nuclear" family, restricted to parents and children, and an "extended" family, comprising an entire community of other relatives. No doubt you have seen many versions of families on television, in movies, and possibly in your own life. Given the interest and involvement that family members have in each other's lives, it shouldn't be surprising that they have opinions about a business owned by one or more members, whether they are officially connected with the company or not.

In this book, the word **family** refers to a group of people bound by a shared history and a commitment to share a future together, while supporting the development and well-being of individual members.[2] This definition acknowledges the considerable differences in the compositions of families. They can vary according to blood relationships, generational representation, legal status, and more. A **family business** can be defined as an organization "in which either the individuals who established or acquired the firm or their descendants significantly influence the strategic decisions and life course of the firm. Family influence might be exerted through management and/or ownership of the firm."[3]

Experts on family businesses try to sort through family relationships and apply labels to firms as they evolve from one generation to another. An **owner-managed business** is a venture that is operated by a founding entrepreneur. If the children of the founder become the owners and managers of the business, that second-generation ownership is referred to as a **sibling partnership**. A **cousin consortium** describes a business in the third and subsequent generations when children of the siblings take ownership and management positions. But whichever generation is leading a company, the influence of other generations is felt, as described in the Spotlight feature that opens this chapter.

family
A group of people bound by a shared history and a commitment to share a future together, while supporting the development and well-being of individual members.

family business
An organization in which either the individuals who established or acquired the firm or their descendants significantly influence the strategic decisions and life course of the firm.

owner-managed business
A venture operated by a founding entrepreneur.

sibling partnership
A business in which children of the founder become owners and managers.

cousin consortium
A business in third and subsequent generations, when children of the siblings take ownership and management positions.

5-1a Family and Business Overlap

Families and businesses exist for fundamentally different reasons. The family's primary function is the care and nurturing of family members, while the business is concerned with the production and distribution of goods and/or services. And while the family's focus is on creating value for family members and emphasizing cooperation, unity, and stability, the business's goal is to create value for customers and emphasize competition, diversity, and flexibility.

Individuals involved in a family business have interests and perspectives that differ according to their particular situations. The model in Exhibit 5.1 (a Venn diagram) shows the ways in which individuals may be involved—as owners, members of the family, employees of the business, and various combinations of these. In addition, the configuration of roles can affect the way these individuals think about the enterprise. For example, whereas a family member who works in the firm and has an ownership interest (segment 7) might favor reinvesting in order to grow the business, a family member with an ownership share but who works elsewhere (segment 5) might want dividend payouts, and an employee with neither family nor ownership interest (segment 2) might seek higher wages.

Competing interests can complicate the management process, creating tension and sometimes leading to conflict. Relationships among family members in a business are more sensitive than relationships among unrelated employees. For example, disciplining an employee who consistently arrives late is much more problematic if he or she is also a family member. Or, consider a performance review session between a parent-boss and a child-subordinate. Or the spouse who wonders when the family will take priority over the business. In 2013, Meg Cadoux Hirshberg concluded a series of columns that she had written about her own relationship with her husband, Greg, founder of Stonyfield Farm, a producer of organic yogurt. Meg had labeled her columns "Balancing Act" and provided numerous examples of the stresses the

EXHIBIT 5.1 The Three-Circle Model of Family Firms

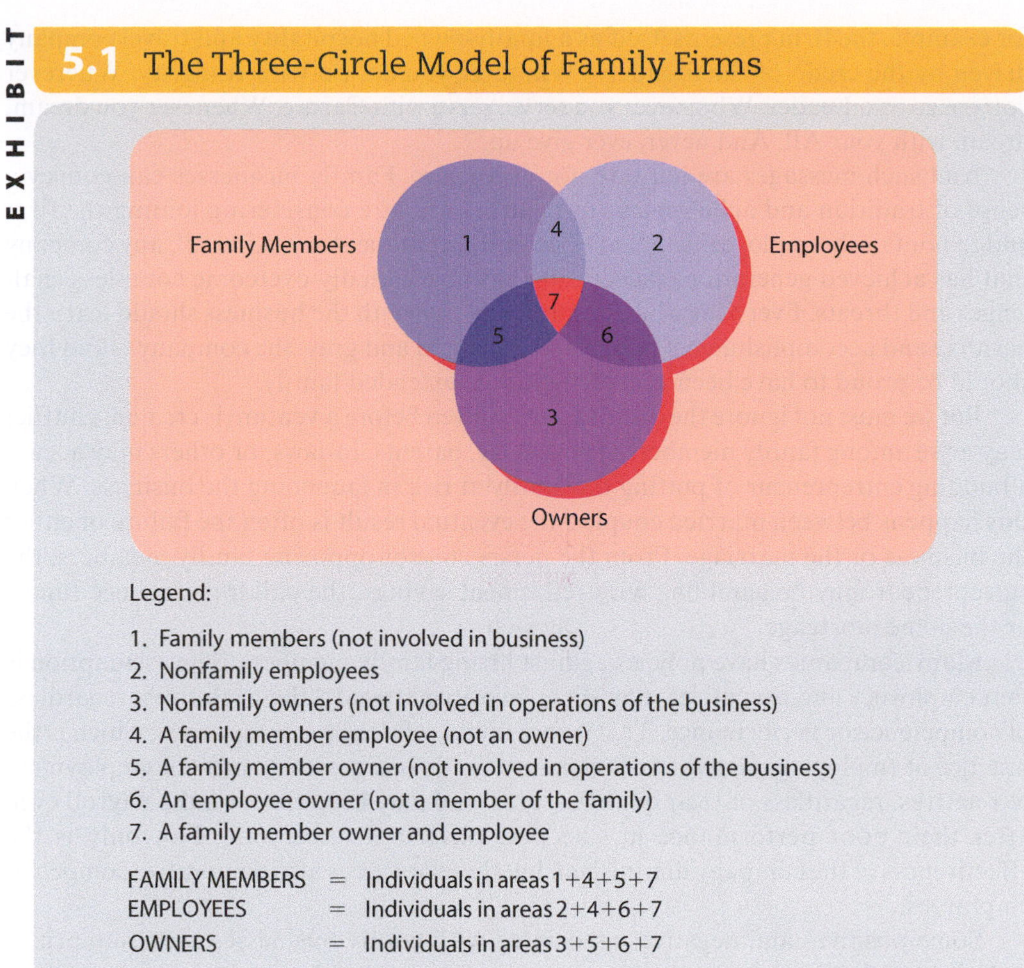

Legend:

1. Family members (not involved in business)
2. Nonfamily employees
3. Nonfamily owners (not involved in operations of the business)
4. A family member employee (not an owner)
5. A family member owner (not involved in operations of the business)
6. An employee owner (not a member of the family)
7. A family member owner and employee

FAMILY MEMBERS = Individuals in areas 1+4+5+7
EMPLOYEES = Individuals in areas 2+4+6+7
OWNERS = Individuals in areas 3+5+6+7

Sources: Based on Frank Hoy and Pramodita Sharma, *Entrepreneurial Family Firms* (Boston: Prentice Hall, 2010); and James J. Chrisman, Franz W. Kellermanns, Kam C. Chan, and Kartono Liano, "Intellectual Foundations of Current Research in Family Business: An Identification and Review of 25 Influential Articles," *Family Business Review*, Vol. 23 (2010), pp. 9-26.

business placed on the family. In her final column, she described the reactions that many others involved in family enterprises had to her stories, giving her a sense that she had helped them open up about the emotional toll the business takes. But in the end, she recognized that Greg would continue to throw himself into new ventures and that she would both challenge and admire him.[4] The existence of a family relationship adds an emotional factor that strongly supports (or vastly complicates) the working relationship.

5-1b Advantages and Disadvantages of a Family Business

Problems with family firms can easily blind people to the unique advantages that come with participating in a family business. The benefits associated with family involvement should be recognized and discussed when recruiting both relatives and nonfamily members to work in the family firm. One primary benefit derives from the strength of family relationships. Family members have a unique motivation: Business success is also family success.

Businesses that are family owned often highlight this feature in their promotional materials to set themselves apart from competitors. On the Carlson Company website, for example, the firm presents itself as a family-owned hospitality and travel company driven by the credo of the founder: "Whatever you do, do with Integrity. Wherever you go, go as a Leader. Whomever you serve, serve with Caring. Whenever you dream, dream with your All. And never, ever give up."[5]

And such messages are not only for customers. Family businesses can convey a sense of tradition and achievement to relatives who are considering joining the firm and to nonfamily employees who have become part of the story. After all, any company that has achieved generational succession has undoubtedly overcome countless challenges and threats. Everyone who accepts a position with the business should learn the heritage and accomplishments of those who created and grew the company—and they should be proud to have been accepted into the extended family.

But we must not ignore the disadvantages. Even before a venture is created, conflict may arise among family members. The spouse, parents, in-laws, or others may accuse a budding entrepreneur of putting the family at risk in launching the business. When this happens between married couples, the eventual result is often the failure of either the business or the marriage. From the perspective of opposing family members, the entrepreneur may be gambling with retirement savings, the children's college funds, or the home mortgage.

Many companies have policies against hiring family members. The assumption is that employees and executives may show favoritism toward their relatives, regardless of competence or performance. This is sometimes referred to as **nepotism**, which is the practice of employing relatives. In fact, many family businesses do provide employment to relatives, regardless of their qualifications, and may keep them on the payroll even after their poor performance has become obvious to everyone. Not only is the effectiveness of the company diminished, but these practices also demoralize competent employees.

nepotism
The practice of employing relatives.

Some positives and negatives associated with family businesses are summarized in Exhibit 5.2. The fact that so many family firms are able to survive generational transitions, however, demonstrates that the negatives can be overcome.

EXHIBIT

5.2 Positives and Negatives of Family Businesses

Positives (+)	Negatives (−)
Trust among family members	Mistrust by nonfamily employees of incompetent family employees
Loyalty to the family by those within the firm	Lack of loyalty to the firm by family members not directly involved in the business
Commitment to the firm by all family	Sense of entitlement by the succeeding generation and those not working in the firm
Knowledge among extended family members	Lack of knowledge among those outside the firm
Long-range thinking by leaders of the firm	Demand for instant gratification from those who feel entitled
Close communication among family members	Failure to communicate across generations and with family not involved in the firm

Sources: Based on Priscilla M. Cale and David C. Tate, *Sink or Swim: How Lessons from the* Titanic *Can Save Your Family Firm* (Santa Barbara, CA: Praeger, 2011); Frank Hoy and Pramodita Sharma, *Entrepreneurial Family Firms* (Boston: Prentice Hall, 2010); and Ritch L. Sorenson, Andy Yu, Keith H. Brigham, and G. T. Lumpkin (eds.), *The Landscape of Family Business* (Cheltenham, UK: Edward Elgar, 2013).

5-2 DYNAMIC FAMILY BUSINESSES

LO 5-2

Explain the forces that can keep a family business moving forward.

On average, family businesses survive longer than nonfamily firms. Recent research findings suggest that companies that are successful in transferring ownership and management from one generation to the next are characterized by entrepreneurial behavior. That means the new leaders need to act on their own, take risks, and introduce or support innovations. For family businesses, a key issue in the transfer of ownership and management is the retention or modification of the **organizational culture**, a pattern of behaviors and beliefs that characterize a particular firm.

The culture of the family firm deserves special attention because it can serve as either an advantage or a disadvantage. On the positive side, it can be a strategic resource that promotes an entrepreneurial orientation. This prevents successive leaders from thinking of themselves simply as administrators who are expected to continue the practices of the founder.

5-2a The Imprint of Founders on the Family Business Culture

Founders leave a deep impression on the family businesses they launch.[6] And the distinctive values that motivate and guide an entrepreneur in the founding of a company may help create a competitive advantage for the new business. Business founders are often innovators who may meet customers' needs in a special way and emphasize customer service as a guiding principle for the company. Founders often imprint their own personalities on their companies. They hire the first employees and, even as the company grows, may know everyone in the organization and their family members.

organizational culture
Patterns of behaviors and beliefs that characterize a particular firm.

Of course, there is always a darker possibility—an overly controlling founder who won't listen to others or share information or allow others to make decisions. Feelings of superiority and complacency with the status quo can harm the business when they spread throughout the organization. At a minimum, such founders fail to prepare others for leadership. While contributions of founders deserve proper acknowledgment, any negative legacy must be avoided.

5-2b The Commitment of Family Members

In family firms, when the founder turns over the reins of leadership (most often, to a new generation), the continuity of the business depends, in large part, on those next-generation family members and their level of commitment to the business. Recent research suggests that family members entering a family business do so for a variety of reasons, and these reasons shape the strength and nature of their commitment to the company.[7]

The Spirit of the Founder
Read the biography of a founder who put his or her name on a company: L.L. Bean, Estée Lauder, Henry Ford. These people and their enterprises have survived and grown from one generation to the next. You will be fascinated by their stories.

The model pictured earlier in Exhibit 5.1 is often used to summarize the complexities of dealing with the family firm's interactive components: the business, the family, and the owner. This model can help founders recognize that they have to balance their obvious interest in the business, their personal aspirations, and the needs of their family. Next-generation family members who choose to pursue a career in the business must also deal with these challenges, and their commitment to the company will likely determine the value of their contributions, the financial benefits they create for the family, and their personal satisfaction in work-related roles.

SOCIOEMOTIONAL WEALTH

One of the newest theories regarding family businesses is the finding that the commitment of family members to the firm relates to what is called **socioemotional wealth**.[8] The idea is that gains and losses in nonfinancial characteristics of the relationship between the family and the business affect strategic and policy decisions regarding the company. The socioemotional involvement of family members can include the exercise of personal authority, the enjoyment of family influence, and close identification with a firm that may be carrying the family name.

Jennifer Silence Rankin worked in her parents' lawn care business when she was a teenager. She hated the sweeping and laundry cleaning, and vowed not to join the company. But after studying marketing and communication in college, she started to look at the company in a different way. As Rankin put it, "It hit me how much sweat, blood and tears my parents have put into this place. . . . I would not be OK with it being handed over to someone else."[9] Rankin chose this business for more than the salary she receives or the wealth it might create.

The socioemotional commitment of family members to the firm occurs along five dimensions, shown in Exhibit 5.3. The acronym for the dimensions is FIBER: *family* control, *identification* with the firm, *binding* social ties, *emotional* attachment, and *renewal* of family bonds through dynastic succession.

THE FEAR OF COMMITMENT

Greg McCann, founding director of the Family Enterprise Center at Stetson University, has learned from students and the family firms that he has coached that members of the succeeding generation in family firms may have emotional resistance to joining the firm. Typical fears include the following:[10]

1. **Fear of failure.** *If I really take ownership of my life, I might fail.* Realize that if emotional resistance prevents your progress, you are destined to fail.
2. **Fear of success.** *If I succeed, then others will expect more of me in the future.* It's true that successful people have to deal with the pressure of high expectations. But isn't this pressure preferable to others having no expectations of you? Or worse yet, having no expectations of yourself?
3. **Fear of commitment.** *If I never really try, then I will never really fail.* Avoiding a decision may feel safe, but many people don't understand that not deciding *is* a decision, and it is a poor one.
4. **Fear of disappointing your parents.** *It would break my dad's heart if I worked for another company instead of the family business.* Your parents want you to be happy, and if you are working to achieve that, almost all parents will be happy

socioemotional wealth
Nonfinancial factors in a family firm that affect the commitment of family members to the business.

EXHIBIT

5.3 Dimensions in Socioemotional Commitment

Family control and influence. Specifically, family members exert control over strategic decisions.
Identification of family members with the firm. The firm may be seen as an extension of the family itself.
Binding social ties. Family members feel closeness and solidarity.
Emotional attachment of family members. The history and knowledge of past events influence and shape current activities.
Renewal of family bonds to the firm through dynastic succession. There is an intention to hand the business down to future generations.

Source: Based on Pascual Berrone, Cristina Cruz, and Luis Gomez-Mejia, "Socioemotional Wealth in Family Firms: Theoretical Dimensions, Assessment Approaches, and Agenda for Future Research," *Family Business Review*, Vol. 25, No. 3 (2012), pp. 258-279.

with your decision. Beyond that, you have to decide whether being authentic is important to you. If it is, you will have to confront this fear.

5. **Fear of disappointing others.** *If I don't go with all my friends to an internship in Chicago, I might lose their friendship.* This fear is similar to the last one, but it plays out with friends, mentors, colleagues, and bosses. It is a real and understandable fear, but you need to look at it more deeply to determine what pleasing others costs you and to question the assumption that you know what they want. Remember, you are responsible for your own happiness.

McCann's final advice is that each individual should make her or his own decisions and not let emotional resistance influence those decisions. How each person handles these fears is often influenced by the sense of unity within her or his family.

COMMITMENT TO CONTINUITY

PricewaterhouseCoopers (PwC) conducts periodic surveys of family-owned enterprises. In 2010, only 55 percent of respondents were optimistic about their companies remaining in the hands of family members. The PwC researchers concluded that the attitude reflected difficult economic conditions that the businesses were experiencing. In the 2012 survey, the results showed 76 percent of family businesses were planning to keep the companies in the family. Just over half intended to have family members both own and manage the businesses.

The biggest concern expressed about retaining family management was the fear there would be a lack of innovation on the part of successors. The most frequently expressed source of innovation was the expectation of the company going international. Technological advances were also expected to trigger innovative behavior.[11]

co-preneurs
Couples teams who own and manage businesses.

5-3 FAMILY ROLES AND RELATIONSHIPS

LO
5-3
Describe the complex roles and relationships involved in a family business.

A *Wall Street Journal* article begins, "There's no easy way to fire a relative." The author proceeds to discuss the risks of family conflicts and the long-run consequences.[12] This dim view of the family enterprise is not shared by everyone. However, significant conflicts can result when family roles and business interests collide, and anticipating these challenges and planning for them can really pay off. This section examines a few of the many possible family roles and relationships that can contribute to managerial complexity in a family business.

5-3a Co-Preneurs

Some family businesses are owned and managed by couples teams. Such couples are popularly known as **co-preneurs**. Their roles vary depending on their backgrounds and expertise. Whatever the arrangement, both individuals are integral parts of the business.

One potential advantage of a couples team is the opportunity to work with someone you really trust and to share more of your lives together. For some couples, however, the benefits can be overshadowed

© PAULPALADIN/SHUTTERSTOCK.COM

by problems related to the business. Differences of opinion about business matters can carry over into family life. And the energy of both parties may be so spent by working long hours in a struggling company that little zest remains for a strong family life. There is a recent trend of couples starting Web-based businesses, often from home. In some of these cases, the co-preneurs have found that there can be too much togetherness, in which case they must establish rules for time apart.[13]

Many couples have had to set boundaries and develop routines to cope with the demands of everyday life (like raising children) and still have sufficient time for the business. Dr. Ken Blanchard is internationally known for writing *The One Minute Manager* and over 30 other books. He and his wife, Dr. Marjorie Blanchard, are co-owners of The Ken Blanchard Companies. They founded their business in 1979, and today it is a global training company. The Blanchards had three simple goals—"to make a difference in people's lives, to drive human worth and effectiveness in the workplace, and to help each organization we work with become the provider, employer, and investment of choice."[14]

Family members may think that simple rules, guidelines, or goals are unnecessary, but for many people working with relatives, such goals can keep a focus on what they want both the business and the family to become.

5-3b Mom or Dad, the Founder

Many entrepreneurs expect to pass the enterprise on to a son or a daughter. The idea is that the business and the family will grow and prosper together. Entrepreneurs with children think naturally in terms of handing the business on to the next generation. Some of the approaches taken to prepare prospective successors for ownership and leadership include the following:

- Demonstrating the founders' commitment to both the business and the family through both actions and words.
- Permitting and supporting entrepreneurial behavior by the children; letting them take calculated risks, and encouraging them to learn from failure.
- Supporting educational efforts that contribute to skills for leading the business while helping the children to develop their own special talents.
- Helping the children recognize that rules and responsibilities have their place in both business and life.

Of all the relationships in a family business, the parent–child relationship has been recognized for generations as the most troublesome. Parents sometimes have difficulty accepting that their children may choose a different path than joining the business. In recent years, the problems inherent in the relationship have been addressed by counselors, seminars, and books too numerous to count. In spite of all this attention, however, the parent–child relationship continues to disrupt many families involved in family businesses.

5-3c Sons and Daughters

Should sons and daughters be recruited for the family business, or should they pursue careers of their own choosing? Experts recommend introducing children to the family firm at an early age. Parents may take small children to the firm on occasion, then hire them as interns on weekends or during summer breaks. This exposes the children to the lives their parents are living and to what the company is contributing to the family.

Parents can make a conscious effort to teach their children that a successful enterprise demands hard work and is not just an inheritance.

Another issue is personal freedom. Our society values the right of the individual to choose his or her own career and way of life. If this value is embraced by a son or a daughter, that child must be granted the freedom to select a career of his or her own choosing. In the entrepreneurial family, the natural tendency is to think in terms of a family business career and to push a child, either openly or subtly, in that direction. Little thought may be given to the child's talent, aptitude, and temperament. He or she may prefer music or medicine to the world of business and may fit the business mold very poorly. It is also possible that the abilities of the son or daughter may simply be insufficient for a leadership role.

A son or daughter may feel a need to work out side the family business, for a time at least, to prove that he or she can make it without help from the family. Family business consultants typically give this advice to parents. Grown children who find they can succeed on their own are likely to have more self-confidence in their abilities if they choose to join the family firm at a later date. And nonfamily employees may have more respect for the new entrant if the son or daughter was hired after demonstrating competence in a different organization.

5-3d Sibling Cooperation, Sibling Rivalry

It is not unusual for more than one child to take positions within the company as they enter the workforce or make a career change. Even if they do not work in the business, brothers and sisters of those who do may be more than casual observers on the sidelines. They may have a stake as heirs or partial owners.

At best, siblings work as a smoothly functioning team, each contributing services according to his or her respective abilities. Just as families can experience excellent cooperation and unity in their relationships with one another, some family businesses benefit from effective collaboration among brothers and sisters.

However, business issues tend to generate competition, and this affects family, as well as nonfamily, members. Siblings, for example, may disagree about business policy or about their respective roles in the business. And, in some cases, the conflicts can spiral seriously out of control.[15]

A strategy taken by some parents is to involve their children directly in the business at young ages. Ty Kester, the third-generation director of the Oklahoma State Horseshoeing School in Ardmore, Oklahoma, explains why he and his sister are running the company:

> *The reason the business still works is because we grew up here. . . . As kids, we were here all the time. We were taught our whole lives how a successful business is managed. From a very young age, it was a constant mentorship from my grandfather, grandmother and father. That's why the school's still going strong.*[16]

Nonfamily members can play a key role in resolving or avoiding conflict among siblings. Sometimes, nonfamily executives become mentors when a family member joins the firm. This can occur formally or informally. Mentoring is often job-related, focusing on developing work and leadership skills. But the mentor can also guide the son or daughter with regard to the culture and values that underlie the company and its success. A member of the firm's board of directors or board of advisors may play a similar role. While these mentors should not be seen as referees, they may be able to coach siblings in how to reach agreement on issues by setting lifetime memories and resentments aside.

Living the Dream

ENTREPRENEURIAL EXPERIENCES

Nature or Nurture?

Was it Cady Zildjian MacPherson's choice to join the family firm, or was her fate chosen for her?

The Avedis Zildjian Company of Norwell, Massachusetts, proudly describes itself on the company website "as the oldest family-owned business in America." The first Avedis founded the company in 1623 in what was then Constantinople (now Istanbul, Turkey), using a "secret alloy to create cymbals of spectacular clarity and power." Avedis III brought the firm to the United States in 1929. Today, the company is led by CEO Craigie Zildjian and her sister Debbie, who is vice president of human resources. They are members of the family's 14th generation.

© LEE MARTIN/ALAMY

Debbie's daughter, Cady, interned at Zildjian while in high school. Her first assignment was as a receptionist. After completing her studies at Colgate University, she worked part time for Zildjian, then joined SmartPak Equine, LLC, as a senior marketing assistant. For three years, Cady was part of a team that included registered pharmacy technicians, in a firm funded by venture capitalists. She found this experience to be valuable in understanding how professionals operate and evolve in their working relationships.

According to Cady, no pressure was placed on her to join the family firm. Although she says that she always knew it would be hard to work with family, she found that the attraction to be part of the Zildjian tradition was irresistible. Cady joined the company in April 2007 and, in 2012, held the position of associate product manager. She says her only regret is that she would have liked more outside experience.

Cady describes the steps that the company leadership has taken as important in enabling family members to work together successfully. The Zildjians relied on outside advisors to help them set up guidelines for the family and firm. They created a family council and developed written policies for entry into the business. Cady considers effective communication to be essential. The company holds quarterly meetings for shareholders, and family members make a point of spending time together that is not for business purposes.

Cady now watches with interest as her sister and her cousin complete their college degrees. Will they be part of the Avedis Zildjian story, or will they follow a different path?

Sources: Based on personal interview with Cady Zildjian MacPherson, May 21, 2012; and http://zildjian.com, accessed July 27, 2012.

Another sibling dilemma has been labeled the *predator/parasite conflict*. Family members working in the firm are sometimes seen by relatives who work outside the company as predators—extracting money from the business that the outsiders believe is rightfully theirs. From the inside, family members external to the firm are seen, in turn, to be parasites. That is, they have ownership rights, receive dividends, or make other claims on the business without contributing to its success.

There are many stories about siblings who destroyed their families' businesses. Adolf and Rudolf Dassler appeared to have complementary skills that should have been perfect for collaboration—one was reserved and a sports fanatic; the other was an outgoing salesperson. But they battled over everything, eventually going separate ways. Adolf founded Adidas and Rudolf launched Puma, and their companies continued the fights.[17] The Disney brothers, Walt and Roy, were similarly known to argue, but they recognized each other's talent and proved to be the right team to build the Disney empire.[18]

Later in the chapter, you will learn that many family enterprises have sought to preempt conflicts by formalizing structures. Some have implemented written guidelines by way of constitutions, while others have formed structures such as family business councils.

5-3e In-Laws In and Out of the Business

You are born or adopted into a *family of origin*, the relatives who form your world in your childhood. When you partner with another individual, you discover yourself with a new *family of attachment*, which refers to the new, separate relationship you just formed plus the family connections you acquire from your partner. Suddenly, the members of your family of origin find themselves linked to your new family, with its own values and traditions. For many family firms, the families of attachment may influence the business in some way. In-laws may become directly or indirectly involved in the firms. They may have been employed in the company and married a family member. They may have accepted a position in the company following the marriage. At a minimum, they will have opinions about the family business and their spouses' relatives, which they are likely to express.

When an in-law joins a company, effective collaboration may be achieved by assigning family members to different branches or roles within the company. But competition for leadership positions may eventually force decisions that distinguish among the children and in-laws employed in the business. Being fair and maintaining family loyalty become more difficult as the number of family employees increases.

In-laws who are on the sidelines also have considerable influence on the business and the family. They are keenly interested in family business issues that impact their spouses. When family frustrations come up at work, spouses tend to hear all about it at home, often just before the couple goes to bed. The family member vents, then feels better, and goes to sleep. The spouse, on the other hand, is just hearing about the situation and spends the rest of the night worried, angry, or both. Then, when everything is sorted out at the office the next morning, no one even thinks about phoning the spouse to let him or her know that everything is fine. Spouses tend to hear only one side of the story—the bad side—and it shades their view of the business. So, the criticism they receive for having a bad attitude about the family and its enterprise is often undeserved.[19]

5-3f The Entrepreneur's Spouse

Couples don't always become co-preneurs. But even if a spouse does not work in the business, he or she may still play a critical role behind the scenes. Traditionally, this role has been fulfilled by the male entrepreneur's wife and the mother of his children. However, many husbands have now assumed the role of entrepreneur's spouse.

As a parent, the spouse helps prepare the children for possible careers in the family business. Researchers have found that one of the most frequent and stressful roles performed by the spouse is to serve as a mediator in business relationships between the entrepreneur and the children.

Ideally, the entrepreneur and her or his spouse form a team committed to the success of both the family and the family business. Such teamwork does not occur automatically—it requires a collaborative effort by both parties in the marriage. Tim Berry, chairman and founder of Palo Alto Software, explained the endorsement he received from his wife when he was weighing whether to start the company:

> *[This was the] biggest boost to starting a business: My wife said, "Go for it; you can do it." And she meant it. At several key points along the way, she made it clear that we would take the risk together. There was never the threat of "I told you so, why did you leave a good job, you idiot!" What she said was, "If you fail, we'll fail together, and then we'll figure it out. We'll be okay."*[20]

5-4 GOOD GOVERNANCE IN THE FAMILY FIRM

Identify management practices that enable a family business to function effectively.

Family businesses sometimes face the stereotype of not being professionally managed. Yet several research studies have shown that publicly traded family firms perform as well as or better than nonfamily corporations.[21] As with all companies facing global competition and rapidly changing markets, family businesses have to look carefully at family members who want leadership positions in the enterprise and determine whether they are up to the task. The complex relationships in family firms require the oversight of competent and professional management, whether from inside or outside the family. Allowing unprepared or incompetent family members to be managers weakens the firm. Compromising in this way runs counter to the interests of both the firm and the family.

The family firm is a competitive business. Practicing good management will help the business thrive and permit the family to function as a family. Failing to do so poses a threat to the business and strains family relationships.

5-4a Nonfamily Employees in a Family Firm

Nonfamily members often discover that they have limited opportunities in a family firm. In some cases, promotions are missed because of the presence of family members who may have the inside track. Few parents will promote an outsider over a competent daughter or son who is being groomed for future leadership, and this is understandable. But this limits the potential for advancement of nonfamily employees, which may lead them to become frustrated, to feel cheated, or to leave the firm.

Those outside the family are sometimes caught in the crossfire between family members who are competing with each other. It is difficult for outsiders to maintain strict neutrality in family feuds. If a nonfamily executive is perceived as siding with one of those involved in the feud, she or he may lose the support of other family members. Hardworking employees often feel that they deserve hazard pay for working in a firm plagued by family conflict.

The extent of limitations on nonfamily employees depends on the number of family members active in the business and the number of managerial or professional positions in the business to which nonfamily employees might aspire. It also depends on the extent to which the owner demands competence in management and maintains an atmosphere of fairness in supervision. To avoid future problems, the owner should make clear, when hiring nonfamily employees, the extent of opportunities available to them and identify the positions, if any, that are reserved for family members.

The leader of a family-owned enterprise might decide to bring in a nonfamily member as an executive with the firm for the following reasons:

- To bridge the gap between generations
- To set a new direction for the firm
- To deal with change
- To provide new skills and expertise

Two Men and a Truck was founded by two brothers. When they left for college, their mother, Mary Ellen Sheets, took charge and grew the company. She recruited her daughter to join the firm and take over as CEO. Eventually, the brothers returned to the company. When their sister decided to devote more time to her family, she passed the CEO position to one of the founding brothers. That brother, Brig Sorber, in turn chose Randy Shacka as his replacement as president of Two Men and a Truck because he recognized that Shacka had a set of organizational skills that he felt were right for moving the company ahead.[22] The rest of the family agreed that Shacka had demonstrated a commitment to values that paralleled their own. Owners often look for certain traits in nonfamily leaders: maturity, facilitation skills, mentoring skills, emotional sensitivity, trustworthiness, and the ability to understand and share the values of the family.

5-4b Family Retreats

It would be great if founders thought about how the business and the family would affect each other from the time they start on their adventure. The truth is, however, that most owners don't start thinking about how the two will interact until some problem comes up, often when the business matures and has created wealth. One of the first steps experts recommend for building a healthy family-to-business relationship is to hold a retreat. A **family retreat** is a meeting of family members (often including in-laws), usually held away from company premises, to discuss family business matters. In most cases, the atmosphere is informal to encourage family members to communicate freely and discuss their concerns about the business in an environment that does not pit family members against each other. The retreat is not so much an *event* as it is the *beginning of a process* of connecting family members. It presents an opportunity to celebrate the founders and their sacrifices, as well as to highlight the legacy they want to pass down to future generations of the family.

The prospect of sitting down together to discuss family business matters may seem threatening to some family members. As a result, some families avoid open communication, fearing it will stir up trouble. They assume that making decisions quietly or secretly will preserve harmony. Unfortunately, this approach often covers up serious differences that become increasingly troublesome. Family retreats are designed to improve lines of communication and to bring about understanding and agreement on family business issues.

family retreat
A gathering of family members, usually at a remote location, to discuss family business matters.

Honest and candid discussion can be difficult, so it is standard for family leaders to invite an outside expert or facilitator to coordinate early sessions. The facilitator can help develop an agenda and set ground rules for discussion. While chairing early sessions, he or she can establish a positive, nonthreatening tone that emphasizes family achievements and encourages rational consideration of sensitive issues. Family members who are able to develop an atmosphere of neutrality, however, may be able to chair the sessions without using an outsider.

To ensure the success of a family business retreat, David Lansky, CEO of a family business consulting firm, suggests that these guidelines be followed:[23]

1. *Be clear about the purpose of the retreat.* Be able to answer this question: "If the meeting accomplished everything you could possibly hope for, what would that look like?"
2. *Set small, attainable goals.* Don't look at the retreat as having to accomplish all possible goals.
3. *Use an agenda, and stick to it.* Schedule the meeting for a fixed period of time, and appoint someone to take notes.
4. *Give everyone a chance to participate.* This is a critical step in establishing trust among the participants. People need to feel that they have been heard.
5. *Know the difference between consensus and agreement.* Participants don't have to see things the same way (agreement) in order to concur on a course of action (consensus).

But the talk at family retreats is not always about business. After a retreat, families often speak of the joy of sharing family values and stories of past family experiences. Thus, retreats can turn into vacations with participants enjoying each other's company socially. When members of an extended family grow to like each other, it strengthens the family as well as the company.

5-4c Family Councils

A logical follow-up to the retreat is the creation of a **family council**, in which family members meet to discuss values, policies, and a direction for the future. A family council is the organizational and strategic planning arm of a family. It provides a forum for listening to the ideas of all members and discovering what they believe in and want from the business. A family council formalizes the participation of the family in the business to a greater extent than a family retreat does. It can also be a focal point for planning the future of individual family members, the family as a whole, and the business, as well as how each relates to the others.

A council isn't a casual get-together. It should be a formal organization that provides governance for family members in their relationship with the business. Council members are normally elected by the extended adult family members. The representatives hold regular meetings, keep minutes, and make suggestions to the firm's board of directors. During the first several meetings, an acceptable mission statement is usually generated, as well as a family constitution.

Family businesses that have such councils find them useful for developing family harmony. Although council members are typically elected, extended family members are often invited to participate in events held in conjunction with the council meetings. The meetings are often fun and informative and may include speakers who discuss items of interest. Time may be set aside for sharing achievements, milestones, and family history. The younger generation is encouraged to participate because much of the process is designed to increase their understanding of family traditions and business interests and to prepare them for working effectively in the business.

family council
An organized group of family members who gather periodically to discuss family-related business issues.

5-4d Family Business Constitutions

As we just explained, family councils may be charged with the responsibility of writing a **family business constitution**, which is a statement of principles intended to guide a family firm through times of crisis and change, including the succession process. This is not usually a legally binding document, but it helps preserve the intentions of the founder and ensures that the business survives periods of change largely intact. When a transfer between generations occurs and there is no guiding document, issues such as ownership, performance, and compensation can become flashpoints for conflict.[24]

When Randall Clifford's father died in 1994, the ownership and control of Ventura Transfer Company, the oldest trucking company in California, were suddenly called into question. Clifford's stepmother sued him and his three brothers for an interest in the business. Then, to make matters worse, the four Clifford brothers began to struggle among themselves for control of the company. After a drawn-out legal battle, the sons decided to enlist the help of a consultant to draft a family business constitution. The resulting document helped the family sort out many of the issues that had plagued the transition process.[25]

A family business constitution, sometimes called a *family creed*, provides the framework for a family's system of governance of the firm and may include the following topics:[26]

- The core values that all family members should follow
- A process for decision making
- The benefits that family members may receive from the business
- A mechanism for introducing younger members to the family business and its governance structures
- A dispute resolution procedure
- The philanthropic ambitions of the family

At the end of her first year as owner of Two Men and a Truck, Mary Ellen Sheets found that she had accumulated a $1,000 profit. She immediately wrote 10 checks to various charities. Not realizing what her business was destined to become, Sheets did not draft a constitution at that point, but she did set the precedent. Today, giving back to the community is a core value of the company.[27]

family business constitution
A statement of principles intended to guide a family firm through times of crisis and change.

A family business constitution cannot foresee every eventuality, but like any such document, it can be amended as needed. The important point is that this document can smooth any transitions, including a change in leadership, which is the subject of the next section.

5-5 THE PROCESS OF LEADERSHIP SUCCESSION

Describe the process of managerial succession in a family business.

The task of preparing family members for careers, leadership, and ownership within the business is difficult and sometimes frustrating. Professional and managerial requirements are intertwined with family feelings and interests. Making the process work can take years.

In a 2014, PricewaterhouseCoopers (PwC) surveyed 2,484 key decision makers of family-owned businesses in over 40 countries. They investigated many characteristics of family businesses and the plans of their owners. Succession was identified as the critical issue. Approximately 32 percent of the responding firms intended to pass ownership to the next generation, but only about 16 percent have a documented succession plan in place.[28]

Because everyone is so uncomfortable with the subject, plans for succession often are not well developed or at least are poorly communicated. It is hard for the entrepreneurial owner to think of not being around and in charge. And the succeeding generation finds it difficult to confront mom and dad with the prospect of death. The successor may feel that she or he is appearing to be mercenary.

But ignoring the prospect of death does not make it go away. Failing to act can result in disaster. Consultants Deb Houden and Wendy Sage-Hayward describe death as an "undiscussable topic" and offer this advice:

> *The question to ask is how do families make an undiscussable topic more discussable? How can they put the tough, messy subjects on the table in such a way that everyone can talk in a meaningful, non-judgmental and calm manner? Families need to name the issue, start small and build capacity to take on these taboo topics. Building capacity takes time, effort and courage; it is hard—but given the consequences from continued avoidance, it is essential.*[29]

5-5a Available Family Talent

Companies that survive long enough to face a generational transition generally have talented, visionary leadership. But the leadership that made the business successful at one time may not be right as conditions change. A business is dependent, therefore, on developing or attracting effective leaders for the future. If the available talent is not sufficient, the owner must bring in outside leadership or supplement family talent to avoid a decline in the business under the leadership of second- or third-generation family members.

The question of competency is both critical and sensitive. With experience, individuals can improve their abilities. Therefore, younger family members should not be judged too harshly early on. In fact, learning from mistakes may be essential for later success. Parents may be overly cautious about delegating authority to their children, but how will those children be ready if they haven't tested their wings? When Richard A. Lumpkin asked his father to authorize him to create a holding company that would allow their firm to break into other businesses, his dad answered, "Son, I wouldn't be for that even if I thought it was a good idea." Lumpkin found the board of directors to be more receptive, and they convinced his father to allow the change. Twenty-five years later, Lumpkin's company, Consolidated Communications, Inc., was the 14th largest telephone company in the United States.[30]

In some cases, a younger family member's skills may actually help to rescue the company, especially when the business becomes mired in the past and fails to keep up with changing technology and emerging markets. Charles Johnson, Jr., and his sister Jessica took control of Johnson Security Bureau shortly before the unexpected death of their father in 2008. The company had been founded by their grandparents in 1962. There had been conflict between the second and third generations before Charles Sr. died. Charles Sr. was informal in bidding on projects and avoided technology, opposing a company website. After taking charge, Jessica and Charles Jr. moved forward with the website and formalized procedures, taking the company to a new level.[31]

A family firm should not accept the existing level of family talent as unchangeable. Using development programs to teach younger family members and improve their skills is imperative. It is not unusual for firms to specify training programs and other requirements in formal documents, such as a family business constitution. Some firms include mentoring as a part of such programs. *Mentoring* is the process by which an experienced person guides and supports the work, progress, and professional relationships of a new or less-experienced employee. In the family business, a mentor and protégé have the opportunity to navigate and explore family as well as business-related roles and responsibilities.[32]

Perhaps the fairest and most practical approach to leadership development is to recognize the right of family members to prove themselves. A period of development and testing may occur either in the family business or, preferably, in another organization. If children show themselves to be capable, they earn the right to increased leadership responsibility. If potential successors are found to have inadequate leadership abilities, preservation of the family business and the welfare of family members demand that they be passed over for promotion. The appointment of competent outsiders to these jobs, if necessary, increases the value of the firm for all family members who have an ownership interest in it.

5-5b Preparing for Succession

Sons or daughters do not typically assume leadership of a family firm at a particular moment in time. Instead, a long, drawn-out process is involved. This process can be intentionally designed and implemented, or it can simply occur as all parties age. In the latter case, no one should be surprised if the next generation is not prepared at the time a transition is necessary. Successful management and ownership transitions require thoughtful action by both the current and the future leadership teams. Family business educator Greg McCann proposed actions for both generations, as discussed in the following subsections.[33]

© AUREMAR/SHUTTERSTOCK.COM

RESPONSIBILITIES OF THE SENIOR GENERATION

Listed below are some topics that the senior generation should consider and some steps it should take:

1. *Communication.* Parents need to listen and ask questions. Communication can be used to build trust and to convey values. Providing support and feedback are important, but not just in a one-way direction.
2. *Planning.* Not only should the company's vision be articulated, but also the family's values and even the plan for settling the estate of the senior generation. Planning should encompass family members, employees, and owners.
3. *Accountability.* The senior generation engages in roles as both parent and business owner. In each case, there should be investments in and support for the development of the succeeding generation. That means holding the next generation accountable for their actions, especially those that relate to credibility and integrity.
4. *Owner development.* To prepare the next generation to participate in the governance of the firm, the senior generation should be specific about the job structure of an active owner-manager or board member.

5. *Long-term planning.* When asking the next generation to develop long-term plans that will prepare them for leadership, the current generation of leaders must simultaneously prepare their own plans. Such plans should take into account future business development, boards of directors and advisors, family councils, and other structures.

Because members of the junior generation sometimes have trouble seeing the senior generation as managers rather than parents, many seniors decide to bring in outside experts to help work through these steps.

RESPONSIBILITIES OF THE JUNIOR GENERATION

If prospective future leaders of the family enterprise expect to advance to executive positions, they must proactively share in their preparation by doing the following:

1. *Be open to communication.* The succeeding generation should understand the values that led to the creation and growth of the family enterprise and to its current mission. If they believe change is necessary, their actions should result from conscious decisions. They should seek to be fully informed about the history and direction of the company.
2. *Develop a personal action plan.* At this stage, prospective successors should seriously assess whether they have addressed the following questions: Who am I? What are my core values? What are the most important areas of my personal and professional life that I should work on?
3. *Implement the personal action plan.* This involves pursuing relevant education, training, and experience. Actions should lead to the establishment of personal credibility and marketability. The junior generation should not be joining the family business simply because they lack alternatives.
4. *Prepare for ownership.* Future leaders need to develop basic management skills, such as the ability to comprehend financial statements and to effectively supervise employees. They must grasp the role of a board of directors in terms of its relationship to the management team of the firm. And they need to understand the relationship between the business and the family.
5. *Design life plans.* Life plans are for both the individual and the business. What should the résumé of the family company CEO look like in five or ten years?

A key responsibility of junior generation members is to keep in mind that they are not entitled to a leadership position. Such positions need to be earned.

5-5c Transfer of Ownership

The succession process for a surviving family firm eventually requires the **transfer of ownership**. Questions of inheritance affect not only the leadership successor but also other family members who have no involvement in the business. In distributing their estate, parent-owners typically wish to treat all their children fairly, both those involved in the business and those on the outside. And for many family-controlled enterprises, nonfamily members may have shares of ownership in the firm.

One step taken by some parents involves changing the ownership structure of the firm. Those children active in the firm's management, for example, might be given common (voting) stock and others given preferred (nonvoting) stock.

transfer of ownership
Passing ownership of a family business to the next generation.

Typically, a variety of legal issues need to be resolved. Tax considerations are relevant, and they tend to favor gradual transfer of ownership to all heirs. As noted, however, transfer of equal ownership shares to all heirs may be inconsistent with the future successful operation of the business. Tax advantages should not be allowed to blind one to possible adverse effects on management.

There are also government regulations to protect minority shareholders. Outside investors, business partners, and even employees who may hold stock are not necessarily interested in watching the value of their stock lie dormant or deteriorate. Careless decisions by family members may lead to actions in civil courts.

Ideally, the founder has been able to arrange his or her personal holdings to create wealth outside the business as well as within it. This is an area where outside experts who grasp financial and estate planning, as well as tax law and accounting, can be invaluable. Planning and discussing the transfer of ownership is not easy, but it is strongly recommended. Over a period of time, the owner must reflect seriously on family talents and interests as they relate to the future of the firm. The plan for transfer of ownership can then be firmed up and modified as necessary when it is discussed with the children or other potential heirs. In discussing exit strategies in Chapter 13, we explain a variety of possible financial arrangements for the transfer of ownership.

In this chapter, we have tried to make one message very clear to prospective family business owners—families and family businesses are interrelated. Trying to separate them would be like trying to unscramble eggs. The better you understand that going in, the more successful you can be in both areas of your life. Despite what many people believe, family members can work together successfully and happily. Advance planning can help avoid a lot of problems, as well as boost the success of the business.

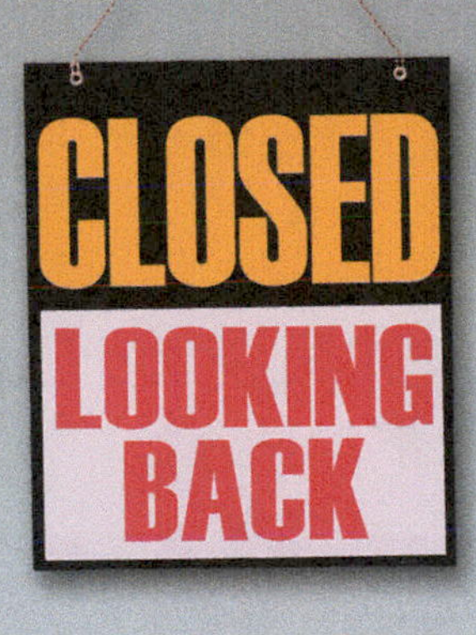

5-1. Define the terms *family* and *family business*.

- The word *family* refers to a group of people bound by a shared history and a commitment to share a future together while supporting the development and well-being of individual members.
- A majority of businesses in the United States and other countries with free-market economies fit some definition of family ownership.
- A *family business* is an organization in which either the individuals who established or acquired the firm or their descendants significantly influence the strategic decisions and life course of the firm.
- A family business can be described as an owner-managed business, a sibling partnership, or a cousin consortium.

5-2. Explain the forces that can keep a family business moving forward.

- The organizational culture of a family business is composed of the patterns of behaviors and beliefs that characterize a particular firm.
- The founder often leaves a deep imprint on the culture of a family firm.
- The long-term survival of the business is dependent on the commitment of family members. They may be committed to the family business for different reasons, and these reasons will likely determine the nature and strength of that commitment.

5-3. Describe the complex roles and relationships involved in a family business.

- Couples known as co-preneurs join in owning and managing a business together, which can strengthen or weaken their relationship.
- A primary and sensitive relationship exists between a founder and her or his son or daughter. Some children decide to work outside the company to gain experience before joining the family business.
- Siblings and other relatives may similarly strengthen or weaken their working and personal relationships through a family business.

- In-laws play a crucial role in the family business, either as direct participants or as sideline observers.
- The role of the founder's spouse is especially important, as he or she often serves as a mediator in family disputes and helps prepare the children for possible careers in the family business.

5-4. Identify management practices that enable a family business to function effectively.

- Good management practices are as important as good family relationships in the successful functioning of a family business.
- Motivation of nonfamily employees can be enhanced by open communication and fairness.
- Family retreats bring all family members together to discuss business and family matters.
- Family councils provide a formal framework for the family's ongoing discussion of family and business issues.
- Family business constitutions can guide a company through times of crisis or change.

5-5. Describe the process of managerial succession in a family business.

- Discussing and planning the transfer of leadership is difficult and sometimes frustrating.
- The quality of leadership talent available in the family determines the extent to which outside managers are needed.
- Succession is a long-term process starting early in the successor's life.
- The succession process requires actions and effective communication on the part of both the senior generation and the succeeding generation.
- Transfer of ownership involves issues of fairness, taxes, and managerial control.

Key Terms

co-preneurs p. 129
cousin consortium p. 124
family p. 124
family business p. 124
family business constitution p. 137
family council p. 136
family retreat p. 135
nepotism p. 126
organizational culture p. 127
owner-managed business p. 124
sibling partnership p. 124
socioemotional wealth p. 128
transfer of ownership p. 140

You Make the Call

Situation 1

Twin brothers Stefan and Dillon inherited the fruit-canning factory founded by their father just before they turned 30. It turned out they made a great team—one outstanding at production and operations, the other a natural at marketing and sales. Over the next three decades, they tripled the size of the enterprise. And they enjoyed each other's company, often vacationing together and making sure that their kids grew up more like siblings than cousins.

The brothers were in excellent health as they approached 60. They weren't thinking about retirement, but they had spent time and effort in developing the next generation for leadership. Then, out of the blue, they received an offer from a multinational corporation to buy their business at a huge premium.

The brothers turned to their children for their opinions. For Stefan's son and daughter, this was a no-brainer—take the money and move on. Dillon's son was of a different mind, though. He had always wanted to lead the family firm in its third generation. Stefan liked the idea of financial security and was happy with his children's reaction. Dillon was ready to step aside for a more comfortable life style, but wanted what was best for his son. A series of conversations and meetings began to turn ugly.

Question 1 What would you do if you were Stefan? What would you do if you were Dillon?

Question 2 What advice would you offer to Stefan and Dillon to maintain strong family relationships?

Situation 2

It took five tries, but Morris and Ellen finally succeeded as co-preneurs. They had tried businesses in different industries, but none was able to do more than put bread on the table—and they had five children to feed! But the fifth venture took off. They started a printing company specializing in designing and producing promotional brochures and grew it into the largest producer in their region.

The time they spent in the businesses took its toll, however. At one time or another, each of their children joined the firm, and at one time or another, each was fired. The couple was distant from three of their children. Two children returned to the family business after working for other firms and learning that their parents were not that different from other business owners. Their oldest son was a good technician but invariably failed with any projects he took on independently. The younger son was recognized by employees and customers as skilled both in management and in interpersonal communication. Unfortunately, he had a felony conviction for drug trafficking and was prohibited from driving motor vehicles.

Morris recently suffered a heart attack and has realized that he cannot continue forever. He and Ellen have to make a decision about the continuity of the business. Compounding their dilemma is the fact that they are in a declining industry, one in which electronic production is rapidly replacing paper.

Question 1 What advice do you have for Morris and Ellen?
Question 2 What recommendations do you have for preparing children to lead changes in a company?

Situation 3

Can owning a business be in your genes? What about if it's a franchise? Brothers Joe and Allen Hertzman mixed coleslaw and mopped floors in their father's Long John Silver's restaurants when they were kids. Today, the brothers own six Long John's Silver's, thirteen Rally's, and twenty-four Papa John's Pizza units. Both have been named franchisee of the year by their franchisors. When asked if they have different management styles, the brothers responded that they have some differences but intentionally have the same message and culture. Their saying is "Operate each store as if it's our only store."

Sources: "Bro Deals: Sibling Franchisees Are Building an Empire," *Entrepreneur*, August 2014, p. 102; and Debbie Selinsky, "Tri-Effective: Joe Hertzman Wins with Three Brands over Three Decades," http://www.franchising.com/articles/trieffective_joe_hertzman_wins_with_three_brands_over_three_decades.html, accessed January 22, 2015.

Question 1 How do you think growing up in a family business affects career decisions by children of the owners?
Question 2 If you were going to run a business with a family member, how would you go about deciding on the organizational culture you want to create?

Case 5

Iaccarino & Son (P. 654)

The case of Iaccarino & Son tracks a family firm through three generations. The Iaccarinos faced discrimination, economic upturns and downcycles, severe competition and more. The case addresses issues in succession, conflict, leadership, communication, and decision making.

Alternative Case for Chapter 5

Video Case 4, Two Men and a Truck, p. 652
Case 22, Pearson Air Conditioning & Service, p. 690

Endnotes

1. "The World's Biggest Public Companies," http://www.forbes.com/global2000, accessed January 18, 2015; and "America's Largest Private Companies," http://www.forbes.com/largest-private-companies, accessed January 18, 2015.
2. Frank Hoy and Pramodita Sharma, *The Entrepreneurial Family Business* (Upper Saddle River, NJ: Pearson Prentice Hall, 2010).
3. *Ibid.*
4. Meg Cadoux Hirshberg, "Goodbye and Thanks for All Your Stories," *Inc.*, September 2013, pp. 82–86.
5. "Carlson Credo," http://carlson.com/our-company/the-carlson-credo.do, accessed January 19, 2015.
6. Michael A. Klein, *Trapped in the Family Business* (Northampton, MA: MK Insights, 2012).
7. Tim Barnett, Kimberly Eddleston, and Franz Willi Kellermanns, "The Effects of Family versus Career Role Salience on the Performance of Family and Nonfamily Firms," *Family Business Review*, Vol. 22, No. 1 (March 2009), pp. 39–52; and Pramodita Sharma and Frank Hoy, "Family Business Roles," in *The Landscape of Family Business, op. cit.*, pp. 113–142.

8. Pascual Berrone, Cristina Cruz, and Luis R. Gomez-Mejia, "Socioemotional Wealth in Family Firms: Theoretical Dimensions, Assessment Approaches, and Agenda for Future Research," *Family Business Review*, Vol. 25, No. 3 (2012), pp. 258–279.
9. Sarah E. Needleman, "Where Every Day Is Father's Day," *The Wall Street Journal*, http://online.wsj.com/article/SB10001424052702303823104576391841138964286.html, accessed January 19, 2015.
10. Greg McCann, *When Your Parents Sign the Paychecks* (Charleston, SC: CreateSpace Publishing, 2013), p. 63.
11. PricewaterhouseCoopers, "Playing Their Hand: U.S. Family Businesses Make Their Bid for the Future," http://www.pwc.com/us/en/private-company-services/publications/assets/pwc-family-business-survey-us-report.pdf, accessed January 19, 2015.
12. Veronica Dagher, "You're Fired . . . But I Hope to See You at the Next Family Reunion," *The Wall Street Journal*, February 3, 2014, p. R7.
13. Kirby Rosplock, "Family Dynamics in the Family Firm," in *The Landscape of Family Business, op. cit.*, pp. 143–166.
14. "The Ken Blanchard Companies: Our Story," http://www.kenblanchard.com/About-Us/Our-Story, accessed March 1, 2015.
15. Otis W. Baskin, "Understanding Conflict in the Family Business (Part I)," http://blog.thefbcg.com/understanding-conflict-in-the-family-business/?utm_source=Blog+Archive+December+2014&utm_campaign=November+2014+Blog+Email&utm_medium=email, accessed January 21, 2015.
16. Matt Alderton, "How to Keep Your Family Business Running Well into the Future," http://www.nfib.com/article/4-family-business-survival-tips-64918, accessed March 1, 2015.
17. Mousumi Saha Kumar, "Success Story of Adolf Dassler, the Founder of Adidas," http://www.successstories.co.in/success-story-of-adolf-dassler-the-founder-of-adidas, accessed January 21, 2015.
18. "In Walt's Own Words: His Brother Roy," http://www.waltdisney.org/storyboard/walts-own-words-his-brother-roy, accessed January 21, 2015.
19. Christopher Hann, "It's a Family: Seven Lessons Family Startups Need to Learn, for Harmony at Home and at the Office," *Entrepreneur*, March 2014, pp. 94–104.
20. "Three Things to Never Tell an Entrepreneur about Her/His Spouse," http://timberry.bplans.com/2014/06/3-things-never-to-tell-an-entrepreneur-about-herhis-spouse.html, accessed January 21, 2015.
21. Raphael Amit and Belen Villalonga, "Financial Performance of Family Firms," in Leif Melin, Matias Nordqvist, and Pramodita Sharma, eds., *The SAGE Handbook of Family Business* (London: SAGE Publications, 2014), pp. 157–178.
22. "Two Men and a Truck: History," http://www.twomenandatruck.com/history-of-two-men-and-a-truck, accessed January 21, 2015.
23. David Lansky, "Family Meetings: Some Guidelines," https://www.ahola.com/Articles/Lansky-Family-Meetings-Some-Guidlines.aspx, accessed January 21, 2015.
24. Massimo Bau, Karin Hellerstedt, Mattias Nordqvist, and Karl Wennberg, "Succession in Family Firms," in *The Landscape of Family Business, op. cit.*, pp. 167–197.
25. Matthew Fogel, "A More Perfect Business," http://www.inc.com/magazine/20030801/familybusiness.html, accessed January 21, 2015.
26. Ken McCracken, Matthew Woods, and Charlie Tee, "Governance and Management," http://www.globelawandbusiness.com/BFG/sample.pdf, accessed January 21, 2015.
27. "Two Men and a Truck: Mary Ellen Sheets," http://www.twomen.com/mary-ellen-sheets, accessed January 21, 2015.
28. PricewaterhouseCoopers, "2014 Family Business Survey," http://www.pwc.com/gx/en/pwc-family-business-survey/about.jhtml, accessed March 9, 2015.
29. Deb Houden and Wendy Sage-Hayward, "Undiscussables: Dealing with Elephants in Family Business," *The Family Business Advisor*, November 2014.
30. Hoy and Sharma, *Entrepreneurial Family Firms, op. cit.*
31. "Johnson Security Bureau: About Us," http://www.johnsonsecuritybureau.com, accessed March 1, 2015; and Adriana Gardella, "This Is Not Your Father's Company," http://boss.blogs.nytimes.com/2011/12/16/this-is-not-your-fathers-company/?scp=1&sq=This%20Is%20Not%20Your%20Father%E2%80%99s%20Company&st=cse, accessed January 22, 2015.
32. For an extended discussion of various aspects of mentoring in the family firm, see Barbara Spector (ed.), *The Family Business Mentoring Handbook* (Philadelphia: Family Business Publishing Co., 2004). Only one of many resources on mentoring, this book contains articles outlining a number of proven mentoring strategies, as well as case examples of family companies that have used these approaches to achieve effective succession transitions. It addresses processes and strategies as they apply specifically to family businesses.
33. Greg McCann, "Cultivating Ownership in the Next Generation," in *The Family Business Shareholder's Handbook, op. cit.*, pp. 120–121.

© DESRUS BENEDICTE/SIPA/NEWSCOM

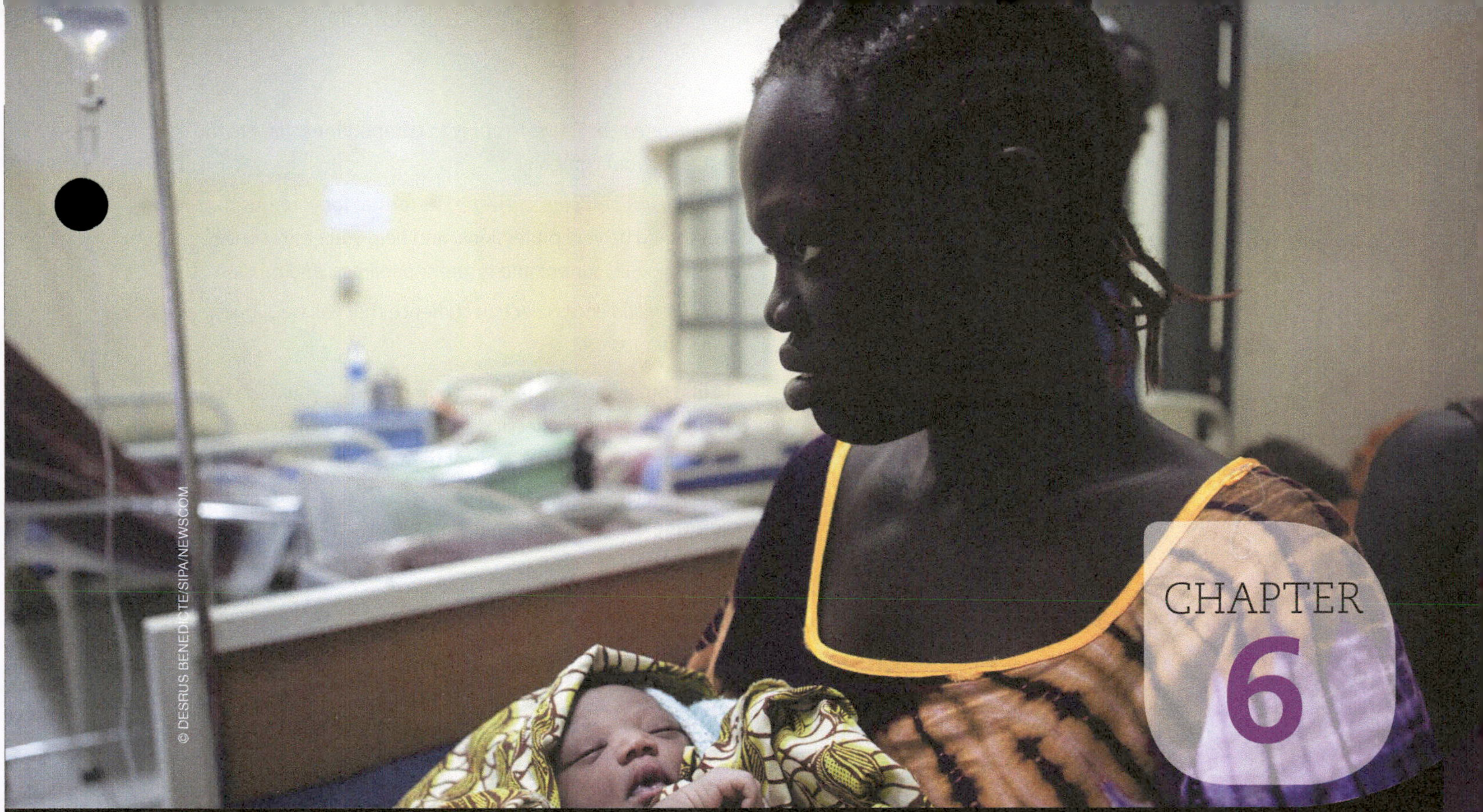

CHAPTER 6

The Business Plan: Visualizing the Dream

According to the World Health Organization (WHO), approximately 1,000 women die every day from preventable causes linked to pregnancy and childbirth. A full 99 percent of these deaths occur in developing countries, with women in poor rural communities most at risk. Most of these problems can be avoided through skilled care during childbirth.

Meg Wirth spent five years with Commons Capital, where she identified challenges in global health. Based on her research, Wirth founded Maternova in 2009 as a mission-driven, for-profit organization. The company adopted a two-pronged approach to driving revenue: (1) the aggregation and sales of select low-tech medical devices in a pioneering e-commerce marketplace, and (2) an innovative open-source platform, where health-care workers can connect globally.

In the SPOTLIGHT
Maternova
http://maternova.net

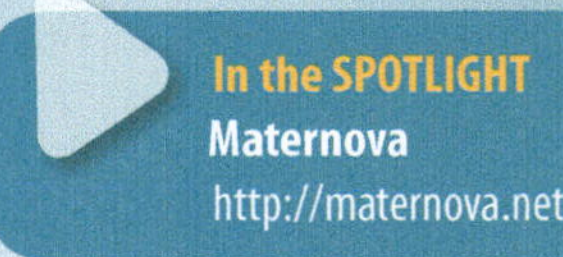

Looking for capital to fund this new enterprise, Wirth and her small team entered business plan competitions and two startup incubators in hopes of gaining visibility and needed cash. In fact, entering business plan competitions has served as part of the team's overall bootstrapping strategy. In the process, they have discovered that the chance to present a business plan to the right audience makes entering these competitions a no-brainer.

OPEN LOOKING AHEAD

After studying this chapter, you should be able to. . .

6-1. Explain the purpose and objectives of business plans.

6-2. Give the rationale for writing (or not writing) a business plan when starting a new venture.

6-3. Explain the concept and process for developing a firm's business model.

6-4. Describe the preferred content and format for a business plan.

6-5. Offer practical advice on writing a business plan.

6-6. Explain how to pitch to investors.

6-7. Identify available sources of assistance in preparing a business plan.

6-8. Maintain the proper perspective when writing a business plan.

Through their participation in business plan competitions, the Maternova team has garnered a number of benefits, including the following:

- Growth in business relationships and an expanded international network of partners
- Valuable press coverage nationally and internationally
- Annual compounded revenue growth of over 200 percent
- Positioning of the company for government contracts
- Expanded product lines and improved online capabilities to drive client revenue

The Maternova team credits online business-planning software called *LivePlan* for helping them turn their business model into a winning business plan. (*LivePlan* was developed by Palo Alto Software to walk an entrepreneur through the process of writing a plan, along with providing advice when needed.)

The Maternova team offers these tips for anyone considering entering a business plan competition:

- *Do your research:* It pays to apply to competitions that are the best fit for your company.
- *Use good business plan software:* The format for your business plan should be very professional and help you easily convey business goals, current and future capabilities, and mission.
- *Know your audience:* Select an audience that will be aligned with your mission.

To find out about business plan competitions, you don't have to look far. Many universities and colleges with business and entrepreneurship programs sponsor them annually. Also, a large number of online resources, including www.bizplancompetitions.com, provide directories and calendars of national and international competitions.

Sources: Written by Sherisa Aguirre, Senior Content Strategist, Palo Alto Software. Resources include http://maternova.net, accessed January 21, 2015; http://www.liveplan.com, accessed January 21, 2015; and http://www.bizplancompetitions.com, accessed January 21, 2015.

When you mention an idea for a new business to a friend who's also a business owner, she says, "You'll need to prepare a business plan." While the business idea sounds great, spending hours writing some formal document is not exactly your idea of fun, and you wonder if it is really necessary. After all, you know an entrepreneur who started and successfully grew a company based on an idea developed on the back of a napkin over dinner at a local restaurant. And isn't it true that the founders of such notable companies as Microsoft, Dell Computers, *Rolling Stone* magazine, and Calvin Klein all started their businesses without business plans?

Explain the purpose and objectives of business plans.

6-1 AN OVERVIEW OF THE BUSINESS PLAN

To answer the question of whether you should write a business plan, you'll first need to understand its purpose and objectives, and that there is no one correct formula for preparing a business plan. Opportunities are so diverse in size as well as growth potential that no single plan will work in all situations. But, in general, a **business plan** is a document that outlines the basic concept underlying a business—specifically, what problem will be solved—and describes how you will execute your plan to solve the problem. A business plan can also be thought of as an entrepreneur's game plan. It gives shape to the dreams and hopes that have motivated the entrepreneur to take the startup plunge. The plan should lay out your basic idea for the venture and include descriptions of where you are now, where you want to go, and how you intend to get there. John Mullins, the author of *The New Business Road Test*, says that the following three key elements should be in every business plan:[1]

business plan
A document that outlines the basic concept underlying a business and describes how that concept will be realized.

- A logical statement of a problem and its solution
- A significant amount of cold, hard evidence
- Candor about the risks, gaps, and assumptions that might be proved wrong

Writing a business plan is an opportunity to assess if a good idea is also a good investment opportunity. It needs to provide evidence that your business can sell enough products or services to make a satisfactory profit. Also, as emphasized in Chapter 1, your personal aspirations and motivations deserve careful thought. *If the business does not align with your personal goals, you are not likely to succeed, and you certainly will not enjoy the journey.*

A business plan, if done well, is a tool to be used by company *insiders* for direction and to aid in the development of relationships with *outsiders* who could help the company achieve its goals. Exhibit 6.1 provides an overview of those who might have an interest in a business plan for a proposed venture.

The first group consists of the internal users of the plan: the entrepreneur, the new firm's management, and its employees. The business plan provides a framework that helps the entrepreneur and the management team focus on important issues and activities for the new venture. And it helps the entrepreneur communicate his or her vision to current and prospective employees of the firm.

The business plan can also be helpful with outsiders. To make the company successful, the entrepreneur must convince outsiders—potential customers, suppliers, lenders, and investors—to become linked with the firm. Why should they do business with your startup, rather than with an established firm? They need evidence that you will be around in the future. Professor Amar Bhide at Tufts University, who conducts extensive research in strategy and entrepreneurship, explains, "Some entrepreneurs may have an innate capability to outperform their rivals, acquire managerial skills, and thus build a flourishing business. But it is difficult for customers (and others) to identify founders with these innate capabilities."[2]

6-2 WILL WRITING A PLAN MAKE A DIFFERENCE?

Give the rationale for writing (or not writing) a business plan when starting a new venture.

Will writing a business plan make a difference? That all depends. The justification often used for not writing a business plan goes something like this: "Companies that start up based on business plans are no more successful than those that do not." It is

EXHIBIT 6.1 Users of Business Plans

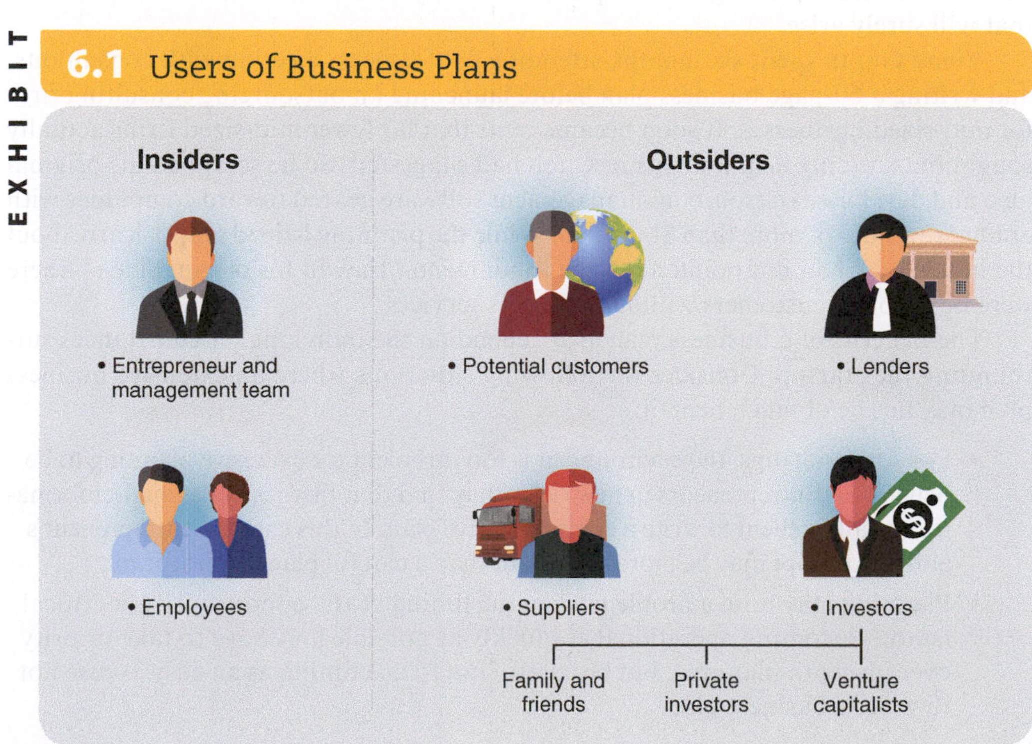

true that studies attempting to measure the success of entrepreneurs with business plans against the success of those without them have produced mixed results. Some findings suggest a relationship; others find none.

6-2a The Balance Between Planning and Executing

Given what we know about companies that were started without business plans, having a plan is clearly not an absolute prerequisite for success. *But this simply tells us that the business plan is not the business.* Some entrepreneurs spend days, if not weeks, writing a 60-page business plan with another 50 pages of appendices but are not effective at executing the plan. In such cases, we can say confidently that writing the plan accomplished little, if anything. Only if you effectively *execute* the business plan does it have a chance of making a difference. Thomas Stemberg, the founder of Staples, who later became a venture capitalist, says it well:

> *In my experience, entrepreneurs often confuse envisioning what a business will be with laying the foundation for what it could be. So they dream big dreams and construct detailed business plans, which is fine. But it's nowhere near as important as putting in place as early as humanly possible the people and systems that will carry them through their journey, no matter what unexpected directions, changing markets or technology force them to take. To me, business plans are interesting chiefly as indications of how an entrepreneur thinks. . . . If you have the right management team and an exciting market, the rest will take care of itself.*[3]

Thus, an entrepreneur must find the right balance between planning and becoming operational. No matter how well your plan has been thought out, unexpected events will happen. One of the key attributes of a successful entrepreneurial team is adaptability, regardless of what the business plan says to do. Boxer Mike Tyson once commented, "Everybody has a plan until they get punched in the face." Starting a business can be a bit like a prizefight.[4] You plan, but then you have to adapt to the obstacles that will surely arise.

Vinay Gupta spent six months attending conferences, meeting with consultants, and writing a 60-page business plan before launching an outsourcing consulting firm for mid-sized businesses. It soon became clear that far fewer mid-sized firms actually sought outsourcing help than his research had suggested. So he scrapped his original idea and developed outsourcing-management software geared toward companies with annual revenues of more than $1 million. While the planning helped Gupta learn about the industry, it had not pointed out the fundamental flaw in his original idea—there were not enough customers willing to buy his services.[5]

The benefits of a business plan also depend on the individual circumstances surrounding the startup. Consider the following situations where an extensive business plan may not be of much benefit:

- For some startups, the environment is too turbulent for extensive planning to be beneficial. Entrepreneurs in new fields may find that there is not enough information to allow them to write a comprehensive plan. In this case, an entrepreneur's ability to adapt may be more important than a careful plan for the future.
- Planning may pose a problem when the timing of the opportunity is a critical factor. Becoming operational as quickly as possible may have to take priority over in-depth planning, but be careful not to use timing as an easy excuse not to write a business plan.

- A business may be so constrained by a shortage of capital that planning is not an option. In a study of firms identified by *Inc.* magazine as the fastest-growing firms in the United States, Amar Bhide concluded that planning may not make sense for some companies: "Capital-constrained entrepreneurs cannot afford to do much prior analysis and research. The limited profit potential and high uncertainty of the opportunity they usually pursue also make the benefits low compared to the costs."[6]

Should You Write a Business Plan?
Before you decide not to write a plan, consider that a lender or other investor might demand to see a business plan before investing in your venture. Wouldn't you require the same before investing your personal savings or, even more important, your family's savings?

Although there are times when writing a carefully documented business plan is not needed, more often than not entrepreneurs resist writing a business plan because they lack the discipline to do so. Frank Moyes, a successful entrepreneur who for many years taught courses on business planning at the University of Colorado, offers the following observation:

> *Perhaps the most important reason to write a business plan is that it requires you to engage in a rigorous, thoughtful, and often painful process that is essential before you start a venture. It requires you to answer hard questions about your venture. Why is there a need for your product/service? Who is your target market? How is your product/service different than your competitor? What is your competitive advantage? How profitable is the business, and what are the cash flows? How should you fund the business?*[7]

So, a business plan may not be needed in some situations, especially if you are the only person working in the business. But if you want to capture the future potential of an opportunity and make a difference in lives, planning is the rule, not the exception. Remember Ewing Marion Kauffman's words from Chapter 1, "You should not choose to be a common company. It is your right to build an uncommon company if you can."[8] Building an uncommon company requires thoughtful planning and then execution. Deciding what you want the business to be and to accomplish is vital and deserves considerable thought. Above all, be intentional, which comes from having to justify your beliefs and assumptions about your startup—that is what a business plan is all about.

6-2b What Form Will the Business Plan Take?

For most entrepreneurs, the issue is not *whether* to plan but *when* and *how* to engage in effective planning, given the situation. As already noted, different situations lead to different needs—and to different levels of planning. In a truly entrepreneurial setting, the rationale for writing a business plan is to assess the feasibility of the opportunity to create economic value for the owners and investors. But many small business owners may not prepare a plan until they are required to do so, probably because somebody else—like the bank's loan officer—wants it from them.

In addition to deciding when to plan, a related issue is the form that the planning will take. When starting a business, an entrepreneur has to make some trade-offs, as preparing a plan requires time and money, two resources that are always in short supply. The entrepreneur has two basic choices when it comes to writing a business plan: the *short plan* or the *comprehensive plan*.

THE SHORT PLAN

As noted earlier, extensive planning may be of limited value when there is a great amount of uncertainty in the environment or when timing is a critical factor in capturing an opportunity. A **short plan** is an abbreviated form of the traditional business plan, which addresses only the most important issues in a firm's success, including the following:

short plan
An abbreviated business plan that presents only the most important issues and projections for the business.

- The problem that needs to be solved for customers
- The strategy that will be developed to solve the problem
- The business model (to be described shortly)
- Measures used to gauge success
- Milestones to be met
- Tasks and responsibilities of the team

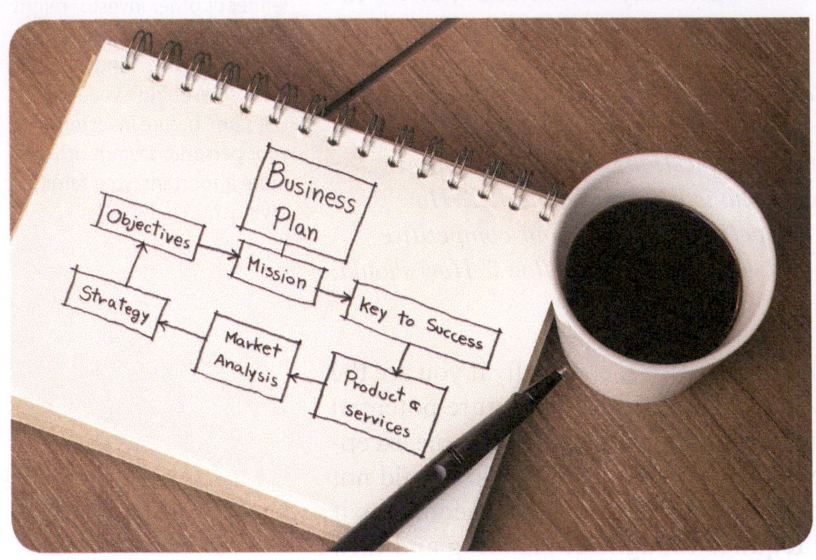

© DT10/SHUTTERSTOCK.COM

A short plan can also be used when trying to attract investors to the business. Some investors will want to begin by reading the full comprehensive business plan on the way to making a decision about the investment. Others will want to see an abbreviated presentation to learn whether the business idea sparks their interest. They might want to hear a 15- to 30-minute presentation, consisting of 10 to 15 PowerPoint slides, or what is called a *pitch* (discussed more fully later in the chapter).

THE COMPREHENSIVE PLAN

When entrepreneurs and investors speak of a business plan, they are usually referring to a **comprehensive plan**, a complete business plan that provides an in-depth analysis of the critical factors that will determine a firm's success or failure, along with all the underlying assumptions. Such a plan is beneficial when you are describing a new opportunity (startup), facing significant change in the business or the external environment (changing demographics, new legislation, developing industry trends), or explaining a complex business situation. But before we examine the content of a comprehensive plan, we need to explain the *business model*, which should be used when preparing a business plan. Think of the business model as a major component of the foundation for the business plan.

comprehensive plan
A complete business plan that provides an in-depth analysis of the critical factors that will determine a firm's success or failure, along with all the underlying assumptions.

6-3 BEGIN WITH THE BUSINESS MODEL[9]

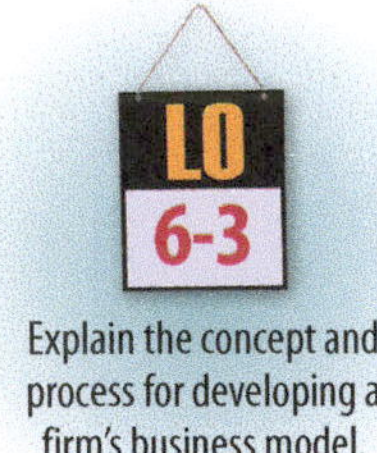

Explain the concept and process for developing a firm's business model.

The term *business model* has become a popular phrase in business, especially among entrepreneurs and their investors. Ramon Casadesus-Masanell and Joan Ricart at Harvard University emphasize the significance of developing an effective business model:

> *There has never been so much interest in business models as there is today; seven out of 10 companies are trying to create innovative business models, and 98 percent are modifying existing ones, according to a recent survey. . . . Strategy has been the primary building block of competitiveness over the past three decades, but in the future, the quest for sustainable advantage may well begin with the business model.*[10]

6-3a What Is a Business Model?

While widely discussed in business circles, business models are little understood by most businesspeople in small and large firms alike. Simply stated, a **business model** explains in a systematic and clear way how a business will generate profits and cash flows. It is the "nuts and bolts" of how a business will make money. As such, it measures the anticipated financial outcomes of the management's strategic decisions and activities that determine a company's profits and cash flows. It is also important to remember that businesses do not operate in a vacuum: The eventual success or failure of a business model depends in large part on how it interacts with the business models of competitors.

Information about Business Models

The following resources offer additional information about business models:

- Andrea Ovans, "What Is a Business Model?" *Harvard Business Review*, January 23, 2015, https://hbr.org/2015/01/what-is-a-business-model.
- Alexander Osterwalder, *Value Proposition Canvas* (Hoboken, NJ: John Wiley & Sons, 2014, http://www.businessmodelgeneration.com/downloads/value_proposition_canvas.pdf.
- Alexander Osterwalder and Yves Pigneur, *Business Model Generation* (Hoboken, NJ: John Wiley & Sons, 2010).

Webinars:

- "Business Model Canvas Explained," https://www.youtube.com/watch?v=QoAOzMTLP5s.
- "How to Design, Test and Build Business Models," https://www.youtube.com/watch?v=RzkdJiax6Tw.

6-3b Developing a Business Model

Some business models are easy to understand. A firm produces a product and/or service and sells it to customers; if sales exceed expenses, the company makes a profit. Other models are less straightforward. For instance, television broadcasting is part of a complex network of distributors, content creators, advertisers, and viewers. How the eventual profits and cash flows are created and shared depends on a number of competing factors, which are not always clear at the outset. Furthermore, e-commerce is giving rise to new business models. Consider auctions, one of the oldest ways for setting prices for such things as agricultural commodities and antiques. Today, the Internet has popularized the auction model and broadened its use to a wide array of goods and services.

In a startup, where there is so much uncertainty, a business model forces an entrepreneur to be disciplined and avoid wishful thinking about financial projections. When it comes time to create a business plan, the entrepreneur needs to know the drivers that will determine the firm's future profits and cash flows. And a business model can provide the best evidence as to whether a business concept can be translated into a viable, profitable business and the size of the investment required to make it happen. Exhibit 6.2 provides a basic overview of the process for building a business model for a company with two sources of revenues.

As shown at the top of Exhibit 6.2, an entrepreneur should begin by developing the venture's mission statement, its strategic goals, and the principles that are to guide its operations. Four key elements then make up the business model: (1) the revenue model, (2) cost structures, (3) the required resources to grow the business, and (4) business model risk. Let's briefly consider each element.

REVENUE MODEL

The **revenue model** identifies the nature and types of a company's sources of revenue. The more common revenue models follow:

- *Volume or unit-based revenue model.* Customers pay a fixed price per unit in exchange for a product or service.
- *Subscription/membership revenue model.* Customers pay a fixed amount at regular intervals, prior to receiving a product or service.
- *Advertising-based revenue model.* Customers pay based on cost per impression, cost per click, or cost per acquisition.
- *Licensing revenue model.* Customers pay a one-time licensing fee to be able to use or resell the product or service.

EXHIBIT 6.2 Basic Business Model Framework

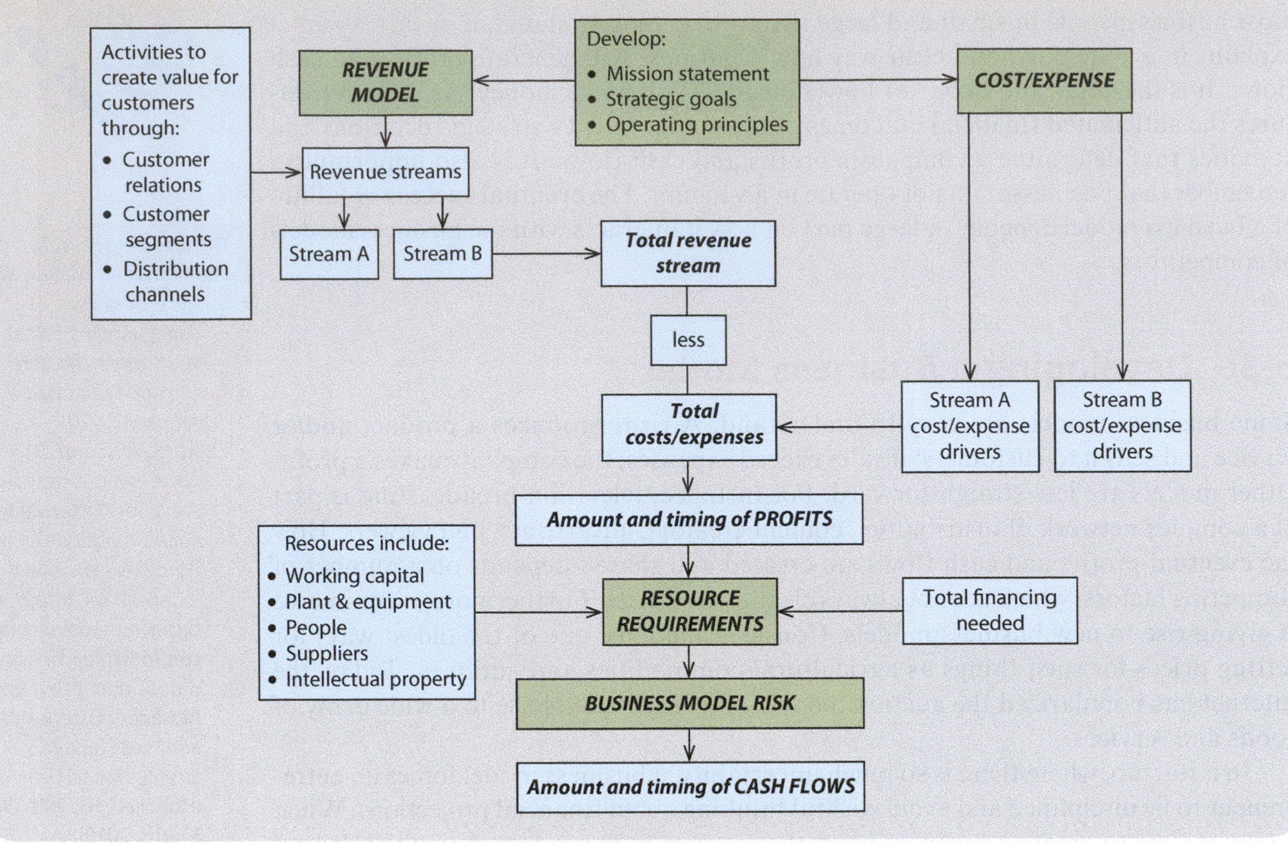

We can further categorize the actual revenue streams as follows:

1. *Single stream*, where a firm's revenues come from a single product or service
2. *Multiple streams*, where a business realizes revenues from a combination of multiple products and services
3. *Interdependent streams*, where a company's revenues come from selling one or more products and/or services as a way to generate revenues from other products and/or services, such as printers and printer cartridges
4. *Loss leader*, where one or several revenue streams are sold at a loss in order to create sales in a profitable revenue stream

These revenue streams are driven by a firm's ability to create value for its customers through activities such as customer relations, customer segmentation, and its choice of channels of distribution.

When forecasting revenues, an entrepreneur will find that the answers to a number of key questions can provide the rationale for future sales estimates:

1. Who are your most likely customers?
2. How are they different from the general population?
3. What events will trigger the need or desire for your type of product or service?
4. When will these events occur? Can they be predicted?

business model
An analysis of how a firm plans to create profits and cash flows given its revenue sources, its cost structures, the required size of investment, and sources of risk.

revenue model
A component of the business model that identifies the nature and types of a company's sources of revenue.

5. How will customers make decisions on whether or not to buy your product or service?
6. What will be the key decision factors?
7. How will your product or service compare to that of the competition on these key factors?
8. Will these differences be meaningful to the customer?
9. Are these differences known to the customer?
10. How can your product or service be exposed to your most likely potential customers?

Again, the goal is to differentiate the value that a company provides for its customers. Without such differentiation, a business has the wrong revenue model and will lack a competitive advantage.

COST STRUCTURES

Cost structures consist of the drivers that affect a firm's costs of goods sold, especially the cost of producing one unit of product or service, and the company's operating expenses, such as payroll, selling activities, administrative costs, and marketing expenses. In other words, you want to know what activities drive these expenses, which can vary with either time or volume of sales. You then need to classify these costs and expenses in terms of the following:

- *Fixed costs*. Costs that do not vary at all with volume, such as rent expenses.
- *Variable costs*. Expenses that vary directly and proportionately with changes in volume—for example, sales commissions.
- *Semi-variable costs*. Expenses that include both variable costs and fixed costs. These costs vary in the direction of, but not proportionately with, changes in the volume of sales, such as certain types of payrolls that change as a firm becomes larger but do not change proportionally with sales changes.

Once an entrepreneur understands the company's revenue model and cost structures, he or she needs to assess the firm's resource requirements.

KEY RESOURCE REQUIREMENTS

Another key component of a business model is the **key resource requirements** to achieve positive cash flows and profits. Resources include the amount of investment in hard assets, such as equipment and buildings, as well as the amount of working capital in the form of operating cash, accounts receivable, and inventory. They also include the people, suppliers, key partners, and intellectual property needed to achieve the business's mission.

BUSINESS MODEL RISK

When designing a business model, an entrepreneur must anticipate **business model risk**; that is, he or she must consider changes that can affect the level of risk in a given business model and how the model can adjust to them. It is not enough to have a business model that provides a competitive advantage given the present circumstances. Consideration must be given as to how the model will be affected by changing circumstances, such as changes in demand for and supply of the products or services offered, and how the competition will respond to the firm's entry into the market. In other words, an entrepreneur must continually be anticipating what can go wrong with the firm's business model and what can be done if it does.

Cost structures
A component of the business model that provides a framework for estimating a firm's cost of goods sold and operating expenses.

key resource requirements
A component of the business model that provides estimates of the types and amounts of resources required to achieve positive profits and cash flows.

business model risk
A component of the business model that identifies risks in the model and how the model can adjust to them.

Living the Dream

ENTREPRENEURIAL EXPERIENCES

Changing the Business Model

When Jen Falso and Lisa Assenza met in 1998, the two quickly became great friends and came up with the idea of painting furniture and glassware to make some extra cash. Falso and Assenza began selling their HuePhoria hand-painted goods at local fundraisers and through word of mouth to get their hobby-turned-business into motion. At the outset, they painted wine glasses that were more creative than what they were seeing in stores—and more durable.

After selling more than 5,000 glasses in two years, they hit a point where they could not keep up with demand. Also, they could not offer the glasses to retail stores at a wholesale price that would keep them in business. So, in 2005, they partnered with another friend, Kathy Berger, to help HuePhoria glassware make the leap into mass production.

The partners thought they had a winning business model, selling their product to upscale gift boutiques. But when U.S. consumer spending shriveled in 2008, upscale gift stores that sold products like HuePhoria's drastically cut back their inventory.

They had been attending about four gift shows a year in New York and Atlanta in order to reach prospective buyers. Each show cost the four-employee company about $10,000. In previous years, the shows had paid off through dozens of new orders. But by late 2008, Berger estimated that nearly 40 percent of their independent retail customers were struggling financially, with some even filing for bankruptcy. So they decided to focus on selling through HuePhoria's website. They added a greater variety of partyware products and developed relationships with customers that were willing to manage the inventory and ship product on-demand. It was a way to expand product offerings without the expense of housing the inventory.

And they looked for ways to capitalize on HuePhoria's loyal customer base of moms. They launched the "Ball Mom" program, which offered women startup kits so that they could host parties and sell HuePhoria products for 25 percent of sales.

The new strategies paid off. Sales in the first quarter of 2011 increased 72 percent from the previous year. The partners credit their improved financials to their willingness to try a new business model when the old one wasn't working.

Sources: Based on Kelly K. Spors, "Banking on a New Business Model," *Entrepreneur*, April 25, 2011, http://www.entrepreneur.com/article/219530, accessed January 5, 2015; and http://www.huephoria.com.

Describe the preferred content and format for a business plan.

6-4 PREPARING A BUSINESS PLAN: THE CONTENT AND FORMAT

Like writing a term paper or report, getting started in writing a business plan is usually the hardest part. Recall that in Chapter 3, we emphasized the importance of first conducting a feasibility analysis and writing a business plan only if your idea seems viable. Three elements must be evident from the feasibility analysis before you move on to the business plan: (1) strong market potential, (2) an attractive industry, and (3) the right individual or team to execute the plan.[11]

Once the business model has been established and the feasibility analysis is completed, it's time to begin the process of writing a business plan. For this, two issues are of primary concern: (1) the content and format of the plan and (2) the effectiveness of the written presentation.

When considering the content of a business plan, continue to think first and foremost about the opportunity, as identified by your feasibility analysis. Strategies and financial plans will follow naturally if the opportunity is a good one. The business plan should give thorough consideration to the following basic factors (presented graphically in Exhibit 6.3):

1. The *opportunity* should reflect the potential and the attractiveness of the market and industry.
2. *Critical resources* include not just money but also human assets (suppliers, accountants, lawyers, investors, etc.) and hard assets (accounts receivable, inventories, etc.). An entrepreneur should think of ways to minimize the resources necessary for startup.
3. The *entrepreneurial team* must possess integrity, as well as breadth and depth of experience.
4. The *financing structure*—how a firm is financed (i.e., debt versus equity) and how the ownership percentage is shared by the founders and investors—will have a significant impact on an entrepreneur's incentive to work hard. The goal is to find a win-win deal.
5. The *context* (or external factors) of an opportunity includes the regulatory environment, interest rates, demographic trends, inflation, and other factors that inevitably change but cannot be controlled by the entrepreneur.

Thus, the business plan will need to demonstrate that the entrepreneur has pulled together the right opportunity, the right resources, the right people, and the right financing structure, all within the right context. Admittedly, there will always be uncertainties and ambiguities; the unanticipated is bound to happen. But by making decisions about these key factors, you can be sure that you are dealing with the important issues, and this will help you in determining the appropriate content to include in the plan.

EXHIBIT 6.3 Key Factors for Success

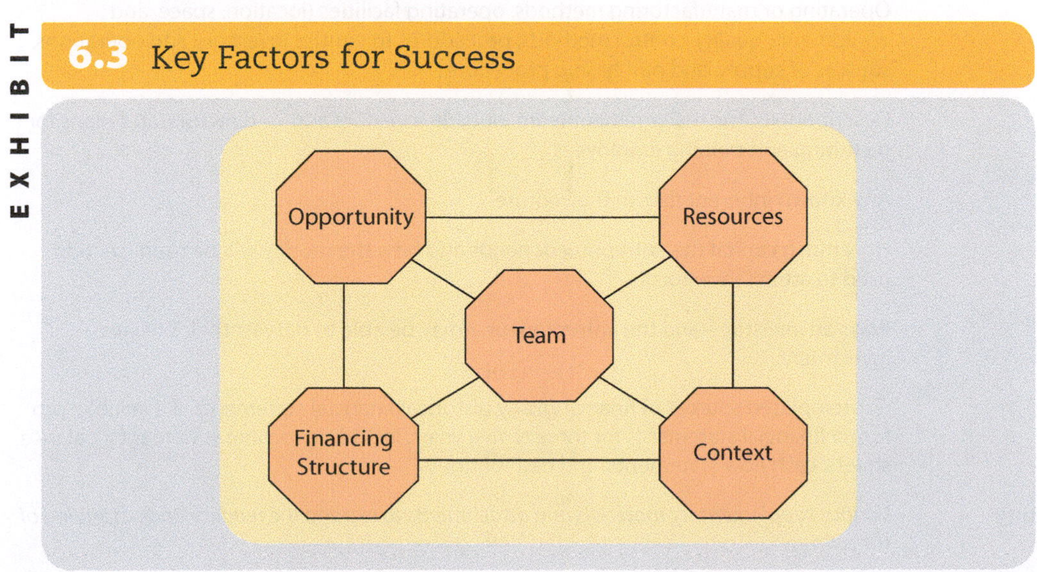

There is no single format to be followed in writing a business plan. However, investors want to see the plan in a format that is familiar to them. Presenting a business plan with a unique format would be a mistake.

Exhibit 6.4 summarizes the major sections common to most business plans. A brief overview of each of these sections follows.[12] (Chapters 7 through 13 take an in-depth look at each section of the business plan.)

6-4a Cover Page

The cover page should contain the following information:

- Company name, address, phone number, fax number, and website
- Tagline and company logo

EXHIBIT

6.4 Abbreviated Business Plan Outline

Section Heading	Information Provided
Cover Page	Company name, logo, tagline, contact information, copy number, date prepared, and disclaimer (if needed)
Table of Contents	Listing of the key sections of the business plan
Executive Summary	One- to three-page overview of the significant points, intended to motivate the reader to continue reading
Company Description	Company objectives, the nature of the business, its primary product or service, its current status (startup, buyout, or expansion) and history (if applicable), and the legal form of organization
Industry, Target Customer, and Competitor Analysis	Key characteristics of the industry, including the different segments, and the niche where you plan to compete
Product/Service Plan	Justification for why people will buy the product or service, based on its unique features
Marketing Plan	Marketing strategy, including the methods of identifying and attracting customers, selling approach, type of sales force, distribution channels, types of sales promotions and advertising, and credit and pricing policies
Operations and Development Plan	Operating or manufacturing methods, operating facilities (location, space, and equipment), quality-control methods, procedures to control inventory and operations, sources of supply, and purchasing procedures
Management Team	Description of the management team, outside investors and/or directors, and plans for recruiting and training employees
Critical Risks	Any known inherent risks in the venture
Offering	How much capital the entrepreneur needs and how the money will be used (section used to attract investors)
Exit Strategy	Ways an investor—and the entrepreneur—may be able to harvest their business investment
Financial Plan	Contemplated sources of financing; any historical financial statements, if available; pro forma financial statements for three to five years, including income statements, balance sheets, cash flow statements, and cash budgets
Appendix of Supporting Documents	*Various supplementary materials and attachments to expand the reader's understanding of the plan*

- Name of contact person (preferably the president) with mailing address, phone number, fax number, and e-mail address
- Date on which the business plan was prepared
- If the plan is being given to investors, a disclaimer that the plan is being provided on a confidential basis to qualified investors only and is not to be reproduced without permission
- Number of the copy (to help keep track of how many copies have been given out)

6-4b Table of Contents

The table of contents provides a sequential listing of the sections of the plan, with page numbers. This allows the reader to spot-read the plan (a common practice) rather than reading it from front to back. Exhibit 6.5 presents the table of contents of the business plan for BlueAvocado, a company that produces environmentally friendly, reusable shopping bags. While the table of contents for BlueAvocado's business plan does not follow exactly the general format presented in Exhibit 6.4, it has much of the same content.

6-4c Executive Summary (Overview)

The **executive summary**, or **overview**, is often thought to be the most important section of the business plan. If you don't catch the readers' attention in the executive summary, most likely they will not continue reading. At the very outset, it must convey a clear and concise picture of the proposed venture and, at the same time, create a sense of excitement regarding its prospects. This means that it must be written—and, if necessary, rewritten—to achieve clarity and create interest. Even though the executive summary comes at the beginning of the business plan, it provides an overview of the

EXHIBIT **6.5** Table of Contents For BlueAvocado Business Plan

Table of Contents	
1.0	Introduction
2.0	The Company
3.0	Market Opportunity
4.0	Product Overview
5.0	Lauren Conrad Partnership
6.0	Technology Initiatives
7.0	Supply Chain
8.0	Marketing/Sales Plan
9.0	Financial Overview
10.0	People
11.0	Sustainability Issues
12.0	Conclusion/Contact Appendices

Source: BlueAvocado, Co. Reprinted with permission.

executive summary (overview)
A section of the business plan that conveys a clear and concise overall picture of the proposed venture and creates interest in the venture.

entire plan and should be written last. In no more than three (preferably two) pages, the executive summary should include the following subsections:

- A description of the opportunity
- An explanation of the business concept
- An industry overview
- The target market
- The competitive advantage you hope to achieve in the market
- The economics of the opportunity
- The management team
- The amount and purpose of the money being requested (the "offering"), if you are seeking financing

Depending on the situation and the preference of the entrepreneur, the executive summary may be in the form of a synopsis or a narrative. A *synopsis* briefly covers all aspects of the business plan, giving each topic relatively equal treatment. It relates, in abbreviated fashion, the conclusions of each section of the completed business plan. Although it is easy to prepare, the synopsis can be rather dry reading for the prospective investor.

Because the *narrative* tells a story, it can convey greater excitement than the synopsis. However, composing an effective narrative requires a gifted writer who can communicate the necessary information and generate enthusiasm without crossing the line into hype. A narrative is more appropriate for businesses that are breaking new ground with a new product, a new market, or new operational techniques. It is also a better format for ventures that have one dominant advantage, such as holding an important patent or being run by a well-known entrepreneur. Finally, the narrative works well for companies with interesting or impressive backgrounds or histories.

Exhibit 6.6 shows the overview that appears in BlueAvocado's business plan. It was written in the narrative form.

6-4d Company Description

The company description informs the reader of the type of business being proposed, the firm's objectives, where the firm is located, and whether it will serve a local or international market. If the business is already in existence, its history should be included. In many cases, legal issues—especially those concerning the firm's form of organization—are addressed in this section of the plan. (Legal issues regarding the form of organization are discussed at length in Chapter 8.) In writing this section, the entrepreneur should answer the following questions:

1. When and where is the business to be started?
2. What is the history (if any) of the company?
3. What are the firm's objectives?
4. What changes have been made in structure and/or ownership?
5. In what stage of development is the firm—for example, seed stage or full product line?
6. What has been achieved to date?
7. What is the firm's competitive advantage or distinctive competence?
8. What are the basic nature and activity of the business?

EXHIBIT

6.6 BlueAvocado Overview

BlueAvocado™ is a woman-owned, sustainable business with a vision to invite millions to reduce their environmental impact and carbon footprint with eco-chic lifestyle products. In 2008, the company introduced a patent-pending reusable shopping bag system, the gro-pak®, to the US market to eliminate the use of 1,000 plastic bags and avoid 35 pounds of carbon dioxide emissions annually. The gro-pak includes 5 stylish, machine-washable bags that include ventilated bags for produce, insulated bag for hot/cold items, and durable hauling bags that collapse into one kit. Since then, the company has expanded its portfolio, offering reusable lunch kits and continues to invest in next-generation products that reduce our environmental waste and inspire joy.

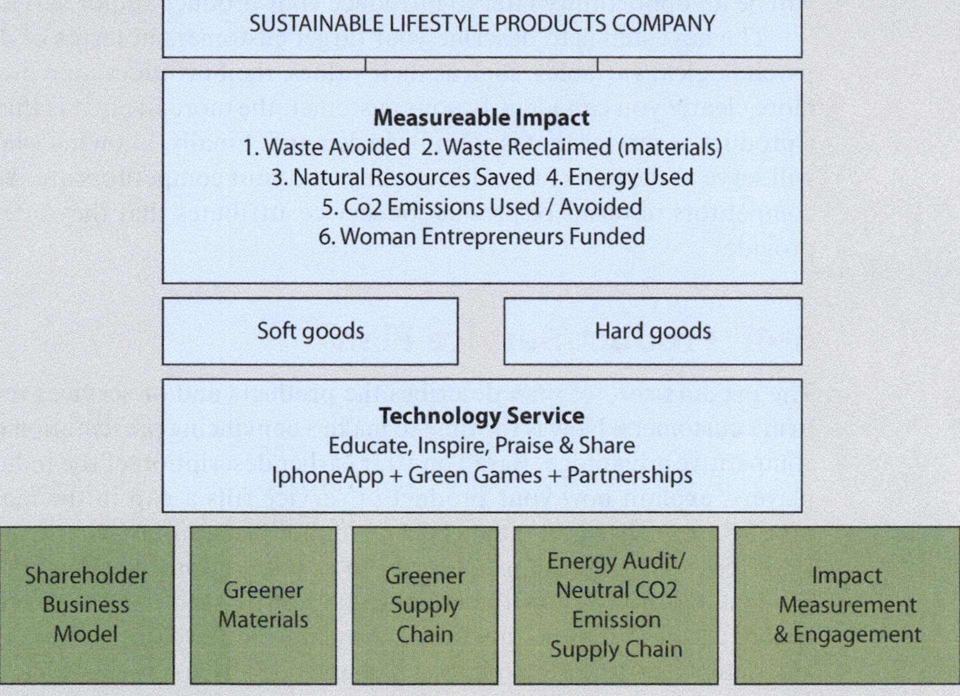

With its unique stylish kit and commitment to sustainability, BlueAvocado has successfully captured mind share and market share throughout the United States. The company and its products have been featured in *Real Simple*, *Better Homes & Gardens*, *InStyle*, *PARADE*, *CNN*, *MSNBC*, *Shape*, *Parenting*, and *USA Today*. The company has received numerous accolades, including a Top Pick at the International Home & Housewares show in the Chicago Tribune (2009) and a top "Green Product Finalist" at the Natural Products Expo (2009). In June 2010, BlueAvocado was featured in *Fast Company* as a green company to watch, after being selected as a finalist at the Sustainable Brands Conference Innovation Open. In August 2012, it was a sustainable brand finalist at the New York International Gift Fair. BlueAvocado products are available in more than 700 retail outlets throughout the US states, Canada, and Italy at key retailers, including The Container Store, Sur La Table, Whole Foods, Amazon, and the Home Shopping Network.

Source: BlueAvocado, Co. Reprinted with permission.

9. What is its primary product or service?
10. What customers will be served?
11. What is the firm's form of organization—sole proprietorship, partnership, limited liability company, corporation, or some other form?
12. What are the current and projected economic states of the industry?
13. Does the firm intend to sell to another company or an investment group? Does it plan to be a publicly traded company, or do the owners want to transfer ownership to the next generation of the family?

6-4e Industry, Target Customer, and Competitor Analysis

The primary purpose of this section is to present the opportunity and demonstrate why there is a significant market to be served. You should describe the broader industry in which you will be competing, including industry size, growth rate, fundamental trends, and major players. Next, identify the different segments of the industry and then describe in detail the niche in which you plan to participate. It is tempting to begin describing your own company at this point. Instead, you should provide the context of the opportunity and demonstrate that a market segment is being underserved. There will be an opportunity later to introduce your product and/or service.

The next step is to describe your target customers in terms of demographics and psychological variables, such as their values, their attitudes, and even their fears. The more clearly you can identify your customer, the more likely it is that you will provide a product or service that is actually in demand. Finally, knowing who your customer is will serve as the basis for understanding who your competitors are. You should analyze competitors in terms of product or service attributes that they offer or are failing to provide.

6-4f Product/Service Plan

The **product/service plan** describes the products and/or services to be offered to the firm's customers. Now is the time to make a convincing presentation of your company's competitive advantage. Based on your earlier description of the industry and its major players, explain how your product or service fills a gap in the market or how your product or service is "better, cheaper, and/or faster" than what is currently available. In the case of a physical product, try to provide a working model or prototype. Investors will naturally show the greatest interest in products that have been developed, tested, and found to be functional. Any innovative features should be identified and any patent protections explained. (Chapter 15 discusses this topic more fully.) Also, your growth strategy for the product or service should be explained in this section, as growth is a primary determinant of a firm's value. If relevant, describe secondary target markets the firm will pursue.

product/service plan A section of the business plan that describes the product and/or service to be provided and explains its merits.

marketing plan A section of the business plan that describes how the firm will reach and service customers within a given market.

operations and development plan A section of the business plan that offers information on how a product will be produced or a service provided, including descriptions of the firm's facilities, labor, raw materials, and processing requirements.

6-4g Marketing Plan

The **marketing plan** describes how the firm will reach and service customers within a given market. In other words, how will you entice customers to make the change to your product or service and to continue using it? This section should present the marketing strategy, including the methods of identifying and attracting customers; pricing strategies, selling approach, type of sales force, and distribution channels; types of sales promotions and advertising; and credit and pricing policies. Sales forecasts will need to be developed, based on this information. Finally, in terms of servicing the customer, this section should describe any warranties, as well as planned product updates. (Chapter 7 provides in-depth coverage of the marketing plan.)

6-4h Operations and Development Plan

The **operations and development plan** offers information on how the product will be produced or the service provided. Here, you will explain how the operations will contribute to the firm's competitive advantage—that is, how its operations will create value for the customer. This section discusses items such as location and facilities, including how much space the business will need and what type of equipment it will require. It is important to describe the choice between in-house production and outsourcing in order to minimize costs. Remember, however, that you should never plan to outsource a part of operations that contributes to your competitive advantage. The operations and development plan should also explain the firm's proposed approach to assuring quality, controlling inventory, and using subcontractors for obtaining raw materials. (Read Chapters 9 and 21 for further discussion the issues to be addressed in this section.)

6-4i Management Team

Prospective investors look for well-managed companies. Of all the factors they consider, the quality of the management team is paramount. Some investors say that they would rather have an "A" management team and a "B" product or service than a "B" team and an "A" product or service. But it can also be said that the right management in the wrong market is likely headed for failure. For success, you must have a good team working in a growth market.

The **management team section** should detail the proposed venture's organizational structure and the backgrounds of those who will fill its key positions. Ideally, a well-balanced management team—one that includes financial and marketing expertise as well as production experience and innovative talent—will already be in place. Managerial experience in related enterprises and in other startup situations is particularly valuable. (The factors involved in preparing the management team section are discussed in greater detail in Chapter 8.)

6-4j Critical Risks

The business plan is intended to tell a story of success, but there are always risks associated with starting a new venture. Thus, the plan would be incomplete if it did not identify the risks inherent in the venture. The **critical risks section** identifies the potential pitfalls that may be encountered by an investor. Common risks include a lack of market acceptance (customers don't buy the product as anticipated), competitor retaliation, longer time and higher expenses than expected to start and grow the business, inadequate financing, and government regulations.

6-4k Offering

If the entrepreneur is seeking capital from investors, an **offering** should be included in the plan to indicate clearly how much money is needed and when. It is helpful to convey this information in a *sources and uses table* that indicates the type of financing being requested (debt or equity) and how the funds will be used. For example, for a firm needing $500,000, including any money borrowed and the founder's investment, the sources and uses table for the first year might appear as follows:

Sources:	
Bank debt	$100,000
Equity:	
New investors	300,000
Founders	100,000
Total sources	$500,000

management team section
A section of the business plan that describes a new firm's organizational structure and the backgrounds of its key employees.

critical risks section
A section of the business plan that identifies the potential risks that may be encountered by an investor.

offering
A section of the business plan that indicates to an investor how much money is needed, and when and how the money will be used.

Uses:	
Product development	$125,000
Personnel costs	75,000
Working capital:	
Cash	20,000
Accounts receivable	100,000
Inventory	80,000
Machinery	100,000
Total uses	$500,000

If equity is being requested, the entrepreneur will need to decide how much ownership of the business she or he is willing to give up—not an easy task in most cases. Typically, the amount of money being raised should carry the firm for 12 to 18 months—enough time to reach some milestones. Then, if all goes well, it will be easier and less costly to raise more money later. (These issues will be explained in greater detail in Chapters 11 and 12.)

6-4l Exit Strategy

If a firm is using the business plan to raise equity financing, investors will want to know the possible options for cashing out of their investment. This should be provided in the **exit strategy section**. Most equity investors absolutely will not invest in a startup or early-stage business if they are not reasonably confident that at some time in the future there will be an opportunity to recover their principal investment, plus a nice return on the investment. (In Chapter 13, we will explain the issue of crafting an exit strategy, or what we call the *harvest*.)

6-4m Financial Plan

The **financial plan** presents financial forecasts as pro forma statements. This section of the business plan should show that the proposed business can be self-supporting and, ultimately, profitable. To do this, the entrepreneur needs to be honest with himself or herself and fully consider the company's financial outlook.

Pro forma statements, which are projections of the company's financial statements, should be presented for at least three years and possibly up to five years. The forecasts ideally include balance sheets, income statements, and statements of cash flows on an annual basis for three to five years, as well as cash budgets on a monthly basis for the first year and on a quarterly basis for the second and third years. It is vital that the financial projections be supported by well-substantiated assumptions and explanations of how the figures have been determined. And as Rudy Garza, a venture capitalist in Austin, Texas, explains, "While I may not have much confidence in the entrepreneur's financial forecasts, the financial plan helps me understand the entrepreneur's thought processes about the opportunity. That is very important in my estimation."[13]

While all the financial statements are important, the pro forma statements of cash flows deserve special attention, because a business can be profitable but fail if it does not produce positive cash flows. A well-prepared statement of cash flows identifies the sources of cash—that is, how much will be generated from operations and how much will be raised from investors. It also shows how much money will be devoted to investments in areas such as inventories and equipment. The statements of cash flows should clearly indicate how much cash is needed from lenders and prospective investors and for what purpose. (The preparation of pro forma statements and the process of raising needed capital are discussed in Chapters 11 and 12.)

exit strategy section
A section of the business plan that focuses on options for cashing out of the investment.

financial plan
A section of the business plan that projects the company's financial position based on well-substantiated assumptions and explains how the figures have been determined.

Pro forma statements
Projections of a company's financial statements for up to five years, including balance sheets, income statements, and statements of cash flows, as well as cash budgets.

6-4n Appendix of Supporting Documents

The appendix should contain various supplementary materials and attachments to expand the reader's understanding of the plan. These supporting documents include any items referenced in the text of the business plan, such as (1) the résumés of the key investors and owners/managers; (2) photographs of products, facilities, and buildings; (3) professional references; (4) marketing research studies; (5) pertinent published research; and (6) signed contracts of sale.

The fact that it appears at the end of the plan does not mean that the appendix is of secondary importance. The reader needs to understand the assumptions underlying the premises set forth in the plan. And nothing is more important to a prospective investor than the qualifications of the management team.

Each chapter in this section (Part 3) of the book, with the exception of Chapter 10, ends with a special set of exercises to walk you through the process of writing a business plan. These exercise sets consist of questions to be thoughtfully considered and answered. They are entitled "The Business Plan: Laying the Foundation," because they deal with issues that are important to starting a new venture and provide guidelines for preparing the different sections of a business plan.

Living the Dream

ENTREPRENEURIAL EXPERIENCES

Jania and Desmin Daniels Believe in Writing a Business Plan

At Rose Petals Cafe, in the Germantown neighborhood of Philadelphia, co-founders Jania and Desmin Daniels are dedicated to creating unique and delicious food. "I'm Puerto Rican and my husband's African-American, so we formulate a dinner menu that merges those things," Jania says of their menu, which is inspired by a fusion of cultures. They also feature an extensive breakfast menu, with creative offerings like catfish and cornbread waffles.

Jania had previously managed a food court establishment. Based on that experience, she believed that writing a business plan should be an early step in starting a business. She says it helped them organize all of their thoughts and ideas about the business, in addition to having concrete financial information to show to potential lenders and investors. And the planning didn't stop there. "It is such a working document. You're always tweaking your concept and your idea," she says.

The Daniels learned that planning is an ongoing process, and when there are curveballs in your business, it helps to go back to your business plan and think things through. Jania uses the example of their decision to open the business in Germantown, a different neighborhood than originally planned. They had to adjust their plan to the new market and possible new competitors.

© VINAY A BAVDEKAR/SHUTTERSTOCK.COM

Source: Adapted from "Building a Future, Honoring the Past: The Story of Rose Petals Café," http://www.liveplan.com/blog/2015/01/building-future-honoring-past-story-rose-petals-cafe, accessed February 5, 2015.

6-5 ADVICE FOR WRITING A BUSINESS PLAN

Offer practical advice on writing a business plan.

An effective written presentation ultimately depends on the quality of the underlying business opportunity. Remember, *the plan is not the business*. A poorly conceived new venture idea cannot be rescued by a good presentation. However, a good concept may be destroyed by a presentation that fails to communicate effectively. Below are recommendations that will help you avoid some of the common mistakes.

6-5a Analyze the Market Thoroughly

In analyzing the market for your product or service, you must answer some basic questions. Investors and lenders require answers to these questions, and so should you.

- What is your target market?
- How large is the target market?
- What problems concern the target market?
- Are any of these problems greater than the one you're addressing?
- How does your product or service fix the problem?
- Who will buy your product or service?
- How much are they willing to pay for it?
- Why do they need it?
- Why would they buy from you?
- Who are your competitors?
- What are their strengths and weaknesses?

As we have already said, your presentation should be the result of evidence-based statements. Nowhere in the business plan is it more important to provide hard evidence to support your claims than when presenting your analysis of the market. Gathering secondary data about the market is important, but if you are not out talking to prospective customers, then your analysis has no credibility.

Be prepared to revise your plan based on what you learn from customers. Eric Ries, an entrepreneur and author of *The Lean Startup*, recommends an iterative process summarized as the *build-measure-learn loop*. You begin small, try it out in the market, and then make changes based on what you learn from customers. Ries contends that if you don't learn quickly about a plan's core assumptions through inexpensive data-driven experiments, the traditional business plan is a waste of time.[14]

Finally, understand that everyone has competitors. Saying "We have no competition," is almost certain to make readers skeptical. You must show in your plan where your business will fit in the market and what your competitors' strengths and weaknesses are. If possible, include estimates of their market shares and profit levels.

Think Lean
For more about the lean startup, see "An Introduction to Lean Planning" at LivePlan, http://www.liveplan.com/blog/2014/11/an-introduction-to-lean-planning.

6-5b Provide Solid Evidence for Any Claims

Factual support must be supplied for any claims or assurances made. In short, the plan must be believable. *Think of your assumptions and original beliefs not as facts, but as hypotheses to be tested.*

Page after page of detailed computer-generated financial projections suggest—intentionally or unintentionally—that the entrepreneur can predict with great accuracy what will happen. Experienced investors know this isn't the case. They want to know what is behind the numbers, as this allows them to see how the entrepreneur thinks and if he or she understands the key factors that will drive success or failure. To determine this information, investors often ask a common question: "What is your business model?"

6-5c Think Like an Investor

Many small firms do not seek outside capital, except in the form of bank loans. But whether or not you are preparing a business plan in order to seek outside financing, you would benefit from understanding the world as an investor sees it—that is, you should think as an investor thinks. As Jeffrey Bussgang, who has been both an entrepreneur and a venture capitalist, advises, "You should think like [an investor] and act like an entrepreneur."[15] In this way, you bring to the analysis both the energy of the entrepreneur and the discipline of an investor.

At the most basic level, prospective investors have a single goal: to maximize potential return on an investment through cash flows that will be received, while minimizing the risk they are taking. Even investors in startups who are thought to be risk takers want to minimize their exposure to risk. For one thing, they look for ways to shift risk to others, usually to the entrepreneur. Given the fundamentally different perspectives of the investor and the entrepreneur, the important question becomes "How do I write a business plan that will satisfy what a prospective investor wants to know?" There is no easy answer, but two facts are relevant: Investors have a short attention span, and certain features attract investors while others repel them.

© DAVID CROCKETT/SHUTTERSTOCK.COM

Because most investors receive so many business plans, they cannot possibly read them all in any detailed fashion. To illustrate, one of the authors delivered an entrepreneur's business plan to a prospective investor with whom he had a personal relationship. The plan was well written, clearly identifying a need. While the investor was courteous and listened carefully, he made a decision not to consider the opportunity in a matter of five minutes. A quick read of the executive summary did not spark his interest, and the discussion quickly changed to other matters.

Furthermore, investors are more *market-oriented* than *product-oriented*, realizing that most patented inventions never earn a dime for the inventors. The essence of the entrepreneurial process is to identify new products or services that meet an identifiable customer need. Thus, it is essential for the entrepreneur to appreciate investors' concerns about target customers' responses to a new product or service and to reach out to prospective customers. (We'll discuss presenting (or pitching) to prospective investors more thoroughly later in the chapter.)

6-5d Don't Hide Weaknesses—Identify Potential Fatal Flaws

One difficult aspect of writing a business plan is effectively dealing with problems or weaknesses—and every business has them. An entrepreneur, wanting to make a good impression, may become so infatuated with an opportunity that he or she cannot see potential fatal flaws.

For instance, an entrepreneur might fail to ask, "What is the possible impact of new technology, e-commerce, or changes in consumer demand on the proposed venture?" If there are weaknesses in the plan, the investors will find them. At that point, an investor's question will be "What else haven't you told me?" The best way to properly handle weaknesses is to consider thoroughly all potential issues, to be open and straightforward about those issues, and to have an action plan that effectively addresses any problems. To put it another way, *integrity matters*.

6-5e Maintain Confidentiality

When presenting your business plan to outsiders (especially prospective investors), prominently indicate that all information in the plan is proprietary and confidential. Number every copy of the plan, and account for each outstanding copy by requiring all recipients of the plan to acknowledge receipt in writing.

When a startup is based on proprietary technology, be cautious about divulging certain information—for example, the details of a technological design or the highly sensitive specifics of a marketing strategy—even to a prospective investor.

While you should be cautious about releasing proprietary information, *do not become fixated on the notion that someone may take your idea and beat you to the market with it.* Remember, the plan is not the key to your success; your execution is what matters! If someone can "out-execute" you, then you may not be the right person to start the business.

6-5f Pay Attention to Details

Paying attention to the details may seem minor to you but likely is not to others who read the plan to determine whether they want to be associated with the firm. The following suggestions will help you attend to the "little things":

1. *Use good grammar.* Nothing turns off a reader faster than a poorly written business plan. Find a good editor, and then review and revise, revise, revise.
2. *Limit the presentation to a reasonable length.* The goal is not to write a long business plan, but to write a good business plan. People who read business plans appreciate brevity and view it as an indication of your ability to identify and describe in an organized way the important factors that will determine the success of your business. In all sections of your plan, especially the executive summary, get to the point quickly.
3. *Go for an attractive, professional appearance.* To add interest and aid readers' comprehension, make liberal but effective use of visual aids, such as graphs, exhibits, and tabular summaries. The plan should be in a three-ring, loose-leaf binder (or on a flash drive) to facilitate future revisions, as opposed to being bound like a book and printed on shiny paper with flashy images and graphs.
4. *Describe your product or service in lay terms.* Entrepreneurs with a technical background tend to use jargon that is not easily understood by individuals who are unfamiliar with the technology or the industry. That is a big mistake! Present your product and/or service in simple, understandable terms, and avoid the temptation to use too much industry jargon.

If you choose to ignore these recommendations, the business plan will detract from the opportunity itself, and you may lose the chance to capture it. We suggest that you have trusted and experienced entrepreneurs critique the business concept and the effectiveness of the business plan presentation; they know the minefields to avoid.

6-6 PITCHING TO INVESTORS

Explain how to pitch to investors.

In addition to having a written business plan, an entrepreneur seeking capital from investors may be asked to give an oral presentation to the investors, or what is called a **pitch**. This is not the time to present the entire business plan but rather to spark the investors' interest in the business. Frequently, the entrepreneur is given 15 to 20 minutes to present, followed by about the same amount of time for questions and answers.

pitch
A verbal presentation of the business idea to investors.

Christopher Mirabile, who is a frequent investor in startups, emphasizes the importance of thinking like an investor. He classifies entrepreneurs into three groups:

> *Competent entrepreneurs can explain their company in terms of what the product does. Good entrepreneurs can explain their company in terms of their customer and their market. Funded entrepreneurs can pitch their company in terms that an investor can relate to.*[16]

Mirabile continues by explaining that most entrepreneurs have difficulty putting their story together from an investor's perspective. They can speak elegantly about the product, the customer, and possibly the market. But they lack the intuition and experience to present the opportunity in a way that lets the investor know if it's a good investment.

What investors want to know is relatively straightforward, as is the order in which they want to see the topics in the pitch. Also, the essential topics that need to be covered are the same for most businesses. Caroline Cummings at Palo Alto Software suggests that you prepare 12 PowerPoint slides to accompany your presentation:

1. Identify the problem to be solved.
2. Introduce your solution to the problem.
3. Discuss your beginning traction for getting sales.
4. Identify the target market.
5. Explain the costs of acquiring customers in your target market.
6. Communicate the value proposition relative to competitors.
7. Describe the basics of the revenue model.
8. Provide financial projections, along with the assumptions.
9. Sell the team.
10. Identify your funding needs, and explain the use of the funds.
11. Describe possible exit strategies—how the investors may be able to cash out.
12. End on a high note—remind investors why your product/service/team is so great.

Guy Kawasaki, the founder of Garage Technology Ventures and the author of *The Art of the Start*, gives his 10/20/30 rule: Have only 10 presentation slides, limit the presentation to 20 minutes, and use a 30-point font in your slides. As Kawasaki explains, the purpose of the pitch is not to close the deal with the investors. Instead, the objective is to get to the next stage of due diligence. The pitch is not the end; it is only the beginning.

Finally, you might note that the topics to be covered in a pitch are very similar to those to be included in the written business plan's executive summary (described earlier in the chapter). No matter which list of topics you decide to use, they should be consistent in terms of content.

Hints on How to Make a Pitch

To learn more about making a pitch to investors, watch the following YouTube videos:

- Caroline Cummings, Vice President of Marketing and Resident Entrepreneur at Palo Alto Software: "How to Deliver a Powerful Pitch to Investors," https://www.youtube.com/watch?v=YJ5D82z3oFA
- Nathan Gold, Chief Coach at DemoCoach (www.democoach.com): "How to Pitch to Investors with 13 Slides in under 10 Minutes," https://www.youtube.com/watch?v=sVXop1o5Kv4 (PowerPoint slides can be seen at http://static1.squarespace.com/static/536fd655e4b0a44be2fb1f44/t/539f20b7e4b037955eafb8d0/1402937527757/13slides.pdf.)
- Guy Kawasaki: "Make a Great Pitch," https://search.yahoo.com/search;_ylt=At6kFgq9hBVakSKUVyqePuKbvZx4?p=guy+kawasaki+making+"'a+great+pitch&toggle=1&cop=mss&ei=UTF-8&fr=yfp-t-901&fp=1

Identify available sources of assistance in preparing a business plan.

6-7 RESOURCES FOR BUSINESS PLAN PREPARATION

In the writing of a business plan, there are an almost unlimited number of books, websites, and computer software packages that offer extensive guidance, even step-by-step instruction. Such resources can be invaluable. However, resist the temptation to adapt an existing business plan for your own use. The following sections provide a brief description of some of these resources.

6-7a Computer-Aided Business Planning

A number of business plan software packages have been designed to help an entrepreneur think through the important issues in starting a new company and organize his or her thoughts to create an effective presentation. Beginning with Maternova, the company presented in this chapter's Spotlight feature, we have referenced LivePlan at various points throughout the chapter. LivePlan is one of the leading business software packages available to entrepreneurs, and there are certainly many to choose from.

While they can facilitate the process, software packages in and of themselves are not capable of producing a unique plan. In fact, they can actually limit an entrepreneur's creativity and flexibility, if not used properly. One of the authors received a business plan that was almost 80 pages long. When questioned about the excessive length, the entrepreneur responded, "By the time I answered all the questions in the software package, that's how it turned out." Only you as the entrepreneur can say what should and should not be in the plan. If you don't know, then you are not ready to write one. Remember, there is no simple procedure for writing a business plan, no "magic formula for success." If you recognize their limitations, however, you can use business plan software packages to facilitate the process.

6-7b Professional Assistance in Business Planning

Company founders are most notably doers—and evidence suggests that they had better be, if the venture is to be successful. But some small business owners lack the breadth of experience and know-how, as well as the inclination, needed for planning.

A small business owner who is not able to answer tough questions about the business may need a business planning advisor—someone accustomed to working with small companies, startups, and owners who lack financial management experience. Such advisors include accountants, marketing specialists, attorneys (preferably with an entrepreneurial mindset), incubator organizations, small business development centers (SBDCs), and regional and local economic development offices.

An investment banker or financial intermediary can draw up a business plan as part of a firm's overall fundraising efforts. Also, a well-chosen advisor will have contacts you lack and may even help you reformulate your business plan entirely. However, using a business planning advisor will cost you. They frequently charge an hourly fee as well as a contingency percentage based on the amount raised.

The Small Business Administration (SBA) and the Service Corps of Retired Executives (SCORE) can also be helpful. Both organizations have programs to introduce business owners to volunteer experts who will advise them. SCORE, in particular, is a source for all types of business advice, such as how to write a business plan, investigate market potential, and manage cash flows. SCORE counselors work out of local chapters throughout the United States and can be found by contacting the national office.

Another source of assistance is the FastTrac entrepreneurial training program sponsored by the Kauffman Center for Entrepreneurial Leadership in Kansas City, Missouri. Located in universities, chambers of commerce, and SBDCs across the country, the FastTrac program teaches the basics of product development, concept recognition, financing strategies, and marketing research, while helping entrepreneurs write a business plan in small, well-organized increments.

You definitely have options when it comes to getting business plan assistance. However, if you choose to hire a consultant, the following suggestions may help you avoid some costly mistakes:[17]

- *Get referrals.* Ask colleagues, acquaintances, and professionals such as bankers, accountants, and lawyers for the names of business plan consultants they recommend. A good referral goes a long way to easing any concerns you may have. In any case, few consultants advertise, so referrals may be your only option.
- *Look for a fit.* Find a consultant who is an expert in helping businesses like yours. Ideally, the consultant should have lots of experience with companies of similar size and age in related industries. Avoid general business experts or those who lack experience in your particular field.
- *Check references.* Get the names of at least three clients the consultant has helped to write business plans. Call the former clients and ask about the consultant's performance. Was the consultant's final fee in line with the original estimate? Was the plan completed on time? Did it serve the intended purpose?
- *Get it in writing.* Have a legal contract outlining the consultant's services. It should state in detail the fee, when it will be paid, and under what circumstances. And make sure you get a detailed written description of what the consultant must do to earn the fee. Whether it's an hourly rate or a flat fee isn't as important as each party's knowing exactly what's expected of them.

Keep in mind that securing help in business plan preparation does not relieve the entrepreneur of the responsibility of being the primary planner. His or her ideas remain essential to producing a plan that is realistic and believable.

6-8 KEEPING THE RIGHT PERSPECTIVE

Maintain the proper perspective when writing a business plan.

Writing a business plan should be thought of as an ongoing process and not as the means to an end. In fact, when it comes to writing a plan, the process is just as important as the final outcome. Some entrepreneurs have difficulty accepting this, given their orientation to "bottom-line" results. But this point deserves to be repeated: *Writing a business plan is primarily an ongoing process and only secondarily the means to an outcome. The process is just as important as—if not more so than—the finished product.*

While your plan will represent your vision and goals for the firm, it will rarely reflect what actually happens. With a startup, too many unexpected events can affect the final outcome. Thus, a business plan is in large part an opportunity for an entrepreneur and management team to think about the potential key drivers of a venture's success or failure. Anticipating different scenarios and the ensuing consequences can significantly enhance an entrepreneur's adaptability—an essential quality, when so much is uncertain.

Now that you are aware of the role of the business plan in a new venture, you are ready to move on to Chapters 7 through 13, which will closely examine each of the plan's components.

6-1. **Explain the purpose and objectives of business plans.**

- A business plan is a document that sets out the basic idea underlying a business and describes related startup considerations. It should explain where the entrepreneur is presently, indicate where he or she wants to go, and outline how he or she proposes to get there.
- A business plan has three key elements: (1) a logical statement of a problem and its solution, (2) a significant amount of hard evidence, and (3) candor about the risks, gaps, and assumptions that might be proved wrong.
- The objectives of a business plan include assessing whether a good idea is also a good investment opportunity, determining whether the business aligns with your personal goals, providing direction for insiders, and convincing outsiders to enter into a relationship with the company.

6-2. **Give the rationale for writing (or not writing) a business plan when starting a new venture.**

- Studies attempting to measure whether entrepreneurs who have business plans do better than those who don't have produced mixed results. Some findings suggest a relationship; others do not.
- What ultimately matters is not writing a plan, but implementing it. The goal is to execute the plan.
- An entrepreneur must find the right balance between planning and becoming operational.
- For some startups, excessive planning isn't beneficial because the environment is too turbulent, fast action is needed to take advantage of an opportunity, or there's a shortage of capital.
- Most entrepreneurs need the discipline that comes with writing a business plan. A written plan helps to ensure systematic, complete coverage of the important factors to be considered in starting a new business.
- A business plan helps an entrepreneur communicate his or her vision to current and prospective employees of the firm.
- By enhancing the firm's credibility, a business plan serves as an effective selling tool with prospective customers and suppliers, as well as investors.
- A short plan is an abbreviated form of a traditional business plan that presents only the most important issues and projections for the business.
- A comprehensive plan is a complete business plan that provides an in-depth analysis of the critical factors that will determine a firm's success or failure, along with the underlying assumptions.

6-3. **Explain the concept and process for developing a firm's business model.**

- The term *business model* has become a popular phrase in business, especially among entrepreneurs and their investors.
- The business model measures the anticipated results of the core business decisions and all the trade-offs that determine a company's profits and cash flows.
- Understanding the business model is especially important in a startup, where there is so much uncertainty.
- A business model explains in a systematic and clear way how a business will generate profits and cash flows, given its revenue sources, its cost structures, the required size of investment, and its sources of risk.

6-4. **Describe the preferred content and format for a business plan.**

- The opportunity, the critical resources, the entrepreneurial team, the financing structure, and the context of an opportunity are all interdependent factors that should be given consideration when thinking about the content of a business plan.
- Key sections of a business plan are the (1) cover page, (2) table of contents, (3) executive summary (overview), (4) company description, (5) industry, target customer, and competitor analysis, (6) product/service plan, (7) marketing plan, (8) operations and development plan, (9) management team, (10) critical risks, (11) offering, (12) exit strategy, (13) financial plan, and (14) appendix of supporting documents.

6-5. **Offer practical advice on writing a business plan.**

- Analyze the market thoroughly.
- Provide solid evidence for any claims.
- Understand how investors think.
- Don't hide weaknesses; try to identify potential fatal flaws.
- Maintain confidentiality, when appropriate.
- Pay attention to the details.

6-6. Explain how to pitch to investors.

- Most entrepreneurs can speak elegantly about the product, the customer, and possibly the market. But they lack the intuition and experience to pitch the opportunity in a way that lets the investor know if it's a good investment.
- What most investors want to know is relatively straightforward, as is the order in which they want to see the topics in the pitch.
- Guy Kawasaki's 10/20/30 rule provides guidelines for the pitch: Have only 10 presentation slides, limit the presentation to 20 minutes, and use a 30-point font in your slides.

6-7. Identify available sources of assistance in preparing a business plan.

- A variety of books, websites, and computer software packages are available to assist in the preparation of a business plan.
- Professionals with planning expertise, such as attorneys, accountants, and marketing specialists, can provide useful suggestions and assistance in the preparation of a business plan.
- The Small Business Administration (SBA), the Service Corps of Retired Executives (SCORE), and the Kauffman FastTrac entrepreneurial training program can also be helpful.

6-8. Maintain the proper perspective when writing a business plan.

- Writing a business plan should be thought of as an ongoing process and not the means to an end.
- The plan rarely reflects what actually happens with the business.
- A business plan can be viewed as an opportunity for the entrepreneur and the management team to think about the potential key drivers of a venture's success or failure.

Key Terms

business model p. 152
business model risk p. 153
business plan p. 146
comprehensive plan p. 150
cost structures p. 153
critical risks p. 161
executive summary (overview) p. 157
exit strategy p. 162
financial plan p. 162
key resource requirements p. 153
management team p. 161
marketing plan p. 160
offering p. 161
operations and development plan p. 160
pitch p. 167
product/service plan p. 160
pro forma statements p. 162
revenue model p. 151
short plan p. 150

You Make the Call

Situation 1

You want to start an online clothing store and need information about the size of the market for the marketing section of your business plan. From an online search, you found that Americans spent $18.3 billion online for apparel, accessories, and footwear last year and that the forecast for their spending on these items in the coming year is $22.1 billion. You have also researched publicly traded apparel companies, like Gap, to discover trends in online sales for these firms.

Question 1 Why is your research thus far inadequate for what you need to know?

Question 2 Do you think it will be difficult to find all the information you need?

Question 3 What else might you do to find the necessary information?

Situation 2

You recently visited with a friend who knew you had taken a small business course when you attended college. During your visit, she made the comment, "I plan to open a business this summer. I won't be applying for a bank loan to fund this company, so I don't have a business plan. Do I need one?"

Question 1 What would you need to know in order to answer her question?
Question 2 If she decides to write a business plan, what advice would you give her?

Situation 3

John Martin and John Rose decided to start a new business to manufacture noncarbonated soft drinks. They believed that their location, close to high-quality water, would give them a competitive edge. Although Martin and Rose had never worked together, Martin had 17 years of experience in the soft drink industry. Rose had recently sold his firm and had funds to help finance the venture; however, the partners needed to raise additional money from outside investors. They spent almost 18 months developing their business plan. The first paragraph of their executive summary reflected their excitement:

> *The "New Age" beverage market is the result of a spectacular boom in demand for drinks with nutritional value from environmentally safe ingredients and waters that come from deep, clear springs free of chemicals and pollutants. Argon Beverage Corporation will produce and market a full line of sparkling fruit drinks, flavored waters, and sports drinks that are of the highest quality and purity. These drinks have the same delicious taste appeal as soft drinks while using the most healthful fruit juices, natural sugars, and the purest spring water, the hallmark of the "New Age" drink market.*

With the help of a well-developed plan, the two men were successful in raising the necessary capital to begin their business. They leased facilities and started production. However, after almost two years, the plan's goals were not being met. There were cost overruns, and profits were not up to expectations.

Question 1 What problems might have contributed to the firm's poor performance?
Question 2 Although several problems were encountered in implementing the business plan, the primary reason for the low profits turned out to be embezzlement. Martin was diverting company resources for personal use, even using some of the construction materials purchased by the company to build a house. What could Rose have done to avoid this situation? What are his options after the fact?

Business Plan

LAYING THE FOUNDATION

Part 3 (Chapters 6 through 13) deals with issues that are important in starting a new venture. This chapter presented an overview of the business plan and its preparation. Chapters 7 through 13 focus on major segments of the business plan, such as the marketing plan, the organizational plan, the location plan, the financial plan, and the exit plan, or what we call the harvest. After you have carefully studied these chapters, you will have the knowledge you need to prepare a business plan.

Since applying what you study facilitates learning, we have included, at the end of each chapter in Part 3 (except Chapter 10), a list of important questions that need to be addressed in preparing a particular segment of a business plan.

Company Description Questions

Now that you have learned the main concepts of business plan preparation, you can begin the process of creating a business plan by writing a general company description. In thinking about the key issues in starting a new business, respond to the following questions:

1. When and where is the business to start?
2. What is the history of the company?
3. What are the company's objectives?
4. What changes have been made in structure and/or ownership?
5. In what stage of development is the company?
6. What has been achieved to date?
7. What is the company's distinctive competence?
8. What are the basic nature and activity of the business?
9. What is its primary product or service?
10. What customers will be served?
11. What is the company's form of organization?
12. What are the current and projected economic states of the industry?
13. Does the company intend to become a publicly traded company or an acquisition candidate, or do the owners want to transfer ownership to the next generation of the family?

Case 6

Hyper Wear®, Inc. (P. 656)

Hyper Wear was founded in 2008 to participate in the functional fitness market, along with such recognized brands as CrossFit and Zumba. The market had been growing at an 11 percent annual rate from 2007 to 2012. In 2011, the firm raised money from outside investors and hired Denver Fredenburg as its CEO. By 2012, sales were approximately $1 million, and the firm needed more money to fund its growth. Fredenburg wrote a business plan to be used in raising the needed money.

Alternative Cases for Chapter 6

Case 3, The Kollection, p. 649

Video Case 6: KindSnacks [website only]

Endnotes

1. John Mullins, *The New Business Road Test* (London: Financial Times Prentice Hall, 2014).
2. Amar Bhide, *The Origin and Evolution of New Businesses* (New York: Oxford University Press, 2000), p. 53.
3. Thomas Stemberg, "What You Need to Succeed," *Inc.*, Vol. 29, No. 1 (January 2007), pp. 75–77.
4. Taken from San Hogg, "Pull No Punches," *Entrepreneur*, July 2012, p. 74.
5. Kelly Spors, "Do Start-Ups Really Need Formal Business Plans?" *The Wall Street Journal*, January 9, 2007, p. B9.
6. Bhide, *op. cit.*, p. 70.
7. Stephen Lawrence and Frank Moyes, "Writing a Successful Business Plan," http://leeds-faculty.colorado.edu/moyes/html/resources.htm, accessed October 10, 2012.
8. Personal conversation with Ewing Marion Kauffman, October 2005.
9. The explanation of business models in this section draws heavily from a variety of sources, primarily Richard G. Hammerers, Paul W. Marshall, and Tax Pirmohamed, "Note on Business Model Analysis for the Entrepreneur," Harvard Business School (9-802-048), January 22, 2002; Karan Girotra and Serguel Netesskine, "How to Build Risk into Your Business Model," *Harvard Business Review*, May 2011, pp. 100-105; Peter Weill, Thomas W. Malone, and Thomas G. Apel, "The Business Models Investors Prefer," MIT Sloan Management, Vol. 52, No. 4 (2011), pp. 17-19; Vivek Wadhwa, "Before You Write a Business Plan," *Bloomberg Businessweek*, http://www.businessweek.com/stories/2008-01-07/before-you-write-a-business-plan-businessweek-business-news-stock-market-and-financial-advice, accessed September 30, 2014; Michael Rappa, "Business Models on the Web," http://www.digitalenterprise.org/models/models.html, accessed September 10, 2014; Vivek Wadhwa, "Countdown to Product Launch (Part II)" *Bloomberg Businessweek*, May 12, 2006, http://www.businessweek.com/print/smallbiz/content/may2006/sb20060512_948264.htm, accessed August 31, 2014; Karen E. Klein, "Do You Really Need a Business Plan?" *Bloomberg Businessweek*, http://www.businessweek.com/stories/2008-03-12/do-you-really-need-a-business-plan-businessweek-business-news-stock-market-and-financial-advice, accessed October 9, 2014; and Rob Adams, "Taking the Trouble to Research Your Market," *Bloomberg Businessweek*, http://www.businessweek.com/smallbiz/content/oct2004/sb20041020_9945.htm, accessed January 16, 2015.
10. Ramon Casadesus-Masanell and Joan E. Ricart, "How to Design a Winning Business Model," *Harvard Business Review*, January–February 2011, p. 100.
11. An alternative framework for a feasibility analysis is provided by Frank Moyes, a former professor at the University of Colorado, at http://leeds-faculty.colorado.edu, accessed February 8, 2015.
12. Portions of the content in this section draw on Andrew Zacharakis, Stephen Spinelli, and Jeffry A. Timmons, *Business Plans That Work* (New York: McGraw-Hill, 2011).
13. Personal conversation with Rudy Garza, November 29, 2013.
14. Eric Ries, *The Lean Startup: How Today's Entrepreneurs Use Continuous Innovation to Create Radically Successful Businesses* (New York: Crown Business, 2011).
15. Jeffrey Bussgang "Think Like a VC, Act Like an Entrepreneur," *Bloomberg Businessweek*, http://www.businessweek.com/stories/2008-08-26/think-like-a-vc-act-like-an-entrepreneur, accessed December 2, 2012.
16. Christopher Mirabile, "What's Your Story? Pitch Deck Flow," Angel Capital Association, January 21, 2015, http://www.angelcapitalassociation.org/blog/whats-your-story-pitch-deck-flow, accessed February 5, 2015.
17. "Get Help with Your Plan," *Entrepreneur*, March 2,2001, www.entrepreneur.com/startingabusiness/businessplans/article38314.html, accessed August 14, 2014.

CHAPTER 7

The Marketing Plan

After studying this chapter, you should be able to . . .

7-1. **Describe small business marketing.**

7-2. **Identify the components of a formal marketing plan.**

7-3. **Discuss the nature of the marketing research process.**

7-4. **Define *market segmentation* and discuss its related strategies.**

7-5. **Explain the different methods of forecasting sales.**

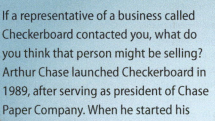

OPEN LOOKING AHEAD

In the SPOTLIGHT

Checkerboard Ltd.: Building a Bigger Share of a Shrinking Market

www.checkernet.com

If a representative of a business called Checkerboard contacted you, what do you think that person might be selling? Arthur Chase launched Checkerboard in 1989, after serving as president of Chase Paper Company. When he started his new business, which prints invitations to special events, Arthur wanted a name that did not tie him exclusively to paper products. He and his wife were brainstorming names for the company with an artist friend who suddenly noticed a coat with a checkerboard pattern hanging in the room and declared, "That's it!" Checkerboard Ltd. was born. So, if you do get a call, it may be about preparing that announcement about your graduation or invitation to your wedding or another important occasion.

Micah Chase joined his father's company in 1992. He had studied artificial intelligence in college and was enjoying his work in Silicon Valley when his father called. His immediate reaction to Arthur's offer was negative, and it stayed that way for quite a while. Finally, Micah agreed to work with his dad, not expecting to stay at Checkerboard forever. But he found himself caught up in his father's vision and in his own ability to introduce new ideas to the firm. Micah became CEO in 1994, eventually buying out his father, who went on to a political career, serving as a state senator in Massachusetts.

Micah found ways to grow Checkerboard, landing it on *Inc.* magazine's list of fastest-growing companies in the United States more than once. Given his technology background, Micah recognized early on that paper invitations were being replaced by electronic ones. He looked into electronic alternatives as the Internet was becoming widely accessed. As a small, independent firm, he could not justify the resource investment that would have been required at that time. In the following years, Micah observed many competitors redefining their purpose or exiting the industry. As a result, Checkerboard increased its market share, but with the realization that the entire market for the paper products that the company offered was in decline. Checkerboard would have to change or die.

Micah knew that he needed new products. And he knew those products would demand a different pricing strategy, alternative distribution channels, and new promotional tactics. All this would not happen overnight. Although he was late to the table, Micah did move the company into electronic invitations, starting eInvite.com as a separate unit. In 2012, Checkerboard introduced a new product line at the International Gift Fair in New York City that included personalized pillows, plates, and wall décor for homes and events.

Checkerboard's culture has been described as unconventional. Micah coined the word "unintuitive" to explain the strategies he has introduced. The focus is on craftsmanship combined with cutting-edge technology. But it may be his grasp of the market and of his customers' changing needs that is most likely to ensure Checkerboard's survival. According to Micah, "We are in the business of communication between people during life's critical moments."

Sources: Based on http://www.checkernet.com, accessed January 13, 2015; personal communication with Arthur Chase, October 31, 2014; and personal communication with Micah Chase, December 8, 2014.

Is Arthur Chase, founder of Checkerboard Ltd., a born salesman? After all, he not only built a company from scratch, selling to customers who could have bought from many other suppliers, but he was also able to sell himself and his political views to voters in order to become a Massachusetts state senator. It's clear that some people are born to be entrepreneurs, but you've discovered in this book that entrepreneurship and small business management are skills that can also be learned. The same thing can be said for selling. However, a critical lesson that business owners must learn is that marketing a product or service involves more than simply selling it. If you want to be a successful business owner, you need to put yourself in the shoes of your customers and figure out why customers buy what they do. In other words, you need a marketing plan.

small business marketing
Business activities that direct the creation, development, and delivery of a bundle of satisfaction from the creator to the targeted user.

The features that we discuss in this chapter are important components of any well-written plan. First, it is appropriate to answer a few basic questions about marketing:

- How can marketing be defined for a small business?
- What are the components of an effective marketing philosophy?
- What does having a consumer orientation imply about a business?

7-1 WHAT IS SMALL BUSINESS MARKETING?

Describe small business marketing.

The practice of marketing has a much broader scope than simply selling a product or service. And it is not just advertising. It consists of many activities, some of which occur even before a product is produced and made ready for distribution and sale. Entrepreneurs need to be sure that a market exists for what they plan to sell before they ever launch their companies.

Small business marketing consists of those business activities that direct the creation, development, and delivery of a bundle of satisfaction from the creator to the targeted user. This definition emphasizes the benefits customers will gain from a

Marketing Advice

When your company is in the startup stage, planning for marketing is different from when your business has been operational for a few years. Check out Startup Professionals (www.startupprofessionals.com), which advises ventures that are just getting underway. It was once a startup itself and presents its own plan on its website.

product or service. It may be helpful to view a *bundle of satisfaction* as having three levels: core product/service, actual product/service, and augmented product/service. The **core product/service** is the fundamental benefit or solution sought by customers. The **actual product/service** is the basic physical product and/or service that delivers those benefits. The **augmented product/service** is the basic product and/or service plus any extra or unsolicited benefits to the consumer that may prompt a purchase. In the case of shoes, for example, the core product is basic protection for the feet; the actual product is the shoe itself. The augmented product might be increased running speed, greater comfort, or less wear and tear on feet and legs. Augmentation could also be reflected in how the customer feels. Do the shoes offer style, prestige, social identity?

Because smaller firms generally cannot afford the talented marketing experts that large corporations employ, they conduct many trials and endure numerous problems. A marketing plan will not enable you to avoid all missteps, but it can drastically reduce the number of errors by forcing you to think through available options, given the resources you have.

To be successful today, a business must solve someone's "pain," or problem. In other words, a business provides a bundle of satisfaction to its customers, not merely the tangible product or intangible service that is the focus of the exchange. By offering a bundle of satisfaction, you don't just make a sale, you retain your customers, resulting in multiple purchases over time. And the solution that you provide may not even be the product or service that you are offering. The homepage of the website for Hendrick Boards announces, "One shirt saves one animal." After adopting a puppy and spending $20,000 on veterinary bills, David Hendrickson felt he had a mission to help rescue animals. As much as 40 percent of the company's revenues go to animal shelters, rescues, and sanctuaries.[1]

7-1a Marketing Philosophies Make a Difference

A firm's marketing philosophy determines how its marketing activities are developed in the marketing plan and used to achieve business goals. Three different marketing perspectives guide most small businesses: the production-oriented, sales-oriented, and consumer-oriented philosophies. The first two philosophies are used most often, as they are associated with the experience and aptitudes of entrepreneurs who may have a manufacturing or technology-based background, or who may have had a career in sales.

A *production-oriented philosophy* emphasizes the product as the single most important part of the business. The firm concentrates resources on developing the product in the most efficient manner, while promotion, distribution, and other marketing activities are given less attention. This is the classic "build a better mousetrap" approach. But do customers understand what makes your mousetrap special, or do they even know about your product? On the other hand, a *sales-oriented philosophy* deemphasizes production efficiencies and customer preferences in favor of a focus on "pushing product." Achieving sales goals becomes the firm's highest priority. In contrast, a firm adopting a *consumer-oriented philosophy* believes that everything, including production and sales, centers on the consumer and his or her needs. The result: All marketing efforts begin and end with the consumer. Needless to say, we believe that a consumer-oriented philosophy leads to success in many areas, not just marketing.

core product/service
The fundamental benefit or solution sought by customers.

actual product/service
The basic physical product and/or service that delivers those benefits.

augmented product/service
The basic product and/or service plus any extra or unsolicited benefits to the consumer that may prompt a purchase.

7-1b A Consumer Orientation—The Right Choice

Consumer orientation is put into practice by applying a two-stage process that underlies all marketing efforts: identifying customer needs and satisfying those needs. This simple formula is easy to understand but difficult to implement, given the competitive nature of most markets. But this is what it takes for a company to be successful in the long term. We strongly recommend that all new businesses begin with a consumer orientation. Customer satisfaction is not a means to achieving a goal—it *is* the goal!

Why don't all firms adopt a consumer orientation when the benefits seem so obvious? The answer lies in three key factors. First, if there is little or no competition and if demand exceeds supply, a firm is tempted to emphasize production. This is usually a short-term situation, however, and concentrating on production to the exclusion of marketing can lead to disaster in due time.

Second, an entrepreneur may have a strong background in production or in selling but be weak other areas. It is natural for an owner to play to his or her strength. Third, some small business owners are simply too focused on the present. What is "hot" today may not be hot five years from now. The better course of action is to identify ways to please consumers in the long term.

We can find many examples of both production- and sales-oriented philosophies that generate short-term success. However, a consumer orientation not only recognizes production efficiency goals and professional selling but also adds concern for customer satisfaction. In effect, a firm that adopts a consumer orientation incorporates the best of each marketing philosophy.

Once a small firm makes a commitment to a customer orientation, it is ready to develop a marketing strategy to support this goal. Marketing activities include taking the steps necessary to locate and describe potential customers—a process called **market analysis**. Marketing activities also encompass product and/or service, pricing, promotion, and distribution, which combine to form the **marketing mix**.

7-2 THE FORMAL MARKETING PLAN

Identify the components of a formal marketing plan.

After an entrepreneur completes a feasibility study (described in Chapter 3) and determines that the venture idea is a viable opportunity, he or she is ready to prepare the formal marketing plan. Each business venture is different, so each marketing plan must be unique. A cloned version of a plan created by someone else should be avoided. But certain subjects—market analysis, the competition, and marketing strategy—must be covered. Exhibit 7.1 depicts the major components of the marketing plan (market analysis, the competition, and marketing strategy) and the marketing activities required to generate the information needed for the plan (marketing research, market segmentation, and sales forecasting).

In the remainder of the chapter, we will take a more in-depth look at these plan components and marketing activities. Note that detailed treatment of marketing activities and strategies for both new and established small businesses is provided in Part 4, in Chapters 14 through 18. The material in those chapters can also help you in writing your marketing plan.

7-2a Market Analysis

A critical section of the marketing plan describes the market the entrepreneur is targeting. A **customer profile** identifies the key demographic and psychological characteristics of the customers you consider most likely to be qualified purchasers of your products and services. Marketing research information, compiled from both secondary and primary data, can be used to construct this profile.

If a business owner envisions several target markets, each segment must have a corresponding customer profile. Likewise, different target markets may call for

market analysis
The process of locating and describing potential customers.

marketing mix
The combination of product/service, pricing, promotion, and distribution activities.

customer profile
A description of potential customers in a target market.

EXHIBIT 7.1 The Marketing Plan and Supporting Marketing Activities

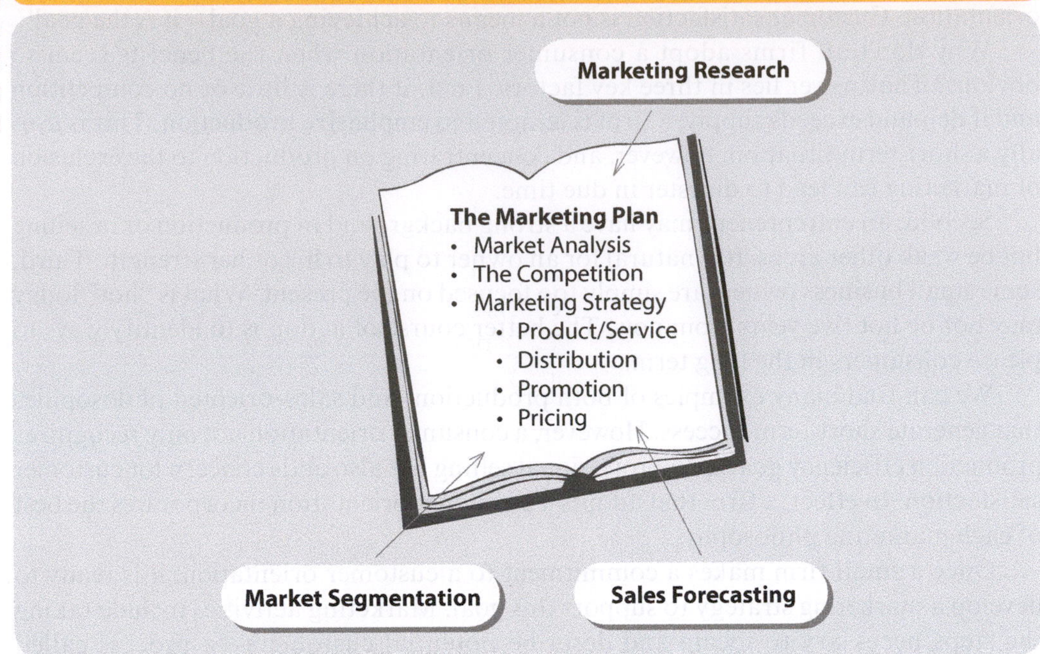

a corresponding number of related marketing strategies. Typically, however, a new venture will initially concentrate on a select few target markets—or even just one. Attempting to reach all potential customers would be way too costly for a small business.

A detailed discussion of the major benefits to customers provided by the new product or service should also be included in this section of the plan. Obviously, these benefits must be reasonable and consistent with statements in the product/service section of the plan.

Spira Footwear produces running and walking shoes that contain a patented WaveSpring technology. Spira's management team can talk at length about the product's lateral stability, height and size, weight and appearance.[2] But they also understand that customers buy their shoes more for the benefits they receive than for the features that the designers love. Excerpts from the company's marketing plan concentrate on those benefits:

> *The WaveSpring® not only cushions with every step, but returns almost the same amount of energy. Up to 96% of the energy is returned to the wearer. This "recycled" energy allows you to participate in your activities with far less stress on the joints, ligaments and the entire body than traditional footwear.*
>
> *The WaveSpring® reduces peak impact forces throughout the gait cycle by 20%. It is during these peaks that injuries usually occur. With the reduction in peak force, injuries can be reduced. Many elite athletes, marathoners, fitness enthusiasts report that they can race, train and work out at a more intense level. Recovery time between activities is often reduced.*

© SPIRA FOOTWEAR

The WaveSpring® is mechanical and works through deflection [as] opposed to compression. This helps to [. . .] keep the "new shoe" cushioned feel throughout the normal life of the shoe.[3]

Another major component of market analysis is the actual sales forecast. It is usually desirable to include three sales forecasts covering the "most likely," "best-case," and "worst-case" scenarios. These alternatives provide investors and the entrepreneur with different numbers on which to base their decisions.

It is always difficult to forecast. Anyone who has followed global business cycles knows that it is not possible to predict all the variables that will affect how a company sells its product or service. Forecasting sales for a new venture is even more difficult. While it is necessary to make assumptions during forecasting, these should be minimized. The forecasting method should be fully described and backed up by data whenever feasible.

7-2b The Competition

Existing competitors should be studied carefully. The more you know about their key management personnel, the better you can anticipate the actions they will take. A brief discussion of competitors' overall strengths and weaknesses should be a part of the competition section of the plan. Also, related products currently being marketed or tested by competitors should be noted. The entrepreneur should also assess the likelihood that any of these firms will enter the targeted market. Performing a SWOT analysis at this point is always a good idea (see Chapter 3). It is important that your company have a clear understanding of its *strengths*, its *weaknesses*, available market *opportunities*, and *threats* from competitors as well as from changes in the company's operating environment (social, technological, economic, political, and other environmental variables).

Every company must address its distinct set of competitors. Spira's founders knew they were up against major competitors who would not politely give up market share in the shoe markets. But they could easily track Nike, Reebok, Asics, New Balance, and others. They could learn how these companies react when existing competitors introduce new products or attempt to enter new markets. On the other hand, Checkerboard, the company featured in this chapter's Spotlight, had to analyze the practices of relatively small, highly segmented firms.

7-2c Marketing Strategy

The information on marketing strategy forms the most detailed section of the marketing plan and, in many respects, is subject to the closest scrutiny from potential investors. Marketing strategy plots the course of the marketing actions that will make or break the owner's vision. It's one thing to know that a large target market exists for a product or service. It's another to be able to explain why customers will buy that product or service from you.

The marketing mix of the "4 Ps" highlights the areas that a company's marketing strategy should address: (1) *product* decisions that will transform the basic product or service idea into a bundle of satisfaction, (2) *place* (distribution) activities that will determine the delivery of the product to customers, (3) *pricing* decisions that will set an acceptable exchange value on the total product or service, and (4) *promotional* activities that will communicate the necessary information to target markets.

The limited resources of small businesses have a direct bearing on the emphasis given to each of these areas. Additionally, a service business will not have the same distribution problems as a product business, and the promotional challenges facing a retail store will be quite different from those faced by a manufacturer. Despite these differences, we can offer a generalized format for presenting strategies in a marketing plan for those who will carry out those strategies.

THE PRODUCT/SERVICE SECTION

The product/service section of the marketing plan includes the name of the product and/or service and the name of the business and why they were selected. Any legal protection that has been obtained for the names should be described. It is also important to explain the logic behind the name selection. An entrepreneur's family name, if used for certain products or services, can sometimes make a positive contribution to sales. Tim Hussey is the sixth-generation CEO of Hussey Seating Company. Founded in 1835 to produce plows and other agricultural implements, today Hussey is the world leader in the production of bleachers and other products for spectator seating. Tim Hussey shares stories he heard from his grandfather about the struggles the company faced during the Great Depression and says he learned from his father that integrity is key.[4]

A good name is simple, memorable, and descriptive of the benefit provided by the product or service. (We will look at this in more depth in Chapters 14 and 15.) Whatever the logic behind the choice of names, the selection should be defended and the names registered with the appropriate agencies so that they are protected.

Sometimes, names selected for a business or a product or service may be challenged, even many years later, particularly if they haven't been registered. In fact, this happened to Apple Computer, a company that can afford all the legal advice that anyone could ever need. The iPad trademark in Europe is owned by STMicroelectronics, a Swiss semiconductor corporation that uses it as an acronym for "integrated passive and active devices."[5] A small business that changes its name or the name of a key product or service may find that advertising, packaging, and other materials become prohibitively expensive.

In the marketing plan, other components of the total product, such as the packaging, should be presented via drawings. It may be desirable to use professional packaging consultants to develop these drawings in some cases. Customer service plans such as warranties and repair policies also need to be discussed in this section. All of these elements of the marketing strategy should be tied directly to customer satisfaction. (Chapter 14 further examines the importance of creating and maintaining good customer relationships.)

Another legal issue that many small business owners face relates to unique features of their products or services. These features affect the reasons customers buy your product and why someone might invest in your company. To protect these special features, companies obtain patents, trademarks, and copyrights, which are used to differentiate products and images from those of competitors and to prevent rivals from stealing a competitive advantage.

Rather than patenting their products or technologies, some enterprises prefer to maintain trade secrets. We all have heard the stories of the secret Coca-Cola formula and of KFC's mysterious 11 herbs and spices. These trade secrets fall under the term *intellectual property*. Many companies build their marketing strategies around their intellectual property, promoting the idea that only they can offer a particular benefit to customers.

PLACE—THE DISTRIBUTION SECTION

Quite often, new ventures use established intermediaries to handle the distribution of their product. This strategy reduces the investment necessary for launch and helps the new company get its products to customers faster. How those intermediaries will be persuaded to carry the new product should be explained in the distribution section of the marketing plan. Any intention the new business may have of licensing its product or service should also be covered in this section.

Some retail ventures require fixed locations; others need mobile stores. For many, the Internet is their location, but they may rely on others in a distribution chain to transport and/or warehouse merchandise. Layouts and configurations of retail outlets should be described in this section of the marketing plan. Questions such as the following should be addressed: Will the customer get the product by regular mail or by express delivery? Will the service be provided from the entrepreneur's home or office or from the location of a licensed representative? How long will it take between order placement and actual delivery?

When a new firm's method of product delivery is exporting, the distribution section must discuss the relevant laws and regulations governing that activity. Knowledge of exchange rates between currencies and distribution options must be reflected in the material discussed in this section. (Distribution concepts are explained in greater detail in Chapter 15, and exporting is discussed in Chapter 18.)

THE PRICING SECTION

At a minimum, the price of a product or service must cover the cost of bringing it to customers. Therefore, the pricing section must calculate both production and marketing costs. Naturally, forecasting methods used for analysis in this section should be consistent with those used in preparing the market analysis section.

Break-even computations, which indicate the points at which revenues and costs are equal, should be included for alternative pricing. However, setting a price based exclusively on break-even analysis is not advisable, as it ignores other important aspects. If the entrepreneur has found a truly unique niche, he or she may be able to charge a premium price—at least in the short run. There's no perfect way of doing it, but your objective is to determine what purchasers are willing to pay for your product or service, then work backward to make sure you can produce and distribute it in a way that allows you to make a profit.

Competitors should be studied to learn what they are charging. To break into a market, an entrepreneur will usually have to price a new product or service within a reasonable range of that of the competition. Many new business owners think their best strategy is to underprice the competition in order to gain market acceptance and boost sales. It is important to keep in mind, however, that existing competitors probably have more resources than you do. If they consider your business to be a threat and engage you in a price war, they can probably outlast you. In addition, do you really want your customers to come to you only because you sell a cheaper product or service? That's no way to build loyalty; you will lose those customers to the next company that prices lower than you do. (Chapter 16 examines break-even analysis and pricing strategy in more depth.)

THE PROMOTION SECTION

The promotion section of the marketing plan should describe the entrepreneur's approach to creating customer awareness of the product or service and explain why customers will be motivated to buy. Among the many promotional options available to the entrepreneur are personal selling (that is, person-to-person selling) and advertising. You will read more about personal selling and advertising in Chapter 17.

If personal selling is appropriate, the section should outline how many salespeople will be employed and how they will be compensated. The proposed system for training

Living the Dream

ENTREPRENEURIAL EXPERIENCES

Direct Sales?

"My first thought was, 'That makes no sense. *Direct sales?* That's a dirty word.'" But Hil Davis was reading how direct sales were a strategy for some of Warren Buffet's most successful enterprises. Davis decided to learn more, so he read *The Pampered Chef: The Story behind the Creation of One of Today's Most Beloved Companies* by Doris Christopher, who told the story of creating and growing a direct sales company, then selling it to Buffet. Davis got excited.

The standard approach in starting a business, including much of what we tell you in this book, is to have a product or service idea and then build the company. Davis and his partner, Veeral Rathod, did just the opposite. Both were in the investment banking business. They decided that direct sales looked like a winning marketing strategy, so the next question was what would they sell?

The answer came from Davis's wife, Holly. One day, she asked him why he didn't buy more custom-made shirts, given that the ones he had were the only shirts he wore. Davis's immediate reaction was that custom-made shirts were too expensive. Then it dawned on him that selling direct to customers could bring the price down. After recruiting some personal stylists, their company, J. Hilburn, was born.

Neither Davis nor Rathod had experience in the apparel industry, so they made nearly every mistake that novices could make. Their initial suppliers did not obtain the quality of fabric that is demanded in custom clothing. More traditional suppliers did not take them seriously and ignored their attempts to order products. Shirts failed to fit properly and had to be returned. Deliveries were delayed. For awhile, Davis thought seriously about giving up and going back to Wall Street.

But the entrepreneurs persevered, recovering from their mistakes. The direct-sales business model proved itself, and J. Hilburn expanded its product line, offering suits, belts, ties, and a line of ready-to-wear items. And customers can now shop online. Davis and Rathod still believe in direct sales, though. On the firm's website, they tell prospective personal stylists that J. Hilburn is ready to help them start their own business, to "Create the Life You've Always Wanted."

Sources: Based on Tom Foster, "Made to Measure: How Hil Davis Took a Business Model People Loved to Hate, Filed Off the Rough Edges, Took It Upscale, and Produced a *Why-Didn't-I-Think-of-That* Innovation," *Inc.*, February 2013, pp. 65–70; https://jhilburn.com, accessed January 17, 2015; Ian Mount, "*Men's Clothing Firm Wants to Expand into Online Sales*, November 2, 2011, http://www.nytimes.com/2011/11/03/business/smallbusiness/j-hilburn-wants-to-sell-online-case-study.html?_r=1, accessed January 17, 2015; and Doris Christopher, *The Pampered Chef: The Story Behind the Creation of One of Today's Most Beloved Companies* (New York: Doubleday, 2005).

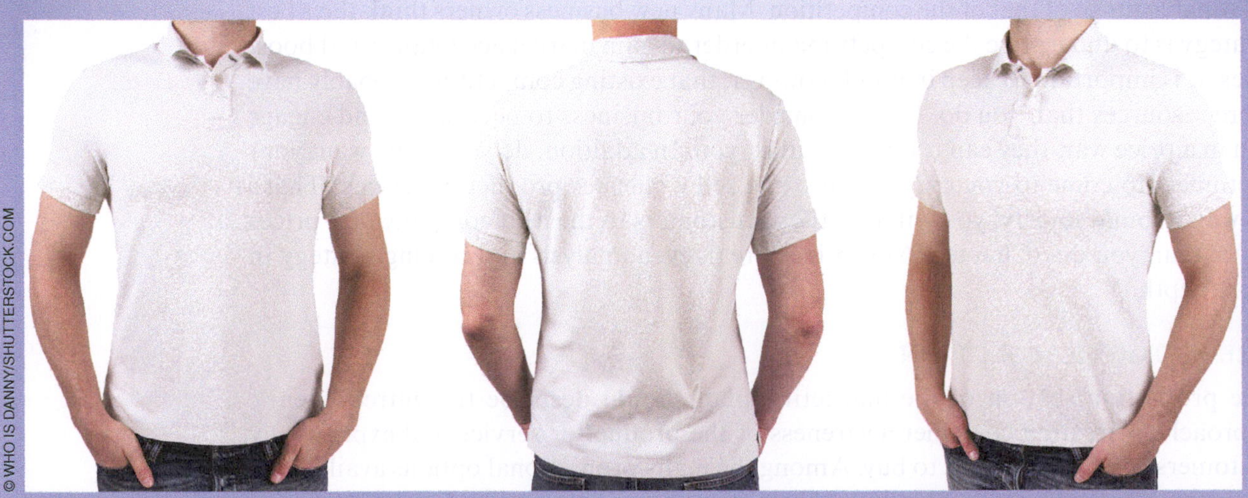

the sales force should also be mentioned. If advertising is to be used, a list of the specific media to be employed should be included and advertising themes should be described. If you will be using the services of an advertising agency, the name and credentials of the agency should be provided, as well as a brief mention of successful campaigns supervised by the agency.

7-3 MARKETING RESEARCH FOR THE SMALL BUSINESS

Discuss the nature of the marketing research process.

Many small business owners base their marketing plans on intuition or on their personal, limited experiences and observations. If you are serious about meeting the needs of your customers, collect and evaluate marketing research data before writing the marketing plan. A plan based on research will be stronger than a plan with intuition and personal observations as its foundation.

7-3a The Nature of Marketing Research

Marketing research may be defined as the gathering, processing, interpreting, and reporting of market information. It is all about finding out what you want to know. A small business typically conducts less marketing research than a big business does, partly because of the expense involved but also because the entrepreneur often does not understand the basic research process. Therefore, our discussion of marketing research focuses on the more widely used and practical techniques that entrepreneurs can employ as they analyze potential target markets and make preparations to develop their marketing plans. A word of caution: Don't use research techniques that you've heard about but haven't really studied. You can mislead yourself and make bad decisions.

© PICTURE ALLIANCE/KARSTEN LEMM/NEWSCOM

Although a small business can conduct marketing research without the assistance of an expert, the cost of hiring such help is often money well spent, as the expert's advice may help increase revenues or cut costs. Marketing researchers are trained, experienced professionals, and prices for their research services typically reflect this. On the other hand, companies such as SurveyMonkey (www.surveymonkey.com) are now reducing overall research costs by taking advantage of the Internet to offer Web-based surveys and online focus groups.

Before committing to research, an entrepreneur should always estimate the projected costs of marketing research and compare them with the benefits expected. Such analysis is never exact, but it will help the entrepreneur to decide how much and what kind of research should be conducted.

marketing research The gathering, processing, interpreting, and reporting of market information.

7-3b Steps in the Marketing Research Process

The typical steps in the marketing research process are (1) identifying the informational need, (2) searching for secondary data, (3) collecting primary data, and (4) interpreting the data gathered.

STEP ONE: IDENTIFYING THE INFORMATIONAL NEED

The first step in marketing research is to identify and define what you need to know. The fact is that small business owners sometimes conduct or commission surveys without pinpointing the specific information they need. Broad statements such as "Our need is to know if the venture will be successful" or "We want to know why our customers make their buying decisions" will do little to guide the research process, but even a more specific goal can easily miss the mark. For example, an entrepreneur thinking about a location for a restaurant may decide to conduct a survey to ascertain customers' menu preferences and reasons for eating out when, in fact, what he or she needs to know most is how often residents of the target area eat out and how far they are willing to drive to eat in a restaurant.

Keep in mind that your marketing plan has to fit with your entire business strategy. What resources do you have to draw from? How efficient are your operations? What is your current competitive advantage, and how long will it last? You must understand how your business operates in order to determine who your customer segments are and should be, and what relationships you want to build with those customers.

STEP TWO: SEARCHING FOR SECONDARY DATA

secondary data
Market information that has been previously compiled.

Information that has already been compiled is known as **secondary data**. Generally, collecting secondary data is much less expensive than gathering new, or primary, data. Therefore, after defining their informational needs, entrepreneurs should exhaust available sources of secondary data before going further into the research process. It may be possible to base much of the marketing plan for the new venture solely on secondary data. A massive amount of information is available in libraries throughout the United States and on the Internet. The libraries of higher education institutions can be especially valuable. Not only do they have access to numerous databases containing business-related information, but they also have librarians with the skills necessary to guide you through those databases.

Secondary Data
Your school library can help you find answers to your small business research questions. And there are many other sources, like the Small Business Administration and state agencies, that you can access. Also take a look at www.411sbfacts.com, from the National Federation of Independent Business. This page will take you to survey responses from thousands of business owners on numerous issues that they have faced.

Software programs and hundreds of websites (many offering free information) can help an entrepreneur research customers for her or his product or service. Like all repositories of information, the Internet is most helpful when used in tandem with other sources. Be very careful to verify the accuracy of all secondary data gathered from the Internet and other sources. Blogs have become a very popular means of conveying information, but not all of that information is factually correct.

A particularly helpful source of secondary data for the small firm is the Small Business Administration, which publishes information on many topics that could prove valuable to you, including marketing research. For example, search for "market research" on the SBA website, and you will be directed to options that include a detailed explanation of how to conduct marketing research.

Unfortunately, the use of secondary data has several drawbacks. One is that the information may be outdated. Another is that the units of measure in the secondary data may not fit the current problem. For example, a firm's market might consist of individuals with incomes between $50,000 and $75,000, while secondary data may report only the number of individuals with incomes between $50,000 and $100,000, skewing the information toward people who may be looking for products and services at a different quality level or in different locations than what you propose to offer.

Finally, the question of credibility is always present. Some sources of secondary data are less trustworthy than others. Mere publication of data does not in itself make the information valid and reliable. It is advisable to compare several different sources to see whether they are reporting similar data. Professional research specialists can also help assess the credibility of secondary sources.

STEP THREE: COLLECTING PRIMARY DATA

If the secondary data are insufficient, a search for new information, or **primary data**, is the next step. Observational methods and questioning methods are two techniques used in accumulating primary data. Observational methods avoid interpersonal contact between respondents and the researcher, while questioning methods involve some type of interaction with respondents. We encourage drawing on the expertise of research specialists when gathering primary data.

Observational Methods Observation is probably the oldest form of research in existence. A simple but effective form of observational research is mystery shopping. Mystery shoppers gather observational data by going into a store (yours or a competitor's) and looking at how items are displayed, checking out in-store advertising, and assessing other features of the store. Mystery shopping can also be used to test employee product knowledge, sales techniques, and more. The results of such activities are used to make important changes in store design and merchandising, as well as to reward good employees.[6]

Jaynie L. Smith is CEO of Smart Advantage, a marketing consulting firm, and author of the book *Relevant Selling*. Smith says that when she asks company executives what they think their customers want and compares their answers to what the customers say, the executives are wrong 90 percent of the time. While business owners often love the features of their products and services, customers want to know how to use the product or service and what benefits they might gain from it.[7] Be careful about seeing only what you want to see and drawing incorrect conclusions about why customers are buying your products.

Questioning Methods Surveys and experimentation are questioning methods that involve contact with respondents. Surveys can be conducted by mail, telephone, the Web, or personal interview. Mail surveys are often used when target respondents are widely dispersed. However, they usually yield low response rates—only a small percentage of the surveys sent out are typically returned. Telephone surveys and personal interview surveys achieve higher response rates. But personal interviews are very expensive, and individuals are often reluctant to grant such interviews if they think a sales pitch is coming. Some marketing researchers, such as iThink, are now specialists in online surveys. For many target-market segments, Internet surveys will be the preferred approach.

© ISTOCKPHOTO.COM/ S-CPHOTO

A questionnaire is the basic instrument guiding the researcher who is administering the survey and the respondent who is taking it. It should be developed carefully and

primary data
New market information that is gathered by the firm conducting the research.

pretested before it is used in the market. Poorly designed questionnaires may lead to results that cause you to make bad decisions. Here are several considerations to keep in mind when designing and testing a questionnaire:

- Ask questions that relate directly to the issue under consideration. A good test of relevance is to assume an answer to each question and then ask yourself how you would use that information.
- Select the form of question, such as open-ended or multiple-choice, that is most appropriate for the subject and the conditions of the survey.
- Carefully consider the order of the questions. Asking questions in the wrong sequence can produce biased answers to later questions.
- Ask the more sensitive questions near the end of the questionnaire. Age and income, for example, are usually sensitive topics.
- Carefully select the words in each question. They should be as simple, clear, and objective as possible.
- Pretest the questionnaire by administering it to a small sample of respondents who are representative of the group to be surveyed.

It is important to remember that formal marketing research is not always necessary. The business owner's first decision should be whether to conduct primary research at all. It may be best not to conduct formal research in the following situations:[8]

- Your company doesn't have the resources to conduct the research properly or to implement any findings generated from the proposed research.
- The opportunity for a new business or product introduction has passed. If you've been beaten to the punch, it may be wise to wait and see how the early entrant to the market fares.
- A decision to move forward has already been made. There's no need to spend good money on a decision that has already been made.
- You can't decide what information is needed. If you don't know where you are going, any road will take you there.
- The needed information already exists (that is, secondary information is available).
- The cost of conducting the research outweighs the potential benefits.

Bloomberg Businessweek journalist John Tozzi suggests several ways entrepreneurs can do their own research with very little money.

1. Conduct your research in the same way that you sell your product or service. Salespeople who make personal calls can gather information while they are out. If sales are over the phone, survey over the phone. If you market primarily online, conduct Web surveys.
2. Mine public sources. Use government sites, such as that of the U.S. Census Bureau. After all, you've paid for this information through your taxes.
3. Enlist students from local colleges to help stretch your limited research budget. In addition, their professors may prove to be good sources of research interpretation expertise.[9]

STEP FOUR: INTERPRETING THE DATA GATHERED

After the necessary data have been gathered, they must be transformed into usable information. Without interpretation, large quantities of data are only isolated facts.

Methods of summarizing and simplifying information for users include tables, charts, and other graphics. Descriptive statistics (for example, the average response) are most helpful during this step in the research procedure. Inexpensive personal computer software, such as Excel, is now available to perform statistical calculations and generate report-quality graphics.

As important as marketing research is, it should be viewed as a supplement to, not a replacement for, good judgment and cautious experimentation in launching new products and services. Ultimately, the marketing plan should reflect the entrepreneur's educated belief about the best marketing strategy for her or his firm.

7-4 UNDERSTANDING POTENTIAL TARGET MARKETS

Define *market segmentation* and discuss its related strategies.

To prepare the market analysis section of the marketing plan, an entrepreneur needs a proper understanding of the term *market*, which means different things to different people. It may refer to a physical location where buying and selling take place ("They went to the market"), or it may be used to describe selling efforts ("We must market this product aggressively"). Still another meaning is the one we emphasize in this chapter: A **market** is a group of customers or potential customers who have purchasing power and unsatisfied needs. Note carefully the three ingredients in this definition of a market:

1. A market must have buying units, or *customers*. These units may be individuals or business entities.
2. Customers in a market must have *purchasing power*. Those who lack money and/or credit do not constitute a viable market because no transactions can occur.
3. A market must contain buying units with *unsatisfied needs*. Customers, for instance, will not buy unless they are motivated to do so—and motivation can occur only when a customer recognizes his or her unsatisfied needs.

In light of our definition of a market, determining market potential is the process of locating and investigating buying units that have both purchasing power and needs that can be satisfied with the product or service that is being offered.

7-4a Market Segmentation and Its Variables

In Chapter 3, cost- and differentiation-based strategies were described as they apply to marketplaces that are relatively homogeneous, or uniform, in nature. As discussed, these strategies can also be used to focus on a market niche within an industry. In his book *Competitive Advantage*, Michael Porter refers to this type of competitive strategy—in which cost- and differentiation-based advantages are achieved within narrow market segments—as a *focus strategy*.[10]

A focus strategy depends on market segmentation and becomes a consideration in competitive markets. Formally defined, **market segmentation** is the process of dividing the total market for a product or service into smaller groups with similar needs, such that each group is likely to respond favorably to a specific marketing strategy. A generation ago, telephones were purely a landline technology. Today, there are cell phone and smartphone configurations targeted at young versus older segments, tech-oriented versus non-tech-oriented customers, business versus home features. And voice communication can be achieved through technologies that bear no resemblance to phones.

market
A group of customers or potential customers who have purchasing power and unsatisfied needs.

market segmentation
The division of a market into several smaller groups, each with similar needs.

In order to divide the total market into appropriate segments, an entrepreneur must consider **segmentation variables**, which are parameters that distinguish one form of market behavior from another. Two broad sets of segmentation variables that represent the major dimensions of a market are benefit variables and demographic variables.

BENEFIT VARIABLES

The definition of a market highlights the unsatisfied needs of customers. **Benefit variables** are related to customer needs since they are used to identify segments of a market based on the benefits sought by customers. For example, a single health club may offer services that are used for different reasons and in different ways by different market segments. Older adults might want cardiovascular exercise, young men might be interested in bodybuilding, and young girls may attend gymnastics classes there.

DEMOGRAPHIC VARIABLES

It is impossible to implement forecasting and marketing strategy with benefit variables alone. Therefore, small businesses commonly use **demographic variables** as part of market segmentation. These variables refer to certain characteristics that describe customers, their purchasing power, their consumption patterns, and other factors. They include age, marital status, gender, occupation, and income.

7-4b Marketing Strategies Based on Segmentation Considerations

There are several types of strategies based on market segmentation efforts. The three types discussed here are the unsegmented approach, the multisegment approach, and the single-segment approach. Few companies engage in all three approaches simultaneously. Small businesses often lack the resources that these strategies tend to require. But for some, a marketing strategy based on segmentation considerations is the best route to take.

THE UNSEGMENTED STRATEGY

When a business defines the total market as its target, it is following an **unsegmented strategy** (also known as **mass marketing**). This strategy can sometimes be successful, but it assumes that all customers desire the same basic benefit from the product or service. This may hold true for water but certainly does not hold true for shoes, which satisfy numerous needs through a wide range of styles, prices, colors, and sizes. With an unsegmented strategy, a firm develops a single marketing mix—one combination of product, price, promotion, and distribution. Its competitive advantage must be derived from either a cost- or a differentiation-based advantage. For example, the moving company Two Men and a Truck (Video Case 4) "offers you any home moving services you need" and does local and long-distance moves. This company targets both commercial and residential customers, offering similar services to each.[11] Exhibit 7.2 represents its strategy.

THE MULTISEGMENT STRATEGY

With a view of the market that recognizes individual segments with different preferences, a firm is in a better position to tailor marketing mixes to various segments. If a firm determines that two or more market segments have the potential to be profitable and then develops a unique marketing mix for each segment, it is following a **multisegment strategy**.

segmentation variables
The parameters used to distinguish one form of market behavior from another.

benefit variables
Specific characteristics that distinguish market segments according to the benefits sought by customers.

demographic variables
Specific characteristics that describe customers, their purchasing power, their consumption patterns, and other factors.

unsegmented strategy (mass marketing)
A strategy that defines the total market as the target market.

multisegment strategy
A strategy that recognizes different preferences of individual market segments and develops a unique marketing mix for each.

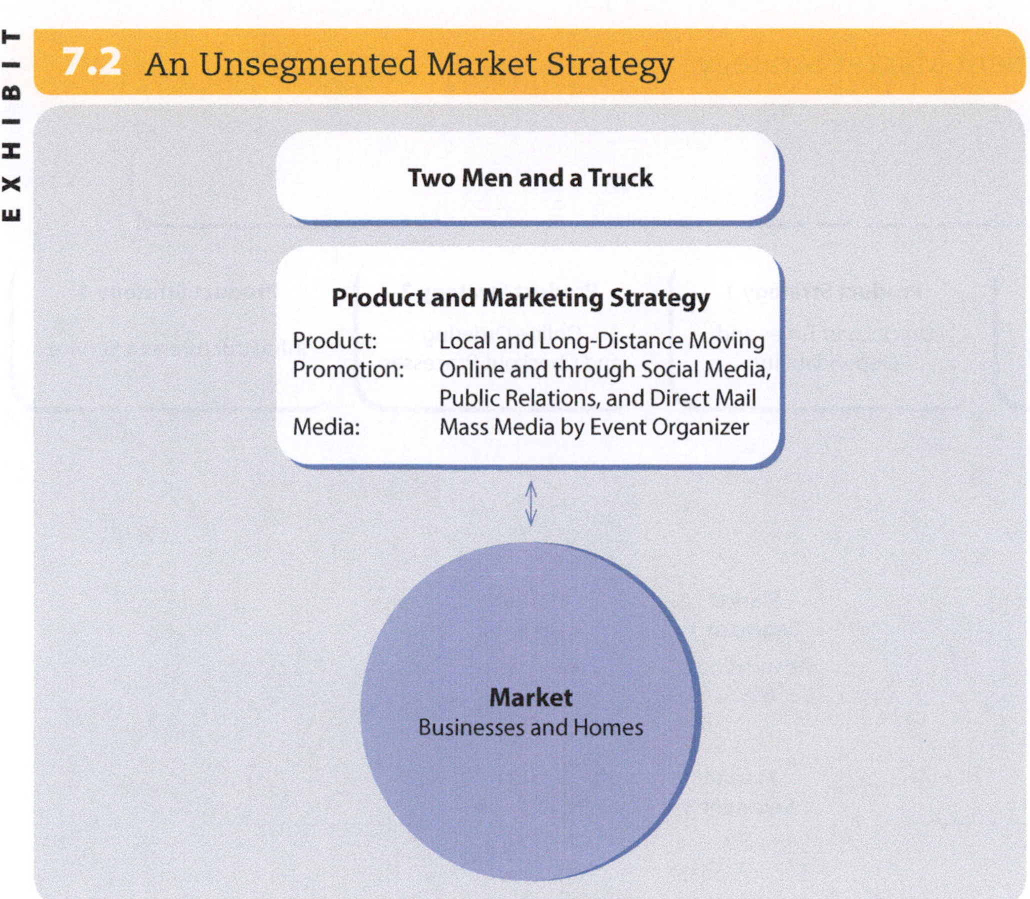

EXHIBIT 7.2 An Unsegmented Market Strategy

In Video Case 16, you will be introduced to Dyn, a global Internet infrastructure service provider. Its clients include both businesses and home users, and it identifies four primary customer segments, as shown in Exhibit 7.3.

THE SINGLE-SEGMENT STRATEGY

When a firm recognizes that several distinct market segments exist but chooses to concentrate on reaching only the most potentially profitable segment, it is following a **single-segment strategy**. Once again, a competitive advantage is achieved through a cost- or differentiation-based strategy. Startup Professionals, a team of experts who help entrepreneurs start and grow their ventures, provides products and services that have value for students, retirees, hobbyists, and more, but the founders chose to focus their energies on high-growth-potential ventures. Its market strategy is illustrated in Exhibit 7.4.[12]

single-segment strategy
A strategy that recognizes the existence of several distinct market segments but focuses on only the most profitable segment.

The single-segment approach is probably the wisest strategy for small businesses to use during initial marketing efforts. It allows a small firm to specialize and make better use of its limited resources. Then, once its reputation has been established, the firm will find it easier to enter new markets.

7-5 ESTIMATING MARKET POTENTIAL

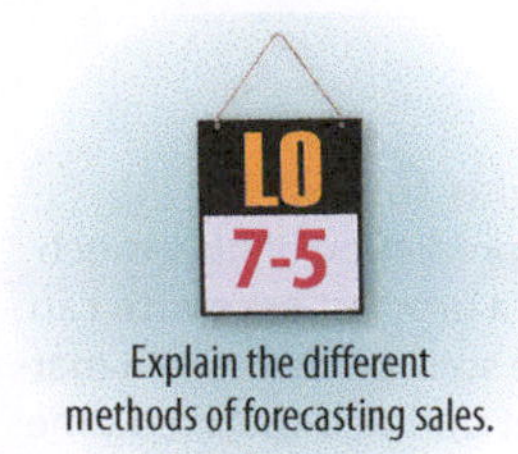

Explain the different methods of forecasting sales.

A small business can be successful only if sufficient market demand exists for its product or service. A sales forecast is the typical indicator of market adequacy, so it is particularly important to complete this assessment prior to writing the marketing

EXHIBIT 7.3 A Multisegment Market Strategy

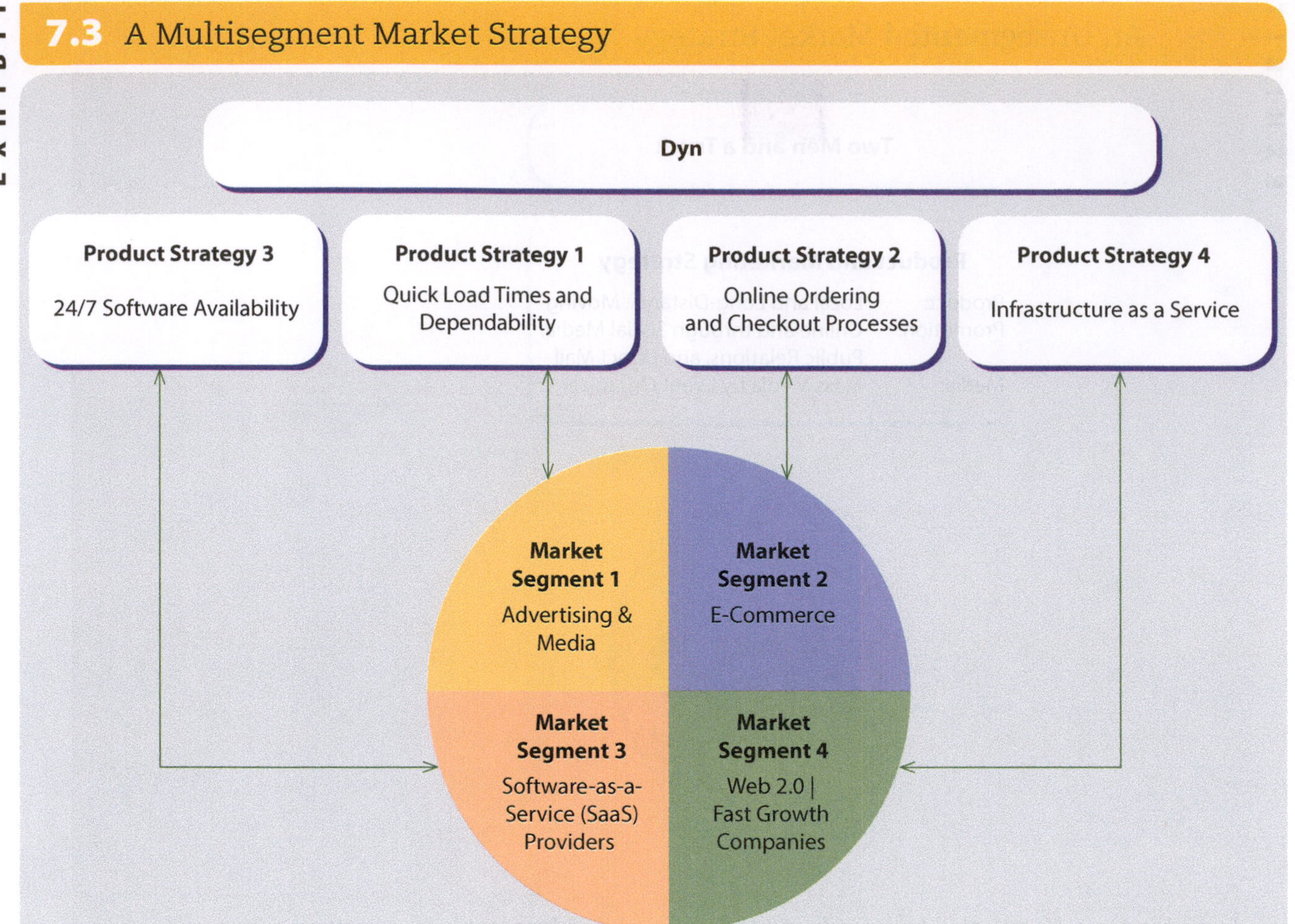

plan. Many types of information are required to gauge market potential. This section discusses these information needs as it examines the forecasting process.

7-5a The Sales Forecast

A **sales forecast** is an estimate of how much of a product or service can be sold within a given market in a defined time period. The forecast can be stated in terms of dollars and/or units.

Because a sales forecast revolves around a specific target market, that market should be defined as precisely as possible. Don't make the mistake of forecasting sales that exceed the size of the market you are serving. If the market for desks is described as "all offices," the sales forecast will be extremely large. But you are probably only selling to a smaller segment, such as "government agencies seeking solid wood desks priced between $800 and $1200." That will result in a much smaller but more useful forecast.

One sales forecast may cover a period of time that is a year or less, while another may extend over several years. Both short-term and long-term forecasts are needed for a well-constructed marketing plan.

sales forecast
A prediction of how much of a product or service can be sold within a given market during a specified time period.

A sales forecast is an essential component of the marketing plan because it is critical to assessing the feasibility of a new venture. If the market is insufficient, the business is destined for failure. A sales forecast is also useful in other areas of business

EXHIBIT 7.4 A Single-Segment Market Strategy

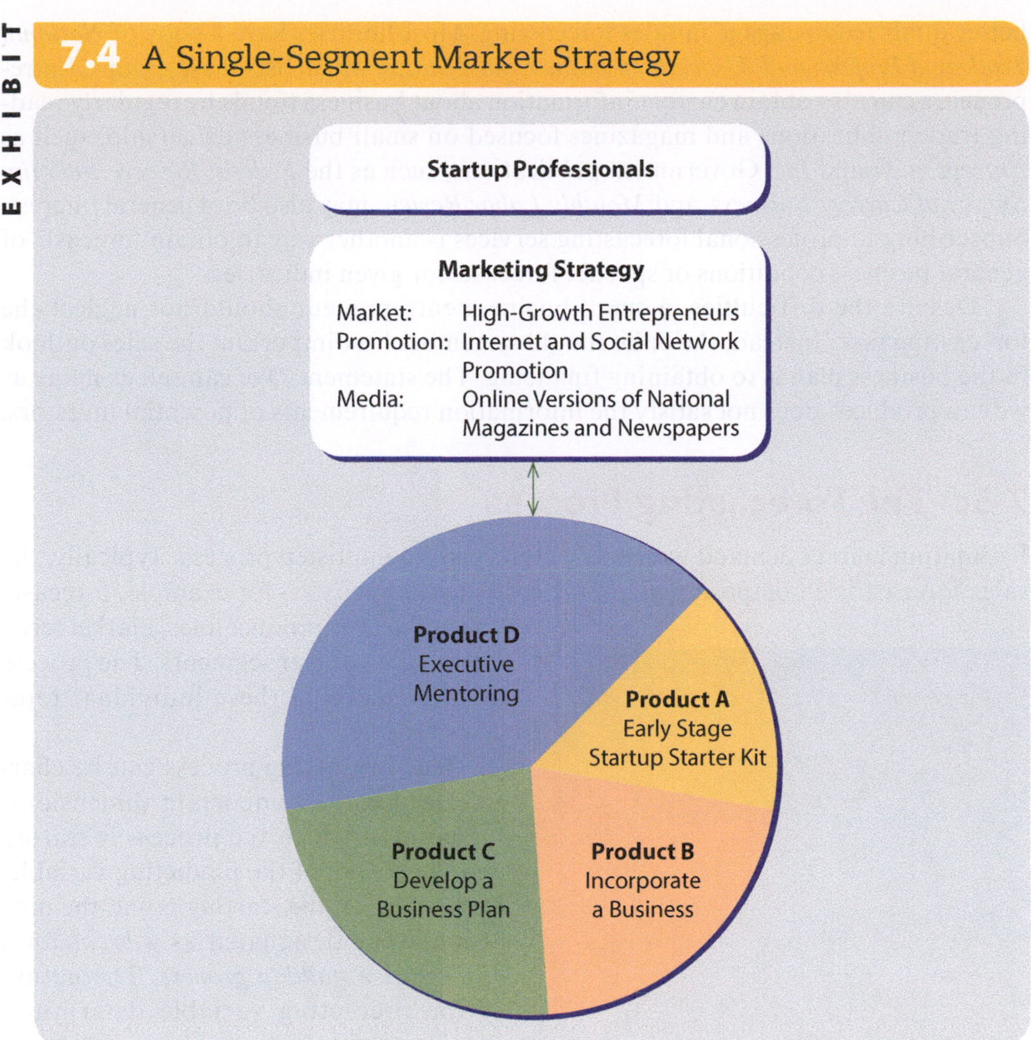

planning. Production schedules, inventory policies, and personnel decisions all start with a sales forecast. Obviously, a forecast can never be perfect, and entrepreneurs should remember that a forecast can be wrong in either direction, by either underestimating or overestimating potential sales.

7-5b Limitations of Forecasting

For a number of practical reasons, forecasting is used less frequently by small firms than by large firms. First, for any new business, forecasting circumstances are unique. Entrepreneurial inexperience, coupled with a new idea, represents the most difficult forecasting situation. An ongoing business that requires only an updated forecast for its existing product is in the most favorable forecasting position.

Second, a small business manager may be unfamiliar with methods of quantitative analysis (analysis of measurable data). Not all forecasting must be quantitatively oriented—qualitative forecasting is often helpful and may be sufficient—but quantitative methods have repeatedly proven their value in forecasting.

Third, the typical small business entrepreneur and his or her team know little about the forecasting process. To overcome this deficiency, the owners of some small firms attempt to keep in touch with industry trends through contacts with appropriate trade associations. The professional members of a trade association are frequently better qualified to engage in sales forecasting. Most libraries have a copy of *National Trade and Professional Associations of the United States*, which lists these groups. Entrepreneurs can also obtain current information about business trends by regularly reading trade publications and magazines focused on small business ownership, such as *Entrepreneur* and *Inc*. Government publications, such as the *Federal Reserve Bulletin*, *Survey of Current Business*, and *Monthly Labor Review*, may also be of general interest. Subscribing to professional forecasting services is another way to obtain forecasts of general business conditions or specific forecasts for given industries.

Despite the difficulties, a small business entrepreneur should not neglect the forecasting task. Instead, she or he should remember how important the sales outlook in the business plan is to obtaining financing. The statement "We can sell as many as we can produce" does not satisfy the information requirements of potential investors.

7-5c The Forecasting Process

Estimating market demand with a sales forecast is a multistep process. Typically, the sales forecast is a composite of several individual forecasts—for example, forecasts for products or product lines, market territories, or customer segments. The process involves merging these individual forecasts properly.

© ISTOCKPHOTO.COM/ RAWPIXEL LTD

The forecasting process can be characterized by two important dimensions: the point at which the process is started and the nature of the predicting variable. Depending on the starting point, the process may be designated as a *breakdown process* or a *buildup process*. The nature of the predicting variable determines whether the forecasting is *direct* or *indirect*.

THE STARTING POINT

The **breakdown process**, sometimes called the **chain-ratio method**, begins with a variable that has a very large scope and systematically works down to the sales forecast. This method is frequently used for consumer products forecasting. The initial variable might be a population figure for the target market. Through the use of percentages, an appropriate link is built to generate the sales forecast.

breakdown process (chain-ratio method)
A forecasting method that begins with a variable that has a very large scope and systematically works down to the sales forecast.

buildup process
A forecasting method in which all potential buyers in a target market's submarkets are identified and the estimated demand is added up.

David Goldsmith cautions his New York University students against making a general forecast of the future, recommending activity-based forecasting instead.[13] This approach breaks the whole into its parts or activities, forecasts each of those, and then brings them together to get a better picture of what's to come.

One source of data available to every small business owner is the U.S. Census Bureau, which compiles statistics on various population segments by, for example, gender, age, geographic location, and household income. Additional data on customer segments may be obtained through state and local government agencies, chambers of commerce, trade associations, and private enterprise sources.

In contrast to the breakdown process, the **buildup process** calls for identifying all potential buyers in a target market's submarkets and then adding up the estimated demand. For example, a local dry-cleaning firm that is forecasting demand for cleaning high school letter jackets might estimate its market share within each area school as 20 percent. Then, by determining the number of high school students obtaining a letter jacket at each school—perhaps from school yearbooks—an analyst could estimate the total demand.

The buildup process is especially helpful for industrial goods forecasting. To estimate potential, forecasters often use data from the Annual Survey of Manufactures by the U.S. Department of Commerce. The information can be broken down according to the North American Industry Classification System (NAICS), which classifies businesses by type of industry. Once the code for a group of potential industrial customers has been identified, the forecaster can obtain information on the number of establishments and their geographic location, number of employees, and annual sales. A sales forecast can be constructed by summing this information for several relevant codes.

THE PREDICTING VARIABLE

In **direct forecasting**, which is the simplest form of forecasting, sales is the forecasted variable. Many times, however, sales cannot be predicted directly and other variables must be used. **Indirect forecasting** takes place when surrogate variables are used to project sales. For example, if a firm lacks information about industry sales of baby cribs but has data on births, the strong correlation between the two variables allows planners to use the figures for births to help forecast industry sales for cribs.

For a new business, there are few things as important as identifying your market—nothing happens until someone buys something from your company. And if you plan to grow your business, understanding your market is essential. In this chapter, we introduced you to the steps necessary for putting together a marketing plan. The plan will be a living document for you as you manage your business. Every day, you will learn more about your market and how you can meet customer needs. And the marketing plan has an impact on many other areas of your business. In later chapters, you will see that your marketing strategy affects how many people you employ and what skills they need, the volume and selection of your inventory, the production processes you use, and many other business functions.

direct forecasting
A forecasting method in which sales is the estimated variable.

indirect forecasting
A forecasting method in which variables related to sales are used to project future sales.

7-1. Describe small business marketing.

- Small business marketing consists of business activities that direct the creation, development, and delivery of a bundle of satisfaction from the creator to the targeted user.
- The product or service as a bundle of satisfaction has three levels: (1) core product/service, (2) actual product/service, and (3) augmented product/service.
- Three distinct marketing philosophies are the production-, sales-, and consumer-oriented philosophies.
- A small business should adopt a consumer orientation to marketing, as that philosophy is most consistent with long-term success.
- Small business marketing activities include analyzing the market and determining the marketing mix.

7-2. Identify the components of a formal marketing plan.

- The formal marketing plan should include sections on market analysis, the competition, and marketing strategy.
- The market analysis should include a customer profile.
- A SWOT analysis is helpful in assessing the competition.
- The "4 Ps" of marketing strategy that should be discussed in the marketing plan are (1) product decisions affecting the total product and/or service, (2) place (distribution) activities, (3) pricing decisions, and (4) promotional activities.

7-3. Discuss the nature of the marketing research process.

- Marketing research involves the gathering, processing, interpreting, and reporting of marketing information.
- The cost of marketing research should be evaluated against its benefits.
- The steps in the marketing research process are identifying the informational need, searching for secondary data, collecting primary data, and interpreting the data gathered.

7-4. Define *market segmentation*, and discuss its related strategies.

- A focus strategy relies on market segmentation, which is the process of dividing the total market for a product or service into smaller groups with similar needs, such that each group is likely to respond favorably to a specific marketing strategy.
- Broad segmentation variables that represent major dimensions of a market are benefit variables and demographic variables.
- Three types of market segmentation strategies are (1) the unsegmented approach, (2) the multisegment approach, and (3) the single-segment approach.
- The unsegmented strategy—when a business defines the total market as its target—is also known as mass marketing.
- A firm that determines that two or more market segments have the potential to be profitable and then develops a unique marketing mix for each segment is following a multisegment strategy.
- A firm that follows a single-segment strategy recognizes that several distinct market segments exist but chooses to concentrate on reaching only the segment that promises the greatest profitability.

7-5. Explain the different methods of forecasting sales.

- A sales forecast is an estimate of how much of a product or service can be sold within a given market during a defined time period.
- The forecasting process may be either a breakdown or a buildup process and may be either direct or indirect, depending on the predicting variable.
- The breakdown process, or chain-ratio method, begins with a variable that has a very large scope and systematically works down to the sales forecast.
- The buildup process calls for identifying all potential buyers in a target market's submarkets and then adding up the estimated demand.
- In direct forecasting, sales is the forecasted variable. In indirect forecasting, surrogate variables are used to project sales.

Key Terms

actual product/service p. 176
augmented product/service p. 176
benefit variables p. 188
breakdown process (chain-ratio method) p. 192
buildup process p. 192
core product/service p. 176
customer profile p. 177
demographic variables p. 188
direct forecasting p. 193
indirect forecasting p. 193
market p. 187
market analysis p. 177
marketing mix p. 177
marketing research p. 183
market segmentation p. 187
multisegment strategy p. 188
primary data p. 185
sales forecast p. 190
secondary data p. 184
segmentation variables p. 188
single-segment strategy p. 189
small business marketing p. 175
unsegmented strategy (mass marketing) p. 188

You Make the Call

Situation 1

What is your strategy for e-commerce? That's a question Michael Maher, Barrett Purdum, and Mike Armenta asked each other when they launched Taylor Stitch, a custom shirt manufacturer and retailer in San Francisco. They decided that their strengths were in designing, manufacturing, and marketing their products, not in designing a Web platform for their business. After researching available options, they chose Shopify, which helps companies set up online stores. It sells or configures domain names, sets up and hosts websites, provides shopping cart features enabling customers to browse and buy, and offers other e-commerce products and consulting services. The owners of Taylor Stitch credit the Shopify platform with spurring sales through a well-integrated system.

Sources: Based on http://www.taylorstitch.com, accessed December 13, 2012; and http://www.shopify.com, accessed December 13, 2012.

Question 1 What factors should business owners consider when deciding to manage their own website and online sales instead of contracting for the service?

Question 2 Taylor Stitch has both a bricks-and-mortar store and an online store. What are the advantages and disadvantages of this strategy?

Situation 2

Every company wants to use "word of mouth" to promote their business. The Internet has taken that to a whole new level. People read endorsements from others through networks they have found reliable. Gregory E. Alden manages the chain of Woodside Hotels in Northern California. Positioned in the luxury hotel category, Woodside properties rely on being ranked high by their customers on such websites as Yelp, TripAdvisor, Expedia, and others. But monitoring all those services can be seriously time consuming. Alden found a better way to monitor how satisfied customers were and what they were communicating about the hotels by contracting with Revinate. Revinate provides a software platform for hotels and other companies in the hospitality industry. The platform allows Alden to track online reviews and to use social media to learn what travelers want. He can spot trends and act on criticisms immediately, bringing customers back and attracting new ones.

Sources: Based on Gwen Moran, "Chatter Master," *Entrepreneur*, December 2012, p. 62; http://www.woodsidehotels.com, accessed March 13, 2015; and http://www.revinate.com, accessed March 13, 2015.

Question 1 How do you think Alden found out about Revinate? Given all the online companies that might help your business connect you with customers, how would you choose one?

Question 2 Do you report your experiences with businesses on any social networks? Why or why not?

Situation 3

Ricardo De La Blanca Brigati is CEO of the DLB Group, a full-service marketing company operating throughout the Americas and in Spain with about $10 million in revenues. He encourages his clients to focus on African American, Hispanic, Asian American, and Native American consumers. He sees the buying power of these segments, but few small businesses are making adjustments to serve them. DLB's website offers examples of how the company helps clients, both in the United States and abroad, develop comprehensive marketing strategies that set them apart by adapting to (and respecting) other cultures.

Sources: Based on http://www.dlbgroup.com, accessed March 13, 2015; and Karen E. Klein, "What Companies Get Wrong When Marketing to Minorities," http://www.businessweek.com/smallbiz/content/dec2010/sb20101213_643259.htm, accessed March 13, 2015.

Question 1 Identify a minority group to which you do not belong. What steps could you take to learn about that market segment in order to sell those consumers a product or service?

Question 2 Suppose that your small business was contacted by a company in another country that wanted to sell your products in its market. What would you want to know about that market before going into it? Choose any country (other than the United States) and determine what changes you would have to make to your marketing plan to adjust to the different culture.

Business Plan

LAYING THE FOUNDATION

As part of laying the foundation for your own business plan, respond to the following questions regarding the marketing plan, marketing research, market segmentation, and sales forecasting.

Marketing Plan Questions

1. How will you identify prospective customers?
2. What is the customer profile for your product and/or service?
3. Who is your competition?
4. Have you conducted a SWOT analysis?
5. What geographic area will you serve?
6. What are the distinguishing characteristics of your product and/or service?
7. What steps have already been taken to develop your product and/or service?
8. What do you plan to name your product and/or service?
9. Will there be a warranty?
10. How will you set the price for your product and/or service?
11. What type of distribution plan will you use?
12. Will you export to other countries?
13. What type of selling effort will you use?
14. What special selling skills will be required?

15. What types of advertising and sales promotion will you use?
16. Can you use the Internet to promote your company and product/service?

Marketing Research Questions

1. What research questions do you need answers to?
2. What types of research should be conducted to collect the information you need?
3. How much will this research cost?
4. What sources of secondary data will address your informational needs?
5. What sources of relevant data are available in your local library?
6. What sources of outside professional assistance would you consider using to help with marketing research?
7. Is there information available on the Internet that might be helpful?
8. What research questions do you need answers to?

Market Segmentation Questions

1. Will you focus on a limited market within the industry?
2. What segmentation variables will you use to define your target market?
3. If you determine that several distinct market segments exist, will you concentrate on just one segment?

Sales Forecasting Questions

1. How do you plan to forecast sales for your product and/or service?
2. What sources of forecasting assistance have you consulted?
3. What sales forecasting techniques are most appropriate to your needs?
4. What is the sales forecast for your product and/or service?
5. How reliable is your sales forecast?

Video Case 7

Readymade Magazine (P. 657)

ReadyMade markets itself as a magazine catering to GenNest, the group of consumers ages 25 to 35 who are just settling down after college. But *ReadyMade* appeals to a wide variety of readers, with subscribers in all age groups. This diversity offers a unique challenge to *ReadyMade* as it tries to promote itself to advertisers who need to know what sort of people will be reached through advertisements in the publication.

Alternative Cases for Chapter 7

Case 1, Dashlocker, p. 646
Video Case 14, Numi Tea, p. 675

Endnotes

1. Jennifer Wang, "Emotional Rescue," *Entrepreneur*, April 2013, p. 69; and http://hendrickboards.com, accessed January 16, 2015.
2. Based on "Spira: Wavespring Technology," http://spira.com/wavespring-technology, accessed January 16, 2015.
3. *Ibid.*
4. Adam Bluestein, "The Success Gene: Why Some Family Businesses Thrive Year after Year after Year," http://www.inc.com/magazine/20080401/the-success-gene.html, accessed January 17, 2015; and http://www.husseyseating.com, accessed January 17, 2015.
5. Brad Stone, "What's in a Name? For Apple, iPad Said More Than Intended," *The New York Times*, January 29, 2010, pp. A1, A3.
6. "Mystery Shopping," http://www.inc.com/encyclopedia/mystery-shopping.html, accessed January 17, 2015.
7. Jason Fried, "A Chat with the Master," *Inc.*, October 2012, p.35.
8. Carl McDaniel, Jr. and Roger Gates, *Marketing Research* (New York: Wiley, 2014).
9. John Tozzi, "Market Research on the Cheap," *Bloomberg Businessweek*, http://www.businessweek.com/smallbiz/content/jan2008/sb2008019_352779.htm, accessed January 17, 2015.
10. Michael Porter, *Competitive Advantage* (New York: Free Press, 1985), p. 5.
11. http://www.twomenandatruck.com, accessed January 17, 2015.
12. http://www.startupprofessionals.com/index.html, accessed January 17, 2015.
13. David Goldsmith, "For a Finer Forecast, Pull Apart the Future," *Fast Company*, http://www.fastcompany.com/3001941/finer-forecast-pull-apart-future, accessed January 17, 2015; and David Goldsmith, *Paid to Think: A Leader's Toolkit for Redefining Your Future* (Dallas, TX: BenBella Books, 2012).

CHAPTER 8

The Organizational Plan: Teams, Legal Structures, Alliances, and Directors

One of the most enduring myths in American business is that of the lone entrepreneur who defies the odds by taking a creative business idea and turning it into reality by sheer force of will and personality. It makes a great story, but it doesn't really reflect reality. Ventures are increasingly being started by teams, with each partner bringing unique skills and competencies to the table.

Rose Cook and Lynn Faughey are co-founders of FlexPro, a specialty consulting company that matches project managers in the life sciences with the pharmaceutical firms that need their expertise. The two women are also identical twins, and both studied engineering at Rutgers University. But before founding FlexPro in 2008, they struggled to maintain a work-life balance that felt right to them. Rising above this shared challenge is the foundation for their business, but it's really their relationship as sisters that defines their partnership. "Nothing between us is much of a surprise," says Cook, "We can finish each other's sentences. It's an unfair advantage." Their tight collaboration may explain why the company is so successful, having made *Inc.*'s list of fastest-growing private companies for three years in a row.

New venture partners are rarely related, but they are almost always connected in some meaningful way. An electronics-repair store based in Orlando, Florida, called uBreakiFix was started by three friends who relied on previous

In the SPOTLIGHT
FlexPro, uBreakiFix, and GreenCupboards
www.theflexprogroup.com
www.ubreakifix.com
www.greencupboards.com

OPEN
LOOKING AHEAD

After studying this chapter, you should be able to. . .

8-1. Describe the characteristics and value of a strong management team.

8-2. Explain the common legal forms of organization used by small businesses.

8-3. Identify factors to consider in choosing among the primary legal forms of organization.

8-4. Discuss the unique features and restrictions of five specialized organizational forms.

8-5. Understand the nature of strategic alliances and their uses in small businesses.

8-6. Describe the effective use of boards of directors and advisory boards.

startup experience to get the venture up and running. Launched in 2009 as an Internet-based, mail-in electronics repair service, the founders soon realized that the demand for quicker turnaround times and face-to-face interactions could only be addressed through a physical location. That prompted the team to set up its first brick-and-mortar shop in Orlando, which has been followed more recently by rapid growth through franchising into locations all across the United States and even in Canada.

Thinking strategically, uBreakiFix has achieved impressive results from its relentless focus on industry-leading customer service, unmatched technical knowledge, and comprehensive warranty policy. But more fundamentally, the partners attribute the company's success to their ability to communicate effectively and develop the business together as a team. Co-founder David Reiff put it this way: "All of us approach problems in different ways. That can cause some friction, but friction is beneficial." In order to resolve the occasional conflict, the team will sit down as a group and discuss the issue. If all else fails, Justin Wetherill, the uBreakiFix CEO, is responsible for the final decision making in the company.

Sometimes, small business owners reach beyond the startup team to find the difference makers they need. For example, professional relationships can also lead to important partnership relationships. Josh Neblett and his wife, Sarah Wollnick, reached out for help to a former professor, Tom Simpson, when they launched GreenCupboards, "an e-tailer of certified organic, fair trade, cruelty free and environmentally friendly products and foods for low-impact and healthy living." After graduating from college, Neblett approached Simpson, seeking direction for the startup, and that conversation led to the professor's signing on permanently as chairman—and he continues to serve as a mentor to the entrepreneurs. Looking back, Neblett asserts that partnering with an experienced advisor has been the smartest move he has made on the path to small business success.

Whether teaming up with family members, talented friends, capable associates, or even a trusted advisor, these entrepreneurs and their experiences provide evidence that the game of business is often best played as a team sport.

Sources: "About uBreakiFix," http://www.ubreakifix.com/about, accessed November 28, 2014; Jennifer Alsever, "For Better and for Worse," *Inc.*, Vol. 35, No. 7 (September 2013), pp. 48–56; "FlexPro: Meet Rose and Lynn," http://www.theflexprogroup.com/our-story, accessed November 28, 2014; and David Mielach, "Behind the Business Plan: GreenCupboards," *BusinessNewsDaily.com*, September 21, 2012, http://www.businessnewsdaily.com/3168-business-plan-greencupboards.html, accessed November 28, 2014.

Popular notions aside, most successful entrepreneurs do not operate as "Lone Rangers" in the startup world. In fact, it seems that an increasing number of new ventures—including those featured in the opening Spotlight to this chapter—are being led by talented and effective *teams* of entrepreneurs. This adjustment may be required to handle the increasing complexity and share the expanding workload involved in getting a startup off the ground.

To be sure, plenty of solo entrepreneurs are starting new businesses, but evidence is mounting that shows team-founded ventures tend to outperform their solo-founded counterparts. Entrepreneurship experts Stephen Spinelli and Robert Adams emphasize this point: "Owning and running the whole show effectively puts a ceiling on growth. . . . It is extremely difficult to grow a higher-potential venture by working single-handedly. Higher-potential entrepreneurs build a team, an organization, and a company."[1]

Unfortunately, team leadership in a small enterprise all too often presents its share of heartaches, especially when partners are hastily chosen, work and reward relationships are unclear, and formal agreements are poorly conceived or confusing. The high hopes of partnership and camaraderie in business can easily be dashed on the rocks of real life. People are imperfect, after all, so working closely with others is bound to lead to a certain amount of disappointment. However, in all but the simplest of businesses, the entrepreneur's personal talents often need to be supplemented with the experience and abilities of other individuals. A venture's prospects typically are most promising when its leadership is composed of competent, resourceful, and tenacious individuals who are committed to doing their best and can get along because they trust one another and share the same values.[2] With that in mind, it is important for an entrepreneur to identify and attract a strong management team. An organizational plan that provides for effective leadership is appealing to both potential investors and prospective managerial personnel.

In this chapter, we also discuss the selection of an appropriate ownership structure, often called a legal form of organization. The direction of the business will be powerfully shaped by an entrepreneur's decision to organize as a sole proprietorship, a partnership, a corporation, or one of the other available forms. The organizational form should match the needs of the business, but getting it right can be a challenge. Also included in the organizational plan are strategic alliances, which are becoming increasingly popular among small businesses and can be vitally important to their performance. Finally, we describe the role of boards of directors or advisory boards for small businesses and provide insights on how to make the most of them.

All of these elements of a small business should be carefully considered in the organizational plan. The quality of an entrepreneur's decisions on these issues can greatly enhance the performance of the company—or doom it to failure. We will show you how to navigate the potentially dangerous waters of planning for these facets of the business and guide you toward improved odds for success.

Division of Ownership
Research by Harvard Business School professor Noam Wasserman found that 73 percent of entrepreneurial teams craft their startup agreements within the first month of founding. This means that the division of equity among partners is set in stone at a time of great optimism and before capabilities and commitments are sorted out. When the balance of contributions changes (often dramatically), tensions rise and unhappiness with the initial equity split nearly triples. For more on this research, see Noam Wasserman, "How an Entrepreneur's Passion Can Destroy a Startup," *The Wall Street Journal*, August 25, 2014, pp. R1–R2.

8-1 BUILDING A MANAGEMENT TEAM

Describe the characteristics and value of a strong management team.

If a firm is extremely small, the founder will probably be the key manager and perhaps the only manager. In most firms, however, others share leadership roles with the owner, which creates opportunities to leverage their combined networks and resources for the good of the company. In general, the **management team** consists of individuals with supervisory responsibilities, as well as nonsupervisory personnel who play key roles in the business.[3] For example, members of a management team might include a financial manager who supervises a small office staff and another person who directs the marketing effort.

If you should find that you don't have your "dream team" in place when you are just getting started, understand that the team arrangement does not have to be permanent. Though it can be difficult to do, sometimes you have to respectfully and appropriately let individuals go when they cannot or will not effectively support the business. New members can be added to the team as the need arises.[4]

Strong management can make the best of a good business idea by securing the resources needed to make it work. Of course, even a highly competent management team cannot rescue a firm that is based on a weak business concept or that lacks adequate resources. But the importance of strong management to startups is evident in the attitudes of prospective investors, who consider the quality of a new venture's management to be one of the most important factors in decisions to invest or to take a pass. In other words, investors know that enterprises typically perform poorly if they are guided by weak or incapable managers.

One reason that a management team often can bring greater strength to a venture than an individual entrepreneur can is that a team can provide a diversity of talent to meet various managerial needs. This can be especially helpful to startups built on new technologies that must manage a broad range of factors. In addition, a team can provide greater assurance of continuity, since the departure of one member of a team is less devastating to a business than the departure of a single owner.

The competence required in a management team depends on the type of venture and the nature of its operations. For example, a software development firm and a restaurant require very different types of business experience. Similarly, service firms and retail businesses tend to be less complicated to launch and operate, which may explain why solo entrepreneurs lean toward these kinds of startups. Whatever the

management team Managers and other key persons who give a company its general direction.

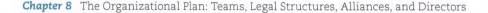

business, a small firm needs managers with an appropriate combination of education, experience, and skills. The qualifications of an applicant for a key position should complement those of members already on the team.

In many cases, a startup owner stacks the management team with family and friends, rather than seeking balanced expertise. This has a definite upside. The owner knows these people well and trusts them, they often work for less compensation (despite the elevated risk of joining a new venture), and they are more likely to make personal sacrifices to keep the business alive. The downside is that the team can quickly become very homogeneous, lack complementary strengths, entertain feelings of entitlement, and carry the baggage of family dysfunction into the enterprise. All of these factors—the negative and the positive—should be taken into consideration when hiring family and friends.

8-1a Achieving Balance

Not all members of a management team need competence in all areas—the key is balance. As one small business observer put it, "You want someone who knows as much as you do, just not about the same things."[5] For example, if one member has expertise in finance, another should have an adequate marketing background. Recent research shows that it's helpful to pair the depth of knowledge of highly specialized experts with big-picture thinkers who are better able to "connect the dots" of the business and its opportunities.[6] Further, the venture most likely will need someone who can supervise employees effectively.[7] This diversity in perspectives and work styles is what enables the completion of complex tasks, but it can also lead to serious conflict, which can squeeze all the energy and enthusiasm out of a venture.[8]

Even when entrepreneurs recognize the need for team members with varying expertise, they frequently look for qualities that reflect their own personalities and management styles. Interpersonal compatibility and cooperation among team members are necessary for effective collaboration, and cohesive teams tend to perform better.[9] However, experience suggests that a functionally diverse and balanced team will be more likely to cover all the business bases, giving the company a competitive edge—especially when softer relational issues of fit and compatibility are also worked out.

To ensure balance, a management team should comprise both competent insiders and outside specialists. For example, a small firm will benefit greatly by developing working relationships with a commercial bank, a law firm, and an accounting firm. (A number of outside sources of managerial assistance are identified and discussed in Chapter 19.) In addition to providing counsel and guidance to the management team, an active board of directors or an advisory board (discussed later in this chapter) can also help connect the venture with external sources of expertise and assistance. It is simply a matter of tapping into board members' existing networks of business relationships. The value of a good board, in this regard, cannot be overstated.

8-1b The Solo Startup Is Still an Option

Despite the advantages of forming a team to start a business, the truth is that many entrepreneurs would rather go it alone. And emerging technologies makes this option increasingly manageable today. Business support services that used to cost thousands of dollars are now available online for free or for a small monthly charge, and hiring help from around the world can require nothing more than a few mouse clicks. These tools can replace the assistance that might otherwise be available only by taking on a skilled business partner or expanding the management team.

Living the Dream

ENTREPRENEURIAL EXPERIENCES

Taking Team Formation to Heart

New venture stories that begin with a strong startup team that is guided by an intelligent division of responsibilities are more likely to have a happy ending. But the steps to building a strong team are best taken with emotional and style considerations in mind, not just strategic concerns—and with a mindset of flexibility that permits adaptation when circumstances change.

In 2010, entrepreneurs Bryan Burkhart and Sonu Panda introduced their new subscription-based floral service, H.Bloom, to New York City. From the beginning, the partners worked closely together to launch their business and gain a foothold in the market. As they learned the intricacies of the business, the pair divided key tasks according to their respective strengths. "We have a clear division of labor and discrete roles and responsibilities," reports Burkhart. "[Panda] does much of the work that is grueling and detail-oriented, things that I find extremely painful but are integral to our success." Tasks related to sales, marketing, and investor relations, on the other hand, are Burkhart's domain. These assignments were the result of long and honest conversations upfront between the partners so that everyone would be happy with the arrangement, and it seems to be paying off for the business. By September of 2014, H.Bloom had expanded to 13 major cities and over 80 employees and was recently declared the fastest-growing company in the $35 billion flower market.

But the division of labor based on tasks is just one option. Partners in other startups may have lifestyle preferences that incline them toward a certain schedule or operating style. Joan Ripple, co-founder of Beantown Bedding, a pioneer in the eco-friendly, disposable bedding industry, acknowledges that her partner Kirsten Lambert does her best work in the evening. But as she sees it, "[That's] a positive thing, because she can do follow-ups in the evening on the things that may be urgent, and I can do the same thing in the morning." The arrangement allows the entrepreneurs to maximize their time and energy while performing business functions.

As in any good relationship, the key to success is communicating often and effectively. When H.Bloom first started to expand into new markets, Burkhart and Panda realized that their diverging roles started to cause them to drift apart. In order to bridge the gap, the pair elected to schedule weekly quality meetings. Ripple and Lambert also talk regularly to ensure that they stay on the same page. "While we share a common vision for the company, sometimes we each want to take a different path to get there," Ripple says. Talking often and remaining flexible has ensured that the team stays on track.

Clear delineation of responsibilities prevents co-founders from duplicating efforts and provides an effective way to maximize the strengths of each partner. It also ensures that co-founders' differing backgrounds, perspectives, and lifestyles remain complementary rather than turning contentious. Ripple and Lambert maintain that their "differences actually bring breadth and perspective and simplify the division of labor." However, this division of labor cannot exist without implicit trust between partners. "Even if we run into disagreements," says Burkhart, "we trust one another to go off to our separate roles and responsibilities and make it happen better than anybody else we know." Combined with a passion for their respective businesses, this trust has unified these two entrepreneurial teams and has allowed them each to achieve success.

Sources: Paula Andruss, "Divide & Conquer," *Entrepreneur*, Vol. 41, No. 4 (April 2013), pp. 87–89; "Beantown Bedding: Our Story," http://www.beantownbedding.com/About, accessed November 30, 2014; Bryan Burkhart, "Introducing Building the Team: Flower Power," *The New York Times*, January 16, 2013, http://boss.blogs.nytimes.com/2013/01/16/introducing-building-the-team-flower-power/?_php=true&_type=blogs&_r=0, accessed November 25, 2014; and "H.Bloom: Our Story," https://www.hbloom.com/Home/AboutUs, accessed November 30, 2014.

Harvey Manger-Weil found a way to go into business without the hassles that come from having a physical location, partners, or other fixed features. As a former enrollment director at Dartmouth College, he had seen many smart students be rejected by the colleges of their choice due to mediocre SAT scores. So, he developed a tutoring method that would allow applicants to improve their exam results dramatically. And after perfecting his system, Manger-Weil used it to launch The College Wizard, an online training company that gets very high marks from those who have used it.[10]

The College Wizard is growing at a healthy clip, but Manger-Weil is able to keep up with it as a solo business owner by following principles that he learned from entrepreneur-in-residence at Yale University and go-it-alone guru Bruce Judson. The secret, says Judson, is relatively simple: "Systematize everything you can. Look at your business and see what pieces you can automate and outsource. Ultimately, every business is a repetitive system, and you need to automate that so you can spend your time doing the things that really add value."[11]

In the final analysis, teams can achieve great things and may, at times, be necessary. But they're not for everyone, as indicated by recent research showing that 44 percent of successfully funded startups were run by a single entrepreneur.[12] Taking on a partner or adding to the management team means giving up the freedom to make your own decisions, being dependent on others to get things done, and pursuing a dream that you may not fully share. In other words, the price can be steep, and many entrepreneurs are unwilling to pay it.

8-1c Expanding Social Networks

Whether starting with a team or choosing to go it alone, it's often not *what* you know but *whom* you know that matters. Management team members help the venture obtain investment and technology resources. But they can also connect the enterprise with a social network that provides access to a wide range of resources beyond the reach of individual team members. A **social network** is the web of relationships that a person has with other people, including roommates or other acquaintances from college, former employees and business associates, and contacts through community organizations like the Rotary Club and religious groups. But it doesn't end there. A friend from college may not have what you need, but he or she may know someone who does. It is often said that business is all about relationships, a principle that is not lost on successful entrepreneurs. And the power of social networks is expanded tremendously as well-connected people are added to the management team.

What does an entrepreneur need from his or her network? That all depends on the situation. Howard Aldrich and Nancy Carter, two highly regarded experts on building management teams and social networks, have found that nearly half of those who are starting businesses use their networks to access information or get advice. About one-fourth use their networks to gain introductions to other people. Finally, a much smaller percentage use connections to obtain money, business services, physical facilities and equipment, help with personal needs, and other forms of assistance.[13] Clearly, a healthy system of personal relationships can help a small business access the knowledge and resources it needs to get established and grow.

Beyond providing access to resources, social networks can be especially helpful in communicating legitimacy and jump-starting sales. Reputable firms may hesitate to do business with a company that doesn't have a demonstrated track record for reliable delivery or quality products or services. But influential advocates can use their pull to help a small business acquire one or more high-profile customers, which may persuade

social network
An interconnected system of relationships with other people.

Living the Dream

ENTREPRENEURIAL EXPERIENCES

Entrepreneurs Get By with a Little Help from Their Network Friends

© PESHKOVA/SHUTTERSTOCK.COM

Many start down the entrepreneurial path because they want the independence it allows, hoping to call their own shots and work things out for themselves. But finding success via this approach may prove elusive—without the help of others along the way, that is.

For Scott Rousseau, owner of Massachusetts-based Beyond the Shaker, this was definitely the case. After earning an MBA that prepared him to pursue his entrepreneurial ambitions, Rousseau decided it was time to leave a lucrative financial services career and try something new. He eventually hit upon the idea of launching a gourmet sea salt company and, as a first step, made the decision to spend around $700 to exhibit his wares and drum up sales at a tradeshow. But no one showed up. "Nine hours a day for three days in a row, and it was a dead loss," remembers Rousseau. In reality, though, the investment was not a total loss after all. He happened to make a connection with another entrepreneur at the show, who recommended that he attend the New England Made tradeshow instead. Despite the hefty $2,000 price tag, Rousseau decided to give it a try. And he is glad he did! That one show netted deals with 15 stores, 2 distributors, and 10 secondary accounts.

Rousseau is not alone. Many others have found similar successes after receiving a tip or a helping hand from others. Consider Ginny Simon, founder of the organic baked-goods line ginnybakes. She started out at small markets frequented by foodies, hoping simply to "help people live better, healthier lives." But all that changed when Eddie Niemes, the manager of a Fresh Market grocery store, tasted her product. Impressed, Niemes sent samples to the chain's headquarters, which led, in turn, to distribution deals with over 120 Fresh Market stores. Capitalizing on the momentum, Simon secured contracts with other large grocery retailers and is now on track to reach $5 million in annual sales. The company has been so successful that Simon's two sons and her husband have joined the business as full-time employees.

In some cases, product exposure is simply not enough to overcome underlying issues. Twenty years ago, Richelieu Dennis founded Sundial Brands with the intent to sell his mother's soaps. Dennis wanted to brand the product as a high-end, multi-ethnic skincare option for consumers. But things didn't quite turn out that way. Buyers ended up pigeonholing the brand as mono-ethnic and cheap. The company eventually found breakout success but only after meeting a Macy's buyer at a diversity conference and following her branding and pricing recommendations. Growth has been rapid since then, with the company expanding from 20 employees to 100.

Time and time again, solo entrepreneurs have learned that advice and coaching can help fill in the gaps in their knowledge and experience and push their ventures to new levels of success. But the key to maximizing the chances of finding this kind of external catalyst is to socialize energetically and network continuously. Interactions with others may not always lead to the results you are expecting, but sometimes unexpected results prove to be the most profitable of all.

Sources: "Beyond the Shaker: About Us," http://beyondtheshaker.com/pages/our-story.html, accessed November 28, 2014; "Featured Alumni Business: Beyond the Shaker," http://blogs.babson.edu/news/2012/09/20/featured-alumni-business-beyond-the-shaker, accessed November 28, 2104; Drew Limsky, "Rising to the Top," *Modern Luxury*, July/August, 2014, http://digital.modernluxury.com/publication/?i=214745&p=178, accessed November 28, 2014; Joe Robinson, "The Turning Point," *Entrepreneur*, Vol. 41, No. 10 (October 2013), pp. 116–118; and "Sundial Brands: About Us," http://www.sundialbrands.com/as-seen-in.html, accessed November 28, 2014.

Creating an Internal Network

Sometimes, the network that is most important to cultivate is the one that exists *inside* the company. When employees have the information they need, they are able to make much better decisions, and that bodes well for the business. Closed social networks—think Facebook or Twitter, but only for your employees—could be just the ticket. Chatter, Yammer, and Jive are some of the better known enterprise social-networking platforms, and these tools and others like them can be very useful for crowdsourcing ideas, facilitating group problem solving, and connecting pockets of expertise in the venture with its most pressing challenges.

others to give a relatively unknown company a shot at their business, too. For an entrepreneur, having a healthy social network and a management team with helpful connections can be critical in establishing a solid reputation.

Some small business owners are tapping into the expanding universe of social media tools, including LinkedIn, Twitter, and Facebook, to attract customers, connect with peers, and share advice about common problems. In fact, a recent study found that the rate of adoption of social media tools by small companies has been doubling each year, which greatly expands the reach of their network-building efforts.[14] While keeping up with the rapid growth of social media is a challenge, an active and robust social network is necessary for building **social capital**, which we refer to as the advantage created by an individual's connections within a network of social relationships. But this advantage doesn't develop overnight or by accident. It takes years to build social capital, and the building blocks that support it are well known—being reliable as a friend, being fair in your dealings, being true to your word.

The principle of reciprocation can be extremely helpful in adding to whatever social capital you already have. In his popular book on influence, Robert Cialdini defines **reciprocation** as a subtle but powerful sense of obligation, deeply embedded in every society, to repay in kind what another person has done for us or provided to us.[15] In general, people naturally feel that they should return favors. You can easily prime the pump of social capital by being the first to lend a hand and then watch those you assist come to your rescue when you run up against a challenge and ask for help. You don't have to fake it; just slow down a bit, and take a genuine interest in the needs of your friends and acquaintances. And helping others doesn't have to be costly. In today's information economy, passing along an important bit of news or insight is easy and free—but it can be as good as gold! So, think ahead, and reach out to help where you can. Your social capital is sure to increase, binding friends and contacts to you and providing a solid foundation for building a business.

Explain the common legal forms of organization used by small businesses.

8-2 COMMON LEGAL FORMS OF ORGANIZATION

When launching a new business, an entrepreneur must choose a legal form of organization, which will determine who the actual owners of the business are. The most basic options are the sole proprietorship, partnership, and C corporation. More specialized forms of organization exist, but many small businesses find one of these common forms suitable for their needs. After outlining the primary options, we look first at some criteria for choosing among them and then introduce a number of specialized forms (see Exhibit 8.1) that offer their own unique features and advantages.

social capital
The advantage created by an individual's connections in a social network.

reciprocation
A powerful sense of obligation to repay in kind what another has done for or provided to us.

sole proprietorship
A business owned by one person, who bears unlimited liability for the enterprise.

8-2a The Sole Proprietorship Option

A **sole proprietorship**, the most basic business form, is a company owned by one person. An individual proprietor has title to all business assets and is subject to the claims of creditors. He or she receives all of the firm's profits but must also assume all losses, bear all risks, and pay all debts. Although this form certainly is not right for everyone, forming a sole proprietorship is nonetheless the simplest and cheapest way to start operation. Most states do not even require such companies to have a business license. Because of the ease of startup, the majority of small businesses (63.9 percent)[16] adopt this legal structure (see Exhibit 8.2).

EXHIBIT 8.1 Forms of Legal Organization for Small Businesses

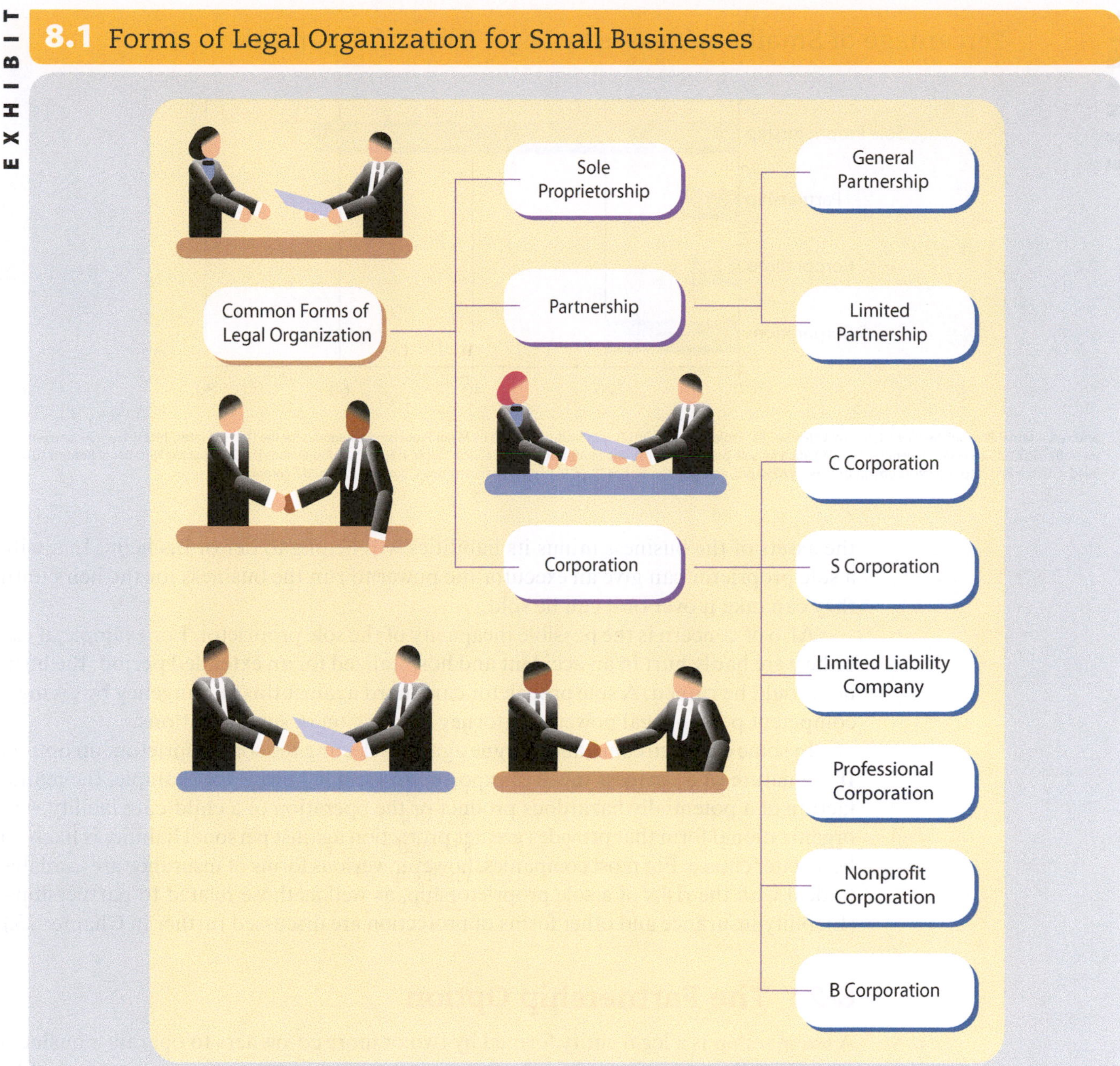

In a sole proprietorship, an owner is free from interference by partners, shareholders, and directors. However, a sole proprietorship lacks some of the advantages of other legal forms. For example, there are no limits on the owner's personal liability—that is, the owner of the business has **unlimited liability**, and thus his or her personal assets can be taken by business creditors if the enterprise fails. For this reason, the sole proprietorship form is usually the practical choice only for very small businesses. In addition, sole proprietors are not employees of the business and cannot benefit from the advantage of many tax-free fringe benefits, such as insurance and hospitalization plans, which are often provided by corporations for their employees.

unlimited liability
Liability on the part of an owner that extends beyond the owner's investment in the business.

The death of the owner terminates the legal existence of a sole proprietorship. Thus, the possibility of the owner's death may cloud relationships between a business and its creditors and employees. It is important that the owner have a will, because

EXHIBIT

8.2 Percentage of Small Businesses by Legal Form of Organization

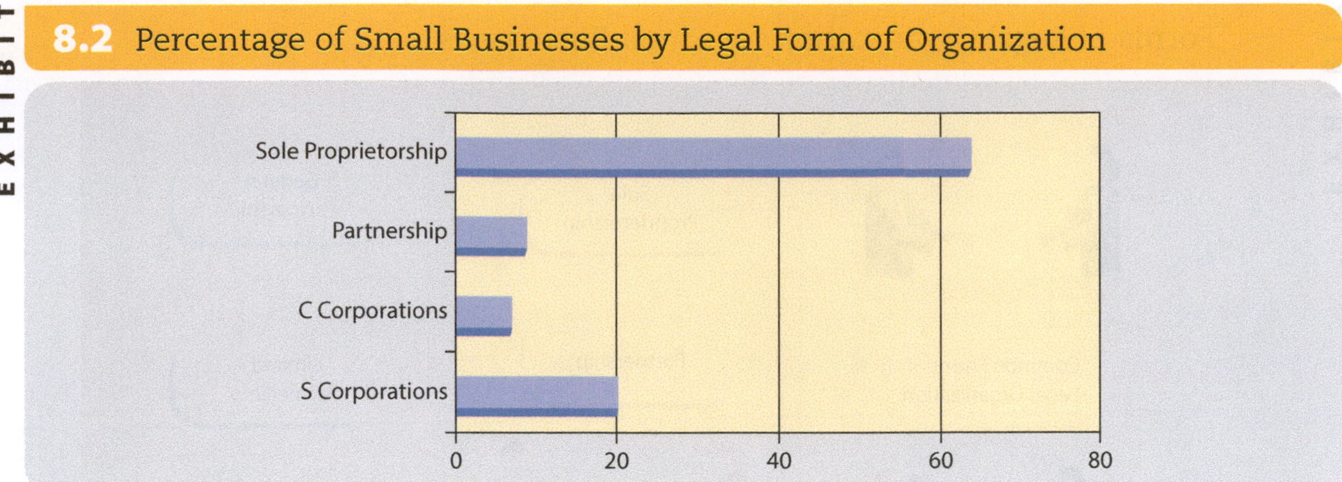

Sources: Internal Revenue Service, "Table 1A: Calendar Year Projections [for 2017] of Individual Returns by Major Processing Categories for the United States," http://www.irs.gov/pub/irs-pdf/p6187.pdf, accessed November 19, 2014 (data for sole proprietorships); and Internal Revenue Service, "Table 1: Fiscal Year Projections [for 2017] of the Number of Returns to Be Filed with the IRS," http://www.irs.gov/pub/irs-pdf/p6292.pdf, accessed November 19, 2014 (data for partnerships, C corporations, and S corporations).

the assets of the business minus its liabilities will belong to her or his heirs. In a will, a sole proprietor can give an executor the power to run the business for the heirs until they can take it over or it can be sold.

Also of concern is the possible incapacity of the sole proprietor. For example, if she or he were badly hurt in an accident and hospitalized for an extended period, the business could be ruined. A sole proprietor can guard against this contingency by giving a competent person legal power of attorney to carry on in such situations.

In some cases, circumstances argue against selecting the sole proprietorship option. If the nature of a business involves exposure to legal liability—for example, the manufacture of a potentially hazardous product or the operation of a child-care facility—an organizational form that provides greater protection against personal liability is likely to be a better choice. For most companies, however, various forms of insurance are available to deal with the risks of a sole proprietorship, as well as those related to partnerships. (Liability insurance and other forms of protection are discussed further in Chapter 23.)

8-2b The Partnership Option

A **partnership** is a legal entity formed by two or more co-owners to operate a business for profit. Because of a partnership's voluntary nature, owners can set it up quickly, avoiding many of the legal requirements involved in creating a corporation. A partnership pools the managerial talents and capital of those joining together as business partners. As in a sole proprietorship, however, the owners share unlimited liability.

Operating a business as a partnership has benefits, but it is also fraught with potential problems, enough that most experts discourage the use of this form of organization as a way to run a business. The benefits of partnerships include the ability to share the workload as well as the emotional and financial burdens of the enterprise and to gain management talent that might otherwise break the budget. And it should not be overlooked that partners can add companionship to life in a small business.

However, many believe that the personal conflicts common in partnerships more than offset the benefits, and partners often fall short of one another's expectations. Of course, decision making is more complicated in partnerships because leadership is shared, and owners must also share their equity position in the business, which naturally dilutes the control of each partner. While some of the difficulties of

partnership
A legal entity formed by two or more co-owners to operate a business for profit.

partnerships are financial in nature, most are relational—for example, coping with a partner's dishonesty or dealing with differing priorities. Partnerships clearly have both disturbing and redeeming qualities. Therefore, *a partnership should be formed only if it appears to be the best option after considering all features of the enterprise.*

QUALIFICATIONS OF PARTNERS

Any person capable of contracting may legally become a business partner. Individuals may become partners without contributing capital or having a claim to assets at the time of dissolution. Such persons are partners only in regard to management and profits. The formation of a partnership involves consideration not only of legal issues but also of personal and managerial factors. A strong partnership requires partners who are honest, healthy, capable, and compatible. The following suggestions may help entrepreneurs make the most of this form of organization:

- *Choose your partner carefully.* Partnerships are like marriages—they work best when you pick the right partner. Many sources are available to help you find that "perfect someone"—trade magazines, client contacts, professional associations, even online matching services like BusinessPartners.com and CoFoundersLab.com. But identifying a promising partner is just a start. You also need to be sure that your goals, values, and work habits are compatible and that your skills are complementary before committing to the deal. Above all, team up with a person you can trust, since the actions of your partner can legally bind you, even if a decision is made without your knowledge or consent.[17]
- *Be open, but cautious, about partnerships with friends.* Valued relationships can take a quick turn for the worse when a business deal gets rocky. A Dr. Jekyll friend can sometimes transform into a Mr. Hyde business associate when money enters the picture.
- *Test-drive the relationship, if possible.* Try more limited forms of business collaboration before jumping in with both feet. For example, you can cooperate on a small project or share a booth at a trade show and observe the behavior, style, and work habits of your prospective partner. This allows you to assess his or her strengths and weaknesses before committing to a long-term relationship.
- *Create a combined vision for the business.* Partners must be on the same page when it comes to forming the business concept they hope to develop together. This takes time, patience, and a lot of conversation. Other specific matters you should discuss before joining forces include the expectations of all partners (contributions of time, money, expertise, etc.), planned division of work, anticipated vacation time, and the sharing of profits and losses.
- *Prepare for the worst.* Keep in mind that more than half of all partnerships fail. That is why most experts recommend having an exit strategy for the partnership from the beginning. What looks like a good business arrangement at the outset can quickly fall apart when market conditions shift, a partner becomes involved in another business venture, or personal circumstances change. For example, the birth of a child, a sudden divorce, or the unexpected death of a spouse can alter everything. If it becomes necessary, exiting a partnership is far more difficult when plans for such an unfortunate outcome were not considered early on.

Failure to take suggestions like these seriously can derail efforts to build an effective working relationship or doom an otherwise workable partnership to an unnecessary or painful demise.

RIGHTS AND DUTIES OF PARTNERS

An oral partnership agreement is legal and binding, but memory is always less than perfect. In his book *Legal Guide for Starting and Running a Small Business*, author and practicing business attorney Fred S. Steingold strongly recommends that partners sign a written **partnership agreement** to avoid problems later on.[18] This document, which explicitly spells out the partners' rights and duties, should be drawn up before the venture is launched. Though the partners may choose to have an attorney draft the agreement in order to ensure that all important features are included, many other sources of assistance also are available to guide you through this process. One such resource is another book by Steingold, *Legal Forms for Starting and Running a Small Business*,[19] which provides a lengthy outline and description of a proper agreement.

Unless the articles of the partnership agreement specify otherwise, a partner is generally recognized as having certain implicit rights. For example, partners share profits or losses equally, unless they have agreed to a different ratio. But these rights are also balanced against serious liabilities. In a general partnership, each party bears **joint and several liability**, which means that a business decision by one partner binds all other partners, even if they were not consulted in advance, didn't approve the agreement or contract in question, or didn't even know about it![20] As with a sole proprietorship, the unlimited personal liability of the partners can be terrifying. The assets of the business are at risk, of course, but so are the personal assets of the partners, including their homes, cars, and bank accounts. Good faith, together with reasonable care in the exercise of managerial duties, is required of all partners in the business.

Unfortunately, complications can arise even if partners have been careful to match their expectations at the start of the partnership and the arrangement has been formalized through a partnership agreement. When problems emerge, partners should move quickly to try to resolve the underlying issues. If they cannot do so, they should consider hiring a business mediator. Working with a mediator can be expensive, but the dissolution of the partnership is likely to be far more costly.

partnership agreement
A document that states explicitly the rights and duties of partners.

joint and several liability
The liability of each partner resulting from any one partner's ability to legally bind the other partners.

TERMINATION OF A PARTNERSHIP

Death, incapacity, or withdrawal of a partner ends a partnership and requires liquidation or reorganization of the business. Liquidation often results in substantial losses to all partners, but it may be legally necessary. A partnership represents a close personal relationship of the parties that cannot be maintained against the desire of any one of them.

© INUENG/SHUTTERSTOCK.COM

When one partner dies, loss due to liquidation may be avoided if the partnership agreement stipulates that surviving partners can continue the business after buying the decedent's interest. This option can be facilitated by having each partner carry life insurance that names the other partners as beneficiaries.

Partnerships sometimes have immediate concerns to address when a partner decides to leave the business, especially if the departure is unexpected. Aaron Keller, Brian Adducci, and a third partner started a marketing and design firm in Minneapolis called Capsule. Eighteen months later, when their partner decided to leave the business and start a competing company (taking several employees and clients with him), Keller and Adducci knew they would have to move quickly to avoid serious losses. As part of a sound response plan, they were advised to take several measures: First, cut off the departing partner's access to bank accounts, physical facilities, and company assets to avoid loss or damage to equipment critical to the business. Then, quickly assess that partner's role in the enterprise and take steps to fill his shoes to get the business back to normal as soon as possible. Once these very pressing matters are under control, sort out any legal issues that remain, such as abiding by any exit agreements that may have been signed. With time and a lot of hard work, Keller and Adducci were able to regain their footing, but the experience helped them to understand just how fragile a partnership can be—and how important it is to have a rapid-response plan when things go wrong.[21]

8-2c The C Corporation Option

In 1819, Chief Justice John Marshall of the United States Supreme Court defined a **corporation** as "an artificial being, invisible, intangible, and existing only in contemplation of the law." With these words, the Supreme Court recognized the corporation as a **legal entity**, meaning that it can file suit and be sued, hold and sell property, and engage in business operations that are stipulated in the corporate charter. In other words, a corporation is a separate entity from the individuals who own it, which means that the corporation, not its owners, is liable for the debts of the business. The implications of this arrangement for risk taking and business formation are profound and far-reaching, prompting one highly influential business executive to declare the creation of the modern corporation to have been the single greatest innovation in the last several hundred years, at least where wealth creation is concerned.[22] The ordinary corporation—often called a **C corporation** to distinguish it from more specialized forms—is discussed in this section.

THE CORPORATE CHARTER

To form a corporation, one or more persons must apply to the secretary of state (at the state level) for permission to incorporate. After completing preliminary steps, including payment of an incorporation fee, the written application (which should be prepared by an attorney) is approved by the secretary of state and becomes the **corporate charter**. This document—sometimes called *articles of incorporation* or *certificate of incorporation*—shows that the corporation exists.

A corporation's charter should be brief, in accordance with state law, and broad in its statement of the firm's powers. Details should be left to the *corporate bylaws*, which outline the basic rules for ongoing formalities and decisions of corporate life, including the size of the board of directors, the duties and responsibilities of directors and officers, the scheduling of regular meetings of the directors and shareholders, the means of calling for a special meeting of these groups, procedures for exercising voting rights, and restrictions on the transfer of corporate stock.

RIGHTS AND STATUS OF STOCKHOLDERS

Ownership in a corporation is evidenced by **stock certificates**, each of which stipulates the number of shares owned by a stockholder. An ownership interest does not confer a legal right to act for the firm or to share in its management. It does, however, provide the stockholder with the right to receive dividends in proportion to stockholdings, but only when the dividends are properly declared by the firm. Ownership of stock typically carries a **preemptive right**, or the right to buy new shares in proportion to the number of shares already owned before new stock is offered for public sale.

The legal status of stockholders is fundamental, of course, but it may be overemphasized. In many small corporations, the owners typically serve both as directors and as managing officers. The person who owns most or all of the stock can control a business as effectively as if it was a sole proprietorship. Thus, this form of organization can work well for individual- and family-owned businesses, where maintaining control of the firm is important.

corporation
A business organization that exists as a legal entity and provides limited liability to its owners.

legal entity
A business organization that is recognized by the law as having a separate legal existence.

C corporation
An ordinary corporation, taxed by the federal government as a separate legal entity.

corporate charter
A document that establishes a corporation's existence.

stock certificates
A document specifying the number of shares owned by a stockholder.

preemptive right
The right of stockholders to buy new shares of stock before they are offered to the public.

LIMITED LIABILITY OF STOCKHOLDERS

For most stockholders, their limited liability is a major advantage of the corporate form of organization. Their financial liability is restricted to the amount of money they invest in the business. Creditors cannot require them to sell personal assets to pay the corporation's debts. However, a bank that makes a loan to a small firm may insist that the owners assume personal liability for the firm's debts. If the corporation is unable to repay the loan, the banker can then look to the owners' personal assets to recover the amount of the loan. In this case, the corporate advantage of limited liability is lost.

Why would owners agree to personally guarantee a firm's debt? Simply put, they may have no choice if they want the money. Most bankers are unwilling to loan money to an entrepreneur who is not prepared to put his or her own personal assets at risk.

DEATH OR WITHDRAWAL OF STOCKHOLDERS

Unlike a partnership interest, ownership in a corporation is readily transferable. Exchange of shares of stock is sufficient to transfer an ownership interest to a different individual.

Stock shares of large corporations are exchanged continually without noticeable effect on the operation of the business. For a small firm, however, a change of owners, though legally similar, can involve numerous complications. For example, finding a buyer for the stock of a small company may prove difficult. Also, a minority stockholder in a small firm is vulnerable. If two of three equal shareholders in a small business sold their stock to an outsider, the remaining shareholder would then be at the mercy of that outsider.

The death of a majority stockholder can have unfortunate repercussions in a small firm. An heir, the executor, or a purchaser of the stock might well insist on direct control, with possible adverse effects for other stockholders. To prevent problems of this nature, legal arrangements should be made at the outset to provide for management continuity by surviving stockholders and fair treatment of a stockholder's heirs. As in the case of a partnership, taking out life insurance ahead of time can ensure the ability to buy out a deceased stockholder's interest.

EXHIBIT **8.3** Comparison of Basic Legal Forms of Organization

Form of Organization	Initial Organizational Requirements and Costs	Liability of Owners	Continuity of Business
Sole proprietorship	Minimum requirements; generally no registration or filing fee	Unlimited liability	Dissolved upon proprietor's death
General partnership	Minimum requirements; generally no registration or filing fee; written partnership agreement not legally required but strongly suggested	Unlimited liability	Unless partnership agreement specifies differently, dissolved upon withdrawal or death of partner
C corporation	Most expensive and greatest requirements; filing fees; compliance with state regulations for corporations	Liability limited to investment in company	Continuity of business unaffected by shareholder withdrawal or death
Form of organization preferred	Proprietorship or partnership	C corporation	C corporation

(continued)

MAINTAINING CORPORATE STATUS

Certain steps must be taken if a corporation is to retain its standing as a separate entity. For example, the corporation must hold annual meetings of both the shareholders and the board of directors, keep minutes to document the major decisions of shareholders and directors, maintain bank accounts that are separate from owners' bank accounts, and file a separate income tax return for the business.

8-3 CONSIDERATIONS IN CHOOSING AN ORGANIZATIONAL FORM

Identify factors to consider in choosing among the primary legal forms of organization.

Choosing a legal form for a new business deserves careful attention because of the various, sometimes conflicting features of each organizational option. Depending on the particular circumstances of a specific business, the tax advantages of one form, for example, may offset the limited liability advantages of another form. Some trade-offs may be necessary. Ideally, an experienced attorney or knowledgeable accountant should be consulted for guidance in selecting the most appropriate form of organization.

Some entrepreneurship experts insist that the two most basic forms of business—sole proprietorship and partnership—should *never* be adopted. While these forms clearly have drawbacks, they are still workable for many small business owners. And, fortunately, there is another basic form to consider—the C corporation. Exhibit 8.3 summarizes the main considerations in selecting one of these three primary forms of ownership.

INITIAL ORGANIZATIONAL REQUIREMENTS AND COSTS

Organizational requirements and costs rise as the formality of the organization increases. That is, a sole proprietorship is typically less complex and less expensive to form than a partnership, and a partnership is less complex and less expensive to form than a corporation. In view of the relatively modest costs, however, this consideration is of minimal importance in the long run.

EXHIBIT 8.3 Comparison of Basic Legal Forms of Organization *(continued)*

Transferability of Ownership	Management Control	Attractiveness for Raising Capital	Income Taxes
May transfer ownership of company name and assets	Absolute management freedom	Limited to proprietor's personal capital	Income from the business is taxed as personal income to the proprietor
Requires the consent of all partners	Majority vote of partners required for control	Limited to partners' ability and desire to contribute capital	Income from the business is taxed as personal income to the partners
Is easily transferred by transferring shares of stock	Shareholders have final control, but usually board of directors controls company policies	Usually the most attractive form for raising capital	The C corporation is taxed on its income and the stockholder is taxed if and when dividends are received
Depends on the circumstances	Depends on the circumstances	C corporation	Depends on the circumstances

LIABILITY OF OWNERS

Liability risks are among the most important factors to consider when selecting an organizational form. As discussed earlier, a sole proprietorship and a partnership have the built-in disadvantage of unlimited liability for the owners. With these forms of organization, there is no distinction between the firm's assets and the owners' personal assets. In contrast, setting up a corporation limits the owners' liability to their investment in the business.

Two cautions are in order regarding liability and organizational forms. First, incorporation will not protect a firm's owners from liability if it is used to perpetuate a fraud, skirt a law, or commit some wrongful act. In such cases, the courts may decide that there is no legal separation between the owners and the corporate entity, a concept known as **piercing the corporate veil**. Protection from financial liability may be jeopardized if, for example, (1) the company is bankrupt, but its owners knowingly take on debt; (2) the board of directors does not meet as required by law or observe other corporate formalities; or (3) business and personal accounts are not kept separate and company funds are used to pay an owner's personal expenses. Legal action is taken most often against smaller, privately held business entities and "sham corporations" that are set up with the specific goal of deceiving others.[23] Of course, some forms of organization offer no shield against liability in the first place.

Second, no form of organization can protect entrepreneurs from *all* forms of liability. For example, if an owner causes a traffic accident and is declared personally liable for damages or injuries in court, he or she will have to pay the judgment, even if it means selling personal assets to satisfy the ruling. If, on the other hand, an employee caused the accident while on company business, the assets of the business will be at risk, but the personal assets of the owner will be shielded from liability—*but only if the business is organized as a corporation or limited liability company* (which will be discussed later in the chapter). This protection does not extend to the owner(s) of a sole proprietorship or a partnership, whose personal assets would also be at risk.

As indicated previously, most banks and many suppliers require small business owners to sign a personal guarantee before loaning money or extending credit to them, regardless of the form of organization. Entrepreneurs have to pay off these obligations if their businesses are unable to, even if doing so requires the use of personal assets. This is the lender's way of trying to ensure that debts are repaid, but it illustrates a practical limitation of organizational forms when it comes to liability protection.[24]

CONTINUITY OF BUSINESS

A sole proprietorship is immediately dissolved on the owner's death. Likewise, a partnership is terminated on the death or withdrawal of a partner, unless the partnership agreement states otherwise. A corporation, on the other hand, offers continuity. The status of an individual investor does not affect the corporation's existence.

TRANSFERABILITY OF OWNERSHIP

Ownership is transferred most easily in a corporation. The ability to transfer ownership, however, is not necessarily good or bad—it all depends on the owners' preferences. In some businesses, owners may want the option of evaluating any prospective new investors. Under other circumstances, unrestricted transferability may be preferred.

MANAGEMENT CONTROL

A sole proprietor has absolute control of the firm. Control within a partnership is normally based on the majority vote, so it follows that an increase in the number of

piercing the corporate veil
A situation in which the courts conclude that incorporation has been used to perpetuate a fraud, skirt a law, or commit some wrongful act and remove liability protection from the corporate entity.

partners reduces each partner's voice in management. Within a corporation, control has two dimensions: (1) the formal control vested in the stockholders who own the majority of the voting common shares and (2) the functional control exercised by the corporate officers in conducting daily operations. In a small corporation, these two forms of control usually rest with the same individuals.

ATTRACTIVENESS FOR RAISING CAPITAL

A corporation has a distinct advantage when raising new equity capital, due to the ease of transferring ownership through the sale of common shares and the flexibility in distributing the shares. In contrast, the unlimited liability of a sole proprietorship and a partnership discourages new investors.

INCOME TAXES

Income taxes frequently have a major effect on an owner's selection of a form of organization. To understand the federal income tax system, you must consider this twofold question: Who is responsible for paying taxes, and how is tax liability determined? The three major forms of organization are taxed in different ways:

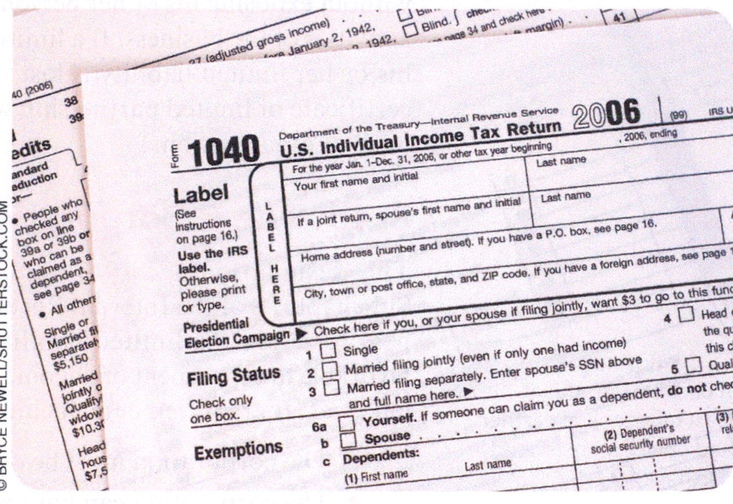

- *Sole proprietorship.* Self-employed individuals who operate a business as a sole proprietorship report income from the business on their individual federal income tax returns. They are then taxed on that income at the rates set by law for individuals.
- *Partnership.* A partnership reports the income it earns to the Internal Revenue Service, but the partnership itself does not pay any taxes. The income is allocated to the partners according to their agreement. The partners each report their own shares of the partnership's income on their personal tax returns and pay any taxes owed.

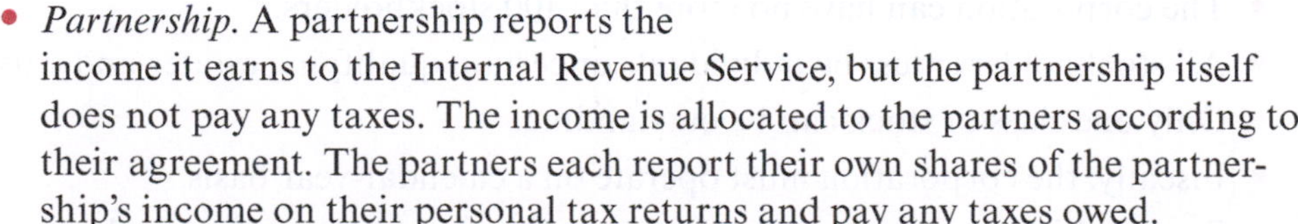

- *C corporation.* The C corporation, as a separate legal entity, reports its income and pays any taxes related to these profits. The owners (stockholders) of the corporation must report on their personal tax returns any amounts paid to them by the corporation in the form of dividends. (They must also report capital gains or losses, but only at the time they sell their stock in the company.) Keep in mind that dividends are, in essence, taxed twice—first as part of a corporation's earnings and then as part of the owners' personal income.

The IRS's small business website at www.irs.gov/businesses/small/index.html provides links to tax information on the different organizational forms, insights related to important small business topics, and answers to industry-specific questions, as well as forms and publications that will help with tax planning and preparation.

8-4 SPECIALIZED LEGAL FORMS OF ORGANIZATION

Discuss the unique features and restrictions of five specialized organizational forms.

The majority of small businesses use one of the three major ownership structures just described—the sole proprietorship, partnership, or C corporation. However, other specialized forms of organization are also used by small firms. Five of these alternatives merit further consideration: the limited partnership, the S corporation, the limited liability company, the professional corporation, the nonprofit corporation, and the B corporation.

8-4a The Limited Partnership

The **limited partnership** is a special form of partnership involving at least one general partner and one or more limited partners. The **general partner** remains personally liable for the debts of the business, but **limited partners** have limited personal liability as long as they do not take an active role in the management of the partnership. In other words, limited partners risk only the capital they invest in the business. An individual with substantial personal wealth can, therefore, invest money in a limited partnership without exposing his or her personal assets to liability claims that might arise through activities of the business. If a limited partner becomes active in management, however, his or her limited liability is lost. To form a limited partnership, partners must file a certificate of limited partnership with the proper state office, as state law governs this form of organization.

8-4b The S Corporation

The designation **S corporation**, or **Subchapter S corporation**, is derived from Subchapter S of the Internal Revenue Code. This organizational form permits a business to retain the limited liability feature of a C corporation while offering more favorable tax treatment on income. To obtain S corporation status, a corporation must meet certain requirements, including the following:[25]

- The corporation must be domestic.
- The corporation can have no more than 100 stockholders.[26]
- All stockholders must be individuals or certain qualifying estates and trusts.[27]
- Only one class of stock can be outstanding.
- Fiscally, the corporation must operate on a calendar-year basis.
- Partnerships, corporations, and nonresident aliens cannot be shareholders.

An S corporation does not pay income taxes but instead passes taxable income or losses on to the stockholders. This allows stockholders to receive dividends from the corporation without double taxation on the firm's profit (once through a corporate tax and again through a personal tax on received dividends). A competent tax attorney should be consulted before selecting S corporation status, as tax law changes have considerable effect on this form.

limited partnership
A partnership with at least one general partner and one or more limited partners.

general partner
A partner in a limited partnership who has unlimited personal liability.

limited partners
A partner in a limited partnership who is not active in its management and has limited personal liability.

S corporation (Subchapter S corporation)
A type of corporation that offers limited liability to its owners and passes taxable income or losses on to stockholders.

limited liability company
A form of organization in which owners have limited liability but pay personal income taxes on business profits.

8-4c The Limited Liability Company

The **limited liability company** has grown in popularity because it offers the simplicity of a sole proprietorship and the protection of a corporation to shield the personal assets of owners. A limited liability company can have an unlimited number of owners (even having a single owner is permitted in most states), and these may include non-U.S. citizens.[28] This form differs from the C corporation in that it avoids double taxation. Like S corporations, limited liability companies are not taxed but simply pass their income on to their owners, who pay taxes on it as part of their personal income.[29]

According to many attorneys, the limited liability company is usually the best choice for new businesses. Compared to most other forms, it is easier to set up, is more flexible, and offers some significant tax advantages. But a limited liability company isn't always the best way to go. For example, under the following conditions, it would be better to use a C corporation:

- *You want to provide extensive fringe benefits to owners or employees.* The C corporation can deduct these benefits, and they are not treated as taxable income to the employees.
- *You want to offer stock options to employees.* Since limited liability companies do not have stock, they cannot offer such incentives.
- *You hope to go public or sell the business at some time in the future.* A C corporation can go public or be sold to another corporation in a tax-free, stock-for-stock exchange.
- *You plan to convert to a C corporation eventually.* You cannot change from a pass-through entity like a limited liability company without paying additional taxes.

8-4d The Professional Corporation

Have you noticed the initials PC or PA as part of the corporate name on the letterhead or signage of your doctor, dentist, or attorney? These letters indicate that the practice is set up as a **professional corporation** in order to offer professional services. Though its meaning varies from state to state, the term *professional* usually applies to those individuals whose professions require that they obtain a license before they can practice, so this would include doctors, chiropractors, lawyers, accountants, engineers, architects, and other highly trained individuals.

But unlike other liability-shielding organizational forms, the professional corporation does not protect a practitioner from her or his own negligence or malpractice. Rather, it shields owners in the practice from one another's liability. In some states, a different business structure called a *limited liability partnership* can serve the same purpose and may have additional advantages. Obviously, the professional corporation applies to a fairly narrow range of enterprises, but it is usually the best option for businesses that fall into that category. In fact, many state laws require this form of organization before a professional practice can operate.

8-4e The Nonprofit Corporation

For some ventures, the most practical form of organization is the **nonprofit corporation**. Most elect to become 501(c)(3) organizations, which are created to serve civic, educational, charitable, or religious purposes. To qualify for 501(c)(3) status, the money-raising concern, fund, or foundation must be a corporation—the IRS will not grant this option to a sole proprietorship or partnership. In the application process, the officers need to submit articles of organization that spell out and limit the range of activities of the enterprise. For a tax exemption to be granted, the organization must pass the **organizational test** ("IRS-speak" for verification that the organization is staying true to the articles filed). A nonprofit corporation must establish a board of directors or trustees to oversee its operations, and if it should dissolve, it is required to transfer its assets to another nonprofit corporation.

There is no question that in some cases nonprofit forms are better than for-profit alternatives. For example, if you hope to seek tax-deductible donations from individuals, foundations, and corporations, then forming as a nonprofit will be necessary. A for-profit business, on the other hand, will have the ability to raise money from private

professional corporation
A form of corporation that shields owners from liability and is set up for individuals in certain professional practices.

nonprofit corporation
A form of corporation for enterprises established to serve civic, educational, charitable, or religious purposes; not for generation of profits.

organizational test
Verification of whether a nonprofit organization is staying true to its stated purpose.

investors, for which it then grants equity in the venture or promises dividends. This is the perhaps the most fundamental difference between the two general forms, but there are others to consider.

In some cases, a hybrid model, which links nonprofit and for-profit entities, is the way for smaller entrepreneurial ventures to go. Story Pirates is a nonprofit that was launched in 2003 by graduates of Northwestern University "to celebrate the words and ideas of young people" and "make learning more engaging and effective."[30] Its after-school story-writing and drama programs have grown in popularity and now are offered at more than 130 schools from coast to coast. Because of its rising popularity, the founders had to figure out how to handle the rapid growth in ticket sales. Forming a for-profit with the same name was a huge step in the right direction. The two organizations now are able to share the name and content through licensing agreements that allow them to make the most of various high-potential opportunities that come their way.[31]

Hybrid forms come with some hassles that must be managed—such as maintaining separate boards and management teams and being prepared to prove that transactions between entities reflect true market value. But as one writer put it, "You get to have your cake and save the whales, too."[32] What more could a small business owner ask for?

8-4f The B Corporation

Are you hoping to use the power of business to solve a social or environmental problem? If so, the **B corporation** (the "B" stands for "benefit") may be exactly the form you need to adopt. The performance and accountability standards are demanding, sustainability must be a primary thrust, and transparency is enforced through B Impact Reports. But, according to the certifying organization (a nonprofit called B Lab), the outcomes more than justify the costs: "Individuals will have greater economic opportunity, society will move closer to achieving a positive environmental footprint, more people will be employed in great places to work, and we will have built stronger communities at home and around the world."[33]

B corporation
A form of corporation that creates a positive social or environmental impact while maintaining high standards of transparency and accountability.

strategic alliance
An organizational relationship that links two or more independent business entities in a common endeavor.

More than 1,000 enterprises had already organized as B corporations by 2014, including business exemplars such as Etsy, Patagonia, and Warby Parker. But taking on this organizational form saddles a company with serious burdens, such as a binding commitment to altruistic policies, and permits shareholders to sue directors if a company falls short of its stated social mission. So why go down this path? Neil Blumenthal, a Warby Parker co-founder, makes the case: "We wanted to build a business that could make profits. But we also wanted to build a business that did good in the world."[34] Forming as a B corporation forces a firm to stay true to its stated mission—even in a down year when investors may pressure management to shift to financial priorities. Further, the deliberate social emphasis helps the business recruit and retain talented employees (who often will work for less to pursue that social purpose), sell products or services to consumers who support the mission, and fend off hostile takeover bids from corporations that care only about profits.

Understand the nature of strategic alliances and their uses in small businesses.

8-5 FORMING STRATEGIC ALLIANCES

A **strategic alliance** is an organizational relationship that links two or more independent business entities in some common endeavor. Without affecting the independent legal status of the participating business partners, it provides a way for companies to improve their individual effectiveness by sharing certain resources. And these alliances can take many forms, from informal information exchanges to formal equity- or contract-based relationships and everything in between. Many small businesses form alliances that involve licensing, outside contracting, marketing, and distribution. These are shown in Exhibit 8.4, along with other less-common options.

Strategic alliances are increasing in importance to small businesses today, and more entrepreneurs are finding creative ways to use these cooperative strategies to their advantage. In fact, statistics show that nearly two-thirds of small businesses use alliances, and three-fourths of these companies report having positive experiences with them.[35] Given the escalating pace of competition and the rising costs of developing essential capabilities, alliances provide a way for small companies to become more competitive, for example, by accessing another firm's first-rate resources, expanding the market range for products or services offered, combining advertising efforts, reaching crucial economies of scale, and sharing risks that might prove crippling if borne by a single small company. Since a competitive advantage often goes to the entrepreneur who is quick to exploit it, many small business owners see strategic alliances as an essential part of their plan for growth. These cooperative strategies represent one way to keep up with the accelerating pace of change in today's business environment. (See Chapter 18 for a discussion of strategic alliances as these apply to global enterprises.)

8-5a Strategic Alliances with Large Companies

Small business owners often assume that their ventures have nothing to offer larger companies, but the truth is that they can play an essential role in helping corporations address some of their most pressing challenges. Typically, these alliances are formed to join the complementary skills and expertise of the partnered firms, in order to promote the competitive edge of both (or all) parties. For example, large manufacturers sometimes team up with innovative small manufacturers in product development efforts, and giant retailers form alliances with smaller suppliers to achieve specific quality requirements and meet demanding delivery schedules. Combining the speed, flexibility, and creative energy of a small business with the industry experience, production capabilities, and market reach of a large corporation can be a winning strategy.

EXHIBIT 8.4 Most Popular Small Business Alliances by Type

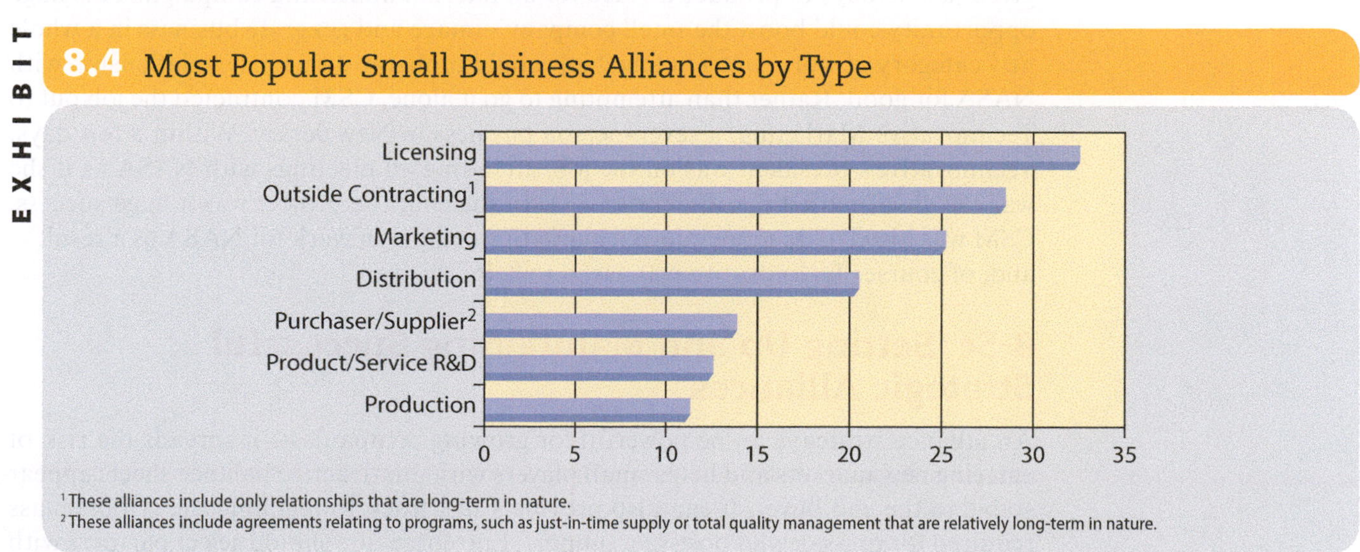

[1] These alliances include only relationships that are long-term in nature.
[2] These alliances include agreements relating to programs, such as just-in-time supply or total quality management that are relatively long-term in nature.

Source: Based on William J. Dennis, Jr. (ed.), "Strategic Alliances," *National Small Business Poll*, Vol. 4, No. 4 (Washington, DC: NFIB Research Foundation, 2004), pp. 1–8.

Building Business Alliances

It is crucial that you select a strategic partner that won't damage your reputation and will help boost your venture's performance. For an excellent primer on partner selection, see Donna Peek's advice in "Evaluating and Selecting a Strategic Partner," at www.entrepreneurship.org/resource-center/evaluating-and-selecting-a-strategic-partner.aspx.

While alliances with large firms can give a tremendous boost to performance, some small businesses discover that bigger isn't always better. The advantages created by joining forces with large firms must be weighed against the risk of being squeezed financially or of running into smothering bureaucratic complications. One small company, for example, jumped at the chance to form an alliance with a major multinational firm in the same industry. Everything seemed to be running smoothly until the small firm learned that a simple invoice discrepancy was holding up a $1.2 million payment that it desperately needed to meet future expansion commitments. The money was small change to the multinational, but it was critical to its small partner. The two companies reached a stalemate, the alliance failed, and the small business was never able to recover $300,000 of the money that it was owed.

Forming alliances with prestigious partners may offer a substantial boost to status and market access, but the parties' strategic priorities may not mesh, and a major corporation can wield enormous power over a small, struggling enterprise. Also, some large firms have a track record of misbehavior as partners, and you need to know this *before* entering an alliance with them. The guidelines provided in Chapter 4 for the evaluation of a franchisor can be helpful when deciding whether to take on a particular strategic partner. For example, it would be wise to investigate whether the corporation has been a good, ethical partner for other small companies. Knowing this in advance will help you to make an informed and profitable decision.

8-5b Strategic Alliances with Small Companies

Small businesses can also form strategic alliances with partners that are similar in size, in ways that enhance mutual competitive strength. Studies have indicated that about half of all small businesses maintain one or more strategic alliances with companies that are smaller or equal in size.[36] When *Inc.* researchers asked dozens of entrepreneurs which alliance partners had performed best for them, they were surprised to learn that the most enthusiastic anecdotes were about other small companies.[37] These partnerships were more flexible, dedicated, creative, and understanding of the specific needs of small businesses. Apparently, it takes one to know one!

The Center for Systems Management (CSM), a small Virginia-based consulting and training company that was recently acquired by Management Concepts, found that it was in over its head when it accepted a contract from NASA. CSM had been given just 45 days to produce a video for an internal marketing campaign. This huge opportunity could boost the small company's image and generate business in a whole new category of work, but a botched job would probably damage its relationship with NASA for good. Rather than attempting to go it alone, CSM contracted the job out to Technovative Marketing, a seven-person business in New Jersey. Within a few days, Technovative's president was on the job, attending all meetings with NASA as if she was the chief marketing officer of CSM. In the end, the project was a huge success. CSM was hired to do more internal marketing campaign work for NASA as a result—and, of course, Technovative was asked to help.[38]

8-5c Setting Up and Maintaining Successful Strategic Alliances

An alliance strategy can be powerful for growing companies—it spreads the risk of entering new markets and helps small players with unattractive balance sheets appear stable to the end buyer. It can also provide a fast track to reaching the critical mass required for pre-sale and post-sale support. Entrepreneurs should select partners with a "division of labor" mentality that allows all parties to focus their efforts on what they do best. For example, identifying intersections between product lines and expertise opens up the potential for cross-selling that creates growth opportunities for everyone involved.

Working closely with other companies can also introduce significant hazards. Because alliance partners are in a unique position to learn about your strategy and customer base, they can become competitors overnight. Therefore, it is crucial to select partners with care and to structure contracts to ensure growth, including an "easy out" clause if the alliance does not work out.

While strategic alliances often are not easy to set up, they can be even more difficult to maintain. Research has shown that many small businesses have been pleased with the results of their strategic alliances,[39] but a number of alliances run into trouble and, in time, fail. Fortunately, when setting up alliances, entrepreneurs can take the following steps to improve their chances for success:

- *Establish a healthy network of contacts.* These people can lead you to still other contacts, and eventually to the one you need. Tap into leads through industry analysts, executive recruiters, public relations agencies, business reporters, and even the government.
- *Identify and contact individuals within a firm who are likely to return your call.* "Dialing high" (calling contacts at the level of vice president or higher) works in small- or medium-sized firms, but in large firms, you may need to call managers or other mid-level employees to get a response.
- *Do your homework and win points just for being prepared.* You should be able to clearly outline the partner's potential financial benefits from the alliance. If possible, show that your firm can deliver value to the alliance across several fronts.
- *Learn to speak and understand the "language" of your partner.* You will not pick up on subtle messages in conversations with partners unless you know how they communicate. This can eventually make or break the alliance.
- *Make sure that any alliance offer is clearly a win-win opportunity.* Only those agreements that benefit all participating parties will endure.
- *Monitor the progress of the alliance to ensure that goals and expectations are being met, and make changes as they become necessary.*

The goal is to form strategic alliances that are beneficial to all partners and to manage these alliances effectively. A key to successful strategic alliances is understanding the true nature of the relationship. Instead of being between companies, relationships in strategic alliances are actually built between people. Cultivating relationships is essential to business success in general, and these can be promoted through an effective board of directors or advisors, the topic to which we turn next.

board of directors
The governing body of a corporation, elected by the stockholders.

8-6 MAKING THE MOST OF A BOARD OF DIRECTORS

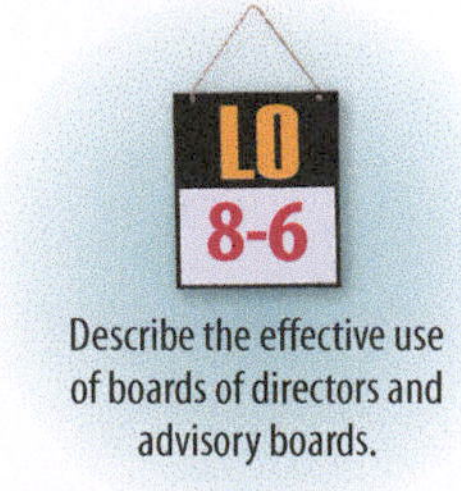

Describe the effective use of boards of directors and advisory boards.

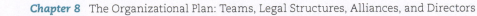

In entrepreneurial firms, the **board of directors** tends to be small (usually five or fewer members)[40] and serves as the governing body for corporate activity. In concept, the stockholders elect the board, which in turn chooses the firm's officers, who manage the enterprise. The directors also set or approve management policies, consider reports on operating results from the officers, and declare any dividends.

© BLUESKYIMAGE/SHUTTERSTOCK.COM

All too often, the majority stockholder in a small corporation (usually the entrepreneur) appoints a board of directors only to fulfill a legal requirement (since corporations are required by law to have a board of directors) or as mere window dressing for investors. Such an entrepreneur often will select personal friends, relatives, or businesspersons who are too busy to analyze the firm's circumstances and are not inclined to disagree with the owner. Entrepreneurs who take a more constructive approach find an active board to be both practical and beneficial, especially when the members are informed, skeptical, and independent.

8-6a Selection of Directors

An entrepreneur who is attempting to assemble a cooperative and experienced group of directors needs to consider the value of an outside board, one with members whose income does not depend on the firm. The firm's attorney and banker, local management consultants, and other business executives might all be considered as potential directors but usually lack the independence needed to critically review an entrepreneur's plans. Also, in many cases, the owner is already paying for their expertise.

Objectivity is a particularly valuable contribution of outside directors. They can look at issues more dispassionately than can insiders who are involved in daily decision making. Outside directors, for example, are freer to evaluate and to question a firm's ethical standards. Some operating executives, without the scrutiny of outside directors, may rationalize unethical or illegal behavior as being in the best interest of the company. In a family business, an outside board can help mediate and resolve issues related to leadership succession, in addition to providing more general direction. As outsiders, they bring to the business a measure of detachment from potentially explosive emotional differences.

Working with outside board members is not always easy, but an entrepreneur who is advised by the board to make tough decisions may find that those decisions are required to move the business forward. For example, the board may keep bringing the conversation back to issues that are easy to avoid, such as the need to build long-term relationships with important individuals in the banking community or the value of converting intentions for the company's future into a formal business plan that can be studied, debated, perfected, and used as a tool to attract crucial resources to the enterprise. Entrepreneurs often spend as much as 20 percent of their time on board-related activities, but the time commitment is worth the cost if the directors are doing their jobs well.

The nature and needs of a business help determine the qualifications required in its directors. For example, a firm that faces an intellectual property problem may benefit greatly from the counsel of a board member with a legal background. Business prominence in the community is not an essential quality for board members, although it may help to give the company credibility and enable it to attract other well-qualified directors. Directors with a broad network of influential business friends and associates can contribute greatly, as long as they are willing to reach out to their contacts on behalf of the company.

After deciding on the qualifications to look for, a business owner must seek suitable candidates as board members. Effective directors are honest and accountable, offer valuable insights based on business experience, and enhance the company's credibility with its stakeholders (especially customers and suppliers). Suggestions for such candidates may be obtained from the firm's accountant, attorney, banker, and other associates in the business community. Owners or managers of other, noncompeting small companies, as well as second- and third-level executives in large companies, are often willing to accept such responsibilities. Before offering candidates positions on the board, however, a business owner would be wise to do some discreet background checking.

8-6b Contributions of Directors

The growing complexity of small businesses, arising in part from globalization and technological developments, makes the expertise of well-chosen directors especially valuable. As mentioned earlier, outsiders in a family business can play a unique role in helping evaluate family talent and mediating differences among family members. And a strong board of directors can help the entrepreneur look beyond the next few months to make important, long-term strategic decisions. In other words, good directors will be able to help entrepreneurs keep their eyes on the big picture.

By virtue of their backgrounds, directors can fill gaps in the expertise of a management team and monitor its actions. The board should meet regularly to provide maximum assistance to the chief executive. In board meetings, ideas should be debated, strategies determined, and the pros and cons of policies explored. In this way, the chief executive is informed by the unique perspectives of all the board members. Their combined knowledge makes possible more intelligent decisions on issues crucial to the firm.

By utilizing the experience of a board of directors, the chief executive of a small corporation is in no way giving up active control of its operations. Instead, he or she is simply drawing on a larger pool of business knowledge. A group will typically make better decisions than will a single individual working alone.

An active board of directors serves management by reviewing major policy decisions, advising on external business conditions and on proper reaction to the business cycle, providing informal advice from time to time on specific problems that arise, and offering access to important personal contacts. With a strong board, a small firm may gain greater credibility with the public, as well as with business and financial communities.

8-6c Compensation of Directors

The compensation paid to board members varies greatly, and some small firms pay no fees at all. If compensation is provided, it is usually offered in the form of an annual retainer, board meeting fees, and pay for committee work. (Directors may serve on committees that evaluate executive compensation, nominate new board members, and oversee the work of the company's auditors.) Estimates vary, but annual retainers for board work at established small firms typically range from $5,000 to $10,000, and board meeting fees can run from $500 to $2,000 per meeting. These costs to the firm are usually in addition to reimbursements for travel expenses related to board meetings and the financial burden of providing directors and officers liability insurance, which protects board members if they should be sued in the course of carrying out their duties as directors.[41] Sometimes, board members are also given a small percentage of the company's profits as a bonus for their participation, and some cash-strapped businesses may grant them stock (often 1 percent, but as high as 2 percent or more to lure top talent) in lieu of compensation.[42]

The relatively modest compensation offered for the services of well-qualified directors suggests that financial reward is not their primary motivation for serving on a board. In fact, it is not uncommon for some directors to serve for free because of their interest in seeing a new or small business prosper. Reasonable compensation is appropriate, however, if directors are making important contributions to the firm's operations. In any case, it is important to keep in mind that you usually get what you pay for.

8-6d An Alternative: An Advisory Board

Some individuals are reluctant to join a board of directors because outside directors may be held responsible for illegal company actions, even though they are not directly involved in wrongdoing. Thus, many small companies use an **advisory board** as an alternative to a board of directors. Qualified outsiders are asked to serve on a board as advisors to the company. This group then functions in much the same way as a board of directors does, except that its actions are only advisory in nature. In other words, it has no legal authority over the owner or the company.

The legal liability of members of an advisory board is not completely clear. However, limiting their compensation and power is thought to lighten, if not eliminate, the personal liability of members. Since its role is advisory in nature, the board also may pose less of a threat to the owner and possibly work more cooperatively than a board of directors.

Without a doubt, a well-selected board of directors or advisors can do a great deal for a small company, but bear in mind that this is only one part of an effective organizational plan. The success of any business depends on the quality of its people, who must also be well organized and skillfully led. That's why having a balanced management team, selecting an organizational form that makes sense for the enterprise and its circumstances, and joining advantageous strategic alliances are all so important. This chapter has touched on each of these topics to help you think through key factors involved in developing a solid organizational plan that will give your business a good running start and help to ensure its long-term success.

advisory board
A group that serves as an alternative to a board of directors, acting only in an advisory capacity.

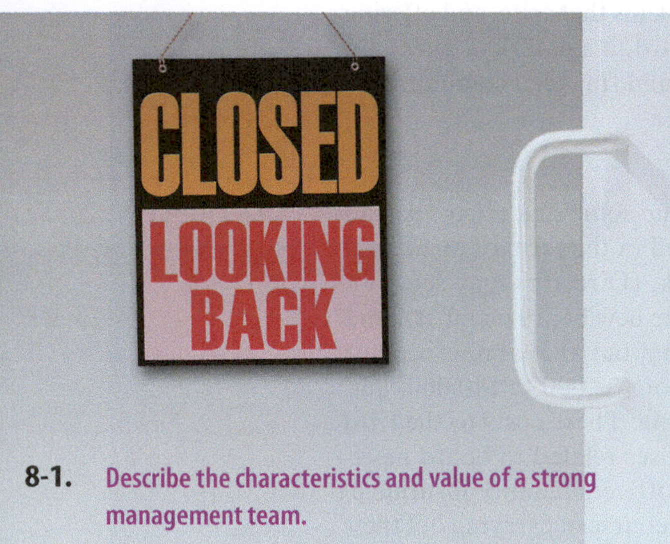

8-1. Describe the characteristics and value of a strong management team.

- A strong management team nurtures a good business idea and helps provide the necessary resources to make it succeed.
- The skills of management team members should complement each other, forming an optimal combination of education and experience.
- A small firm can enhance its management by drawing on the expertise of competent insiders and outside specialists.
- Social media tools can be very helpful in attracting customers, connecting with peers, and sharing advice about common problems.
- Building social capital through networking and goodwill is extremely helpful in developing a small business.

8-2. Explain the common legal forms of organization used by small businesses.

- The most basic legal forms of organization used by small businesses are the sole proprietorship, partnership, and C corporation.

- In a sole proprietorship, the owner receives all profits and bears all losses. The principal disadvantage of this form is the owner's unlimited liability.
- In a partnership, which should be established on the basis of a written partnership agreement, success depends on the partners' ability to build and maintain an effective working relationship. The partners share unlimited liability.
- C corporations are particularly attractive because of their limited liability feature. The fact that ownership is easily transferable makes them well suited for combining the capital of numerous owners.
- Currently, 63.9 percent of all new businesses are organized as sole proprietorships, 8.9 percent are set up as partnerships, and 7 percent are established as C corporations.

8-3. Identify factors to consider in choosing among the primary legal forms of organization.

- The key factors in choosing an organizational form are initial organizational requirements and costs, liability of the owners, continuity of the business, transferability of ownership, management control, attractiveness for raising capital, and income tax considerations.
- Self-employed individuals who operate businesses as sole proprietorships report income from the businesses on their individual tax returns.
- A partnership reports the income it earns to the Internal Revenue Service, but the partnership itself does not pay income taxes. The income is allocated to the owners according to their partnership agreement.
- A C corporation reports its income and pays any taxes due on this corporate income. Individual stockholders must also pay personal income taxes on dividends paid to them by a corporation.

8-4. Discuss the unique features and restrictions of five specialized organizational forms.

- In a limited partnership, general partners have unlimited liability, while limited partners have only limited liability as long as they are not active in the firm's management.
- S corporations, also called Subchapter S corporations, enjoy a special tax status that permits them to avoid the corporate tax but requires individual stockholders to pay personal taxes on their proportionate shares of the business profits.
- In limited liability companies, individual owners have the advantage of limited liability but pay only personal income taxes on the firm's earnings.
- Professional corporations are set up for those who offer professional services (usually those that require a license), to protect them from the liability of other owners in the practice.
- Some enterprises (especially those with a social focus) benefit from greater credibility and authenticity when they organize as nonprofit corporations, such as 501(c)(3) organizations.
- The B corporation may be the best form of organization for entrepreneurs who are intending to use the power of business to solve a social or environmental problem.

8-5. Understand the nature of strategic alliances and their uses in small businesses.

- Strategic alliances allow business firms to combine their resources without compromising their independent legal status.
- Strategic alliances may be formed by two or more independent businesses to achieve some common purpose. For example, a large corporation and a small business or two or more small businesses may collaborate on a joint project.
- Entrepreneurs can improve their chances of creating and maintaining a successful alliance by establishing productive connections, identifying the best person to contact, being prepared to confirm the long-term benefits of the alliance, learning to speak the partner's "language," ensuring a win-win arrangement, and monitoring the progress of the alliance and making any necessary changes.

8-6. Describe the effective use of boards of directors and advisory boards.

- To be most effective, a board of directors should include properly qualified, independent outsiders, who provide a good fit with the nature and needs of the business.
- Boards of directors can assist small businesses by offering objective counsel and assistance to their chief executives.
- Directors can fill gaps in the expertise of a management team and monitor its activities.
- One alternative to an active board of directors is an advisory board, whose members are not personally liable for the company's actions.

Key Terms

advisory board p. 222
B corporation p. 216
board of directors p. 219
C corporation p. 209
corporate charter p. 209
corporation p. 209
general partner p. 214
joint and several liability p. 208
legal entity p. 209
limited liability company p. 214
limited partners p. 214
limited partnership p. 214
management team p. 199
nonprofit corporation p. 215
organizational test p. 215
partnership agreement p. 208
partnership p. 206
piercing the corporate veil p. 212
preemptive right p. 209
professional corporation p. 215
reciprocation p. 204
S corporation (Subchapter S corporation) p. 214
social capital p. 204
social network p. 202
sole proprietorship p. 204
stock certificate p. 209
strategic alliance p. 216
unlimited liability p. 205

You Make the Call

Situation 1

Just recently, Donny Eckols came up with the idea of starting an online service that would help investors who are looking for rental properties on the cheap to get connected with homeowners who really need to sell their houses fast. This opportunity holds special appeal for Eckols, whose parents have been involved in the real estate industry for decades. Eckols doesn't want to start this new business by himself, however, so he keeps prodding his friend John Starner to partner with him.

While Starner thinks this potential startup could very well turn out to be a smash hit, he just can't quite see himself in the real estate business. To him, it sounds a lot like sales, and that's more Eckols's thing, with his upbeat style and his natural ability to read people and anticipate their reactions. Starner's personality is very different, focusing on technology more than people and on ideas more than interactions. So far, he and Eckols have had a great friendship, but Starner is beginning to wonder if the good times will continue to roll once money is on the line and the pressure begins to mount. He knows that Eckols leans heavily on Starner's computer skills, even as Starner looks to Eckols to make life interesting and keep him connected.

Starner also fears that Eckols might begin to take over the business once it gets going. After all, he would bring a lot of industry insight to the new venture, given his family background, and it was his idea in the first place. How could he not take on a sense of ownership? Starner knows that his programming skills and ease with technology will fill in important gaps in what Eckols brings to the table, but will that be enough to keep him in the game? He has to decide soon. Eckols wants to launch the new company before the end of the month.

Question 1 How relevant are the individual personalities to the success of this entrepreneurial team? Do you think Starner and Eckols have a chance to survive a potential partnership? Why or why not?

Question 2 Do you consider it an advantage or a disadvantage that the members of this team are about the same age?

Question 3 On balance, is it good or bad that the company will be started by two men who are also very close friends? What are the potential benefits and drawbacks of mixing business and friendship in this case?

Situation 2

This is a true story related by David Allen, Director of the John F. Baugh Center for Entrepreneurship at Baylor University. The names have been changed to hide the identities of the individuals involved.

> *One morning years ago, while working in the office of my outdoor advertising company, I received a telephone call from an old high school acquaintance. He had started a humidor shop in partnership with his older brother, the older brother supplying the finances and the younger managing the shared venture. Gary asked me to call on him to discuss billboard advertising in order to make the local market aware of the new enterprise. After I explained the benefits of outdoor advertising to achieve his goals, Gary contracted with my company to display a number of small billboards throughout the market.*
>
> *After designing the posters, ordering the printing work, and scheduling the specific locations which*

would best reach Gary's target market, the materials arrived and were posted on the agreed upon date. About mid-morning on the posting date, the older brother, Jerry, called me and mentioned that he had seen some of the posters on billboards in the area. He wanted to know what was going on, because he had no idea that the displays had been ordered. I explained what had taken place and that Gary had contracted for the advertising space. Jerry expressed his displeasure over the telephone, in no uncertain terms, so I asked him if he was dissatisfied with the design or the locations that had been assigned. He said that he actually was quite pleased with the showing, but he was simply upset with his brother for contracting for it without consulting with him first or even informing him as to what he had done. Jerry was, after all, the partner who had to pay the bills.

This incident has stayed in my memory over the years as a caution against starting a business using the partnership as the legal form of organization. Jerry understood that while he had not agreed to the transaction and, indeed, did not even know what his brother had done, he was nonetheless liable for paying the entire bill, because his partner had signed on behalf of the business. Over the years, I have seen too many partnerships destroyed because the partners failed to understand this crucial feature of general partnerships. Partnerships can work, but only when there is a strong partnership agreement in place to specify the precise duties and responsibilities of each partner within the firm. In addition, the partners need to be in complete agreement on the goals and direction of the partnership and the methods that will be employed to achieve them; otherwise, the venture can go off the rails in very short order.

The good news of the incident that I just related is that the advertising did its job; the business found its footing quickly and was making profits in a very short time. Jerry was pleased with the outcome, but he had a long talk with Gary regarding the need for the two of them to confer before signing any contracts. Going a step further, they found a local attorney who understood the potential pitfalls of partnerships and worked out a partnership agreement that defined the roles and responsibilities of the two partners. The business thrived for several years until it eventually was sold to a third party.

While this particular story had a happy ending, too many good businesses falter and, in time, fail because partners are completely unaware of the joint and several liability aspect of their chosen form of organization.

Question 1 What are the advantages and disadvantages of running a business as a partnership?

Question 2 What other legal forms of organization could have been used for this business? Which form would you recommend? Why?

Situation 3

Julie Patton is co-founder and president of PM Meals, a food-services business that prepares and sells boxed meals and convenience snacks to hotels, convention operators, corporate clients, and community event planners. Patton makes most of the business decisions related to the company and is in charge of generating new accounts. The firm's other co-founder, Angela Marks, has culinary training and oversees the meal-preparation side of the operation. The food they offer represents relatively simple fare, but it is flavorful and attractively presented, exceeding by far what most clients would expect from a boxed-meal provider.

The company has entered a growth phase, which has attracted the attention of a high-potential investor. PM Meals could certainly use the money to support its growing business, but the investment would come with major strings attached. For example, even though the company has been performing nicely without a board of directors, the investor insists that it form one and that he be given a seat on the new board. In his words, "If I am going to put up money for the business, I want to be able to influence how my money is being used."

Patton and Marks are concerned that forming a board and including at least one outside investor (the one who insists on having a seat) will undermine their control and paralyze the business. As they weigh alternatives, they are leaning toward forming a three-person board and accepting the new investment—but they are far from certain as to what they should do.

Question 1 Would you accept the investment and the conditions that go along with it, or refuse it and go a different direction?

Question 2 Can one outside member on a board of three make any real difference in the way the board operates?

Question 3 If you were the owners, whom would you include on the board?

Question 4 If Patton and Marks decide to form a board of directors, what will determine its usefulness or effectiveness? Do you predict that it will be helpful? Why or why not?

Business Plan

LAYING THE FOUNDATION

As part of laying the foundation to prepare your own business plan, respond to the following questions regarding your management team, legal form of organization, strategic alliances, and board of directors.

Management Team Questions

1. Who are the members of your management team? What skills, education, and experience do they bring to the team?
2. What other key managers do you plan to recruit?
3. Do you plan to use consultants? If so, describe their qualifications.
4. What are your plans for future employee recruitment?
5. What will be the compensation and benefit plans for managers and other employees?
6. What style of management will be used? What will be the decision-making process in the company? What mechanisms are in place for effective communication between managers and employees? If possible, present a simple organizational chart.
7. How will personnel be motivated? How will creativity be encouraged? How will commitment and loyalty be developed?
8. What employee retention and training programs will be adopted? Who will be responsible for job descriptions and employee evaluations?

Organizational Form Questions

1. Who will have an ownership interest in the business?
2. Will the business function as a sole proprietorship, partnership, or corporation? If a corporation, will it be a C corporation, an S corporation, a limited liability company, a professional corporation, a nonprofit corporation, or a B corporation?
3. What are the liability implications of this form of organization?
4. What are the tax advantages and disadvantages of this form of organization?
5. If a corporation, where will the corporation be chartered and when will it be incorporated?
6. What attorney or legal firm has been selected to represent the firm? What type of relationship exists with the company's attorney or law firm?
7. What legal issues are presently or potentially significant?
8. What licenses and/or permits may be required?

Strategic Alliances Questions

1. What strategic alliances are already in place, and what others do you plan to establish in the future? Describe the nature of these alliances.
2. What are the responsibilities of and benefits to the parties involved in these strategic alliances?
3. What are the exit strategies if an alliance should fail?

Board of Directors Questions

1. Who are the directors of the company?
2. What are the qualifications of the board members?
3. How will the directors be compensated?

Case 8

Couchsurfing International: A Story of Startup, Growth, and Transformation (P. 658)

This case highlights important features of high-performing ventures, including the make-up and coordinated roles of the founding team, the selection of an organizational form, and the formation of a board of directors or advisors.

Alternative Cases for Chapter 8

Video Case 12, Moonworks, p. 668
Case 13, Network Collie, p. 670

Endnotes

1. Stephen Spinelli and Robert Adams, *New Venture Creation: Entrepreneurship for the 21st Century* (New York: Irwin McGraw-Hill, 2012), p. 46.
2. Our position is consistent with recent research showing that the quality of business ideas generated in a business idea competition was related to the characteristics of the entrepreneurial teams that came up with those ideas. The quality was higher for larger teams, those with more years of work experience, and those that received outside assistance from experienced venture founders. For more on this research, see Maw-Der Foo, "Member Experience, Use of External Assistance and Evaluation of Business Ideas," *Journal of Small Business Management*, Vol. 48, No. 1 (January 2010), pp. 32–43.
3. Management team members are typically defined as those with financial ownership and significant decision-making responsibilities in the venture [see Gaylen N. Chandler, "New Venture Teams," in Andrew Zacharakis and Stephen Spinelli, Jr. (eds.), *Entrepreneurship: The Engine of Growth* (Westport, CT: Praeger Perspectives, 2007), pp. 75–76]. Other definitions are more restrictive and emphasize such factors as being a founder of the venture [see Iris Vanaelst, Bart Clarysse, Mike Wright, Andy Lockett, Nathalie Moray, and Rosette S'Jegers, "Entrepreneurial Team Development in Academic Spinouts: An Examination of Team Heterogeneity," *Entrepreneurship Theory and Practice*, Vol. 30, No. 2 (March 2006), p. 251]. At the other end of the spectrum, some entrepreneurs consider all employees and advisors to be a part of the team. Because our discussion here is focused on those who hold important leadership positions in the small business but may not share ownership in the firm, we use the broader term *management team* rather than *entrepreneurial team*.
4. For an interesting study of the addition of members to the management team, see Daniel P. Forbes, Patricia S. Borchert, Mary E. Zellmer-Bruhn, and Harry J. Sapienza, "Entrepreneurial Team Formation: An Exploration of New Member Addition," *Entrepreneurship Theory and Practice*, Vol. 30, No. 2 (March 2006), pp. 225–248.
5. Ross McCammon, "We're Better Together," *Entrepreneur*, Vol. 40, No. 6 (June 2012), pp. 20–21.
6. Knowledge@Wharton, "Goodbye Dilbert: The Rise of the Naked Economy," January 4, 2014, http://knowledge.wharton.upenn.edu/article/goodbye-dilbert-rise-naked-economy, accessed November 19, 2014.
7. Research has not always supported the view that functional balance leads to improved venture performance. Some studies have found that functional heterogeneity is correlated with small firm growth, while others offer no evidence to indicate a relationship with team performance (see Chandler, *op. cit.*).
8. Andy Lockett, Deniz Ucbasaran, and John Butler, "Opening Up the Investor-Investee Dyad: Syndicates, Teams, and Networks," *Entrepreneurship Theory and Practice*, Vol. 30, No. 2 (March 2006), p. 119.
9. Chandler, *op. cit.*, p. 71.
10. "The College Wizard: About Harvey," http://thecollegewizard.net/about.html, accessed November 19, 2014; and personal communication with Harvey Manger-Weil on October 5, 2012.
11. Jason Daley, "Well Enough Alone," *Entrepreneur*, Vol. 40, No. 4 (April 2012), pp. 81–85.
12. Elaine Pofeldt, "Going It Alone," *Inc.*, Vol. 36, No. 1 (February 2014), pp. 22–23.
13. Howard E. Aldrich and Nancy M. Carter, "Social Networks," in William B. Gartner, Kelly G. Shaver, Nancy M. Carter, and Paul D. Reynolds (eds.), *Handbook of Entrepreneurial Dynamics: The Process of Business Creation* (Thousand Oaks, CA: Sage, 2004), p. 331.
14. Jennifer Van Grove, "How Small Business Is Using Social Media," http://mashable.com/2010/03/02/small-business-stats, accessed November 19, 2014.
15. Robert B. Cialdini, *Influence: Science and Practice* (Needham Heights: MA: Allyn & Bacon, 2009).
16. This percentage from the IRS includes enterprises organized as limited liability companies (LLCs), an organizational form that is introduced later in the chapter. This inclusion is probably inconsequential, as other sources indicate the number of startups formed as LLCs is still quite small. See Internal Revenue Service, "Table 1A: Calendar Year Projections [for 2017] of Individual Returns by Major Processing Categories for the United States," http://www.irs.gov/pub/irs-pdf/p6187.pdf, accessed November 19, 2014.
17. Fred S. Steingold, *Legal Guide for Starting and Running a Small Business* (Berkeley, CA: Nolo Press, 2013).
18. *Ibid.*
19. Fred S. Steingold, *Legal Forms for Starting and Running a Small Business* (Berkeley, CA: Nolo Press, 2012).
20. Ira Nottonson, *Forming a Partnership: And Making It Work* (Irvine, CA: Entrepreneur Press, 2007), pp. 6–7.
21. Nichole L. Torres, "Left in the Lurch?" *Entrepreneur*, Vol. 34, No. 5 (May 2006), p. 108.
22. John Seely Brown, as quoted in Stephen J. Dubner, "How Can We Measure Innovation? A Freakonomics Quorum," April 25, 2008, http://freakonomics.com/2008/04/25/how-can-we-measure-innovation-a-freakonomics-quorum/?hp&_r=0, accessed November 20, 2014.
23. "Piercing the Corporate Veil," http://www.residual-rewards.com/piercingthecorporateveil.html, accessed November 20, 2014.
24. David Newton, "Personal Loan Guarantees," http://www.entrepreneur.com/article/55544, accessed November 20, 2014.
25. Internal Revenue Service, "S Corporations," http://www.irs.gov/Businesses/Small-Businesses-&-Self-Employed/S-Corporations, accessed November 21, 2014.
26. For tax years beginning after 2004, the law increased the maximum number of shareholders permitted in an S corporation from 75 to 100. (Note that husband and wife count as one stockholder.)
27. The rules have been modified in recent years to allow more types of trusts to hold Subchapter S stock.
28. Internal Revenue Service, "Limited Liability Company (LLC)," http://www.irs.gov/Businesses/Small-Businesses-&-Self-Employed/Limited-Liability-Company-LLC, accessed November 21, 2014.
29. For a description of the tax advantages of the limited liability company, see Steingold, *Legal Guide, op. cit.*
30. "Story Pirates," http://storypirates.org, accessed November 21, 2014.
31. Issie Lapowsky, "The Social Entrepreneurship Spectrum: Hybrids," *Inc.*, Vol. 33, No. 4 (May 2011), pp. 86–88.
32. *Ibid.*
33. "B Corp: A New Kind of Corporation," http://strongertogether.coop/fresh-from-the-source/b-corp-a-new-kind-of-corporation, accessed

November 24, 2014. To learn more about the advantages and limitation of B corporations, visit http.www.bcorporation.net, or consult resources such as *The B Corp Handbook*, by Ryan Honeyman.

34. James Surkowiecki, "Companies with Benefits," *The New Yorker* (August 4, 2014), http://www.newyorker.com/magazine/2014/08/04/companies-benefits, accessed November 24, 2014.

35. William J. Dennis, Jr. (ed.), "Strategic Alliances," *NFIB National Small Business Poll*, Vol. 4, No. 4 (Washington, DC: NFIB Research Foundation, 2004), p. 4.

36. *Ibid.*, pp. 9–14.

37. Michael Fitzgerald, "Turning Vendors into Partners," *Inc.*, http://www.inc.com/magazine/20050801/vendors.html, accessed November 25, 2014.

38. *Ibid.*

39. Dennis, *op. cit.*, p. 7.

40. In many states, the number of board members required depends on the number of shareholders in the business. A corporation with one shareholder may need only one director to satisfy this demand, with two directors being required when there are two shareholders and three directors when there are three. However, no state requires a corporation to have more than three directors on its board (see Steingold, *Legal Guide, op. cit.*).

41. The compensation figures provided here are consistent across many sources, but the ranges are wide enough to indicate that the variation among small businesses is considerable.

42. Kent Romanoff, "Board of Directors Compensation," http://theperfectpayplan.typepad.com/the_salary_sage/board-compensation, accessed November 25, 2014.

CHAPTER 9

The Location Plan

While many small companies still operate out of a fixed place of business, the list of location alternatives grows longer each year. For example, more and more, small business owners are choosing their homes as the center of their entrepreneurial world. But even at home, the true location varies—from a bedroom office one day, to the back patio the next, and to the kitchen table the day after that. And for entrepreneurs who start businesses on the Internet, everyday work life may be a mix of tapping into the wireless at a local Starbucks and renting office or conference room space on an as-needed basis. The point is that small businesses have many options from which to choose.

In San Francisco, a group of business owners decided to stretch the boundaries of the conventional location with an

In the SPOTLIGHT
The Icebreaker
www.icebreaker-sf.com

innovative approach to affordable and collaborative work space that they called the Icebreaker. They took up offices in a former Icelandic car ferry docked at San Francisco's Pier 50. The 40-year-old ship became the work home of a group of entrepreneurs, from NASA physicists to tech visionaries, who were determined to grow their businesses in the San Francisco Bay area. The ship's bridge was converted from a nautical command center to a hangout for computer coders, complete with bean bag chairs and dry-erase boards.

A wide array of businesses operated out of the ship. Procurement firm

After studying this chapter, you should be able to. . .

9-1. **Describe the five key factors in locating a brick-and-mortar startup.**

9-2. **Discuss the challenges of designing and equipping a physical facility.**

9-3. **Recognize both the attraction and the challenges of creating a home-based startup.**

9-4. **Understand the potential benefits of locating a startup on the Internet.**

SupplyBetter is all about the sale of custom mechanical parts, whereas startup Imaginary Number develops educational games that teach mathematics. Other startups that were "in the neighborhood" have been responsible for producing Internet chat software, an electric Porsche, and 3D gesture-control modules. Rent agreements were also varied, with some companies offering equity or maintenance services in exchange for office space.

However, this group of entrepreneurs had more to worry about than just the success of their ventures. Eventually, port officials contacted the ship's owners to inform them that the port is reserved solely for functioning ships, not floating offices. In order to bypass the threat of eviction, the vessel would have to "leave the dock and complete a cruise around Alcatraz and return to the dock." But this was a problem, because the ship hadn't set sail for a number of years. Although it had a functioning engine, it still needed a suitable anchor, fuel, and an experienced crew to navigate the bay. The owners estimated that it would have cost around $30,000 to prepare the ship for its short voyage around the harbor.

With a history rich in free thinking, San Francisco has been home to many unconventional movements in politics, social issues, and technology. With the presence of the Icebreaker, it seemed that the city would be able to add working space to the list. But, unfortunately, the owners of the Icebreaker were unable to meet all of the port authority's demands and had to close down their experiment in office-space creativity. It remains to be seen whether the ship will get a new life at some point in the future, but for now it seems that their unusual startup workspace may sadly have been lost at sea.

Sources: Nellie Bowles, "Startup Incubator on Old Ship Tries to Stay Afloat," *SFGate*, October 10, 2013, http://www.sfgate.com/technology/article/Startup-incubator-on-old-ship-tries-to-stay-afloat-4882815.php, accessed December 4, 2014; Rakesh Sharma, "A Ship, a Couple of Startups and the Bay," *Forbes*, October 7, 2013, http://www.forbes.com/sites/rakeshsharma/2013/10/07/a-ship-a-couple-of-startups-and-the-bay, accessed December 4, 2014; "The Icebreaker," http://www.icebreaker-sf.com, accessed December 8, 2014; and Danny Yardon, "Seagoing Office Space Doesn't Float San Francisco's Boat," *The Wall Street Journal*, November 18, 2013, p. A1, A14.

It is not until an entrepreneur works through all of the basic parts of the business plan that a new venture idea really begins to take shape. And that idea becomes even more real as resources are committed to the implementation of the plan, including the selection of a business location and any facilities and equipment. But, as you can see from this chapter's Spotlight feature, the location-related possibilities for small businesses are growing in number and variety. At the leaner end of the spectrum, these can be nothing more than a cell phone, some desk space at home, and a website. And locating on the Internet has changed everything for many startups. It offers global market reach at minimal cost, which provides a tremendous boost to budding ventures that desperately need customers but are short on funding. The rise of the Internet-based venture has been a game-changing phenomenon.

Entrepreneurs at the other end of the location continuum, however, might need a new building and/or a fully stocked warehouse facility, and perhaps even forklifts and other equipment to get their planned operations off the ground. It all depends on the nature of the business. But, regardless of the specific resources involved, every location decision should be based on certain fundamental principles that can guide the process and minimize mistakes.

Those who purchase an existing business or a franchise usually receive considerable location guidance from members of the acquired firm or the franchisor. But entrepreneurs who choose to start a venture from scratch will quickly find that the location decision can be very time consuming. To help make the task more manageable, this chapter addresses some of the major factors that should be considered when choosing a location and setting up physical facilities. And because starting a home-based business and launching on the Internet have become such popular options, these alternatives are also covered in some detail. (Although we recognize that the Internet can be an integral part of operations for both a traditional and a home-based business, we treat e-commerce ventures in a separate category because of the Internet's significance as the sole sales outlet for these small businesses.)

Regardless of how the selection is made, a discussion of key location factors and how they support the location decision should be included in the business plan. This chapter will guide you through that process. But keep in mind that the depth of this discussion will vary from plan to plan, depending on the nature and specific needs of the new venture.

9-1 LOCATING THE BRICK-AND-MORTAR STARTUP

Describe the five key factors in locating a brick-and-mortar startup.

The choice of a location for a physical facility is often a one-time decision, but a small business owner may later relocate a venture to reduce operating costs, be closer to customers, or tap other advantages. One survey found that 42 percent of entrepreneurs in the United States believe that their current location is best for their business, but nearly half of those polled said they would consider a move if it would help their companies.[1] That ability to be flexible led Marty and Avery Walker to relocate their Volvo Rents business from Austin to College Station, Texas. Since their venture rents and sells heavy equipment to construction companies and other businesses, it made sense to move 100 miles from the saturated rental market in Austin to be closer to the steady building activity in College Station. And the Walkers cashed in on their change of address, with company revenues increasing from $1.1 to $4 million in less than two years.[2] Location decisions can be complicated, but if carefully planned and wisely made, the payoff can be fantastic.

9-1a The Importance of the Location Decision

The importance of the initial decision as to where to locate a traditional physical building—a **brick-and-mortar facility**—is underscored by both the high cost of such a place and the hassle of pulling up stakes and moving an established business. Also, if the site is particularly poor, the business may never become successful, even with adequate financing and superior managerial ability. The importance of location is so clearly recognized by national chains that they spend hundreds of thousands of dollars investigating sites before establishing new facilities.

The choice of a good location is much more vital to some businesses than to others. For example, the site chosen for an apparel store can make or break the business because it must be convenient for customers. The physical location of a painting contractor's office, on the other hand, is of less importance, since customers do not need frequent access to the facility. But even painting contractors may suffer if their business site is poorly chosen. For example, some communities are more willing or able than others to invest resources to keep their properties in good condition, thereby providing greater opportunities for painting jobs.

9-1b Key Factors in Selecting a Good Location

Five key factors, shown in Exhibit 9.1, guide the location selection process: customer accessibility, business environment conditions, availability of resources, the entrepreneur's personal preference, and site availability and costs. Other factors relevant to the location decision include the following:[3]

- *Neighbor mix:* Who's next door?
- *Security and safety:* How safe is the neighborhood?

brick-and-mortar facility
The traditional physical facility from which businesses have historically operated.

EXHIBIT 9.1 Five Key Factors in Determining A Good Business Location

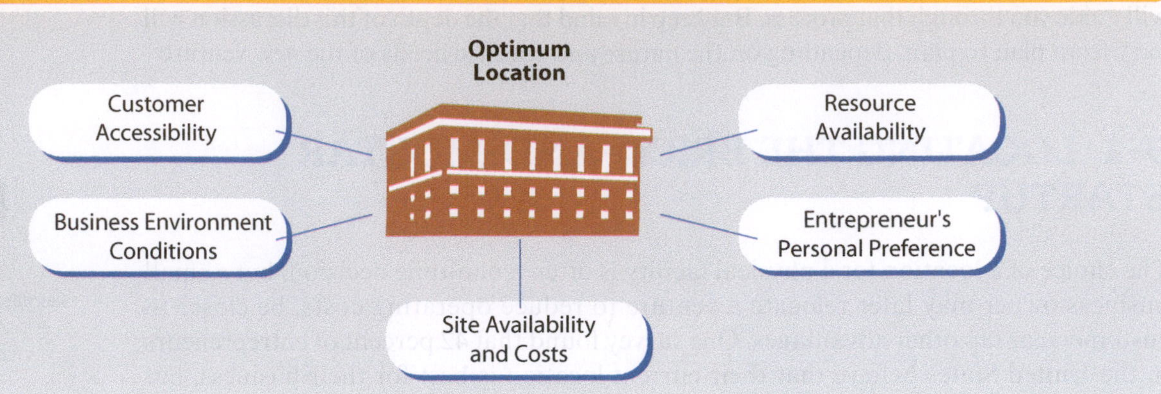

- *Services:* Does the city provide trash pickup, for example?
- *Past tenants' fate:* What happened to previous businesses in that location?
- *Location's life-cycle stage:* Is the area developing, stagnant, or in decline?

For a particular business and its unique situation, one factor may carry more weight than others. However, each of the five key factors should always have some influence on the final location decision.

CUSTOMER ACCESSIBILITY

For many businesses, customer accessibility is an extremely important consideration in selecting a location. It is vital in industries in which the cost of shipping the finished product is high relative to the product's value. Products such as packaged ice and soft drinks, for example, must be produced near consuming markets because of the excessive transportation costs involved. Retail outlets and service firms (such as tire repair companies and hair stylists) must be located where they can provide handy access for targeted purchasers to avoid losing business to more conveniently placed competitors.

Rarely will customers be willing to travel long distances on a repeat basis just to shop. That's why Glenn Campbell and Scott Molander decided to sell hats in high-traffic areas through their startup, Hat World, Inc. (selling mostly under the Lids brand). Each store, located in a shopping mall or airport, offers a vast assortment of officially licensed baseball-style hats. And this positioning works. From its start in 1995, and after some consolidation moves, the total operation has grown to more than 1,000 stores nationwide and in Canada and Puerto Rico.[4]

Choosing the best location for a retail store used to be a hit-or-miss proposition. The recent emergence and growing popularity of site-selection software has removed much of the guesswork. Some products worth a look include MapInfo AnySite, geoVue's iSITE package, REGIS Online software by SitesUSA, or even location-analytics startup PiinPoint. But no matter which of these you may want to consider, try to arrange a test run, if possible, before you invest your hard-earned dollars to see if the software is right for your business. And always ask about Web-based versions, which often are less expensive.

Site-selection programs can give users access to demographic information such as age, income, and race for specific neighborhoods, as well as details about other businesses located nearby, climate conditions, traffic flow, and much more. Just keep in mind that these software packages also have their limitations. For example, many emphasize traffic counts and geographic distance, which can easily overlook factors like slowdowns from rush-hour traffic conditions, the potential of railroads or interstates to divide buying clusters, and similar issues.

If you want to go it alone but still capture the power of detailed data to make your decision, it may be helpful to visit the United States Census Bureau at www.census.gov. Don't let all of the options presented on this site discourage you. If you are patient and work your way through some of the links, you will be amazed by the depth of helpful information you can uncover. We also suggest that you visit the website of *Site Selection* magazine (www.siteselection.com), which offers online tools for researching locations and demographics.

Convenient access for customers is one reason that many small businesses have successfully established a strong presence on the Internet. With a suitable computer connection, customers can access a small company's home page from anywhere in the world. (Locating a startup on the Internet is discussed later in this chapter.)

BUSINESS ENVIRONMENT CONDITIONS

A startup business is affected in a number of ways by the environment in which it operates. Weather is one important environmental feature that influences the location decision, as well as the demand for products such as air conditioners and outdoor swimming pools. Such factors are particularly important to entrepreneurs like Trey Cobb, owner of a high-performance car-parts maker called COBB Tuning. In 2002, Cobb took the bold step of moving his entire small company from Texas to a custom-built facility in Utah. This particular move was all about climate—in this case, improving product-testing conditions. Cobb recognized the advantages of locating the company in an area that provided access to the varied geographic and weather conditions that would be necessary to fully test the car parts that his company manufactures.[5]

Competition, legal requirements, and tax structure are a few of the other critical environmental factors. Since entrepreneurs need profits to sustain their businesses, all factors affecting the financial picture are of great concern. State and local governments can help or hinder a new business by forgiving or levying taxes. State corporate income tax rates vary considerably across the United States, with only a few states having no such tax. To rank the states in terms of the costs of their tax systems on small business (based on a composite score pulled from 18 different tax measures), the Small Business & Entrepreneurship Council publishes a "Business Tax Index" each year. In its 2014 report, the council found that the five states with the most favorable tax systems, in order, were (1) Nevada, (2) South Dakota, (3) Texas, (4) Wyoming, and (5) Washington.[6]

Tax relief for the business is important, but don't forget to factor in the impact of a state's personal income tax rates, which will affect the pay your employees ultimately receive for their labor. These taxes will determine how far wage dollars will go and, in turn, the benefit and satisfaction your workers receive from the business.[7] And there are other important elements in the equation, such as the overall cost of living. A lower *cost* of living can mean a higher *standard* of living for employees. To do cost-of-living research yourself, search for "cost-of-living calculator" on your search engine, or contact local economic development agencies and request data on this and other factors, which they will provide free of charge.[8]

Governments don't always do everything they could to help new businesses get started and flourish. And the barriers can run far beyond issues of taxation. Consider these "wrinkles in the law" that have thwarted entrepreneurial aspirations:[9]

- Esmeralda Rodriguez had to pay rent while waiting for permits to open a play center in Chicago. After a year of delays, and with her savings running out, she had to give up.

- James Tia, a former lawyer, sold meatless burritos in Washington, D.C.—that is, until the city shut the operation down "because his rice was not on the list of approved foods." It took a year and a half of lobbying, guided by Tia's expert legal skills, and favorable test results from a food-safety expert to finally get the business back on track.
- In Miami, jitney van services flourished briefly because of an accidental legal loophole. But the county responded swiftly, closing the gap in the law by requiring jitney startups to first prove that they would not be cutting into the business of existing competitors.
- Philadelphia required Ramesh Naropanth to spend $8,000 to install unnecessary gates on his convenience store before approving a permit for him to sell sandwiches.

Stories like these are not all that uncommon. And such setbacks can easily doom a small business, especially if it is new, lacks momentum, and is short on resources.

Still, most state and city governments go to great lengths to support startups; after all, their economic futures depend on new venture creation. Nonetheless, nearly all cities have regulations that restrict new business operations under certain circumstances. For example, some cities have **zoning ordinances** that may limit the operations of home-based businesses. These ordinances often apply to factors related to traffic and parking, signage, nonrelated employees working in a home, the use of a home more as a business than as a residence, the sale of retail goods to the public, and the storage of hazardous materials and work-related equipment.[10]

AVAILABILITY OF RESOURCES

Access to raw materials, suitable labor, crucial suppliers, and transportation are some of the factors that have a bearing on location selection. Proximity to important sources of raw materials and an appropriate labor supply are particularly critical considerations in the location of most manufacturing businesses, whereas access to key suppliers is more likely to influence site selections for retail outlets and restaurant operations.

© SEAN PAVONE/SHUTTERSTOCK.COM

If raw materials required by a company's operations are not readily available in all areas, then regions in which these materials abound will offer significant location advantages. This is especially true for businesses that are dependent on bulky or heavy raw materials that lose much of their size or weight in the manufacturing process. A sawmill is an example of a business that must stay close to its raw materials in order to operate economically.

The suitability of the labor supply for a manufacturer depends on the nature of its production process. Labor-intensive operations need to be located near workers with appropriate skills and reasonable wage requirements. A history of acceptable levels of labor productivity and peaceful relations with employers are also important factors. Companies that depend on semiskilled or unskilled workers usually locate in an area with surplus labor, while other firms may need to be close to a pool of highly skilled labor. If the required talent is unavailable, relocation may be necessary, even it if means

zoning ordinances
Local laws regulating land use.

moving to another state. According to Sharon K. Ward, an economic development consultant, finding a suitable workforce is currently the most pressing need that is driving firms to relocate, especially for those depending on technical expertise.[11]

Access to good transportation is important to many companies. For example, good highways and bus systems provide customers with convenient access to retail stores, which encourages sales. For small manufacturers, quality transportation is especially vital. They must carefully evaluate all trucking routes, considering the costs of both transporting supplies to the manufacturing location and shipping the finished product to customers. It is critical that they know whether these costs will allow their products to be competitively priced.

PERSONAL PREFERENCE OF THE ENTREPRENEUR

As a practical matter, many entrepreneurs tend to focus primarily on their personal preference and convenience when locating a business. Statistics hint at this, showing that nearly half of all entrepreneurs (47 percent) live no more than a five-minute drive from their venture's location.[12] And, despite a world of alternatives, small business owners often choose to stay in their home community. Just because an individual has always lived in a particular town, however, does not automatically make the town a satisfactory business location.

On the other hand, locating a business in one's home community may offer certain unique advantages that cannot be found elsewhere. From a personal point of view, an entrepreneur will generally appreciate and feel comfortable with the atmosphere of his or her home community. As a practical business matter, he or she may find it easier to establish credit with hometown bankers who know that entrepreneur's personal background and reputation. Having personal connections in the local business community can also lead to invaluable business advice. If local residents are potential customers, the prospective entrepreneur probably has a better idea of their tastes and preferences than would an outsider. And it doesn't hurt that friends and relatives in the community may be quick to buy the product or service and gladly spread positive reports about it to others. Though such decisions are usually based on emotion, there are clearly some potential benefits of locating a startup close to home.

The personal preferences that drive the location decision are as varied as the entrepreneurs who make it. Sometimes entrepreneurs choose a location offering unique lifestyle advantages, such as being close to a favorite golf course or a trustworthy babysitter. But while personal preference is important and should not be ignored, it would be unwise to allow this to take priority over obvious location weaknesses that are almost certain to limit or even doom the success of the enterprise. The location decision must take all relevant factors into consideration.

SITE AVAILABILITY AND COSTS

Once an entrepreneur has settled on a certain area for her or his business, a specific site must still be chosen. Many small business owners recognize the value of seeking professional assistance (for example, from local realtors) in determining site availability and appropriateness.

If an entrepreneur's top location choices are unavailable, other options must be considered. One alternative is to share facilities with other enterprises. In recent years, business incubators have sprung up in all areas of the country. A **business incubator** is a facility that rents space to new businesses or to people wishing to start businesses.[13] Incubators are often located in repurposed buildings, such as abandoned warehouses or schools. They serve fledgling businesses by making space available, offering management advice, and providing other forms of assistance (including clerical support),

business incubator
A facility that provides shared space, services, and management assistance to new businesses.

all of which help reduce operating costs. An incubator tenant can be fully operational the day after moving in, without buying phones, renting a copier, or hiring office employees.

Most incubators can accommodate different kinds of early-stage ventures, but some are beginning to focus on a specific business niche, such as fashion, food, or design. Many provide access to industry-specific resources. HBK (Hot Bread Kitchen) Incubates, for example, provides food startups with access to "seven kitchens complete with industrial trial-size convection ovens, deep fryers, blenders, kettles, grills, and a host of other devices."[14] Client businesses also receive recipe scale-up assistance, training in kitchen-use efficiency, supervised production time, general business training, and solid partnership opportunities with other startups in the incubator.[15] To avoid renting space to new ventures that are apt to compete directly with one another, most specialty incubators accept no more than two startups that target the same market. Nonetheless, this arrangement can still lead to its share of complications—for example, similar businesses sometimes try to tie up crucial pieces of equipment for their own use and advantage. But despite the drawbacks, locating in a niche incubator must be worth the trouble, because spaces are so often in short supply.

The purpose of business incubators is to see new businesses hatch, grow, and then move on, so the situation is temporary *by design*. But it appears that many businesses are looking for permanent shared-office arrangements. Regus, a leading provider of shared office space, finds that its business is booming. The firm currently operates more than 2,000 business centers in 750 cities spread over nearly 100 countries.[16]

Perhaps you are more of a free spirit. One variation on the shared-office-space theme is the "co-working" movement, which involves shared working spaces (sometimes an office) that allow mostly freelancers, consultants, artists, and other independent workers to work and connect in the same location. Many such facilities are now available around the world, providing a clean and safe place to work, plentiful networking opportunities, a sense of camaraderie, and access to good coffee. This arrangement is not for everyone, but it provides a good working alternative for many entrepreneurs. And these days it is easy to find and book such a work or meeting space by using a shared-space marketplace like ShareDesk, which can point you to one of more than 2,400 listed venues in all corners of the globe.[17]

Beginning on a Budget
When searching for a location to lease for your business, be sure to use a broker who understands your business, knows what you can afford, and is on your side. Pair the broker with an attorney who can ensure that you understand the lease implications, and your team is ready to go! For more information and important recommendations on leasing, see Robert Moskowitz, "How to Negotiate a Better Commercial Lease," http://quickbooks.intuit.com/r/money/how-to-negotiate-a-better-commercial-lease.

When it comes to site selection—whether permanent or more flexible—the process should factor in all relevant costs. Unfortunately, an entrepreneur is frequently unable to afford the *best* site. The costs involved in building on a new site may be prohibitive, or the purchase price of an existing structure may exceed the entrepreneur's budget.

Assuming that suitable building space is available, the entrepreneur must decide whether to lease or buy. More small business owners choose to purchase rather than lease their buildings (57 percent, according to one study[18]), but the benefits of leasing can sometimes outweigh the gains of owning:

- A large cash outlay is avoided, which can be especially important for a new small firm that lacks adequate financial resources.
- Risk is reduced by minimizing investment and by postponing commitments for space until the success of the business is assured and facility requirements are better known.
- It is usually more affordable to lease in a high-image area than to buy in a prime location.
- Leasing allows the entrepreneur to focus on running the business rather than managing properties.

But there are clearly disadvantages to leasing as well. For example, those who buy will benefit financially when a well-selected property appreciates in value, and their facilities costs will be stable and predictable over time. Just as important, they won't need to ask permission to make future changes or additions to the property.

If entering a lease agreement seems to be the way to go, the entrepreneur first should check the landlord's insurance policies to be sure there is proper coverage for various types of risks. If not, the lessee should seek coverage under his or her own policy. It is also wise to have the terms of the lease agreement reviewed by an attorney. She or he may be able to add special provisions to a lease, such as an escape clause that allows the lessee to exit the agreement under certain conditions. An attorney can also ensure that an entrepreneur will not be unduly exposed to liability for damages caused by the gross negligence of others. Consider the experience of one firm that wished to rent 300 square feet of storage space in a large complex of offices and shops. On the sixth page of the landlord's standard lease, the firm's lawyer found language that could have made the firm responsible for the entire 30,000-square-foot complex if it burned down, regardless of blame! Competent legal counsel may not be cheap, but the services that it provides can certainly save an entrepreneur a lot of money and heartache.

9-2 DESIGNING AND EQUIPPING THE PHYSICAL FACILITIES

LO 9-2

Discuss the challenges of designing and equipping a physical facility.

A well-written location plan should describe the physical space in which the business will be housed and include an explanation of any equipment needs. The plan may call for a new building or an existing structure, but ordinarily a new business that needs physical space will occupy an existing building, perhaps after some minor or major remodeling.

9-2a Challenges in Designing the Physical Facilities

When specifying building requirements, an entrepreneur must avoid committing to a space that is too large or too luxurious for the company's needs. At the same time, the space should not be so small or limiting that operations are hindered or become inefficient. Buildings do not produce profits directly; they merely house the operations and personnel that do so. Therefore, the ideal building will be practical, not extravagant.

The general suitability of a building for a given type of business operation depends on the functional requirements of the enterprise. For example, a restaurant should ideally be on one level to make service manageable; a manufacturer's interlinked production processes should be in the same building and located near one another in order to be efficient. Other important factors to consider include the age and condition of the building, potential fire hazards, the quality of heating and air conditioning systems, the adequacy of lighting and restroom facilities, and appropriate entrances and exits. Obviously, these factors are weighted differently for a factory than for a wholesale or retail operation. But in every case, the comfort, convenience, and safety of the business's employees and customers should be taken into consideration.

9-2b Challenges in Equipping the Physical Facilities

The final step in arranging for physical facilities is the purchase or lease of equipment and tools. The National Federation of Independent Business has reported that, overwhelmingly, owners of small businesses would rather own their equipment than lease it (see Exhibit 9.2). The majority believe that, in the long run, it is cheaper to buy than

EXHIBIT

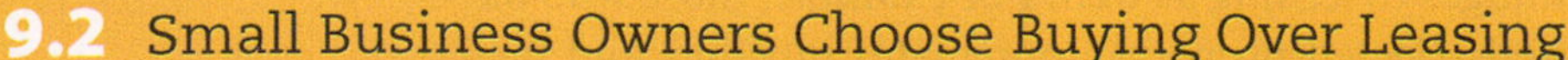

9.2 Small Business Owners Choose Buying Over Leasing

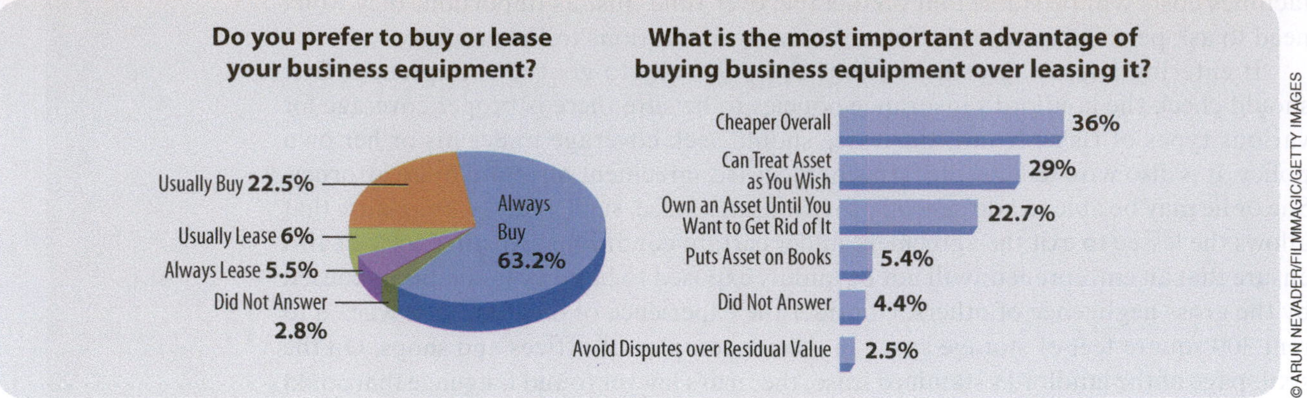

Source: Based on data from National Federation of Independent Business, "411Small Business Facts: Reinvesting in the Business," http://www.411sbfacts.com/files/reinvesting.pdf, accessed December 11, 2014.

to lease. Having the flexibility to use the equipment as they wish and to keep it until it is no longer needed are also important reasons why small business owners prefer to own rather than lease. Still, the leasing option has advocates as well. So what should a small business owner do? To make an informed decision on this, use an equipment lease-versus-buy calculator, which can be found online with a simple Internet search. It's also a good idea to check with an accountant to be sure that any tax consequences of your decision to lease or buy are considered.

MANUFACTURING EQUIPMENT

Machines used in factories can include either general-purpose or special-purpose equipment. **General-purpose equipment** requires minimal investment and is easily adapted to various operations. Small machine shops and cabinet shops, for example, use this type of equipment, which can be set up to handle two or more shop operations using the same piece of machinery. This offers flexibility, which is most important to industries in which products are so new that the technology is not yet well developed or there are frequent design changes. **Special-purpose equipment**, such as bottling machines and manufacturing robots used in factories, offers a more narrow range of possible applications and is more expensive to buy or lease. But a small firm can use special-purpose equipment economically only if it makes a standardized product on a fairly large scale. Upgrades via special tooling can lead to greater output per machine-hour of operation and reduce the labor cost per unit of product even further. On the downside, though, it is important to remember that this equipment has little or no resale value, due to its narrow range of possible applications.

General-purpose equipment
Machines that serve many functions in the production process.

Special-purpose equipment
Machines designed to serve specialized functions in the production process.

RETAILING EQUIPMENT

Small retailers need merchandise-display racks or counters, storage racks, shelving, mirrors, seating for customers, shopping carts, cash registers, and other items to facilitate selling. Such equipment may be costly, but it is usually less expensive than that necessary for a factory operation. And enterprising entrepreneurs often find ways to reduce startup or expansion costs by purchasing used equipment, making their own, or finding other ways to improvise.

If a store is intended to serve a high-income market, its fixtures should signal this by displaying the elegance and style expected by such customers. For example, polished mahogany showcases with bronze fittings can help to create an upscale setting. Indirect lighting, thick rugs, and oversized easy chairs also communicate luxury to clients. In contrast, a store that caters to lower-income customers should concentrate on simplicity. Luxurious fixtures and plush seating would suggest an atmosphere that is inconsistent with low prices and only add to the cost of the operation, making it more difficult to keep prices down.

© JEFFREY LIAO/SHUTTERSTOCK.COM

OFFICE EQUIPMENT

Every business office—even a home office—needs furniture, filing and storage cabinets, and other such items. Major manufacturers of office furniture can certainly provide the necessary desks, chairs, and cabinetry, but so can scores of smaller vendors. Check out local sources of used office furniture, which may have items for sale that are still very presentable but a lot less expensive. And always make your decisions with the future in mind. If you select furnishings that are simple, free-standing, and detachable, you can easily move them all to a larger facility when your business takes off.

Selecting office equipment that can help a business operate efficiently can be challenging. Be sure to choose computers, multifunction printers, and telephone systems that reflect the latest technological advances applicable to a particular business.

A company's major equipment needs should be identified in the location plan. This can ensure that the financial section of the plan will include funds for their purchase.

9-2c Business Image

All new ventures should be concerned with projecting the most appropriate image to customers and the public at large. The look and "feel" of the workplace should create an impression that says something about the quality of a firm's product or service and about the way the business is operated in general. For a small firm, and especially a startup, it is important to use the physical facilities to convey the image of a stable, professional company.

Factors as basic as color and interior design should be considered. Even before the first customer shows up, companies sometimes find that their financial backers are unwilling to hand over investment dollars until an office or retail store is perceived as attractive and inviting. If the image aspect of the facilities equation is beyond your expertise and insight, you may need to consult a design professional with a trained eye who can help you to make decisions that work.

Image is the engine of sales, so carefully consider how to mold your space to create a distinct and appropriate impression, yet still provide plenty of space, allow easy traffic flow, pass building inspections, and more—all in keeping with your budget and business goals. If you are planning office space, you also need to think about the impact that something as simple as seating arrangements can have on personnel interactions and learning. The way your facilities, customers, and employees come together will be critical to the success of your new business.

Equipping a New Business on a Shoestring

You don't need the flashiest equipment and the best of furnishings to get started, just stuff that works. With deals on sites like Craigslist and FreeCycle, you could save a bundle. If you need computers and would prefer to buy new rather than used, you can usually save money by going to sites like Techbargains.com and BradsDeals.com. And you can often find a wide selection and good deals on new furniture on Overstock's website.

Living the Dream

ENTREPRENEURIAL EXPERIENCES

Hanging Out with the Right People Makes a Big Difference!

Seating arrangements matter. High school students have to navigate a complex social web every time they decide where to eat lunch in a cafeteria. During college, assigned seats can dramatically impact academic experience. Neighbors can become best friends, study partners, or a source of unending distraction.

According to Dr. Ben Waber, a human group dynamics scientist and the chief executive of workplace analytics provider Sociometric Solutions, physical location has a profound effect in the workplace as well. The evidence for this claim is not just anecdotal. By using wearable electronic sensors, Sociometric Solutions has been able to track employee movements and identify social patterns in a variety of companies, and this has led to a number of important insights. For instance, the data show that 40 to 60 percent of employee interactions (face-to-face, electronic, and on the phone) occur with colleagues seated immediately nearby, whereas employees have a mere 5 to 10 percent chance of interacting with co-workers located only two rows away. This shows that seating arrangements can have a profound effect on organizational effectiveness. Grouping employees by department can increase focus and improve efficiency, but mixing workers across different functions of the business can foster innovation and encourage breakthrough ideas to develop and spread.

© MONKEY BUSINESS IMAGES/SHUTTERSTOCK.COM

Many companies have already experimented with this. At MODCo Media, a New York-based advertising agency, management has tried three different seating arrangements to mix and match employees from different departments. For example, they placed a number of accountants near media buyers to see if they would somehow come to share the same skills and insights. The experiment worked impressively—especially for the media buyers, who started to understand the financial dimensions of the business and learned how to factor those insights into their daily decision making. This created efficiencies that ultimately saved MODCo hundreds of thousands of dollars. In a test at another firm, similar adjustments led to a 10 percent increase in the interactions of sales staff with people outside their team, which caused sales to go up by 10 percent. Employee location and office traffic flow clearly make a difference.

One final caution is in order, however: Seating arrangements should be planned only after giving careful thought to the company's organizational culture. "Think about who your people are and how they work before you start making decisions about how to get them to interact with other employees," advises Waber. "If you make changes without taking that into consideration, it could be a waste of time." But with a reasonable plan, an intelligent office layout can yield extraordinary results.

Sources: "Sociometric Solutions," http://www.sociometricsolutions.com, accessed December 18, 2014; Rachel Feintzeig, "Bosses Take a Stand on Where Workers Sit," *The Wall Street Journal*, October 9, 2013, p. B8; Gwen Moran, "Swap Seats, Change Your Company? Why Where You Sit Matters," *Entrepreneur*, November 5, 2013, http://www.entrepreneur.com/article/229683, accessed December 18, 2014; and Joshua Brustein, "The Case for Wearing Productivity Sensors on the Job," *Bloomberg Businessweek*, December 19, 2013, http://www.businessweek.com/articles/2013-12-19/sociometric-solutions-ben-waber-on-workers-wearing-sensors, accessed December 18, 2014.

9-3 LOCATING THE STARTUP IN THE ENTREPRENEUR'S HOME

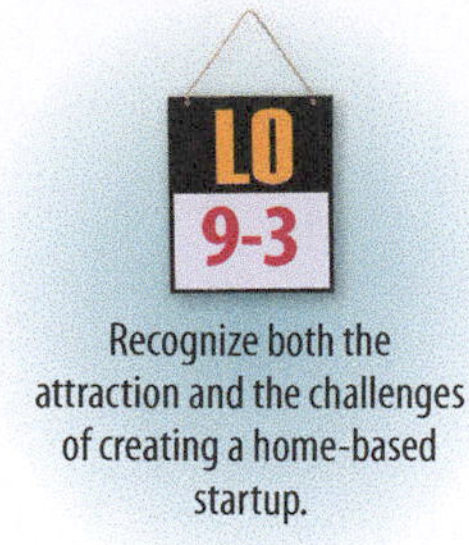

Recognize both the attraction and the challenges of creating a home-based startup.

Rather than lease or buy a commercial site, many entrepreneurs choose instead to use their basement, garage, or spare room for their operations, creating a **home-based business**. In the past, a home location for a business was almost always considered second-rate. But times have changed. Despite the limitations and potential for image problems, home-based entrepreneurs no longer feel embarrassed about their location. In fact, research has shown that home-based businesses may actually enjoy an advantage over other companies when it comes to certain dimensions of financial performance (for example, achieving a first sale[19]). The home office, once viewed as a passing phase on the path to growth for many businesses, has become a viable permanent option for some.

home-based business A business that maintains its primary facility in the residence of its owner.

9-3a The Attraction of Home-Based Businesses

According to government surveys, more than half of all U.S. business owners choose to run their businesses primarily out of a home.[20] Why do many entrepreneurs find operating a business at home so appealing? Motivations vary, but the main attractions of a home-based business relate to financial and family lifestyle considerations, such as the following:[21]

- To get a business up and running quickly and cheaply
- To have something interesting to do, and get paid for doing it
- To be your own boss, and reap the rewards from your efforts
- To spend more time with family and friends
- To save time and money wasted on daily commutes

FINANCIAL CONSIDERATIONS

Like most ventures, a home-based business has an important goal—earning money—and locating at home helps increase profits by reducing costs. For example, a freelance writer of magazine articles may need only a computer, a few office supplies, and an Internet connection to launch a business from home. Since most writers own a computer, the true startup costs for such a business may be only a few hundred dollars.

This option can certainly limit the cost and therefore the risk of testing market demand for a new product or service. With the ups and downs of the advertising industry, Donnovan Andrews and Stephen Smyk thought it would be best to start their fledgling agency, called Performance Bridge, in their home. "[We] built the business slowly and were conservative until we got to the point where we had excess capital," says Andrews. This cautious approach worked well. Andrews and Smyk were able to move into office space in a professional building only four months after they started the business.[22]

FAMILY LIFESTYLE CONSIDERATIONS

Many young entrepreneurs remain in a family business because of close ties to relatives. Similarly, entrepreneurs who locate business operations in the home are frequently motivated by the desire to spend more time with family members, sometimes even including them in the work.

Marissa Shipman founded and served as CEO of Shipman Associates, Inc., a cosmetics business that she launched from her home in 2001. She enjoyed working from her residence, despite the constant change and disruption that were necessary to accommodate her growing business. In time, the venture became a true family affair when Shipman's sister, Jordana, signed on as executive vice president with marketing responsibilities. At one point, even her father was added to the payroll. Shipman eventually shut down the business to move on to other career aspirations, but she had already concluded that a home is a great place to launch a startup. "If you have something you think could work," she says, "do it on a small scale and see."[23]

9-3b The Challenges of Home-Based Businesses

Just as most businesses located at commercial sites have their problems, home-based businesses face special challenges because of their location. We briefly examine two of these issues—business image and legal considerations. A third challenge—family and business conflicts—was discussed in Chapter 5.

PROFESSIONAL IMAGE

Maintaining a professional image when working at home is a major challenge for many home-based entrepreneurs. Allowing young children to answer the telephone, for example, may undermine a company's image. Likewise, a baby crying or a dog barking in the background during a phone call can be distracting to a client and discourage sales.

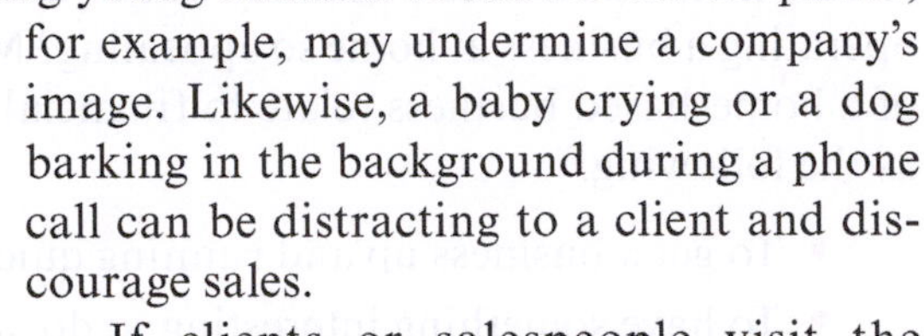

© MONKEY BUSINESS IMAGES/SHUTTERSTOCK

If clients or salespeople visit the home-based business, it is critical that a professional office area be maintained. Space limitations sometimes make this difficult. For example, when you own a home-based business, house guests can create a real problem. Unless you want Aunt Zerelda wandering into a client meeting in her bathrobe or your nephew Jimmie playing his electric guitar during a work call, ground rules need to be set for house guests. Otherwise, major disruptions to the business are bound to occur. But establishing appropriate boundaries between home and business is easier said than done. Consider one successful work-at-home small business owner's take on this:

> *The moment you create a business, you step into a twilight zone where the barrier between what is work and what is not starts to break down. The deterioration accelerates for entrepreneurs who work out of their homes. You may start off with a home-based business but soon find yourself with a business where you and your family also happen to live.*[24]

So, it's not just a matter of preventing family members from spoiling business opportunities. Family life is paramount and should be shielded, in reasonable ways, from the creeping reach of the company's operations. The groan of extra car traffic, the presence of strangers (customers and employees) wandering through the house, inconvenient stacks of inventory and packing materials cluttering common areas, brusquely rejected invitations to break the focus on work to join one's spouse for lunch—these

and many other hassles and inconveniences are everyday fare for the family of a home-based entrepreneur. And they call for patience and an extra dose of understanding from everyone involved.

LEGAL CONSIDERATIONS

Local laws can sometimes pose serious problems for home-based businesses. Zoning ordinances, discussed earlier, regulate the types of enterprises permitted to operate within certain areas, and some cities outlaw any type of home-based business within city limits.

Municipalities have been easing zoning restrictions since the 1990s, but the pace of deregulation accelerated following the 2008 financial crisis to respond to adverse economic realities. Nonetheless, these zoning laws, some dating as far back as the 1930s, can still create burdensome restrictions for a small business. The intent of such laws is to protect a neighborhood's residential quality by forbidding commercial signs, limiting noise, and preventing parking problems. The neighborhood you live in may have a homeowners' association that can limit your ability to run a home-based business. Some entrepreneurs first become aware of these zoning laws when neighbors complain or initiate zoning enforcement actions.

There are also tax issues related to a home-based business. For example, a separate space must be clearly devoted to the activities of the business if an entrepreneur is to claim a tax deduction. A knowledgeable accountant can help explain these tax regulations.

And don't forget the insurance considerations that may affect a home-based business. A homeowner's policy is not likely to cover an entrepreneur's business activities, liabilities, and equipment. Therefore, he or she should always consult a trustworthy insurance agent about policy limitations to avoid unpleasant surprises down the road.

The bad news for home-based businesses is that they often face significant hassles and restrictions, such as those just outlined. The good news is that these ventures now have access to powerful business-application technologies that can help them compete, even against rivals with a commercial site. With this in mind, we examine the potential of the Internet as a place to host a new business in the next section.

9-4 E-COMMERCE: LOCATING A STARTUP ON THE INTERNET

LO 9-4

Understand the potential benefits of locating a startup on the Internet.

What does the term *e-commerce* really describe? **E-commerce** refers to electronic commerce, or the buying and selling of products or services over the Internet. It is an alternative means of conducting business transactions that traditionally have been carried out by telephone, by mail, or face to face in a brick-and-mortar facility. After the crash of Web-based enterprises more than a decade ago, Internet businesses are now growing in new ways and faster than ever—and with good reason. Locating on the Web can fundamentally reshape the way small firms conduct business. Far more than a simple alternative to the brick-and-mortar facility, the Internet can significantly boost a small company's financial performance.

9-4a Benefits of E-Commerce for Startups

E-commerce
Electronic commerce, or the buying and selling of products or services over the Internet.

Electronic commerce can benefit a startup in many ways. It certainly allows a new venture to compete with bigger businesses on a more level playing field. Because of their limited resources, small firms often cannot reach beyond local markets. So those small

Living the Dream

ENTREPRENEURIAL EXPERIENCES

In the Zone or Out of Bounds?

Studies have revealed that 69 percent of new businesses are started at home, with the Small Business Administration estimating that home-based ventures account for more than half of the 28 million small businesses in the United States. And that number is almost certain to increase. Responding to stubbornly high unemployment and sagging municipal tax revenues since the 2008 financial crisis, many cities and districts have accelerated the relaxing of zoning restrictions to make it easier for displaced workers to start businesses of their own.

Typical zoning laws in years past have allowed professional services firms, like medical or legal offices, to operate from residential areas. But now, more municipalities are granting the option to a wider range of enterprises so that, for example, food makers and landscapers can also run ventures out of their homes. This shift appears to be widespread. According to James Duncan, founding partner of Duncan Associates, a planning consulting firm, "Almost all communities are loosening their regulations on home businesses."

One lucrative home-based opportunity that attracts many small business hopefuls involves the preparation of food products. Nearly every state now has provisions, called Cottage Food Laws, which regulate this kind of business, but a great number have recently changed these rules to accommodate startups. For example, Louisiana and Texas recently amended their requirements to allow the production and sale of a greater variety of home-prepared edible goods. The amendments also increase the number of places where these goods can be sold. These changes have enabled entrepreneurs like Roxane Daigle of Fancy Cakes LLC to expand their home-based food operations. Many continue to advocate for additional reforms, which would further curb current restrictions. Daigle, for instance, has been lobbying Louisiana politicians to increase the revenue cap from \$20,000 to \$50,000 for businesses that sell food products in that state, knowing that this may be the only way for her to expand and stay in business.

Despite fewer restrictions, home-based business owners still face a number of challenges when operating from a residential property. "Almost all zoning is enforced by complaints," says Don Elliott of consulting group Clarion Associates. Some of the most common protests directed against home-based businesses involve traffic, noise, and visual nuisances. If objections should surface, business owners need to be prepared to scale back their volume or rethink their business models. This may not be easy, but it may very well be the only way for a small company to keep the neighbors happy and its doors open.

Sources: Alli Condra, "Cottage Food Laws in the United States," http://blogs.law.harvard.edu/foodpolicyinitiative/files/2013/08/FINAL_Cottage-Food-Laws-Report_2013.pdf, accessed December 19, 2014; Small Business Administration, "Home-Based Businesses," https://www.sba.gov/content/home-based-businesses, accessed December 19, 2014; Nicole Hong, "More and More, There's No Place Like Home," *The Wall Street Journal*, September 30, 2013, p. R5; Forrager: Cottage Food Community, "Louisiana," August 7, 2014, http://forrager.com/law/louisiana, accessed December 19, 2014; and "One Woman's Fight to Change Louisiana's Cottage Food Law," *Small Food Business*, January 24, 2013, http://www.smallfoodbiz.com/2013/01/24/one-womans-fight-to-change-louisianas-cottage-food-law, accessed December 19, 2014.

firms confined to the brick-and-mortar world typically can serve only a restricted region. But the Internet blurs geographic boundaries and expands a small company's reach. In fact, e-commerce allows any business access to customers almost anywhere.

The experience of Beauty Encounter, a company that sells perfumes and beauty products, shows how the Internet is proving to be a great equalizer, giving small firms a presence comparable to that of marketplace giants. The business is an extension of three physical stores that were started by a Vietnamese couple who immigrated to the United States in 1980. Their daughter, Jacquelyn Tran, recognized the limitations of such operations and decided to carve out her own space in the global marketplace by establishing an online presence in 1999. Since then, the company has done nothing but grow. It now offers 40,000-plus products representing more than 1,000 brands, with new items being added daily, proving that small companies now can play in the big leagues.[25] Going online can unlock the door of opportunity for small companies, regardless of the industry.

It should also be pointed out that an e-commerce operation can help the startup with early cash flow problems by compressing the sales cycle—that is, reducing the time between receiving an order and converting the sale to cash. E-commerce systems can be designed to generate an order, authorize a credit card purchase, and contact a supplier and shipper in a matter of a few minutes, all without human assistance. The shorter cycle translates into quicker payments from customers and improved cash flows to the business.

9-4b E-Commerce Business Models

One of the fundamental features of an online operation is the business model upon which it is built. As discussed in Chapter 6, a business model is an analysis of how a firm plans to create profits and cash flows given its revenue sources, its cost structures, the required size of investment, and sources of risk. Online companies differ in their decisions concerning which customers to serve, how best to become profitable, and what to include on their websites. Exhibit 9.3 shows some possible alternatives for e-commerce business models. None of these models can currently be considered dominant, and some of the more complex Internet operations cannot be described by any single form. In reality, the world of e-commerce contains endless combinations of business models. To help you grasp the possibilities, we first outline e-commerce business models according to the type of customer served and then describe models based

EXHIBIT 9.3 Basic E-Commerce Business Models

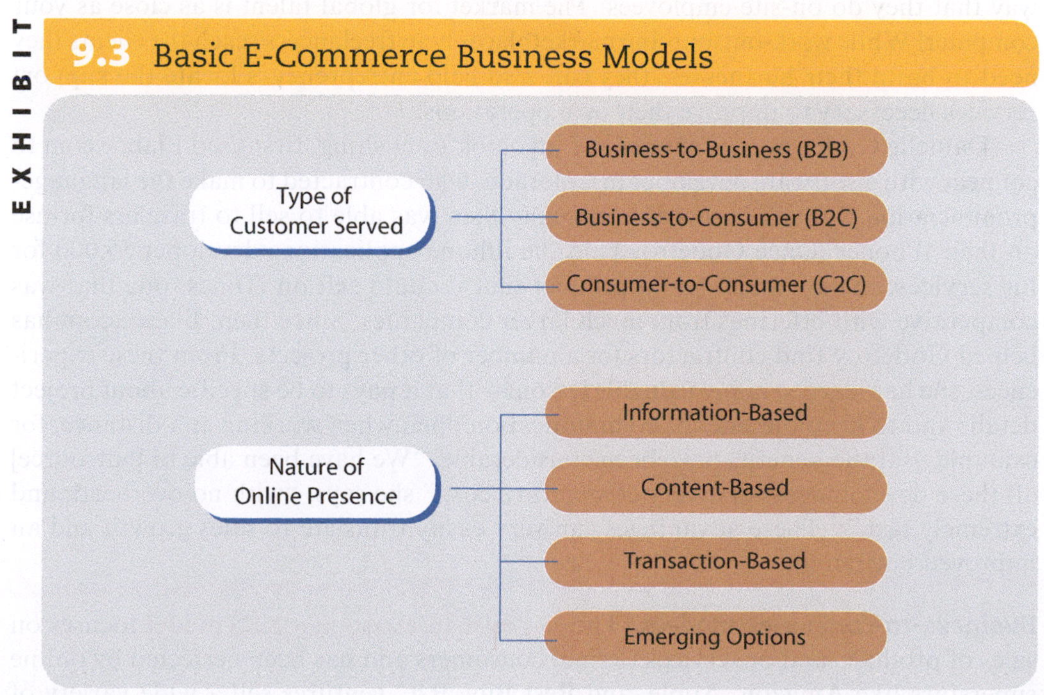

on the nature of a company's online presence. As you consider a direction for your small business and its online aspirations, keep in mind that a poorly devised business model is often the primary cause of an online company's failure.

TYPE OF CUSTOMERS SERVED

Marketing frameworks classify traditional brick-and-mortar facilities as manufacturers, wholesalers, or retailers, depending on the customers they serve. E-commerce businesses also are commonly distinguished according to customer focus. There are three major categories of e-commerce business models: business-to-business (B2B), business-to-consumer (B2C), and consumer-to-consumer (C2C). In this section, we examine some strategies used by e-commerce firms within these three categories.

Business-to-business models The dollar amounts generated by firms using a **business-to-business (B2B) model** (selling to business customers) are significantly greater than those for firms with a business-to-consumer (B2C) model (selling to final consumers). Because B2B success stories generally receive less publicity than B2C ventures do, the potential of B2B opportunities is often overlooked. But aspiring entrepreneurs should be sure to consider B2B options.

B2B operations "come in all shapes and sizes," but the most popular form of this strategy emphasizes sales transactions. By using online capabilities, a B2B firm can achieve greater efficiency in its buying and selling activities. For example, by dealing directly with its business clients online, Hewlett-Packard is able to build its computer systems and related products to meet the specific needs of its customers. The company relies heavily on the Internet to deliver its business solutions, but it also has an extensive sales force and IT consulting services to deliver value to its many customers worldwide.

A unique form of B2B trade involves work outsourcing, which helps connect freelancers and other specialists with companies that need their services. These online marketplaces are increasing in number and availability, and some sites are reporting sales growth as high as 60 percent a year.[26] Some of the better-known sites include Elance.com, Freelancer.com, oDesk.com, Guru.com, and PeoplePerHour.com, which allow businesses to find, hire, manage, and pay remote contractors in much the same way that they do on-site employees. The market for global talent is as close as your computer! While work-outsourcing marketplaces help freelancers reach the clients they need to build their businesses, they can also help entrepreneurs locate the support services necessary to improve their own operations.

Danielle Godefroy, co-founder of Lingolook Publishing, first used Elance.com to connect with a software developer in Colorado, who contracted to make the language-pronunciation flashcards that the company then was able to sell to travelers for use on their iPhones. Once Godefroy paid the iPhone applications developer $5,000 for his services, the company had a product that it could sell on iTunes, one that was competitive with offerings from much larger companies. Since then, Elance.com has helped Godefroy find contractors for a number of other projects. From these experiences, she has learned many valuable lessons—that it pays to be specific about project details and to keep the lines of communication open when working at a distance, for example. But the benefits have been considerable. "We have been able to [outsource] all these developments at a very competitive cost," she says, "with no overhead, and extremely fast."[27] These advantages can very easily translate to sales growth and an improved bottom line.

business-to-business (B2B) model
A business model based on selling to business customers electronically.

business-to-consumer (B2C) model
A business model based on selling to final consumers electronically.

Business-to-consumer models. The **business-to-consumer (B2C) model** focuses on sales of products and/or services to final consumers and has been perfected by online superstars like Amazon, Apple, and Best Buy. B2C ventures sell a wide variety of products, with offerings ranging from clothing to pet items, computer software to groceries, and much more. The B2C model offers three main advantages over brick-and-mortar retailing: convenient use, immediate transactions, and round-the-clock access to a broad array of products and services.

Opening up an online business has never been easier, thanks to the "online storefront" option and support services offered by giant operators like Amazon, Yahoo, and eBay. Some companies do business only through such a storefront, though many others also establish their own independent website and sell through both. When he launched his online store, Oliver's Pet Care, Shaheed Khan signed up for Amazon Webstore (www.webstore.amazon.com), which provides all of the tools needed to build an online business. It allows sellers to list their items alongside those offered by Amazon and to use the Fulfillment by Amazon program to handle product packing and shipping. The fulfillment program makes it possible for Khan's customers to combine orders of his products with those of Amazon and to receive free shipping, customer service, and returns support directly from Amazon. Khan says these services make his life manageable and have greatly boosted Oliver's Pet Care sales.[28]

Some small business owners prefer to steer clear of big Internet marketplaces and establish their own presence online. There now are a number of e-commerce platform providers that make it relatively easy for even a one-person online store to appear to be a polished, sophisticated retail operation. These providers include Bigcommerce, Shopify, Tictail, Storenvy, and Big Cartel, which specialize in helping people set up their own virtual storefronts. These companies typically charge around $10 a month for their services, with some tacking on transaction fees ranging from 1 to 2 percent of sales. But they make getting started a snap: Sign up and select a name, choose one of the preset designs and themes, upload images of products to be offered, and then let the selling begin. Most of these services even provide a dashboard that allows owners to see order numbers and examine sales analytics. These powerful tools can deliver impressive results.[29]

No matter which platform they adopt, B2C e-commerce businesses certainly face unique challenges (payment security risks, customers who refuse to purchase a product without first seeing it or trying it on, etc.). But they also enjoy the advantages of flexibility. For example, they are able to change merchandise mixes and prices quickly, and they can easily modify the appearance of their online store. Traditional merchants located in brick-and-mortar stores would find such changes to be very costly and time-consuming, making it nearly impossible for them to keep up with fast-moving markets.

Gilt Groupe, started in 2007, exploits the flexibility edge that online businesses can have. As one of a number of popular "flash sale" websites, this fashion retailer makes e-commerce fun and exciting by offering instant access to some of the most popular designer labels available, but on an invitation-only basis and at insider prices.[30] Gilt's website provides its members with a unique selection of apparel, accessories, and lifestyle items that change every day—and that is the secret to the company's success. Susan Lyne, who serves on the firm's board, explains what sets Gilt Groupe apart from the competition:

> *Most online shopping mirrors brick-and-mortar stores. They're not taking advantage of what's uniquely possible online, the heightened sense of entertainment and competition. A big part of the Gilt brand promise is discovery: you come every day and it's new every day.*[31]

By changing its product offerings daily, customers are drawn to the website often to see what's new, and the pages can be changed to keep up with shifts in consumer demand and product availability. This capacity for flexibility provides a substantial edge over brick-and-mortar operations—at least for those online businesses that position themselves to take advantage of it.

Many producers and wholesalers today are choosing to bypass retailers and take their product or service directly to the final consumer through online operations, a strategy sometimes referred to as **disintermediation**. This decision is driven mostly by the increasingly slim margins that they get when selling through big retailers. And the model can work like a charm—think Zappos and Warby Parker.

When Andres Niño and Nicholas Hurtado launched Beckett Simonon in 2012, it was with the specific intent to offer their line of men's shoes directly to the end user. This direct-to-customer model allows them to sell $300 shoes for $79 to $130 and to offer a much higher level of customer care. "It's a lot more work to grow a brand this way," observes Niño, "but being able to talk to [buyers] and build personal relationships enables us to build a better brand."[32] The company's sales have been growing rapidly (up a whopping 114 percent from January to March in 2014!), showing that its concept is right on the money. That's the power of the online option—it offers market reach and flexibility that would not otherwise be available.

As B2C e-commerce models continue to develop and evolve, new alternatives will emerge, which is bound to catch established rivals off guard. Even some very large competitors find it difficult to keep up with the online game. For example, Google's creative service offerings have forced Microsoft to reconsider how it prices its software, and full-service travel agencies are still trying to figure out how to adjust their approaches to deal with more recent competitors like Kayak.com and CheapOAir.com. An alert entrepreneur will monitor movement in the marketplace to be able to respond quickly to potential risks and identify emerging opportunities.

Consumer-to-consumer models A growing number of entrepreneurs who sell their wares over the Internet do so without creating either a website or a storefront. Instead, they use auction sites, which fall under what is sometimes called the **consumer-to-consumer (C2C) model**. This model is usually set up around Internet **auction sites** that allow individuals and companies to list products available for sale to potential bidders.

Online auctions have become one of the most celebrated success stories on the Internet. And eBay, founded in 1995 by computer programmer Pierre Omidyar, is the 900-pound gorilla of auction sites. Here are a few statistics to show you what an amazing phenomenon eBay has become: The company has more than 145 million active users around the world and sells over $2,642 in goods *every second*. It may also surprise you to know that goods totaling a mind-blowing $20.5 billion were sold on eBay in a recent three-month period.[33]

You can buy or sell nearly anything on eBay, and it's incredibly easy. For a fee, auction-site consultants will coach you on how to be a successful seller. You can also attend eBay University, in person or via online tutorials, to learn the ins and outs of operating an eBay business. To show you how simple it is to get started, Exhibit 9.4 provides a simple four-step procedure for selling items on eBay. As easy as it is to sell a few items on eBay, it is a very different matter to actually make money as an ongoing business on the site. As in the more conventional forms of retailing, a well-thought-out business plan is helpful in turning your business idea (or hobby) into a money-making proposition.

Auction sites like eBay generate most of their revenue through listing fees and commissions. To continue its rapid growth, eBay is expanding its services and entering additional markets across the globe through new sites, acquisitions, and shared ventures—it now does business in 39 countries, including the United States.[34] But it is no longer

disintermediation
The bypassing of a middleman by a producer or wholesaler in order to sell its product or service directly to the final consumer.

consumer-to-consumer (C2C) model
A business model usually set up around Internet auction sites that allow individuals and companies to list items available for sale to potential bidders.

auction sites
Web-based businesses offering participants the ability to list products for consumer bidding.

EXHIBIT

9.4 Selling Your Item on Ebay

Step 1: Set up an eBay seller's account, which is free of charge.
Step 2: Create a listing for the item to be offered for sale.
Step 3: Manage your listing to see if anyone has bid on or purchased your item.
Step 4: Wrap up with the sale with your buyer by receiving payment, shipping the item, and leaving feedback.

Source: Adapted from "Getting Started Selling on eBay," http://pages.ebay.com/help/sell/sell-getstarted.html, accessed December 12, 2014.

the only show in town. Today, eBay faces competition from the likes of UBid.com, eBid.com, OnlineAuction.com, and a number of other significant challengers.

The company is also taking steps to expand the eBay Stores side of its business, which gives sellers access to millions of shoppers worldwide. This option helps eBay Store sellers achieve success by providing powerful tools to help them build, manage, promote, and track their eBay presence. And they can create a listing, with full search exposure, after paying a reasonable subscription fee.[35] To hold on to its position at the top of the heap, the company has harnessed the power of the smartphone revolution by perfecting a new generation of powerful mobile-shopping technologies, with impressive results.[36]

NATURE OF ONLINE PRESENCE

A second broad way of categorizing e-commerce models relates to a firm's intended level of online presence. The role of a website can range from merely offering information and basic content to enabling complex business transactions.

Information-based model A website built on the **information-based model** simply offers information about a business, its products, and other related matters. It is typically just a complement to an existing brick-and-mortar facility. Many small businesses use this model for their online operations. Your dentist or plumber may have a website that simply describes the services offered but probably will require a phone call to set up an appointment. These sites often feature a "Contact Us" link that will take the user to a separate Web page displaying the company's address and phone number and, in many cases, offer "click-through" access that allows the user to get in touch with the business via e-mail.

The Internet has become the first stop for consumers who need information on a local business. So it makes sense for small companies to create websites that can then be picked up by consumer searches. They should also list their businesses on local platforms offered by major search engines, which can be done by going to www.google.com/business or www.local.yahoo.com, to mention only two available options.

Content-based model The **content-based model** of e-commerce is a variation of the information-based alternative in that it also features a website that provides access to information but not the ability to make purchases. Rather than selling products or services, a content-based website provides information (content) for those who visit it, usually with the hope of attracting a healthy stream of visitors.

In most cases, this online traffic can be "monetized" (turned into a source of revenue), assuming that is what the creator has in mind. For example, it is easy enough to have Google place ads or banners on your website; you would then earn money each

information-based model
A business model in which a website simply provides information about a business, its products, and other related matters.

content-based model
A business model in which a website provides information (content) that attracts visitors, usually with the hope of generating revenue through advertising or by directing those visitors to other websites.

time a visitor clicks on them (see www.google.com/adsense for details). Ad revenue is usually disappointingly low, but another option is to become an online affiliate. Affiliate programs (sometimes called *associate programs*) arrange for online merchants to pay a commission to websites for any traffic that they can send to them. For example, Amazon's Associates Program pays referral fees of up to 10 percent on qualified sales of its products that are initiated through links on an affiliate's website. As a bonus, the program is easy to use, and the company will show you countless options for building links and ads for Amazon products on your site.[37] But this is just one example of hundreds of affiliate programs that you could choose to join.

transaction-based model
A business model in which a website provides a mechanism for buying or selling products or services.

Transaction-based model In a **transaction-based model** of e-commerce, a website is set up to provide a mechanism for buying or selling products or services. The transaction-based model could be considered the center of the e-commerce universe, with online stores where visitors go to shop, click, and buy.

Many Internet ventures sell a single product or service. For example, Huber and Jane Wilkinson market their reading comprehension program, IdeaChain, through their MindPrime, Inc., website (www.mindprime.com). Other ventures are direct extensions of a brick-and-mortar store, creating what is sometimes called a bricks-and-clicks or a clicks-and-mortar strategy. If you wanted to purchase a new printer, for instance, you might research options on Office Depot's website and then either buy your selection online or pick up the printer at your neighborhood Office Depot store. Although Office Depot is a large corporation with millions of customers, many small businesses are following the same general model, and with excellent results.

Many e-commerce companies generate a lot of sales by merging the content- and transaction-based models into one website. Launched in 1999, Bodybuilding.com is the most visited bodybuilding and fitness website in the world. The endless volume of educational content on the site, most of which plugs products that are sold through its transaction features, attracts more than 1.1 million unique visitors each day.[38]

But this raises a thorny ethical question: How can an online company feature content that is so closely tied to its own products? To maintain integrity in this situation, the company should be transparent and make sure that all claims are legitimate. After all, the long-term performance of the company will depend on it. According to Peter Nguyen, an Internet-business superstar, websites that get extraordinary results usually do at least one of the following three things:[39]

- Create *meaningful value* in the form of valuable information, incentives, or services.
- Provide *remarkable experiences* that create entertainment that can be shared.
- Offer *impactful solutions* that help people improve themselves, their businesses, or their communities.

It follows that online entrepreneurs who create the most benefit for their customers are far more likely to succeed. Websites that make false or overstated claims are usually short-lived, as the news of their misdeeds spreads quickly on the Internet. As with brick-and-mortar operations, enduring and impactful online businesses must have integrity and deliver genuine value to their customers.

START UP ACTION

From the Online Shopping Cart to Purchase

It may surprise you to know that about two-thirds of online shoppers put items in their shopping cart and abandon them later. Here are some ways to fix that:

- Be sure that your checkout button is easy to find.
- Find ways to assure shoppers that their personal information is secure.
- Streamline the checkout process, and make the page easy to navigate.
- Allow users to check out as guests—they can set up their accounts later.
- Make it easy for shoppers to know your return policy—this encourages sales.

Source: Kasey Wehrum, "Their Carts Are Full, So Why Won't They Buy?" *Inc.*, Vol. 35, No. 10 (December 2013/January 2014), p. 28.

Emerging options The Internet world is known for how fast it moves, and entrepreneurial minds are constantly finding new ways to cash in on its potential. In most cases, these are variations on the content-based model discussed earlier.

Bloggers produce online journals to trade comments with friends and other readers, but these can also be managed as a money-making venture. Small firms have found blogs easy to use and thus an attractive platform from which to promote the sale of an overstocked item or to give an employee special recognition. But Web traffic on a blog can also generate considerable income from advertising and paid links. The amount earned is dependent on such factors as how much traffic the site generates, the trustworthiness of the content offered, and how relevant the ads are to those who visit. Rhett Butler quit his job as a production manager when he realized that he could make a very comfortable living from his environmental conservation blog, Mongabay. "The rainforest has always been my passion," says Butler, "but I never expected to make a living off of it." At one point, he was making between $15,000 and $18,000 a month in ad revenue, and his website continues to attract more than one million unique visitors each month.[40]

Another option is to create podcasts, audio or video files that are distributed over the Internet and can draw a listenership of around 38 million. Comedian, former radio personality, and multimedia ranter Adam Carolla launched his podcast venture in 2009 and now records humorous, sometimes offensive, episodes that he archives online. Millions of listeners tune in each month to see what he has to say, and that translates to substantial profits. Carolla and other podcasters can make money by peddling ads and sponsorships, asking for donations, selling subscriptions, and charging for access to live events.[41]

Still other entrepreneurs are cashing in on the Web by exploiting the reach of YouTube or Pinterest to create a following that can be turned into profit. YouTube has organized a Partner Program that allows content creators to display advertisements on their videos and earn 55 percentage of the revenue generated from showing them. According to the managing editor of online video marketer's guide ReelSEO, the top 1,000 channels on YouTube generate an impressive $23,000 a month from advertising.[42] But that's not the end of the profit potential the platform can create. Online style guru Michelle Phan has used her YouTube celebrity to push her book to best-seller status, launch her own L'Oreal cosmetics line, and attract endorsement deals from commercial heavyweights like Dr Pepper and Toyota.[43]

Pinterest first launched its social image bookmarking website in 2010, but it is only now beginning to figure out how to make money from it.[44] A number of its more popular "pinners," however, have been finding ways to cash in on the site for some time. For example, fast-rising designer Satsuki Shibuya has more than a million followers, exposure that has prompted some companies to pay her anywhere from $150 to $1,200 just for pinning an image of one of their products. "It's a smart move [for the paying brands]," she says. "They're already putting ads in magazines, and there are 10 times as many people looking at Pinterest."[45] As these examples demonstrate, new online business concepts are being created all the time, and alert entrepreneurs are finding ways to make the most of them.

9-4c Internet-Based Businesses and the Part-Time Startup Advantage

When an entrepreneur launches a new company, many times she or he has to decide whether to give up an existing job and jump full-time into the startup or hold on to the job while getting a part-time business going on the side. There are advantages and drawbacks to each approach, of course, but research shows that many entrepreneurs prefer to launch a part-time enterprise to keep the income flowing until they can afford to make a complete transition to the new business. This is especially true for those who tend to be more risk averse and less self-confident.[46] Though many kinds of businesses can be started on a part-time basis, a growing number of small business owners are finding that the flexibility and low cost of launching an online business make this a very attractive option.

Holding on to a full-time career while launching a new venture on the side can be a very satisfying, but grueling, experience. It is not unusual for these hardy souls to work 90 to 100 hours a week while the company is in its startup phase, with only about half of those hours being spent in regular employment. In other words, it is important to understand that a "part-time" business has a way of tying up weekends and evenings, and it may take years to grow the startup to the point where the founder(s) can afford to set aside regular employment and work for the new company full time. On the upside, though, the part-time approach can take much of the risk out of making the transition to life as an entrepreneur, with research showing that such ventures tend to survive longer than those launched by owners who choose to jump in with both feet from the start.[47] But perhaps more important to our discussion here, the Internet is often the enabling platform that makes it possible to convert these part-time startup dreams into full-time entrepreneurial reality.

Clearly, the location decision is complicated, but it is extremely important to get it right. If your business needs a physical facility, can you find a location that is convenient to customers, offers a supportive business climate, and provides access to necessary resources? As the owner of the business, would you be happy to show up to work at that location, day after day and year after year? When you think of the costs involved, does the location make sense? If you have decided to locate your business at home, can you keep the business and your home life manageably separate? Also, can you abide by zoning restrictions and maintain a favorable company image? If the Internet is the right place for your startup, can you identify the type of customer you will serve and the business model you will adopt? There are many questions to be answered, but there are also many sources of information to help you decide on the location that will work best for your planned venture. Don't get impatient—just take your time, do your research, and make a wise choice. A world of endless business opportunities awaits you.

9-1. Describe the five key factors in locating a brick-and-mortar startup.

- Customer accessibility is a key location factor in industries with high transportation costs, as well as those that must provide handy access for targeted customers to avoid losing those customers to more conveniently located competitors.
- Business environment factors affecting the location decision are climate, competition, legal requirements, and the tax structure.
- Availability of resources such as raw materials, suitable labor, crucial suppliers, and transportation can be important to location decisions.
- Though it can interfere with sound decision making, the entrepreneur's personal preference is a practical consideration in selecting a location.
- An appropriate site must be available and priced within the entrepreneur's budget.

9-2. Discuss the challenges of designing and equipping a physical facility.

- The general suitability of a building depends on the functional requirements of the business; it should be neither too large and extravagant nor too small and restrictive.
- The comfort, convenience, and safety of the business's employees and customers must not be overlooked.
- Deciding whether to purchase or lease equipment is an important choice many entrepreneurs face.
- Most small manufacturing firms must use general-purpose equipment, but some can use special-purpose equipment for specialized operations.
- Small retailers must have merchandise display racks and counters, storage racks, shelving, mirrors, shopping carts, cash registers, and other equipment that facilitates selling.
- Fixtures and other retailing equipment should create an atmosphere appropriate for customers in the retailer's target market.
- Entrepreneurs should select office equipment that reflects the latest advances in technology applicable to a particular business.
- All new ventures, regardless of their function, should project an image that is appropriate to and supportive of the business and its intentions.

9-3. Recognize both the attraction and the challenges of creating a home-based startup.

- Home-based businesses are started both for financial reasons and to accommodate family lifestyle considerations.
- Operating a business at home can pose challenges beyond family and business conflict, particularly in the areas of professional image and legal considerations.
- Technology, especially the Web, has made it possible to operate many types of businesses from almost any location.

9-4. Understand the potential benefits of locating a startup on the Internet.

- E-commerce offers small firms the opportunity to compete with bigger companies on a more level playing field.
- Internet operations can help small firms with early cash flow problems by compressing the sales cycle.
- Business-to-business (B2B) companies generate far more sales than ventures following alternative models.
- The three main advantages of online business-to-consumer (B2C) firms are convenient use, immediate transactions, and continuous access to products and services.
- Internet auction sites, like eBay, are based on the consumer-to-consumer (C2C) model and can help even the smallest of businesses access a worldwide market with great convenience.
- The role of a website can range from merely offering information and content to permitting the buying and selling of products and services online.
- Emerging platforms for online ventures include blogging, podcasting, and creating a following on YouTube or Pinterest to generate revenue from ads and sponsorships, donations, subscription charges, or fees for access to live events.
- Internet-based businesses can be started on a part-time basis, which reduces the personal risk of the entrepreneur if the venture should fail.

Key Terms

auction sites p. 248
brick-and-mortar facility p. 231
business incubator p. 235
business-to-business (B2B) model p. 246
business-to-consumer (B2C) model p. 246
consumer-to-consumer (C2C) model p. 248
content-based model p. 249
disintermediation p. 248
e-commerce p. 243
general-purpose equipment p. 238
home-based business p. 241
information-based model p. 249
special-purpose equipment p. 238
transaction-based model p. 250
zoning ordinances p. 234

You Make the Call

Situation 1

Entrepreneurs Joe Stengard and his wife, Jackie Piel, had a decision to make. Located just outside of St. Louis, Missouri, their five-year-old company, S&P Crafts, was growing rapidly, and they were in desperate need of more space to make their custom-ordered craft kits.

A move always involves a certain measure of risk, so the couple was hesitant to transfer the company's operations. However, an economic development organization in Warren County, Missouri, offered attractive incentives in the form of tax breaks and financial assistance if they would move to a new facility in the rural town of Hopewell. Initial research indicated that a local workforce was readily available and had skills appropriate to the operation, so Stengard and Piel decided to move.

Since the change of address, company sales have tripled. And the new facility has grown from 10,000 square feet to 40,000 square feet in just two short years.

Question 1 How important was the location decision for these two entrepreneurs? Why?
Question 2 What types of permits and zoning ordinances did Stengard and Piel need to consider before deciding to relocate?
Question 3 How could Stengard and Piel use the Internet to expand their business?

Situation 2

You may be noticing a lot more "pop-up stores" opening up these days. They may look like regular stores, but they are open for only a few months—and that is by design. But these small shops are starting to have a significant impact of local economies, with estimates indicating that they bring in around $2 billion during the holiday rush alone.

Small business owners use pop-up stores for a number of reasons, such as to spread the word on a brand, to test a new line of products, or to try out a new sales channel. Denise Maple took this step to increase exposure for her company and its products. Maple is owner of VaVaVroom, a fashion company that sells to "female motorcycling enthusiasts who crave the best-designed, best-made, and most fashionable cycling clothing on the planet." To rev up sales, she joined a few other fashion designers and launched a pop-up store on Chicago's Michigan Avenue, a trendy shopping area. The 16-day pop-up was all about exposure—that is, getting new customers to see her designs so that they might become long-term buyers in the years ahead. Maple is counting on this move to drive new sales at her website, VaVaVroom.com.

Sources: Kate Rogers, "Pop Up Stores Prep for Winter Sales Lift," *CNBC*, December 5, 2014, http://www.cnbc.com/id/102232200#, accessed December 17, 2014; National Federation of Independent Business, "Should You Open a Pop-Up Store?" December 19, 2011, http://www.nfib.com/article/should-you-open-a-pop-up-store-59022, accessed December 17, 2014; and "VaVaVroom: About Us," http://www.vavavroomonline.com/index.php/about-us.html, accessed December 17, 2014.

Question 1 What are the major advantages that Maple is likely to enjoy as the result of operating out of a pop-up store?
Question 2 What are the major disadvantages and special challenges that the company is likely run into as a result of following this strategy?
Question 3 Do you think it was a good idea for Maple to try this approach? Can you think of any other options that might have worked even better for her?

Situation 3

Eliza Roundtree, a single parent, wants to start an interior design business to help support her two young children. She works in the banking industry but has always had a desire to start a business. She enjoys decorating her own home and is often asked, "Have you ever considered doing this professionally? You have such a good sense of colors and how they blend together with fabrics, furnishings, and design."

Roundtree is unsure whether she should locate in a commercial site or in her home, which is in rural central Texas.

She is leaning toward locating at home because she wants more time with her children. However, she is concerned that the home-based location is too far from the closest city, which is where most of her potential customers live.

Initially, her services would include planning for mid-market residential interior design projects, which would involve estimating project options and costs and consulting with clients on colors, fabrics, and furnishings. Eventually, she would like to specialize in creating luxury interiors for owners of upscale homes. But she has a lot to learn before she will be ready for that.

Question 1 What are some potential problems that Roundtree will face if she locates her new business at home?

Question 2 What do you see as the major benefits for Roundtree of a home-based business?

Question 3 How could Roundtree use technology to help operate a home-based business?

Business Plan

LAYING THE FOUNDATION

As part of laying the foundation for preparing your own business plan, respond to the following questions regarding location.

Brick-and-Mortar Startup Location Questions

1. How important are your personal reasons for choosing a location?
2. What business environment factors will influence your location decision?
3. What resources are most critical to this decision?
4. How important is customer accessibility to your location decision?
5. How will the formal site evaluation be conducted?
6. What laws and tax policies of state and local governments need to be considered?
7. What is the cost of the proposed site?

Physical Facility Questions

1. What are the major considerations in choosing between a new and an existing building?
2. What is the possibility of leasing a building or equipment?
3. How feasible is it to locate in a business incubator?
4. What is the major objective of your building design?
5. What types of equipment do you need for your business?

Home-Based Startup Location Questions

1. Will a home-based business be a possibility for you?
2. For the venture you are planning, what would be the advantages and disadvantages of locating the business in your home?
3. Have you given consideration to family lifestyle issues?
4. Will your home project the appropriate image for the business?
5. What zoning ordinances, if any, regulate the type of home-based business you want to start?

Internet Startup Questions

1. What type of customers will be served by the Internet startup?
2. What technical limitations (such as the cost of designing and developing a website or constantly changing software needs) might hinder the company you plan to launch?
3. How will you deal with nontechnical issues (privacy concerns, website security, global languages and cultures, etc.) that may limit the success of your online business?
4. Do you plan to open a storefront hosted by Amazon, eBay, or one of the other online giants, or would an independent website be better suited to the needs of your business?
5. What will be the nature of the online presence you hope to establish—information-based, content-based, transaction-based, or some other form?
6. Will you start the Internet business on a part-time basis, or do you plan to be involved full-time?

Case 9

Cookies-n-Cream (P. 661)

This case highlights the importance of the location decision to the success of a small business, illustrating specifically how nontraditional location options, like the use of mobile vending trucks, can open up opportunities for a startup.

Alternative Cases for Chapter 9

Case 3, The Kollection, p. 649

Endnotes

1. Jessica Bruder, "The Best Places to Launch," *Fortune Small Business*, Vol. 19, No. 9 (November 2009), pp. 56, 58.
2. Jason Daley, "Move, or Lose," *Entrepreneur*, Vol. 39, No. 6 (June 2011), p. 122.
3. Adapted from Gail P. Hiduke and J. D. Ryan, *Small Business: An Entrepreneur's Business Plan*, 9th ed. (Mason, OH: South-Western Cengage Learning, 2014), pp. 159–161.
4. "Lids: About Us," http://www.lids.com/HelpDesk/Corporate/About, accessed December 8, 2014.
5. "COBB Tuning: History," http://www.cobbtuning.com/company-info-history-s/50300.htm, accessed December 10, 2014.
6. Small Business & Entrepreneurship Council, "Business Tax Index 2014," http://www.sbecouncil.org/2014/04/15/sbe-councils-small-business-tax-index-ranks-state-tax-systems, accessed December 10, 2014.
7. Jacquelyn Lynn, "Tax Relief," *Entrepreneur*, Vol. 36, No. 7 (July 2008), p. 24.
8. Jacquelyn Lynn, "What's It Worth?" *Entrepreneur*, Vol. 36, No. 3 (March 2008), p. 32.
9. As reported in Chip Mellor and Dana Berliner, "Small Businesses Losing Out to Red Tape," *USA Today*, October 25, 2010, http://usatoday30.usatoday.com/news/opinion/forum/2010-10-21-mellor26_st_N.htm, accessed December 10, 2014.
10. Rieva Lesonsky, *Start Your Own Business: The Only Start-Up Book You'll Ever Need* (Irvine, CA: Entrepreneur Press, 2007), p. 251.
11. Mark Henricks, "How to Relocate Your Business," http://www.entrepreneur.com/article/81406, accessed December 10, 2014. See also Craig S. Galbraith, Carlos L. Rodriguez, and Alex F. DeNoble, "SME Competitive Strategy and Location Behavior: An Exploratory Study of High-Technology Manufacturing," *Journal of Small Business Management*, Vol. 46, No. 2 (April 2008), pp. 183–202.
12. National Federation of Independent Business, "411 Small Business Facts: Local Business Climate," http://www.411sbfacts.com/sbpoll.php?POLLID=0048&KT_back=1, accessed December 10, 2014.
13. For the sake of clarity, we need to point out that an *accelerator* is different from an *incubator*. Both typically offer access to networks, a program of seminars and classes, and mentoring support. However, incubators house startups for a longer period of time (one to five years versus as little as three months), and they don't usually provide financial support. Most accelerators grant funding in exchange for equity stakes in the startup and are designed to position startups to attract seed funding. For a useful but brief comparison of these two options, see Robin D. Schatz, "Accelerate Me!" *Inc.*, Vol. 36, No. 6 (July/August 2014), pp. 18–19.
14. Sarah E. Needleman, "Start-Up Programs Find Niche," *The Wall Street Journal*, November 18, 2010, p. B7.
15. "HBK Incubates," http://hotbreadkitchen.org/hbk-incubator, accessed October 2, 2012.
16. "Regus: Work Your Way," http://www.regus.com/procurement, accessed December 10, 2014
17. "ShareDesk: About," https://www.sharedesk.net/#!/about, accessed December 11, 2014.
18. National Federation of Independent Business, "411 Small Business Facts: Energy Consumption," http://www.411sbfacts.com/sbpoll-about.php?POLLID=0047, accessed December 11, 2014.
19. See Candida G. Brush, Linda F. Edleman, and Tatiana S. Manolova, "The Effects of Initial Location, Aspirations, and Resources on Likelihood of First Sale in Nascent Firms," *Journal of Small Business Management*, Vol. 46, No. 2 (April 2008), pp. 159–182.
20. Chuck Green, "My Home Is Not Your Home," *The Wall Street Journal*, November 14, 2011, http://www.wsj.com/news/articles/SB10001424052702303365804576432051484597620?mg=reno64-wsj, accessed December 11, 2014.
21. Adapted from Ken Harthun, "Top 5 Reasons for Starting a Home-Based Business," April 14, 2010, http://www.examiner.com/article/top-5-reasons-for-starting-a-home-based-business, accessed December 11, 2014.
22. Nicole L. Torres and April Y. Pennington, "Home Court Advantage," http://www.entrepreneur.com/article/78450, accessed December 11, 2014.
23. Nicole L. Torres, "Shipman Associates," http://www.entrepreneur.com/article/78440, accessed December 12, 2014.
24. Meg Cadoux Hirshberg, "Bed and Boardroom," *Inc.*, Vol. 32, No. 1 (February 2010), pp. 31–33.
25. "Beauty Encounter: About Us," http://www.beautyencounter.com/about-us, accessed December 11, 2014.
26. Elaine Pofeldt, "A Fresh Take on the Freelance Marketplace," *Forbes*, May 30, 2013, http://www.forbes.com/sites/elainepofeldt/2013/05/30/a-fresh-take-on-the-freelance-marketplace, accessed December 11, 2014.
27. Raymund Flandez, "Help Wanted—and Found," *The Wall Street Journal*, October 13, 2008, http://www.wsj.com/news/articles/SB122347721312915407?mg=reno64-wsj, accessed December 11, 2014.
28. "New Video about Oliver's Pet Care," http://blog.oliverspetcare.com/amazon-interview, accessed October 10, 2012; and "Amazon: FBA

Overview," http://www.amazon.com/gp/help/customer/display.html?nodeId=200229160, accessed December 11, 2014.

29. Jenna Wortham, "Buying the Bricks for Your Online Storefront," *The New York Times*, November 16, 2014, p. BU4.

30. "Gilt: About Gilt," http://www.gilt.com/company/main, accessed December 11, 2014.

31. Jennifer Vilaga, "21_Gilt-Groupe," http://www.fastcompany.com/3017920/most-innovative-companies-2010/21gilt-groupe, accessed December 11, 2014.

32. Amy Westervelt, "The New Black? Direct Sales," *The Wall Street Journal*, August 25, 2014, p. R5.

33. "EBay: The Company," http://pages.ebay.in/community/aboutebay/news/infastfacts.html, accessed December 12, 2014.

34. *Ibid.*

35. "EBay Store Fees," http://pages.ebay.com/help/sell/storefees.html, accessed December 12, 2014.

36. Bloomberg News, "Amazon and eBay Target Mobile Shoppers with Thanksgiving Deals," November 26, 2014, https://www.internetretailer.com/2014/11/26/amazon-and-ebay-target-mobile-shoppers-thanksgiving-deals, accessed December 12, 2014.

37. "Amazon Associates," https://affiliate-program.amazon.com, accessed December 12, 2014.

38. "BodyBuilding.com: Come Join Our Team," http://www.bodybuilding.com/fun/bbcomcareer.htm, accessed December 12, 2014.

39. Peter Nguyen, *Advertiser360: Learning the Essentials* (Irvine, CA: Ad Ventures Group, 2011), p.19.

40. "About Mongabay," http://www.mongabay.com/about.html, accessed December 12, 2014; and Kelly K. Spors, "New Services Help Bloggers Bring in Ad Revenue," *The Wall Street Journal*, January 15, 2008, http://www.wsj.com/articles/SB120036638439890355, accessed December 12, 2014.

41. Ann O'Neill, "Battle over Adam Carolla Podcast Ends 30-Year Friendship," http://www.cnn.com/2014/09/02/showbiz/adam-carolla-podcast-lawsuit, accessed December 12, 2014; and Ellen McGirt, "Pod Star," *Fast Company*, No, 144 (April 2010), pp. 79–83.

42. Carla Marshall, "What It Takes to Make a Living from YouTube's Partner Earnings," http://www.reelseo.com/youtube-partner-earnings, accessed December 16, 2014.

43. Rolfe Winkler, "YouTube Offering Its Stars Bonuses," *The Wall Street Journal*, December 8, 2014, p. R4.

44. Eric Blattberg, "Pinterest Launches Its Way to Make Money: Promoted Pins," http://venturebeat.com/2014/05/12/pinterest-launches-its-way-to-make-money-promoted-pins, accessed December 16, 2014.

45. Max Chafkin, "Starring Ben Silbermann As the Pinup Kid," *Fast Company*, No. 169 (October 2012), pp. 90–96, 146–147.

46. Joseph Raffiee and Jie Feng, "Should I Quit My Day Job? A Hybrid Path to Entrepreneurship," *Academy of Management Journal*, Vol. 57, No. 4 (2014), pp. 936–963.

47. *Ibid.*

CHAPTER 10

Understanding a Firm's Financial Statements

After studying this chapter, you should be able to. . .

10-1. Describe the purpose and content of an income statement.

10-2. Describe the purpose and content of a balance sheet.

10-3. Explain how viewing the income statement and balance sheets together gives a more complete picture of a firm's financial position.

10-4. Use the income statement and balance sheets to compute a company's cash flows.

10-5. Analyze the financial statements using ratios to see more clearly how decisions affect a firm's financial performance.

Johnny Stites is CEO of J&S Construction Company, Inc., in Cookeville, Tennessee. After graduating from college, Johnny served in the U.S. Navy for three years and then returned home to work in the family business. Several years later, his younger brother, Jack, joined him in the business and now serves as the company's president .

Johnny and Jack have grown the business into one of the most successful construction firms in the Southeast, if not the United States. A visitor to their business is immediately struck by the passion and attention they give to detail in operating their company. When asked how they use financial information to run the business, Johnny made the following observations:

In the SPOTLIGHT
J&S Construction Company
www.jsconstruction.com

When you start and run your own business, it no longer matters whether you were a marketing, management, finance, or any other specific major. As an entrepreneur, you have to know how a business operates, which requires more than having knowledge in a specific academic field. So whatever your major, you had best know the basics of accounting and finance. You do not need to be an accountant, but you had better be able to read and understand financial statements. Sure, you can hire an accountant, but if you do not understand what the numbers are telling you, you are in big trouble.

The construction industry is one of the riskiest industries you can enter, second only to the restaurant industry. For years, we would bid a job based on our best understanding of the costs that would be incurred. Then we would have to wait to the completion of the job to see if we made or lost money—not exactly an ideal situation to be in. Today, we have the ability to know how we are doing in terms of profits and costs on a daily basis. Not having accurate and timely accounting information would be deadly. We simply could not exist in such a competitive industry, and certainly not profitably, without understanding where we are financially.

Like many others, when faced with the recession of 2008, we believed we could survive, but we also realized there was very little opportunity for error. That makes a thorough understanding and an in-depth analysis of the financial situation critical. It was how we determined we should cut salaries by 15 percent instead of laying off our core personnel. When the economy turned, we were ready with the nucleus of our team to grab market share.

So, do accounting and finance matter to you as an entrepreneur? Only if you want to have a good understanding of your business.

Source: Personal interview with Johnny Stites, February 1, 2015.

Entrepreneurs do not start companies so that they can learn accounting—that's for certain. In fact, for many students and aspiring entrepreneurs, accounting is not their favorite subject. But if you have or plan to start a business, you had better learn some accounting, sooner rather than later. Norm Brodsky, a serial entrepreneur and noted columnist for *Inc.*, puts it plainly:

> *When I started out, I thought that CEOs ran businesses with the help of their top executives. What I didn't realize is that a business is a living entity with needs of its own, and unless the leaders pay attention to those needs, the business will fail. So how do you know what those needs are? There's only one way: by looking at the numbers and understanding the relationships between them. They will tell you how good your sales are, whether you can afford to hire a new salesperson or office manager, how much cash you will need to deal with new business coming in, how your market is changing, and on and on. You can't afford to wait until your accountant tells you these things. Nor do you have to become an accountant. You do have to know enough accounting, however, to figure out which numbers are most important in your particular business, and then you should develop the habit of watching them like a hawk.*[1]

Understanding accounting has to do more with experience than ability. In this chapter, you will learn how to construct an *income statement*, a *balance sheet*, and a *cash flow statement*. Equally important, you will learn some basics of interpreting what these **financial statements**, or **accounting statements**, tell you about your business. This chapter is presented as simply as possible, without sacrificing the content that a small business owner needs.

Before we begin a systematic study of financial statements, we will lay a foundation by telling a story about two young sisters who started their own small business, a lemonade stand.

THE LEMONADE KIDS

Cameron and Ashley Bates, ages 13 and 15, wanted to buy an iPad to share, which they estimated would cost $360. Their parents said they would pay most of the cost, but that the two girls would need to contribute $100 to the purchase price.

financial statements (accounting statements)
A firm's income statement, balance sheets, and cash flow statement.

To earn money, the girls decided to operate a lemonade stand for two Saturdays in a nearby park frequented by walkers and runners. To start the business, they each invested $5 from their savings. Their mom, Krista, liked the girls' idea and said she would loan them any additional money they would need with two conditions: (1) The girls would have to repay her in two weeks, and (2) she would keep the books for their business and expect them to learn what the numbers meant. Krista thought that this would provide the girls a valuable opportunity to learn about business.

Setting Up the Business

A balance sheet, Krista explained to the girls, is a table that shows on a specific date (1) the dollar amount of the assets owned by the business and (2) the sources of the money used to pay for the assets. She continued to say that there are two sources of money to pay for assets. The girls could either borrow money or, as the owners of the business, they could put their own money into the business. The first means of paying for assets is called *debt* and the second is the *owner's equity.* It's a bit like buying a house for $100,000, borrowing $70,000 from a bank, and then using $30,000 from your savings to pay the remaining part of the purchase price. The $30,000 is your equity in the home. Similarly, companies usually borrow money (debt) to supplement the owners' investment of their own money in the business (equity). Thus, a company's total assets will always equal the total debt plus the owners' equity they have invested in the business; that is,

Total assets = Money borrowed from others + Money invested by the owners

or

Total assets = Debt + Owners' equity

For instance, the girls' beginning $10 in cash represented their only asset and, since it was their own money, it was also their equity in the business. Krista then wrote out a simple balance sheet:

Assets		**Loans (Debt) and Owners' Equity**	
		Loans	$ 0
Cash	$10	Cameron & Ashley's equity	10
Total assets	$10	Total loans & equity	$10

After thinking about what they would need in supplies to operate the lemonade stand, the girls requested a $40 loan from their mother. After the loan was made, the new balance sheet appeared as follows:

Assets		**Loans (Debt) and Owners' Equity**	
		Loan from Mom	$40
Cash	$50	Cameron & Ashley's equity	10
Total assets	$50	Total loans & equity	$50

$50 = $10 beginning cash + $40 in cash from loan

$40 increase in debt

In preparing for their opening day, the girls bought $40 of "premium pink lemonade mix" and paper cups. Krista explained that the lemonade mix and cups constituted their *inventory* of supplies. After the girls paid for the inventory, the resulting balance sheet was as follows, where cash decreased and inventory increased by $40:

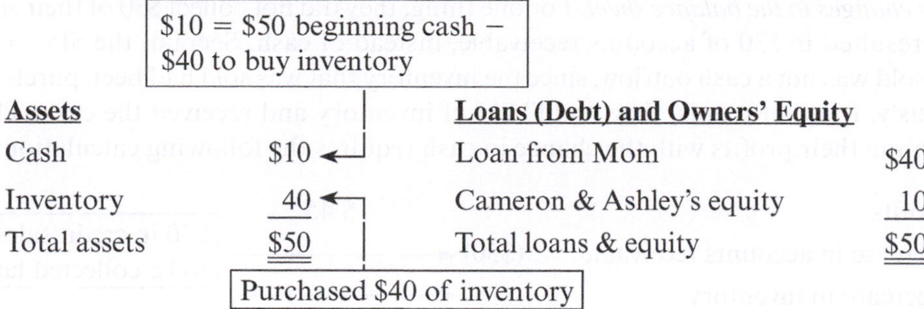

Assets		**Loans (Debt) and Owners' Equity**	
Cash	$10	Loan from Mom	$40
Inventory	40	Cameron & Ashley's equity	10
Total assets	$50	Total loans & equity	$50

Opening Day

Being astute young entrepreneurs, Cameron and Ashley were aware that not all passersby carried cash. So they created a sign-up sheet where customers could record their contact information for payment later in the week. They then chose a prime location for their lemonade stand and prepared to serve some very fine ice-cold pink lemonade.

By the end of the day, they had sold 60 cups at $1 each—30 cups that were bought on "credit" and 30 with cash. Since the lemonade only cost the girls 25 cents a cup, they made 75 cents per cup in profits, for a total of $45 in profit [$45 = ($1 sale price per cup − $0.25 cost per cup) × 60 cups]. Krista told the girls that an income statement reports the results of a firm's operations over a period of time—in this case, for a day. So the income statement for their first Saturday of selling looked like this:

Sales (60 cups × $1 per cup sales price)	$60
Cost of lemonade sold (60 cups × $0.25 cost per cup)	(15)
Profits	$45

Their balance sheet at the end of the day was as follows:

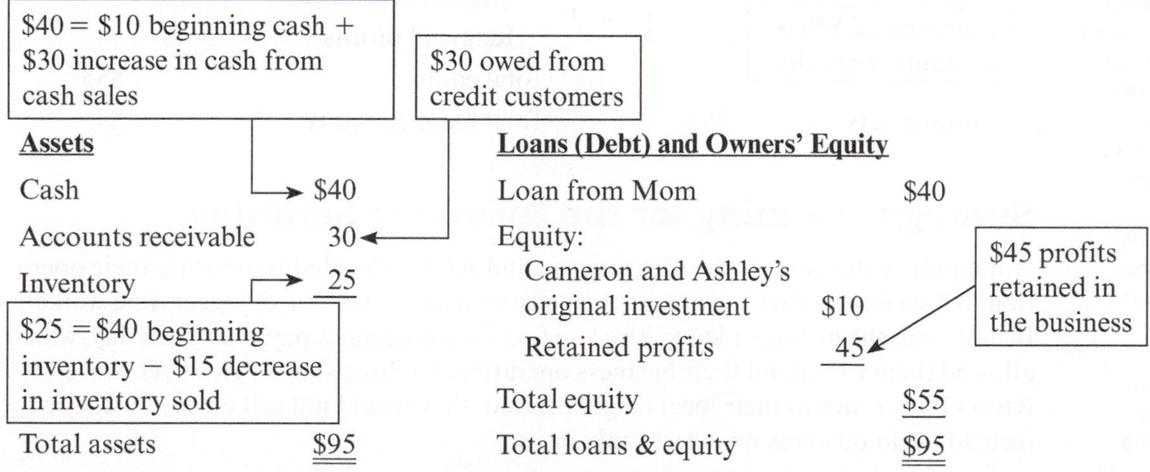

Assets		**Loans (Debt) and Owners' Equity**		
Cash	$40	Loan from Mom		$40
Accounts receivable	30	Equity:		
Inventory	25	Cameron and Ashley's original investment	$10	
		Retained profits	45	
		Total equity		$55
Total assets	$95	Total loans & equity		$95

This time, cash increased from $10 to $40, as a result of the cash sales of $30—even though they had sold $60 of lemonade. The remaining $30 was still owed by their credit customers; the girls hoped to collect this money during the coming week. These assets, they learned, were called "accounts receivable." Also, there was a $15 decline in inventory, the result of the lemonade sold. Finally, the girls' equity increased by $45, the amount of the day's profits.

Avoiding Failure

Jeff Sandefer, a successful entrepreneur and the founder of the highly ranked Acton School of Business MBA in Entrepreneurship, puts it this way:

Have you ever thought, "I don't need to know anything about finance and accounting. Once my business is up and running, I'll just hire someone to handle all of the numbers"?

If so, . . . here's a time-tested recipe for failure in business:

1. *Begin with a good idea.*
2. *Have a great deal of drive and determination.*
3. *Raise money from investors.*
4. *Grow your revenues as quickly as possible.*
5. *Fail to acquire basic financial skills.*
6. *Hire someone else to "run the numbers" for you.*

It's a proven formula for destroying a promising business. And the faster sales rise, the more fiery the crash when you run out of cash.

Do you want to build a business that can survive minor financial setbacks? Do you want to avoid the embarrassment (and the possibility of criminal charges) that comes from losing large sums of other people's money?

If so, you must learn to ask the fundamental questions of finance and master the tools you need to answer them. If you do this and minimize investments, grow at a controlled rate

(continued)

When Ashley looked at the income statement and balance sheet, she questioned why cash had only increased $30, even though profits were $45 for the day. Why were they not the same? Krista told her that she was about to learn an important lesson: *Computing a company's cash flows will require you to look at both the income statement and the changes in the balance sheet.* For one thing, they did not collect $30 of their sales, which resulted in $30 of accounts receivable, instead of cash. Second, the $15 cost of goods sold was not a cash outflow, since the inventory that was sold had been purchased previously. In other words, they "sold" $15 of inventory and received the cash. Thus, reconciling their profits with the change in cash requires the following calculation:

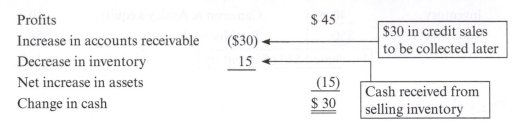

Profits		$ 45	
Increase in accounts receivable	($30)		← $30 in credit sales to be collected later
Decrease in inventory	15		← Cash received from selling inventory
Net increase in assets		(15)	
Change in cash		$ 30	

Collecting Accounts Receivable

Not wanting to let their accounts receivable go uncollected too long, the girls hired their younger sister, Erin, for $5 to make calls during the week on their credit customers. To their delight, by Friday night Erin (accompanied by a few of her friends) had collected all the money they were owed. With the money collected, cash increased $30 with a corresponding $30 decrease in accounts receivable. As a result, the balance sheet appeared as follows:

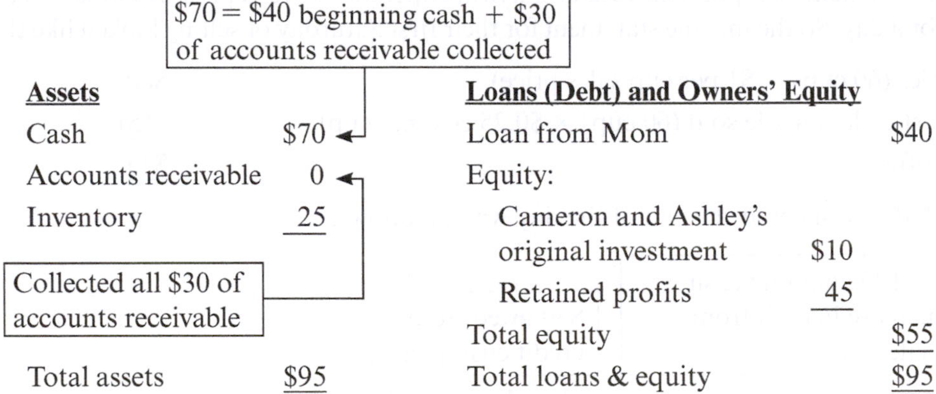

Assets		**Loans (Debt) and Owners' Equity**		
Cash	$70	Loan from Mom		$40
Accounts receivable	0	Equity:		
Inventory	25	Cameron and Ashley's original investment	$10	
		Retained profits	45	
		Total equity		$55
Total assets	$95	Total loans & equity		$95

Strategic Planning for the Following Saturday

Anticipating the next weekend, Cameron and Ashley decided to relocate their operation to Two Rivers Park, an area in their city with a high volume of joggers and walkers. In addition, the girls decided to hire two friends, agreeing to pay each $10 a day, which allowed them to expand their business operations to three stands. However, since Two Rivers Park is not in their local neighborhood, they would not sell on credit, choosing instead to do business on a cash-only basis.

The Second Saturday of Business

Cameron and Ashley arrived at Two Rivers Park with their two friends early Saturday morning and soon found themselves surrounded by customers. By mid-afternoon, they had sold 100 cups of lemonade, depleting their entire inventory! After paying their two friends $10 dollars each and Erin $5 for her collection work, the girls were delighted to see that they had made $50 in profits. Their income statement for the second day looked like this:

Sales ($1 sales price per cup × 100 cups)	$100
Cost of lemonade ($0.25 cost per cup × 100 cups)	(25)
Salaries (2 friends × $10 + $5 paid to Erin)	(25)
Profits	$50

The balance sheet at the end of the day appeared as follows:

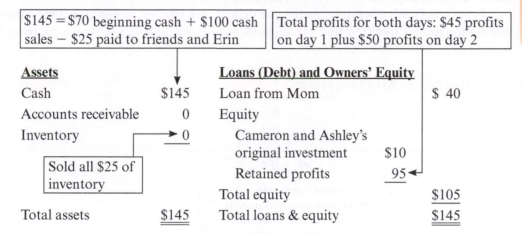

$145 = $70 beginning cash + $100 cash sales − $25 paid to friends and Erin

Total profits for both days: $45 profits on day 1 plus $50 profits on day 2

Assets		Loans (Debt) and Owners' Equity		
Cash	$145	Loan from Mom		$ 40
Accounts receivable	0	Equity		
Inventory	0	Cameron and Ashley's original investment	$10	
		Retained profits	95	
		Total equity		$105
Total assets	$145	Total loans & equity		$145

Sold all $25 of inventory

Cash assets had now increased to $145, a $75 increase as a result of the $100 in cash sales less the $25 paid to Erin and the girls' two friends. Inventory was now zero, and the girls' equity once again increased by the day's profits, in this case, $50.

The girls had accomplished their goal! They had enough to pay for their portion of the iPad ($100), repay the $40 loan to their mom; and still had $5 to split. When they went to bed that night, they discussed the possibility of starting a summer business. The entrepreneurial flame had been lit, and they had big dreams for their next venture.

The hypothetical story of Cameron and Ashley and their lemonade stand provides an uncomplicated way of thinking about accounting statements. If you understand—really understand—the Lemonade Kids' financial results, you are ready to move on to the next step. This will not make you an accountant, but it will give you the skill needed to manage a small business by the numbers. Our starting point is the income statement.

(continued)

with plenty of cash on hand for emergencies, and keep your business processes simple and focused on satisfying customers, you'll be much more likely to build a healthy business or, at a minimum, avoid an embarrassing collapse.

Source: Jeff Sandefer, "Searching for the Mythical Numbers Guru," Acton Foundation for Entrepreneurship Excellence, March 2012, p. 1.

10-1 THE INCOME STATEMENT

Describe the purpose and content of an income statement.

An **income statement**, or **profit and loss statement**, indicates the amount of profits or losses generated by a firm *over a given time period*, usually monthly, quarterly, or yearly. In its most basic form, the income statement may be represented by the following equation:

Sales (revenue) − Expenses = Profits (income)

income statement (profit and loss statement) A financial report showing the amount of profits or losses from a firm's operations over a given period of time.

(In this text, we generally use the term *profits*, instead of *earnings* or *income*, but all three terms can be used interchangeably. For example, *profits before taxes* are the same thing as *earnings before taxes*.)

cost of goods sold
The cost of producing or acquiring goods or services to be sold by a firm.

gross profits
Sales less the cost of goods sold.

operating expenses
Costs related to marketing and selling a firm's product or service, general and administrative expenses, and depreciation.

A more complete overview of an income statement is presented in Exhibit 10.1. As shown in the exhibit, you begin with sales (for example, the number of lemonade drinks sold times the sales price per cup). You then subtract the **cost of goods sold** (e.g., the cost per cup of lemonade times the number of cups sold) from sales to compute the firm's **gross profits**. Next, **operating expenses**, consisting of marketing and selling expenses, general and administrative expenses, and depreciation expense are deducted from gross profits to determine **operating profits**. (The amount that Cameron and Ashley paid their friends and Erin to work for them was an operating expense.) As shown in the exhibit, operating profits reflect only the decisions the owner has made relating to sales, cost of goods sold, and operating expenses. How the firm is financed (debt versus equity) has no effect on operating profits.

From the firm's operating profits, we deduct any **interest expense** incurred from borrowing money (debt) to find **profits before taxes**, or **taxable profits**—a company's

EXHIBIT **10.1** The Income Statement: An Overview

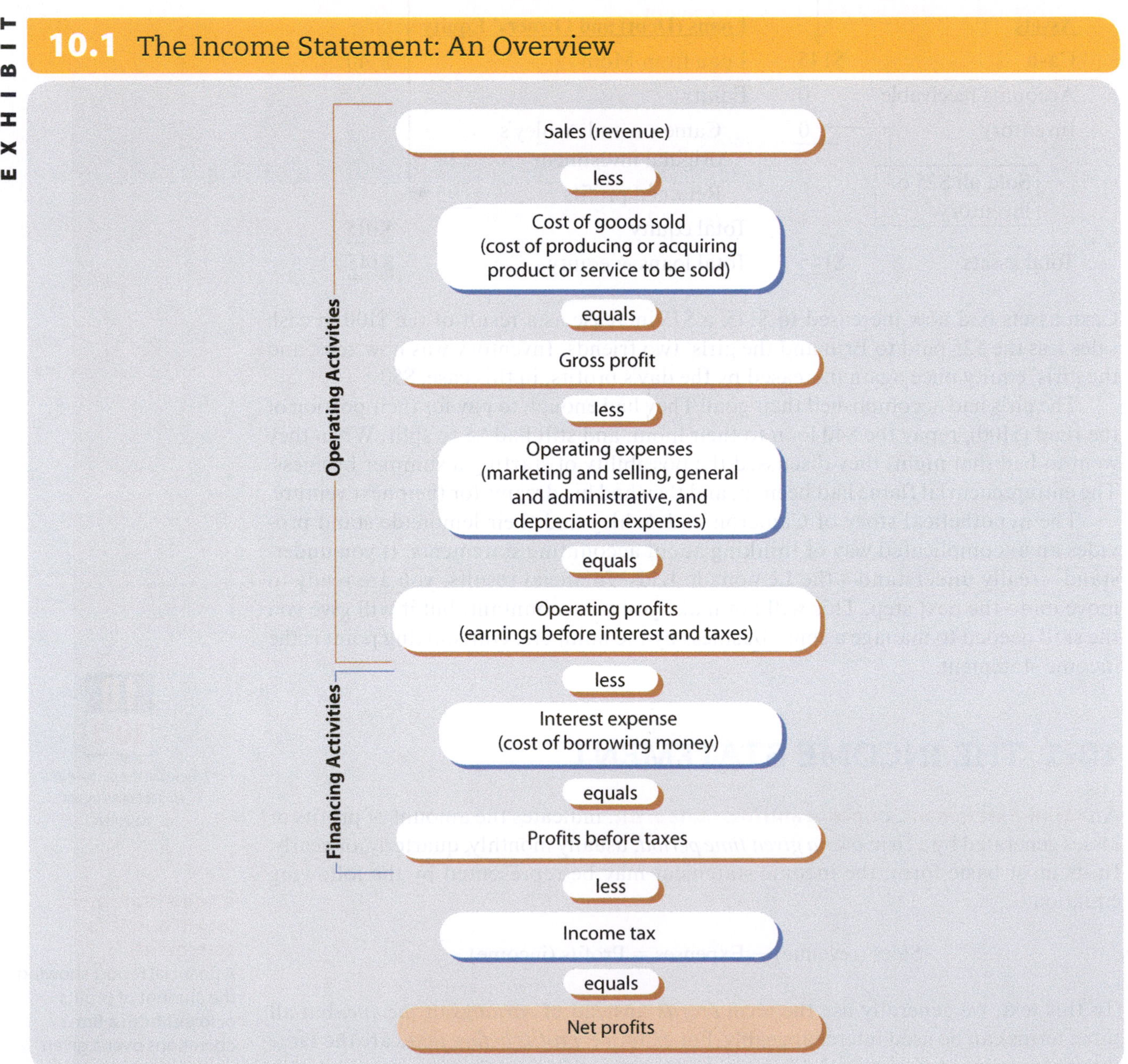

taxable income. A firm's income taxes are calculated by multiplying profits before taxes by the applicable tax rate. For instance, if a firm has profits before taxes of $100,000 and its tax rate is 28 percent, then it will owe $28,000 in taxes (0.28 × $100,000 = $28,000).

The number that results when taxes are subtracted from profits before taxes represents **net profits**, or profits that may be reinvested in the firm or distributed to the owners—provided, of course, the cash is available to do so. As you will come to understand, *positive net profits in an income statement does not necessarily mean that a firm has generated positive cash flows.*

Exhibit 10.2 shows the 2015 income statement for Dickey & Associates, Inc., a medical supply company owned by sisters Hannah and Rebekah Dickey. The company had sales of $850,000 for the 12-month period ending December 31, 2015. The cost of goods sold was $550,000, resulting in a gross profit of $300,000. The company had $200,000 in operating expenses, which included marketing expenses, general and administrative expenses, and depreciation expense. **Depreciation expense** is the cost of a firm's equipment and building, allocated over the asset's useful life. For example, if a business paid $10,000 for a piece of equipment with a four-year life expectancy, the depreciation expense each year would be $2,500 ($10,000 ÷ 4 years = $2,500). So, after total operating expenses were subtracted, the company's operating profits would amount to $100,000. To this point, we have calculated profits based *only* on expenses related to the firm's operations—and not those affected by how the firm finances its assets.

Dickey & Associates' interest expense of $20,000 (the expense it incurred from borrowing money) is deducted from operating profits to arrive at the company's profits before taxes, or taxable income, of $80,000. Given a 25 percent tax rate, the company paid $20,000 in income taxes ($80,000 profits before tax × 0.25 tax rate = $20,000), leaving net profits of $60,000.

operating profits
Gross profits less operating expenses.

interest expense
The cost of borrowed money.

profits before taxes (taxable profits)
Operating profits less interest expense.

net profits
Earnings that may be distributed to the owners or reinvested in the company.

depreciation expense
The cost of a firm's building and equipment, allocated over the asset's useful life.

EXHIBIT **10.2** Income Statement for Dickey & Associates, Inc., for the Year Ending December 31, 2015

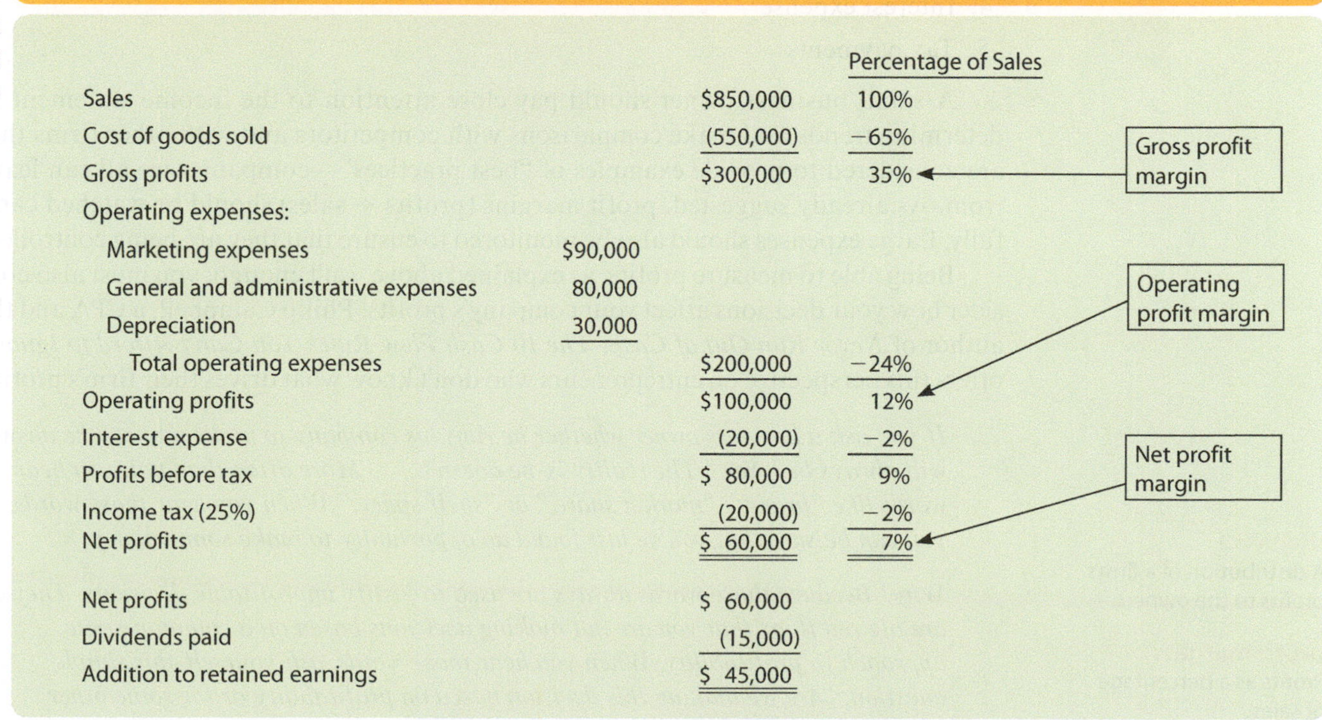

			Percentage of Sales	
Sales		$850,000	100%	
Cost of goods sold		(550,000)	−65%	
Gross profits		$300,000	35%	← Gross profit margin
Operating expenses:				
Marketing expenses	$90,000			
General and administrative expenses	80,000			
Depreciation	30,000			
Total operating expenses		$200,000	−24%	
Operating profits		$100,000	12%	← Operating profit margin
Interest expense		(20,000)	−2%	
Profits before tax		$ 80,000	9%	
Income tax (25%)		(20,000)	−2%	
Net profits		$ 60,000	7%	← Net profit margin
Net profits		$ 60,000		
Dividends paid		(15,000)		
Addition to retained earnings		$ 45,000		

The net profits of $60,000 are the profits that the business earned for its owners after paying all expenses—cost of goods sold, operating expenses, interest expense, and income taxes. Now the owners have to decide what to do with these profits. They can let the company pay them a **dividend** out of the profits, which represents a withdrawal of capital from the business (assuming cash is available to do so). Or, they can retain the profits in the business to help finance the firm's growth. Of course, they can combine the two choices by taking a smaller dividend and retaining the rest of the profits in the business.

In the last column in Exhibit 10.2, we have expressed each amount in the income statement as a percentage of sales. Also, we show what is called **profit margins**—gross profit margins, operating profit margins, and net profit margins—which simply express a firm's profits as a percentage of sales. Specifically, Dickey & Associates has a gross profit margin of 35 percent, an operating profit margin of 12 percent and a net profit margin of 7 percent. For every $100 of sales, the company earns $35 in gross profits, $12 in operating profits, and $7 in net profits. Company owners need to track these numbers very carefully.

So what did the Dickey sisters, as the firm's owners, do with their profits? As shown at the bottom of Exhibit 10.2, $15,000 in dividends was distributed to them; the remaining $45,000 ($60,000 net profits less $15,000 in dividends) was retained by the firm—an amount you will see later in the balance sheet. *Dividends paid to a firm's owners, unlike interest expense, are not considered an expense in the income statement.* Instead, they are viewed as a return of principal to the owners.

In summary, the income statement answers the question "How profitable is the business?" In providing the answer, the income statement reports financial information related to five broad areas of business activity:

1. Sales (revenue)
2. Cost of producing or acquiring the goods or services sold by the company
3. Operating expenses, such as marketing expenses, rent, managers' salaries, and depreciation expense
4. Interest expense
5. Tax payments

A small business owner should pay close attention to the income statement to determine trends and make comparisons with competitors and with other firms that are considered to provide examples of "best practices"—companies we all can learn from. As already suggested, profit margins (profits ÷ sales) should be watched carefully. Large expenses should also be monitored to ensure that they are being controlled.

Being able to measure profits, as explained above, isn't enough; you must also consider how your decisions affect your company's profits. Philip Campbell, a CPA and the author of *Never Run Out of Cash: The 10 Cash Flow Rules You Can't Afford to Ignore*, offers this perspective on entrepreneurs who don't know what drives their firm's profits:

> *If you ask a business owner whether he runs his company to make money, the answer will always be "Yes." The reality is, he doesn't. . . . More often than not, you hear words like "brand," "market share," or "shelf space." When you hear those words, you can be sure that you've just found an opportunity to make some money.*
>
> *Why? Because those words always are used to justify unprofitable decisions. They are big red flags that you are not making decisions based on a common-sense approach to profitability. When you hear those words, ask yourself this simple question, "Are we making this decision based on profitability or for some other (possibly hidden) reason?"*[2]

dividend
A distribution of a firm's profits to the owners.

profit margins
Profits as a percentage of sales.

Let's Check for Understanding

Understanding the Income Statement

Answer the following two questions:

1. What is the difference between gross profits, operating profits, profits before taxes, and net profits?
2. a. Construct an income statement, using the information provided below.
   b. What are the firm's gross profits, operating profits, and net profits?
   c. What are the firm's profit margins?
   d. Which expense is a *noncash* expense?

Interest expense	$10,000
Cost of goods sold	$160,000
Marketing expenses	$70,000
Administrative expenses	$50,000
Sales	$400,000
Stock dividends	$5,000
Income tax	$20,000
Depreciation expense	$20,000

(The answers to the questions above are shown below.)

How Did You Do?

Understanding the Income Statement

1. What is the difference between gross profits, operating profits, profits before taxes, and net profits?

   To understand a firm's profits, think about the process. For instance, a retailer buys merchandise from a wholesaler. The merchandise is then placed on display shelves in the store, where sales personnel, a bookkeeper, and a maintenance person work. The retailer sells the merchandise, hopefully for a profit. The difference between what the retailer received from customers (sales) and the cost of the merchandise is the gross profits. The expenses of operating the store represent the business's operating expenses. So deducting the operating expenses from gross profits gives the operating profits. If the retailer borrowed money from a bank, he or she would have to pay interest expense. Subtracting any interest expense from operating profits gives profits before taxes. The retailer then pays income taxes on those taxable profits. The remaining earnings are the company's net profits, which are the profits that are left for the owners. (See Exhibit 10.1 for a graphical representation of the process.)

2. Construct an income statement, using the information provided. What are the firm's gross profits, operating profits, and net profits? What are the firm's profit margins? Which expense is a noncash expense?

Sales		$400,000	
Cost of goods sold		160,000	
Gross profits		$240,000	
Operating expenses:			
Marketing expenses	$ 70,000		
Administrative expenses	50,000		
Depreciation expense	20,000		← Noncash expense
Total operating expenses		$140,000	

(continued)

(continued)

Operating profits	$100,000
Interest expense	10,000
Profits before taxes	$ 90,000
Income tax	20,000
Net profits	$ 70,000

The gross profit margin is 60 percent (60.0% = 0.60 = $240,000 gross profits ÷ $400,000 sales).

The operating profit margin is 25.0 percent (25.0% = 0.25 = $100,000 operating profits ÷ $400,000 sales).

The net profit margin is 17.5 percent (17.5% = 0.175 = $70,000 net profits ÷ $400,000 sales).

Note: The $5,000 in dividends is not shown as an expense in the income statement but is considered to be a return of the owner's capital. Thus, the net profits of $70,000 less the $5,000 in dividends, or $65,000, will be added to the firm's retained earnings in the balance sheet.

Living the Dream

ENTREPRENEURIAL EXPERIENCES

The Little Things Are the Big Things When It Comes to Managing Finances

As an entrepreneur, you have to be an effective manager of your time AND your firm's finances. No one will watch your company's money like you will or should. After all, it's your money.

According to Russell Allred, a business growth consultant, "If you don't know where you're wasting money this month, it's too late to figure it out at the end of the year."

By checking his monthly expenses closely, Eli Mechlovitz, co-founder of GlassTileStore.com, found a number of unnecessary subscriptions, warranty programs, fee-based website analytics programs, utility bill errors, and other incorrect or unwanted charges. According to Mechlovitz, eliminating these wasteful expenses has saved his company approximately $4,000 per month.

So, it's important that entrepreneurs not only understand what the financial statements tell them but also act on what they learn.

Source: Adapted from Gwen Moran, "How to Clean Up Your Business," *Entrepreneur*, May 2011, pp. 76-78.

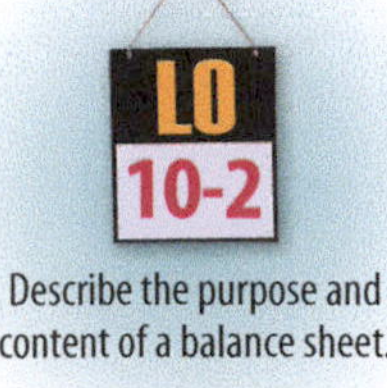

Describe the purpose and content of a balance sheet.

10-2 THE BALANCE SHEET

While an income statement reports the results of business operations over a period of time, a **balance sheet** provides a snapshot of a business's financial position at a *specific point in time*. Thus, a balance sheet captures the cumulative effects of all earlier financial decisions up to a specific date. It shows the assets a firm owns, the liabilities (or debt) outstanding or owed, and the amount the owners have invested in the business (owners' equity) on that date. In its simplest form, a balance sheet follows this formula:

$$\text{Total assets} = \text{Debt} + \text{Owners' equity}$$

This is more than just an equation. It is an identity. It must happen, or the company will cease to exist. That is, for every dollar of assets, there *must* be a dollar of financing in the form of debt or owner's equity.

Exhibit 10.3 illustrates the elements in the balance sheet of a typical firm. Each of the three main components of the balance sheet—assets, debt, and owners' equity—is discussed in the following sections.

10-2a Assets

Assets, shown on the left side of Exhibit 10.3, are what the company owns that has a monetary value. They are always grouped into three categories: (1) current assets, (2) fixed assets, and (3) other assets.

balance sheet
A financial report showing a firm's assets, liabilities, and owners' equity at a specific point in time.

EXHIBIT 10.3 The Balance Sheet: An Overview

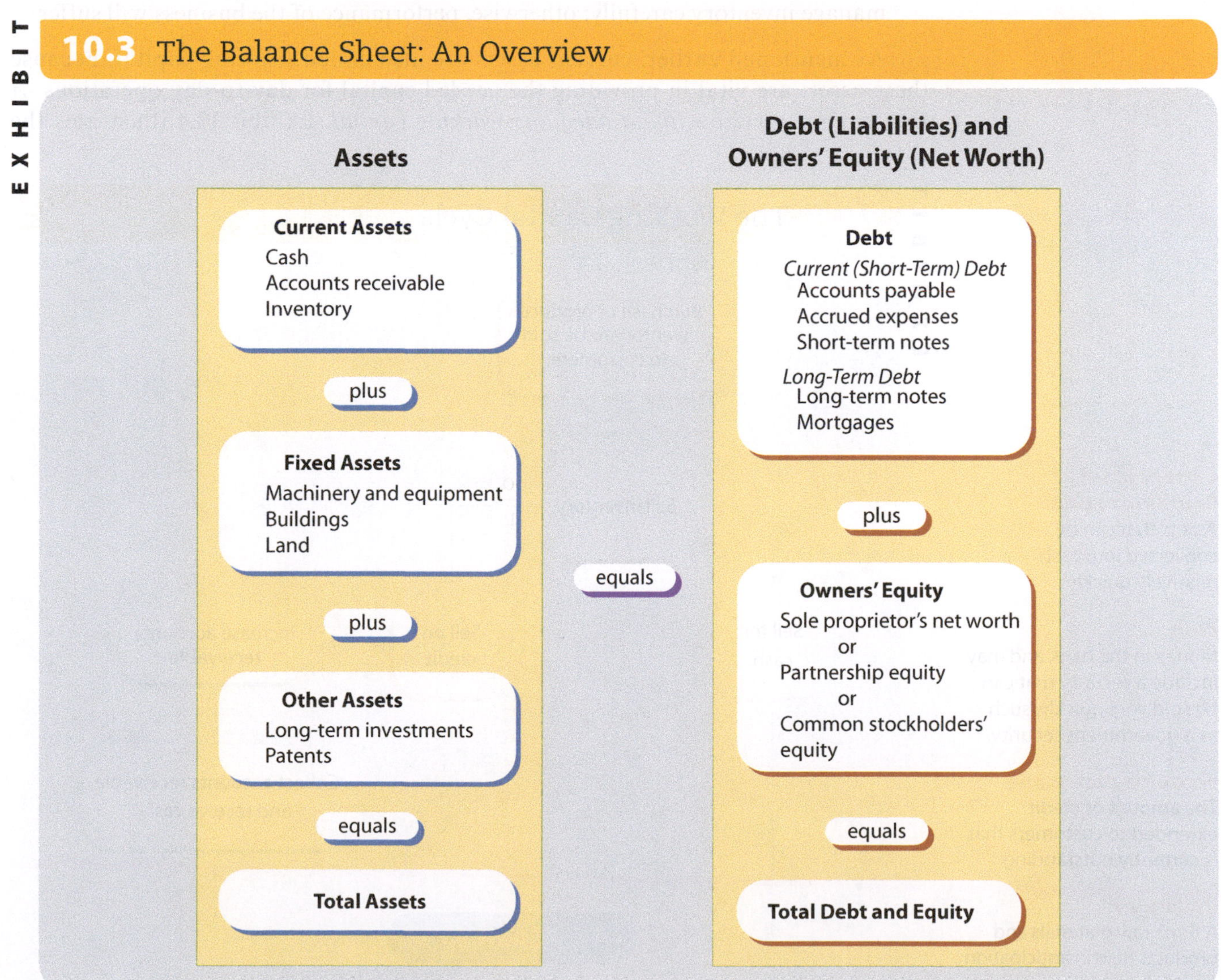

CURRENT ASSETS

Current assets (working capital), which are always listed first in a balance sheet, include those assets that are relatively liquid—that is, assets that can be converted into cash relatively quickly. Current assets primarily include cash, accounts receivable, and inventory.

1. **Cash** is money in the bank and may include some type of marketable security, such as a short-term government security, that can be sold very quickly. Every firm must have cash for current business operations.
2. **Accounts receivable** occur when a product or service is sold but paid for later. When a firm sells its products or services, customers may pay in cash or be given credit terms, such as being allowed 30 days to pay for the goods being purchased. Accounts receivable need to be monitored carefully, since they have a lot to do with the cash that will (or will not) come into the business. Creditors are likely to be watching it as well.
3. **Inventory** comprises the raw materials and the products being held by a firm for sale in the ordinary course of business. Service companies typically have little or no inventory, but nearly every other company—manufacturers, wholesalers, retailers—does. As with accounts receivable, the business owner had better manage inventory carefully; otherwise, performance of the business will suffer.

As mentioned earlier, current assets are also called working capital, because these assets are vital in providing the needed capital for day-to-day operations. *A firm cannot survive without adequate working capital.* Exhibit 10.4 illustrates the

current assets (working capital)
Assets that can be converted into cash relatively quickly.

cash
Money in the bank and may include a security that can be sold very quickly, such as a government security.

accounts receivable
The amount of credit extended to customers that is currently outstanding.

inventory
A firm's raw materials and products held in anticipation of eventual sale.

EXHIBIT **10.4** The Working Capital Cycle

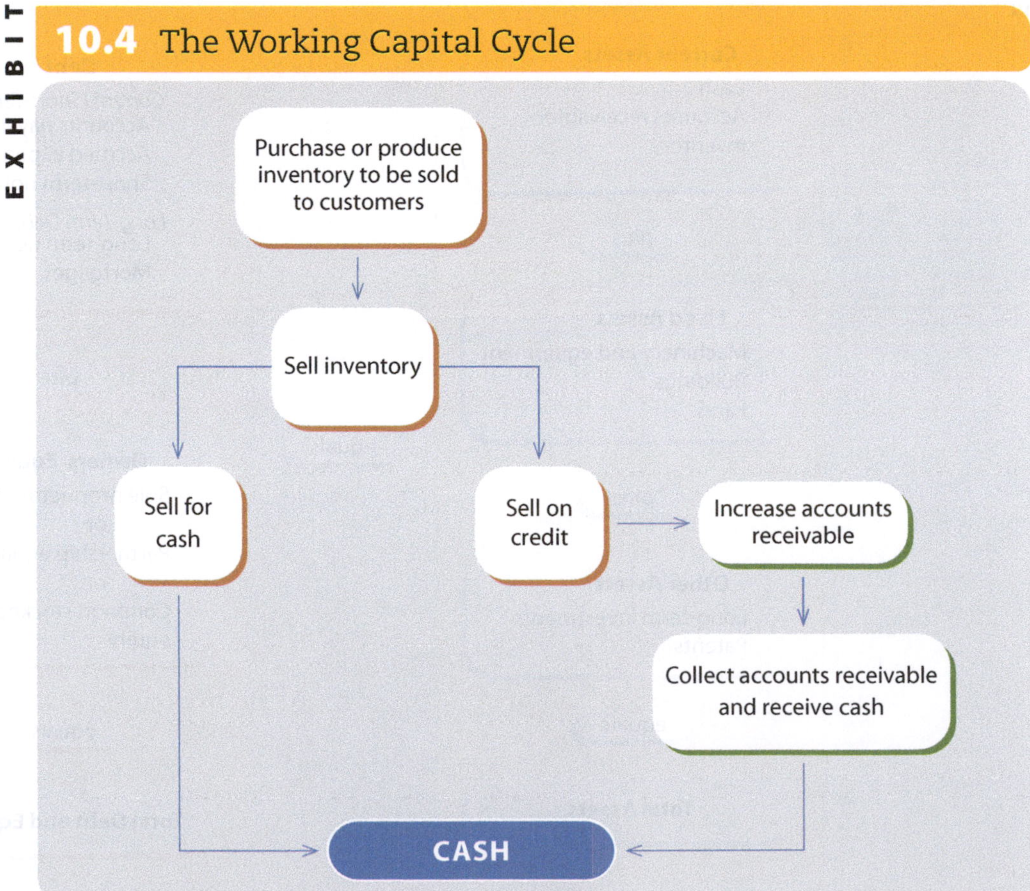

working capital cycle, a process where inventory is purchased or produced, and then sold for cash or on credit (accounts receivable). The accounts receivable are later converted into cash when collected. The cycle is then repeated, over and over.

FIXED ASSETS (PROPERTY, PLANT, AND EQUIPMENT)

The second type of assets in the balance sheet is the set of more permanent assets in a business. **Fixed assets**, also called **property, plant, and equipment (PPE)**, include land, buildings, machinery, trucks, computers, and every other physical asset a company owns that will be used in the business for more than one year. The balance sheet lists a firm's facilities and equipment at the original cost, when they were purchased. Some businesses are more capital-intensive than others—for example, a manufacturer is more capital-intensive than a gift store—and, therefore, it will have a greater amount invested in fixed assets.

Most fixed assets are also **depreciable assets**; that is, they wear out or become obsolete over time. The original cost of these assets is shown on the balance sheet when they are purchased. Each year, the assets are depreciated over their expected useful life.

Assume, for example, that a business purchased a truck for $20,000 with an expected useful life of four years. When the firm buys the truck, the original cost of $20,000 is shown on the balance sheet as a **gross fixed asset**. We would then depreciate the cost of the truck over its useful life of four years. A depreciation expense of $5,000 would be shown annually in the income statement ($20,000 ÷ 4 years = $5,000). Each year, the cumulative depreciation expense, or what is called **accumulated depreciation**, is subtracted from the original cost of the fixed asset to yield the **net fixed asset**. In this instance, the balance sheet at the end of each year would appear as follows:

	Year 1	Year 2	Year 3	Year 4
Gross fixed asset	$20,000	$20,000	$20,000	$20,000
Accumulated depreciation	(5,000)	(10,000)	(15,000)	(20,000)
Net fixed asset	$15,000	$10,000	$ 5,000	$ 0

OTHER ASSETS

The third category of assets, **other assets**, includes patents, copyrights, and goodwill. For a startup company, organizational costs—costs incurred in organizing and promoting the business—may also be included in this category.

10-2b Debt and Equity

The right side of the balance sheet in Exhibit 10.3, showing debt and equity, indicates how a firm is financing its assets. Financing comes from two main sources: debt (liabilities) and owners' equity (net worth). Debt is money that has been borrowed and must be repaid at some predetermined date. Owners' equity, on the other hand, represents the owners' investment in the company—money they have personally put into the firm without any specific date for repayment. Owners recover their investment by withdrawing money from the firm in the form of dividends or by selling their ownership in the firm.

DEBT

Debt is financing provided by a creditor. As shown in Exhibit 10.3, it is divided into (1) current, or short-term, debt and (2) long-term debt.

working capital cycle
The process of converting inventory to cash.

fixed assets (property, plant, and equipment [PPE])
Physical assets that will be used in the business for more than one year, such as equipment, buildings, and land.

depreciable assets
Assets whose value declines, or depreciates, over time.

gross fixed assets
Depreciable assets at their original cost, before any depreciation expense has been taken.

accumulated depreciation
Total (cumulative) depreciation expense taken over an asset's life.

net fixed assets
Gross fixed assets less accumulated depreciation.

other assets
Intangible assets, such as patents, copyrights, and goodwill.

debt
Financing provided by creditors.

current debt (short-term liabilities) Borrowed money that must be repaid within 12 months.

accounts payable (trade credit) Outstanding credit that is owed to suppliers.

accrued expenses Operating expenses that have been incurred but not paid; shown as an expense in the income statement and as a liability in the balance sheet.

matching principle The principle that requires the matching of expenses with the revenues they helped to earn in the same time period.

short-term notes Agreements to repay cash amounts borrowed from banks or other lending sources within 12 months or less.

long-term debt Loans from banks or other sources with repayment terms of more than 12 months.

long-term note Agreements to repay cash amounts borrowed from banks or other lending sources, plus interest, for periods longer than 12 months.

Current Debt **Current debt (short-term liabilities)** is borrowed money that must be repaid within 12 months. Sources of current debt may be classified as follows:

- **Accounts payable (trade credit)** represent credit extended by suppliers to a firm when it purchases inventory. For example, when a firm buys $10,000 in inventory, the supplier (seller) may allow the purchasing company 30 or 60 days to pay for it. Thus, along with the $10,000 increase in inventory in the balance sheet, accounts payable would increase by a like amount.
- **Accrued expenses** are operating expenses that have been incurred and are owed but not yet paid. The amount of the expense is included in the income statement and then also shown as a liability (accrued expense) in the balance sheet. For example, consider an employee who is owed $4,000 for work performed in April but who will not be paid until May 1. The $4,000 would be recorded as an expense in the income statement for April, but since no payment is made in April, it would be shown as a liability (accrued wages) in the balance sheet on April 30. When the employee is paid on May 1, the accrued expenses are decreased by $4,000, along with a $4,000 decrease in cash. In accounting jargon, this is called the **matching principle**, which requires the recording of expenses in the same accounting period that they contribute to a company's income, not necessarily when they are actually paid.
- **Short-term notes** represent cash amounts borrowed from a bank or other lending source for 12 months or less. Short-term notes are a primary source of financing for most small businesses. Assume, for example, that you borrow $50,000 from a bank for 90 days (one quarter of a year) to purchase inventory during a peak season. If the interest rate on the loan is 8 percent, you will incur $1,000 in interest ($\$1,000 = \$50,000$ principal owed $\times$ 0.08 interest rate $\times$ ¼ year). The interest paid on the loan would be shown as interest expense in the income statement and the principal amount borrowed as a liability in the balance sheet.

Long-Term Debt Loans granted for longer than 12 months from banks or other financial institutions comprise **long-term debt**. When a firm borrows money for five years to buy equipment, it signs an agreement—a **long-term note**—promising to repay the loan plus interest over five years. As with short-term notes, the interest is an expense shown in the income statement and the amount of the principal is a liability reported on the balance sheet.

© BKMCPHOTOGRAPHY/SHUTTERSTOCK.COM

When a firm borrows money, say, for 30 years to purchase a warehouse or office building, the real estate usually serves as collateral for the long-term loan, which is called a **mortgage**. If the borrower is unable to repay the loan, the lender can take the real estate in settlement.

OWNERS' EQUITY

Owners' equity is money that the owners invest in a business, whether it is a sole proprietorship, partnership, or corporation. For corporations, shares of **common stock** are issued to the investors, representing their ownership in the corporation. In addition to investing directly in a business by writing a check to the company, owners can invest indirectly simply by leaving all or part of their profits (the net profits or net income) in the business to be reinvested. The total of *all* net profits that have been retained and reinvested in a business over the entire life of the company—profits not paid out to the owners in dividends—is called **retained earnings**. That is,

$$\text{Retained earnings} = \begin{array}{c}\text{Cumulative total}\\ \text{of all net profits}\\ \text{over the life of the business}\end{array} - \begin{array}{c}\text{Cumulative total}\\ \text{of all dividends paid}\\ \text{over the life of the business}\end{array}$$

mortgage
A long-term loan to purchase a building or land.

Owners' equity
Owners' cash investments in a company plus the net profits that have been retained in the firm.

common stock
Stock shares that represent ownership in a corporation.

retained earnings
Profits not paid out as dividends over the life of a business.

We then can calculate the owners' total equity as follows:

$$\text{Owners' equity} = \text{Owners' investment} + \overbrace{\text{Cumulative profits} - \text{Cumulative dividends paid to owners}}^{\textbf{Earnings retained within the business}}$$

Exhibit 10.5 presents balance sheets for Dickey & Associates for December 31, 2014, and December 31, 2015, along with dollar changes in the balance sheets for the same time periods. By referring to the columns representing the two balance sheets, you can see the financial position of the firm at the beginning *and* at the end of 2015.

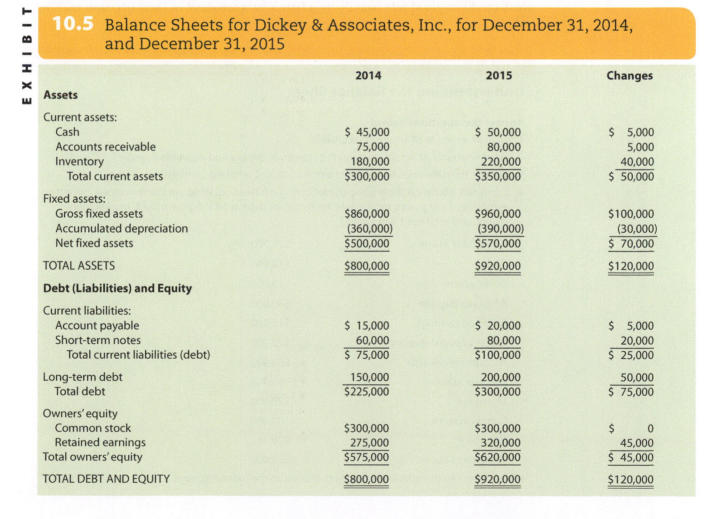

EXHIBIT 10.5 Balance Sheets for Dickey & Associates, Inc., for December 31, 2014, and December 31, 2015

	2014	2015	Changes
Assets			
Current assets:			
Cash	$ 45,000	$ 50,000	$ 5,000
Accounts receivable	75,000	80,000	5,000
Inventory	180,000	220,000	40,000
Total current assets	$300,000	$350,000	$ 50,000
Fixed assets:			
Gross fixed assets	$860,000	$960,000	$100,000
Accumulated depreciation	(360,000)	(390,000)	(30,000)
Net fixed assets	$500,000	$570,000	$ 70,000
TOTAL ASSETS	$800,000	$920,000	$120,000
Debt (Liabilities) and Equity			
Current liabilities:			
Account payable	$ 15,000	$ 20,000	$ 5,000
Short-term notes	60,000	80,000	20,000
Total current liabilities (debt)	$ 75,000	$100,000	$ 25,000
Long-term debt	150,000	200,000	50,000
Total debt	$225,000	$300,000	$ 75,000
Owners' equity			
Common stock	$300,000	$300,000	$ 0
Retained earnings	275,000	320,000	45,000
Total owners' equity	$575,000	$620,000	$ 45,000
TOTAL DEBT AND EQUITY	$800,000	$920,000	$120,000

The 2014 and 2015 year-end balance sheets for Dickey & Associates show that the firm began 2015 (ended 2014) with $800,000 in total assets and ended 2015 with total assets of $920,000. We see how much has been invested in current assets (cash, accounts receivable, and inventory) and in fixed assets. We also observe how much debt and equity were used to finance the assets. Note that about half of the equity came from investments made by the owners (common stock), and the other half came from reinvesting profits in the business (retained earnings). Referring back to the income statement in Exhibit 10.2, note that the $45,000 increase in retained profits, shown in the Changes column in Exhibit 10.5, is the firm's net profits for the year ($60,000) less the dividends paid to the owners ($15,000).

Finally, a balance sheet helps the small business owner know the financial strength and capabilities of the business—something that cannot be known in any other way. It helps answer such key questions as the following:

- Is the business in a position to expand?
- Can the firm easily handle the ebb and flow of sales and expenses?
- Is the firm collecting its accounts receivable as planned and efficiently managing inventory?
- Can accounts payable be paid more slowly to forestall an inevitable cash shortage, without hurting the entrepreneur's credit reputation?

The entrepreneur is not the only one who needs to be well versed about the balance sheet. Lenders such as bankers, investors, and suppliers, who are considering how much credit to grant rely heavily on a firm's balance sheet in their decision making.

Let's Check for Understanding

Understanding the Balance Sheet

Answer the questions below:

1. Give an example of accounts receivable.
2. What relationship would you expect between inventory and accounts payable?
3. What is the difference between common stock and retained earnings?
4. Construct a balance sheet using the following information. What are the firm's total current assets, net fixed assets, total assets, total current debt, total long-term debt, total owners' equity, and total debt and equity?

Gross fixed assets	$75,000
Cash	$10,000
Other assets	$15,000
Accounts payable	$40,000
Retained earnings	$15,000
Accumulated depreciation	$20,000
Accounts receivable	$50,000
Long-term note	$5,000
Mortgage	$20,000
Common stock	$100,000
Inventory	$70,000
Short-term notes	$20,000

(The answers to the questions above are shown on the following page.)

How Did You Do?

Understanding the Balance Sheet

On the previous page, you were asked four questions. Your answers should be similar to those provided below.

1. Give an example of accounts receivable.

   Accounts receivable represent money owed by customers to a company for goods or services that have already been received by the customers but not yet paid for. For example, an auto repair shop may purchase parts for $200 from a parts supplier and be given 30 days to pay for the parts. At the time of the transaction, the supplier records the $200 sale and the same amount in accounts receivable. When the repair shop pays the $200, the accounts receivable are decreased by $200 and cash increases by $200.

2. What relationship would you expect between inventory and accounts payable?

   Accounts payable are the amounts owed suppliers for inventory purchased on credit. When a business purchases inventory on credit, inventory increases along with a corresponding increase in accounts payable.

3. What is the difference between common stock and retained earnings?

   Both common stock and retained earnings represent an owner's equity in a firm. Common stock is cash that has been invested in a firm by its owners. Retained earnings are the amount of profits that have been reinvested in a business as opposed to distributing the profits in the form of dividends.

4. Based on the financial data provided, your balance sheet should read as follows:

Assets	
Cash	$ 10,000
Accounts receivable	50,000
Inventory	70,000
Total current assets	$130,000
Gross fixed assets	$ 75,000
Accumulated depreciation	(20,000)
Net fixed assets	$ 55,000
Other assets	15,000
TOTAL ASSETS	$200,000

Debt and Equity	
Accounts payable	$ 40,000
Short-term notes	20,000
Total current debt	$ 60,000
Long-term note	5,000
Mortgage	20,000
Total long-term debt	$ 25,000
Total debt	$ 85,000
Common stock	$100,000
Retained earnings	15,000
Total owners' equity	$115,000
TOTAL DEBT AND EQUITY	$200,000

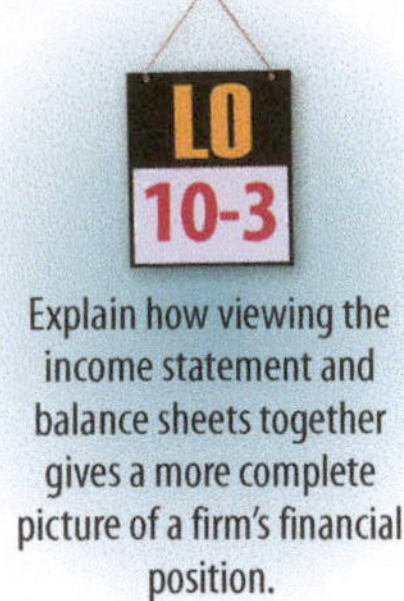

Explain how viewing the income statement and balance sheets together gives a more complete picture of a firm's financial position.

10-3 VIEWING THE INCOME STATEMENT AND BALANCE SHEET TOGETHER

Thus far, we have discussed the income statement and the balance sheet as separate reports. But they actually complement each other to give an overall picture of the firm's financial situation. Because the balance sheet is a snapshot of a firm's financial condition at a specific point in time, such as on the exact day of December 31, and the income statement reports results over a given period, such as the period from January 1 through December 31, both are required to determine a firm's financial position.

Exhibit 10.6 shows how the income statement and the balance sheet fit together. To understand how a firm performed during 2015, you must know the firm's financial position at the beginning of 2015 (balance sheet on December 31, 2014), its financial performance during the year (income statement for 2015), and its financial position at the end of the year (balance sheet on December 31, 2015).

Note that this exhibit shows the financial statements for a one-year period; however, most companies produce financial statements monthly and quarterly, as well as annually. Owners do not want to wait an entire year before knowing how the business is doing financially.

Use the income statement and balance sheets to compute a company's cash flows.

10-4 THE CASH FLOW STATEMENT

An entrepreneur once told us how intimidated she felt when her accountant presented the firm's monthly financial reports and she had difficulty understanding cash flows. Our advice was to get a new accountant—one who would explain the statements carefully—and to spend the time necessary to gain a solid understanding of the financial statements and the firm's cash flows.

EXHIBIT 10.6 The Fit of the Income Statement and Balance Sheet

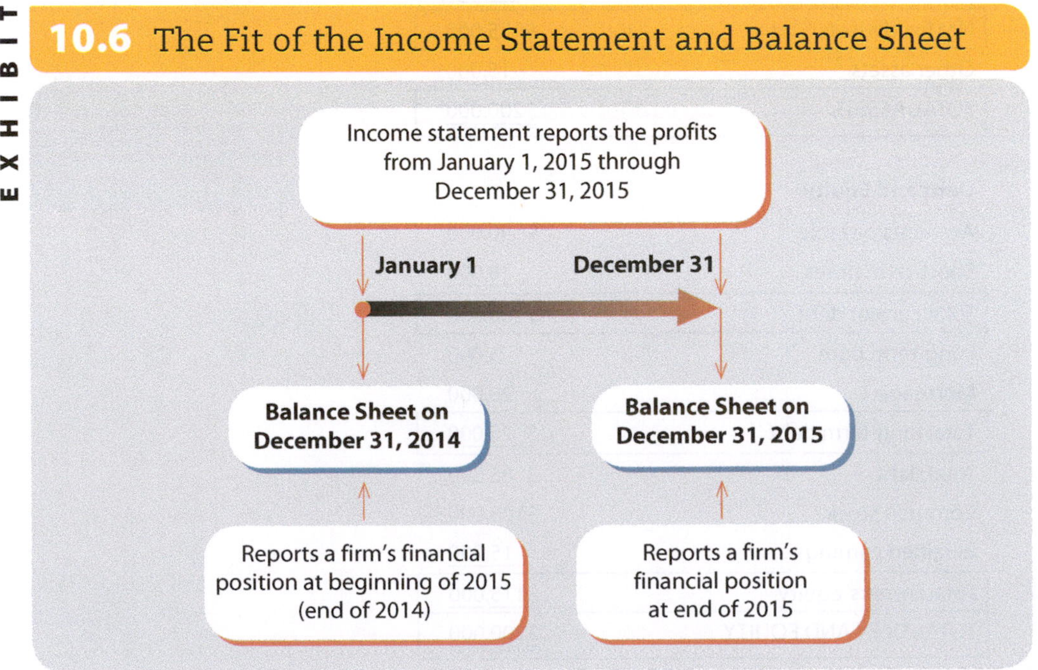

Living The Dream

ENTREPRENEURIAL EXPERIENCES

Surviving Tough Times Means Effectively Managing Your Finances

In 2006, after managing a commercial interior design business, Rose Corrick founded Art of Cloth, a producer of hand-dyed fashion textiles. By the summer of 2008, sales had never been higher, as an increasing number of boutiques were buying Corrick's clothing. In preparation for anticipated growth, she moved from her basement into a 4,500-square-foot facility, signing a three-year lease. She then bought the necessary equipment to manufacture her clothes in greater quantities.

© EVIKKA/SHUTTERSTOCK.COM

But when the recession hit in late 2008, customers began canceling orders, even though Art of Cloth had already made some custom products. The result was $30,000 in lost revenues. Corrick felt she had little legal recourse, as she did not want to cut off customers who might return in better economic times. The business began having major cash flow issues. As Corrick explained, "All of a sudden, we couldn't pay our bills. Being such a small company, it was very painful."

In response to the changing conditions and the cash flow problems, Corrick negotiated more favorable payment terms with several of her suppliers. She stopped paying herself a salary and was forced to lay off people. Finally, she used her personal credit card to pay for some company expenses, such as travel to trade shows. Corrick established three priorities: (1) Cut expenses that would affect revenues the least, (2) make the firm's products more marketable, given the economic realities, and (3) carefully monitor the company's cash flows.

Accordingly, she cut prices on several higher-priced items by 15 to 30 percent, based on feedback from her customers. To offset the lost revenues, she found a way to cut manufacturing costs and improve efficiency by speeding up the dyeing process. But she continued to attend design shows in major U.S. cities to gain exposure to prospective buyers, spending $1,000 to $4,000 to attend each one.

By late 2009, her efforts were paying off. Although the number of boutiques carrying her apparel had decreased slightly, sales remained at about the same level as in 2008—$362,000. But by 2014, the firm had achieved $1.5 million in sales.

If there is a moral to Corrick's story, it would have to be the importance of understanding the relationship between revenues and different types of expenses. When times are good, inefficiencies can develop and not even be noticed. But when times are bad, only those who understand the finances of their business can survive.

Sources: Based on interview with Sally Pruitt at Art of the Cloth, April 7, 2015; Kelly K. Spoors, "A Fashion Startup Survives Cash-Flow Problems and Redesigns Itself for a Comeback," *Entrepreneur*, May 9, 2011, http://www.entrepreneur.com/article/219579, accessed January 12, 2015; and John Sung Kim, "How Rose Corrick Made Her Small Business Comeback," May 17, 2011, http://www.halloo.com/Blog/index.php/how-rose-corrick-made-her-small-business-comeback, accessed January 19, 2015.

Effectively managing cash flows is critical for small business owners. In the words of Philip Campbell, "Despite the fact that cash is the lifeblood of a business—the fuel that keeps the engine running—most business owners don't truly have a handle on their cash flow. Poor cash-flow management is causing more business failures today than ever before."[3]

For this reason, a small firm owner must understand the sources and uses of the firm's cash. A **cash flow statement** is a financial report that shows the sources of a firm's cash and its uses of the cash. In other words, it answers the questions "Where did the cash come from?" and "Where did the cash go?"

10-4a Profits versus Cash Flows

Entrepreneurs need to be aware that *the profits shown on a company's income statement are not the same as its cash flows!* In the words of author Jan Norman, "Even profitable companies can go broke. That's a difficult truth for some business owners to swallow. But the sooner you learn that when you're out of cash, you're out of business, the better your chances for survival will be."[4] Many a business that showed a profit on its income statement has had to file for bankruptcy because the amount of cash coming in did not compare positively with the amount of cash going out. Without adequate cash flows, little problems become major problems!

An income statement is not a measure of cash flows because it is calculated on an *accrual* basis rather than a *cash* basis. This is an important point to understand. In **accrual-basis accounting**, profits are recorded when earned—whether or not the profits have been received in cash—and expenses are recorded when they are incurred—even if money has not actually been paid out. In **cash-basis accounting**, profits are reported when cash is received and expenses are recorded when they are paid. For a number of reasons, profits based on an accrual-basis accounting system will differ from the firm's cash flows:

1. Sales reported in an income statement include both *cash* sales and *credit* sales. Thus, total sales do not correspond to the actual cash collected. A company may have had sales of $1 million for the year but may not have collected on all of them. If accounts receivable increased $80,000 from the beginning of the year to the end of the year, then we would know that only $920,000 of the sales had been collected ($920,000 = $1,000,000 sales − $80,000 increase in accounts receivable).
2. Cash spent for inventory doesn't represent all inventory purchases since some inventory is financed by credit. Consider a business that purchased $500,000 in inventory during the year, but the supplier extended $100,000 in credit for the purchases. The actual cash paid for inventory would be only $400,000 ($400,000 = $500,000 total inventory purchases − $100,000 credit granted by the supplier).
3. The depreciation expense shown in the income statement is a noncash expense. It reflects the costs associated with using an asset that benefits the firm's operations over a period of several years, such as a piece of equipment used over five years. Thus, if a business had profits of $250,000 that included depreciation expenses of $40,000, then the cash flows would be $290,000 ($290,000 = $250,000 profits + $40,000 depreciation expense).

So the question—and its answer—that every small business owner should ask and understand is "How do I compute my firm's cash flows?"

cash flow statement
A financial report showing a firm's sources of cash as well as its uses of cash.

accrual-basis accounting
An accounting method of recording profits when earned and expenses when incurred, whether or not the profits have been received in cash or the expenses paid.

cash-basis accounting
An accounting method of recording profits when cash is received and recording expenses when they are paid.

10-4b Measuring a Firm's Cash Flows

It's time to return to our young entrepreneurs, Cameron and Ashley, and their lemonade stand. To develop a report that explained the cash flows from their lemonade business, you could simply list all the cash inflows and outflows and see what happened to their cash balance. Here is what it would look like:

Cameron and Ashley's initial investment	$ 10
Loan from their mom	40
Purchased inventory	(40)
Cash collected from the first Saturday's sales	30
Collection of accounts receivable	30
Cash collected from the second Saturday's sales	100
Salaries expense	(25)
Ending cash	$145

They began with a $10 investment in the business and ended with $145 in cash, before repaying their mom the $40 loan and contributing $100 toward the iPad purchase. This works quite well in the world of lemonade stands. But the report would become overwhelming in a business of any significant size, where thousands of transactions (or more) are recorded in the financial statements each year. Also, there's a better approach to learning what activities contribute to a firm's cash flows. We can explain the cash inflows and outflows of a business by looking at three **cash flow activities**:

cash flow activities Operating, investing, and financing activities that result in cash inflows or outflows.

1. *Generating cash flows from day-to-day business operations (operating activities).* It is informative to know how much cash is being generated in the normal course of operating a business on a daily basis, beginning with purchasing inventory on credit, selling on credit, paying for the inventory, and finally collecting on the sales made on credit.
2. *Buying or selling fixed assets (investing activities).* When a company buys (or sells) fixed assets, such as equipment and buildings, cash outflows (or inflows) result. These cash flows are not part of the regular day-to-day operations and, consequently, are not included in the income statement. They appear only as changes from one balance sheet to the next.
3. *Financing the business (financing activities).* Cash inflows and outflows occur when the company borrows or repays debt; when it distributes money to the owners, such as when dividends are paid; or when the owners put money into the business in the form of additional equity.

© ISTOCKPHOTO.COM/JASON_V

If we know the cash flows from the activities listed above, we can explain a firm's total cash flows. To illustrate how this is done, we use Dickey & Associates' income statement (Exhibit 10.2) and balance sheets (Exhibit 10.5).

ACTIVITY 1: CASH FLOWS FROM DAY-TO-DAY BUSINESS OPERATIONS

To convert the company's income statement from an *accrual* basis to a *cash* basis, we take two steps: (1) Add back depreciation to net profits, since depreciation is not a cash expense, and (2) subtract any uncollected sales (increase in accounts receivable) and payments for inventory (increases in inventory less increases in accounts payable).

The reason we add back depreciation should be clear. The changes in accounts receivable, inventory, and accounts payable may be less intuitive. Two comments might be helpful for your understanding:

1. A firm's sales are either cash sales or credit sales. If accounts receivable increase, that means customers did not pay for everything they purchased. Thus, any increase in accounts receivable needs to be subtracted from total sales to determine the cash that has been collected from customers. Remember the Lemonade Kids: On their first day, they sold $60 in lemonade, but they only collected $30. The remainder was accounted for by an increase in accounts receivable.
2. The other activity occurring in the daily course of business is purchasing inventory. An increase in inventory shows that inventory was purchased, but if accounts payable (credit extended by a supplier) increase, then we may conclude that the firm did not pay for the entire inventory purchased. The net payment for inventory is equal to the increase in inventory less what has not yet been paid for (increase in accounts payable).

Referring back to Dickey & Associates' income statement (Exhibit 10.2) and balance sheets (Exhibit 10.5), we can perform the conversion from accrual basis to cash basis as follows:

Net profits	$60,000	
Add back depreciation	30,000	
Profits before depreciation		$90,000
Less increase in accounts receivable (uncollected sales)		(5,000)
Less payments for inventory consisting of:		
Increase in inventory	($40,000)	
Less increase in accounts payable (inventory purchased on credit)	$ 5,000	
Cash payments for inventory		(35,000)
Cash flows from operations		$50,000

ACTIVITY 2: INVESTING IN FIXED ASSETS

The second cash flow activity occurs when a company purchases or sells fixed assets, such as equipment or buildings. These activities are shown as a change in *gross* fixed assets (not *net* fixed assets) in the balance sheet. An increase means the company spent cash buying fixed assets, while a decrease means it received cash from selling fixed assets. For instance, Dickey & Associates spent $100,000 on new plant and equipment in 2015, based on the change in gross fixed assets from $860,000 to $960,000, as shown in its balance sheets (Exhibit 10.5).

ACTIVITY 3: FINANCING THE BUSINESS

The cash flows associated with financing a business are as follows:

1. A cash inflow when a company borrows more money (increases short-term and/or long-term debt).
2. A cash outflow when a firm repays debt (decreases short-term and/or long-term debt).
3. A cash inflow when the owners invest in the business to increase their equity.

4. A cash outflow when the owners withdraw money from the business. In sole proprietorships and partnerships, the owner(s) would simply write a check on the firm's bank account to take the money out. In a corporation, the company would either pay a dividend to the owners or would repurchase some of the owners' stock.

Note that when we talk about borrowing or repaying debt when financing the business, accounts payable and accrued expenses are not included. These sources of financing were included in activity 1, when we computed cash flows from operations. Here, in activity 3, only debt from such sources as banks in the form of short-term notes and long-term debt is included.

The income statement of Dickey & Associates (Exhibit 10.2) shows that $15,000 in dividends was paid to the owners. From its balance sheets (Exhibit 10.5), we see that short-term debt increased $20,000 and long-term debt increased $50,000, both sources of cash flow. Thus, in net, Dickey & Associates raised $55,000 in financing cash flows:

Increase in short-term notes	$20,000
Increase in long-term debt	50,000
Less dividends paid to owners	(15,000)
Financing cash flows	$55,000

TIPS FOR COMPUTING CASH FLOWS

When measuring cash flows, follow these suggestions:

1. Work on the three parts of the cash flow statement individually, and then put it all together. That helps you focus on what needs to be done without being overwhelmed.
2. Use only depreciation expense and net profits from the income statement.
3. It is necessary that you understand how the changes in a firm's balance sheets have implications for its cash flows.
   - A *decrease in an asset is a source of cash*—for example, selling inventory or collecting receivables.
   - *An increase in an asset is a use of cash*—for example, investing in fixed assets or buying inventory.
   - *An increase in liabilities or equity is a source of cash*—for example, borrowing funds or selling stock.
   - *A decrease in liabilities or equity is a use of cash*—for example, paying off a loan or buying back stock.
4. Use every change in the company's balance sheets, with two exceptions:
   (a) Ignore accumulated depreciation and net fixed assets since they involve the noncash item of depreciation, and use only the change in *gross* fixed assets.
   (b) Ignore the change in retained earnings since it equals net profits and dividends paid, two items that are captured elsewhere.

To summarize, Dickey & Associates generated $50,000 in cash flows from operations, invested $100,000 in gross fixed assets (gross property, plant, and equipment), and received a net $55,000 from financing activities, for a net increase in cash of $5,000. This change in cash can be verified from the balance sheets (see Exhibit 10.5), which show that the firm's cash increased by $5,000 during 2015 (from $45,000 to $50,000).

Stated somewhat differently, Dickey & Associates had positive cash flows from (1) its day-to-day business operations (cash flow from operations) and (2) borrowing money from a bank. These cash inflows were used to pay for fixed assets and to increase the firm's cash. The complete cash flow statement for Dickey & Associates is presented in Exhibit 10.7.

EXHIBIT

10.7 Cash Flow Statement for Dickey & Associates, Inc., for the Year Ending December 31, 2015

Operating activities:		
Net profits	$60,000	
Add back depreciation	30,000	
Profits before depreciation		$ 90,000
Less increase in accounts receivable (uncollected sales)		($ 5,000)
Less payments for inventory consisting of:		
Increase in inventory	(40,000)	
Less increase in accounts payable (inventory purchased on credit)	5,000	
Payments for inventory		($ 35,000)
Cash flows from operations		$ 50,000
Investment activities:		
Less increase in gross fixed assets		($100, 000)
Financing activities:		
Increase in short-term notes	20,000	
Increase in long-term debt	50,000	
Less dividends paid to owners	(15,000)	
Financing cash flows		$ 55,000
Increase in cash		$ 5,000
Beginning cash (December 31, 2014)	$45,000	
Ending cash (December 31, 2015)	$50,000	

Let's Check for Understanding

Understanding Cash Flows

The Maness Corporation's financial statements are shown below, along with the changes in the balance sheets between 2014 and 2015 (numbers you will need). Use this data to prepare a cash flow statement, and then answer the following questions:

1. How much of Maness Corporation's cash flows are from operating activities, from investment activities, and from financing activities?
2. What was the change in cash between December 31, 2014, and December 31, 2015?
3. Look at your answers for questions 1 and 2, and describe what you learned about the company's cash flows.

Balance Sheets as of December 31, 2014, and December 31, 2015

	2014	2015	Changes
Assets			
Cash	$ 150,000	$ 125,000	$ (25,000)
Accounts receivable	350,000	375,000	25,000
Inventory	475,000	550,000	75,000
Total current assets	$ 975,000	$1,050,000	$ 75,000
Gross fixed assets	$2,425,000	$2,750,000	$ 325,000
Accumulated depreciation	(1,000,000)	(1,200,000)	(200,000)
Net fixed assets	$1,425,000	$1,550,000	$ 125,000
TOTAL ASSETS	$2,400,000	$2,600,000	$ 200,000
Debt (Liabilities) and Equity			
Accounts payable	$ 200,000	$ 150,000	$ (50,000)
Short-term notes	0	150,000	150,000
Total current liabilities	$ 200,000	$ 300,000	$ 100,000
Long-term debt	600,000	600,000	$ 0
Total debt	$ 800,000	$ 900,000	$ 100,000
Owners' equity			
Common stock	$ 900,000	$ 900,000	$ 0
Retained earnings	700,000	800,000	100,000
Total owners' equity	$1,600,000	$1,700,000	$ 100,000
TOTAL LIABILITIES AND OWNERS' EQUITY	$2,400,000	$2,600,000	$ 200,000

Income Statement January 1–December 2015

Sales	$1,450,000
Cost of goods sold	(850,000)
Gross profits	$ 600,000
Operating expenses	(240,000)
Operating profits	$ 360,000
Interest expense	(64,000)
Profits before taxes	$ 296,000
Taxes	(118,000)
Net profits	$ 178,000
Net profits	$ 178,000
Dividends paid	(78,000)
Increase in retained earnings	$ 100,000

(The answers to the questions above are shown on the following page.)

How Did You Do?

Understanding Cash Flows

On the previous page, you were asked three questions. Your answers should be similar to those provided below.

(continued)

(continued)

The answers to the first two questions follow. The three types of cash flow activities and the company's change in cash for the year are as follows for Maness:

Cash flows from operations	$ 228
Cash flows from investing in fixed assets	(325)
Cash flows from financing	72
Change in cash balance	$ (25)

The computations are as follows:

Cash Flow Statement		
Cash flows from operating activities		
Net profits		$ 178
Plus depreciation		200
Profits before depreciation		$ 378
Less increase in accounts receivable (uncollected sales)		$ (25)
Less payments for inventory consisting of:		
Increase in inventory	$ (75)	
Less decrease in accounts payable (reduced accounts payable)	(50)	
Cash payments for inventory		$ (125)
Cash flows from operations		$ 228
Cash flows from investing activities		$ (325)
Cash flows from financing activities		
Borrow money (increase in short-term notes)	$ 150	
Dividend payments	(78)	
Total financing cash flows		$ 72
Change in Maness's cash balance		$ (25)

The third question asked what you learned about the firm's cash flows: The Maness Corporation primarily received cash flows from day-to-day operations and to a lesser extent from borrowing on a short-term note (probably from the bank). It also used some of its cash in the bank (decreased cash). All cash flows were used to buy fixed assets and to pay dividends to the owners.

10-5 EVALUATING A FIRM'S FINANCIAL PERFORMANCE

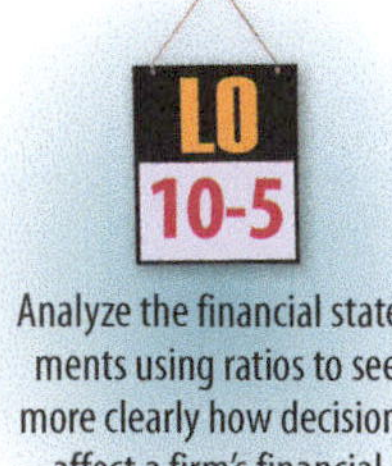

Analyze the financial statements using ratios to see more clearly how decisions affect a firm's financial performance.

Once a firm's owner understands the content of the accounting statements, she or he wants to know how management decisions impact the financial situation of a business. An entrepreneur's decisions play out primarily in four ways when it comes to finances:

1. *The firm's ability to pay its debt as it comes due.* In other words, does the company have the capacity to meet its short-term (one year or less) debt commitments?
2. *The company's profitability from assets.* Is the business providing a good rate of return on its assets? There is no more important question when it comes to determining if a business is strong economically.

3. *The amount of debt the business is using.* Using debt increases a firm's risk, but it may also increase the expected rate of return on the owners' equity investment.
4. *The rate of return earned by the owners on their equity investment.* All decisions ultimately affect the rate of return earned by the owners on their equity investment in the business.

Exhibit 10.8 provides a list of financial ratios as they relate to the four issues just listed. The name of each ratio is given, along with how it is computed. We illustrate the ratios by using the 2015 financial data for Dickey & Associates, as presented in Exhibit 10.2 (income statement) and Exhibit 10.5 (balance sheets). Finally, the last column shows an industry average for each ratio, which comes from financial publications, such as Risk Management Association's *Annual Statement Studies.* Let's look at the ratios as they apply to Dickey & Associates.

10-5a Liquidity (Ability to Pay Debt)

A business—or a person, for that matter—that has enough money to pay off any debt owed is described as being *liquid.* The **liquidity** of a business depends on the availability of cash to meet maturing debt obligations. The **current ratio** is traditionally used to measure a company's liquidity. This ratio compares a firm's *current assets* to its *current liabilities*, as follows:

$$\text{Current ratio} = \frac{\text{Current assets}}{\text{Current liabilities}}$$

As you can see in Exhibit 10.8, for Dickey & Associates, the current ratio is 3.50, compared to an industry norm of 2.70. In other words, the firm has \$3.50 in current assets for every \$1 of short-term debt, compared to an industry average of \$2.70 of current assets for every \$1 in short-term debt. Thus, based on the current ratio, Dickey & Associates is more liquid than the average firm in the industry.

liquidity
The degree to which a firm has working capital available to meet maturing debt obligations.

current ratio
A measure of a company's relative liquidity, determined by dividing current assets by current liabilities.

EXHIBIT **10.8** Financial Ratio Analysis for Dickey & Associates, Inc.

Financial ratios	Dickey & Associates	Industry Norm
1. Ability to pay debt as it comes due:		
Current ratio = $\frac{\text{Current assets}}{\text{Current liabilities}}$	$\frac{\$350,000}{\$100,000} = 3.50$	2.7
2. Company's profitability on its assets:		
Return on assets = $\frac{\text{Operating Profits}}{\text{Total assets}}$	$\frac{\$100,000}{\$920,000} = 10.87\%$	13.2%
Operating profit margin = $\frac{\text{Operating Profits}}{\text{Sales}}$	$\frac{\$100,000}{\$850,000} = 11.76\%$	11.0%
Total asset turnover = $\frac{\text{Sales}}{\text{Total assets}}$	$\frac{\$850,000}{\$920,000} = 0.92$	1.2
3. The amount of debt the company uses:		
Debt ratio = $\frac{\text{Total debt}}{\text{Total assets}}$	$\frac{\$300,000}{\$920,000} = 32.61\%$	40.0%
4. Rate of return earned by the owners on their equity investment:		
Return on equity = $\frac{\text{Net profits}}{\text{Owners' equity}}$	$\frac{\$60,000}{\$620,000} = 9.68\%$	12.5%

10-5b Profitability on Assets

A vitally important question to a firm's owners is whether a company's operating profits are sufficient relative to the total amount of assets invested in the company. A firm's assets are invested for the express purpose of producing operating profits. A comparison of operating profits to total assets reveals the rate of return that is being earned on the firm's total assets, which represent the total amount of investment in the business. We compute the **return on assets** as follows:

$$\text{Return on assets} = \frac{\text{Operating profits}}{\text{Total assets}}$$

As shown in Exhibit 10.8, Dickey & Associates' return on assets of 10.87 percent is less than the industry norm of 13.2 percent, indicating that Dickey & Associates is generating less operating profits on each dollar of assets than its competitors. That is not good!

To gain more understanding about why Dickey & Associates is not doing very well in generating profits on the firm's assets, you can separate the return on assets into two components: (1) the operating profit margin and (2) the total asset turnover. The equation for the return on assets can be restated as follows:

$$\text{Return on assets} = \frac{\text{Operating profits}}{\text{Total assets}} = \underbrace{\frac{\text{Operating profits}}{\text{Sales}}}_{\textbf{Operating profit margin}} \times \underbrace{\frac{\text{Sales}}{\text{Total assets}}}_{\textbf{Total asset turnover}}$$

The first component of the expanded equation, the **operating profit margin** (operating profits ÷ sales), shows how well a firm is controlling its cost of goods sold and operating expenses relative to a dollar of sales. The second component of a firm's return on assets, the **total asset turnover** (sales ÷ total assets), indicates how efficiently management is using the firm's assets to generate sales.

The operating profit margin and total asset turnover for Dickey & Associates, along with industry averages, are presented in Exhibit 10-8 and shown again below. You can also see how they relate to Dickey & Associates' return on assets, as well as to the industry:

		Operating profit margin	×	total asset turnover	=	return on assets
Dickey	=	11.76%	×	0.92	=	10.87%
Industry	=	11.00%	×	1.20	=	13.20%

Based on the operating profit margin, Dickey & Associates is competitive when it comes to managing its income statement—that is, keeping costs and expenses low relative to sales. However, Dickey & Associates' total asset turnover shows why the firm is not earning a good return on its assets. The firm is not using its assets efficiently. The company's problem is that it generates $0.92 in sales per dollar of assets, while the competition produces $1.20 in sales from every dollar in assets. Management needs to assess what is causing the problem, looking carefully at how they are managing the different types of assets, namely, the accounts receivable, inventory, and fixed assets.

return on assets
A measure of a firm's profitability relative to the amount of its assets, determined by dividing operating profits by total assets.

operating profit margin
A measure of how well a firm is controlling its cost of goods sold and operating expenses relative to sales, determined by dividing operating profits by sales.

total asset turnover
A measure of how efficiently a firm is using its assets to generate sales, calculated by dividing sales by total assets.

The low total asset turnover, showing that Dickey & Associates is using more assets per sales dollar than its competitors, possibly indicates one or more of the following problems:

1. The firm is not collecting its accounts receivable as quickly as the competition. By collecting its receivables on a more timely basis, it would release money that is currently tied up.
2. Given the amount of sales, the owners have too much money tied up in inventory, which suggests that some inventory is slow moving or even obsolete.
3. It is possible that the company has overinvested in fixed assets (such as facilities) compared to the competition.

Clearly, the Dickey sisters need to investigate why their firm is not competitive when it comes to managing assets. After all, entrepreneurship is about doing more with less when it comes to managing resources.

10-5c Use of Debt Financing

How much debt, relative to the total assets, is used to finance a business is extremely important. For one thing, the more debt a business uses, the more risk it is taking because the debt has to be repaid no matter how much profit the firm earns; it is a fixed cost. However, if a company earns a higher return on its investments than the interest rate being paid on its debt, the owners benefit from using debt.

The **debt ratio** tells us what percentage of the firm's assets is financed by debt and is computed as follows:

$$\text{Debt ratio} = \frac{\text{Total debts}}{\text{Total assets}}$$

Refer again to Exhibit 10.8, which shows Dickey & Associates' debt ratio as 32.61 percent, compared to an industry norm of 40.0 percent. Since Dickey & Associates uses less debt than the average firm in the industry, it has less risk. After all, borrowed money must be repaid regardless of how much money the business makes. All is well if the company prospers and repays the loan. But if not, *watch out!*

10-5d Return on Owners' Equity

The last financial ratio considered here is the rate of return that the owners are receiving on their equity investment, or the **return on equity**. It is computed as follows:

$$\text{Return on equity} = \frac{\text{Net profits}}{\text{Total owners' equity}}$$

As you can see in Exhibit 10.8, the return on equity for the Dickey sisters is 9.68 percent, while the industry average for return on equity is 12.5 percent. Thus, it appears that the Dickey sisters are not receiving a return on their investment equivalent to that of owners of comparable businesses. Why not? To answer this question, consider the following:

1. A firm with a high (low) return on *assets* will have a high (low) return on *equity*. It simply is not possible to have a good return on equity if you are not earning a good return on your assets.
2. As the amount of a firm's debt increases, its return on equity will increase, *provided that the return on assets is higher than the interest rate paid on any debt.*

debt ratio
A measure of what percentage of a firm's assets is financed by debt, determined by dividing total debt by total assets.

return on equity
A measure of the rate of return that owners receive on their equity investment, calculated by dividing net profits by owners' equity.

In the case of Dickey & Associates, the firm has a lower return on *equity* in part because it has a lower return on *assets*. It also uses less debt than the average firm in the industry, causing its return on equity to be lower than that of other firms. However, using less debt does reduce the firm's risk.

Here's another example: If a business earns a 15 percent return on *assets* but only has to pay 6 percent on its bank debt, the owners will receive 15 percent on the amount of their equity investment plus the 9 percent difference between the return on assets and what they pay the bank (15% − 6% = 9%). The more debt and the less equity they use, the more the owners' return on equity will be; it's called **financial leverage**.

It's very important to understand that the return on equity will be lower if the return on assets falls below the interest rate on the loan (e.g., if the return on assets is 8 percent, but the interest rate on debt is 10 percent). That is called negative financial leverage. These relationships will be explained further in Chapter 12, when we discuss sources of financing.

Our analysis of financial statements is now complete. Hopefully, you are now better prepared to know what financial statements can tell you about a business—knowledge that can be found in no other way than by interpreting the numbers.

In this chapter, we focused on understanding financial statements related to a firm's historical financial performance. We were essentially looking back to see how a business performed in a previous time period. In the next chapter, we will continue to work with financial statements, but this time we will be looking forward. In writing a business plan, you need to show convincingly how your plans will play out in terms of the firm's financial future.

Let's Check for Understanding

Understanding How to Evaluate a Firm's Financial Performance

Let's return once again to Maness Corporation's financial data to illustrate how to use financial ratios to evaluate a firm's performance. Using the data for 2015, which are shown below, and the industry norms, compute the financial ratios that were discussed in this chapter (current ratio, return on assets, operating profit margin, total asset turnover, debt ratio, and return on equity). Once you have computed the ratios, answer the following questions:

1. Is Maness Corporation more or less liquid than the average company in the industry?
2. Is the company doing a good job of earning a return on its assets? Explain.
3. How does the owner finance the business in terms of debt and equity?
4. Is Maness receiving a good return on equity? Explain.

Balance Sheet as of December 31, 2015

Assets	**2015**
Cash	$ 125,000
Accounts receivable	$ 375,000
Inventory	550,000
Total current assets	$ 1,050,000
Gross fixed assets	2,750,000
Accumulated depreciation	(1,200,000)
Net fixed assets	$ 1,550,000
TOTAL ASSETS	$ 2,600,000

financial leverage
The impact (positive or negative) of financing with debt rather than with equity.

Debt (Liabilities) and Equity	
Accounts payable	$ 150,000
Short-term notes	150,000
Total current liabilities	$ 300,000
Long-term debt	600,000
Total debt	$ 900,000
Common stock	$ 900,000
Retained earnings	800,000
Total owners' equity	$ 1,700,000
TOTAL LIABILITIES AND OWNERS' EQUITY	$ 2,600,000

Income Statement for the Year ending December 31, 2015	
Sales	$ 1,450,000
Cost of goods sold	(850,000)
Gross profits	$ 600,000
Operating expenses	(240,000)
Operating profits	$ 360,000
Interest expense	(64,000)
Profits before taxes	$ 296,000
Taxes	(118,000)
Net profits	$ 178,000

Industry Norms	
Current ratio	3.25
Return on assets	15.0%
Operating profit margin	20.0%
Total asset turnover	0.75
Debt ratio	0.20
Return on equity	9.0%

(The answers to the questions are shown on the following page.)

How Did You Do?

Understanding How to Evaluate a Firm's Financial Performance

On the previous page, you were asked four questions about Maness's financial performance. Your answers should be similar to those provided below. The results of ratio computations follow:

	Maness	Industry
Current ratio	3.50	3.25
Return on assets	13.8%	15.0%
Operating profit margin	24.8%	20.0%
Total asset turnover	0.56	0.75
Debt ratio	0.35	0.20
Return on owners' equity	10.5%	9.0%

(continued)

(continued)

Answers to questions:

1. Is the Maness Corporation more or less liquid than the average company in the industry?

   Based on the current ratio, Maness has $3.50 in liquid assets (current assets) for every $1 in current liabilities, compared to $3.25 for the industry, which suggests that Maness is slightly more liquid.

2. Is the company doing a good job at earning a return on its assets? Explain.

   For every $100 in assets, Maness generates $13.80 in operating profits (based on return on assets of 13.8 percent), compared to $15 in profits for the competition. Thus, Maness is not competitive on its profits on assets. Looking at the operating profit margin, we see that Maness actually does quite well in generating profits on sales—24.8 percent compared to 20 percent for the industry. Clearly, Maness is effective at controlling costs and expenses in the income statement. The problem lies with the total asset turnover, which measures how well the business's assets are being managed. Maness only produces $0.56 in sales for every $1.00 of assets, which is less than the $0.75 for the industry. Maness's team needs to dig deeper into their asset management policies and procedures.

3. How does the owner finance the business in terms of debt and equity?

   Maness uses more debt relative to total assets than does the industry—35 percent compared to 20 percent. Thus, the firm will encounter more financial risk than the average company in the industry. (As we will see later, debt is risky!)

4. Is Maness receiving a good return on equity? Explain.

   Maness's return on owners' equity is higher than for owners in other companies, earning 10.5 percent relative to 9 percent for the industry. But there is good news and bad news. The higher return on equity is not the result of being better at generating profits on the company's total assets—always a good thing to do if you do not have to assume more risk. The lower return on assets described in question 2 will result in a lower return on owners' equity. Maness's higher return on equity is the consequence of using more debt, which is fine as long as the company does well. But things could get tough if a significant downturn in the economy occurs, such as happened in 2008. Maness would be at a greater risk of not being able to meet his debt commitments.

10-1. Describe the purpose and content of an income statement.

- An income statement (also known as a profit and loss statement) indicates the amount of profits or losses generated by a firm over a given time period.
- An income statement is, in its most basic form, represented by the equation:

  Sales (revenue) − Expenses = Profits (income)

- An income statement answers the question "How profitable is the business?" by looking at five broad areas of business activity: (1) sales, (2) cost of producing or acquiring goods or services, (3) operating expenses, (4) interest expense, and (5) tax payments.

10-2. Describe the purpose and content of a balance sheet.

- A balance sheet provides a snapshot of a firm's financial position at a specific point in time.
- It shows the assets a firm owns, its liabilities, and the amount of owners' equity on a specific date.
- In its most simple form, the balance sheet is represented by the formula:

  Total assets = Debt + Owners' equity

- Total assets include current, fixed, and other assets.
- Debt is financing provided by creditors. It can be current (short-term) debt and/or long-term debt.
- Owners' equity is the owners' investment in the business, both in terms of actual cash invested and earnings that have been retained in the business.

10-3. Explain how viewing the income statement and balance sheets together gives a more complete picture of a firm's financial position.

- Because the balance sheet offers a snapshot of a firm's financial condition at a specific point in time and the income statement reports a firm's performance over a period of time, both are needed to fully evaluate a firm's financial position.
- Three financial reports are needed to evaluate a firm's performance over a given time period: a balance sheet showing a firm's performance at the beginning of a year, a balance sheet for the end of the year, and an income statement spanning the time period between the two balance sheets.

10-4. Use the income statement and balance sheets to compute a company's cash flows.

- A cash flow statement shows the sources of a firm's cash as well as its uses of cash.
- A cash flow statement is comprised of three sections: (1) cash flows from daily operations (operating activities), (2) cash flows related to the investment in fixed assets (investing activities), and (3) cash flows related to financing the firm (financing activities).
- Cash flows from operations are calculated by adding back the depreciation expense to the net profits and then subtracting any uncollected sales and payments for inventory. Only depreciation expense and net profits are used from the income statement.
- Investments in fixed assets are recorded in the statement of cash flows as a change in gross fixed assets, as shown in a firm's balance sheets.
- Financing a business involves borrowing money, repaying debts, investing by owners, and paying dividends or selling/repurchasing stock.
- In a cash flow statement, the only changes ignored in a firm's balance sheets are changes in accumulated depreciation, net fixed assets, and retained earnings.

10-5. Analyze the financial statements using ratios to see more clearly how decisions affect a firm's financial performance.

- Financial ratios help examine a firm's (1) ability to pay debt as it comes due, (2) profitability from assets, (3) use of debt, and (4) rate of return to owners.
- A firm's ability to pay debt as it comes due (its liquidity) is most often evaluated by looking at a firm's current ratio (current assets divided by current liabilities).
- A company's profitability on assets is measured by calculating a company's return on assets (operating profits divided by total assets).
- The debt ratio is used to evaluate the total amount of debt used by the company to finance its assets (total debt divided by total assets).
- The return on equity is the rate of return earned by owners on their equity investment (net profits divided by total owners' equity).

Key Terms

operating profits p. 264
other assets p. 271
owners' equity p. 272
profit margins p. 266
profits before taxes (taxable profits) p. 264
retained earnings p. 273
return on assets p. 286
return on equity p. 287
short-term notes p. 272
total asset turnover p. 286
working capital cycle p. 271

You Make the Call

Situation 1

The Donahoo Western Furnishings Company was formed on December 31, 2014, with $1,000,000 in equity plus $500,000 in long-term debt. On January 1, 2015, all of the firm's capital was held in cash. The following transactions occurred during January 2015:

- January 2: Donahoo purchased $1,000,000 worth of furniture for resale. It paid $500,000 in cash and financed the balance using trade credit that required payment in 60 days.
- January 3: Donahoo sold $250,000 worth of furniture that it had paid $200,000 to acquire. The entire sale was on credit terms of net 90 days.
- January 15: Donahoo purchased more furniture for $200,000. This time, it used trade credit for the entire amount of the purchase, with credit terms of net 60 days.
- January 31: Donahoo sold $500,000 worth of furniture, for which it had paid $400,000. The furniture was sold for 10 percent cash down, with the remainder payable in 90 days. In addition, the firm paid a cash dividend of $100,000 to its stockholders and paid off $250,000 of its long-term debt.

Question 1 What did Donahoo's balance sheet look like at the outset of the firm's life?

Question 2 What did the firm's balance sheet look like after each transaction?

Question 3 Ignoring taxes, determine how much income Donahoo earned during January. Prepare an income statement for the month. Recognize an interest expense of 1 percent for the month (12 percent annually) on the $500,000 long-term debt, which has not been paid but is owed.

Question 4 What was Donahoo's cash flow for the month of January?

Situation 2

At the beginning of 2015, Mary Abrahams purchased a small business, the Maitz Company, whose income statement and balance sheets are shown below.

Income Statement for the Maitz Company for 2015

Sales		$175,000
Cost of goods sold		(105,000)
Gross profits		$ 70,000
Operating expenses:		
Depreciation	$ 5,000	
Administrative expenses	20,000	
Selling expenses	26,000	
Total operating expenses		$ (51,000)
Operating profits		$ 19,000
Interest expense		(3,000)
Profits before taxes		$ 16,000
Taxes		(8,000)
Net profits		$ 8,000

Balance Sheets for the Maitz Company for 2014 and 2015

Assets	**2014**	**2015**
Current assets:		
Cash	$ 8,000	$ 10,000
Accounts receivable	15,000	20,000
Inventory	22,000	25,000
Total current assets	$45,000	$ 55,000
Fixed assets:		
Gross fixed assets	$50,000	$ 55,000
Accumulated depreciation	(15,000)	(20,000)
Net fixed assets	$35,000	$ 35,000
Other assets	12,000	10,000
TOTAL ASSETS	$92,000	$100,000
Debt (Liabilities) and Equity		
Current debt:		
Accounts payable	$10,000	$ 12,000
Accruals	7,000	8,000
Short-term notes	5,000	5,000
Total current debt	$22,000	$ 25,000
Long-term debt	15,000	15,000
Total debt	$37,000	$ 40,000
Equity	$55,000	$ 60,000
TOTAL DEBT AND EQUITY	$92,000	$100,000

The firm has been profitable, but Abrahams has been disappointed by the lack of cash flows. She had hoped to have about $10,000 a year available for personal living expenses. However, there never seems to be much cash available for purposes other than business needs. Abrahams has asked you to examine the financial statements and explain why, although they show profits, she does not have any discretionary cash for personal needs. She observed, "I thought that I could take the profits and add back depreciation to find out how much cash I was generating. However, that doesn't seem to be the case. What's happening?"

Question 1 Given the information provided by the financial statements, what would you tell Abrahams? (As part of your answer, calculate the firm's cash flows.)

Question 2 How would you describe the cash flow pattern for the Maitz Company?

Situation 3

Philip Spencer, the owner of Wholesome Foods, has hired you to evaluate his firm's financial performance. The firm's financial data is provided below, along with an average for the financial ratios that Spencer collected on several competing peer firms.

Question 1 Compute the financial ratios discussed in the chapter for Wholesome Foods for 2014 and 2015.

Question 2 Prepare a cash flow statement for the firm for 2014 and 2015.

Question 3 Interpret your findings, both for the firm's financial ratios compared to those of the peer group and for the cash flow statement.

Assets	**2013**	**2014**	**2015**
Cash	$ 21,000	$ 20,200	25,000
Accounts receivable	42,000	33,000	46,000
Inventory	51,000	84,000	96,000
Prepaid rent	1,200	1,100	2,000
Total current assets	$ 115,200	$ 138,300	$ 169,000
Gross property, plant, and equipment	650,000	664,000	740,000
Accumulated depreciation	(364,000)	(394,000)	(434,000)
Net property, plant, and equipment	$ 286,000	$ 270,000	$ 306,000
TOTAL ASSETS	$ 401,200	$ 408,300	$ 475,000

Debt (Liabilities) and Equity	**2013**	**2014**	**2015**
Accounts payable	$ 48,000	$ 57,000	$ 52,400
Accrued expenses	9,500	9,000	12,000
Short-term notes	11,500	9,000	20,000
Total current liabilities	$ 69,000	$ 75,000	$ 84,400
Long-term debt	160,000	150,000	185,000
Common stock	$ 22,200	$ 22,200	$ 34,500
Retained earnings	150,000	161,100	171,100
Total owners' equity	$ 172,200	$ 183,300	$ 205,600
TOTAL DEBT AND EQUITY	$ 401,200	$ 408,300	$ 475,000

Income Statement	**2014**	**2015**
Sales	$ 600,000	$ 650,000
Cost of goods sold	(460,000)	(487,500)
Gross profits	$ 140,000	$ 162,500
Operating expenses:		
General and administrative expenses	$ 30,000	$ 37,500
Depreciation expense	30,000	40,000
Total operating expenses	$ 60,000	$ 77,500

Income Statement	2014	2015
Operating profits	$ 80,000	$ 85,000
Interest expense	(10,000)	(12,000)
Profits before taxes	$ 70,000	$ 73,000
Taxes	(27,100)	(30,000)
Net profits	$ 42,900	$ 43,000
Net profits	$ 42,900	$ 43,000
Dividends paid	(31,800)	(33,000)
Addition to retained earnings	$ 11,100	$ 10,000

Financial Ratios (Averages)	Peer Companies
Current ratio	1.80
Return on assets	16.8%
Operating profit margin	14.0%
Total asset turnover	1.20
Debt ratio	0.50
Return on equity	18.0%

Case 10

Harper & Reiman, LLC (P. 662)

Haprer & Reiman, LLC caters to non-profit organizations. The company has experienced significant growth, with sales approaching $29 million in 2014—far beyond anything Harper & Reiman could have imagined. For one thing, the firm distinguished itself in the industry by designing a payment system that serves non-profits by allowing them to make payments in seasons when donations are the highest. This case allows students to evaluate the firm's financial performance. This case was prepared by Lauren Houser, April 2013.

Alternative Case for Chapter 10

Video Case 10, B2B CFO [website only]

Endnotes

1. Norm Brodsky, "Secrets of a $110 Million Man," *Inc.*, October 2008, p. 77.
2. Philip Campbell, "Are You Really Focused on Profits?" *Inc.*, June 2008, http://www.inc.com/resources/finance/articles/20060601/campbell.html, accessed December 15, 2012.
3. Quoted in "How to Manage Cash Flows," http://www.inc.com/encyclopedia/cashflow.html, accessed February 3, 2011.
4. Jan Norman, "You're Making Sales, but Are You Making Money?" *Entrepreneur*, March 2004, http://www.entrepreneur.com/article/15728, accessed January 11, 2013.

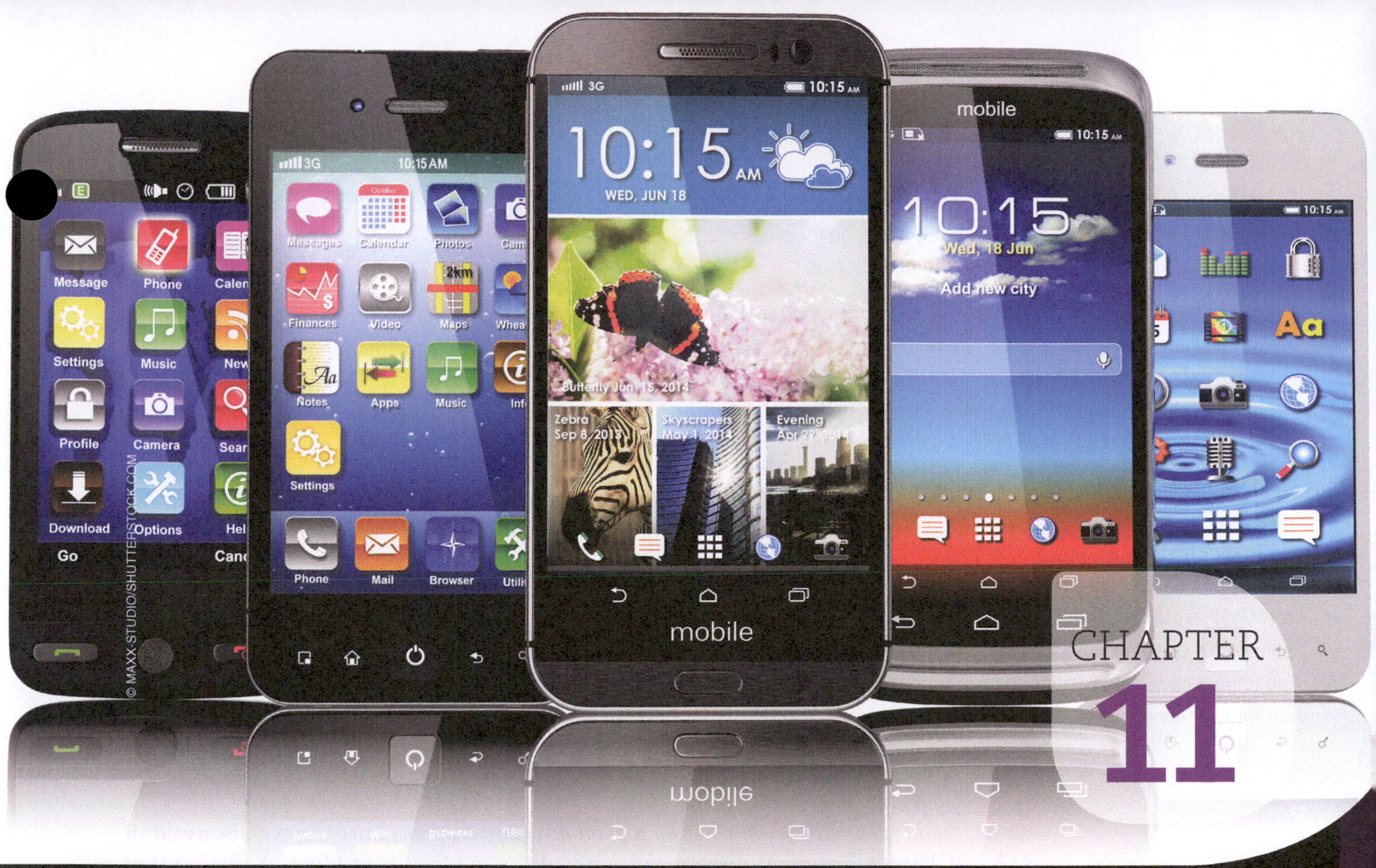

CHAPTER 11

Forecasting Financial Requirements

Managing rapid growth can become an entrepreneur's worst nightmare. Unhappy customers and employees, a lack of cash, and the inability to fill orders can overwhelm a small business owner who hasn't prepared for the challenges that growth brings. "They're too busy working in the business to work on the business," observes Jeff DeGraff, professor at the Ross School of Business at the University of Michigan. But taking the time to plan for growth, especially when it's unexpected, can keep a small business on track.

When Ahmed Khattak arrived at Yale University as an international student with no credit and no ability to access the traditional cell phone market, he was unable to call his family in Pakistan. In response to the problem, Khattak revolutionized the cell phone industry through his company, GSM Nation, providing not only himself but also others like him an easy way to purchase a cell phone without the hassle of a binding contract.

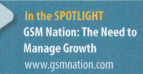

In the SPOTLIGHT
GSM Nation: The Need to Manage Growth
www.gsmnation.com

Khattak's first hurdle was to obtain seed funding for his startup. An initial loan of $30,000 came from his family and friends, followed by an investment from GSM Nation's co-founder, Junaid Shams. The new venture proved to be successful from the very beginning. Khattak says,

> *It's hard to put a finger on a particular occasion when I thought we were going to be successful because we have surpassed our wildest imaginations. I mean, think of it, in excess of $50 million in sales in just over two years. We have*

After studying this chapter, you should be able to…

11-1. Describe the purpose of financial forecasting.

11-2. Develop a pro forma income statement to forecast a new venture's profitability.

11-3. Determine a company's asset and financing requirements using a pro forma balance sheet.

11-4. Forecast a firm's cash flows.

11-5. Provide some suggestions for effective financial forecasting.

taken such huge leaps that every six months we have a new aim and we literally treat that as our starting point.

The fast-paced growth, however, brought with it significant financial forecasting challenges, particularly involving the projection and management of cash flow. According to Shams,

> *[T]he biggest mistake we made in the early going was not having as much funding as we originally thought we needed. We were growing so fast the first 6 to 12 months, faster than what even we had expected, that we didn't have the funding at the time necessary to allow us to grow at the same pace.*

GSM Nation now sells to a wide variety of retailers and end-users in the United States, Europe, Asia-Pacific, and Australia. In recent years, the company has again experienced high demand and growth as it has moved into the mobile virtual network operator (MVNO) realm to complement its cell phone offerings. MVNO plans allow customers to scale their text and data usage according to their needs and to purchase more, if necessary. Although currently offering beta service to about 500 customers, Khattak says that experts predict usage to increase to 100,000 customers within 12 to 14 months.

Today, the co-founders' concerns are still about managing growth, making certain that the products keep moving, and cash flows stay positive. The challenge for the company will be to apply lessons learned as a startup to its next round of rapid expansion.

© ZEYNEP DEMIR/SHUTTERSTOCK.COM

Sources: Excerpts from Marty Jerome, "Young Entrepreneur Changes the U.S. Cell Phone Market," *Entrepreneur*, December 2012, http://www.entrepreneur.com/article/224539, accessed January 27, 2015; Elaine Pofeldt, "They're Young, They're Smart—And You Probably Couldn't Pay Them Enough to Work at Your Company," http://www.forbes.com/sites/elainepofeldt/2012/03/20/theyre-young-and-smart-and-you-probably-couldnt-pay-them-enough-to-work-at-your-company, accessed January 11, 2015; "GSM Nation—About Us," http://www.gsmnation.com/about-us, accessed January 28, 2015; and Mike Dano, "Phone Retailer GSM Nation Launches US Mobile MVNO to Target $25/Month Market," *Fierce Wireless*, September 26, 2014, http://www.fiercewireless.com/story/phone-retailer-gsm-nation-launches-us-mobile-mvno-target-25month-market/2014-09-26, accessed February 27, 2015.

A good idea may or may not be a good investment opportunity. As we discussed in Chapter 3, a good investment opportunity requires a product or service that meets a definite customer need and creates a sustainable competitive advantage. To be attractive, an opportunity must generate strong profits relative to the required amount of investment. Therefore, projections of a venture's profits, its asset and financing requirements, and its cash flows are essential in determining whether a venture is economically viable.

11-1 THE PURPOSE OF FINANCIAL FORECASTING

Describe the purpose of financial forecasting.

In Chapter 10, we followed the Lemonade Kids to see the accounting implications of what was happening in their venture. In that very simple world, there was really no need to plan for the future. Everything just worked out okay. But that is not the case when starting and operating a business with any complexity. In the real world, you need to forecast, as best you can, the financial outcomes that could result from your decisions.

Granted, the numbers never work out the way you planned. But the process allows you to understand what drives your numbers, and that's very important to lenders and investors. Whether you are applying for your first (or tenth) bank loan or pitching to investors, sooner or later you will have to prepare a set of financial projections. Lenders will look at what the numbers say about the likelihood of repayment. Investors will attempt to value your company based on the numbers.

pro forma financial statements
Statements that project a firm's financial performance and condition, including a firm's projected profits, assets and financing requirements, and cash flows.

The purpose of **pro forma financial statements** is to answer three questions:

1. How profitable can you expect the firm to be, given the projected sales levels and the expected sales-expenses relationships?

2. How much and what type of financing (debt or equity) will be needed to finance a firm's assets?
3. Will the firm have adequate cash flows? If so, how will they be used? If not, where will the additional cash come from?

Preparing historical financial statements, such as income statements, balance sheets, and cash flow statements, is not a difficult task. However, *projecting* what may happen to a business in the future in terms of profits and cash flows is another matter.

For an established firm, you at least have the benefit of past data, in terms of both past revenues and what your costs and expenses have been. You basically need to anticipate how your market could change, what you will be doing differently in the future, and how the changes will affect the financial numbers. The main difficulty here is predicting sales, which can be greatly affected by influences outside of the business itself.

When starting a new business, however, there is limited, if any, past experience on which to base your numbers. You make assumptions, which may feel like no more than educated guesses. But it can be done, as business plan consultant Rhonda Abrams explains:

> *The best place to start is by speaking with others in your industry, attending trade shows, and contacting your industry association. Another excellent source is the Risk Management Association Annual Statement Studies, which look at actual financial statements of companies in certain industries.*[1]

Once financial projections have been prepared, the process should not stop there. Because of the uncertainty of what can happen, the small business owner should always be asking, "What could go wrong, and if it does happen, what will I do?" For instance, you want to plan how to respond if sales are significantly lower or higher than projected. A firm can get into trouble not only when sales are inadequate, but also when the firm is experiencing high growth.

When seeking financing, an entrepreneur must be able to give informed answers about the firm's needs, including the amount of money required, the purposes for which it will be used, and when and how the lender or creditor will be paid back. Only careful financial planning can provide answers to these questions.

Let's take a look at the process for projecting a firm's profitability, asset and financing requirements, and cash flows. This process should be based on a carefully developed *business model* (see Chapter 6).

11-2 FORECASTING PROFITABILITY

Develop a pro forma income statement to forecast a new venture's profitability.

Profits reward an owner for investing in a company and constitute *a primary source of financing for future growth if reinvested in the business.* Therefore, it is essential for an entrepreneur to truly understand the factors that drive a company's profits (see Exhibit 10.1 for an overview of the income statement). To forecast profitability, an entrepreneur needs to know what will determine the five following components of an income statement going forward:

1. *Amount of sales.* The dollar amount of sales equals the price of the product or service times the number of units sold or the amount of service rendered.
2. *Cost of goods sold.* Cost of goods sold is the cost of producing or purchasing the firm's products or services. These costs can either be *fixed* (those that do not vary with a change in sales volume) or *variable* (those that change proportionally with sales).

3. *Operating expenses.* These expenses relate to marketing and distributing the product, general and administrative expenses, and depreciation expenses. Like cost of goods sold, operating expenses can be fixed or variable in nature.
4. *Interest expense.* An entrepreneur who borrows money agrees to pay interest on the loan principal. For example, a loan of $25,000 for a full year at a 12 percent interest rate results in an interest expense of $3,000 for the year ($\$3{,}000 = 0.12 \times \$25{,}000$).
5. *Taxes.* A firm's income taxes are figured as a percentage of profits before taxes, or what is also called taxable profits.

A hypothetical example demonstrates how to estimate a new venture's profits.[2] David Allen is planning to start a new business called D&R Products, Inc., which will do wood trim work for luxury homes. In thinking about how to build a company that is economically viable in terms of profits and cash flows, Allen envisions a *revenue model* based on two complementary revenue streams: product design and product sales/installations.

1. *Product design.* For customers who want to be engaged in the creation of their own wood trim for new homes or renovations, D&R will provide user-friendly design software. In addition, the firm has developed alliances with professional interior designers who will work with the customer to create a design that is not only aesthetically pleasing but also architecturally sound. Finally, an open platform will allow customers to interface with other customers who are designing their own wood trim. D&R will receive 10 percent of the interior designers' revenue stream resulting from working with D&R contacts. While Allen does not see this revenue stream as a major source of sales, he does expect it to lead to increased product sales and installations.

© PICS721/SHUTTERSTOCK.COM

2. *Product sales/installations.* The primary source of revenues for D&R will be the actual sale and installation of product in new and renovated homes, with plans to eventually expand to larger commercial projects.

In terms of the company's *cost structure,* Allen has carefully identified expected fixed and variable costs of goods sold and operating expenses. The firm will have a cost advantage in the form of a newly developed lathe that will allow it to adapt to varying design specifications in a very economical manner. Finally, Allen has determined the asset investments that will be required in order to gain positive cash flows.

After extensive interviews with prospective customers, building contractors, and suppliers, along with industry research, Allen has made the following estimates for the first two years of operations:

1. *Amount of sales.*
   a. *Year 1:* Allen already has contracts for 10 jobs and expects to acquire another 10, or 20 jobs in total, by the end of the first year at an average price

of \$12,500 per job. Thus, revenue from product sales and installations is projected to be \$250,000 in the first year, computed as follows:

$$20 \text{ jobs} \times \$12,500 \text{ average price per job} = \$250,000$$

Allen further estimates that revenue from product design will only amount to \$10,000 in this first year. So total revenues for year 1 are projected to be \$260,000:

Product sales and installations	\$250,000
Product design	10,000
Total revenues	\$260,000

b. *Year 2:* Allen forecasts 30 jobs in the second year, again believing that the average revenue per job will be \$12,500. He also expects \$25,000 in product design sales, for total revenues of \$400,000:

Product sales and installations	\$375,000
Product design	25,000
Total revenues	\$400,000

2. *Cost of goods sold.* For product and installation sales, the fixed cost of goods sold (including production costs and employee salaries) is expected to amount to \$100,000 per year, while the variable costs of production will be around 20 percent of product sales and installations. In addition, there will be fixed costs of \$10,000 per year related to product design.
3. *Operating expenses.* The firm's fixed operating expenses (marketing expenses, general and administrative expenses) are estimated to be \$46,000 per year. In addition, depreciation will be \$4,000 annually. The variable operating expenses will be approximately 30 percent of product sales and installations. There will be no operating costs for product designs.
4. *Interest expense.* Based on the anticipated amount of money to be borrowed and the corresponding interest rate, Allen expects interest expense to be \$8,000 in the first year, increasing to \$12,000 in the second year.
5. *Taxes.* Income taxes will be 25 percent of profits before taxes (taxable profits).

Given the above estimates, we can forecast D&R Products' profits, as shown in the pro forma income statement in Exhibit 11.1. We first enter our assumptions in a spreadsheet (rows 3–18). Then, in rows 20–44, we see the two years of pro forma income statements (columns B and C) and the equations used to compute the numbers (columns D and E), where

- Rows 22 and 23 show the projected revenues for product sales and installations (row 22) and for product design activities (row 23).
- Row 24 shows total sales.
- Rows 28–30 provide the cost of goods sold for product sales and installations.
- Row 31 gives us the expected costs of \$10,000 for product design.
- Row 32 then sums the costs of goods sold for both product sales and installations and product design to arrive at the total cost of goods sold.
- Row 33 gives us gross profits, which equals total sales less total cost of goods sold.

EXHIBIT **11.1** Pro Forma Income Statements For D&R Products, Inc.

	A	B	C	D	E
3	INCOME STATEMENT ASSUMPTIONS:				
4		**Year 1**	**Year 2**		
5	Product sales and installations:				
6	Number of projected jobs	20	30		
7	Average selling price per job	$ 12,500	$ 12,500		
8	Fixed cost of goods sold	$100,000	$100,000		
9	Fixed operating expenses	$ 46,000	$ 46,000		
10	Depreciation expense	$ 4,000	$ 12,000		
11	Interest expense	$ 8,000	$ 8,000		
12	Variable cost of goods sold	20%	20%		
13	Variable operating expenses	30%	30%	**Equations based on assumptions**	
14	Product design:				
15	Projected design revenues	$ 10,000	$ 25,000		
16	Fixed design costs	$ 10,000	$ 10,000		
17					
18	Income tax rate	25%	25%		
19				*Equations for:*	
20				***Year 1***	***Year 2***
21	Sales:				
22	Product sales and installations	$250,000	$375,000	=B6*B7	=C6*C7
23	Product design	10,000	25,000	=B15	=C15
24	Total sales	$260,000	$400,000	=SUM(B22:B23)	=SUM(C22:C23)
25					
26	Cost of goods sold				
27	Cost of goods sold: product sales and installations				
28	Fixed cost of goods sold	$100,000	$100,000	=B8	=C8
29	Variable cost of goods sold (20% of product sales)	50,000	75,000	=B22*B12	=C22*C12
30	Total cost of goods sold: product sales and installations	$150,000	$175,000	=SUM(B28:B29)	=SUM(C28:C29)
31	Total cost of goods sold: product design	10,000	10,000	=B16	=C16
32	Total cost of goods sold	$160,000	$185,000	=SUM(B30:B31)	=SUM(C30:C31)
33	Gross Profits	$100,000	$215,000	=B24-B32	=C24-C32
34					
35	Operating expenses: product sales and installations				
36	Fixed operating expenses	$ 46,000	$ 46,000	=B9	=C9
37	Variable operating expenses (30% of product sales)	75,000	112,500	=B13*B22	=C13*C22
38	Depreciation expense	4,000	4,000	=B10	=C10
39	Total operating expenses: product sales and installations	$125,000	$162,500	=SUM(B36:B38)	=SUM(C36:C38)
40	Operating profits	$ (25,000)	$ (52,500)	=B33-B39	=C33-C39
41	Interest expense (interest rate 12%)	8,000	12,000	=B11	=C11
42	Profits before taxes	$ (33,000)	$ 40,500	=B40-B41	=C40-C41
43	Taxes (25% of profits before tax)	0	10,125	0	=C42*C18
44	Net profits	$ (33,000)	$ 30,375	=B42-B43	=C42-C43

- Rows 36–39 present the anticipated operating expenses associated with product sales and installations; there are no operating expenses related to product design.
- Row 40, operating profits, equals gross profits less total operating expenses.
- Row 41 shows the interest expense for borrowing money.
- Row 42 is profits before taxes (operating profits less interest expense).
- Row 43 equals the tax expense. Since D&R Products is expected to have a loss in the first year, the taxes will be zero. The taxes in the second year are calculated as the tax rate (25 percent) multiplied by the profits before taxes. (In reality, the firm would not expect to pay taxes in the second year either, since tax laws allow a firm to carry losses in one year forward into future years. However, we are ignoring this reality in order to provide a simple example.)
- Row 44 shows the firm's projected net profits—profits before taxes minus income taxes.

These computations indicate that D&R Products is expected to have a $33,000 net loss in its first year, followed by a positive net profit of $30,375 in its second year. A startup typically experiences losses for a period of time, frequently as long as two or three years.[3] In a real-world situation, an entrepreneur should project the profits of a new company at least three years into the future (or five years into the future, if it can be done with some degree of confidence).

Let's now shift our attention from forecasting profits to estimating asset and financing requirements.

11-3 FORECASTING ASSET AND FINANCING REQUIREMENTS

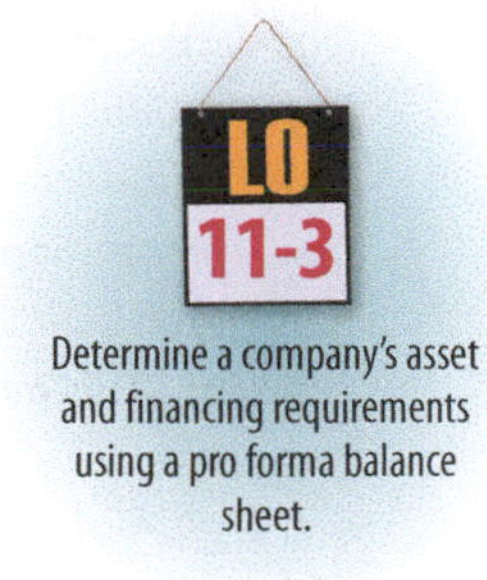

Determine a company's asset and financing requirements using a pro forma balance sheet.

The amount and types of assets required for a new venture will vary, depending on the nature of the business. High-technology businesses—such as computer manufacturers, designers of semiconductor chips, and pharmaceutical companies—often require millions of dollars in investment. Most service businesses, on the other hand, require minimal initial capital. For example, IRM Corporation, an information technology firm serving the food and beverage industry, has little in the way of assets. The firm leases its office space and has no inventory. Its only asset of any significance is accounts receivable.

Most firms of any size need both working capital (cash, accounts receivable, inventory, etc.) and fixed assets (property, plant, and equipment). For instance, a food store requires operating cash, inventory, and possibly limited accounts receivable. In addition, the owner will have to acquire cash registers, shopping carts, shelving, office equipment, and a building. The need to invest in assets results in a corresponding need for financing.

Working capital is another term used in the business world for current assets—namely, cash, accounts receivable, and inventory that are required in the day-to-day operations of the business. *It has nothing to do with property, plant, and equipment.* Also, the term is sometimes used loosely to mean current assets less current liabilities, which is really **net working capital**. Net working capital is a measure of a company's liquidity. The greater a firm's net working capital, the greater its ability to pay on any debt commitment as it comes due.[4]

net working capital
A measure of a company's liquidity; current assets less current liabilities.

Too frequently, small business owners tend to underestimate the amount of capital the business requires. Consequently, the financing they get may be inadequate. Without the money to invest in assets, they try to do without anything that is not absolutely essential and to spend less money on essential items. When Dan Cassidy

Living the Dream

ENTREPRENEURIAL EXPERIENCES

Financial Planning Makes a Difference at REEcycle

REEcycle was founded by three students from the University of Houston, led by Casey McNeil as the firm's CEO. The company reclaims precious materials known as *rare earth elements* from recycling companies that have no use for them.

A primary example of these unwanted materials is earth magnets, which are used in computer hard drives. After purchasing unwanted magnets from e-waste companies, REEcycle uses a patented process to extract the critical rare earth elements locked inside. The firm then sells the recycled elements to companies that will use these materials to design cutting-edge technologies, including electric cars, wind turbines, and even missile guidance systems.

The owners discovered early on just how difficult it would be to raise funding, such as venture capital, for such a high-risk venture. In part, it was a *chicken-and-egg problem:* without funding, large prototypes could not be built; but without a prototype, funds could not be raised. So, the three founders decided to compete in various business plan competitions across the United States. They successfully raised over $300,000 in cash and in-kind prizes for the company. This money was quickly put to use.

© ARTEM_KA/SHUTTERSTOCK.COM

One of the problems that REEcycle faced was finding investors interested in funding a company at such an early stage. Furthermore, the business was not working on a problem that could be solved in a garage; it required large facilities and extensive use of heavy equipment. Another issue was the price volatility of their product. It experienced some of the most volatile swings ever seen in commodities markets. Businesses were literally living and dying by the swings of the market. Thus, timing the market correctly was an important risk factor.

To get the odds in their favor, the management team needed to purchase the most critically necessary elements for their product in a way that would balance supply and demand. For this to happen, they needed the ability to forecast the financial consequences of their decisions. For example, they decided to use three-year averages for the prices of the elements the company produced, allowing them to set a "floor" price point that the company would have to stay above in order to be successful. This allowed the company to set benchmarks for the efficiencies that had to be met in all aspects of the process and forced the founders to develop strategies for keeping all costs at a bare minimum. This way of thinking prevented REEcycle from becoming overzealous in its financial projections, which might lead to a lack of trust by investors and, ultimately, the company's demise.

The company now operates out of the University of Houston's Energy Research Park. Because of the significant risk involved in scaling up the scientific processes used by the company, REEcycle plans on using funds from competitions and grants to completely scale the company before any investor funding is taken. This not only mitigates the risk taken by investors, but also significantly increases the amount of control that the founders will have over the company for years to come.

Source: Written by Casey McNeil, founder and CEO, Reecycle, Inc., March 15, 2015.

started Baha's Fajita Bar, a restaurant aimed at serving college students, his goal was to raise $100,000 in capital. However, he opened the restaurant when he had raised only $70,000. In six months, he ran out of cash and had to close the restaurant. The problem became critical when students went home for spring break and were slow to eat at restaurants in the week following their return to school. Cassidy's unfortunate experience shows just how risky it can be for a small business to ignore the potential for unexpected challenges and underestimate its capital needs.[5]

© AFRICA STUDIO/SHUTTERSTOCK.COM

While being undercapitalized is rarely, if ever, a good decision, the goal of the entrepreneur should be to minimize and control, rather than to maximize and own resources. To the greatest extent possible, the entrepreneur should use other people's resources—for instance, leasing equipment rather than buying, negotiating with suppliers to provide inventory "just in time" to minimize tied-up inventory, and arranging to collect money owed the firm before having to pay its bills. As discussed in Chapter 1, this is called *bootstrapping*, and it's one of the most common ways entrepreneurs accomplish more with less. When Cecilia Levine, the owner of MFI International, a manufacturing firm, had the opportunity to get a contract to make clothing for a Fortune 500 company, she became a master of bootstrapping.

> *I never expected the fast growth and demand that my services would have. To finance the growth, debt financing would have been helpful, but it was not an option. The definition of credit in the dictionary reads, "The ability of a customer to obtain goods or services before payment, based on the trust that payment is going to be made in the future." What it does not say is that for a banker, trust means having collateral, and without collateral you don't get credit. But I still had children to feed and the desire to succeed so I looked for another form of financing—bootstrapping.*
>
> *I had a major customer who believed in me, and who had the equipment I needed. He sold me the equipment and then would reduce his weekly payment of my invoices by an amount to cover the cost of the equipment. Also, the customer paid me each Friday for what we produced and shipped that week. Everyone who worked for me understood that if we didn't perform and finish the needed production for the week, we didn't get paid by our customer. When I received the payment from the customer, I was then able to pay my employees. We were a team, and we understood the meaning of cash flow. Therefore, we performed.*[6]

Working with a limited amount of capital makes forecasting all the more important because you have less room for error. Moreover, the uncertainties surrounding an entirely new venture make estimating asset and financing requirements difficult. Even for an established business, forecasts are never perfect. There are always surprises—you can count on it.

In gathering needed information for financial forecasting, an entrepreneur should search for relevant information from a variety of sources. Risk Management Association, Dun & Bradstreet, banks, trade associations, and similar organizations compile financial information for a variety of industries.

Along with public data, common sense and educated guesswork should also be used. Continually ask yourself, "Does this make economic sense?" and "What could go wrong?" However, no source of information can compare with talking to prospective customers. Sitting in a room with your computer, without ever getting out and talking to potential customers, is a certain way to miss the obvious.

The key to effectively forecasting financing requirements is first to understand the relationship between a firm's projected sales and its assets. A firm's sales are the

"What If" Scenarios

When it comes to financial forecasting and budgeting, you should always prepare at least three scenarios: one with an aggressive forecast for sales increases, another using more conservative assumptions, and a third with worst-case scenarios. This is particularly important in an environment where future demand is unclear, as in the last economic downturn. Remember that a spreadsheet is a great tool to evaluate "what if" scenarios when forecasting profits and cash flows.

EXHIBIT **11.2** Assets-To-Sales Financing Relationships

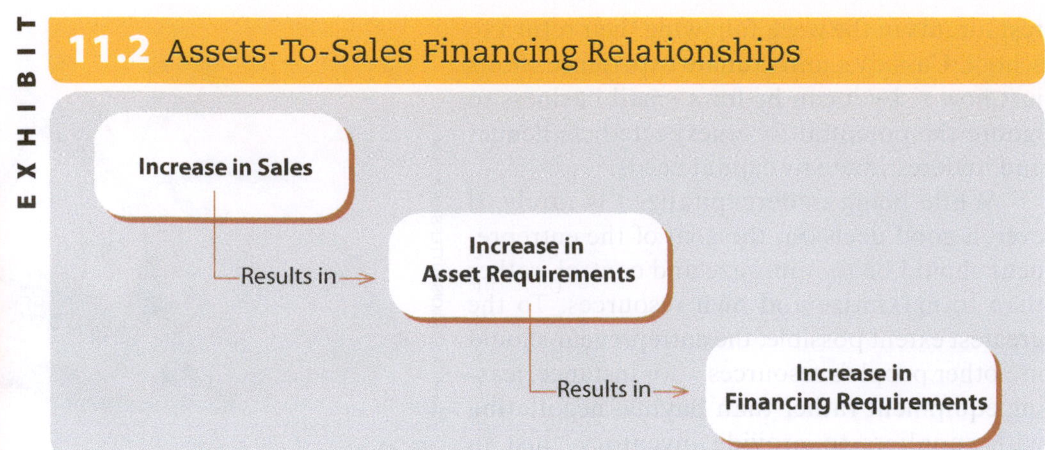

primary force driving future asset needs. Exhibit 11.2 depicts this relationship, which can be expressed simply as follows: *The greater a firm's sales, the greater the asset requirements will be and, in turn, the greater the need for financing.*

11-3a Determining Asset Requirements

Since asset needs increase as sales increase, a firm's asset requirements are often estimated as a percentage of sales. Therefore, if future sales have been projected, a ratio of assets to sales can be used to estimate asset requirements. Suppose, for example, that a firm's sales are expected to be $1 million. If assets in the firm's particular industry tend to run about 50 percent of sales, the firm's asset requirements would be estimated to be 0.50 × $1,000,000, or $500,000.

Although the assets-to-sales relationship varies over time and with individual businesses, it tends to be relatively constant within an industry. For example, assets as a percentage of sales average 20 percent for grocery stores, compared with 65 percent for oil and gas companies. This method of estimating asset requirements is called the **percentage-of-sales technique**. It can also be used to project figures for individual assets, such as accounts receivable and inventory.

percentage-of-sales technique A method of forecasting asset requirements.

To illustrate the percentage-of-sales technique, let's return to D&R Products, Inc., where we will estimate the firm's asset requirements for the first two years, given the company's sales projections. In Exhibit 11.1, the firm's pro forma income statements, product and installation sales (not including the $10,000 of design revenues) were forecasted to be $250,000 and $375,000 in years 1 and 2, respectively. After considerable investigation of the opportunity, Allen estimated the firm's current asset requirements (cash, accounts receivable, and inventory) as a percentage of product and installation sales:

Current Assets	Current Assets as a Percentage of Sales
Cash	4%
Accounts receivable	10%
Inventory	25%

Allen will need equipment that will cost $10,000. Also, he has found a building suitable for a manufacturing facility for $40,000. Combined, these two items total $50,000 and will be reflected in a balance sheet as *gross fixed assets*.

Net fixed assets are equal to gross fixed assets minus accumulated depreciation. Since the depreciation expense reported in the income statement (Exhibit 11.1) is $4,000 per year, then the accumulated depreciation will be $4,000 in year 1, increasing (accumulating) to $8,000 the next year. Given the anticipated sales and the assets-to-sales relationships, Allen is able to forecast the asset requirements for his venture. If product and installation sales are $250,000 in year 1 and $ 375,000 in year 2, Allen estimates the following:

Assets	Assumptions	Year 1	Year 2
Product and installation sales		$250,000	$375,000
Cash	4% of sales	$ 10,000	$ 15,000
Accounts receivable	10% of sales	25,000	37,500
Inventory	25% of sales	62,500	93,750
Total current assets		$ 97,500	$146,250
Gross fixed assets	Equipment and building costs	$ 50,000	$ 50,000
Accumulated depreciation	$4,000 annually	(4,000)	(8,000)
Net fixed assets		$ 46,000	$ 42,000
TOTAL ASSETS		$143,500	$188,250

So Allen expects to need $143,500 in assets by the end of the first year and $188,250 by the conclusion of the second year. However, at this point, he should test how sensitive the results of the model are to changes in the assumptions being made. He needs to determine which assumptions have the greatest impact on the outcomes. Then he can focus his research on what matters most.

At this point, Allen has a sense of the asset investments required to achieve the forecasted profits. Now, he needs to consider how these assets will be financed.

11-3b Determining Financing Requirements

There must be a corresponding dollar of financing for every dollar of assets. Stated another way, debt plus equity must equal total assets. To forecast a company's financing needs effectively, an entrepreneur must understand certain basic principles that govern the financing of firms, which can be stated as follows:

1. The more assets a business needs, the greater its financing requirements. Thus, a firm that is experiencing rapid sales growth requires more assets and, consequently, faces greater pressure to find financing—and that pressure can be unbearable if not managed carefully.
2. A company should finance its growth in such a way as to maintain adequate liquidity. (*Liquidity* measures the degree to which a firm has current assets available to meet maturing short-term debt.) The need for adequate liquidity in small firms deserves special emphasis. As already mentioned, a common weakness in small business financing is the tendency to maintain a disproportionately small investment in liquid assets, or what was defined earlier as *net working capital* (current assets − current liabilities). Even more specifically, in Chapter 10 we used the *current ratio* (current assets ÷ current liabilities) as a measure of liquidity that compares a firm's current assets to its current liabilities on a relative basis. To ensure payment of short-term debts as they come due, small business owners should, as a general rule, maintain a current ratio of at least 2—that

is, have current assets of at least two times the amount of current liabilities—or have a good reason for not doing so.

3. The amount of money that a firm can borrow is dependent in part on the amount of money the owners put into the business in the form of owners' equity. A bank would never provide *all* of the necessary financing for a firm. For example, a bank might specify that at least half of the firm's financing must come from owners' equity, while the rest can come from debt. In other words, the owners would have to limit the firm's *debt ratio* (total debt ÷ total assets) to 50 percent.
4. Some types of short-term debt—specifically, *accounts payable* and *accrued expenses*—maintain a relatively constant relationship with sales. For example, as sales increase, more inventories will be required. If the inventory is purchased on credit, accounts payable will increase as well. As a result, accounts payable will track increases in sales. If sales increase by $1, accounts payable might increase by $0.15, or 15 percent of sales. So, if you expect a $1,000 increase in sales, you can also expect accounts payable to increase by $150, which is 15 percent of the increase in sales. The same holds true for accrued expenses. More business means more expenses, some of which will be accrued as liabilities, rather than being paid immediately. Given the "spontaneous" relationship of these types of liabilities with sales, they are sometimes called **spontaneous debt financing**. While not the more formal type of debt, such as bank loans, these accrued liabilities can be a significantly large source of financing for many small companies. The rest of debt financing must come from loans by banks and other lending sources.
5. Owners' equity in a business comes from two sources: (1) investments the owners make in the business, and (2) profits that are retained within the company rather than being distributed to the owners, or *retained earnings*. Recall from Chapter 10 that

$$\text{Retained earnings} = \begin{matrix}\text{Cumulative total}\\ \text{of all net profits}\\ \text{over the life of the business}\end{matrix} - \begin{matrix}\text{Cumulative total}\\ \text{of all dividends paid}\\ \text{over the life of the business}\end{matrix}$$

We then can calculate the owners' total equity as follows:

$$\text{Owners' equity} = \begin{matrix}\text{Owners'}\\ \text{investment}\end{matrix} + \overbrace{\begin{matrix}\text{Cumulative}\\ \text{profits}\end{matrix} - \begin{matrix}\text{Cumulative dividends}\\ \text{paid to owners}\end{matrix}}^{\text{Earnings retained within the business}}$$

For the typical small firm, retained earnings are the primary source of equity capital for financing growth. (Be careful not to think of retained earnings as a cash resource. As already noted, a firm may have significant profits but no cash to reinvest.)

So the essence of the foregoing principles can be captured in the following equation:

$$\begin{matrix}\text{Total asset}\\ \text{requirement}\end{matrix} = \begin{matrix}\text{Total sources}\\ \text{of financing}\end{matrix} = \begin{matrix}\text{Spontaneous}\\ \text{debt financing}\end{matrix} + \begin{matrix}\text{Loans from}\\ \text{banks}\end{matrix} + \begin{matrix}\text{Owners'}\\ \text{Investment}\end{matrix} + \begin{matrix}\text{Retained}\\ \text{Earnings}\end{matrix}$$

Small business owners who thoroughly understand these five principles and their relationships with each other will be effective in forecasting their firm's financial requirements—and they will be effective in acquiring needed financing.

spontaneous debt financing
Short-term debts, such as accounts payable, that automatically increase in proportion to a firm's sales.

Recall that Allen projected asset requirements of $143,500 and $188,250 for years 1 and 2, respectively. He then made estimates of the financing requirements, based on the following facts and assumptions:

1. Allen negotiated with a supplier to receive 30 days' credit on inventory purchases, which results in accounts payable running about 8 percent of sales.
2. Allen also estimates that accrued expenses that will be shown as short-term liabilities in the balance sheet will amount to about 4 percent of sales. This approximation comes from his evaluation of accrued expenses in similar businesses.
3. Allen plans to invest $110,000 of his personal savings to provide the needed startup equity for the business. He will receive common stock in return for his investment.
4. A bank has agreed to provide a short-term line of credit of $25,000 to D&R Products. A **line of credit** is simply a short-term loan to help with temporary needs, such as seasonal increases in inventory. It works like a credit card—the company has the option to borrow up to the limit (in this case, $25,000) as needed and then pay it down when it is no longer needed.
5. The bank has also agreed to help finance the purchase of a building for manufacturing and warehousing the firm's products. Of the $40,000 needed to purchase the building, the bank will lend the firm $30,000, with the building serving as collateral for the loan. The loan will be repaid over 10 years in equal principal payments of $3,000 plus interest on the remaining note balance each year.
6. As part of the loan agreement, the bank has imposed two restrictions: (1) The firm's current ratio must remain at 2.0 or above, and (2) no more than 50 percent of the firm's financing may come from debt, both short-term and long-term (that is, total debt should be no more than 50 percent of total assets). Failure to comply with either of these conditions will cause the bank loan to come due immediately.

With this information, Allen can now estimate the sources of financing for D&R Products. If sales resulting from product and installations are $250,000 in year 1 and $375,000 in year 2, Allen estimates the following available sources of financing:

Sources of Financing	Assumptions	Year 1	Year 2
Accounts payable	8% of sales	$20,000	$ 30,000
Accrued expenses	4% of sales	$10,000	$15,000
Mortgage	$30,000 – $3,000 annual payments	$27,000	$24,000
Common stock	Owner's investment	$110,000	$110,000

Any remaining financing, up to $25,000, can come from the bank line of credit. If the line of credit is inadequate to meet the firm's needs, Allen will have to put more equity into the business.

Based on this information, Allen can now develop pro forma balance sheets for D&R Products. Exhibit 11.3 shows the assumptions made, the equations underlying the numbers, and the actual balance sheets, as developed in a spreadsheet. To help you visualize the results more easily, the balance sheets are also shown graphically in Exhibit 11.4. In looking at this exhibit, you need to remember two things:

1. Total assets and total sources of financing (debt and equity) must always balance. Note that D&R Products' total asset requirements of $143,500 for the first year and $188,250 for the second year are the same as the firm's total debt and equity.

line of credit
A short-term loan.

EXHIBIT

11.3 Pro Forma Balance Sheets For D&R Products, Inc.

	A	B	C	D	E
3	*BALANCE SHEET ASSUMPTIONS*	**Year 1**	**Year 2**		
4	Projected revenues: product sales and installations	$250,000	$375,000		
5	Cash/sales	4%	4%		
6	Account receivable/sales	10%	10%		
7	Inventory/sales	25%	25%		
8	Gross fixed assets	$ 50,000	$ 50,000	**Equations based on assumptions**	
9	Accounts payable/sales	8%	8%		
10	Accrued expenses/sales	4%	4%		
11	Cost of equipment	$ 10,000	$ 10,000		
12	Building cost	$ 40,000	$ 40,000		
13				*Equations for:*	
14	**Assets**			***Year 1***	***Year 2***
15	Cash	$ 10,000	$ 15,000	=B4*B5	=C4*C5
16	Accounts receivable	25,000	37,500	=B4*B6	=C4*C6
17	Inventory	62,500	93,750	=B4*B7	=C4*C7
18	Total current assets	$ 97,500	$146,250	=SUM(B15:B17)	=SUM(C15:C17)
19	Gross fixed assets	$ 50,000	$ 50,000	=B8	=C8
20	Accumulated depreciation	(4,000)	(8,000)	Depreciation expense for year 1	Accumulated depreciation expense for years 1 and 2
21	Net fixed assets	$ 46,000	$ 42,000	=B19+B20	=C19+C20
22	TOTAL ASSETS	$143,500	$188,250	=B18+B21	=C18+C21
23					
24	**Debt Liabilities and Equity**				
25	Accounts payable	$ 20,000	$ 30,000	=B4*B9	=C4*C9
26	Accrued expenses	10,000	15,000	=B4*B10	=C4*C10
27	Short-term line of credit	9,500	11,875	Required financing	Required financing
28	Total current liabilities	$ 39,500	$ 56,875	=SUM(B25:B27)	=SUM(C25:C27)
29	Mortgage	27,000	24,000	Original loan of $30,000-annual payment of $3,000	Year 1 balance of $27,000-annual payment of $3,000
30	Total debt	$ 66,500	$ 80,875	=SUM(B28:B29)	=SUM(C28:C29)
31	Ownership equity				
32	Common stock	$110,000	$110,000	Given	Given
33	Retained earnings	(33,000)	(2,625)	Year 1 loss	Year 1 loss + year 2 profit
34	Total ownership equity	$ 77,000	$107,375	=SUM(B32:B33)	=SUM(C32:C33)
35	TOTAL DEBT AND EQUITY	$143,500	$188,250	=SUM(B30:B33)	=SUM(C30:C33)
36					
37	Current ratio	$ 2.47	$ 2.57	=B18/B28	=C18/C28
38	Debt ratio	46%	43%	=B30/B35	=C30/C35

EXHIBIT **11.4** Pro Forma Balance Sheets for D&R Products, Inc.

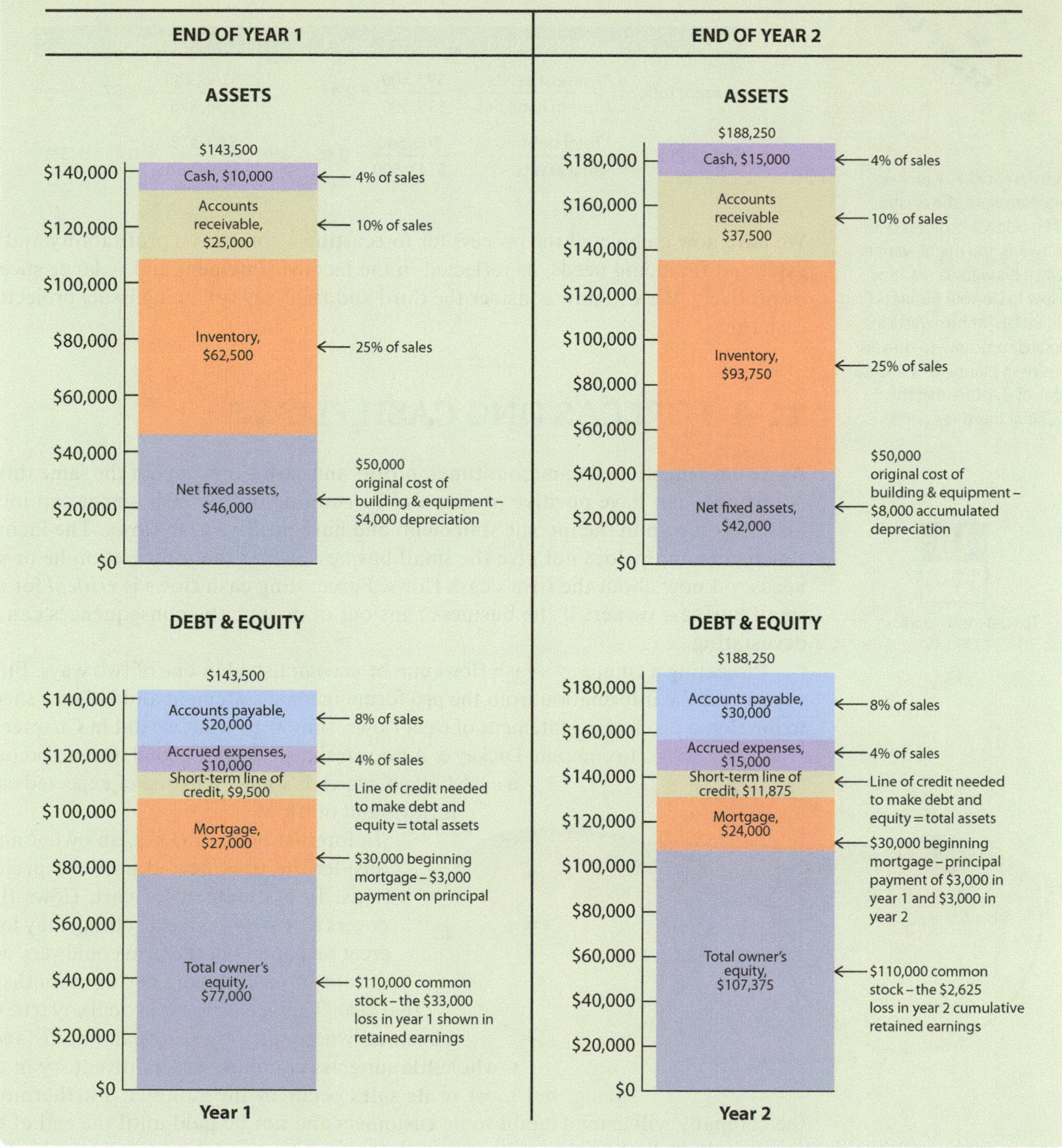

2. To bring sources of financing into balance with total assets, D&R Products will need to borrow on the company's $25,000 line of credit. By the end of the first year, $9,500 of the line of credit is needed to bring the total debt and equity to $143,500. In the second year, line-of-credit borrowing will increase to $11,875 to gain the $188,250 in total financing needed.

Finally, based on Allen's projections, the firm should be able to satisfy the bank's loan restrictions, maintaining both a current ratio of 2.0 or more and a debt ratio of less than 50 percent. The computations are as follows:

Ratio	Computation	Year 1	Year 2
Current ratio =	$\frac{\text{Current assets}}{\text{Current liabilities}}$ =	$\frac{\$97,500}{\$39,500} = 2.47$	$\frac{\$146,250}{\$56,875} = 2.57$
Debt ratio =	$\frac{\text{Total debt}}{\text{Total assets}}$ =	$\frac{\$66,500}{\$143,500} = 0.46 = 46\%$	$\frac{\$80,375}{\$188,250} = 0.43 = 43\%$

How to Do Your Business Plan Financials

Tim Berry works with Palo Alto Software, the creator of LivePlan, a business plan software. You might want to watch his webinar entitled, "How to Do Your Business Plan Financials" at http://articles.bplans.com/how-to-do-your-business-planning-financials-pt-1-of-3. (Note that the webinar has three parts.)

We have now completed the process for forecasting a company's profitability and its asset and financing needs, as reflected in the income statement and balance sheets, respectively. We will now consider the third and final key financing issue: projecting cash flows.

11-4 FORECASTING CASH FLOWS

Forecast a firm's cash flows.

As we have mentioned numerous times, profits and cash flows are not the same thing. A business can have positive profits and be running out of cash—or it can incur losses, as shown in the income statement, and have positive cash flows. The income statement simply does not give the small business owner the information he or she needs to know about the firm's cash flows. Forecasting cash flows is *critical* for the small business owner: If the business runs out of money, the consequences can be devastating.

Projecting a company's cash flows can be accomplished in one of two ways. First, we can use the information from the pro forma income statement and balance sheets to develop a pro forma statement of cash flows, similar to what we did in Chapter 10 to compute Dickey & Associates' cash flows. Second, we can prepare a cash budget, which is simply a listing of expected cash inflows and outflows.

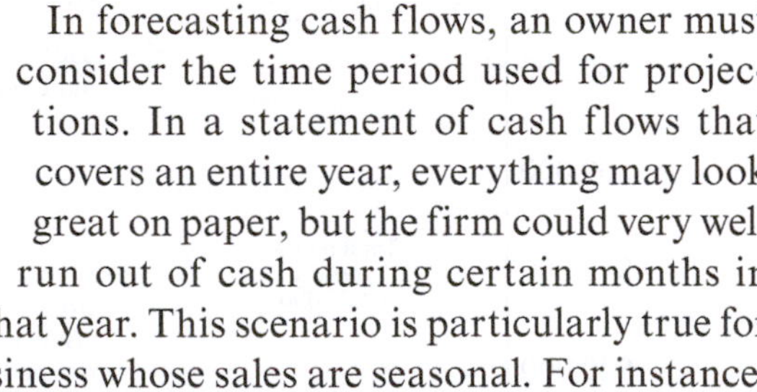

© VICTORIA BRASSEY/SHUTTERSTOCK.COM

In forecasting cash flows, an owner must consider the time period used for projections. In a statement of cash flows that covers an entire year, everything may look great on paper, but the firm could very well run out of cash during certain months in that year. This scenario is particularly true for a business whose sales are seasonal. For instance, a wholesale sunglass company orders inventory in the spring, but most of its sales occur in the summer. Furthermore, the company will extend credit to its customers and not be paid until the end of the summer. If we look at the company's cash flows on an annual basis, all may be well. But during the spring and early summer, there will be large investments in accounts receivable and inventory, putting extreme pressure on the firm's cash flows. In this instance, the owner would want to forecast cash flows on a monthly basis—maybe even on a weekly basis

In the next two sections, we use D&R Products, Inc., to illustrate how to forecast cash flows. First, we prepare pro forma statements of annual cash flows. Then, we illustrate how to prepare a monthly cash budget.

11-4a Pro Forma Statement of Cash Flows

The pro forma income statement and balance sheets for D&R Products, Inc., that we prepared earlier are now used to prepare a pro forma statement of cash flows, which is shown in Exhibit 11.5. (Recall that the process for preparing the *historical* statement of cash flows was explained in Chapter 10.) As you look at Exhibit 11.5, pay particular attention to (1) cash flows from operating activities, (2) cash flows from investing activities, and (3) cash flows from financing activities, which are shown in boxes in the exhibit. Looking at these numbers, we can see the following:

1. In the first year, the business is expected to have negative cash flows from operations of $86,500 and will be investing $50,000 in the building and equipment. To cover these negative cash flows, Allen expects to raise $146,500 in financing from his personal investment of $110,000, $9,500 on the line of credit from the bank, and $27,000 from the mortgage on the building after making the annual $3,000 payment on the principal. The firm would then end the year with $10,000 in cash. (Note that the change in the pro forma balance sheet for year 1 is the same as the year-end balance shown in the balance sheet, since the business did not exist in the prior year. The balance at the beginning of year 1 would have been zero.)
2. In the second year, the firm's cash flow operations are expected to be $5,625. (Notice that while the business is expected to have $5,625 in cash flows from operations, Allen anticipates having profits of $30,375. Remember, *cash flows and profits are not the same thing*.) Moreover, there are no plans to invest in fixed assets in the second year. Given his underlying assumptions, Allen would need

EXHIBIT **11.5** Pro Forma Cash Flow Statements For D&R Products, Inc.

		Year 1		Year 2	Sources of Information
Operating activities:					
Net profits		($ 33,000)		$30,375	***Pro forma income statement***
Depreciation		4,000		4,000	
Increase in accounts receivable (cash outflow)		($ 25,000)		($12,500)	
Increase in inventory (cash outflow)	($62,500)		($31,250)		***Changes in projected balance sheets from founding of business to year 1 and from year 1 to year 2***
Increase in accounts payable (cash inflow)	$20,000		$10,000		
Cash payments for inventory (cash outflow)		($ 42,500)		($21,250)	
Increase in accrued expenses (cash inflow)		10,000		5,000	
Cash flows from operations		**($ 86,500)**		**$5,625**	
Investing activites:					
Increase in gross fixed assets (cash outflow)		($ 50,000)		$ 0	
Cash flows from investing		**($50,000)**		**$ 0**	
Financing activities:					
Increase in short-term line of credit		**$ 9,500**		**$ 2,375**	
Increase (decrease) in mortgage		27,000		(3,000)	
Increase in stock		110,000		0	
Cash flows from financing		$146,500		($625)	
Increase (decrease) in cash		$ 10,000		$5,000	
Beginning cash		$ 0		$10,000	
Ending cash (as shown in the balance sheets)		$ 10,000		$15,000	

to increase the line of credit (short-term debt) from the bank from $9,500 in year 1 to $11,875 in year 2, for an increase of $2,375, and pay $3,000 on the mortgage. The resulting balance of all the cash flows would be a $5,000 increase in cash, for an ending cash balance of $15,000.

Allen now has a good estimate of the cash flows for each year as a whole and an idea of what contributes to the cash inflows and outflows. But there is also a need to track the firm's cash flows for a shorter time period, usually on a monthly basis.

11-4b The Cash Budget

The **cash budget** is one of the primary tools that a small business owner can use to manage cash flows. The budget is concerned specifically with dollars both received and paid out. *No single planning document is more important in the life of a small company, either for avoiding cash flow problems when cash runs short or for anticipating short-term investment opportunities if excess cash becomes available.*

To help you understand the process of preparing a cash budget, let's continue with the example of D&R Products. In the previous section, we prepared a pro forma statement of cash flows for the year. But Allen realizes that he also needs to have a sense of the timing of the cash flows throughout the year, so he has decided to prepare a monthly cash budget for the first year of operations. We will look at only the first three months of the cash budget to understand how it was prepared. While Allen predicts that the firm will have $250,000 in annual sales in the first year, his sales projections for the first three months are as follows:

January	$4,000
February	6,000
March	9,000

In addition, the following assumptions will be made:

1. Of the firm's sales dollars, 40 percent are collected the month of the sale, 30 percent one month after the sale, and the remaining 30 percent two months after the sale.
2. Inventory will be purchased one month in advance of the expected sale and will be paid for in the month in which it is sold.
3. Inventory purchases will equal 60 percent of projected sales for the next month's sales.
4. The firm will spend $3,000 each month for advertising.
5. Salaries and utilities for the first three months are estimated as follows:

	Salaries	Utilities
January	$5,000	$150
February	6,000	$200
March	6,000	$200

6. Allen will be investing $110,000 in the business from his personal savings.
7. The firm will be investing $10,000 for needed equipment and $40,000 for the purchase of a building, for a total investment of $50,000. However, the bank has agreed to finance $30,000 of the building purchase price in the form of a mortgage.

cash budget
A listing of cash receipts and cash disbursements, usually for a relatively short time period, such as a week or a month.

Based on this information, Allen has prepared a monthly cash budget for the three-month period ending March 31. Exhibit 11.6 shows the results of his computations, which involve the following steps:

Step 1. Determine the amount of collections each month, based on the projected sales patterns just provided.

Step 2. Estimate the amount and timing of the following cash disbursements:

a. Inventory purchases and payments. The amount of the purchases is shown in the boxed area at the top of the table. However, the actual payment for inventory will not be made until one month later.

b. Advertising, wages and salaries, and utilities are paid in the month incurred.

Step 3. Calculate the cash *flows from operating activities*, which equals the cash receipts (collections from sales) less cash disbursements.

Step 4. Recognize the $110,000 investment in the business by Allen.

Step 5. Note the $50,000 investment in the building and equipment.

Step 6. Show the $30,000 loan from the bank to help pay for the building.

EXHIBIT 11.6 Three-Month Cash Budget For D&R Product, Inc., For January–March

Assumptions:

Anticipated sales collections:

In the month of sale	40%
1 month later	30%
2 month later	30%

	December	January	February	March
Monthly Sales	$ 0	$4,000	$6,000	$9,000
Inventory purchases on credit	$2,400	$3,600	$5,400	

		December	January	February	March
	Monthly Sales	$0	*$ 4,000	$ 6,000	$ 9,000
	Cash receipt				
Step 1:	Collection of sales				
	In month of sale		$ 1,600	$ 2,400	$ 3,600
	1 month later			1,200	1,800
	2 months later				1,200
	Total cash receipts		$ 1,600	$ 3,600	$ 6,600
Step 2:	**Operating cash disbursements**				
Step 2a:	Payments on inventory purchases		$ 2,400	$ 3,600	$ 5,400
	Advertising		3,000	3,000	3,000
Step 2b:	Wages and salaries		5,000	6,000	6,000
	Utilities		150	200	200
	Total operating cash disbursements		$10,550	$12,800	$14,600
Step 3:	**Cash flows from operations**		($ 8,950)	($ 9,200)	($ 8,000)
Step 4:	Allen's personal investment		110,000		
Step 5:	Purchases of equipment and building		(50,000)		
Step 6:	Mortgage (loan from the bank to buy the building)		30,000		
Step 7:	Beginning cash balance		0	81,050	71,850
Step 8:	**Ending cash balance**		$81,050	$71,850	$ 63,850

*For example, January sales of $4,000 are collected as follows: (40%) $1,600 in January, (30%) $1,200 in February, (30%) $1,200 in March.

Step 7. Determine the beginning-of-month cash balance (ending cash balance from the prior month).

Step 8. Compute the end-of-month cash balance.

Evaluate Your Suppliers
Budgeting season is the perfect time to scrutinize vendor relationships. Your suppliers are in all likelihood mapping out their expectations for the year, and you can help them do so by providing your outlook. As a best practice, you should share your budget and the variety of scenarios you might face with your suppliers to see whether they can handle each level of demand. If they can't accommodate your needs, you are dealing with the wrong suppliers.

Based on the cash budget, Allen now has a sense of what to expect for the first three months of operations, which could not be seen from the annual pro forma statement of cash flows presented in Exhibit 11.5. He knows now that he will be "burning" somewhere between $8,000 and $9,200 of cash per month for the first three months of operations. Given that he will have almost $64,000 in cash remaining at the end of March, he will run out of cash in about seven or eight months if the cash flows from operations continue to be negative $8,000 or $9,000 each month. At that time, he will have to start borrowing on the bank line of credit.

One final thought about the cash budget. Once it has been prepared, an entrepreneur has to decide how to use it. Entrepreneurship is about seeking opportunities, and there is a real danger that a cash budget may lead to inflexibility. A strict cost-containment strategy in order to "make the budget" can discourage managers from being creative and shifting their approach when it makes sense to do so. An inflexible budget can also lead to a "use it or lose it" mentality, where managers spend remaining budgeted money at year's end so that allocations will not be cut the following year. Such a mindset negatively impacts the entrepreneurial process.

11-5 USE GOOD JUDGMENT WHEN FORECASTING

Provide some suggestions for effective financial forecasting.

The forecasting process requires an entrepreneur to exercise good judgment in planning, particularly when the planning is providing the basis for raising capital. The overall approach to forecasting is straightforward—entrepreneurs make assumptions and, based on these assumptions, determine financing requirements. But entrepreneurs may be tempted to overstate their expectations in order to acquire much needed financing. So how do you get it right? Here are some practical suggestions about making financial forecasts:[7]

1. *Develop realistic sales projections.* Entrepreneurs often think they can accomplish more than they actually are able to, especially when it comes to forecasting future sales. When graphed, their sales projections for a new venture often resemble a hockey stick—the sales numbers are flat or rise slightly at first (like the blade of a hockey stick) and then soar upward (like a hockey stick's handle). Such projections are always suspect—only the most astonishing changes in a business or market can justify such a sudden, rocket-like performance.
2. *Build projections from clear assumptions about marketing and pricing plans.* Don't be vague, and don't guess. Spell out the kinds of marketing you plan to do—for example, state specifically how many customers you expect to attract.
3. *Do not use unrealistic profit margins.* Projections are immediately suspect if profit margins (profits ÷ sales) or expenses are significantly higher or lower than the average figures reported by firms in the industry with similar revenues and numbers of employees. In general, a new business should not expect to exceed the industry average in profit margins. Entrepreneurs frequently assume that as their company grows it will achieve economies of scale, and gross and operating profit margins will improve. In fact, as the business grows and increases its fixed costs, its operating profit margins are likely to suffer in the short run. If you

insist in your projections that the economies can be achieved quickly, you will need to explain your position.

4. *Don't limit your projections to an income statement.* Entrepreneurs frequently resist providing a projected balance sheet and cash flow statement. They feel comfortable projecting sales and profits but do not like having to commit to assumptions about the sources and uses of capital needed to grow the business. Investors, however, want to see those assumptions in print. They are particularly interested in the firm's cash flows—and you should be as well.

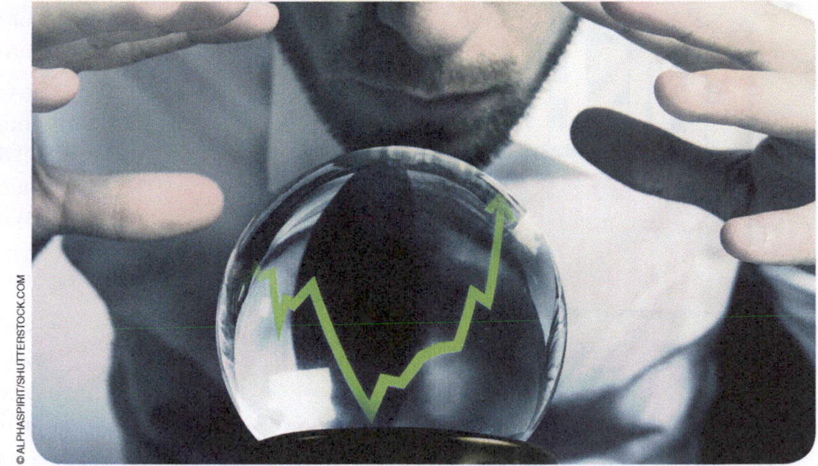
© ALPHASPIRIT/SHUTTERSTOCK.COM

5. *Provide monthly data for the upcoming year and annual data for succeeding years.* Many entrepreneurs prepare projections using only monthly data or annual data for an entire three- or five-year period. Given the difficulty in forecasting accurately beyond a year, monthly data for the later years are not particularly believable. From year 2 on, annual projections are adequate.
6. *Avoid providing too much financial information.* Computer spreadsheets are extremely valuable in making projections and showing how different assumptions affect the firm's financials. But do not be tempted to overuse this tool. Instead, limit your projections to two scenarios: the most-likely scenario (base case) and the break-even scenario. The base case should show what you realistically expect the business to do; the break-even case should show what level of sales is required to break even.
7. *Be certain that the numbers reconcile—and not by simply plugging in a figure.* All too often, entrepreneurs plug a figure into equity to make things work out. While everyone makes mistakes, that's one you want to avoid because it can result in a loss of credibility.
8. *Follow the plan.* After you have prepared the pro forma financial statements, check them against actual results at least once a month, and modify your projections as needed.
9. *Don't forget that you have to live.* While our focus is on ascertaining the financial needs of the business, a small business owner should not disregard his or her personal finances. Particularly during the early stages of the business, the owner may have to make some significant personal sacrifices and assume some personal risks. Even so, your personal living expenses have to be considered alongside the financing needs of the business, even if at a minimal level. Inadequate provision for your living expenses could lead to the temptation of diverting assets from the business for personal needs and a departure from the plan.

These suggestions, if followed, will help you avoid overpromising and underdelivering when starting a business. But even then, entrepreneurs at times simply have to have faith that they will be able to deliver on what they promise, even though it may not be clear exactly how this will be accomplished. Risk is part of the equation, and often things will not go as planned. But integrity requires you to honor your commitments, and that cannot be done if you have made unrealistic projections about what you can accomplish.

The information on financial planning provided in this chapter and in Chapter 10 will serve as a foundation for the examination of an entrepreneur's search for specific sources of financing in Chapter 12.

11-1. Describe the purpose of financial forecasting.

- The purpose of pro forma financial statements is to determine (1) future profitability based on projected sales levels and expected sales-expenses relationships, (2) how much and what type of financing will be needed, and (3) whether the firm will have adequate cash flows.
- Accurate financial forecasting is important not only for ensuring that a firm has the resources it needs to grow, but also for managing growth.

11-2. Develop a pro forma income statement to forecast a new venture's profitability.

- In order to develop a pro forma income statement, an entrepreneur must understand the drivers of a firm's profits, which include (1) amount of sales, (2) cost of goods sold, (3) operating expenses, (4) interest expense, and (5) taxes.
- In a real-world situation, an entrepreneur should project the profits of a company for at least three years into the future.

11-3. Determine a company's asset and financing requirements using a pro forma balance sheet.

- The amount and type of assets required for a venture will vary according to the nature of the business. However, all firms need to understand how much working capital and fixed assets will be required.
- An entrepreneur should try to bootstrap as many resources as possible in order to minimize a firm's investment while simultaneously ensuring adequate resources.
- A direct relationship exists between sales growth and asset needs: As sales increase, more assets are required.
- For every dollar of assets needed, there must be a corresponding dollar of financing.
- To forecast a firm's financing requirements, an entrepreneur must understand (1) its asset requirements, (2) the need to maintain adequate liquidity, (3) the debt ratio, (4) sources of spontaneous debt financing, and (5) sources of owners' equity.

11-4. Forecast a firm's cash flows.

- Forecasting cash flows can be accomplished in two ways: (1) by preparing a pro forma statement of cash flows, and/or (2) by developing a cash budget. Ideally, an entrepreneur would do both.
- A firm's cash flows involve three activities: operating, investing, and financing activities.
- A cash budget is concerned specifically with dollars both received and paid out.
- A cash budget should provide boundaries but not limit creativity and flexibility. The entrepreneurial process is all about seizing opportunity.

11-5. Provide some suggestions for effective financial forecasting.

- Develop realistic sales projections based on clear assumptions about marketing and pricing plans.
- Do not use unrealistic profit margins. In general, new businesses do not exceed industry average profit margins in their first years.
- Do not limit your projections to an income statement. Investors want to see pro forma balance sheets and a cash flow statement as well.
- Provide monthly data for the upcoming year and annual data for succeeding years.
- Avoid providing too much financial information. Limit projections to the most-likely scenario (base case) and the break-even scenario.
- Be certain that the numbers reconcile.
- Follow the plan, and measure how actual performance compares with forecasted performance so that modifications to future forecasts will be more accurate.
- Funding for a new venture should cover asset requirements and also the personal living expenses of the owner.

Key Terms

cash budget p. 312
line of credit p. 307
net working capital p. 301
percentage-of-sales technique p. 304
pro forma financial statements p. 296
spontaneous debt financing p. 306

You Make the Call

Situation 1

D&R Products, Inc., used as an example in this chapter, is an actual firm (although some of the facts were changed to maintain confidentiality). David Allen bought the firm from its founding owners and moved its operations to his hometown. Although he has estimated the firm's asset needs and financing requirements, he cannot be certain that these projections will be realized. The figures merely represent the most-likely case. Allen also made some projections that he considers to be the worst-case and best-case sales and profit figures. If things do not go well, the firm might have sales of only $200,000 in its first year. However, if the potential of the business is realized, Allen believes that sales could be as high as $325,000. If he needs any additional financing beyond the existing line of credit, he could conceivably borrow another $5,000 in short-term debt from the bank by pledging some personal investments. Any additional financing would need to come from Allen himself, thereby increasing his equity stake in the business.

Question If all of D&R Products' other relationships hold, how will Allen's worst-case and best-case projections affect the income statement and balance sheet in the first year?
To help you in your analysis, D&R Product's pro forma statements, as presented in Exhibits 11.1, 11.3, and 11.4, are available at CengageBrain.com (select the Longenecker text).

Situation 2

Philip Spencer of the Spencer Corporation wants you to forecast the firm's financing needs over the fourth quarter (October through December). He has made the following observations relative to planned cash receipts and disbursements:

- Interest on a $75,000 bank note (principal due next March) at an 8 percent annual rate is payable in December for the three-month period just ended.
- The firm follows a policy of paying no cash dividends.
- Actual historical and future predicted sales are as follows:

Historical Sales		Predicted Sales	
August	$150,000	October	$200,000
September	175,000	November	220,000
		December	180,000
		January	200,000

- The firm has a monthly rental expense of $5,000.
- Wages and salaries for the coming months are estimated at $25,000 per month.
- Of the firm's sales, 25 percent is collected in the month of the sale, 35 percent one month after the sale, and the remaining 40 percent two months after the sale.
- Merchandise is purchased one month before the sales month and is paid for in the month it is sold. Purchases equal 75 percent of sales.
- Tax prepayments are made quarterly, with a prepayment of $10,000 in October based on earnings for the quarter ended September 30.
- Utility costs for the firm average 3 percent of sales and are paid in the month they are incurred.
- Depreciation expense is $20,000 annually.

Question 1 Prepare a monthly cash budget for the three-month period ending in December.
Question 2 If the firm's beginning cash balance for the budget period is $7,000, and this is its desired minimum balance, determine when and how much the firm will need to borrow during the budget period. The firm has a $50,000 line of credit with its bank, with interest (10 percent annual rate) paid monthly. For example, interest on a loan taken out at the end of September would be paid at the end of October and every month thereafter, as long as the loan was outstanding.

Situation 3

Karen Lamont is in the process of starting a new business and wants to forecast the first year's income statement and balance sheet. She has made a number of assumptions, which are shown below:

a. Lamont has projected the firm's sales will be $1 million in the first year.
b. She believes that the operating and gross profit margins will be 20 percent and 50 percent, respectively.
c. For working capital, Lamont has estimated the following:
   - Accounts receivable as a percentage of sales: 12%
   - Inventory as a percentage of sales: 15%
   - Accounts payable as a percentage of sales: 7%
   - Accruals as a percentage of sales: 5%

d. A bank has agreed to loan her $300,000, consisting of $100,000 in short-term debt and $200,000 in long-term debt. Both loans will have an 8 percent interest rate.

e. The firm's tax rate will be 30 percent.

f. Lamont will need to purchase $350,000 in plant and equipment.

Lamont will provide any other financing needed.

Question 1 Based on Lamont's assumptions, prepare a pro forma income statement and balance sheet.

Question 2 If her estimates are correct, what will be the firm's current ratio and debt ratio? Explain the meaning of these ratios.

Business Plan

LAYING THE FOUNDATION

As part of laying the foundation to prepare your own business plan, you will need to develop the following:

1. A business model that recognizes the different revenue streams, cost structures, and key resources to grow the business.
2. Historical financial statements (if applicable) and three to five years of pro forma financial statements, including balance sheets, income statements, and statements of cash flows.
3. Monthly cash budgets for the first year and quarterly cash budgets for the second year.
4. The rationale and explanation for the underlying assumptions for your pro forma financial statements.
5. Current and planned financing to be provided by the owners and other investors.
6. Justification of the intended use of funds being raised from lenders and investors.
7. Profit and cash flow break-even analysis. (See Chapter 16 for an explanation of break-even analysis.)

Case 11

Ashley Palmer Clothing Inc. (P. 665)

Ashley Palmer Clothing, Inc. designs apparel for the modern woman's shape rather than using a standardized size as traditionally done. The firm was launched in June 2009 by Ashley Jantz and Amanda Palmer, both graduates of a liberal arts college in Boston, followed by graduate studies in business. The firm has experienced significant growth over the past four years. But Jantz and Palmer are expecting the growth rate to double in 2014. The case is aimed at forecasting the firm's financial requirements for 2014.

Alternative Cases for Chapter 11

Case 22, Pearson Air Conditioning & Service, p. 690
Video Case 10, B2B CFO [website only]

Endnotes

1. Rhonda Abrams, "How Can I Make Financial Projections in My Business Plan When I Have No Solid Numbers?" *Inc.*, September 2000, http://www.inc.com/articles/2000/09/20226.html, accessed December 15, 2014.
2. This example is based on an actual situation; however, the name of the founder has been changed, as have some of the numbers.
3. Investors also look to financial projections to determine the sales level necessary for the firm to break even. A firm's break-even point, while important from a financial perspective, is also important for pricing its products or services. The issue of pricing and the break-even point are discussed in Chapter 16.
4. In Chapter 10, we used the *current ratio* to measure a company's ability to meet maturing obligations, which was measured as current assets *divided* by current liabilities. Thus, the current ratio is a relative measure (current assets *relative* to current liabilities), which allows us to compare firms of different sizes. *Net working capital* (current assets *less* current liabilities) is an *absolute* dollar measure of liquidity used by many bankers.
5. Personal communication with Dan Cassidy, October 6, 2012.
6. Personal communication with Cecilia Levine, November 21, 2014.
7. Information in this section was largely taken from Linda Elkins,"Real Numbers Don't Deceive," *Nation's Business*, Vol. 85, No. 3 (March 1997), pp. 51–52; and Paul Broni, "Persuasive Projections," *Inc.*, Vol. 22, No. 4 (April 2000), pp. 183–184.

CHAPTER 12

A Firm's Sources of Financing

After studying this chapter, you should be able to. . .

12-1. Describe how a firm's characteristics affect its available financing sources.

12-2. Evaluate the choice between debt financing and equity financing.

12-3. Identify the typical sources of financing used at the outset of a new venture.

12-4. Discuss the basic process for acquiring and structuring a bank loan.

12-5. Explain how business relationships can be used to finance a small firm.

12-6. Describe the two types of private equity investors who offer financing to small firms.

12-7. Describe how crowdfunding can be used by some small businesses to raise capital.

12-8. Distinguish among the different government loan programs available to small companies.

12-9. Explain when large companies and public stock offerings can be sources of financing.

In the Spotlight
Emmy's Organics
http://emmysorganics.com

Because of a serious illness in 2008, Ian Gaffney left Brooklyn, New York, where he had been working as a graphic designer. Back at home, in Ithaca, New York, he met Samantha Abrams, a recent graduate of Ithaca College. As an experienced raw vegan chef, Gaffney impressed Abrams with his various clean food dishes. After an especially delicious batch of macaroons, Abrams had a sudden flash of brilliance—sell the macaroons in prepackaged sets. Gaffney's mother, Emmy, let the couple use her kitchen, where they created four new macaroon flavors. Their new business, Emmy's Organics, was born.

When Gaffney and Abrams decided to expand their company, they turned to an unlikely source for business advice: Gaffney's brother's rock band, the Makepeace Brothers. The band had just successfully paid for the recording of their latest album using Indiegogo, a crowdfunding site that lets users raise money for "projects." Gaffney thought the site would be a good fit for their company. Within a month, the campaign raised more than its $15,000 goal, giving Emmy's the necessary capital to redesign its logo, create new packaging, and launch new branding.

After getting their kitchen certified, Gaffney and Abrams reached out to a local co-op and several other stores in the area. In 2009, the couple started selling their products at Ithaca's farmer's market. As their products' local popularity grew, Gaffney and Abrams pursued venders in New York City. Orders piled up at a dizzying rate.

For the next two years, Gaffney and Abrams poured their hearts and souls into the business. Demand continued to surge, which meant they would have to invest in machinery. So they turned to Alternatives Federal Credit Union (AFCU) in Ithaca for a loan. AFCU's chief lending officer, Carol Chernikoff, was pleased to learn about the company's interest in working with AFCU. "We had known Sam and Ian previously from their engagement with the community," Chernikoff adds. The loan was approved.

With the new equipment in hand, macaroon production skyrocketed, which eventually meant that Gaffney and Abrams would have to renovate their warehouse. In order to do that, though, they would have to obtain a second, this time larger, loan. They went to M&T Bank, one of the largest Small Business Administration lenders in the nation, according to Kara Taylor, vice president of the bank. In her words:

In our first meeting, we spent a lot of time getting to know each other and specifically discussing the story behind Emmy's Organics. It's important for us to really understand and know the businesses we work with, and what we would need to do to help them get to the next logical step in their business cycle.

Once again, Gaffney and Abrams were successful in getting a loan. That was millions of macaroons ago. Thanks to partnerships with AFCU and M&T Bank, Emmy's Organics currently sells its products in 2,500 locations in 40 states. Eager to expand even more, Gaffney and Abrams plan on developing new products before tackling international markets in 2014 and beyond.

Sources: Adapted from "Emmy's: Our Story," http://emmysorganics.com/pages/our-story, accessed March 10, 2015; Tony Armstrong, "Small Business Loan Success Stories: Emmy's Organics' Collaboration with Alternatives Federal Credit Union and M&T Bank," June 20, 2014, http://www.nerdwallet.com/blog/small-business/small-business-loan-success-stories-emmys-organics-collaboration-alternatives-federal-credit-union-mt-bank, accessed March 10, 2015; and Tim Donnelly, "How to Use Indiegogo to Fund Your Innovation," *Inc.*, March 2011, http://www.inc.com/guides/201103/how-to-use-indiegogo-to-fund-your-innovation.html, accessed March 10, 2015.

In Chapter 11, we addressed *how much* financing is needed and *what types* of financing are available for small businesses. In this chapter, we describe the different sources of financing. But first, it's important to understand how a firm's characteristics affect the way in which it will be financed.

12-1 FIRM CHARACTERISTICS AND SOURCES OF FINANCING

Describe how a firm's characteristics affect its available financing sources.

At times, financing a business can weigh heavily on small business owners. In recent years, acquiring needed financing became increasingly difficult for small firms as financial institutions struggled and the economy faltered. But even when the economy improved, aspiring entrepreneurs needed persistence and discipline to get a business off and running.

Four basic firm characteristics significantly affect how a business is financed: (1) the firm's economic potential, (2) the size and maturity of the company, (3) the nature of its assets, and (4) the personal preferences of the owners with respect to the trade-offs between debt and equity. Without understanding how these characteristics come into play in financing your business, you stand little chance of getting appropriate financing (see Exhibit 12.1).

12-1a Firm's Economic Potential

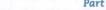

A firm with potential for high growth and large profits has more possible sources of financing than does a firm that provides a good lifestyle for the owner but little in the way of returns to investors. Only firms with a high rate of return on investment create

EXHIBIT

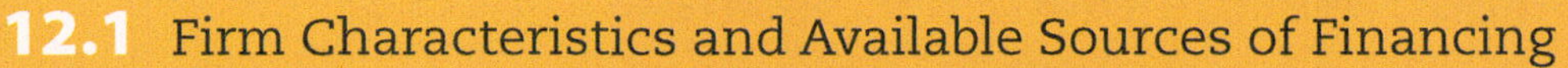

12.1 Firm Characteristics and Available Sources of Financing

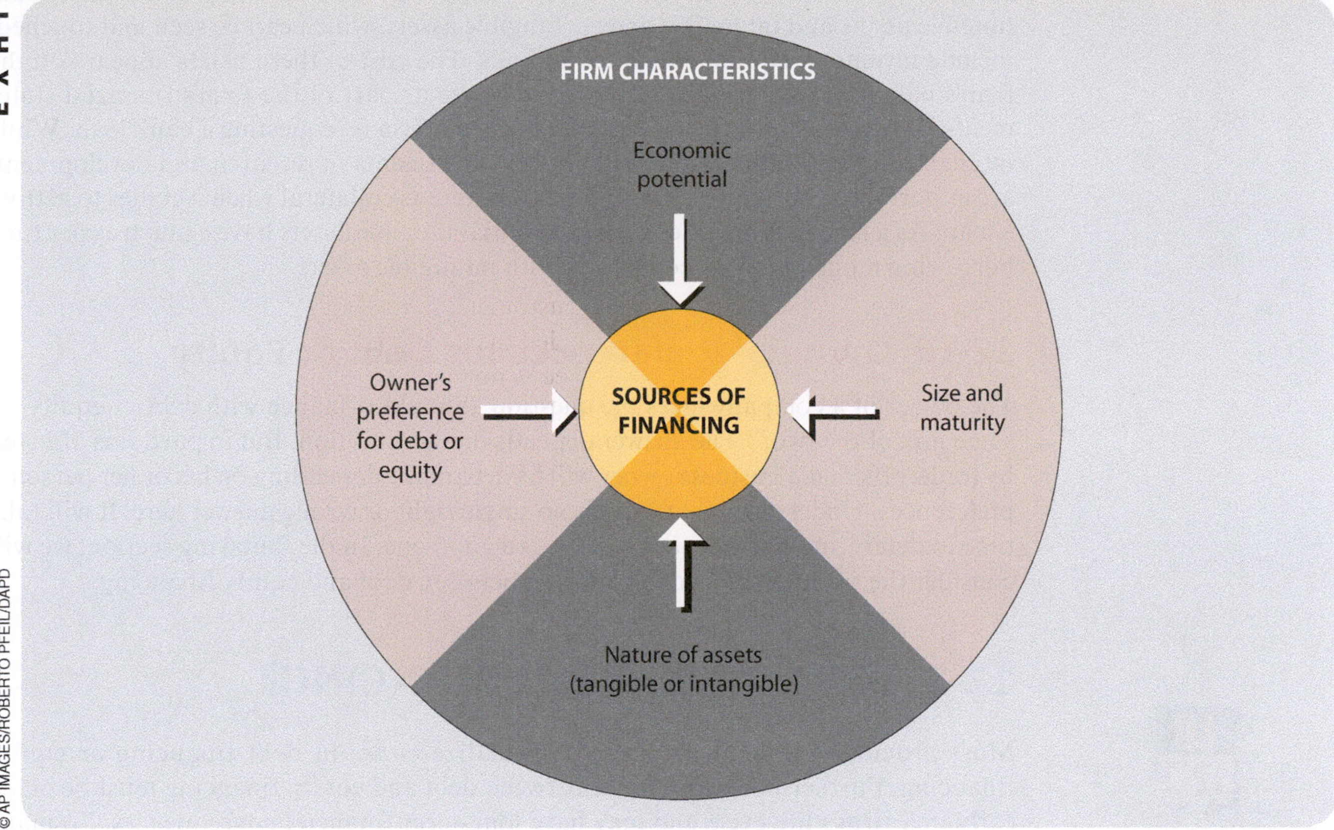

value for the investor. In fact, most investors in startup companies focus on firms that offer potentially high returns within a 5- to 10-year period. Clearly, a company that provides a comfortable lifestyle for its owner but insufficient profits to attract outside investors will find its options for alternative sources of financing limited.

12-1b Company Size and Maturity

Larger and older firms have access to bank credit that may not be available to younger and smaller companies. Also, smaller firms tend to rely more on personal loans and credit cards for financing. In the early years of a business, most entrepreneurs bootstrap their financing—that is, they depend on their own initiative to come up with the necessary capital. Only after the business has an established track record will most bankers and other financial institutions be willing to provide financing.

You have probably read about venture capitalists who helped finance firms such as Yahoo, eBay, and Apple. But even venture capitalists limit how much they will invest in startup companies. Many such investors believe that the additional risk associated with startups is too great relative to the returns they expect to receive. On average, about three-fourths of a venture capitalist's investments are in later-stage businesses—only a few focus heavily on startups. Similarly, bankers demand evidence that the business will be able to repay a loan—and that evidence usually must be based on what the firm has done in the past and not what the owner says it will achieve in the future. So, a firm's life-cycle position is a critical factor in raising capital.

START UP ACTION

Banker/Investor Checklist

Before approaching a banker or investor, be sure that you have (1) cleaned up your personal credit, if there was a problem, (2) assessed the qualifications of your management team, (3) written an effective business plan, (4) decided on what type of financing you need, and (5) made certain that you are approaching the right lender or investor given the circumstances.

12-1c Nature of Firm's Assets

A banker specifically considers two types of assets when evaluating a firm for a loan: tangible assets and intangible assets. Tangible assets, which can be seen and touched, include inventory, equipment, and buildings. The cost of these assets appears on the firm's balance sheet, which the banker receives as part of the firm's financial statements. Tangible assets are great collateral when a firm is requesting a bank loan. While intangible assets, such as goodwill or past investments in research and development, are important to an investor, they have little value as collateral when it comes to getting a loan. As a result, companies with substantial tangible assets have a much easier time borrowing money than do companies with intangible assets.

12-1d Owners' Preferences for Debt or Equity

The owner of a company faces the question "Should I finance with debt or equity, or some mix of the two?" The answer depends on the situation. But in part, it is affected by trade-offs that a business owner will have to make depending on his or her personal preferences. Understand that there is no single right or wrong answer here. It will take time to determine whether the choice was a good one. In the following section, we will consider the trade-offs faced in choosing between debt and equity financing.

12-2 DEBT OR EQUITY FINANCING?

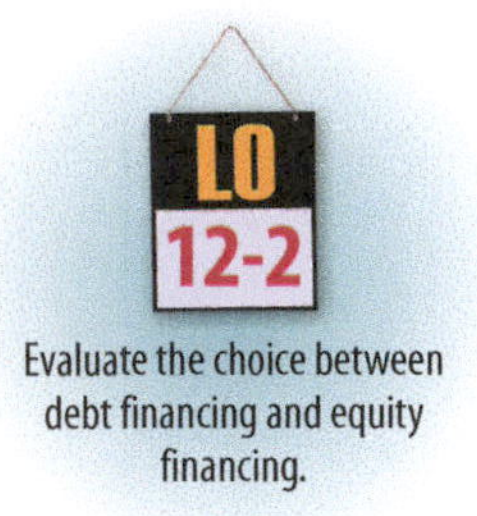

Evaluate the choice between debt financing and equity financing.

Most providers of financial capital specialize *either* in debt financing *or* equity financing. Furthermore, the choice between debt and equity financing must be made early in a firm's life cycle and may have long-term financial consequences. To make an informed decision, a small business owner needs to recognize and understand the trade-offs between debt and equity with regard to the following three factors:

- Potential profitability for the owners
- The business's financial risk
- Voting control of the business

These three trade-offs are shown visually in Exhibit 12.2. Let's consider each trade-off in turn.

12-2a Potential Profitability

Anyone who owns a business wants it to be profitable, *and* they want it to provide a good return on their investment. Both outcomes are important—dollar profits and the percentage return earned on investment in the business. But an acceptable dollar amount cannot be determined independent of the size of the business owner's investment in the business. Making $100,000 in profits may sound great, but not if the owner must invest $10 million to earn it. That is only a 1 percent return on the investment (1% = 0.01 = $100,000 ÷ $10,000,000). It would be better to purchase a certificate of deposit that earns, say, 1.5 percent. Any rate over 1 percent would provide income greater than $100,000.

To see how the choice between debt and equity affects owners' profitability, consider the Asbil Corporation, a new firm that's still in the process of raising needed capital.

- The owners have already invested $100,000 of their own money in the new business. To complete the financing, they need another $100,000.

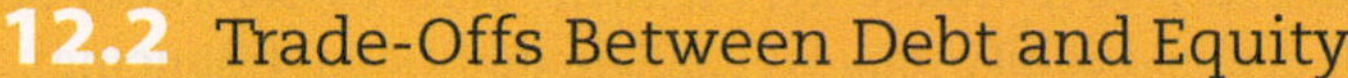

EXHIBIT 12.2 Trade-Offs Between Debt and Equity

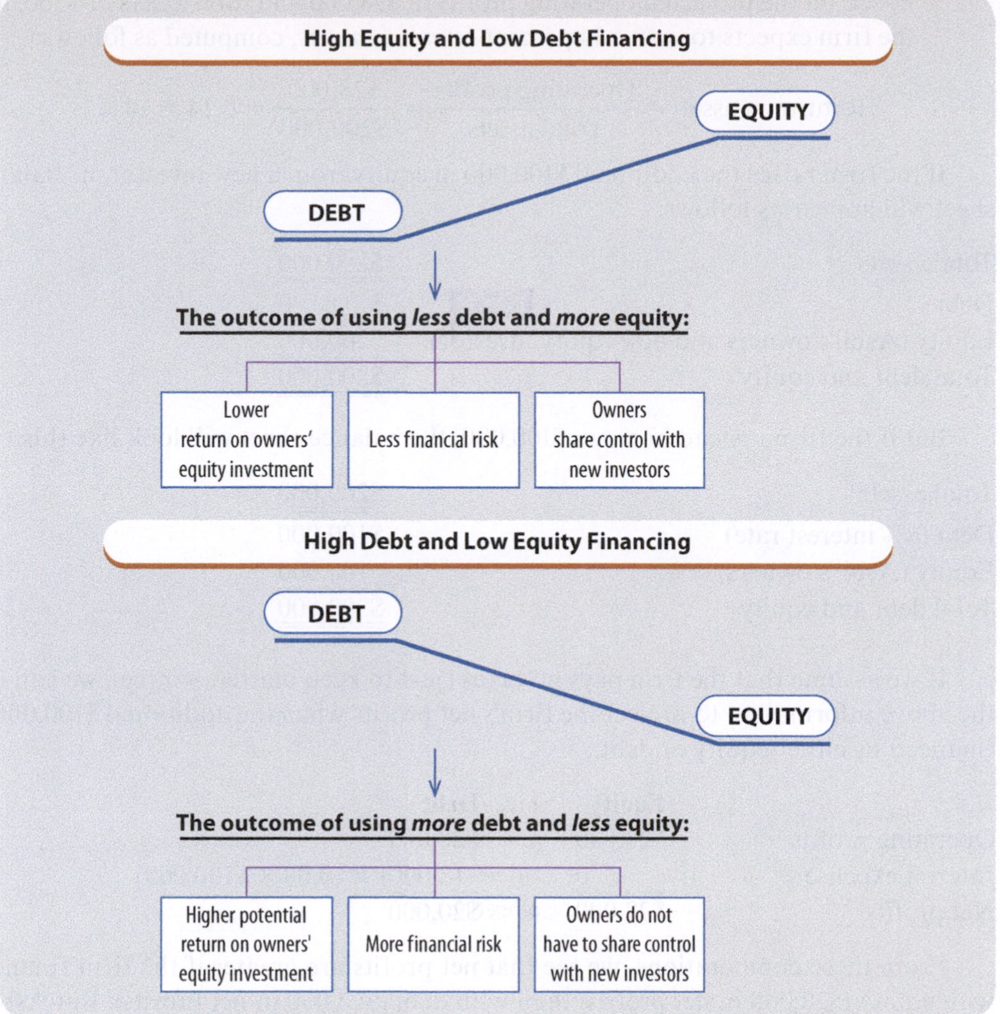

- They are considering one of two options for raising the additional $100,000: (1) new equity investors (common stockholders) who would provide $100,000 for a 30 percent share of the firm's outstanding stock; or (2) a bank that would lend the money at an interest rate of 8 percent, so the interest expense each year would be $8,000 ($8,000 = 0.08 × $100,000). In the first instance, Asbil would have to give up 30 percent of the company's equity ownership. If debt financing is used instead, there would be no loss of ownership, but the firm would have a fixed interest cost of $8,000, no matter how well the business does.
- The firm's operating profits (the profits or earnings before any interest expense and taxes are paid) are expected to be $28,000, shown as follows:

Sales	$150,000
Cost of goods sold	80,000
Gross profit	$ 70,000
Operating expenses	42,000
Operating profits	$ 28,000

- With the additional \$100,000 in financing, the firm's total assets would be \$200,000 (\$100,000 original equity plus \$100,000 in additional financing).
- Based on the projected operating profits of \$28,000 and total assets of \$200,000, the firm expects to earn a 14 percent *return on assets*, computed as follows:[1]

$$\text{Return on assets} = \frac{\text{Operating profits}}{\text{Total assets}} = \frac{\$28{,}000}{\$200{,}000} = 0.14 = 14\%$$

If the firm raises the additional \$100,000 in equity from a new investor, its balance sheet will appear as follows:

Total assets	\$200,000
Debt	\$ 0
Equity (Asbil's owners and new equity investor)	200,000
Total debt and equity	\$200,000

But if the firm instead borrows \$100,000, the balance sheet will look like this:

Total assets	\$200,000
Debt (8% interest rate)	\$100,000
Equity (Asbil's owners)	100,000
Total debt and equity	\$200,000

If we assume that the firm pays no taxes (just to keep matters simple), we can use the above information to project the firm's net profits when the additional \$100,000 is financed by either equity or debt:

	Equity	**Debt**	
Operating profits	\$28,000	\$28,000	
Interest expense	0	(8,000)	= (0.08 × \$100,000)
Net profits	\$28,000	\$20,000	

From these computations, we see that net profits are greater if the firm finances with equity (\$28,000 in net profits) than with debt (\$20,000 in net profits). But Asbil's owners would have to invest *twice* as much money (\$200,000 rather than \$100,000) to avoid the \$8,000 interest expense and get the higher net profits.

Should the owners finance with equity to get higher net profits, in this case \$28,000 as compared to \$20,000? Not necessarily. The return on the owners' investment, or *return on equity*, is a better measure of performance than the absolute dollar amount of net profits. Remember from Chapter 10 that an owner's return on equity is calculated as follows:

$$\text{Return on equity} = \frac{\text{Net profits}}{\text{Total owner's equity}}$$

So when the firm uses *all* equity financing, the return on equity is 14 percent, computed as follows:

$$\text{Return on equity} = \frac{\text{Net profits}}{\text{Total owner's equity}} = \frac{\$28{,}000}{\$200{,}000} = 0.14 = 14\%$$

But if the additional financing comes from debt, leading to an interest expense of \$8,000 with an equity investment of only \$100,000, the rate of return on equity is 20 percent, calculated as follows:

$$\text{Return on equity} = \frac{\text{Net profits}}{\text{Total owner's equity}} = \frac{\$20{,}000}{\$100{,}000} = 0.20 = 20\%$$

Thus, the owners' return on equity is higher if half of the firm's financing comes from equity and half from debt. By using only equity, the owners will earn $0.14 for every $1 of equity invested. By using debt, they will earn $0.20 for every $1 of equity invested. So, in terms of a rate of return on their own investment, Asbil's owners get a better return by borrowing money at 8 percent interest than by bringing in a new equity investor. That makes sense, because the firm is earning 14 percent on all the assets of $200,000, but only paying creditors at an 8 percent rate on the loan of $100,000. The owners benefit from the difference. These relationships are shown in Exhibit 12.3.

As a general rule, *as long as a firm's rate of return on its assets (operating profits ÷ total assets) is greater than the cost of the debt (interest rate), the owners' rate of return on equity will increase as the firm uses more debt.*

12-2b Financial Risk

If debt is so beneficial in terms of producing a higher rate of return, why shouldn't Asbil's owners use as much debt as possible—even 100 percent debt—if they can? Then their rate of return on the equity investment would be even higher—unlimited, in fact, if they did not have to invest any money.

That's the good news. The bad news: *Debt is risky.* If the firm fails to earn profits, creditors still insist on being repaid, regardless of the firm's actual performance. In extreme cases, creditors can force firms into bankruptcy if they fail to honor their financial obligations. Equity, on the other hand, is less demanding. If a firm is not profitable, an equity investor must accept the disappointing results and hope for better results next year. Equity investors cannot demand more than what is earned.

EXHIBIT **12.3** Debt Versus Equity at the Asbil Corporation

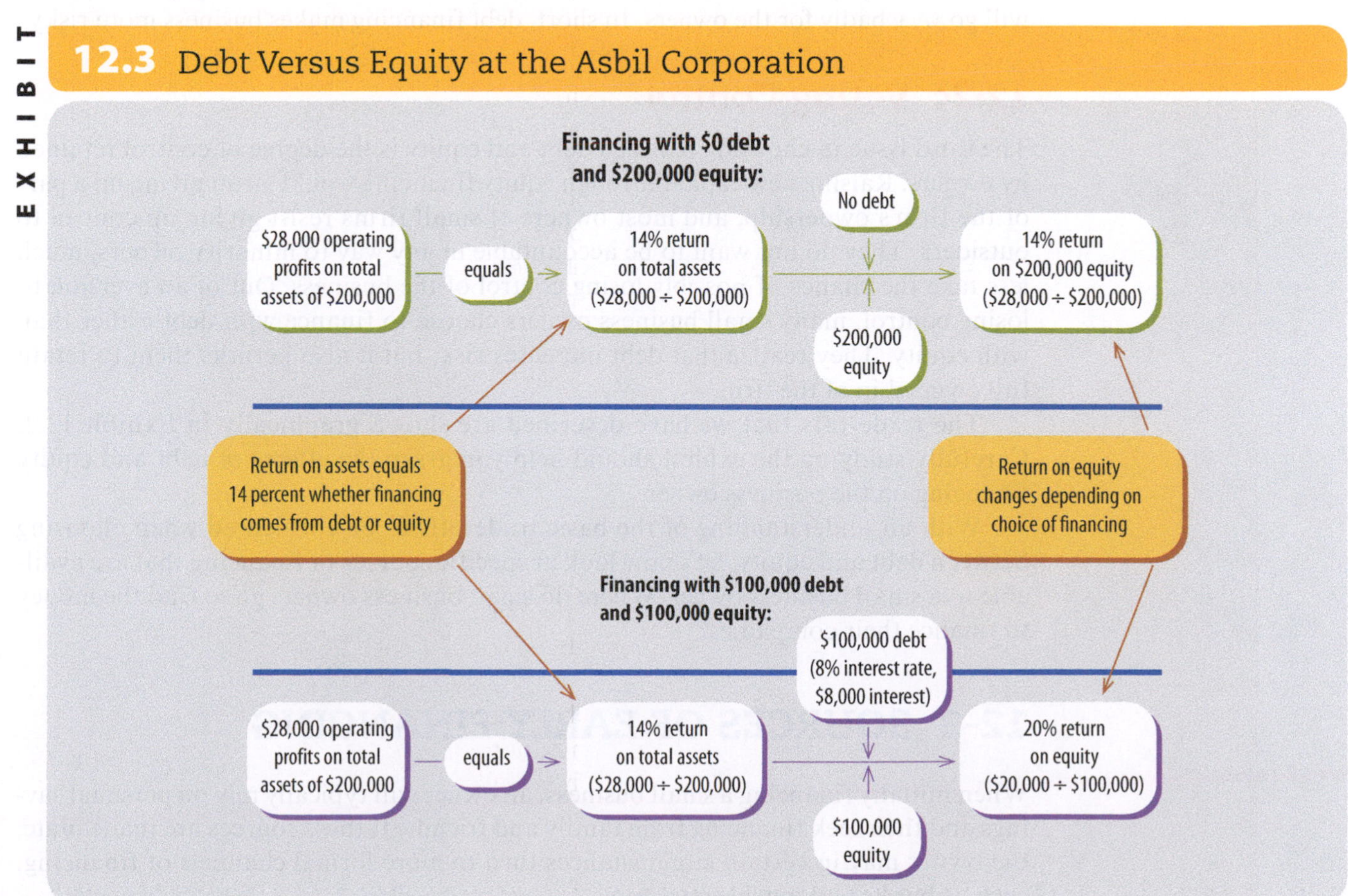

Another way to view the negative side of debt is to contemplate what happens to the return on equity if a business has a bad year. Suppose that instead of earning 14 percent on its assets, or $28,000 in operating profits, the Asbil Corporation earns a mere $2,000—only 1 percent on its assets of $200,000 ($1\% = .01 = \$2{,}000 \div \$200{,}000$). The return on equity would again depend on whether the firm used debt or equity to finance the second $100,000 investment in the company. The results would be as follows:

	Equity	Debt	
Operating profits	$2,000	$2,000	
Interest expense	0	(8,000) = (0.08 × $100,000)	
Net profits	$2,000	($6,000) ←	Ouch! Now Asbil lost $6,000!

If the added financing came in the form of equity, the return on equity would be a disappointing 1 percent:

$$\text{Return on equity} = \frac{\text{Net profits}}{\text{Total owner's equity}} = \frac{\$2{,}000}{\$200{,}000} = 0.01 = 1\%$$

But if debt were used, the return on equity would be a painful negative 6 percent:

$$\text{Return on equity} = \frac{\text{Net profits}}{\text{Total owner's equity}} = \frac{-\$6{,}000}{\$100{,}000} = -0.06 = -6\%$$

So if only 1 percent is earned on the firm's assets, the owners would be better off if they financed solely with equity. Thus, debt is a double-edged sword. If debt financing is used and things go well, they will go *very* well for the owners. But if things go badly, they will go *very* badly for the owners. In short, debt financing makes business more risky.

12-2c Voting Control

The third issue in choosing between debt and equity is the degree of control retained by owners. Raising new capital through equity financing would mean giving up a part of the firm's ownership, and most owners of small firms resist giving up control to outsiders. They do not want to be accountable in any way to minority owners, much less take the chance of possibly losing control of the business. Out of an aversion to losing control, many small business owners choose to finance with debt rather than with equity. They realize that debt increases risk, but it also permits them to retain full ownership of the firm.

The trade-offs that we have described are shown graphically in Exhibit 12.2. Carefully studying the exhibit should help you grasp the effects of debt and equity financing on the business owner.

With an understanding of the basic trade-offs to be considered when choosing between debt and equity, let's now look at specific sources of financing that are available to a small business owner. Where do small business owners go to find the money to finance their companies?

12-3 SOURCES OF EARLY FINANCING

When initially financing a small business, an owner will typically rely on personal savings and then seek financing from family and friends. If these sources are inadequate, the owner may in certain circumstances turn to more formal channels of financing, such as banks and outside investors.

Exhibit 12.4 gives an overview of the sources of financing of smaller companies. As indicated earlier, some sources of financing—such as banks, business suppliers, asset-based lenders, and the government—essentially provide only debt capital. Equity financing for most small business owners comes from personal savings and, in rare instances, from selling stock to the public. Other sources—including friends and family, other individual investors, venture capitalists (rarely), and large corporations—may provide either debt or equity financing, depending on the situation. Keep in mind that the use of these and other sources of funds are not limited to a startup's initial financing. Such sources will also be used to finance a firm's day-to-day operations and business expansions.

Let's now consider specific sources of financing for smaller companies, beginning with sources "close to home"—personal savings, friends and family, and credit cards.

Money Isn't Everything

Successfully raising needed money to scale a business is vital. But do not expect money to solve all your problems. "Some entrepreneurs mistake feedback from investors and VCs as a substitute for getting out there and talking to real customers," says Guy Turner of Hyde Park Venture Partners in Chicago. "Just because a VC likes it, doesn't mean customers do."[2]

12-3a Personal Savings

It is imperative for an entrepreneur to have some personal investment in the business, which typically comes from personal savings. Indeed, personal savings is by far the most common source of equity financing used to start a new business, which needs equity to allow for a margin of error. In its first few years, a firm can ill afford large fixed outlays for debt repayment. Also, a banker—or anyone else—is unlikely to loan money if the owner does not have his or her own money at risk.

A problem for many people who want to start a business is that they lack sufficient personal savings for this purpose. It can be very discouraging when the banker asks, "How much will you be investing in the business?" or "What do you have for collateral to secure the loan you want?" There is no easy solution to this problem, which is faced by an untold number of entrepreneurs. Nonetheless, many individuals who lack personal savings for a startup find ways to own their own companies without spending large amounts of money. And they figure out how to grow the business—perhaps by using the cash flows being generated from the firm's operations, by using other people's resources, or by finding a partner or friends and relatives who will provide the necessary financing.

EXHIBIT **12.4** Sources of Funds

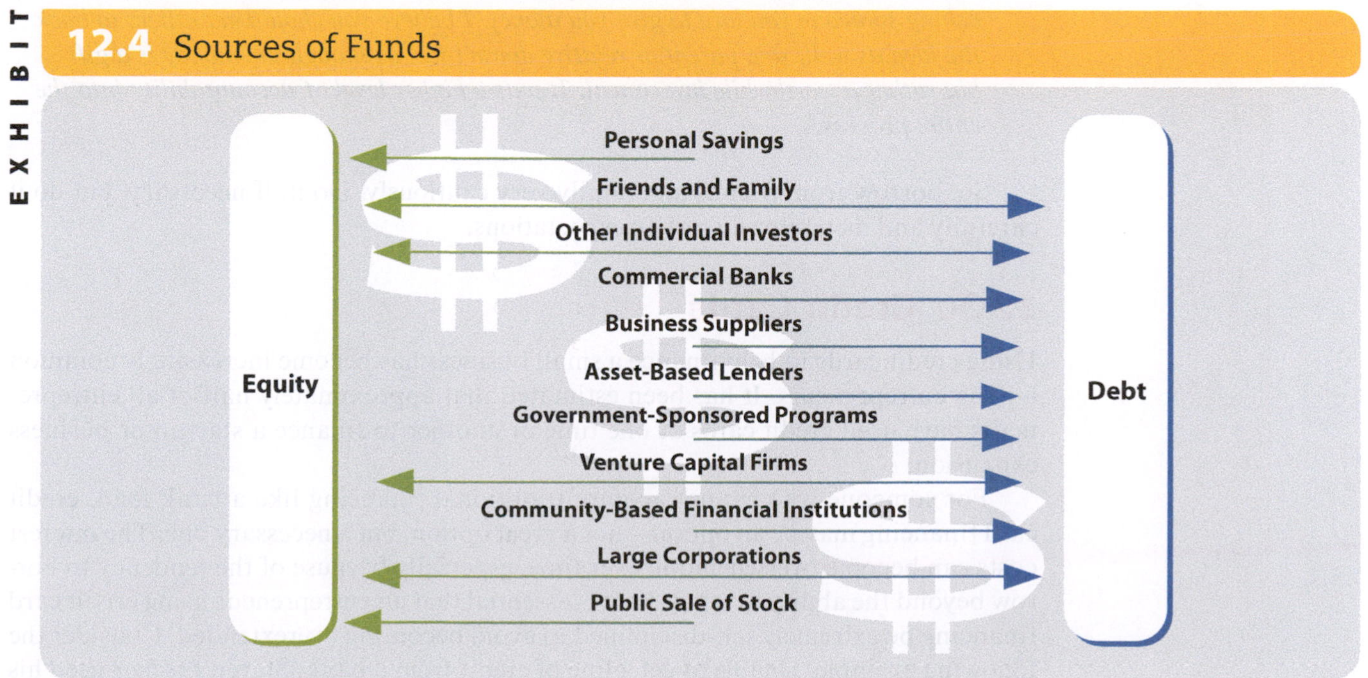

12-3b Friends and Family

While personal savings serve as the *primary* source of financing for most small business startups, friends and family are a distant second. They are the leading source of startup capital beyond the entrepreneur's personal savings.

Entrepreneurs who acquire financing from friends and family are putting more than just their financial futures on the line—they are putting personal relationships at risk. For that reason, you should think of it as a high risk source of money, especially if not done right. Seeking advice from an experienced entrepreneur who has raised family and friend money in the past would be time well spent.

At times, loans from friends or relatives may be the only available source of new financing. Such loans can often be obtained quickly, because they are based more on personal relationships than on financial analyses. *But you should accept money from a friend or relative only if that person will not be hurt financially to any significant extent if the entire amount is lost.* In other words, do not borrow money from your brother if he cannot afford the loss, much less from your grandmother's retirement savings.

Friends and relatives who provide business loans sometimes feel that they have the right to offer suggestions concerning the management of the business. And hard business times may strain the relationship. But if relatives and friends are the only available source of financing, the entrepreneur may have no other alternative. To minimize the chance of damaging important personal relationships, the entrepreneur should plan to repay such loans as soon as possible. In addition, any agreements should be put in writing. It is best to clarify expectations up front, rather than be disappointed or angry later.

Some good advice comes from James Hutcheson, president of Regeneration Partners, a consulting group that specializes in family-owned businesses. He says that entrepreneurs should approach their relatives only after they have secured investments or loans from unbiased outside sources.

> *Go and get matching funds. If you need $25,000, then first get $12,500 from others before asking your family for the rest. If you can't do it that way—and if you don't have your own skin in the game—then you need to think twice about why you're asking someone you love to give you money. I believe you should get others to back the idea as well, so a parent or relative doesn't feel as though the money is a gift but rather a worthwhile investment. It puts a higher level of accountability into the entire process.*[3]

So, borrow from friends and family very cautiously. Do it, if necessary, but do it carefully and meticulously clarify expectations.

12-3c Credit Cards

Using credit cards to help finance a small business has become increasingly common among entrepreneurs. It has been estimated that approximately half of all entrepreneurs have used credit cards at one time or another to finance a startup or business expansion.

For someone who cannot acquire traditional financing like a bank loan, credit card financing may be an option—not a great option, but a necessary one. The interest costs can become overwhelming over time, especially because of the tendency to borrow beyond the ability to repay. So it is essential that an entrepreneur using credit card financing be extremely self-disciplined to avoid becoming overextended. Consider the following example. Unable to get a line of credit from a bank, Steven Fischer used his personal credit cards to keep his business operating after he was unable to collect receivables from some of his clients. He anticipated using his cards to keep his company afloat until they were paid. However, paying wages and bills proved to be more expensive than he had anticipated. Also, mixing his personal credit cards with business loans and expenses created problems. In the end, Fischer's company didn't survive.[4] After laying off employees and paying all of the business's bills, Fischer found himself personally liable for $80,000 in credit card debt.

So why use credit cards? At times the only option open to a small business entrepreneur, credit cards also have the advantage of speed. A lender at a bank has to be convinced of the merits of the business opportunity and that involves extensive preparation on the part of the entrepreneur. Credit card financing, on the other hand, requires no justification of the use of the money.

In practice, credit cards are a significant source of financing for a number of entrepreneurs, particularly early in the game. But the eventual goal is to use credit cards as a method of payment and not as a source of credit. In other words, the sooner you can pay your credit card balance in full each month, the sooner you can grow a profitable business.

12-4 BANK FINANCING

Discuss the basic process for acquiring and structuring a bank loan.

While commercial banks are primary providers of debt capital to *established* firms, they are generally less interested in financing startup businesses. Quite simply, bankers want firms with proven track records and plenty of collateral in the form of hard assets. Bankers are reluctant to loan money to finance losses, which are characteristic of early-stage companies. Neither are they very interested in financing R&D expenses, marketing campaigns, and other "soft" assets. Such expenditures usually have to be financed by equity sources. Nevertheless, it is wise to cultivate a relationship with a banker sooner rather than later, and well in advance of making a loan request.

12-4a Types of Loans

Bankers primarily make business loans in one of three forms: lines of credit, term loans, and mortgages.

LINES OF CREDIT

A **line of credit** is an informal agreement or understanding between a borrower and a bank as to the maximum amount of funds the bank will provide the borrower at any one time. Under this type of agreement, the bank has no legal obligation to provide the capital. (A similar arrangement that does legally commit the bank is a *revolving credit agreement*.) The entrepreneur should arrange for a line of credit in advance of an actual need, as banks are reluctant to extend credit on the spur of the moment.

line of credit
An informal agreement between a borrower and a bank as to the maximum amount of funds the bank will provide at any one time.

TERM LOANS

Under certain circumstances, banks will loan money on a 5- to 10-year term. Such **term loans** are generally used to finance equipment with a useful life corresponding to the loan's term. Since the economic benefits of investing in such equipment extend beyond a single year, banks can be persuaded to lend on terms that more closely match the cash flows to be received from the investment. For example, if equipment has a useful life of seven years, it might be possible to repay the money needed to purchase the equipment over, say, five years. It would be a mistake for a firm to borrow money for a short term, such as six months, when the equipment being purchased is expected to last for seven years. *Failure to match the loan's payment terms with the expected cash inflows from the investment is a frequent cause of financial problems for small firms.* The importance of synchronizing cash inflows with cash outflows when structuring the terms of a loan cannot be overemphasized.

Some loans call for term payments that include principal and interest, others for interest only with lump sum principal reductions. If in doubt, ask your banker for advice: "I want to expand. Here's the loan I think I need. What do you think?"

MORTGAGES

Mortgages, which represent a long-term source of debt capital, can be one of two types: chattel mortgages and real estate mortgages. A **chattel mortgage** is a loan for which certain items of inventory or other movable property serve as collateral. The borrower retains title to the inventory but cannot sell it without the banker's consent. A **real estate mortgage** is a loan for which real property, such as land or a building, provides the collateral. Typically, these mortgages extend up to 25 or 30 years.

12-4b Understanding a Banker's Perspective

To be effective in acquiring a loan, an entrepreneur needs to understand that a banker has three priorities when making a loan. They are listed below in their order of importance to the banker:

1. *Recouping the principal of the loan.* A banker is not rewarded adequately to assume large amounts of risk and will, therefore, design loan agreements so as to reduce the risk to the bank. First and foremost, the banker has to protect depositors' capital.
2. *Determining the amount of income the loan will provide the bank*, both in interest income and in other forms of income, such as fees.
3. *Helping the borrower be successful and then become a larger customer.* Only if the relationship is a win-win for both parties will the bank do well.

In making a loan decision, bankers give serious consideration to what they call the "five C's of credit": (1) the borrower's *character*, (2) the borrower's *capacity* to repay

term loans
Money loaned for a 5- to 10-year period, corresponding to the length of time the investment will bring in profits.

chattel mortgage
A loan for which items of inventory or other movable property serve as collateral.

real estate mortgage
A long-term loan with real property held as collateral.

the loan, (3) the *capital* being invested in the venture by the borrower, (4) the *collateral* available to secure the loan, and (5) the *conditions* of the industry and economy. Of course, no banker would ever make a loan to a borrower whose character is in question. Here, the borrower's relationships and credit scores are used as indicators. But while good character is vital, it is not sufficient to receive a loan. In fact, members of a loan committee will spend little time talking about a prospective borrower's character unless they become aware of some reason to question it. The conversation about the person will more likely center on her or his ability and achievements, and the nature of the borrower's relationship with the bank. Exhibit 12.5 illustrates the coming together of the five C's for a decision. While we place character at the center, all the criteria (C's) are important, as reflected in the exhibit.

These issues are apparent in the six questions that Jack Griggs, a banker and long-time lender to small businesses, wants answered before he will make a loan:[5]

- Does the borrower have strong character and reasonable ability?
- Do the purpose and amount of the loan make sense, both for the bank and for the borrower? For example, the loan may be too small to be profitable for the bank or may be in an industry in which the bank has no lending experience.
- Does the loan have a certain primary source of repayment? This usually means proven cash flows.
- Does the loan have a certain secondary source of repayment? This would be the collateral that the borrower can offer in case the loan cannot be repaid.
- Can the loan be priced profitably for the customer and for the bank?
- Are the loan and the relationship good for both the customer and the bank?

A banker's review of a loan request includes an analysis of financial considerations. When seeking a loan, a small business owner will be required to provide certain

EXHIBIT **12.5** Five C's: The Foundation For Getting a Loan

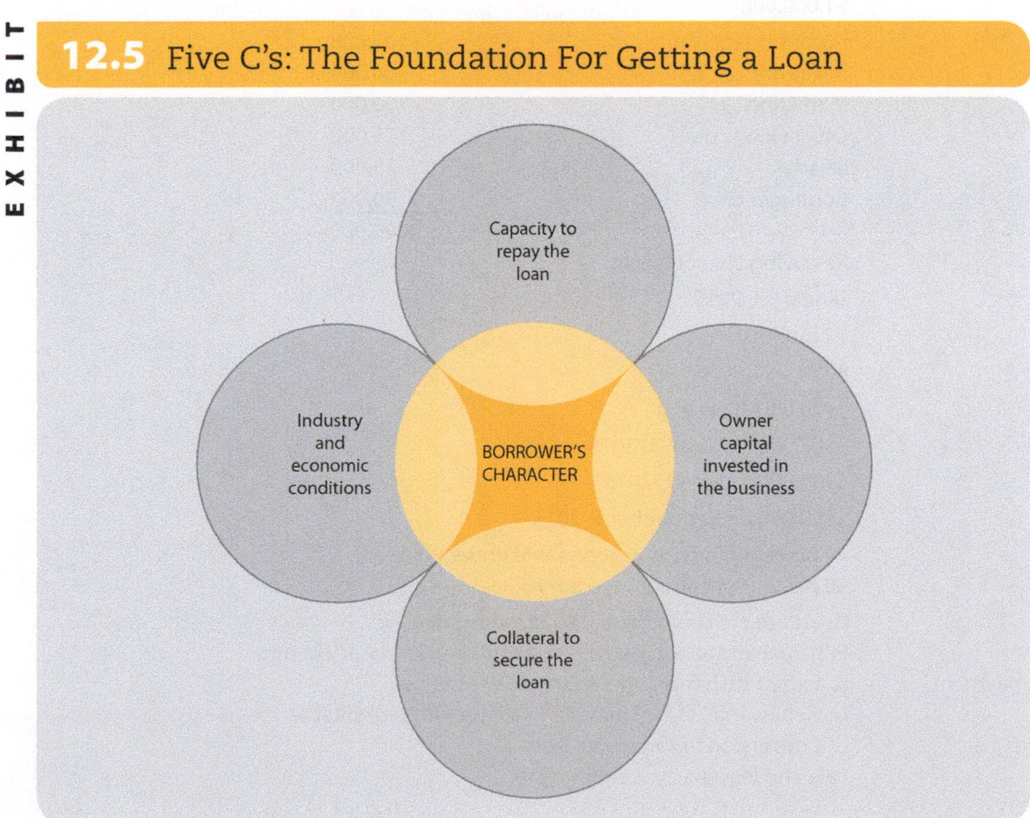

information in support of the request. Failure to provide this information will almost certainly result in rejection by the banker. Presenting inaccurate information or not being able to justify assumptions made in forecasting financial results is sure to make the banker question the entrepreneur's business acumen.

A well-prepared loan request is absolutely necessary. It reflects the entrepreneur's ability to capture the firm's history and future in writing, suggesting that the entrepreneur has given thought to where the firm has been and where it is going. As part of the presentation, the banker will want to know early on the answers to the following questions:

- How much money is needed?
- What is the venture going to do with the money?
- When is the money needed?
- When and how will the money be paid back?

An example of a written loan request is provided in Exhibit 12.6. A banker also will want to see, if at all possible, the following detailed financial information:

- Three years of the firm's historical financial statements, if available, including balance sheets, income statements, and cash flow statements.

Bankers Don't Like Surprises

Never surprise your banker with bad news. Tell your banker immediately if you are having a problem, and let him or her work with you. Avoiding your banker when things go wrong may cause you to be perceived as not being forthright, and you may lose his or her trust.

EXHIBIT

12.6 Sample Written Loan Request

Date of Request:	December 15, 2014	
Borrower:	Prestige & DeLay, Inc.	
Amount:	$1,000,000	
Use of Proceeds:	Accounts receivable	$ 400,000
	Inventory	200,000
	Marketing	100,000
	Officer loans due	175,000
	Salaries	75,000
	Contingencies	50,000
		$1,000,000
Type of Loan	Revolving Line of Credit	
Closing Date	January 3, 2015	
Term	12 months	
Rate	8.5%	
Takedown	$400,000 at closing	
	$300,000 at March 1, 2015	
	$200,000 at June 1, 2015	
	$100,000 on September 1, 2015	
Collateral	70 percent of accounts receivable under 90 days	
	50 percent of current inventory	
Guarantees	Guarantees to be provided by Prestige & DeLay	
Repayment Schedule	Principal and all accrued interest due on anniversary of note	
Source of Funds for Repayment	a. Excess cash from operations (see cash flow)	
	b. Renewable and increase of line if growth is profitable	
	c. Conversion to three-year note	
Contingency Source	Sale and leaseback of equipment	

- The firm's pro forma financial statements (balance sheets, income statements, and cash flow statements), in which the timing and amounts of the debt repayment are included as part of the forecasts
- Personal financial statements showing the borrower's net worth (assets − debt) and estimated annual income. A banker simply will not make a loan without knowing the personal financial strength of the borrower.

Joe Worth, who has served as a chief financial officer (CFO) for both private and public firms, offers this perspective:

> *[Y]ou'll get approved more readily and with better terms if you give the banks precisely what they need to make a decision: tax returns and audited (if possible) financial statements (P&L [income statements], balance sheets and cash flow) for the year to date and the previous three years; monthly statements for the previous 12 months; a business plan explaining what you do, how you do it, and why your company would be a good risk; a detailed projection showing how you will generate the funds to pay down the line; and a backup plan (collateral) to repay the bank if the projections don't pan out.*[6]

12-4c Selecting a Banker

For a typical small firm, the provision of checking-account facilities and the extension of short-term (and possibly long-term) loans are the two most important services of a bank. Normally, loans are negotiated with the same bank in which the firm maintains its checking account. In addition, the firm may use the bank's safe-deposit vault or its services in collecting notes or securing credit information. An experienced banker can also provide management advice, particularly in financial matters, to a new entrepreneur.

For convenience in making deposits and conferring about loans and other matters, a bank should be located in the same general vicinity as the firm. All banks are interested in their home communities and, therefore, tend to be sympathetic to the needs of local business firms. Except in very small communities, two or more local banks are usually available, thus permitting some freedom of choice.

Banks' lending policies are not uniform. Some bankers are extremely conservative, while others are more willing to accept some limited risks. If a small firm's loan application is neither obviously strong nor patently weak, its prospects for approval depend heavily on the bank's approach to small business accounts. Differences in willingness to lend have been clearly established by research studies, as well as by the practical experience of many business borrowers.

12-4d Negotiating the Loan

In negotiating a bank loan, a small business owner must consider the terms that will accompany the loan. Four key terms are included in all loan agreements: the interest rate, the loan maturity date, the repayment schedule, and the loan covenants.

INTEREST RATE

The interest rate charged by banks to small companies is usually stated in terms of the prime rate or, occasionally, the LIBOR. The **prime rate**, or **base rate**, is the rate of interest charged by banks on loans to their most creditworthy customers. The **LIBOR (London Interbank Offered Rate)** is the interest rate that London-based banks charge other banks in London, which is considerably lower than the prime rate.

prime rate (base rate)
The interest rate charged by commercial banks on loans to their most creditworthy customers.

LIBOR (London Interbank Offered Rate)
The interest rate on loans that London-based banks charge other banks in London.

Living the Dream

ENTREPRENEURIAL EXPERIENCES

Able Lending

When Hayley Groll, a professional hairstylist, was given the opportunity to buy an existing hair salon, the Shag Salon, she jumped at it. Groll had only one problem; she did not have the money required to make the purchase.

Groll first tried to borrow the money from an online lender, but to no avail. She then approached Able Lending, which is based in Austin, Texas, and within three weeks she was granted a $105,000 loan with a 9 percent interest rate. The loan was to be repaid over three years. The money gave her enough to buy the business and extend her building lease well into the future.

Will Davis and Evan Baehr, the founders of Able Lending, describe themselves as "collaborative lenders," offering business owners loans for up to three years for amounts between $25,000 and $250,000. But here is the catch—borrowers must raise the first 25 percent of the loan from friends and family. Davis says that Able is trying to find the people who are being missed by traditional banks and even nontraditional online lenders. The concept is described on Able's website:

> *Able helps entrepreneurs grow their small business through a collaborative loan involving Backers—those friends and family who are willing to help fund your Able loan. Three to five Backers fund 25 percent of the total loan amount, which unlocks the remaining 75 percent from Able and lets us lend to you at lower rates than other lenders.*

After a business owner completes an online application, Able uses its proprietary technology to assess the company's bank accounts, cash flows, and credit history. Then, taking a unique path, Able tracks a company's social media presence on Yelp, Facebook, Twitter, and LinkedIn. Davis doesn't reveal how a business's online footprint helps to evaluate an applicant, but he does claim that Able receives a more complete picture of a company's creditworthiness than any bank can acquire.

Depending on how fast the borrower lines up backers, funding can arrive within two weeks of applying—"much quicker than traditional bank financing," Davis says.

Able Lending has so far made 50 loans ranging from $5,000 to $150,000, mostly in the Austin area. But the firm has received nearly $40 million in loan requests nationwide.

Sources: Adapted from Michelle Goodman, "This Startup Will Give You a Loan—But There's a Twist," *Entrepreneur*, November 3, 2014, p. 86; and http://blog.ablelending.com, accessed February 12, 2015.

If a banker quotes a rate of "prime plus 2" and the prime rate is 3 percent, the interest rate for the loan will be 5 percent(3% + 2%). Alternatively, a banker might state the rate as "prime plus 200 basis points." A **basis point** is 1/100th of 1 percent; thus, 200 basis points are the same as 2 percent.

The interest rate can be a floating rate that varies over the loan's life—that is, as the prime rate changes, the interest rate on the loan changes—or it can be fixed for the duration of the loan. A banker may also impose a floor on the interest rate so that it cannot go below a given rate. For instance, the floor might be set at 3.5 percent, no matter the prime rate. If a banker does impose a floor, you might request a ceiling that the rate cannot go above. If the bank agrees to a ceiling of 6.5 percent, for example, you will know that your interest rate cannot go any higher than that.

basis point
1/100th of 1 percent, when quoting an interest rate.

Although a small firm should always seek a competitive interest rate, concern about the interest rate should not override consideration of the loan's maturity date, its repayment schedule, and any loan covenants.

LOAN MATURITY DATE

As already noted, a loan's term should coincide with the use of the money—short-term needs require short-term financing, while long-term needs demand long-term financing. For example, since a line of credit is intended to help a firm with only its short-term needs, it is generally limited to one year. Some banks require that a firm "clean up" a line of credit one month each year. Because such a loan can be outstanding for only 11 months, the borrower can use the money to finance seasonal needs but cannot use it to provide permanent increases in working capital, such as accounts receivable and inventory.

REPAYMENT SCHEDULE

With a term loan, the loan is set to be repaid over 5 to 10 years, depending on the type of assets used for collateral. However, the banker may have the option of imposing a **balloon payment** before the loan is fully repaid. A balloon payment allows the bank to require the borrower to pay off the balance of the loan in full at a specified time, rather than waiting the full term for the loan to be repaid. Assume, for example, that you borrow $50,000 at an interest rate of 6 percent, and the loan is to be repaid in equal monthly repayments over 84 months (seven years). The amount of each payment is determined to be $730 in order to pay off the loan in full by the end of the seven years.[7] However, the banker may include a term in the loan agreement giving the bank the right to "call" the loan at the end of three years, meaning that you would have to pay off what is still owed at that time ($31,100). The banker would have the choice of (1) requiring you to pay off the $31,100 at the end of the third year or (2) allowing you to have the remaining four years to pay off the loan. This provision permits the banker to reassess the borrower's creditworthiness at the end of the third year if the business is not doing well.

balloon payment
A very large payment that may be required about halfway through the term over which payments were calculated, repaying the loan balance in full.

LOAN COVENANTS

In addition to setting the interest rate and specifying when and how the loan is to be repaid, a bank normally imposes other restrictions on the borrower. These restrictions, or **loan covenants**, require certain activities (positive covenants) and limit other activities (negative covenants) of the borrower to increase the chance that the borrower will be able to repay the loan. Some types of loan covenants that a borrower might encounter include the following:

loan covenants
Bank-imposed restrictions on a borrower that increase the chance of timely repayment.

1. The company must provide financial statements to the bank on a monthly basis or, at the very least, quarterly (positive covenant).
2. As a way to restrict a firm's management from siphoning cash out of the business, the bank may limit managers' salaries. It also may prohibit any personal loans from the business to the owners (negative covenant).
3. A bank may put limits on various financial ratios to make certain that a firm can handle its loan payments. For example, to ensure sufficient liquidity, the bank may require the firm's current assets to be at least twice its current liabilities—that is, the current ratio (current assets ÷ current liabilities) must be equal to or greater than 2. Or the bank might limit the amount of debt the firm

© GOODLUZ/SHUTTERSTOCK.COM

can borrow in the future, as measured by the debt ratio (total debt ÷ total assets) (negative covenant).

4. The borrower will normally be required to personally guarantee the firm's loan. A banker wants the right to use both the firm's assets and the owner's personal assets as collateral. Even when a business is structured as a corporation and the owner can escape personal liability for the firm's debts—that is, the owner has *limited liability*—most banks still require the owner's personal guarantee (negative covenant).[8]

It is imperative that you pay close attention to the loan covenants being imposed by a banker. Ask for a list of the covenants before the closing date, and make certain that you can live with the terms. If you have an existing company, determine whether you could have complied with the covenants, especially key ratios, if the loan had been in place during the recent past. Then, if necessary, negotiate with your banker and suggest more realistic covenants. Bankers will negotiate, although they may sometimes try to convince you otherwise. After all, making loans is a primary source of profits for the bank.

You also need to be aware of what happens when you violate a loan covenant. Ultimately, the banker can make you repay the loan in full immediately. More often, the banker will increase the interest rate or require you to repay the loan in a shorter period of time. What happens will also depend on which covenant is violated. As Jack Griggs noted, "Some covenants are like yield signs, while others are stop signs."[9] In other words, bankers use covenants as warning lights to address any potential problems before they become fatal.

Explain how business relationships can be used to finance a small firm.

12-5 BUSINESS SUPPLIERS AND ASSET-BASED LENDERS

Companies that have business dealings with a new firm are possible sources of funds for financing inventory and equipment. Both wholesalers and equipment manufacturers/suppliers may provide accounts payable (trade credit) or equipment loans and leases.

12-5a Accounts Payable (Trade Credit)

Credit extended by suppliers is very important to a startup. In fact, trade (or mercantile) credit is the source of short-term funds most widely used by small firms. As mentioned in Chapter 10, *accounts payable (trade credit)* is of short duration—30 days is the customary credit period. Most commonly, this type of credit involves an unsecured, open-book account. The supplier (seller) sends merchandise to the purchasing firm; the buyer then sets up an account payable for the amount of the purchase.

The amount of trade credit available to a new company depends on the type of business and the supplier's confidence in the firm. For example, wholesale distributors of sunglasses—a very seasonal product line—often provide trade credit to retailers by granting extended payment terms on sales made at the start of a season. Sunglass retailers, in turn, sell to their customers during the season and make the bulk of their payments to the wholesalers after they have sold and collected the cash for the sunglasses. Thus, the retailer obtains cash from sales before paying the supplier. More often, however, a firm has to pay its suppliers prior to receiving cash from its customers. In fact, this can be a serious problem for many small firms, particularly those that sell to large companies. (This issue will be addressed in a discussion of asset management in Chapter 22.)

12-5b Equipment Loans and Leases

Some small businesses, such as restaurants, use equipment that is purchased on an installment basis through an **equipment loan**. A down payment of 25 to 35 percent is usually required, and the contract period normally runs from three to five years. The equipment manufacturer or supplier typically extends credit on the basis of a conditional sales contract (or mortgage) on the equipment. During the loan period, the equipment cannot serve as collateral for another loan.

Instead of borrowing money from suppliers to purchase equipment, some small businesses choose to lease equipment, especially computers, photocopiers, and fax machines. Leases typically run for 36 to 60 months and cover 100 percent of the cost of the asset being leased, with a fixed rate of interest included in the lease payments. However, manufacturers of computers and industrial machinery, working hand in hand with banks or financing companies, are generally receptive to tailoring lease packages to the particular needs of customers.

It has been estimated that 80 percent of all firms lease some or all of their business equipment. Three reasons are commonly given for the popularity of leasing: (1) the firm's cash remains free for other purposes, (2) available lines of credit can be used for other purposes, and (3) leasing provides a hedge against equipment obsolescence. A business owner can make a good choice about leasing, however, only after carefully comparing the interest charged on a loan to the implied interest cost of a lease, calculating the tax consequences of leasing versus borrowing, and examining the significance of the obsolescence factor. Also, the owner must be careful about contracting for so much equipment that it becomes difficult to meet installment or lease payments.

12-5c Asset-Based Lending

As its name implies, an **asset-based loan** is a line of credit secured by working capital assets, such as accounts receivable, inventory, or both. The lender cushions its risk by advancing only a percentage of the value of a firm's assets—generally, 65 to 85 percent against receivables and up to 55 percent against inventory. Also, assets such as equipment (if not leased) and real estate can be used as collateral for an asset-based loan. Asset-based lending is a viable option for young, growing businesses.

Of the several categories of asset-based lending, the most frequently used is factoring. **Factoring** is an option that makes cash available to a business before accounts receivable payments are received from customers. Under this option, a factor (an entity often owned by a bank holding company) purchases the accounts receivable, advancing to the business 70 to 90 percent of the amount of an invoice. The factor, however, has the option of refusing to advance cash on any invoice it considers questionable. The factor charges a servicing fee, usually 2 percent of the value of the receivables, and an interest charge on the money advanced prior to collection of the receivables. The interest charge may range from 2 to 3 percent above the prime rate.

Another way to finance working capital is to sell purchase orders. With **purchase-order financing**, the lender advances the amount of the borrower's cost of goods sold for a specific customer order less a fee, typically somewhere between 3 and 8 percent. For instance, for a purchase order of $20,000, with the cost of goods sold being $12,000, the lender will advance the $12,000 less the fee charged. According to Jason Goldberg, first vice president of Crestmark Bank, this type of financing "attempts to address the issue of a company growing so rapidly that cash flow can't sustain growth." With a signed

equipment loan
An installment loan from a seller of machinery used by a business.

asset-based loan
A line of credit secured by working capital assets.

factoring
Obtaining cash by selling accounts receivable to another firm.

purchase-order financing
Obtaining cash from a lender who, for a fee, advances the amount of the borrower's cost of goods sold for a specific customer order.

purchase order from a creditworthy customer, a business owner can often get financing for almost the entire process, provided the gross profit margin(gross profits ÷ sales) is at least 35 percent. Although the fee is not insignificant, it makes sense when the entrepreneur would not otherwise be able to accept an order from a large customer. In times when credit is scarce, Goldberg says, it's an opportunity "to leverage the ability to sell product."[10]

12-6 PRIVATE EQUITY INVESTORS

Describe the two types of private equity investors who offer financing to small firms.

Over the past two decades, private equity markets have been the fastest-growing source of financing for entrepreneurial ventures with the potential for becoming significant businesses. For an entrepreneur, these sources fall into two categories: business angels and venture capitalists.

12-6a Business Angels

Business angels are private individuals who invest in early-stage companies.[11] They are the oldest and largest source of early-stage equity capital for entrepreneurs. According to the Center for Venture Research at the University of New Hampshire, angel investments in 2013 amounted to $24.8 billion. A total of 70,730 businesses received funding from an estimated 298,800 angel investors.[12] The type of financing they provide has come to be known as **informal venture capital** because no established marketplace exists in which business angels regularly invest.

Business angels generally make investments in firms that are relatively small—over 80 percent of business angels invest in startup firms with fewer than 20 employees. They invest locally, usually no more than 50 miles from their homes. Some limit their investments to industries in which they have had experience, while others invest in a wide variety of business sectors.

Along with providing needed money, business angels frequently contribute know-how to new businesses. Because many of these individuals invest only in the types of businesses in which they have had experience, they can be very demanding. While they are generally more "friendly" as investors than some venture capitalists, initially their personal relationship with the entrepreneur has little impact on their decision to invest. Thus, the entrepreneur must be careful in structuring the terms of any such investors' involvement.

The traditional way to find informal investors is through contacts with business associates, accountants, and lawyers. Other entrepreneurs are also a primary source of help in identifying prospective investors. In addition, there are now a large number of formal angel networks and angel alliances in all major cities, both in the United States and abroad. Each angel group has its own process for evaluating deals. Some, for example, require entrepreneurs who are seeking funding to post their business plan on Gust.com, a global platform for startup funding. The group screens the plans and selects those entrepreneurs who will be allowed to present to the group. In most cases, individual angels then make personal decisions about whether or not to invest, regardless of what the other angels do. If enough angels are interested, a detailed evaluation is undertaken before a final decision is made.[13]

Finally, angels are beginning to search for investment opportunities on the emerging equity crowdfunding websites. The number of these websites are increasing almost daily. More will be said about crowdfunding later in the chapter.

business angels
Private individuals who invest in early-stage ventures.

informal venture capital
Funds provided by wealthy private individuals, usually to small, local startups.

Guy Kawasaki, the founder of Garage Technology Ventures, is now a venture capitalist and the author of *The Art of the Start* (a must-read for anyone wanting to start a new business). He offers the following suggestions about dealing with business angels:[14]

1. *Make sure the investors are accredited.* "Accredited" is legalese for "rich enough to never get back a penny." You can get into trouble for selling stock to those who aren't accredited—so don't.
2. *Make sure they're sophisticated.* Sophisticated angel investors have "been there and done that." You want angels' money, but you also want their knowledge and expertise.
3. *Don't underestimate them.* The idea that angel investors are easy marks is simply wrong. Angels care as much about how they will get their money back as venture capitalists do—maybe even more, because they're investing their personal, after-tax money.
4. *Understand their motivation.* Angel investors differ from venture capitalists in that business angels typically have a double bottom line. They've made it, so they want to pay back society by helping the next generation of entrepreneurs. Thus, they're often willing to invest in riskier deals to help entrepreneurs get to the next stage.
5. *Enable them to live vicariously.* One of the rewards of angel investing is the ability to live vicariously through an entrepreneur's efforts. Angels want to relive the thrills of entrepreneurship, while avoiding the firing line. They enjoy helping you, so seek their guidance frequently.
6. *Make your story comprehensible to the angel's spouse.* An angel's "decision-making committee" usually consists of one person: a spouse. So, if you've got a highly technical product, you must make it understandable for the angel's spouse when he or she asks, "What are we investing $100,000 in?"

ADAM ROSE/ABC/DISNEY ABC TELEVISION GROUP/GETTY IMAGES

7. *Sign up people the angel has heard of.* Angel investors are also motivated by the social aspect of investing with buddies in startups run by bright people who are changing the world. Once you've brought one angel on board, you're likely to attract a whole flock of other angels, too.
8. *Be nice.* Not infrequently, angel investors fall in love with entrepreneurs. An entrepreneur may remind an investor of a son or daughter, or even fill the position of the son or daughter the investor never had. Venture capitalists will sometimes invest in a schmuck as long as that schmuck is a proven moneymaker. If you're seeking angel capital, then you're probably not a proven moneymaker, so you can't get away with acting like a schmuck. Always be respectful to your investors.

formal venture capitalists
Individuals who form limited partnerships for the purpose of raising venture capital from large institutional investors.

12-6b Venture Capital Firms

In addition to business angels who provide informal venture capital, small businesses also may seek out **formal venture capitalists**, groups of individuals who form limited

Living the Dream

ENTREPRENEURIAL EXPERIENCES

"Shark Tank": Changing the Game of Angel Investing

"Shark Tank," the wildly successful television show, is quickly changing the angel-investing landscape. The show features a variety of hopeful entrepreneurs with capital-hungry start-ups. They enter the "shark tank" one by one, with the hope of securing an investment from one of the show's seasoned investors.

© CBPIX/SHUTTERSTOCK.COM

In many ways, the show accurately represents the process of obtaining capital from investors. The deals are structured like typical investments in which the entrepreneur exchanges a percentage of his or her company's equity for cash. The entrepreneurs must prepare a concise and compelling business plan and must be able to pitch it in a manner that demonstrates competency and keeps the investors' attention. This can often be a challenging process.

> *[T]he Sharks have a goal, too. They want a return on their investment and [to] own a piece of the next big business idea. . . . But if the pitch is poor, the Sharks will tear into the ill-prepared presenters and pass on the idea with a simple "I'm out!"*

Getting in front of an investor has traditionally been a lengthy and difficult process. Building a network and obtaining an introduction takes time. Since the show has aired, however, the gap is closing between entrepreneurs and potential investors.

> *More and more entrepreneurs are finding that angel investors are open to hearing their pitch if they present it in a quick, contest-style format. Sure, there are still plenty of angel connections happening from networking and pitching individual investors. But the opportunities to get in front of an angel without an introduction at a competition are growing.*

Small-scale angel investing competitions are becoming increasingly popular nationwide. One example is the Guppy Tank, southern California's own small-scale version of "Shark Tank." A group of angels with $500,000 select 2 to 10 local startups in which to invest their money.

Obtaining quick capital sounds like an entrepreneurial dream come true. However, it is important to realize that "Shark Tank" and competitions like it are just the starting point in entrepreneur-investor negotiations.

> *The contract for [Shark Tank] stipulates that "making an offer" on the show is definitely not a guarantee of investment. An offer on Shark Tank is an agreement to "negotiate in good faith," using the terms from the show as a starting point. This sounds unfair, but this is how it is done in the real world as well. "Shark Tank" is a reality show, but it is not a "game show." This is business. No one gets $100,000 from a 15-minute meeting.*

Sources: Based on "Shark Tank: About the Show," http://abc.go.com/shows/shark-tank/about-the-show, accessed February 18, 2015; Carol Tice, "How Shark Tank Is Changing Angel Investing," *Entrepreneur*, October 5, 2012, http://www.entrepreneur.com/blog/224597, accessed February 18, 2015; and Nate Berkopec, "How Exactly Are the Investments on "Shark Tank" Executed? Do the Producers Get a Cut?" May 29, 2012, http://www.huffingtonpost.com/quora/how-exactly-are-the-inves_b_1554151.html, accessed February 18, 2015.

partnerships for the purpose of raising capital from large institutional investors, such as pension plans and university endowments. Within the group, a venture capitalist serves as the general partner, with other investors constituting the limited partners. As limited partners, such investors have the benefit of limited liability.

A venture capitalist attempts to raise a predetermined amount of money, called a *fund.* Once the money has been committed by the investors, the venture capitalist evaluates investment opportunities in high-potential startups and existing firms. For example, the Sevin Rosen Funds raised $600 million for the Sevin Rosen Fund VIII. The money was then used to invest in a portfolio of companies.

For the investment, the venture capitalist receives the right to own a percentage of the entrepreneur's business. Reaching agreement on the exact percentage of ownership often involves considerable negotiation. The primary issues are the firm's expected profits in future years and the venture capitalist's required rate of return. Once an investment has been made, the venture capitalist carefully monitors the company, usually through a representative who serves on the firm's board.

Most often, investments by venture capitalists take the form of preferred stock that can be converted into common stock if the investor so desires. In this way, venture capitalists ensure that they have senior claim over the owners and other equity investors in the event the firm is liquidated but can convert into common stock and participate in the increased value of the business if it is successful. These investors generally try to limit the length of their investment to between 5 and 7 years, though it is frequently closer to 10 years before they are able to cash out.

Although venture capital as a source of financing receives significant coverage in the business media, *few small companies, especially startups, ever receive this kind of funding.* No more than 1 or 2 percent of the business plans received by any venture capitalist are eventually funded—not exactly an encouraging statistic. Failure to receive funding from a venture capitalist, however, does not indicate that the venture lacks potential. Often, the venture is simply not a good fit for the investor. So, before trying to compete for venture capital financing, an entrepreneur should assess whether the firm and its management team are suitable for a particular investor.

12-7 CROWDFUNDING

Describe how crowdfunding can be used by some small businesses to raise capital.

Perhaps you need $50,000 to fund a new business project and have tried the conventional sources of financing without success. You should check into crowdfunding.

Crowdfunding is the process of raising money online, frequently in small amounts per investor, but from a large number of investors. It has mushroomed with the advent of crowdfunding websites, also called *portals* or *platforms.* According to a study by Massolution, the dollar amount of crowdfunding increased from $530 million in 2009 to $1.3 billion in 2011. It was approximately $5.1 billion in 2013.[15]

crowdfunding
The process of raising small investments from a large number of investors via the Internet.

There are four basic approaches to crowdfunding: (1) donations, (2) rewards, (3) pre-purchases, and (4) equity investing. Only the last type of crowdfunding provides investors with equity ownership in the business.

Individuals who *donate* make a contribution to support a given project without receiving anything tangible in return. This approach is more akin to a charitable contribution than an investment. Interestingly, there are people who enjoy helping a business at times, without any promise of something in return.

In the second approach, *rewards,* supporters make a monetary contribution in return for a reward of some type. For example, BodBot, a startup providing exercise and nutrition recommendations on the Web, set a goal to raise $20,000 by crowdfunding. (It actually raised $61,410 from 1,092 participants.[16]) In return for participating, depending on the amount of the contribution, the company offered different packages of workouts and other benefits, beginning at $20 and continuing up to $15,000!

Living the Dream

ENTREPRENEURIAL EXPERIENCES

Parke New York: A Success at Crowdfunding

Solomon Liou is the founder of Parke New York, an online luxury clothing brand based in downtown New York City. Liou describes his business concept as follows:

> *Parke New York is a new vertically integrated, online denim brand, targeting a $13 billion market in the U.S. and $66 billion worldwide. Created with quality and aesthetics in mind, Parke combines premium fabrics and artisanal craftsmanship to provide the perfect fitting jeans. Additionally, by selling direct to consumers online, we can offer prices that are 50 percent less than traditional brands.*

In 2012, Liou chose to use crowdfunding as a way to gauge consumer support for the brand and to raise capital. His plans were to launch the business in July 2013, based on the outcome of the crowdfunding effort.

> *As part of an effort to secure consumer support and demonstrate market demand, Parke New York hosted a rewards crowdfunding campaign on Kickstarter for 30 days (from December 19, 2012, to January 18, 2013). This campaign received an immense amount of support and revealed clear support within the fashion/denim niche.*

The offer was for backers to "receive premium jeans and luxury basics at accessible prices through an online-only, pre-order model." The campaign raised $90,535 from 634 individuals. Following this success, Liou and his team were prepared to expand manufacturing and distribution capabilities to sell Parke New York jeans to consumers across the United States.

Sources: Based on "Parke New York: Profile," http://www.fundable.com/parke-new-york, accessed February 15, 2013; and http://www.parkenewyork.com, accessed February 15, 2015.

A similar approach to receiving a reward is a *pre-purchase*, in which the financial contribution is essentially the conditional pre-purchase of the entrepreneur's planned product. If the product launch is successful, contributors are sent the actual product.

Donations, rewards, and pre-purchases are not considered investments. The contributors are not loaning the firm money, nor are they receiving any ownership in the business. *Equity-based crowdfunding*, however, does offer participants partial ownership in the business. Since the participants are investors, the company is subject to securities laws. As of early 2015, any participant in equity-based crowdfunding had to be an accredited investor, which requires a net worth of at least $1 million, not including her or his primary residence, or income of at least $200,000.[17] For instance, Syntellia developed an app to assist visually impaired individuals with typing on a smartphone. Along with funds provided by angel investors, the firm raised $900,000 with equity-based crowdfunding. But anyone participating had to be an accredited investor.[18]

There are three types of equity-based crowdfunding:[19]

1. Type 1 allows for accredited investors to view private investment opportunities on a password-protected website. The entrepreneur can raise an unlimited amount of capital from an unlimited number of accredited investors. This type of crowdfunding allows the entrepreneur to avoid public exposure of confidential material.

2. Type 2 allows entrepreneurs to publicly solicit funding and to raise an unlimited amount of capital from an unlimited number of accredited investors. This type is quickly becoming the most popular type of equity crowdfunding,
3. Type 3, when approved by the SEC, will allow *unaccredited* investors to invest online. Then, entrepreneurs will be able to reach out to almost any and all investors in America, accredited or not.

An entrepreneur who is considering crowdfunding as a way to raise money can use a number of websites designed for this purpose. Two of the more popular websites are Kickstarter and Indiegogo. Both facilitate crowdfunding based on donations, rewards, and pre-purchases. As of early 2015, they did not provide equity crowdfunding. Kickstarter describes itself as follows:

> *We're a home for everything from films, games, and music to art, design, and technology. Kickstarter is full of projects, big and small, that are brought to life through the direct support of people like you. Since our launch in 2009, 8.2 Million people have pledged more than $1.6 Billion, funding 80,000 creative projects. Thousands of creative projects are raising funds on Kickstarter right now.*[20]

Two portals, among others, that do focus on equity-based crowdfunding are AngelList and Crowdfunder. These websites allow entrepreneurs to reach investors interested in purchasing equity in their companies. In contrast to Kickstarter, Crowdfunder describes itself as follows: "If you would benefit from fundraising tools that empower you to create a powerful online pitch and reach new investors . . . then Crowdfunder would be a good fit for you."[21]

Crowdfunder even allows investors to co-invest with angels and venture capitalists as long as they commit to share between 5 percent and 20 percent of any gains—assuming that there are some. But, again, securities laws prohibit private companies from advertising or selling shares to investors who are not relatively wealthy—that is, "accredited," as defined by legislation.

Small businesses that raise equity through crowdfunding should be aware of potential problems that can arise. First, if crowdfunding investors receive voting rights, that fact may become a deterrent to raising money from angels and venture capitalists in the future. Such investors usually would not be interested in sharing voting rights with a large group of small investors. Second, a company should be wary about sharing detailed financial information and trade secrets with a multitude of crowdfunding investors.

In short, when it is a good fit, crowdfunding is a viable option for small businesses that need to raise capital. And all signs suggest that this approach will become even more popular in the future.

12-8 GOVERNMENT LOAN PROGRAMS

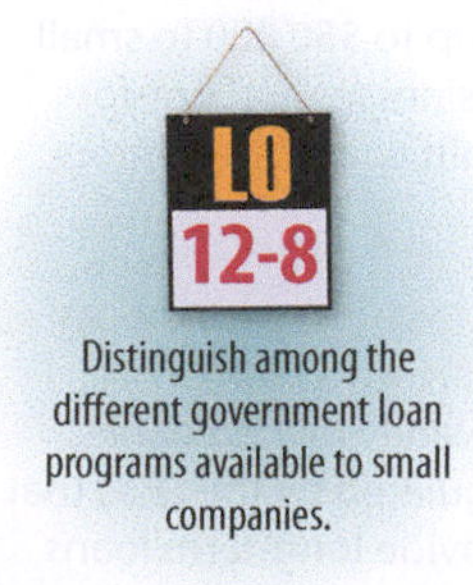

Distinguish among the different government loan programs available to small companies.

Several government programs provide financing to small businesses. Over the past decade, federal and state governments have allocated increasing, but still limited, amounts of money to financing new businesses. Local governments have likewise increased their involvement in providing financial support to startups in their areas. Though funds are available, they are not always easy to acquire. Time and patience on the part of the entrepreneur are required. Let's take a look at some of the more familiar government loan programs offered by various agencies.

12-8a The Small Business Administration

The federal government has a long history of helping new businesses get started, primarily through the programs and agencies of the Small Business Administration (SBA). For the most part, the SBA does not loan money but serves as a guarantor of loans made by financial institutions. The five primary SBA programs are (1) the 7(a) Loan Guaranty Program, (2) the Certified Development Company (CDC) 504 Loan Program, (3) the 7(m) Microloan Program, (4) small business investment companies (SBICs), and (5) the Small Business Innovative Research (SBIR) Program.

7(A) LOAN GUARANTY PROGRAM

The **7(a) Loan Guaranty Program** serves as the SBA's primary business loan program to help qualified small businesses obtain financing when they might not be eligible for business loans through normal lending channels. Guaranty loans are made by private lenders, usually commercial banks, and may be for as much as $750,000. The SBA guarantees 85 percent of loans not exceeding $150,000 and 75 percent up to $3.75 million.

To obtain a guaranty loan, a small business must submit a loan application to a lender, such as a bank. After an initial review, the lender forwards the application to the SBA. Once the loan has been approved by the SBA, the lender disburses the funds. The loan proceeds can be used for working capital, machinery and equipment, furniture and fixtures, land and building, leasehold improvements, and debt refinancing (under special conditions). Loan maturity is up to 10 years for working capital and generally up to 25 years for fixed assets.

7(a) Loan Guaranty Program
The SBA's primary business loan program, which helps qualified small companies obtain financing when they might not be eligible through normal lending channels.

CERTIFIED DEVELOPMENT COMPANY 504 LOAN PROGRAM

The **Certified Development Company (CDC) 504 Loan Program** provides long-term, fixed-rate financing for small businesses to acquire real estate or machinery and equipment for expansion or modernization. The borrower must provide 10 percent of the cost of the property, with the remaining amount coming from a bank and a certified development company funded by the SBA.

Certified Development Company (CDC) 504 Loan Program
An SBA loan program that provides long-term, fixed-rate financing for small businesses to acquire real estate or machinery and equipment.

7(M) MICROLOAN PROGRAM

The **7(m) Microloan Program** grants short-term loans of up to $50,000 to small businesses and not-for-profit child-care centers for working capital or the purchase of inventory, supplies, furniture, fixtures, and machinery and equipment. The SBA makes or guarantees a loan to an intermediary, which in turn makes the microloan to the applicant. As an added benefit, the lender provides business training and support programs to its microloan borrowers.

Most banks regard microloans as too costly to administer directly to small business owners. Therefore, some nonprofit organizations, such as the Northeastern Pennsylvania Alliance and the Detroit Micro-Enterprise Fund, work with banks and foundations to make these microloans.[22]

7(m) Microloan Program
An SBA loan program that provides short-term loans of up to $50,000 to small businesses and not-for-profit child-care centers.

SMALL BUSINESS INVESTMENT COMPANIES

Small business investment companies (SBICs) are privately owned banks that provide long-term loans and/or equity capital to small businesses. SBICs are licensed and regulated by the SBA, from which they frequently obtain a substantial part of their capital at attractive rates of interest. SBICs invest in businesses with fewer than 500 employees, a net worth of no more than $18 million, and after-tax income not exceeding $6 million during the two most recent years.

small business investment companies (SBICs)
Privately owned banks, regulated by the SBA, that provide long-term loans and/or equity capital to small businesses.

SMALL BUSINESS INNOVATIVE RESEARCH PROGRAM

The **Small Business Innovative Research (SBIR) Program** helps finance small firms that plan to transform laboratory research into marketable products. Eligibility for the program is based less on the potential profitability of a venture than on the likelihood that the firm will provide a product of interest to a particular federal agency.

Small Business Innovative Research (SBIR) Program
An SBA program that helps to finance companies that plan to transform laboratory research into marketable products.

12-8b State and Local Government Assistance

State and local governments have become more active in financing new businesses. The nature of the financing varies, but each program is generally geared to augment other sources of funding. Examples of such programs include the Golden Circle Loan Guarantee Fund, established by the city government of Des Moines, Iowa, to guarantee bank loans of up to $250,000 to small companies, and loans made to business owners by the New Jersey Economic Development Authority at the U.S. Treasury rate, significantly lower than interest rates typically charged at banks.

Most of these loans are made in conjunction with a bank, which enables the bank to take on riskier loans for entrepreneurs who might not qualify for traditional financing. "And some loans have a lower down payment requirement," explains Donna Holmes, former director of the Penn State Small Business Development Center. "The bank may do 50 percent, the state program another 40 percent, and the borrower only has to come up with 10 percent; with a straight bank loan, the bank might be looking for 20 percent or 25 percent."[23]

While such government programs may be attractive to an entrepreneur, they are frequently designed to enhance specific industries or to facilitate certain community goals. Consequently, you need to determine that a program is in sync with your specific business objectives.

12-8c Community-Based Financial Institutions

Community-based financial institutions are lenders that serve low-income communities and receive funds from federal, state, and private sources. They are increasingly becoming a source of financing for small companies that otherwise would have little or no access to startup funding. Typically, community-based lenders provide capital to businesses that are unable to attract outside investors but do have the potential to make modest profits, serve the community, and create jobs. An example of a community-based financial institution is the Delaware Valley Community Reinvestment Fund, which provides financing for small companies in Philadelphia's inner-city area.

community-based financial institution
A lender that uses funds from federal, state, and private sources to provide financing to small businesses in low-income communities.

12-9 WHERE ELSE TO LOOK

Explain when large companies and public stock offerings can be sources of financing.

The sources of financing that have been described thus far represent the primary avenues for obtaining money for small firms. The remaining sources are generally of less importance but should not be ignored by a small business owner in search of financing.

12-9a Large Corporations

Large corporations at times make funds available for investment in smaller firms when it is in their best interest to maintain a close relationship with such a firm. For instance, some large high-tech firms, such as Intel and Microsoft, prefer to invest in smaller firms that are conducting research of interest, rather than conduct the research themselves.

12-9b Stock Sales

Another way to obtain capital is by selling stock to outside individual investors through either private placement or public sale. Finding outside stockholders can be difficult when a new firm is not known and has no ready market for its securities, however. In most cases, a business must have a history of profitability before its stock can be sold successfully.

Whether it is best to raise outside equity financing depends on the firm's long-range prospects. If there is opportunity for substantial expansion on a continuing basis and if other sources are inadequate, the owner may logically decide to bring in other owners. Owning part of a larger business may be more profitable than owning all of a smaller business.

PRIVATE PLACEMENT

One way to sell common stock is through a **private placement**, in which the firm's stock is sold to select individuals—usually the firm's employees, the owner's acquaintances, members of the local community, customers, and suppliers. When a stock sale is restricted to private placement, an entrepreneur can avoid many of the demanding requirements of the securities laws.

PUBLIC SALE

When small firms—typically, larger small firms—make their stock available to the general public, this is called going public, or making an **initial public offering (IPO)**. The reason often cited for a public sale is the need for additional working capital.

In undertaking a public sale of its stock, a small firm subjects itself to greater governmental regulation, which escalated dramatically following the rash of corporate scandals in publicly owned companies such as Enron, Tyco, and WorldCom. In response to such corporate malfeasance, the U.S. Congress passed legislation, including the Sarbanes-Oxley Act, to monitor public companies more carefully. This resulted in a significant increase in the cost of being a publicly traded company—especially for small firms. Then in 2010, Congress enacted the Dodd-Frank Act for the purpose of averting a financial crisis similar to the one experienced in 2008–2009. The legislation primarily relates to the financial sector but also includes strict regulations for all companies to ensure transparency and accountability, again increasing costs. Finally, publicly traded firms are required to report their financial results quarterly in 10Q reports and annually in 10K reports to the Securities and Exchange Commission (SEC). The SEC carefully scrutinizes these reports before they can be made available to the public. At times, SEC requirements can be very burdensome.

Common stock may also be sold to underwriters, which guarantee the sale of securities. Compensation and fees paid to underwriters typically make the sale of securities in this manner expensive. Fees frequently range from 20 to 25 percent (or higher) of the value of the total stock issued. The reasons for the high costs are, of course, the uncertainty and risk associated with public offerings of the stock of small, relatively unknown firms.

We have now completed our discussion of what an entrepreneur needs to understand when seeking financing for a company, in terms of a firm's financial statements and forecasts (Chapters 10 and 11) and the different sources of financing typically used by small firms (Chapter 12). Our detailed explanations should help you avoid mistakes commonly made by small business owners when trying to get financing to grow a business.

private placement
The sale of a firm's capital stock to select individuals.

initial public offering (IPO)
The issuance of stock to be traded in public financial markets.

12-1. Describe how a firm's characteristics affect its available financing sources.

- Four basic firm characteristics determine how a firm is financed: (1) the firm's economic potential, (2) the size and maturity of the company, (3) the nature of the firm's assets, and (4) the personal preferences of the owners with respect to the trade-offs between debt and equity.
- An entrepreneurial firm with high-growth economic potential has more possible sources of financing than does a firm that provides a good lifestyle for its owner but little in the way of attractive returns to investors.
- Older and larger companies have more access to bank financing, while smaller firms tend to rely more on personal loans and credit cards.
- Tangible assets serve as great collateral when a business is requesting a bank loan, while intangible assets have little value as collateral for lenders.

12-2. Evaluate the choice between debt financing and equity financing.

- The choice between debt and equity financing involves trade-offs with regard to potential profitability, financial risk, and voting control.
- Borrowing money (debt) rather than issuing common stock (owners' equity) creates the potential for higher rates of return to the owners and allows them to retain voting control of the company, but it also exposes them to greater financial risk.
- Issuing common stock rather than borrowing money results in lower potential rates of return to the owners and the loss of some voting control, but it does reduce their financial risk.

12-3. Identify the typical sources of financing used at the outset of a new venture.

- The aspiring entrepreneur tends to stay "close to home" for sources of early financing, which include (1) personal savings, (2) friends and family, and (3) credit cards.
- The primary source of equity financing used in starting a new business is personal savings. A banker or other lender is unlikely to loan venture money if the entrepreneur does not have her or his own money at risk.
- Loans from friends and family may be the only available source of financing and are often easy and fast to obtain, although such borrowing can place the entrepreneur's most important personal relationships in jeopardy.
- Credit card financing provides easily accessible financing, but the high interest costs may become overwhelming at times.

12-4. Discuss the basic process for acquiring and structuring a bank loan.

- Bankers primarily make business loans in one of three forms: lines of credit, term loans, and mortgages.
- The priorities of a banker when making a loan are (1) recouping the principal of the loan, (2) determining the amount of income the loan will provide the bank, and (3) helping the borrower be successful and become a larger customer.
- In making a loan decision, a banker always considers the "five C's of credit": (1) the borrower's *character*, (2) the borrower's *capacity* to repay the loan, (3) the *capital* being invested in the venture by the borrower, (4) the *collateral* available to secure the loan, and (5) the *conditions* of the industry and economy.
- Obtaining a bank loan requires a well-prepared loan request that addresses: (1) how much money is needed, (2) what the venture is going to do with the money, (3) when the money is needed, and (4) when and how the money will be paid back.
- A banker may request other detailed financial information, including three years of the firm's historical financial statements, the firm's pro forma financial statements, and personal financial statements showing the borrower's net worth and estimated annual income.
- An entrepreneur should carefully evaluate available banks before choosing one, basing the decision on factors such as the bank's location, the services provided, and the bank's lending policies.
- In negotiating a bank loan, the owner must consider the accompanying terms, which typically include the interest rate, the loan maturity date, the repayment schedule, and the loan covenants.

12-5. Explain how business relationships can be used to finance a small firm.

- Business suppliers may offer trade credit (accounts payable), which is the source of short-term funds most widely used by small firms.

- Suppliers may also offer equipment loans and leases, which allow small businesses to use equipment purchased on an installment basis.
- An asset-based loan is financing secured by working capital assets, such as accounts receivable, inventory, or both.

12-6. Describe the two types of private equity investors who offer financing to small firms.

- Business angels are private individuals, generally with substantial business experience, who invest in early-stage ventures.
- Formal venture capitalists are groups of individuals who form limited partnerships for the purpose of raising capital from large institutional investors. The money is then invested in high-potential startups and existing firms for an ownership share.

12-7. Describe how crowdfunding can be used by some small businesses to raise capital.

- Crowdfunding is the process of raising small investments from a large number of investors via the Internet.
- There are four basic approaches to crowdfunding: (1) donations, (2) rewards, (3) pre-purchases, and (4) equity investing.

12-8. Distinguish among the different government loan programs available to small companies.

- The federal government helps new businesses get started through the programs and agencies of the Small Business Administration (SBA), which include the 7(a) Loan Guaranty Program, the Certified Development Company (CDC) 504 Loan Program, the 7(m) Microloan Program, small business investment companies (SBICs), and the Small Business Innovative Research (SBIR) Program.
- State and local governments finance new businesses with programs that are generally geared to augmenting other sources of funding.
- Community-based financial institutions are lenders that use funds from federal, state, and private sources to serve low-income communities and small companies that otherwise would have little or no access to startup funding.

12-9. Explain when large companies and public stock offerings can be sources of financing.

- Large companies may finance smaller businesses when it is in their self-interest to have a close relationship with the smaller company.
- Stock sales, in the form of either private placements or public sales, may provide a few high-potential ventures with equity capital.

Key Terms

7(a) Loan Guaranty Program p. 344
7(m) Microloan Program p. 344
asset-based loan p. 337
balloon payment p. 335
basis point p. 334
business angels p. 338
Certified Development Company (CDC) 504 Loan Program p. 344
chattel mortgage p. 330
community-based financial institution p. 345
crowdfunding p. 341
equipment loan p. 337
factoring p. 337
formal venture capitalists p. 339
informal venture capital p. 338
initial public offering (IPO) p. 346
LIBOR (London InterBank Offered Rate) p. 333
line of credit p. 329
loan covenants p. 335
prime rate (base rate) p. 333
private placement p. 346
purchase-order financing p. 337
real estate mortgage p. 330
Small Business Innovative Research (SBIR) Program p. 345
small business investment companies (SBICs), p. 344
term loan p. 330

You Make the Call

Situation 1

David Bernstein needs help financing his six-year-old, $3.5 million company, Access Direct, Inc. "We're ready to get to the next level," says Bernstein, "but we're not sure which way to go." Access Direct cleans and then sells used computer equipment for corporations. It is looking for up to $2 million in order to expand. "Venture capitalists, individual investors, or banks," says Bernstein, who owns the company with four partners, "we've thought about them all."

Question 1 What is your impression of Bernstein's perspective on raising capital to "get to the next level"?

Question 2 What advice would you offer Bernstein as to both appropriate and inappropriate sources of financing in his situation?

Situation 2

John Dalton is well on his way to starting a new venture—Max, Inc. He has projected a need for $350,000 in initial capital. He plans to invest $150,000 himself and either borrow the additional $200,000 or find a partner who will buy stock in the company. If Dalton borrows the money, the interest rate will be 6 percent. If, on the other hand, another equity investor is found, he expects to have to give up 60 percent of the company's stock. Dalton has forecasted earnings of about 16 percent in operating profits on the firm's total assets.

Question 1 Compare the two financing options in terms of projected return on the owner's equity investment. Ignore any effect from income taxes.

Question 2 What if Dalton is wrong, and the company earns only 4 percent in operating profits on total assets?

Question 3 What should Dalton consider in choosing a source of financing?

Situation 3

Mike Smith seeks your counsel about a problem that has grown out of a decision he made three years earlier to buy a warehouse. Up until then, he had rented three warehouses, where he stored containers and did pick-and-pack for retailers importing goods from abroad. Figuring it was time to consolidate, Smith found a building, negotiated a price of $3.5 million, put down $300,000, and borrowed $3.2 million from a bank at 7 percent interest.

It seemed like a good idea at the time. Then a recession hit. As his sales dropped, he struggled to make his monthly payment of $27,000. At present, he's behind in his payments and scared. Furthermore, the situation seems unlikely to improve anytime soon. To make matters worse, he signed a personal guarantee on the loan and thinks he might lose his house. The bank is assessing the situation to decide what to do.

In a panic, Smith tells you, "I'm going to tell the bank I need eight months. It can take the money I'll owe for that time, plus what I owe now, and tack it onto the end of the mortgage. What do you think?"

"How do you know that's what the bank is looking for?" you ask.

"I have to offer them something," Smith says. "My wife and I could lose everything!"

"You aren't going to lose everything," you say, "and you're making a mistake to assume that you know what the bank wants."

Question 1 What guidance will you give Smith in negotiating with the bank?

Question 2 Why might you advise him not to go into a meeting with bank officers with a plan already in mind?

Business Plan

LAYING THE FOUNDATION

As part of laying the foundation for your own business plan, respond to the following questions regarding the financing of your venture:

1. What is the total financing required to start the business?
2. How much money do you plan to invest in the venture? What is the source of this money?
3. Will you need financing beyond what you personally plan to invest?
4. If additional financing is needed for the startup, how will you raise it? How will the financing be structured—debt or equity? What will the terms be for the investors?
5. According to your pro forma financial statements, will there be a need for additional financing within the first five years of the firm's life? If so, where will it come from?

Video Case 12

Moonworks (P. 668)

Moonworks began installing Gutter Helmet® in Rhode Island, but soon the business began expanding further into the New England states and New York. Now it offers industry-leading home improvement products. Moonworks has had a long relationship with the Bank of Rhode Island, and this case tells the story of the company's financing and how it has changed along with the company over 15 years.

Endnotes

1. We learned about *return on assets* and how it is computed in Chapter 10. In that discussion, we said that operating profits (operating income, or earnings before interest and taxes) should be used in the numerator, instead of net profits. Operating profits are the profits from investing in the firm's assets before distribution to the lenders and owners and is, therefore, a better measure of the firm's overall profitability on the assets.
2. Quoted in Elaine Pofeldt, "Why Money Isn't Always Your Biggest Problem," *Inc.*, March 2015, http://www.inc.com/magazine/201404/elain-pofeldt/too-much-startup-funding-causes-problems.html, accessed March 10, 2015.
3. Quoted in Ilan Mochari, "The Numbers Game," *Inc.*, October 2002, http://www.inc.com/magazine/20021015/24778.html, accessed February 16, 2015.
4. Asheesh Advani, "The Angel in Your Pocket," *Entrepreneur*, November 2009; and Steven Fischer, "The Perils of Using Personal Credit Cards to Fund Your Business," http://unintentionalentrepreneur.com, accessed December 2014.
5. Personal communication with Jack Griggs, president and CEO of Southwestern Bancorp, Inc., and chairman of the board of Texas Heritage Bank, September 20, 2014.
6. Joe Worth, "What You Need to Know about Credit Lines," *Entrepreneur*, January 2015, p. 68.
7. To compute the $730 monthly payment, you can use a financial calculator or a computer spreadsheet:

   PV (present value) = $50,000 (current loan)

   N (number of payments) = 84 (7 years × 12 months = 84)

   I / yr (interest rate/month) = 0.5% (6% interest rate per year ÷ 12 months = 0.005 = 0.5%)

   FV (future value) = 0 (in 7 years)

   PMT (payment) = $730.43
8. Mochari, op. cit., p. 64.
9. Comment by Jack Griggs, October 1, 2014.
10. Quoted in C. J. Prince, "New Money," *Entrepreneur*, March 2008, http://www.entrepreneur.com/magazine/entrepreneur/2008/march/190066.html, accessed October 2, 2014.
11. For an excellent source on business angels, see Bill Payne, *The Definitive Guide to Raising Money from Angels*, http://billpayne.com/services/definitive-guide-raising-money-from-angel-investors, accessed January 5, 2015.
12. Jeffrey Sohl, "The Angel Investor Market in 2013: A Return to Seed Investing," *Center for Venture Research*, April 30, 2014, http://paulcollege.unh.edu/sites/paulcollege.unh.edu/files/2013%20Analysis%20Report%20FINAL.pdf, accessed February 16, 2015.
13. For a description of how angel networks function, visit the Angel Capital Association website at http://angelcapitalassociation.org.
14. Guy Kawasaki, "Garnering Angels," *Entrepreneur*, January 2008, http://www.entrepreneur.com/magazine/entrepreneur/2008/january/187614.html, accessed February 28, 2015.
15. Katherine Noyes, "Why Investors Are Pouring Millions into Crowdfunding," *Fortune*, April 17, 2014, http://fortune.com/2014/04/17/why-investors-are-pouring-millions-into-crowdfunding, accessed March 12, 2015.
16. "Bodbot," https://www.fundable.com/bodbot, accessed April 4, 2015.
17. In 2012, in order to make more capital available to small businesses, Congress passed the Jumpstart Our Business Startups, or JOBS, Act, which will remove the requirement that investors have to be accredited in order to invest in private companies. However, as of March 2015, the Securities and Exchange Commission was finalizing the regulation dealing with nonaccredited investors, which would allow these persons to invest up to $5,000 in a company.
18. See "Syntellia," https://www.fundable.com/fleksy, accessed April 4, 2015.
19. Taken from Eric T. Wagner, "Equity Crowdfunding 101: Is It Right for Your Startup?" *Forbes*, March 18, 2014, http://www.forbes.com/sites/ericwagner/2014/03/18/equity-crowdfunding-101-is-it-right-for-your-startup, accessed March 3, 2015.
20. See https://www.kickstarter.com/hello, accessed April 3, 2015.
21. See https://www.crowdfunder.com/startup-funding?gclid=CNqxt-2P5cQCFY47gQoddlkAzg, accessed April 7, 2015.
22. Asheesh Advani, "Finally, Someone Wants to Give You Money," *Entrepreneur*, March 2010, http://www.entrepreneur.com/article/205058, accessed October 16, 2014.
23. Quoted in C. J. Prince, "Alternate Financing Routes," *Entrepreneur*, March 2007, pp. 66–68.

© WATCHARAKUN/SHUTTERSTOCK.COM

CHAPTER 13

Planning for the Harvest

The following story of Tapestry Medical, Inc., is told by Robert Knorr, its founder and CEO. He discusses building the company and then "finishing well," by executing what proved to be a successful harvest.

For as long as I can remember, I felt the entrepreneurial spirit burning within me. In the early part of my professional career, my desire was satisfied by creating new businesses for my employer, Johnson & Johnson. Within the security of a corporate environment, I had easy access to funding and talented people who helped me create several successful new businesses. Although in many ways I operated as an entrepreneur within a large corporation, ultimately Johnson & Johnson bore all the risks AND received all the rewards of each new business I created.

In the SPOTLIGHT
Tapestry Medical, Inc.

After almost 20 years, I decided to leave Johnson & Johnson and venture out on my own. At that point in my career, I had the industry knowledge to start my own company in the healthcare field. I also had the confidence to use my own money to fund my company that began in my garage. By "bootstrapping"

© GST/SHUTTERSTOCK.COM

After studying this chapter, you should be able to . . .

13-1. Explain the importance of having a harvest, or exit, plan.

13-2. Describe the options available for harvesting.

13-3. Explain the issues in valuing a firm that is being harvested and deciding on the method of payment.

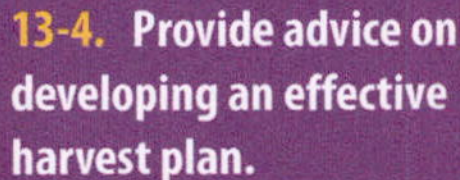

13-4. Provide advice on developing an effective harvest plan.

my company, I and a few members of the management team were able to maintain tight control of the company's ownership and control all decision making. Most importantly, this time I would bear the risks but also receive the rewards of my new business [Tapestry Medical]. Within a few years, Tapestry had established itself as the leading company in this small but growing field of remote patient monitoring. In fact, within four years Tapestry was among the fastest-growing private healthcare companies in the U.S.

Although Tapestry's sales were growing rapidly, additional working capital was needed to sustain growth beyond what we could provide. Also, several competitors were interested in consolidating Tapestry's market share and best-in-class operations into their own companies. Following the financial crisis of late 2008, I decided that the time was right to sell Tapestry to a larger healthcare company with the resources to take the business to the next level. Potential acquirers included diversified healthcare companies interested in entering Tapestry's marketplace.

At the time, Tapestry was still a privately funded startup company competing against three large, well-funded publicly traded companies. However, just prior to putting Tapestry up for sale, I signed an important co-marketing agreement with a leading healthcare software company that provided access to 500,000 potential new customers.

With impressive past results and a promising future, I engaged an investment banker who helped negotiate the best acquisition terms. After several months of intense negotiations, Tapestry was eventually acquired by its principal competitor, a leading healthcare company that had made several other acquisitions in this industry. I, along with key members of my management team, remained on board and was immediately given responsibility for merging Tapestry into the acquiring company's operations. The first year after the acquisition, sales of the new combined entity rose dramatically as a result of adopting best practices across both organizations and leveraging customer relationships.

Although Tapestry was founded and then sold within five years, there were periods of great uncertainty and risk. Looking back on the company sale, Knorr offers three pieces of advice:

- Do whatever you can to detach yourself emotionally from selling your company.
- Establish a short list of "must haves" prior to beginning negotiations and remain flexible on all secondary points.
- Remember to thank (and when appropriate, reward) everyone who helped you achieve your goals.

Knorr's positive experience with selling Tapestry and then becoming an executive of the acquiring firm is not the norm, at least not without a lot of frustration. Being prepared for the harvest process and life after exiting your business is something that deserves your thoughtful attention.

Source: Personal communication with Robert Knorr, founder and CEO, Tapestry Medical, Inc., September 28, 2014.

As you will learn in this chapter, exiting your business, or what we call the *harvest*, can be the best of times and the worst of times, depending in large part on how well you understand yourself, your business, and what is required to exit your business effectively. You may wonder why we address the issue of exiting a business so early in the text, choosing to delay instruction on managing a business to subsequent chapters. We do so because of our strong conviction that it is better for an entrepreneur to consider the exit sooner rather than later.

In previous chapters, we have talked about recognizing business opportunities and developing strategies for capturing these opportunities. Such activities represent the cornerstone for everything a company does. But, for entrepreneurs, that's not the end of the story. Experience suggests that an entrepreneur who is developing a company strategy should think about more than just starting (founding or acquiring) and growing a business. The entrepreneurial process is not complete until the owners and any other investors have exited the venture and captured the value created by the business. This final—but extremely important—phase can be enhanced through an effective harvest, or exit, plan. In other words, the goal is to create value during the entrepreneurial journey by making a difference and then *finishing well!*

13-1 THE IMPORTANCE OF THE HARVEST

Explain the importance of having a harvest, or exit, plan.

Most small business owners do not like to think about the harvest, even though few events in the life of an entrepreneur, and of the firm itself, are more significant. Consequently, the decision to harvest is frequently the result of an unexpected event, possibly a financial crisis, rather than a well-conceived strategy.

Harvesting, or **exiting**, is the method that owners and investors use to get out of a business and, ideally, reap the value of their investment in the firm. Many entrepreneurs successfully grow their businesses but fail to develop effective harvest plans. As a result, they are unable to capture the full value of the business they have worked so hard to create.

An entrepreneur needs to understand that harvesting encompasses more than merely selling and leaving a business. It involves capturing value (cash flows), reducing risk, and creating future options—the reason we prefer the term *harvest* over *exit*. In addition, there are personal, nonfinancial considerations for entrepreneurs. Owners may receive a lot of money for their firms but still be disappointed with the harvest if they are not prepared for a change in lifestyle. Thus, carefully designing an intentional harvest strategy is as essential to an entrepreneur's personal success as it is to his or her financial success.

In this chapter, we offer suggestions for achieving a "successful" harvest. It is a mistake to define success only in terms of the harvest; the entrepreneurial journey should be successful as well. So, throughout the chapter, we encourage you to think about what success means to you. Arriving at the end of the journey only to discover that your ladder was leaning against the wrong wall is one of life's tragedies.

The harvest is vitally important to a firm's investors as well as to its founder. Investors who provide high-risk capital—particularly angels and venture capitalists—generally insist on a well-thought-out harvest strategy. They realize that it is easy to put money into a business but difficult to get it out. As a result, a firm's appeal to investors is driven, in part, by the availability of harvest options. If investors are not convinced that opportunities will exist for harvesting their investment, they will be unlikely to invest.

While it is important to think sooner rather than later about the harvest, don't lose focus on the business itself. Attention must always be on running a successful business, including continuing to deliver high-quality products and services and creating a great workplace environment. A well-balanced business plan takes exit planning into account while simultaneously contemplating market entry and developing financial projections.

Planning for a Successful Harvest

The earlier you begin planning for a harvest, the more successful your eventual exit will most likely be. In fact, some of the steps involved in planning for the harvest, such as fine-tuning your company's strategies, focusing on internal growth, improving your financial systems, and creating an independent board, are the same as those required to build a successful company.

13-2 METHODS OF HARVESTING A BUSINESS

Describe the options available for harvesting.

The four basic ways to harvest an investment in a privately owned company are (1) selling the firm, (2) distributing the cash flows generated by the business to its owners instead of reinvesting the cash, (3) offering stock to the public through an initial public offering (IPO), and (4) undertaking a private equity recapitalization. These options are shown graphically in Exhibit 13.1.

13-2a Selling the Firm

In any harvest strategy, the financial questions associated with the sale of a firm include how to value the firm and how to structure the payment for the business. Most frequently, an entrepreneur's motivation for selling a company relates to retirement

harvesting (exiting) The process used by entrepreneurs and investors to reap the value of their investment in a business when they leave it.

EXHIBIT 13.1 Methods for Harvesting a Business

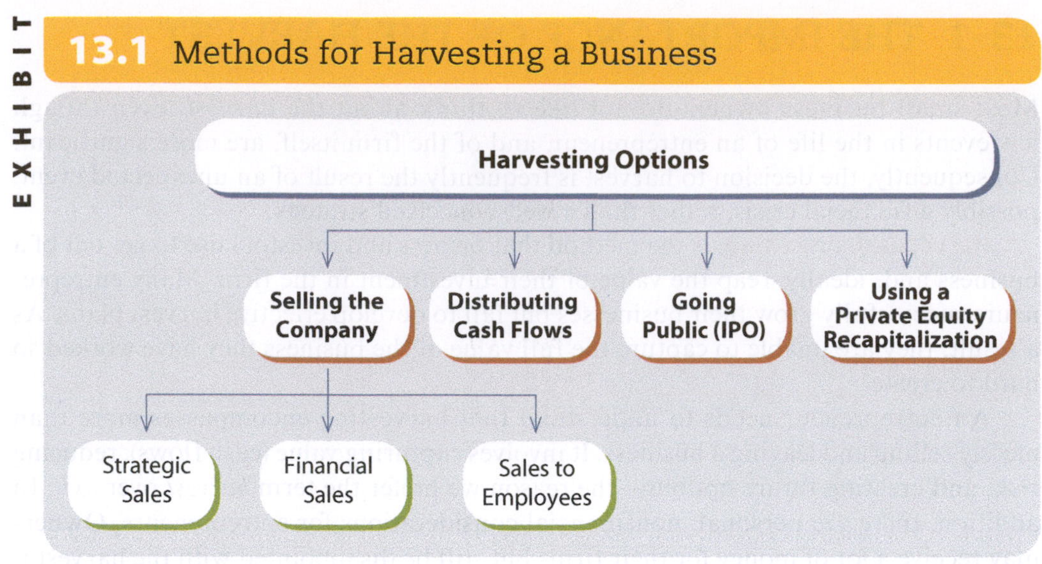

and estate planning and a desire to diversify investments. Thus, in choosing a possible buyer, entrepreneurs should understand what they want to accomplish from the sale.

Potential buyers for a company can come from a number of places, including customers, suppliers, employees, friends and family, or even a competitor. An owner may also want to use a business broker. A **business broker** is a professional who assists in the buying and selling of a business. In addition to finding possible buyers, a business broker can provide valuable guidance to the selling entrepreneur and help facilitate the negotiations. Brokers can, however, be relatively expensive, charging 5 to 10 percent of the selling price. Care has to be taken when selecting a broker. Not all brokers act professionally, and some make false claims regarding their qualifications. It is not unusual for an entrepreneur to be disappointed with a broker's contribution to the sale. For example, Robert Hall, the owner of Visador Corporation, hired a business broker to help sell his business. At one point in the negotiations, Hall gave the broker the firm's latest financial information that reported a downturn in sales in the previous month. Hall felt that ethics required that the buyer be given this information. The broker, as Hall learned later, chose not to give the information to the buyer so that the deal would not be adversely affected. After all, the broker received a fee only if the sale was consummated.

In the search for potential buyers, it is essential that the selling entrepreneur understand the different types of buyers. In the sections that follow, we will look at three buyer groups in particular: (1) strategic buyers, (2) financial buyers, and (3) employees.

SALES TO STRATEGIC BUYERS

Usually, a strategic buyer is a firm in a similar line of business in a different market or in need of new products and services to sell to existing customers. Another possibility is a buyer in an unrelated business that wants to acquire a seller's strengths to help the buyer's existing business. For example, IBM acquired a privately owned company, HealthLink, Inc., that provided information technology in the healthcare industry. Since IBM had not developed a presence in this niche area, acquiring HealthLink quickly gave it a way to compete in that space.

Strategic buyers value a business based on the synergies they think they can create by combining the acquired firm with another business. Since the value of a business to a buyer is derived from both its stand-alone characteristics and its synergies, strategic

business broker
A professional who assists in the buying and selling of a business.

buyers may pay a higher price than would other buyers, who value the business only as a stand-alone entity. Thus, in strategic acquisitions, the critical issue is the degree of strategic fit between the firm to be harvested and the potential buyer's other business interests. If the prospective buyer is a current rival and if the acquisition would provide long-term, sustainable competitive advantages (such as lower production costs or superior product quality), the buyer may be willing to pay a premium for the company.

SALES TO FINANCIAL BUYERS

Unlike strategic buyers, buyers in financial acquisitions look primarily to a firm's stand-alone, cash-generating potential as its source of value. A financial buyer hopes to increase future sales growth, reduce costs, or both. This fact has an important implication for the owner of the business being purchased. The buyer often will make changes in the firm's operations that translate into greater pressures on the firm's personnel, resulting in layoffs that the current owner might find objectionable.

A **leveraged buyout (LBO)** is a financial acquisition involving a very high level of debt financing, where the future cash flows of the target company are expected to be sufficient to meet debt repayments. In the past, acquisitions frequently were financed with \$9 in debt for every \$1 in equity—thus, the name *leveraged* buyout. The LBO has sometimes been called a **bust-up LBO**, in which the new owners pay the debt down rapidly by selling off the acquired firm's assets.

Because buyers rely heavily on debt to finance the acquisition, the acquired company must have the following characteristics: (1) steady earnings over time, (2) attractive growth rates, (3) an effective management team already in place, and (4) assets that can be used as collateral on the debt. Otherwise, the risk is too great, and the transaction simply will not work.

Consider Visador Corporation, which was sold to a financial buyer for \$67 million. The buyer financed the purchase as a leveraged buyout, incurring a lot of debt. The firm's total assets and debt and equity (as presented in the balance sheet) before and after the sale were as follows:

	Before the Sale	After the Sale
Total assets	\$18,000,000	\$67,000,000
Total debt	\$ 5,000,000	\$60,000,000
Equity	13,000,000	7,000,000
Total debt and equity	\$18,000,000	\$67,000,000

Visador's before-sale and after-sale numbers differ in two important respects. First, the total assets (and total debt and equity) increased from \$18 million to \$67 million. In other words, the founders of Visador had invested just over \$18 million in the firm during their years of ownership, up to the point of the acquisition. However, the buyer was willing to pay \$67 million for the business, based on future cash flows that were expected to be generated.

Second, before the sale, the assets were financed with 28 percent debt (\$5 million total debt ÷ \$18 million total assets) compared to 90 percent debt (\$60 million total debt ÷ \$67 million total assets) after the sale. Consequently, the firm was exposed to significantly more financial risk. If sales had decreased, the company may not have been able to service its debt. This is typical for bust-up leveraged buyouts.

More recently, the bust-up LBO has been replaced by the build-up LBO. As the name suggests, a **build-up LBO** involves pulling together a group of smaller firms to create a larger enterprise that might eventually be sold or taken public via an initial public offering.

leveraged buyout (LBO)
A purchase heavily financed with debt, where the future cash flows of the target company are expected to be sufficient to meet debt repayments.

bust-up LBO
A leveraged buyout involving the purchase of a company with the intent of selling off its assets.

build-up LBO
A leveraged buyout involving the purchase of a group of similar companies with the intent of making the firms into one larger company for eventual sale or to be taken public.

Consider Visador Corporation, designer/producer of residential staircases, which was sold to a financial buyer for $67 million. The buyer financed the purchase as a leveraged buyout.

The process of a build-up LBO begins with the acquisition of a company, which then acquires a number of smaller businesses that in some way complement it. These subsequent acquisitions may expand capacity in related or completely different businesses. The newly formed combination is operated privately for five years or so in order to establish a successful track record, and then it is sold or taken public. These acquisitions continue to rely heavily on debt financing, but to a lesser extent than bust-up LBOs. Build-up LBOs have occurred in a number of industries where smaller companies frequently operate, such as funeral services and automobile dealerships.

Sometimes, the selling firm's own management initiates an LBO to buy the business from the entrepreneur—in which case the arrangement is referred to as a **management buyout (MBO)**. An MBO can contribute significantly to a firm's operating performance by increasing management's focus and intensity. Thus, an MBO is a potentially viable means of transferring ownership from the founder to the management team. In many entrepreneurial businesses, managers have a strong incentive to become owners but lack the financial capacity to acquire the firm. An MBO can solve this problem through the use of debt financing, which is often underwritten in part by the selling entrepreneur.

SALES TO EMPLOYEES

Established by Congress in 1974, **employee stock ownership plans (ESOPs)** have gradually been embraced by more than 12,000 companies. Once established, an ESOP uses employees' retirement contributions to buy company stock from the owner and holds it in trust. Over time, the stock is distributed to employees' retirement plans.

It is common for an entrepreneur to start an ESOP by selling only a portion of the company. But even if the owner sells all of her or his stock, the owner can still retain her or his management position with the firm, thereby effectively maintaining control of the business. And an ESOP creates significant tax advantages for the seller. For instance, if the entrepreneur sells at least 30 percent of the company, taxes that may be owed as a result of the sale can frequently be deferred and not paid until a later date—in some cases, indefinitely. For example, after the owner-managers of BFW Construction Company created an ESOP, they sold the business and rolled over the money from the shares into their personal retirement accounts. As a result, they have not paid taxes from the time the shares were put into the ESOP, and they will not have to pay them until they are required to begin withdrawing the money, when they are 70½ years old.[1]

A reason frequently given for selling to employees is to create an incentive for them to work harder—by giving them a piece of the profits. However, employee ownership is not a panacea. Although advocates maintain that employee ownership improves motivation, leading to greater effort and reduced waste, the value of increased employee effort resulting from improved motivation varies significantly from firm to firm. Selling all or part of a firm to employees works only if the company's employees have an owner's mentality—that is, they do not think in "9-to-5" terms. An ESOP may provide a way for the owner to sell the business, but if the employees lack the required mindset, it will not serve the business well in the future.

Employee education is necessary if an ESOP is to be effective. Consider the experience of Mick Slinger, chief financial officer of Van Meter Industrial, Inc., who

management buyout (MBO)
A leveraged buyout in which the firm's top managers become significant shareholders in the acquired firm.

employee stock ownership plan (ESOP)
A harvesting method by which a firm is sold either in part or in total to its employees.

thought his company's employee stock program was a great perk for employees. But at a company meeting, an employee said he didn't care at all about the stock fund, asking, "Why don't you just give me a couple hundred bucks for beer and cigarettes?" It was a wake-up call for Slinger, who says that many employees at the 100-percent employee-owned company "didn't know what stock was, didn't know what an [employee] owner was. I made the mistake of thinking that everyone thinks like me." So, the company created an employee committee to raise awareness of stock ownership and how it affects employees' net worth. Today, employees are much more engaged in the program, and the firm's management believes it has made a significant contribution to increasing its stock price and lowering employee turnover. But it required a lot of effort to make the plan work as desired.[2]

The approaches that have been described in this section for selling a company represent the primary ways in which small business owners exit their businesses. But the opportunity to sell a business can be affected by market conditions. For instance, during the last recession, there were not many buyers—but neither were there many sellers. Entrepreneurs who had been considering an exit were holding back in the hope of an economic recovery.

By 2014, as the economy was coming out of the recession, the number of willing buyers had increased considerably with more attractive offers being made by buyers. But it continued to be difficult for buyers to get financing from traditional sources. As a result, **seller financing**, in which a seller loans the buyer part of the purchase price of the business, became more prevalent. For instance, an entrepreneur purchased a business for $3.5 million and paid $2.7 million in cash, with the seller taking a note for the remaining $800,000 to be paid off over the next seven years. The $2.7 million in cash came from a bank loan of $2 million and $700,000 of the buyer's personal money. The loan from the seller was subordinated to the bank loan, so that if the buyer missed a payment to the bank, she could not make any payments to the seller until the bank loan was current.

13-2b Distributing the Firm's Cash Flows

A second harvest strategy involves the orderly withdrawal of the owners' investment in the form of the firm's cash flows. The withdrawal process could be immediate if the owners simply sold off the assets of the firm and liquidated the business. However, for a value-creating firm—one that earns attractive rates of return for its investors—this does not make economic sense. The mere fact that a firm is earning high rates of return on its assets indicates that the business is worth more as a going concern than a dead one. Instead, the owners might simply stop growing the business. By doing so, they would increase the cash flows that can be returned to investors.

In a firm's early years, all of its cash is usually devoted to growing the business. Thus, the company's inflow of cash during this period is zero—or, more likely, negative—requiring its owners to seek outside cash to finance its growth. As the firm matures and opportunities to grow the business decline, sizable cash flows frequently become available to its owners. Rather than reinvest all the cash in the business, the owners can begin to withdraw the cash, thus harvesting their investment. If they decide to adopt this approach, only the amount of cash necessary to maintain current markets is retained and reinvested. There is little, if any, effort to grow the present markets or expand into new markets.

Harvesting by slowly withdrawing a firm's cash from the business has two important advantages: The owners can retain control of the business while they harvest their investment, and they do not have to seek out a buyer or incur the expenses associated

seller financing
Financing in which the seller accepts a note from a buyer in lieu of cash in partial payment for a business.

with consummating a sale. There are disadvantages, however. Reducing investment when the firm faces valuable growth opportunities could leave a firm unable to sustain its competitive advantage. The end result may be an unintended reduction in the value of the business. Also, there may be tax disadvantages to an orderly liquidation, compared with other harvest methods. For example, if a corporation distributes cash as dividends, both the company and the stockholders will be taxed on the income; this is known as **double taxation**. (However, there is no double taxation for a sole proprietorship, partnership, limited liability company, or S corporation.)

Finally, for the entrepreneur who is simply tired of day-to-day operations, siphoning off the cash flows over time may require too much patience. Unless other people in the firm are qualified to manage it, this strategy may be destined to fail.

13-2c Initial Public Offering (IPO)

A third method of harvesting a firm is an initial public offering. As briefly discussed in Chapter 12, an **initial public offering (IPO)** occurs when a private firm sells its shares for the first time to the general public. This requires registering the stock issue with the Securities and Exchange Commission (SEC) and adhering to blue sky laws that govern the public offering at a state level. The purpose of these federal and state laws is to ensure adequate disclosure to investors and to prevent fraud. Businesses intending to conduct an IPO must file a detailed registration statement with the SEC, which includes in-depth financial, management, and operational information.

double taxation
Taxation of income that occurs twice—first as corporate earnings and then as stockholder dividends.

initial public offering (IPO)
The first sale of shares of a company's stock to the public.

In the 1990s, entrepreneurs frequently considered the prospect of an initial public offering to be the ultimate outcome for their efforts, bringing with it increased prestige in many business circles. Some called it the "holy grail" of entrepreneurial success. However, that is not the case today, especially for smaller IPOs. Exhibit 13.2 shows the number of IPOs and dollars raised from 2000 through 2014. Fewer dollars were raised for IPOs in 2002 and 2003, following a dot-com bubble, and again in 2008–2009, at the height of the Great Recession. The most active year for IPOs since 2000 was 2014, when the amount of capital raised increased 55 percent over 2013. However, much of this increase was due to the Chinese e-commerce giant Alibaba's public offering in

EXHIBIT 13.2 IPOs 2000–2014

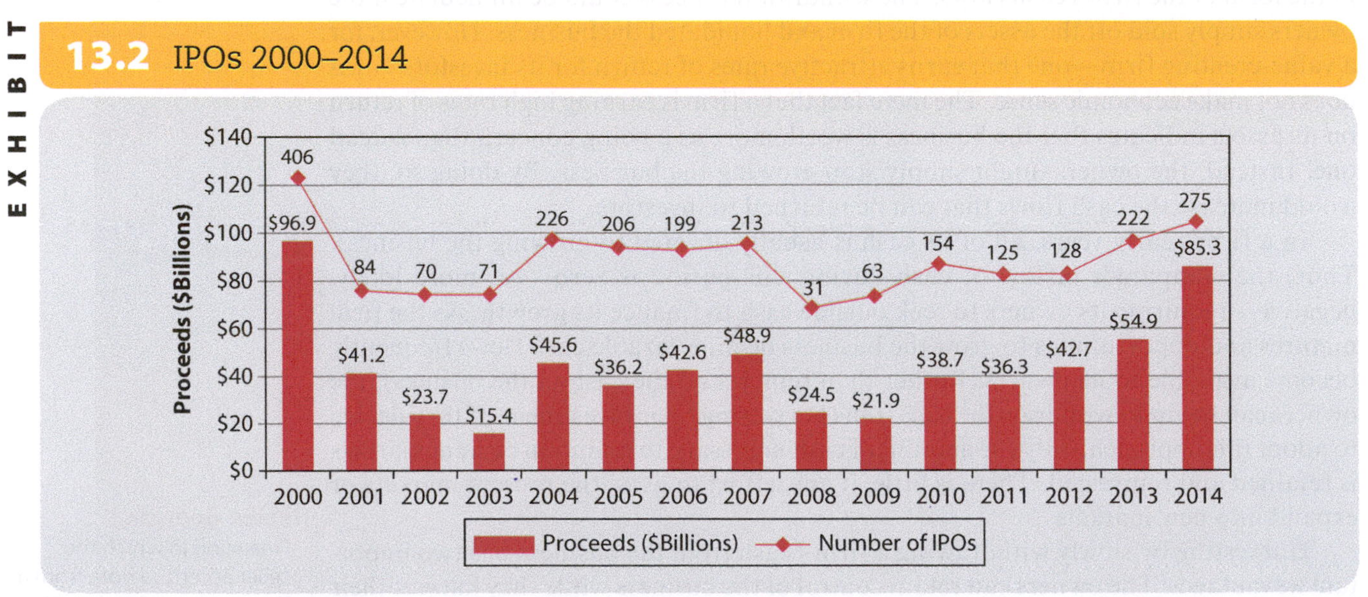

Source: "2014 Was Another Big Year for IPO Offerings," https://www.fidelity.com/viewpoints/active-trader/IPO-opportunities?imm_pid=1&immid=00926&imm_eid=e41740581&buf=999999, accessed March 22, 2015.

Living the Dream

ENTREPRENEURIAL EXPERIENCES

Two Friends Build and Successfully Exit Their Business

Jorge Fernandez and Bruce Goodhartz met 22 years ago, when both were working for a large commercial electrical contractor. Sharing a number of common goals, they decided to start their own business. Goodhartz describes building their company and their experience in finally exiting the business:

Experiencing early successes, we grew ESA Construction into one of the more recognizable names in dental construction in the [Dallas-Fort Worth] metroplex in less than three years. However, we knew that to stay competitive, we would need to strengthen our position. So we were the first of our competitors to build a website that showcased our previous dental projects; although at this early stage, it primarily served as a marketing tool and not for searches.

Jorge and I often wondered how we would ever "exit" from our business when the time came. Also, we had no idea as to the value of the business, other than what was on the books. So we hired an independent business valuation company and were shocked to learn that we indeed owned a company that had substantial value to others.

© ISTOCKPHOTO.COM/DESERT_FOX99

Based on recommendations for improving our value and becoming more marketable, we spent the next five years enhancing our brand recognition and removing the "Jorge and Bruce" from ESA Construction. We promoted our employees to key front-line positions with our customers and vendors; we aggressively increased our market share; we set up and maintained a Facebook page; and [we] reworked our website for maximum Google optimization.

[In 2011,] we had two confidential meetings over a six-month period with larger contractors and actually received a "Letter of Intent" from one of them, although it was an offer that we declined. Following these unsuccessful negotiations, we decided to take a break from marketing ESA and focus back on building our business and maintaining our market share—things that had started to slip as we were trying to sell the company. Then in fall 2012, we approached our largest subcontractor, a younger, successful, and aggressive drywall contractor, about the idea of his buying a portion of our company. We saw it as a way to strengthen and grow the company into new markets. He would then be allowed to completely buy us out in five years.

While we agreed on terms, he could not get a bank to finance the deal. As it turned out, no bank would loan him the money unless he owned 100 percent of the company. Thus, he countered with an offer to buy the firm in total. We went through about four months of negotiations, bank appraisals, and valuations. To get the deal done, we had to reduce our asking price by about 8 percent, but we received the full amount in cash at the time of the sale.

We closed the sale on February 15, 2013, with Jorge and me receiving an employment agreement for one year at our former base salary, benefits, and the same job description as before, with the added role to help in the transition to the new ownership. The sale turned out to be good for Jorge and me as the former owners. But equally important, all of the ESA employees retained their positions and salaries, with new excitement and synergy at the office.

What's next for Jorge and me beyond our one-year employment is up in the air. We are having to learn how to work for someone else, which is different. Also, I want to take this time to do some special things with family—including being a new granddad. But I know that I would not be happy not working. So Jorge and I are open to the idea of continuing with the company and the new owner, whom we consider to be a good friend. In fact, we are in discussions about assisting ESA in opening offices in other Texas markets and possibly beyond. But where will we be in five years, only time will tell.

Source: Written by Bruce Goodhartz, co-founder and co-owner, ESA Construction, October 12, 2014. Reprinted with permission.

September 2014 for $22 billion. Finally, the average size of IPOs has increased significantly over the past years; thus, offerings by smaller firms have not been nearly as prevalent.

Evaluate Your Business as a Buyer Would

Take time periodically to look at your company as though you were a prospective buyer. You'll notice things that you might otherwise overlook, such as improvements that you can make and best practices that you can adopt.

THE COSTS OF MANAGING AN IPO

An entrepreneur must consider more than just the initial costs of an IPO, which can be as much as 20 percent of the issue. He or she must also think hard about the costs of running a publicly traded company, which include significant ongoing costs associated with reporting its financial results to investors and to the SEC. These costs significantly increased in 2002, when the U.S. Congress passed the Sarbanes-Oxley Act. The act placed a much greater burden on companies to have good accounting practices and controls that will prevent egregious offenses by managers. In 2009, Congress passed the Dodd-Frank Act, which was primarily aimed at banks and other financial institutions to help avoid a repeat of the most recent financial crisis. However, it also added costly requirements for all publicly traded companies. Furthermore, these regulatory costs are disproportionate to a small firm and no small consideration in the decision to go public.

REASONS FOR GOING PUBLIC

The purpose of the IPO process is to create a ready market for publicly trading the company's stock. An IPO offers a number of benefits:

1. It can enhance the reputation of the business if done successfully.
2. It provides an additional source of capital to grow the business.
3. A stock that is publicly traded can create an ongoing interest in the company and its continued development.
4. Publicly traded stock is more attractive to key personnel whose incentive pay includes the firm's stock.

While there are several reasons for going public, the primary reason is to raise capital. In most cases, money raised from selling a firm's stock to the public is used for expansion, paying down debt, and increasing the firm's liquidity (cash). In fewer instances, initial public offerings result from entrepreneurs' desire to sell their stock. Thus, IPOs are seldom intended as an *immediate* exit strategy but rather as a way to raise capital for growth. Eventually, however, entrepreneurs can and frequently do sell their shares as a way to cash out of their companies.

13-2d Private Equity Recapitalization

A fourth method of harvesting is a **private equity recapitalization**, also called a *private equity recap*, where private equity investors provide a combination of debt and equity to the business that allows the entrepreneur to cash out part of his or her investment in the company. The entrepreneur will most likely continue to manage the business. Private equity investors offer two key advantages that public investors do not: immediacy and flexibility. With private equity, an entrepreneur can sell most of her or his stock immediately, an option not available when a company is taken public. Also, private equity investors can be more flexible in structuring their investment to meet an entrepreneur's needs.

private equity recapitalization
Provision of debt and equity by private equity investors that allows an entrepreneur to cash out part of his or her investment.

Although the situation is complicated by the different needs of each generation, a private equity recap is particularly effective for family-owned businesses that need to transfer ownership to the next generation. In that transfer of ownership, there must be a trade-off among three important goals: (1) liquidity (cash) for the selling family members, (2) continued financing for the company's future growth, and (3) the desire of the younger generation to maintain control of the firm. In other words, the older generation wants to get cash out of the business, while the younger generation wants to retain the cash needed to finance the firm's growth and yet not lose ownership control.

© MARCEL MOOIJ/SHUTTERSTOCK.COM

To understand how a private placement might work, consider the following approach taken by New Heritage Capital, a firm that works with family-owned businesses:[3] Assume that a company could be sold for \$20 million through a leveraged buyout (LBO), which would most likely be financed through at least 80 percent debt and 20 percent equity. Many entrepreneurs would find such an arrangement intolerable. They simply would not want their company subjected to the risk associated with a large amount of debt financing. Also, with an LBO, the family generally loses control of the business.

As an alternative, the retiring generation might sell to New Heritage Capital for \$18 million—10 percent less than the LBO price—of which \$15 million would be paid to the retiring generation and \$3 million reinvested in the business by the younger generation. For the \$3 million investment, the younger generation would receive 51 percent of the equity. The remaining \$15 million of the purchase price would be financed from two sources: \$7 million in debt and \$8 million from New Heritage Capital, consisting of \$4 million in preferred stock and \$4 million in common stock. The preferred stock would provide an annual dividend to the investors, while the common stock would give 49 percent of the firm's ownership to the new investor (see Exhibit 13.3).

EXHIBIT 13.3 Private Placement—An Illustration

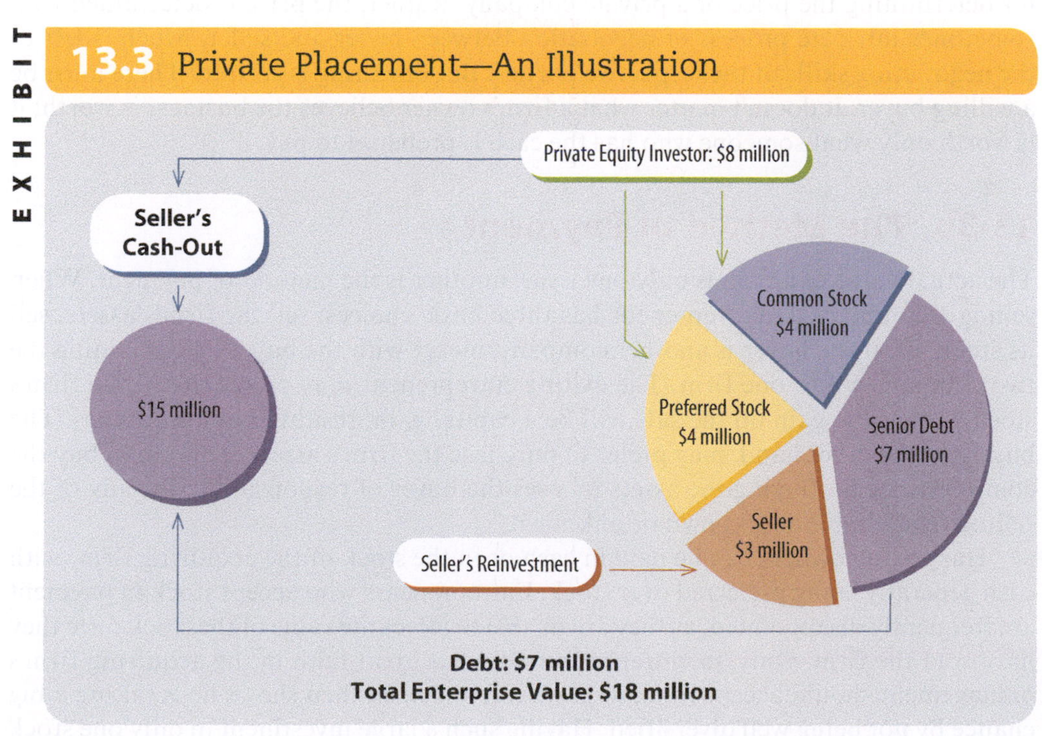

The differences between the two capital structures are clear. The debt ratio is much lower with the recapitalization than with the LBO, possibly allowing for a lower interest rate on the debt given less risk, and permitting the firm's cash flows to be used to grow the firm rather than to pay down debt. This arrangement allows the senior generation of owners to cash out, while the next generation retains control and the cash to grow the firm—a win-win situation. The younger generation also has the potential to realize significant economic gains in the future if the firm performs well after the sale.

Small Business Owners' Exit Plans

In a survey by Harris Poll and Bank of the West, 62 percent of small business owners identified their exit plan as follows:

- Plan to leave it to their children or relatives—21%
- Expect to sell it to the highest bidder—19%
- Plan to liquidate—11%
- Would sell to employees—7%
- Would leave it to their current business partner—4%

Source: "Paying It Forward: Small Business Owners Share Their Experiences and Insights," Bank of the West Survey of Small Business, 2014.

13-3 FIRM VALUATION AND PAYMENT METHODS

Explain the issues in valuing a firm that is being harvested and deciding on the method of payment.

As a firm moves toward the harvest, two issues are of primary importance: the harvest value (what the firm is worth) and the method of payment when a firm is sold.

13-3a The Harvest Value

Valuing a company may be necessary on numerous occasions during the life of the business—but it is never more important than at the time of the exit. Owners can harvest only what they have created. Value is created when a firm's return on invested capital is greater than the investors' **opportunity cost of funds**, which is the rate of return that could be earned on an investment of similar risk.

opportunity cost of funds
The rate of return that could be earned on another investment of similar risk.

Growing a venture to the point of diminishing returns and then selling it to others who can carry it to the next level is a proven way to create value. How this incremental value is shared between the old and the new owners depends largely on the relative strengths of each party in the negotiations—that is, who wants the deal the most or who has the best negotiating skills.

Business valuation is part science and part art, so there is no precise formula for determining the price of a private company. Rather, the price is determined by a sometimes intricate process of negotiation between buyer and seller. Much is left to the negotiating skills of the respective parties. But one thing is certain: There must be a willing buyer. It doesn't matter what a firm's owner believes the business is worth; it is worth only what someone who has the cash is prepared to pay.

13-3b The Method of Payment

The actual value of a firm is only one issue; another is the method of payment. When selling a company, an entrepreneur has three basic choices: sell the firm's assets, sell its stock, or, if the buyer is another company, merge with the buyer by combining the two companies into one firm. The exiting entrepreneur may prefer to sell the firm's stock so that the gain on the sale will be a capital gain, resulting in lower taxes. The buyer, on the other hand, may prefer to purchase the firm's assets rather than buy the company's stock. Buying the assets relieves the buyer of responsibility for any of the selling firm's liabilities, known or unknown.

Harvesting owners can be paid in cash or in the stock of the acquiring firm, with cash generally being preferred over stock. Entrepreneurs who accept stock in payment are frequently disappointed, as they are unable to affect the value of the stock once they have sold the firm. Only an entrepreneur who has great faith in the acquiring firm's management should accept stock in payment, and even then she or he is taking a big chance by not being well diversified. Having such a large investment in only one stock is risky, to say the least.

Living the Dream

ENTREPRENEURIAL EXPERIENCES

Why My Exit Strategy Failed

Michael Flatt felt deep disappointment after selling his business, and his experience is not unusual for many entrepreneurs. His counsel: Get good advice before selling, and understand that the money realized from the sale may not be of primary importance when compared to other considerations.

Exiting the company you founded is a natural part of entrepreneurship, and it can provide great financial rewards. It has great consequences for your successors in management and the employees you leave behind. And I made sure to attend to those. But the exit also has consequences for you. I took them too lightly.

In my case, everything pointed toward the wisdom of selling the natural disaster mitigation and reconstruction business I had founded 26 years earlier. I had built the company into a valuable, profitable powerhouse, but I felt I was burning out. My partners were aging. I sensed opportunities elsewhere, and my efforts to keep the staff together and engaged were wearing me out. I knew I could sell, which made all these headaches seem unnecessary.

Shortly after announcing the sale, we were contacted by three interested parties. Everything went smoothly. We even managed to miss the 2008 recession and, according to our consultants, we received an above-market price. As a businessman, I had done everything right. Inside, though, I was wracked by regret. What I forgot to consider were the things I enjoyed at work. I didn't ask myself the hard questions about why I was selling, what I wanted to gain—and most important, what I would miss if I sold.

My advice to you—before you do what I did—is to stop and think. Go back to the fundamentals of your business, way back if you need to. You must first understand why you created your business. And I don't mean just the value proposition. I mean why are YOU there? What do you gain from continuing to stay with the company and what would you lose if you left? Be honest. If you can fully realize what you will be giving up, you will be able to envision the future.

Finally, go one step further and ask what else matters to you. What else do you want to accomplish in life, and will it be easier to do that with or without your company? This is by no means an easy question, but even success can't extinguish true passion: This is your chance to chase after your dreams. . . . [A]fter I sold the company, I soon realized that to be captain of my own ship was my dream. I missed leading my team, charting the company's course, and responding to challenges at a moment's notice. Today, four years after selling, I have learned that the riches of a successful exit can't replace the rewards of leadership.

In hindsight, I should have looked to someone outside the organization [who] could offer me perspective. A coach, perhaps, someone to ask me why I was selling, what I wanted to gain afterward, and most importantly, what I would be missing.

Source: Michael Flatt, "Why My Exit Strategy Failed," *Inc.*, March 5, 2012, accessed June 15, 2014. *Inc.*: the magazine for growing companies by Goldhirsh Group. Reproduced with permission of Goldhirsh Group via Copyright Clearance Center.

13-4 DEVELOPING AN EFFECTIVE HARVEST PLAN

We have discussed why planning for the harvest is important and also described the methods for harvesting. However, understanding what the options are for exiting a company in no way guarantees a successful harvest. More times than not, owners who harvest their businesses are disappointed with the process and the outcome. In the sections that follow, we provide suggestions for crafting an effective exit strategy.[4]

13-4a Anticipate the Harvest

Entrepreneurs frequently do not appreciate the difficulty of harvesting a company. One investor commented that exiting a business is "like brain surgery—it's done a lot, but there are a lot of things that can go wrong." Harvesting, whether through a sale or a stock offering, takes a lot of time and energy on the part of the firm's management team and can be very distracting from day-to-day affairs. The result is often a loss of managerial focus and momentum, leading to poor performance.

Uncertainties accompanying an impending sale often lower employee morale. The stress can affect the whole organization, as employees become anxious about the prospect of a new owner. Len Baker, at Sutter Hill Ventures, offers this advice: "Don't start running the company for the liquidity event. Run the business for the long haul." There is also a risk of becoming so attentive to "playing the harvest game" that an entrepreneur may forget to keep first things first.

Investors are always concerned about how to exit, and entrepreneurs need to have a similar mindset. Peter Hermann, general partner at New Heritage Capital, notes, "People generally stumble into the exit and don't plan for it." However, for Hermann, "The exit strategy begins when the money goes in." Similarly, Gordon Baty, managing partner of Zero Stage Capital and an angel investor, enters each investment with a clear understanding of its investment horizon and harvest plan: "We plan for an acquisition and hope for an IPO." Jack Kearney, at BDO Capital Advisors, LLC, indicates that an exit strategy should be formulated in advance, unless "the entrepreneur expects to die in the CEO chair. . . . The worst of all worlds is to realize, for health or other reasons, that you have to sell the company right now." Jim Knister, formerly with the Donnelly Corporation, advises entrepreneurs to start thinking two or three years ahead about how they are going to exit so that they can correctly position their companies.

This type of advice is particularly important when the entrepreneur is planning an IPO. Running a public company requires information disclosures to stockholders that are not required of a privately held firm. Specifically, this means (1) maintaining an accounting process that cleanly separates the business from the entrepreneur's personal life, (2) selecting a strong board of directors that can and will offer valuable business advice, and (3) managing the firm so as to produce a successful track record of performance.

Having a harvest plan in place is also very important because the window of opportunity can open and close quickly. Remember that the opportunity to exit is triggered by the arrival of a willing and able buyer, not just an interested seller. For an IPO, a hot market may offer a very attractive opportunity, and a seller must be ready to move when the opportunity arises.

In summary, an entrepreneur should always anticipate the harvest. In the words of Ed Cherney, an entrepreneur who has sold two companies, "Don't wait to put your package together until something dramatic happens. Begin thinking about the exit strategy and start going through the motions, so that if something major happens, you will have had time to think through your options."

13-4b Expect Conflict—Emotional and Cultural

Having purchased other companies does not prepare entrepreneurs for the sale of their own company. Entrepreneurs who have been involved in the acquisition of other firms are still ill-prepared for the stress associated with selling their own businesses. Jim Porter, who has been involved in a number of acquisitions, says, "It's definitely a lot more fun to buy something than it is to be bought." One very real difference between selling and buying comes from the entrepreneur's personal ties to the business that he or she helped create. A buyer can be quite unemotional and detached, while a seller is likely to be much more concerned about nonfinancial considerations.

For this reason and many others, entrepreneurs frequently do not make good employees. The very qualities that made them successful entrepreneurs can make it difficult for them to work under a new owner. In fact, an entrepreneur who plans to stay with the firm after a sale can become disillusioned quickly and end up leaving prematurely. As Len Baker observes, "There is a danger of culture conflict between the acquiring versus the acquired firm's management. The odds are overwhelming that somebody who's been an entrepreneur is not going to be happy in a corporate culture."

Conflicts occur to varying degrees whenever an entrepreneur remains with the company after the sale. Although the nature of the conflict varies, the intensity of the feelings does not. An entrepreneur who stays with the company should expect culture conflict and be pleasantly surprised if it does not occur.

13-4c Get Good Advice

Entrepreneurs learn to operate their businesses through experience gained in repeated day-to-day activities. However, they may engage in a harvest transaction only once in a lifetime. "It's an emotional roller-coaster ride," says Ben Buettell, who frequently represents sellers of small and mid-size companies.[5] Thus, entrepreneurs have a real need for good advice, both from experienced professionals and from those who have personally been through a harvest. In seeking advice, be aware that the experts who helped you build and grow your business may not be the best ones to use when it's time to sell the company, as they may not have the experience needed in that area. So choose your advisors carefully.

© YURI ARCURS/SHUTTERSTOCK.COM

Jack Furst, at HM Capital Partners, believes that advisors can give entrepreneurs a reality check. He contends that, without independent advice, entrepreneurs frequently fall prey to thinking they want to sell unconditionally, when in fact they really want to sell only if an unrealistically high price is offered.

Professional advice is vital, but entrepreneurs stress the importance of talking to other entrepreneurs who have sold a firm or taken it public. No one can better describe what to expect—both in events and in emotions—than someone who has had the experience. This perspective nicely complements that of the professional advisor.

Perhaps the greatest misconception among entrepreneurs is that an IPO is the end of the line. They often feel that taking their firm public through an IPO means they have "made it." The fact is that going public is but one transition in the life of a firm. Many entrepreneurs are surprised to learn that a public offering is just the beginning, not an end.

An entrepreneur will not be able to cash out for some time after the completion of the IPO. In a sense, investors in the new stock offering have chosen to back the entrepreneur as the driving force behind the company—that is, they have invested in the entrepreneur, not the firm. While the daily stock price quotes will let the management team keep score, the business will have to reach another plateau before the founder can think about placing it in the hands of a new team and going fishing. Under these circumstances, getting good advice is a must.

13-4d Understand What Motivates You

For an entrepreneur, harvesting a business that has been an integral part of life for a long period of time can be a very emotional experience. When an entrepreneur has invested a substantial part of her or his working life in growing a business, a real sense of loss may accompany the harvest. Walking away from employees, clients, and one's identity as a small business owner may not be the wonderful ride into the sunset that was expected.

So, entrepreneurs should think very carefully about their motives for exiting and what they plan to do after the harvest. Frequently, entrepreneurs have great expectations about what life is going to be like with a lot of liquidity, something many of them have never known. The harvest does provide the long-sought liquidity, but some entrepreneurs find managing money—in contrast to operating their own company—less rewarding than they had expected.

Peter Hermann believes that "seller's remorse" is definitely a major issue for a number of entrepreneurs. His advice: "Search your soul and make a list of what you want to achieve with the exit. Is it dollars, health of the company, your management team or an heir apparent taking over?" The answers to these and similar questions determine to a significant extent whether the exit will prove successful in all dimensions of an entrepreneur's life.

Entrepreneurs are also well advised to be aware of potential problems that may arise after the exit. There are stories about people selling a firm or going public and then losing everything. Ed Cherney says, "It is more difficult to handle success than it is to handle struggling. People forget what got them the success—the work ethic, the commitment to family, whatever characteristics work for an entrepreneur. Once the money starts rolling in, people forget and begin having problems."

And for the entrepreneur who believes that it will be easy to adapt to change after the harvest, even possibly to start another company, William Unger, at the Mayfield Fund, quotes from Machiavelli's *The Prince:* "It should be remembered that nothing is more difficult than to establish a new order of things."

As a way to provide an overview of the issues we have discussed for developing an effective harvest strategy, take a look at the *harvest framework* provided in Exhibit 13.4. While we cannot address fully all the issues that need to be considered, this framework will hopefully give you a good starting point on which to build.

A Caveat for All Entrepreneurs

For many entrepreneurs, their *total* retirement plan is summed up in these words: *Sell the business.* According to a report by the Small Business Administration, small business owners are "significantly less likely" than employees to have diversified retirement assets, increasing their financial vulnerability as they grow older.

"There is a risk of significant consequences if the business goes bad," says Jules Lichtenstein, the SBA senior economist who authored the report. "There's a double-whammy if something happens to that company because you'll lose your income and your retirement assets."

No doubt investing everything in your business may be the only option if you are to succeed. But there comes a time when you need to stop betting everything on the company.

For more on this issue, see Karen F. Klein, "Risking Retirement on Selling the Business," *Businessweek*, December 15, 2012, http://www.businessweek.com/articles/2012-12-15/risking-retirement-on-selling-the-business, accessed February 28, 2015.

13-4e What's Next?

Entrepreneurs by their very nature are purpose-driven people. So, after the exit, an entrepreneur who has been driven to build a profitable business will need something to bring meaning to her or his life. Many entrepreneurs have a sense of gratitude for the benefits they have received from living in a capitalist system. As a result, they want to give back, with both their time and their money.

Judy Johnston is a great example of an entrepreneur who asked the question "What's next?" For Johnston, it will be a nonprofit venture. She used her life savings of $50,000 to found her first business, PrintPaks, which she sold to Mattel three years later for $26 million. Blue Lake Children's Publishing, Johnston's most recent startup, was founded in 2002—she hopes to sell it in the next five years. Her children's magazine, *Tessy & Tab*, will eventually need a video program, she says, but that's for a successor to figure out. "I know it has to be done, but somebody else needs to own the company when it happens," she says. "There's only so far I can take it, because I'm not motivated by just making more money. I'm not qualified or interested in running a really big company."

EXHIBIT

13.4 The Harvest Framework

Why do I want to exit?	Is now the right time to sell?	What is the business worth?	How do I decide on the harvest method?	How do I get the best price?	Do I stay with the business?
What are my goals for the harvest?	Why is now the right time to sell?	What is my business worth in the market today? in the long term? to a strategic buyer in a hot market? to me?	What method is best? Why?	How do I make "the pie" bigger?	Why would I want to stay with the business after the harvest?
Whose interests matter most: mine? those of shareholders? those of employees?	Why is now not the right time to sell?	What valuation method is most appropriate?	What will it cost financially?	What are the best negotiating tactics?	Why wouldn't I want to stay with the business?
What will I do in the next phase of my life? (Golfing, fishing, and traveling are not adequate answers.)	Has the business been run in a way that makes it an attractive acquisition?	Do we want to be paid in cash or stock?	Will the harvest hurt the company? Will we have to provide access to proprietary information?	How do we increase the pressure to close the deal?	If I stay, what role would I want to have? Will I be able to enjoy and contribute to the new culture?

Blue Lake will likely be Johnston's last for-profit startup, but not her last startup endeavor. "I want to do something that doesn't involve having to return capital to investors," she says. Nonprofits are still fair game.[6]

The good news is that there is no limit to the number of worthy charitable causes, including universities, churches, and civic organizations. And it may be that, when all is said and done, the call to help others with a new venture may be too strong for an individual with an entrepreneurial mindset to resist. But whatever you decide to do, do it with passion and let your life benefit others in the process.

13-1. Explain the importance of having a harvest, or exit, plan.

- Harvesting, or exiting, is the method entrepreneurs and investors use to get out of a business and, ideally, reap the value of their investment in the firm.
- Harvesting is about more than merely selling and leaving a business. It involves capturing value (cash flows), reducing risk, and creating future options.
- A firm's appeal to investors is driven, in part, by the availability of harvest options.

13-2. Describe the options available for harvesting.

- There are four basic ways to harvest an investment in a privately owned company: (1) selling the firm, (2) distributing the firm's cash flows to its owners, (3) offering stock to the public through an IPO, and (4) using a private equity recapitalization.
- In a sale to a strategic buyer, the value placed on a business depends on the synergies that the buyer believes can be created.
- Financial buyers look primarily to a firm's stand-alone, cash-generating potential as the source of its value.

- In leveraged buyouts (LBOs), high levels of debt financing are used to acquire firms.
- With bust-up LBOs, the assets of the acquired firm are sold to repay the debt. With build-up LBOs, a number of related businesses are acquired to create a larger enterprise, which may eventually be taken public via an initial public offering (IPO). A management buyout (MBO) is an LBO in which management is part of the group buying the company.
- In an employee stock ownership plan (ESOP), employees' retirement contributions are used to purchase shares in the company.
- The orderly withdrawal of an owner's investment in the form of the firm's cash flows can be achieved by simply stopping the firm's growth.
- An initial public offering (IPO) is used primarily as a way to raise additional equity capital to finance company growth, and only secondarily as a way to harvest the owner's investment.
- A private equity recapitalization is a form of outside financing that can allow the original owners to cash out part of their investment but possibly continue to operate the business.
- Trying to finance liquidity and growth while retaining control is perhaps the most difficult task facing family firms.

13-3. Explain the issues in valuing a firm that is being harvested and deciding on the method of payment.

- Value is created when a firm's return on invested capital is greater than the investors' opportunity cost of funds.
- If a seller has grown the venture to the point of diminishing returns, the firm will have greater value in the hands of new owners who can take it to the next level.
- Cash is generally preferred over stock and other forms of payment by those selling a firm.

13-4. Provide advice on developing an effective harvest plan.

- Investors are always concerned about exit strategy.
- Entrepreneurs frequently do not appreciate the difficulty of selling or exiting a company. Having purchased other companies does not prepare entrepreneurs for the sale of their own firm.
- Entrepreneurs who plan to stay with a business after a sale can become disillusioned quickly and end up leaving prematurely.
- Getting good advice is essential, from both experienced professionals and those who have personally been through a harvest.
- Entrepreneurs must carefully consider their motives for exiting and their plans for after the harvest.

Key Terms

build-up LBO p. 355
business broker p. 354
bust-up LBO p. 355
double taxation p. 358
employee stock ownership plan (ESOP) p. 356
harvesting (exiting) p. 353
initial public offering (IPO) p. 358
leveraged buyout (LBO) p. 355
management buyout (MBO) p. 356
opportunity cost of funds p. 362
private equity recapitalization p. 360
seller financing p. 357

You Make the Call

Situation 1

After multiple conversations with investment bankers, 37-year-old David Sloan, co-owner of Li'l Guy Foods, a family-owned Mexican-food manufacturing business, realized that "there weren't a whole lot of people wanting to jump into this industry."

The 35-employee company was facing huge financial pressure from the rising costs of commodities like corn and plastic packaging. "We were under an assault on margins," Sloan says, something that made outside investors nervous. Still, the business enjoyed a strong base of customers that paid a premium for its products.

That was enough to attract the attention of a large, more sophisticated competitor, Tortilla King Inc., which had hedging policies in place that allowed it to lock in prices, guarding against increases. And since Tortilla King was already familiar with the industry and the company's customer base in the region, it was willing to take risks that outside investors were not. With costs high and consumer spending on the wane, Tortilla King president Juan Guardiola saw the acquisition of Li'l Guy Foods as a way to reduce competition and increase market share. "We were fighting in the market, cutting each other's margins," he says, "so it made a lot of sense to merge."

The two companies hammered out a deal, and a bank agreed to provide financing but backed out just as the deal was about to close—part of the broad pullback in business lending during 2008. So Sloan's company agreed to finance the purchase. Sloan says he would have preferred to walk away without being so invested in the combined company's future but felt it would be too difficult to continue running the small business. So he went along with the deal. "It wasn't the most ideal transaction for us," he says.

Sources: Based on Arden Dale and Simona Covel, "Sellers Offer a Financial Hand to Their Buyers," The Wall Street Journal, November 13, 2008, p. B–1; http://www.lilguyfoods.com, accessed January 15, 2011; and Suzanna Stagemeyer, "Li'l Guy Sells to Tortilla King, Moves Manufacturing to Wichita," *Kansas City Business Journal*, September 14, 2008, http://www.bizjournals.com/kansascity/stories/2008/09/15/story2.html, accessed January 15, 2011.

Question 1 What would be the reasons for and against Sloan working for Tortilla King?
Question 2 What advice would you offer Sloan?

Situation 2

Ed and Barbara Bonneau started their wholesale sunglass distribution firm 30 years ago with $1,000 of their own money and $5,000 borrowed from a banker in Ed's hometown. The firm grew quickly, selling sunglasses and reading glasses to such companies as Walmart, Eckerd Drugs, and Phar-Mor.

Although the company had done well, the market had matured recently and profit margins narrowed significantly. Walmart, for example, was insisting on better terms, which meant significantly lower profits for the Bonneaus. Previously, Ed had set the prices that he needed to make a good return on his investment. Now, the buyers had consolidated, and they had the power. Ed didn't enjoy running the company as much as he had in the past, and he was finding greater pleasure in other activities, such as serving on a local hospital board and being actively involved in church activities.

Just as Ed and Barbara began to think about selling the company, they were contacted by a financial buyer, who wanted to use their firm as a platform and then buy up several sunglass companies. After negotiations, the Bonneaus sold their firm for about $20 million. In addition, Ed received a retainer fee for serving as a consultant to the buyer. Also, the Bonneaus' son-in-law, who was part of the company's management team, was named the new chief operating officer.

Question 1 Do you agree with the Bonneaus' decision to sell? Why or why not?
Question 2 Why did the buyers retain Ed as a consultant?
Question 3 Do you see any problem with having the Bonneaus' son-in-law become the new chief operating officer?

Situation 3

An entrepreneur addresses the difficult question of when to sell his business:

> *I started my telecommunications business when I was 18, and I'm going to be 47 this summer. It's a successful business and provides me with a good living. . . . Yet each day I feel more and more unfulfilled in what I'm doing. . . . I have a lot of business knowledge that I feel is being wasted here, just doing the same thing year after year. I've tried some side ventures. . . . I've also considered selling the business, but it's too large to be bought by a local competitor . . . and too small to attract the attention of large companies. Besides, I don't know what I'd do if I did sell it. And will whatever I do next allow me to earn as much money as I'm earning now? More important, will I like it, or will I regret letting go of the one thing I've had all my adult life?*

Source: Quoted in Norm Brodsky, "Street Smarts: Ask Norm," *Inc.*, July 2008, pp. 69-70.

Question 1 Do you agree that the entrepreneur's company is not sellable?
Question 2 Are there any other options for the entrepreneur besides selling his business?
Question 3 What would you recommend the entrepreneur do? Why?

Business Plan

LAYING THE FOUNDATION

1. What are my goals for the harvest?
2. When will be the right time to harvest?
3. What options are realistic for harvesting my business?
4. Why would a prospective investor be interested in acquiring my company?
5. Who specifically would be interested in acquiring my business?
6. How would an investor value my business?

Case 13

Network Collie (P. 670)

In 2008, William Casey, along with three college friends, founded Network Collie. The company provided support for businesses wanting to use social networking at a time when this space was beginning to grow rapidly. While the founders had full-time jobs away from Network Collie, they were committing significant time to the new company. However, by late 2009, they knew something needed to happen if they were going to achieve the success in their original plans. At about the same time, two companies expressed interest in acquiring the firm, forcing the young owners to consider four options:

- quit their current jobs and commit to Network Collie on a full-time basis,
- hire someone to run the company,
- try and sell the company, or
- walk away and move on to the next idea.

EndNotes

1. Personal conversation with Bob Browder, former CEO, BFW Construction, Inc., June 20, 2014.
2. Simona Covel, "How to Get Workers to Think and Act Like Owners," *The Wall Street Journal*, February 7, 2008, p. B–1.
3. This example was provided by Peter Hermann of Heritage Partners (now New Heritage Capital), a Boston venture capital firm, which obtained a registered trademark for the process it calls a Private IPO®.
4. The unattributed quotes in this part of the chapter are taken from personal interviews conducted as part of a research study on harvesting, sponsored by the Financial Executives Research Foundation and cited in J. William Petty, John D. Martin, and John Kensinger, *Harvesting the Value of a Privately Held Company* (Morristown, NJ: Financial Executives Research Foundation, 1999). For more information on Financial Executives Research Foundation, visit http://www.financialexecutives.org.
5. Quoted in Jeff Bailey, "Selling the Firm—and Letting Go of the Dream," *The Wall Street Journal*, December 10, 2002, p. B–6.
6. Jennifer Wang, "Confessions of Serial Entrepreneurs," *Entrepreneur*, January 8, 2009, http://www.entrepreneur.com/startingabusiness/successstories/article199436.html, accessed March 18, 2015.

CHAPTER 14

Building Customer Relationships

The Cut & Color Room, a boutique hair styling salon in Orlando, Florida, stands head and shoulders above the competition. This salon sets itself apart by focusing intently on customer satisfaction. The goal is to deliver high-quality hair salon products and services in a "no-attitude" environment, which allows clients to feel relaxed and comfortable. From its extensive hair care inventory to its friendly staff, The Cut & Color Room focuses on the customer experience above all else.

But despite a concerted effort to deliver distinctive products and services, co-owner Jeff Morris realized that his salon still had a problem: a lack of customer loyalty. Customers would take his stylists' expert suggestions to nearby retailers and purchase the recommended products to earn customer-rewards points at those

In the SPOTLIGHT
The Cut and Color Room
www.cutandcolorroom.com

stores. "Losing that business lit the match underneath us," recalls Morris. "We knew we needed to work on something to keep those sales in-house."

Recognizing that a new approach was needed, the owners of The Cut & Color Room decided to introduce their own rewards program, one designed to engage customers in a unique way and capture more sales. But Morris felt strongly that they needed to avoid the generally ineffective "buy 10, get 1 free" punch-card model for rewarding repeat customers, which so often leads to the giving away of free products to customers already inclined to buy.

After studying this chapter, you should be able to . . .

14-1. Define *customer relationship management (CRM)*, and explain its importance to a small business.

14-2. Discuss the significance of providing extraordinary customer service.

14-3. Understand how technology can be used to improve customer relationships and the techniques used to create a customer database.

14-4. Explain how consumers are decision makers and why this is important in understanding customer relationships.

14-5. Identify certain psychological influences on consumer behavior.

14-6. Recognize certain sociological influences on consumer behavior.

The quest to find a better way led the company to collaborate with Perka, a mobile and cardless loyalty marketing system that was created with the needs of small companies in mind. The model offers increasing perks based on purchasing volume, giving credit as well for booking follow-up appointments and referring new customers. The mobile app at the center of this loyalty program is designed around "gamification," which makes it fun to participate, even as it promotes consumer engagement that can be pointed toward specific outcomes. For The Cut & Color Room, the objective was to generate increased traffic and sales.

The success of the salon's loyalty project became quickly apparent, as more than 600 customers enrolled in the first five months. And Perka clients come to the shop every four to five weeks, while those who are not in the program visit only every six weeks. The program offers other advantages as well. For example, staff at Perka, which is based in New York City, can set up a new program in about an hour and can assist client firms in creating a mix of customized incentives to help maximize customer response. Rewards can be designed to reach both regular and VIP customers, incentivize new customers, and boost traffic during normally slow hours.

Perka now supports over 2,000 small businesses and has made it possible for them to implement rewards programs that can cost as little as $1,000 a year. And it certainly has worked out well for The Cut & Color Room. Since only about 10 percent of businesses offer any kind of rewards programs, the salon's work with Perka has helped to set it apart from the competition, even while strengthening its relationships with customers. That has created a new level of loyalty—this time between The Cut & Color Room and the rewards program it has created.

Sources: Jason Ankeny, "Playing for Keeps," *Entrepreneur*, September 2013, Vol. 41, No. 9, pp. 63-64; "Perka: Our Story," http://getperka.com/about, accessed January 2, 2015; John Swanciger and Jed Williams, "Why Small Businesses Should Be Utilizing Customer-Loyalty Programs," *Entrepreneur*, April 25, 2014, http://www.entrepreneur.com/article/233362, accessed January 2, 2015; and http://www.cutandcolorroom.com, accessed January 2, 2015.

Managing customer relationships pays great dividends. Long-term customers usually stay with a company because they trust it, and that trust naturally translates to increased sales. Loyal customers tend to buy a company's more expensive products, are less sensitive to price increases, and bring their friends in to do business, too.[1] If companies increase their customer retention by a mere 5 percent per year, they could see their net profits rise by as much as 80 percent.[2] Keeping customers is critical, so it's essential that firms do it effectively.

But as was the case for The Cut & Color Room (see the Spotlight feature), maintaining customer loyalty can be challenging. In this age of highly social and very mobile media, customers find it easier to sidestep traditional advertising channels by surveying social networks for advice on their purchases. They can make on-the-go price comparisons with laser-like precision and great convenience, thanks to the wealth of information online and simple technologies like barcode-scanning comparison apps. And if they don't like the way they have been treated by a brand or business, they can quickly report their displeasure to their Facebook friends and through online forums and user review websites like Yelp. Savvy small businesses are learning how to use the tools now available to establish strong and healthy customer relationships and to build great companies. If they want to stay ahead of the game, they really have no choice.

This chapter shows you how to create and maintain vital connections that will satisfy your customers, enhance the reputation of your business, and generate superior company performance. Chapters 15 through 18 discuss additional marketing topics essential to growth, based on the crucial customer focus that provides the foundation for this chapter.

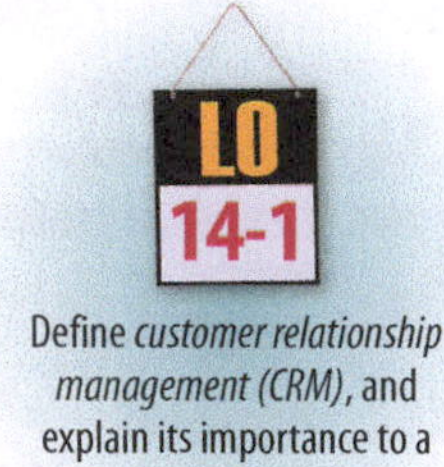

Define *customer relationship management (CRM)*, and explain its importance to a small business.

14-1 WHAT IS CUSTOMER RELATIONSHIP MANAGEMENT?

Customer relationship management (CRM) means different things to different firms. To some, it means having employees simply smile and say "thank you" and "come again" to customers who have just made a purchase. For others, CRM is nothing short of complete customization of products and/or services to fit individual customer needs. The goals of a CRM program for most small companies fall somewhere between these two perspectives.

Formally defined, **customer relationship management (CRM)** is a "company-wide business strategy designed to optimize profitability, revenue, and customer satisfaction by focusing on precisely defined customer groups."[3] It is a process or method that can be used to learn more about the needs and behaviors of customers with the specific purpose of building stronger relationships with them so that a firm can succeed. CRM involves treating customers the way the entrepreneur would want to be treated if he or she was a customer—the business version of the Golden Rule.[4]

Regardless of the level of a firm's commitment to customer relationship management, the central message of every CRM program is "Cultivate customers for more than a one-time sale." For decades, entrepreneurs have recognized the importance of treating customers well. "The customer is king" is, after all, an age-old mantra. What is new, however, is defining the concept more precisely and using the latest techniques and innovative technologies to implement effective customer relationship management practices.

14-1a Benefits of CRM to a Small Firm

Building relationships with customers is serious business for most small companies. This is underscored by a survey of entrepreneurs, who indicated that it is precisely because of the small size of their companies that they are able to respond quickly to customer-service issues. And being able to move quickly and effectively is enormously important. Indeed, of those surveyed, 84 percent said that this is one of the greatest advantages of running a small business.[5]

As depicted in Exhibit 14.1, a firm's next sale comes from one of two sources—a current customer or a new customer. Marketing efforts devoted to bringing in new customers sometimes leave current customers feeling taken for granted and neglected. But keeping existing customers happy should be a high priority. CRM programs address this.

Brian Vellmure, the founder and CEO of Initium Technology, a provider of CRM solutions to small firms, has identified five major economic benefits of maintaining relationships with current customers:[6]

1. It costs much more to acquire a new customer than to hold on to an old customer.
2. Long-time customers trust you and thus spend more money than new customers do.
3. Happy customers refer their friends and colleagues, leading to even more sales.

EXHIBIT 14.1 Sources of the Next Sale

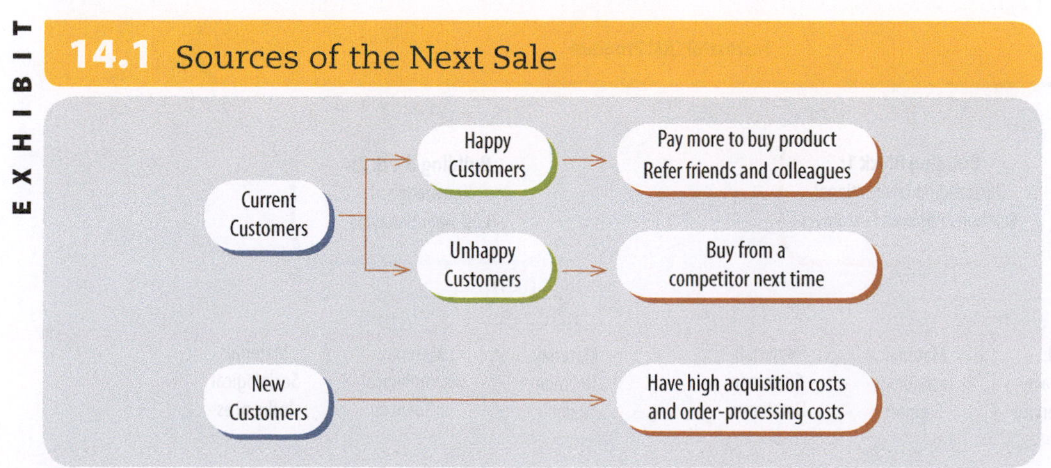

customer relationship management (CRM) A company-wide business strategy designed to optimize profitability, revenue, and customer satisfaction by focusing on specific customer groups.

4. It costs less to process orders for established customers, because they are already in the system and know how it works.
5. Current customers buy without discounts, so they are willing to pay more for products.

These factors contribute to profits and may explain why 47 percent of small firms report that they sell their products or services primarily to repeat customers.[7]

14-1b Essential Materials for a CRM Program

Assembling a CRM program requires an entrepreneur to know about and understand the basic foundations upon which a successful initiative can be established. In the remainder of this chapter, we consider the two crucial building blocks involved: (1) outstanding relationships with customers and (2) knowledge of consumer behavior. We will also examine the basic materials from which these building blocks can be constructed (see Exhibit 14.2).

Discuss the significance of providing extraordinary customer service.

14-2 OUTSTANDING CUSTOMER RELATIONSHIPS THROUGH EXTRAORDINARY SERVICE

To be successful in the long run, small companies need to concentrate on building positive transactional relationships with customers (see Building Block 1 in Exhibit 14.2). A **transactional relationship** is an association between a business and a customer that begins (or ends) with a purchase or a business exchange. Clearly, the nature of such relationships can vary greatly. But consumers who have positive interactions with a business are much more likely to become loyal customers. Four basic beliefs underlie our emphasis on providing exceptional customer service:

transactional relationship An association between a business and a customer that begins (or ends) with a purchase or a business deal.

1. Small businesses possess greater potential for providing superior customer service than do large firms.
2. Superior customer service leads to customer satisfaction.

EXHIBIT 14.2 Essential Materials of a Successful CRM Program

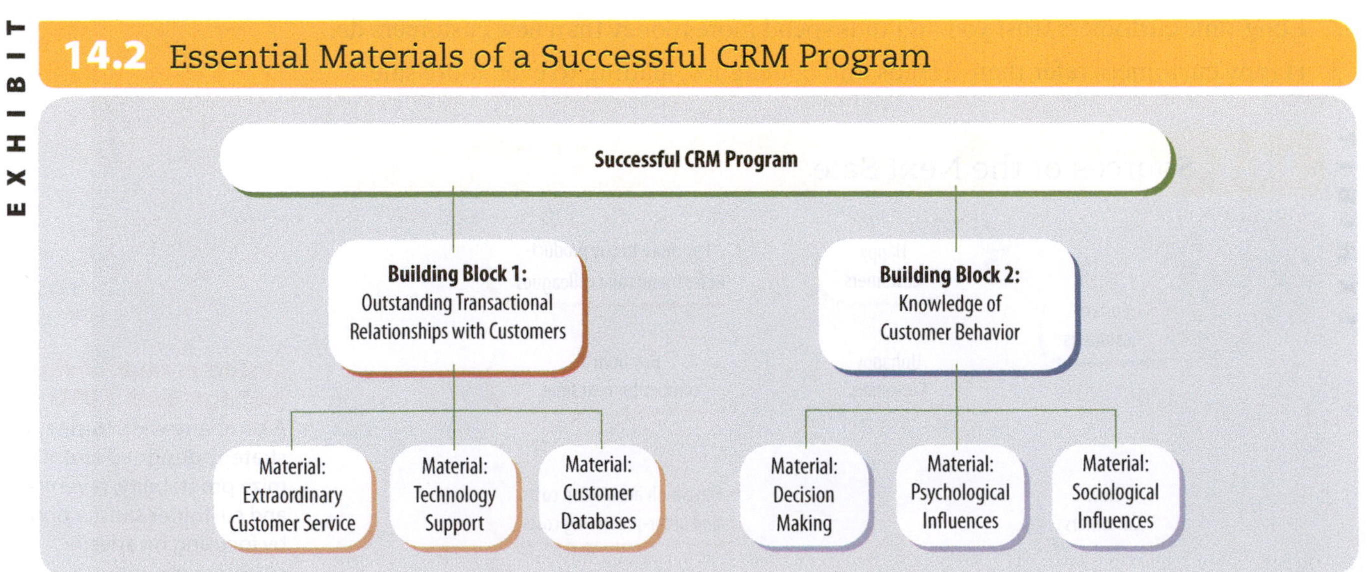

3. Customer satisfaction results in a positive transactional relationship.
4. Positive transactional relationships lead to increased profits.

As you can see, failure to emphasize customer service jeopardizes any effort to maintain a positive customer relationship. Edward Reilly, president and CEO of the American Management Association, said it best when he offered the following warning: "My message to small companies is that big companies are coming after you with better customer service, so you'd better be paying attention."[8]

There is plenty of room for improvement—for businesses of all sizes. One survey found that only 22 percent of customers describe their transaction experiences with companies as "excellent."[9] And 64 percent of customers say they have walked out of a store in the previous 12 months because of poor customer service.[10] This creates opportunities for entrepreneurs like Marx Acosta-Rubio, who started his toner cartridge and office supplies company, OneStop, based on what he refers to as a "customer intimacy model." As part of its attentive service efforts, OneStop representatives call clients before they run out of supplies, maintaining a sense of personal connection by using the phone rather than expecting clients to place their orders online, which is the norm in the industry. As a result, OneStop has been able to generate tremendous sales with a limited sales staff, and its salespeople are nearly five times as productive as those working for its major competitors.[11]

14-2a Managing Customer Satisfaction

Why is customer satisfaction so important? Because happy customers are loyal customers, and that often leads them to cross-buy products with higher margins, react less to price increases, encourage their friends to buy the same products, and engage in other behaviors that tend to enhance the firm's profits. Research conducted by Ruth Bolton, professor of marketing at Arizona State University, has shown that, on average, a mere 10 percent increase in customer satisfaction leads to an 8 percent increase in the duration of customer relationships. This translates to an 8 percent increase in revenues generated over the long term.[12]

Companies control a number of factors that affect customer satisfaction. For example, customers have basic expectations regarding the benefits they should receive from any firm selling the product or service that your company provides. Your offering must meet these most basic expectations to satisfy customers and earn their repeat business. Beyond that, customers anticipate that your business will provide assistance to them at the time they make a purchase and again later if they should encounter problems. Keep in mind that those who buy prestige products, such as a Louis Vuitton purse or a Rolex watch, will expect more intensive assistance.

PERSONAL ATTENTION

Personal attention is the "gold standard" against which the quality of customer service is judged. Firms that provide the best response to the needs of a specific buyer in a given situation are sure to have satisfied and loyal customers—and plenty of them. It follows, however, that personalized service will be an option only for those companies that listen intently to their customers and thus understand their precise needs.

Because small companies like flower shops, for example, have fewer customers and fewer layers of employees between the customer and the business owner, they are able to build stronger and closer relationships with

© HANNAMARIAH/SHUTTERSTOCK.COM

those they serve and to hold on to them as customers. The following are some of the more common signposts on the road to extraordinary, and very personal, customer service:[13]

- *Doing business on a first-name basis.* Small ventures that know their customers by name and greet them as friends establish a bond that is powerful and encourages loyalty.
- *Keeping in touch.* Face-to-face and phone conversations are much more effective than e-mail messages or mass mailings. Asking for feedback during these interactions is helpful to your business and shows that you are committed to getting customers' approval. It also confirms that you care about more than selling.
- *Finding ways to help.* Helping customers doesn't always lead to an immediate sale, but it can be good for business, and at minimal cost. Send them articles and information of interest with a kind note attached, remind them of important dates (like birthdays and anniversaries), and so on.
- *Customizing your service to meet customer preferences.* By remembering your customers' personal preferences and adjusting your service to meet them, you increase the value of what you offer.
- *Addressing problems promptly.* When an issue arises, take steps to resolve it quickly. Doing so lets a customer know that he or she is important to you. Contact lost customers to find out why they went elsewhere and use that information to correct deficiencies.

Denny Fulk, a serial entrepreneur, emphasizes the importance of building and maintaining personal customer relationships to business success:

> *If you operate a business, no matter how small or large, customers like to feel there is a person who really cares about their needs. Whether the information shared is by telephone or e-mail, promptness and a personal approach are keys to the customer's having a good feeling about your company. Regardless of whether your business is a startup or a very established company, a customer who receives a prompt, accurate, and understanding response will be very likely to continue doing business with your company.*[14]

Guy Kawasaki, author of *The Art of the Start*, is a convincing advocate of returning calls and e-mails promptly. To test Kawasaki's commitment, an entrepreneur e-mailed him at 10:00 p.m. one evening and received a reply in about 10 minutes![15]

CUSTOMER EXPERIENCE MANAGEMENT

In recent years, some small business owners have begun to go beyond simple CRM, to **customer experience management (CEM)**. This approach recognizes that, with every interaction, customers learn something about a business that will either strengthen or weaken their satisfaction and desire to return, spend more, and recommend the company to others. One marketing expert summed it up this way: "You literally can't afford to ignore [CEM], because your customers take it personally every time they touch your products, your services, and your support."[16]

customer experience management (CEM)
An approach that recognizes that, with every interaction, customers learn something about a company that will affect their desire to do business there in the future.

Having a positive experience with a business can actually become part of a firm's value equation—it's almost like money in the bank. Research has shown that 86 percent of customers would pay as much as 25 percent more for an excellent buying experience.[17] But stumble in this area and they will make you pay for it. A survey by market research firm Harris Interactive found that 26 percent of respondents have posted negative comments online, which can mushroom into disastrous financial effects, and 89 percent began doing business with a competitor after an unpleasant customer experience.[18]

Relationship-enhancing interactions can begin with very low-tech and inexpensive gestures that customers will perceive as "high touch." According to Spike Jones, a managing director and senior vice president at public relations giant Edelman, getting started "can be as simple as having [customer-service] employees use photos of themselves as their online profile picture rather than the company logo" in order to add a personal touch.[19] Don't count on this alone to produce a good experience, but it can certainly help to get the relationship off on the right foot.

One problem that can jeopardize the customer experience is long wait times. Because the public's tolerance for waiting has decreased significantly over the years, these are very likely to lead to serious frustration and lost sales—that is, unless you can find a way to shorten these delays or, better yet, turn them into an advantage. Many firms are experimenting with new strategies that will help them do exactly that. Consider the following examples:[20]

- Need to get your car's oil changed *and* wash the dog? An auto service shop in Plano, Texas, set up a dog wash station on the premises so that you can do both at the same time.
- Galpin Motors, Inc., a car dealership, put a Starbucks café in its waiting area to help customers pass the time more pleasantly.
- Surgeon Vishal Mehta launched MedWaitTime, a mobile app that lets patients know if the waiting room outlook is green (no wait), yellow (moderate wait), or red (long wait).
- Porter Airlines, a regional Canadian carrier, opened free business-style lounges so that all of its passengers can relax in comfort while waiting for their next flight to depart.

These strategies significantly improved customers' experiences and boosted their loyalty to the products and services offered, with the results flowing to the bottom line of the companies involved.

HONEST RELATIONSHIPS AND SERVICE AFTER THE SALE

It's common for sales staff to work hard to cultivate a relationship with a client or customer to get them to buy and then quickly move on once they have earned their commission or sales reward, but this is very shortsighted. Research has shown that customers are significantly more satisfied and loyal to a company, and tend to give it even more business, if they receive continued attention after a sale—especially if that contact is in person or via the telephone.[21]

Most entrepreneurs truly care about their customers. The problem is that they often get so focused on building their businesses that their minds naturally move on to the next sale, and they may not even understand why following up is so important or know how to go about doing it. Fortunately, a number of helpful methods can help enhance customer relationships after a sale is completed. They include building value for a customer though post-sale follow-up; monitoring delivery and installation to make sure the customer is satisfied; checking in with a customer in person or via phone, e-mail, handwritten note, etc; and resolving any customer complaints to clear the way for future business.[22]

Keep in mind that it costs far more to replace a customer than to keep one. Providing exceptional customer service gives small firms a competitive edge, regardless

Living the Dream

ENTREPRENEURIAL EXPERIENCES

When It Comes to Posting Online Reviews, Some Customers Can't Yelp Themselves

Like your personal reputation, your business reputation is critical. Word of mouth can make or break a company. Today, customers increasingly use social media outlets to voice their opinions and evaluations of businesses. But one such outlet, Yelp, has recently come under fire by a Virginia-based small business owner named Joe Hadeed. Hadeed, who owns and operates a carpet-cleaning service, filed a lawsuit against Yelp after the company refused to reveal the identities of anonymous users who posted critical reviews of the firm online. Because of the implications for First Amendment free speech rights, the issue has been hotly contested and, after a series of appeals, has made its way to the Virginia Supreme Court.

The crux of the case stems from a series of negative reviews that Hadeed's company received on Yelp. In early 2012, Hadeed logged onto the website and found an anonymous post describing his carpet-cleaning business: "Lots of hype, mediocre cleaning and a hassle at the end. Don't go with Joe!" Days later, another anonymous contributor added fuel to the fire by discouraging customers from using Hadeed's service. "I will never use them again," wrote M.P., "and advise others to proceed with caution!" Over time, the company suffered a string of damaging comments, with about 10 percent of the 80 posted reviews being decidedly negative. Hadeed contends that at least seven of those negative reviews are fraudulent, since he has not been able to link the comments to any prior customers.

Yelp's online service can have a significant impact on companies and their financial performance. This certainly seems to have been the case for Hadeed's business, which saw annual revenues sink from $12 million to $9.5 million after the negative reviews were posted. This prompted him to file a complaint for defamation and conspiracy to defame against the seven negative reviewers on July 2, 2012, and he petitioned Yelp to turn over their true identities. Perhaps more important, Hadeed also sought $1.1 million in punitive and compensatory damages, attorney's fees and court costs, and a permanent injunction.

© GONGTO/SHUTTERSTOCK.COM

Both the Alexandria Circuit Court and the Virginia Court of Appeals have sided with the carpet-cleaning service and have held Yelp in contempt for failing to release the requested information. The appeals court has acknowledged that dissatisfied customers "have a constitutional right to speak anonymously over the Internet" but that this "right must be balanced against Hadeed's right to protect its reputation." Yelp, on the other hand, views these issues in a different light. In the petition for appeal, it argued that "consumers and others, who have valuable contributions to make to public debate, but who worry about retaliation, will be chilled into silence." The company has been supported by other social media giants, as should be expected given that they have a vested interest in protecting their user bases from possible retaliation.

Small businesses should heed the growing importance of their online image and be proactive in order to shield their reputations from damage. The extent to which firms can insulate themselves remains unclear, but there is no question about the power of social media to shape the way potential customers perceive and respond to a company's brand. *Caveat venditor* ("Let the seller beware").

Sources: Frank Green, "Va. Supreme Court to Hear Defamation Case Involving Yelp," *Richmond Times-Dispatch*, October 27, 2014 http://www.timesdispatch.com/va-supreme-court-to-hear-defamation-case-involving-yelp/article_4f471a7d-b106-5da8-8be8-2105e6277820.html, accessed January 2, 2015; Angus Loten, "Yelp Reviews Brew a Fight over Speech and Fairness," *The Wall Street Journal*, April 3, 2014, p. A1; John Villasenor, "When Should the Authors of Anonymous Online Reviews Be Revealed? Yelp Challenges a Court 'Unmasking' Order," *Forbes*, February 2014, http://www.forbes.com/sites/johnvillasenor/2014/02/07/when-should-the-authors-of-anonymous-online-reviews-be-revealed-yelp-challenges-a-court-unmasking-order, accessed January 2, 2015; and "Yelp: Hadeed Carpet," http://www.yelp.com/biz/hadeed-carpet-alexandria, accessed January 2, 2015.

of the nature of the business. They typically know their customers' needs better than larger firms do, and they can offer more personalized service. In addition, more tools are available than ever before to make this possible.

14-2b Evaluating a Firm's Customer Service Health

Establishing an effective customer service program begins with determining how well a firm is currently serving its customers (sometimes referred to a firm's *customer service quotient*). Strategies can then be developed to improve the effectiveness of customer service efforts. Exhibit 14.3 lists some popular approaches to creating customer service strategies and provides space for evaluating how well a small firm is currently performing in each area and what it can do to improve its customer service.

Although customer service issues may be identified through a formal review process within a small firm, they often surface via customer complaints in the course of normal daily business operations. Every firm strives to eliminate customer complaints. When they occur, however, they should be analyzed carefully to uncover possible weaknesses in product quality and/or customer service.

EXHIBIT **14.3** Customer Service Strategies

Which of the following can be used to support your marketing objectives?	How well is your company doing?	What improvements will you pursue further?
Provide an exceptional experience throughout every transaction. Ensure that customers are acknowledged, appreciated, and find it easy to do business with you. (List the typical chain of contacts between you and your customers, and evaluate your company's performance at each contact point.)		
Provide sales materials that are clear and easy to understand, including website information, marketing materials, retail displays, and sales conversations.		
Respond promptly to customers' requests and concerns. Have a service recovery plan in place.		
Listen to customers, and respond accordingly. Solicit feedback, encourage interaction, stay engaged throughout transactions, and take the appropriate action to please the customer.		
Stand behind products and/or services. Provide guarantees and warranties, ensuring customers that you deliver on your promises. Also, create products and deliver services that exceed expectations.		
Treat customers as family members and best friends by valuing them the same way you honor those you care most about.		
Stay in the hearts and minds of customers. Don't take them for granted, and find ways to let them know you have their best interests in mind.		

Source: Adapted from "Exceptional Customer Experiences Worksheet," Ewing Marion Kauffman Foundation, http://www.entrepreneurship.org/resource-center/exceptional-customer-experiences-worksheet.aspx, accessed on January 2, 2015.

Improving Your Serve
Offering excellent customer service may not come naturally to some small business owners. For an excellent primer to help you consider all the angles, take a look at "How to Deliver Great Customer Service," which can be found on *Inc.* magazine's website (http://www.inc.com/magazine/20100901/how-to-deliver-great-customer-service.html).

Small companies are *potentially* in a much better position than are large firms to respond to such grievances and to achieve greater customer satisfaction as a result. Most problems can be solved simply by dealing with issues as they arise, thus giving customers more attention and respect. And showing respect is often easier for a small company because it has fewer employees and can give each of them the authority to act in customers' best interests. In contrast, large corporations may assign that responsibility to a single manager, who has limited contact with customers. John Stites, CEO and co-owner of a family-owned construction company, points out that "the owner [of a small business] is closer to the customers and more likely to get accurate feedback, unfiltered by layers of management."[23] This makes possible more timely and accurate responses to problems that may come up.

What do consumers do when they are displeased? As Exhibit 14.4 shows, buyers have several alternatives for dealing with their dissatisfaction, and most of these options threaten repeat sales. Small business owners can learn about customer service concerns through personal observation and other research techniques. By talking directly to customers or by playing the customer's role anonymously—for example, by making a telephone call to one's own business to see how customers are treated—an entrepreneur can evaluate service quality. Some restaurants and motels invite feedback on customer service by providing comment cards to those they serve.

Implementation of some forms of customer service can be inexpensive—or even free, such as when customer-contact personnel just need to be encouraged to smile and greet visitors warmly—but offering a full program of superior customer service before, during, and after a sale can be a costly undertaking. These costs often can be passed along to the purchaser as part of the price of a product or service, or they can sometimes be recouped separately, based on the amount of service requested (through extended product warranties, for example). Many customers are willing to pay a premium price, as long as good service is part of the buying experience.

EXHIBIT **14.4** Consumer Options for Dealing with Product or Service Dissatisfaction

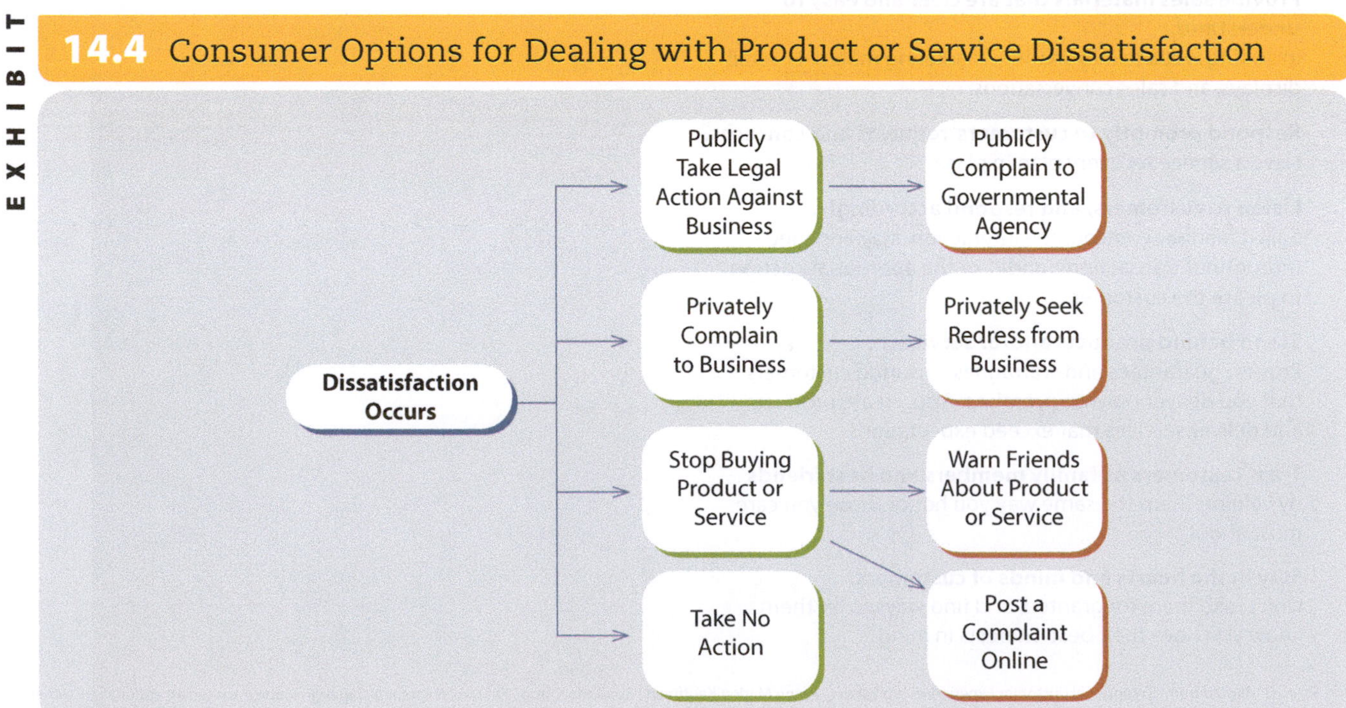

14-3 USING TECHNOLOGY TO SUPPORT CUSTOMER RELATIONSHIP MANAGEMENT

Understand how technology can be used to improve customer relationships and the techniques used to create a customer database.

When it comes to analyzing and making use of customer data, a small business has options. A startup can easily manage the amount of data available, but this situation changes as the company grows and the contacts and accounts become more complex. For that reason, it's best to start thinking about available analytical technologies—from basic spreadsheets to very sophisticated CRM software packages—from the very beginning.

Many small companies keep track of their CRM numbers in a simple spreadsheet that can be expanded and updated as the business grows. The next step up would be to use a database management package like Microsoft Access. This offers greater utility and flexibility, as it can store large amounts of data and match data from multiple tables. Though not designed specifically for CRM programs, Access can certainly help you manage the data needed to guide customer care, basic advertising campaigns, and other marketing-related initiatives.

The most powerful tools available for customer relationship management are software programs designed specifically for CRM. Responding to one survey, 42 percent of small businesses said they had a CRM system already in place, and another 25 percent were planning to deploy such a program in the near future.[24] These packages allow companies to gather all customer contact information into a single data management program. Web-based marketers, in particular, are attracted to such technology, because it helps to make their complex job far more manageable. Most online shoppers expect to receive excellent customer service, and companies are much better positioned to give it if they use the options for interaction and personal attention that are designed into the software. Experts point out that customers typically appreciate the conveniences that are built into many company websites, but they can quickly become frustrated when the experience does not go exactly as planned. The burden of coordination is greatly eased when software is used to help manage it.

Deciding which marketing activity should get initial CRM support is not always easy. However, the sales department is a popular place to start because its personnel nearly always generate the most customer contact. CRM emphasizes such sales activities as filling orders promptly and accurately, managing follow-up contacts to ensure customer satisfaction, and providing user-friendly call centers to handle all inquiries, including complaints. It's a complex mix of tasks, but technologies are available to support all of these activities and many others.

To find the CRM software package that may provide the best fit for you and your firm, consider the included features, accessibility of buyer data, integrated sales and marketing tools, ease of use, and the help and support provided by the manufacturer. It might be wise to narrow your search from the start by checking recommendations from the editors of *CRM* magazine, especially those specifically for small businesses (see Exhibit 14.5). These experts have declared Microsoft Dynamics to be the overall "king of the CRM software hill" because of its depth of functionality, interface and mobile-support improvements, and extremely competitive pricing.[25] But there are a number of other highly recommended alternatives, including niche products that can do precisely what you may need them to do. For example, both CAR-Research XRM and Reynolds Web Solutions provide CRM software solutions for car dealers, with high-performance features designed specifically for that industry.

Concerns about having ample resources to support CRM programs have led some small business owners to outsource certain applications. For example, hosted call centers, which handle phone, e-mail, and other online communications for clients,

EXHIBIT

14.5 Recommended CRM Software Packages for Small Businesses

CRM Package	Summary Description
Infusion Soft	Developed specifically for small businesses, intuitive and easy to use, strong contact management and marketing automation functionality, optional sales and e-commerce add-on features, excellence guidance and service support.
Microsoft Dynamics	Very well supported, popular because of its superior depth of functionality, hosted ("in the cloud") and on-premises options or a hybrid of the two, interfaces with Microsoft Outlook and Web browser, very competitively priced.
NetSuite CRM+	Best for larger small businesses, excellent built-in e-commerce applications, powerfully connects CRM and back-office ERP, more expensive than other options, additional charges for various add-ons.
Salesforce.com	A very popular package, considered a top innovator by CRM experts, many features and highest ratings for functionality, expandable to accommodate business growth, complexity causes some to find it confusing to use.
SugarCRM	Ample depth of functionality, readily customizable (though this can make upgrading more difficult), competitive mobile product, very user-friendly.
Zoho	Highly flexible, competitively priced, easy to configure, robust software functionality, can be integrated with Dropbox, free e-mail hosting, available cloud synchronization.

Sources: Based on Editors of *CRM*, "The 2014 CRM Market Leaders," http://www.destinationcrm.com/Articles/ReadArticle.aspx?ArticleID=98228&PageNum=2, accessed January 2, 2015; and Jay Ivey, "Compare Small Business CRM Software," http://www.softwareadvice.com/crm/small-business-comparison/#reasons-to-shop, accessed January 2, 2015.

may be more cost effective than comparable in-house centers, a crucial consideration for many cash-strapped small firms. In addition to cost, a lack of internal expertise can justify using these outside services.

Many companies have decided to control the cost of customer assistance by using alternatives like automated Web-based, self-service systems, sometimes called *customer information management systems.* When a call-center customer care representative handles telephone calls, it typically will cost the company about $20 to $35 an hour—sometimes more, depending upon the complexity of the product or service being supported.[26] The expense is similar for a number of other service channels, including e-mail, regular mail, and click-to-call. These costs can be cut by nearly half, however, when representatives conduct online chats, assuming they can manage to toggle between multiple sessions going on at the same time. But self-service inquiries handled on the Internet are the least-expensive alternative by far, costing around one-tenth as much as a call.[27] One popular self-service option is to post a list of Frequently Asked Questions (FAQs), but even this simple tool is becoming more sophisticated. For example, a company can buy smart software that recognizes the questions that its website visitors are most interested in and places those questions at the top of the list. Such systems can reduce the cost of serving customers while taking some of the repetition out of tending to their needs.[28]

The list of tools supporting CRM grows longer every day, and they are becoming much more user-friendly as time goes on. Executives and managers in enterprises of all sizes are tapping the power of the Internet to set up the blogs, wikis, social media sites, and other online communities that allow people to build social as well as business connections, to share information, and to collaborate on projects. According to recent research, the real power of these Web applications comes in the form of building relationships with customers:

> *According to the 2014 Customer Collaboration report, 38 percent of consumers are most satisfied when they are given the ability to interact with a brand regarding the*

promotions and offers it provides. Further, consumers actually want to be involved in the product side of a company. Nearly a quarter of consumers (22%) want to collaboratively engage with brands about future products being offered. The ability to share their opinions on product usage guidelines also ranked important to Americans (18%).[29]

In other words, online communities can provide a rich source of feedback and ideas for product development, and in a form that is much faster and cheaper to use than the focus groups and surveys that have been a staple of common marketing practices. But perhaps more important, Web tools can be used to give customers a sense of connection with the enterprise, an identity that results from their active participation in the company's business. For this, there is no substitute.

Using Social Media to Address Customer Needs
Despite their widespread use among customers, companies have been slow to harness the power of social media for customer care. This creates a competitive opening for small companies. Twitter is the tool of choice for this application, but all forms of social media can be tapped. To learn more about the ins and outs of social media customer care, read "The Ignored Side of Social Media: Customer Service," *Knowledge@Wharton*, January 2, 2014, http://knowledge.wharton.upenn.edu/article/ignored-side-social-media-customer-service.

14-3a Creating a CRM Database

The best way to stay in touch with customers and to identify their needs is to talk to them. Such conversations lead to an understanding of each customer and provide a foundation on which to build a **customer database**. These databases are essential to a successful CRM program and typically include the following categories of information, with examples of specific data items provided:[30]

- *Personal information.* Name, address, phone number, e-mail address, clothing sizes, birthday, hobbies, memberships, etc.
- *Demographics.* Background information that can be used for market segmentation and other data analysis purposes, such as age, marital status, names and ages of family members, geographic location.
- *Lifestyle and psychographic data.* Homeowner versus renter status, car ownership (model and year), media preferences, payment methods of choice, recreational interests, etc.
- *Internet information.* Time spent on the Internet, frequency of visits to the company's website, and other online habits.
- *Transaction data.* Complete transaction history, including details such as prices paid, SKUs (which identifies specific products purchased), form of order (Web, phone, in-store, etc.), mode of payment, and delivery dates.
- *Profile of past responses.* Sales calls and service requests—including all customer- and company-initiated contacts—responses to past product or service promotions, and incentives redeemed.
- *Complaints.* Complete history of complaints regarding past purchases or service.

CRM data can almost always be collected at any **touch point**, which provides an occasion for contact between the business and its customers, whether in-person or online. Touch points can include interactions resulting from a phoned-in request for product information, completed and returned warranty cards, responses to online surveys, a visit from a salesperson, orders placed on the company's website—even a text message from a customer service representative. As indicated previously, some small companies prefer to collect data and feedback from customers using comment cards or questionnaires. While these can be effective, contact via the Internet is fast becoming the touch point of choice for companies as well as the customers they serve.

customer database
A collection of information about a customer as defined by CRM goals, including personal, demographic, lifestyle, and transaction data; online habits; past responses; and complaint history.

touch point
An interaction between a business and its customers.

Instead of wasting time with phone numbers and mail surveys, companies are publicizing their Web sites as the first touch point for customer interactions. Web users can evaluate and purchase products, make reservations, indicate preferential data, and provide customer feedback on services and products. Data from these Web-based interactions are then captured, compiled, and used to segment customers, refine marketing efforts, develop new products, and deliver a high degree of individual customization to improve customer relationships.[31]

In a CRM system, a customer's selection of a channel for interaction can be an important source of information in itself. For example, if the customer first contacts the company via e-mail, this provides an insight into his or her preferred method of communication, and the astute firm will consider that in all of its follow-up efforts.

14-3b Using a CRM Database

In a nutshell, an effective CRM program will (1) capture relevant customer data on interactions across important touch points, (2) analyze those data to better understand customers, and (3) use those insights to improve relationships with customers so that they are satisfied, loyal to the company and its products or services, and more willing to do business with it. The database for your company should include information on every customer you have ever had, as well as others whom you consider to be high-potential prospects. As time goes on and your database grows, you may want to organize it further according to region, economic status, customer focus, or any other variable that makes sense to your business and its marketing goals.

© JIRSAK/SHUTTERSTOCK.COM

The Seattle Mariners baseball organization has used this process to "better understand the fans" and identify ways to boost attendance at games. The club launched a loyalty card program to collect data from as many touch points as possible. Now, every time a fan uses the card to snag a hotdog and a soda at a concession stand, buy a jersey from the online store, or purchase a bobblehead of a favorite player at a shop in the ballpark, the club is able to track the fan's attendance, as well as his or her activities and preferences. From collecting these data, the club knows to take measures like sending an e-mail message to a fan who is close to reaching "season ticketholder" status, which boosts sales.

The loyalty program is also useful in monitoring complaints that can flag adjustments needed to boost fan satisfaction. As an example of how specific this can get, the CRM system found that one fan had complained about the smell of garlic fries. Knowing this, the organization was able to relocate him to a section "where there were no frequent consumers of garlic fries."[32] Such programs send a powerful message to customers, who are then inclined to do even more business with the company. But it takes a well-constructed database to get the process started.

On a more general level, you can use these data to set up a **customer segmentation strategy**, a process of identifying customers that fit into smaller, more homogeneous groups. By focusing on those with similar demographic, psychographic, and lifestyle tendencies and sorting them by their previous purchases and payment histories, a marketing appeal can be crafted to meet their specific needs and generate greater sales. For example, a small real estate company could identify young, tech-comfortable

customer segmentation strategy
A process of identifying customers that fit into smaller, more homogeneous groups.

customers and reach out to them with an online-intensive sales campaign, while trying to sell upscale homes to older, more-affluent prospects using in-person appeals.

There are many other ways through which the data you gather can be used to form and strengthen relationships with customers and increase sales. One of these builds on the usefulness of the **80/20 principle**, which maintains that 80 percent of a company's sales will come from 20 percent of its customers. These percentages are not meant to be exact, but experience has shown that the idea generally holds true for most businesses. If a company has created a customer database and organized its data appropriately, it then becomes possible to identify the 20 percent who are the most loyal and who also deliver the greatest profitability to the company.

Often, these "best customers" can be identified by running a **recency-frequency-monetary analysis**, which reveals those who are most likely to buy from you in the future because they have made purchases recently, frequently, and in amounts that exceed some appropriate minimum. Whatever method is used to identify them, you should go the extra mile with these customers to keep them happy and coming back to do more business. This might include anticipating their needs and tailoring product or service offerings to suit them, providing intensive customer service, or offering loyalty rewards to build long-term relationships. As for those who require intensive and costly effort but offer little to no potential to generate profits, it is best to find a way to reduce their cost to the company, perhaps by steering them to low-cost, self-service options online. Some businesses may even chose to end the relationship altogether.

It is also very important to estimate the **Customer Lifetime Value (CLV)** of those who buy from your business if you are to create an effective CRM plan. The CLV is the total profit expected from all future sales to a customer and underscores the *long-term* value of each customer, which can then be communicated to others. Losing a sale today might not seem all that costly—until you factor in the likely loss of all future sales that can result from one interaction gone wrong. And since it can cost a lot more to acquire a new customer than to hold on to the ones you have, the loss can be greatly compounded. Everyone in the company needs to understand this so that they will be more committed to treating customers well.[33]

The CLV can also give sales and service employees a better idea of how much they should spend to acquire and retain customers. Let's say that you own a pizzaria and one of your loyal diners gets upset over a $12 meal. Before you decide how to handle the situation, keep in mind that his CLV could be as much as $8,000 (Pizza Hut's estimated CLV for its best customers).[34] That's why having good data and knowing what to do with them can be so important.

80/20 principle
A principle that maintains that 80 percent of a company's sales will come from 20 percent of its customers.

recency-frequency-monetary analysis
An analysis that reveals customers most likely to buy from a firm in the future because they have made purchases recently, frequently, and in amounts that exceed some established minimum.

customer lifetime value (CLV)
The total profit expected from all future sales to a customer.

14-3c Data Use and Privacy Concerns

Having so much data on customers puts considerable power in an entrepreneur's hands, and it is imperative that it be used responsibly. Customers may not be comfortable with everything required to gain the depth of insight necessary for successful CRM. For example, firms often watch customers' online shopping behavior very closely, taking note of the items they look at, for how long, and in what order. Some even analyze what

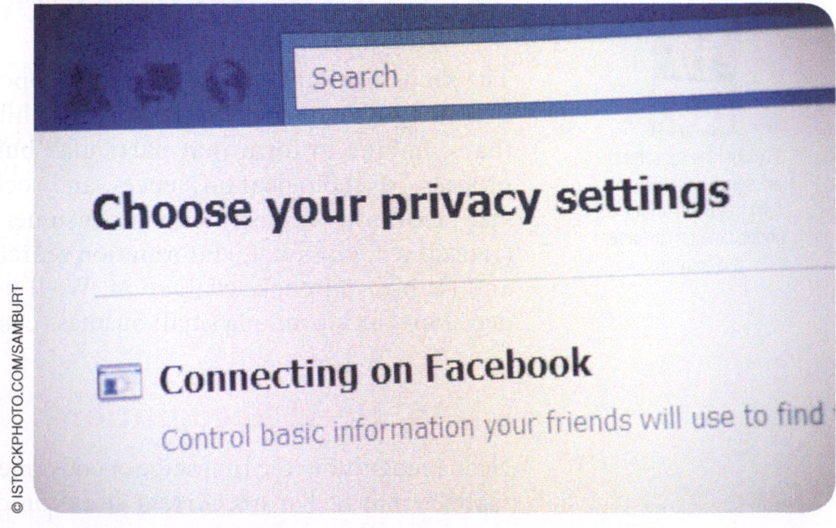

© ISTOCKPHOTO.COM/SAMBURT

customers say through social media, including comments left on blogs, frustrations expressed via Twitter, and more-private Facebook reflections. And this is just the start. The number of database-building options available to firms is great and growing.

There is no question that well-designed CRM systems provide value to customers (such as getting notices on sales that are both timely and relevant) and companies (such as predicting and planning for what customers will want next and generating higher response rates to e-mail offers), but there is still potential for abuse. To address privacy concerns, the process must be honest and transparent, the company must comply with applicable information-use laws, and permission to use personal data must be requested whenever appropriate. Because it can be very profitable to sell customer data to other companies or to purchase data from third parties to fill gaps in any database being built, it can be quite tempting to misuse the information. But the trust of the customer is at stake, as well as the reputation of the company, and these must be protected. The long-term success of a CRM program depends on it.

Privacy concerns have grown tremendously with the rapidly expanding reach of computer applications and the mind-boggling growth of e-commerce, which make data collection easy and nearly cost-free. The risks to the customer are considerable, as some CRM experts have reported:

> *Online users have complained of being "spammed," and Web surfers, including children, are routinely asked to divulge personal information to access certain screens or purchase goods or services. Internet users are disturbed by the amount of information businesses collect on them as they visit various sites in cyberspace. Indeed, many users are unaware of how personal information is collected, used, and distributed.*[35]

Because of the sharp escalation in data collection and use, online and offline privacy practices are coming under increasing scrutiny. Though U.S. companies have, for the most part, been able to get away with self-policing, increased regulatory attention is coming. More than 50 nations now have or are in the process of enacting legislation designed to safeguard the handling of customer data in firms that do business internationally. Those that do business in the European Union or trade with a European company, for example, must comply with strict laws regulating these practices. Many countries are modeling their own systems after the European standard, so the burden of privacy protection is sure to rise.[36]

Explain how consumers are decision makers and why this is important in understanding customer relationships.

14-4 CUSTOMERS AS DECISION MAKERS

The second primary building block supporting a successful CRM program involves knowledge of customer behavior (see Exhibit 14.2). The three interrelated "materials" that combine to form that particular building block include the decision-making process, psychological influences, and sociological influences. Offering an expanded view, Exhibit 14.6 illustrates how consumer decision making flows through four stages: (1) need recognition, (2) information search and evaluation, (3) the purchase decision, and (4) post-purchase evaluation. We'll use this widely accepted model to examine decision making among small business customers.

14-4a Need Recognition

Need recognition (the first stage of consumer decision making) occurs when a consumer realizes that her or his current situation differs significantly from some ideal state.

EXHIBIT 14.6 Simplified Model of Consumer Behavior

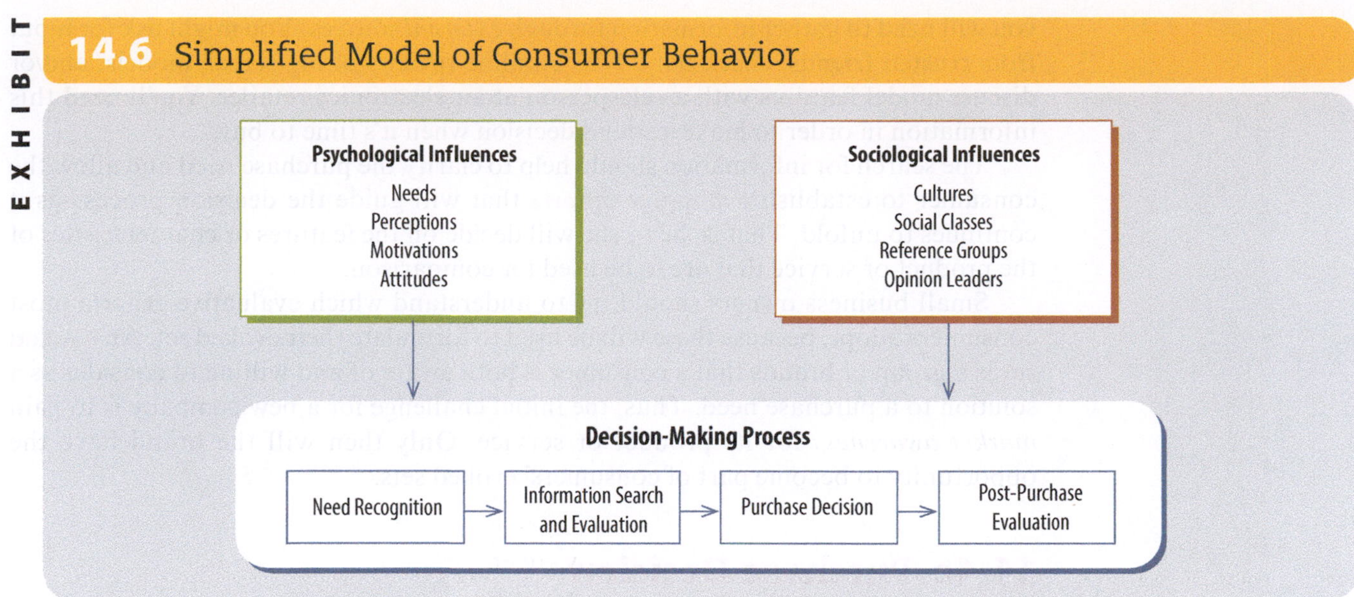

Some needs are routine conditions of depletion, such as a lack of food when lunchtime arrives. Other needs arise less frequently and may evolve slowly. Recognition of the need to replace the family dining table, for example, may take years to develop.

A consumer must recognize a need before purchase behavior can begin; thus, the need-recognition stage cannot be overlooked. Many factors influence consumers' recognition of a need, either by changing the actual situation or by affecting the desired state. Here are a few examples:

- A change in financial status (job promotion with a salary increase)
- A change in household characteristics (birth of a baby)
- Normal depletion (using up the last tube of toothpaste)
- Product or service performance (breakdown of a DVD player)
- Past decisions (poor repair service on a car)
- The availability of products (introduction of a new product)

An entrepreneur must understand the need-recognition stage in order to decide on the appropriate marketing strategy to use. In some situations, a small business owner will have to *influence* need recognition. In other situations, she or he may simply be able to *react* to needs that consumers have identified on their own.

14-4b Information Search and Evaluation

The second stage in consumer decision making involves the collection and evaluation of appropriate information. Internal sources of insight (usually from previous experiences with a product or brand) typically are considered first. However, prospective buyers usually turn to external sources (for example, input from friends and family, product-rating data from *Consumer Reports*, or feature descriptions from advertisements or salespeople) when their own past experience or knowledge is limited and the cost of gathering outside information is low.

To illustrate, suppose you are in the market for a big-screen television. If you work in the consumer electronics industry or have personal experience with some of the brands and models available (two *internal* sources of information), you probably know enough already to make a purchase decision. However, if you are like most people, you will need to gather information through *external* sources. You might ask for input from trusted friends, check out CNET's online reviews of big-screen models, and/or discuss model features with a salesperson at an electronics retailer. You'll need this information in order to make a sound decision when it's time to buy.

The search for information should help to clarify the purchase need and allow the consumer to establish **evaluative criteria** that will guide the decision process as it continues to unfold. That is, he or she will decide on the features or characteristics of the product or service that are to be used for comparison.

Small business owners should try to understand which evaluative criteria most consumers adopt, because these will be used to formulate their evoked set. An **evoked set** is a group of brands that a consumer is both aware of and willing to consider as a solution to a purchase need. Thus, the initial challenge for a new company is to gain *market awareness* for its product or service. Only then will the brand have the opportunity to become part of consumers' evoked sets.

14-4c Purchase Decision

Once consumers have evaluated brands in their evoked set and made their choice, they must still decide how and where to make the purchase (stage 3). A substantial volume of retail sales now comes from nonstore settings, such as the Internet, TV shopping channels, and catalogs. These outlets have created a complex and challenging environment in which to develop marketing strategy. And consumers attribute many different advantages and disadvantages to various shopping outlets, making it difficult for the small firm to devise a single correct strategy. Sometimes, however, simple recognition of these factors can be helpful.

Of course, not every purchase decision is planned prior to entering a store or looking at a mail-order catalog. Studies show that most types of purchases from traditional retail outlets are not planned or intended prior to the customers' entering the store. This fact underscores the tremendous importance of such features as store layout, sales personnel, and point-of-purchase displays.[37] There are some interesting new technologies that can be used to help identify problems with these features.

14-4d Post-Purchase Evaluation

The consumer decision-making process does not end with a purchase. Small businesses desire repeat purchases from customers and thus need to understand the fourth stage of the process, post-purchase behavior. Exhibit 14.7 illustrates several consumer activities that occur during post-purchase evaluation. Two of these activities—post-purchase dissonance and consumer complaints—are directly related to customer satisfaction.

Post-purchase dissonance is the psychological tension or anxiety that occurs immediately following a purchase decision when consumers have second thoughts as to the wisdom of their purchase. This dissonance can influence how a consumer evaluates a product and his or her ultimate level of satisfaction with it.

A consumer who is unhappy with the purchase process or the product during and after use may complain to the company, or even post a negative review on an online forum like Yelp. Despite the frustration or concern a complaint may cause, it creates an important opportunity for a business to make things right—a well-handled complaint may prevent the loss of a valuable customer. The outcome of the post-purchase process is a final level of customer satisfaction that affects customer loyalty and the likelihood of repeat purchases and product usage. It can also lead to brand switching and discontinued use of the product.

evaluative criteria
The features or characteristics of a product or service that customers use for comparison.

evoked set
A group of brands that a consumer is both aware of and willing to consider as a solution to a purchase need.

post-purchase dissonance
The psychological tension or anxiety that occurs when a customer has second thoughts immediately following a purchase.

Living the Dream

ENTREPRENEURIAL EXPERIENCES

Little Brother Is Watching—But He Only Wants to Help

Prism Skylabs is in the business of recycling—but not the kind of recycling you probably have in mind. The San Francisco–based startup provides innovative technology that reuses security camera footage and converts it into real-time analytics for businesses. The venture provides statistics, graphics that reveal the most frequently used footpaths in the shop, and heat maps of customer interest to help business owners analyze demographics and in-store traffic flows so that they can determine whether to, say, shift employee hours to handle peak demand or reorganize the sales floor to make shopping more convenient. One of the primary applications of the service is to help companies improve relationships with their customers.

Small businesses that understand customer patterns can more effectively manage staffing levels, security, and product placement. But the technology also functions outside the retail environment. For example, patrons can quickly check availability at a local restaurant by going online through Prism Skylab's software, which will also allow them to assess the popularity of the venue or even estimate wait times. These insights can help to adjust expectations and smooth demand patterns, which tend to improve the customer experience and boost satisfaction.

With plans costing as little as $99 per month, Prism's technology provides a service that even small companies can afford. Business owners also do not need to purchase any new hardware or surveillance systems to use the service, which connects with existing security equipment and allows users to access data over a cloud-based system.

This kind of technology does have its critics, however. A similar service called SceneTap came under fire amid concern that its offering invaded the privacy of bar and restaurant patrons. SceneTap allows users to access real-time data on the number of people, average age, and gender ratios at a venue as computed from facial-detection algorithms. When customers first learned about the system, they organized to boycott establishments using it and criticized the service online. But patrons' concerns were quieted once they got used to the service and learned that the technology would not collect or report data on individuals.

Privacy advocates remain unconvinced. They argue that data captured by these systems could easily be manipulated or combined with data from other services to reveal private information. In response, Prism Skylabs says that it is rewriting the software to obscure faces and bodies from generated images, replacing them with ghost-like shapes instead. These efforts, it says, prove that the firm is taking privacy concerns seriously and will make sure that this is not a problem. Regardless, the discussion highlights how CRM technology tools can cut both ways—they can be used to enhance and improve customer experiences, even as they erode the trust relationships that provide their foundation.

Sources: Jamie Condliffe, "This CCTV System Actually Edits People Out," Gizmodo, November 10, 2014, http://gizmodo.com/this-cctv-system-actually-edits-people-out-1656745407, accessed April 2, 2015; Gretchen Gavett, "How Data Visualization Answered One of Retail's Most Vexing Questions," *Harvard Business Review*, May 9, 2014, https://hbr.org/2014/05/how-data-visualization-answered-one-of-retails-most-vexing-questions, accessed April 2, 2015; Derrick Harris, "With Privacy Concerns Rising in Retail, Prism Skylabs Says Video Analytics Are the Future," Gigaom Research, July 10, 2014, https://gigaom.com/2014/07/10/with-privacy-concerns-rising-in-retail-prism-skylabs-says-video-analytics-are-the-future, accessed January 2, 2015; and Amy Westervelt, "Lights. Camera. Data.," *The Wall Street Journal*, August 19, 2013, p. R8.

The best way to preserve customer satisfaction is to deal with issues and complaints as soon as possible and in the most effective way possible. This calls for a well-trained, informed, and cooperative work force. At the Angus Barn, owner Van Eure encourages employees to use the "20-Foot Rule"—that is, any restaurant employee within 20 feet of a problem should get involved in addressing it to make sure that all customers leave completely satisfied. For example, waiters might provide dessert to a diner free

EXHIBIT 14.7 Post-Purchase Activities of Consumers

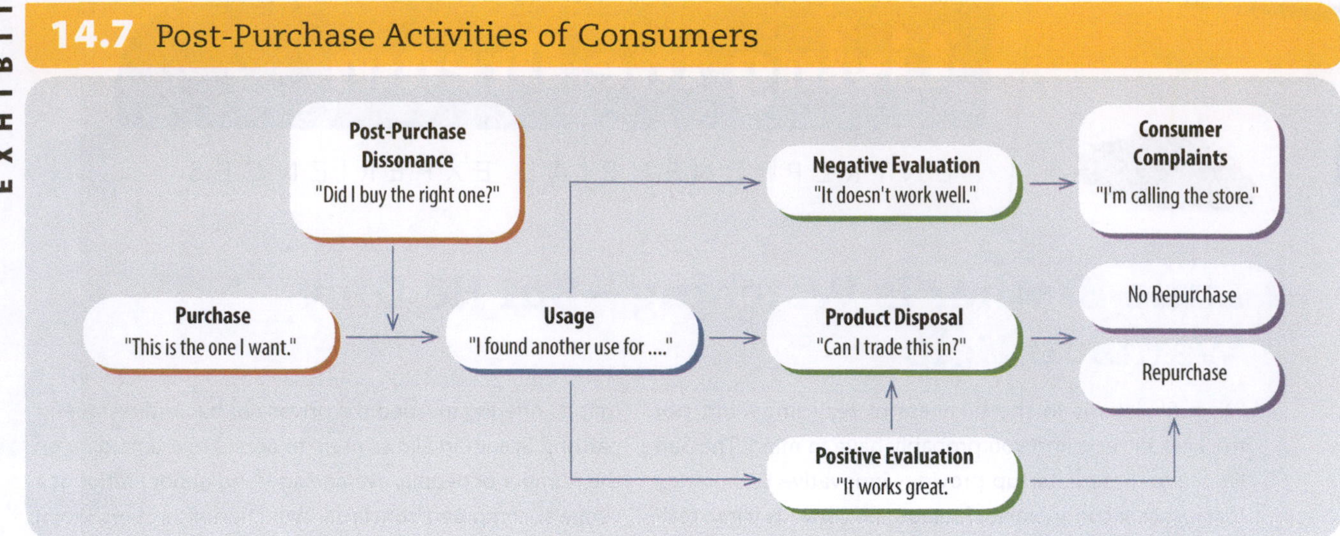

of charge or accommodate a customer's needs by altering the seating chart. Because they are so central to the success of the operation, Eure takes very good care of those who work for her, as reflected by a very low turnover rate. Her approach to resolving customer concerns may underlie the high satisfaction quotient of both her customers and her employees.[38]

Identify certain psychological influences on consumer behavior.

14-5 UNDERSTANDING PSYCHOLOGICAL INFLUENCES ON CUSTOMERS

Another major component of the consumer behavior model, as presented in Exhibit 14.6, is psychological influences. The four psychological influences that have the greatest relevance to small businesses are needs, perceptions, motivations, and attitudes.

14-5a Needs

Needs are often described as the starting point for all behavior. Without needs, there would be no behavior. Although consumer needs are innumerable, they can be identified as falling into four categories—physiological, social, psychological, and spiritual.

Consumers' needs are never completely satisfied, thereby ensuring the continued existence of business. One of the more complex characteristics of needs is the way in which they function together in shaping behavior. In other words, various needs operate simultaneously, making it difficult to determine which need is being satisfied by a specific product or service. Nevertheless, careful assessment of the needs-behavior connection can be very helpful in developing marketing strategy. But you should keep in mind that purchases of the same product can satisfy different needs. For example, consumers purchase food products in supermarkets to satisfy physiological needs, but they also purchase food in status restaurants to satisfy their social and/or psychological needs. Also, certain foods are demanded by specific market segments to satisfy religious or spiritual needs. A needs-based strategy would result in a different marketing approach in each of these situations.

needs
The starting point for all behavior.

14-5b Perceptions

© ALEXANDER IVANOV/SHUTTERSTOCK.COM

A second psychological factor, **perception**, encompasses those individual processes that ultimately give meaning to the stimuli consumers encounter. When this meaning is severely distorted or entirely blocked, consumer perception can cloud a small company's marketing effort and make it ineffective. For example, a retailer may mark its fashion clothing "on sale" to communicate a price reduction from usual levels, but customers' perceptions may be that "these clothes are out of style."

Perception depends on the characteristics of both the stimulus and the perceiver. Consumers attempt to manage huge quantities of incoming stimuli through **perceptual categorization**, a process by which things that are similar are perceived as belonging together. Therefore, if a small business wishes to position its product as being comparable to an existing brand, the marketing mix should reflect an awareness of perceptual categorization. For example, comparable quality can be communicated through similar prices or a package design with a color scheme bearing a resemblance to that of an existing brand. These techniques will help a consumer fit the new product into the desired product category.

Small businesses that attach an existing brand name to a new product are relying on perceptual categorization to pre-sell the new product. If, on the other hand, the new product is physically different or is of a different quality, a new brand name should be selected to create a distinctive perceptual categorization in the consumer's mind.

If a consumer has strong brand loyalty to a product, it will be difficult for other brands to penetrate his or her perceptual barriers. That individual is likely to have distorted images of competing brands because of a pre-existing attitude. Consumer perceptions thus present a unique communication challenge.

14-5c Motivations

Everyone is familiar with hunger pains, which are manifestations of the tension created by an unsatisfied physiological need. What directs a person to obtain food so that the hunger pains can be relieved? The answer is motivation. **Motivations** are goal-directed forces that organize and give direction to the tension caused by unsatisfied needs. Marketers cannot create needs, but they can offer unique motivations to consumers. If an acceptable reason for purchasing a product or service is provided, it will probably be internalized by the consumer as a motivating force. The key for the marketer is to determine which motivations the consumer will perceive as acceptable in a given situation. The answer is found through an analysis of other consumer behavior variables.

Like physiological needs, the other three classes of needs—social, psychological, and spiritual—can be connected to behavior through motivations. For example, a campus clothing store might promote styles that communicate that the college student wearing those clothes has obtained membership in a social group, such as a fraternity or sorority.

Understanding motivations is not easy. Several motivations may be present in any situation, and they are often subconscious. However, they must be investigated if the marketing effort is to succeed.

perception
The individual processes that give meaning to the stimuli confronting consumers.

perceptual categorization
The process of grouping things that are perceived as being similar.

motivations
Goal-directed forces that organize and give direction to the tension caused by unsatisfied needs.

14-5d Attitudes

Like the other psychological variables, attitudes cannot be observed, but everyone has them. Do attitudes imply knowledge? Do they imply feelings of good or bad, favorable or unfavorable? Does an attitude have a direct impact on behavior? The answer to each of these questions is a resounding "Yes." An **attitude** is an enduring opinion, based on a combination of knowledge, feelings, and behavioral tendencies.

An attitude may act as an obstacle or a driver in bringing a customer to a product. For example, consumers with the belief that a local, family-run grocery store has higher prices than a national supermarket chain may avoid the local store. Armed with an understanding of the structure of a particular attitude, a marketer can approach the consumer more intelligently.

Recognize certain sociological influences on consumer behavior.

14-6 UNDERSTANDING SOCIOLOGICAL INFLUENCES ON CUSTOMERS

Sociological influences, as shown in Exhibit 14.6, comprise the last component of the consumer behavior model. Among these influences are cultures, social classes, reference groups, and opinion leaders. Note that these influences represent different degrees of group aggregation: Culture involves large masses of people, social classes and reference groups represent smaller groups of people, and opinion leaders are individuals who exert influence.

14-6a Cultures

In marketing, **culture** refers to the behavioral patterns and values that characterize a group of customers in a target market. These patterns and beliefs have a tremendous impact on the purchase and use of products. Marketing managers often overlook the cultural variable because its influences are so subtly embedded within a society. International marketers who have experienced more than one culture, however, can readily attest to the impact of cultural influence.

The prescriptive nature of cultures should concern the entrepreneur. Cultural norms create a range of product-related acceptable behaviors that influence what consumers buy. However, because a culture changes by adapting slowly to new situations, what works well as a marketing strategy today may not work a few years from now.

An investigation of a culture within a narrower boundary—defined by age, religious preference, ethnic orientation, or geographical location—is called *subcultural analysis*. Here, too, unique patterns of behavior and social relationships must concern the marketing manager. For example, the needs and motivations of the youth subculture are far different from those of the senior citizen subculture. Small business managers who familiarize themselves with cultures and subcultures are able to create better marketing mixes.

attitude
An enduring opinion, based on a combination of knowledge, feelings, and behavioral tendencies.

culture
Behavioral patterns and values that characterize a group of consumers in a target market.

social classes
Divisions within a society having different levels of social prestige.

14-6b Social Classes

Another sociological factor affecting consumer behavior is social class. **Social classes** are divisions within a society having different levels of social prestige. Occupation is probably the single most important determinant of social class. Other determinants include possessions, sources of income, and education. The social class system has important implications for marketing. Different lifestyles correlate with different levels of social prestige, and certain products often become symbols of a type of lifestyle. For products like grocery staples, social class analysis will probably not be very useful. For products like home furnishings, however, such analysis may help to explain variations in shopping and communication patterns.

© BECKY STARES/ SHUTTERSTOCK.COM

Efforts designed to encourage appropriate conduct are often based on appeals to legitimate power at the societal level, suggesting that some behaviors are simply the right thing to do.

14-6c Reference Groups

Technically, social class could be considered a reference group. However, marketers are generally more concerned with smaller groups such as families, work groups, neighborhood groups, and recreational groups. **Reference groups** are those small groups that an individual allows to influence his or her behavior.

The existence of group influence is well established. The challenge to the marketer is to understand why this influence occurs and how it can be used to promote the sale of a product or service. Individuals tend to accept group influence because of the benefits they perceive as resulting from it, and these perceived benefits give influencers various kinds of power. Five widely recognized forms of power—all of which are available to the marketer—are reward, coercive, referent, expert, and legitimate power.

Reward power and *coercive power* relate to a group's ability to give and to withhold rewards. Rewards may be material or psychological; recognition and praise are typical psychological rewards. A Pampered Chef in-home party is a good example of a marketing technique that takes advantage of reward power and coercive power. The ever-present possibility of pleasing or displeasing the hostess-friend encourages guests to buy.

Referent power and *expert power* involve neither rewards nor punishments. They exist because an individual attaches great importance to being part of a group or perceives the group as being knowledgeable. Referent power (based on one's admiration or respect for the power holder) influences consumers to conform to a group's behavior and to choose products selected by group members. Children are often affected by referent power, so marketers can create a desire for products by using cleverly designed advertisements or packages that appeal to this inclination. And a person perceived as an expert can be an effective spokesperson for a host of products because consumers trust his or her judgment.

Legitimate power involves authority and the approval of what an individual ought to do. We are most familiar with legitimate power at the societal level, but it can also be used in smaller groups. Social marketing efforts are an attempt to encourage a certain behavior as the right thing to do (for example, wear your seat belt, don't drink and drive).

14-6d Opinion Leaders

According to widely accepted communication principles, consumers receive a significant amount of information through individuals called **opinion leaders**, group members who play a key communications role.

Generally speaking, opinion leaders are knowledgeable, visible, and have exposure in the mass media. A small business firm can enhance its own image by identifying with such leaders. For example, a farm-supply dealer may promote its products in an agricultural community by holding demonstrations of these products on the farms of highly successful local farmers, who are typically the community's opinion leaders.

reference groups
Small groups that an individual allows to influence his or her behavior.

opinion leaders
A group member who plays a key communications role.

When Phil Knight established Nike, Inc., in the early 1970s, he used a marketing strategy that followed what he called the Five Cool Guys Principle. The idea was that if he could get five of the best and most popular athletes on a high school campus to wear his shoes, then others would want to buy the shoes for themselves. The "cool guys" would set the trend. Of course, the strategy can be applied at higher and more visible levels, which is why Nike has paid so much money over the years to get world-class athletes to don the company's products. Nike's tremendously successful marketing efforts are an illustration of the influence of opinion leaders.

In the modern era of social media, this effect can be magnified many times over to the benefit of small businesses. One mention of your company in a celebrity's "tweet" or even the briefest exposure of your product on a viral YouTube video can push customer interest through the roof. In fact, some small businesses find that such occurrences can increase demand so much that they have a very difficult time coming up with enough product to satisfy it. This is a great problem to have, but it may be more challenging to deal with than you realize.

Customer relationship management will be at the heart of any business that is destined for success. A satisfied customer is likely to be a repeat customer who will tell others about your company. But establishing an effective CRM program is hard work—it requires a thorough knowledge of the major components of customer satisfaction, the development of a suitable customer database, wise handling of complaints, and an understanding of the customer decision-making process. Of course, it all starts with maintaining a helpful and positive attitude toward customers, but the more small business owners know about their customers, the better they will be able to meet those customers' needs.

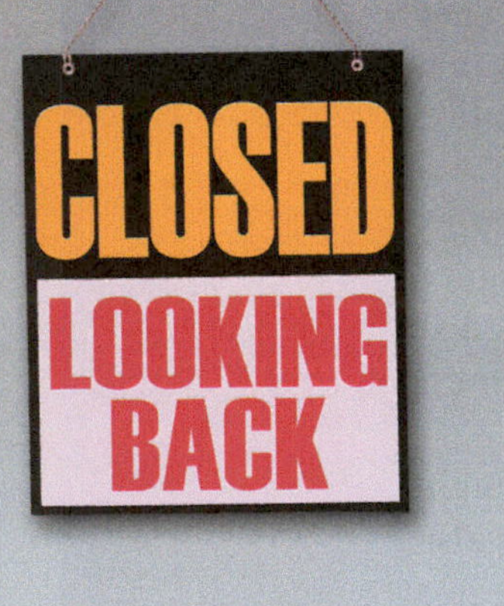

14-1. Define *customer relationship management (CRM)*, and explain its importance to a small business.

- Customer relationship management (CRM) is a company-wide strategy that can be used to learn more about the needs and behaviors of customers with the specific purposes of building stronger relationships with them, thereby optimizing profitability.
- The central message of every CRM program is "Cultivate customers for more than a one-time sale."
- A CRM program recognizes the importance of keeping current customers satisfied to ensure their loyalty, given the high costs associated with attracting new customers.
- Being able to respond quickly to customer service issues is one of the greatest advantages of small firms.
- Two vital building blocks of any CRM program are outstanding transactional relationships with customers and knowledge of consumer behavior.

14-2. Discuss the significance of providing extraordinary customer service.

- To be successful in the long run, small firms must build positive transactional relationships in order to develop and maintain loyal customers.
- Providing exceptional customer service before and after a sale can give small firms a competitive edge, regardless of the nature of the business.
- Satisfied customers are loyal, which translates to increased revenue.
- Personal attention is the "gold standard" against which the quality of customer service is judged, and this can be strengthened by doing business on a first-name basis, keeping in touch with customers, findings ways to help them, customizing services offered, and addressing problems promptly.
- Customer experience management (CEM) recognizes that relationships with customers can be strengthened or weakened depending on the quality of the experience they have with a company.

- Establishing an effective customer service program begins with determining how well the firm is currently serving its customers, or its *customer service quotient*.
- Although many types of customer service cost very little to offer, there are definite costs associated with superior levels of customer service.

14-3. Understand how technology can be used to improve customer relationships and the techniques used to create a customer database.

- It is best to start thinking about a small company's need for CRM technologies—from basic spreadsheets to sophisticated software packages—from the start.
- CRM software programs allow companies to gather all customer contact information into a single data management program.
- Options for interactions with and providing personal attention to customers are built into the software.
- CRM emphasizes such sales activities as filling orders promptly and accurately, managing follow-up contacts to ensure customer satisfaction, and providing user-friendly call centers to handle all inquiries, including complaints.
- Concern about having ample support resources for CRM information technology has led some entrepreneurs to outsource certain applications.
- Tools for CRM management are growing in number and are becoming cheaper, more sophisticated, and easier to use.
- Blogs, wikis, social networking sites, and online communities offer ways of gathering customer feedback and ideas for product development.
- Customer databases are essential to a successful CRM program, as they represent building material for the required knowledge of customers.
- Categories of useful customer information include personal information, demographics, lifestyle and psychographic data, Internet information, transaction data, profile of past responses, and a history of complaints.
- CRM data can be collected at any touch point (places where customer contact occurs) and used to guide customer segmentation strategies.
- According to the 80/20 principle, most of a company's sales will come from a relatively small number of its best customers, and a recency-frequency-monetary analysis using the database can help to identify them.
- It is very important to think beyond any single transaction in order to focus on the Customer Lifetime Value, representing all future expected sales from a customer.
- If a small company chooses to set up a customer database, then it is essential that all collected data be used ethically and responsibility to protect customer privacy.

14-4. Explain how consumers are decision makers and why this is important in understanding customer relationships.

- The four stages of consumer decision making are closely tied to ultimate customer satisfaction.
- Need recognition (stage 1) occurs when a consumer realizes that her or his current situation differs significantly from some ideal state.
- Stage 2 in consumer decision making involves consumers' collection and evaluation of appropriate information from both internal and external sources.
- Once consumers have evaluated brands in their evoked set and made their choice, they must still decide how and where to make the purchase (stage 3).
- Post-purchase evaluation (stage 4) may lead to psychological dissonance or anxiety and complaint behavior, which can negatively influence customer satisfaction with the product or service and the business that provides it.
- The best way to preserve customer satisfaction is to deal with issues and complaints as soon as they come up.

14-5. Identify certain psychological influences on consumer behavior.

- The four psychological influences that have the greatest relevance to small businesses are needs, perceptions, motivations, and attitudes.
- Needs are often described as the starting point for all behavior.
- Perception encompasses those individual processes that ultimately give meaning to the stimuli confronting consumers.
- Motivations are goal-directed forces that organize and give direction to the tension caused by unsatisfied needs.
- An attitude is an enduring opinion, based on a combination of knowledge, feelings, and behavioral tendencies.

14-6. Recognize certain sociological influences on consumer behavior.

- Among the sociological influences are cultures, social classes, reference groups, and opinion leaders.
- In marketing, the term *culture* refers to the behavioral patterns and values that characterize a group of customers in a target market.
- Social classes are divisions within a society having different levels of social prestige.
- Reference groups are those small groups that an individual allows to influence his or her behavior.
- Consumers receive a significant amount of information through opinion leaders, group members who play a key communications role.

Key Terms

80/20 principle p. 385
attitude p. 392
culture p. 392
customer database p. 383
customer experience management (CEM) p. 376
Customer Lifetime Value (CLV) p. 385
customer relationship management (CRM) p. 373
customer segmentation strategy p. 384
evaluative criteria p. 388
evoked set p. 388
motivations p. 391
needs p. 390
opinion leaders p. 393
perception p. 391
perceptual categorization p. 391
post-purchase dissonance p. 388
recency-frequency-monetary analysis p. 385
reference groups p. 393
social classes p. 392
touch point p. 383
transactional relationship p. 374

You Make the Call

Situation 1

Jeremy Argyle launched his own clothing label in 2009, vowing to sell his original shirts, sweaters, and ties only through his own stores and on the Internet. To further boost the success his company has had so far, he realizes that it is crucial to keep customers coming back for more. So, like entrepreneurs everywhere, Argyle wants to employ customer retention techniques that will establish a strong foundation for repeat business. You will find his venture's website at www.jeremyargyle.com, which has software capabilities to support customer interactions.

Sources: "Gallivant: Jeremy Argyle," http://gallivant.com/shop/jeremy-argyle, accessed January 2, 2015; Jeff Haden, "Building His Brand His Way," *Inc.*, July/August 2013, Vol. 35, No. 6, p. 68; and "About Jeremy Argyle," http://www.jeremyargyle.com/t-about.aspx, accessed January 2, 2015.

Question 1 What customer loyalty techniques would you recommend to Argyle?

Question 2 What information would be appropriate to collect about customers in a database?

Question 3 What specific computer-based communication could be used to achieve Argyle's goal?

Situation 2

Sometimes a creative twist on standard marketing research methods can improve their effectiveness. This was certainly true for Jason Belkin, owner of Hampton Coffee Company, with two coffeehouse locations in New York and a mobile espresso van. At one time, Belkin used a mystery shopper service (which hires individuals to pose as real customers to evaluate a company's true service performance) to assess customer experiences, but he decided to turn to comment cards for the information he wanted. He now offers a free cup of coffee to customers who fill out a card. The comment card asks a number of questions, which you can see at http://hamptoncoffeecompany.com/assets/uploads/CommentCard-front.pdf.

Sources: John Bobey, "Hampton Coffee Company: A Great Cup of Joe," *Hampton's Magazine*, http://hamptons-magazine.com/dining/articles/hampton-coffee-company-coffee-beans, accessed January 2, 2015; "Hampton Coffee Company: Our Story," http://hamptoncoffee-company.com/about-us/story, accessed January 2, 2015; and Heather Larson, "Coffee Talk," *MyBusiness*, http://www.nfib.com/article/?cmsid=53793, accessed January 2, 2015.

Question 1 What are the advantages and disadvantages of the two approaches Belkin has used to assess customer experiences at his coffee shops? Which one would you recommend?

Question 2 Do you see any problems with offering a free cup of coffee as an incentive for filling out a comment card? Would you suggest any other options for encouraging customers to provide feedback?

Question 3 Take a look at the comment card that Belkin has posted online. What are the best features of the card? How might it be improved?

Situation 3

Jay Goltz owns a Chicago-based decorative frame company, Artists Frame Service, and three other businesses. And in his mind, customer service today is more important than ever. "Smiling and being pleasant is not enough," Goltz observes. He goes out of his way to hire great employees and trains them to handle even the most challenging questions and service requests. Then he goes a step or two further by making the following claims on his company's website:

- Our framing consultants have art backgrounds and an average of ten years of experience in the industry.
- We offer an extraordinary selection of frame mouldings sourced personally and passionately from around the world.
- We take framing seriously. It's about details, higher standards, and meeting our own level of expectation.
- With a huge inventory and a large staff of artisans, we get the job done when you need it. We deliver on this promise.

To ensure that all goes as planned, Goltz keeps extensive documentation on every job. If complaints arise, he can figure out what happened and deal with the problem quickly. Taking this approach, he can tell if a customer's dissatisfaction stems from, say, an employee's carelessness, inadequate equipment, or some other problem. If the cause is an employee's poor workmanship, Goltz will provide coaching to help improve that associate's performance. After that, if the problem still is not solved, the employee is fired. As Goltz sees it, "The company's first mission isn't having employees, it's staying in business. Customer service is the main advantage small businesses have over their big competitors, so you have to get that right—no matter what it takes."

Sources: Jay Goltz, "The True Price of Customer Service," *The New York Times*, August 21, 2014, http://boss.blogs.nytimes.com/2014/08/21/the-true-price-of-customer-service/#more-87996, accessed January 2, 2104; Megan Pacella, "Strong Support," *MyBusiness*, http://www.nfib.com/article/?cmsid=54314, accessed January 2, 2015; and "We Know Framing. You Know the Difference," http://www.artistsframe.com/why-us, accessed January 2, 2015.

Question 1 As a long-run strategy, will Goltz's approach to superior customer service quality be successful?

Question 2 Would you want to work for a company with such policies? What would be the pros and cons of working there?

Question 3 What suggestions would you have for Goltz? Can you see any ways to improve his system?

Video Case 14

Numi Tea (P. 675)

Numi Tea was started in 1999 by the brother and sister team of Ahmed and Reem Rahim. Keeping it in the family is important at Numi. Every member of the Tea'm, as they call it, is committed to the company's core values of sustainability, creativity, and quality organics. This extends to their corporate customers and their producers as well. Like their teas, every relationship is carefully cultivated and maintained.

Alternative Case for Chapter 14

Video Case 2, PortionPac Chemicals, p. 647

Endnotes

1. "The Neglected Moneymaker: Customer Retention," April 25, 2007, http://research.wpcarey.asu.edu/marketing/the-neglected-moneymaker-customer-retention, accessed January 2, 2015.
2. Frederick Reichheld, *The Loyalty Effect: The Hidden Force behind Growth, Profits, and Lasting Value* (Boston: Harvard Business School Press, 2008).
3. Charles W. Lamb, Joseph F. Hair, and Carl McDaniel, *Marketing*, 12th ed. (Cincinnati: Cengage Learning, 2013), p. 771.
4. Research has shown that the entrepreneur-customer relationship is actually reciprocal [see Dirk De Clercq and Deva Rangarajan, "The Role of Perceived Relational Support in Entrepreneur-Customer Dyads," *Entrepreneurship Theory & Practice*, Vol. 32, No. 4 (2008), pp. 659–683]. In other words, just as customers recognize that the way an entrepreneurial company treats them has an impact on their level of satisfaction with and commitment to the company, so does the customer's reputation and the reliability of the customer's exchanges with the company influence the entrepreneur's satisfaction with and commitment to that customer. One builds upon the other.
5. "Crunching the Numbers: Customer Service" *Inc.*, Vol. 33, No. 4 (May 2011), p. 30.
6. Brian Vellmure, "Let's Start with Customer Retention," http://www.initiumtechnology.com/newsletter_120602.htm, accessed October 26, 2012.
7. National Federation of Independent Business, "411 Small Business Facts: Marketing Perspectives," http://411sbfacts.com/sbpoll-tables-res.php?POLLID=0054&QID=00000001624&KT_back=1, accessed January 2, 2015.
8. Amy Barrett, "True Believers," http://www.businessweek.com/stories/2006-12-24/true-believers, accessed January 2, 2015.
9. Lynne Meredith Schreiber, "CRM: You (Should) Love Your Customers, Now Work to Keep Them," http://www.startupnation.com/articles/crm-you-should-love-your-customers-now-work-to-keep-them, accessed January 2, 2015.
10. "Crunching the Numbers" *op. cit.*, p. 24.
11. Lindsay Holloway, "Marx Acosta-Rubio," *Entrepreneur*, Vol. 36, No. 9 (September 2008), pp. 66–67.
12. "The Neglected Moneymaker," *op. cit.*
13. Some of these suggestions were adapted from Lesley Spencer Pyle, "Keep Your Customers from Straying," *Entrepreneur*, June 12, 2008, http://www.entrepreneur.com/article/194784, accessed January 2, 2015.
14. Personal communication with Denny Fulk, May 7, 2007.
15. John Greathouse, "Personal Pitch," http://www.infochachkie.com/personal-pitch, accessed October 26, 2012.
16. Harley Manning, "You Are in the Customer Experience Business, Whether You Know It or Not," *Forbes*, August, 28, 2012, http://www.forbes.com/sites/forrester/2012/08/28/you-are-in-the-customer-experience-business-whether-you-know-it-or-not, accessed January 2, 2015.
17. Oracle Corporation, "Seven Power Lessons for Customer Experience Leaders," February 2012, http://www.oracle.com/us/corporate/acquisitions/rightnow/seven-power-lessons-wp-1502937.pdf, accessed January 2, 2015.

18. *Ibid.*

19. Franci Rogers, ""Protecting Your Rep," *Baylor Business Review*, Spring 2012, pp. 42–45.

20. These examples were adapted from Alina Dizik, "Fun for the Whole Family: The Long Wait in Line," *The Wall Street Journal*, August 10, 2011, pp. D1–D2.

21. Howard Stevens and Theodore Kinni, *Achieve Sales Excellence* (Avon, MA: Platinum Press, 2007).

22. Adapted from Thomas N. Ingram, Raymond W. LaForge, Ramon A. Avila, Charles H. Schwepker, and Michael R. Williams, *Sell* (Mason, OH: Cengage Learning, 2013).

23. Personal communication with John Stites, October 23, 2007.

24. Editors of *CRM Magazine*, "The 2012 CRM Market Leaders," http://www.destinationcrm.com/Articles/Editorial/Magazine-Features/The-2012-CRM-Market-Leaders-83897.aspx, accessed January 2, 2015.

25. Editors of CRM magazine, "The 2014 CRM Market Leaders," http://www.destinationcrm.com/Articles/ReadArticle.aspx?ArticleID=98228&PageNum=2, accessed January 2, 2015.

26. Joanna L. Krotz, "Should You Outsource Your Customer Service?" *Entrepreneur*, January 23, 2013, http://www.entrepreneur.com/article/225510, accessed January 2, 2015.

27. Francesco Banfi, Boris Gbahoué, and Jeremy Schneider, "Higher Satisfaction at Lower Cost: Digitizing Customer Care," http://www.mckinsey.com/client_service/marketing_and_sales/latest_thinking/digitizing_customer_care, accessed January 2, 2015.

28. Darren Dahl, "What Seems to Be the Problem? Self Service Gets a Tune-Up," *Inc.*, Vol. 30, No. 2 (February 2008), pp. 43–44.

29. Elise Ferguson, "Walmart and Apple Are Least Collaborative Brands in America," *Top Level Designs*, http://tldesign.co/walmart-and-apple-are-least-collaborative-brands-in-america, accessed January 2, 2015.

30. Adapted from Dawn Iacobucci, *MM*[3] (Mason, OH: Cengage Learning, 2013), p. 192.

31. Lamb et al., *op. cit.*, p. 778.

32. *Ibid.*, pp. 774–775.

33. Chris Zane, *Reinventing the Wheel* (Dallas: BenBella Books, 2011), pp. 32–34.

34. Lamb et al., *op. cit.*, p. 785.

35. *Ibid.*, p. 793.

36. *Ibid.*

37. See, for example, Del I. Hawkings and David L. Mothersbaugh, *Consumer Behavior: Building Marketing Strategy*, 12th ed. (New York: McGraw-Hill Irwin, 2012), Chapter 17.

38. "Angus Barn: Our History," http://www.angusbarn.com/ohistory.htm, accessed January 2, 2015.

© SERGEY NIVENS/SHUTTERSTOCK.COM

CHAPTER 15

Product Development and Supply Chain Management

Many entrepreneurs are on a mission, a quest to create breakthrough products that can launch entire new industries and the technologies or services that evolve from them. But this path is risky, because introducing new software or gadgets can be incredibly expensive. The risk is further compounded by the sheer volume of competitors, each desperate to secure their piece of a new revolution. Some small businesses succeed with highly creative ambitions, but many more get better results pursuing what could be called incremental innovation—that is, by coming up with smart improvements to existing products or services.

In 2010, former Apple engineers launched a company called Nest Labs, with the stated purpose of pursuing this alternative vision, and they are now reaping the rewards. Simply put, the company identifies problems with decades-old products and solves them. Nest's co-founder, Tony Fadell, says, "[These are] products that have been unloved, that are basically the same as when we were growing up."

In the SPOTLIGHT
Nest Labs
www.nest.com

Nest's first product, a home thermostat, certainly fits that description. Conventional units are boxy and offer plenty of gimmicky features that add no real value. Nest's version clearly stands apart from the field, providing a sleek look and an energy-saving intuition that actively learns a user's heating and cooling preferences. Sensors in the device

After studying this chapter, you should be able to . . .

15-1. Recognize the challenges associated with the growth of a small business.

15-2. Explain the role of innovation in a company's growth

15-3. Identify stages in the product life cycle and the new product development process

15-4. Describe the building of a firm's total product

15-5. Understand product strategy and the alternatives available to small businesses

15-6. Discuss how the legal environment affects product decisions

15-7. Explain the importance of supply chain management and the major considerations in structuring a distribution channel upload the data over a cloud-based network that analyzes these patterns. The thermostat then changes home temperatures accordingly. Homeowners can interact with the thermostat, if they wish, using their smartphone or tablet to manually override or set temperatures.

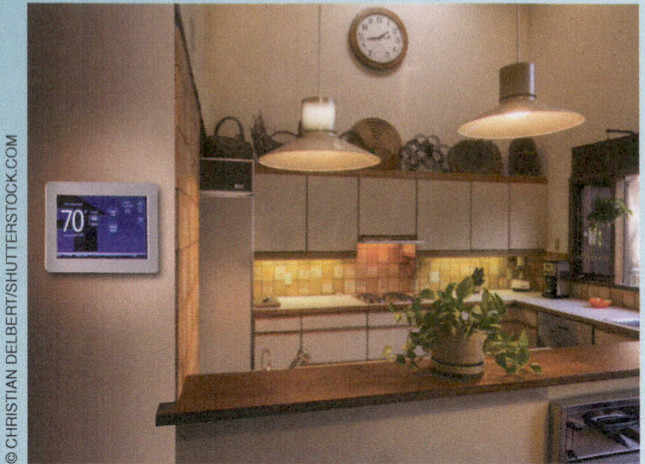

© CHRISTIAN DELBERT/SHUTTERSTOCK.COM

"It's not just about connecting things. It's about the experience," says Fadell. Part of that user experience is saving money. The thermostat costs $249, but it can yield energy savings of around $173 a year. "We have tens of thousands of people who are getting paid when they use their thermostats, because they're saving money on energy," reports Fadell.

Revolutionizing the thermostat business was only the beginning for Nest. In the firm's second round of innovation, the focus shifted to smoke detectors and the frustrations these devices cause. Dubbed "Nest Protect," the $129 product is able to detect intelligently the location of a threat and verbally warn a homeowner about potential concerns. While the underlying functionality may be similar, the quality of the user experience surpasses that of any other device currently on the market.

Nest has reinvented two markets previously known for undifferentiated products that are usually selected based on cost. But the company still sees the home as a target-rich environment. "I can tell you 10 things, minimally, that can get changed in the house," Fadell observes. "They are all great markets with large incumbents who haven't innovated in years."

Nest might very well become the home-devices incumbent of the future. This is especially true now that it has access to the abundant resources of Google, which acquired the startup in 2014. But even with these deep pockets to support future product development efforts, Nest will almost certainly stay the course and continue on the path of incremental innovation. And why not? It has certainly been a winning strategy so far.

Sources: Quentin Hardy, "Nest's Tony Fadell on Smart Objects, and the Singularity of Innovation," *The New York Times*, November 7, 2013, http://bits.blogs.nytimes.com//2013/11/07/nests-tony-fadell-on-smart-objects-and-the-singularity-of-innovation, accessed January 8, 2015; Robert Hof, "Nest's Tony Fadell on How to Create Magical Product Experiences," *Forbes*, November 5, 2013, http://www.forbes.com/sites/roberthof/2013/11/05/nests-tony-fadell-on-how-to-create-magical-product-experiences, accessed January 8, 2015; Farhad Manjoo, "Big Innovation in Small Annoyances," *The Wall Street Journal*, October 10, 2013, p. B1-B2; and "How Nest Helps You Save," https://nest.com/thermostat/saving-energy, accessed January 8, 2015.

You have probably heard the terms *supply* and *demand* used in conversations about the economy, and with good reason—these fundamental forces of the marketplace determine how high the prices of products and services are likely to be. *Supply* refers to the willingness of businesses to put a certain product or service up for sale, while *demand* represents the interest and ability of buyers to purchase it. If a product is in short supply, its price will almost always rise as demand takes over and motivated buyers scramble to purchase the limited goods available at that time.

Supply and demand also affect the operation of a small business, though in a slightly different way. Robert Kiyosaki, entrepreneur and celebrated author of the *Rich Dad Poor Dad* series of books, explains why these concepts are so important:

> *Think of demand as sales and marketing. It's your sales and marketing department's job to create demand by making sure that your customers know and buy what your company has to offer. Meanwhile, supply is represented by manufacturing, warehousing and distribution, aka the supply chain. It's your supply chain's job to be prepared to fulfill the demand created by the sales side.*[1]

This simplifies the formula but clearly explains the need for balance in these key areas of the company's operations.

In Chapter 14, you learned about customer decision making (demand) and the need for an entrepreneur to make a strong commitment to customer relationship management (CRM) to ensure that new customers are drawn to the company and connections to current customers are preserved. You also learned that marketing programs must reflect consumer behavior concepts if CRM efforts are to sustain the firm's competitive advantage. In this chapter, we discuss the demand side of the equation further, explaining how product innovation—like the improvements made by Nest Labs, which are discussed in this chapter's Spotlight—can lead to business growth from increased demand. But you will also get a healthy dose of supply-side thinking. That is, we address product and supply chain management decisions, which together have a significant impact on the total bundle of satisfaction targeted to customers. Business growth can be a wonderful thing, but supply-demand balance is critical to enterprise success.

15-1 TO GROW OR NOT TO GROW

Recognize the challenges associated with the growth of a small business.

Once a new venture has been launched, the newly created firm settles into day-to-day operations. Its marketing plan reflects current goals as well as any expansion or growth that will impact marketing activities.

Entrepreneurs differ in their desire for growth. Some want to grow rapidly, while others prefer a modest expansion rate. Many find that maintaining the status quo is challenge enough, and this becomes the driving force behind their marketing decisions. However, growth sometimes happens unexpectedly, and the entrepreneur is forced to concentrate all efforts on meeting demand. Consider what happened to an entrepreneur who showed a new line of flannel nightgowns to a large chain-store buyer, and the buyer immediately ordered 500 of them, with delivery expected in five days! The entrepreneur accepted the order, even though he had material on hand for only 50 gowns. He emptied his bank account to purchase the necessary material and frantically begged friends to join him in cutting and sewing the gowns. After several sleepless nights, he filled the order.[2]

As you can see, growing quickly can be a stressful proposition if you are not prepared. Many paths can lead a small business owner to similar situations. For example, a new entrepreneur may price a product too low, prompting some buyers to exploit the opportunity by placing large orders. This can be especially hard on a startup, because the final costs of production can exceed total revenues from sales. Also, if a small business is unable to deliver on time or with the level of quality promised, or if it must turn down an order because it can't handle the volume, its reputation can be damaged significantly.

Successful growth seldom happens on its own; it will occur only when a number of factors are carefully considered and well managed. When a business experiences rapid growth in sales volume, its income statements will generally reflect growing profits. However, rapid growth in sales and profits may be hazardous to the company's cash flows. A *growth trap* can occur because growth tends to demand additional cash faster than it can be generated in the form of increased profits.

Inventory, for example, must be expanded as sales volume increases. Additional dollars must be spent on merchandise or raw materials to accommodate the higher level of sales. Similarly, accounts receivable must be expanded proportionately to meet the increased sales volume. A profitable business can quickly find itself in a financial bind, growing profitably while its bank accounts dwindle. (For more on forecasting financial requirements, including those related to raw materials and inventory, see

Chapter 11. You can also refer to Chapter 22 to learn about effective methods for managing assets, such as accounts receivable, cash flows, and inventory.)

The growth problem is particularly acute for small companies. Increasing sales by 100 percent is easier for a small venture than for a Fortune 500 firm, but doubling sales volume makes an enterprise a much different business. Combined with difficulty in obtaining external funding, this may have unfavorable effects if cash is not managed carefully. In short, a high-growth firm's need for additional financing may exceed its available resources, even though the venture is profitable. Without additional resources, the company's cash balances may decline sharply, leaving it in an uncertain financial position.

Growth also places huge demands on a small company's personnel and the management style of its owners. When orders escalate rapidly—sometimes doubling, tripling, or more in one year's time—managerial and sales staff can become overwhelmed. At that point, major adjustments may be required immediately. But too many owners resist the idea that their "startup baby" is quickly morphing into a very different business—they may not be ready for the change or the new responsibilities. If they fail to adjust, they are likely to find that the increased demand will stretch their staff too thin, resulting in burnout, apathy, and poor overall performance.

Despite these and other challenges, the entrepreneurial spirit continues to carry small companies forward in pursuit of growth. Business expansion can occur in many ways. One common path to growth is paved by innovation.

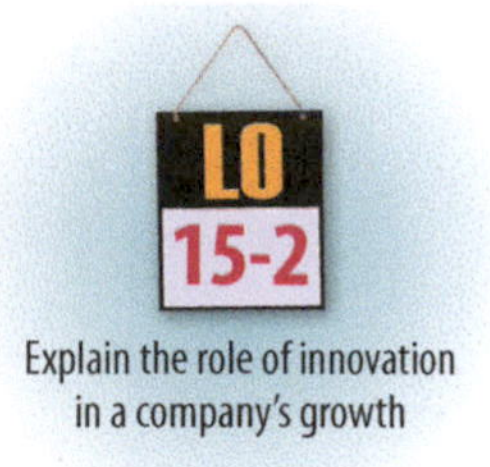

Explain the role of innovation in a company's growth

15-2 INNOVATION: A PATH TO GROWTH

Studies have shown that small entrepreneurial firms produce twice as many innovations per employee as large firms. These innovations account for half of all those created and an amazing 95 percent of all *radical* innovations.[3] It could be said that innovation provides the soil in which a startup's competitive advantage can take root and grow, taking on a life of its own. Some widely recognized examples of small firm innovations are soft contact lenses, the zipper, overnight delivery services, the personal computer, and social media services like Facebook.

There is a certain glamour associated with innovation, but creating and then perfecting new products or services is often difficult to pull off. Clayton M. Christensen, a Harvard Business School professor and the author of a number of books on innovation, points out that the road to new product development is rarely straight, and it is filled with potholes. His research bears this out. According to Christensen, "[Ninety-three percent] of all innovations that ultimately become successful started off in the wrong direction; the probability that you'll get it right the first time out of the gate is very low."[4] But remember, Christensen is talking about successful products and does not take into account tortured attempts to massage life into the 80 percent of all new products that end up failing or performing well below expectations.[5] Nobody said it would be easy.

15-2a Gaining a Competitive Advantage

From a menu of growth options, entrepreneurs generally choose the one they think will lead to the most favorable outcomes, such as superior profitability, increased market share, and improved customer satisfaction. These are some of the "fruits" of competitive advantage, and they all contribute to the value of the venture. However, when innovation is the goal, failure is always a risk. With that in mind, we offer a few "rules of thumb" that may help to reduce the risk in gaining a competitive advantage through innovation:

- *Base innovative efforts on your experience.* Innovative efforts are more likely to succeed when you know something about the product or service technology.
- *Focus on products or services that have been largely overlooked.* You are more likely to strike "pay dirt" in a vein that has not already been fully mined and in which competitors are few.
- *Be sure there is a market for the product or service you are hoping to create.* A new product or service is doomed to failure if the pool of potential customers is too shallow to generate enough sales for the company to recover its cost of innovation, along with a reasonable profit.
- *Pursue innovation that customers will perceive as adding value to their lives.* It is not enough to create a product or service that *you* believe in; people become customers when *they* believe your product or service will provide value they cannot find elsewhere.
- *Focus on new ideas that will lead to more than one product or service.* Success with an initial product or service is critical, of course, but investment in innovation packs even more of a punch when it also leads to other innovative products or services.
- *Raise sufficient capital to launch the new product or service.* Many formal investors will take on *market* risks, but they will not accept *product* risks. In other words, they want to see at least a working prototype, and preferably a developed product, before they invest in a new venture. To get to that point, the entrepreneur will most likely need to rely on more informal sources of capital, such as personal savings and investment from family and friends. This requires forward planning on investment.

Small companies that are "one-hit wonders" may find that the ride comes to an abrupt and unpleasant ending. While one innovation can provide a launch pad for a new and interesting business, continued innovation is critical to sustaining competitive advantage in the years to follow. A survey by *Inc.* magazine found that 13 of 30 company founders reported that their business turned out to be nothing like their original venture concept.[6]

15-2b Achieving Sustainability

The importance of a company's competitive advantage was underscored in Chapter 3, but this strength needs to be long-lasting to have great impact. A company can sustain its competitive advantage through the use of various strategies. For example, some entrepreneurs with sophisticated technologies obtain patents to protect them. Because obtaining a patent requires the disclosure of intellectual property to the public, they may choose instead to guard it by maintaining trade secrets (that is, taking steps to keep private a formula, a process, collected data, and more that give the company a competitive advantage).

Others will try to operate "below the radar screen" of competitors, but unfortunately the effort to avoid attracting attention limits the growth potential of the enterprise. In some cases, businesses find protection through long-term contracts or alliances with larger and more powerful partners, which can lead to exclusive and secure deals as a distributor, vendor, or user of an important technology.[7] But regardless of the protective strategy selected, the goal is to develop the competitive muscle of the enterprise while establishing protective features as a safeguard against being swept aside by resource-rich rivals.

A business can take steps to block threats from competitors, but no competitive advantage lasts forever. Research has emphasized the importance of **sustainable competitive advantage**, a value-creating position that is likely to endure over time. To incorporate sustainability into strategy, an entrepreneur should use the firm's unique capabilities in a way that competitors will find difficult to imitate. However, since rivals will discover a way to copy any value-creating strategy sooner or later, it is important to plan for its transformation over the long run.

Exhibit 15.1 illustrates the competitive advantage life cycle, which has three stages: develop, deploy, and decline. Simply put, a firm must invest resources to *develop* a competitive advantage, which it can later *deploy* to boost its performance. But that position will eventually *decline* as rival firms build these advantages into their own strategies, new and better technologies emerge, customer preferences change, or other factors come into play.

To understand how this works, consider the Blue Buffalo Company, a maker of holistic pet food products. The company is small but growing, and it is unique in that only Blue Buffalo products contain LifeSource Bits, which provide "a precise blend of vitamins, minerals, and antioxidants."[8] But how long will the sales growth continue, given that the company's competitive advantage seems to be based mostly on its proprietary blends? When competitors come up with similar ingredients, Blue Buffalo's competitive advantage and the sales growth it generates may very well stabilize and eventually fall into decline. That's when it pays to be very forward-thinking.

In order to maintain performance over time, companies must continue to reinvent themselves—and it is very important that they do this *before* the business stalls. Research has shown that firms that wait until they hit a slump before making adjustments run a serious risk of failing to realize a complete recovery. In one study, only 7 percent were able to return to healthy levels of growth.[9]

So how can a small business maintain its performance? A firm is more likely to avoid a slump if it keeps a close eye on "hidden curves" related to its competition, its internal capabilities, and its people—and takes corrective measures before these hidden trends become apparent in the company's financial results. Specifically, high performers have a way of (1) spotting changes in customer needs early on and adjusting to them ahead of their rivals, (2) upgrading capabilities to maintain marketplace advantages, and (3) developing and

Inspiration for Innovation

Having trouble generating useful product or service ideas and getting them up and running? Try crowdsourcing to tap into the collective insight of online communities. The "crowd" can help with all kinds of challenges, such as coming up with a new product or business name (Squadhelp.com), designing a logo or website (99designs.com or crowdSPRING.com), coming up with a marketing campaign (zooppa.com), testing website usability (uTest.com), assessing a new product idea (IdeaScale.com), and improving your interactions with customers (getsatisfaction.com).

EXHIBIT **15.1** The Competitive Advantage Life Cycle

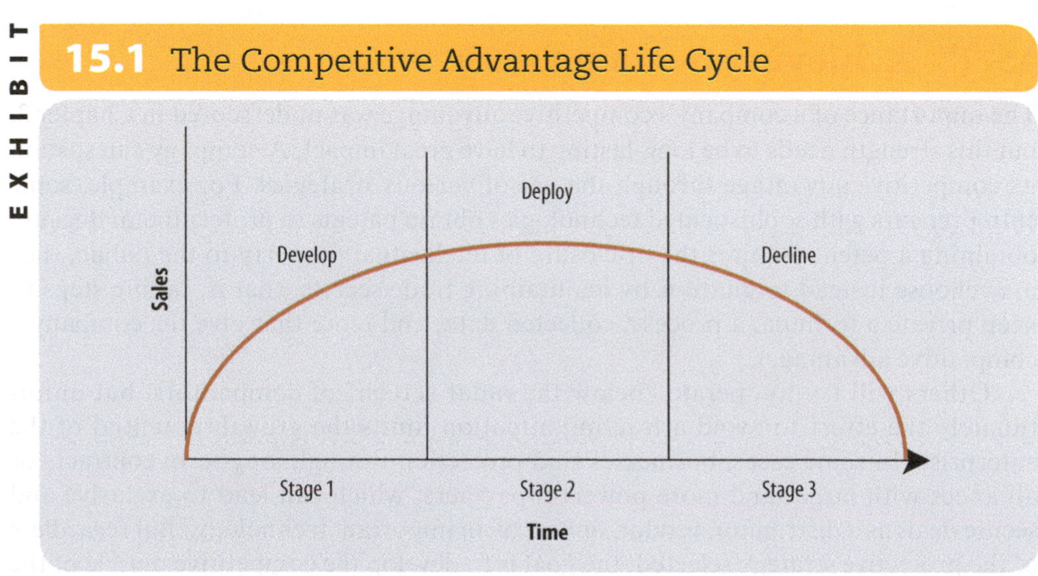

sustainable competitive advantage
A value-creating position that is likely to endure over time.

retaining people with "both the capabilities and the will to drive new business growth."[10] By taking these steps, a firm can extend its competitive advantage *before* the current strategy has run its course. So, small business owners can maintain their venture's performance and stay one step ahead of competitors if they keep an eye on the future and continuously improve their product and/or service offerings to meet the rising expectations of customers, all the while developing the capabilities and the people who make this possible.

© HAGIT BERKOVICH/SHUTTERSTOCK.COM

But staying ahead of competitors may require a small business owner to make some gutsy decisions. Jason Fried is co-founder of a Chicago-based Web applications company called Basecamp (formerly 37signals), which was launched in 1999 as a Web design venture. The firm took a huge step forward in 2004 when it introduced a project-management and collaboration tool (also called Basecamp). Similar software packages that existed at the time were designed mostly around charts, graphs, statistics, and one-way communication. Basecamp broke from this standard model by providing its users with "a consistent place to work on projects and tools to swap ideas, share feedback, make revisions, and deliver the final product online."[11]

Given that the product has since been used by millions of people, 96 percent of whom say they would recommend it to others, there is no question that it has been a success. Users, however, had become attached to the existing product, making it very difficult to design in any changes beyond the incremental. Fried decided to start over, despite the costs and the risks involved—but with a twist. The company now offers Basecamp Classic for users who need or just prefer the security of the tried-and-true, but it also sells a completely revamped product. It was the only way to keep it fresh and stave off the aggressive advances of innovative rivals.[12] A marketplace advantage is sustainable only for businesses that are already planning for the future and taking smart risks to beat all challengers to the competitive punch.

15-3 THE PRODUCT LIFE CYCLE AND NEW PRODUCT DEVELOPMENT

LO 15-3

Identify stages in the product life cycle and the new product development process.

What creates the need for innovation in a specific business, and how can innovation be managed? We will examine these questions by looking at the product life cycle concept and a four-stage approach to new product development.

15-3a The Product Life Cycle

An important concept underlying sound product strategy is the product life cycle, which allows us to visualize the sales and profits of a product from the time it is introduced until it is no longer on the market. The **product life cycle** provides a detailed picture of what happens to the sales and profits of an *individual* product or service over time. (Although its shape is similar to that of the competitive advantage life cycle, shown in Exhibit 15.1, the two models are very different in that the product life cycle reflects the sales and profit trend for a specific product or service, whereas the competitive advantage life cycle is based on the competitive edge of the company overall and can influence the sales of

product life cycle
A detailed picture of what happens to a specific product's sales and profits over time.

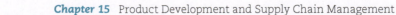

multiple products or services.) The product life cycle sales curve, shown in Exhibit 15.2, depicts slow and, ideally, upward movement in the initial stages. The stay at the top is exciting but relatively brief. Then, suddenly, the decline begins, and the downward movement can be rapid. Also note the shape of the typical profit curve. The introductory stage is dominated by losses, with profits peaking late in the growth stage—that is, the point around which new firms, having been lured into the market because of its evident potential, begin to compete and drive per-unit prices, and thus total profits, down.

The product life cycle concept is important to a small business owner for three reasons. First, it helps the entrepreneur to understand that promotion, pricing, and distribution policies should all be adjusted to reflect a product's position on the curve. Second, it highlights the importance of revitalizing product lines, whenever possible, to extend their commercial potential. Third, it is a continuing reminder that the natural life cycle for most products rises and then falls; therefore, innovation is necessary for a firm's survival. Good business practice calls for forward-thinking product planning, which should begin before the curve of the existing life cycle peaks. This parallels the point made earlier about the need to extend the firm's competitive advantage *before* the current strategy has run its course.

Keep in mind that products and/or services and competitive advantages that are on the verge of decline can be reinvigorated using any number of different strategies. For example, companies may choose to modify a product or service by adding new features (such as advanced "digital filters" on smartphones to allow users to alter photos) or proposing alternative uses (such as suggesting that baking soda placed in refrigerators can kill odors). Similarly, a competitive advantage can be refreshed through research and development that yields new patents (for instance, Palmetto Biomedical, Inc., is a very small firm that has more than 60 patents or patents pending to protect the medical devices it invents). It can also be energized by expanding into complementary products (such as Oreck Corporation's addition of lightweight steam mops to its vacuum offerings) or by redefining the business (such as The Walt Disney Company's shift from animation to a broader identity as an entertainment services provider). The point is that the downward-trending sections of the life cycles presented in Exhibits 15.1 and 15.2 can be extended or reversed using these strategies, among many others.

EXHIBIT **15.2** The Product Life Cycle

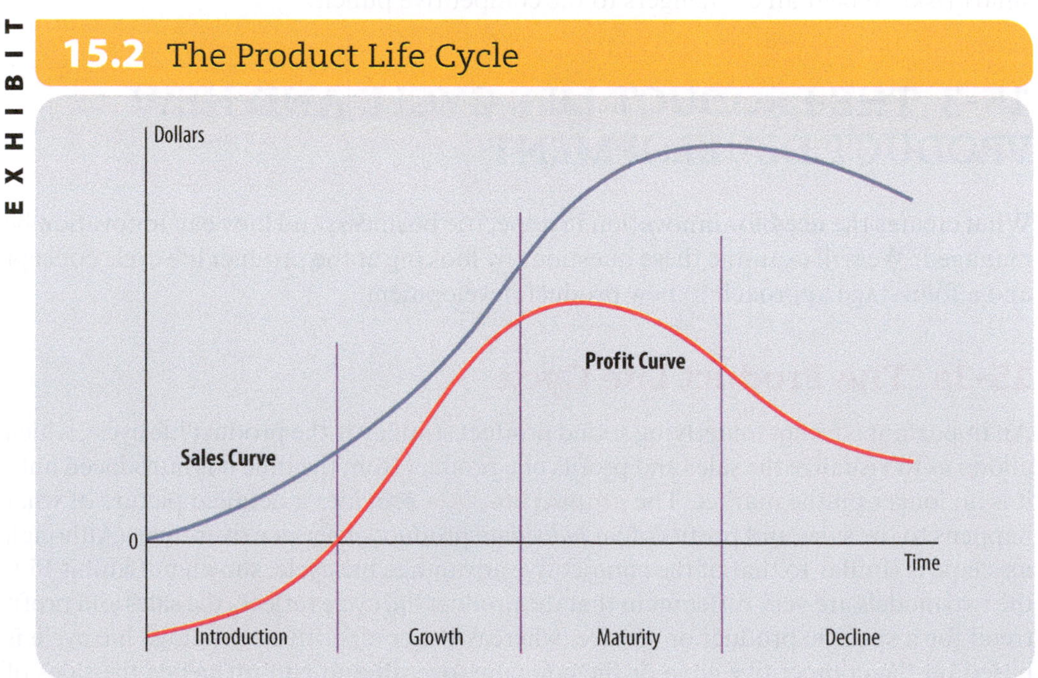

15-3b The New Product Development Process

It is usually up to the small business owner to find, evaluate, and introduce the new products that the company needs. This responsibility requires setting up a process for new product development. As in large firms, where committees or entire departments are created for that purpose, new product development in small businesses is best handled through a structured process, as long as enough flexibility is maintained to allow for adjustments when unforeseen circumstances arise.

Entrepreneurs tend to view new product development as a monumental task—and it can be in some cases. But many find that following the common four-stage, structured approach—idea accumulation, business analysis, development of the physical product, and product testing—is the best way to tackle new product development. (Some of these stages may seem similar to those related to the launch of a new venture, as outlined in Chapter 3, but the focus here shifts to expanding an *existing* business through new product development.)

IDEA ACCUMULATION

The first stage of the new product development process—idea accumulation—involves increasing the pool of ideas under consideration. New products start with ideas, and these ideas have varied origins. The many possible sources include the following:

- Sales staff, engineering personnel, or other employees within the firm
- Government-owned patents, which are generally available on a royalty-free basis
- Privately owned patents listed by the U.S. Patent and Trademark Office
- Other small companies that may be available for acquisition or merger
- Competitors' products and their promotional campaigns
- Requests and suggestions from customers (increasingly gathered through online channels such as blogs, online surveys, and similar tools)
- Brainstorming
- Marketing research (primary and secondary)

In a recent survey, 500 CEOs indicated that they have found the best sources of promising ideas for new products or services to be customers (38 percent), followed by the CEO himself or herself (24 percent) and employees (20 percent).[13] But figuring out which ideas are the *most* promising is often the greatest challenge. Small firms can feel the strain of the weight of too many ideas, and it is the job of the entrepreneur to figure out which ones to eliminate and which to pursue.

BUSINESS ANALYSIS

Business analysis, the second stage in new product development, requires that every new product idea be carefully studied in relation to several financial considerations. Costs and revenues are estimated and analyzed with techniques such as break-even analysis (a concept that is described in greater detail in Chapter 16). Any idea failing to show that it can be profitable is discarded during the business analysis stage. The following four key factors need to be considered in conducting a business analysis:

1. *The product's relationship to the existing product line.* Some firms intentionally add very different products to their product mix. In most cases, an added product item or line should be somehow related to the existing product mix. For example, a new product may be designed to fill a gap in a firm's product line or in the range of prices of the products it currently sells. If the product is

completely new, it should have at least a family relationship to existing products to save on costs of manufacturing, distribution, promotion, and/or sales strategy.

2. *Cost of development and introduction.* Considerable capital outlays may be necessary when adding a new product. These include expenditures for design and development, marketing research to establish sales potential, advertising and sales promotion, patents, and additional equipment. One to three years may pass before profits are realized on the sale of a new product.
3. *Available personnel and facilities.* Obviously, having adequate skilled personnel and sufficient production capabilities is preferable to having to add employees and buy equipment. Thus, introducing new products is typically more appealing if the personnel and the required equipment are already available.
4. *Competition and market acceptance.* The potential competition facing a proposed product in its target market must not be too severe. It has been suggested that a new product can be introduced successfully only if 5 percent of the total market can be secured. The ideal solution, of course, is to offer a product that is sufficiently different from existing products or that is in a price bracket where it avoids direct competition.

DEVELOPMENT OF THE PHYSICAL PRODUCT

The next stage of new product development entails sketching out the plan for branding, packaging, and other supporting efforts, such as pricing and promotion. But before getting to that point, an actual prototype (usually a functioning model of the proposed new product) may be needed. After these components have been evaluated, the new product idea may be judged a misfit and discarded, or it may be moved to the next stage for further consideration.

Many small business owners are intimidated by the thought of having to develop a prototype, but new approaches and rapidly emerging technologies are changing all of that. This was certainly true for Celestina Pugliese of Melville, New York, who was able to bring her Ready Check Glo product to market in only seven months and for a mere $11,800 in *total* costs, not just those related specifically to product development.[14]

The inspiration for the product hit Pugliese in the summer of 2009 as she and a guest were dining at a restaurant. After the server dropped off the check, he returned repeatedly to ask, "Are you ready to pay the check?" and it began to annoy the two friends. After the fourth interruption, Pugliese started thinking out loud about the need for a check presenter with a light that would signal servers when diners were ready to pay the check. Out of these musings was born the idea for the Ready Check Glo Illuminating Guest Check Presenter. To move forward with it, however, Pugliese would have to find ways to make the most of the limited funds she had for a new venture.[15]

To get her company off the ground, Pugliese arranged much of the work required through Internet sites that allowed her to find the talent she needed for a fraction of the normal price. For example, rather than spending around $100,000 to have an engineer build the product (not an uncommon amount), Pugliese opted to use guru.com to hire a freelance engineer in Ohio, who was willing to design her product for just $500. She also used the site to contract with an attorney, who filed a provisional patent application for her for a very affordable $500 charge. In time, she found a legitimate inventors' network online that led her to deals with capable and reliable manufacturers, who are handling production at a reasonable cost.[16] It took some ingenuity, but using such strategies clearly saved Pugliese a small fortune.

But the options for physical product development certainly do not end there.[17] Today, there are countless new tools and services that can support and radically reduce costs for entrepreneurs who want to bring a new product or service to market. Suppose that you've created a mock-up of an idea for a product. You could then use one of the free or relatively low-cost versions of SketchUp (www.sketchup.com) to create or revise your model. Once you've perfected a digital model, you could use a 3-D printing marketplace like Shapeways (www.shapeways.com) to build your creation using a variety of materials, including plastic (in various colors and grades of transparency), metal (brass, bronze, silver, or gold), and sandstone. Or you could buy a 3-D rapid-prototyping printer for as little as $1,375 from MakerBot (www.makerbot.com) and produce your own creations. Does your product need to be interactive? With the Arduino open-source electronics prototyping platform (www.arduino.cc), it has never been easier to embed a product with an electronic controller. This very inexpensive and easy-to-use control board allows your product to link to a variety of sensors to gauge its environment and then respond by controlling lights, motors, and other actuators.

If you think that you might need more help, several workshops give entrepreneurs and do-it-yourselfers access to tools, equipment, instruction, and a community of like-minded individuals. Check out TechShop (http://techshop.ws) and WeWork (www.wework.com) for two possibilities. If you need more information to protect your intellectual property as you are getting started, LegalZoom (www.legalzoom.com) may be just the ticket for you. If you like the sound of all this but think you need a little more hand-holding, companies such as Big Idea Group (www.bigideagroup.net) can walk you through the process from ideation to business incubation. The whole point is that small businesses can turn to many sources of assistance as they move through the new product development process.

PRODUCT TESTING

The last step in the product development process, product testing, should determine whether the physical product is acceptable (safe, effective, durable, etc.). While the product can be evaluated in a laboratory setting, a limited test of market reaction should also be conducted.

Though using a structured process to handle new product development can be very helpful, it is much more likely to succeed if it is outwardly focused on customers. Inwardly focused firms—those that are only in it to please themselves or to beat rivals—are apt to fall short of the mark.[18] More than 80 percent of the high-performing companies in one study reported that they test and validate customer preferences periodically during the development process, compared with only 43 percent of the low performers. According to this analysis, the high performers were also twice as likely to research what, precisely, customers want.[19] Taking such steps provides the only reliable path to creating value for customers, which, in turn, can boost the company's performance.

15-4 BUILDING THE TOTAL PRODUCT

Describe the building of a firm's total product.

A major responsibility of marketing is to transform a basic product concept into a total product. Even when an idea for a unique new pen has been developed into physical reality in the form of the basic product, for example, it is still not ready for the marketplace. The total product offering must be more than the materials molded into the shape of the new pen. To be marketable, the basic product must be named, have a package, perhaps have a warranty, and be supported by other product features. Let's examine a few of the components of a total product offering: branding, packaging, labeling, and warranties.

15-4a Branding

An essential element of a total product offering is a **brand**, which is a means of identifying the product—verbally and/or symbolically. The most effective branding efforts are carefully designed and executed.

The brand identity of most small businesses will have the three components identified in Exhibit 15.3. The first of these features, the intangible **brand image** component—that is, people's overall perception of a brand—may be even more important to acceptance of a firm's total product offering than the tangible brandmark and brand name elements. Consumers tend to resist heavy-handed marketing appeals. They are far more likely to respond positively to businesses that craft and communicate interesting and consumer-relevant images that encourage an emotional connection to the firm.[20] A recent analysis found that the most effective American brands generate trust in the minds of buyers by conveying to them a sense of personal connection (Amazon), happiness (Coca-Cola), dependability (FedEx), and/or consistency (Ford). Being seen as cool (Apple), focused on the customer (Nordstrom), offering fantastic experiences (Target), or even a little quirky (Southwest Airlines) can also be powerful.[21] Regardless of the type of appeal, branding is increasingly important because consumers will give their business to a company based more on the way they feel about it than on the facts and figures of the firm's selling proposition or its hard-hitting marketing campaigns.

The tangible components of brand identity are brand names and brandmarks. A **brand name** is a brand that can be spoken—like the name Dell. Since a product's brand name is so important to the image of the business and its products, careful attention should be given to its selection. In general, six rules apply in naming a product:

1. *Select a name that is easy to pronounce and remember.* You want customers to remember your product. Help them do so with a name that can be spoken easily—for example, Two Men and a Truck (the moving service mentioned in Chapter 5). Before choosing to use your own family name to identify a product, evaluate it carefully to ensure its acceptability.
2. *Choose a descriptive name.* A name that is suggestive of the major benefit of the product can be extremely helpful. As a name for a sign shop, Sign Language correctly suggests a desirable benefit. But Rocky Road would be a poor name for a business selling mattresses or paving materials.

EXHIBIT **15.3** Components of a Brand Identity

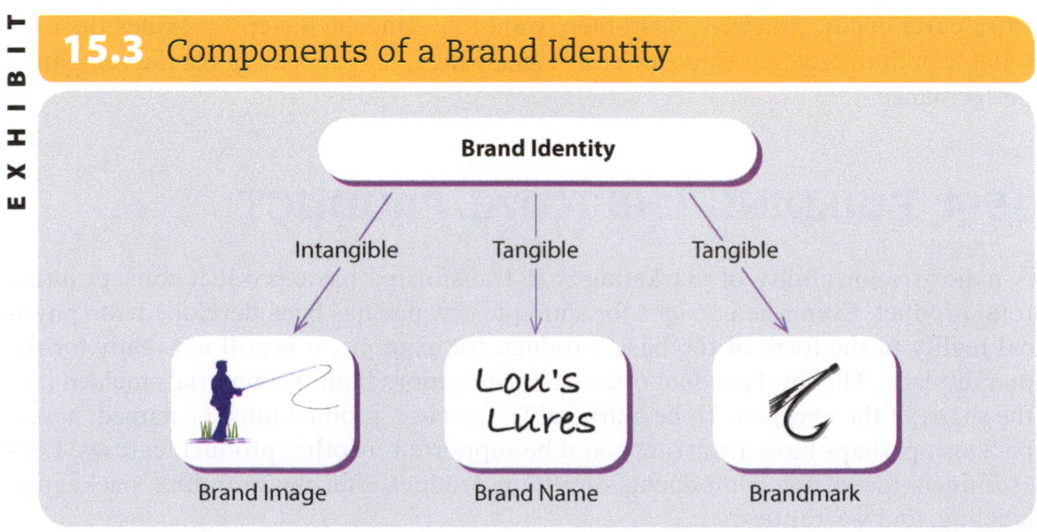

brand
A verbal and/or symbolic means of identifying a product.

brand image
The overall perception of a brand.

brand name
A brand that can be spoken.

3. *Use a name that is eligible for legal protection.* Be careful to select a name that can be defended successfully. Do not risk litigation by copying or adapting someone else's brand name. For example, a new retailer named Wally-Mart would certainly be challenged by industry giant Walmart—even if the new store was actually started by someone named Wally.
4. *Select a name with promotional possibilities.* Long names are not compatible with good copy design on signs and billboards, where space is at a premium. A competitor of the McDonald's hamburger chain called Bob's has a name that will easily fit on any sign or billboard.
5. *Select a name that can be used on several product lines of a similar nature.* Customer understanding can be lost when a name doesn't fit a new line. The name Just Brakes is excellent for an auto service shop that repairs brakes, but the company had to help the car-owning public see past its name when it expanded into factory-scheduled maintenance services in 2011.
6. *In cases where online presence is crucial, consider the cost of domain name acquisition.* Common domain names like Diamonds.com and VacationRentals.com can cost millions of dollars to secure. Selecting a quirky name like Kaggle and Shodogg (which are now in use) may be the only way to avoid the high costs.

If you haven't already chosen a strong brand name, you might consider licensing one, especially if you have a product for which an appropriate name is available. Winston Wolfe, founder of Olympic Optical, a maker of industrial safety sunglasses for the shooting sports industry, harnessed the power of this approach for his business. By licensing the names Remington, Smith & Wesson, and Zebco, he was able to boost sales of his high-end sporting glasses dramatically by riding the wave of popular enthusiasm for these established brands. As he puts it, "Licensing the right name can be magic. It can separate you from the crowd and give you a great sales advantage. It can also allow you greater profit margins, since most consumers are willing to pay more for a brand name they know."[22]

© ISTOCK.COM/GETTY IMAGES PLUS/GETTY

A **brandmark** is the other tangible component of brand identity. It is a brand that *cannot* be verbalized—like the golden arches of McDonald's. A brandmark also has tremendous value. The Nike swoosh and the Chevy badge are marks widely associated with their owners. A small company's special "signature," or logo, should symbolize positive images of the firm and its products. Because of the impact a brandmark can have, it's important to get it right. According to Elinor Selame, who co-founded the brand management firm BrandEquity International, "The logo can be your company's hardest-working employee. For a small company with a limited budget, the returns get higher each year you use it correctly."[23]

Developing an effective logo can be an expensive undertaking. The following tips may help you to design a logo without breaking the bank:[24]

brandmark
A brand that cannot be spoken; a company logo.

1. *Be simple.* The best logos are often the least complicated. Think of Target, whose red circle with a red dot in the center conveys the essence of affordable, hip

Living the Dream

USING TECHNOLOGY

What's in a (Quirky) Name? Plenty, Especially for Online Startups

Imgur. Spotify. Uber. A few years ago, these words would have been considered mere gibberish, but today they are household names. And this is important because brand name recognition, particularly online, directly impacts the bottom line.

Inspired by the success of these online heavyweights, many startups have redoubled their efforts to establish and promote a meaningful online presence. Finding a useful and impactful name for their websites, however, has become increasingly difficult.

Fifteen years ago, the Internet was mostly a developing technology, filled with uncharted territory and plenty of domain names that were up for grabs. Today, there are more than 252 million registered domain names. The scarcity of prime domain names has driven up their value, sometimes to staggering levels. For example, a number have sold for seven figures, including Wine.com ($3.3 million), Hotels.com ($11 million), and Insure.com ($16 million). Drawn by the potential for huge profits, some speculators actually buy up domain names and trade them like stocks. The advent of smartphones and the proliferation of apps have driven prices down somewhat, but average, "sellable" Web addresses still fetch between $5,000 and $20,000. Many startups still find these price points to be prohibitively high, however, and have had to come up with less-conventional alternatives.

Creating a new word often provides the best solution for new ventures. The founders of creative music app studio Mibblio, for example, merged the word "music" and the Latin root of "book" when they settled on a name. David Leiberman, co-founder of the company, felt that the name offered linguistic ease and would leave a lasting impression on users. The new word also greatly reduced the likelihood that the startup would unintentionally commit trademark violations.

Unfortunately, poorly crafted names can drive away online traffic. A few years ago, Wesabe.com and Mint.com were competing for dominance in the personal investment industry, and Mint eventually won. According to Noah Kagan, a former employee at Wesabe, it was the startup's awkward name that led to its eventual demise.

Memorable, short, or quirky names, by themselves, will not guarantee success. It took Mibblio's founders nearly a year to select a name, as they deliberately meshed themes central to their business concept to find the right tone. The name is certainly unique, inexpensive, modern—and it was cheap. The effort seems to have paid off, at least if the deal the founders recently signed with Disney is any indication. And if their luck holds out, perhaps Mibblio will one day join the ranks of other startups that have become household names.

Sources: Lindsay Gellman, "Why Startups Are Sporting Increasingly Quirky Names," *The Wall Street Journal*, July 18, 2013, p. B4; "Mibblio: Play It All," http://www.mibblio.com, accessed January 8, 2015; David Teten, "Should a Startup Spend VC Funding on a Domain Name?" *Forbes*, May 1, 2013, http://www.forbes.com/sites/davidteten/2013/05/01/should-a-startup-spend-vc-funding-on-a-domain-name/2, accessed January 8, 2015; and Martin Zwilling, "Get a Domain Name without Bankrupting Your Startup," *Forbes*, January 14, 2013, http://www.forbes.com/sites/martinzwilling/2013/01/14/get-a-domain-name-without-bankrupting-your-startup, accessed January 8, 2015.

practicality. H&R Block uses a green square in association with its name. Simple things are easy to remember and slower to appear dated.

2. *Design for visibility.* Nike paid Carolyn Davidson, a graphic design student, $35 to design the bold red swoosh that has been the firm's brandmark since its unveiling at the U.S. Track & Field Olympic Trials in 1972. One of its most positive qualities is that you simply cannot miss it wherever it is displayed.
3. *Leave it open to interpretation.* The logo should not explain, at a glance, the complete nature of your company. One of the reasons the Nike swoosh is

so effective is that it stands as an "empty vessel." Because it has no obvious meaning, Nike can build any image around it that serves the firm's purposes and will be associated only with its products.

4. *Be relentlessly consistent*. Companies with strong graphic identities have built that recognition through years of use. Pick a typeface. Pick a color. Use them over and over again *on everything*. Eventually, you will be able to establish an identifiable look and feel.
5. *Recognize the importance of logo design*. Logos and colors are often considered "cosmetic," unimportant features of doing business. But most design-driven companies got to be that way through the efforts of highly placed advocates, such as Steve Jobs at Apple. Design programs work best when others know that they are championed by important people.
6. *Get good advice*. You can go pretty far with common sense. But sooner or later, you'll need the services of a professional graphic designer. The website of the American Institute of Graphic Arts (www.aiga.org), the largest professional organization for graphic designers, offers useful information about how to find and work with experienced professionals.
7. *Don't expect miracles*. Your company's image is the sum total of many factors. Make sure that your company looks, sounds, and feels smart in every way, every time it goes out in public.

Trademark and **service mark** are legal terms indicating the exclusive right to use a brand to represent products and services, respectively. Once an entrepreneur has found a name or symbol that is unique, easy to remember, and related to the product or service, it is time to run a name or symbol search and then to register the brand name or symbol. The protection of trademarks and service marks is discussed later in this chapter.

Designing an Effective Logo

Coming up with the perfect logo is not easy to do. Market reaction can be difficult to predict and the laws that apply to logo design overlap with those regulating both trademarks and copyrights. Websites that provide insights on and assistance with logo design and intellectual property rights include www.thelogofactory.com, http://theperfectdesign.com, www.uspto.gov/trademarks, and www.copyright.gov. But a good intellectual property rights or copyright attorney may be the best source of information and up-to-date advice.

15-4b Packaging

In addition to protecting the basic product, packaging is a significant tool for increasing the value of the total product. Consider some of the products you purchase. How many do you buy mainly because of a preference for package design and/or color? The truth is that innovative packaging is often the deciding factor for consumers. If two products are otherwise similar, packaging may create the distinctive impression that makes the sale.

Adrian Bryce Diorio is the founder of BRYCE, an online organic skincare company that offers all-natural products that are infused with fresh vegetable and fruit purees. Despite the novelty and high quality, sales of BRYCE products were slow. When Diorio surveyed friends and customers to find out why, he discovered that packaging his products in cobalt blue bottles with clear labels, though attractive, didn't allow potential buyers to recognize the uniqueness of his skincare creations. They couldn't see the difference between his offerings and the slew of available lower-priced, generic creams.[25] He knew that he needed a solution to the problem.

> *To make his lotions and cleansers pop off the page, Diorio switched to clear containers that showed off exactly how colorful and original Bryce products are, made with "seeds, pulp, everything." He also incorporated each concoction's signature ingredient into the photography, such as a ripe pomegranate next to a jar of Mediterranean Pomegranate Exfoliating Polishing Scrub . . . in an effort to "scream that it was fresh, fresh, fresh!"*[26]

trademark
A legal term indicating that a firm has exclusive rights to use a brand to promote a product.

service mark
A legal term indicating that a company has the exclusive right to use a brand to identify a service.

Within six months of making these adjustments, sales of Diorio's products had increased 150 percent.[27] Nothing changed in the products themselves, but the look and design of the packaging and presentation increased consumer interest, showing just how important these features can be to a small business and its total product offering.

Financial constraints often prevent small businesses from pursuing creative packaging strategies that would boost sales. Entrepreneurs who can't afford the expensive equipment required for such packaging innovations can often work with "contract packagers," who are able to handle such orders at a low per-unit cost.[28] It certainly pays to consider what goes on the outside of your product, not just what's in it.

15-4c Labeling

Labeling serves several important purposes for manufacturers, which apply most labels. One purpose is to display the brand, particularly when branding the basic product would be undesirable. For example, a furniture brand is typically shown on a label and not on the basic product. On some products, brand visibility is highly desirable; Louis Vuitton handbags would probably not sell as well if the name label were only inside the purse.

A label is also an important informative tool for consumers. It often includes information on product care and use and may even provide instructions on how to dispose of the product.

Laws concerning labeling requirements should be reviewed carefully. A number of government agencies issue regulations that must be followed to remain within the law, including the Food and Drug Administration (www.fda.gov), the Federal Trade Commission (www.ftc.gov), and the U.S. Department of Agriculture (www.usda.gov). Their websites can be consulted to read up on any requirements, including any recent changes, by entering "labeling requirements" in the search window. Small businesses are exempt from many of these requirements, but it is wise to consider including information that goes beyond the specified minimum legal requirements if doing so would give an advantage to your company and the way your products are positioned in the marketplace.

SATISFACTION GUARANTEE
LIFETIME WARRANTY
100%
SATISFACTION GUARANTEE

15-4d Warranties

A **warranty** is simply a promise, written or unwritten, that a product will do certain things or meet certain standards. All sellers make an implied warranty that the seller's title to the product is good. A merchant seller, who deals in goods of a particular kind, makes the additional implied warranty that those goods are fit for the ordinary purposes for which they are sold. A written warranty on a product is not always necessary. In fact, many firms operate without written warranties, believing that offering one would likely confuse customers or make them suspicious.

Warranties are important for products that are innovative, comparatively expensive, purchased infrequently, relatively complex to repair, or positioned as high-quality goods. When assessing the merits of a proposed warranty policy, a firm should consider important factors, such as cost, service capability, competitive practices, customer perceptions, and legal implications.

warranty
A promise, written or unwritten, that a product will perform at a certain level or meet certain standards.

15-5 PRODUCT STRATEGY

Understand product strategy and the alternatives available to small businesses.

Product strategy includes decisions about branding and other elements of the core component of the bundle of satisfaction, whether a product or service. To be more specific, a **product strategy** describes the manner in which the product component of the marketing mix is used to achieve the objectives of a firm. This involves several supporting features:

- A **product item** is the lowest common denominator in a company's product mix. It refers to an individual item, such as one brand of bar soap.
- A **product line** is the sum of the related individual product items, but the relationship is usually defined generically. So, two brands of bar soap are two product items in one product line.
- A **product mix** is the collection of all product lines within a firm's ownership and control. A firm's product mix might consist of a line of bar soaps and a line of household cleansers.
- **Product mix consistency** refers to the closeness, or similarity, of the product lines. The more product items in a product line, the greater its depth; the more product lines in a product mix, the greater its breadth.

To illustrate how these features can come together, Exhibit 15.4 shows the product lines and product mix of the firm 180s, LLC, which makes innovative performance apparel and accessories.

product strategy
The way in which the product component of the marketing mix is used to achieve a firm's objectives.

product item
The lowest common denominator in the product mix—the individual item.

product line
The sum of related individual product items.

product mix
The collection of a firm's total product lines.

product mix consistency
The similarity of product lines in a product mix.

15-5a Product Marketing versus Service Marketing

Traditionally, marketers have used the word *product* as a generic term to describe both goods and services. However, certain characteristics—tangibility, amount of time separating production and consumption, standardization, and perishability—lead to a number of differences between the strategies for marketing goods and those for

EXHIBIT 15.4 Product Lines and Product Mix for 180s LLC

Depth of Product Lines	Breadth of Product Mix					
	Ear Warmers	Gloves	Jackets/ Thermals	Booties	Hats/Masks	Scarves
Casual Wear	15 Men's Styles, 17 Women's Styles	9 Men's Styles, 10 Women's Styles				
Training Gear			11 Men's Styles, 14 Women's Styles		2 Men's Styles, 4 Women's Styles	4 Women's Styles
College Sports Apparel	16 Teams	16 Teams		4 Teams		13 Teams
LED Outdoor Gear	1 Men's Style, 1 Women's Style	3 Men's Styles, 3 Women's Styles			1 Men's Style, 1 Women's Style	
Bluetooth and MP3 Gear	2 Men's Styles, 2 Women's Styles					

Source: Compiled from http://www.180s.com, accessed January 6, 2015.

marketing services (see Exhibit 15.5). Based on these characteristics, for example, the marketing of sunglasses fits the pure goods end of the scale and the marketing of haircuts fits the pure services end.

Although marketing services obviously presents unique challenges that are not faced when marketing goods, space constraints prevent us from describing it separately. Therefore, from this point on in the chapter, a **product** will be considered to include the total bundle of satisfaction offered to customers in an exchange transaction, whether this involves a good, a service, or a combination of the two. In addition to the physical product or core service, a product also includes complementary components, such as its packaging or a warranty. The physical product or core service is usually the most important element in the total bundle of satisfaction, but that main feature is sometimes perceived by customers to be similar for a variety of products. In that case, complementary components become the most important features of the product. For example, a particular brand of cake mix may be preferred by consumers not because it is a better mix, but because of the unique website mentioned on the package that offers creative baking suggestions. Or a certain dry cleaner may be chosen over others because it treats customers with great care, not because it cleans clothes exceptionally well.

15-5b Product Strategy Options

Failure to clearly understand product strategy options will lead to ineffectiveness and conflict in the marketing effort. The major product strategy alternatives of a small business can be condensed into six categories, based on the nature of the firm's product offering and the number of target markets:

1. One product/one market
2. One product/multiple markets
3. Modified product/one market
4. Modified product/multiple markets
5. Multiple products/one market
6. Multiple products/multiple markets

product
A total bundle of satisfaction—whether a service, a good, or both—offered to consumers in an exchange transaction.

Each alternative represents a distinct strategy, although two or more of these strategies can be attempted at the same time. However, a small company will usually pursue the alternatives in the order listed. Also, keep in mind that once a product strategy has been implemented, sales can be increased through certain additional

EXHIBIT 15.5 Services Marketing Versus Goods Marketing

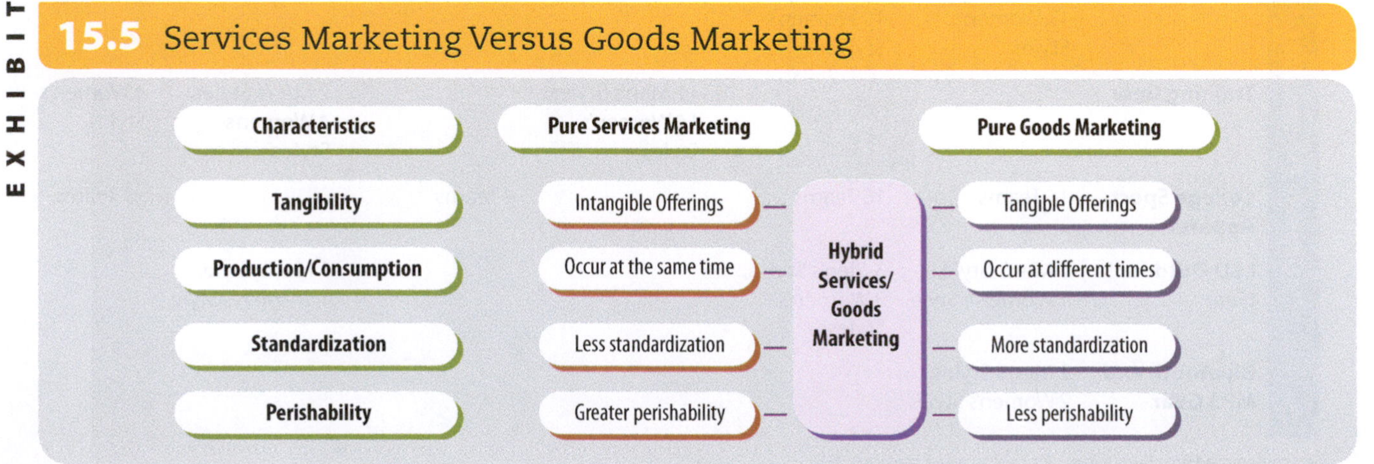

growth tactics. For example, within any market, a small firm can try to increase sales of an existing product by (1) convincing nonusers in the targeted market to become customers, (2) persuading current customers to use more of the product, and/or (3) alerting current customers to new uses for the product.

When small businesses add products to their product mix, they generally select related products. But there are also strategies that involve unrelated products. For example, a local dealer selling Italian sewing machines might add a line of microwave ovens, an entirely unrelated product. This type of product strategy can be more difficult to pull off. However, it is occasionally used by small businesses, especially when the new product fits existing sales and distribution systems or requires similar marketing knowledge.

Adding an unrelated product to the mix to target a new market can be even more challenging to manage, as a business is attempting to sell an unfamiliar product in an unfamiliar market. However, if well planned, this approach can offer significant advantages. For example, a company that sells both snow skis and surfboards expects that demand will be high in one market or the other at all times, smoothing the sales curve and maintaining a steady cash flow throughout the year. It is tempting to take on new product opportunities—sometimes to the point of becoming overextended—but staying manageably focused is critical.

15-6 THE LEGAL ENVIRONMENT

Discuss how the legal environment affects product decisions.

Strategic decisions about growth, innovation, product development, and the total product offering are always made within the guidelines and constraints of the legal environment of the marketplace. Let's examine a few of the laws by which the government protects both the rights of consumers and the marketing assets of companies.

15-6a Consumer Protection

Federal regulations on such subjects as product safety and labeling have important implications for product strategy. For example, to protect the public against unreasonable risk of injury or death, the federal government enacted the Consumer Product Safety Act of 1972. This act created the Consumer Product Safety Commission to set safety standards for toys and other consumer products and to ban goods that are exceptionally hazardous, which ultimately increase the costs of doing business. This law was extended by the Consumer Product Safety Improvement Act of 2008, but its focus remains the same.[29] (To learn more about compliance requirements, consult the webpage of the U.S. Consumer Product Safety Commission that has been specifically constructed for small businesses at www.cpsc.gov/Business-Manufacturing/Small-Business-Resources/Small-Business-Program.)

The Nutrition Labeling and Education Act of 1990 requires every food product covered by the law to have a standard nutrition label, listing the amounts of calories, fat, salt, and nutrients in the product. The law also addresses the accuracy of advertising claims such as "low salt" and "fiber prevents cancer." Although these legal requirements may seem to be a minor burden, some experts estimate that labeling costs can easily amount to thousands of dollars per product. As indicated earlier in this chapter, you can access a wealth of applicable information on the Food and Drug Administration website (www.fda.gov) by entering the words "labeling requirements" in the search window. Similarly, you can search on "small business exemptions" to learn more about your specific obligations under the law. These guidelines should be carefully followed to avoid problems.

15-6b Protection of Marketing Assets

The four primary means used by firms to protect certain marketing assets are trademarks, patents, copyrights, and trade dress.

Nutrition Facts
Serving Size 2/3 cup (51g)
Servings Per Container About 9
Cereal with 1/2 cup Skim Milk
Amount Per Serving
Cereal
Calories 240 280
Calories from Fat 70 70
% Daily Value**
Total Fat 8g* 12% 12%
Saturated Fat 2.5g 13% 13%
Trans Fat 0g
Cholesterol 0mg 0% 0%
Sodium 50mg 2% 5%
Total Carbohydrate 37g 12% 14%
Dietary Fiber 3g 12% 12%
Sugars 13g
Protein 4g 8% 16%
Vitamin A 0% 4%
Vitamin C 0% 0%
Calcium 2% 15%
Iron 6% 6%

© ISTOCKPHOTO.COM/CHRIS SADOWSKI

TRADEMARKS

Trademark or service mark protection is important, because it safeguards a company's distinctive use of a name, word, phrase, slogan, symbol, design, logo, picture, or any combination of these. In some cases, even a sound or scent (submitted for registration application in the form of a detailed written description) can be part of a trademark or service mark, but these *nontraditional marks* can be difficult to defend in court.[30] In essence, trademarks or service marks represent the way people identify your business.

Because names that refer to products or services are often registered, potential names should be investigated carefully to ensure that they are not already in use. Entrepreneurs can conduct their own searches online at www.uspto.gov or by using any of the more than 80 Patent and Trademark Resource Centers that can be found in nearly every U.S. state.[31] Small business owners often seek the advice of an attorney for assistance with trademark search and registration, which may be necessary, especially if complications arise (for example, if the desired trademark is similar to one that is already registered). Applications for registration can be submitted online using the USPTO's Trademark Electronic Application System (www.uspto.gov/trademarks/teas/index.jsp); filing, search, and examination fees will be charged according to the schedule listed on the website.[32]

Common law recognizes a property right in the ownership of trademarks. However, reliance on common-law rights is not always adequate. For example, Microsoft Corporation claimed it had common-law rights to the trademark *Windows* because of the enormous industry recognition of the product. Nevertheless, the U.S. Patent and Trademark Office rejected Microsoft's trademark application, claiming the word was a generic term and, therefore, in the public domain.

Registration of trademarks is permitted under the federal Lanham (Trademark) Act, making protection easier if infringement is encountered. The act was revised in 1989 and now allows trademark rights to begin with merely an "intent to use" the mark, along with the filing of an application and payment of fees. Prior to this revision, a firm had to have already used the mark on goods shipped or sold. A company's federally registered trademark rights can last indefinitely, as long as the owner uses the mark continuously on or in connection with the goods and/or services to which it applies and renews the registration with the USPTO in accordance with the mandatory schedule (usually every 10 years thereafter).[33]

According to the law, a business must use a trademark in order to protect it, but it is also important to *use it properly*. Inform the public that your trademark is exactly that by labeling it with the symbol ™ (℠ for a service mark). If that trademark or service mark is registered, the symbol ® should be used.

patent
The registered, exclusive right of an inventor to make, use, or sell an invention.

utility patent
Registered protection for a new or improved process, machine, manufactured product, or "composition of matter."

design patent
Registered protection for the appearance of a product and its inseparable parts.

PATENTS

A **patent** is the registered, exclusive right of an inventor to make, use, or sell an invention. The two primary types of patents are utility patents and design patents. A **utility patent** covers the discovery or improvement of a new and useful process, machine, manufactured product, or "composition of matter." A **design patent** covers the appearance of a product and everything that is an inseparable part of the product. Utility patents are granted for a period of 20 years, while design patents are effective for 14 years. Patent law also provides for **plant patents**, which cover the invention or discovery and reproduction of any distinct, new variety of living plant.[34]

To get answers to most of your patent-related questions, we suggest that you first visit the Patent and Trademark Office's "Patents for Inventors" webpage (www.uspto.gov/inventors/patents.jsp). But because the process can be so complicated, it is advisable to use a patent attorney to prepare a patent application. Even when a patent is secured, however, the protection it provides will not be perfect. If patent infringement can be proved, the court can require monetary damages and hand down injunctions to prevent further misuse. However, as Choon Ng, creator of Rainbow Loom jewelry kits, has learned, just fighting these challenges can burn through cash that could be better used to fuel enterprise growth (see the Living the Dream feature). Unfortunately, the cost of even getting to that point is often more than a small company can afford.

The patent-approval process has been overhauled in a way that is not always kind to small companies. Among other changes, the America Invents Act of 2011 redefined what is and is not patentable and amended the procedure for challenging a patent during the review process. But more important to small firms, all patent applications are now prioritized according to a new "first-to-file" rule that replaces the longstanding "first-to-invent" specification. This new standard may allow big corporations with deep pockets and more familiarity with the process to "patent early and challenge often," potentially separating resource-strapped and less-connected small companies and garage tinkerers from the inventions that they create.[35] So, inventors need to be very careful about discussing their ideas with others, including potential investors, who might be in a position to file quickly and secure patents on those inventions first.[36] The new system is clearly a game-changer.

Filing a Patent Application

Should you hire an attorney to file a patent application for you or attempt to do it yourself? A few easy-to-access resources can help you decide. Along with the U.S Patent and Trademark Office (www.ustpo.gov), Google (www.google.com/patents) and *Inventors Digest* (http://inventorsdigest.com) can get you started. If you think you are ready to step out on your own, software programs like PatentWizard (www.patentwizard.com) can help you draft and file a provisional patent.

plant patents
Registered protection for any distinct, new variety of living plant.

COPYRIGHTS

A **copyright** is the exclusive right of a creator (such as an author, composer, designer, photographer, or artist) to reproduce, publish, perform, display, or sell work that is the product of that person's intelligence and skill. Works created on or after January 1, 1978, receive copyright protection for the duration of the creator's life plus 70 years. A "work made for hire" (work created by an employee for an employer) is protected for 95 years from its publication or 120 years from its creation, whichever is shorter.[37] Copyrights are registered in the U.S. Copyright Office of the Library of Congress, whose website (www.copyright.gov) provides an extensive supply of useful information about copyrights.

© TIMQUO/SHUTTERSTOCK.COM

Under the Copyright Act of 1976, copyrightable works are automatically protected from the moment of their creation. However, any work distributed to the public should contain a copyright notice. This notice consists of three elements (all of which can be found on the copyright page in the front of this textbook): (1) the symbol©, (2) the year the work was published, and (3) the copyright owner's name.

The law provides that copyrighted work may not be reproduced by another person without authorization. Even photocopying such work is prohibited, although an individual may copy a limited amount of material for such purposes as research, criticism, comment, and scholarship. A copyright holder can sue a violator for damages.

copyright
The exclusive right of a creator to reproduce, publish, perform, display, or sell his or her own works.

Living the Dream

USING TECHNOLOGY

Banding Together to Fight Patent Infringement

Choon Ng founded Rainbow Loom in 2010 to sell rubber-band jewelry kits. He started the company in his garage after struggling to craft rubber-band bracelets with his daughters. He found that his fingers were too large to weave the bands together, so he set out to find a solution to the problem. By cutting up old credit cards, Ng was able to create small clips that fastened and held each band together to create unique geometric shapes.

Impressed, his daughters encouraged him to sell the invention. Ng invested his life savings, $10,000 in total, and several years of hard work before his creation became a success. But his efforts have paid off for Rainbow Loom, which has grown so much that it now employs 12 people and operates out of a 7,500-square-foot warehouse in Wixom, Michigan. For Ng, it was a dream come true. "Every basement inventor has the fantasy that his invention will go big," he says.

In response to the success of Rainbow Loom, however, a host of competitors have entered the rubber-band jewelry market with their own knockoff devices. Rainbow's easy-to-replicate design has allowed these manufacturers to quickly create looms of their own and steal market share away from Ng. The widespread availability of 3-D printing technology, fast-manufacturing capabilities, and affordable e-commerce platforms have only compounded the problem.

Rainbow Loom has successfully defended its patents against competitors, but victory in court comes at a price. Ng has filed more than eight patent lawsuits in the last two years alone, diverting cash flows that could otherwise be used to fuel the company's growth. The company's financial success to date has allowed it to absorb these liabilities and survive, but startups that have no such financial cushion may not be able to weather the storm. For now, patents provide hopeful entrepreneurs with a measure of protection. However, as inexpensive manufacturing capabilities become more widespread, it may just be a matter of time before lawsuits simply cannot stem the fast-rising tide of infringement.

Sources: Catherine Clifford, "Rainbow Loom Maker Sues Rival Toymaker over Patents," *Entrepreneur*, September 12, 2013, http://www.entrepreneur.com/article/228363, accessed January 8, 2015; Sarah Needleman and Adam Janofsky, "Patent Fight Erupts over Kids' Fad," *The Wall Street Journal*, September 11, 2013, p. B1; "Rainbow Loom," http://www.rainbowloom.com, accessed January 8, 2015; and Camille Sweeney, "How a DIY Dad Took the Toy World by Storm with Rainbow Loom," *Fast Company*, August 21, 2013, http://www.fastcompany.com/3016092/how-to-be-a-success-at-everything/how-a-diy-dad-took-the-toy-world-by-storm-with-rainbow-loom, accessed January 8, 2015.

TRADE DRESS

The valuable intangible asset called **trade dress** describes those elements of a firm's distinctive operating image not specifically protected under a trademark, patent, or copyright. Trade dress is the "look" that a firm creates to establish its marketing advantage. For example, if the employees of a small pizza chain dress as prison guards and inmates, a "jailhouse" image could become uniquely associated with this business and, over time, become its trade dress. Trade dress can be protected under trademark law if it can be shown that the design or appearance of one product is so similar to that of another that the typical consumer would be likely to confuse the two.[38] This is only one small part of the intellectual property rights picture, however. A small business needs to take measures to protect its legitimate claims to all such entitlements—that is, trademarks, service marks, patents, copyrights, and trade dress.

trade dress
Elements of a firm's distinctive image not protected by a trademark, patent, or copyright.

15-7 SUPPLY CHAIN MANAGEMENT

Explain the importance of supply chain management and the major considerations in structuring a distribution channel.

The focus of this chapter so far has been on product development and total product strategy. However, a company's offerings are of use only to the extent that consumers have access to them. **Supply chain management** is a system of management through which a company integrates and coordinates the flows of materials and information needed to produce a product or service and deliver it to customers. It also coordinates the flow of payments between entities in the chain of transactions.

Recent attention directed toward supply chain management has motivated firms of all sizes to create a more competitive, customer-driven supply system. Effective supply chain management can potentially lower the costs of inventory, transportation, warehousing, and packaging, while increasing customer satisfaction. This has never been more true than it is today as the Internet, with its simple, universally accepted communication standards, brings suppliers and customers together in a way never before thought possible.

In this section, we look briefly at some of the important features of supply chain management.[39] This includes the functions of intermediaries, the various distribution channels that can be folded into supply chain operations, and the basics of logistics.

supply chain management
A system of management through which a company integrates and coordinates the flows of materials and information needed to produce a product or service and deliver it to customers.

merchant middlemen
Intermediaries that take ownership of the goods they distribute.

agents/brokers
Intermediaries that do not take ownership of the goods they distribute.

distribution
The physical movement of products and the establishment of intermediary relationships to support such movement.

channel of distribution
The system of relationships established to guide the movement of a product.

physical distribution (logistics)
The activities of distribution involved in the physical relocation of products.

direct channel
A distribution system without intermediaries.

indirect channel
A distribution system with one or more intermediaries.

15-7a Intermediaries

Intermediaries can often perform marketing functions better than the producer of a product can. A producer can handle its own distribution operations—including delivery—if the geographic area of the market is small, customers' needs are specialized, and risk levels are low. This might be the case for, say, a donut maker. However, intermediaries generally provide more efficient means of distribution if customers are widely dispersed or if special packaging and storage are needed.

Some intermediaries, called **merchant middlemen**, take ownership of the goods they distribute, thereby helping a company to share or shift business risk. Other intermediaries, such as **agents** and **brokers**, do not take title to goods and, therefore, assume less market risk than do merchant middlemen.

15-7b Channels of Distribution

An effective distribution system is just as important as a unique package, a clever name, or a creative promotional campaign. In the context of supply chain operations, **distribution** encompasses both the physical transfer of products and the establishment of intermediary (middleman) relationships to achieve product movement. The system of relationships established to guide the movement of a product is called the **channel of distribution**, and the activities involved in physically moving a product through the channel of distribution are called **physical distribution (logistics)**. Distribution is essential for both goods (tangible products) and services (intangible products). However, since distribution activities are more visible for goods, our comments here will focus primarily on tangible products. Most services are delivered straight to the user—for example, an income tax preparer and a hairdresser serve their clients directly. Nonetheless, even the distribution of labor can involve channel intermediaries, such as when an employment agency provides a firm with temporary personnel.

A channel of distribution can be either direct or indirect. In a **direct channel**, there are no intermediaries—the product goes directly from producer to user. An **indirect channel** of distribution has one or more intermediaries between producer and user.

Exhibit 15.6 depicts the various options available for structuring a channel of distribution. E-commerce (online merchandising) and mail-order marketing are direct channel systems for distributing consumer goods. As a very cost-conscious airlines, Southwest Airlines is an example of a company that uses a direct channel to customers. Rather than sell tickets through travel agents and online travel service distributors, it sells flights directly to consumers through its own website and in-airport ticket counters and self-service kiosks, which significantly reduces the firm's operating costs.[40]

Indirect channels of distribution are shown on the right-hand side of Exhibit 15.6. Channels with two or more stages of intermediaries are most typically used by small firms that produce products with geographically large markets. This practice is called **dual distribution**.

Small businesses that successfully employ a single distribution channel may switch to dual distribution if they find that an additional channel will improve overall profitability. Alex Romanov, owner of Chagrin Shoe Leather & Luggage Repair, saw sales increase by 25 percent after the U.S. economy slowed in 2008 and Americans decided that it would be cheaper and wiser to repair their shoes than to buy new ones. But his son, Ilya, had no interest in being a cobbler, so he launched American Heelers, an online business that receives by mail about 100 pairs of shoes for repair each week. These shoes are serviced in the elder Romanov's shop and returned to their owners. Establishing this father-son partnership has expanded the business by opening up two fronts for sales: a physical operation that takes orders directly from customers and an e-commerce operation that generates revenue from customers who live in other areas.[41]

dual distribution
A distribution system that involves more than one channel.

EXHIBIT **15.6** Channels of Distribution

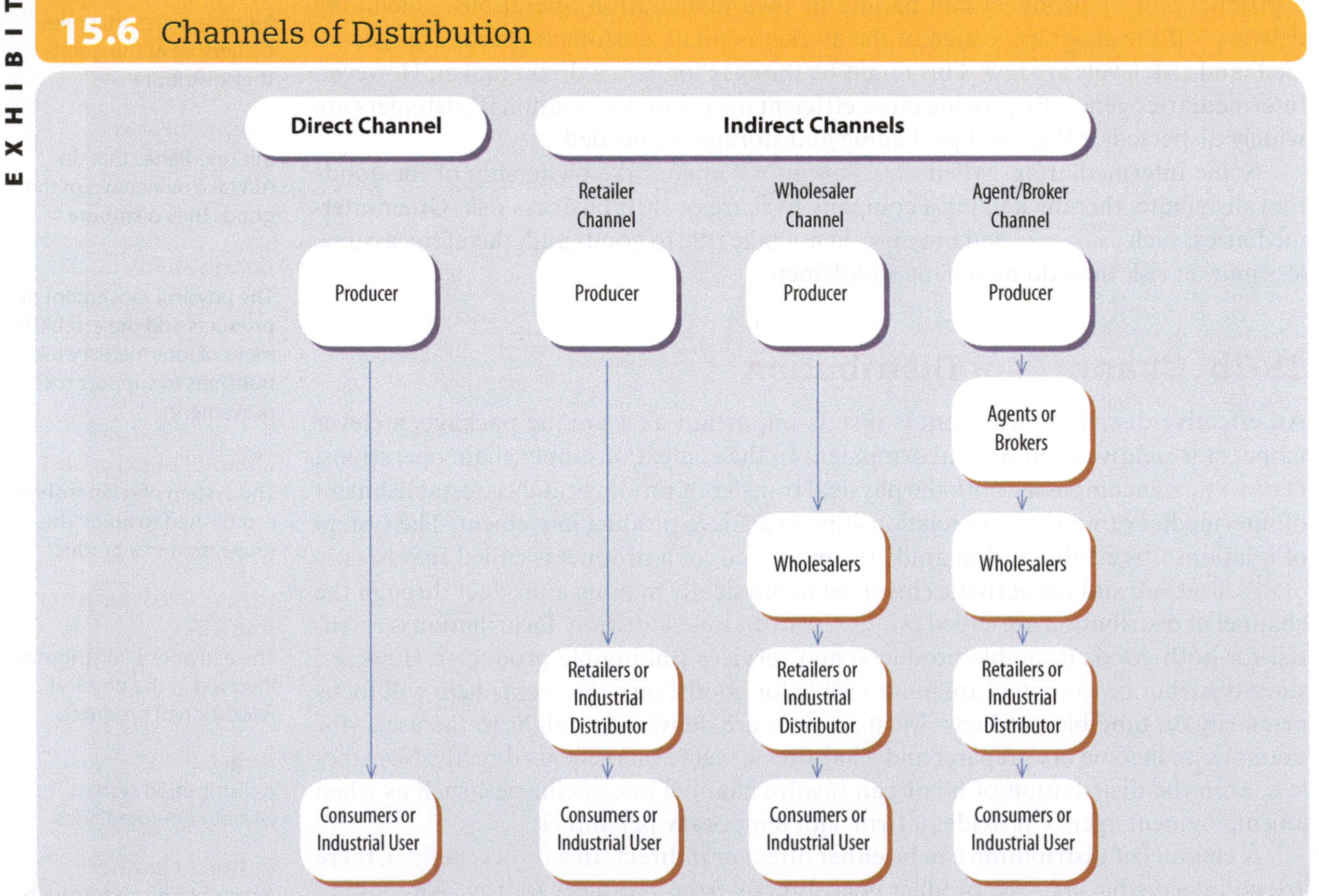

A logical starting point in structuring a distribution system is to study systems used by competing businesses. Such an analysis should reveal some practical alternatives, which can then be evaluated. The three main considerations in evaluating a channel of distribution are costs, coverage, and control.

COSTS

In many cases, the least-expensive channel may be indirect. For example, a firm producing handmade dolls may choose not to purchase trucks and warehouses to distribute its product directly to customers if it costs less to use established intermediaries that already own such equipment and facilities. Small companies should look at distribution costs as an investment—spending money in order to make money—and ask themselves whether the cost of using intermediaries (by selling the product to them at a reduced price) is more or less expensive than distributing the product directly to customers.

COVERAGE

Small businesses can often use indirect channels of distribution to increase market coverage. Suppose a small manufacturer's internal sales force can make 10 contacts a week with final users of the venture's product. Creating an indirect channel with 10 industrial distributors, each making 10 contacts a week, could expose the product to 100 final users a week.

CONTROL

A direct channel of distribution is sometimes preferable because it provides more control. To ensure that the product is marketed with care, an entrepreneur must deliberately select intermediaries that provide the desired support.

A small business that chooses to use intermediaries to market and distribute its product must be sure that the intermediaries understand how the product is best used and why it's better than competitors' offerings. Additionally, if a wholesaler carries competing products, an entrepreneur must be sure that her or his product gets its fair share of marketing efforts. An intermediary's sloppy marketing support and insufficient product knowledge can undermine the success of even the best product.

15-7c The Scope of Physical Distribution

As mentioned earlier, in addition to the intermediary relationships that make up a channel of distribution, there must also be a system of *physical distribution (logistics)*, the activities that physically move a product through a channel. The main component of physical distribution is transportation. Other components include storage and materials handling, delivery terms, and inventory management. (Inventory management is discussed in Chapter 21.)

TRANSPORTATION

The major decision regarding physical transportation of a product is which method to use. Available modes of transportation are traditionally classified as airplanes, railroads, trucks, pipelines, and waterways. Each mode has unique advantages and disadvantages. For example, the train operator CSX Corporation runs radio ads that boldly announce, "Nature is spectacular, and we want to keep it that way. That's why CSX trains move one ton of freight nearly 500 miles on a single gallon of fuel."[42] The purpose of the ad campaign is twofold—to let potential customers know that the company offers inexpensive transportation services that also minimize environmental impact.

But the choice of a specific mode of transportation is usually based on several criteria: relative cost, transit time, reliability, capability, accessibility, and traceability.

Transportation intermediaries are legally classified as common carriers, contract carriers, and private carriers. **Common carriers** are available for hire by the general public, without discrimination. Like common carriers, **contract carriers**, which engage in individual contracts with shippers, are subject to regulation by federal and/or state agencies; however, they have the right to choose their clients at will. Transport lines owned by shippers are called **private carriers**.

STORAGE AND MATERIALS HANDLING

Lack of space is a common problem for small businesses. But when a channel system uses merchant middlemen or wholesalers, ownership of the goods is transferred, as is responsibility for the storage function. With other options, the small business must plan for its own warehousing. If a firm is too small to own a private warehouse, it can rent space in a public warehouse. When storage requirements are simple and do not involve much special handling equipment, a public warehouse can provide inexpensive storage.

Even if it is in the right place at the right time, a damaged product is worth very little. Therefore, a physical distribution system must arrange for suitable materials-handling methods and equipment. Forklifts, as well as special containers and packaging, are part of a materials-handling system.

DELIVERY TERMS

A small but important part of a physical distribution system is the delivery terms, specifying which party is responsible for several aspects of the distribution. Delivery terms include paying the freight costs, selecting the carriers, bearing the risk of damage in transit, and selecting the modes of transport.

The simplest delivery terms—and the most advantageous to a small business as the seller—is F.O.B. (free on board) origin, freight collect. This shifts all of the responsibility for freight costs to the buyer. Ownership of the goods and risk of loss also pass to the buyer at the time the goods are shipped.

Logistics companies specialize in transportation and distribution services, providing trucking, packaging, and warehousing services for small and medium-size companies with limited in-house staff. Many small businesses believe that using **third-party logistics firms (3PLs)** is more cost effective than carrying out the same functions on their own. For example, one cosmetics company uses APL Logistics to handle the packaging and shipping of its health and beauty-aid products. Products produced in plants around the country go to the APL warehouse in Dallas, Texas, and are then shipped to distribution outlets nationwide.[43] More familiar firms offering 3PL services include household names such as FedEx and UPS, both of which offer customized assistance for small businesses that would prefer to focus on their primary operations and leave the transportation and distribution challenges to others.

common carriers
Transportation intermediaries available for hire to the general public.

contract carriers
Transportation intermediaries that contract with individual shippers.

private carriers
Lines of transport owned by shippers.

third-party logistics firms (3PLs)
A company that provides transportation and distribution services to firms that prefer to focus their efforts on their primary operations.

As this chapter explains, innovation and growth are critical to competitive advantage and small business success. For this reason, a company's efforts to maintain existing products and develop new ones should be wisely managed according to a carefully devised product strategy. But it doesn't stop there. Thought must also be given to all facets of the physical flow of inputs and outputs. Managing the supply chain requires planning for how and where the firm will get components for the products it produces and how it will deliver the finished products to customers. Though many channels of distribution exist, each of these has benefits and drawbacks and must therefore be considered carefully. In the end, if all of these vitally important tasks are not managed effectively, the performance of the company is almost certain to decline.

15-1. Recognize the challenges associated with the growth of a small business.

- Some entrepreneurs find that maintaining the status quo is challenge enough and thus choose not to grow their ventures.
- A business's reputation may be damaged if it is unable to deliver on time or with the level of quality promised, or if it must turn down an order because it can't handle the volume.
- A growth trap may occur when a firm's growth soaks up cash faster than it can be generated.
- Growing a business too quickly can be stressful for a small firm's owners and personnel.

15-2. Explain the role of innovation in a company's growth.

- Small entrepreneurial firms produce twice as many innovations per employee as large firms, accounting for half of all those created and an amazing 95 percent of all *radical* innovations.
- The risk of failure increases when innovation is the goal.
- An entrepreneur can reduce the risk of innovation by basing innovative efforts on experience, targeting products or services that have been overlooked, ensuring a market for the product or service, emphasizing value creation for customers, pursuing new ideas that will lead to more than one product or service, and raising sufficient capital before launching a new product or service.
- Innovation is a means by which a firm can achieve and sustain a competitive advantage.
- The competitive advantage life cycle has three stages: develop, deploy, and decline.
- High-performing companies have an awareness of "hidden curves" related to their competitors, their own internal capabilities, and the capabilities and motivations of their people.

15-3. Identify stages in the product life cycle and the new product development process.

- The product life cycle portrays the sales and profits of an individual product from introduction through growth and maturity to sales decline.
- The new product development process has four stages: idea accumulation, business analysis, development of the physical product, and product testing.
- When conducting a business analysis on a new product, the following four factors should be considered: its fit with existing product lines, its development and introduction costs, the personnel and facilities available to get it started, and its competition and market acceptance potential.
- New technologies are making the creation of a working prototype for a new product much more manageable.
- Product testing determines whether a product is safe, effective, durable, etc.
- A new product development process is much more likely to succeed if it is focused on the firm's customers.

15-4. Describe the building of a firm's total product.

- Components of a total product offering include branding, packaging, labeling, and warranties.
- The intangible brand image component is important to consumers' acceptance of a firm's total product offering.
- A brand name should be easy to pronounce and remember, descriptive, eligible for legal protection, full of promotional possibilities, and suitable for use on several product lines. It should also lead to a domain name that is relatively inexpensive to acquire.
- In order to develop an effective but inexpensive logo, be simple, design for visibility, leave room for interpretation, emphasize consistency, recognize the importance of logo design, get good design advice, and don't expect miracles.
- Trademark and service mark are legal terms referring to a company's exclusive right to use a brand to represent products and services.
- Packaging is a significant tool for increasing total product value.
- A label is an important informative tool, providing brand visibility and instructions on product care and use.
- A warranty is important for products that are innovative, comparatively expensive, purchased infrequently, complex to repair, or positioned as high-quality goods.

15-5. Understand product strategy and the alternatives available to small businesses.

- Product strategy describes how a product is used to achieve a firm's goals and involves the product item, product line, product mix, and product mix consistency.
- Marketing services presents unique challenges not faced when marketing goods.
- There are six categories of major product strategy alternatives, which are based on the nature of the firm's product offering and the number of target markets.

15-6. Discuss how the legal environment affects product decisions.

- Federal legislation regarding labeling and product safety was designed to protect consumers.
- Meeting the legal requirements for labeling can cost thousands of dollars per product.
- The legal system provides protection for a firm's marketing assets through trademarks and service marks, patents, copyrights, and trade dress.
- According to the law, businesses must use a trademark or service mark in order to protect it, but they must also use it properly.
- New procedures in the patent-approval process are not always kind to small businesses, and lawsuits concerning patent infringement can be costly.
- Copyrighted work may not be reproduced without authorization.
- A firm can use the law related to trade dress to protect its unique operating image.

15-7. Explain the importance of supply chain management and the major considerations in structuring a distribution channel.

- Effective supply chain management can potentially lower the costs of inventory, transportation, warehousing, and packaging, while increasing customer satisfaction.
- Intermediaries provide an efficient means of distribution if customers are widely dispersed or if special packaging and storage are needed.
- Distribution encompasses both the physical movement of products and the establishment of intermediary relationships to guide the movement of products from producer to user.
- A distribution channel can be either direct or indirect, and many firms successfully employ more than one channel of distribution.
- Costs, coverage, and control are the three main considerations in evaluating a channel of distribution.
- Transportation, storage and materials handling, delivery terms, and inventory management are the main components of a physical distribution system.
- Small companies with limited in-house staff sometimes find it helpful to use logistics firms for their transportation and distribution needs, as these vendors provide trucking, packaging, and warehouse services.

Key Terms

agents/brokers p. 421
brand p. 410
brand image p. 410
brandmark p. 411
brand name p. 410
channel of distribution p. 421
common carriers p. 424
contract carriers p. 424
copyright p. 419
design patent p. 419
direct channel p. 421
distribution p. 421
dual distribution p. 422
indirect channel p. 421
merchant middlemen p. 421
patent p. 419
physical distribution (logistics) p. 421
plant patents p. 419
private carriers p. 424
product p. 416
product item p. 415
product life cycle p. 405
product line p. 415
product mix p. 415
product mix consistency p. 415
product strategy p. 415
service mark p. 413
supply chain management p. 421
sustainable competitive advantage p. 404
third-party logistics firms (3 PLs) p. 424
trade dress p. 420
trademark p. 413
utility patent p. 419
warranty p. 414

You Make the Call

Situation 1

The world's first elliptical bike, called the ElliptiGo, was invented by mechanical engineer and Ironman athlete Brent Teal and his friend, fellow cyclist and triathlete Bryan Pate, who had so much pain from knee and hip injuries that he was forced to limit his exercise activity to low-impact options. Because Pate wanted to continue exercising but hated being locked away in a gym, he and Teal came up with a new product concept for "a low-impact running device that [Pate] could ride on the street." The ElliptiGo is a mix between an elliptical trainer and a standard bicycle, but with 3- and 11-speed models that can make the ride as leisurely as a stroll or as aggressive as a full-out cycling workout. One observer describes it as having "the sleek curves of a high-end road bike, the clean lines of a Razor scooter, a pair of shiny carbon-fiber elliptical pedals, a smooth hub-and-crank stride mechanism and a steering column that collapses for easy storage." Check it out for yourself at www.elliptigo.com.

Sources: Based on "ElliptiGo: Our Story," http://www.elliptigo.com/History, accessed January 8, 2015; John Pozadzides, "The ElliptiGo Elliptical Training Bike," September 10, 2012, http://geekbeat.tv/review-the-elliptigo-elliptical-training-bike-photos-video, accessed January 8, 2015; and Jennifer Wang, "A Profitable Alternative to the Bicycle," http://www.entrepreneur.com/article/207532, accessed January 8, 2015.

Question 1 Using the rules of thumb for reducing the risks related to introducing an innovative new product, how well are Teal and Pate likely to do with the ElliptiGo?

Question 2 What are the primary benefits and drawbacks of this innovation?

Question 3 What can Teal and Pate do to sustain or extend their competitive advantage with this new product?

Situation 2

Project Home (formerly Tomboy Tools) provides tools for women who want to do their own home improvement and repair projects. Friends Sue Wilson, Mary Tatum, and Janet Rickstrew, all of Denver, Colorado, were concerned that the tools they used for home repair projects were designed for men, not women. So they started their venture to "empower women through hands-on education, quality tools, and . . . an internal culture that supports women and teaches them to feel confident using tools. . . ." What is most interesting is how the products are sold—exclusively at in-home workshops led by Project Home's independent sales representatives. Instead of Tupperware or cosmetics, guests see basic home repair tools in action and learn simple home repair and improvement techniques. The company's founders chose the in-home approach to market their products because of its proven success with consumers, particularly women.

Source: Based on "Project Home: About Us," http://www.projecthome.us/about-us, accessed January 8, 2015.

Question 1 What are the advantages and disadvantages of the in-home method of selling Project Home products?

Question 2 What other channels of distribution might Project Home use?

Question 3 What do you think about the name "Project Home"? Does it create a positive impression for the company?

Situation 3

Chris Sugai owns Niner Bikes, a nine-year-old mountain bike company in Fort Collins, Colorado. With a price range from around $1,650 to $10,000, the bikes he sells are not garden-variety two-wheelers. These bikes are for the serious rider who is really into mountain biking and the buzz and conversation that goes along with being a part of the Niner community. There must be many such enthusiasts out there, because business has increased impressively in recent years. In fact, in 2014 alone the company's total sales increased from $15 million to a very impressive $17 million.

But with such growth comes new hassles, especially on the supply chain end of things. Sugai has been depending on a third-party logistics provider to store and deliver his bikes, but he thinks it may be time to bring the operation in-house. With 34 employees, the company should be able to handle the change, even though it will cost about $85,000 to buy the software, scanners, forklifts, and more that will be needed. Sugai might have to hire a few more employees to make the transition possible, but that should be very manageable for a company that is growing at such a rapid pace, and the up-front investment would probably pay for itself in no time. It would definitely make life more complicated, though.

Sources: Angus Loten and Ruth Simon, "Small Business Optimism Surges with Solid Economy," *The Wall Street Journal*, January 2, 2015, pp. B1, B5; "Niner Bikes," *Colorado Cyclist*, http://www.coloradycyclist.com/niner-bikes, accessed January 9, 2015; and http://www.ninerbikes.com, accessed January 9, 2015.

Question 1 What are the advantages that Sugai will likely gain if he decides to bring inventory storage and bike delivery in-house?

Question 2 What complications might arise if Sugai makes this change? What might he have to give up if he should chose the new approach?

Question 3 On balance, do you think that converting to an in-house operation would be the way to go? Why or why not? Put together the best case you can to support your decision.

Video Case 15

Graeter's Ice Cream (P. 677)

This case demonstrates how one company expanded its business through its own growing chain of ice cream shops, distribution via partnerships with major supermarket and grocery store companies, and selective diversification into related ice cream products and baked goods.

Alternative Cases for Chapter 15

Case 3, The Kollection, p. 649
Case 5, Iaccarino & Son, p. 654
Case 18, Auntie Anne's Pretzels in China, p. 682
Video Case 23, Jack's Restaurant, p. 693

Endnotes

1. Robert Kiyosaki, "Even Steven," *Entrepreneur*, Vol. 36, No. 8 (August 2008), p. 36.
2. Debra Kahn Schofield, "Grow Your Business Slowly: A Cautionary Tale," http://www.gmarketing.com/articles/179-grow-your-business-slowly-a-cautionary-tale, accessed January 5, 2015.
3. Stephen Spinelli and Robert J. Adams, *New Venture Creation: Entrepreneurship for the 21st Century* (Boston: McGraw-Hill/Irwin, 2012), p. 14.
4. Reported in an interview with Martha E. Mangelsdorf, "Hard Times Can Drive Innovation," *The Wall Street Journal*, December 15, 2008, p. R2.
5. Neale Martin, *Habit: The 95% of Behavior Marketers Ignore* (Upper Saddle River, NJ: FT Press, 2008), p. 5.
6. Leigh Buchanan, "*Inc.* 500," *Inc.*, Vol. 32, No. 7 (September 2010), p. 148.
7. Some of the strategies outlined here are mentioned in Anne Field, "Creating a Sustainable Competitive Advantage for Your Small Business," http://www.startupnation.com/articles/creating-a-sustainable-competitive-advantage-for-your-small-business, accessed January 5, 2015.
8. "The Blue Story," http://bluebuffalo.com/why-choose-blue/blue-story, accessed January 5, 2015.
9. Matthew S. Olson and Derek van Bever, *Stall Points: Most Companies Stop Growing—Yours Doesn't Have To* (New Haven, CT: Yale University Press, 2008), p. 28.
10. Paul Nunes and Tim Breene, "Reinvent Your Business before It's Too Late," *Harvard Business Review*, Vol. 89, No. 1/2 (January/February 2011), pp. 80–87.
11. Jason Fried, "Starting Over," *Inc.*, Vol. 34, No. 1 (February 2012), p. 40.
12. *Ibid.*
13. For more on the survey, see "Idea Factories," *Inc.*, Vol. 35, No. 7 (September 2013), pp. 104–105.
14. Personal communication with Celestina Pugliese, January 7, 2013.
15. "Ready Check Glo: Our Story," http://www.readycheckglo.com/our-story2, accessed January 6, 2015.
16. Pugliese, *op. cit.*
17. The descriptions of tools and services in this section are based on the websites mentioned, all of which were accessed on January 6, 2015.
18. Jennifer Wang, "Be Disruptive," *Entrepreneur*, Vol. 39, No. 9 (January 2011), p. 20.
19. Mike Gordon, Chris Musso, Eric Rebentisch, and Nisheeth Gupta, "The Path to Developing Successful New Products," *The Wall Street Journal*, November 30, 2009, p. R5.
20. Paula Andruss, "Branding's Big Guns," *Entrepreneur*, Vol. 40, No. 4 (April 2012), pp. 50–55.
21. *Ibid.*
22. Personal communication with Winston Wolfe, February 8, 2011.
23. Tahl Raz, "Re: Design—Not Just a Pretty Typeface," *Inc.*, http://www.inc.com/magazine/20021201/24907.html, accessed January 6, 2015.
24. Adapted from Gwen Moran, "Best and Worst Marketing Ideas . . . Ever," *Entrepreneur*, Vol. 37, No. 1 (January 2009), p. 48; and Raz, *op. cit.*
25. Jennifer Wang, "Skincare Startup's Lesson for Online Brands: Looks Matter" *Entrepreneur*, Vol. 40, No. 3 (March 2012), p. 48.
26. *Ibid.*
27. *Ibid.*
28. Laura Tiffany, "The Whole Package," *Entrepreneur*, Vol. 36, No. 2 (February 2008), p. 24.
29. "Public Law 110-314—August 14, 2008," http://www.cpsc.gov//PageFiles/113865/cpsia.pdf, accessed January 7, 2015.
30. Eleni Mezulanik, "The Status of Scents as Trademarks: An International Perspective," *INTABulletin*, January 1, 2012, http://www.inta.org/INTABulletin/Pages/TheStatusofScentsasTrademarksAnInternationalPerspective.aspx, accessed January 7, 2015.
31. "The United States Patent and Trademark Office: Patent and Trademark Resource Centers," April 11, 2014, http://www.uspto.gov/products/library/ptdl/locations, accessed January 7, 2015.
32. "United States Patent and Trademark Office Fee Schedule," http://www.uspto.gov/web/offices/ac/qs/ope/fee010114.htm, accessed January 7, 2015.
33. The United State Patent and Trademark Office, "Maintain/Renew a Registration: How to Keep a Registration Alive," http://www.uspto.gov/trademarks/process/maintain/prfaq.jsp, accessed January 8, 2015.
34. The United State Patent and Trademark Office, "Patents," http://www.uspto.gov/patents, accessed January 8, 2015.
35. Jonathan Blum, "Protect Yourself," *Entrepreneur*, Vol. 39, No. 8 (August 2011), pp. 64–68.

36. Rachel Z. Arndt, "The Real Cost of Patent Reform," *Fast Company*, No. 162 (February 2012), p. 104.

37. "Copyright Basics," http://www.copyright.gov/circs/circ01.pdf, accessed January 8, 2015.

38. "Nolo's Plain-English Law Dictionary: Trade Dress," http://www.nolo.com/dictionary/trade-dress-term.html, accessed January 8, 2015.

39. A comprehensive discussion of supply chain management is beyond the scope of this book, but many excellent resources provide helpful information on this subject. We recommend John J. Coyle, C. John Langley, Robert A. Novak, and Brian J. Gibson, *Supply Chain Management: A Logistics Perspective*, 9th ed. (Mason, OH: Cengage Learning, 2013); and Joel D. Wisner, Keah-Choon Tan, and G. Keong Leong, *Principles of Supply Chain Management: A Balanced Approach*, 4th ed. (Mason, OH: Cengage Learning, 2016).

40. "Southwest Airlines: Finding Low Fares," http://www.southwest.com/html/travel-experience/finding-low-fares/index.html, accessed January 8, 2015.

41. Sarah E. Needleman, "In a Sole Revival, the Recession Gives Beleaguered Cobblers New Traction," *The Wall Street Journal*, February 2, 2009, pp. A1, A13.

42. "CSX TV Spot: Fireworks," http://www.ispot.tv/ad/7L9w/csx-fireworks, accessed January 8, 2015.

43. Personal communication with Dr. Pedro Reyes, associate professor of operations management, Baylor University, March 14, 2011.

CHAPTER 16

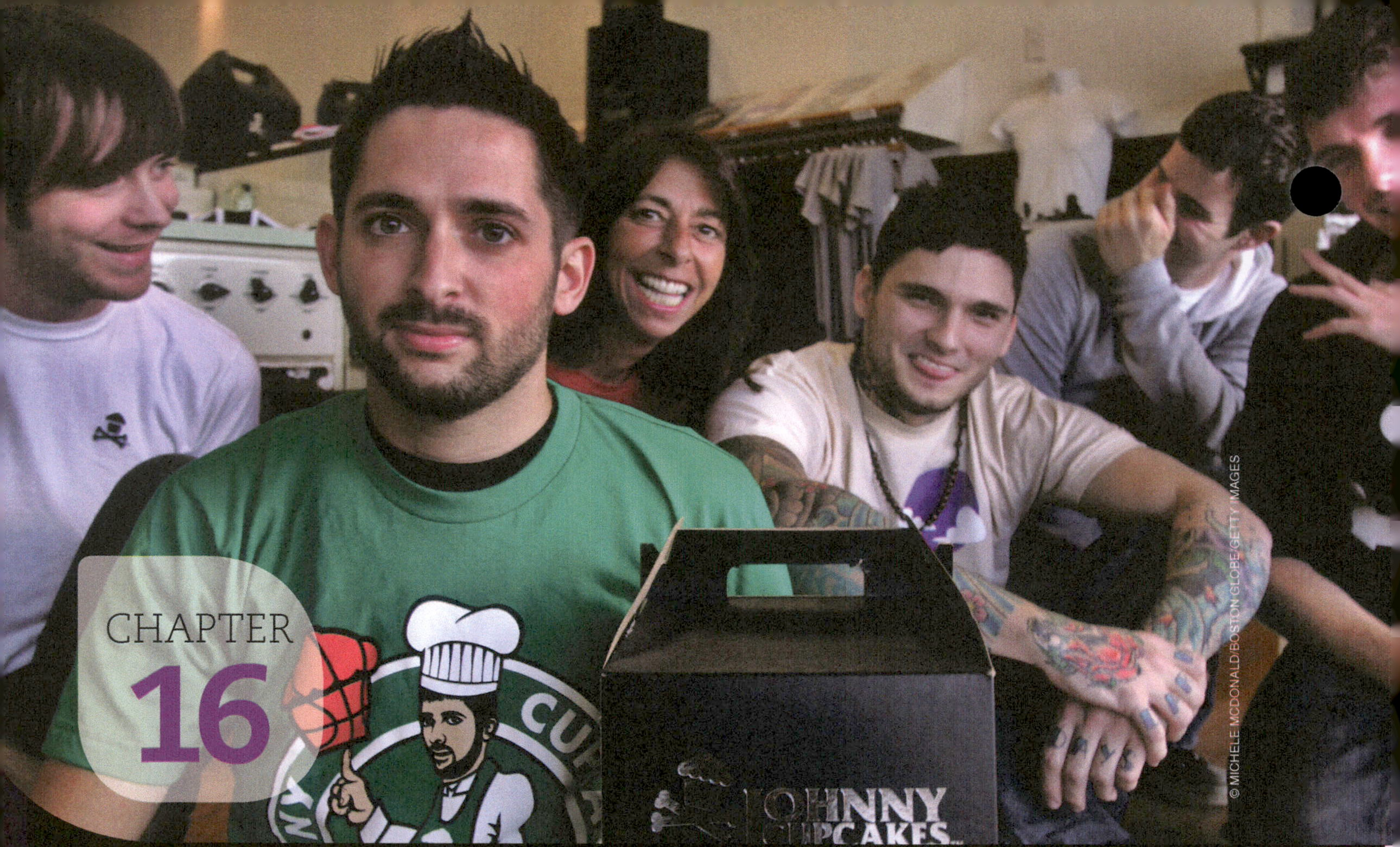

Pricing and Credit Decisions

After studying this chapter, you should be able to. . .

16-1. Discuss the role of cost and demand factors in setting a price.

16-2. Apply break-even analysis and markup pricing.

16-3. Identify specific pricing strategies.

16-4. Explain the benefits of credit, factors that affect credit extension, and types of credit.

16-5. Describe the activities involved in managing credit.

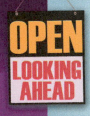

In the SPOTLIGHT
Johnny Cupcakes: It's a Brand, Not a Fad!
www.johnnycupcakes.com

How much was that last t-shirt that you bought? Was it $25? Or $30? May be $40? Those prices look crazy to people who think that t-shirts are commodities—items that you buy at the discount store and wear when you need them. But for others, those prices are just starting points. T-shirts can make statements, and one entrepreneur felt they could make a statement about his entire business. So he created a brand that customers would want to pay for.

Some would say Johnny Earle was born to be an entrepreneur. He started with lemonade stands and yard sales. By the time he was 16, he had started 16 companies. After high school, he worked in a record store and started a hardcore metal band. His co-workers at the store teased him by giving him nicknames. One day, someone called him "Johnny Cupcakes," and the name stuck. Earle liked it enough to get t-shirts made with the nickname on it. People immediately asked him where they could get one of those shirts.

Earle recognized the opportunity and started designing t-shirts with graphics that poked fun at pop culture. He saw what he labeled "tough guys" wearing skull-and-crossbones t-shirts. He replaced the skull with a cupcake and started selling them from the trunk of his car and from a suitcase he carried while on tour with his band. In 2001, at age 19, Earle decided that he was more passionate about selling the t-shirts than the band, so he launched his company.

But can you make a living selling t-shirts? Earle made some early decisions to ensure that his products would be seen by customers as something special, something worth coming back for, something that would not just be a fad. He decided that the t-shirts would be sold only through his own stores, and he called the stores *bakeries*. The designs on the shirts are critical, and once a design sells out, they do not print any more. Some shirts are numbered and come in special packaging. As you can imagine, operating this business is not cheap! How do you price products like these?

When he started the company, Earle offered most of his products in the $20 range. He knew his shirts were not just another commodity. He wanted them to be seen as something special, so there had to be a premium price. Plus, there were costs associated with the unique designs, specialized packaging, and brick-and-mortar outlets. Prices fluctuated with the company's financial responsibilities. By 2015, Johnny Cupcakes had a range of prices for its t-shirts, with most hovering around $30.

Earle and his staff track the prices charged by competitors. They take into consideration the time, energy, resources, and money that go into the creation and release of each product. Earle's strategy is to grow the company by introducing the brand to new customers. He says that Johnny Cupcakes strives "to always have fair-priced items for newcomers, while also balancing in some limited-edition collectors' t-shirts at higher price-points."

Sources: Based on "World's First T-Shirt Bakery," http://www.johnnycupcakes.com, accessed March 1, 2015; Johnny Earle, "Lecture Series Demo Reel," http://www.youtube.com/user/JohnnyCupcakes, accessed March 1, 2015; personal communication with Johnny Earle, October 14, 2014, and January 3, 2015; Tracy Brown, "Johnny Cupcakes' Crypt Tour to Visit L.A. Store Wednesday," http://articles.latimes.com/2012/oct/14/image/la-ig-johnny-cupcakes-20121014, accessed March 1, 2015.

There are countless guidelines and formulas for determining the prices of the products and services that a small business sells, but none of the rules are hard and fast. Even though he had run several businesses before starting Johnny Cupcakes, Johnny Earle still went through some trial and error as he devised his pricing strategy.

Very few business owners have any formal training in how to set the prices for the products and services they sell. Many times, their prices are based on what competitors are charging, some percentage above their costs, or what their suppliers suggest. All too often, new business owners think that their path to success is to undercut competitors' prices. Later in this chapter, we will explain why that can be dangerous. Keep in mind that pricing and credit decisions are vital to the success of a company because they influence the relationship between the business and its customers. These decisions also directly affect both revenue and cash flows. If you find that you started with prices too low to cover your costs, for example, you can expect that your customers won't be happy with price increases or restrictive credit policies. Therefore, a business owner needs to set prices and design credit policies as carefully as possible, to avoid the need for frequent changes.

value
The extent to which a good or service is perceived by a customer as meeting his or her needs or wants, measured by the customer's willingness to pay for it.

price
A specification of what a seller requires in exchange for transferring ownership or use of a product or service.

credit
An agreement between a buyer and a seller that allows for delayed payment for a product or service.

Keep one thing in mind: value should be at the heart of a pricing strategy. In marketing terms, **value** is "the extent to which a good or service is perceived by its customer to meet his or her needs or wants, measured by a customer's willingness to pay for it. It commonly depends more on the customer's perception of the worth of the product than on its intrinsic value."[1] The **price** of a product or service specifies what the seller requires for giving up ownership or use of that product or service. Often, the seller must extend credit to the buyer in order to make the exchange happen. **Credit** is an agreement between a buyer and a seller specifying that payment for a product or service will be received at some later date. This chapter examines both the pricing decisions and the credit decisions of small firms.

16-1 SETTING A PRICE

Discuss the role of cost and demand factors in setting a price.

In setting a price, an entrepreneur decides on the most appropriate value for the product or service being offered for sale. The task seems easy, but it isn't. The first pricing lesson is to remember that total sales revenue depends on just two components—sales volume and price—and even a small change in price can drastically influence revenue. Consider the following situations for products being sold, *assuming no change in demand*:

Situation A

Quantity sold	×	Price per unit	=	Gross revenue
250,000	×	$3.00	=	$750,000

Situation B

Quantity sold	×	Price per unit	=	Gross revenue
250,000	×	$2.80	=	$700,000

The price per unit is only $0.20 lower in Situation B than in Situation A. However, the total difference in revenue is $50,000! Clearly, a small business can lose significant revenue if a price is set too low.

Pricing is also important because it indirectly affects sales quantity. Setting a price too high for the value being offered may result in lower quantities sold, reducing total revenue. In the example just provided, quantity sold was assumed to be independent of price—and it very well may be for such a small price difference. However, a larger price increase or decrease might substantially affect the quantity sold. It makes no sense to lower a price if you wind up selling the same number of products. On the other hand, it makes no sense to raise your price if the result is a big cut in sales. Pricing, therefore, has a dual influence on total sales revenue. It is important *directly* as part of the gross revenue equation and *indirectly* through its impact on demand.

16-1a Pricing Starting with Costs

For a business to be successful, its pricing must cover the costs of providing products or services plus a profit margin that sustains the company and moves it forward. You cannot stay in business for long if your prices are below your costs.

Costs react differently as the quantity produced or sold increases or decreases. Recall from Chapter 10 that the *cost of goods sold* increases as the quantity of products sold increases. Material costs and sales commissions are typical variable costs incurred as a product is made and sold. For instance, material costs may be $10 per unit. If the company sells 1,000 units, the total costs of goods sold would be $10,000, but that figure would change if the number of units increases or decreases. *Operating expenses* are those that remain constant at different levels of quantity sold, or fixed costs. For example, marketing expenses, factory equipment costs, and salaries of office personnel are operating expenses. Service organizations will handle operating expenses in ways similar to product companies. Their *cost of sales* is often harder to define than the cost of goods sold. One metric that is often used is to calculate a figure for the time spent providing a service to the customer. Some owners combine hourly personnel costs with a percentage of the operating expenses.[2]

An understanding of the nature of different kinds of costs can help a seller minimize pricing mistakes. Although cost of goods sold and cost of sales and operating expenses do not behave in the same way, small businesses often treat them identically. An approach called **average pricing** exemplifies this practice. With average pricing, the total cost (cost of goods sold plus operating expenses) over a previous period is divided by the quantity sold in that period to arrive at an average cost, which is then used to set the current price. For example, consider the cost structure of a firm selling 25,000 units of a product in 2015 at a sales price of $8 each (see Exhibit 16.1). The

average pricing
An approach in which the total cost for a given period is divided by the quantity sold in that period to set a price.

EXHIBIT **16.1** Cost Structure of a Hypothetical Firm, 2015

Sales revenue (25,000 units @ $8)	$200,000
Cost of goods sold ($2 per unit)	(50,000)
Gross profits	$150,000
Operating expenses	(75,000)
Net profits (before interest and taxes)	$ 75,000

$$\text{Average cost} = \frac{(50,000 + 75,000)}{25,000} = \$5$$

average unit cost would be $5 (that is, $125,000 ($50,000 + $75,000) in total costs ÷ 25,000 units sold). The $3 markup provides a profit at this sales volume (25,000 units sold × $3 markup = $75,000).

However, Exhibit 16.2 shows that the impact on profit will be very negative if sales in 2016 reach only 10,000 units and the selling price has been set at the same $3 markup, based on the average cost in 2015. At the lower sales volume (10,000 units sold), the average unit cost increases to $9.50 (that is, $95,000 ÷ 10,000). This increase is, of course, attributable to the need to spread operating expenses over fewer units. *Average pricing overlooks the reality of higher average costs at lower sales levels.* Be cautious about taking this approach.

On rare occasions, pricing at less than total cost can be used as a special short-term strategy. Operating expenses tend to be ongoing, regardless of how much production or provision of services is occurring. When sales revenues are down, pricing should cover all marginal or incremental costs—that is, those costs incurred specifically to get additional business. Keep in mind the old business saying, "If you price below cost, you can't make it up in volume!" For example, you might bid on a contract that appears to offer a high price only to discover that you have to add personnel, equipment, or materials whose costs are more than that attractive price. Sometimes, business owners offer *loss leaders*, merchandise they intentionally sell below the direct product cost with the expectation that customers will buy more as they learn of other products and services the business has available. It can be unpleasant to discover that the loss leader was the only thing customers bought—no profit there. In the long run, all costs must be covered.

EXHIBIT **16.2** Cost Structure of a Hypothetical Firm, 2016

Sales revenue (10,000 units @ $8)	$ 80,000
Cost of goods sold ($2 per unit)	(20,000)
Gross profits	$ 60,000
Operating expenses	(75,000)
Net profits (before interest and taxes)	$(15,000)

$$\text{Average cost} = \frac{(20,000 + 75,000)}{10,000} = \$9.50$$

Some businesses may use a **freemium** (a combination of the words "free" and "premium") **strategy**, with the idea that customers will accept basic features at no cost and then seek advanced products or services at a subscription price. As with loss leaders, it is critical that enough customers upgrade—in this case, to offset what the company gives away.[3]

16-1b Pricing Starting with Customers

Cost analysis can identify a level below which a price should not be set under normal circumstances. However, it does not show by how much the final price might exceed that minimum figure and still be acceptable to customers. Demand factors must be considered before making this determination.

ELASTICITY OF DEMAND

Customer demand for a product or service is often sensitive to the price level. *Elasticity* is the term used to describe this sensitivity, and the effect of a change in price on the quantity demanded is called **elasticity of demand**. A product or service is said to have **elastic demand** if an increase in its price *lowers* demand for the product or service or a decrease in its price *raises* demand. A product or service is said to have **inelastic demand** if demand does not change significantly when there is a change in the price of the product or service.

In some markets, the demand for products or services is very elastic. With a lower price, the amount purchased increases sharply, thus providing higher revenue. For example, with many electronic products, a decrease in price will frequently produce a more than proportionate increase in quantity sold, resulting in higher total revenues. For products such as milk, however, demand is highly inelastic. Regardless of price, the quantity purchased will not change significantly, because consumers use a fixed amount of milk.

The concept of elasticity of demand is important because the degree of elasticity sets limits on or provides opportunities for higher pricing. A small firm should seek to distinguish its product or service in such a way that small price increases will incur little resistance from customers and thereby yield increasing total revenue. Keep in mind the word we introduced at the beginning of this chapter, *value*. Customers are ready to pay higher prices when they perceive a product or service offering greater value than their other choices. Some business owners experiment beyond small price increases or decreases. One tactic that is gaining more and more attention is *surge*, or dynamic, pricing. Movie theaters that offer low prices during the day and then boost them at night when more people are in attendance provide an example of surge pricing. A company receiving a lot of attention for its surge pricing policy is Uber, a company that connects riders and drivers via their app. Passengers are accustomed to seeing meters in taxis that calculate charges, often regulated by a municipality. Uber, on the other hand, raises the price dramatically during periods of high demand.[4]

freemium strategy
A strategy that offers customers basic features at no cost with the idea that they will upgrade to advanced products or services at subscription prices.

elasticity of demand
The degree to which a change in price affects the quantity demanded.

elastic demand
Demand that changes significantly when there is a change in the price of a product or service.

inelastic demand
Demand that does not change significantly when there is a change in the price of a product or service.

PRICING AND A FIRM'S COMPETITIVE ADVANTAGE

Several factors affect the attractiveness of a product or service to customers. One factor is the firm's competitive advantage—a concept discussed in Chapter 3. If consumers perceive the product or service as an important solution to their unsatisfied needs, they are likely to demand more of it.

Companies want prospective buyers to see their products as special. But even if two products are physically similar, other factors typically differ. Speed of service, credit terms offered, delivery arrangements, personal attention from a salesperson, and warranties are but a few of the factors that can be used to distinguish one product from another. A unique and attractive combination of products and services may well justify a higher price.

A pricing tactic that often reflects a competitive advantage is **prestige pricing**, or setting a high price to convey an image of high quality or uniqueness. Liz Lange kept hearing from pregnant friends that they could not find attractive clothes. Everything they saw in stores was unfashionable or made them look like they were wearing a tent. With work experience at *Vogue* magazine and in a clothing design firm, Lange decided to go out on her own and started Liz Lange Maternity. She discovered a big market that was ready for designer maternity clothes. The high end of this market proved so profitable that Lange was able to launch a less-expensive line for Target.[5]

A strong brand image is typically associated with prestige pricing, and some business owners think that a clever name is sufficient to establish the brand in people's minds. Do not underestimate the time and expense that are necessary to create a positive brand image. The influence of prestige pricing varies from market to market, from product to product, and from service to service. Liz Lange recognized that higher-income buyers are usually less sensitive to price variations than those with lower incomes and that prestige pricing typically would work better in high-income markets.

16-2 APPLYING A PRICING SYSTEM

Apply break-even analysis and markup pricing.

In order to properly evaluate a pricing system, a small business owner must understand potential costs, revenue, and product demand for the venture. A key to that understanding is the ability to determine when enough products and services have been sold to cover the operating expenses of running your business—or, more simply, the ability to recognize the break-even point.

16-2a Break-Even Analysis

Break-even analysis has two phases: (1) examining cost-revenue relationships and (2) incorporating sales forecasts into the analysis. It allows the entrepreneur to compare alternative cost and revenue estimates in order to determine the acceptability of each price. Break-even analyses are usually represented by formulas and graphs, which help owners visualize how their businesses are functioning.

EXAMINING COST AND REVENUE RELATIONSHIPS

The objective of the first phase of break-even analysis is to determine the sales volume level at which the product, at an assumed price, will generate enough revenue to start earning a profit. Exhibit 16.3(a) presents a simple break-even chart reflecting this comparison. *Fixed costs*, or operating expenses, as represented by a horizontal line in the bottom half of the graph, are $300,000. The section for the *variable costs* of making and selling the products, or cost of goods sold, is a triangle that slants upward, depicting the direct relationship of variable costs and expenses to output. In this example, variable costs are $5 per unit. The entire area below the upward-slanting total cost line represents the combination of fixed and variable costs and expenses. The distance between the sales and total cost lines reveals the profit or loss position of the company at any level of sales. The point of intersection of these two lines is called the **break-even point**, because total sales revenue equals total costs and expenses at this sales volume. As shown in Exhibit 16.3(a), the break-even point is approximately 43,000 units sold, which means that the break-even point in dollar revenue is roughly $514,000.

prestige pricing
An approach based on setting a high price to convey an image of high quality or uniqueness.

break-even analysis
The examination of cost-revenue relationships and the incorporation of sales forecasts into the analysis.

break-even point
Sales volume at which total sales revenue equals total costs and expenses.

Living the Dream

ENTREPRENEURIAL EXPERIENCES

Have You Had Your Brick for the Day?

That's the way Michael Houlihan expressed it to his staff, "Every day, bam, smacked in the head by a brick. You think you've got something figured out, then, bam, there's a new brick." Houlihan turned the problem into a rallying cry: "Have you had your brick for the day?" The message he was sending to his staff was "Keep your eyes open; there's always a surprise coming."

When you take a course in small business management or entrepreneurship, you are told to get knowledge and experience about the business you want to own. Know your product, your industry, your customer. Michael Houlihan did none of that. Houlihan and his partner, Bonnie Harvey, found themselves somewhat accidental owners of a winery. Houlihan had done some consulting with wine companies, helping them with contracts, finding financing, and negotiating with government agencies. Harvey had owned an office management company, and one of her clients supplied grapes to wineries. A customer of the grape producer was going into bankruptcy and could not pay the producer's bill. Houlihan and Harvey offered to take over the facility and produce the wine to offset the debt. Without intending to create a permanent business, in 1986, they found themselves the owners of what is today Barefoot Cellars.

As Houlihan and Harvey later described their entrepreneurial venture, they never wasted a good mistake. And they made plenty as they learned about state and federal regulations, manufacturing processes, dealing with distributors, promotional strategies, and more. Cost control and product pricing proved to be challenging.

The first lesson the owners learned was about what customers were willing to pay. Their brand was unknown, and they were not going after the high-end market. The target customer was a housewife shopping for a $5.00 bottle of wine to take home to serve at dinner. That meant Houlihan and Harvey had to work backward to make sure that they could produce a bottle for less than the retail price. And they discovered that controlling costs was more than just turning grapes into wine and putting it in bottles.

© JOHN HOLLAND/ZUMA PRESS/CORBIS WIRE/CORBIS

States have their own regulations for wine sales, and some retail outlets will buy directly from producers while others choose to work only with distributors. Houlihan and Harvey discovered the industry practice of legally paying extra commissions, called *spiffs*, to distributor representatives to get special attention. And they learned about something they labeled the Velocity Price Point. This was the discovery that their products could sell vastly more at certain price points than others. Initially, selling a bottle at $4.99 generated far more sales than their experiments at $5.99 or $6.99. They also found it necessary to give away bottles to gain access to some stores, and that giving away bottles at charity events helped them build brand image. But the sales revenues had to cover the costs of the giveaways.

The team built a successful business over time, leading the company to become attractive to others in the industry. In 2005, Barefoot was acquired by E. & J. Gallo Winery. Houlihan and Harvey continue to represent Barefoot Cellars, publishing a book about their experiences and going on the talk circuit to share their insights as entrepreneurs.

Sources: Michael Houlihan and Bonnie Harvey with Rick Kushman, *The Barefoot Spirit: How Hardship, Hustle, and Heart Built America's #1 Wine Brand* (Ashland, OH: Evolve Publishing, 2013); "About the Barefoot Wine Founders," http://thebarefootspirit.com/about, accessed March 5, 2015; "Barefoot Cellars: About Us," http://barefootwine.com/our-story/about-us#, accessed March 5, 2015; and Robert Reis, "The Incredible Story of Starting the World's Largest Wine Brand," http://www.forbes.com/sites/robertreiss/2014/12/09/the-incredible-story-of-starting-the-worlds-largest-wine-brand-barefoot-wines, accessed March 5, 2015.

EXHIBIT 16.3 Break-Even Graphs for Pricing

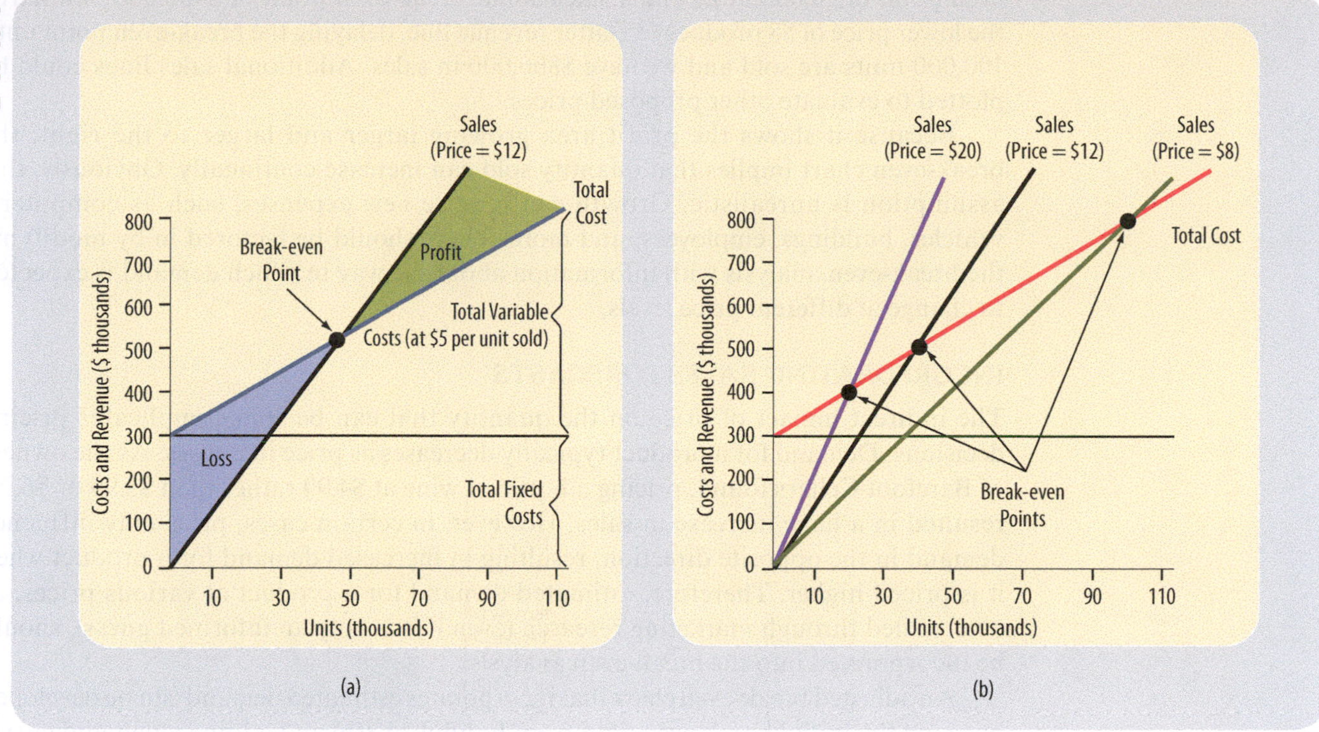

Exhibit 16.3(a) shows how you can visualize the break-even concept. Another way to think of it is as a simple math equation:

$$\text{Break-even point} = \frac{\text{Total fixed operating costs and expenses}}{\text{Unit selling price} - \text{Unit variable costs and expenses}}$$

$$\text{Break-even point} = \frac{\$300{,}000}{\$12 - \$5} = 42{,}857 \text{ units}$$

We can now see that the exact break-even point in units sold is 42,857. And given the $12 sales price, the dollar break-even point is $514,284 ($12 sales price per unit × 42,857 break-even units sold).

This example shows that the break-even point is a function of (1) the firm's total fixed operating costs and expenses (numerator) and (2) the unit selling price less the unit variable costs and expenses (denominator). The higher the total *fixed* costs, the more units we must sell to break even; the greater the difference between the unit selling price and the unit *variable* costs and expenses, the fewer units we must sell to break even. The difference between the unit selling price and the unit variable costs and expenses is the **contribution margin**; that is, for each unit sold, a contribution is made toward covering the company's fixed costs.

contribution margin The difference between the unit selling price and the unit variable costs and expenses.

To evaluate other break-even points, the entrepreneur can plot additional sales lines for other prices on the chart. Don't be intimidated about drawing a graph or crunching the numbers to get a break-even point. The key issue is that calculating the break-even point helps you to determine whether you have a chance to make a profit by selling your products at certain prices. Every business owner must determine a way to represent these critical numbers so that she or he can understand them and run the business successfully. On the flexible break-even chart shown in Exhibit 16.3(b), the higher price of $20 yields a much more steeply sloped sales line, resulting in a break-even point of 20,000 units and a sales dollar break-even point of $400,000. Similarly, the lower price of $8 produces a flatter revenue line, delaying the break-even point until 100,000 units are sold and we have $800,000 in sales. Additional sales lines could be plotted to evaluate other proposed prices.

Because it shows the profit area growing larger and larger to the right, the break-even chart implies that quantity sold can increase continually. Obviously, this assumption is unrealistic. Growth can require new expenses, such as computers, vehicles, buildings, employees, and more. These should be factored in by modifying the break-even analysis with information about the way in which demand is expected to change at different price levels.

INCORPORATING SALES FORECASTS

The indirect impact of price on the quantity that can be sold complicates pricing decisions. Demand for a product typically decreases as price increases. As the owners of Barefoot Cellars found, pricing a bottle of wine at $4.99 rather than $5.99 or $6.99, resulted in a huge increase in sales. However, in certain cases, price may influence demand in the opposite direction, resulting in increased demand for a product when it is priced higher. Therefore, estimated demand for a product at various prices, as determined through marketing research (even if it is only an informed guess), should be incorporated into the break-even analysis.

An adjusted break-even chart that incorporates estimated demand can be developed by using the initial break-even data from Exhibit 16.3(b) and adding a demand curve, as done in Exhibit 16.4. This graph allows a more realistic profit area to be identified.

We see that the break-even point in Exhibit 16.4 for a unit price of $20 corresponds to a quantity sold that appears impossible to reach at the assumed price (the break-even point does not fall within the demand curve). No customers are willing to pay $20 for

EXHIBIT 16.4 A Break-Even Graph Adjusted for Estimated Demand

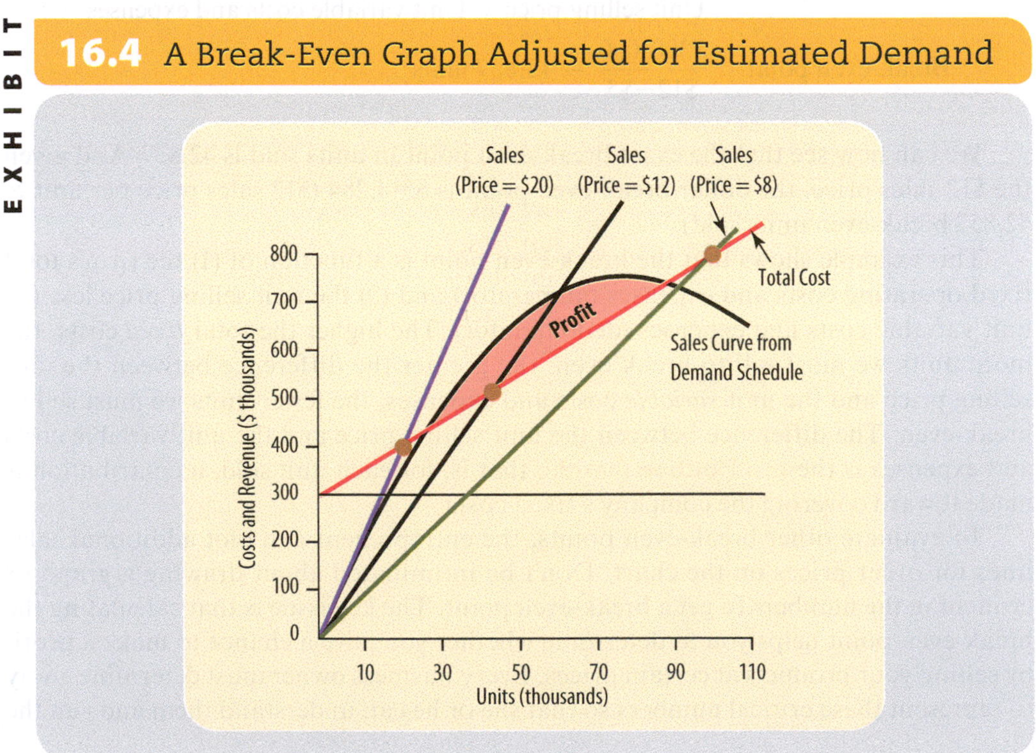

any quantity—the demand curve line is always below the $20 sales line. So, at the low price of $8, we would never break even—the more we sell, the greater the loss would be. Only at $12 does the revenue from the demand curve rise above the total cost line. The potential for profit at this price is indicated by the shaded area in the graph.

16-2b Markup Pricing

In the retailing industry, where businesses often carry many different products, **markup pricing** has emerged as a manageable pricing system. This cost-plus approach to pricing is used both in brick-and-mortar stores and by online product vendors. Retailers are able to price hundreds of products much more quickly than they could by using individual break-even analyses. Manufacturers will often recommend a retail price for their products that retailers and wholesalers can use as guidelines. In calculating the selling price for a particular item, a retailer adds a markup percentage (sometimes referred to as a *markup rate*) to cover (1) operating expenses, (2) subsequent price reductions—for example, markdowns and employee discounts, and (3) the desired profit. It is important to have a clear understanding of markup pricing computations. Markups may be expressed as a percentage of either the *selling price* or the *cost*. For example, if an item costs $6 and sells for $10, the markup of $4 represents a 40 percent markup of the selling price [($4 markup ÷ $10 selling price) × 100] or a 66⅔ percent markup of the cost [($4 markup ÷ $6 cost) × 100]. Two simple formulas are commonly used for markup calculations:

$$\frac{\text{Markup}}{\text{Selling price}} \times 100 = \text{Markup expressed as a percentage of selling price}$$

or

$$\frac{\text{Markup}}{\text{Cost}} \times 100 = \text{Markup expressed as a percentage of cost}$$

16-3 SELECTING A PRICING STRATEGY

Identify specific pricing strategies.

Break-even analysis and similar techniques give owners an idea of how much they need to sell to cover their costs. But their seemingly precise nature can be very misleading. Such analyses should not by themselves determine the final price. Price determination must also consider characteristics of targeted customers and the firm's total marketing strategy. Pricing strategies that reflect these additional considerations include prestige or premium pricing (which we discussed earlier), penetration pricing, price skimming, follow-the-leader pricing, variable pricing, price lining, and optional product and service pricing.[6]

markup pricing
An approach based on applying a percentage to a product's cost to obtain its selling price.

16-3a Penetration Pricing

A firm that uses a **penetration pricing strategy** prices a product or service at less than its normal, long-range market price in order to gain more rapid market acceptance or to increase existing market share. This strategy can sometimes discourage new competitors from entering a market niche if they mistakenly view the penetration price as a long-range price. Obviously, a firm that uses this strategy sacrifices some profit margin to achieve market penetration.

penetration pricing strategy
A technique that sets lower than normal prices to hasten market acceptance of a product or service or to increase market share.

16-3b Price Skimming

A **price skimming strategy** sets prices for products or services at high levels for a limited time period before reducing them to more competitive levels. This strategy assumes that certain customers will pay a higher price because they view a product or service as a prestige item. Use of a skimming price is most practical when there is little threat of short-term competition or when startup costs must be recovered rapidly. Another reason for using this strategy is the high cost of introducing a new product. The company may not have achieved economies of scale in production, so higher prices might be charged to customers who could be labeled *early adopters*. Some buyers like to be the first to own or use new products or services, so they are willing to pay a premium price. To reach a larger market, however, the price usually needs to be reduced.

16-3c Follow-the-Leader Pricing

© 237/MARTIN BARRAUD/OCEAN/CORBIS

A **follow-the-leader pricing strategy** uses a particular competitor as a model in setting a price for a product or service. The probable reaction of competitors is a critical factor in determining whether to cut prices below a prevailing level. A small business in competition with larger firms is seldom in a position to consider itself the price leader. Different brands may have different characteristics, but customers often do not perceive sufficient differences to pay premium prices. Thus, small businesses selling commodities (products purchased primarily based on price) tend to be better off holding down costs so that they can price their merchandise in the same range as their larger competitors.

16-3d Variable Pricing

Some businesses use a **variable pricing strategy** to offer price concessions to certain customers, even though they may advertise a uniform price. Lower prices are offered for various reasons, including a customer's knowledge and bargaining strength. In some fields of business, therefore, firms make two-part pricing decisions: They set a standard list price but offer a range of price concessions to particular buyers—for example, those that purchase large quantities of their product.

16-3e Price Lining

A **price lining strategy** establishes distinct price categories at which similar items of retail merchandise are offered for sale. For example, men's suits (of differing quality) might be sold at $250, $450, and $800. The amount of inventory stocked at different quality levels would depend on the income levels and buying desires of a store's customers. A price lining strategy has the advantage of simplifying the selection process for the customer and reducing the necessary minimum inventory.

16-3f Optional Product and Service Pricing

Companies seek to increase the amount customers spend by offering optional products or services that increase the total price paid by the customer. An office management company may rent office space by the square foot but provide receptionist services, access to printers and copiers, delivery services, and more at additional costs.

price skimming strategy
A technique that sets very high prices for a limited period before reducing them to more competitive levels.

follow-the-leader pricing strategy
A technique that uses a particular competitor as a model in setting prices.

variable pricing strategy
A technique that sets more than one price for a product or service in order to offer price concessions to certain customers.

price lining strategy
A technique that sets a range of several distinct merchandise price levels.

Local, state, and federal laws must be considered in setting prices. For example, the Sherman Antitrust Act generally prohibits price fixing. Direct competitors cannot agree on the prices they will charge customers. Fixing prices can lead to prison sentences and fines or civil court lawsuits, resulting in significant legal expenses and possibly damage payments.[7] On the other hand, a Supreme Court decision gave manufacturers the authority to impose minimum prices at which retailers must sell their products. Large discount retailers objected, claiming that such policies are anticompetitive. But the Court concluded that smaller businesses might give better service to customers through the information they provide about products, only to see those customers then buy from a discounter that provides less service. Resale price maintenance is assumed to encourage stores to offer a better shopping experience.[8]

When a small business markets a line of products, some of which may compete with each other, pricing decisions must take into account the effects of a single product price on the rest of the line. This often results in **product line pricing**, placing different prices on a range of products or services to reflect the benefits to the customer of parts of the range.[9] The next time you are shopping for shoes, check out the prices charged for various styles offered under the same brand. Why are different prices charged? Is it quality of materials or something else? Are they offering special prices if you buy two or more pairs?

Continually adjusting a price to meet changing marketing conditions can be both costly to the seller and confusing to buyers. Thanks to the Internet, companies can monitor product sales in real time and determine immediately if dropping a price might lead to more sales or if raising it might make sense for a product in high demand. Discounting can also be designed to meet a variety of needs. For example, a seller may offer a trade discount to a buyer (such as a wholesaler) that performs a certain marketing function for the seller (such as distribution). The stated, or list, price is unchanged, but the seller offers a lower actual price by means of a discount.

Small firms should not treat bad pricing decisions as uncorrectable mistakes. Remember, pricing is not an exact science. *If the initial price appears to be off target, make any necessary adjustments and keep on selling!*

16-4 OFFERING CREDIT

Explain the benefits of credit, factors that affect credit extension, and types of credit.

In a credit sale, the seller provides products or services to the buyer in return for the buyer's promise to pay later. The major reason for granting credit is to make sales; credit encourages decisions to buy by providing an incentive for customers who can buy now but would prefer to pay later. But businesses want to make sure their customers will fully pay for what they are buying. An added bonus to the seller is that credit provides records containing customer information that can be used for sales promotions, such as direct-mail appeals to customers.

16-4a Benefits of Credit

If credit buying and selling did not benefit both parties in a transaction, their use would cease. Buyers obviously enjoy the availability of credit, and small firms, in particular, benefit from being able to buy on credit from their suppliers. Credit provides small firms with working capital, often allowing marginal businesses to continue operations. A delay in paying a bill is the equivalent of obtaining an interest-free loan until the time the bill is due. Additional benefits of credit to buyers are (1) the ability to satisfy immediate needs and pay for them later, (2) better records of purchases on credit billing

product line pricing
A technique that places different prices on a range of products or services to reflect the benefits to the customer of parts of the range.

statements, (3) better service and greater convenience when exchanging purchased items, and (4) the ability to establish a credit history. Suppliers, on the other hand, extend credit to customers in order to facilitate increased sales volume and also to earn money on unpaid balances. They expect the increased revenue to more than offset the costs of extending credit, so that profits will increase. Other benefits of credit to sellers are (1) a closer association with customers because of implied trust, (2) easier selling through telephone- and mail-order systems and over the Internet, (3) smoother sales peaks and valleys, since purchasing power is always available, and (4) easy access to a tool with which to stay competitive.

16-4b Factors That Affect Selling on Credit

A business owner must decide whether to sell on credit or for cash only. In many cases, credit selling cannot be avoided, as it is standard trade practice in many types of businesses. It is important to note that in today's marketplace, credit-selling competitors will almost always outsell a cash-only firm.

Although a seller always hopes to increase profits by allowing credit sales, it is not a risk-free practice. Small firms frequently shift or at least share credit risk by accepting credit cards carried by customers rather than by offering their own credit. For example, the franchisee of a DoubleTree Hotel, part of the Hilton chain, may accept Hilton credit cards and other major credit cards, thereby avoiding the hassles of credit management. The business will pay a fee to the credit card company, but that cost may be less than the expense of managing its own independent credit system, especially when losses from bad debts are factored in. A retailer following this strategy must obtain merchant status with individual credit card companies. This is not an automatic process and can be problematic, particularly for home-based businesses.

© OLEGDOROSHIN/SHUTTERSTOCK.COM

Unfortunately, the cost of accepting major credit cards for payment over the Internet has increased. To deal with Internet fraud, small online retailers have turned to third-party firms (like PayPal, Charge.com, and TransFirst) that specialize in handling Internet credit card payments. For example, PayPal offers a variety of plans with transaction fees of 2.9 percent plus 30 cents or less, depending on monthly sales volume.[10] Also, if a small firm makes credit sales online, it is subject to "chargebacks" whenever buyers dispute a transaction. Some credit card companies assess fines and threaten account termination if the number of chargebacks is excessive.

For a variety of reasons, a small business may or may not decide to sell on credit. There are five factors related to the entrepreneur's decision to extend credit: the type of business, credit policies of competitors, customers' ages and income levels, the availability of working capital, and economic conditions.

1. *Type of business.* Retailers of durable products typically grant more credit than do retailers that sell perishables or small service firms with primarily local customers. Most consumers find it necessary to buy big-ticket items on an installment basis, and the life span of such a product makes installment selling feasible.

2. *Credit policies of competitors.* Most firms in an industry offer comparable credit terms unless they have a competitive advantage that causes customers to be willing to pay cash. Wholesale hardware companies and retail furniture stores are examples of businesses that face stiff competition from credit sellers.
3. *Ages and income levels of customers.* Customers' ages and income levels are significant factors in determining credit policy. For example, a drugstore adjacent to a high school might not extend credit to high school students, who are typically undesirable credit customers because of their lack of both maturity and steady income.
4. *Availability of working capital.* Credit sales increase the amount of working capital needed by the business doing the selling. Open-credit and installment accounts tie up money that may be needed to pay business expenses.
5. *Economic conditions.* Business cycles are real. Owners sometimes have short memories when times are good, and they receive and extend credit without concern for an economic downturn. The recession of 2008 caused the bankruptcy of many that were overextended. But free enterprise systems are also characterized by recoveries and prosperity. Good credit management is critical to long-term success.

16-4c Types of Credit

There are two broad classes of credit: consumer credit and trade credit. **Consumer credit** is granted by retailers to final consumers who purchase for personal or family use. A small business owner sometimes uses his or her personal consumer credit to purchase supplies and equipment for the business. **Trade credit** is extended by nonfinancial firms, such as manufacturers and wholesalers, to business firms that are customers. Consumer credit and trade credit differ with respect to types of credit instruments, the paperwork, sources for financing receivables, and terms of sale.

consumer credit
Financing granted by retailers to individuals who purchase for personal or family use.

trade credit
Financing provided by suppliers to client companies.

CONSUMER CREDIT

The three major kinds of consumer credit accounts are open charge accounts, installment accounts, and revolving charge accounts. Many variations of these credit accounts are also used. Credit cards (a type of revolving charge account) are discussed separately because of their widespread use.

Open charge accounts When using an **open charge account**, a customer takes possession of products (or services) at the time of purchase, with payment due when billed. Customers typically have a month to pay their bills from the time their statements are sent. There is no finance charge for this kind of credit if the balance on the account is paid in full at the end of the billing period. Customers are not generally required to make a down payment or to pledge collateral. Small accounts at department stores are good examples of open charge accounts.

open charge account
A line of credit that allows the customer to obtain a product or service at the time of purchase, with payment due when billed.

Installment accounts An **installment account** is a vehicle for long-term consumer credit, useful for large purchases, such as a car, home appliance, or home renovation. A down payment is normally required, and annual finance charges can be a significant percentage of the purchase price. Payment periods are commonly from 12 to 36 months, although automobile dealers often offer an extended payment period of 60 months or even longer.

installment account
A line of credit that requires a down payment, with the balance paid over a specified period of time.

Revolving charge accounts A **revolving charge account** is a variation of the installment account. A seller grants a customer a line of credit, and charged purchases may not

revolving charge account
A line of credit on which the customer may charge purchases at any time, up to a pre-established limit.

exceed the credit limit. A specified percentage of the outstanding balance must be paid monthly, forcing the customer to budget and limiting the amount of debt that can be carried. Finance charges are computed on the unpaid balance at the end of the month.

CREDIT CARDS

A **credit card** provides assurance to a seller that a buyer has a satisfactory credit rating and that the seller will receive payment from the financial institution that issued the card. Credit cards are usually based on a revolving charge account system. Depending on the issuer, we can distinguish three basic types of credit cards: bank credit cards, travel and entertainment credit cards, and retailer credit cards.

Bank credit cards The best-known credit cards issued by banks or other financial institutions are MasterCard and Visa. Bank credit cards are widely accepted by retailers that want to offer credit but don't provide their own credit cards. Most small business retailers fit into this category. In return for a set fee (usually 25 percent of the purchase price) paid by the retailer, the bank takes the responsibility for making collections. Some banks charge annual membership fees to their cardholders. Also, cardholders are frequently able to obtain cash up to the credit limit of their card.

Retailer credit cards Many companies—for example, department stores and oil companies—issue their own credit cards specifically for use in their outlets or for purchasing their products or services from other outlets. Customers are usually not charged annual fees or finance charges if the balance is paid each month.

TRADE CREDIT

Firms selling to other businesses may specify terms of sale, such as 2/10, net 30. This means that the seller is offering a 2 percent discount if the buyer pays within 10 days of the invoice date. Failure to take this discount makes the full amount of the invoice due in 30 days. For example, with these terms, a buyer paying for a $100,000 purchase within 10 days of the invoice date would save 2 percent, or $2,000.

Sales terms for trade credit depend on the product sold, as well as the buyer's and the seller's circumstances. The credit period often varies directly with the length of the buyer's inventory turnover period, which obviously depends on the type of product sold. The larger the order and the higher the credit rating of the buyer, the better the sales terms will be, assuming that individual terms are fixed for each buyer. The greater the financial strength and the more adequate and liquid the working capital of the seller, the more generous the seller's sales terms can be. Of course, no business can afford to allow competitors to outdo it in reasonable generosity of sales terms. In many types of businesses, terms are so firmly set by tradition that a unique policy is difficult, if not impossible, for a small firm to implement.

credit card
An alternative to cash whose use provides assurance to a seller that a buyer has a satisfactory credit rating and that payment will be received from the issuing financial institution.

16-5 MANAGING THE CREDIT PROCESS

Describe the activities involved in managing credit.

A small clothing store or online craft shop that accepts Visa or MasterCard is transferring much of the credit risk to another party. In effect, the fee that the business pays the credit card company covers the credit management process. Banks and their business customers are often in conflict over the fees charged. In 2013, American Express settled two lawsuits with retailers who were adding a surcharge to customers' bills for credit card use.[11] Many small business owners find that the fees cut their profits significantly. Those small firms that want to offer their own credit to customers need to understand the credit function. Let's take a look at some of the major considerations in developing and operating a comprehensive credit management program for a small business.

16-5a Evaluation of Credit Applicants

In most retail stores, the first step in credit investigation is having the customer complete an application form. The information obtained on this form is used as the basis for examining an applicant's creditworthiness. Since the most important factor in determining a customer's credit limit is her or his ability to pay the obligation when it becomes due, it is crucial to evaluate the customer's financial resources, debt position, and income or revenue level. The mobile content company, Amp'd Mobile, received $360 million from investors, then tried to save money by not running credit checks on customers. When it declared bankruptcy, 80,000 of its 175,000 customers were unable to pay their bills.[12]

The amount of credit requested also requires careful consideration. Drugstore customers usually need only small amounts of credit. On the other hand, business customers of wholesalers and manufacturers typically expect large credit lines. In the special case of installment selling, the amount of credit should not exceed the repossession value of the goods sold. Automobile dealers follow this rule as a general practice.

THE FOUR CREDIT QUESTIONS

In evaluating the credit status of applicants, a seller must answer the following questions:

1. Can the buyer pay as promised?
2. Will the buyer pay?
3. If so, when will the buyer pay?
4. If not, can the buyer be forced to pay?

The answers to these questions have to be based in part on the seller's estimate of the buyer's ability and willingness to pay. Such an estimate constitutes a judgment of the buyer's creditworthiness. For credit to be approved, the answers to questions 1, 2, and 4 should be "yes," and the answer to question 3 should be "on schedule."

Every applicant is creditworthy to some degree. A decision to grant credit merely recognizes the buyer's credit standing. But the seller must consider the possibility that the buyer will be unable or unwilling to pay. When evaluating an applicant's credit status, therefore, the seller must decide how much risk of nonpayment to assume.

THE TRADITIONAL FIVE C'S OF CREDIT

As explained in Chapter 12, the ability to repay a loan is frequently evaluated in terms of the five C's of credit: character, capacity, capital, collateral, and conditions. These factors are also indicators of a firm's ability to repay trade credit and deserve repeating:

- *Character* is the fundamental integrity and honesty that should underlie all human and business relationships. For business customers, character is embodied in the business policies and ethical practices of the firm, generally measured by their credit history.
- *Capacity* refers to the customer's ability to conserve assets, and to faithfully and efficiently follow a financial plan. A business customer should have sufficient cash flow to pay bills.

- *Capital* can be defined as net worth but really consists of the cash and other liquid assets owned by the customer. A prospective business customer should have sufficient capital to underwrite planned operations, including an appropriate amount invested by the owner.
- *Collateral* represents enough assets to secure the debt. It is a secondary source for loan repayment in case the borrower's cash flows are insufficient for repaying a loan.
- *Conditions* refer to both the overall economy and the borrower. Economic factors include business cycles and changes in price levels, which may be either favorable or unfavorable to the payment of debts. Adverse factors that might limit a business customer's ability to pay include strong new competition, labor problems, and fires and other natural disasters.

16-5b Sources of Credit Information

One of the most important, and most frequently neglected, sources of credit information is a customer's previous credit history. Properly analyzed, credit records show whether a business customer regularly takes cash discounts and, if not, whether the customer's account is typically slow.

Manufacturers and wholesalers can frequently use a firm's financial statements as an additional source of information. Obtaining maximum value from financial statements requires a careful ratio analysis, which will reveal a firm's working capital position, profit-making potential, and general financial health (as discussed in Chapter 10).

trade-credit agencies Privately owned organizations that collect credit information on businesses.

credit bureaus Privately owned organizations that summarize a number of firms' credit experiences with particular individuals.

Although you should collect financial data and credit histories directly from customers who apply for credit, pertinent data should also be obtained from outsiders. For example, arrangements may be made with other sellers to exchange credit data. Such credit information exchanges are quite useful for learning about the sales and payment experiences others have had with the seller's own customers or credit applicants.

Another source of credit information for the small firm, particularly about commercial accounts, is the customer's banker. Some bankers willingly supply credit information about their depositors, considering this to be a service that helps those firms or individuals obtain credit in amounts they can successfully handle. Other bankers believe that credit information is confidential and should not be disclosed.

Organizations that may be consulted regarding credit standings are trade-credit agencies and credit bureaus. **Trade-credit agencies** are privately owned organizations that collect credit information on businesses only, not individual consumers. After analyzing and evaluating the data, trade-credit agencies make credit ratings available to client companies for a fee. Dun & Bradstreet, Inc. (www.dnb.com), a nationwide trade-credit agency, offers a wide array of credit reports, such as the Small Business Risk Account Score.[13]

© NETPHOTOS/ALAMY

Credit bureaus are the most common type of consumer reporting agency. These private companies maintain credit histories on individuals, based on reports from banks, mortgage companies, department stores, and other creditors. These companies make possible the exchange of credit information on persons with previous credit activity. Some credit bureaus do not require a business firm to be a member in order to get a credit report. The fee charged to nonmembers, however, is considerably higher than that charged to members. The three primary online credit bureaus are Experian, Equifax, and TransUnion.[14]

16-5c Aging of Accounts Receivable

Many small businesses can benefit from an **aging schedule**, which categorizes accounts receivable based on the length of time they have been outstanding. Typically, some accounts are current and others are past due. Regular use of an aging schedule allows troublesome collection trends to be spotted so that appropriate actions can be taken.

Exhibit 16.5 presents a hypothetical aging schedule for accounts receivable. According to the schedule, four customers have overdue credit, totaling $200,000. Only customer 005 is current. Customer 003 has the largest amount overdue ($80,000). In fact, the schedule shows that customer 003 is overdue on all charges and has a past record of slow payment (indicated by a credit rating of C). Immediate attention must be given to collecting from this customer. Customer 002 should also be contacted, because, among overdue accounts, this customer has the second largest amount ($110,000) in the "Not due" classification. Customer 005, however, could quickly have the largest amount overdue and should be watched closely.

Customers 001 and 004 require a special kind of analysis. Customer 001 has $10,000 more overdue than customer 004. However, customer 004's overdue credit of $40,000, which is 60 days past due, may well have a serious impact on the $100,000 not yet due ($10,000 in the beyond-discount period plus $90,000 still in the discount period). On the other hand, even though customer 001 has $50,000 of overdue credit, this customer's payment is overdue by only 15 days. Also, customer 001 has only $50,000 not yet due ($30,000 in the beyond-discount period plus $20,000 still in the discount period), compared to the $100,000 not yet due from customer 004. Both customers have an A credit rating. In conclusion, customer 001 is a better potential source of cash. Therefore, collection efforts should be focused on customer 004 rather than on customer 001, who may simply need a reminder of the overdue amount of $50,000.

16-5d Billing and Collection Procedures

Timely notification of customers regarding the status of their accounts is essential for keeping credit accounts current. Most credit customers pay their bills on time if the

aging schedule
A categorization of accounts receivable based on the length of time they have been outstanding.

EXHIBIT **16.5** Hypothetical Aging Schedule for Accounts Receivable

	Customer Account Number					
Account Status (Days past due)	**001**	**002**	**003**	**004**	**005**	**Total**
120 days	—	—	$50,000	—	—	$ 50,000
90 days	—	$ 10,000	—	—	—	10,000
60 days	—	—	—	$40,000	—	40,000
30 days	—	20,000	20,000	—	—	40,000
15 days	$50,000	—	10,000	—	—	60,000
Total overdue	$50,000	$ 30,000	$80,000	$40,000	$ 0	$200,000
Not due (beyond discount period)	$30,000	$ 10,000	$ 0	$10,000	$130,000	$180,000
Not due (still in discount period)	$20,000	$100,000	$ 0	$90,000	$220,000	$430,000
Credit rating	A	B	C	A	A	—

Source: http://www.consumer.ftc.gov/articles/0155-free-credit-reports, accessed March 6, 2015.

creditor provides them with information verifying their credit balance. Failure on the seller's part to send invoices delays payments.

Overdue credit accounts tie up a seller's working capital, prevent further sales to the slow-paying customer, and lead to losses from bad debts. Even if a slow-paying customer is not lost, relations with this customer are strained for a time at least.

A firm that is extending credit must have adequate billing records and collection procedures if it expects prompt payments. Also, a personal relationship between seller and customer must not be allowed to tempt the seller into being less than businesslike in extending further credit and collecting overdue amounts. Given the seriousness of the problem, a small firm must decide whether to collect past-due accounts directly or turn the task over to an attorney or a collection agency.

Perhaps the most effective weapon in collecting past-due accounts is reminding the debtors that their credit standing may be in jeopardy. A lower credit rating is certain to happen if the account is turned over to a collection agency. Delinquent customers will typically attempt to avoid damage to their credit standing, particularly when it would be known to the business community. This concern underlies and strengthens the various collection efforts of the seller.

A small firm should deal compassionately with delinquent customers. There are people who will intentionally abuse a relationship and drag out or even refuse to make a payment. However, a collection technique that is too threatening not only may fail to work but also could cause the firm to lose a customer worth keeping or to become subject to legal action.

Effective collection practices usually consist of a series of steps, each somewhat more forceful than the preceding one. Historically, the process has started with a gentle written reminder; subsequent steps may include additional letters, telephone calls, registered letters, personal contacts, and referral to a collection agency or attorney. The timing of these steps should be carefully standardized so that each one automatically follows the preceding one in a specified number of days. More recently, some businesses have started to send text messages and e-mails as reminders, especially when they have a significant percentage of younger customers.

© ISTOCKPHOTO.COM/DNY59

Various ratios can be used to monitor expenses associated with credit sales. The best known and most widely used expense ratio is the **bad-debt ratio**, which is computed by dividing the amount of bad debts by the total amount of credit sales. The bad-debt ratio reflects the efficiency of credit policies and procedures and can help you track how well you are managing the credit you have extended to customers. To compare the effectiveness of your firm's credit management with that of other firms, look for sources that provide industry financial ratios. (These are often available in university libraries.) Two examples are Dun & Bradstreet's *Industry Norms and Key Business Ratios* and the *Almanac of Business & Industrial Financial Ratios*. A relationship exists among the bad-debt ratio, profitability, and the size of the firm. Many times, small profitable retailers have a higher bad-debt ratio than large profitable retailers do.

bad-debt ratio
Bad debts divided by credit sales.

16-5e Credit Regulation

The use of credit is regulated by a variety of federal laws, as well as state laws that vary considerably from state to state. The most significant piece of credit legislation is the federal Consumer Credit Protection Act, which includes the 1968 Truth-in-Lending Act. Its two primary purposes are to ensure that consumers are informed about the terms of a credit agreement and to require creditors to specify how finance charges are computed. The act requires that a finance charge be stated as an annual percentage rate and that creditors specify their procedures for correcting billing mistakes.

Other federal legislation related to credit management includes the following:

- The *Fair Credit Billing Act* provides protection to credit customers in cases involving incorrect billing. A reasonable time period is allowed for billing errors to be corrected. The act does not cover installment credit.
- The *Fair Credit Reporting Act* gives certain rights to credit applicants regarding reports prepared by credit bureaus. Amendments such as the Fair and Accurate Credit Transactions Act (FACTA), signed into law in December 2003, have strengthened privacy provisions and defined more clearly the responsibilities and liabilities of businesses that provide information to credit-reporting agencies.
- The *Equal Credit Opportunity Act* ensures that all consumers are given an equal chance to obtain credit. For example, a person is not required to reveal his or her sex, race, national origin, or religion to obtain credit.
- The *Fair Debt Collection Practices Act* bans the use of intimidation and deception in collection, requiring debt collectors to treat debtors fairly.

It should be apparent by now that pricing and credit decisions are of prime importance to a small firm because of their direct impact on its financial health. However, small business owners can fall into the trap of giving all their attention to costs of products, materials, and operations when setting prices. Be sure that your pricing decisions are driven by a customer focus: What is the customer willing and able to pay, and does that price enable you to make a profit? Providing value for your customers and putting them first is the way to move your business forward.

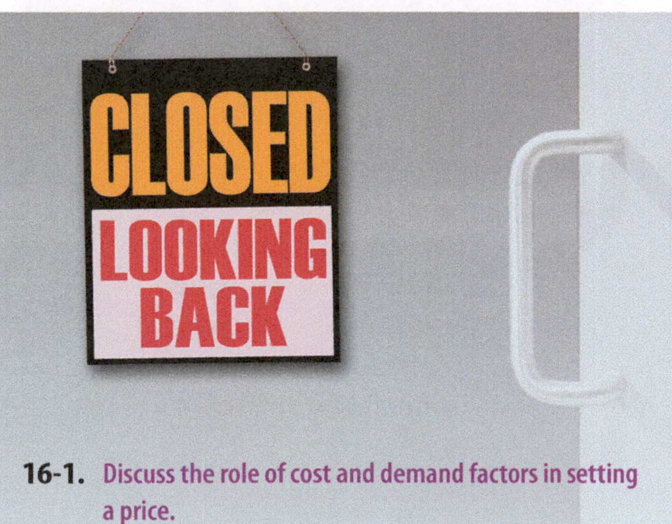

16-1. Discuss the role of cost and demand factors in setting a price.

- The total sales revenue of a firm is a direct reflection of two components: sales volume and price.
- The price must be sufficient to cover total cost plus some margin of profit.
- Pricing at less than total cost can be used as a special short-term strategy to increase demand.
- A firm should examine elasticity of demand—the effect of price on quantity demanded—when setting a price.
- A product's competitive advantage is a demand factor in setting price.

16-2. Apply break-even analysis and markup pricing.

- Break-even analysis has two phases: (1) examining the cost-revenue relationship and (2) incorporating sales forecasts into the analysis.
- Analyzing costs and revenue under different price assumptions identifies the break-even point, the quantity sold at which total costs and expenses equal total sales revenue.

- Markup pricing is a generalized cost-plus system of pricing used by intermediaries with many products.
- Markups may be expressed as a percentage of either the selling price or the cost.

16-3. Identify specific pricing strategies.

- Penetration pricing and price skimming are short-term strategies used when new products are first introduced into the market.
- Follow-the-leader and variable pricing are special strategies that reflect the nature of the competition's pricing and concessions to customers.
- A price lining strategy simplifies choices for customers by offering a range of several distinct prices.
- Local, state, and federal laws must be considered in setting prices, as well as any impact that a price may have on other product line items.

16-4. Explain the benefits of credit, factors that affect credit extension, and types of credit.

- Credit provides small firms with working capital. Its other benefits to borrowers are the ability to immediately satisfy needs and pay for it later, better records of purchases, convenience when exchanging purchased items, and the ability to establish a credit history.
- Benefits of credit to sellers include easier selling and shared risk.
- Type of business, credit policies of competitors, ages and income levels of customers, availability of adequate working capital, and economic conditions affect the decision to extend credit.
- The two broad classes of credit are consumer credit and trade credit.

16-5. Describe the activities involved in managing credit.

- Evaluating the credit status of applicants begins with the completion of an application form.
- A seller must know whether the buyer can pay as promised, whether the buyer will pay, when the buyer will pay, and if the buyer can be forced to pay.
- A customer's ability to pay is often evaluated in terms of the five C's of credit: character, capacity, capital, collateral, and conditions.
- Pertinent credit data can be obtained from several sources, including credit bureaus, financial statements, bankers, and formal trade-credit agencies such as Dun & Bradstreet.
- An accounts receivable aging schedule can be used to improve the credit collection process.
- A small firm should establish a formal procedure for billing and collecting from credit customers.
- It is important that a small firm follow all relevant credit regulations.

Key Terms

aging schedule p. 447
average pricing p. 432
bad-debt ratio p. 448
break-even analysis p. 435
break-even point p. 435
consumer credit p. 443
contribution margin p. 437
credit p. 431
credit bureaus p. 446
credit card p. 444
elastic demand p. 434
elasticity of demand p. 434
follow-the-leader pricing strategy p. 440
freemium strategy p. 434
inelastic demand p. 434
installment account p. 443
markup pricing p. 439
open charge account p. 443
penetration pricing strategy p. 439
prestige pricing p. 435
price p. 431
price lining strategy p. 440
price skimming p. 440
product line pricing p. 441
revolving charge account p. 443
trade-credit agencies p. 446
value p. 431
variable pricing strategy p. 440

You Make the Call

Situation 1

Frolic! is a membership-based indoor playground in Brooklyn, New York. Owners Carey Balogh and Julia Dawson see Frolic! as a community of families with babies and young children. They bill it as "the ultimate rock 'n' roll play space for the urban 'under six' crowd and their parents." When Frolic! opened, the owners considered what competitors were asking and charged a little less. But Frolic! offers more than space. Balogh and Dawson provide music lessons, organize birthday parties, and offer a coffee lounge and a boutique. In the early days of the business, the company lost money week after week.

Sources: "Frolic!—About Us," http://frolicplayspace.com/about.html, accessed March 16, 2013; Norm Brodsky, "There's a Funny Thing about Entrepreneurs: They're Often Way Too Optimistic about Sales and Way Too Pessimistic about Prices," *Inc.*, Vol. 34, No. 5, (2012) p. 40.

Question 1 Are Balogh and Dawson offering too many services? What do you advise?

Question 2 Are Balogh and Dawson charging too low a price? What would you suggest to them?

Question 3 If the owners raise their prices, how do you think their customers will react?

Situation 2

Giving customers time to pay their bill generates more sales. But when a recession hits, they may have trouble making payments. If you have businesses as clients, they may have slow-paying customers, which means that they'll be slow to pay you. That is what happened to Terry Croom's business, BizCon Group, a business services company, with a discount card as its primary product. Croom estimated that 50 percent of his customers—other small businesses—were behind in paying what they owed him. Croom needed those customers to keep his business operating, so he was hesitant to demand payment on past due accounts.

Source: Emily Maltby, "How Firms Cope with Slow Payers," *The Wall Street Journal*, November 14, 2011, p. R5.

Question 1 Should a small business owner push customers to pay when times are tough? Why or why not?

Question 2 What problems do you think a business services company might have when its customers do not pay?

Situation 3

Warren Keating is an artist in Los Angeles who was an early seller on eBay, following the pattern of many artists who believe that auctioning their work is the way art should be sold. He has concluded that his market is made up of collectors, who would not want to see the value of what they are buying decline due to price cutting. Keating leans toward full retail pricing, and when he sells on eBay, it's through the "Buy It Now" listing or the more negotiable "Buy It Now or Make Offer." He thinks the biggest mistake an artist can make is inconsistent pricing that causes the buyer to lose confidence in the product's value. According to Keating, you should act with "courage and conviction."

Sources: www.warrenkeating.com, accessed April 7, 2015; and Warren Keating, "Sell More Art Online with New Pricing Strategies," http://youcansellartonline.blogspot.com/2011/01/sell-more-art-online-with-new-pricing.html, accessed April 7, 2015.

Question 1 What do you think makes selling works of art different from selling other kinds of products? What makes it the same?

Question 2 Have you bought anything on eBay? If so, did you receive good value for the price you paid? If not, ask someone who has shopped successfully on eBay for advice on how to shop on that site, and report on what that person tells you.

Question 3 How would you price a work of art? What do you think the advantages and disadvantages of using an auction would be?

Sources: http://www.warrenkeating.com, accessed March 20, 2011; and Warren Keating, "Sell More Art Online with New Pricing Strategies," http://artistmarketingsalon.wordpress.com/2011/01/24/sell-more-art-online-with-new-pricing-strategies, accessed March 20, 2011.

Video Case 16

DYN (P. 679)

The story of Dyn is not unlike many tech startup stories. The difference is that it started during the dot.com boom, survived the bust, thrived after the dust settled, and surges ahead today. At the beginning of Dyn's history, pricing structure was evaluated monthly, but now that it's more established, forecasting is done depending on client needs.

Alternative Case for Chapter 16

Case 22, Pearson Air Conditioning & Service, p. 690

Endnotes

1. "Value," http://www.businessdictionary.com/definition/value.html, accessed March 4, 2015.
2. Heather Clancy, "Pricing Strategies for Services: Managing Solution Provider Margins," http://searchitchannel.techtarget.com/feature/Pricing-strategies-for-services-Managing-solution-provider-margins, accessed March 4, 2015.
3. Vineet Kumar, "Making 'Freemium' Work," https://hbr.org/2014/05/making-freemium-work, accessed March 4, 2015.
4. "Uber: Moving People," https://www.uber.com, accessed March 4, 2015; and James Surowiecki, "In Praise of Efficient Price Gauging," http://www.technologyreview.com/review/529961/in-praise-of-efficient-price-gouging, accessed March 4, 2015.
5. Lyve Alexis Pleshette, "Liz Lange: Success in Fashion Design," http://www.womenhomebusiness.com/success-stories/liz-lange-success-in-fashion-design.htm, accessed March 4, 2015.
6. For a comprehensive explanation of pricing strategies, see William M. Pride and O. C. Ferrell, *Marketing*, Chapter 21 (Mason, OH: Cengage Learning, 2014).
7. Ann C. Logue, "Sticker Shock," *Entrepreneur*, Vol. 40, No. 7 (2012), p. 64.
8. NAW Legal Advisory, "Supreme Court Rules Greater Supplier Control over Minimum Resale Pricing," http://www.naw.org/govrelations/advisory.php?articleid=490, accessed March 5, 2015.
9. Tim Friesner, "Pricing Strategies," http://www.marketingteacher.com/pricing-strategies, accessed March 5, 2015.
10. "Paypal: Usually Free. Always Fair," https://www.paypal.com/webapps/mpp/paypal-fees, accessed March 5, 2015.
11. "American Express Agrees to Settle Class Action Litigations," http://about.americanexpress.com/news/pr/2013/amex-agrees-to-settle-class-action.aspx, accessed March 6, 2015.
12. "The 20 Worst Venture Capital Investments of All Time," www.insidecrm.com/articles/crm-blog/the-20-worst-venture-capital-investments-of-all-time-53532, accessed March 6, 2015.
13. "D&B: Small Business Risk Account Score," http://www.dnb.com/business-credit/enterprise-solutions/small-business-risk-insight/small-business-risk-account-score.html, accessed March 6, 2015.
14. Information regarding how to obtain free credit reports is available on the website of the Federal Trade Commission, "Free Credit Reports," http://www.consumer.ftc.gov/articles/0155-free-credit-reports, accessed March 6, 2015.

CHAPTER 17

Promotional Planning

Marketing Goddess. That's what one of her first clients called her. It's not the title Shari Worthington had in mind when she graduated from St. Lawrence University with her bachelor's degree in biology and psychology. But as so often happens with college graduates, multiple careers awaited her.

Worthington's first job out of school was in psychology. It didn't pay much, so she added a part-time job as a file clerk in the sales department of a computer company. She had no business training, but her boss saw that she had impressive communication skills. She was moved to telemarketing, where her training in biology and psychology proved to be a perfect fit as she was selling to scientists and engineers. From there, it was on to product management.

In the SPOTLIGHT
Telesian Technology Inc.
www.telesian.com

Worthington's psychology background again became valuable, as she began managing online discussion groups as a way to interact with customers and prospects. This provided tremendous insights that could then be applied to new product launches.

When the computer industry became a bit unstable, Worthington started a consulting business on a part-time basis. It didn't take long before she realized that she was making more money in her part-time venture than in her full-time job. And she found that she liked being her own boss. Before she knew it, Worthington had five different businesses going at once.

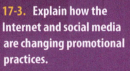

After studying this chapter, you should be able to. . .

17-1. **Describe the communication model and the factors that determine a promotional mix.**

17-2. **Explain methods of determining the appropriate level of promotional expenditures.**

17-3. **Explain how the Internet and social media are changing promotional practices.**

17-4. **Describe personal selling activities.**

17-5. **Identify advertising options for a small business.**

17-6. **Discuss the use of sales promotional tools.**

After a while, Worthington woke up to the fact that she had a specialty: marketing to "techies." She landed a contract with Apple, managing an association of scientists and engineers who used Apple products. She also worked on several in-house projects with Apple's marketing team, including creating an "Apple in Science and Engineering" sales kit of materials. This enabled her to concentrate on one business, Telesian Technology Inc., which has now been operating for over 25 years. According to the company's website, "We create compelling go-to-market strategies, brands, and messaging for our clients' products and services. These are then delivered via a unique mix of paper, face-to-face, and electronic means, including magalogs, microsites, blogs, and more."

Telesian reaches out to clients and prospects in multiple ways. Worthington explains that print materials still are viewed as the most trusted source of information. Nevetheless, she has moved forward with blogs, podcasts, online newsletters, TED talks, and other means by which prospective clients can find her and existing clients can feel they are gaining added value.

In Shari Worthington's words, "Marketing is a continuing series of experiments!"

Sources: Based on http://telesian.com/index.cfm, accessed March 10, 2015; personal interview with Shari Worthington, January 6, 2015; Shari Worthington, "Why Most People Don't Get Marketing," https://www.youtube.com/watch?v=LkL4VQK74Fo, accessed March 10, 2015; and Gary Mintchell, "Podcast Conversation with Shari Worthington on ISA Marketing Manufacturing Solutions," http://themanufacturingconnection.com/2013/10/podcast-conversation-shari-worthington-isa-marketing-manufacturing-solutions, accessed March 10, 2015.

Imagine what life was like a generation ago, before the Internet and social media. Think about how expensive it had to be for startups to get the word out about their products and services, and to make people aware of their company names and brands. Check out the prices for advertising on television, on billboards, in magazines. Compare those with what you are spending on Twitter, on Pinterest, on Google+. Promotional strategies and technologies are advancing daily, giving you countless alternatives for getting your message out. Your venture can be an international player from the day you launch. You can see and communicate with foreign customers and suppliers via Skype, WebEx, Adobe Connect, and others. This has got to be the best of all times for small businesses to compete with large companies.

Promotion consists of marketing communications that inform potential consumers about a firm or its product or service and try to persuade them to buy it. Small businesses use promotion in varying degrees. In this chapter, we discuss promotion on the Internet and social media, but we do not ignore valuable traditional methods, including personal selling, advertising, and sales promotional tools.

A key decision in developing a promotional strategy is determining what you want to get out of it. Do you want to attract customers to your store or website? Are you asking them to buy a specific product or service? Or do you just want to plant the name of your business firmly in customers' minds so that they will think of you when they are ready to buy? This decision will drive what you choose to communicate to prospective customers and the means for getting your message out to them.

promotion
Marketing communications that inform and persuade consumers.

First, let's look at the basic communication model that characterizes promotion. An entrepreneur who understands that promotion is a special form of communication will be better able to grasp the entire process.

17-1 PROMOTION IS COMMUNICATION

Describe the communication model and the factors that determine a promotional mix.

The basic communication model is simple—someone sends a message through a channel, and someone else receives it and understands it. Of course, in practice, communication is much more complicated. Through your promotional activities, you seek to have an existing or prospective customer take action as a result of the message you send. So, has your message actually reached your target customer? Did the customer actually understand the message? Did he or she take the action you desired?

Playworld Systems produces and installs commercial playground equipment. Its management team chose to use Facebook as a way to communicate directly with those who might use their products. Playworld launched a social media campaign inviting community representatives to submit essays on why they wanted to encourage more play in their towns and to include photos showing where a playground might be located. The company selected six finalists, then invited consumers who had "liked" the Playworld Facebook page to vote for their favorites. There was a winner in Mason City, Iowa, and one in Northbrook, Illinois. By offering this communication exchange, Playworld was able to increase its Facebook fan base from 600 to 9,000 during the two-month contest. And the firm enjoyed a lot of free publicity through news stories in community news outlets.[1]

The promotional efforts of a small firm can encompass nonpersonal (advertising), personal (personal selling), combined (social media), and special (sales promotion) forms of communication. A business combines these promotional methods in a **promotional mix**, aimed at a target market. The particular mix of the various promotional methods—advertising, personal selling, social media, and sales promotional tools—is determined by many factors, one of which is geography. A widely dispersed market generally requires mass coverage through advertising or social media, in contrast to the more costly individual contacts of personal selling. On the other hand, if the market is local or if the number of customers is relatively small, personal selling and point-of-display promotion may be more feasible. But based on current behavior both by consumers and by businesses, social media must not be ignored.

Another factor is the size of the promotional budget. Small firms may not select certain forms of promotion, especially time-honored media options, because the costs are just too high. Television advertising, for example, is generally more expensive than radio advertising. Pets.com became the poster child for spending too much on advertising. Started in 1998 as an online business selling pet accessories and supplies, it shut down in 2000 after earning $619,000 in sales while spending $11,800,000 on advertising. The company spent $1,200,000 on a single Super Bowl ad.[2] The lower costs and more targeted nature of company websites have led many small firms to choose electronic media and inbound marketing strategies.

A third factor that heavily influences the promotional mix is a product's characteristics. If the product is of high unit value, such as manufacturing machinery, personal selling will be a vital ingredient in the mix. Personal selling is also an effective method for promoting highly technical products, such as industrial insulation products, because a customer's knowledge about them is usually limited. On the other hand, nonpersonal advertising is more effective for a relatively inexpensive item, like disposable razors.

Do not underestimate what you can learn from competitors. It is natural to want to stand out from the competition and try different tactics from those that established companies are using. You may discover, though, that your competitors have already tried your idea and found that it did not attract buyers. So, if everyone in your industry is using the same types of promotions, there may be a reason.

Finally, listen to your customers. Keep in mind that successful communication includes feedback. Find out whether your customers are posting negative comments about your company or your products online. Pay attention to the comments posted about other businesses to learn why customers are purchasing from them instead of from you. Consider meeting with a group of customers from time to time to get recommendations on how you can serve them better. No promotional activities will be successful day in and day out, for extended periods of time. You need to stay alert in order to make changes when tried-and-true techniques start wearing out.

Communicating with customers and prospects does not come without a price. Virtually every option you consider will have a cost. Think about all the promotional

promotional mix
A blend of nonpersonal, personal, combined, and special forms of communication aimed at a target market.

messages that come your way every day and all the sources from which they come. There are many stories about failed businesses that wasted money on marketing efforts. This is an area where you need to take budgeting seriously.

17-2 DETERMINING THE PROMOTIONAL BUDGET

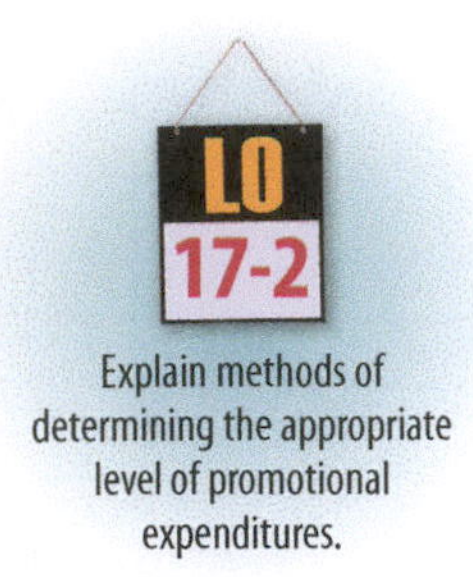

Explain methods of determining the appropriate level of promotional expenditures.

In Chapter 16, you learned that there is no magic formula for determining the right price for what you are selling. The same is true when figuring out how much a small business should spend on promotion. Four approaches that small business owners often use include the following:

1. Budgeting a fixed percentage of sales
2. Deciding how much is left over after other expenses are covered
3. Spending at the same level as competitors
4. Determining how much is needed to achieve objectives

17-2a Budgeting a Fixed Percentage of Sales

Many small businesses operate in stable markets with predictable revenue streams. In such cases, the simplest method of determining how much to budget for promotion is to earmark promotional dollars based on a percentage of sales. A firm's own past experiences should be evaluated to establish a promotion-to-sales ratio. If 2 percent of sales, for example, has historically been spent on promotion with good results, the firm can safely budget 2 percent of forecasted sales for future promotion. Secondary data on industry averages can also be used for comparison. Professional and industrial associations typically collect these data and report them to their members. A variation on the percentage-of-sales approach is to use a percentage of profits.

A major shortcoming of allocating a percentage of sales is a tendency to spend more on promotion, when sales are increasing and less when they are declining. When the economy is booming, do you really need to spend more to attract customers? In a recession, however, using promotion to stimulate sales may be the most important way to let people know why they should be doing business with you. Of course, this strategy does not make sense for new firms with no historical sales figures on which to base their promotional budgets.

Budgeting Marketing Dollars
You can find a free template for compiling a marketing budget at the SCORE website (www.score.org/resources/annual-marketing-budget-template).

17-2b Deciding How Much Is Left Over after Other Expenses Are Covered

Spending whatever is left over when all other activities have been funded occurs all too often in small businesses. This is sometimes described as the "all you can afford" method. The decision about promotional spending might be made only when a media representative sells an owner on a special deal that the business can afford.

Small business owners should have objectives for the money that they spend. And they should be alert for new media opportunities.

17-2c Spending at the Same Level as Competitors

As mentioned earlier, sometimes competitors are doing things right. You should always ask yourself why competitors are using a particular ad medium and spending money in a certain pattern throughout the year. The answer may be that they've learned something about people's shopping and buying habits. By duplicating the promotional efforts of close competitors, a business will be spending at least as much as the competition in the hope of reaching the same customers. If the competitor is a large business, this method is clearly not feasible. However, it can be used to react to short-run promotional tactics by small competitors.

Of course, this approach may result in copying competitors' mistakes as well as their successes. And the biggest pitfall can be that it makes you lazy. You don't want to ignore something that could really move your business forward. And if you design a new promotional strategy, competitors may try to copy it. They may increase their budgets to keep you from stealing their customers, and you may find yourself in an ad war.

17-2d Determining How Much Is Needed to Achieve Objectives

With your promotional budget, you may be trying to increase sales or profits, get more prospects to visit your website, gain better name or brand recognition for your company or your product, or simply increase the number of people reached by your message. Determining how much you need to accomplish your goals requires a comprehensive analysis of the market with a link to the firm's objectives. You should know how your target market is getting information. Is a new social medium becoming popular? Do your customers need to be introduced to your product, or are they looking for it? The options for spending promotional budgets are increasing every day.

Next, we consider specific options for promoting products and services, beginning with some of the newer ones. Advancements in communications technologies have led to new products and new methods for connecting businesses with their markets.

17-3 PROMOTION USING THE INTERNET AND SOCIAL MEDIA

LO 17-3

Explain how the Internet and social media are changing promotional practices.

In 2014, the Pew Research Center reported that 87 percent of American adults use the Internet.[3] Of those adults, 74 percent were using social networking sites.[4] Companies that fail to recognize how the Internet and social media are changing the way that people communicate and process information are not likely to prosper. To gain a better understanding of what this means for small business owners, we look first at creating and managing websites, and then discuss the promotional opportunities offered by social media.

17-3a The Small Business Website

If you are not thinking about marketing when you set up and manage your company's website, you are missing opportunities and doing damage to your business. Numerous decisions must be made prior to launching a site. Three critical startup tasks are related to the likely promotional success of a corporate website: (1) creating and registering a site name, (2) building a user-friendly site, and (3) promoting the website.

CREATING AND REGISTERING A SITE NAME

The Domain Name System (DNS) allows users to find their way around the Internet. Selecting the best domain name for a corporate website is an important promotional

© PURESOLUTION/SHUTTERSTOCK.COM

decision. Popular domain designations are .com, .net, .biz, .info, and .org. Domain names have a minimum of 3 and a maximum of 63 characters preceding the domain designation. They must begin with a letter or number and end with a letter or number. They may not include a space. Follow the rules carefully to avoid problems when you register. The United States Small Business Administration provides details on registering a domain name and meeting other requirements for online business practices.[5]

Since a domain name gives a small business its online identity, it's desirable to select a descriptive and appealing name. An entrepreneur's first thought might be to use the name of her business, but she may discover it has already been taken. There is plenty of advice available on the Internet for creative approaches to selecting a name.[6] Like real estate, website names can be bought and sold. In 2014, mi.com sold for $3.6 million.[7]

BUILDING A USER-FRIENDLY WEBSITE

First impressions are important, and high-quality Web design gives a small e-commerce business the opportunity to make a good first impression on each visitor. Many technical specialists are available to help design and build a site. One such company, Telesian Technology Inc. (profiled in the opening Spotlight), details how business owners need to grasp website development, e-commerce, website hosting, strategic planning, and marketing to make the site a success.[8] Our purpose in this chapter is simply to provide some useful ideas about website design (see Exhibit 17.1).

EXHIBIT

17.1 Website Design Guidelines

- **Select and register your domain name.** Comply with registration rules, and choose a descriptive and user-friendly name.
- **Choose a Web host.** Determine the primary purpose of your website, and then locate a host that best fits that purpose (types of hosts include e-commerce, blogging, business, and similar options).
- **Decide on the layout.** Design a site that balances attractiveness with the ability to interact.
- **Provide easy navigation.** Do not overload a page. Enable users to access any content with as few clicks as possible.
- **Stay consistent in style.** Inconsistency in headings, fonts, page layouts, color schemes, and terms only confuses visitors and appears amateurish.
- **Make sure the website can be accessed by multiple devices.** Users may also search for your company from smartphones and tablets, as well as desktops and laptops.
- **Engage in search engine optimization (SEO).** Serious competitors are applying SEO strategies to improve their websites' visibility. Don't be left behind.
- **Keep the website fresh.** Review your site frequently to remove outdated material, introduce new links, experiment with new formats, and make other changes.
- **Include a call to action.** Think again about your purpose, and invite users to take the action you are seeking.
- **Supply contact information.** Be sure that visitors know who you are and how to get in touch with you.

Sources: Based on http://www.webhostinggeeks.com, accessed March 11, 2015; http://www.register.com, accessed March 11, 2015; http://www.hostindex.com, accessed March 11, 2015; and Sue Smith, "Website Design Guidelines," http://www.ehow.com/info_8160582_website-design-guidelines.html, accessed March 11, 2015.

Websites fail to retain customers for many reasons. One of the most frequent problems is slow downloads. Online shoppers are impatient, and the slightest inconvenience sends them away. If your firm is conducting a considerable amount of online business, a slow website translates into lost sales revenue. Lost revenue can be direct (for example, missed sales if you're selling online) or indirect (for example, loss of customer confidence if you're providing Web-based solutions to clients). The more important a website is to your business, the less you can afford to have it perform slowly or, worse, experience downtime.

Websites will also fail if they do not satisfy visitors' information needs. Frequently, this is because designers look inward to the business for Web design ideas, rather than outward to customer needs. Some experts recommend that firms integrate social networking into their websites from the beginning. Designer Rebecca Minkoff, for example, introduced a new line of fashion clothing by posting photos on Snapshot, which were used by prospective customers to find her website.[9]

User-Friendly Design

Small business owners should seek low-cost but high-expertise advice. Government agencies often provide such services. The U.S. Department of Health and Human Services published an entire book on website design, *Research-Based Web Design & Usability Guidelines*, which you can find at www.usability.gov/sites/default/files/documents/guidelines_book.pdf. Let others do the research for you.

PROMOTING THE WEBSITE

A Web address can be promoted both to existing customers and to prospects by including the URL on print promotions, business cards, letterhead, and packaging. Johnny Earle, also known as Johnny Cupcakes, introduced in Chapter 16's Spotlight, found packaging to be a great form of promotion.[10] And the Spotlight personality for this chapter, Shari Worthington, contends that print is still the most trusted advertising medium.[11] Special direct mail and radio campaigns can also be designed for this purpose. Additionally, a website can be promoted by placing banner advertisements on other websites, where a quick click will send users to the advertised site. When building HubSpot, Inc., Brian Halligan and Dharmesh Shah explained to clients that traditional promotion acts like a megaphone, broadcasting from one to many. Their idea for inbound marketing was for a firm's website to become a hub, enabling like-minded people to connect.[12]

Search engine optimization (SEO) is the process of increasing the volume and quality of traffic to a particular website. The higher your small business ranks in search engine results, the more visitors it will attract. An important goal is to make your website as search engine–friendly as possible.

Keep in mind, too, that there are many specialized search engines. Your company might benefit from being registered with an engine such as Go.com, a Disney property that represents itself as family friendly.[13] You can find guidelines for designing and submitting your website by visiting search engine websites.[14]

17-3b Social Media

Social media comprise social networking and microblogging websites, as well as other means of online communication, where users share personal messages, information, videos, and other content. The pervasiveness of social media has resulted in the introduction of new terms and new definitions of some words. Inbound marketing company HubSpot offers lists 120 social media marketing terms.[15] One term especially relevant to this chapter is **social networking**, which refers to interacting online with other users who share common interests. Smartphones, tablets, and other mobile devices are helping business owners find entirely new ways of reaching customers and prospects.

social media
Social networking and microblogging websites, as well as other means of online communication, where users share personal messages, information, videos, and other content.

social networking
Interacting online with other users who share common interests.

Among the many lessons for small business owners is that they cannot absolutely control how their businesses are viewed by consumers. Today's customers are often members of communities that are sharing real-time information about the products and services being offered. Entrepreneurs may find that they need qualified experts to guide them through the social media maze, just as many expect accountants to coach them through their financial statements.

Promoting businesses, products, and services through social media can be intimidating, if only because of the vast array of options available. But the same entrepreneurial attitude that helps an owner create and manage a small business can be applied in order to reach customers through online communication. Stay tuned for the rapid changes these technologies will continue to bring.

SOCIAL NETWORKING SITES

Hundreds of social networks are available and accessible for small businesses to join communities, make contacts, introduce products and services, build customer relationships, and otherwise promote their ventures. Deciding which networks to use, learning how to use them, and staying active and involved by sharing information and monitoring what others are doing require resources that very few small businesses have.[16]

Which networks will connect you with current and prospective customers and help you discover what your competitors are doing, what new technologies may affect your business, and what social and cultural changes may affect your sales? Some networks are more general in nature, while others specialize. Look at the websites of your competitors to determine which networks they are encouraging visitors to click and join. Those are the ones your competitors think work best for them. A few examples the most popular sites are:[17]

- *Facebook*, a network that links you with friends and others with whom you might be connected through work, study, or mutual interests. Businesses often set up fan pages in order to interact with customers.
- *Twitter*, a short-messaging service that businesses can use to provide real-time notifications to their followers.
- *LinkedIn*, a business-oriented network with the mission of connecting professionals and enabling companies to improve their competitiveness.
- *Pinterest*, a place to discover ideas for all projects and interests, with help from other users with similar interests.
- *Google+*, a network that increases search visibility for business users; comparable to Facebook.
- *Tumblr*, a network that enables users to set up blogs and to find blogs that they may want to follow.

DIRECT E-MAIL PROMOTION

Before social networking sites became dominant, **e-mail promotion**, in which electronic mail is used to deliver a firm's message, provided and still provides a low-cost way to pinpoint customers and achieve high response rates. As more and more businesses began using e-mail for this purpose, however, customer inboxes become cluttered. And recipients are reluctant to open some e-mail messages, fearing they may contain computer viruses. Nevertheless, businesses continue to rely on this strategy with many increasing their budgets for e-mail marketing.[18] According to a Salesforce Marketing Cloud 2015 survey, 73 percent of marketers reported e-mail advertising was a core strategy.[19]

Two obstacles to e-mail promotion have arisen. First, Congress passed the Can-Spam Act of 2003, which took effect on January 1, 2004, and established standards regarding the use of commercial e-mail, enforceable by the Federal Trade Commission (FTC).[20] Second, anti-spam software, which sometimes also blocks legitimate e-mails,

e-mail promotion
Delivery of a firm's message by electronic mail.

became popular. Before sending a promotional message by e-mail, marketers should consider testing their message by putting it through a preview tool. MailWasher and SpamButcher are examples of software packages that permit previews. Previewing allows you to see advertisements that may be delivered as e-mails without customers having to download them to their computers.

RECIPROCAL ADVERTISING AND HYPERLINKS

A **hyperlink** is a word, phrase, or image that a user may click on to go to another part of a document or website or to a new document or website.[21] As promotional tools, hyperlinks are typically reciprocal. This enables readers to move from one website to another that may have information that relates to their original search or complements what the original website is offering. Companies, therefore, can give visitors more information by linking them to websites maintained by others. Hyperlinks may be free to the linked parties if those parties believe that the connections are mutually beneficial. Otherwise, one company may have to pay a per-click charge to the other if it is seeking to obtain business from those using the primary website.

BLOGS

The word *blog* is a contraction of the term *weblog*. **Blogs** are online journals that offer a writer's experiences, opinions, etc. (The term may refer to the website itself.) Bloggers often include hyperlinks to complement or supplement the ideas they have presented. The websites are generally intended to be interactive, allowing readers to leave comments. Many business owners have set up blogs related to their companies and products. This can be done for free on such websites as WordPress.com or Blogger.com. An owner can then comment on other blogs that may have related topics, each time including links back to his or her company blog.

Telesian Technology has put together a blog team to introduce marketing ideas to clients and prospective clients. It provides hyperlinks to other sites in order to expose visitors to president Shari Worthington's blog to other points of view.[22]

MOBILE DEVICES

Technological changes and consumer and commercial uses of mobile devices have exploded in recent years, along with the opportunities that these products offer to small firms. According to the Pew Research Center, in 2014, 90 percent of adults in the United States owned a cell phone, 58 percent had a smartphone, and 42 percent owned computer tablets.[23]

A *mobile device* is a generic term used to refer to a variety of wireless handheld computing devices that allow people to access information from wherever they are. When you are ready to promote your company and its products and services on mobile devices, keep in mind that your website may need to be reformatted to fit smaller portable screens. You want a clear layout with easy navigation. You may need a professional checkout service provider so that your customers don't have to worry about pulling out their credit cards and entering numbers in public locations.[24]

APPS

App is shorthand for *application*, specifically a small, specialization software program. You may be well acquainted with apps for a variety of uses, including how to get along in a college community. With the widespread use of smartphones, individuals, businesses, nonprofit organizations, and even government agencies offer apps to stay in contact and provide information to people on the go. For an example, take a look at the United States government's list of apps that can be downloaded at www.usa.gov/mobileapps.shtml.

hyperlink
A word, phrase, or image that a user may click on to go to another part of a document or website or to a new document or website.

blogs
An online journal that offers a writer's experiences, opinions, etc.

app
Abbreviation for a small, specialized software program.

Large corporations use apps to make sure that their customers can reach them. Small business owners must take this method of communication seriously to compete and promote their companies. An app should not cost your business more than the revenue it brings in. While you don't have to invest in the most technologically advanced app, you should think about how people can have fun when they click on your app. For example, Flickr can be used to share photos, perhaps showing what a good time your customers are having with your products. And don't forget that when people use their mobile devices, they want responses and information *now*!

Small business owners avoid social media promotion at their risk. Exhibit 17.2 offers some do's and don'ts for social media marketing. Strategies and technologies are changing so fast, though, that you cannot assume what is working for you today will still work tomorrow. And keep in mind that until recently, an unsuccessful advertisement could be quickly pulled and forgotten. Now it lives on online, tarnishing the image of the company that spent good money to create it.

QUICK RESPONSE CODES

Another tool for electronic communication that small business owners have been discovering is the **quick response (QR) code**. A QR code is a square barcode that connects to a website, a video, or some other Web content. The barcode makes it easy for someone to access your site without typing in a URL. Prospective customers just scan the QR code with their phone camera or webcam. Business owners are finding lots of value in these codes. A QR code on a business card can be scanned to an address list. QR codes can announce events or promotions for a company, providing days, times, locations, and other information. They may include an e-mail message that encourages a response. Connecting people to videos may generate the most attention.

quick response (QR) code
A square bar code that connects to a website, a video, or some other Web content.

EXHIBIT **17.2** Do's and Don'ts of Social Media Marketing

Do's	Don'ts
• Do tell stories personalizing your brand and company. Post videos of customers using and enjoying your products.	• Don't overpromote. Provide more useful than promotional information.
• Do build relationships with opinion leaders, including journalists. Show an interest in what others are writing about. Bloggers and reporters often ask questions that you or someone in your company may be able to answer.	• Don't waste your time on the wrong network. Just because everyone seems to be on Facebook doesn't mean that your customer will look there for what you are selling. Make sure you know your target customers and where they get their information.
• Do ask your customers to review the products they buy from you. People trust the endorsements and recommendations of other customers more than those of someone who works for you.	• Don't expect your customers to be perfect. They will make spelling errors typing in keywords. Keep common misspellings associated with your product and business in your search engine list to help people find you.
• Do keep it quick and short. Even 140 characters can be too long at times.	• Don't use hype, slang, or abbreviations. They all look like spam and make your brand look cheap.
• Do take keywords seriously. Keywords bring people to your site. Emphasize the keywords that your customers search for in your URL, in title tags, and in headings.	• Don't overinvest in social media at the expense of building content on your own website.

Sources: Based on "Intel Social Media Guidelines," http://www.intel.com/content/www/us/en/legal/intel-social-media-guidelines.html, accessed March 12, 2015; Thomson Reuters, "Social Media Guidelines," http://site.thomsonreuters.com/site/social-media-guidelines, accessed March 12, 2015; Emily Maltby, "Some Social-Media Tips for Business Owners," http://online.wsj.com/article/SB10001424127887323701904578274090683864964.html?KEYWORDS=social+media, accessed March 12, 2015; and Caron Beesley, "Putting the 'Social' into Social Media Marketing: 3 Tips for Interacting with Your Customers," http://www.sba.gov/community/blogs/community-blogs/small-business-matters/putting-social-social-media-marketing-3-tips, accessed March 12, 2015.

Living the Dream

ENTREPRENEURIAL EXPERIENCES

An e-Commerce Revolutionary

Founded in 2009. Over a million Facebook Likes by 2015. How did this small, rural children's clothing company do it?

Stay-at-home mom Brandi Tysinger-Temple sewed clothes for her three daughters because she couldn't find what she felt would be both tasteful and fun and would allow the girls to match when the occasion called for it. Having purchased too much fabric, she made some extra dresses and sold them on eBay. They were snapped up quickly, encouraging Temple to produce more and leading her to hire more sewers to meet the demand. On what she labeled a "fluke," Temple offered some remnants on Facebook. The response took her breath away. Her next step was to move all of her offerings from eBay to Facebook.

Temple's company, Lolly Wolly Doodle, proceeded to double in growth each year. In 2013, the company received a $20 million investment from AOL co-founder Steve Case through his venture fund, Revolution Growth. Although much larger firms had attempted to use Facebook as a sales platform, most had had mediocre results and chose to invest in more traditional approaches.

What has worked so well for Temple? The strategy she has adopted is to conduct a preview sale on Facebook of an item that the company is considering producing. They test multiple new designs every day. Facebook fans of Lolly Wolly Doodle can request a limited amount of customization, such as monograms. Only when the customer pays does the company manufacture the clothing items in-house. This is pure just-in-time production. That means no excess inventory for initial product runs. Feedback from customers determines the next action to take. How do the attributes that customers like—pattern, color, neckline, ruffles, etc.—relate to the sales performance of previous products? Should they modify the clothing, discontinue the experiment, or generate stock and make the item permanent?

This startup has become the largest company in the world transacting business on Facebook. In addition, Lolly Wolly Doodle makes sales through its own website, www.lollywollydoodle.com.

Temple is proud that her business has had an impact where it is located. The state of North Carolina helped finance the construction of a 19,000-square-foot facility in Lexington where the company was started. The town had an unemployment rate nearly twice the national average, so the growth experienced by Lolly Wolly Doodle is having many positive effects.

Sources: Based on "Hi, and Welcome to Lolly Wolly Doodle," http://www.lollywollydoodle.com/pages/what-a-journey, accessed March 12, 2015; https://www.facebook.com/?_rdr#!/LollyWollyDoodle, accessed March 12, 2015; and Tom Foster, "Along Came Lolly: From the Unlikeliest of Places, an e-Commerce Revolution with Ruffles," *Inc.*, June 2014, pp. 25–29.

17-4 PERSONAL SELLING IN THE SMALL FIRM

Describe personal selling activities.

As much as social media seem to be taking over the world, face-to-face contact still counts. Through personal selling, you can use body language to convey your message, answer questions and resolve problems immediately, and build confidence. When you are starting a new business, this may be your most important marketing tool. Small business owners should always think of themselves as personal sales representatives for their companies. Wherever you go as a business owner, you are the company to the people you meet. Your interpersonal skills may come into play in any number of ways. People you meet inside or outside of your business form judgments based on how they react to you. They also form judgments based on their interactions with any of your employees. So everyone working for you should know that he or she is making an impression that could lead to sales or could send a customer to someone else.

For many products, **personal selling**—a face-to-face meeting with a customer—is the best way to make a presentation and close a sale. Of course, the face you see may be on a computer screen or a smartphone or some other device. Personal selling includes the activities of both inside salespeople of retail, wholesale, and service establishments and outside sales representatives, who call on business customers and final consumers. In a small business, every person in the company is a salesperson. A customer who walks into a business or places a phone call or sends an e-mail to a business should not have to wait very long to be taken care of by the owner or a certain employee—everyone must be ready to meet the customer's needs. The entrepreneur's responsibility is to make sure that all employees are prepared to do personal selling.

Before hiring a sales force for your company, calculate the costs and expected returns. This can be an expensive form of promotion per sale. For a small business, personal selling is labor intensive. It takes you and your employees away from the many other activities that may be critical to keeping your business alive.

17-4a The Importance of Product Knowledge

Effective selling is built on a foundation of product knowledge. A salesperson is expected to give individual attention to a prospect, perhaps being ready to negotiate and customize a product or service to fit a special need. With thorough knowledge, the salesperson can explain the product's or service's advantages, uses, and limitations, and can educate customers by answering questions and countering objections. Communication in this form of promotion should be interactive. Customers are seldom experts on the products they buy. However, they can immediately sense a salesperson's knowledge or ignorance. Personal selling degenerates into mere order-taking when a salesperson lacks product knowledge.

17-4b The Sales Presentation

The heart of personal selling is the sales presentation to a prospective customer. Being a good listener is essential, but you should have a good idea of what you or your sales representatives will be ready to say. At this crucial point, an order is either secured or lost. There are some standard practices that have been found to lead to success.

PROSPECTING

A preliminary step leading to an effective sales presentation is **prospecting**, which is the systematic process of continually looking for new customers. With expanding options and rapid changes in communication technology, it is better to think of prospecting as both looking for customers and making it easy for customers to find you. Prospecting also includes consideration of whether a potential customer can be well served by the company. This is especially important in distinguishing true prospects from casual browsers when they initiate contact with you. Small business owners must use their limited resources wisely.

One of the most important skills a small business owner can have is the ability to network.[25] You will read more about *networking*, the process of developing and

personal selling
A face-to-face meeting with a customer.

prospecting
A systematic process of continually looking for new customers.

engaging in mutually beneficial relationships in Chapter 19. For now, we want to point out how building relationships through business and social interactions can lead to *personal referrals*. If you are able to demonstrate to friends, customers, and other business contacts that you deliver on your promises, that you have solutions to their problems and the products and/or services that can make their lives better, those contacts may open other doors for you. They may let you use their names when introducing yourself to others. At a minimum, they can provide word-of-mouth endorsements, often the strongest recommendation you can get.

Another source of prospects is *impersonal referrals* from media publications, public records, and directories. Newspapers and magazines, particularly trade magazines, often identify prospects by reporting on new companies and new products. Engagement announcements in a newspaper can serve as impersonal referrals for a local bridal shop. Public records of property transactions and building permits can be impersonal referrals for a garbage pick-up service, which might find prospective customers among home buyers or those planning to build houses or apartment buildings.

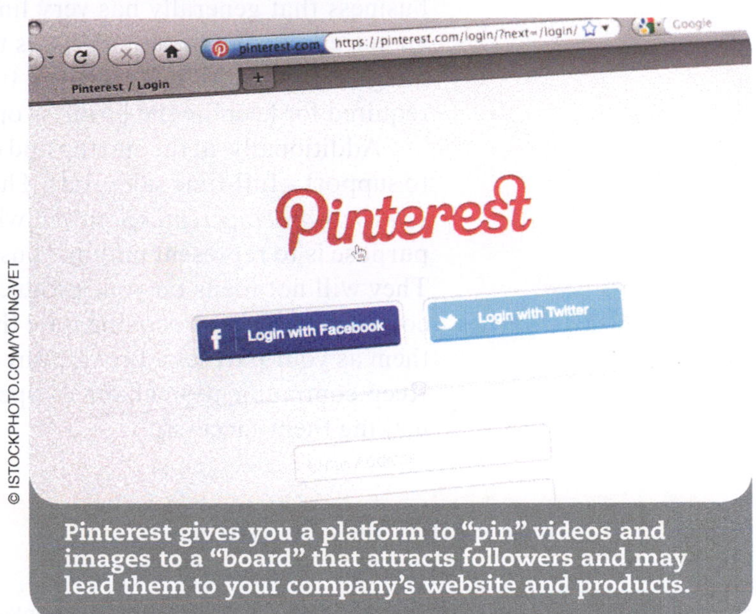

© ISTOCKPHOTO.COM/YOUNGVET

Pinterest gives you a platform to "pin" videos and images to a "board" that attracts followers and may lead them to your company's website and products.

A high-tech variation of impersonal referrals is taking place on various social websites such as Facebook and Pinterest, where more and more subscribers are providing reviews of the establishments they patronize. With Google+, for example, you can target niche circles that users have created, finding prospects with special interests in welding or vacation home ownership or video gaming and more. Keep in mind that reviews posted on social networking websites can be positive or negative. Develop a strategy for responding to online criticisms.[26]

Prospects can also be identified without referrals through *marketer-initiated contacts*. Telephone calls or mail surveys, for example, help locate possible buyers. Finally, inquiries by a potential customer that do not lead to a sale can still create a "hot prospect." Small furniture stores often require their salespeople to fill out a card for each person visiting the store. These *customer-initiated contacts* can then be systematically followed up by telephone calls, and prospects can be notified of special sales. Some customers may become followers on your Twitter account and receive notification through Twitter of special offers. Contact information should be updated periodically. Firms with websites can similarly follow up with visitors who have made inquiries online.

PRACTICING THE SALES PRESENTATION

Nothing substitutes for practice before making a sales presentation. Everything may be clear in your mind, but that does not guarantee that the right words will come out of your mouth. Successful salespersons recognize that style can count as much as content. One way to learn about your own style is to record the presentation in order to study it later and improve your delivery.

The best salespeople have done their homework. They have not only practiced their presentations, but they have also studied their prospective customers. They have thought about possible customer objections to the product and are prepared to handle them. Knowing something about customers' wants and needs will prepare you for most of their likely objections. Most objections can be categorized as relating to (1) price,

(2) product, (3) timing, (4) source, (5) service, or (6) need. Training can be helpful in teaching salespeople how to deal with customers' objections.

Successful salespeople develop techniques, like those shown in Exhibit 17.3, for attracting a customer's attention, presenting reasons to buy, responding to objections, and closing a sale.

17-4c Cost Control in Personal Selling

We have already explained that personal selling efforts can be expensive. You may not be spending as much on a salesperson as on an advertising campaign, but neither are you reaching as many people. Cost considerations are especially important for a new business that generally has very limited resources. While nothing can substitute for an entrepreneur's personal efforts to sell products and services and to represent the image and reputation of the firm, time spent selling is time away from other activities required for keeping the business open and operating.

Additionally, in the startup and early growth stages, a business may not have funds to support a full-time sales staff. The most cost-efficient mode of selling may be to use *sales or marketing representatives*, who are self-employed or work for a company whose purpose is to represent multiple businesses, thereby spreading out the costs of selling. They will not focus on your products alone, as your own employees would, but your company will have to compensate them only as merchandise is actually sold. Think of them as your partners. Provide any sales aids they may need to make their job easier. Keep communication channels open, and let them know that you are committed to making them successful.

EXHIBIT 17.3 Successful Sales Techniques

- **Be honest.** Your prospect has to discover only one misrepresentation to lose all trust and confidence in you. You want customers who will come back to you and tell others how good you are.
- **Know your audience.** Are you talking with the decision maker, or does this person need approval from someone else? How is your product or service used by this customer?
- **Know how much time you have, and get to the point.** Many people recognize that time is their most valuable asset. Be sure to respect that. If you can't make clear in the first sentence or two why you're there, you'll lose your prospect's interest.
- **Prepare an outline, and rehearse.** Be sure to cover all critical issues and logically order your presentation. Then test your ideas on others. Do they understand your message?
- **Be relevant, and engage the customer.** Ask enough questions to know what is important to your prospective customer and how you can help him or her. Think of your presentation as a *conversation*. Be a better listener than a speaker.
- **Believe in what you are selling, and be enthusiastic.** Be able to genuinely convey what makes your product or service better for the customer than anyone else's. But recognize that the world's best salespeople still hear no more than yes. Do not let that burn you out.
- **Use visuals.** Size, technology requirements, safety, and other issues might limit your ability to show your product. Nevertheless, visual representations help project customers into a situation where they better understand what the product will do for them.
- **Get reactions from the prospect.** If the prospect does not ask questions, it is a sign that you have not communicated your message successfully. Be ready with questions of your own, questions that will solicit more than yes-or-no answers. You want to know what is preventing you from getting the results that you seek. You want to know how to make the prospect happy.

Sources: Based on Kelley Robertson, "Creating a Powerful Sales Presentation," http://www.businessknowhow.com/marketing/sales-presentation.htm, accessed March 12, 2015; "Sales Presentation," http://www.m62.net/sales-presentation, accessed March 12, 2015; Kevin Davis, "10 Tips for Winning Sales Presentations," http://www.businessknowhow.com/marketing/winslspres.htm, accessed March 12, 2015; and "The Keys to Great Sales Presentations," www.allbusiness.com/sales/selling-techniques/809-1.html#axzz2jtCKGWqf; accessed March 12, 2015.

17-4d The Compensation Program for Salespeople

Salespeople will not be motivated for the same reasons that an owner is. You may be in love with your product or service; you may be seeking to change the world. But your employees want to get paid. Nevertheless, they can be motivated by nonfinancial compensation as well as money. Research studies on small businesses have identified noncash incentives that relate to firm performance.[27]

NONFINANCIAL COMPENSATION

Personal recognition and the satisfaction of reaching a sales quota are examples of nonfinancial rewards that motivate many salespeople. Small retail businesses sometimes post a photograph of the top salesperson of the week or month for all to see. An engraved plaque or other recognition may also be given as a more permanent record of sales achievements.

Nonfinancial compensation may also relate to personal and career advancement. Rewards for being a desired employee include opportunities for promotion, advanced education and training, and job security. Business owners should be aware that effective sales personnel are often competitive. They gain a sense of accomplishment by measuring their achievements against those of their peers. Some companies run internal competitions, which can be motivational. If the competition creates hostility among sales personnel, however, consider alternatives such as measuring performance against past achievements, or industry measures or competitions that may be conducted by professional associations.

FINANCIAL COMPENSATION

As much as employees may believe in your vision for the firm, they have to take care of themselves and their families. Two basic plans used for financial compensation are commissions and straight salary. Each plan has specific advantages and limitations for the small firm.

Many small businesses prefer to use commissions as compensation, because such an approach is simple and directly related to productivity. A certain percentage of the sales generated by a salesperson represents his or her commission. Revenue is generated for the firm, so the money is readily available to pay the salesperson. Such a plan incorporates a strong incentive for sales effort—no sale, no commission! On the negative side, a salesperson's job is always more than making the sale. Personnel on commission might be less likely to provide follow-up service or complete after-sale paperwork or other tasks that the business needs to have done.

The straight salary form of compensation provides salespeople with income security, regardless of sales made. However, working for a straight salary can potentially reduce a salesperson's motivation by providing income despite low performance or no sales at all.

Many businesses combine the salary and commission forms of compensation. Salary usually represents the larger part of compensation for a new salesperson. As the salesperson gains experience, the ratio is adjusted to provide more money from commissions and less from salary. And do not put a cap on what a salesperson can earn through commission. Many companies have lost their top producers by limiting incentives. Why would you stop rewarding someone who is making money for your business?

Whatever plan you choose should incorporate sales volume targets with a time frame for accomplishment, typically a month or a year. Additionally, the sales staff should know what the minimum expectations are for their performance. Beyond sales, these expectations can also include customer development, repeat sales, service efforts following sales, and other activities that contribute to the success of the company.

Identify advertising options for a small business.

17-5 ADVERTISING PRACTICES

Along with personal selling, advertising is likely to be part of the promotional strategy for your business. Ideas in advertising are communicated to businesses and consumers through media, such as television, radio, magazines, newspapers, direct mail, billboards, and the Internet.

17-5a Advertising Objectives

advertising
A strategy to sell by informing, persuading, and reminding customers of the availability or superiority of a firm's products or services.

product advertising
A presentation designed to make potential customers aware of a specific product or service and create a desire for it.

institutional advertising
A presentation of information about a particular firm, designed to enhance the firm's image in order to make its product advertising more credible and effective.

To use your money wisely, you should decide what your goals are when you advertise. **Advertising** is a strategy to sell by informing, persuading, and reminding customers of the availability or superiority of a firm's products or services. Without product or service strengths, such as quality and efficiency, advertising will not be enough to help your business survive and grow. Advertising must always be viewed as a complement to a good product and never as a replacement for a bad product.

The importance of honesty in advertising cannot be overstated. An entrepreneur should avoid creating misleading expectations, as such expectations are likely to leave customers dissatisfied. There is nothing wrong in speaking glowingly of a product or service that you believe in. But no false claims should be made.

At times, advertising may seem to be a waste of money. It is expensive and adds little direct value to a product or service. Many startup companies believe that Internet exposure will generate sales immediately. Google has found, however, that many ads are never viewed.[28] It and other Internet providers offer advice and services that small businesses should be adopting to improve their chances for success. Small business owners need to stay up to date with changes in technology and societal behavior.

17-5b Types of Advertising

The two basic types of advertising are product advertising and institutional advertising. **Product advertising** is designed to make potential customers aware of a particular product or service and create a desire for it. **Institutional advertising**, on the other hand, conveys information about the business itself. It is intended to make the public aware of the company and enhance its image so that its product advertising will be more credible and effective.

Most small business advertising is of the product type. Small retailers' ads often stress products, such as weekend specials at a supermarket or sportswear sold exclusively in a women's clothing store. It is important to note, however, that the same advertisement can convey both product and institutional themes. With advertising, you are prospecting for customers who want your product, so the ideal solution is that they clearly understand the best place to buy it is from your company. This may be approached in a variety of ways. A firm may stress its product in newspaper advertisements, for example, while using institutional advertising on websites. Decisions regarding the type of advertising to be used should be based on the nature of the business, industry practice, available media, and the objectives of the firm.

© BLOOMUA/SHUTTERSTOCK.COM

17-5c Advertising Specialists

An entrepreneur cannot be an expert in everything. Small business owners often contract with outside companies and individuals for accounting services, legal advice, transportation, and more. It is not unusual to rely on others' expertise to create promotional messages. Advertising agencies, suppliers, trade associations, and advertising media can provide this specialized assistance.

Advertising agencies provide many services, including the following:

- Graphic design, artwork, and even printing for specific advertisements and/or commercials
- Recommendations for media with the greatest "pulling power" for your product or service
- Copywriting for traditional ads, as well as for blogs, press releases, and other promotional materials
- Assistance with trade shows and merchandise displays
- Website design and social media management
- Mailing and e-mail list management

Since advertising agencies charge fees for their services, an entrepreneur must be sure that the return from those services will be greater than the fees paid. Of course, with the high level of computer technology currently available, creating print advertising in-house is becoming increasingly common among small firms. Some business owners are assisted by suppliers who furnish display aids and even entire advertising programs to their dealers. Trade associations also provide helpful assistance. In addition, advertising media themselves can provide some of the same services offered by an ad agency. And, as illustrated by Telesian Technology Inc. in this chapter's Spotlight, consultants who specialize in Internet marketing can help firms shape their online promotional strategies.

17-5d Frequency of Advertising

Determining how often to advertise is an important and highly complex issue for a small business. Obviously, advertising should be done regularly, and attempts to stimulate interest in a firm's products or services should be part of an ongoing promotional program. Continuity reinforces the presence of the company as the place for customers to buy when they are ready. One-shot advertisements that are not part of a well-planned promotional effort lose much of their effectiveness in a short period. Of course, some noncontinuous advertising may be justified, such as advertising to prepare consumers for the acceptance of a new product. Such an approach may also be used for holidays and seasonal events. Many products and services have some seasonal demand—landscaping services in warm months, snow removal in cold ones, costumes at Halloween, flowers on Valentine's Day. Deciding on the frequency of advertising involves a host of factors, both objective and subjective. This is another reason for entrepreneurs to seek professional advice.

Enchanting Customers and More

Through his books, website, social media, and other means, Guy Kawasaki introduces countless ideas to entrepreneurs about starting and growing their ventures. Good places to look for promotional ideas include his books *The Art of the Start*, *Selling the Dream*, and *Enchantment*. More information is available on his website at www.guykawasaki.com.

17-5e Where to Advertise

Not everyone is a serious prospect for your business. You have to identify the market segment most likely to buy the products and services you offer and to buy them from you rather than other sources. This means restricting your advertising, perhaps by geography or customer type. You cannot afford to be all things to all people. From among the many media available, a small business owner must choose those that will provide the greatest return for the advertising dollar.

The most appropriate combination of advertising media depends on the type of business and its current circumstances. Furniture retailers and auto dealers use television and newspaper ads. Television keeps their name and products in front of the consumers, making them easy to remember when customers are ready to shop and buy. And when someone is ready to purchase a car or some furniture, she or he is likely to look in newspapers to compare products and prices. Hotels and restaurants near busy highways rely on billboards to attract patrons to their locations. Retirement communities and assisted-living facilities may obtain mailing lists from senior citizen centers and use direct mail to reach their target market. The current stage of communication technology demands the inclusion of a website in any combination of advertising media. Websites are the first step in identifying prospective sources of products and services by many consumers and businesses.

To make an informed selection, entrepreneurs should learn about the strengths and weaknesses of each medium, as shown in Exhibit 17.4. Study this information carefully, noting the particular advantages and disadvantages of each medium.

EXHIBIT

17.4 Advantages and Disadvantages of Major Advertising Media

Medium	Advantages	Disadvantages
Internet	Fastest-growing medium, including smartphones and tablets; ability to target demographics; easy to update; relatively short lead time required for creating Web-based advertising; natural fit with social networking	Possible difficulty in measuring ad effectiveness and return on investment; not all consumers have access; rapidly changing technologies may result in product obsolescence; service issues
Newspapers	Geographic selectivity and flexibility; short-term advertiser commitments; news value and immediacy; year-round readership; high individual market coverage; co-op and local tie-in availability; short lead time	Little demographic selectivity; limited color capabilities; low pass-along rate; may be expensive
Magazines	Good reproduction, especially for color; demographic selectivity; regional selectivity; local market selectivity; relatively long advertising life; high pass-along rate	Long-term advertiser commitments; slow audience buildup; limited demonstration capabilities; lack of urgency; long lead time
Radio	Low cost; immediacy of message; can be scheduled on short notice; relatively no seasonal change in audience; highly portable; short-term advertiser commitments; entertainment carryover	No visual treatment; short advertising life of message; high frequency required to generate comprehension and retention; distractions from background sound; commercial clutter
Television	Ability to reach a wide, diverse audience; low cost per thousand viewers; creative opportunities for demonstration; immediacy of messages; entertainment carryover; demographic selectivity with cable stations	Short life of message; some consumer skepticism about claims; high campaign cost; little demographic selectivity with network stations; long-term advertiser commitments; long lead times required for production; commercial clutter
Direct Mail	Ability to target respondents; provides a detailed and personalized message	May be tossed out as "junk" mail; rising costs per qualified prospect
Outdoor Media	Repetition; moderate cost; flexibility; geographic selectivity	**Short message; lack of demographic selectivity; high "noise" level distracting audience**

17-6 SALES PROMOTION

Discuss the use of sales promotional tools.

A more traditional marketing practice, which is also used on websites and mobile devices, is sales promotion. Generally, **sales promotion** includes any promotional technique, other than personal selling or advertising, that stimulates the purchase of a particular product or service. The term is defined in BusinessDictionary.com as the stimulation "of sales achieved through contests, demonstrations, discounts, exhibitions or trade shows, games, giveaways, point-of-sale displays and merchandising, special offers, and similar activities."[29]

For best results, sales promotion typically is used in combination with personal selling and advertising. Social media companies enable small firms to compete head-on with their large competitors in cost-efficient ways through sales promotion. Many businesses make use of Foursquare, which enables businesses to introduce online loyalty programs. For example, for an anniversary celebration, Park City Mountain Resort in Utah offered discounts on rentals and outerwear to customers who checked in on Foursquare.[30]

We briefly examine four of the most widely used promotional tools: specialties, trade show exhibits, coupons, and publicity.

17-6a Specialties

There are countless specialty items: calendars, pens, key chains, coffee mugs, and shirts. Almost anything can be used as a specialty promotion, as long as each item is imprinted with the firm's name or other identifying slogan. Contact information is also often included.

The distinguishing characteristics of specialties are their enduring nature and tangible value. The key to an effective specialty item is that it lasts—the customer or client has the tangible, visible item for months or years, keeping the name of your company or product in front of them. As functional products, they are worth something to recipients. Specialties can be used to promote a product directly or to create goodwill for a firm. They are excellent reminders of a firm's existence.

Finally, specialties are personal. They are distributed directly to the customer in a personal way, they can be used personally, and they have a personal message. A small business needs to retain its unique image, and owners often use specialties to achieve this objective. More information on specialties is available on the website of Promotional Products Association International at www.ppai.org.

17-6b Trade Show Exhibits

Advertising often cannot substitute for trial experiences with a product, and a customer's place of business is not always the best environment for product demonstrations. Trade show exhibits allow potential customers to get hands-on experience with a product.

Trade show exhibits are of particular value to manufacturers. The greatest benefit of these exhibits is the potential cost savings over personal selling. Trade show groups claim that the cost of an exhibit is less than one-fourth the cost of sales calls, and many small manufacturers agree that exhibits are more cost-effective

sales promotion
An inclusive term for any promotional technique other than personal selling and advertising that stimulates the purchase of a particular product or service.

than advertising. Experienced exhibitors offer the following helpful tips regarding trade shows:[31]

- *Check out the trade show's history.* Does the show regularly attract large crowds? Will the show be adequately promoted to your potential customers?
- *Apply for a speaking opportunity.* Many shows have keynote speakers and breakout sessions on special topics. Also, having a customer speak on your behalf makes a great impression.
- *Pick a good location for the booth.* It will cost you extra, but a good location could be critical in a large show. Corner booths are best.
- *Prepare a professional-looking display.* You do not need to have the biggest, flashiest booth on the trade show floor to attract attendees. But signs, photographs of your products, and other business-related elements used in the display should appear to be professionally prepared.
- *Have a sufficient quantity of literature on hand.* Have plenty of professional-looking brochures or other handouts to distribute, and have them prepared well in advance of the show.
- *Bring the right staff.* You want someone who believes in the product and who enjoys talking with strangers.
- *Have the right giveaways.* Consider using the specialty promotion items just described. Don't waste money on novelty items that no one will use.
- *Find a partner.* You can cut your costs by paying for a portion of the space in another vendor's booth.
- *Follow up.* Have a plan for following up on leads as soon as you get home from the show.

17-6c Coupons

Coupons have been used as promotional tools for over a hundred years. Coca-Cola is credited with being the first company to use coupons. Asa Candler, a co-founder of the Coca-Cola Company, gave handwritten notes to customers that they could exchange for a free glass of Coke. The first official coupon was issued by C. W. Post, offering one cent off the price of a box of Grape-Nuts cereal. Consumers continue to cut coupons from newspapers and magazines, use coupons received through direct mail, and download them from the Internet.[32] Not only do they attract customers to purchase products, but coupons also have value even if they are not used. A study by University of Virginia professors found that consumers who received but did not redeem coupons actually increased their purchasing from the stores associated with the coupons.[33]

© R.NAGY/SHUTTERSTOCK.COM

The world of couponing changed with Groupon. The company was launched in 2008, in response to the frustration that its founder, Andrew Mason, felt when trying to get a reply from a major corporation. Mason decided that collective action from large numbers of customers would get more attention and designed a platform that uses social media to gain commitment from individuals until a critical mass is reached. Groupon negotiates deals with businesses for reduced prices on merchandise and services that go into effect once the tipping point is reached—that is, when enough people have signed up for a coupon to obtain the discounted item.[34]

Groupon has spawned competitors, such as LivingSocial and SocialTwist. Many small businesses use these platforms to attract business in the hope of gaining returning customers. Some, however, have actually lost money, offering too large a discount and not retaining customers for the long term.[35] But others have taken actions to reduce their risks and build sales.

START UP TOOLS

Deliver the Message

Small business owners must be effective communicators. BizLaunch is a company that offers free seminars to help owners build skills. It provides a PowerPoint presentation that guides you through the process of getting free publicity at www.slideshare.net/rogerpierce/how-to-get-free-publicity?next_slideshow=1.

17-6d Publicity

Of particular importance to small firms is **publicity**, which provides visibility for a business at little or no cost. Publicity can be used to promote both a product and a firm's image. It is a vital part of public relations for the small business. A good publicity program requires regular contacts with the news media. As explained in Exhibit 17.2, journalists are opinion leaders. You can help them as much as they can help you if you and your business are the source of good stories.[36]

Examples of publicity efforts that incur some expense include underwriting school yearbooks and sponsoring youth athletic programs. While the benefits are difficult to measure, publicity is nevertheless important to a small business and should be used at every opportunity. The return on a relatively small investment can be substantial.

publicity
A promotional strategy that provides visibility for a business at little or no cost.

17-6e When to Use Sales Promotion

A small firm can use sales promotion to accomplish various objectives. For example, small manufacturers can use it to stimulate channel members—retailers and wholesalers—to market their product. Wholesalers can use sales promotion to induce retailers to buy inventory earlier than they normally would, and retailers, with similar promotional tools, may be able to persuade customers to make a purchase.

At its core, successful promotion is all about effective communication. The source (a small business) must have a message that intended recipients (in the target market) receive or find, understand, and act on. But this is not a simple exercise. Many decisions must be made along the way—decisions regarding the size of the promotional budget, the promotional mix, the nature and placement of advertising, the identification of high-potential prospects, participation in trade shows, and the list goes on. Rapid changes in technologies and in social behavior mean that companies of all sizes will make promotional errors along the way—and you will, too. Your job is to learn from those mistakes. Keep your eyes and ears open for better ways to serve your customers and to get the word out about why they should do business with you.

17-1. Describe the communication model and the factors that determine a promotional mix.

- The basic communication model involves a source, a message, a channel, and a receiver.
- A promotional mix is a blend of nonpersonal, personal, combined, and special forms of communication aimed at a target market.
- A promotional mix is influenced primarily by three important factors: the geographical nature of the market, the size of the promotional budget, and the product's characteristics.
- An entrepreneur should also learn from competitors and listen to customers when deciding on a promotional mix.

17-2. Explain methods of determining the appropriate level of promotional expenditures.

- Earmarking promotional dollars based on a percentage of sales is a simple method for determining expenditures.
- Spending only what can be spared after other expenses have been covered is a widely used approach to promotional budgeting.
- Spending as much as the competition does is a way to react to short-run promotional tactics of competitors.
- The preferred approach to determining promotional expenditures is to decide what it will take to do the job through a comprehensive analysis of the market.

17-3. Explain how the Internet and social media are changing promotional practices.

- Companies that fail to recognize how the Internet and social media are changing how people communicate and process information are not likely to prosper.
- Websites should have a descriptive and appealing name and be user-friendly.
- Efforts must be taken to promote websites to both existing and prospective customers.
- Search engine optimization is a necessary activity to attract visitors to a small business website.
- Through social networking and microblogging, customers share real-time information about products and services.
- There are many tools available for engaging in marketing and promotion through social media, such as e-mail, reciprocal advertising, hyperlinks, blogs, and apps. Your website may need to be reformatted to fit the smaller screens of mobile devices.
- Small business owners must stay informed about growing social media options, such as quick response (QR) codes.

17-4. Describe personal selling activities.

- Effective selling is based on a salesperson's knowledge of the product or service, as well as his or her study of prospective customers.
- A sales presentation is a process involving prospecting, practicing the presentation, and then making the presentation.
- Prospecting is the systematic process of continually looking for new customers.
- Cost control is very important in personal selling.
- An entrepreneur is first and foremost a salesperson for the enterprise.
- The most attractive compensation plan for salespeople combines commissions and straight salary.

17-5. Identify advertising options for a small business.

- Common advertising media include television, radio, magazines, newspapers, direct mail, billboards, and the Internet.
- Product advertising is designed to promote a product or service, while institutional advertising conveys information about the business itself.
- Sources for assistance with advertising include advertising agencies, suppliers, trade associations, and advertising media.
- A small firm must decide how often and where to advertise.

17-6. Discuss the use of sales promotional tools.

- Sales promotion includes any promotional technique, other than personal selling and advertising, that stimulates the purchase of a particular product or service.
- Typically, sales promotional tools are used in combination with advertising and personal selling.
- Four widely used sales promotional tools are specialties, trade show exhibits, coupons, and publicity.

Key Terms

advertising p. 468
app p. 461
blog p. 461
e-mail promotion p. 460
hyperlink p. 461
institutional advertising p. 468
personal selling p. 464
product advertising p. 468
promotion p. 454
promotional mix p. 455
prospecting p. 464
publicity p. 473
quick response (QR) code p. 462
sales promotion p. 471
social media p. 459
social networking p. 459

You Make the Call

Situation 1

Michael Di Pippo owns Pen Fishing Rods. He launched the company to sell his inventions, the world's smallest fishing rods and reels. The Pen Rod Goliath opens to 61 inches, but when it's closed, it's only 8 inches. Di Pippo will ship his products anywhere in the world. How does he let people know about his products? YouTube! He introduces his products using taglines such as "fishing," "camping," and "outdoors." If you visit the company's website, you can link to multiple YouTube videos or watch some right on the site. Even customers are posting videos on YouTube, showing themselves using Pen Fishing Rods products. It didn't take long before over 100 videos related to this company's products were online.

Sources: Based on http://www.perkyjerky.com, accessed March 2, 2013; and Jason Fell, "Building a (Nearly) Million-Dollar Brand on a Startup Budget," http://www.entrepreneur.com /article/219395#, accessed March 2, 2013; Pen Fishing Rods, http://penfishingrods.com/shop/index.php, accessed April 10, 2015.

Question 1 Why do you think Di Pippo chose videos to market his products?
Question 2 What risks do you think Di Pippo faces with customers posting videos about his products?
Question 3 Take a look at some of the videos showing Pen Fishing Rods products and some that were posted by customers? Why has this approach worked? What would you recommend to make it better?

Situation 2

Working in pet care and education, Michael Landa realized that he was seeing more and more overweight pets. He started Nulo, Inc., in an effort to turn things around. His strategy to break into the pet food industry, which is dominated by huge corporations, was to launch an online community, giving pet owners a chance to share information on weight loss and nutrition. Nulo prides itself on offering fresh, simple recipes in small batches with nutritionally rich ingredients. The company stays active on Facebook, Twitter, and YouTube. It was the official pet food company for the 2012 Emmy Awards.

Sources: Based on http://nulo.com, accessed March 3, 2013; and Gwen Moran, "Build Up Your Pack," *Entrepreneur*, Vol. 39, No. 4 (2011), p. 48.

Question 1 If you were starting a company in an industry with large competitors, what steps would you take to prepare your advertising budget?
Question 2 If Landa had come to you for advice, what would you have told him about building an online community?
Question 3 Can Nulo's online community be sustained? What kinds of information should the company be sharing on its website?

Situation 3

On the company website, Birchbox is labeled "the leading discovery commerce platform." Founded by Hayley Barna and Katia Beauchamp, the company is an e-commerce venture specializing in beauty, grooming, and lifestyle products, with a subscription-based marketing strategy. Each month, subscribers receive samples in a mix of categories, determined by a profile that subscribers complete. Birchbox lists their business partners on a brand page on their website. If subscribers like the products they sample, they can then purchase more through Birchbox. The company has a point system that enables subscribers to enjoy discounts and other benefits. As one subscriber expressed it, "They send products I wouldn't necessarily spend money on, but once I get them, I realize I really like them."

Sources: Based on http://www.birchbox.com, accessed March 2, 2013; and Suzy Evans, "Marketing Makeover: How Birchbox Sells Benefit, Kiehl's, Marc Jacobs, and More," *Fast Company*, No. 152 (2011), p. 35.

Question 1 What risks are Barna and Beauchamp taking by giving away samples every month?
Question 2 If you owned a beauty product company, would you partner with Birchbox to market your products? Why or why not?
Question 3 What questions would you want to ask Birchbox before signing up to pay the subscription fee?

Video Case 17

Hubspot, Inc. (P. 681)

HubSpot is an Internet marketing company that caters to small businesses. It used to be that the size of your firm's sales force was the key to finding new customers, but that is not necessarily the case today, thanks to the Internet.

Alternative Case for Chapter 17

Video Case 14, Numi Tea, p. 675

Endnotes

1. Jason Ankeny, "Infectious Behavior," *Entrepreneur*, May 2014, pp. 33–38; and Playworld, http://playworldsystems.com, accessed March 11, 2015.
2. "The 20 Worst Venture Capital Investments of All Time," http://www.insidecrm.com/articles/crm-blog/the-20-worst-venture-capital-investments-of-all-time-53532, accessed March 11, 2015.
3. Pew Research Center, "Internet Use over Time," http://www.pewinternet.org/data-trend/internet-use/internet-use-over-time/, accessed March 11, 2015.
4. Pew Research Center, "Social Networking Fact Sheet," http://www.pewinternet.org/fact-sheets/social-networking-fact-sheet, accessed March 11, 2015.
5. U.S. Small Business Administration, "Online Businesses," https://www.sba.gov/content/start-online-business, accessed March 11, 2015.
6. Shopify, "5 Rules for Choosing a Good & Brandable Domain Name," http://www.shopify.com/blog/3033082-5-rules-for-choosing-a-memorable-domain-name, accessed March 11, 2015.
7. Domaining, "Top Domain Name Sales," http://www.domaining.com/topsales, accessed March 11, 2015.
8. Telesian Technology Inc., "Web Design & Development," http://telesian.com/ebusiness/web_design.cfm, accessed March 11, 2015.
9. Ann Handley, "Trends 2014," *Entrepreneur*, December 2013, pp. 50–51.
10. Johnny Cupcakes, "Ch. 5 2006: Press," http://kitchen.johnnycupcakes.com/story, accessed March 11, 2015.
11. Personal interview with Shari Worthington, January 2015.
12. Brian Halligan and Dharmesh Shah, *Inbound Marketing: Get Found Using Google, Social Media, and Blogs* (Hoboken, NJ: John Wiley & Sons, 2009), pp. 12–13.
13. http://go.com, accessed March 11, 2015.
14. An extensive list of search engines with brief descriptions can be found at http://www.thesearchenginelist.com.
15. Kipp Bodner, "The Ultimate Glossary: 120 Social Media Marketing Terms Explained," http://blog.hubspot.com/blog/tabid/6307/bid/6126/The-Ultimate-Glossary-120-Social-Media-Marketing-Terms-Explained.aspx, accessed March 12, 2015.
16. Michelle Manafy, "How to Choose the Best Social Media Site for Your Business," http://www.inc.com/michelle-manafy/how-to-choose-the-best-social-media-sites-to-market-your-business.html, accessed March 12, 2015.
17. eBizMBA, "Top 15 Most Popular Social Networking Sites," http://www.ebizmba.com/articles/social-networking-websites, accessed March 12, 2015.
18. Jayson DeMers, "5 Reasons You Need to Increase Your Email Marketing Budget," http://www.forbes.com/sites/jaysondemers/2015/03/11/5-reasons-you-need-to-increase-your-email-marketing-budget, accessed March 12, 2015.
19. Jenna Hanington, "The 2015 Email Marketing Landscape Described in 16 Stats," http://www.pardot.com/blog/the-2015-email-marketing-landscape, accessed March 12, 2015.
20. Federal Trade Commission, "CAN-Spam Act: A Compliance Guide for Business," https://www.ftc.gov/tips-advice/business-center/guidance/can-spam-act-compliance-guide-business, accessed March 12, 2015.
21. "Hyperlink," http://www.webopedia.com/TERM/H/hyperlink.html, accessed March 12, 2015.
22. "The Blog Team," http://blog.telesian.com/the-blog-team, accessed March 12, 2015.
23. Pew Research Center, "Device Ownership over Time," http://www.pewinternet.org/data-trend/mobile/device-ownership, accessed March 12, 2015.
24. Sarita Harbour, "Best Practices for Navigation on the Mobile Web," http://www.webdesignerdepot.com/2012/11/best-practices-for-navigation-on-the-mobile-web, accessed March 12, 2015.
25. Mark Hunter, "21 Tips to Use at a Networking Event," http://thesaleshunter.com/resources/articles/networking/21-tips-to-use-at-a-networking-event, accessed March 12, 2015.
26. Tim Devaney and Tom Stein, "Handling Haters: How to Respond to Negative Online Reviews," http://www.forbes.com/sites/sage/2014/03/03/handling-haters-how-to-respond-to-negative-online-reviews, accessed March 12, 2015.
27. Dawn S. Carlson, Nancy Upton, and Samuel Seaman, "The Impact of Human Resource Practices and Compensation Design on Performance: An Analysis of Family-Owned SMEs," *Journal of Small Business Management*, Vol. 44, No. 4 (2006), pp. 531–543; and José L. Barbero, José C. Casillas, and Howard D. Feldman, "Managerial Capabilities and Paths to Growth as Determinants of High-Growth Small and Medium-Sized Enterprises," *International Small Business Journal*, Vol. 29, No. 6 (2011), pp. 671–694.
28. Google, "5 Factors of Viewability," http://think.storage.googleapis.com/docs/5-factors-of-viewability_infographics.pdf, accessed March 12, 2015.

29. BusinessDictionary.com, "Sales Promotion," http://www.businessdictionary.com/definition/sales-promotion.html, accessed March 12, 2015.

30. Park City Mountain Resort, "We're Celebrating 50 Years with 50 Days of Giveaways," http://www.parkcitymountain.com/site/blog/authors/colette-maddock/we-re-celebrating-50-years-with-50, accessed March 12, 2015.

31. Hilary Genga, "How I Saved . . . $6,500," *Entrepreneur*, December 2013, p. 78; Michelle Goodman, "It's Showtime!," *Entrepreneur*, July 2014, p. 72; Janet Attard, "Trade Show Dos and Don'ts," http://www.businessknowhow.com/tips/tradesho.htm, accessed March 12, 2015; and David Lavenda, "10 Ways to Make Sure Your Trade Show Isn't a Bust," http://www.fastcompany.com/1841035/10-ways-make-sure-your-trade-show-isnt-bust, accessed March 12, 2015.

32. The Coupon Company, "Coupon History," http://www.couponcompany.co.za/About_Coupons_History.html, accessed March 12, 2015.

33. Rajkumar Venkatesan and Paul Farris, "Unused Coupons Still Pay Off," *Harvard Business Review*, May 2012, p. 32.

34. "About Groupon," http://www.groupon.com/about, accessed March 13, 2015; and Jolie O'Dell, "The History of Groupon," http://www.forbes.com/sites/mashable/2011/01/07/the-history-of-groupon/, accessed March 13, 2015.

35. Stefanie O'Connell, "5 Things You Should Know about Groupon," http://money.usnews.com/money/the-frugal-shopper/2014/02/20/5-things-you-should-know-about-groupon, accessed March 13, 2015.

36. Diana Spechler and Jim O'Grady, "The Scoop," *Entrepreneur*, October 2013, pp. 57–60.

© AEKKAPHOB/SHUTTERSTOCK.COM

CHAPTER 18

Global Opportunities for Small Businesses

After studying this chapter, you should be able to . . .

18-1. Describe the potential of small businesses as global enterprises.

18-2. Identify the basic forces prompting small companies to engage in global expansion.

18-3. Understand and compare strategy options for global businesses.

18-4. Explain the challenges that global enterprises face.

18-5. Recognize the sources of assistance available to support international business efforts.

Matthew Griffin, a former Army Ranger, wanted to bring economic stability to war-torn countries. With that objective in mind, he founded Combat Flip Flops after a deployment to Afghanistan. The idea behind the startup, recalls Griffin, was to "create an environment that gives people living in post-conflict nations the opportunity to peacefully rebuild their economy." At first, the company manufactured only one style of flip-flops, but it was truly unique, featuring decorative AK-47 casings and military-grade soles. Today, the firm distributes an array of products produced entirely in Afghanistan, Colombia, or Laos.

But as with any startup that goes global so early on, the road to success for Combat Flip Flops had plenty of potholes. When Griffin founded his venture in 2009,

In the SPOTLIGHT
Combat Flip Flops in Afghanistan
www.combatflipflops.com

he intended to produce flip-flops in an Afghan manufacturing plant. To get production started, he secured inexpensive raw materials from China, which were to be shipped to Kabul via Pakistan. But before the order could arrive, the Pakistani government closed its border with Afghanistan in protest of American military actions in the region. Undeterred, Griffin rerouted the shipment through Tajikistan. This adjustment paid off, and soon his venture was up and running.

But then Griffin ran into another setback: The Kabul factory's first 2,000 pairs of flip-flops were so poorly made that Griffin could not sell them in Western markets. He had no choice but to just give them away. To fix the problem, he contracted with a second factory—which unfortunately went out of business before the first sandal even came off the production line. A more effective solution clearly was needed, so Griffin decided to relocate production from Kabul to his home garage in Issaquah, Washington, where he and his friends were able to churn out 3,400 pairs of sandals.

Despite the frustrating setbacks, Griffin has had some important wins. For example, he attempted to attract investment through social media and Kickstarter campaigns, but both drives yielded only modest results. Then he partnered with newly founded VetLaunch, a crowdfunding site set up exclusively for veteran-owned businesses. The effort paid off, with the company pulling in over $17,000 in just six weeks. At around the same time, the decision was made to move sandal production to a factory in Bogota, Colombia, which has worked out very well so far.

Capitalizing on the venture's newfound momentum, Griffin began to turn his attention back to Afghanistan, choosing to work directly with the Department of Defense's Cashmere Task Force to develop the great but largely untapped potential of the cashmere industry there. He also broadened the range of products sold by offering sarongs (to help finance education for women in Afghanistan) and bracelets (to support the removal of dangerous unexploded ammunition in Laos). These changes further enhanced the sense of meaning for the venture.

Griffin has come a long way with his global startup, taking nearly five years to get this far, and his future success is far from assured. This is not the exception for small firms doing business overseas, but the rule. Nonetheless, he remains upbeat about his prospects. "After multiple production runs, stops, and starts, [with] community support and a refusal to accept defeat," he says, "we've turned the corner." So, this may be just the beginning for Combat Flip Flops—and other new ventures that are traveling the same road to global adventure.

Sources: Peter Clark, "Combat Flip Flops Expands Its Catalog through Crowdfunding," *The Issaquah Press*, August 26, 2014, http://www.issaquahpress.com/2014/08/26/combat-flip-flops-expands-its-catalog-through-crowd-funding, accessed January 19, 2015; "Combat Flip Flops: Our Story," http://www.combatflipflops.com, accessed January 19, 2015; "Combat Flip Flops Rock the Cashmagh Campaign," August 18, 2014, http://campaigns.vetlaunchusa.com/campaigns/combat-flip-flops-rock-the-cashmagh, accessed January 19, 2015; and Dion Nissenbaun, "Afghan Business Tale: Don't Try This," *The Wall Street Journal*, October 10, 2013, p. B5.

Our changing world creates extraordinary new opportunities for small businesses, even as it gives rise to emerging challenges, like those Matthew Griffin ran into when he started Combat Flip Flops (see this chapter's Spotlight feature). There was a time when national economies were isolated by trade and investment barriers, differences in language and culture, distinctive business practices, and various government regulations. However, these dissimilarities are fading as market preferences converge, trade barriers fall, and national economies integrate to form a global economic system. This process is central to the trend of **globalization**. Though the drift toward convergence tapered off during the recent economic slowdown, increasing globalization is still the norm, creating many new opportunities and competitors that did not exist even a few years ago. And with the astounding rate of economic growth in countries such as China and India, it would be unwise for a small business owner to ignore these emerging market opportunities—and the new competitors that come with them.

globalization The expansion of international business, encouraged by converging market preferences, falling trade barriers, and the integration of national economies.

As you read in the pages that follow about the challenges of international business and the many decisions that are involved in expanding abroad, you may become convinced that being a global entrepreneur is not for you. This is a normal reaction. But the opportunities are tremendously rewarding, and available resources can help you overcome any obstacles that may stand in your way. Later in this chapter, you will read about the numerous forms of assistance that can help you achieve your global ambitions. As you will see, many small businesses are showing that it can be done. You can do it, too!

18-1 SMALL BUSINESSES AS GLOBAL ENTERPRISES

Describe the potential of small businesses as global enterprises.

The potential of global businesses is clear, but does that potential extend to small companies?[1] Evidence indicates that recent startups and other small businesses continue to expand overseas, despite the recent global economic slowdown.[2]

As illustrated in Exhibit 18.1, most of the firms on *Inc.* magazine's list of the 500 fastest-growing private companies have set up shop in various countries around the world, from Canada to New Zealand. In fact, many small companies, often called **born-global firms**,[3] are being launched with cross-border business activities in mind. "Whatever the reason, 'born global' companies are becoming the new normal," observes Karen Gerwitz, president of World Trade Center Denver. "Companies waiting until they are 'mature' enough to start thinking globally are falling behind."[4]

You are probably familiar with Skype, which was acquired by Microsoft in 2011. In 2003, the company was just a startup, and it was clearly an international business right out of the gate.

> *[Niklas] Zennstrom, who is Swedish, and his partner Janus Friis, a Dane, launched their Internet telephony company Skype in Luxembourg, with sales offices in London. But they outsourced product development to Estonia, the same fertile womb that had earlier gestated their music-sharing system, Kazaa.*[5]

As access to affordable technology increases, talent becomes more mobile, the cost of global travel and communication falls, and trade agreements pry open national markets to foreign competition, entrepreneurs are focusing more and more on international expansion opportunities. In some cases, they may be forced to enter foreign markets in order to compete with firms in their industry that have already done so.[6] But the upshot is clear: Size does not necessarily limit a firm's international activity. Small companies can build upon their unique resources to become global competitors.[7]

born-global firms
Small companies launched with cross-border business activities in mind.

The global option is practically unavoidable in some cases. For example, when Howard Pedolsky began to market his innovative, eco-friendly refrigeration technology, he found that European supermarkets were far more interested in it than were their

EXHIBIT **18.1** Where in the World Are Entrepreneurial Companies Doing Business?

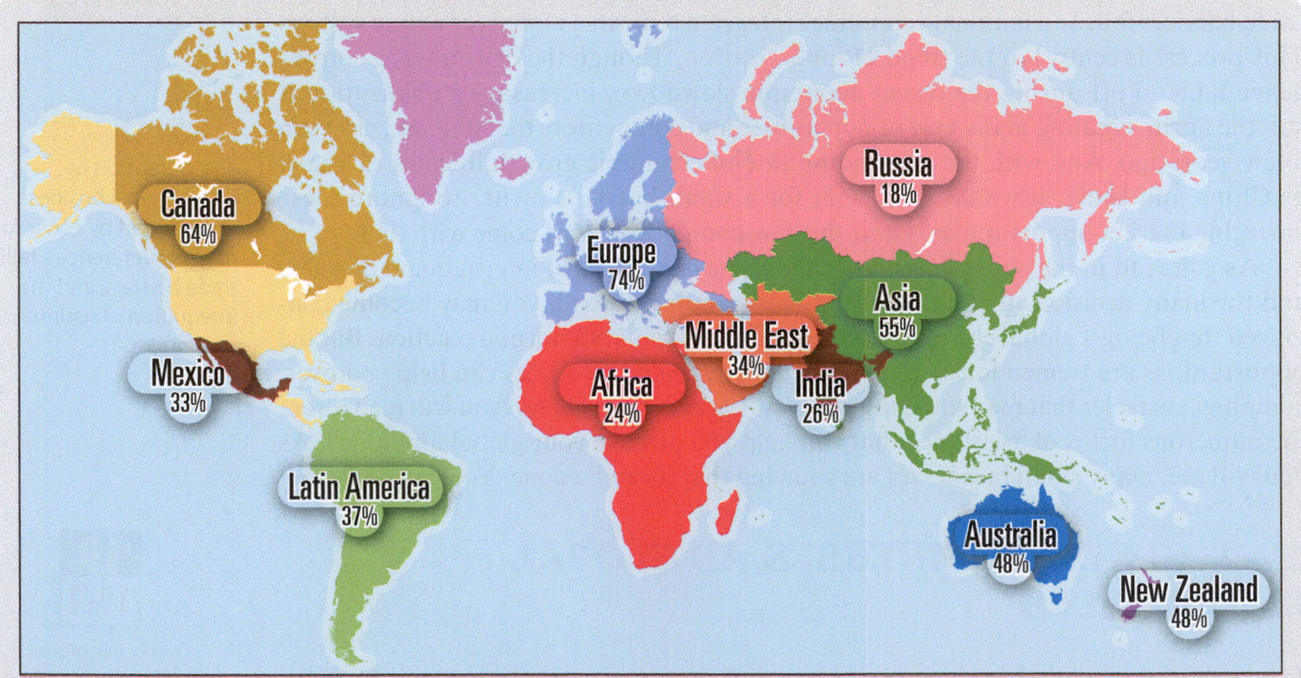

Source: Based on Issie Lapowsky, "Planting the Flag," http://www.inc.com/magazine/201109/inc-500-global-map.html, accessed January 14, 2015.

American counterparts. It turned out that their attraction was the result of strict European standards, so Pedolsky realized that he would need to focus on developing a customer base in Europe first: "The European environment was just much stronger in our direction, and [supermarkets there] tend to spend more money on our products."[8]

The fact that many firms are going global does not mean that it is easy. The challenges that small businesses face in the international marketplace are considerable. First, a small business owner must decide whether the company is up to the task. To help entrepreneurs assess the impact of going global on their small businesses, the U.S. Department of Commerce publishes *A Basic Guide to Exporting*. This handbook outlines important questions entrepreneurs should consider when assessing their readiness for the challenges of global business (see Exhibit 18.2).

Once small business owners decide to expand internationally, they should study the social, technological, economic, and political forces in foreign markets to figure out how best to adapt their business practices, as well as their product or service, to local circumstances, and make other adjustments that are necessary to ensure smooth market entry. For example, doing business in the Middle East can require significant changes in what many small business owners would consider to be "standard business procedures."

> *In Saudi Arabia, the workweek begins on Saturday and ends on Wednesday, appointments are generally scheduled around five daily prayer times, and many businesses are closed in the afternoon. Most real business is conducted face to face, with far less reliance on documents and contracts than is typical in the Western world; therefore, the time it takes to do business is relative.*[9]

And that's just the beginning! When you consider that collecting or paying interest is forbidden in many Islamic countries—along with a host of other fundamental differences—it becomes clear that navigating the unique hurdles of an international market like that of Saudi Arabia can be a serious challenge.

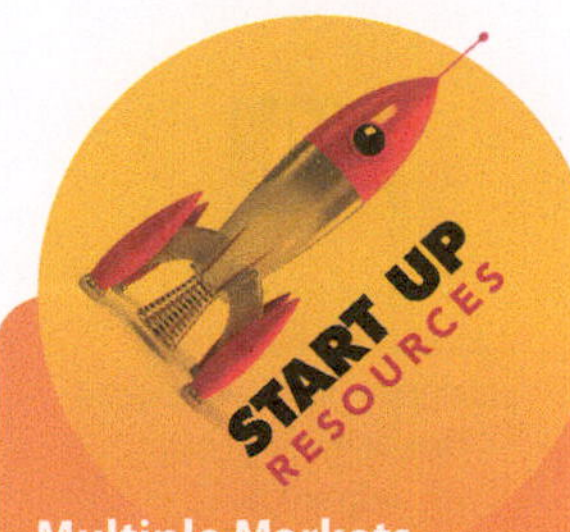

Multiple Markets

To be sure that you understand the often-complicated forms, trade laws, and payment issues that are involved in going global, consult the SBA's U.S. Export Assistance Centers (www.sba.gov/content/us-exports-assistance-centers). It would also be wise to check out websites such as BuyUSA.gov and USTDA.gov, which are shaping their assistance to better meet the needs of small businesses as they search for customers and suppliers and generally expand abroad.

EXHIBIT

18.2 Questions To Consider Before Going Global

Management Objectives	• What are the company's reasons for going global? • How committed is top management to going global? • How quickly does management expect its international operations to pay off?
Management Experience and Resources	• What in-house international expertise does the firm have (international sales experience, language skills, etc.)? • Who will be responsible for the company's international operations? • How much senior management time should be allocated to the company's global efforts? • What organizational structure is required to ensure success abroad?
Production Capacity	• How is the present capacity being used? • How much additional production capacity will be needed at home and abroad? • What product designs and packaging options are required for international markets?
Financial Capacity	• How much capital can be committed to international production and marketing? • Will the company be able to cover the initial expenses of going global (e.g., the costs of finding customers abroad, expanding production to support international sales)? • What other financial demands might compete with plans to internationalize? • By what date must the global effort pay for itself?

Source: Adapted from International Trade Administration, *A Basic Guide to Exporting: The Official Government Resource for Small- and Medium-Sized Businesses*, as cited in John B. Cullen and K. Praveen Parboteeah, *Multinational Management: A Strategic Approach*, 7th ed. (Cincinnati, OH: Cengage Learning, 2017), Exhibit 7.4.

Identify the basic forces prompting small companies to engage in global expansion.

18-2 THE FORCES DRIVING GLOBAL BUSINESSES

Given the difficulty of international business, why would any entrepreneur want to go global? Among the reasons are some that have motivated international trade for centuries. In 1271, Marco Polo traveled to China to explore the trading of Western goods for exotic Oriental silks and spices, which would then be sold in Europe. Clearly, the motivation to take domestic products to foreign markets and to bring foreign products to domestic markets is as relevant today as it was in Marco Polo's day. Consider, for example, the clothing designer who sells Western wear in Tokyo or the independent rug dealer who scours the markets of Turkey to locate low-cost sources of high-quality products.

Complementing these age-old reasons for going global are motivations that epitomize the core of entrepreneurial drive. A writer for *Inc.* magazine describes the impulse to go global as follows:

> *Because it's what entrepreneurs do. . . . Globalization is risky. Entrepreneurs embrace risk. Therefore entrepreneurs embrace globalization. . . . [T]he chance to try new things in new places is like a jumper cable to the entrepreneurial engine.*[10]

In other words, many entrepreneurs are looking to do more than simply expand a profitable market. They recognize that their enterprises are no longer insulated from global challengers and that they must consider the dynamics of the new competitive environment.[11]

© POGONICI/SHUTTERSTOCK.COM

One way to adjust to these emerging realities is through innovation, which is essential to competitiveness in many industries. Small businesses that invest heavily in research and development often can outperform their large competitors. But as R&D costs rise, they often cannot be recouped from domestic sales alone. Increasing sales in international markets may be the only viable way to recover a firm's investment. In some cases, this may require identifying dynamic markets that are beginning to open around the world and then locating in or near those markets.[12]

As you can see, the motives for global expansion vary. But these basic forces can be divided into four general categories: expanding markets, gaining access to resources, cutting costs, and capitalizing on special features of location. Within each category fall some tried and true motivations, as well as some newer angles that have emerged in more recent years.

18-2a Expanding Markets

More than 95 percent of the world's population lives outside the United States, so it follows that globalization greatly increases the size of an American firm's potential market. One study of small companies found that their primary interest in globalization was in reaching new markets and growing their business, as opposed to seeking resources abroad, gaining access to technologies, and avoiding regulatory pressures at home.[13] But this research focused on U.S. firms expanding into Europe; the primary motivation for involvement in other parts of the world may be different. For example, many American small companies doing business in Asia are also seeking new markets, even as they are looking to access low-cost component sources or to relocate business processes via outsourcing.

COUNTRIES TARGETED

Because the primary motivation for going global is to develop market opportunities outside the home country, the focus of globalization strategies tends to be on countries with the greatest commercial potential. In the past, these were developed countries, with high levels of widely distributed wealth. In more recent years, companies have been paying greater attention to emerging markets, where income and buying power have been growing more rapidly.

The term *BRIC*s is often used to refer to the fast-growing economies of *B*razil, *R*ussia, *I*ndia, and *C*hina. These markets have definitely captured the attention of many entrepreneurs. And that interest seems to be growing, as mainstay markets like Europe, Japan, and the United States continue to struggle with economic stagnation while China and India, in particular, have mounted more impressive recoveries (see Exhibit 18.3). The smaller BRIC countries, Russia and Brazil, have also been doing well in recent years (despite economic downturns in each starting in 2014), but they have not enjoyed the same level of growth and vigor as China and India.

Because of their immense populations and potential market demand, China and India have become the focus of many international firms. Combined, these two nations account for an astounding 40 percent of the world's 7 billion inhabitants, thus providing fertile ground for international expansion. Small firms are among the countless competitors battling for position in these emerging markets as they attempt to sell to their new, fast-growing "consuming class."

PRODUCTS PROMOTED

International business authority Raymond Vernon observed in the mid-1960s that firms tended to introduce new products in the United States first and then sell them in less-advanced countries later, as demand in the home market declined.[14] In other words, they were using international expansion to extend a product's life cycle. Although this approach is effective under some circumstances, it has become less viable as customer preferences, income levels, and delivery systems have become more similar and product life cycles have contracted. Furthermore, consumers in the developing world have

EXHIBIT **18.3** Bric Markets

Country	2013 Population (in millions)	2013 Wealth (GNI per capita)*	2013 Economic Growth (GDP growth, %)**
Brazil	200	11,690	2.5
China	1,357	6,560	7.7
India	1,252	1,570	5.0
Russia	143	13,850	1.3
World	**7,125**	**10,679**	**2.2**

* GNI = Gross National Income (Atlas Method, Current U.S. Dollars)
** GDP = Gross Domestic Product

Source: From data provided by the World Bank, "World DataBank," http://databank.worldbank.org, accessed January 16, 2015.

become more sophisticated in their tastes and expectations and are no longer the "late adopters" that they were in years past.

Today, products that sell at home are more likely to be introduced very quickly abroad, with little or no adaptation in many cases. Television programs, movies, print media, and the Internet are shaping cultural tastes throughout the world, and this is facilitating the entry of small businesses into international markets. American interests have long held a starring role in the cultural arena, inspiring widespread purchases of products such as jeans and fast food, and generating international fascination with U.S. sports and celebrities. By informing consumers about the lifestyles of others, globalization is creating more common consumer preferences.

Highly specialized products can also do well in international markets. As technology makes possible increasingly advanced goods, markets are demanding more differentiated products to satisfy their unique needs and interests. This increases the cost of doing business; however, expanded sales allow the makers of such products to recover the higher costs of product development. Many small companies follow focused business strategies, despite limited domestic market potential. For them, exploiting the advantage of specialized products across several international markets may be even more important than for their large corporate counterparts.[15]

MAKING THE MOST OF EXPERIENCE

No matter which countries are targeted or products promoted, international expansion has the potential to provide benefits beyond the standard per-unit profits on additional items sold. As a venture expands and volume grows, it usually can find ways to work smarter or generate efficiencies. Analysts first observed such **experience curve efficiencies** in the aircraft manufacturing industry. They noticed that each time a manufacturer doubled its total output, the production cost per aircraft dropped by 20 percent. In other words, per-unit costs declined by 20 percent when the firm manufactured four units instead of two, declined by another 20 percent when the firm made eight units instead of four, and so on.

What can explain this gain in efficiency? Most credit the outcome to learning effects and economies of scale. **Learning effects** occur when the insight an employee gains from experience leads to improved work performance. Learning effects can also take place at the level of the firm if the experiences of individual employees are shared, leading to improved practices and production routines across the organization. These gains from learning are greatest during the startup period and gradually decline over time. Efficiencies from **economies of scale**, on the other hand, continue to rise as the business grows and volume increases, because these savings derive from spreading investment costs across more units of output and acquiring more specialized (and thus more efficient) plants, equipment, and employee skills.

Though experience curve efficiencies also apply to purely domestic enterprises, small firms can accelerate gains from them by emphasizing international expansion, assuming they can manage the growth. The benefits of learning effects and economies of scale are especially apparent in startups based on complex technologies. The possibility of achieving experience curve efficiencies through accelerated globalization of emerging technologies is likely to stimulate the interest of startups and small companies in doing business abroad.

experience curve efficiencies
Per-unit savings gained from the repeated production of the same product.

learning effects
Insights, gained from experience, that lead to improved work performance.

economies of scale
Efficiencies from expanded production that result from spreading fixed costs over more units of output.

18-2b Gaining Access to Resources

Small firms today may leave the United States to gain access to essential raw materials and other factors of production. For example, the oil fields of Kuwait are tended not only by employees of global oil giants but also by hundreds of support personnel who work for small companies that have contracted to assist their large clients. These small players choose to locate operations in Kuwait (or Mexico, Nigeria, Saudi Arabia, etc.) for one simple reason: That's where the oil is! The same principle holds for manufacturers that require scarce inputs. For example, because aluminum processing requires so much energy, a number of these producers have relocated to Iceland to tap the country's abundant and inexpensive hydroelectric and geothermal power.[16]

Though small firms have traditionally pursued international ventures to obtain raw materials, increasingly the focus of their search is skilled labor.[17] For example, a rising number of technology companies are relocating their operations in Russia to get access to the people they need. Despite the fact that the installation of a telephone can take months and crime bosses sometimes pay visits to demand protection money, these firms are lured to Russia by its highly educated human capital, a necessary resource that is in short supply in the United States. Of the 43 percent of Russians with university degrees, about a third are trained in science- or technology-related disciplines and thus are very well suited for highly skilled jobs.[18] As something of a bonus for small firms, computer programmers and information technology professionals in Russia earn less than 25 percent of what their American counterparts make.[19]

There is no question that skilled labor around the world is within the reach of startups and other very small businesses. Consider Efrem Meretab, an Eritrean-born stock analyst who started his own investment research venture to offer PowerConnect. This investment research tool mines and compares information from thousands of company reports, pulling it instantly into an analysis that can inform and guide investment decisions.[20] His Montclair, New Jersey-based company, MCAP Research LLC, has been able to harness the power of the Internet to find and hire employees around the globe. For example, when Meretab needed software developers to create PowerConnect, he reconnected with programmers with whom he had worked in the past, including talented coders living in far-off countries like Belarus, Ukraine, and Pakistan. These contract workers were able to get the job done, and at a very reasonable cost.[21] Of course, small businesses that take this approach don't create many jobs in the United States, but they are still important new enterprises—and they are becoming more common as time goes on.

18-2c Cutting Costs

Many firms go global to reduce the costs of doing business. Among the costs that firms have traditionally reduced by venturing abroad are those related to raw materials, labor, and manufacturing overhead.

While some startups are launching as global enterprises, other small businesses are shifting their operations over time to international markets in order to exploit the same advantages. In fact, American businesses of all sizes have been slashing costs by contracting with independent providers overseas (an arrangement called **international outsourcing**) or by relocating their stateside operations abroad (which is sometimes referred to as **offshoring**). These initiatives have been especially popular in countries such as India and China, where highly skilled labor can be accessed at relatively little cost.

For a long time, hardware-based startups have had difficulty getting market traction, but that is definitely changing as opportunities to shift operations overseas have greatly reduced the cost of bringing products to market, which is enormously important to cash-strapped new ventures. As some have observed, the new business plan is to "raise enough money to create prototypes in the U.S. that can be manufactured in Asia and sold online."[22]

international outsourcing
A strategy that involves accessing foreign business operations through contracts with independent providers.

offshoring
A strategy that involves relocating operations abroad.

Living the Dream

ENTREPRENEURIAL EXPERIENCES

Making the Most of Chinese Partnerships

In today's global economy, locating production overseas can provide an enormous competitive edge. American firms that manufacture their products in China, for instance, can often charge consumers as much as 30 to 50 percent less than those using domestic plants. Even though costs have been rising there, producers from all over the world continue to flock to China to cash in on the potential savings.

But setting up shop in China can definitely present its share of challenges. According to Mike Bellamy, founder of PassageMaker Sourcing Solutions, there are a number of measures a business should take in order to ensure a successful relocation approach. Bellamy understands the issues that buyers face in China better than most. "I was fed up with middlemen and poorly run factories distorting pricing, failing to control quality, and allowing intellectual property (IP) to be knocked off, so I decided to do something about it," he says. He founded his company to show others how to address these problems, and today the firm generates over $20 million in revenue a year doing exactly that.

Bellamy contends that researching manufacturers and requesting references can help protect intellectual property. Producers should also look to secure Chinese patents for items they plan to manufacture and sell. American patents cannot be enforced in China, but Chinese-issued patents can and frequently are upheld. And perhaps just as important, 70 percent of all patent lawsuits go to trial in China, compared to only 10 percent in the United States. While a mere 5 percent of these cases involve foreigners, Chinese legal procedures frequently favor the plaintiff, and defendants typically pay about $160,000 in damages. These costs can easily ruin a new business.

Another critically important issue, quality control, requires extra diligence and deliberate management. Bellamy recommends making contracts extremely detailed to provide recourse should a shipment fail to meet expectations. In many cases, placing a company representative at a manufacturing plant in order to take partial ownership of the production process may be the best way to ensure that quality standards are met.

© ROMAN SIGAEV/SHUTTERSTOCK.COM

Recognizing, understanding, and adjusting to the great cultural differences in China can be challenging, but it is key to business success there. For example, Americans tend to bypass pleasantries during meetings and focus on hashing out agreements, whereas their Chinese counterparts generally prefer to build a personal connection over time before committing to a joint venture or business partnership. Bellamy reports that these communication issues often create serious problems: "So many foreign buyers have told me they just don't trust the Chinese anymore . . . but it often turns out that the buyer and seller were not on the same page from day one." He goes on to say that when the business relationship is developed with care and patience, most Chinese suppliers are a pleasure to work with. In the final analysis, outsourcing can be an excellent alternative for a small company—as long as the business relationship is managed wisely.

Sources: Saaira Chaudhuri, "Outsourcing to China? Here Are the Best Ways to Protect Yourself," *The Wall Street Journal*, August 18, 2013, pp. R3; Michael Evans and Jack Toolan, "Manufacturing in China Can Give Your Business the Competitive Advantage," *Forbes*, February 7, 2014, http://www.forbes.com/sites/allbusiness/2014/02/07/manufacturing-in-china-can-give-your-business-the-competitive-advantage, accessed January 23, 2015; Chris Neumeyer, "China's Great Leap Forward in Patents," *IPWatchdog*, April 4, 2014, http://www.ipwatchdog.com/2013/04/04/chinas-great-leap-forward-in-patents/id=38625, accessed January 23, 2015; and "What Is PassageMaker?" http://www.psschina.com/about/ourhistory/home, accessed February 6, 2015.

Abe and Lisa Fetterman are the inventors of a new cooking appliance for amateur chefs. Called Nomiku, it is an inversion circulator that can be used to cook *sous-vide*—that is, to cook meats and vegetables in sealed bags by submerging them in a water bath that is raised to a precisely controlled temperature.[23] Gadget critics say the new product promises to deliver "perfectly cooked meals, every time, with less fuss than you would expect."[24]

"We've thrown everything to the wind to commit to this," says Lisa,[25] and the effort is paying off. However, there have been complications. For example, development and manufacturing of the first model of the product were located in Shenzhen, China, to hold costs down. But while the couple still outsources component production for the new WiFi-enabled version of the Nomiku, they decided to locate both the prototyping process and the final product assembly in the San Francisco area. "China is great if you have your design down pat," says Lisa, but companies "can iterate much faster [in the U.S.]." In other words, outsourcing mass production may work well in China, but it doesn't suit small runs of more customized products—like the final assembly of their product. And since China's manufacturing costs gap with the United States has narrowed considerably (as wages in China have doubled since 2008), locating production at home is becoming a more realistic option for more American ventures.[26]

Nomiku may not be an ordinary startup, but in many ways it fits the common outsourcing pattern. Most entrepreneurs who choose to outsource internationally, or relocate offshore, are seeking two things that are so often important to the success of small companies: access to employee talent and/or reduced costs. For some of its operations, at least, Nomiku is going abroad to tap into both.

The advantages of globalization in reducing labor costs have long been recognized. However, countries have been forming regional free-trade areas in which commerce has been facilitated by reducing tariffs, simplifying commercial regulations, or even—in the case of the European Union—adopting a common currency. These cost-cutting measures can be a powerful inducement to small firms to move into the prescribed area. Since the enactment of the North American Free Trade Agreement (NAFTA), for instance, many foreign firms have chosen to locate production facilities in Mexico to take advantage of reduced tariffs on trade within that region and easy access to the American market.

18-2d Capitalizing on Special Features of Location

Some of the benefits of location are simply the result of unique features of a local environment. For example, Italian artisans have long been well known for their flair for design, and Japanese technicians have shown an extraordinary ability to harness optical technologies for application in cameras, copiers, and other related products. Small companies that depend on a particular strength or resource often find that it makes sense to set up in a region that provides the best location for that type of business. This explains why one Korean-American entrepreneur opened his chopstick-making company in Americus, Georgia, where abundant supplies of wood allowed him to shave 20 percent off his costs when compared to production in China.[27]

In some cases, there is no way to be authentic apart from being local. Colin Flahive, who grew up in Denver, Colorado, and three of his friends found that the Western food in China was absolutely dreadful, but locals were still eating it up. So, in 2004, with $30,000 in investment money, they started Salvador's Food and Beverage Co., Ltd. In a coffeehouse in Kunming (a city of more than 6 million people), they now offer Western products—including ice cream, bagels and cream cheese, and Mexican food—to local customers.[28]

The way forward has not always been easy, and the team has had much to learn. Early on, they ran into a bureaucratic brick wall, which required the outsiders to turn to a common practice in China—building their *guanxi*, or personal connections—to get the government approvals they needed.[29] But the effort has paid off. Though still young, the enterprise has been wonderfully successful, which allows it to support some grass-roots initiatives that are very important to the community, including Green Kunming, an organic grocery market, and Village Progress, a nonprofit that organizes art and health-education programs for rural villagers. Flahive takes great pleasure in helping others, but he also believes his humanitarian efforts are win-win contributions, because they benefit the communities that are served even as they promote his business.[30]

© ISTOCKPHOTO.COM/AIMSTOCK

Small companies are sometimes pulled toward doing business abroad because of the unique advantages that are available in international locations

Sometimes, the appeal of a location is a matter of cache or brand image. For example, while Chanel might like to manufacture its designer handbags in Asia to reduce costs, the company insists on producing them in Italy and France. These are both high-cost countries, but they have reputations that match Chanel's luxury image. These nations also have developed unique competencies, honed by hundreds of years of experience, that can accommodate the advanced designs and high quality that give the company its edge. Customers know that the high quality of the brand is scrupulously protected and thus are willing to pay a premium to buy Chanel's products, which covers the high manufacturing costs. But this is just one example. Other country settings provide their own location-specific strengths—including Colombia (high-quality coffee), Japan (anime-based video games), and Switzerland (precision watches)—and firms locate there to tap into those strengths.

Finally, some small businesses are following large client firms to their new locations. As major corporations locate their operations abroad, their small suppliers find it necessary to go global with the client firms to ensure the continuation of important sourcing contracts. A small business owner may have no personal desire to expand internationally, but dependence on a major customer relocating abroad might leave the owner with no alternative. For example, some small companies moving into China are doing so with limited interest in the country's cheap labor and enormous market. But being there is necessary in order to feed the supply chains of corporate customers with ample delivery speed and efficiency.

The motivations for small businesses to go global are numerous, but the ultimate incentive is this: If you fail to seize an international market opportunity, someone else will. Under these conditions, the best defense is a good offense. Establishing a position outside of the domestic setting may preempt rivals from exploiting those opportunities and using them against you in the future.

18-3 STRATEGY OPTIONS FOR GLOBAL FIRMS

Understand and compare strategy options for global businesses.

Once an entrepreneur has decided to go global, the next step is to plan a strategy that increases the potential of the firm. For most small businesses, the first step toward globalization is a decision to export a product to other countries or to import goods from abroad to sell in the market at home. These initial efforts are often followed by more sophisticated nonexport strategies, such as licensing, franchising, forming strategic alliances with international partners, or even locating facilities abroad.

18-3a Exporting

Exporting involves the sale of products produced in the home country to customers in another country. The U.S. Small Business Administration (SBA) recently announced that small firms represent more than 98 percent of American exporters, contributing 33 percent of the value of exported goods.[31] In some cases, this activity is a reflection of the reality of international competition. That is, some U.S. companies are steadily moving toward overseas markets because they recognize that foreign-owned companies are already competing against them in the United States. The SBA describes conditions in today's global marketplace as follows:

> *The division between domestic and international markets is becoming increasingly blurred. In a world of . . . global communication networks, next-day airfreight deliveries worldwide and CNN, it no longer makes sense to limit your company's sales to the local or even to the national market. Your business cannot ignore these international realities if you intend to maintain your market share and keep pace with your competitors.*[32]

exporting
Selling products produced in the home country to customers in another country.

As the SBA statistics reveal, entrepreneurs are taking note and accepting the challenge. In fact, exporting is one of the most popular international strategies among small businesses because it provides a low-cost way to expand into the international arena. Taking this approach, small export companies can market and distribute their products in other countries without incurring the expense of supporting costly operations in those markets. If the financial benefits from international sales more than offset shipping costs and tariffs, exporting is a favorable option.

The Internet has fueled vigorous growth in export activity. Small firms now see the Web as a powerful tool for increasing their international visibility, allowing them to connect with customers who were previously beyond their reach. Entertainment Earth is an online retailer, started in 1995, that specializes in action figures, gifts, and other collectibles. It wasn't long before the founders decided to expand their reach by selling over the Internet, and the move has really paid off. Over the years, Entertainment Earth has sold collectibles to millions of clients all around the world.[33]

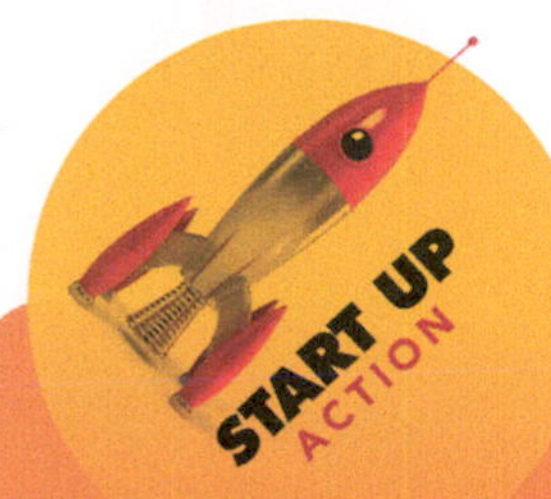

A First Step for Small Online Businesses

If you want to sell globally through your online business but aren't ready to take on the complexity of adapting your website to multiple foreign markets, consider starting with a Spanish-language version. This would increase your business's potential in Spanish-speaking countries and would certainly help in reaching the 35.5 million Americans who speak both English and Spanish. And don't forget that there are also 2.1 million Spanish speakers in the United States who aren't fluent in English and could potentially do business with you, but only if your website can speak to them.

Source: "The Stat: 2.1 Million," *Entrepreneur*, Vol. 41, No. 11, 2013, p. 60.

But you don't have to go it alone. Just ask Charlene Anderson, the Jackson Hole, Wyoming-based jewelry and textile artist and owner of e-commerce sales company Purveyor of All Things Creative.[34] Although Anderson's company is just a small operation, the world is her sales floor. How did she manage to go global? It's simple: eBay and Amazon. These e-commerce giants can help even the tiniest of businesses connect with customers anywhere in the world, and getting started takes about as much time as it would to apply for a passport!

"My international sales went big very quickly because so many people don't do it," Anderson reports. "They are uncomfortable selling internationally and think it's too much of a hassle, which is totally wrong!"[35] Not exactly convinced? Then you might be surprised to learn that 40 percent of the company's sales through eBay are international. But Anderson does even more global business on Amazon. "If you are already selling through [Fulfillment by Amazon], you'd be crazy not to sell internationally," insists the online entrepreneur. "You check one box, upload an image of your signature for customs forms, and you are selling internationally. . . . It's ridiculously easy!"[36] To learn more about how to get started selling to the world, check out eBay's "Selling Internationally" tutorial at http://pages.ebay.com/help/sell/intl-ov.html or visit the Amazon Global Selling website at http://services.amazon.com/global-selling.

Of course, exporting can be very challenging. Suddenly, you have to worry about communicating in a language other than English, translating payments into other

To Export or Not to Export?
Still not sure that your small business should be exporting? Watch the video at www.inc.com/exporting, and let small business owners and government experts help you see the global light.

currencies, and setting up international shipping. Products may have to be modified to meet government standards or the unique interests of buyers abroad, poor government connections may very well put your company at a great disadvantage in negotiations, and unfavorable exchange rates can make it difficult or even impossible to offer products at competitive prices and still make a profit. In some countries, the government may not allow a company to enter its market unless it is willing to reveal the specifics of its core technologies, which are often the bedrock of its competitive advantage.

Nonetheless, export success is clearly within the reach of small companies. Many measures adopted by the U.S. government have prompted observers to predict that small and medium-size businesses will account disproportionately for export growth in the years to come. Indeed, the number of these firms that export has increased more than two-and-a-half-fold since 1992, reaching 300,000 today, which shows that many small companies are having considerable success selling their products and services abroad.[37] To fuel the fire of growth, the U.S. government launched an online portal to information and services called BusinessUSA, in order to help boost the competitiveness of American companies in the global economy (see http://business.usa.gov/export). One important feature of this resource is a set of links that can help small businesses find the assistance they need to begin exporting or to expand an existing program.

Small firms that have excelled at exporting typically have had to do their homework in figuring out what products would sell in targeted markets—for example, what products local companies could not yet make for themselves. Then, they got close to the market and developed personal connections with influential decision makers, getting assistance wherever they could find it. A good place to start in your search for customers abroad is the U.S. Department of Commerce's Trade Information Center website (export.gov). Or, get in touch with the foreign embassy community (embassy.org), select a country where you want to do business, and e-mail or call the country specialist for assistance. You may be surprised at the leads this can generate. Finally, check with officials from your state to see if they provide assistance. In many cases, an Internet search on "[insert name of your state here] foreign trade office" will lead you where you need to go.

18-3b Importing

The flip side of exporting is **importing**, which involves selling products from abroad in the firm's home market. When a small company finds a product overseas that has market potential at home or identifies a product that would sell at home but cannot find a suitable domestic producer, an import strategy may be the best solution.

Connecting with vendors at international trade shows can also open the door to opportunity. Using imported products found at such shows, Holly Pennington sells fashion accessories through her 12 Compass Trading Company stores. Because of the depth of its merchandise, the company can accommodate both classic styles that create a professional look and cutting-edge designs featured in trendy fashion magazines, along with many styles in between. Best of all, its products sell for a fraction of the prices charged for similar goods at high-end retailers. And customers like what they are getting, which is why this small company has been growing so quickly.[38]

Regardless of the import strategy used, one of the most important factors for success is finding a good product vendor. This sounds easy enough to do, especially in this era of Internet-enabled matching services, online communication tools, and flexible and affordable travel. Though websites like Alibaba.com, MadeInChina.com, and GlobalSources.com seem to bring the goods you need right to your doorstep, finding and managing international suppliers for long-term relationships can be

importing
Selling products produced in another country to buyers in the home country.

challenging. But some are not sold on the idea. "I don't care if it's China or Timbuktu," says one entrepreneur with vast experience in setting up international sourcing for small businesses. "The Internet does not suffice."[39] In other words, it often takes an in-person visit to a prospective sourcing partner to know if it can meet the selection, quality, and quantity standards that can support your business.

© CHARLIE EDWARD/SHUTTERSTOCK.COM

Importing is not an easy option. However, it holds tremendous potential, especially if you follow a few simple guidelines:

- Learn as much as you can about the culture and business practices of the country from which you will be sourcing to avoid making deal-breaking mistakes.
- Do your research, and be sure to select a source that is not a competitor or a company that hopes to learn from your operations in order to compete against you in the future.
- Protect your intellectual property so that your suppliers cannot easily take it from you. Some entrepreneurs require their sourcing partners to sign nondisclosure agreements so that they cannot patent the item in the country where the sourcing takes place.
- Don't rush the process of forming a relationship with a sourcing partner. You need time to ask difficult questions about important factors such as quality standards and capabilities, manufacturing flexibility, and time to order fulfillment.
- Work out transportation logistics ahead of time. A good freight forwarder can assist you with the mechanics of shipping, as well as help you with the confusing jumble of required documents. To get a sense of the process, review the rules and regulations on the U.S. Customs and Border Protection website at cbp.gov, and read the SBA's notes on importing by searching on that term at sba.gov.

At times, the process may seem so complicated that you may wonder if small companies should even be attempting to source from abroad. But it can be done, and with great benefit to your business.

18-3c Foreign Licensing

Importing and exporting are the most popular international strategies among small firms, but there are also other options. Because of limited resources, many small firms are hesitant to go global. One way to deal with this constraint is to follow a licensing strategy. **Foreign licensing** allows a company in another country to purchase the rights to manufacture and sell a firm's products in overseas markets. The firm buying these rights is called the **licensee**. The licensee makes payments to the **licensor**, or the firm selling those rights, normally in the form of **royalties**, which is a fee paid for each unit produced.

International licensing has its drawbacks. The foreign licensee makes all the production and marketing decisions, and the licensor must share returns from international sales with the licensee. However, foreign licensing is the least expensive way to go global, since the licensee bears all the costs and risks related to setting up a foreign operation.

Small companies tend to think of tangible products when they explore international licensing options, but licensing intangible assets such as proprietary technologies,

foreign licensing
A strategy that allows a company in another country to purchase the rights to manufacture and sell a company's products in international markets.

licensee
The company buying licensing rights.

licensor
The company selling licensing rights.

royalties
Fees paid by the licensee to the licensor for each unit produced under a licensing contract.

copyrights, and trademarks may offer even greater returns. Just as Disney licenses its famous Mickey Mouse character to manufacturers around the world, for example, a small branded apparel retailer called Peace Frogs used licensing when it introduced its copyrighted designs in Spain. As Peace Frogs' founder, Catesby Jones, has explained, the company exported its T-shirts directly into larger markets like Japan, but that strategy didn't make as much sense in some countries. For example, Spain's lower per capita income, stronger domestic competition, and high tariffs made licensing a more attractive option there. So Peace Frogs licensed the rights to manufacture its product to a Barcelona-based apparel maker.[40] From that agreement, Peace Frogs was able to generate additional revenue, but with almost no added expense.

Foreign licensing can also be used to protect against **counterfeit activity**, or the unauthorized use of a company's intellectual property or manufacture of its products. If a firm in a foreign market is granted licensing rights, it can become a powerful local champion to help ensure that other firms do not use protected assets in an inappropriate way.

18-3d International Franchising

International franchising is a variation on the licensing theme. As outlined in Chapter 4, the franchisor offers a standard package of products, systems, and management services to the franchisee, which provides capital, market insight, and hands-on management. Although international franchising was not widely used before the 1970s, today it is the fastest-growing market-entry strategy of U.S. firms, with Canada as the dominant market, followed by Japan and the United Kingdom. This approach is especially popular with U.S. restaurant chains that want to establish a global presence. McDonald's, for example, has raised its famous golden arches in more than 100 countries around the world.[41] But small companies are being pulled toward international franchising as well, especially in countries where credit is readily available, financing barriers are weak, and demand for American goods and services is strong.[42]

Danny Bensusan is the owner of Blue Note, a premier jazz club in Manhattan that opened its doors in 1981. Considered one of the top venues in the world for jazz and other forms of music, this club attracted the attention of international businesspeople who have opened two franchises in Japan and one in Italy. As a result, the club has successfully established itself as the world's only franchised jazz club network.[43] Blue Note has proved that there is more than one way for a small business to globalize.

counterfeit activity
The unauthorized use of a company's intellectual property or manufacture of its products.

international franchising
A strategy to sell a standard package of products, systems, and management services to a company in another country.

international strategic alliance
An organizational relationship that allows companies in different countries to pool resources and share risks as they enter new markets.

18-3e International Strategic Alliances

Moving beyond licensing and franchising, some small businesses have expanded globally by joining forces with large corporations in cooperative efforts. An **international strategic alliance** allows firms to share risks and pool resources as they enter a new market, usually matching the local partner's understanding of the target market (culture, legal system, competitive conditions, etc.) or its access to low-cost labor with the technology or product knowledge of its alliance counterpart. One of the advantages of this strategy is that both partners take comfort in knowing that neither of them is "going it alone."

Strategic alliances can be used in many different ways by small companies to gain advantage internationally. At one time, Behlen Manufacturing Company, a maker of agricultural grain bins, drying systems, and metal-frame buildings, exported products to China. But then-CEO Tony Raimondo suspended shipments when he found out that Chinese copycats were making the same products, using local advantages such as cheaper labor to undercut Behlen on cost and sell at much lower prices. For a time, it looked as if the company would no longer be able to tap into this huge market. But then Raimondo hit on the idea of forming Behlen China, a 50/50 joint venture (a form of alliance in which two companies share equal ownership in a separate business) in Beijing. "In order for us to sustain market share," says Raimondo, "we had to be on the inside."[44] Making product within China made it possible for Behlen to capitalize on the same advantages that Chinese factories had, and that has made all the difference. Behlen's success in China has spread to other international business initiatives, and the company still does a substantial share of its business overseas.[45]

Global Manufacturing Hotspots

You may have decided that it would save money to produce your products in China. Some experienced entrepreneurs are suggesting that you should think about going to Mexico instead. Find out why by reading Chris Anderson, "Mexico: The New China," *The New York Times*, January 27, 2013, p. SR7.

18-3f Locating Facilities Abroad

A small business may choose to establish a foreign presence of its own in strategic markets, especially if the firm has already developed an international customer base. Most small companies start by locating a production facility or sales office overseas, often as a way to reduce the cost of operations. Amanda Knauer concluded that launching a new venture in the United States was too expensive, so she set her sights on Argentina. After doing some research, she went to Buenos Aires. A few months later, she was running her own business, Qara Argentina, a luxury leather goods manufacturer. But it wasn't easy. Knauer has had to learn the local Spanish dialect, negotiate a complicated and very different legal landscape, and master a new set of business practices. But the work paid off, allowing her to establish her company in Buenos Aires, a city that is so interesting and beautiful that it is often called "the Paris of South America."[46]

Opening an overseas sales office can be a very effective strategy, but most small business owners should wait until sales in the local market are great enough to justify the move. An overseas office is costly to establish, staff, manage, and finance, so anticipated advantages are sometimes difficult to achieve. However, U.S. firms often locate their first international sales office in Canada, though European expansion is also common, with the English-speaking United Kingdom and Ireland being very popular locations. Still others have selected Asia, because of its economic dynamism and fast-growing consumer demand.

Some small firms have grander ambitions and may purchase a foreign business from another firm through what is known as a **cross-border acquisition**. Some may even start a **greenfield venture**, by forming from scratch a new wholly owned subsidiary in another country. Unfortunately, either option is likely to be fraught with difficulties.

cross-border acquisition
The purchase by a business in one country of a company located in another country.

greenfield venture
A wholly owned subsidiary formed from scratch in another country.

Go-it-alone strategies are complex and costly. They offer maximum control over foreign operations and eliminate the need to share generated revenues, but they also force companies to bear the entire risk of the undertaking. With a greenfield venture, a firm may have much to learn about running an enterprise in a foreign country, managing host-country nationals, and developing an effective marketing strategy. The commercial potential of a wholly owned international subsidiary may be great, but the hassles of managing it can be even greater. This option is not for the faint of heart.

18-4 CHALLENGES TO GLOBAL BUSINESSES

Explain the challenges that global enterprises face.

Small businesses face challenges. *Global* small businesses face challenges on a much larger scale. But, the success of enterprising entrepreneurs in international markets proves that small firms can do better than survive—they can thrive! However, success requires careful preparation. Small business owners must recognize the unique complications facing global firms and adjust their plans accordingly. Beyond managing cultural differences, entrepreneurs need to pay attention to political risks, economic risks, and the relative ease of doing business in countries where they want to extend operations.

18-4a Political Risk

The potential for a country's political forces to negatively affect the performance of businesses operating within its borders is referred to as **political risk**. Often, this risk is related to the instability of a host nation's government. Potential problems range from threats as trivial as new regulations that restrict the content of television advertising to a government takeover of private assets. Political developments can threaten access to an export market, require a firm to reveal trade secrets, or even demand that work be completed in-country.

Many large corporations maintain a risk assessment office with staff trained to determine the risk profile of the individual countries for which they have planned projects. Because small firms cannot afford the cost of staffing such an office, some turn to inexpensive tools for risk assessment. One helpful resource is *Euromoney* magazine's annual "Country Risk Rankings," which provides a general sense of the political risks that companies will face when doing business abroad. Small businesses can develop international growth plans using these insights and make appropriate adjustments to their strategies. It's not a perfect method, but it is low cost and far better than planning a global strategy with no information at all.

political risk
The potential for political forces in a country to negatively affect the performance of businesses operating within its borders.

economic risk
The probability that a country's government will mismanage its economy in ways that hinder the performance of firms operating there.

exchange rates
The value of one country's currency relative to that of another country.

18-4b Economic Risk

Economic risk is the probability that a country's government will mismanage its economy and affect the business environment in ways that hinder the performance of firms operating there. Economic risk and political risk are therefore related.[47] Two of the most serious problems resulting from economic mismanagement are inflation and fluctuations in exchange rates. While a more complete discussion of these factors is beyond the scope of this book, it is important to recognize that inflation reduces the value of a country's currency on the foreign exchange market, thereby decreasing the value of cash flows that the firm receives from its operations abroad.

Exchange rates represent the value of one country's currency relative to that of another country—for example, the number of Mexican pesos that can be purchased with one U.S. dollar. Sudden or unexpected changes in these rates can be a serious problem for small international businesses, whether they export to that market or have a local presence there.

Mary Ellen Mooney of Mooney Farms recognized the potential of exporting her sun-dried tomato products to France and came close to striking a deal with a local distributor some years ago, but the negotiations fell through when the exchange rate between the dollar and the euro changed.[48] To understand her dilemma, suppose the French distributor was willing to pay €5 (5 euros) for a package of sun-dried tomatoes. If the dollar and the euro were exchanged one to one, Mooney could convert €5 to $5. If $4.50 covered costs of production, transportation, insurance, and so on, then Mooney would earn a $.50 profit ($5.00 − $4.50) per unit. But if the dollar were to *increase* in value relative to the euro, the situation would change drastically. Assume that the exchange rate changed to $.80 per €1. Then units selling for €5 would yield only $4 each (5 × $.80), which would result in a $.50 loss on every sale.

© LUCIA PITTER/SHUTTERSTOCK.COM

Living the Dream

ENTREPRENEURIAL EXPERIENCES

Having the Energy to Take Daring Risks

When most entrepreneurs think of locations around the world for their businesses, many steer clear of countries that are known to be politically or economically unstable. But these tumultuous regions are precisely where young and daring oil companies like Genel Energy have chosen to focus their efforts. In early 2012, representatives of the venture flew 500 miles north of Somalia's capital, Mogadishu, to meet with leaders of a breakaway region known as Somaliland. After a meeting with the resources minister, Genel Energy was granted permission by the new government to begin prospecting for oil in the region. The agreement represents a larger strategy of certain firms to seek revenue sources in challenging environments, even if it means dealing with unrecognized governments.

Genel Energy is not a small company—except when you compare it to the industry giants against which it competes, that is. But its entrepreneurial spirit definitely pulls it toward political frontiers where few other energy companies dare to operate. Firms like Genel often swim against the political stream in their own home countries and the United Nations, which assert that international firms can cause or amplify regional instability if they decide to do business in disputed territories. One executive of the venture dismisses the claim, arguing that when "people have the opportunity to earn money and buy a BMW, rather than run around the hills with a Kalashnikov, they'll do it."

Where others see political instability and turn back, entrepreneurial firms like Genel Energy see immense opportunity and choose to engage. In this regard, Somaliland is very appealing because it controls an area that is geologically promising and larger and more established firms are not in active production in the area. But there is a problem. In many cases, these new contracts overlap with leases granted previously to oil companies that did business there in the past. More specifically, the zone falling under Genel's agreement with the breakaway government of Somaliland cuts into the area covered by an existing ConocoPhillips lease that was negotiated with the Somali government in Mogadishu. Although ConocoPhillips is not currently exploring the area, both the oil giant and the central government have strongly protested Genel's deals.

After signing the agreement with Somaliland, Genel began seismic tests in the region with the hope of finding deep oil reserves. But after a security threat, all exploration teams were forced to pull out of the region. Despite the uncertainty, Genel refused to give up, opening up discussions with the Somaliland government to find a way to resume exploration, while ensuring the safety of its personnel. So far, the situation looks bleak, but the company knew that it was taking on significant risk when it signed on to deals there.

Despite these developments, Genel Energy has plans to push the political frontier in other regions of the world as well. The political risk involved is great, but that drives rivals away and leaves a competitive gap for smaller and more risk-accepting companies. That is exactly the kind of opening that plucky startups like Genel Energy are looking for.

Sources: "Genel Energy: Our Operations in Somaliland," http://www.genelenergy.com/operations/somaliland.aspx, accessed February 6, 2015; "Genel Energy: Briefing, Somaliland, Oil and Security," 4-traders, August 7, 2014, http://www.4-traders.com/GENEL-ENERGY-PLC-9445424/news/Genel-Energy--Briefing-Somaliland-oil-and-security-18868869, accessed January 25, 2015; Justin Scheck, "Former BP Chief's New Quest: Wildcatting on the Edge of Danger," *The Wall Street Journal*, November 11, 2013, pp. A1, A14; and Rachel Williamson, "High Hopes and Dirty Deals," *Beacon Reader*, July 27, 2014, https://www.beaconreader.com/rachel-williamson/high-hopes-and-dirty-deals, accessed April 15, 2015.

Clearly, a good deal can quickly fall apart if exchange rates take a turn for the worse. This risk is especially serious for small companies that are just getting established in international markets. To protect against exchange rate shifts, many small American firms choose to state their contracts in U.S. dollars, but this can give competitors an edge if they are willing to sell in the buyer's currency.

It can also lead to nonpayment if unfavorable shifts make goods or services too expensive for a foreign customer. The International Trade Administration of the U.S. Department of Commerce recommends that small firms use more sophisticated financial strategies and risk management tools, including forward contracts and options, which can be manageable (see www.trade.gov/publications/pdfs/tfg2008ch12.pdf for details).

18-4c The Ease of Doing Business Index

Since 2003, the World Bank has been publishing the "Ease of Doing Business Index" to underscore to businesses and governments the large impact that regulatory conditions have on economic growth and development. The index is based on a survey of more than 10,600 local experts, including "lawyers, business consultants, accountants, freight forwarders, government officials, and other professionals routinely administering or advising on legal and regulatory requirements."[49] Following a very careful methodology, the process uses data related to 11 key sets of indicators—including the difficulty of starting a business, getting credit, and enforcing contracts—to create a ranking for 189 countries. This information can easily be used to shape the international expansion decisions of small businesses.

In Exhibit 18.4, countries are color-coded to indicate the relative ease of doing business in each—green represents "go" countries, which are relatively business friendly; yellow signifies countries that are somewhat more challenging, where companies should "proceed with caution"; and red identifies "stop and think very carefully" countries, where small businesses are likely to have even more difficulty. While color coding is not a part of the index, the data provided are very helpful for planning. Conducting

EXHIBIT **18.4** Ease of Doing Business in Different Countries

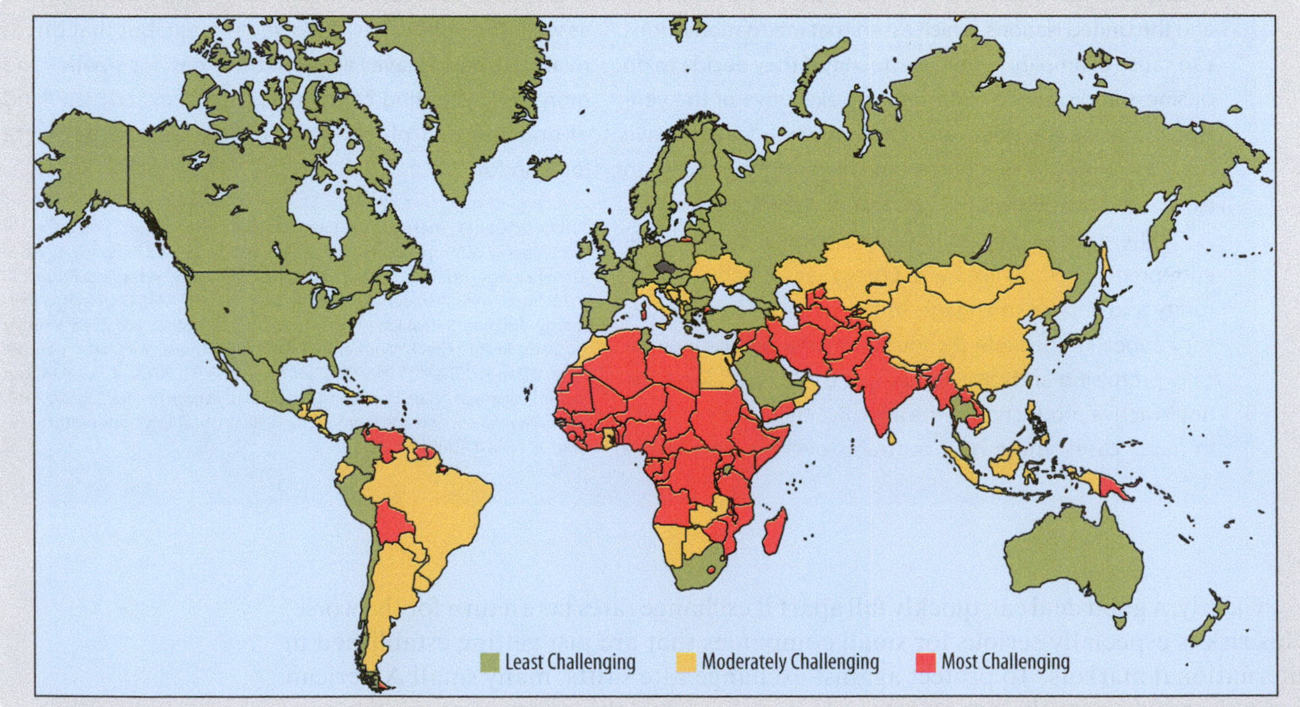

Source: World Bank Group, "Economy Rankings: Ease of Doing Business," http://www.doingbusiness.org/rankings, accessed February 4, 2015.

business internationally will never be as easy as doing business at home—it is likely to stretch managerial skills and resources to the limit. Global commerce can complicate every task and raise difficult questions related to every function of the firm. However, the motivations to go global are sound, and others have already proved that it can be done. You can do it, too, if you plan carefully and take advantage of the resources available to help you achieve your global aspirations.

18-5 ASSISTANCE FOR GLOBAL ENTERPRISES

Recognize the sources of assistance available to support international business efforts.

Help is available to small companies with international aspirations—you need only open your eyes to find it. Once you decide to enter the global marketplace, you will be amazed at how many resources there are to assist you.

18-5a Analyzing Markets and Planning Strategy

Among the many activities required to prepare a small firm for the challenges of going global, two are especially fundamental to success abroad: finding international markets that fit the company's unique potentials and putting together a game plan for entry into targeted markets.

A small business should begin its research by exhausting secondary sources of information. The U.S. government offers a number of publications on how to identify and tap into global market opportunities. Also, the Small Business Administration stands ready to help small companies expand abroad. Many of the international programs and services of the SBA are delivered through U.S. Export Assistance Centers (USEACs).

One excellent source of information about global business for small companies is an SBA-sponsored, nuts-and-bolts, self-paced course entitled "Take Your Business Global: An Introduction to Exporting." Available online free of charge,[50] this course provides an overview of exporting that is useful for both new and experienced exporters. It is designed to guide small firms through the complexities of doing business abroad, with sections focused specifically on the benefits of going global, researching markets and making connections abroad, developing an export strategy, managing transactions, financing trade, accessing key international trade resources, and other important topics.

Though not focused on small businesses alone, a website maintained by the International Trade Administration of the U.S. Department of Commerce (trade.gov) supplies helpful insights about international expansion. General business publications, such as *The Economist, Financial Times,* and *The Wall Street Journal*, can also be useful, as they provide timely, in-depth analyses of world trade markets and business issues. They are available at subscription rates that start at a fairly reasonable $10 a month. Beyond these resources, many state and private organizations supply trade information, trade leads, and company databases. One such source, TradePort (tradeport.org), offers information to promote international trade with California-based companies.

Talking with someone who has lived in or even visited a potential foreign market can be a valuable way to learn about it. For example, conversations with experienced global business professionals or even international students at a local university can be very helpful. However, the best way to study a foreign market is to visit the country personally. A representative of a small firm can do this either as an individual or as a member of a group that is organized for the purpose of exploring new international business possibilities.

18-5b Connecting with International Customers

Numerous resources are available to help a small company connect with customers in targeted international markets. They include trade leads, trade missions, and trade intermediaries.

TRADE LEADS

Trade leads are essential in identifying potential customers overseas. Accessed most often via the Internet, they offer an inexpensive way to establish vital links with buyers and suppliers in target markets. One good online source of trade leads is provided by the globalEDGE portal created by the International Business Center at Michigan State University (see http://globaledge.msu.edu/global-resources/trade-leads). This website offers a wealth of international business resources, including leads that can direct a company to valuable partners in most of the world's markets. The website of the Federation of International Trade Associations (www.fita.org) will also help you identify trade leads. In addition, it provides news, announced events, and links to over 8,000 trade-related websites.

TRADE MISSIONS

Joining a trade mission is another excellent way to evaluate a foreign market and connect with overseas customers. A **trade mission** is a planned visit to a potential international market, designed to introduce U.S. firms to prospective foreign buyers and to establish strategic alliances. These missions usually involve groups of five to ten business executives and are set up to promote international sales. Members of the group typically pay their own expenses and share in the operating costs of the mission. Foreign governments sometimes sponsor trade missions in order to promote business links with U.S. firms.

trade mission
A trip organized to help small business owners meet with potential foreign buyers and establish strategic alliances in an international market.

© ISTOCKPHOTO.COM/POP_JOP

TRADE INTERMEDIARIES

Perhaps the easiest way to break into international markets is to use a **trade intermediary**. Similar to the assistance wholesalers provide with domestic sales, trade intermediaries distribute products to international customers on a contract basis. These agencies tap their established network of contacts, as well as their local cultural and market expertise. In short, an intermediary can manage the entire export end of a business, taking care of everything except filling the orders—and the results can be outstanding. For example, American Cedar, Inc., wanted to expand the market for its cedar wood products overseas. With the assistance of a trade intermediary, the firm was able to generate 30 percent of its total sales from exporting. Then-company president Julian McKinney recalls how the story unfolded: "We displayed our products at a trade show, and an export management company found us. They helped alleviate the hassles of exporting directly. Our products [were] distributed throughout [Europe] from a distribution point in France."[51] An export management company is only one of the many types of trade intermediaries. Exhibit 18.5 describes the trade intermediaries that can best provide the assistance needed by small businesses.

18-5c Financing

The more information small firms have about direct and indirect sources of financing, the more favorably they tend to view foreign markets. Sources of this information include private banks and the Small Business Administration.

PRIVATE BANKS

Commercial banks typically have a loan officer who is responsible for handling foreign transactions. Large banks may have an entire international department. Exporters use banks to issue commercial letters of credit and to perform other financial activities associated with exporting.

trade intermediary An agency that distributes a company's products on a contract basis to customers in another country.

EXHIBIT **18.5** Trade Intermediaries Most Suited for Small Businesses

Confirming House (Buying Agent)	• Works for foreign firms that are interested in buying U.S. products. • "Shops" for lowest possible price for requested items. • Is paid a commission for its services. • Is sometimes a foreign government agency or quasi-governmental firm.
Export Management Company	• Acts as the export department for one or several producers of products or services. • Solicits and transacts business in the names of the producers it represents or in its own name in exchange for a commission, salary, or retainer plus commission. • May provide immediate payment for the products or services by arranging financing or directly purchasing products for resale. • Usually has well-established networks of foreign distributors already in place.
Export Trading Company	• Acts as the export department for producers or takes title to the product and exports it under its own name. • May be set up and operated by producers. • Can be organized along multiple- or single-industry lines. • Can represent producers of competing products.
Export Agent, Merchant, or Remarketer	• Purchases products directly from the manufacturer, packing and marking the product according to its own specifications. • Sells the products overseas under its own name through contacts and assumes all risks. • Requires the producer to give up control of the marketing and promotion of its product.
Piggyback Marketer	• Is a manufacturer or service firm. • Distributes another firm's product or service.

Source: Adapted from International Trade Administration, *A Basic Guide to Exporting*, Chapter 5, "Methods and Channels," http://export.gov/basicguide/eg_main_038338.asp, accessed February 4, 2015.

Planning to Go Global
Most small businesses make their first move into global business via exporting, and the SBA has created the *Export Business Planner* to help improve their odds of success. But whether you plan to export or follow some other strategy, this publication is very thorough and can be extremely helpful as you make your move. You can find the planner at www.sba.gov/exportbusinessplanner.

A **letter of credit** is an agreement to honor a draft or other demand for payment when specified conditions are met. It helps to ensure that a seller will receive prompt payment. A letter of credit may be revocable or irrevocable. An irrevocable letter of credit cannot be changed unless both the buyer and the seller agree to the change. The process of establishing a letter of credit is quite involved and can be very confusing. However, banks and other financial institutions that offer this service have expert staff who can explain how these documents work and will walk you through the process.

A guarantee from a reputable bank that the exporter will indeed be paid is critical to a small business that has stretched its resources to the limit just to enter the global game and thus cannot afford an uncollected payment. But what if the small business is on the import end of the exchange? How will its interests be protected? The letter of credit provides security for the receiving firm as well, because the exporter does not receive payment from the bank until it has released the title, or proof of ownership, of the delivered goods. Once the product has been shipped and the title transferred, the exporter receives a document called a **bill of lading** to confirm this. This document must be received before the bank will pay on the letter of credit. In brief, the letter of credit ensures that the exporter will receive payment only when the goods are delivered in-country, and it also guarantees that the exporter will be paid.

letter of credit
An agreement issued by a bank to honor a draft or other demand for payment when specified conditions are met.

bill of lading
A document indicating that a product has been shipped and the title to that product has been transferred.

SMALL BUSINESS ADMINISTRATION

The Small Business Administration (SBA) serves small U.S. firms primarily through its regional, district, and branch offices. Small businesses that are either already exporting or interested in doing so can receive valuable information from the SBA through conferences and seminars, instructional publications, and export counseling. An informative list of the financial assistance programs offered by the SBA to small firms is posted on the agency's website at https://www.sba.gov/category/navigation-structure/starting-managing-business/starting-business/preparing-your-finances/understanding-basics.

A growing number of small firms are choosing to participate in international business for various reasons, with new motivations continuing to emerge in the forever-evolving competitive landscape. Whatever your reasons are for entering the global arena, your company is certain to confront serious challenges that purely domestic firms do not have to face. But assistance is available in abundance from a number of private and public sources. With a little help and a lot of hard work, your company can succeed in the global marketplace.

18-1. Describe the potential of small businesses as global enterprises.

- Many startups and even the smallest of businesses continue to expand internationally, despite a slowed global economy.
- Some small companies called born-global firms are being launched with cross-border business activities in mind.
- Before going global, it is important for a small business owner to determine whether her or his company is up to the task.
- Small business owners who decide to go global must study the social, technological, economic, and political forces in a foreign market to determine how best to adapt their business practices, as well as their products or services, to ensure smooth market entry.

18-2. Identify the basic forces prompting small companies to engage in global expansion.

- The basic forces behind global expansion are expanding markets, gaining access to resources, cutting costs, and capitalizing on special location features.

- Since more than 95 percent of the world's population lives outside the United States, globalization greatly expands the size of a firm's potential market.
- The fast-growing markets of the BRIC countries (*B*razil, *R*ussia, *I*ndia, and *C*hina) are attracting small firms that wish to tap their enormous market potential (especially in India and China).
- Because of converging preferences and delivery systems around the world, products that sell at home are more likely to be introduced very quickly abroad, often with little or no adaptation necessary.
- Small businesses with a highly differentiated product may need international markets in order to increase sales enough to recover product development costs.
- Going global can accelerate gains from experience curve efficiencies (resulting from learning effects and economies of scale), especially for startups based on complex technologies.
- Small businesses may go global to gain access to resources, including raw materials and skilled workers. They can also cut their costs in these areas and in manufacturing overhead.
- Businesses of all sizes have been slashing costs by contracting with independent providers overseas (international outsourcing) or relocating their stateside operations abroad (offshoring).
- Small businesses may want to capitalize on the special features of an international location to create authenticity by being local, to enhance a brand's reputation, or to follow a large client firm.

18-3. Understand and compare strategy options for global businesses.

- Exporting can be facilitated by using the Internet to increase firms' international visibility.
- Importing should be used when products manufactured abroad have market potential at home.
- Other international strategies include foreign licensing, international franchising, international strategic alliances, and locating facilities abroad.
- Some small firms may purchase a foreign business from another firm through a cross-border acquisition. Others may even start a greenfield venture by forming from scratch a new wholly owned subsidiary in another country.

18-4. Explain the challenges that global enterprises face.

- Political risk is the potential for a country's political forces to negatively affect the performance of small businesses operating there. It varies greatly across nations.
- Economic risk is the probability that a government will mismanage its economy and affect the business environment in ways that hinder the performance of firms operating there (most notably through inflation and fluctuations in exchange rates).
- The World Bank's "Ease of Doing Business Index" can help a small company anticipate the overall level of difficulty of entering a specific country market, based on legal and regulatory requirements.

18-5. Recognize the sources of assistance available to support international business efforts.

- Numerous public and private organizations provide assistance to small businesses in analyzing markets and planning an entry strategy.
- Small businesses can connect with international customers by reviewing sources of trade leads, joining trade missions, and using the services of trade intermediaries.
- For assistance in financing its entry into a foreign market, a small firm can turn to private banks (which can issue letters of credit) and programs initiated by the Small Business Administration

Key Terms

bill of lading p. 500
born-global firms p. 480
counterfeit activity p. 492
cross-border acquisition p. 493
economic risk p. 494
economies of scale p. 484
exchange rates p. 494
experience curve efficiencies p. 484
exporting p. 489
foreign licensing p. 491
globalization p. 479
greenfield venture p. 493
importing p. 490
international franchising p. 492
international outsourcing p. 485
international strategic alliance p. 492
learning effects p. 484
letter of credit p. 500
licensee p. 491
licensor p. 491
offshoring p. 485
political risk p. 494
royalties p. 491
trade intermediary p. 499
trade mission p. 498

You Make the Call

Situation 1

Jesse Acevas recognized the advantages of outsourcing software development work when he decided to start Victoris Consulting International, an information technology company. He has considered linking up with a service provider in Bangalore, India, because the wages are very low, the pool of well-trained employees is deep, and technical skills are strongly emphasized in the system of higher education there. But India is a long way from the company's home office in Phoenix, Arizona, which means greater travel costs, dealing with the hassle of working between times zones that are nearly opposite one another, and communication delays. There have also been reports of problems with infrastructure limitations (including poor or dropped Internet and phone connections), as well as the cost and quality of completed work. Finally, the cultural gap would be significant, even though most educated workers in India speak English.

Acevas has also been in touch with an operation in Guadalajara, Mexico. His contacts there tell him that the skilled workers he needs are available, the cultural gap is limited, turnover is very low, and technical staff will not need special visas to travel between Mexico and project sites in the United States. However, wages there are significantly higher than in Bangalore, university graduates in Mexico receive little practical training, and the law makes it very difficult to fire staff once they are hired.

The clock is ticking. Acevas needs to line up employees for three big contracts he is currently negotiating, and his potential clients all want to get their projects started within a month or so of a final decision. If he even closes two of the three deals, he will have much more work than his staff in the United States can handle. He will need additional employees—he's just not certain where to go for outsourcing support.

Question 1 What additional information would be helpful to Acevas as he ponders this decision?

Question 2 What additional advantages and disadvantages should Acevas consider when choosing between offshoring this work to India and "nearshoring" it to Mexico?

Question 3 Which location would you choose—India or Mexico? Build a case to support your final decision.

Situation 2

Frank Shipper and several other small business owners joined a trade mission to China to explore market opportunities there. The group learned that China has a population of over 1.3 billion and is one of the fastest-growing export markets for small and medium-size U.S. companies. Average annual income varies greatly across the country, but it is increasing rapidly. Annual per capita incomes range from a low of about $1,400 for rural workers to just over $4,300 in urban areas—even higher in Shanghai, Beijing, and other major cities.

The World Bank estimates that the economy in China will continue to expand by around 7 percent each year, and recent analyses indicate that the number of Internet users there has been growing rapidly, reaching around 650 million. Furthermore, as the customer base in China continues to grow and quality-of-life expectations rise, the demand for various kinds of services increases significantly. Members of the group learned that 95 percent of the people in China have cell phones, and nearly 86 percent of these people have mobile access to the Internet. On the downside, they also found that counterfeit goods (from clothing and leather goods to software and DVDs) were readily available at a fraction of the cost of legitimate merchandise and that local merchants have expressed interest in doing business only with vendors with whom they have established relationships.

Sources: Paul Carsten, "China's Internet Population Hits 649 Million, 86 Percent on Phones," *Reuters*, February 3, 2015, http://www.reuters.com/article/2015/02/03/us-china-internet-idUSKBN0L713L20150203, accessed February 5, 2015; Lee Rainie and Jacob Poushter, "Emerging Nations Catching Up to U.S. on Technology Adoption, Especially Mobile and Social Media Use," Pew Research Center: FactTank, February 13, 2014, http://www.pewresearch.org/fact-tank/2014/02/13/emerging-nations-catching-up-to-u-s-on-technology-adoption-especially-mobile-and-social-media-use, accessed February 5, 2015; Kenneth Rapoza, "Average Chinese Getting Richer," *Forbes*, February 24, 2015, http://www.forbes.com/sites/kenrapoza/2014/02/25/average-chinese-getting-richer, accessed February 5, 2015; and The World Bank, "China Overview," http://www.worldbank.org/en/country/china/overview, accessed February 5, 2015.

Question 1 What types of businesses would prosper in China? Why?

Question 2 What are the challenges and risks associated with doing business in China?

Question 3 What steps should Shipper take to address these challenges and risks in order to increase his chance of success in that market?

Situation 3

Aaron Altmann is the founder of Sacred Earth, which imports 16-ounce bags of soil from Israel for use at groundbreakings, burials, and other ceremonial events. The product holds special significance for people of various religious faiths, and each parcel of Sacred Earth is certified to be genuine by a rabbi in Jerusalem. The company sells the soil for $29.95 per bag.

The obstacles the company has had to overcome have been numerous. For example, import operations can be very difficult to set up, especially if they involve organic matter. Soil products cannot be imported without the permission of the U.S. Department of Agriculture, which requires that they be treated, tested, and formally approved. The new venture had to bear these costs on top of normal business expenses, such as obtaining the soil and then shipping, packaging, storing, marketing, and delivering it to buyers. Altmann worked with scientists to come up with a soil-cleaning process that satisfies U.S. import regulations, giving his startup a competitive advantage over would-be rivals.

Altmann is now considering ways to expand the market and potential of his young company. For example, he is thinking about marketing his soil product to Christian Evangelicals, as well as a number of other applications that include using the soil to feed potted plants, to promote good luck, or even to save as a keepsake. The future looks promising, but for now Altmann can take pleasure in knowing that his import operation is finally off the ground . . . in more ways than one.

Question 1 In your opinion, what new country markets would be likely to hold the greatest potential for additional sales for Altmann's company?

Question 2 Of the major strategy options mentioned in this chapter, which is Altmann currently following? Which of the other strategies would offer the safest path to further global expansion? the fastest path? the best path? Why?

Question 3 What are the greatest challenges Altmann is likely to face in the future? What sources of assistance would you suggest that he use as he takes on those challenges?

Case 18

Auntie Anne's Pretzels in China (P. 682)

This case describes the challenges that two first-time entrepreneurs encountered when taking the Auntie Anne's Pretzels franchise into China.

Alternative Case for Chapter 18

Case 5, Iaccarino & Son, p. 654

Endnotes

1. Data published by the SBA indicate that a large number of small enterprises are already exporters. The numbers become even more impressive when other forms of globalization are considered. See "SBA: Frequently Asked Questions," https://www.sba.gov/sites/default/files/advocacy/FAQ_March_2014_0.pdf..
2. Sabine Vollmer, "A Rising Number of Small and Midsize Companies Go International," *Journal of Accountancy*, January 31, 2013, http://www.journalofaccountancy.com/issues/2013/feb/20125941.html, accessed January 14, 2015.
3. Terms other than *born-global firms* are sometimes used. They include *born-international firms, global startups, international new ventures*, and *instant exporters*.
4. Karen Gerwitz, "'Born Global Companies'—The New Normal?" *World Trade Center Association News*, September 4, 2013, http://www.wtcdenver.org/wtcblog/1381603, accessed January 14, 2015.
5. Leigh Buchanan, "The Thinking Man's Outsourcing," *Inc.*, Vol. 28, No. 5 (May 2006), pp. 31–33.
6. See John A. Matthews and Ivo Zander, "The International Entrepreneurial Dynamics of Accelerated Internationalisation," *Journal of International Business Studies*, Vol. 38, No. 3 (May 2007), pp. 387–403.
7. Buchanan, *op. cit.*
8. Rich Sloan and Jeff Sloan, "Taking Your Startup to a Foreign Market," http://www.startupnation.com/articles/taking-your-startup-to-a-foreign-market, accessed January 14, 2015.
9. Shelby Scarbrough, "A Whole New World," *Entrepreneur*, Vol. 36, No. 6 (June 2008), p. 21.
10. Leigh Buchanan, "Gone Global," *Inc.*, Vol. 29, No. 4 (April 2007), pp. 88–91.
11. For more on this point, including a sophisticated analysis of internationalization drivers, see Stephanie A. Fernhaber, Patricia P. McDougall, and Benjamin M. Oviatt, "Exploring the Role of Industry Structure in New Venture Internationalization," *Entrepreneurship Theory and Practice*, Vol. 31, No. 4 (July 2007), pp. 517–542.
12. Svante Andersson, "Internationalization in Different Industrial Contexts," *Journal of Business Venturing*, Vol. 19, No. 6 (2004), pp. 851–875; "Don't Laugh at Gilded Butterflies," *The Economist*, Vol. 371, No. 8372 (April 22, 2004), pp. 71–73; and Oliver Burgel, Andreas Fier, Georg Licht, and Gordon C. Murray, "The Effect of Internationalization on Rate of Growth of High-Tech Start-Ups—Evidence for UK and Germany," in Paul D. Reynolds et al. (eds.), *Frontiers for Entrepreneurship Research*, proceedings of the 20th Annual Entrepreneurship Research Conference, Babson College, June 2002.
13. For an extended discussion of this study, see Edmund Prater and Soumen Ghosh, "Current Operational Practices of U.S. Small and Medium-Sized Enterprises in Europe," *Journal of Small Business Management*, Vol. 43, No. 2 (April 2005), pp. 155–169.
14. As described in Charles W. L. Hill, *Global Business Today* (New York: McGraw-Hill/Irwin, 2014), pp. 168–170.
15. Leslie E. Palich and D. Ray Bagby, "Trade Trends in Transatlantica: A Profile of SMEs in the United States and Europe," in Lester Lloyd-Reason and

Leigh Sears (eds.), *Trading Places—SMEs in the Global Economy: A Critical Research Handbook* (Cheltenham, UK: Edward Elgar Publishing, 2007), pp. 64–65.

16. Lowana Veal, "Iceland Renews Push for Aluminum Plant," *Inter Press Service News Agency*, June 9, 2013, http://www.ipsnews.net/2013/06/iceland-renews-push-for-aluminium-plant, accessed January 29, 2015.
17. In an attempt to prevent dangerous individuals from entering the country, the U.S. government has tightened visa and work permit restrictions, which has made it more difficult for companies to bring in the foreign talent they need. Also, many international students from countries like China and India train at the best universities in the United States and then return home, hoping to use their skills to get in on the ground floor of opportunities that are emerging in their rapidly developing home countries.
18. Robert Thornock and Wesley Whitaker, "Skolkovo: Russia's Emerging Silicon Valley," http://knowledge.wharton.upenn.edu/article/skolkovo-russias-emerging-silicon-valley, accessed February 9, 2015.
19. These data, converted to U.S. dollars, are from PayScale Human Capital, "Salary Data and Career Research Center," http://www.payscale.com/research/RU/Country=Russia/Salary, accessed January 29, 2015.
20. "About MCAP Research," http://powerconnectpro.com/About.php, accessed January 29, 2015.
21. Mark Whitehouse, "Starting a Global Business, with No U.S. Employees," *The Wall Street Journal*, January 19, 2010, p. B8.
22. Pui-Wing Tam and Jessica A. Vascellaro, "Forget the Web, Start-Ups Get Real," *The Wall Street Journal*, August 18, 2012, p. B1.
23. http://www.nomiku.com, accessed February 6, 2015.
24. "Nomiku," http://uncrate.com/stuff/nomiku, accessed February 6, 2015.
25. *Ibid.*
26. Kim-Mai Cutler, "Lean-Hardware Strategy Lets Kickstarter Breakout Nomiku 'In-Shore' Manufacturing Back to the U.S.," *TechCrunch*, August 18, 2014, http://techcrunch.com/2014/08/18/nomiku-2, accessed February 6, 2015.
27. Rachel Z. Arndt, "Georgia Chopsticks," *Fast Company*, No. 165 (May 2012), p. 92.
28. Electra Draper, "Denver Native Colin Flahive Finds Success Serving Comfort Food to China," *The Denver Post*, February 27, 2013, http://www.denverpost.com/ci_22666138/serving-comfort-food-china, accessed April 14, 2015; Mike Ives, "Colin Flahive Opened a Restaurant in China That's a Beacon of Enlightened Management," *The Christian Science Monitor*, July 11, 2013, http://www.csmonitor.com/World/Making-a-difference/2013/0711/Colin-Flahive-opened-a-restaurant-in-China-that-s-a-beacon-of-enlightened-management, accessed April 14, 2015; and "Salvador's Coffee House—Kunming, China," http://www.salvadors.cn/history.html, accessed April 14, 2015.
29. *Ibid.*
30. Ives, *op. cit.*
31. SBA Office of Advocacy, "Frequently Asked Questions," https://www.sba.gov/sites/default/files/FAQ_March_2014_0.pdf, accessed February 2, 2015.
32. U.S. Small Business Administration, *Take Your Business Global: A Small Business Guide to Exporting*, Chapter 1, "Making the Export Decision," http://www.mass.gov/export/pdf/oit_business_global_workbook.pdf, accessed April 15, 2015.
33. "About Entertainment Earth," http://www.entertainmentearth.com/help/aboutee.asp, accessed February 2, 2015.
34. "Charlene Anderson: Purveyor of All Things Creative," http://charanderson.com/about-me, accessed February 2, 2015.
35. Erica J., "You'd Be Crazy Not to Sell Internationally," *The Daily Shipper*, July 8, 2014, http://www.shipstation.com/blog/handling-your-business/youd-crazy-sell-internationally-says-ebay-fba-seller, accessed February 2, 2015.
36. *Ibid.*
37. United States Chamber of Commerce, "Help Small Businesses to Export," February 6, 2014, http://www.uschamber.com/issue-brief/help-small-businesses-export, accessed February 3, 2015.
38. "Shop Compass," http://www.compasstradingco.com/compass-trading-co, accessed January 4, 2013; and personal communication with Compass Trading Company store management, February 8, 2008.
39. Christopher Hann, "Get the Goods Rolling," *Entrepreneur*, Vol. 40, No. 7 (July 2012), p. 25.
40. U.S. Small Business Administration, *Breaking into the Trade Game: A Small Business Guide to Exporting*, ed. Kathy Parker (Darby, PA: Diane Publishing, 1997), Chapter 7, "Strategic Alliances and Foreign Investment Opportunities," http://www.foreign-trade.com/reference/trad12.htm, accessed April 15, 2015.
41. "McDonald's: About Us," http://www.aboutmcdonalds.com/mcd/our_company.html, accessed February 4, 2015.
42. Angus Loften, "Smaller Franchisers Expand Their Horizons," *The Wall Street Journal*, November 14, 2011, p. R7.
43. "About Blue Note," http://www.bluenote.net/about/index.shtml, accessed February 4, 2015.
44. Elizabeth Wasserman, "Happy Birthday, WTO?" http://www.inc.com/magazine/20050101/wto.html, accessed February 6, 2015.
45. Robert Sberna, "How I Cracked the China Market" National Association of Manufacturers, August 2013, http://www.robertsberna.com/wp-content/uploads/2013/08/china1.pdf, accessed February 6, 2015.
46. Karen E. Klein, "An American in South America's Paris," http://www.bloomberg.com/bw/stories/2006-06-15/an-american-in-south-americas-parisbusinessweek-business-news-stock-market-and-financial-advice, accessed February 6, 2015; and Nichole L. Torres, "Change of Scenery," *Entrepreneur*, Vol. 34, No. 8 (August 2006), p. 90.
47. One form of risk that is not within the control of a government but may have very serious effects on business performance is what some researchers call *environmental risk*. This suggests that climate change risks vary across global regions and should be a recognized decision-making factor. See Peter Romilly, "Business and Climate Change Risk: A Regional Time Series Analysis," *Journal of International Business Studies*, Vol. 38, No. 3 (May 2007), pp. 474–480.
48. Personal communication with Mary Ellen Mooney, April 18, 2011.
49. World Bank Group, "Doing Business 2015 Data Note," http://www.doingbusiness.org/methodology/methodology-note#Easeof DB, accessed February 4, 2015.
50. "Take Your Business Global: An Introduction to Exporting" can be found at http://www.sba.gov/tools/sba-learning-center/training/take-your-business-global-introduction-exporting.
51. "Foreign Market Entry," http://www.foreign-trade.com/reference/trad8.htm, accessed February 4, 2015.

CHAPTER 19

Professional Management and the Small Business

Liam Martin found himself overwhelmed by the workload he faced as his tutoring-service business grew. Exhausted from the burden, the founder asked his assistant to handle customer refunds that needed to go out. That was a big mistake! One customer had requested a $1,500 refund for a few unused tutoring sessions; the assistant accidentally refunded $10,000, amounting to fees received for the entire semester. From this experience, Martin learned that he was not very good at delegation, and shifting tasks to others was causing his anxiety levels to go up, not down.

Martin later launched an Ottawa-based temporary-employment agency called Staff.com. But despite the disaster at the tutoring-service venture, Martin understood that he would have to get comfortable with delegating responsibilities to his employees in order to have time to guide his startup. Effective delegation was especially crucial at Staff.com because the company relies heavily on off-site staff. "When you delegate tasks to others, the orders shouldn't be easy to understand—they should be impossible to misunderstand," Martin now realizes. In order to streamline delegation and ensure quality control, he created a wiki that details procedures to be followed if any of 500 common operational issues should come up. Now Martin spends less time managing business activities and more time developing and implementing strategic initiatives.

In the SPOTLIGHT
Effective Delegation at Staff.com
www.staff.com

OPEN LOOKING AHEAD

After studying this chapter, you should be able to. . .

19-1. **Understand the entrepreneur's leadership role.**

19-2. **Explain the small business management process and its unique features.**

19-3. **Identify the managerial tasks of entrepreneurs.**

19-4. **Describe the problem of time pressure and suggest solutions.**

19-5. **Outline the various types of outside management assistance.**

Harvard Business School professor Linda Hill says that entrepreneurs understand managerial efficiency, but many have difficulty actually achieving it: "[They] won't delegate until they're so exhausted and burned out that they have to." The danger is that small business owners can become so embroiled in day-to-day operations that they have too little time to do what their employees cannot do—that is, to provide strategic direction for the organization.

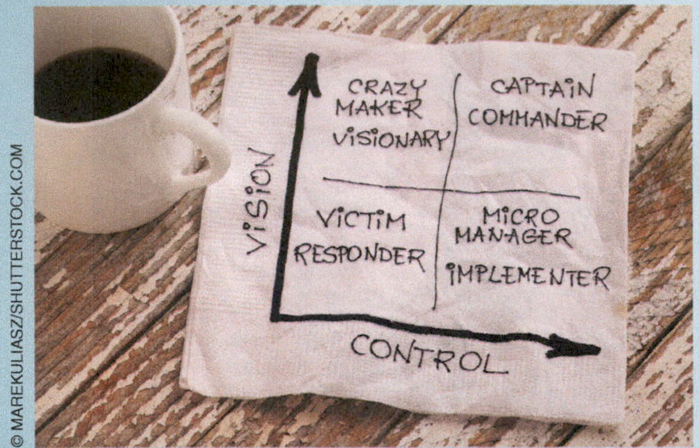

© MAREKULIASZ/SHUTTERSTOCK.COM

There are a number of strategies and techniques that entrepreneurs can use to address this issue. Some have opted to follow the 80 percent rule. Trevor Sumner, founder of marketing firm LocalVox, describes the rule this way: "When a [subordinate] can do a task 80 percent as well as you can, you need to let him do it on his own." Other small business owners may find that certain tasks cannot be adequately handled by their current staff, in which case it may be necessary to hire professional contractors who can efficiently tackle those specific duties.

Even more important, employees need the space to face obstacles on their own. Adam Robinson, co-founder and CEO of hiring-management software producer Hireology, puts it very succinctly: "Hire great people and then get the heck out of their way!" Great advice, but not always easy to follow. Nonetheless, entrepreneurs must learn to delegate responsibility and empower employees if they want their enterprises to grow. And if they can't seem to make this transition, it may become necessary to hire a professional manager to keep their growing business on track. That may be the only way to kick the micromanagement habit!

Sources: Sarah Brown, "Staff.com and Time Doctor Co-Founder Liam Martin on the Future of Contract and Remote Work," http://www.trada.com/blog/staff-com-time-doctor-co-founder-liam-martin-future-contract-remote-work, accessed February 19, 2015; Govindh Jayaraman, "Get Out of Their Way!" http://papernapkinwisdom.com/get-way-adam-robinson-founder-ceo-hireology, accessed February 19, 2015; Scott Liebs, "Just Trust," *Inc.* Vol. 36, No. 2 (March 2014), pp. 18-19; and Young Entrepreneurial Council, "12 Tips for Founders Who Hate to Delegate," *Inc.*, November 18, 2013, http://www.inc.com/young-entrepreneur-council/12-tips-for-founders-who-hate-to-delegate.html, accessed February 19, 2015.

As you can see from the opening Spotlight feature, Liam Martin has learned two important lessons: (1) ineffective delegation can be very costly and (2) effective delegation can give you the flexibility you need to have time to develop and pursue the strategic initiatives that will drive your company forward. But this is only one facet of leading a growing business that you will need to get right if your venture is to have any hope of flourishing.

Unless you plan to remain a tiny one-person business forever, you are sure to encounter leadership and management problems. When they occur, you must find ways to integrate the efforts of employees and give new direction to the business. This is absolutely necessary if production employees, salespeople, administrative staff, and other personnel are to work together effectively. Even long-established businesses need vigorous leadership if they are to avoid stagnation or failure. This chapter examines the leadership challenges facing entrepreneurs and the managerial activities required as firms mature and grow.

Understand the entrepreneur's leadership role.

19-1 SMALL BUSINESS LEADERSHIP

Leadership roles differ greatly, depending on the size of the business and its stage of development. For example, an enterprise that is just getting started will face problems and uncertainties unlike those of a family firm that has been functioning well over two or three generations. We must begin, therefore, with the recognition that leadership cannot be reduced to simple rules or processes that fit all situations.

19-1a What Is Leadership?

The question of how to define leadership is simple, but the answer is not. Eric Paley, managing partner of venture capital firm Founder Collective, offered the following description:

> *Being a leader means focusing your team on the key priorities. You need to build consensus on these priorities, set goals, evaluate performance against those goals, and change course when necessary. Great leaders build credibility with their team by making a plan, executing it effectively, and demonstrating that it was the right plan.*[1]

In other words, leadership involves pointing the way and getting others to follow willingly. It is far more focused on the destination than on the details of getting there. An entrepreneur must convey his or her vision of the firm's future to all other participants in the business so that they can contribute most effectively to the accomplishment of the mission. Although leaders must also engage in more routine processes, particularly as the company grows, the first task of the small business owner is to create and communicate a vision for the company.

19-1b Leadership Qualities of Founders

An entrepreneur is a trailblazer who enlists others, both team members and outsiders, to work with him or her in a creative endeavor. Others may then buy into this vision for the business as they join their efforts with those of the entrepreneur.

In a totally new venture, the founder faces major uncertainties and unknowns. Therefore, individuals who are launching promising startups, with the prospect of attaining significant size or profitability, need to have certain qualities. One of the most important traits is tolerance for ambiguity. Because of the uncertainty involved in starting a new business, entrepreneurs must also be adaptable, able to adjust to unforeseen problems and opportunities. These two basic qualities can be useful in many business settings, but they are never more important than in the startup situation.

19-1c What Makes a Leader Effective?

Many people assume that a business leader must have a flashy, highly charismatic, "I'm-in-charge" personality to be effective, but this is not the norm, and it certainly is not required. In fact, charisma has little to do with effective leadership. It's not so much about wanting to *be* in charge as it is having the ability to *take* charge and inspire others to follow one's lead. This is exactly the point made by Judith Cone, an innovator in entrepreneurship education:

> *A leader is able to explain a vision in a compelling way that motivates people to follow or to become a part of that vision. [Leaders] are solid, smart, they have integrity, people respect them, and people want to follow them because of the quality person[s] they are.*[2]

Clearly, effective leadership is based not on a larger-than-life personality but, instead, on a focus on reaching business goals. In most small firms, leadership is personal. The owner-manager is not a faceless unknown, but an individual whom employees see and relate to in the course of their normal work schedules. This situation is entirely different from that of large corporations, where most employees never see

Stand Up Straight

If you want to be a leader, pay attention to your posture. Faculty at the Harvard Business School have found that standing straight and tall or sitting with shoulders and arms open actually changes a person's body chemistry and causes them to look and feel more like a leader. To learn more, see Leigh Buchanan, "Leadership Advice: Strike a Pose," at www.inc.com/magazine/201205/leigh-buchanan/strike-a-pose.html.

the chief executive. If the employer-employee relationship is good, employees in small enterprises develop strong feelings of personal loyalty to their employer.

In a large corporation, the values of top-level executives must be filtered through many layers of management before they reach those who make and sell the products. As a result, the influence of those at the top tends to be diluted by the process. In contrast, personnel in a small company receive the leader's messages directly. This face-to-face contact facilitates their understanding of the leader's vision as well as her or his stand on integrity, customer service, and other important issues. In the end, this infused sense of purpose, high standards, and achievement can actually create a competitive advantage for the small business over its corporate rivals.

19-1d Leadership Styles

Leaders use many different styles of leadership. Some styles may be better suited to certain situations, but most leaders choose from a variety of approaches as they deal with different issues. Psychologist Daniel Goleman and his colleagues have identified six distinct leadership styles. In their study of nearly 4,000 managers, they found that effective leaders shift fluidly and often between the first four styles listed below, and they make very limited but skillful use of the last two styles.[3]

1. The *visionary* mobilizes people toward a shared vision.
2. The *coach* develops people by establishing a relationship and trust.
3. The *team builder* promotes emotional bonds and organizational harmony.
4. The *populist* builds consensus through participation.
5. The *paragon* sets challenging and exciting standards and expects excellence.
6. The *general* demands immediate compliance.

An entrepreneur may use different styles at different times as she or he attempts to draw out the best of the organization and its employees. Although it should be used sparingly, general-style leadership might be necessary and expected in a genuine emergency situation, but it would not be appropriate in most settings.

For most entrepreneurial firms, leadership that recognizes and values individual worth is strongly recommended. Some decades ago, many managers were hard-nosed autocrats, giving orders and showing little concern for those who worked under them. Over the years, this style of leadership has given way to more sensitive and effective approaches, and there is solid evidence to indicate that employees find these styles to be far more motivating. For example, consulting-firm CEO and leadership researcher John Gerzema conducted a massive survey of 64,000 people in 13 countries, asking them to identify the traits of modern leaders that they find to be the most desirable. Rising to the top of the list were qualities like patience, expressiveness, flexibility, and empathy. And this stands to reason. In today's super-charged business environment, companies have to demand more and more output from fewer and fewer people just to stay in the game, and the stress is taking its toll.

To maintain a sense of balance, leaders must attend to the emotional needs of their anxious employees by helping them see that they are part of something important and by communicating appreciation, concern, and support.[4] To get results in a business world transformed by the speed of the Internet and increasingly saturated with competitors from every corner of the globe, you need to take a caring approach with employees. An editor at *Inc.* magazine put it this way: "It takes a tender person to lead a tough company."[5]

Danny Meyer appears to have struck the right balance. Making it in the restaurant business is tough, but it seems that just about everything Meyer starts in the industry turns to gold. He owns some of New York's best and most popular restaurants, along with a few barbecue establishments, a burger chain called Shake Shack, and even a catering business. His success is undeniable, but the road to results required some fundamental adjustments. Meyer recalls a time early on when his managers and waiters were continually testing him by disregarding his standards for excellent service. Responding to advice from a highly respected and successful mentor, Meyer came up with his own unique management approach. In fact, he has a name for it: *constant, gentle pressure*. Problems are going to arise, conspiring to throw everything out of balance, but Meyer is committed to moving things "back to center," where they should be. That's the "constant" feature of his approach. But he always responds in a way that nudges his employees in the right direction to keep them motivated in a positive way. That's why he calls it "gentle." He also insists on excellent performance, however, overseeing the details of every table—even to the point of moving an out-of-place saltshaker to its proper place. That's where the "pressure" comes in. It's a management style that works.[6]

In many cases, progressive managers seek some degree of employee participation in decisions that affect personnel and work processes. Often, the focus is on important features of the business, such as shaping the mission of the firm or establishing everyday workplace practices. Managers may carry this leadership approach to a level called **empowerment**. The manager who uses empowerment goes beyond solicitation of employees' opinions and ideas by increasing their authority to act on their own and to make decisions about the processes they're involved with. This sends the message that their superiors trust them to do the right thing, which tends to elevate employee morale as well as performance. It also frees up time for owners and managers to take care of other pressing business challenges.

Some companies actually carry employee participation a step further by creating **self-managed work teams**. Each work team is assigned a given task or operation; its members manage that task or operation without direct supervision and assume responsibility for the results. When work teams function properly, the number of supervisors needed decreases sharply. While this approach may not be appropriate for some small businesses, it certainly provides a powerful model for the management of many ventures.

The research is clear: Effective leaders create tremendous business value. According to Bill Passmore, senior vice president at the Center for Creative Leadership, "Leaders who make choices to operate in a more participative way—who operate on principles of high engagement, versus bureaucracies that treat people as if they were cogs in a machine—see a 30 percent improvement in performance."[7] That's because engaged employees are more productive and customer-focused, which leads to greater firm profitability. This does not mean that more "masculine" leadership traits such as decisiveness, resilience, and confidence are no longer valued—the same research has shown that these are also desirable leadership qualities—but they must be balanced with a more sensitive touch if a leader is to have greater impact.[8]

empowerment
Authorization of employees to make decisions or take actions on their own.

self-managed work teams
Groups of employees with freedom to function without direct supervision, but with responsibility for results.

19-1e Shaping the Culture of the Organization

Over time, an organization tends to take on a life of its own. As indicated in Chapter 2, an organizational culture begins to emerge in every small business, establishing a tone that helps employees understand what the company stands for and how to go about their work. It is the factor that determines the "feel" of a business, the "silent teacher" that sets the mood for employee conduct, even when managers are not present.

A company's culture does not emerge overnight. It unfolds over the lifetime of the business and usually reflects the character and style of the founder. (You may recall that we discussed the founder's imprint on organizational culture in the family business in Chapter 5.) Because of its power to shape how business is conducted, the culture of the organization should not be left to chance. If a founder is honest in his or her dealings, supportive of employees, and quick to communicate, he or she will likely set a standard that others will follow. An entrepreneur can create an innovative cultural environment by setting aside his or her ego and opening up to the ideas of others, supporting experimentation through the elimination of unnecessary penalties for failure, and looking for and tapping into the unique gifts of all employees. Like empowerment, creating an organizational culture that fosters innovation tends to draw employees into the work of the company and often provides a boost to commitment and employee morale.

Deliberate physical design efforts can also influence the organizational culture, thereby helping to shape the way people in the organization think, how they interact, and what they achieve together. John Ferrigan, a freelance interior designer who has helped a number of Silicon Valley companies, from startups to tech giants like Google, emphasizes that intentional steps can be taken to set the tone of business. For example, a collaborative climate can be cultivated in open-office layouts by seating team members near one another. This creates more occasions for employees to run into one another and start idea-generating conversations, though the noise and lack of privacy created can inhibit concentration and deep thinking.[9] Aware of the drawbacks, Ferrigan notes that collaboration can still be emphasized by creating "enclaves" where teams can gather and discuss ideas without disrupting others in the same general area. At the same time, giving "higher-ups" private offices while everyone else has to work out in the open can send the wrong message. It also cuts off the flow of ideas and communication. Executives who heed Ferrigan's advice and come out of their offices often say, "Wow, I've learned more about my own company in the last three weeks than I did in the past three years."[10] Relatively simple adjustments in physical space can have a profound effect on the mindset that employees assume at work.

Another important factor in shaping culture is hiring new employees based on their attitude, style, and fit with the personality of the company. Tony Hsieh built Zappos.com into a billion-dollar firm in less than a decade and then sold it to Amazon in 2009 (which asked Hsieh to stay on as CEO).[11] The online shoe retailer now also sells apparel, bags, housewares, electronics, and cookware, but at its core is a strong and carefully crafted culture. It's a little quirky—values such as "embrace and drive change" and "create fun and a little weirdness" top the list[12]—but it's hard to argue with the company's approach, given its success. During the interview process, potential new employees are screened for their fit with the Zappos culture, and many very smart and talented prospects are rejected if there is no match. This emphasis is backed up by the firm's performance review process for existing employees, which Hsieh says is "50 percent based on whether [they are] living the Zappos culture or inspiring it in others."[13] This sends a clear signal regarding the perceived importance of culture at the online superstar.

© JARED MCMILLEN/AURORA PHOTOS/CORBIS

It should be clear by now that, in large part, business management is a mental sport, and those who have the right frame of mind are most likely to win. Therefore, every leader should strive to incorporate a positive, "can-do" attitude into the organizational culture. You can work on your own attitude and inspire others to follow your lead. Attitude often is everything, in life and in business. Whether an event is mentally framed as a setback or a positive life experience is entirely up to you. If all the parking spaces close to the store are full, taking one farther away can be seen as a chance to get some exercise. A new competitor can present a fresh reminder of why it is so important to serve your customers to the best of your ability. And a lost sale can show you how to improve your product or adjust your presentation so that many more sales can be generated in the future. Develop a positive mindset, and let it shape the culture of those you have hired to work alongside you.

19-2 THE SMALL FIRM MANAGEMENT PROCESS

Explain the small business management process and its unique features.

Small business owners face challenges that differ greatly from those of corporate executives. Some of those challenges may arise with necessary changes to leadership and management processes as the firm moves from a startup to the point where it may employ a full staff of **professional managers**, trained in the use of more advanced management methods.

19-2a From Founder to Professional Manager

The way businesses and other organizations are managed can vary greatly. The extremes of very unskilled and highly professional types of management represent the ends of a continuum. At the less-developed end are entrepreneurs and other managers who rely largely on past experience, rules of thumb, and personal whims in giving direction to their businesses. In most cases, their mental models for managing are based on the way they were treated in earlier business experiences or in family relationships. Other entrepreneurs and managers take a more sophisticated approach. They are analytical and systematic in dealing with management problems and issues. Because they emphasize getting the facts and working out logical solutions, their routines are sometimes described as more methodical in nature.

The challenge for small firm leaders is to develop a professional approach, while still retaining the entrepreneurial spirit of the enterprise. This can be especially difficult because founders of new businesses are not always good organization members. As discussed in Chapter 1, they are creative, innovative, risk-taking individuals who have the courage to strike out on their own. Indeed, they are often propelled into entrepreneurship by precipitating events, sometimes involving their difficulty in fitting into conventional organizational roles. But even very capable entrepreneurs may fail to appreciate the need for good management practices as a company grows.

Scott Leibs, executive editor of *Inc.* magazine, points out that many experts believe it is extremely difficult, indeed often impossible, for entrepreneurs to make the transition from founder to professional manager:

> *Some founders . . . can get a company through the first couple of stages of growth, but no further. They don't know their weaknesses, or understand the real reasons for their company's success, and they want to make every decision rather than cede control as the company outgrows what any one person can manage.*[14]

professional managers
A manager who uses systematic, analytical methods of management.

When an entrepreneur cannot make the transition as the venture grows and becomes more complex, and refuses to hand the reins of control to someone better suited to take over, the enterprise is very likely to fail. This is a common problem—so common that investors actually have a name for it: "founderitis," or "founder's syndrome."

Some entrepreneurs recognize the problem early on and make adjustments. Sara Blakely, founder of shapewear trendsetter SPANX, reports that building a team to run her company was one of her greatest challenges. Before becoming an entrepreneur, Blakely had no formal business training or experience in the fashion industry, but starting a new venture meant taking on the responsibility of her employees and their livelihoods. She soon felt very overwhelmed, but then she realized, "It's OK if you're not good at this; hire someone who is." So she hired a CEO two years after startup ("one of the smartest business decisions I ever made") and gave up control of tasks that did not align with her natural skills so that she could concentrate on those that played to her strengths. With "adult supervision" in place, Blakely shifted her focus to being the public face of SPANX, an evangelist for the company and its products, but she continued to work on product development and marketing ideas as well. That turned out to be a much more comfortable and practical arrangement for her.[15] "The person who starts a company from the ground up is not always the best person to grow it," declares Blakely. "I think this is the most important lesson an entrepreneur can learn."[16] Following this principle has certainly been good for Spanx, leading to Blakely's spectacular rise as the world's youngest self-made female billionaire.[17]

Although many entrepreneurs are professional in their approach to management and many corporate managers are entrepreneurial in that they are truly innovative and are willing to take risks, a founder's more simplistic methods can act as a drag on business growth. Ideally, the founder should be able to add a measure of professional management without sacrificing the entrepreneurial spirit and basic values that have given the business a successful start.

EXPANDING BEYOND THE COMFORT ZONE

Although some large corporations experience poor management, small enterprises seem particularly vulnerable to this weakness. Many small firms are marginal or unprofitable businesses, struggling to survive from day to day. At best, they earn only a meager living for their owners.

It is common to hear about businesses that become successful, are praised for their problem-solving wizardry, and start to take on high-prestige customers. But it is precisely at that point when many companies start to lose their business grip. When these ventures were small, with perhaps a few dozen employees and a handful of projects in the pipeline, they were able to perform quite well. But when they expanded beyond some comfortable point, problems began to mount. Suppliers started to gripe about late payments, customers became unhappy because of delayed deliveries and shoddy workmanship, and employee morale began to drift. This can easily be the beginning of the end, and bankruptcy is all too often the final outcome. In the postmortem, it becomes clear that the cause of failure in many cases was a lack of professional management. The good news, however, is that poor management is neither universal nor inevitable.

MANAGING THE CONSTRAINTS THAT HAMPER SMALL BUSINESSES

Managers of small firms, particularly new and growing companies, are constrained by conditions that do not trouble the average corporate executive—they must face the grim reality of small bank accounts and limited staff. A small firm often lacks the money for slick sales brochures, and it cannot afford much in the way of marketing research. The shortage of cash also makes it difficult to employ an adequate number of support staff. Such limitations are painfully apparent to managers who move from large firms into positions in small companies.

Michael Fertik, a serial Internet entrepreneur and experienced CEO, reflects on some of the major differences between managing in a large corporation and in a startup. In a new venture situation, he says,

> *You can't wait around for someone from "IT" to set up your computer. There is no IT department! You should plan to schedule your own meetings and organize your own recruiting pipeline. If you're going to do something bigger like investigate a new channel opportunity, research it yourself, call prospective customers personally, make some mock-ups (if you can't use Adobe, draw on paper; if you can't draw, sketch; if you can't sketch, ask your nephew), model the growth, and create the PowerPoint deck.*[18]

Because small firms typically have few specialized staff members, most small business managers have no choice but to be generalists. Lacking the support of experienced specialists in such areas as marketing research, financial analysis, advertising, and human resource management, the manager of a small firm often must make decisions in these areas without the expertise that is available in a larger business. This limitation may be partially overcome by using outside management assistance (the sources of which are discussed later in this chapter). But coping with a shortage of internal professional talent is part of the reality of managing an entrepreneurial company.

19-2b Firm Growth and Managerial Practices

As a newly formed business becomes established and grows, its organizational structure and pattern of management will need to be adjusted. To some extent, management in any organization must adapt to growth and change. However, the changes involved in the early growth stages of a new business are much more extensive than those that occur with the growth of a relatively mature business.

A number of experts have proposed models related to the growth stages of business firms.[19] These models typically describe four or five stages of growth and identify various management issues related to each step. The model that we offer focuses mostly on the managerial challenges that go along with each of these phases of expansion.

Exhibit 19.1 shows four stages of organizational growth characteristic of many small businesses. As firms progress from Stage 1 to Stage 4, they add layers of management and increase the formality of operations. Though some firms skip the first stage or two by starting as larger businesses, thousands of small firms make their way through each of the stages pictured in the exhibit.

In Stage 1, the startup is simply a one-person operation. Some firms begin with a larger organization, but the solo venture is by no means rare; in fact, many businesses remain one-person endeavors indefinitely. In Stage 2, the entrepreneur becomes a player-coach, which implies continuing active participation in business operations. In addition to performing the basic work—whether making the product, selling it, writing checks, keeping records, or other activities—the entrepreneur must also coordinate the efforts of others.

A major milestone is reached in Stage 3, when an intermediate level of supervision is added. In many ways, this is a turning point for a small firm, because the entrepreneur must rise above direct, hands-on management and work through an intervening

EXHIBIT 19.1 Organizational Stages of Small Business Growth

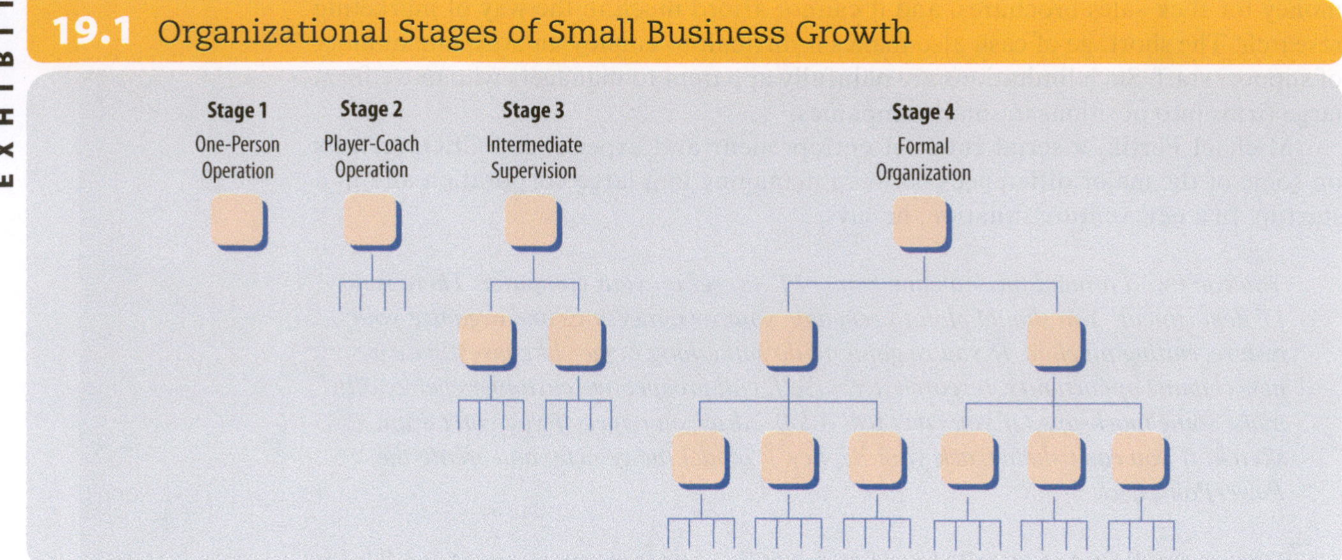

layer of management. Conversion to formalized management in Stage 4 typically requires that the company begin to adopt written policies, prepare plans and budgets, standardize personnel practices, computerize records, put together organizational charts and job descriptions, schedule training conferences, set up control procedures, and so on. While some formal managerial practices may be adopted prior to Stage 4, the steps shown in Exhibit 19.1 outline a typical pattern of development for successful firms. Flexibility and informality may be helpful when a business is first started, but growth requires greater formality in planning and control. Tensions often develop as the traditional easygoing patterns of management become dysfunctional. The entrepreneur will need to demonstrate great skill if he or she wants to preserve a "family" atmosphere while introducing professional management.

From Stage 1 to Stage 4, the pattern of entrepreneurial activities changes. The small business owner becomes less of a doer and more of a leader and manager. Those with strong "doing" skills often have weak managing skills, and this is understandable. Most entrepreneurs build businesses on their specialized capabilities; for example, they may know software development inside and out, have a knack for raising money, or possess enviable selling skills. But when it comes to tasks like assessing talent in others, they often come up short. This limitation can be a serious problem, although sometimes the personal talent or brilliance of the entrepreneur can enable a business to survive while necessary skills are being acquired.

Small firms that hesitate to move through the various organizational stages and acquire the necessary professional management often limit their rate of growth. On the other hand, a small business may attempt to grow too quickly. If an entrepreneur's primary strength lies in product development or selling, for example, a quick move into Stage 4 may saddle the entrepreneur with managerial duties and deprive the organization of her or his valuable talents.

An entrepreneur plays a different role in starting a business than in operating the firm as it becomes more fully developed. And the personal qualities involved in starting a venture differ from the qualities required to manage over the long haul. This helps to explain why so few new ventures actually become established businesses with staying power. Growing a business requires maturation and adaptation on the part of the entrepreneur.

19-3 MANAGERIAL RESPONSIBILITIES OF ENTREPRENEURS

Identify the managerial tasks of entrepreneurs.

So far, our discussion of the management process has been very general. Now it is time to look more closely at how entrepreneurs organize and direct a company's operations.

19-3a Planning Activities

Beyond creating an initial business plan to guide the *launch* of a new venture (the focus of Chapter 6), most entrepreneurs also plan for the ongoing operation of their enterprises. However, the amount of planning is typically less than ideal and tends to be haphazard and focused on specific and pressing issues—for example, how much inventory to have on hand, whether to buy a new piece of equipment, and so on. Circumstances affect the degree to which formal planning is needed, but most businesses can function more profitably by increasing the amount of planning done by managers and making it more systematic.

long-range plan (strategic plan)
A firm's overall plan for the future.

short-range plans
A plan that governs a firm's operations for one year or less.

budget
A document that expresses future plans in monetary terms.

A firm's basic path to the future is spelled out in a document called a **long-range plan**, or **strategic plan**. As noted in Chapter 3, strategy decisions concern issues such as identifying niche markets and establishing features that differentiate a firm from its competitors. But planning is important, even in established businesses, to ensure that changes in the business environment can be addressed as they occur.

Short-range plans are action plans designed to deal with activities in production, marketing, and other areas over a period of one year or less. An important part of a short-range operating plan is the **budget**, a document that expresses future plans in monetary terms. A budget is usually prepared each year (one year in advance), with a breakdown of figures for each month or quarter. (Budgeting is explained in much greater detail in Chapter 22.)

Planning pays off in many ways. First, the process of thinking through the issues confronting a company and developing a plan to deal with those issues can improve productivity. Second, planning provides a focus for a firm: Managerial decisions over the course of the year can be guided by the annual plan, and employees can work consistently toward the same goal. Third, evidence of planning increases credibility with bankers, suppliers, and other outsiders.

Winning the Race against Time
In business, time is money. But feeling pressed for time can diminish your focus, cause your rational decision-making skills to break down, and erode your health. Look for signs—like a churning stomach, a pounding heart, or talking a mile a minute—that signal a need to take a deep breath and slow down. For more suggestions, see Joe Robinson, "How to Deal with Deadline Panic," which can be found at www.entrepreneur.com/article/217408.

Managing time during the course of the business day is another important planning activity for small business managers, who all too often succumb to what is sometimes called the "tyranny of the urgent." In other words, they can easily become distracted by fighting the everyday fires of business. This makes it easy to ignore or postpone planning to free up time and energy to concentrate on more urgent issues in areas such as production and sales. And, just as quarterbacks who are focusing on a receiver may be blindsided by blitzing linebackers, managers who have neglected to plan may be bowled over by competitors. (Personal time management is discussed in more depth later in the chapter.)

19-3b Creating an Organizational Structure

While an entrepreneur may give direction through personal leadership, she or he must also define the relationships among the firm's activities and among the individuals on the firm's payroll. Without some kind of organizational structure, operations eventually become chaotic and morale suffers.

THE UNPLANNED STRUCTURE

In very small companies, the organizational structure tends to evolve with little conscious planning. Certain employees begin performing particular functions when the company is new and retain those functions as it matures.

This natural evolution is not necessarily bad. In fact, a strong element of practicality often characterizes these arrangements. The structure is forged through the experience of working and growing, rather than being pulled out of thin air or copied from another firm's organizational chart. But unplanned structures are usually far from perfect, and growth typically creates a need for organizational change. The entrepreneur should therefore examine structural relationships periodically and make adjustments as needed for effective teamwork.

THE CHAIN OF COMMAND

A **chain of command** refers to superior-subordinate relationships with a downward flow of instructions, but it involves much more. It is also a channel for two-way communication. As a practical matter, strict adherence to the chain of command is not advisable. An organization in which the primary channel of communication is rigid will be bureaucratic and inefficient. At the same time, frequent and flagrant disregard of the chain of command quickly undermines the position of the bypassed manager. There is need for balance, and getting this right requires reasonable care and heads-up management.

In a **line organization**, each person has one supervisor to whom he or she reports and looks for instructions. All employees are directly engaged in the firm's work, producing, selling, and performing office or financial duties. Most very small firms—for example, those with fewer than 10 employees—use this form of organization.

A **line-and-staff organization** is similar to a line organization in that each person reports to a single supervisor. However, a line-and-staff structure also has staff specialists who perform specific services or act as management advisors in particular areas (see Exhibit 19.2). Staff specialists may include a human resource manager, a production control technician, a quality control expert, and an assistant to the president. The line-and-staff organization, in some form, is used in many small businesses.

chain of command
The official, vertical channel of communication in an organization.

line organization
A simple organizational structure in which each person reports to one supervisor.

line-and-staff organization
An organizational structure that includes staff specialists who assist management.

EXHIBIT **19.2** Line-and-Staff Organization

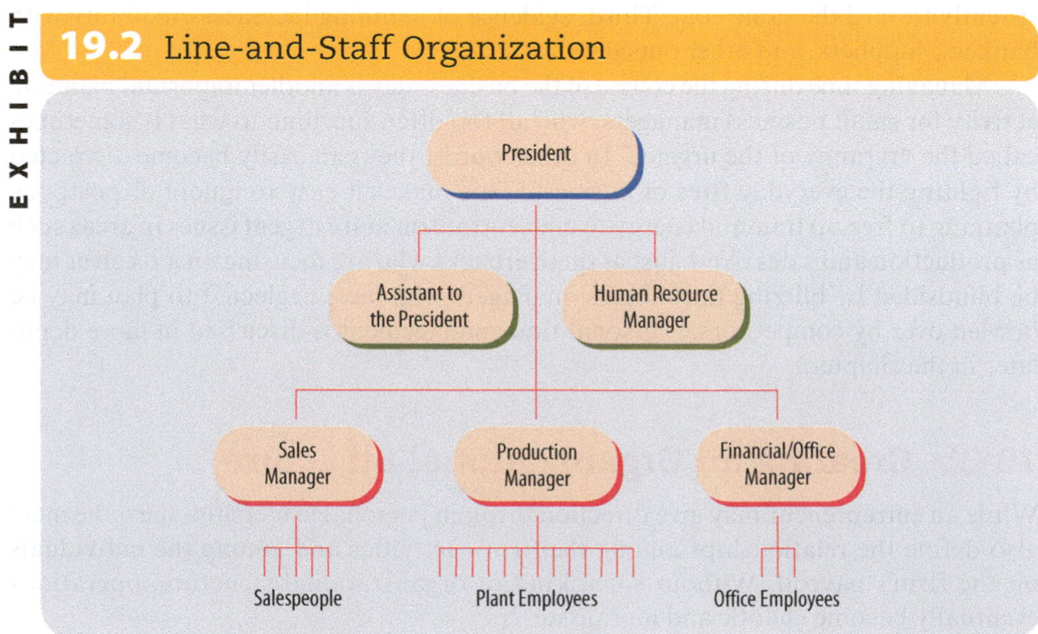

SPAN OF CONTROL

The **span of control** is the number of employees who are supervised by a manager. Although some experts have stated that six to eight people are all that one individual can supervise effectively, the optimal span of control is actually a variable that depends on a number of factors. Among these factors are the nature of the work and the manager's knowledge, energy, personality, and abilities. In addition, if the abilities of subordinates are better than average, the span of control may be broadened accordingly.

As a very small firm grows and adds employees, the small business owner's span of control is extended. Eventually, the attempted span of control exceeds the entrepreneur's reach, demanding more time and effort than she or he can devote to the business. It is at this point that the entrepreneur must establish intermediate levels of supervision and dedicate more time to management, moving beyond the role of player-coach.

19-3c Delegating Authority

Through **delegation of authority**, a manager grants to subordinates the right to act or to make decisions. Turning over some functions to subordinates by delegating authority frees the superior to perform more important tasks.

Although failure to delegate may be found in any organization, it is often a special problem for entrepreneurs, given their backgrounds and personalities. Because they frequently must pay for mistakes made by subordinates, owners are inclined to keep a firm hold on the reins of leadership in order to protect the business. Some of the problem is simply a matter of habit and momentum. Many entrepreneurs have become accustomed to doing everything themselves, which makes it difficult to turn over some tasks to others when the business grows and they truly need help with their expanded responsibilities. Some owners also may simply feel the need to continue doing those things that made the firm successful or conclude that they just do them better than their employees. Regardless of the underlying concern, the end result is the same: insufficient delegation and the piling up of work that needs more focused attention.

© ZUDY/SHUTTERSTOCK.COM

Inability or unwillingness to delegate authority can become apparent in a number of ways. For example, subordinates who have to clear even minor decisions with the boss may flood the owner with a constant stream of requests in order to resolve issues that they lack the authority to settle. This keeps the owner exceptionally busy—rushing from assisting a salesperson to helping iron out a production bottleneck to setting up a new filing system. Entrepreneurs often work long hours, and those who have difficulty delegating compound the problem.

Despite the profound business results that Jason Fried, co-founder of Web applications company Basecamp, has been able to achieve, he still finds delegation difficult. When Fried and his partner decided it was time to hire an executive assistant to handle many of the administrative tasks that were distracting them from their most important initiatives, he realized that he was bothered by the plan.

> *Even though the paperwork and other chores were piling up, I still had a hard time letting go. I have a feeling I am not alone in this. . . . For more than a decade I had*

span of control
The number of employees who are supervised by one manager.

delegation of authority
The process of granting to subordinates the right to act or make decisions.

been involved in every decision at this company, from which hosting company to use to what brand of paper towel goes into the kitchen. When you're used to having every decision run through you, it can be a bit unnerving to surrender control. I understand that it's silly to believe that every small decision needs to be run through you. But it's such a primal instinct when your business is your baby.[20]

After months of interviews, Fried and his colleague finally found and hired the perfect assistant. He still wasn't sure he could let go, but the stacks of files and boxes around his desk reminded him of the need to release his grip. Once Fried was able to turn over a few tasks to his new assistant, it became easier to let go of others. And he is really glad that he did. She was able to make a number of problems go away. This allowed Fried and his partner to spend their time more profitably, focusing their attention on work that is driving the business forward.[21] That's what delegation is all about.

As one small business writer has observed, "By delegating authority, entrepreneurs unleash the same force in their subordinates that makes them so productive: the thrill of being in charge."[22] This is not to say that delegation is a cure-all for management challenges. In fact, turning over duties can easily lead to its own problems as a result of a subordinate's carelessness or some other failure. But this can be minimized, if the handover is managed well. We offer the following suggestions to ease the transition:

- Accept the fact that you will not be able to make all of the decisions anymore. If you don't, you will blunt the venture's potential to grow and develop.
- Prepare yourself emotionally for the loss of control that small business owners feel when they first start to delegate. This is completely natural.
- Manage carefully the process of finding, selecting, hiring, and retaining employees who are trustworthy enough to handle greater responsibility. In other words, keep an eye on the future when you hire new staff.
- Move forward one step at a time. Start by delegating those functions that you are most comfortable giving up. Even then, continue to provide reasonable oversight to smooth the transition and to ensure the quality of the work.
- Plan to invest the time needed to coach those who are taking over new responsibilities so that they can master required skills. The first thing to do is to write job descriptions to help minimize confusion.
- Make delegation meaningful. Focus on results, and give subordinates the flexibility to carry out assignments. To realize the benefits of delegation, you must build leadership in subordinates, who can then take on more advanced and complex tasks.

If you want to turbocharge the success of your delegation efforts, think carefully about those you ask to join your venture. In response to one entrepreneur who admitted having a hard time turning tasks over to others completely, Phil Libin, co-founder and CEO of popular notetaking and archiving startup Evernote, offered the following solution: "Hiring people smarter than yourself is the long-term answer to your micromanagement problem."[23] If they can do the job better than you could ever hope to do it, delegating will actually *reduce* your stress level, and you will be able to focus your time and attention on the things you do best.

19-3d Controlling Operations

Despite good planning, organizations never function perfectly. As a result, managers must monitor operations to discover deviations from plans and make corrections when necessary. These managerial activities serve to keep the business on course.

The control process begins with the establishment of standards, which are set through planning and goal setting. Planners translate goals into norms (standards) by making them measurable. A goal to increase market share, for example, could be expressed as a projected dollar increase in sales volume for the coming year. Such an annual target may, in turn, be broken down into quarterly target standards so that corrective action can be taken early if performance begins to fall below the projected level.

As Exhibit 19.3 shows, performance measurement occurs at various stages of the control process: at the input stage, perhaps to determine the quality of materials purchased; during the process stage, perhaps to determine if a machine is operating within predetermined tolerances; and at the output stage, perhaps to check the quality of a completed product.

Corrective action is required when performance deviates significantly from the standard in an unfavorable direction. To prevent the problem from recurring, such action must be followed by an analysis of the cause of the deviation. If the percentage of defective products increases, for example, a manager must determine whether this is caused by substandard raw materials, untrained workers, equipment failure, or some other factor. For a problem to be effectively controlled, corrective action must identify and deal with the true cause.

19-3e Communicating

Another key to a healthy organization is effective communication—that is, getting managers and employees to talk with one another and openly share problems and ideas. The result is two-way communication—a far cry from the old-fashioned idea that managers give orders and employees simply carry them out.

Solid research proves that effective staff communication is crucial to small business success. One study found that companies following sound communication practices report higher levels of "employee engagement" and lower turnover. And this has implications for the bottom line. For example, the study's researchers estimated that firms that communicate effectively are worth, on average, nearly 20 percent more than their interaction-challenged counterparts.[24] Still, workplace communication is rarely adequate—indeed, there is always room for improvement.

EXHIBIT 19.3 Stages of the Control Process

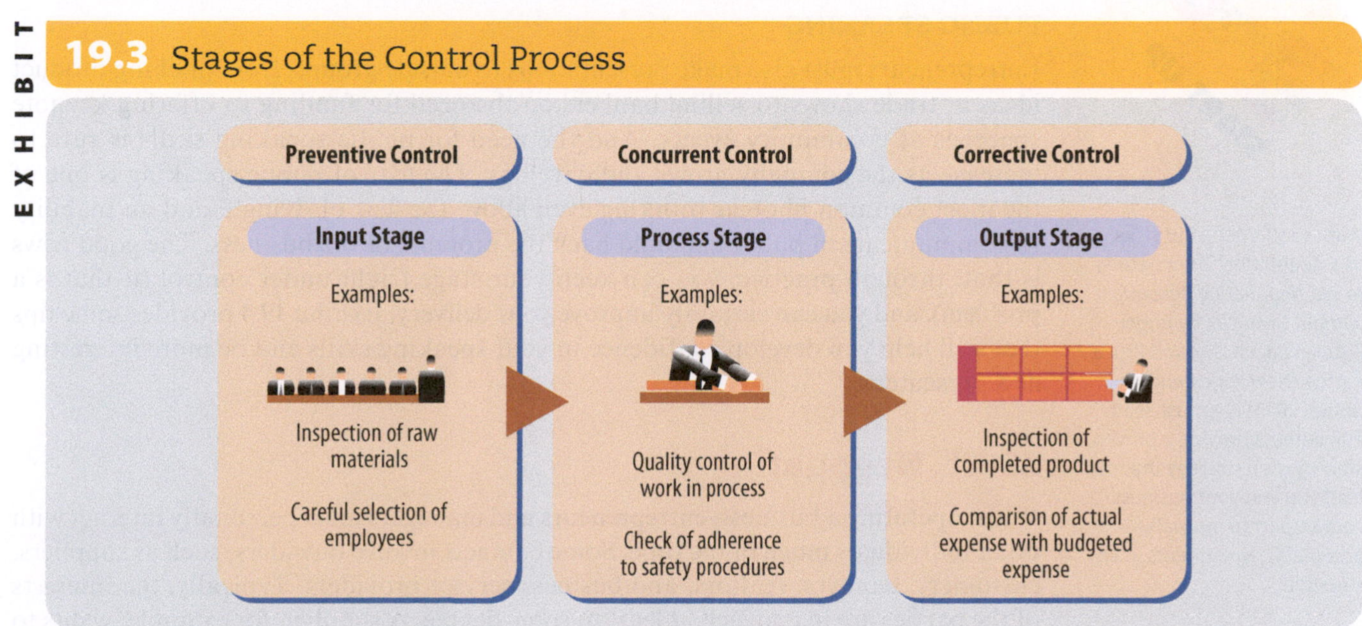

To communicate effectively, managers must tell employees where they stand, how the business is doing, and what the firm's plans are for the future. While negative feedback may be necessary at times, giving positive feedback to employees is the primary tool for establishing good human relations. Perhaps the most fundamental concept managers need to keep in mind is that employees are people, not machines. They can quickly detect insincerity but respond to honest efforts to treat them as mature, responsible individuals. In short, an atmosphere of trust and respect contributes greatly to good communication.

COMMUNICATIONS TOOLS

Many practical tools and techniques can be used to stimulate two-way communication between managers and employees. Here are some that may work for you and your enterprise:

- Periodic performance review sessions to discuss employees' ideas, questions, complaints, and job expectations
- Physical or virtual bulletin boards to keep employees informed about developments affecting them and/or the company
- Blogs for internal communication, especially in companies that have open organizational cultures and truly want transparent dialogue
- Microblogging tools (like Twitter and Yammer) to enable employees to communicate, collaborate, and share brief thoughts and observations about the business in real time
- Physical or virtual suggestion boxes to solicit employees' ideas on possible improvements
- Wikis set up to bring issues to the surface and draw feedback from employees
- Formal staff meetings to discuss problems and matters of general concern
- Breakfast or lunch with employees to socialize and just talk

These methods and others can be used to supplement the most basic of all channels for communication—the day-to-day interactions between each employee and his or her supervisor.

Powerful Persuaders
Want to sharpen your skills as a negotiator? Then *Getting to Yes: Negotiating Agreement without Giving In*, by Roger Fisher, William Ury, and Bruce Patton (New York: Penguin Books, 2011) is a must-read. The authors provide a proven, step-by-step strategy that can lead you and your business counterpart to mutually acceptable agreements in any situation.

PUBLIC SPEAKING

Entrepreneurs must also make presentations to outside groups, from pitching product ideas at trade shows to selling bankers on the need for funding to offering keynote speeches at community events. And the need for public speaking skills is sure to increase as the company grows and develops. The fear of public speaking is one of the most common phobias (ranking even above the fear of dying!), and an inability to communicate in public can hold back the progress of the business. The good news is that, through practice, you can keep your stage fright under control (if that is a problem), and you can certainly improve your delivery. Exhibit 19.4 provides some tips that will help you develop confidence in your speaking skills and be more interesting as a presenter.

19-3f Negotiating

When operating a business, entrepreneurs and managers must personally interact with other individuals much of the time. Some contacts involve outsiders, such as suppliers, customers, bankers, realtors, and business service providers. Typically, the interests of the parties are in conflict, at least to some degree. A supplier, for example, wants to

EXHIBIT 19.4 Presentation Tips

1. **Do your homework.** Know the purpose of the presentation and to whom you will be presenting. If you can find out in advance who will be attending your presentation, you will be able to adapt your comments to their needs and concerns.
2. **Know your material.** The better you know what you plan to talk about, the more you can concentrate on the delivery. And being prepared inspires confidence.
3. **Be interactive.** Listeners may be lulled into disinterest when they are not engaged. Find ways to get the audience involved in what you have to say. Don't, for example, read from your notes for extended periods of time—doing so will ensure that the communication goes in only one direction, and your audience will know it immediately.
4. **Make vivid mental connections in the minds of listeners.** Telling stories helps, but so can other tools and techniques. For example, use props to focus attention, or employ a metaphor throughout the presentation to draw listeners back to a central theme. Humor is entertaining and can provide comic relief, but it can also be used to make a point unforgettable.
5. **Emphasize relevance.** Your listeners are busy people, so be sure to deliver information that they will find useful and worth their time.
6. **Be dynamic, but be yourself.** Let your listeners know that you are passionate about the topic by the way you invest yourself in the presentation. It is much easier for an audience to remain engaged when the presenter is energetic and uses inflections, gestures, movement, and facial expressions to show it. Maintaining eye contact communicates that you want to connect with each individual in the room, which is motivating. However, if your level of energy and your use of voice and body are less than authentic, listeners will quickly pick up on that and may write off the talk as insincere.
7. **Use PowerPoint with care.** Text-laden slides can produce the same effect as sleeping pills. If a picture paints a thousand words, then adding pictures and graphics can certainly help the audience access the ideas you want to convey (as long as they are not flashy to the point of distraction). Limit the text on each slide, and do not read from the slides you are showing. Try to imagine how you would respond to the slides if you were not particularly interested in the topic, and then make adjustments accordingly.
8. **Dress appropriately.** Although your audience may be wearing more casual clothing, dress in business professional attire. Avoid distracting clothing (like a tie that draws attention away from what you have to say), and check to be sure that everything you're wearing is in order before standing up to speak.
9. **Avoid food and drink that make speaking difficult for you.** Caffeinated drinks and sugary foods can make you jittery, which will only add to your nervousness. If you find that you need to clear your throat often after consuming certain foods or beverages, avoid them before speaking engagements.
10. **Practice, practice, practice.** The more presentations you give, the more you will feel confident while giving them. And one of the best ways to conquer stage fright is to spend time speaking in front of others. Recognize that your discomfort with public speaking is likely to fade with experience at the podium.

sell a product or service for the highest possible price, and the buyer wants to purchase it for the lowest possible price. To have a successful business, a manager must be able to reach agreements that both meet the firm's requirements and contribute to good relationships over time.

Even within the business, personal relationships pit different perspectives and personal interests against one another. Subordinates, for example, frequently desire changes in their work assignments or feel that they are worth more to the company than their salary levels indicate. Managers in different departments may compete for services offered by a maintenance department or a computer services unit.

The process of developing workable solutions through discussions or interactions is called **negotiation**. We are all negotiators in our daily lives, both inside and outside our family relationships. Conflicting interests, desires, and demands require that we reconcile, or negotiate, differences in order to live together peacefully.

negotiation
The process of developing workable solutions through discussions or interactions.

Many people consider negotiation to be a win-lose game; that is, one party must win, and the other must lose. The problem with this concept of negotiation is that if parties feel that they have lost, they may go away with thoughts of getting even in subsequent dealings. Clearly, such feelings do not contribute to good long-term relationships. In contrast, other negotiators advocate a win-win strategy. A win-win negotiator tries to find a solution that will satisfy at least the basic interests of both parties.

Implementing a win-win strategy in relationships involves thinking about one's own interests while also exploring those of the other party. After clarifying the interests of the involved parties and their needs, the negotiator can explore various alternatives to identify their overall fit, looking for a solution that will produce a plan that is workable for all. There are situations in which a win-win solution is impossible, but a positive solution should be pursued whenever it is feasible to do so. And, of course, a foundation for successful negotiation is created by developing strong relationships between the negotiating parties, which can facilitate cooperation.

19-4 PERSONAL TIME MANAGEMENT

Describe the problem of time pressure and suggest solutions.

A typical small business owner spends much of the workday on the front lines—meeting customers, solving problems, listening to employee complaints, talking with suppliers, and the like. She or he tackles such problems with the assistance of only a small staff. As a result, the owner-manager's energies and activities are diffused, and time becomes a scarce resource. This highlights the importance of *time management*. However, as author and personal achievement expert Barry Farber points out, "When you think about time management, realize that you don't really manage time—you manage activities."[25] It's an interesting way to think about one of the challenges you are sure to face.

19-4a The Problem of Time Pressure

Survey results reported by *Inc.* magazine indicate that 43 percent of small business owners work 40 to 80 hours in a typical week. Another 13 percent of those surveyed actually put in more than 80 hours a week![26] Such schedules often lead to inefficient work performance, especially when the entrepreneur has not made the necessary effort to set priorities in life and work. Owner-managers may be too busy to see sales representatives who could supply market information on new products and processes, too busy to read technical reports or trade literature that would tell them what others are doing and what improvements might be adapted to their own use, too busy to listen carefully to employees' opinions and grievances, and too busy to give employees the instructions they need to do their jobs correctly.

Need an Idea, and Fast?
Leaders often find themselves on the spot, needing a creative solution to a very pressing problem—but with no time to spare. When you find yourself in this situation, it's best to be able to think on your feet. As Gerald Haman, president of innovation-training agency SolutionPeople, explains, research shows that standing up increases oxygen flow to the brain, which stimulates thinking. See "How to ... Lead a Late-Afternoon Brainstorm," *FastCompany*, No. 172 (February 2013), p. 28.

Getting away for a vacation seems impossible for some small business owners, and more than a third of them report having taken less than a week off during the past year.[27] In extremely small firms, owners may find it necessary to close the business during their absence. Even in somewhat larger businesses, owners may fear that the firm will not function properly if they are not there. Unfortunately, keeping one's nose to the grindstone in this way may cost an entrepreneur dearly in terms of personal health, family relationships, and effectiveness in business leadership.

19-4b Time Savers for Busy Managers

Part of the solution to the problem of time pressure is the application of the managerial approaches discussed in the preceding section. For example, when possible, the manager should assign duties to subordinates who can work without close supervision. For such delegation to work, though, a manager must first select and train qualified employees.

The greatest time saver is the effective use of time. Little will be achieved if an individual flits from one task to another and back again. On the other hand, using smartphones, e-mail, the Internet, and other technologies can be very helpful in allowing a manager to make the most of his or her time. (A note of caution: Because these tools can become a distraction, they need to be used wisely. For example, checking and responding at length to incoming e-mail messages throughout the day can distract from the tasks at hand and should be minimized.)

E-mails—Getting to the Point

Do you find that answering e-mail is taking up way too much of your day? A tool called five.sentenc.es (found at exactly that URL) helps curb the length of your e-mails and explains why in the footer of the messages you send out. Want to save even more time? There are also four.sentenc .es, three.sentenc.es, and two .sentenc.es options.

The first step in time management should be to analyze how much time is normally spent on various activities. Relying on general impressions is unlikely to be accurate. Instead, for a period of a few days or (preferably) weeks, the owner-manager should record the amounts of time she or he spends on various activities during the day. An analysis of these figures will reveal a pattern, indicating which projects and tasks consume the most time and which activities are responsible for wasted time. It will also uncover chronic time wasting due to excessive socializing, work on trivial matters, coffee breaks, and so on.

If your habits are typical, you will probably find that the workplace "time wasters" in your life will include such things as time lost from telephone interruptions, drop-in visitors, ineffective delegation, losing things in desk clutter, procrastination, and frequent or lengthy meetings. (Some entrepreneurs and experts argue that efficiency losses from messy desks are more than offset by the creativity they generate, but this is clearly debatable.) Knowing the distractions that others find to be time wasters may help you to pinpoint those that are creating a problem for you. Only by identifying these distractions can you take steps to deal with them.

After eliminating practices that waste time, a manager can carefully plan his or her use of available time. A planned approach to a day's or week's work is much more effective than a haphazard, do-whatever-comes-up-first style. This is true even for small firm managers, whose schedules are continually interrupted in unanticipated ways.

Many time management specialists recommend the use of a daily written plan of work activities, often called a "to-do" list. A survey of 2,000 executives from mostly small companies found that around 95 percent of them keep a list of things to do. Those executives may have 6 to 20 items on their list at any given time, though fewer than 1 percent of them complete all listed tasks on a daily basis.[28] Many entrepreneurs use Microsoft Outlook or a day planner to create and manage these lists, but others might use a to-do list mobile app, note cards, or even sticky notes—there are many options. Regardless of the medium selected, you should highlight priorities among listed items. By classifying duties as first-, second-, or third-level priorities, you can focus attention on the most crucial tasks.

To prioritize action items more precisely, you could adopt the approach used by Dwight D. Eisenhower, 34th president of the United States. He observed, "What is important is seldom urgent, and what is urgent is seldom important." In other words, many things that do not seem to be all that pressing actually deserve your immediate focus, and others that cry out for your attention are not all that important and should not be acted on first, though they often are. Your time and attention should be prioritized as follows:[29]

1. Give your attention first to critical activities (urgent and important). Leave enough slack time in your schedule to deal with unexpected issues and activities.
2. Next, deal with important concerns (not urgent, but important). These will not seem pressing, but they support the long-term goals of the company and should be given sufficient time.

Living the Dream

ENTREPRENEURIAL EXPERIENCES

Cluttered Desk, Creative Mind?

Most desks at TheSquareFoot.com, an online real estate and brokerage company in New York, are clean and well organized. There is, however, one exception. Co-founder Jonathan Wasserstrum's desk and cubicle are covered with paper, files, and old tech-gear. "I like being near my stuff rather than fishing for it in a cabinet somewhere," he says.

But the clutter is causing friction in the office. The startup's other co-founder, Justin Lee, finds his colleague's stuff to be a distraction and difficult to work around. From time to time, "some of his crud will spill over onto my desk," Lee protests. Other co-workers often find themselves printing additional copies of documents to avoid food-smeared paperwork coming from Wasserstrum's desk.

Conventional wisdom maintains that working in an organized cubicle boosts focus and productivity. This notion is consistent with findings of a CareerBuilder survey in which 28 percent of employers reported that they would be less likely to promote an employee with a poorly organized workspace. Research has also shown that a messy individual's workspace may distract neighbors and lead to a dip in performance. The issue is especially important in companies with open-office design plans, expanded shared workspaces, and shrinking office footprints (which have decreased in size by 21 percent over the last decade and a half).

But the conventional wisdom may be overlooking the upside of a cluttered office. From a study of 48 students, researchers from the University of Minnesota learned that people working in disorganized environments are more likely to propose creative ideas. "Being creative is breaking away from tradition, order and convention, and a disorderly environment seems to help people do just that," they assert in a *Psychological Science* article. For those who have maintained that clutter fuels innovation, these conclusions are not surprising. Even Albert Einstein, notorious for his messy desk, is said to have quipped, "If a cluttered desk is a sign of a cluttered mind, then what are we to think of an empty desk?"

© MICOLAS/SHUTTERSTOCK.COM

Many firms, such as Google, actively encourage workspace disorganization with the aim of capitalizing on clutter-fueled creative impulses. The company even issued $50 incentives to employees with explicit instructions to buy desk decorations. Backed up by the results of the *Psychological Science* study, the firm's practice suggests that Wasserstrum's desk, while disorganized, may actually yield positive outcomes.

The tricky balance for managers then is to weigh the needs of both messy and organized workers in order to maximize the productivity and potential of each group. "The appearance of your desk or work area is hugely important," says Judith Bowman, a coach and author on corporate etiquette. "But it's so personal. Criticizing someone's messy desk is like telling someone they're dressed sloppily or have a dirty house." Instead, she recommends inspiring employees by consistently exhibiting an organized desk and periodically holding an office-wide "de-junking" day. That is certainly a gentler approach to the problem.

Sources: "About TheSquareFoot," http://www.thesquarefoot.com/about, accessed February 25, 2015; Dale Buss, "Messy-Deskers Unite: New Study Hints That We're More Creative," *Forbes*, September 19, 2013, http://www.forbes.com/sites/dalebuss/2013/09/19/messy-deskers-unite-new-study-hints-that-were-more-creative, accessed February 25, 2015; Richard Feloni, "Why Google Encourages Having a Messy Desk," *Business Insider*, September 26, 2014, http://www.businessinsider.com/why-google-encourages-having-a-messy-desk-2014-9, accessed February 25, 2015; and Sue Shellenbarger, "Clashing over Office Clutter: I'm Not Messy, I'm Creative," *The Wall Street Journal*, March 19, 2014, pp. D1–D2.

3. Interruptions (urgent, but not important) can keep you from completing important work. Reschedule or delegate these tasks, if possible, and be prepared to respond to requests with a polite "no" when necessary.
4. Finally, avoid distractions (not urgent and not important) as much as possible. If they are not pressing and do not matter, attend to them only as you have spare time.

Following these guidelines will help you to focus your time and attention in order to achieve the most productive outcomes.

There are countless guides to time management, and they offer many valuable tips: Get a good time management system and use it, try to make meetings more efficient, unsubscribe from magazines and catalogs you never read, create a file folder for active projects, keep your desk and office organized, use deadlines to promote focus, manage e-mail effectively, and so on. However, the one bit of advice that seems to show up on just about every list of suggestions is to set aside time to work undisturbed. As the pace of business and the flow of information pick up speed, and new technologies and media channels increasingly compete for your attention, preserving time for focused work on important projects becomes more and more difficult—but it is critical that you do so. The health and future of your company may very well depend on it!

In the final analysis, effective time management requires firmly established priorities and self-discipline. An individual may begin with good intentions but then lapse into habitually attending to whatever he or she finds to do at the moment. Procrastination is another common problem—many managers delay unpleasant and difficult tasks, retreating to trivial and less-threatening activities with the rationalization that they are getting those duties out of the way in order to better concentrate on the more important tasks. It is essential to identify such "time thieves" and correct them as soon as possible.

19-5 OUTSIDE MANAGEMENT ASSISTANCE

Outline the various types of outside management assistance.

Because entrepreneurs tend to be better doers than they are managers, they should consider the use of outside management assistance. Such support can supplement the manager's personal knowledge and the expertise of the few staff specialists on the company's payroll.

19-5a The Need for Outside Assistance

Entrepreneurs often lack opportunities to share ideas with peers, given the small staff in most new enterprises. Consequently, they may experience a sense of loneliness. Some small business owners reduce their feelings of isolation by joining groups such as the Entrepreneurs' Organization (eonetwork.org) and the Young Presidents' Organization (ypo.org), which allow them to meet with peers from other firms and share problems and experiences.

Peer groups and other sources of outside managerial assistance can offer a detached, often objective point of view and new ideas. They may also possess knowledge of methods, approaches, and solutions beyond the experience of a particular entrepreneur.

19-5b Sources of Management Assistance

Entrepreneurs seeking management assistance can turn to any number of sources, including SBA-funded programs, management consultants, and personal and business networks. Many colleges and universities also offer support that can help entrepreneurs navigate small business challenges.

U.S. SMALL BUSINESS ADMINISTRATION (SBA)

For many aspiring small business owners, the U.S. Small Business Administration (SBA) is an important gateway to information and support for startups and other small companies, and it is often the first place they go for assistance. The federal government specifically tasks the SBA with connecting entrepreneurs with the resources they need to start and/or grow their companies. In accord with its mandate, the agency helps small businesses across the country through a variety of support programs. The SBA offers the Service Corps of Retired Executives program and its small business development centers to provide consulting and other forms of assistance. However, it also funds a much broader range of useful counseling programs, which you can find by visiting its main website at sba.gov.

© B CHRISTOPHER/ALAMY

Service Corps of Retired Executives (SCORE) By contacting any SBA field office, small business managers can obtain free management advice from the **Service Corps of Retired Executives**, or **SCORE** (score.org). SCORE has more than 13,000 working and retired business executives who serve as volunteer consultants to assist nearly 500,000 small business clients each year.[30] As a resource partner of the SBA, SCORE provides an opportunity for retired executives to contribute to the business community and, in the process, help small business managers to solve their problems. The relationship is mutually beneficial.

Small Business Development Centers (SBDCs) Patterned after the Agricultural Extension Service, most **small business development centers (SBDCs)** are affiliated with colleges or universities as a part of the SBA's overall program of assistance to small business. Operating from some 900 delivery points, SBDCs provide a wide range of services, including business plan consultation, export and import support, help with market research, and financial lending assistance. The staff typically includes faculty members, SCORE counselors, professional staff, and graduate student assistants.[31]

EDUCATIONAL INSTITUTIONS

Many colleges and universities have student consulting teams willing to assist small businesses. These teams of upper-class and graduate students, under the direction of a faculty member, work with owners of small ventures in analyzing their business problems and proposing appropriate solutions to them.

Service corps of retired executives (SCORE)
An SBA-sponsored group of retired executives who give free advice to small business owners.

These programs offer mutual benefits: They provide students with a practical view of business management and supply small firms with answers to their problems. The students who participate are typically combined in teams that provide a diversity of academic backgrounds. An individual team, for example, may include students specializing in management, marketing, accounting, and finance.

small business development centers (SBDCs)
University-affiliated centers offering consulting, education, and other support to small business owners.

Some colleges and universities offer training directly to aspiring small business owners. For example, more than 300,000 entrepreneurs have gone through a business development program called FastTrac, which is available across the United States and in select countries around the world. This program, developed by the Ewing Marion Kauffman Foundation, is offered through a wide variety of affiliates, including colleges and universities, chambers of commerce, business development centers, and consulting firms. FastTrac is a practical, hands-on program designed to show entrepreneurs how to hone the practical skills they will need to start and grow a successful business. Participants don't just learn about business—they live it by working on their own business ideas.[32]

MANAGEMENT CONSULTANTS

Management consultants serve small businesses as well as large corporations, and they do this with operations that can range from large global firms to one- and two-person ventures. The results they deliver can provide a substantial boost to a small business. For example, 69 percent of the companies in an *Inc.* magazine survey reported that they had used consultants. Of these, 90 percent found their services helpful.[33] But many small firm managers are still reluctant to use outside advisors, for a host of reasons. Some believe that they can solve problems themselves, that an outsider could never truly understand the business, or that bringing in an outside advisor would simply cost too much. But some small businesses need analysis by consultants and find that the additional revenue resulting from improved performance can easily cover the cost of such services. Results definitely vary, but a growing number of small firms are accessing high-powered talent at a very low cost by using online services like HourlyNerd.com to find and hire well-trained MBA students from top-tier business schools to manage limited projects or to cover short-term needs.

For small companies that decide to pursue the consulting option directly, the owner and the consultant should reach an understanding on the nature of the assistance to be provided before it begins. This can help to ensure satisfaction for both the provider and the client. Any consulting fees should be specified, and the particulars of the agreement should be put in writing. Fees are often quoted on a per-day basis and can easily range from $500 to $5,000, or more. Although the cost may seem high, it must be evaluated in terms of the expertise that it buys.

Directories are available to help entrepreneurs find the right management consultant. One such source is published by the Institute of Management Consultants USA (imcusa.org). The code of ethics to which institute members subscribe, as posted on the website, is an indication of their desire to foster professionalism in their work.

There are now some websites that provide access to expert advice by the minute, which can be very helpful if you have a focused problem that can be addressed over the phone. One of these services, Clarity, caters specifically to the needs of entrepreneurs. Getting the ear of most of the 30,000+ experts on the site will cost you around $1.50 per minute, but the price can go way up from there—for example, it will set you back a hefty $167 per minute if you feel that you just have to talk with Mark Cuban.[34] The service is very easy to use: Simply register on the site, search the community of available experts, select a few dates/times that will work for you, and then connect, talk, and pay.[35]

SMALL BUSINESS NETWORKS

Entrepreneurs can also gain management assistance from peers through **networking**, the process of developing and engaging in mutually beneficial informal relationships. When business owners meet, they can discover a commonality of interests leading to an exchange of ideas and experiences. The settings for such meetings may be trade associations, civic clubs, fraternal organizations, or any other situation that brings businesspeople into contact with one another.

networking
The process of developing and engaging in mutually beneficial informal relationships.

But if networking is going to be of benefit to both parties, then it needs to be about more than just showing up at an event and handing out a lot of business cards. You

Living the Dream

ENTREPRENEURIAL EXPERIENCES

Piecemeal Professionals: Renting Management Talent on the Cheap

Small businesses have many short-term needs, but hiring additional staff for a small project is usually out of the question because of the high cost. They certainly can't afford to call in a top-shelf consulting firm, like McKinsey, Bain, or the Boston Consulting Group. So when these companies need fresh insight or a new marketing plan, they usually have to muddle through on their own.

But that may soon be changing. HourlyNerd, a Boston-based online marketplace, wants to meet this growing demand for expertise by connecting small businesses with MBA students who could use the money and are up for the challenge of tackling short-term projects. HourlyNerd's platform maximizes flexibility for firm and consultant alike, while lowering the cost of such services by as much as 80 percent.

The startup is the brainchild of Rob Biederman, Peter Maglathlin, and Patrick Petitti, who developed the concept as part of a class assignment while attending Harvard Business School. HourlyNerd features a database of current MBA students at top-tier business schools around the world. The co-founders agreed from the start that the quality of students and their business acumen would be key to building credibility and forming a successful business model.

After graduation, the trio committed themselves to launching the company and secured money from investors to get it off the ground. As an early signal of its potential, the startup has grown quickly, using social media and word-of-mouth from happy customers to acquire new clients. The business has served an array of customers, ranging from a very small Boston-area florist to giant firms like Microsoft and GE.

HourlyNerd attracts clients with the promise of cutting personnel costs while accessing valuable and objective insights and skills from well-trained MBA student-consultants. Because of the protracted economic slump, this model offers particular appeal, as cost-cutting measures have been widely pursued. "Small businesses need to start growing revenue again because there's no more [room for] cost-cutting," says co-founder Biederman. "They need to explore ways of growing revenue without committing to a full-time hire."

The arrangement works well for the student-consultants as well. Pursuing an MBA degree can be a very costly undertaking, adding financial strain to students who have to put their professional lives on hold for years while completing their studies. During this period, some students have enough free time to take on short-term projects. HourlyNerd simply provides a platform that allows them to flex their business acumen and earn extra income while pursuing their degrees.

HourlyNerd has experienced 35 percent compounded growth, month over month to date, having connected more than 4,500 companies with nearly 10,000 MBA students. "We recognized there was a real need for small businesses to have something like this," says co-founder Petitti, "It seemed like a no-brainer." It certainly creates an opportunity for small companies to access the talent they need, and at a price they can afford.

Sources: Iris Dorbian, "Boston Startup HourlyNerd Snaps Up $7.8 Mln," https://www.pehub.com/2015/02/boston-startup-hourlynerd-snaps-up-7-8-mln, accessed February 25, 2015; "HourlyNerd: Simple Process. Amazing Results," https://hourlynerd.com/how-it-works, accessed February 25, 2015; Melissa Korn, "For Small Work Projects, Try Renting an M.B.A.," *The Wall Street Journal*, February 6, 2014, p. B7; Louis Lavelle, "Why Hire When You Can Rent by the Hour," *Bloomberg Business*, April 11, 2013, http://www.bloomberg.com/bw/articles/2013-04-11/mbas-why-hire-when-you-can-rent-by-the-hour, accessed February 25, 2015; Gwen Moran, "MBAs by the Hour," *Entrepreneur*, Vol. 42, No. 8 (August 2014), p. 84; and Heesun Wee, "HourlyNerd Offers MBA Students for Hire for Small Businesses," *CNBC*, April 10, 2013, http://www.cnbc.com/id/100627530#, accessed February 25, 2015.

need to be prepared to create value for your counterpart on some level. Serial entrepreneur and investor Gary Vaynerchuk emphasizes that being the first to give value to the relationship reverses "the game that everyone instinctually plays" so that you stand out from the crowd, are appreciated, and are easy to remember. Vaynerchuk reports that these "pay it forward" interactions, from which he expected nothing in return, have done far more than anything else to promote his career and his companies.[36]

Harnessing a personal network, when managed wisely, can provide a tremendous boost to the launch of a new business. For example, fellow garden club members could serve as a focus group to assess startup ideas or as a PR team to spread news of your new landscaping and water pond business. Alumni connections from your college days may lead you to professionals who can take care of your legal, banking, or other needs. They may even become loyal and effective business partners, if the fit is right.

OTHER BUSINESS AND PROFESSIONAL SERVICES

A variety of other business and professional groups provide management assistance. In many cases, such assistance is part of the business relationship. Sources of management advice include bankers, certified public accountants (CPAs), attorneys, insurance agents, suppliers, trade associations, and chambers of commerce.

It takes initiative to draw on the management assistance available from such groups, so it is important to explore the possibilities. For example, rather than limiting a business relationship with a certified public accountant to audits and financial statements, many small business owners ask their CPAs to advise them on a much broader range of subjects.

A good accountant can offer advice on tax matters, as well as recommending an appropriate severance package when it comes time to fire someone. If you are thinking about opening a new branch, an accountant can tell you if your cash flow will support it. Considering the launch of an additional business? An accountant's insight will help you determine whether the margins will be adequate. Accountants can help you make informed assessments of your insurance needs, the impact of taking on a big account (as well as the downside of losing it), and the bottom-line effects of cutting expenses.

As you can see from these examples, potential management assistance often comes disguised as service from professionals and firms encountered in the normal course of business activity. By taking advantage of such opportunities, an entrepreneur can strengthen a small firm's management and improve its operations with little, if any, additional cost. But that doesn't mean it will be easy. Leading and overseeing the operations of a small business may eventually require a professional management approach, which can be developed only through great effort and attention to details. Reaching this state is a challenge, but the insights in this chapter can help guide you toward the competencies you will need to make it happen.

19-1. Understand the entrepreneur's leadership role.

- Entrepreneurs must establish and communicate a vision of the firm's future to all of the other participants in the business.
- Founding entrepreneurs need a tolerance for ambiguity and a capacity for adaptation.
- Leading a business to success requires a focus on reaching business goals more than a flashy personality.
- An entrepreneur exerts strong personal influence in a small firm, which can create a competitive advantage over corporate rivals.
- Progressive managers use various leadership styles, incorporating participative management by employees, empowerment, and even self-managed work teams.
- Entrepreneurs should deliberately shape the organizational culture, which can greatly influence how business is conducted in the company and how the company performs.

19-2. Explain the small business management process and its unique features.

- Many founders tend to manage more from gut instinct and are less analytical and systematic in their approach when compared to professional managers.
- A founder's less-sophisticated management style can adversely affect business growth, and many find it difficult to adopt more effective models.
- Small companies are particularly vulnerable to managerial inefficiency, which may even lead to a firm's failure.
- Small firm managers face special financial and personnel constraints.
- As a new business grows, it adds layers of supervision and increases formality of management, a trend that moves through four or five stages.
- A firm's growth requires the entrepreneur to become more of a manager and less of a doer.

19-3. Identify the managerial tasks of entrepreneurs.

- Both long-range planning and short-range planning are required, but they are often postponed or neglected.
- An organizational structure must be created to provide for orderly direction of operations.
- Successful delegation of authority allows entrepreneurs to devote more time to important duties that drive the business forward.
- Managers exercise control by monitoring operations in order to detect and correct deviations from plans.
- Effective two-way communication is important in building a healthy organization.
- Entrepreneurs need to develop their public speaking skills to meet the demands of being the leader of a growing business.
- Managers must be able to negotiate with both insiders and outsiders and should focus on win-win strategies, which will satisfy the basic interests of both parties.

19-4. Describe the problem of time pressure and suggest solutions.

- Time pressure creates inefficiencies in the management of a small firm because the entrepreneur's energies are scattered.
- The greatest time saver is the effective use of time, which requires firmly established priorities and self-discipline.
- A manager can reduce time pressure through such practices as eliminating unnecessary activities and planning work carefully, using such tools as a "to-do" list and prioritizing activities according to their urgency and importance.

19-5. Outline the various types of outside management assistance.

- Outside management assistance can be used to remedy staff limitations and reduce an entrepreneur's sense of isolation, among other things.
- The U.S. Small Business Administration (SBA) is an important source of information and support for small companies, and it is often the first place that small business owners turn for help.
- Three government- and/or university-sponsored sources of management assistance are the Service Corps of Retired Executives (SCORE), small business development centers (SBDCs), and educational institutions.
- Assistance may also be obtained by engaging management consultants and by networking with other small business owners.
- Professionals such as bankers and CPAs can also provide valuable management assistance.

Key Terms

budget p. 515
chain of command p. 516
delegation of authority p. 517
empowerment p. 509
line-and-staff organization p. 516
line organization p. 516
long-range plan (strategic plan) p. 515
negotiation p. 521
networking p. 527
professional manager p. 511
self-managed work teams p. 509
Service Corps of Retired Executives (SCORE) p. 526
short-range plans p. 515
small business development centers (SBDCs) p. 526
span of control p. 517

You Make the Call

Situation 1

John Smithers learned all about leadership in the military, and he is hoping to apply those skills to running John's Deals to Go, his small automobile-leasing company. One interesting feature of life in the armed services is that considerable responsibilities are delegated to young men and women who have very little work experience. Smithers was only 27 when he was assigned duties as a purchasing manager at Kandahar Airport, Afghanistan, in 2003. As a young Marine, he was directly responsible for nearly $50 million in purchasing contracts, which forced him to grow up—and really fast!

To parallel his military experience, Smithers and his small management team have decided to use various methods to delegate decision making to employees at the operating level in his company. New employees are trained thoroughly after they are first hired, but supervisors will not monitor their work closely once they have learned their duties. Management is willing to jump in and help if truly needed, but they purposely leave workers alone when they take on their assigned duties. Managers will not look over employees' shoulders to be sure that they are doing their jobs as assigned, and they certainly do not monitor the work just to try to catch someone making a mistake. Smithers's managerial philosophy is that people work best when they sense that their superiors trust their abilities and their business integrity.

Smithers and his team sometimes leave for day-long meetings and allow the employees to run the business by themselves. Job assignments are defined rather loosely, but management expects employees to assume responsibility and to take necessary action whenever they see that something needs to be done. To reinforce the message of trust, employees who ask for direction are sometimes simply told to solve the problem in whatever way they think best.

Question 1 Is such a loosely organized firm likely to be as effective as a firm that defines jobs more precisely and monitors performance more closely? What are the advantages and the limitations of the managerial style described above?

Question 2 How might such managerial methods affect morale?

Question 3 Would you like to work for this company? Why or why not?

Situation 2

A few years after successfully launching a new outdoor advertising business, Sean Richeson found himself spending 16-hour days running from one appointment to another, negotiating with customers, drumming up new business, signing checks, and checking up as much as possible on his six employees. The founder realized that his own strength was in selling, but general managerial responsibilities were very time consuming and interfered with his sales efforts. Richeson even slept in the office one or two nights a week just to try to keep up with his work.

Despite his diligence, however, Richeson knew that his employees weren't organized and that many problems needed to be addressed. For example, he lacked the time to set personnel policies or to draw up specific job descriptions for his six employees. Just last week, he had been warned that one employee would sometimes take advantage of the lax supervision and skip work. Invoices often were sent out late to customers, and delivery schedules were not always kept. Fortunately, the business is profitable, in spite of the numerous problems.

Question 1 Is Richeson's problem one of time management or general managerial ability?

Question 2 If Richeson asked you to recommend some type of outside management assistance, would you recommend a SCORE counselor, a student consulting team, a CPA firm, a management consultant, or some other type of assistance? Why?

Question 3 If you were asked to improve this company's management system, what steps would you take first? What would be your initial goal?

Situation 3

Krissi Barr is founder of Barr Corporate Success, in Cincinnati, Ohio. Her results-oriented consulting company shows businesses of all sizes how to make the most of their resources. Barr describes a simple technique that she uses for time management: "If I think something is going to take me an hour, I give myself 40 minutes. By shrinking your mental deadlines, you work faster and with greater focus." So, think less and get more.

Scott Lang, CEO of Silver Spring Networks, a smart-grid (energy) solutions company located in Redwood City, California, takes a very different approach. He leaves big blocks of his calendar open each day (usually 20 to 50 percent of his total time) so that he can be ready for the unanticipated. When the CEO of an important new partner arrived at his office unexpectedly, Lang was able to find an open window of time to talk with him because of his scheduling habits. And it's a good thing he did—during an hour-long visit, the two identified new markets that would allow the company to expand globally. But notice that Lang squeezes more results from his hours by freeing up his schedule, whereas Barr gets more done by allotting less time to her work. These clearly are very different approaches.

Sources: Based on "Barr Corporate Success: Who We Are," http://barrcorporatesuccess.com/whoweare.php, accessed February 19, 2015; "15 Ways to Be More Productive," http://www.inc.com/ss/15-ways-be-more-productive#14, accessed February 19, 2015; and "Silver Spring Networks: We Create Technology Platforms That Empower Networks to Perform Brilliantly," http://www.silverspringnet.com/company, accessed February 19, 2015.

Question 1 Which of these two time management methods is more likely to work best in a small business?

Question 2 What are the advantages and disadvantages of these two approaches? What personality characteristics or natural work habits might sync up best with each of them?

Question 3 Which of these two methods would help you, personally, to be most productive? Why?

Case 19

Andew Mason and the Rise and Fall of Groupon (P. 685)

This case points out how a CEO's leadership style and the culture that he or she instills in the organization may work well while the venture is young but can lead to its downfall if significant adjustments are not made as the enterprise grows and develops.

Alternative Case for Chapter 19

Case 5, Iaccarino & Son, p. 654

Endnotes

1. Eric Paley, "Go Beyond Visionary. Be a Leader," *Inc.*, Vol. 36, No. 1 (February 2014), p. 43.
2. As quoted in Brent Bowers, *The 8 Patterns of Highly Effective Entrepreneurs* (New York: Currency Doubleday, 2006), p. 61.
3. Daniel Goleman, Richard E. Boyatzis, and Annie McKee, *Primal Leadership: Unleashing the Power of Emotional Intelligence* (Cambridge, MA: Harvard Business Review Press, 2013), Chapter 4: "The Leadership Repertoire." The precise labels used here are based on the work of Goleman et al. as presented in Adam Bluestein, "What Kind of Leader Are You?" *Inc.*, Vol. 35, No. 8 (October 2013), pp. 58–59.
4. As reported in Leigh Buchanan, "Between Venus and Mars," *Inc.*, Vol. 35, No. 5 (June 2013), pp. 64–74, 130.
5. *Ibid.*
6. Philip Delves Broughton, "A Classic Recipe for Business Success," *Financial Times*, June 4, 2013, p. A4.
7. Rob Reuteman, "Value Lessons: Just How Much Is Good Leadership Worth?" *Entrepreneur*, Vol. 42, No. 3 (March 2014), pp. 38–47.
8. Buchanan, *op. cit.*
9. Jason Feifer and Anjali Mullany, "Are Open Offices Bad for Work?" *FastCompany*, No. 183 (March 2014), pp. 39–42.
10. John Ferrigan, "How to Fix Open Offices," *FastCompany*, No. 183 (March 2014), p. 42.
11. Tony Hsieh, "Why I Sold Zappos," *Inc.*, Vol. 32, No. 5 (June 2010), pp. 101–104.
12. "Zappos Family Core Values," http://about.zappos.com/our-unique-culture/zappos-core-values/create-fun-and-little-weirdness, accessed February 18, 2015.
13. Tony Hsieh, "Even If You're a Superstar at Your Job, If You're Bad for Culture, We'll Fire You," *Inc.*, July 17, 2013, http://www.inc.com/tony-hsieh/zappos-culture-values-fire-if-bad-for-culture.html, accessed February 18, 2015.

14. Scott Leibs, "Bound Up in Complexity," *Inc.*, Vol. 36, No. 8 (October 2014), pp. 112, 114.
15. Clare O'Conner, "Top Five Startup Tips from Spanx Billionaire Sara Blakely," *Forbes*, April 2, 2012, www.forbes.com/sites/clareoconnor/2012/04/02/top-five-startup-tips-from-spanx-billionaire-sara-blakely, accessed February 18, 2015; and personal communication with Sara Blakely, May 3, 2007.
16. Blakely, *op. cit.*
17. Monica Shipper, "The World's Most Powerful Female Billionaires: Oprah, Torey Birch, Sara Blakely, and Miuccia Prada," *Forbes*, May 28, 2014, http://www.forbes.com/forbeslife/#/sites/natalierobehmed/2014/05/28/the-worlds-most-powerful-female-billionaires-oprah-tory-burch-sara-blakely-melinda-gates, accessed February 18, 2015.
18. Michael Fertik, "Seven Keys to Switching from a Big Company to a Small One," *Harvard Business Review*, October 28, 2010, https://hbr.org/2010/10/seven-keys-to-switching-from-a, accessed February 17, 2015.
19. In their book *New Venture Creation: Entrepreneurship for the 21st Century* (Boston: McGraw-Hill Irwin, 2012), Stephen Spinelli and Robert Adams offer the following creative names for the stages that entrepreneurial businesses go through: Wonder, Blunder, Thunder, Plunder, and Asunder. The authors also note specifically the perils that companies face at different points in their growth and development.
20. Jason Fried, "The Art of the Handoff," *Inc.*, Vol. 33, No. 4 (May 2011), pp. 41–42.
21. *Ibid.*
22. Bowers, *op. cit.*, p. 67.
23. Phil Libin, "How I Wised Up," *Inc.*, Vol. 35, No. 2 (March 2013), p. 26.
24. These findings are based on a study conducted by the human resource consulting firm Watson Wyatt (now Towers Watson), as reported in "How to Communicate with Employees," *Inc. Guidebook*, Vol. 2, No. 2 (May 2010), pp. 55–58.
25. Barry Farber, "Putting Ideas into Action," *Entrepreneur*, Vol. 37, No. 2 (February 2009), p. 62.
26. Andrew Shafer, "Crunching the Numbers," *Inc.*, Vol. 33, No. 6 (July/August 2011), p. 30.
27. "The Inc. 500 CEO Survey," *Inc.*, Vol. 35, No. 7 (September 2013), p. 208.
28. As reported in Mark Henricks, "Just 'To-Do' It," http://www.entrepreneur.com/article/71810, accessed February 18, 2015.
29. Adapted from a number of sources, including MindTools, "Eisenhower's Urgent/Important Matrix: Using Time Effectively, Not Just Efficiently," http://www.mindtools.com/pages/article/newHTE_91.htm, accessed February 18, 2015.
30. "SBA: SCORE," http://www.sba.gov/offices/headquarters/oed/resources/148091, accessed February 19, 2015.
31. To learn more about the SBA's network of small business development centers, go to http://www.sba.gov/offices/headquarters/osbdc/resources/11409.
32. "Kauffman FastTrac," http://www.kauffman.org/what-we-do/programs/entrepreneurship/kauffman-fasttrac, accessed February 18, 2015.
33. See Leigh Buchanan, "Inc. 500," *Inc.*, Vol. 32, No. 7 (September 2010), p. 178.
34. John Brandon, "Need Some Advice?" *Inc.*, Vol. 35, No. 4 (May 2013), p. 52.
35. "Clarity: Make Better & Faster Decisions to Grow Your Business," https://clarity.fm/how-it-works, accessed February 18, 2015.
36. Gary Vaynerchuk, "The Art of Networking," *The Wall Street Journal*, March 20, 2014, p. B4.

TALENT

© OLIVIER LE MOAL/SHUTTERSTOCK.COM

CHAPTER 20

Managing Human Resources

After studying this chapter, you should be able to. . .

20-1. **Explain the importance of employee recruitment, and list some useful sources for finding suitable applicants.**

20-2. **Identify the steps in evaluating job applicants.**

20-3. **Describe the roles of training and development for both managerial and nonmanagerial employees.**

20-4. **Explain the various types of compensation plans, including the use of incentive plans.**

20-5. **Discuss the human resource issues of co-employment, legal protection, labor unions, and the formalizing of employer-employee relationships.**

Securing talented employees can drive a business toward success, but few startups manage the hiring process effectively. In fact, Matt Mickiewicz founded talent marketplace Hired.com to help businesses overcome exactly that problem. "U.S. companies dole out more than $70 billion every year to find people to work for them, and yet they're just not very good at it," he contends. "They frequently toss out the platitude that smart hiring is a priority, yet it's rare [for them] to actually *act* like hiring is important." Instead, small firms frequently make choices that turn the hiring process into a frustrating, time-consuming, and inefficient process.

Failure to expedite the hiring process could very well be the most common and counterproductive mistake small companies make. Qualified job candidates may submit their resumes and wait days, weeks, or even months before they get a response. Some may not hear back at all. And even after a successful interview, many companies fail to provide offers in a timely fashion. "We have seen hundreds of cases where companies just forget to follow up with candidates," Mickiewicz says. "They'll reschedule interviews three times because of other priorities." Hired.com removes this obstacle, providing information about specifically chosen candidates to prospective employers. The firms have only one week to review the profiles and arrange interviews before they lose access to the listed talent. The narrow window forces the company to focus their hiring efforts very deliberately.

In the SPOTLIGHT
Hired.com
www.hired.com

© G-STOCKSTUDIO/SHUTTERSTOCK.COM

Disputes over salary can also derail the process. For this reason, Hired.com requires employers to submit full pay and benefits details to job seekers during initial contact. This requirement compels firms to carefully deliberate and commit to a set amount. But Mickiewicz warns against bidding too low, since a 20 percent increase in salary can provide access to over 30 percent more candidates. Startups, in particular, tend to overestimate the value of the equity they can offer, believing stocks can offset lower salary offerings. Mickiewicz says that this belief does not hold true in his experience.

Hired.com provides a unique payment option for budget-conscious startups, recognizing that many cannot afford to pay large finder's fees. Many headhunting firms charge tens of thousands of dollars for services rendered, and these fees are typically due after a scouted employee has been employed for two months. Hired.com lets firms choose to pay 1 percent of the employee's salary for up to 24 months instead. And if the employee leaves before that time, Hired.com discontinues the recurring fee.

Ultimately, businesses need to commit to identifying, contacting, and securing job seekers who meet the company's needs. Startups, in particular, should deliberately focus on hiring the best candidate for a position to ensure that the expenses incurred will maximize the value that the new employee adds. According to Mickiewicz, "20-25% of your time should be spent interviewing. . . . If you view hiring as a core competency you need to develop in the business, then you'll do whatever it takes." And you will end up with the workforce foundation you need to build the enterprise you want.

Sources: Annlee Ellingston, "Q&A: Tech Job Marketplace Brings Hired Help to Los Angeles," *L.A. Biz*, October 2, 2014, http://www.bizjournals.com/losangeles/news/2014/10/02/q-a-tech-job-marketplace-brings-hired-help-to-la.html?page=all, accessed March 2, 2015; "Hiring.com: About Us," https://hired.com/about, accessed March 2, 2015; Matt Mickiewicz, "Lessons Learned from a Startup Founder Since Age 14," *The Wall Street Journal*, June 23, 2014, http://blogs.wsj.com/accelerators/2014/06/23/matt-mickiewicz-lessons-learned-from-a-startup-founder-since-age-14, accessed March 2, 2015; and Phillip Thomas, "Interview with Matt Mickiewicz, CEO and founder of Hired.com," *Telegraph Research*, February 17, 2014, http://www.telegraphresearch.com/mickiewicz-interview, accessed March 2, 2015.

Jack Tompkins is owner and CEO of Fit Athletic Club, a comprehensive fitness facility and social venue that is consistently voted the best health club in Houston, Texas. How does he manage to pull that off year after year? He knows how important his employees are to the success of his small company. In fact, he acknowledges their vital role through a principle that stands at the core of his well-honed management philosophy:

> *Business owners know that a well-run organization happens because of the people who manage the business. This is not magic, but an executive who finds the right people to do the right thing at the right time will discover that management is so easy, he feels as if he's not working.*[1]

In other words, the entrepreneur who wants to build a competitive business needs to think carefully about how to find and hire the best people available and then hold on to them. This, said the senior executives of 146 of the highest-performing companies in the United States, is the greatest driver of business growth.[2] It therefore stands to reason that employees need to be managed intelligently if they are to boost a venture's performance.

The term **human resource management (HRM)** refers to the management of employees, individually and collectively, in a way that enables them to help the business reach its strategic objectives. This can only be achieved if highly capable employees are recruited, trained, assessed, and given incentives to reach their greatest potential. To complicate things a bit, HRM looks very different in large firms than in small companies. A small entrepreneurial concern neither can nor should duplicate the personnel

human resource management (HRM) The management of employees in a way that enables them to help a company reach its strategic objectives.

Hiring Your First Employee

This chapter provides a very useful framework to help you set up an effective human resource management program and hire your very

(continued)

(continued)

first employee. The Small Business Administration (SBA) makes it easy for you to get started by offering the following eight steps, which will help to ensure that you will be in compliance with the confusing array of federal and state regulations.

Step 1. Obtain an employer identification number.
Step 2. Set up records for tax withholding.
Step 3. Verify that the employee is eligible to work in the United States.
Step 4. Register with your state's new hire reporting program.
Step 5. Obtain workers' compensation insurance.
Step 6. Post required notices.
Step 7. File your taxes.
Step 8. Get organized, and keep yourself informed.

The need to comply with so many regulations may seem so overwhelming that you consider giving up on plans to grow your new venture. Don't let that happen! It's easier than you think, because the SBA leads you through each step at www.sba.gov/content/hire-your-first-employee.

policies and procedures of a Google or a General Motors. Instead, it should carefully manage its employees in a way that is best suited for the 10, 50, or 100 employees on its payroll.

While the HRM practices of small businesses should be well planned and professional, research has shown that this often is not the case.[3] If you are concerned that you may not know enough to hire suitable employees for your startup or business expansion, this chapter will help you by presenting HRM practices that work best for entrepreneurial companies.

20-1 RECRUITING PERSONNEL

Explain the importance of employee recruitment, and list some useful sources for finding suitable applicants.

Recruitment brings applicants to a business. The goal is to obtain a pool of potential employees large enough to contain a number of talented prospects. In a subsequent stage of the selection process, management decides which applicants are "keepers." But attracting and retaining skilled employees may be more difficult than you realize. In fact, the CEOs of Inc. 500 companies identified this as their greatest challenge.[4] Despite painstaking recruitment efforts, 42 percent of small business owners indicate that they simply cannot find prospects with the skills and qualifications that they need.[5]

20-1a The Need for Quality Employees

If you want your venture to grow, then it is important to think of employees not as expenses but as revenue generators. But as Willan Johnson of VivoPools (see the Living the Dream feature) has learned, it makes no sense to hire more employees unless the total costs involved will be more than offset by the additional sales it yields. (It's important to keep cash flows in mind, since it will take some time for the revenue to come in.) Some small companies are finding ways to get by with very few employees or none at all, thereby simplifying their operations and avoiding payroll increases. In fact, research reveals that startups are launching with far fewer employees today than they did in the past.[6]

A startup called Near Networks shows how this can work. The Los Angeles–based online video production studio is led by a small team with many years of experience in the entertainment industry and supported by a community of talented filmmakers from around the world. In 2011, it was launched with only four employees. How was this possible, given the high-tech nature of the venture and its complexity? As Sam Rogoway, who heads Near Networks, explains it, work that once required more employees can now be handled with tools that are readily available online. "You don't need an IT person or an accountant. [The tools have] become so streamlined and user-friendly," says Rogoway. "We all wore different hats and collaborated on everything."[7]

The approach that Near Networks has settled on may work up to a point, but many companies cannot forgo hiring without choking off their growth. When expansion is necessary, there is no substitute for having high-quality employees on board—and the more capable and motivated, the better. Joel Spolsky, co-founder of a software development company, describes the remarkable impact that excellent employees can have on a business:

> *In our field, the top 1 percent of the workforce can easily be 10 times as productive as the average developer. The best developers invent new products, figure out shortcuts that save months of work, and, when there are no shortcuts, plow through coding tasks like a monster truck at a tea party.*[8]

Living the Dream

ENTREPRENEURIAL EXPERIENCES

Knowing When It's Time to Turn to a Hire Power

Willan Johnson has a problem that just won't go away. To be specific, the founder and owner of Los Angeles pool-cleaning company VivoPools finds it very difficult to anticipate future demand for his business, which throws off his hiring decisions. As he puts it, "Determining when and how many employees to hire is a bit tricky for our business as the demand for services varies based on account growth, seasonality, geography of homeowner addresses, and customer requests."

To figure out when it makes sense to hire a new employee, Johnson consults a spreadsheet that allows him to size up the latest client information, including their service needs. The typical home pool only requires vacuuming or scrubbing and can be properly serviced in about 30 minutes, but larger commercial pools usually involve chemical cleaning treatments that can take as long as two hours. Based on all of the data gathered, Johnson projects the number of hours that will be needed to tend to all accounts and divides that figure by a 40-hour work week. If the total exceeds his current staffing levels, he concludes that he will need to hire new employees.

Navigating hiring choices can be more difficult for small business owners than for large firms. Smaller companies have fewer resources available, and they may be more sensitive to economic shifts. Since the recent economic slowdown, many small businesses have been hesitant to bring on new hires because they have concluded that market demand is too uncertain, which creates follow-on complications. For instance, Johnson requires all of his service staff to undergo extensive training and secure third-party certifications, so going through repeated hiring-and-firing cycles cuts into VivoPools' technical expertise, and this can impair customer service. In order to minimize these losses, Johnson refuses to take on new employees unless he is confident that the company will need them for the foreseeable future.

Johnson is not the only small business owner who struggles to balance demand-fueled growth against uneven economic progress. Many small companies are choosing alternatives like hiring part-time workers or authorizing overtime to meet demand increases. But while these options provide flexibility in the short term, they can lead to long-term problems, like sagging employee morale and burnout. There are no easy choices—at least for now.

The recent economic recovery, however, may begin to boost employer confidence and ease hiring-decision uncertainty. According to the "ADP National Employment Report," small business employment has risen faster than any other segment, and some experts have predicted that the economy is on a solid path to employment health. That's good news for Johnson, who has started to franchise VivoPools as part of his expansion plan. With eight deals already completed, convincing more prospective franchisees to sign on will get easier as a stable economy makes market demand and human resource needs more predictable. It stands to reason that they will be more inspired to join the business to clean up pools if they believe that they might clean up financially, as well.

Sources: J. D. Harrison, "Who Actually Creates Jobs: Start-ups, Small Businesses or Big Corporations?" *The Washington Post*, April 25, 2013, http://www.washingtonpost.com/business/on-small-business/who-actually-creates-jobs-start-ups-small-businesses-or-big-corporations/2013/04/24/d373ef08-ac2b-11e2-a8b9-2a63d75b5459_story.html, accessed March 1, 2015; Suzanne Sataline, "Figuring Out What Time Is Right to Start Hiring," *The New York Times*, August 28, 2013, pp. B1, B7; Nate Traylor, "More Service Companies Franchising," *Pool & Spa News*, July 26, 2013, http://www.poolspanews.com/economic-conditions/more-service-companies-franchising.aspx, March 1, 2015; "VivoPools: Experienced Pool Management Professionals," http://www.vivopools.com, accessed March 1, 2015; and ADP Research Institute, "ADP National Employment Report: March 2015," http://www.adpemploymentreport.com/2015/March/NER/NER-March-2015.aspx, accessed April 21, 2015.

So, having the right people "on board" can provide an enormous boost to the overall performance of a company. The presence of even one capable and motivated worker tends to raise expectations of all the others, and interactions between two or more high-impact employees will often lead to outcomes significantly greater than the sum of their already excellent individual contributions.

Recruitment and selection of employees establish a foundation for the ongoing human interactions in a company. In a sense, the quality of a firm's employees determines the firm's potential. A solid, effective organization can be built only with a talented, ambitious workforce. And since payroll is one of the largest expense categories for most businesses, wise employment decisions can have a direct impact on the company's bottom line. By recruiting the best personnel possible, an entrepreneurial firm can improve its return on each payroll dollar.

Most successful companies have moved ahead of their competition because they recognize that employees *are* the business, and vice versa. There is no getting around this, especially for entrepreneurial firms that are expanding. "You cannot separate the need to grow from the number of people you will need to hire," observes Matthew Guthridge, an associate principal at global management consulting firm McKinsey & Company. "And that at the very basic level is the essence of what [an employment] strategy should be about."[9] Hiring and holding on to the right people can easily make or break a small business.

20-1b The Lure of Entrepreneurial Firms

Competing for well-qualified business talent requires small firms to identify their distinctive advantages, especially when recruiting outstanding prospects for managerial and professional positions. Fortunately, there are many good reasons to work for an entrepreneurial business. This is especially true of growing enterprises led by individuals or teams with a compelling vision of a desirable and attainable future.

Chris Resto, Ian Ybarra, and Ramit Sethi, co-authors of the book *Recruit or Die*, have concluded that entrepreneurial firms can compete with such ace recruiters as Microsoft, McKinsey & Company, and Whole Foods Market when it comes to attracting and hiring promising employees. The secret is coming up with a strategy that will convince the best and brightest to join a small company. Offering competitive salaries helps (more on that later in the chapter), but many recruits are even more interested in opportunities for high-level achievement, job variety, interesting experiences, personal recognition, and the potential to do work that they believe is important.[10] Many small businesses are in an excellent position to offer such attractive opportunities to prospective employees.

Because of their small size and limited staff, entrepreneurial companies allow new managers to work more closely with the CEO (often the founder), which can lead to quicker action. A small business can also provide opportunities for the general high-level management or professional experience that achievement-oriented hires find attractive. Rather than toiling in obscure, low-level, specialized positions in a large firm while "paying their dues" and working their way up the corporate ladder, capable newcomers can quickly move into positions of responsibility in a well-managed small business, where they know that they are making a difference in the company's success.

Small firms can also structure the work environment to offer professional, managerial, and technical personnel greater job variety and freedom than they would normally have in a larger business. In this type of environment, individual contributions can be recognized rather than hidden under numerous layers of bureaucracy. In addition, compensation packages can be structured to create powerful incentives for outstanding performance. These are just some of the "selling points" that small companies can use to attract candidates who would likely be moving toward a career in a large corporation. In fact, a recent *Inc.* magazine study found that 43 percent of college graduates surveyed would prefer to work for a startup or a small or medium-size business, which is much higher than the 27 percent who would rather work for a large corporation.

The remaining respondents indicated that they hope to work for a government agency (19 percent) or a nonprofit (11 percent).[11]

© ANDREY_POPOV/SHUTTERSTOCK.COM

To be sure, there are drawbacks to working for a small company—for example, managerial blunders are harder to absorb and thus tend to be obvious to everyone, support systems from legal or human resource staff may not be readily available, and limited employee benefits can lead to high levels of turnover and constant changes in personnel. But many small employers can offset these disadvantages with appealing trade-offs, such as flexible work scheduling, job-sharing arrangements, less (or more) travel, and other potential advantages. With a little thought and some careful positioning, entrepreneurs can actually win the competitive challenge to lure the best talent available.

20-1c Sources of Employees

To recruit effectively, the small business manager must know where and how to find qualified applicants. Sources are numerous, and it is impossible to generalize about the best pool in view of the differences in companies' personnel needs and the quality of the applicants from one locality to another. Some of the more popular sources of employees among small firms are discussed in the following sections.

INTERNET OPTIONS

Small businesses are turning increasingly to the Internet to find the employees they need. A variety of websites, like CareerBuilder.com and Monster.com, allow applicants to submit their résumés online and permit potential employers to search those résumés for qualified applicants. And because the Internet opens up a wealth of connections to potential applicants, many firms are posting job openings on their own websites.

Using the Internet for recruiting is convenient, but it can also carry some significant limitations and unanticipated costs. One small business owner posted a job opening that required a very specific marketing skill set. From that single listing, the company heard back from a slew of interested job seekers, "which included a U.S. Postal Service worker, a bench chemist, a talent agent, and a movie director . . . none with the requisite skills." The final results were very disappointing. In the words of the entrepreneur, "[From] the 141 applicants, we interviewed two and didn't hire any. That cost me hours of my time and my hire manager's time."[12] The point is that the initial cost of posting a position online can be low—sometimes even free—but that doesn't mean the *overall process* will be inexpensive, and it may not even be useful in the end.

Beyond these options, social media tools can be indispensable to recruitment efforts, and their use for this purpose is growing rapidly. According to David Lewis, the president and CEO of human resources outsourcing and consulting firm OperationsInc, "[S]ocial media has radically changed how recruiting is done. With three minutes of work and a couple of clicks, you're connected with a trusted audience of hundreds."[13] One survey found that 93 percent of recruiters use or plan to use social media and networking sites to find the employees they need. Of those who do, most (94 percent) use LinkedIn, though many also use Facebook (66 percent) and/or Twitter

(52 percent). Many say that they find social recruiting to be very efficient and have concluded that it yields more applicants and higher-quality candidates.[14] As a result, many companies are shifting increasingly to social media in order to save time and money, and to avoid some the hassles associated with other sources.[15]

SCHOOLS

Secondary schools, career schools, colleges, and universities are desirable sources of personnel for certain positions, particularly those requiring no specific work experience. Some secondary schools and colleges have internship programs that enable students to gain practical experience in firms, which can be very helpful. Applicants from career schools often have useful educational backgrounds to offer a small business. Colleges and universities can supply candidates for positions in management and in various technical and professional fields. In addition, many college students can work as part-time employees.

Some small businesses have decided that the best way to get the employees they need is to have input into the preparation provided at local trade schools and colleges. By working out partnerships with institutions that are interested in ensuring that the coursework they offer provides the skills for which companies will be hiring in the future, some small businesses have been given a hand in fine-tuning course content related to project management, engineering, architecture, and many other subjects. This then offers the possibility of hiring some of the students as interns, a strategy that gives the company access to inexpensive part-time help for the present and the inside track on hiring high performers as full-time employees after they graduate. The firm wins with this strategy, but so do the students and the training institutions.

PUBLIC EMPLOYMENT OFFICES

At no cost to small businesses, employment offices in each state administer the state's unemployment insurance program and offer information on applicants who are actively seeking employment. These offices, located in all major cities, are a useful source of clerical workers, unskilled laborers, production workers, and technicians. They do not actively recruit but only counsel and assist those who come in. Until recently, the individuals they work with have been, for the most part, untrained or only marginally qualified. However, because of the sluggish economy, individuals with more advanced skills who have been laid off have been seeking assistance from their local state employment office. The role of such agencies is likely to become more important as time goes on, especially where the employment needs of small businesses are concerned.[16]

PRIVATE EMPLOYMENT AGENCIES

Numerous private firms offer their services as employment agencies. In some cases, employers receive these services without cost because the applicants pay a fee to the agency. More often, however, the hiring firms are responsible for the agency fee. Private employment agencies tend to specialize in people with specific skills, such as accountants, computer operators, and managers.

TEMPORARY HELP AGENCIES

The temporary help industry, which is growing rapidly, supplies employees (or temps)—such as customer service representatives, accountants, home health aides, maintenance and repair workers, computer support specialists, and sales clerks—for short periods of time. By using an agency such as Kelly Services or Manpower Inc., small firms can deal with seasonal fluctuations and absences caused by vacation or illness. For example, a temporary replacement might fill the position of an employee who is taking leave following the birth of a child—a type of family leave mandated by law for some employees. In addition, the use of temporary employees provides management with an introduction to individuals whose performance may justify an offer of permanent employment. Staffing with temporary employees is less practical when extensive training is required or continuity is important.

EMPLOYEE REFERRALS

Recommendations of suitable candidates from good employees may provide excellent prospects. Ordinarily, employees will hesitate to recommend applicants unless they believe in their ability to do the job. Also, the family and friends of current workers can be among the best and most loyal employees available, because these individuals are well known and trusted. Statistics show that this is a particularly efficient way to go about recruiting; while only 7 percent of all applicants come from referrals, they account for a surprising 40 percent of hires.[17] Because it works so well, some employers go so far as to offer financial rewards for employee referrals that result in the hiring of new employees.

Scott Glatstein is often looking to hire skilled management consultants for his small consulting company, Imperatives, but he has not had much luck using standard recruiting tools. Not that he hasn't tried! After using a variety of approaches, including Internet advertising, he found only one that yields the results he is looking for: recommendations from his current employees. Glatstein estimates that he hires nearly all of his employees through referrals. Doing so saves money (costing around 70 percent less than advertising or employment agencies) and reduces turnover. But perhaps the most important advantage is that these new hires become productive in less time and tend to have superior skills. Glatstein has been known to pay $300 for each referral hired.[18] But if $300 would be a budget-buster for your company, adjust the figure down or use a different incentive. You may very well end up with the same result.

Hiring based on referrals is really just a way of tapping into the personal networks of employees. However, network recruiting becomes more important as the responsibilities associated with the position increase, as it provides the best connections to individuals with the background, skills, and integrity that are essential to a position of great responsibility in the company.

EXECUTIVE SEARCH FIRMS

When filling key positions, small companies sometimes turn to executive search firms, often called **headhunters**, to locate qualified candidates. The key positions for which such firms seek applicants are those paying a minimum of $50,000 to $70,000 per year. The cost to the employer typically runs from 20 to 35 percent of the first year's salary. Because of the high cost, the use of headhunters may seem unreasonable for small, entrepreneurial firms. At times, however, the need for a manager who can help a firm move to the next level justifies the use of an executive search firm. A headhunter is usually better able than the small business to conduct a wide-ranging search for individuals who possess the right combination of talents for the available position.

WALK-INS AND HELP-WANTED ADVERTISING

A firm may receive unsolicited applications from individuals who walk into the place of business to seek employment. Walk-ins are an inexpensive source of personnel, particularly for hourly work, but the quality of applicants varies. If qualified applicants cannot be hired immediately, their applications should be kept on file for future reference. In the interest of good community relations, all applicants should be treated courteously, whether or not they are offered jobs.

headhunters
A search firm that identifies qualified candidates for executive positions.

A "Help Wanted" sign in the window is one traditional form of recruiting used by some small firms (mostly retailers and fast-food restaurants). A similar but more aggressive form of recruiting consists of advertising in the classifieds section of local newspapers. For some technical, professional, and managerial positions, firms may advertise in trade and professional journals. Although the effectiveness of help-wanted advertising has been questioned by some, many small businesses recruit in this way.

20-1d Diversity in the Workforce

Over time, the composition of the U.S. workforce has changed with respect to race, ethnicity, gender, and age. The U.S. Bureau of Labor Statistics projects that the general trend will continue, but the change will come disproportionately from an increase in the number of Hispanic workers:

© RAWPIXEL/SHUTTERSTOCK.COM

> *From 2010 to 2050, people of Hispanic origin are projected to add 37.6 million [workers] to the labor force, accounting for about 80 percent of the total growth of the labor force. In comparison, non-Hispanics are projected to add only 9 million workers. (Although Hispanics may be of any race, more than 80 percent report that their race is White.)*[19]

The balance is shifting steadily toward greater **workforce diversity** (based on gender, age, ethnicity, and race), even as the labor force participation rate is expected to decrease from 63.7 percent in 2012 to 61.6 percent in 2022. While the overall size of the labor force will continue to grow, mostly as a result of the aging of the population, the *rate* of growth will fall from 0.7 percent per year in the previous decade to 0.5 percent in the decade to come.[20] As a result, the challenge for human resource management is to adapt to a pool of potential employees that is changing along a number of dimensions. To remain fully competitive, business owners need to be open to innovative ways to access the available applicant pool. In many cases, hiring more workers from diverse groups can help a company maintain good relations with an increasingly heterogeneous customer base.

Many small businesses are tapping immigrants as a source of workers, and this presents a potential problem. While most of these employees are authorized immigrants, a certain portion of them are not. Hiring illegal or undocumented workers is a punishable offense and can lead to fines or the suspension or revocation of a company's business license. To steer clear of such hiring violations, it is wise to consult the U.S. Department of Labor website at www.foreignlaborcert.doleta.gov for information on certifying foreign workers and other applicable laws. Your company may also be required to use the E-Verify system to confirm a potential new employee's eligibility. These limitations make it all the more important to cast the employment net as broadly as possible to find the best people available. By developing an awareness of the potential of various parts of the talent pool, small firms can improve the effectiveness of their recruitment methods.

workforce diversity
Differences among employees on such dimensions as gender, age, ethnicity, and race.

Adapting to diversity is important not only because the workforce is becoming more varied, but also because diversity itself can be a good thing, through the innovation

Living the Dream

ENTREPRENEURIAL EXPERIENCES

Where in the World Did All of the Talent Go?

As the largest economy in the world, the United States owes its size and dynamism, in significant measure, to the entrepreneurial drive and effort of immigrants. Research has revealed that four of the ten largest companies in the United States—a list that includes Google, Intel, and eBay—were founded by immigrants or their children, and that three out of four patents awarded to teams from the top 10 American universities included a foreign-born inventor. But the competitive advantage that derives from a diverse and multicultural talent pool may be waning. Many highly qualified, international job seekers face career uncertainty as a result of U.S. immigration law.

Critics of the current policy point out that government inefficiencies, complex legal processes, and visa caps hinder American businesses from hiring the talent that they very desperately need. H-1B visas, which pair internationals with specific employers, are currently limited to 85,000. Large companies, such as the heavy hitters in Silicon Valley, have the means and legal expertise needed to quickly take up these visas. But smaller firms do not have the same depth of resources and have trouble navigating the bureaucratic labyrinth. Limited supply and accessibility, according to immigration reformers, puts many startups and small businesses at a distinct disadvantage.

American policy stands in stark contrast to immigration law in several other countries. Australia issues the same number of employment-based green cards as the United States, despite the fact that its economy is only 1/14th the size. Germany amended 40 percent of its immigration laws in 2013 in order to attract international talent. But studies have shown that for every foreign-born green-card holder in the United States with a graduate degree in a technical field, 2.6 additional jobs are created. So when qualified and entrepreneurially motivated professionals are prevented from taking these additional positions because of immigration restrictions, economic growth is directly and unfavorably impacted.

Consider the case of Hamdi Ulukaya, founder of Chobani Greek Yogurt. The Turkish immigrant started the company in 2005 with a small business loan and a handful of employees. Since then, Ulukaya has grown his business into a production and distribution powerhouse with annual sales of over $1 billion. The firm's plant directly employs 1,300 workers and indirectly creates thousands of jobs through contracts with distributors, vendors, and advertisers. Ulukaya has been successful, but only because he was able to stay in the United States long enough to turn his dream into reality. How many others like him might choose to pursue their entrepreneurial dreams elsewhere because of current immigration law?

© RICHARD LEVINE/ALAMY

Shifting economic forces and escalating globalization are only intensifying the competition for much needed talent. Other countries, seeking to gain a competitive advantage, actively court foreign-born professionals—and this is to be expected. Historically, the United States has enjoyed economic success because it offered the most financially rewarding path for immigration. That is changing as current legislation and mounting competition convince immigrants to take a different path. This trend leaves concern about the future of U.S. small businesses in its wake.

Sources: Steve Case, "As Congress Dawdles, the World Steals Our Talent," *The Wall Street Journal*, October 9, 2013, p. A17; Catherine Clifford, "White House Plays Offense: Says Immigration Reform Will Turbocharge Entrepreneurship," *Entrepreneur*, July 10, 2013, http://www.entrepreneur.com/article/227353, accessed March 1, 2015; Megan Durisin, "Chobani CEO: Our Success Has Nothing to Do with Yogurt," *Business Insider*, May 3, 2013, http://www.businessinsider.com/the-success-story-of-chobani-yogurt-2013-5, accessed March 1, 2015; Steve Forbes, "Why Immigration Reform Would Boost Economy," *Forbes*, May 6, 2013, http://www.forbes.com/sites/steveforbes/2013/06/05/why-immigration-reform-would-boost-economy, accessed March 1, 2015; and Brian Gruley, "At Chobani, the Turkish King of Greek Yogurt," *Bloomberg Business*, January 31, 2013, http://www.bloomberg.com/bw/articles/2013-01-31/at-chobani-the-turkish-king-of-greek-yogurt, accessed March 1, 2015.

it introduces to the workplace and the positive effect it has on problem solving. For example, researchers at Northwestern University studied the value of diversity by asking 50 groups of subjects to solve a murder mystery. Groups that included individuals from different social backgrounds were more likely to solve the case. Homogeneous groups were both more often wrong and more confident that they were right.[21] Venture capitalists are very much aware of this phenomenon and thus are less likely to invest in a company when the management team more closely resembles the results of a cloning experiment than a group of individuals who bring unique perspectives to bear on business challenges. Workplace diversity is clearly beneficial, especially when innovation is important to a firm's competitiveness.

20-1e Job Descriptions

A small business manager should analyze the activities or work to be performed to determine the number and types of jobs to be filled. Knowing the job requirements permits more intelligent selection of applicants for specific positions.

Certainly, an owner-manager should not select personnel simply to fit rigid specifications of education, experience, or personal background. Rather, he or she must concentrate on the overall ability of an individual to fill a particular position in the business. Making this determination requires an outline, or summary, of the work to be performed, which is often referred to as a **job description**. (To see sample descriptions for a number of different jobs, go to www.samplejobdescriptions.org.)

Duties listed in a job description should not be defined too narrowly. It is important that such descriptions minimize overlap but also avoid creating a "that's not my job" mentality. Technical competence is as necessary in small firms as it is in large businesses, but versatility and flexibility may be even more important. Engineers may occasionally need to make sales calls, and marketing people may need to pinch-hit in production.

Any analysis of a position should include a list of the knowledge, skills, abilities, and other characteristics that an individual must have to perform the job. This statement of requirements is called a **job specification** and may be a part of the job description. A job specification for the position of stock clerk, for example, might state that the individual must be able to lift 50 pounds and have completed 10 to 12 years of schooling.

Job descriptions are very important human resource management tools, but only if they are taken seriously. There are sound legal reasons for developing great—not just good—job descriptions. For example, if you do not specify important aspects of the job and how it is to be done *in detail*, the Americans with Disabilities Act presumes that an employee can go about the actual job duties in any way he or she wants to, regardless of company policy or what you think is the best and proper way of doing them.[22] Getting the job description right can avert serious legal hassles, saving you money and giving you one less worry when you go to bed at night.

While job descriptions are primarily an aid in personnel recruitment, they also have other practical uses. For example, they can bring focus to the work of employees, provide direction in training, and supply a framework to guide performance reviews.

job description
An outline, or summary, of the work to be performed for a particular position.

job specification
A list of the knowledge, skills, abilities, and other characteristics needed to perform a specific job.

20-2 EVALUATING PROSPECTS AND SELECTING EMPLOYEES

Identify the steps in evaluating job applicants.

Recruitment activities identify prospects for employment. Additional steps are needed to evaluate these candidates and extend job offers. To reduce the risk of taking an uninformed gamble on applicants of unknown quality, an employer can follow the steps described in the next sections.

20-2a Step 1: Use Application Forms

By using an application form, an employer can collect enough information to determine whether a prospect is minimally qualified and to provide a basis for further evaluation. Typically, an application asks for the applicant's name, address, Social Security number, educational history, employment history, and references.

Although an application form need not be lengthy or elaborate, it must be carefully written to avoid legal complications. In general, a prospective employer cannot seek information about gender, race, religion, color, national origin, age, and disabilities. The information requested should be focused on helping the employer make a better job-related assessment. For example, an employer is permitted to ask whether an applicant has graduated from high school. However, a question regarding the year the applicant graduated would be considered inappropriate because the answer would reveal the applicant's age.

20-2b Step 2: Interview the Applicant

An interview permits the employer to get some idea of the applicant's job knowledge, intelligence, and personality. Any of these factors may be significant to the job to be filled.

Although the interview can be a useful step in the selection process, it should not be the only step. Some managers have the mistaken idea that they are infallible judges of human character and can choose good employees on the basis of interviews alone. Even when conducted with care, an interview can lead to false impressions. Applicants who interview well have a talent for quick responses and smooth talk, for instance, but this skill set may not be helpful when it comes to managing processes or technologies. The interview may reveal little about how well they work under pressure or when part of a team, what motivates them, and other important issues. In fact, research has shown that the typical job interview (unstructured and unfocused) is of limited value in predicting success on the job.[23]

In light of a growing concern regarding the value of interviews as they are typically used, many firms have adopted more effective approaches that are variations on the interview theme. For example, companies have found **behavioral interviews** to be 55 percent predictive of a candidate's future behavior on the job, representing a five-fold improvement over the results of traditional interviews.[24] This kind of interview doesn't focus on asking people about their accomplishments; rather, it explores their reactions to hypothetical situations, looks for patterns in how they spend their free time, gauges the core values that they embody, etc., based on the notion that past behavior is a good predictor of future behavior. Although it can be a taxing process that may come across to the applicant as a barrage of challenging questions, the behavioral interview is designed to get a sense of the applicant's past performance and likely responses in future situations. The nature of the method makes bluffing difficult, and the focus on facts rather than feelings leads to a more accurate impression of what a person is *capable* of doing, as well as what he or she is *likely* to do on the job.

Companies that use behavioral interviews must select a set of questions that will uncover the insights they need to make an informed hiring decision. To give you a sense of how such an interview can be structured, here are some questions that are often asked:[25]

- Can you share a specific example of a time when you used good judgment and logic when solving a problem?
- Tell me about a time when you set a goal and were able to achieve it.

behavioral interviews An approach that assesses the suitability of job candidates based on how they would respond to hypothetical situations.

© MONKEY BUSINESS IMAGES/SHUTTERSTOCK.COM

- Can you recall a time when you had to conform to a company policy with which you did not agree? How did you handle that situation?
- How do you typically deal with workplace conflict? Describe an experience that required you to make such an adjustment.
- Give me an example of a time when your integrity was tested and yet prevailed in a workplace situation.

As you can see from these questions, the focus is on patterns of performance and behaviors in past situations similar to situations that are likely to come up in the job for which the applicant is being considered. Designing this emphasis into the interview process will lead to more effective hiring decisions.

Regardless of the interview method you choose, remember that serious legal consequences can result from a poorly conceived process. Just as in application forms, it is very important to avoid asking questions in an interview that conflict with the law (see Exhibit 20.1 for examples of topics that should be avoided). Some companies believe that applicants should be interviewed by two or more individuals in order to provide a witness to all interactions and to minimize bias and errors in judgment, but this is not always possible—and it certainly makes the process more expensive. In any case, careful planning up front can prevent serious trouble in the future from discrimination lawsuits and poor employee selection.

Time spent in interviews, as well as in other phases of the selection process, can save the company time and money in the long run. In today's litigious society, firing

EXHIBIT

20.1 Topics to Avoid in an Interview

Children. Asking about children may indicate an employer's concern about child care needs, and it singles out women.

Age. The Age Discrimination in Employment Act prevents employers from asking applicants their age or even about life events that could indicate age, such as their year of high school graduation.

Disabilities. The Americans with Disabilities Act does not allow discussions regarding mental or physical disabilities until after a job offer has been made.

Physical Characteristics. Talking about height, weight, or other physical attributes can lead to discrimination based on those features.

Maiden Name. It is okay to ask an applicant's name, but asking for a maiden name can lead to discrimination based on marital status and, potentially, ethnic background.

Citizenship. The Immigration Reform and Control Act allows a company to ask if applicants have a legal right to work in the United States, but inquiring about citizenship can lead to claims of discrimination based on national origin.

Lawsuits. It is against federal and state laws to ask applicants if they have filed suit against a previous employer, a measure intended to protect whistleblowers from potential retaliation.

Arrest Records. Applicants can be asked if they have ever been convicted of a crime, but an arrest record does not necessarily reflect criminal activity (if the charges were later found to be groundless, for instance).

Smoking. Applicants can be asked if they know the company's policy on smoking at work, but they should not be asked if they smoke to avoid being seen as attempting to discriminate against those who may be more prone to absenteeism and higher medical claims.

Medical Conditions. It would violate the Americans with Disabilities Act as well as federal and state civil rights laws to ask if an applicant has any medical conditions, including AIDS or HIV.

Source: Adapted from Chuck Williams, MGMT, 8th edition (Mason, OH: South-Western Cengage Learning, 2017), p. 228.

an employee can be quite difficult and expensive. A dismissed employee may bring suit even when an employer had justifiable reasons for the dismissal. Note, however, that released employees are much less likely to file a lawsuit if they conclude that their employer has been fair throughout the process and has provided ample opportunity for them to improve their work performance before termination.[26]

It's important to remember that employment interviewing is actually a two-way process. The applicant is evaluating the employer while the employer is evaluating the applicant. In order for the applicant to make an informed decision, she or he needs a clear idea of what the job entails and an opportunity to ask questions.

Interviewing High-Potential Prospects

When it comes to identifying high-potential job candidates in interviews, sometimes it's as much about what a prospect does as it is what he or she says. A survey of *Inc.* 500 CEOs showed that they would never hire a person who hasn't done or doesn't do the following:

- Researched the business before interviewing (66 percent)
- Make eye contact during the interview (62 percent)
- Communicate well in writing (51 percent)
- Worked during the previous six months (8 percent)

For more on the findings of the survey, see "Bosses Are Creating a New Generation of Leaders," *Inc.*, Vol. 36, No. 7 (September 2014), p. 78.

20-2c Step 3: Check References and Other Background Information

Careful checking with former employers, school authorities, and other references can help an employer avoid hiring mistakes. Suppose, for example, that you hired an appliance technician who later burglarized a customer's home. If you failed to check the applicant's background and she had a criminal record, it might be considered a negligent hiring decision. Trying to prevent such scenarios from arising is becoming more important, since the number of negligent hiring lawsuits continues to rise and the average settlement is nearly $1 million.[27]

It is becoming increasingly difficult to obtain more than the basic facts about a person's background from previous employers because of the potential for lawsuits brought by disappointed applicants. For this reason and others, firms have been turning increasingly to social media to evaluate job applicants. In fact, a survey conducted by the Society of Human Resource Management found that companies are using LinkedIn (92 percent), Facebook (58 percent), and Twitter (31 percent) to screen job candidates.[28] Many are rejected because of what is revealed. An *Inc.* magazine analysis reported that the most objectionable turnoffs are, in order, posting inappropriate information or photos, exposing evidence of drinking or illicit drug use, demonstrating poor communication skills, and badmouthing a previous employer.[29]

The practice of using social media activity to evaluate job applicants is not without its problems, however. Some employers actually ask for passwords so that they can directly access Facebook accounts, but this is very controversial—even illegal in more than half of the U.S. states.[30] Beyond the privacy issues involved, demanding login details would force the applicant to violate his or her contract with Facebook, since the company's statement of rights and responsibilities specifically prohibits the sharing of this information. Access to a Facebook account may also expose sensitive details regarding age and race, which could open up the evaluating company to charges of unlawful discrimination. But despite the potential drawbacks, many experts argue that using social media to evaluate job candidates is smart and appropriate, so long as the company is searching for legitimate evidence to effectively assess a potential hire.[31]

Although standard reference checks on a prior employment record do not constitute infringements on privacy, third parties are often reluctant to divulge negative information, and this limits the practical usefulness of reference checking. To encourage former employers to be honest, ask for consent for a check from applicants first. Then, ask only for appropriate information, such as employment dates, duties, strengths and weaknesses, and whether the individual is eligible for rehire.

At the same time, gathering information online about an applicant's financial, criminal, and employment history has never been easier. While some employers conduct their own background checks by accessing databases that are readily available, most outsource this function to one of hundreds of vendors that specialize in performing this service. A number of companies advertise that they will provide *free* background checks over the Internet. This certainly sounds appealing. But given the importance of the task, we suggest that you check with the National Association of Professional Background Screeners (napbs.com) before selecting a company for this purpose.

A few final cautions about background checks are in order. First, keep in mind that if a prospective employer requests a credit report to establish an applicant's employment eligibility, the Fair Credit Reporting Act requires that the applicant be notified in writing that such a report is being requested. But this is good practice, in general, when it comes to background checks. Most experts suggest that you require applicants to sign a written consent (detailing how and what you plan to check) before you conduct a check, to ensure legal compliance and to give the applicant the opportunity to withdraw from further consideration. If an applicant refuses to sign the consent form, it is legal for the company to decide against hiring him or her based on that refusal.[32]

Getting access to data is critical to making an informed hiring decision. However, you may be legally prevented from using some of the insights revealed to reject an applicant. Be sure to make your selection based on recent information that is clearly related to job duties.

A Background Check Dilemma

According to Society for Human Resource Management research, 69 percent of employers do background checks on all job candidates, 18 percent only check some prospects, and the rest don't check any.

But what should a small business do with applicants who have criminal records? Using this knowledge and denying employment can lead to charges of discrimination, but ignoring it can set the company up for liability lawsuits if serious misconduct occurs on the job. It's a tough call. To learn more about the dilemma, read John R. Emshwiller and Gary Fields, "Hiring Managers Bedeviled by Flood of Arrest Records," *The Wall Street Journal*, December 13, 2014, pp. A1, A10.

20-2d Step 4: Test the Applicant

Many jobs lend themselves to performance testing. For example, an applicant for a secretarial or clerical position may be given a standardized typing test. With a little ingenuity, employers can develop practical tests that are clearly related to the job in question, and these can provide extremely useful insights for selection decisions.

Psychological examinations may also be used by small businesses, but the results can be misleading because of difficulty in interpreting the tests or adapting them to a particular business. In addition, the U.S. Supreme Court has upheld the Equal Employment Opportunity Commission's requirement that any test used in making employment decisions must be job-related.

To be useful, tests of any kind must meet the criteria of **validity** and **reliability**. For a test to be *valid*, its results must correspond well with job performance—that is, the applicants with the best test scores must generally be the best employees. For a test to be *reliable*, it must provide consistent results when used at different times or by various individuals.

Ideally, testing should include consideration of an applicant's match with the work culture of the company and the team of employees already in place. For this reason, Jen Bilik, founder of an irreverent stationary and gift venture called Knock Knock, prefers to think about hiring as casting for a play or movie:

> *We do a work-style assessment test that's more like a personality test to figure out how we all work together. We look at a person's traits: What kind of person is this? How will he or she work within the specific department? Is this somebody who will butt heads with a particular co-worker we already have in place? You hire a résumé, but you work with a person.*[33]

Because turnover is so costly, even if all indications from testing are positive, it still pays to look deeper if it is practical to do so. Jason Fried, co-founder of the Web applications company Basecamp, follows a unique hiring approach. A job candidate who fares well in the company's very intentional interview process is still given a "test drive." That is, Fried hires prospective employees for a one-week project, or a month-long assignment in some cases, to see how they work, communicate, handle pressure,

validity
The extent to which a test assesses true job performance ability.

reliability
The consistency of a test in measuring job performance ability.

etc. According to Fried, "These real-work tests have saved us a few mismatched hires and confirmed a bunch of great people."[34] That makes such tests more than worth the trouble.

20-2e Step 5: Require Physical Examinations

A primary purpose of physical examinations is to evaluate the ability of applicants to meet the physical demands of specific jobs. However, care must be taken to avoid discriminating against those who are physically disabled. The Americans with Disabilities Act requires companies with 15 or more employees to make "reasonable" adaptations to facilitate the employment of such individuals.

Although some small businesses require medical examinations before hiring an applicant, in most cases, the company must first have offered that individual a job.[35] As part of the physical examination process, the law permits drug screening of applicants. But most small business owners have concluded that drug testing is expensive and unnecessary, despite overwhelming evidence indicating that drug use is prevalent and creates unnecessary risks and costs for employers. According to the U.S. Department of Labor, 65 percent of all on-the-job accidents can be traced back to substance abuse,[36] and employees who abuse drugs file six times more workers' compensation claims than those who don't.[37] It follows that a drug screening program can be a bargain for small businesses, reducing problem hires and long-term costs.

As you can see, a sound program for evaluating and selecting employees involves a number of "moving pieces," but many small companies pull all of the pieces together very skillfully. Rick Davis, founder and CEO of DAVACO Inc., describes how he and the staff at his retail services company pull out all the stops in order to ensure the quality of the hiring process:

> *Recruiting the best people is the single most important thing DAVACO can do. Not only do I make every effort to meet all employees before they are hired, but our human resources team also takes every measure to assure that we've recruited and selected the top candidate for every position to maximize their, and the company's, success. We incorporate practices into our recruiting efforts based on position, including telephone screening, face-to-face interviews, background checks, credit checks, drug screening, personality and behavior testing, skills assessment, and motor vehicle record checks.*[38]

In addition to emphasizing job-related expertise, the company also believes that strength of character is just as important as skills, if not more so. Skills can be taught, but Davis recognizes that ethics, loyalty, and high standards are inherent qualities that are difficult to pass on in a business setting, and he believes that the hiring process must take all of this into account.[39]

20-3 TRAINING AND DEVELOPING EMPLOYEES

Describe the roles of training and development for both managerial and nonmanagerial employees.

Once an employee has been recruited and added to the payroll, the process of training and development must begin. The purpose of this process is to transform a new recruit into a well-trained and effective technician, salesperson, manager, or other employee. Such programs can be well worth the cost. Beyond the benefits of the knowledge and skills conveyed, one study found that employees of small and medium-size enterprises who participated in training and development events were less likely to quit their jobs and more likely to show up for work, arrive on time, and give greater effort to their work.[40] These outcomes offer obvious advantages to any firm.

20-3a Basic Components of Training and Development

Though the terms are often combined, a training and development program can be separated into its two basic components. **Employee training** refers to planned efforts to help workers master the knowledge, skills, and behaviors that they need to perform the duties for which they were hired. In contrast, **management development** is more focused on preparing employees for future roles in business and emphasizes the education, job experiences, network development, and performance assessment necessary to reach long-term career goals and fulfill managerial potential. While the two components are different, they are obviously related.

Most positions require at least some training. If an employer fails to provide such instruction, a new employee must learn by trial and error, which usually leads to a waste of time, materials, and money—and sometimes alienates customers. At the same time, training to improve basic capabilities should not be limited to new hires. The performance of existing employees can often be improved through additional training. Due to constant changes in products, technology, policies, and procedures in the world of business, continual training often is necessary to update knowledge and skills—in firms of all sizes. Only with such training can employees meet the changing demands being placed on them.

Preparation for advancement usually involves developmental efforts, which typically are quite different than the support needed to sharpen skills for current duties. Because most able employees are particularly concerned about their personal development and progress, a small business can profit from careful attention to this phase of the personnel program. Opportunities for growth in an organization not only attract potential applicants, but they also help to improve the morale of current employees and reduce turnover.[41]

20-3b Orientation for New Personnel

The training and development process often begins with an individual's first two or three days on the job. It is at this point that the new employee tends to feel lost and confused, confronted with a new physical layout, a different job title, unknown co-workers, a different type of supervision, changed hours or work schedule, and a unique set of personnel policies and procedures. Any events that conflict with the newcomer's expectations are interpreted in light of his or her previous work experience, and these interpretations can either foster a strong commitment to the new employer or lead to feelings of alienation.

Recognizing the new employee's sensitivity at this point, the employer can contribute to a positive outcome through proper orientation. Some phases of the orientation can be accomplished by informal methods. For example, a company might choose to introduce newcomers to the rest of the staff by strategically placing a tray of bagels and muffins near a new employee's desk on his or her first morning of work. This would encourage co-workers to come by and get acquainted.

Other phases of the orientation must be structured or formalized. In addition to explaining specific job duties, supervisors should outline the firm's policies and procedures in as much detail as possible. A clear explanation of performance expectations and the way in which an employee's work will be evaluated should be

employee training
Planned efforts to help workers master the knowledge, skills, and behaviors they need to perform their duties.

management development
Preparation of employees for career advancement through education, job experiences, network development, and performance assessment.

included in the discussion. The new employee should be encouraged to ask questions, and time should be taken to provide careful answers. Since new hires are faced with an information overload at first, it is a good idea to follow up with the employee after a week or two has passed.

One way to support the orientation process is by providing new hires with a written description of company practices and procedures, which is often referred to as an employee handbook. The handbook may include an expression of the company's philosophy—an overall view of what the firm considers important, such as standards of excellence or quality considerations. This document typically covers topics such as recruitment, selection, training, and compensation, as well as more immediately practical information about work hours, paydays, breaks, lunch hours, absences, holidays, overtime policy, and employee benefits. Such policies should be written carefully and clearly to avoid misunderstandings. Also, bear in mind that an employee handbook is considered part of the employment contract in some states.

20-3c Employee Training

Employee training is an integral part of comprehensive quality management programs. Although quality management is usually associated with machines, materials, processes, and measurements, it also focuses on human performance. Training employees for quality performance is, to a considerable extent, part of the ongoing supervisory role of all managers.

A well-planned training program will begin on the first day on the job, and it will be multidimensional. For starters, you should clearly define what quality means in your company and explain how it is measured. But it will also help to describe some of the company's past problems, outline corrective actions that were taken, and summarize how it is currently reaching its quality goals. In addition, special classes and seminars can be used to teach employees about the importance of quality control and ways in which to produce high-quality work. Staff writers at *Inc.* magazine suggest making the training personal:

> *Train workers to see the connection between their actions and, more broadly, their work ethic, and the company's overall performance. By tying individual behavior to an overall system of work, and then showing where that system can on occasion break down, you will be giving workers the information they need to be good stewards of your business.*[42]

Job descriptions or job specifications can be used to identify abilities or skills required for particular jobs. To a large extent, such requirements determine the appropriate type of training. Instruction at the place of employment that is supervised by a professional trainer or an experienced employee is referred to as **on-the-job training**, or direct instruction. For some jobs, federal law actually *requires* this form of preparation.

More training is accomplished on the job than through any other method. However, on-the-job training of nonmanagerial employees may be haphazard unless it follows a sound, systematic method of teaching, such as **Job Instruction Training**. The steps in this program, shown in Exhibit 20.2, are intended to help supervisors become more effective in training employees.

Effective training programs often turn out to be very straightforward, sometimes linking external training to internal instruction through organized programs. For example, Digineer, a small IT consulting firm, has created a system that encourages

on-the-job training
Instruction at the place of employment, supervised by a professional trainer or experienced employee.

Job Instruction Training
A systematic, step-by-step method for on-the-job training of nonmanagerial employees.

EXHIBIT 20.2 Steps In Job Instruction Training

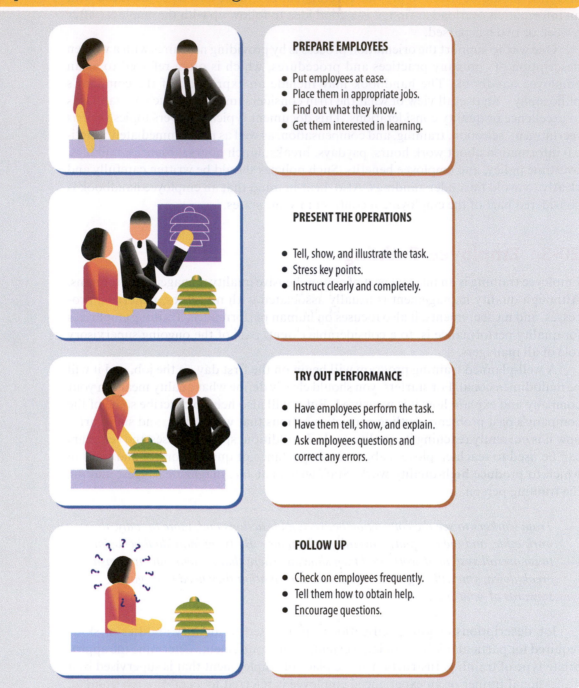

PREPARE EMPLOYEES

- Put employees at ease.
- Place them in appropriate jobs.
- Find out what they know.
- Get them interested in learning.

PRESENT THE OPERATIONS

- Tell, show, and illustrate the task.
- Stress key points.
- Instruct clearly and completely.

TRY OUT PERFORMANCE

- Have employees perform the task.
- Have them tell, show, and explain.
- Ask employees questions and correct any errors.

FOLLOW UP

- Check on employees frequently.
- Tell them how to obtain help.
- Encourage questions.

employees who have received external training to pass it on to their colleagues. This peer-to-peer training platform, which the company calls Digi-U, allows the firm to take full advantage of its investment in training for one employee by extending it to others. For example, one recent training program on project management turned out to be so effective that the company scheduled two Digi-U follow-up sessions to ensure that the instruction would be passed along to the participant's coworkers. Given the advantage that Digi-U offers, Digineer pays all expenses related to useful external training programs and provides up to two weeks of paid time off to attend them.[43]

20-3d From Training to Implementation

Regardless of the level of the position involved, the goal of a training program is to teach employees new knowledge, skills, and behaviors that will lead, in turn, to improved job performance. A recent study found that spending on training by U.S. corporations soared 15 percent to $70 billion in 2014, a trend that includes explosive growth in technology training tools that involve online and mobile platforms.[44] But unfortunately, much of the training provided to employees each year is never actually applied on the job. As one researcher summed it up, "It's clear that a big chunk of the tens of billions of dollars that organizations spend annually on staff development is going down the drain."[45]

Many of the barriers to the implementation of training in the workplace are rooted in human nature. For starters, training suggests that change is necessary, but many people find that change provokes anxiety, so they often fall back on more familiar methods. Old habits and routines are hard to break, and workplace pressures or time demands can easily lead employees to turn to tried-and-true approaches. For example, an employee may find it easier to use an old software program that always worked in the past than to take the time to master an updated version offering new features that could improve performance and efficiency over the long run.

So, what should a small business owner do? To get a better return on training and development spending, the owner must create a workplace environment that encourages people to use that training once they're back on the job:[46]

- *Put it on paper.* People are more likely to do what they write down, so employees should develop a personal action plan for implementing the training they receive. One manufacturing company requires its training participants to spell out what they will do to apply the concepts they have learned and when. They also are asked to describe the results they expect, how those results will be measured, and when they expect to see them. Finally, they must identify the assistance needed to implement their plan.
- *Measure results.* Employees will be more likely to put training to use if they know their performance will be evaluated in light of the new concepts learned. Companies can do this by measuring skills addressed in the training or by assessing the productivity improvement of work groups.
- *Get peers to help.* Peer support has the greatest impact on the effective translation of training to workplace application. When trainees get together to discuss the use of training concepts, they are more inspired to give them a try.
- *Involve supportive superiors.* Management involvement increases the odds that trainees will use what they learn. When supervisors meet with trainees, they can communicate expectations, promote focus on concepts, provide encouragement, and eliminate obstacles that can block success.
- *Provide access to experts.* Companies can assist employees with their action plans by helping to fill in gaps in their understanding. Lingering questions can be answered by providing access to reference materials, additional information on training topics, and experts within the company or from outside sources. Employees who have follow-up meetings with instructors are more likely to apply their training.

Companies that make sure their employees apply the concepts they learn in training to their work are likely to outperform their competitors. In fact, an enterprise that bears the expense of an extensive training program but fails to enjoy any of the fruits of that investment is much more likely to fail in a competitive marketplace.

20-3e Development of Managerial and Professional Employees

A small business has a particularly strong need to develop managerial and professional employees. Whether the firm has only a few key positions or many, it must ensure that the individuals who hold these positions perform effectively. Ideally, other staff members should be trained as potential replacements in case key individuals retire or leave for other reasons. Although an owner-manager often postpones grooming a personal replacement, this step is crucial in ensuring a smooth transition in the firm's management.

Establishing a management development program requires serious consideration of the following factors:

- *The need for development.* What vacancies are expected? Who needs to be developed? What type of training and how much training are needed to meet the demands of the job description?
- *A plan for development.* How can the individuals be developed? Do their current responsibilities permit them to learn? Can they be assigned additional duties? Should they be given temporary assignments in other areas—for example, should they be shifted from production to sales? Would additional schooling be beneficial?
- *A timetable for development.* When should the development process begin? How much can be accomplished in the next six months or one year?
- *Employee counseling.* Do the individuals understand their need for development? Are they aware of their prospects within the firm? Has an understanding been reached as to the nature of the development program? Have the employees been consulted regularly about progress in their work and the problems confronting them? Have they been given the benefit of the owner's experience and insights without having decisions made for them?

Management development strategies often work wonderfully, but they do have their limits. For example, in many situations, the best development strategy is not to promote an employee beyond the position he or she is best suited to perform. Mike Faith, founder, CEO, and president of the online retailer Headsets.com, learned how this can work when he moved the first employee hired by the company up to a management position. Notice how Faith praises his employee before and after the misstep, but not while he was actually in his elevated position.

> *[T]his guy is a genius. Really. He can see the big picture and take an idea and make it work. Because he was so good at what he did . . . we moved him into a management position, and it was a disaster. My A player quickly became a B player; management became a millstone around his neck. Recognizing our mistake, we moved him out of management. Now he takes on a variety of projects and is back to being a genius.*[47]

Faith remains steadfast in his belief that everyone has the ability to be an A player if he or she is placed in the right job. But it's important to remember that a top player in one position can be a less-than-satisfactory player in another.

20-4 COMPENSATION AND INCENTIVES FOR EMPLOYEES

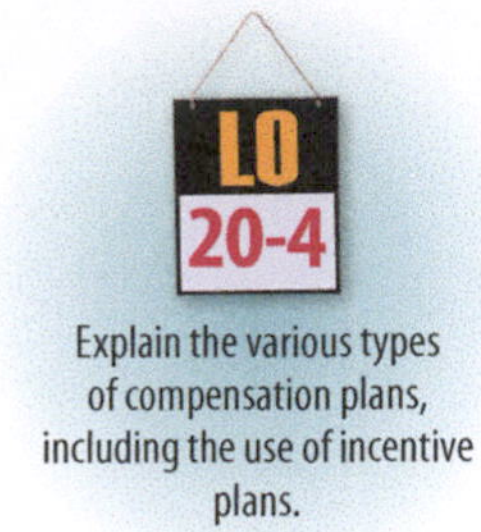

Explain the various types of compensation plans, including the use of incentive plans.

Compensation is important to all employees, and small firms must acknowledge the role of the paycheck in attracting and motivating personnel. In addition, small firms can offer several nonfinancial incentives that appeal to both managerial and nonmanagerial employees.

20-4a Wage and Salary Levels

In general, small firms must be roughly competitive in wage and salary levels in order to attract well-qualified personnel. Payments to employees either are based on increments of time—such as an hour, a day, or a month—or vary with the output of the employees. Compensation based on time is most appropriate for jobs in which performance is not easily measured. Time-based compensation is also easier to understand and is used more widely than incentive systems that are based on specific dimensions of employee performance.

Small businesses often struggle to pay their lowest-level employees even the minimum wage required by law. However, some employers choose to improve the lives of their employees and express their support by paying wages that exceed that legal minimum. For example, In-N-Out Burger has grown quickly over the years by following a few simple practices, including caring for its employees by paying above-minimum wages. According to the company's website, "We start all our new Associates at a minimum of $10.50 an hour for one simple reason . . . you are important to us! And our commitment to a higher starting wage is just one of the ways in which we show it."[48] Such businesses often benefit along with the employees. Many see an improvement in recruiting and retention, particularly in hard-to-fill positions. These businesses may also enjoy an improved public image with customers and the community. In other words, they can earn a respectable return on their investment—on more than one front!

piecework
Financial incentive based on number of units produced.

20-4b Financial Incentives

Incentive plans are designed to motivate employees to increase their productivity. Incentive wages may constitute an employee's entire earnings or merely supplement regular wages or salary. The commission system for salespeople is one type of incentive compensation (see Chapter 17 for an expanded discussion of this topic). In manufacturing, employees are sometimes paid according to the number of units they produce, a practice called **piecework**. Although most incentive plans apply to employees as individuals, they may also involve the use of group incentives and team rewards.

General bonus or profit-sharing plans are especially important for managers and other key personnel, although they may also include lower-level employees. These plans provide employees with "a piece of the action" and may or may not involve assignment of shares of stock. Many profit-sharing plans simply entail distribution of a specified share of all profits or profits in excess of a target amount. Profit sharing serves more directly as a work-related incentive in small companies than in large corporations, because the connection between individual performance and success can be more easily appreciated in a small business.

Determining the Best Pay Rates
Concerned about how much pay to offer to attract the employees you need? Websites such as CBSalary.com, PayScale.com, and Salary.com offer free reports of what workers with a particular job in your area get paid. You can get similar wage information from the U.S. Bureau of Labor Statistics at www.bls.gov/bls/proghome.htm.

Performance-based compensation plans must be designed carefully if they are to work successfully. Such plans should be devised with the aid of a consultant and/or an accountant's insight. Keys to developing effective bonus plans include the following:

- *Set attainable goals.* Performance-based compensation plans work best when workers believe that they can meet the targets. Complex financial measures or jargon-heavy benchmarks should be avoided—employees are motivated only by goals that they understand.
- *Include employees in planning.* Employees should have a voice in developing performance measures and changes to work systems. Incentive plans should be phased in gradually so that employees have a chance to get used to them.
- *Keep updating goals.* Performance-based plans must be continually adjusted to meet the changing needs of workers and customers. The life expectancy of such a plan may be no more than three or four years.

20-4c Stock Incentives

In young entrepreneurial ventures, stock options are sometimes used to attract and hold key personnel. The option holders get the opportunity to share in the growing—perhaps even skyrocketing—value of the company's stock. If the business prospers sufficiently, such personnel can become millionaires.

But stock ownership need not be reserved only for executives or key personnel. Some small firms have created *employee stock ownership plans (ESOPs)*, which give employees a share of ownership in the business.[49] These plans may be structured in a variety of ways. For example, a share of annual profits may be designated for the purchase of company stock, which is then placed in a trust for employees. When coupled with a commitment to employee participation in business operations, ESOPs can motivate employees, resulting in improvements in productivity.

ESOPs also can provide a way for owners to cash out and withdraw from a business without selling the firm to outsiders. See Chapter 13 for a discussion of this topic.

20-4d Employee Benefits

Employee benefits include payments by the employer for such items as Social Security, vacation time, holidays, health insurance, and retirement compensation. All told, these benefits are expensive. According to the Bureau of Labor Statistics, their cost for the average firm is equal to about 31 percent of salary and wage payments.[50] And while increases in the cost of some benefits have slowed in recent years, their escalation continues to outpace the rate of inflation in the economy overall.[51] In general, small companies are less generous than large firms when it comes to providing benefits for employees.[52] Even so, the cost of such benefits is a substantial part of total labor costs for these businesses.

employee benefits
Supplements to compensation, designed to be attractive and useful to employees.

flexible benefit programs (cafeteria plans)
Benefit programs that allow employees to select the types of benefits they wish to receive.

Though employee benefits are expensive, a small company cannot ignore them if it is to compete effectively for good workers. Research has also shown that firms offering well-designed benefits packages—that is, plans that are tailored to the unique needs and preferences of their workers—enjoy higher levels of employee loyalty, retention, and engagement.[53] But this is where small companies really shine, because they are closer to their employees and can have greater flexibility when it comes to accommodating different preferences. To ensure fit, a limited but growing number of small businesses now use **flexible benefit programs** (or **cafeteria plans**), which allow employees to select the types of benefits they wish to receive. All employees receive a core level of coverage, such as basic health insurance, and then are allowed to choose how an employer-specified amount is to be divided among additional options—for example, dependent care assistance, group term life insurance, and additional health insurance.[54]

For small companies that wish to avoid the detailed paperwork associated with administering cafeteria plans, outside help is available. Many small firms—some with fewer than 25 employees—turn over the administration of their flexible benefit plans to outside consulting, payroll accounting, or insurance companies that provide such services for a monthly fee.

A number of firms have devised relatively affordable but meaningful "perks" that are customized to their particular situation but still signal appreciation for workers. Buying pizza for everyone on Fridays and giving each employee a paid day off for her or his birthday are just two examples. These small benefits make employment more attractive for employees and are motivating because they are often thoughtful and sometimes even personalized. Indeed, recent studies have shown that employees respond more positively to such rewards than to cash, and they lead to greater productivity boosts.[55] With a little creativity, these perks can be used to build morale, promote loyalty, and encourage healthy behaviors.[56]

John Roberson is very committed to growing his experiential marketing business. But he also cares about his employees and their physical and emotional health, and he has ways of persuading them to get involved in programs that support wellness. Tailoring rewards to his employees' specific interests, he has given away a guitar, yoga lessons, time with a personal trainer, paid time off to build orphanages in Central America—even a pair of cowboy boots! This has been good for both the workers and the company. Says Roberson, "We attract employees who see we are about more than just profits."[57]

20-5 SPECIAL ISSUES IN HUMAN RESOURCE MANAGEMENT

Discuss the human resource issues of co-employment, legal protection, labor unions, and the formalizing of employer-employee relationships.

So far, this chapter has dealt with the recruitment, selection, training, and compensation of employees. Several related issues—co-employment agreements, legal protection of employees, labor unions, the formalizing of employer-employee relationships, and the need for a human resource manager—are the focus of this final section.

20-5a Co-Employment Agreements

Entrepreneurs can choose to outsource part of the burden of managing employees through an arrangement known as **co-employment**. Today, an estimated 700 co-employment companies, also known as **professional employer organizations (PEOs)**, operate in all 50 states and assist small businesses with their human resource management needs. For a fee of 2 to 6 percent of payroll, a PEO will manage a company's increasingly complex employee-related matters, such as overseeing health benefit programs, handling workers' compensation claims, ensuring payroll tax compliance, processing unemployment insurance claims, and filing reports required by government agencies. Although small companies using this service avoid a certain amount of paperwork, they do not escape the tasks of recruitment and selection. In most cases, the entrepreneur or the venture's management still determines who works, who gets promoted, and who gets time off.

co-employment
An arrangement to outsource part of personnel management to an organization that handles paperwork and administers benefits for those employees.

professional employer organizations (PEOs)
A company that sets up co-employment agreements.

Many employees like the co-employment arrangement. It may allow small employers to provide better benefit packages, since PEOs generally cover hundreds or thousands of employees and thus qualify for better rates. Of course, the small business must bear the cost of insurance and other benefits obtained through a co-employment partner, in addition to paying a basic service fee. However, this may be the only way the company can afford to offer the benefits necessary to attract and keep high-quality employees, and the savings often will more than offset the cost of using a PEO. The fact that the co-employment partner also assumes the burden of managing payroll and other administrative processes makes this arrangement even more attractive.

When a company decides to use the services of a PEO, both parties share legal obligations as a result. That is, the law holds both companies responsible for payment of payroll taxes and workers' compensation insurance and compliance with government regulations—the client company cannot simply offload these obligations to the PEO. This highlights the importance of selecting a PEO carefully to ensure that you will be dealing with a responsible firm. It is wise to follow the guidelines offered by the National Association of Professional Employer Organizations (napeo.org) to be sure you are contracting with a service provider that is honest, dependable, and right for your company.

Using a PEO can also change the application of government regulations to small businesses. Very small ventures are often excluded from specific rules. For example, companies with fewer than 15 employees are exempt from the Americans with Disabilities Act (with some exceptions—for example, where state law holds even small ventures to a high standard). However, when these employees officially become part of a large PEO, the small company using the co-employed workers becomes subject to this law. It always pays to treat your employees with care and respect, of course, but taking on added legal obligations by working with a PEO can actually make managing a small company much more complicated.

20-5b Legal Protection of Employees

Employees are afforded protection by a number of federal and state laws. The United States Department of Labor (DOL) provides a summary of the principal labor statutes that it administers and enforces,[58] but it can be difficult to sort out which of these will apply to your particular business. For that reason, the DOL has created the *FirstStep* Employment Law Advisor (which can be found at www.dol.gov/elaws/FirstStep), and we strongly recommend that you use it. By answering a few brief questions about your business, this interactive e-tool will direct you to summaries of the statutes that will affect ventures such as yours. It also provides guidance on recordkeeping, reporting, and notification requirements that you must follow.

This information still does not cover everything that you need to know, including state laws that may apply. To fill in any gaps, we recommend that you gather as much information as you can from the DOL's "Employment Law Guide" (www.dol.gov/compliance/guide) and "State Labor Laws" (www.dol.gov/whd/state/state.htm) Web pages. But even with these facts in hand, it is best to consult with an attorney to be sure that you are in compliance. It is also advisable to be familiar with some of the broader statutes that shape and influence the wide scope of labor law in the United States.

Civil Rights Act
Legislation prohibiting discrimination based on race, color, religion, sex, or national origin.

One of the most far-reaching statutes is the **Civil Rights Act**, originally enacted in 1964, and its amendments. This law, which applies to any employer with 15 or more people, prohibits discrimination on the basis of race, color, religion, sex, or national origin. Other laws, like the Americans with Disabilities Act and the Age Discrimination in Employment Act, extend similar protection to disabled and older employees. Every employment condition is covered, including hiring, firing, promotion, transfer, and compensation.

The Civil Rights Act includes protection against sexual harassment, an issue that must be addressed by small businesses as well as large corporations. Education and prompt response to complaints are the best tools for avoiding sexual harassment and the possibility of liability claims. The following practical action steps can help a small company prevent sexual harassment from occurring in its workplace and avoid liability if a claim should arise:[59]

© RAWPIXEL/SHUTTERSTOCK.COM

1. Establish clear policies and procedures regarding sexual harassment in the workplace, and publish this information in an employee handbook.
2. Define *sexual harassment* in the handbook and state in no uncertain terms that it will not be tolerated and that wrongdoers will be disciplined or fired.
3. Communicate a clear procedure for filing sexual harassment claims, and require employees to report incidents of harassment to management immediately.
4. Explain that any and all complaints of sexual harassment will be investigated fairly and fully (while assuring claimant confidentiality) and that retaliation against anyone who complains about sexual harassment will not be tolerated.
5. Conduct sessions at least once a year to teach employees and managers (separately) about sexual harassment and the company's complaint procedure, and encourage them to use the procedure if harassment should occur.

Of course, even a well-designed and carefully implemented action plan cannot guarantee that a sexual harassment claim will never be filed. And if that should happen, it would be wise to contact an attorney and proceed according to his or her counsel.

Employees' health and safety are protected by the **Occupational Safety and Health Act** of 1970. This law, which applies in general to firms of any size doing business in the United States and/or its territories, created the Occupational Safety and Health Administration (OSHA) to establish and enforce necessary safety and health standards. But when it comes to determining the requirements that will be applied to your small company, keep in mind that your state might apply even more demanding workplace safety rules than those mandated under federal law. To learn more about how OSHA requirements apply to startups, see "OSHA Help for Small Businesses" at www.osha.gov/OshDoc/data_General_Facts/newbusinesses-factsheet.html.

Compensation of employees is regulated by the minimum wage and overtime provisions of the **Fair Labor Standards Act (FLSA)**, as well as by other federal and state laws. The FLSA applies to employers involved in interstate or foreign commerce with two or more employees. It sets the minimum wage (which is periodically increased by Congress) and specifies no less than time-and-a-half pay for nonsupervisory employees who work more than 40 hours per week. Penalties for noncompliance can be severe, so it is advisable to review the details of the law as posted by the U.S. Department of Labor (www.dol.gov/whd/flsa).

Occupational Safety and Health Act
Legislation that regulates the safety of workplaces and work practices.

Fair Labor Standards Act (FLSA)
Federal law that establishes a minimum wage and provides for overtime pay.

The **Family and Medical Leave Act** was passed and signed into law in February 1993. The law requires firms with 50 or more employees to allow workers as much as 12 weeks of unpaid leave for childbirth, the adoption of a child, serious employee or family health conditions, or other specified family needs.[60] The worker must have been employed by the firm for at least 12 months and have worked at least 1,250 hours over the previous 12 months. Furthermore, the employer must continue health care coverage during the leave and guarantee that the employee can return to the same job or one that is comparable.[61]

20-5c Labor Unions

As a general rule, entrepreneurs prefer to operate independently and to avoid using union laborers. Indeed, most small businesses are not unionized. To some extent, this results from the predominance of small business in services, where unionization is less common than in manufacturing. Also, unions typically focus their attention on large corporations.

Though uncommon, labor unions are not unknown in small firms. Many types of small businesses—building and electrical contractors, for example—negotiate labor contracts and employ unionized personnel. The need to work with a union formalizes and, to some extent, complicates the relationship between a small company and its employees.

If employees wish to bargain collectively—that is, to be represented in negotiations by a union—the law requires the employer to participate in such bargaining. The demand for labor union representation may arise from employees' dissatisfaction with their pay, work environment, or employment relationships. By following constructive human resource policies, a small company can minimize the likelihood of labor organization and improve the relationship between management and employees.

20-5d Formalizing Employer-Employee Relationships

As explained earlier in this chapter, the management systems of small companies are typically less formal than those of larger firms. A degree of informality can be a virtue in small organizations. As personnel are added, however, the benefits of informality decline and its costs increase. Large numbers of employees cannot be managed effectively without some system for regulating employer-employee relationships. This situation can be best understood in terms of a family relationship. House rules are generally unnecessary when only two people are living in the home. But when several children are added to the mix, Mom and Dad soon start sounding like a government regulatory agency.

Growth, then, creates pressure to formalize personnel policies and procedures. Determining how much formality to introduce and how soon involves managerial judgment. Some employee issues should be formalized from the very beginning. On the other hand, excessive regulation can become paralyzing.

Personnel management procedures are standardized in many companies, using performance assessment systems that follow a set timetable for reviews—often on an annual basis. But effective performance review programs tend to bear certain hallmarks. For example, they are guided by clearly established benchmarks that are based on goals that are SMART—that is, *S*pecific, *M*easurable, *A*chievable, *R*ealistic, and *T*ime-bound. They also tend to follow a well-planned process that emphasizes continual communication between managers and employees and ongoing performance tracking. Effective review meetings require sufficient time (from 40 minutes to an hour) and undivided attention, and they should begin with positive feedback before

Family and Medical Leave Act
Legislation that assures employees of unpaid leave for childbirth or other family needs.

summarizing objective judgments of attitudes and behaviors in need of improvement. Used correctly, employee reviews can be a powerful tool for building a small business.[62]

A recent analysis by Deloitte Consulting revealed that many firms are modifying their performance review processes to accommodate rapidly changing work conditions and shifting employee needs and attitudes. Some of these adjustments include more frequent setting and resetting of goals (e.g., quarterly goals have been found to lead to 31 percent better performance than annual goals) and addressing performance problems immediately rather than waiting for a scheduled formal review. A growing number of these firms are also asking their employees to assess their own performance (to determine expectations) and are adopting (mostly) online tools, such as Achievers and Globoforce, to create a setting in which employees feel comfortable providing feedback to one another on a continuous basis.[63] To compete successfully these days, companies are realizing that they need to become more agile and work harder to attract and retain top talent, and that calls for improved performance review strategies.

20-5e The Need for a Human Resource Manager

A venture with only a few employees cannot afford a full-time specialist to deal with personnel problems. Some of the human resource techniques used in large corporations may be far too complicated for small businesses. As a small company grows in size, however, its personnel problems will increase in both number and complexity.

The point at which it becomes logical to hire a human resource manager cannot be precisely identified. In view of the increased overhead cost, the owner-manager of a growing business must decide whether circumstances make it profitable to employ a personnel specialist. Hiring a part-time human resource manager—a retired personnel manager, for example—is a possible first step in some instances. Conditions such as the following favor the appointment of a human resource manager in a small business:

- There are a substantial number of employees (100 or more is often suggested as a guideline[64]).
- Employees are represented by a union.
- The labor turnover rate is high.
- The need for skilled or professional personnel creates problems in recruitment or selection.
- Supervisors or operations employees require considerable training.
- Employee morale is unsatisfactory.
- Industry competition for personnel is keen.

Until a human resource manager is hired, however, the owner-manager typically functions in that capacity. His or her decisions regarding employee selection and compensation, as well as other personnel issues, will have a direct impact on the operating success of the firm.

As this chapter points out, the human resource management function is simple in concept, but it can be challenging to put into practice. From recruitment to prospect evaluation and selection to training and development programs to the administration of compensation and benefit plans—there is so much to do! And these activities must be conducted within the constraints of some very specific laws. While this may seem overwhelming, keep in mind that working with the people who join your enterprise is likely to be the most fulfilling feature of being in business. If they are managed carefully and motivated to do their best, capable employees can take your business to new heights. There is no limit to what can be done with the right people in the right enterprise with the right care and handling.

20-1. Explain the importance of employee recruitment, and list some useful sources for finding suitable applicants.

- Startups have been launching with fewer employees in recent years, but recruiting good employees can boost the overall performance of a small business.
- Small companies can attract applicants by stressing unique work features and opportunities.
- Recruitment sources include the Internet, schools, public and private employment agencies, temporary help agencies, employee referrals, executive search firms, and walk-ins and help-wanted advertising.
- The composition of the U.S. workforce is becoming more diverse over time with respect to race, ethnicity, gender, and age, but the varied perspectives of a diverse workforce can offer advantages, such as improved decision making.
- Well-developed job descriptions can help with employee recruitment, but they can also be useful in other ways, such as bringing focus to work performed, providing direction to training, and serving as a guide for performance reviews.

20-2. Identify the steps in evaluating job applicants.

- In the first step, application forms help the employer obtain preliminary information from applicants. (Employers must avoid questions about gender, race, religion, color, national origin, age, and disabilities.)
- Additional evaluation steps are interviewing the applicant (with behavioral interviews offering the best insights), checking references and other background information, and testing the applicant.
- The final evaluation step is often a physical examination, which may include drug screening.

20-3. Describe the roles of training and development for both managerial and nonmanagerial employees.

- Employee training enables workers to perform their current jobs effectively. Management development prepares them for career advancement.
- An orientation program helps introduce new employees to the firm and its work environment.
- Training is an integral component of a comprehensive quality management program.
- More training is accomplished on the job than through any other method. Following the steps in Job Instruction Training should make training more effective.
- Training is more likely to be put to use if it is written down, measured for results, structured for peer support, encouraged by management, and supported with ongoing advice from experts.
- A management development program should be guided by an understanding of the need for development, a plan for development, and a timetable for development. It should also provide appropriate employee counseling.

20-4. Explain the various types of compensation plans, including the use of incentive plans.

- Small companies must be roughly competitive in salary and wage levels in order to attract well-qualified personnel.
- Payments to employees either are based on increments of time or vary with employee output.
- Incentive systems relate compensation to various measures of performance.
- Employee stock ownership plans enable employees to own a share of the business and provide motivation for improved productivity.
- Employee benefit costs often equal 31 percent of payroll costs and can include flexible benefit programs, which allow employees to select the types of benefits they wish to receive.

20-5. Discuss the human resource issues of co-employment, legal protection, labor unions, and the formalizing of employer-employee relationships.

- Small businesses can reduce paperwork by transferring personnel to the payroll of a professional employer organization (PEO) through a co-employment arrangement, but legal obligations remain and may actually increase.
- Depending on their size, small businesses may have to observe laws that prohibit discrimination and sexual harassment, protect employee health and safety, establish a minimum wage, and provide for family and medical leave.
- Some small businesses must work with labor unions, which may involve collective bargaining.
- As small firms grow, they must adopt more formal human resource management methods, including regular performance reviews.
- Employment of a human resource manager usually becomes necessary as a company grows in size.

Key Terms

behavioral interviews p. 545
Civil Rights Act p. 558
co-employment p. 557
employee benefits p. 556
employee training p. 550
Fair Labor Standards Act (FLSA) p. 569
Family and Medical Leave Act p. 560
flexible benefit programs (cafeteria plans) p. 556
headhunters p. 541
human resource management (HRM) p. 535
job description p. 544
Job Instruction Training p. 551
job specification p. 544
management development p. 550
Occupational Safety and Health Act p. 559
on-the-job training p. 551
piecework p. 555
professional employer organizations (PEOs) p. 557
reliability p. 548
validity p. 548
workforce diversity p. 542

You Make the Call

Situation 1

While trying to find a new accounts receivable person for his Chicago-based postcard printing business, Javier Gomez decided that he had surely found "Mr. Perfect." On paper, this applicant had the right background, and he was asking for less money than Gomez was willing to pay. The interview went well, the reference check was positive, and the drug test came back clear. A few odd twists in Mr. Perfect's story, though, have created some questions for Gomez. First, Mr. Perfect was asked during the hiring process to show his driver's license, but he could produce only an Illinois state I.D. card. (A driver's license is needed to operate a motor vehicle legally, but the state also issues I.D. cards to help Illinois residents prove their identity when banking, traveling, and in other situations.) Second, Mr. Perfect stated that he had worked for his previous employer for 12 years and thus could provide only one appropriate reference. Gomez always asks for three references so that he can contact them all and look for patterns of behavior. Finally, Mr. Perfect mentioned in passing that if he were hired, he would like to perform tasks beyond those listed in the job description for the position. Specifically, he wondered if he might be asked to drop the company's mail off at the post office as needed. Gomez has had plenty of employees ask if they could take on new responsibilities, but doing post office runs was never one of them.

As Gomez pondered his hiring decision, he kept coming back to the fact that if Mr. Perfect were hired, the accounts receivable job would give him access to cash, blank checks, and financially sensitive information. And if he were allowed to take the company's mail to the post office, he would have access to that, too. In so many ways, Mr. Perfect seemed to be exactly what Gomez was looking for, but given the strange details of his story, Gomez is wondering if hiring him for the position would be wise.

Question 1 With the information available at this point, do you think Gomez should hire Mr. Perfect? How much weight should be given to the fact that he doesn't, for example, have a driver's license?

Question 2 How important are reference checks in the hiring process? Should having only one reference cause any concern? Why or why not? What potential problems can you see in this?

Question 3 Mr. Perfect seems to be just the person for the job in so many ways. Does it make sense to think about restructuring the job (for example, limiting access to cash and blank checks as much as possible) to minimize the concerns that have surfaced because of his story? Should a job ever be structured for any single individual?

Situation 2

Cassandra Kinsley is the hiring manager at an advertising agency, and she must choose between two final candidates, Bradley Adams and Jennifer Rensi, for a senior media analyst position in the firm. Both applicants are equally qualified. However, Adams started out with an edge because of reports Kinsley was getting about his very strong leadership and communication skills and the boundless energy he commits to his work. But when she Googled both candidates, a different impression emerged. The search on Rensi revealed only work-related sites that seemed solid. Entries on Adams were more noteworthy, including references to nonprofit work and an award for exemplary community service. Unfortunately for Adams, though, one of his friends failed to enable the privacy settings on his Facebook page, opening a back door that led Kinsley to pictures of Adams drinking and partying with friends from his college days. The reference to "smokin' blunts" was particularly damaging, and the overall profile convinced Kinsley that it would be best to hire Rensi, which is exactly what she did.

It is very efficient to conduct online searches, which is why Kinsley has come to prefer them to the laborious task of checking references. However, she is very much aware that there may be problems with this method, and that is causing her to wonder if she should really be using it. For example, Adams is only one of many job candidates in recent years on whom she has taken a pass because of the reputational damage caused by the online behavior of friends—damage that could have been prevented if they had been more careful with their privacy settings. And there is a question of fairness as well. Adams was prudent enough to select appropriate privacy settings on his own Facebook page, but it was his friend who let the cat out of the misbehavior bag. The photos seemed to provide evidence of wild behavior, but what if the friend's posts were exaggerated and misleading? Adams will never know that this was the reason that he was passed over for the job, so he won't have an opportunity to explain. Such are the drawbacks to using social media in the hiring process.

Source: Adapted from Bidhan Parmar, "Should You Check Facebook before Hiring?" *The Washington Post*, January 22, 2011, http://www.washingtonpost.com/wp-dyn/content/article/2011/01/22/AR2011012203193.html, accessed March 31, 2015.

Question 1 What are the major advantages and disadvantages for employers that choose to use social media to screen job candidates? What are the major benefits and drawbacks for job candidates who are evaluated in this way?

Question 2 What are the most important ethical questions that should be addressed if a small company should decide to use social media tools in its assessment of prospective employees? Can all of these questions be addressed to your satisfaction? Why or why not?

Question 3 The use of social media in employee recruitment and evaluation is rapidly increasing over time. Since there is no question that these tools are going to be even more widely used in the future, what guidelines would you recommend to any small business that chooses to take this path?

Situation 3

John Abelson had a promising idea for a new business. Sizing up the situation at the time, he concluded that the few retailers that specialized in the sale of men's ties had it all wrong. They were always behind when it came to keeping up with the latest fabrics, patterns, and style trends. He wanted to come up with a concept that would become the go-to website for men's ties, mixing style news, social networking, and personalized neckwear recommendations with e-commerce. So, in 2011, he and a partner started TiesInStyle.com to fill the void. But given their limited startup capital, they had to come up with a creative way to staff their new venture on a shoestring.

How were they going to get people to work for a new company for free—especially when they would have to live in New York, the most expensive city in the United States? Simple—they would "hire" interns. As it turns out, they found that there are plenty of young men with diplomas from excellent universities or fashion institutes and dreams of a career amidst the glitz and glamour of the men's fashion world, but with scant job prospects in a sluggish economy. Many of them have accepted Abelson's offer, seeing it as a chance to get a foot in the door of a competitive industry and to make contacts for future opportunities. At last count, TiesInStyle.com had 21 unpaid part-time interns signed up to assist the firm's seven regular employees.

Question 1 Do you think interns make the best employees for a small business like TiesInStyle.com? Does the fact that the company is a startup create any potential complications that you can think of?

Question 2 What adjustments would a small company need to make to its selection practices if it decided to take on unpaid interns in place of hiring regular, paid employees?

Question 3 Do you see any ethical issues that should be considered when hiring unpaid interns? Read the U.S. Department of Labor's Fact Sheet #71, "Internship Programs under the Fair Labor Standards Act" (www.dol.gov/whd/regs/compliance/whdfs71.htm). Do you think Abelson's use of interns is in compliance with these regulations?

Case 20

Jason Fried and Hiring Practices at 37signals (P. 688)

One of the most important features of a company's human resource management program involves its selection practices. This case highlights the unorthodox approaches that one successful small business uses to identify and hire the employees who will serve it best.

Alternative Cases for Chapter 20

Video Case 2, PortionPac Chemicals, p. 647
Case 5, Iaccarino & Son, p. 654

Endnotes

1. "Thinking Outside the Big Box," *Baylor Business Review*, Fall 2014, pp. 26–27.
2. "The Build Quarterly Report on: Talent Management," *Inc.*, Vol. 35, No. 10 (December 2013/January 2014), special section, pp. 2–3.
3. See Jan M. P. de Kok, Lorraine M. Uhlaner, and A. Roy Thurik, "Professional HRM Practices in Family Owned-Managed Enterprises," *Journal of Small Business Management*, Vol. 44, No. 3 (May 2006), pp. 441–460.
4. "CEO Survey," *Inc.*, Vol. 36, No. 7 (September 2014), p. 200.
5. Matt Alderton, "How to Hire Smarter in 2015," *MyBusiness*, November/December 2014, pp. 19–20.
6. Angus Loten, "With New Technologies, Start-Ups Go Lean," *The Wall Street Journal*, September 15, 2011, p. B5.
7. *Ibid.*
8. Joel Spolsky, "Recruiting the Top 1 Percent: There's a Better Way to Find and Hire the Very Best Employees," *Inc.*, Vol. 29, No. 5 (May 2007), pp. 81–82.
9. Chris Penttila, "Talent Scout," *Entrepreneur*, June 30, 2008, http://www.entrepreneur.com/article/194508, accessed February 27, 2015.
10. Chris Resto, Ian Ybarra, and Ramit Sethi, *Recruit or Die: How Any Business Can Beat the Big Guys in the War for Young Talent* (New York: Penguin Group, 2008).
11. "Data Bank: You're Hired," *Inc.*, Vol. 34, No. 6 (July/August 2012), p. 24
12. Personal communication with Scott Glatstein, April 25, 2011.
13. Julie Strickland, "The Good Hires? They're in Your Network," *Inc.*, Vol. 35, No. 4 (May 2013), p. 24.
14. "Jobvite: 2014 Social Recruiting Survey," https://www.jobvite.com/wp-content/uploads/2014/10/Jobvite_SocialRecruiting_Survey2014.pdf, accessed March 2, 2015.
15. Joe Light, "Recruiters Troll Facebook for Candidates They Like," *The Wall Street Journal*, August 8, 2011, pp. B1, B8.
16. To get an idea of the kinds of services that public employment offices in your state can provide, search for "[name of your state] state employment offices," using any search engine.
17. Strickland, *op. cit.*
18. http://www.imperativesllc.com, accessed March 2, 2015; and Glatstein, *op. cit.*
19. Mitra Toossi, "Projections of the Labor Force to 2050: A Visual Essay," *Monthly Labor Review*, October 2012, http://www.bls.gov/opub/mlr/2012/10/art1full.pdf, accessed March 2, 2015.
20. Bureau of Labor Statistics, "Labor Force Projections to 2022: The Labor Force Participation Rate Continues to Fall," *Monthly Labor Review*, December 2013, http://www.bls.gov/opub/mlr/2013/article/labor-force-projections-to-2022-the-labor-force-participation-rate-continues-to-fall-1.htm, accessed March 2, 2015.
21. Dee Gill, "Dealing with Diversity," *Inc.*, Vol. 27, No. 11 (November 2005), p. 38.
22. U.S. Department of Justice, "Americans with Disabilities Act: Questions and Answers" (see "Q: Does the ADA require employers to develop written job descriptions?"), http://www.ada.gov/q&aeng02.htm, accessed March 3, 2015.
23. Katherine Hansen, *The Quintessential Guide to Behavioral Interviewing* (Kettle Falls, WA: Quintessential Careers Press, 2012).
24. *Ibid.*
25. Adapted from "Quintessential Careers: Sample Behavioral Interview Questions for Job-Seekers," http://www.quintcareers.com/sample_behavioral.html, accessed March 18, 2015.
26. Research indicates that around 27 percent of small businesses find it necessary to fire employees each year. See William J. Dennis, Jr. "Unemployment Compensation," *National Federation of Independent Business Quarterly Research Report*, Vol. 7, No. 1, (2007), for details.
27. "HireRight: Industry Fast Facts," http://www.hireright.com/resources/industry-fast-facts, accessed March 18, 2015.
28. Mary Axelson, "The Candidate Selfie: How to Evaluate Job Skills Using Social Networks," *SkilledUp*, December 22, 2014, http://www.skilledup.com/insights/the-candidate-selfie-how-to-evaluate-job-skills-using-social-networks, accessed March 20, 2015.
29. "Data Bank: You're Hired," *Inc.*, Vol. 34, No. 6 (July/August 2012), p. 24.
30. Bernhard Warner, "Social Media, by the Book," *Inc.*, Vol. 36, No. 6 (July/August 2014), pp. 60–61.
31. Nancy Flynn, "Keeping an Eye on Employees Helps Companies Protect Themselves," *The Wall Street Journal*, May 12, 2014, p. R1.
32. "Nolo: Background Checks FAQ," http://www.nolo.com/legal-encyclopedia/background-checks-faq.html, accessed March 19, 2015.
33. Jen Bilik, "I'm More of a Creative Monarch Than a Democratic Team Leader," *Inc.*, Vol. 33, No. 8 (October 2011), pp. 114–116.
34. Jason Fried, "Never Read Another Résumé," *Inc.*, Vol. 32, No. 5 (June 2010), pp. 36–37.
35. As with many governmental regulations that affect small businesses, this applies only to those companies that have *at least* 15 employees.
36. Joe Reilly, "Drug Testing & Safety: What's the Connection?" *Occupational Health & Safety*, September 1, 2014, http://ohsonline.com/Articles/2014/09/01/Drug-Testing-and-Safety.aspx?Page=1, accessed March 19, 2015.
37. "Hiring Your First Employee," http://www.entrepreneur.com/article/83774, accessed March 19, 2015.
38. Personal communication with Rick Davis, August 21, 2007.
39. *Ibid.*
40. See Karl Pajo, Alan Coetzer, and Nigel Guenole, "Formal Development Opportunities and Withdrawal Behaviors by Employees in Small and Medium-Sized Enterprises," *Journal of Small Business Management*, Vol. 48, No. 3 (July 2010), pp. 281–301.
41. Ilan Mochari, "At This Company, Employees Get an Annual Allowance of $1,500 That They Can Spend to Learn (Almost) Anything," *Inc.*, Vol. 35, No. 10 (December 2013/January 2014), p. 14 (Supplement).
42. "Five Ways to Improve Quality," *Inc.*, September 2, 2010, http://www.inc.com/guides/2010/09/5-ways-to-improve-quality.html, accessed March 19, 2015.
43. Gwen Moran, "Not-So-Basic Training," *Entrepreneur*, Vol. 39, No. 11 (November 2011), pp. 87–90.

44. Josh Bersin, "Spending on Corporate Training Soars: Employee Capabilities Now a Priority," *Forbes*, February 4, 2014, http://www.forbes.com/sites/joshbersin/2014/02/04/the-recovery-arrives-corporate-training-spend-skyrockets, accessed March 20, 2015.

45. Ira G. Asherman, "Employee Training: Getting Your Money's Worth," *Regulatory Focus*, August 2010, p. 25.

46. Adapted from Harry J. Martin, "The Key to Effective Training Isn't Necessarily What Happens in the Classroom. It's What You Do Afterwards," *The Wall Street Journal*, December 15, 2008, p. R11.

47. Mike Faith, "A Systems Approach to Hiring the Right People," http://www.entrepreneurship.org/resource-center/a-systems-approach-to-hiring-the-right-people.aspx, accessed March 20, 2015.

48. "In-N-Out Burger: Employment," http://www.in-n-out.com/employment/restaurant.aspx, accessed March 20, 2015.

49. Get more information about ESOPs from the website of the National Center for Employee Ownership at http://www.nceo.org.

50. Bureau of Labor Statistics, "Employer Cost for Employee Compensation," March 11, 2015, http://www.bls.gov/news.release/ecec.nr0.htm, accessed March 23, 2015.

51. The Henry J. Kaiser Family Foundation, "2014 Employer Health Benefits Survey," http://kff.org/report-section/ehbs-2014-summary-of-findings, accessed March 23, 2015.

52. Bureau of Labor Statistics, "Table 8, by Establishment Employment Size," http://www.bls.gov/news.release/ecec.t08.htm, accessed March 23, 2015.

53. Ilan Mochari, "Recruitment and Retention," *Inc.*, Vol. 35, No. 9 (November 2013), pp. 120–121.

54. For IRS guidelines on cafeteria plans, see "Publication 15-B," http://www.irs.gov/publications/p15b/ar02.html#en_US_publink1000101745, accessed March 23, 2015.

55. Adam Vaccaro, "Incentives," *Inc.*, Vol. 35, No. 10 (December 2013/January 2014), p. 129.

56. To get ideas flowing for a low-cost perk program, see Paula Andruss, "Perk Up Your Business," *Entrepreneur*, Vol. 40, No. 5 (May 2012), pp. 56–58.

57. Karen E. Spaeder, "All Well and Good," *Entrepreneur*, Vol. 36, No. 11 (November 2008), p. 24.

58. For more detailed information on laws protecting employees, see the website of the United States Department of Labor, http://www.dol.gov/opa/aboutdol/lawsprog.htm, accessed March 24, 2015.

59. Adapted from Sachi Barreiro, "Preventing Sexual Harassment in the Workplace," http://www.nolo.com/legal-encyclopedia/preventing-sexual-harassment-workplace-29851.html, accessed March 24, 2014.

60. In 2008, the 12-week leave was expanded to 26 weeks in a 12-month period for an employee who needs time to care for a member of the U.S. military who has a serious injury or illness, as long as that individual is the spouse, son, daughter, parent, or next of kin to that service member.

61. For more information on the provisions of the Family and Medical Leave Act, consult the U.S. Department of Labor, "Family & Medical Leave," http://www.dol.gov/dol/topic/benefits-leave/fmla.htm, accessed March 24, 2014.

62. See "How to Conduct Annual Employee Reviews," *Inc. Guidebook*, Vol. 1, No. 9 (December 2008), special supplement.

63. For more on the details of the Deloitte Consulting study, see Josh Bersin, "Time to Scrap Performance Appraisals?" *Forbes*, May 5, 2013, http://www.forbes.com/sites/joshbersin/2013/05/06/time-to-scrap-performance-appraisals, accessed March 26, 2015.

64. For one of the sources that proposes this guideline, see *The Wall Street Journal*, "Employee Retention—How to Retain Employees," http://guides.wsj.com/small-business/hiring-and-managing-employees/how-to-retain-employees, accessed March 26, 2015.

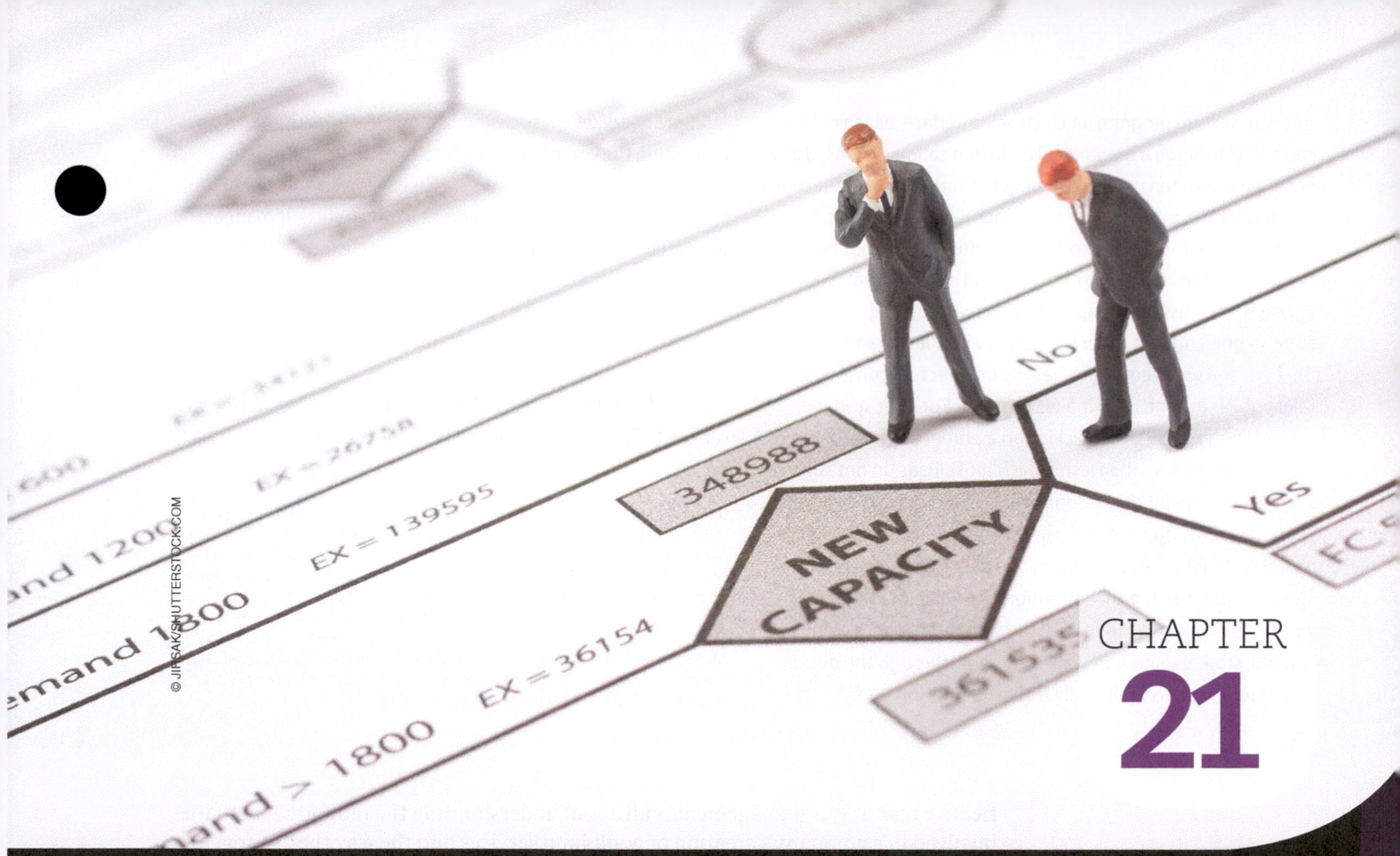

CHAPTER
21

Managing Small Business Operations

The conventional wisdom goes something like this: A firm can give its customers variety and choice, or it can sell them products or services at low prices—it would simply cost too much to give them both at the same time.

Matt Peterson, founder and CEO of Big Shot Bikes, has proved that premise wrong. He has made it his mission to offer maximum customization without incurring elevated costs from the production inefficiencies normally associated with it. His company makes use of the latest technology to provide an online portal through which customers can fully customize their bicycles. After they have selected the desired options and specifications, the bike is then ordered. This strategy, known as mass customization, satisfies the market's demand for highly personalized yet very affordable products.

In the SPOTLIGHT
Big Shot Bikes
www.bigshotbikes.com

Big Shot Bikes is located in Fort Collins, Colorado, and specializes in the production and sale of fixed-gear, single-speed "fixie" bikes. Peterson, a software engineer by profession, launched the company in 2009 with the goal of providing consumers with made-to-order bikes at a price they can afford. To meet this goal, he used his

After studying this chapter, you should be able to . . .

21-1. Understand how operations enhance a small company's competitiveness.

21-2. Discuss the nature of the operations process for both products and services.

21-3. Identify ways to control inventory and minimize inventory costs.

21-4. Recognize the contributions of operations management to product and service quality.

21-5. Explain the importance of purchasing and the nature of key purchasing policies.

21-6. Describe lean production and synchronous management, and discuss their importance to operations management in small businesses.

software skills to program an electronic interface, which guides customers through a menu of bike-customization options. Users get to pick from ten unique components and nine different colors, which can be combined to provide one-of-a-kind bicycles. Big Shot Bikes assembles the product only after the sale has been completed, thus minimizing wasteful and expensive manufacturing costs. The customer reaps the benefit and can expect an order to be shipped right to his or her door—all for less than $500.

Peterson's strategy relies heavily on direct-to-consumer sales, which the software makes possible. But after studying the ordering process, the CEO found a potentially fatal flaw: His application used Adobe Flash, which most iPads do not support. Because 10 percent of the company's customers use iPads, the venture was losing potential sales. Peterson fixed the problem by redeveloping the application, and iPad sales growth surged. The innovation also provided a highly scalable model that allowed the company to branch out into retail spaces. With iPad in hand, store owners can walk customers through the design and purchase process. It really is that straightforward.

Big Shot Bikes' mass customization efforts have paid off, prompting the company recently to expand from 7,000 to 12,000 square feet. "The new space will allow us to streamline production [and] fulfill our orders in a more efficient manner, ultimately allowing our bikes to reach the customer more quickly," says Peterson. The firm has also introduced a new cruiser product line as part of the expansion push. Sales passed 10,000 units in 2013, leaving the startup with over $5 million in revenues.

The company's success offers proof that mass customization can work. Options and affordability no longer have to be mutually exclusive.

Sources: BRAIN Staff, "Big Shot Bikes Expands Its Colorado Facility," *Bicycle Retailer*, March 17, 2014, http://www.bicycleretailer.com/north-america/2014/03/17/big-shot-bikes-expands-its-colorado-facility#.VOV5dfnF_4I, accessed March 2, 2015; "Big Shot Bikes: FAQ," http://www.bigshotbikes.com/faq.html, accessed March 2, 2015; Joshua Lindenstein, "Big Shot Bikes Expands Shop in Fort Collins," *BizWest*, March 18, 2014, http://bizwest.com/big-shot-bikes-expands-shop-in-fort-collins, accessed March 2, 2015; John Patrick Pullen, "Color Wheels," *Entrepreneur*, Vol. 41, No. 10, (October 2013), pp. 20–21; and Michael Shea, "Big Shot Bikes Celebrates 10,000 Bicycles Sold," *Outdoor Industry Association*, March 18, 2013, http://outdoorindustry.org/news/industry.php?newsId=18098, accessed March 3, 2015.

Effective operations management is all about understanding the individual activities involved in a company's creation of goods and services and the way they fit together in an orderly sequence—and then managing these activities with efficiency in mind. The name of the game is coordination, but entrepreneurs tend to underestimate the amount of effort required to keep the people and processes in a business involved and working smoothly together. If one link fails, the work of the entire team comes up short.

Dan and Chip Heath, co-authors of multiple bestselling books on business, describe an experiment that showed just how easy it is to overlook coordination demands in a firm's operations. In this particular test, students were asked to build a giant LEGO® man. Because time was limited, participants decided to split up and work on different parts separately—one had "arm duty," another worked on the torso, and so on. The team ended up with highly developed parts, but the hodgepodge of pieces they created would not fit together. The lesson, say the Heath brothers, is that work groups tend to be better at specialization than coordination.[1] This notion offers a useful place to begin our discussion of operations management, but we apply the principles involved in a distinct way—to the small business.

Many of the concepts presented in this chapter were pioneered and perfected by large corporations. However, this does not mean that they have no place in the world of small business. In some cases, the concepts can be applied directly; in others, they must be adapted before they can meet the needs of small companies. Entrepreneurs who work to improve their operations will find that their companies are better able to withstand the escalating pressures of the competitive marketplace—including those coming from the Microsofts, AT&Ts, and Ford Motor Companies of the world. Besides, understanding and adopting the best practices of industry giants may give your small company a pattern to follow as it grows to become a market leader of the future. Whether they are used in a manufacturing business or a service-based company, these principles can drive profits.

21-1 COMPETING WITH OPERATIONS

Understand how operations enhance a small company's competitiveness.

In very simple terms, **operations** refers to the processes used to create and deliver a product or service. By now, it should be clear that companies vary considerably in how they compete for customers, and the planning and management of operations almost always play a major role in this. You may be familiar with high-profile examples, such as Apple's superior design efforts, Walgreens's emphasis on convenient locations, and Walmart's highly efficient supply chain and distribution capabilities—these are truly world-class players. In the end, however, the formula for gaining competitive strength is surprisingly similar for all firms: Companies gain power to the degree that they excel in satisfying customer needs and wants more precisely and/or efficiently than their competitors.

To be successful, a company's operations must involve all of the activities required to create value for customers and earn their dollars. A bakery, for example, purchases ingredients, combines and bakes them, and makes its products available to customers at some appropriate location. For a service business like a hair salon, activities include the purchase of supplies and shampooing, haircutting, and other tasks and processes involved in serving its clients. A bakery cannot offer its products if it does not operate its ovens, and a hair salon cannot serve its clients without actually styling hair. (Outsourcing these activities presents one possible, but highly impractical scenario.) In the end, *all* necessary activities must be handled in some form if the company's operations are to function.

Operations management refers to the planning and control of a conversion process that includes bringing together inputs (such as raw materials, equipment, and labor) and turning them into outputs (products and services) that customers want. An operations process is required whether a firm produces a tangible product, such as a deli sandwich, or an intangible service, such as dry cleaning.

Operations are at the heart of any business; indeed, a company would not be able to exist without them. It should come as no surprise, then, that their design and effectiveness can determine the success of an enterprise. The following questions can help you to identify operations factors that will impact firm performance and to recognize adjustments that need to be made:

- How much flexibility is required to satisfy your customers over time?
- What is customer demand today? What is the demand trend for the future? Are existing facilities and equipment adequate to keep up with current and future demand?
- What options are available for satisfying your customers? For example, should you set up in-house fabrication, outsource production, or enter a joint venture for manufacturing or service delivery?
- What operations-related skills or capabilities set your firm apart from its competitors? How can you best take advantage of these distinctive features in the marketplace?
- Does the competitive environment require certain capabilities that your enterprise lacks?

Our focus in this chapter is on examining the ways a business can function economically and profitably, providing a high-quality product or service that keeps customers coming back for more. But even more significantly, we discuss how operations management is an important means of building competitive strength in the marketplace. For this, there is no substitute.

operations
The processes used to create and deliver a product or service.

operations management
The planning and control of a conversion process that includes turning inputs into outputs that customers desire.

Discuss the nature of the operations process for both products and services.

21-2 THE OPERATIONS PROCESS

Product-oriented and service-oriented operations are similar in that they change inputs into outputs. Inputs can include money, raw materials, labor, equipment, information, and energy—all of which are combined in varying proportions, depending on the nature of the finished product or service. Outputs are the products and/or services that a business provides to its customers. Thus, the operations process may be described as a conversion process, as shown in Exhibit 21.1.

© DMITRIJS DMITRIJEVS/SHUTTERSTOCK.COM

Managing the operations of a service business will be very different from managing the operations of a product-based venture, mostly because of the intangible nature of services and the extensive employee–customer interactions they require.

21-2a The Operations Process in a Service Business

The operations of firms that provide services differ from those of firms that provide products in a number of ways. One of the most obvious is the intangible nature of services—that is, the fact that you cannot easily see or measure them. Managers of businesses such as auto repair shops and hotels face special challenges in assuring and controlling the quality of their services, given the difficulty inherent in measuring and controlling intangibles.

Another distinctive feature of most service businesses is the extensive personal interactions of employees with customers. In a physical fitness facility, for example, the customer is directly involved in the process and relates personally to trainers and other service personnel. In a small movie theater operation, it only makes sense to

EXHIBIT **21.1** The Operations Process

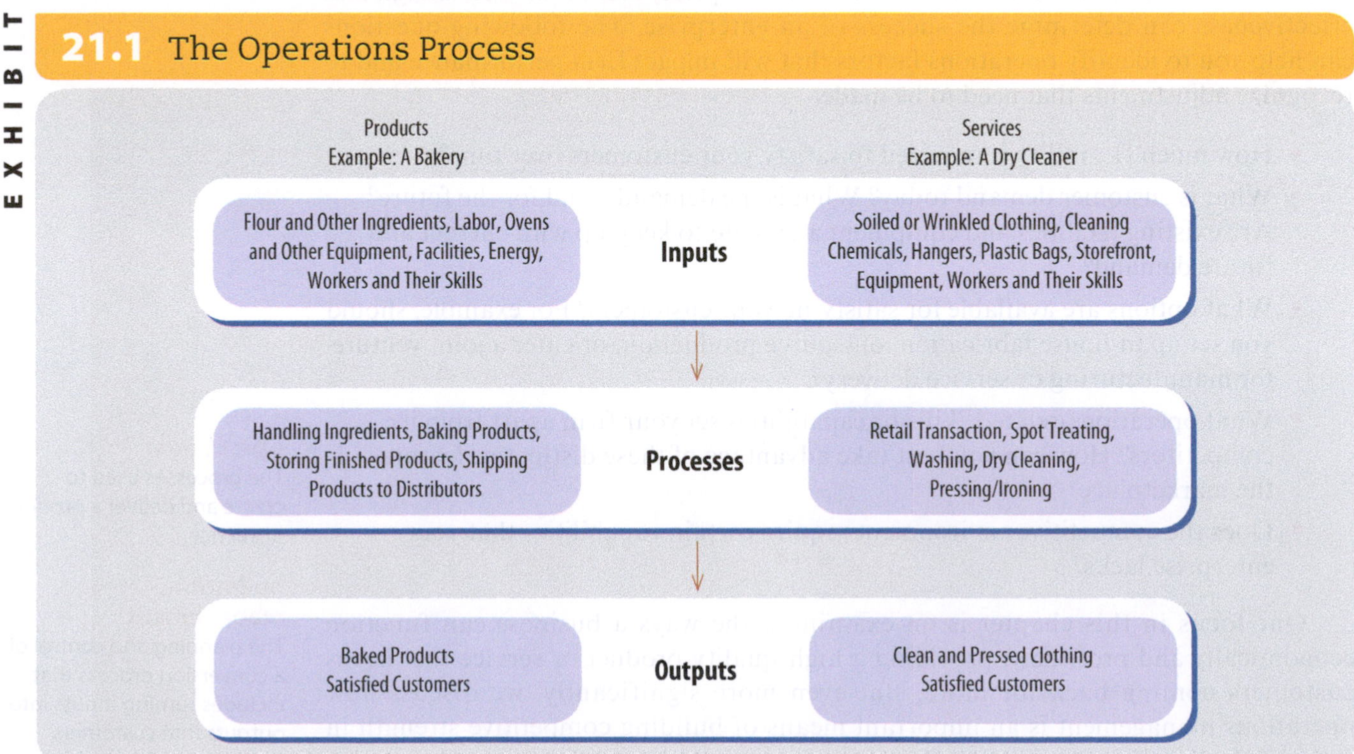

show a film when patrons are present to watch it. This naturally allows for customer input and feedback into creation and delivery processes. In addition, services are created and delivered on demand. That is, neither a workout nor a movie viewing experience can be entered into finished products inventory.

Some service companies have taken unique steps to understand the service provider–customer connection. Firms like Southwest Airlines, for example, want their managers to get close enough to customers to hear what they have to say about various facets of the operation. To that end, they are sent into the field periodically to fill customer-contact positions, which allows them to return to their normal responsibilities with much greater insights into the strengths and weaknesses of services offered. Closer interactions with customers enable employees to understand and report customer sentiments more accurately.

For a service business, the critical importance of its relationship with customers carries implications for managing personnel. An open position that involves a great deal of sensitive interaction with clients requires that those making hiring decisions select individuals with strong interpersonal skills for that vacancy. Employee training must emphasize the skills needed to serve customers well and encourage employees to find ways to improve customer satisfaction.

Various technologies have enabled customers of many businesses to provide more of their own services. More and more hotels are offering their guests self-check-out options, and many telephone systems allow or even encourage customers to obtain information without speaking to a salesperson or other staff. The extent to which such systems are satisfactory from a customer's point of view depends on whether they are more convenient than traditional systems and whether they function efficiently and accurately in meeting customer needs.

In some cases, technology can provide even better service than the traditional model. Consider traditional brick-and-mortar bookstores and their online counterparts. When browsing Amazon's website, for example, a shopper is provided with customer-driven information, such as the following:[2]

- Customers Who Bought This Item Also Bought . . .
- Customer Reviews
- What Other Items Do Customers Buy after Viewing This Item?
- Looking for Similar Products in This Category?

The insights provided by these options can help visitors find services that interest them, and that leads to increased customer satisfaction. The most well-informed employee of a traditional bookstore would have trouble providing similar data.

21-2b The Operations Process in a Manufacturing Business

Manufacturing operations can take many forms, depending on the degree to which they are repetitive. For example, a master craftsman furniture maker who makes customized pieces follows a very different process than do auto workers who assemble hundreds of cars on a production line each day. The former deals with great variety and must maintain flexible operations, whereas the latter follow a set routine that allows them to build cars more efficiently. Most manufacturing operations can be classified as one of three types—job shops, project manufacturing, and repetitive manufacturing.

Job shops are designed for short production runs. Skill sets are grouped, and work moves in batches from location to location. Only a few products are produced before the general-purpose machines are shifted to a different production setup. Machine shops represent this type of operation.

job shops
Manufacturing operations designed for short production runs of small quantities of items.

project manufacturing
Manufacturing operations used to create unique but similar products.

repetitive manufacturing
Manufacturing operations designed for long production runs of high-volume, standardized products.

continuous manufacturing
A form of repetitive manufacturing with output that more closely resembles a product stream than individual products.

Perfectly Unique Goods for the Masses

Flexible manufacturing is being pushed to the extreme as entrepreneurs learn that buyers will pay much more for products that are highly customized. They have taken the process to a whole new level by using do-it-yourself platforms that allow customers to actually design and create what they buy. Using fast-emerging technologies like 3-D modeling and printing, startups are now offering customers the ability to express themselves in their footwear (Shoes of Prey), tablet and smartphone cases (DODOcase), and a wide range of other products (Shapeways)—and sales have been brisk.

To learn more about the ins and outs of this do-it-yourself customization trend, see John Brandon, "Do-It-Yourself Design," *Inc.*, Vol. 35, No. 9, (November 2013), pp. 72–73.

When most people think about manufacturing, they often picture a factory operation, but this is not always the case. **Project manufacturing** is used to create unique but similar products, such as site-built homes and grandstands for sporting facilities. In some cases, these operations may not even seem to belong to the manufacturing family. Creative work, such as composing music or painting portraits, can fall into this category, as can professional work, such as processing tax returns or drafting specific legal documents. Because each project is unique, this type of operation has to be highly flexible to meet the requirements of the job and the demands of customers. However, because of the similarity involved, a company can achieve operational efficiencies by using manufacturing methods that, in some ways, resemble those of repetitive manufacturing, or mass production.

Firms that produce one or relatively few standardized products use **repetitive manufacturing**. This is considered mass production because it requires long production runs. Repetitive manufacturing is associated with the assembly-line production of high-volume products, such as smartphones and apparel items. Highly specialized equipment can be employed because it is used over and over again in making the same item. When the output created more closely resembles a stream of product (such as water from a purification plant or power generated by a hydroelectric dam) than individual goods, this form of repetitive manufacturing is sometimes referred to as **continuous manufacturing**.

Most businesses do not implement a pure version of any of these process types, but rather mix and match them in order to gain the benefits of each. For instance, home builders will frequently blend job shop operations (building several houses using specialized subcontractors for plumbing, painting, and electrical work) with project manufacturing features (being unique, individualized, and customized). To meet the increasing market demands for unique products that are low in price, many companies have turned to **flexible manufacturing systems**, which usually involve computer-controlled equipment that can turn out a variety of products in smaller or more flexible quantities. In other words, machine automation, while expensive, can help cut manufacturing costs while giving customers exactly what they want.

21-2c Capacity Considerations

A small company's capacity to offer products or services is a critical factor. It puts a ceiling on the firm's ability to meet demand and match competitors, but it may also determine startup costs and usually represents a long-term commitment.

Here's an illustration of how this works: Manufacturers of coffee makers have to accommodate seasonal demand. Customers want to buy 50 percent of all coffee makers during the Christmas season, with another 25 percent of sales occurring during May and June (demand for gifts for Mother's Day, Father's Day, weddings, and other seasonal activities). The last 25 percent of sales are spread out over the remaining nine months of the year. In order to handle peak seasonal demand, coffee maker producers like Keurig, Inc.(recently changed to Keurig Green Mountain, Inc.), have to set their production capacity to meet the average level of this demand, manufacture extra products during the slow months, and store these units in inventory to smooth out production for the year and satisfy orders when they come in.[3] This works well for manufacturers. However, service companies cannot hold inventory in the same way, so a competitor such as Starbucks must have the capacity to meet peak demand throughout the day.

Capacity for a coffee maker manufacturer is determined by factory space, machinery, workers, and other such factors. Although capacity at Starbucks is similarly determined by store space, equipment, and workers, adjusting capacity to meet market changes would look very different for these two firms.

21-2d Planning and Scheduling

In manufacturing, production planning and scheduling procedures are designed to achieve the orderly, sequential flow of products through a plant at a rate that matches deliveries to customers. To reach this objective, the manufacturer must avoid production disruptions and utilize machines and personnel efficiently. Simple, informal control procedures are often used in small plants. If a procedure is straightforward and the output is very limited, a manager can keep things moving smoothly with a minimum of paperwork. However, any manufacturing venture that experiences growth will eventually have to establish formal procedures to ensure production efficiency.

Because service firms are closely tied to their customers, they are limited in their ability to produce services and hold them in inventory. An automobile repair shop must wait until a car arrives before starting its operations, and a community bank cannot function until a client is available. A retail store can perform some of its services, such as transporting and storing inventory, but it, too, must wait until the customer arrives to perform other services.

Part of the scheduling task for service firms relates to planning employees' working hours. Restaurants, for example, schedule the work of servers to coincide with variations in diner traffic. In a similar way, stores and medical clinics increase their staff to handle the crush of customers or patients during periods of peak demand. Other strategies of service firms focus on scheduling customers. Appointment systems are used by many automobile repair centers and beauty shops. Service firms such as dry cleaners and plumbers take requests for service and delay delivery until the work can be scheduled. Still other firms, including banks and movie theaters, maintain a fixed schedule of services and tolerate some idle capacity.

To smooth out and delay investment in additional capacity, companies are turning increasingly to **demand management strategies**. These strategies are used to stimulate customer demand when it is normally low, and the options are limited only by the entrepreneur's imagination. Some businesses attempt to spread out customer demand by offering incentives for customers to use services during off-peak hours—examples of this would include early-bird dinner specials at restaurants and lower-price tickets for the afternoon showing of a movie. Other approaches are sometimes more sophisticated. Six Flags theme parks have implemented the FLASH Pass rider reservation system, where a pager-like device holds your place in line so that you can be waiting for a popular ride while enjoying other activities in the park. When a place on the ride becomes available for you, the pager indicates that you can go to the attraction to claim it. Gold and platinum levels of service have been added in recent years, which also hold your spot in line but reduce your wait time by an additional 50 and 90 percent, respectively. Of course, Six Flags charges an extra fee for this privilege—even more for the premium options—but the net result is both a smoothing and a prioritization of demand. Those customers willing to pay more also get more value from their time in the park.[4]

flexible manufacturing systems
Manufacturing operations that usually involve computer-controlled equipment that can turn out products in smaller or more flexible quantities.

demand management strategies
Operational strategies used to stimulate customer demand when it is normally low.

21-3 INVENTORY MANAGEMENT AND OPERATIONS

Identify ways to control inventory and minimize inventory costs.

It may not be glamorous, but inventory management can make the difference between success and failure for a small firm. When examined carefully, inventory management can help an entrepreneur understand the vital balance between two competing pressures in the business. As shown in Exhibit 21.2, the company may need *more* inventory to satisfy customers (meeting customer demand and providing high-quality

EXHIBIT 21.2 Service Level and Balance Sheet Considerations

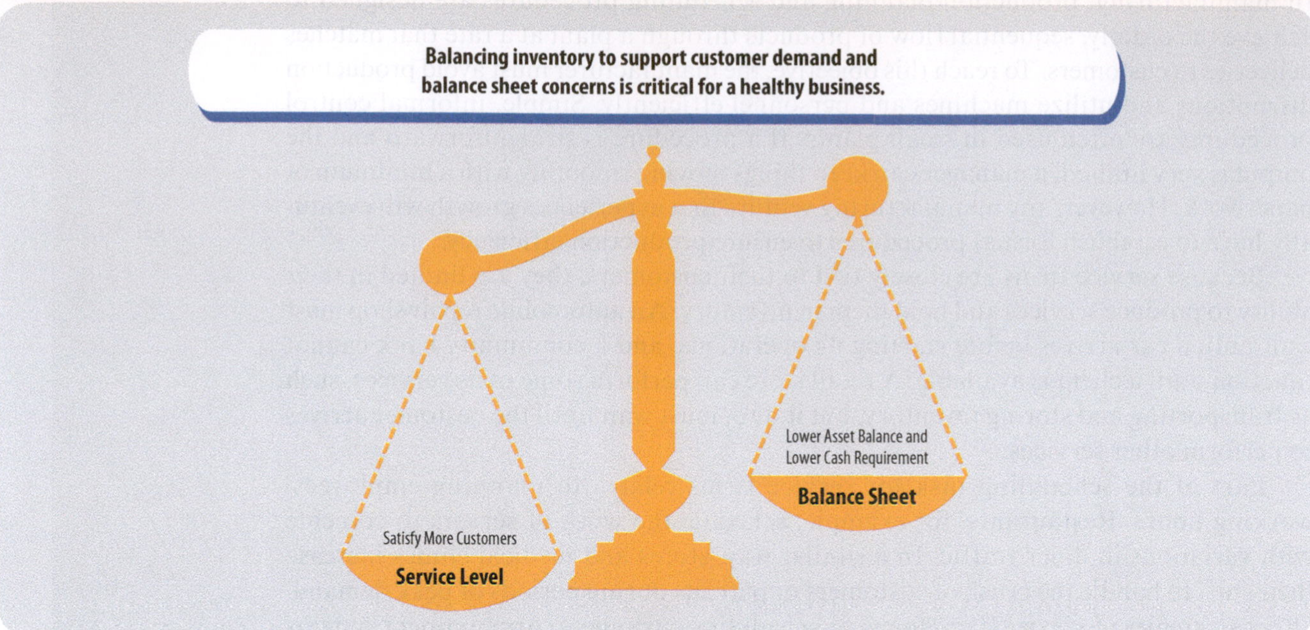

service), but it will want to maintain *less* inventory to keep the company's balance sheet healthy. Inventory management is particularly important in small retail or wholesale companies because inventory typically represents a major financial investment by these businesses.

21-3a Objectives of Inventory Management

The reasons for carrying inventory are numerous. A kitchen pantry analogy can help you to see why this is the case. Why do you keep more boxes of your favorite cereal in the pantry than you need today?

- To eat (to meet customer demand)
- To avoid going to the grocery store for each breakfast meal (to be less dependent on the source)
- To have breakfast supplies for guests to eat (to protect against stockouts)
- To benefit from price discounts (to gain from sales or quantity-based cost reductions)
- To have them in stock before prices go up (to protect against price increases)

© BALONCICI/SHUTTERSTOCK.COM

This exercise shows that you probably store extra cereal boxes for a number of reasons. Having something to eat for breakfast is likely only one of your objectives for keeping the pantry well stocked.

Ensuring continuous operations is particularly important in manufacturing because delays caused by lack of materials or parts can be costly. Furthermore, sales can be maximized by completing production in a timely manner and by stocking an appropriate assortment of merchandise for distribution to wholesale establishments and retail stores. Protecting inventory from theft, misplacement, and deterioration likewise contributes to operational efficiency and business profits.

You may conclude that carrying more stock is the key to maintaining high-quality service. However, research shows that a surprising 72 percent of the root causes of running out of stock can be found in the store—that is, they derive from varied problems such as incorrect forecasting, lost or misplaced inventory, poor shelving or storage systems, and inadequate stock measurements.[5] Having more inventory on hand would increase costs but would not improve service quality in these cases because customers would still be prevented from accessing that stock efficiently due to these other fundamental problems.

21-3b Inventory Cost Control

Maintaining optimal inventory—the level that minimizes stockouts and eliminates excess inventory—saves money and contributes to operating profits. Traditional methods of determining ideal inventory levels may be sufficient for your business. One such method is calculating the **economic order quantity**, a relatively simple index that determines the purchase quantity of an item (some of which will be carried in inventory) that will minimize total inventory costs.[6]

Preferring more advanced methods, many small companies have turned to **statistical inventory control**, which accommodates the variability of supply and demand using a targeted service level. This method allows you to determine statistically the appropriate amount of inventory to carry, and it is easier to use than you might imagine. In fact, the tools required for this computation are built into many inexpensive, off-the-shelf business software packages that have been designed for small businesses, such as Microsoft Dynamics GP or SAP Business One.

If a firm could order merchandise or raw materials and carry inventory with no expenses other than the cost of the items, there would be little concern about order quantity at any given time. However, this is not the case. Inventory comes with many other related costs, which are easy to overlook. At a minimum, you should consider the following:

- Storage (land and buildings, as well as shelving and organization systems)
- Theft, weathering, spoilage, and obsolescence
- Cost of capital (from tying up cash in inventory that could be better used elsewhere)
- Transaction costs (from ordering, receiving, inspecting, transporting, and distributing inventory)
- Insurance and security
- Disposal costs (of inventory that cannot be sold)

Your business may have to bear these costs and others. While some are fixed costs, others will rise and fall based on the quantity of inventory held. Inventory cost management can be a complex challenge, but there are approaches that can help you to minimize these costs, including the ABC method and the just-in-time inventory system.

ABC INVENTORY CLASSIFICATION

Some inventory items are more valuable or critical to a firm's operations than others. That is, some items have a greater effect on the costs and profits of a business. As a general rule, managers will be most attentive to those inventory items requiring the largest investment. Managing inventory according to its priority can help boost a company's performance.

economic order quantity
An index that determines the quantity to purchase in order to minimize total inventory costs.

statistical inventory control
A method of controlling inventory that uses a targeted service level, allowing statistical determination of the appropriate amount of inventory to carry.

One approach to inventory analysis, the **ABC method**, classifies items into three categories based on *dollar velocity* (purchase price × annual quantity consumed). Its purpose is to focus managerial attention on the most important items. The number of categories could easily be expanded to four or more, if that seemed more appropriate for a particular firm.

Category A holds a few high-value inventory items that account for the largest percentage of total dollars or are otherwise critical in the production process and, therefore, deserve close control. These might be monitored using an inventory system that keeps a running record of receipts, withdrawals, and balances of each item. In this way, a company can avoid an unnecessarily heavy investment in costly inventory items.

Category B items are less costly but deserve moderate managerial attention because they still make up a significant share of the firm's total inventory investment. Category C contains low-cost or noncritical items, such as paper clips in an office or nuts and bolts in a repair shop. The carrying costs of such items are not large enough to justify close control. These items might simply be checked periodically to ensure that a sufficient supply is available.

JUST-IN-TIME INVENTORY SYSTEMS

The **just-in-time inventory system** is designed to cut inventory carrying costs by making or buying what is needed just as it is needed. First popularized by the Japanese, the just-in-time approach has led to cost reductions in many countries. New items are received, presumably, just as the last item of that type from existing inventory is placed into service. The just-in-time concept rests on a few basic principles, but chief among these is emphasis on the *pull* of inventory over the *push* of the same. That is, inventory items are made or bought in response to demand (pull), rather than in response to what is planned or anticipated (push). This method prevents the buildup of unnecessary inventory.

Many large firms have adopted some form of the just-in-time system for inventory management, but small businesses can also benefit from its use. It's important to note that this approach requires careful coordination with suppliers. Supplier locations, production schedules, and transportation timetables must be carefully considered, as they all affect a firm's ability to obtain materials quickly and in a predictable manner—a necessary condition for using this approach. The just-in-time method also requires a flexible production system, with short set-up and turnaround times.

The benefits of just-in-time management go beyond reducing in-house inventory and creating a healthier balance sheet. Quality problems become more evident sooner, which reduces waste. Storage space, insurance costs, and revolving credit are freed up for other purposes. The ultimate objective of this method is a smooth and balanced system that responds nimbly to market demand.

The just-in-time inventory system has been used by businesses of all sizes, with good results. You may be familiar with McAlister's Deli, a franchised chain of more than 341 restaurants in 24 states. The operation of each franchise is carefully dictated by the firm's operations manual. Its prescribed approach specifies that each restaurant is to set up four sandwich-making workstations or production cells and to use as many of these as needed, based on the hour of the day and the flow of customers. Each station has a single operator who receives sandwich orders in batches. So, if a party of eight comes in, one workstation would prepare sandwiches for all eight diners.[7]

A McAlister's restaurant in central Texas is one of the higher-volume outlets, and it was granted permission to experiment with the production system by making two changes. First, to accommodate the high volume, the four cells were changed to two

ABC method
A system of classifying items in inventory by dollar velocity (purchase price × annual quantity consumed).

just-in-time inventory system
A method of cutting inventory carrying costs by making or buying what is needed just as it is needed.

assembly lines with specialized workers. Only one of the lines is used most of the time, but it is operated by four to six workers. The second modification, and one that is consistent with the spirit of the just-in-time approach, is that the batch size has been changed to *one sandwich*, regardless of the order size. That is, even when both assembly lines are operating, the sandwiches in a large order will be split, based on available capacity. The result has been reduced order lead time and variability, fewer mistakes, and higher efficiency. Because this new arrangement worked so well, the local owner was happy with the change, and so was the franchisor.[8]

21-3c Inventory Recordkeeping Systems

The larger the company, the greater the need for recordkeeping, but even a very small business needs a system for keeping tabs on its inventory. Because manufacturers are concerned with three broad categories of inventory (raw materials and supplies, work in process, and finished goods), their inventory records are more complex than those of wholesalers and retailers. Small firms should emphasize simplicity in their control methods. Too much control can be as wasteful as it is unnecessary.

In most small businesses, inventory records are computerized. Many different software programs are available for this purpose. The owner or manager, in consultation with the company's accounting advisors, can select the software best suited for the particular needs of the business.

Inventory checks can be carried out in different ways. A **physical inventory system** depends on an actual count of items on hand. The counting is done in physical units, such as pieces, gallons, or boxes. By using this method, a firm can create an accurate record of its inventory level at a given point in time. Some businesses have an annual shutdown to count everything—a complete physical inventory. Others use **cycle counting**, scheduling different segments of the inventory for counting at different times during the year. This simplifies the process and makes it less of an ordeal for the business as a whole.

A **perpetual inventory system** provides an ongoing, current record of inventory items. It does not require a physical count. However, a physical count of inventory should be made periodically to ensure the accuracy of the system and to make adjustments for such factors as loss or theft.

The simplest method is called a **two-bin inventory system**. For each item in inventory, the business sets up two containers, each holding enough to cover lead time. When one is emptied, it is replaced with the second and a new container is ordered. In fact, you may already be using this approach at home. For example, you use sugar out of one bag, but you keep a second bag in the pantry. When the first is empty, you open the second and buy a new one at the grocery store. As a result, your "sweet tooth" is always taken care of.

physical inventory system A method that provides for periodic counting of items in inventory.

cycle counting A method for counting different segments of the physical inventory at different times during the year.

perpetual inventory system A method for keeping an ongoing current record of inventory.

two-bin inventory system A method of inventory control based on the use of two containers for each item in inventory, one to meet current demand and the other to meet future demand.

© ISTOCKPHOTO.COM/VAAKA

21-4 QUALITY AND OPERATIONS MANAGEMENT

Recognize the contributions of operations management to product and service quality.

Owners of successful small firms realize that quality management is serious business and that a strong commitment to the achievement of quality goals is essential. But quality can be achieved only to the extent that operations lead to the outcomes that customers want. Following this logic, companies that fail to produce quality in their operations will not have the buyers they need to stay in business for long.

21-4a Quality as a Competitive Tool

Quality may be defined as the characteristics of a product or service that determine its ability to satisfy stated and implied needs. Quality obviously has many dimensions. For example, a restaurant's customers base their perceptions of its quality on the taste of the food, the attractiveness of the décor, the friendliness and promptness of servers, the cleanliness of silverware, the appropriateness of background music, and many other factors. The operations process establishes the level of quality as a product is being produced or as a service is being provided. Although costs and other considerations cannot be ignored, quality must remain a primary focus of a firm's operations.

International competition is increasingly turning on quality differences. Automobile manufacturers, for example, now place much greater emphasis on quality in their attempts to compete effectively with foreign producers. In examining the operations process, small business managers also must direct special attention to achieving superior product or service quality.

The American Society for Quality (ASQ) has been the leading quality improvement organization in the United States for more than 65 years and has introduced many quality improvement methods throughout the world. Among these is an approach known as **total quality management (TQM)**, an aggressive effort by a company to achieve superior quality. Total quality management is an all-encompassing, quality-focused management approach that is *customer driven* (customer needs and wants are at the core), emphasizes *organizational commitment* (management leads, but the entire organization participates), and focuses on a *culture of continuous improvement.* The most successful quality management efforts incorporate these three features.

Companies that are particularly serious about meeting the highest standards of quality can apply to receive the Malcolm Baldrige National Quality Award (see www.nist.gov/baldrige for details), which has been described as "a kind of decathlon gold medal for organizational excellence."[9] Thousands of those that choose not to apply still use the award's criteria and questions to run a check on their operations. But no matter how it unfolds, the process is grueling. One small business observer describes it this way:

> *The experience of completing the application, even as an academic exercise, is akin to writing a textbook about your company or undergoing a business version of psychoanalysis. This course of self-evaluation and improvement requires that companies fling up their window shades, yank open every cupboard and closet, and see—really see—where their thinking is murky and their efforts inadequate or wholly lacking.*[10]

This may be a little beyond your reach for now. But, at some point, you may want to go through the process with your small business in order to chart a clear path toward outstanding quality performance.

quality
The features of a product or service that enable it to satisfy customers' stated and implied needs.

total quality management (TQM)
An all-encompassing management approach to providing high-quality products and services.

21-4b The Customer Focus of Quality Management

A firm's quality management efforts should begin with a focus on the customers who purchase its products or services. Without this focus, the quest for quality can easily degenerate into an aimless search for some abstract, elusive ideal. To get started, the entrepreneur should determine the products and services that will satisfy customers' needs and expectations. Customers have expectations regarding the quality of products (such as durability and attractiveness) and services (such as speed and accuracy).

A customer is concerned with *product* quality when purchasing a camera or a loaf of bread, but his or her primary concern is *service* quality when having an automobile repaired or a suit tailor-made. Frequently, a customer expects some combination of product *and* service quality—for example, the buyer of a flatscreen TV may be concerned with the performance of the model selected, knowledge and courtesy of the salesperson, credit terms offered, and warranty coverage.

At times, it can be easy to misread what customers want, but what they desire is usually very simple. For example, a car owner who takes his automobile to a repair shop hopes to receive competent service (that is, a successful repair), to get a reasonable explanation of what had to be done, and to be treated with respect. Similarly, a hotel patron anticipates being provided with a clean room, having reasonable security, and being treated like a valued guest. Such uncomplicated expectations open up avenues of opportunity. Exceeding these basic expectations can leave a lasting, favorable impression on customers, which often results in repeat business and free promotion through positive word of mouth. As a bonus, a genuine concern for customer needs and satisfaction can be a powerful force that energizes the total quality management effort of a company.

RETAIL IS DETAIL

Perhaps you've heard the quote "Retail is detail." This means that operating details are crucial to the success of a business, especially in retail industries. Consider Five Guys Burgers and Fries, the restaurant chain started by Jerry Murrell and his sons in 1986. They may love the food, but few of its faithful customers recognize the meticulous attention to detail that makes the eatery the phenomenal success that it is today. It all begins with facility design. "I wanted people to know that we put all of our money into the food," insists Murrell. "That's why the décor is so simple—red and white tiles."[11]

For the Murrells, making high-quality burgers and fries is nothing short of an obsession. Consider some of the painstaking detail that has been planned into the chain's operations.[12]

- Five Guys fries are made only from potatoes grown in Idaho and north of the 42nd parallel, which grow slower and are much higher in quality. It doesn't matter that these spuds are considerably more expensive.
- Most chains dehydrate their frozen fries to eliminate moisture that splatters when it hits the oil. Five Guys actually *soaks its fries in water first* and then pre-fries them to force the steam out and create a seal. Then, when fried a second time, they don't absorb oil and get greasy.
- The chain toasts all buns on the grill to create a caramelized taste, despite the fact that using a bun toaster would be faster and cheaper.
- The beef used is 80 percent lean and always fresh, never frozen.
- All burgers are made to order, with 17 possible toppings, which is why the company will not allow drive-through operations.

Its "retail is detail" emphasis has definitely paid off, with Five Guys expanding from only 5 stores in 2002 to more than 1,000 locations in 47 states and 6 Canadian provinces a little more than a decade later.[13]

CUSTOMER FEEDBACK

Listening attentively to customers' opinions can provide information about their level of satisfaction. Employees having direct contact with customers can serve as the eyes and ears of the business in evaluating existing quality levels and customer needs.

Living the Dream

ENTREPRENEURIAL EXPERIENCES

Five Guys Gets Five Stars on Food Quality

Since Jerry Murrell founded Five Guys Burgers and Fries in Arlington, Virginia, the company has expanded very rapidly. And the physical growth has generated great financial results, as well, with revenues rising by as much as 32.8 percent in a single year.

The secret to the company's success? A laser-like focus on quality ingredients and customer service. "It's a simple story," says Murrell. "Sell good burgers, and people will pay for them." Steadfast devotion to that guiding principle has allowed Five Guys to succeed, despite shifting consumer tastes and increasing concerns about nutrition.

Murrell founded Five Guys after his eldest sons revealed that they did not have any interest in going to college. "I suggested they open a burger joint," he recalls. From the start, the new business owners vowed to use only fresh, premium ingredients. Because of the higher costs, they had to charge higher prices, but hungry diners flocked to the restaurant anyway. That was a sign that the Murrells might be onto something big, and their business results have borne that out. Once they had nearly a decade of successful operations under their belts, Murrell and his sons began franchising the brand. But in the expansion, they have remained absolutely uncompromising in their emphasis on quality control.

One of the unique ways that Five Guys ensures high standards is through an innovative incentive plan. The company employs third-party auditors who secretly evaluate each location's cleanliness, customer service, and adherence to policy. Crews that pass the review receive $1,000, which they split; for employees earning $9 an hour, this additional money is a very attractive incentive. At the end of 2014, Five Guys paid out between $11 and $12 million in bonuses to employees for their commitment to the company's high-quality standards.

© ZUMA PRESS, INC/ALAMY

Rather than launching expensive promotional campaigns, Five Guys relies on word-of-mouth advertising, which originates from its satisfied customer base. This approach is grounded in the philosophy that high-quality food and exceptional customer service will lead consumers to recommend the chain to their friends, family, and co-workers. Given the success that the company has achieved to date, it seems that the strategy is working very well.

Five Guys' kitchens do not have freezers, a cornerstone appliance in other fast-food chains. The decision not to freeze ingredients reflects a strict adherence to the firm's most fundamental guiding principle: If it's not fresh, don't use it. Five Guys locations also do not use drive-thru lanes, a feature that sets the company apart from most of their burger-flipping rivals. Again, it was commitment to quality that drove the decision. Since the burgers are made to order, the process takes too long to work with a drive-thru operation. Murrell is unapologetic about the decision and once even posted a sign inside the stores that read: "If you're in a hurry, there are a lot of really good hamburger places within a short distance from here." Customers seem to get the point, and they keep returning to Five Guys for exactly that reason.

The temptation to cut costs is ever-present, but the company has remained steadfast in its commitment to a high-quality approach. "I once suggested using one tomato slice instead of two," Murrell admits. "My sons staged a revolt." The restaurant continued to use two slices, but simply raised the price for a burger. The recipe for Five Guys is really quite simple: "We don't spend our money on décor. Or guys in chicken suits," says Murrell. "But we'll go overboard on food."

Sources: Bodek and Rhodes, "Outside the Box: Five Guys and Fries," *The B+R Blog*, October 13, 2014, https://bodekandrhodes.wordpress.com/2014/10/13/outside-the-box-five-guys-burgers-and-fries, accessed March 4, 2015; Alexia Chianis, "BUZZBATTLE: Five Guys vs. In-N-Out—Which Burger Joint Feeds Your Office?" *BusinessBee*, June 3, 2013, http://www.businessbee.com/resources/news/operations-buzz/buzzbattle-five-guys-vs-in-n-out-which-burger-joint-feeds-your-office, accessed March 4, 2015; "Five Guys Burgers and Fries: About Us," http://www.fiveguys.com/about-us.aspx, accessed March 4, 2015; Laurie Hurley, "What Five Guys Burgers and Fries Teaches about Social Media Management," *The Social Networking Navigator*, February 3, 2014, http://thesocialnetworkingnavigator.com/five-guys-burgers-fries-can-teach-social-media-management, accessed March 4, 2015; Jerry Murrell, "Five Guys Burgers and Fries," *Inc.*, Vol. 36, No. 1 (February 2014), p. 34; and "5 Reasons Why Five Guys Is a Big Success," http://www.inc.com/ss/five-guys-burgers-and-fries#1, accessed March 4, *2015*.

Unfortunately, many managers are oblivious to the often subtle feedback from customers. Preoccupied with operating details, managers may not listen carefully to, let alone solicit, customers' opinions. Employees having direct contact with customers—such as servers in a restaurant—are seldom trained or encouraged to obtain information about customers' quality expectations. Careful training and management of servers could make them more alert to diners' tastes and attitudes, and provide a mechanism for reporting these reactions to management.

Experts now recommend that firms work hard to involve and empower customers in efforts to improve quality. The marketing research methods of observation, interviews, and customer surveys, as described in Chapter 7, can be used to investigate customers' views regarding quality. Some businesses, for example, provide comment cards for their customers to use in evaluating service or product quality.

Another approach to gathering customer-based information is to "mine" company sales data, statistically analyzing it in search of useful insights on customer behavior. Consider operations superstar Walmart and its response to severe weather events. From carefully studying its own sales data, the firm is well aware of customer buying patterns preceding storms. Before a serious weather event strikes, customers stock up on the expected: water, flashlights, and generators. But in the aftermath of such a storm, customers buy yard and home cleanup items, such as mops and trash bags. Some items that are commonly purchased are less predictable, such as Pop-Tarts (a quirk in buying behavior).[14] By recognizing past trends and adjusting operations to match them (including having an ample supply of Pop-Tarts available after a storm), Walmart can help those most in need and make a profit by serving its customers' known, and perhaps unknown, needs with great precision.

Most business management software programs now include "business intelligence" modules that can help even the smallest of companies to discover customer buying patterns so that they can respond accordingly. Data-mining techniques that provide powerful insights to guide small business operations should not be overlooked.

Small Business Analytics

The use of predictive analytics seems to be transforming every facet of business, including anticipating customer trends and buying behavior. You need a business intelligence tool to make this work, but many are available. Free open-source tools like Revolution R from Revolution Analytics offer one option, but these can be difficult to program. Systems offered by SAS and SAP may be too complex and expensive for many small businesses. More suitable are inexpensive dashboard tools like Geckoboard, Leftronic, and IBM Cognos, which allow you to visualize your data. These tools can help you make sense of your numbers at a subscription price that won't break the bank—less than $100 a month. For a very brief explanation of the use of predictive analytics for small companies, see Mikal E. Belicove, "Fortunetellers," *Entrepreneur*, Vol. 42, No. 7 (July 2014), p. 66.

21-4c "The Basic Seven" Quality Tools

Another important element in effective quality management consists of the various tools, techniques, and procedures needed to ensure high-quality products and services. Once the focus is shifted to the customer and the entire organization is committed to continuous improvement, operating methods become critical concerns. Kaoru Ishikawa, the father of "quality circles," contended that 95 percent of a typical company's quality problems can be solved by using the following seven tools (sometimes called "The Basic Seven"):[15]

1. A *cause-and-effect diagram* (also known as an *Ishikawa chart*, or a *fishbone chart*) identifies potential causes for an effect or problem while sorting them into categories.
2. A *check sheet* provides a structured, prepared form for collecting and analyzing data.
3. A *control chart* transforms data into graphs that can be used to determine if a process errs in some predictable, and correctable, way.
4. A *histogram* is the most commonly used graph for showing how often each different value in a set of data occurs.
5. A *Pareto chart* presents bar graphs that reveal which causes are significant, separating the "vital few" from the "useful many."

6. A *scatter diagram* (or *scattergram*) graphs pairs of different sets of variables, allowing a search for quality relationships or patterns.
7. A *flow chart* (or *run chart*) visually represents the series of steps required to complete an operation.

While this list may seem overwhelming, most of these tools are straightforward and require almost no training, except for control charts, which are discussed in more detail later in this section. You can learn more about how to use all seven of these tools through online resources.

21-4d Quality Inspection versus Poka-Yoke

Management's traditional method of maintaining product quality has been **inspection**, which consists of examining a part or a product to determine whether or not it is acceptable. An inspector often uses gauges to evaluate important quality variables. For effective quality control, the inspector must be honest, objective, and capable of resisting pressure from shop personnel to pass borderline cases.

Although the inspection process is usually discussed with reference to product quality, comparable steps can be taken to evaluate service quality. Follow-up calls to customers of an auto repair shop, for example, might be used to measure the quality of the firm's repair services. Customers can be asked whether recent repairs were performed in a timely and satisfactory manner.

The problem with inspection is that it occurs after the fact—that is, after faulty goods or inadequate services have been created or offered for sale. At that point, considerable resources have already been consumed in a company's operations, but with nothing of quality to show for it. This can lead to both internal costs (those related to repair, inspection, prevention, and training) and external costs (those related to the loss of reputation and repeat customers). Knowing this inspired quality guru Philip Crosby to declare, "Quality is free!" In other words, the *savings* associated with getting quality right more than offset the *cost* of a total quality management program.

© DENIS SELIVANOV/SHUTTERSTOCK.COM

Quality inspection processes are helpful, but **poka-yoke** (Japanese for the notion of designing business processes to prevent defects) is a more proactive approach that seeks to mistake-proof a firm's operations. For example, a microwave oven may be designed so that it will not work with the door open, thereby preventing radiation leakage. Fryers at many fast food restaurants now raise the product out of the hot grease using a timed machine, rather than relying on a vigilant employee and an audible alarm. This innovation prevents food waste (from over- or under-cooked foods) and removes an opportunity for grease-burn injuries.

inspection
The examination of a part or a product to determine whether it meets quality standards.

poka-yoke
A proactive approach to quality management that seeks to mistake-proof a firm's operations.

21-4e Statistical Methods of Quality Control

The use of statistical methods and control charts often can make controlling product and service quality easier, less expensive, and more effective. Because some knowledge of quantitative methods is necessary to develop a quality control method using statistical analysis, a properly qualified employee should be available to lead this part of the process. The savings made possible by use of an efficient statistical method usually will more than justify the cost of setting it up and managing it.

Acceptance sampling involves taking random samples of products and measuring them against predetermined standards. Suppose that a small business receives a shipment of 10,000 parts from a supplier. Rather than evaluate all 10,000 parts, the purchaser might check the acceptability of a small sample of parts and then accept or reject the entire order based on the results. The smaller the sample, the greater the risk of either accepting a defective lot or rejecting a good lot due to *sampling error*. A larger sample reduces this risk but increases the cost of inspection. A well-designed plan strikes a balance, simultaneously avoiding excessive inspection costs and minimizing the acceptance/rejection risk.

The use of statistical analysis makes it possible to establish tolerance limits that allow for inherent variation due to chance. When measurements fall outside these tolerance limits, however, the quality controller knows that a problem exists and must search for the cause. A control chart graphically shows the limits for the process being controlled. As current data are entered, it is possible to tell whether a process is under control or out of control (random or nonrandom). Control charts may be used for either attribute or variable inspections.

Attributes are product or service parameters that can be counted as being either present or absent. A light bulb either lights or doesn't light; similarly, a water hose either leaks or doesn't leak. **Variables** are measured parameters that fall on a continuum, such as weight or length. If a large can of cashews is to be sold as containing a minimum of two pounds of nuts, an inspector may judge the product acceptable if its weight falls within the range of 32 to 33 ounces.

A problem might be caused by variations in raw materials, machine wear, or changes in employees' work practices. Consider, for example, a candy maker that is producing one-pound boxes of chocolates. Although the weight may vary slightly, each box must weigh at least 16 ounces. A study of the operations process has determined that the actual target weight must be 16.5 ounces, to allow for normal variation between 16 and 17 ounces. During the production process, a set of boxes is weighed every 15 or 20 minutes. If the average weight of a box falls outside the tolerance limits—below 16 or above 17 ounces—the quality controller must immediately try to find the problem and correct it.

Continuing improvements in computer-based technology have advanced the use of statistical control processes in small enterprises. In fact, many off-the-shelf enterprise resource planning systems (computer software that coordinates all major facets of a firm's operations) for smaller businesses now include statistical quality control tools. Some of the systems best suited to the needs of small companies include NetSuite, Sage, SYSPRO, and Epicor. Selecting the package that is right for a specific venture can be a complex decision, which should be made with great care and the help of a knowledgeable advisor.

21-4f International Certification for Quality Management

A firm can obtain international recognition of its quality management program by meeting a series of standards, known as **ISO 9000**, developed by the International Organization for Standardization (ISO) in Geneva, Switzerland. The certification process requires full documentation of a firm's quality management procedures, as well as an audit to ensure that the firm is operating in accordance with those procedures. In other words, the firm must show that it does what it says it does.

ISO 9000 certification is particularly valuable for small firms because they usually lack a global image as producers of high-quality products. Buyers in other countries,

acceptance sampling
The use of a random, representative portion of products to determine the acceptability of an entire lot.

attributes
Product or service parameters that can be counted as being present or absent.

variables
Measured parameters that fall on a continuum, such as weight or length.

ISO 9000
The standards governing international certification of a firm's quality management procedures.

especially in Europe, view this certification as an indicator of supplier reliability. Some large U.S. corporations, such as the major automobile makers, require their domestic suppliers to conform to these standards. Small firms, therefore, may need ISO 9000 certification either to sell more easily in international markets or to meet the demands of their domestic customers.

Environmental concerns and a focus on social responsibility have created new opportunities and challenges for entrepreneurs. Although no general certifications have been offered, the International Organization for Standardization also offers an ISO 14001 certification. This certification reflects how efficiently companies have set up and improved their operations processes in order to control the impact of vehicle and smokestack emissions, noise, and other fallout on air, water, and soil.

ISO certification is challenging to earn, but the payoff from achieving it can make it all worthwhile. Advertising agency Partners + Napier took the ISO 9000 challenge, which lasted six months and cost about $20,000. But the result was significant gains, and the agency's creative output seems to have blossomed as well. Partners + Napier is managing to turn out higher-quality work in significantly less time. These improvements now translate directly to the firm's bottom line.[16]

21-4g Quality Management in Service Businesses

For many types of service firms, quality control constitutes management's most important responsibility. When all that a firm sells is service, its success depends on customers' perceptions of the quality of that service.

While customer satisfaction with service businesses overall has been greater in recent years, there is still plenty of room for improvement. For example, some large corporations adjust the quality of the services they provide to the profitability of the customer—with better customers getting better service—and this can easily lead to general dissatisfaction. But poor service from larger businesses (automated telephone answering systems that do not allow callers to speak to a live representative, long lines, reluctance to respond to customer problems, and so forth) opens the door for small service-oriented companies. Although some services are too costly to be used as powerful competitive weapons, providing high-quality service may sometimes involve nothing more than simple attention to detail.

Gathering relevant and useful measurements can be problematic when assessing the quality of a service. It is easier to measure the length of a section of pipe than the quality of motel accommodations. However, methods can be devised for measuring service quality. For example, a motel manager might maintain a record of the number of problems with travelers' reservations, complaints about the cleanliness of rooms, and so on. Frequently, the "easy to measure" becomes the only measure. It is critical that assessment measures are chosen carefully to find parameters most relevant to customers' perspectives on quality.

21-5 PURCHASING POLICIES AND PRACTICES

Explain the importance of purchasing and the nature of key purchasing policies.

Although its role varies with the type of business, purchasing constitutes a key part of operations management for most small businesses. Through purchasing, firms obtain materials, merchandise, equipment, and services to meet production and marketing goals. For example, manufacturing firms buy raw materials or components, merchandising firms purchase products to be sold, and all types of firms obtain supplies.

21-5a The Importance of Purchasing

The quality of a finished product depends on the quality of the raw materials used. If a product must be made with great precision and close tolerances, the manufacturer must acquire high-quality materials and component parts. Then, if a well-managed production process is used, excellent products will result. Similarly, the acquisition of high-quality merchandise makes a retailer's sales to customers easier and reduces the number of necessary markdowns and merchandise returns.

Purchasing also contributes to profitable operations by ensuring that goods are delivered when they are needed. Failure to receive materials, parts, or equipment on schedule can cause costly interruptions in production operations. In a retail business, failure to receive merchandise on schedule may mean a loss of sales and, possibly, a permanent loss of customers.

Another aspect of effective purchasing is securing the best possible price. Cost savings go directly to the bottom line, so purchasing practices that seek out the best prices can have a major impact on the financial health of a business.

Note, however, that the importance of the purchasing function varies according to the type of business. In a small, labor-intensive service business—such as an accounting firm—purchases of supplies are responsible for a very small part of the total operating costs. Such businesses are more concerned with labor costs than with the cost of supplies or other materials that they may require in their operations process.

MAKE OR BUY?

Many firms face **make-or-buy decisions**. Such choices are especially important for small manufacturing companies that have the option of making or buying component parts for products they produce. A less obvious make-or-buy choice exists with respect to certain services—for example, purchasing janitorial or car rental services versus providing for those needs internally. Some reasons for making component parts, rather than buying them, follow:

- More complete utilization of plant capacity permits more economical production.
- Supplies are assured, with fewer delays caused by design changes or difficulties with outside suppliers.
- A secret design may be protected.
- Expenses are reduced by an amount equivalent to transportation costs and the outside supplier's selling expense and profit.
- Closer coordination and control of the total production process may facilitate operations scheduling and control.
- Parts produced internally may be of higher quality than those available from outside suppliers.

Reasons for buying component parts, rather than making them, include the following:

- An outside supplier's part may be cheaper because the supplier specializes in the production of that particular part.
- Additional space, equipment, personnel skills, and working capital are not needed.
- Less-diversified managerial experience and skills are required.
- Greater flexibility is provided, especially in the manufacture of a seasonal item.

make-or-buy decisions
A choice that companies must make when they have the option of making or buying component parts for products they produce, or the option of purchasing necessary services or providing them in-house.

- In-plant operations can concentrate on the firm's specialty—finished products and services.
- The risk of equipment obsolescence is transferred to outsiders.

The decision to make or buy should be based on long-run cost and profit optimization because it can be expensive to reverse. Underlying cost differences need to be analyzed carefully, as small savings from either buying or making may greatly affect profit margins.

OUTSOURCING

Sometimes it makes sense for a business to contract with an external provider (that is, an independent party with its own employees) to take on and manage one or more of its functions. This is called **outsourcing**. (You may recall that international outsourcing was discussed in Chapter 18.) As mentioned earlier, firms can sometimes save money by working with outside suppliers specializing in a particular type of work, especially tasks such as accounting, payroll, janitorial, and equipment repair services. The expertise of these outside suppliers may enable them to provide better-quality services by virtue of their specialization.

outsourcing
Contracting with a third party to take on and manage one or more of a firm's functions.

cooperative purchasing organizations (coops)
An organization in which small businesses combine their demand for products or services in order to negotiate as a group with suppliers.

According to a survey by the Human Capital Institute, a global association for talent and leadership management, 90 percent of U.S. companies engage in outsourcing in some form. And the amount of work that they outsource has been growing, from an average of 6 percent of total operations in 1990 to more than 27 percent two decades later.[17] Similarly, a 2014 study by Deloitte Consulting forecasts that growth in *international* outsourcing will continue, especially when it comes to the information technology, legal, and real estate and facilities management functions.[18]

Despite the trend, there clearly can be drawbacks to outsourcing—for example, no one knows a small business as well as its owner or works as hard for its success. Entrepreneur Bruce Judson warns against outsourcing the company's unique skill or core product, but he contends that everything else should be on the table. As Judson sees it, turning these tasks over to others frees up the entrepreneur's time to focus on his or her greatest strengths.[19]

Outsourcing Decisions
Outsourcing options can work wonders for a small business, but they also come with inherent risks. Many experts suggest that you have a backup plan in case a supplier fails to deliver and that you continually monitor the progress of those companies with which you choose to work. These steps require time, effort, and expense but can help to ensure that your firm is spared the operational disasters that can easily arise from outsourcing.

Outsourcing can take many forms. Chapter 20 explained the practice of co-employment, through which a small company can transfer its employees to a professional employer organization, which then leases them back to the firm. In that case, the small business is outsourcing the payroll preparation process. But the explosive growth in outsourcing among smaller companies may be mostly due to their taking advantage of the broad reach of the Internet to tap the services of hungry freelancers. Websites with names like guru.com, 99designs.com, and Freelancer.com connect businesses with a global market of freelancers and receive a small cut of the final transaction for the services they provide. In the end, everyone comes out ahead.

COOPS AND THE INTERNET

Some small companies find that they can increase their buying power if they join **cooperative purchasing organizations** (often called **coops**). In this type of arrangement, several smaller businesses combine their demand for products and services with the goal of negotiating, as a group, for lower prices and better service from suppliers. Coops, which have been around for a long time, usually focus on a specific industry to maximize the benefits to participating businesses, and they can be very effective.

The Internet, however, has leveled the playing field for many small companies. Today's connected small business owners can line up hundreds of suppliers, large and small, to bid for their business—with just a few mouse clicks. They can also outsource a variety of tasks, from business planning and product design to sales presentations and warranty service. Technology has opened the door to a world of outsourcing alternatives that was unimaginable just a few decades ago.

DIVERSIFICATION OF SUPPLY

Small businesses often must decide whether it is better to use more than one supplier when purchasing a given item. The somewhat frustrating answer is "It all depends." A small company might concentrate purchases with one supplier for any of the following reasons:

- A particular supplier may be superior in its product quality.
- Larger orders may qualify for quantity discounts.
- Orders may be so small that it is impractical to divide them among several suppliers.
- The purchasing business may, as a good customer, qualify for prompt treatment of rush orders and receive management advice, market information, and flexible financial terms in times of crisis.
- The franchise contract might require purchasing from the franchisor.

The following reasons favor diversifying rather than concentrating sources of supply:

- Shopping among suppliers allows a company to locate the best source in terms of price, quality, and service.
- A supplier, knowing that competitors are getting some of its business, may provide better prices and service.
- Diversifying supply sources provides insurance against interruptions caused by strikes, fires, or similar problems with individual suppliers.

Some companies compromise by following a purchasing policy of concentrating enough purchases with a single supplier to justify special treatment and, at the same time, diversifying purchases sufficiently to maintain alternative sources of supply. The point is that a small business can adopt any of a number of different approaches in order to diversify its sourcing strategy.

21-5b Measuring Supplier Performance

What measures of a supplier's performance matter most? The Supply Chain Council has an answer to that question. It has developed the **Supply Chain Operations Reference (SCOR) model**, a list of critical factors that provides a helpful starting place when assessing a supplier's performance. Five attributes stand out:[20]

- *Reliability:* Does the supplier provide what you need and fill orders accurately?
- *Responsiveness:* Does the supplier deliver inputs when they are needed?
- *Agility:* Does the supplier respond quickly to changes in your order?
- *Costs:* Does the supplier help you control your cost of goods sold, your total supply chain management costs, and your warranty/returns costs?
- *Assets:* Does the supplier help you improve efficiencies by shortening the cash cycle, inventory holding time, and demand on assets?

These factors can also prove helpful when first selecting a supplier. Since they are commonly used performance measures, some suppliers have data to show potential

Supply Chain Operations Reference (SCOR) model
A list of critical factors that help in assessing a supplier's performance.

new customers how they stack up (along with references to verify their claims). Just remember that an outstanding rating on a measure that is not important to your business does not provide an advantage—in fact, it can be a form of waste.

When choosing a supplier, also consider the services it offers. The extension of credit by suppliers provides a major portion of the working capital of many small businesses. Some suppliers also plan sales promotions, provide merchandising aids, and offer management advice.

Clearly, it is vitally important to choose suppliers carefully. If a supplier fails to deliver what you need when you need it and with the quality you require, the entire operation breaks down—and so may your business.

21-5c Building Good Relationships with Suppliers

Good relationships with suppliers are essential for firms of any size, but they are particularly important for small businesses. A small company may be only one among dozens, hundreds, or perhaps thousands buying from that supplier. And the small company's purchases are often very limited in volume and, therefore, of less concern to the supplier.

To implement a policy of fair play and to cultivate good relations with suppliers, a small business should try to observe the following purchasing practices:

- Pay bills promptly.
- Give sales representatives a timely and courteous hearing.
- Minimize abrupt cancellation of orders merely to gain a temporary advantage.
- Avoid attempts to browbeat a supplier into special concessions or unusual discounts.
- Cooperate with the supplier by making suggestions for product improvements and/or cost reductions, whenever possible.
- Provide courteous, reasonable explanations when rejecting bids, and make fair adjustments in the case of disputes.

Some large corporations, such as UPS, Dell, FedEx, and Office Depot, have made special efforts to reach out to small business purchasers. By offering various kinds of assistance, such suppliers can strengthen small companies, which then continue as customers. Of course, it still makes sense to shop around, but low prices can sometimes be misleading. If a low bid looks too good to be true, perhaps it is. Low bids often exclude crucial items. Nonetheless, building strong relationships with the right large suppliers can clearly help small businesses become more competitive.

21-5d Forming Strategic Alliances

Some small firms have found it advantageous to develop strategic alliances with suppliers. This form of partnering enables the buying and selling firms to work much more closely together than is customary in a simple contractual arrangement. But the choice of partner can quickly determine whether the arrangement succeeds or fails—so choose carefully. Look first at companies with which you already have a relationship, such as a faithful supplier or distributor. Then, make sure that they offer the right fit, are trustworthy, and have track records of true performance.[21] If a strategic alliance is well planned and executed, everyone involved comes out ahead.

Some potential alliance partners design their businesses specifically to help small firms. In 2005, Michael Prete started a venture called Gotham Cycles to sell parts

Living the Dream

ENTREPRENEURIAL EXPERIENCES

Saving Face and Saving Money

Ava Anderson founded her company, Ava Anderson Non Toxic, in 2009 when she was only 15. As a young high school student, she became aware of the considerable differences between American and European cosmetic offerings. "There are only 10 banned ingredients in the U.S., but more than 1,300 in the EU," she notes. "People are justifiably disturbed by this."

Determined to address the problem, Anderson decided to develop her own alternative—which she worked on in the evenings, after finishing her homework. The result was a line of six skincare products that became the premier offerings used to build her business. Since its launch, Ava Anderson Non Toxic has been expanding rapidly and now has 10 non-toxic lines. Anderson produces many of these in her hometown of Warren, Rhode Island, while sourcing the remainder from other manufacturing facilities across the country.

Anderson originally planned to sell her products online but eventually abandoned the idea after realizing that this option would not allow her to educate consumers about the uniqueness of her cosmetics. As she sees it, "There just isn't enough room on the back of a bottle to explain the issue of toxic chemicals in conventional products." So Anderson decided to adopt a "party plan" direct-sales approach instead. Her representatives organize social events in living rooms across the country, explaining the advantages of using her products and offering consumers the opportunity to place orders on the spot. Because consultants can get started in the business for less than $100, many have signed up with the company. In fact, it only took a few years for their ranks to grow to more than 6,000 representatives.

Aggressive growth, however, requires focused attention to detail and cost control. One of Anderson's first challenges came early on, when an order-fulfillment vendor failed to meet her exacting expectations. The contractor elected to use substandard packaging, including butcher paper and Scotch tape, which was clearly out of step with a premium brand. Adding insult to injury, the company charged extra fees whenever brochures or information sheets were added to orders. Frustrated, Anderson decided to handle shipping within her own company. "Our original fulfillment house charged us $1.55 per order," she recalls. "Now our orders cost approximately $1 each to ship, so our savings are well over $5,000 a month."

The savings, combined with 99.6 percent order-fulfillment accuracy, allowed the fledgling firm to concentrate on controlled growth. Today, Ava Anderson Non Toxic grosses over $5 million annually. The young entrepreneur has also become an outspoken advocate for industry-wide reforms. She has already made two trips to Washington, D.C., to testify before Congress about potentially hazardous chemicals found in American cosmetic lines. Without her decision to take back some of the company's logistical operations, Anderson may not have been able to accomplish so much so quickly. Cutting costs and ensuring that quality standards are met have helped the entrepreneur become a successful millionaire before the age of 20.

Sources: Ava Anderson, "How I Saved . . . $60,000," *Entrepreneur*, Vol. 42, No. 2 (February 2014), p. 66; Megan Brame, "Exclusive Interview with Ava Anderson of Ava Anderson Non Toxic," *Examiner.com*, September 4, 2013, http://www.examiner.com/article/exclusive-interview-with-ava-anderson-of-ava-anderson-nontoxic?cid=rss, accessed March 3, 2015; Samantha Escobar, "Meet Ava Anderson, the Teen CEO of an All-Natural Cosmetics Company," *Blisstree*, June 4, 2013, http://www.blisstree.com/2013/06/04/public-health-2/ava-anderson-teenage-ceo-of-ava-anderson-non-toxic-cosmetics-company/2, accessed March 3, 2015; Robert Farrington, "Starting a Million Dollar Business at 14 with Ava Anderson," *The College Investor*, August 19, 2013, http://thecollegeinvestor.com/8955/starting-million-dollar-business-14-ava-anderson, accessed March 3, 2015; "REAL PEOPLE: Interview with Ava Sprauge Anderson," *Glitter Magazine*, November 2, 2014, http://glittermagrocks.com/connect/2014/11/02/real-people-interview-with-ava-sprague-anderson, accessed March 3, 2015; and Joan Warren, "Barrington-Based Business Enjoys Success, Expanding," *EastBayRI*, December 10, 2014, http://www.eastbayri.com/news/barrington-based-business-enjoys-success-expanding, accessed March 3, 2015.

online for Italian-made Ducati motorcycles. But it wasn't long before he was selling to a loyal worldwide customer base. How did he get off to such a fast start? He hired a very important employee: eBay.[22] Of course, the online auction site isn't exactly an employee—it's more like an army of employees (more than 33,500 strong, in fact[23]) that can help an online company with many of its needs. Sellers who lean on eBay's rich stable of resources to automate their operations are able to focus on building their businesses. A powerful partner for a small company, eBay offers sophisticated tools that can help with shipping, handling e-mail messages and feedback for buyers, and managing listings. It can even help you decide which tools are right for your business (click on "Learn to Sell" at the bottom of eBay's homepage for details).

21-5e Forecasting Supply Needs

How much cash is needed for the next quarter? How much inventory must be carried to support the next season? How much lead time is needed to fill orders? Forecasting can help with understanding where the business is going and the level of resources—from personnel to capital funding—that will be required. Forecasting techniques can be as simple as projecting what will happen based on what happened last year, last week, or an average of several previous periods. Some businesses may require greater accuracy and thus need a more complex model for forecasting.

Associative forecasting takes a variety of driving variables into account when determining expected sales. The amount of sales expected at a local ice cream parlor, for example, is a product of many underlying predictors, such as the day of the week or season of the year, weather (rain versus sunshine, hot versus cool), local events (such as the timing of sporting events or movie premieres), and promotions (which could include sales or coupons). Each of these factors has a different impact on expected sales. Using forecasting tools such as regression, a small business owner can determine the impact of each variable on sales in the past and then use that association to predict future demand.

21-5f Using Information Systems

In recent years, small firms have greatly improved operational efficiency by using computers, new business software, and Internet links with suppliers and customers. Tedious, paper-based processes for tracking orders, work in process, and inventory have been replaced by simplified and accelerated computer-based processes.

A recent study revealed that the use of electronic invoicing and billing worldwide is growing more than 20 percent a year. The analysis also determined that adopting electronic and automated systems can cut the cost of processing invoices by 60 to 80 percent, compared to standard paper-based practices.[24] For a company that handles thousands of invoices per month, this savings can have a substantial impact on costs. The software can be purchased off the shelf, so changing how things are done and training personnel on a new system may actually be more challenging than the installation of the new software itself.

Management information systems are continually being reinvented and improved. Microsoft alone spends exceedingly large sums of money to build software that will automate practically every aspect of a small company's business (including order processing and inventory management) and create a base layer of technology upon which smaller software makers can build applications. This software is also designed to work for a variety of businesses, from retail to manufacturing and distribution.[25] The information systems options and other tech-based tools available to small companies just keep getting better, more powerful, and less expensive.

associative forecasting
Forecasting that considers a variety of variables to determine expected sales.

lean production
An approach that emphasizes efficiency through elimination of all forms of waste in a company's operations.

21-6 LEAN PRODUCTION AND SYNCHRONOUS MANAGEMENT

LO 21-6

Describe lean production and synchronous management, and discuss their importance to operations management in small businesses.

A revolution in operations management practices is changing the way business is done in many firms. With a focus on eliminating waste, lean production and synchronous management have made their mark on both large and small companies.

21-6a Lean Production

Companies are widely adopting principles of lean production, an influential model that is fundamentally reshaping the way operations are planned and managed. **Lean production** is more than a simple set of practices—it is a guiding philosophy and management approach that emphasizes efficiency through the elimination of all forms of waste in a company's operations.

The ideas at the center of lean production certainly are not new. In fact, the seeds of the concept were sown more than a century ago by Henry Ford, a leading visionary in the automobile industry and an outspoken advocate of efficiency in manufacturing. Later, Shoichiro Toyoda, former president of Toyota Motors, built on Ford's concepts and focused on eliminating waste, in all of its many forms, from his production system. He defined *waste* as "anything other than the minimum amount of equipment, materials, parts, space, and workers' time, which are absolutely essential for adding value to the product."[26] In other words, the goal of lean production is to use the minimum amount of resources necessary to achieve a total bundle of satisfaction for the customer.

The lean production mindset that has been integrated into the operations of most major corporations, including the Toyota Production System (TPS), makes the elimination of waste a top priority by emphasizing the following principles:[27]

- *Defects* are costly because they have to be repaired or scrapped.
- *Overproduction* must be stored and may never be sold.
- *Transportation* costs can be minimized by locating close to suppliers and customers.
- *Waiting* can be wasteful because resources are idle.
- *Inventory* in excess of the minimum required is unproductive and costly.
- *Motion*, whether by-product, people, or machinery, is wasted when it's unnecessary.
- *Processing* itself is wasteful if it is not productive.

As companies of all sizes around the world have subscribed to the principles of lean production, the supply chain (introduced in Chapter 15) has become susceptible to disruption, and this can be a problem. Toyota, for example, keeps only two hours of inventory in their assembly plants, so there is little margin for error on the supply side of the equation. However, this incredibly low amount of inventory also leads to a variety of benefits, ranging from capital efficiency to a smooth production process.

21-6b Synchronous Management

Going a step beyond lean production, **synchronous management** views the assets and activities of an organization as interdependent and suggests that they be managed in a way that optimizes the performance of the entire company. This approach presumes that the goal of the organization, and the definition of performance that flows from it,

START UP TOOLS

Robots for Small Factories

There was a time when the use of robots in manufacturing was something that only huge corporations could consider, but now that high-potential machines priced as low as $20,000 have hit the market, that is no longer the case. Small companies recognize the value of robots that can handle a wide range of unbearably tedious and unpleasant tasks, and with greater precision and fewer errors than human beings. The new breed of robots, called "collaborative machines" because they are able to work closely with people, can be programmed with the flexibility that small businesses need to handle various tasks. And they ultimately promote lean production and waste reduction by increasing efficiencies, minimizing scrap and rework, and replacing more expensive human labor. To learn more about the advantages of using robots in small businesses, see Timothy Aeppel, "Robots Work Their Way into Small Factories," *The Wall Street Journal*, September 18, 2014, pp. B1, B7.

is known and influences all decision making. It requires an understanding of how a shift in one area of operations can affect the rest of the organization—that is, it provides insight regarding interrelationships between assets, changes in activities, and achievement of the firm's goals.

Although these ideas are not original, they are finally being understood and implemented, in many cases for the first time. Henry Ford concluded early on that the key to manufacturing efficiency lies in a synchronized flow of materials and products into, through, and out of the plant in concert with market demand. It's clear to see that companies that understand crucial interactions between their assets and activities are likely to produce greater profits.[28]

Identifying bottlenecks is imperative to making synchronous management work. A **bottleneck** is any point in an operations system where limited capacity reduces the production capability of an entire chain of activities so that it cannot satisfy market demand for products or services. For example, a bottleneck can be created by a machine that cannot operate fast enough to keep up with the rest of the equipment on an assembly line. In a more complex production system, it is possible to have more than one bottleneck (that is, more than one resource whose capacity is lower than the market demand for what is being produced). In this case, the most restrictive of the bottlenecks is called a **constraint**. Since the constraint determines the capacity of the entire system, it is imperative to synchronize all other organizational activities with it.

Finding the bottlenecks in an organization can be a challenging exercise. But once a bottleneck or constraint is found, what can be done to address it? The three basic options shown in Exhibit 21.3 provide common ways to deal with bottlenecks and constraints.

Any loss of throughput at a bottleneck or constraint translates to lower production for the entire line or organization. It follows that these points in an operations system deserve special attention, for the sake of the company and its performance. For resources that do not contribute to a bottleneck or constraint in a production line or service firm, it is far less important to make investments to improve their functioning and increase their efficiency.

Hopefully, it is apparent to you by now that operations management is very important to the functioning and performance of all types of businesses, whether large or small. Best practices typically are perfected in large corporations, but the principles

Employee Suggestions for Operations Problems

Harness the brain power of your employees to identify and address bottlenecks and constraints and other operations-centered problems by setting up a simple suggestions box. You might be amazed at the quality of the ideas that your staff can come up with if you offer a small incentive (like a cash prize for the best suggestion). Or, you might use an idea management system like Imaginatik, SpigitEngage, or Brightidea to collect and rank employee ideas.

synchronous management
An approach that recognizes the interdependence of assets and activities and manages them to optimize the entire company's performance.

bottleneck
Any point in the operations process where limited capacity reduces the production capability of an entire chain of activities.

constraint
The most restrictive of bottlenecks, determining the capacity of the entire system.

EXHIBIT **21.3** Avoiding Bottlenecks and Constraints

Add Capacity	• Expand resources. • Subdivide the work. • Outsource production to a company with more capacity.
Increase Efficiency	• Arrange schedules so that the resources take no breaks (for example, have employees take breaks during setup, teardown, or maintenance activities). • Schedule maintenance on nights, weekends, and holidays rather than during productive time. • Increase productivity through employee training, upgraded tools, or automation.
Filter Production	• Inspect quality prior to a constraint. • Allow only work that achieves firm goals and contributes to performance (that is, a finished goods inventory would be unnecessary).

and approaches they refine can usually be adapted to the management of smaller enterprises, at least at some level. In a competitive marketplace, effective and efficient operations are necessary to survival. And where this is not the case, best practices can still add to customer benefits, firm performance, and the satisfaction of the company's owners. Practices such as managing inventory wisely, treating suppliers well, and ensuring the quality of products made or services offered protect and enhance the reputation of the company. This is only possible when sound operations management practices are used. The commitment of time and energy required to reach excellence certainly pays off over the long run.

21-1. Understand how operations enhance a small company's competitiveness.

- The term *operations* refers to the processes used to create and deliver a product or service, which can be used to compete for customers.
- Companies gain power to the degree that they excel in satisfying customer needs and wants more precisely and/or efficiently than their competitors.
- To be successful, a company's operations must involve all of the activities required to create value for customers and earn their dollars.
- *Operations management* refers to the planning and control of a conversion process that includes bringing together inputs and turning them into outputs (products and services) that customers want.

21-2. Discuss the nature of the operations process for both products and services.

- Product-oriented and service-oriented operations are similar in that they change inputs into outputs.
- Managers of service businesses face special challenges in assuring and controlling quality, given the difficulty inherent in measuring and controlling intangibles.
- In service businesses, employees interact extensively with customers.
- The adoption of various technologies has enabled customers of many businesses to provide more of their own services.
- Manufacturing operations can be classified as one of three types—job shops, project manufacturing, and repetitive manufacturing.
- Flexible manufacturing systems can help cut manufacturing costs while giving customers exactly what they want.
- A small company's capacity to offer products or services is a critical factor.
- Planning and scheduling procedures are designed to achieve the orderly sequential flow of products through a plant at a rate that matches deliveries to customers.
- Demand management strategies are used to stimulate customer demand when it is normally low.

21-3. Identify ways to control inventory and minimize inventory costs.

- Inventory management can help an entrepreneur understand the vital balance between two competing pressures in the business—increasing inventory to satisfy customer demand and reducing inventory to maintain a healthy balance sheet.
- The reasons for carrying inventory include the following: to meet customer demand, to be less dependent on a supplier, to protect against stockouts, to benefit from sales or quantity-based discounts, and to protect against price increases.
- One method of determining ideal inventory levels is economic order quantity, an index that determines the purchase quantity of an item that will minimize total inventory costs.
- Statistical inventory control accommodates the variability of supply and demand using a targeted service level.
- The ABC method classifies items into three categories based on dollar velocity.
- Just-in-time inventory systems are designed to cut inventory carrying costs by making or buying what is needed just as it is needed.
- Types of inventory recordkeeping systems are physical inventory systems, perpetual inventory systems, and two-bin inventory systems.

21-4. Recognize the contributions of operations management to product and service quality.

- *Quality* can be defined as the characteristics of a product or service that determine its ability to satisfy customers' stated and implied needs.
- Total quality management is an all-encompassing, quality-focused management approach that is customer driven, emphasizes organizational commitment, and focuses on a culture of continuous improvement.
- A company's quality management efforts should begin with a focus on meeting the expectations of customers who purchase its products or services.
- Paying careful attention to the details of a firm's operations and correcting any weaknesses, as well as listening to customer feedback, helps ensure that customers get the quality they expect.
- One useful approach to gathering customer-based information is to "mine" company sales data to learn more about customer behavior.
- An important element in effective quality management consists of the various tools, techniques, and procedures needed to ensure high-quality products and services.
- Product quality can be maintained by inspection or by using the poka-yoke approach, which seeks to mistake-proof a firm's operations.
- Acceptance sampling is one statistical method of quality control.
- ISO 9000 certification requires full documentation of a firm's quality management procedures and is particularly valuable for small firms.
- Though it is easier to measure the quality of products, effective methods for measuring the quality of services can also be devised.

21-5. Explain the importance of purchasing and the nature of key purchasing policies.

- The quality of a finished product depends on the quality of the raw materials used.
- Purchasing contributes to profitable operations by ensuring that goods are delivered when they are needed.
- Purchasing practices that seek out the best prices can have major impact on the financial health of a business.
- The decision to make or buy should be based on long-run cost and profit optimization because it can be expensive to reverse.
- Companies can sometimes save money by outsourcing to suppliers specializing in a particular type of work.
- Cooperative purchasing organizations help smaller firms negotiate as a group for lower prices and better service from suppliers.
- The Internet provides small business owners with connections to hundreds of suppliers.
- Diversifying purchases from suppliers can help a small business maintain alternative sources of supply.
- Critical factors in assessing supplier performance are reliability, responsiveness, agility, costs, and assets.
- Good relationships with suppliers are essential for small businesses.
- Developing strategic alliances, forecasting supply needs, and using information systems are elements of other purchasing policies used by small companies.

21-6. Describe lean production and synchronous management, and discuss their importance to operations management in small businesses.

- Lean production emphasizes efficiency through the elimination of all forms of waste in a company's operations.
- Maintaining a very low amount of inventory can lead to a variety of benefits, ranging from capital efficiency to a smooth production process.
- Synchronous management suggests that the assets and activities of an organization are interdependent and should be managed in a way that optimizes the performance of the entire company.
- Understanding how a shift in one area of operations can affect the rest of the organization underlies synchronous management and is likely to produce the greatest profits.
- Bottlenecks and constraints must be managed carefully because these determine the capacity of the entire production system.

Key Terms

ABC method p. 576
acceptance sampling p. 583
associative forecasting p. 590
attributes p. 583
bottleneck p. 592
constraint p. 592
continuous manufacturing p. 572
cooperative purchasing organizations (coops) p. 586
cycle counting p. 577
demand management strategies p. 573
economic order quantity p. 575
flexible manufacturing systems p. 573

inspection p. 582
ISO 9000 p. 583
job shops p. 571
just-in-time inventory system p. 576
lean production p. 590
make-or-buy decisions p. 585
operations p. 569
operations management p. 569
outsourcing p. 586
perpetual inventory system p. 577
physical inventory system p. 577
poka-yoke p. 582
project manufacturing p. 572
quality p. 578
repetitive manufacturing p. 572
statistical inventory control p. 575
Supply Chain Operations Reference (SCOR) model p. 587
synchronous management p. 592
total quality management (TQM) p. 578
two-bin inventory system p. 577
variables p. 583

You Make the Call

Situation 1

Christina Poole owns two pizza restaurants in a city with a population of 150,000 and is studying her company's operations to be sure they are functioning as efficiently as possible. About 70 percent of the venture's sales represents dine-in business, and 30 percent comes from deliveries. Poole has always attempted to produce a high-quality product and to minimize the waiting time of customers both on- and off-premises.

Poole recently read a magazine article suggesting that quality is now generally abundant and that quality differences between businesses are narrowing. The writer advocated placing emphasis on saving time for customers rather than producing a high-quality product. Poole is contemplating the implications of this article for her pizza business. Realizing that her attention should be focused, she wonders whether to concentrate primary managerial emphasis on delivery time.

Question 1 Is the writer of the article correct in believing that quality levels now are generally high and that quality differences among businesses are minimal?
Question 2 What are the benefits and drawbacks of placing the firm's primary emphasis on minimizing customer wait time?
Question 3 If you were advising Poole, what would you recommend?
Question 4 How would your answers to the previous questions be different if Poole sold a $6 pizza? What if the pizza cost $25?

Situation 2

Jonathan Tandy, owner of a small furniture manufacturing firm, is trying to deal with the firm's thin working capital situation by carefully managing payments to the company's major suppliers. These suppliers extend credit for 30 days, and customers are expected to pay within that time period. However, the suppliers do not automatically refuse subsequent orders when a payment is a few days late. Tandy's strategy is to delay payment of most invoices for 10 to 15 days beyond the due date. He believes that the suppliers will go along with him rather than risk losing future sales. This practice enables Tandy's firm to operate with sufficient inventory, avoid costly interruptions in production, and reduce the likelihood of an overdraft at the bank.

Question 1 What are the ethical issues raised by Tandy's payment practices?
Question 2 What impact, if any, might these practices have on the firm's supplier relationships? How serious would this impact be?
Question 3 What changes in company culture, employee behavior, or relationships with other business partners may result from Tandy's practices?

Situation 3

Tyler Smithson owns Joe on the Run, a small chain of three coffee shops, all of which are facing a challenge that is common to most service businesses: They have to deal with highly variable demand, with two or three very busy times each day. If a waiting line develops, we can assume that a constraint exists somewhere in the product or service delivery. Typical workstations behind the counter include the barista station (where specialty drinks are made), the drive-thru station, and the cashier station. Because the goal of the company is to satisfy the most customers possible (and thus increase profits), a constraint at one of these workstations must be addressed quickly.

Question 1 What can be done to improve capacity?
Question 2 What can be done to improve efficiency?
Question 3 What could be done at a store level to improve the performance of the business?

Video Case 21

River Pools & Spas (p. 689)

This case focuses on operational adjustments that a small company had to make in response to growth in market demand and later decreases in sales that resulted from the recession and subsequent slow growth of the U.S. economy.

Endnotes

1. Dan Heath and Chip Heath, "Blowing the Baton Pass," *FastCompany*, No. 147 (July/August 2010), pp. 46–47.
2. http://www.amazon.com, accessed April 3, 2015.
3. Richard Sweeney, co-founder of Keurig, Inc., keynote speech at the annual meeting of the United States Association for Small Business and Entrepreneurship, Hilton Head, South Carolina, January 14, 2011.
4. "Six Flags: The FLASH Pass," https://www.sixflags.com/greatadventure/store/flash-pass, accessed April 3, 2015.
5. "Delving into the Mystery of Customer Satisfaction: A Toyota for the Retail Market?" http://knowledge.wharton.upenn.edu/article/delving-into-the-mystery-of-customer-satisfaction-a-toyota-for-the-retail-market, accessed April 4, 2015.
6. Most books on operations management offer formulas and calculations for determining the economic order quantity. One exceptionally good resource for this and many other operations management computations is Wallace J. Hopp and Mark L. Spearman, *Factory Physics*, 3rd ed. (Long Grove, IL: Waveland Press, 2011), pp. 49–57.
7. "McAlister's Deli: About Us," http://www.mcalistersdeli.com/our-story/about-us, accessed April 3, 2015; and personal communication with McAlister's management, Waco, Texas, March 6, 2009.
8. McAlister's management, *op. cit*.
9. Leigh Buchanan, "We Will Be the Best-Run Business in America," *Inc.*, Vol. 34, No. 1 (February 2012), p. 72–78.
10. *Ibid*., p. 74.
11. Adapted from "Five Guys: Handcrafted Burgers and Fries Since 1986," http://www.fiveguys.com, accessed April 3, 2015; and Liz Welch, "Five Guys Burgers and Fries," *Inc.*, Vol. 32, No. 3 (April 2010), p. 78.
12. *Ibid*.
13. "Five Guys Burgers and Fries: About Us," http://www.fiveguys.com/about-us.aspx, accessed April 3, 2015.
14. Victor Mayer-Schonberger and Kenneth Cukier, *Big Data: A Revolution That Will Transform How We Live, Work, and Think* (New York: Eamon Dolan/Mariner Books, 2014).
15. Adapted from "Quality Tools—The Basic Seven," http://src.alionscience.com/pdf/QualityTools.pdf, accessed April 3, 2015; and "The 7 Basic Quality Tools for Process Improvement," http://asq.org/learn-about-quality/seven-basic-quality-tools/overview/overview.html, accessed April 3, 2015.
16. Linda Tischler, "Partners in *Time*," *FastCompany*, No. 143 (March 2010), p. 40.
17. Kate Lister, "Free-Lance Nation," *Entrepreneur*, Vol. 38, No. 9 (September 2010), pp. 89–97.
18. Deloitte Consulting LLP, "2014 Global Outsourcing and Insourcing Survey Results," http://www2.deloitte.com/content/dam/Deloitte/us/Documents/strategy/us-sdt-2014-global-outsourcingInsourcing-survey_051914.pdf, accessed April 7, 2015.
19. Jennifer Wang, "Employees. Who Needs 'Em?" *Entrepreneur*, Vol. 38, No. 3 (March 2010), p. 18.
20. Adapted from "APICS Supply Chain Council: SCOR Metrics," http://www.apics.org/sites/apics-supply-chain-council/benchmarking/scor-metrics, accessed April 8, 2015.
21. Laurel Delaney, "Howdy Partner," *Entrepreneur*, Vol. 35, No. 4 (April 2007), p. 87.
22. "About Gotham Cycles," http://www.gothamcycles.com/About-Us.html, accessed April 8, 2015.
23. "eBay," *Forbes*, May 2014, http://www.forbes.com/companies/ebay, accessed April 8, 2015.
24. For a summary of the report, see Bruno Koch, "E-Billing/E-Invoicing: Key Stakeholders as Game Changers," Billentis, May 6, 2014, http://www2.lindorff.nl/e-invoicing-e-billing, accessed April 9, 2015.
25. "Microsoft Dynamics," http://www.microsoft.com/en-us/dynamics/default.aspx, accessed April 13, 2015.
26. Larry Robinson, "Connecting the Dots: Aligning Lean Operational and Financial Metrics," *Next Generation Manufacturer Newsletter*, http://www.massmac.org/newsline/0708/article04.htm, accessed March 4, 2013.
27. This list was adapted from John J. Coyle, C. John Langley, Brian J. Gibson, Robert A. Novack, and Edward J. Bardi, *Supply Chain Management: A Logistics Perspective* (Mason, OH: Cengage Learning, 2017).
28. Henry Ford first discussed these ideas in his seminal book from 1926, *Today and Tomorrow*, more recently published in 1988 by Productivity Press.

CHAPTER 22

Managing the Firm's Assets

Nathan Perry, owner of The Cutting Edge Elite in New York City, puts maximum effort into building great relationships with his customers. The catering business, now eight years old, uses professional models and actors who are experienced and educated in the art of service. Their mission is to be poised and charismatic when working an event. Coming from all walks of life and ethnic backgrounds, they add diversity and a unique energy to every event.

The firm's website describes the management's business philosophy as follows:

> *The Cutting Edge Elite is dedicated not to building business, but to building relationships. Along with our roster of incredible personalities, we endeavor to maintain a consistency and attentiveness to every client's needs. Focused on creating a seamless partnership, we compose an individual profile for each of our patrons. The nuance, style, and uniqueness recorded, we pass that knowledge on to our staff, making them indistinguishable from your own. Votives stay lit till the last guest leaves, serving from the right, Grandma Mabel allergic to peanuts; all details that never go unnoticed.*

In the SPOTLIGHT
The Cutting Edge Elite, Inc.
www.ceenyc.com

Perry hasn't always been able to focus on building unique experiences with customers, however. In the past, he has had to devote energy to collecting up to $30,000 in accounts receivable at any given time. He begrudges spending his time

After studying this chapter, you should be able to. . .

22-1. Describe the working capital cycle of a small business.

22-2. Identify the important issues in managing a firm's cash flows.

22-3. Explain the key issues in managing accounts receivable.

22-4. Discuss the key financial issues in managing inventory.

22-5. Describe the key issues in managing accounts payable.

22-6. Calculate and interpret a company's cash conversion period.

22-7. Discuss the techniques commonly used in making capital budgeting decisions.

22-8. Describe the capital budgeting practices of small firms.

in this way, finding it to be a major distraction from where his passions lie. But he needs the cash for operations.

"When someone tells you the check is in the mail, it doesn't mean anything," observes Perry. Until recently, almost all small service businesses would complete work for a customer, send a bill, and then have to wait for weeks (even months) to receive payment, possibly tying up thousands of dollars in accounts receivable. In fact, it is not unusual for a small business to give a customer 30 days to pay an invoice but for the customer to take 60 to 90 days before actually paying.

Perry, along with an increasing number of other small business owners, is now relying on mobile payment devices and other technologies to collect what is owed immediately. Instead of sending an invoice after a job and waiting 30 days or longer to be paid, customers now pay as soon as the work is completed by using a mobile payment service. The result: Perry can use the money to pay salaries and to purchase supplies, which means that he has less of his own money tied up in working capital. That, in turn, lets him be more competitive.

But there are no free lunches. Generally, the fees associated with mobile payments are comparable to credit card processing fees. As customers increasingly use their smartphones for more tasks, paying the small fee is balanced by the advantage of having the mobile payment option available in your business. While there are certainly trade-offs, evidence is clear that the payment revolution powered by mobile devices will continue to grow, to the benefit of many small business owners like Nathan Perry.

Sources: Adapted from Angus Loten and Emily Maltby, "Mobile Payments Brighten Cash Flow for Small Business," http://online.wsj.com/article/SB10001424127887323699704578328851902509698.html?mod=WSJ_SmallBusiness_LEFTTopStories, accessed March 15, 2015; http://www.ceenyc.com/start_1.htm, accessed March 15, 2015; and Roger Yu, "Mobile Payment Options Grow for Small Companies," http://usatoday30.usatoday.com/money/smallbusiness/story/2012-08-05/mobile-payments-technology/56757650/1, accessed March 15, 2015.

The Spotlight story of Nathan Perry's efforts to collect what customers owe him on a timely basis, so that more of his time can be focused on cultivating customers, could be told by almost all small businesses that extend credit to their customers. Collections are a never-ending challenge. In fact, most novice entrepreneurs are shocked by how much time and energy they must commit to collections. Controlling all of a firm's assets requires the same commitment from that firm's management. This chapter discusses this important issue.

22-1 THE WORKING CAPITAL CYCLE

Describe the working capital cycle of a small business.

In Chapters 10 and 11, respectively, we defined *working capital* as a firm's current assets (primarily cash, accounts receivable, and inventory), and *net working capital* as current assets less current or short-term liabilities. **Working capital management**—managing current assets and short-term sources of financing (current liabilities)—is extremely important to most small companies. In fact, no financial management process is more important and, yet, more misunderstood. Good business opportunities can be irreparably damaged by ineffective management of current assets and short-term liabilities. We have made this point repeatedly when discussing the importance of managing cash.

A firm's **working capital cycle** is the flow of resources through the company's accounts as part of its day-to-day operations. As shown in Exhibit 22.1, the steps in a firm's working capital cycle are as follows:

working capital management
The management of current assets and current liabilities.

working capital cycle
The daily flow of resources through a firm's working capital accounts.

Step 1: Purchase or produce inventory for sale, which increases inventory on hand and (a) decreases cash if cash is used to pay for the inventory or (b) increases accounts payable if the inventory is purchased on credit.

Step 2: a. Sell the inventory for cash, which increases cash, or
b. Sell the inventory on credit, which increases accounts receivable.

Step 3: a. Pay the accounts payable, which decreases accounts payable and decreases cash.
b. Pay operating expenses and taxes, which decreases cash.

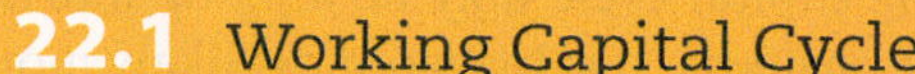

EXHIBIT 22.1 Working Capital Cycle

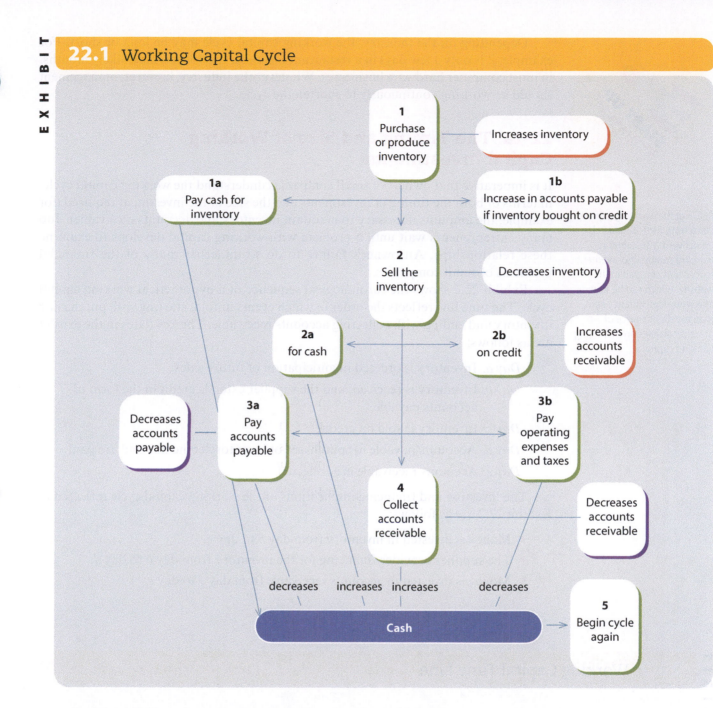

1 Purchase or produce inventory
Increases inventory
1a Pay cash for inventory
1b Increase in accounts payable if inventory bought on credit
2 Sell the inventory
Decreases inventory
2a for cash
2b on credit
Increases accounts receivable
Decreases accounts payable
3a Pay accounts payable
3b Pay operating expenses and taxes
4 Collect accounts receivable
Decreases accounts receivable
decreases
increases
increases
decreases
Cash
5 Begin cycle again

Step 4: Collect the accounts receivable when due, which decreases accounts receivable and increases cash.

Step 5: Begin the cycle again.

Note that the only current liability included in the working capital cycle is accounts payable, which affects the timing of payments for inventory. Accrued expenses, although shown on financial statements as a short-term liability, primarily result from an accountant's effort to match revenues and expenses. Little can be done to "manage" accruals, and so we ignore them as part of the working capital cycle. Also, a short-term bank note, while shown as a current liability is not considered to be part of the working capital cycle. *In this context, think of working capital as the liquid assets (cash and those soon to be converted into cash) that are required to run and grow the business less any credit provided by suppliers in the form of accounts payable.*

Depending on the industry, the working capital cycle may be long or short. For example, it is only a few days in a restaurant business. It is longer, most likely months, in most computer hardware businesses. Whatever the industry, however, management should be working continuously to shorten the cycle.

Want to Know More about Managing Working Capital?
REL, a global working capital consulting firm, is focused on delivering sustainable working capital improvement to its client companies. Its website, which can be found at www.relconsultancy.com, is an excellent source of practical articles on managing working capital.

22-1a The Timing and Size of Working Capital Investments

It is imperative that owners of small companies understand the working capital cycle, in terms of both the timing of investments and the size of the investment required (for example, the amounts necessary to maintain inventory and accounts receivable). Too many entrepreneurs wait until a problem with working capital develops to examine these relationships. An owner's failure to do so underlies many of the financial problems of small companies.

Exhibit 22.2 shows the chronological sequence of a hypothetical working capital cycle. The time line reflects the order in which events unfold, starting with purchasing inventory and ending with collecting accounts receivable. The key dates in the exhibit are as follows:

Day a: Inventory is ordered in anticipation of future sales.

Day b: Inventory is received, and the supplier extends credit in the form of accounts payable.

Day c: Inventory is sold on credit.

Day d: Accounts payable for purchases of inventory come due and are paid.

Day e: Accounts receivable are collected.

The investing and financing implications of the working capital cycle reflected in Exhibit 22.2 are as follows:

- Money is invested in inventory from day *b* to day *c*.
- The supplier provides financing for the inventory from day *b* to day *d*.
- Money is invested in accounts receivable from day *c* to day *e*.

EXHIBIT **22.2** Working Capital Time Line

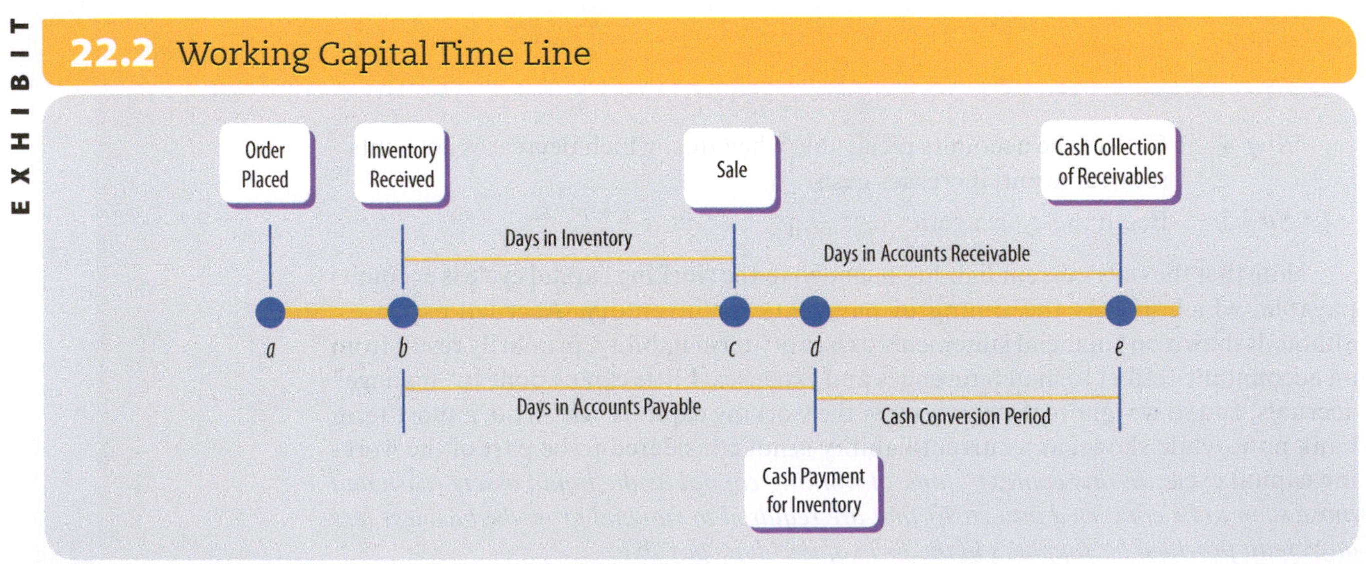

- Financing of the firm's investment in accounts receivable must be provided from day *d* to day *e*. This time span, called the **cash conversion period**, represents the number of days required to complete the working capital cycle, which ends with the conversion of accounts receivable into cash. During this period, the firm no longer has the benefit of supplier financing (accounts payable). The longer this period lasts, the greater the potential cash flow problems for the firm.

22-1b Examples of Working Capital Management[1]

Exhibit 22.3 offers an example of working capital management for two hypothetical firms with contrasting working capital cycles: Pokey, Inc., and Quick Turn Company. On August 15, both firms ordered inventory that they received on August 31, but the similarity ends there.

Pokey, Inc., must pay its supplier for the inventory on September 30, before eventually reselling it on October 15. It collects from its customers on November 30. As you can see, Pokey, Inc., must pay for the inventory two months prior to collecting from its customers. Its cash conversion period—the time required to convert the paid-for inventory and accounts receivable into cash—is 60 days. The firm's managers must

cash conversion period The time required to convert paid-for inventory and accounts receivable into cash.

EXHIBIT **22.3** Working Capital Time Lines For Pokey, Inc., and Quick Turn Company

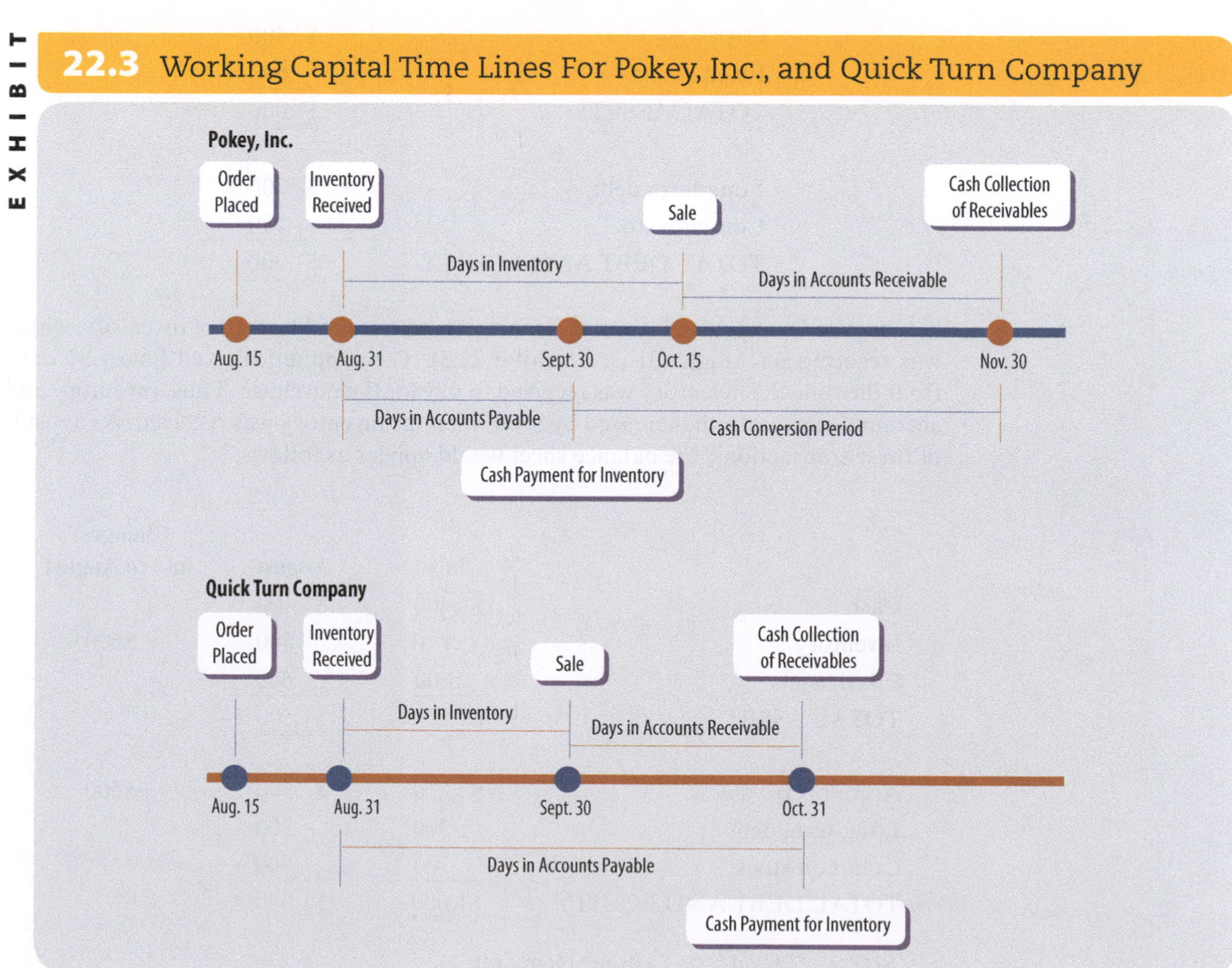

find a way to finance this investment in inventory and accounts receivable or else the company will experience cash flow problems. Furthermore, although increased sales should produce higher profits, the cash flow problems will be compounded because the company will have to finance the investment in inventory until the accounts receivable are collected 60 days later.

Now consider Quick Turn Company's working capital cycle, shown in the bottom portion of Exhibit 22.3. Compared to Pokey, Quick Turn Company has an enviable working capital position. By the time Quick Turn must pay for its inventory purchases (October 31), it has sold its product (September 30) and collected from its customers (October 31). Thus, there is no cash conversion period because the supplier is essentially financing Quick Turn's working capital needs.

To gain an even better understanding of the working capital cycle, let's see what happens to Pokey's balance sheet and income statement. To do so, we will need more information about the firm's activities. A month-by-month listing of its activities and their effects on its balance sheet follow. Pay close attention to the firm's working capital, especially its cash balances.

July: Pokey, Inc., is a new company, having started operations in July with $1,000, financed by $300 in long-term debt and $700 in common stock. At the outset, the owner purchased $600 worth of fixed assets, leaving the remaining $400 in cash. At this point, the balance sheet would appear as follows:

Cash	$ 400
Fixed assets	600
TOTAL ASSETS	$1,000
Long-term debt	$ 300
Common stock	700
TOTAL DEBT AND EQUITY	$1,000

August: On August 15, the firm's managers ordered $500 worth of inventory, which was received on August 31 (see Exhibit 22.3). The supplier allowed Pokey 30 days from the time the inventory was received to pay for the purchase. Thus, inventory and accounts payable both increased by $500 when the inventory was received. As a result of these transactions, the balance sheet would appear as follows:

	July	**August**	**Changes: July to August**
Cash	$ 400	$ 400	
Inventory	0	500	+$500
Fixed assets	600	600	
TOTAL ASSETS	$1,000	$1,500	
Accounts payable	$ 0	$ 500	+$500
Long-term debt	300	300	
Common stock	700	700	
TOTAL DEBT AND EQUITY	$1,000	$1,500	

So far, so good—no cash problems yet.

September: On September 30, the firm paid for the inventory. Both cash and accounts payable decreased by $500, shown as follows:

	July	August	September	Changes: August to September
Cash	$ 400	$ 400	($ 100)	−$500
Inventory	0	500	500	
Fixed assets	600	600	600	
TOTAL ASSETS	$1,000	$1,500	$1,000	
Accounts payable	$ 0	$ 500	$ 0	−$500
Long-term debt	300	300	300	
Common stock	700	700	700	
TOTAL DEBT AND EQUITY	$1,000	$1,500	$1,000	

Now Pokey, Inc., has a cash flow problem in the form of a cash deficit of $100.

October: October was a busy month for Pokey. On October 15, merchandise was sold on credit for $900. Sales (in the income statement) and accounts receivable increased by that amount. The firm incurred operating expenses (selling and administrative expenses) in the amount of $250, to be paid in early November. Thus, operating expenses (in the income statement) and accrued operating expenses (current liabilities in the balance sheet) increased by $250. (An additional $25 in accrued expenses resulted from accruing taxes that will be owed on the firm's earnings.) Finally, in October, the firm's accountants recorded $50 in depreciation expense (to be reported in the income statement), resulting in accumulated depreciation on the balance sheet of $50. The results are as follows:

	July	August	September	October	Changes: September to October
Cash	$ 400	$ 400	($ 100)	($ 100)	
Accounts receivable	0	0	0	900	+$900
Inventory	0	500	500	0	−500
Fixed assets	600	600	600	600	
Accumulated depreciation	0	0	0	(50)	−50
TOTAL ASSETS	$1,000	$1,500	$1,000	$1,350	
Accounts payable	$ 0	$ 500	$ 0	$ 0	
Accrued operating expenses	0	0	0	250	+$250
Income tax payable	0	0	0	25	+25
Long-term debt	300	300	300	300	
Common stock	700	700	700	700	
Retained earnings	0	0	0	75	+75
TOTAL DEBT AND EQUITY	$1,000	$1,500	$1,000	$1,350	

The October balance sheet shows all the activities just described, but there is one more change in the balance sheet: It now shows $75 in retained earnings, which had been $0 in the prior balance sheets. As you will see shortly, this amount represents the firm's income. Note also that Pokey, Inc., continues to be overdrawn by $100 on its cash. None of the events in October affected the firm's cash balance. All the transactions were the result of accruals recorded by the firm's accountant, offsetting entries to the income statement. The relationship between the balance sheet and the income statement is as follows:

Change in the Balance Sheet		Effect on the Income Statement
Increase in accounts receivable of $900	—>	Sales of $900
Decrease in inventory of $500	—>	Cost of goods sold of $500
Increase in accrued operating expenses of $250	—>	Operating expenses of $250
Increase in accumulated depreciation of $50	—>	Depreciation expense of $50
Increase in accrued taxes of $25	—>	Tax expense of $25

November: In November, the accrued expenses were paid, which resulted in a $250 decrease in cash along with an equal decrease in accrued expenses. At the end of November, the accounts receivable were collected, yielding a $900 increase in cash and a $900 decrease in accounts receivable. Thus, net cash increased by $650. The final series of balance sheets is as follows:

	July	August	September	October	November	Changes October to November
Cash	$ 400	$ 400	($ 100)	($ 100)	$ 550	+$650
Accounts receivable	0	0	0	900	0	−900
Inventory	0	500	500	0	0	
Fixed assets	600	600	600	600	600	
Accumulated depreciation	0	0	0	(50)	(50)	
TOTAL ASSETS	$1,000	$1,500	$1,000	$1,350	$1,100	
Accounts payable	$ 0	$ 500	$ 0	$ 0	$ 0	
Accrued operating expenses	0	0	0	250	0	−$250
Income tax payable	0	0	0	25	25	
Long-term debt	300	300	300	300	300	
Common stock	700	700	700	700	700	
Retained earnings	0	0	0	75	75	
TOTAL DEBT AND EQUITY	$1,000	$1,500	$1,000	$1,350	$1,100	

As a result of the firm's activities, Pokey, Inc., reported $75 in profits for the period. The income statement for the period ending November 30 is as follows:

Sales revenue		$ 900
Cost of goods sold		(500)
Gross profit		$ 400
Operating expenses:		
Cash expense	($250)	
Depreciation expense	(50)	
Total operating expenses		$ (300)
Operating income		$ 100
Income tax (25%)		(25)
Net income		$ 75

The $75 in profits is reflected as retained earnings on the balance sheet to make the numbers match.

The somewhat contrived example of Pokey, Inc., illustrates an important point that deserves repeating: An owner of a small firm must understand the working capital cycle of his or her firm. Although the business was profitable, Pokey ran out of cash in September and October (−$100) and didn't recover until November, when the accounts receivable were collected. This 60-day cash conversion period represents a critical time when the firm must find another source of financing if it is to survive. Moreover, when sales are ongoing throughout the year, the problem can be an unending one, unless financing is found to support the firm's sales. Also, as much as possible, a firm should arrange for earlier payment by customers (preferably in advance) and negotiate longer payment schedules with suppliers (preferably over several months).

An understanding of the working capital cycle provides a basis for examining the primary components of working capital management: cash flows, accounts receivable, inventory, and accounts payable.

22-2 MANAGING CASH FLOWS

Identify the important issues in managing a firm's cash flows.

Cash flows are critical at every point in a company's life—when buying inventory, making a capital improvement, or hiring a new employee. Also, without the needed cash on hand, an owner cannot attract financing or secure a line of credit. As Anish Rajparia, then-president of ADP Small Business Services, a global payroll and human resource management services company, said:

> *It's like the blood in the human body. . . . If you don't have a handle on your cash flow—how much you have in the bank on a given day, what you're expecting to get in contrast to what you're going to pay out—it challenges your ability to run your business effectively.*[2]

The examples of Pokey, Inc., and Quick Turn Company in the previous section illustrate that monitoring cash flows is at the core of working capital management. Cash is continually moving through a business. It flows in as customers pay for products or services, and it flows out as payments are made to other businesses and individuals who provide products and services to the firm, such as suppliers and employees. The typically uneven nature of cash inflows and outflows makes it imperative that they be properly understood and managed for the firm's well-being.

According to a study by REL Consultancy, preserving cash flows was the number-one priority of businesses during the Great Recession:

> *Executives realize that in a volatile era, there is no substitute for cash. No matter how much revenue you recognize or how many assets you have on your books, the simple and enduring truth is that the only enterprises that survive are those that generate enough cash to keep their operations running.*[3]

The authors further noted in a related report that cash-focused businesses—what they call "companies with a cash culture"—have certain similarities.

> *[These firms are more likely to] give their best vendors and customers favorable terms, their employees are compensated based on their efficiencies of working capital use, their metrics [for measuring working capital performance] are clear, and their cash policies are carefully considered. As a result of this discipline, companies with a cash culture need 52 percent less working capital.*[4]

Living the Dream

ENTREPRENEURIAL EXPERIENCES

Cash Flow Matters—A Lot

Like many small business owners, Richard Sinclair struggled mightily in 2009 and 2010. Sinclair is the president of Applied Process Equipment, Inc., a water and wastewater treatment company in Scottsdale, Arizona. The Great Recession and subsequent sluggish recovery not only dried up Sinclair's business but also spooked his local bank. When the bank announced that it was eliminating all lines of credit less than $5 million, Sinclair was suddenly without the lifeline that he had counted on for 13 years, and one that he needed now more urgently than ever. "You want a real wake-up call?" he asks. "That brought us home."

Sinclair says there were instances during those two years when he believed his company could go under. Business remained stagnant, and he could not count on his old bank for financing. Now, nearly three years after his credit line vanished, Sinclair has no doubt about what saved his business: proper cash flows.

"If we hadn't had that degree of knowing to the last dollar exactly where we were, there's a very good possibility we may not have survived," he says.

Since Sinclair's business emerged from survival mode in 2011, he has been able to take advantage of opportunities that would not have been possible without a strict handle on cash flows. "Last year, we were able to take advantage of two opportunities that brought several thousand dollars to our bottom line," Sinclair says of two partnerships he was able to make with other local businesses. "Our cash flow was absolutely essential [to that]."

Source: Michael Beller, "Go with the Flow," *MyBusiness*, May–June, 2013, pp. 26–27, http://www.nfib.com/article/go-with-the-flow-62772, accessed March 12, 2015.

Wow! A small company that is able to reduce its investments in working capital by 52 percent would have a huge competitive advantage!

A firm's net cash flow may be determined quite simply by examining its bank account. Monthly cash deposits less checks written during the same period equal a firm's net cash flow. If deposits for a month add up to $100,000 and checks total $80,000, the firm has a net positive cash flow of $20,000. That is, the cash balance at the end of the month is $20,000 higher than it was at the beginning of the month.

Exhibit 22.4 graphically represents the flow of cash through a business. It includes not only the cash flows that arise as part of the firm's working capital cycle (shown in Exhibit 22.1) but other cash flows as well, such as those from purchasing fixed assets and issuing stock. More specifically, cash sales, collection of accounts receivable, payment of expenses, and payment for inventory reflect the inflows and outflows of cash that relate to the working capital cycle. The other items in Exhibit 22.4 represent other, longer-term cash flows.

As we have emphasized on several occasions, calculating cash flows requires that a small business owner be able to distinguish between sales revenue and cash receipts—they are seldom the same. Revenue is recorded at the time a sale is made but does not affect cash flows at that time unless the sale is a cash sale. Cash receipts, on the other hand, are recorded when money actually flows into the firm, often a

EXHIBIT 22.4 Flow of Cash Through a Business

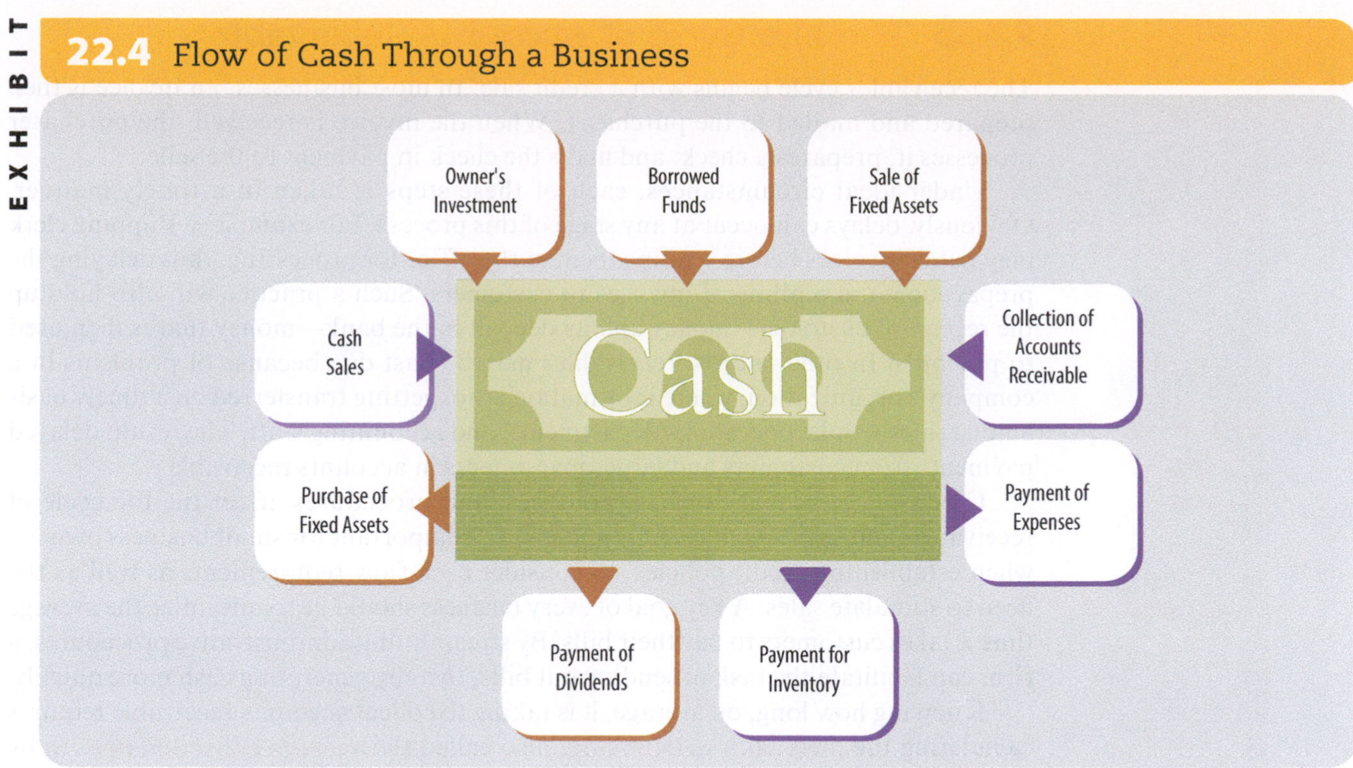

month or two after the sale. Similarly, it is necessary to distinguish between expenses and disbursements. Expenses occur when materials, labor, or other items are used. Payments (disbursements) for these expense items may be made later, when checks are issued. Depreciation, while shown as an expense, is not a cash outflow.

Given the difference between cash flows and profits, it is absolutely essential that the entrepreneur develop a cash budget to anticipate when cash will enter and leave the business. (The cash budget was explained in Chapter 11 when we described financial forecasting.)

22-3 MANAGING ACCOUNTS RECEIVABLE

Explain the key issues in managing accounts receivable.

Chapter 16 discussed the extension of credit by small firms, and the managing and collecting of accounts receivable. This section considers the impact of credit decisions on working capital and particularly on cash flows. The most important factor in managing cash well within a small firm is the ability to collect accounts receivable quickly.

22-3a How Accounts Receivable Affect Cash

Granting credit to customers, although primarily a marketing decision, directly affects a firm's cash account. By selling on credit and thus allowing customers to delay payment, the selling firm delays the inflow of cash.

The total amount of customers' credit balances is carried on the balance sheet as accounts receivable—one of the firm's current assets. Of all noncash assets, accounts receivable are close to becoming cash. Sometimes called *near cash*, or *receivables*, accounts receivable typically are collected and become cash within 30 to 60 days following a sale.

22-3b The Life Cycle of Accounts Receivable

The receivables cycle begins with a credit sale. In most businesses, an invoice is then prepared and mailed to the purchaser. When the invoice is received, the purchaser processes it, prepares a check, and mails the check in payment to the seller.

Under ideal circumstances, each of these steps is taken in a timely manner. Obviously, delays can occur at any stage of this process. For example, a shipping clerk may batch invoices before sending them to the office for processing, thus delaying the preparation and mailing of invoices to customers. Such a practice will also hold up the receipt of customers' money and its deposit in the bank—money that is then used to pay bills. In other words, receivables may be past due because of problems in a company's organization, where information is not getting transferred on a timely basis among salespeople, operations departments, and accounting staff. The result: delayed payments from customers and larger investments in accounts receivable.

Credit management policies, practices, and procedures affect the life cycle of receivables and the flow of cash from them. It is important for small business owners, when establishing credit policies, to consider cash flow requirements as well as the need to stimulate sales. A key goal of every business should be to minimize the average time it takes customers to pay their bills. By streamlining administrative procedures, a firm can facilitate the task of sending out bills, thereby generating cash more quickly.

Knowing how long, on average, it is taking to collect accounts receivable requires calculating the **days sales outstanding**, also called the **average collection period**, by dividing a firm's accounts receivable by daily credit sales, as follows:

$$\text{Days sales outstanding} = \frac{\text{Accounts receivable}}{\text{Annual credit sales} \div 365 \text{ days}}$$

Consider the following information about two businesses, Fast Company and Slow Company:

	Fast Company	Slow Company
Total sales	$1,000,000	$1,000,000
Credit sales	$ 700,000	$ 700,000
Average credit sales per day	$ 1,918	$ 1,918
Accounts receivables	$ 48,000	$ 63,300

These two companies are very similar in that they both have $1 million in annual sales, including $700,000 in credit sales. Thus, on average, they both have average daily credit sales of $1,918 ($700,000 total credit sales ÷ 365 days). However, there is an important difference between the two firms. Fast Company has only $48,000 in accounts receivable, while Slow Company has $63,300 in accounts receivable. Why the difference? It is simple: Fast Company collects its credit sales every 25 days on average, while Slow Company takes 33 days to collect its accounts receivable, calculated as follows:

Fast Company:

$$\text{Day sales outstanding} = \frac{\text{Accounts receivable}}{\text{Annual credit sales} \div 365 \text{ days}} = \frac{\$48{,}000}{\$700{,}000 \div 365} = 25 \text{ days}$$

Slow Company:

$$\text{Days sales outstanding} = \frac{\text{Accounts receivable}}{\text{Annual credit sales} \div 365 \text{ days}} = \frac{\$63{,}300}{\$700{,}000 \div 365} = 33 \text{ days}$$

days sales outstanding (average collection period)
The number of days, on average, that a firm extends credit to its customers.

In other words, Slow Company takes longer to convert its accounts receivable into cash. It could very well have a cash flow problem if it does not have the ability to finance the greater investment in accounts receivable. This illustration, while hypothetical, is a real problem for many small businesses. Most business owners never think about the difficulties in collecting receivables when they start their own business.

For Ann LaWall, president and CEO of Ann LaWall & Co., chasing customers over delinquent payments to her consulting business was a burden that distracted her from managing the growth of her company. Worse, she feared the dreaded collection calls would jeopardize professional and personal relationships that she cherished. “I got tired of telling people I am not their banker,” says LaWall. “Sometimes you are dealing with friends or people you run into at the golf course, and you don’t want to be hunting them down for money.”[5]

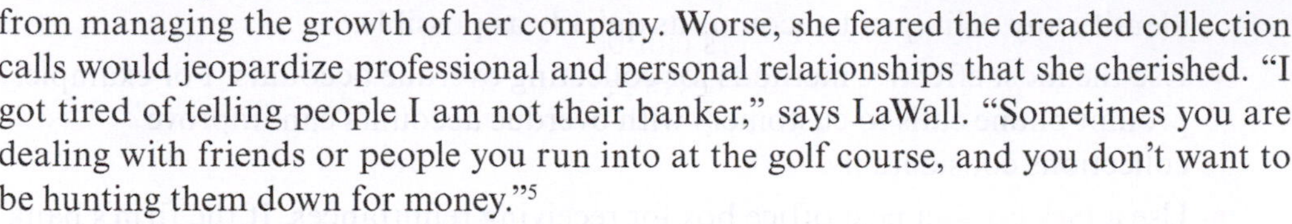

Through delegation and implementation of preemptive measures, LaWall’s stress over collections has disappeared. She says that some of the approaches cost her a little revenue, but she insists that they’ve been worth the expense. To lower the stress involved, LaWall suggests taking the following actions:[6]

- Hire someone else to handle collections one day per week.
- Accept credit cards.
- Sell the receivables to a third party.
- Where possible, require prepayment.
- For a service business, write a detailed work and payment schedule and have it signed by the customer.

In a recent meeting, Johnny Stites, CEO of J&S Construction, told an interesting story. Without saying anything, he posted a graph that was visible to the employee responsible for collecting receivables. The graph showed how quickly accounts receivable were being collected over time and Stites’s goal for how long he wanted it to take. He had intended to discuss the graph with the employee but failed to do so. Nevertheless, without anything else being done, the time that accounts receivable were outstanding began to decline. By providing a clear picture of actual performance versus desired performance, Stites enabled the employee to take ownership of achieving the goal. The outcome: Cash became available for other purposes.[7]

When dealing with large corporations, small companies are especially vulnerable to problems caused by slow collections. Some large firms have a practice of taking 60 or 90 days to pay an invoice, regardless of the credit terms stated in the invoice. Many small companies have had to file for bankruptcy because they could not get a large customer to pay according to the terms of the sale. Susana Ortiz, founder of Caroline’s Desserts, was surprised to find that many large retail customers were paying late during the 2008 economic slowdown. “If you’re small,” she says, “big companies think they can wait to pay you.”[8] It follows that what you do before you deliver a product or service on credit is far more important than what you do after you are owed. Consider this perspective:

> *In attempting to improve their cash position, most companies focus on activities that take place after product and service delivery. In fact, they have the order exactly backward, because the structure of the sale shapes everything that follows. To no small degree, whether an account ends up being easy to collect or difficult depends on what goes on before the contract is signed.*[9]

Mobile Payment Devices

If you want to turn sales into cash more quickly, consider using (1) *mobile card readers* (dongles), which typically attach to the audio jack of a smartphone, enabling merchants to swipe credit and debit cards from anywhere; (2) *electronic invoicing*, which can help automate invoices, receipts, and late notices; and/or (3) *photo card processing* (iPhone app), which enables merchants to take a photo of a customer’s credit card or debit card digits and instantly process payments on the go.

The following credit management practices can also have a positive effect on a firm's cash flows:

- Minimize the time between shipping, invoicing, and sending notices on billings.
- Review previous credit experiences to determine impediments to cash flows, such as the continued extension of credit to slow-paying or delinquent customers.
- Provide incentives for prompt payment by granting cash discounts or charging interest on delinquent accounts.
- Age accounts receivable on a monthly or even a weekly basis in order to identify any delinquent accounts as quickly as possible.
- Use the most effective methods for collecting overdue accounts. For example, prompt phone calls to customers with overdue accounts can improve collections considerably.
- Use a **lock box**—a post office box for receiving remittances. If the firm's bank maintains the lock box to which customers send their payments, it can immediately deposit any checks received into the company's account.

22-3c Accounts Receivable Financing

Some small businesses speed up the cash flow from accounts receivable by borrowing against them. By financing receivables, these firms can often secure the use of their money 30 to 60 days earlier than would be possible otherwise. Although this practice was once concentrated largely in the apparel industry, it has expanded to many other types of small businesses, such as manufacturers, food processors, distributors, and home building suppliers. Such financing is provided by commercial finance companies and some banks.

Two types of accounts receivable financing are available. The first type uses a firm's **pledged accounts receivable** as collateral for a loan. Payments received from customers are forwarded to the lending institution to pay off the loan. In the second type of financing, a business sells its accounts receivable to a finance company, a practice known as *factoring* (discussed in Chapter 12). The finance company thereby assumes the bad-debt risk associated with the receivables it buys.

lock box
A post office box for receiving remittances from customers.

pledged accounts receivable
Accounts receivable used as collateral for a loan.

The obvious advantage of accounts receivable financing is the immediate cash flow it provides for firms that have limited working capital. As a secondary benefit, the volume of borrowing can be quickly expanded proportionally in order to match a firm's growth in sales and accounts receivable.

A drawback to this type of financing is its high cost. Rates typically run several points above the prime interest rate, and factors charge a fee to compensate them for their credit investigation activities and for the risk that customers may default in payment. Another weakness of accounts receivable financing is that pledging receivables may limit a firm's ability to borrow from a bank by removing a prime asset from its available collateral.

Discuss the key financial issues in managing inventory.

22-4 MANAGING INVENTORY

Inventory is a "necessary evil" in the financial management system. It is "necessary" because supply and demand cannot be managed to coincide precisely with day-to-day operations; it is an "evil" because it ties up funds that are not actively productive.

22-4a Reducing Inventory to Free Cash

Inventory is a bigger problem for some small businesses than for others. The inventory of many service companies, for example, consists of only a few supplies. A manufacturer, on the other hand, has several types of inventory: raw materials, work in process, and finished goods. Retailers and wholesalers—especially those with high inventory turnover rates, such as firms in grocery distribution—are continually involved in solving inventory management problems.

Chapter 21 discussed several ideas related to purchasing and inventory management that are designed to minimize inventory carrying costs and processing costs. The emphasis in this section is on practices that will minimize average inventory levels, thereby releasing funds for other uses. The correct minimum level of inventory is the amount needed to maintain desired production schedules and/or a certain level of customer service. A concerted management effort can trim excess inventory and pay handsome dividends.

22-4b Monitoring Inventory

When it comes to managing inventory, small business owners have a tendency to overstock. Consider the following scenario, which plays out far too often:

> *A store manager might know intellectually that holding a lot of inventory is not a good idea, yet still justify hanging on to a few more TVs than the store will probably need—"just in case." Even though a department manager knows some oversupply might drag down overall efficiency a bit, in the scheme of things, the sacrifice for the department doesn't seem nearly as great as the potential pain of a stock-out. A little oversupply seems a smaller risk than the major disaster of having to shut down an assembly line or leave a store shelf empty.*[10]

One of the first steps in managing inventory is to discover what's in inventory and how long it's been there. Too often, items are purchased, warehoused, and essentially forgotten. A yearly inventory for accounting purposes is inadequate for proper inventory control. Items that are slow movers may sit in a retailer's inventory beyond the time when they should have been marked down for quick sale. Software programs can provide assistance in inventory identification and control. Although a physical inventory may still be required, its use will only serve to supplement the computerized system.

A commonly used statistic for monitoring inventory is **days in inventory**, which is the number of days, on average, that a business holds its inventory. Similar in concept to days sales outstanding (described earlier), it is calculated as follows:

$$\text{Days in inventory} = \frac{\text{Inventory}}{\text{Cost of goods sold} \div 365\text{ days}}$$

Recall that both Fast Company and Slow Company had $1 million in annual sales. Let's assume that they also had the same cost of goods sold of $600,000. So, they both sold their products for $1 million, and it cost them $600,000 to produce the products that were sold. If we restate the annual cost of goods sold to a daily cost of goods sold, we find it to be $1,644 ($600,000 cost of goods sold ÷ 365 days) for both companies. But while they sold the same amount of product at identical cost, Fast Company carries only $46,000 in inventory compared to Slow Company, which maintains an inventory of $57,500.

days in inventory
The number of days, on average, that a company holds inventory.

	Fast Company	Slow Company
Total sales	$1,000,000	$1,000,000
Cost of goods sold	$ 600,000	$ 600,000
Daily cost of goods sold	$ 1,644	$ 1,644
Inventory	$ 46,000	$ 57,500

Why would Slow Company have more inventory than Fast Company, given that they both have the same amount of sales? The answer is that Slow Company takes longer to sell its inventory. Fast Company, on average, carries inventory for 28 days, compared to 35 days for Slow Company.

Fast Company:

$$\text{Days in inventory} = \frac{\text{Inventory}}{\text{Cost of goods sold} \div 365 \text{ days}} = \frac{\$46{,}000}{\$600{,}000 \div 365 \text{ days}} = 28 \text{ days}$$

Slow Company:

$$\text{Days in inventory} = \frac{\text{Inventory}}{\text{Cost of goods sold} \div 365 \text{ days}} = \frac{\$57{,}500}{\$600{,}000 \div 365 \text{ days}} = 35 \text{ days}$$

In other words, Slow Company's slow rate of moving its inventory can lead to cash flow problems if it does not have the ability to finance the larger inventory.

22-4c Controlling Stockpiles

Small business managers tend to overbuy inventory for several reasons. First, enthusiasm may lead the manager to forecast greater demand than is realistic. Second, the personalization of the business–customer relationship may motivate a manager to stock everything customers want. Third, a price-conscious manager may be overly susceptible to a vendor's appeal to "buy now, because prices are going up."

Managers must exercise restraint when stockpiling. Improperly managed and uncontrolled stockpiling may greatly increase inventory carrying costs and place a heavy drain on the funds of a small business.

Living The Dream

USING TECHNOLOGY

Taking Stock of Inventory Management

Managing inventory effectively can make the difference between making or losing money—and maybe even bankruptcy. For example, Stephen Carroll owns Walking Equipment Company, a $3 million company located in Largo, Florida. His firm sells assistive walking products, such as walkers, wheelchairs, and canes, and ships up to 500 packages a day.

(continued on next page)

The company's inventory is divided into three different categories: domestically produced, overseas resellers items, and manufactured overseas items. He knows he needs about three turns on inventory for items manufactured, two turns for products from overseas, and one turn for items he can get domestically.

Carroll uses Stone Edge software from Monsoon Commerce. The software lets employees know where an item is and when it was taken off the shelves and shipped. In addition, it helps to create purchase orders based on past order history and to automate the order fulfillment process. Carroll says, "I no longer sit on inventory I don't need, which really helps my cash flow."

© MONKEY BUSINESS IMAGES/SHUTTERSTOCK.COM

Recently, Carroll started using add-on software to ensure that orders are packaged correctly. With the add-on, warehouse packing employees use handheld barcode readers that make the packing process more efficient. Carroll explains,

> *I now can hire new employees, and within a few minutes they can be ready to pack an order. Previously, I had to rely on employees who memorized the product locations in the warehouse.*

The new system allows the order packers to scan a barcode on an order, which will indicate the items needed and the location in the warehouse. They then scan the barcode on the item and can hear an audible notification to indicate if it is the correct item on the order. It also will give an audible notification when all the items on the order have been picked.

By closely managing inventory, Carroll says his company saves tens of thousands of dollars annually.

Source: Personal communication with Stephen Carroll, September 26, 2014.

22-5 MANAGING ACCOUNTS PAYABLE

Describe key issues in managing accounts payable.

Cash flow management and accounts payable management are intertwined. As long as a payable is outstanding, the buying firm can keep cash equal to that amount in its own checking account. When payment is made, however, that firm's cash account is reduced accordingly.

All else being the same, a small business owner would want to delay payment as long as possible, without damaging the firm's reputation by failing to live up to its agreements. Although payables are legal obligations, they can be paid at various times or even renegotiated in some cases. Any business is subject to an emergency situation and may find it necessary to ask creditors to postpone payment on its payable obligations. Usually, creditors will cooperate in working out a solution because it's in their best interest for a client firm to succeed.

"Buy now, pay later" is the motto of many entrepreneurs. By buying on credit, a small business is using creditors' funds to supply short-term cash needs. The longer creditors' funds can be borrowed, the better. Payment, therefore, should be delayed as long as acceptable under the agreement. As we did with accounts receivable and inventory, we can compute **days in payables**, which tells us how many days a company takes to pay its accounts payable. We compute it as follows:[11]

days in payables The number of days, on average, that a business takes to pay its accounts payable.

$$\text{Days in payables} = \frac{\text{Accounts in payable}}{\text{Cost of goods sold} \div 365 \text{ days}}$$

Mistakes to Avoid in Managing Working Capital

The following mistakes can cost your company dearly:

1. Managing only the income statement, while ignoring the balance sheet.
2. Rewarding the sales force for increasing sales, without regard for controlling costs.
3. Overemphasizing quality in production when it requires large amounts of cash without measurably enhancing the firm's reputation.
4. Using only the current ratio (current assets ÷ current liabilities) to measure your company's liquidity, which encourages you to hold larger amounts of accounts receivable and inventory and lower amounts of accounts payable.
5. Becoming complacent if the metrics being used for comparison make you look better than your competitors.

Using the information already provided for Fast Company and Slow Company, and knowing that they have $65,800 and $49,300 in accounts payable, respectively, we can compute the days in payables for each firm as follows:

Fast Company:

$$\text{Days in payables} = \frac{\text{Accounts payable}}{\text{Cost of good sold} \div 365\text{days}} = \frac{\$65{,}800}{\$600{,}000 \div 365\text{days}} = 40 \text{ days}$$

Slow Company:

$$\text{Days in payables} = \frac{\text{Accounts payable}}{\text{Cost of good sold} \div 365 \text{ days}} = \frac{\$49{,}300}{\$600{,}000 \div 365 \text{ days}} = 30 \text{ days}$$

Typically, accounts payable (trade credit) involve payment terms that include a cash discount. With trade discount terms, paying later may be inappropriate. For example, terms of 3/10, net 30, offer a 3 percent potential discount. Exhibit 22.5 shows the possible settlement costs over the credit period of 30 days. Note that for a $20,000 purchase, a settlement of only $19,400 is required if payment is made within the first 10 days ($20,000 less the 3 percent discount of $600). Between day 11 and day 30, the full settlement of $20,000 is required. After 30 days, the settlement cost may exceed the original amount, as late-payment fees are added.

The timing question then becomes "Should the account be paid on day 10 or day 30?" There is little reason to pay $19,400 on days 1 through 9, when the same amount will settle the account on day 10. Likewise, if payment is to be made after day 10, it makes sense to wait until day 30 to pay the $20,000.

By paying on the last day of the discount period, the buyer saves the amount of the discount offered. The other alternative of paying on day 30 allows the buyer to use the seller's money for an additional 20 days by forgoing the discount. As Exhibit 22.5 shows, the buyer can use the seller's $19,400 for 20 days at a cost of $600. The percentage annual interest rate can be calculated as follows:

$$\begin{aligned}\text{Percentage annual interest rate} &= \frac{\text{Days in year}}{\text{Net period} - \text{Cash discount period}} \times \frac{\text{Cash discount\%}}{100\% - \text{Cash discount\%}} \\ &= \frac{365}{30 - 10} \times \frac{3\%}{100\% - 3\%} \\ &= 18.25 \times 0.030928 \\ &= 0.564, \text{ or } 56.4\%\end{aligned}$$

By failing to take a discount, a business typically pays a higher rate for use of a supplier's money—56.4 percent per year in this case. Payment on day 10 appears to be the most logical choice. Recall, however, that payment also affects cash flows. If funds are extremely short, a small firm may have to wait to pay until the last possible day in order to avoid an overdraft at the bank.

EXHIBIT **22.5** An Accounts Payable Timetable For Terms Of 3/10, Net 30

Timetable (days after invoice date)	Settlement Costs for a $20,000 purchase
Days 1 through 10	$19,400
Days 11 through 30	$20,000
Day 31 and thereafter	$20,000 + possible late penalty and deterioration in credit rating

22-6 CASH CONVERSION PERIOD REVISITED

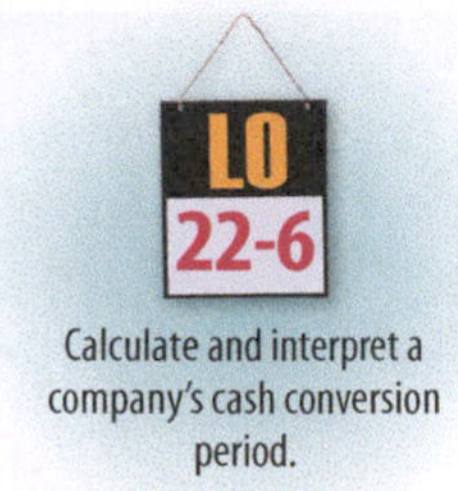

Calculate and interpret a company's cash conversion period.

Earlier in the chapter, we presented the working capital cycle, explaining that the cash conversion period should be a key concern for any small business. As you will recall, the cash conversion period is the time span during which the firm's investment in accounts receivable and inventory must be financed or, more simply, the time required to convert paid-for inventory and accounts receivable into cash. To reinforce this concept, we can use the information we have for Fast Company and Slow Company to compute these two firms' cash conversion periods:

$$\text{Cash conversion period} = \text{Days in inventory} + \text{Days sales out standing} - \text{Days in payables}$$

	Fast Company	Slow Company
Days in inventory	28	35
Days sales outstanding	25	33
Days in inventory and receivables	53	68
Less days in payables	(40)	(30)
Cash conversion period (days)	13	38

Time Is Money!

Each component of working capital (accounts receivable, inventory, and accounts payable) has two dimensions: *time* and *money*. If you can move money faster through the cycle, the business will generate more cash more quickly. Also, if you can negotiate improved terms with suppliers, receiving a longer time to pay or an increased credit limit, you effectively create free financing to help fund future growth.

So, the time from inventory being purchased until it is sold on credit and the accounts receivable are collected is 53 days for Fast Company and 68 days for Slow Company. But both firms are granted trade credit from their suppliers. Fast Company has negotiated credit terms of 40 days before having to pay for its purchases, compared to Slow Company's 30 days. Essentially, Fast Company's suppliers have granted it a loan for 40 days, while Slow Company has a loan for only 30 days.

We see that Fast Company will need to finance 13 days with working capital, while Slow Company will have to finance 38 days. Thus, as both firms grow, Slow Company will have much more pressure on its cash flows than will Fast Company.

22-7 CAPITAL BUDGETING TECHNIQUES

Discuss the techniques commonly used in making capital budgeting decisions.

We turn now to the management of a small firm's long-term assets—equipment and plant—or what is called *capital budgeting*.

Some capital budgeting decisions that might be made by a small firm include (1) developing a new product that shows promise but requires additional study and improvement, (2) replacing a firm's delivery trucks with newer models, (3) expanding sales activity into a new territory, (4) constructing a new building, and (5) hiring additional salespersons to intensify selling in the existing market.

Capital budgeting analysis forms the framework for a company's long-term future development and can have a profound effect on a company's future earnings and growth. For this reason, it is important that a small business owner makes capital budgeting decisions based only on careful analysis.

Capital budgeting analysis
An analytical method that helps managers make decisions about long-term investments.

ZADOROZHNYI VIKTOR/SHUTTERSTOCK.COM

The three major techniques for making capital budgeting decisions are (1) the accounting return on investment technique, (2) the payback period technique, and (3) the discounted cash flow technique, using either net present value or internal rate of return. They all attempt to answer the same basic question: Do the future benefits from an investment exceed the cost of making the investment? However, each technique addresses this general question by focusing on a different specific question:

1. *Accounting return on investment:* How many dollars in average profits are generated per dollar of average investment?
2. *Payback period:* How long will it take to recover the original investment outlay?
3. *Discounted cash flows:* How does the present value of future benefits from the investment compare to the investment outlay?

Three simple rules are used in judging the merits of an investment. Although they may seem trite, the rules state in simple terms the best thinking about the attractiveness of an investment.

1. The investor prefers more cash rather than less cash.
2. The investor prefers cash sooner rather than later.
3. The investor prefers less risk rather than more risk.

With these criteria in mind, let's now look at each of the three capital budgeting techniques in detail.

22-7a Accounting Return on Investment

A small business invests to earn profits. The **accounting return on investment technique** compares the average annual after-tax profits a firm expects to receive with the average book value of the investment.

Average annual after-tax profits can be estimated by adding the after-tax profits expected over the life of the project and then dividing that amount by the number of years the project is expected to last. The average book value of an investment is equivalent to the average of the initial outlay and the estimated final projected salvage value. In making an accept-reject decision, the owner compares the calculated return to a minimum acceptable return, which is usually determined based on past experience.

To examine the use of the accounting return on investment technique, assume that you are contemplating buying a piece of equipment for $10,000 and depreciating it over four years to a book value of $0 (it will have no salvage value). Further assume that you expect the investment to generate after-tax profits each year as follows:

Year	After-Tax Profits
1	$1,000
2	2,000
3	2,500
4	3,000

accounting return on investment technique
A capital budgeting technique that compares expected average annual after-tax profits to the average book value of an investment.

The accounting return on the proposed investment is calculated as follows:

$$\text{Accounting return on invesment} = \frac{\text{Average annual after} - \text{tax profits}}{\text{Average book value of the investment}}$$

$$\text{Accounting return on invesment} = \frac{\left(\frac{\$1{,}000 + \$2{,}000 + \$2{,}500 + \$3{,}000}{4}\right)}{\left(\frac{\$10{,}000 - \$0}{2}\right)}$$

$$= \frac{\$2{,}125}{\$5{,}000} = 0.425\text{, or } 42.5\%$$

For most people, a 42.5 percent profit rate would seem outstanding. Assuming the calculated accounting return on investment of 42.5 percent exceeds your minimum acceptable return, you will accept the project. If not, you will reject the investment—provided, of course, that you have confidence in the technique.

Although the accounting return on investment is easy to calculate, it has two major shortcomings. First, it is based on accounting profits rather than actual cash flows received. An investor is more interested in the future cash produced by the investment than in the reported profits. Second, this technique ignores the time value of money. Thus, although popular, the accounting return on investment technique fails to satisfy any of the three rules concerning an investor's preference for receiving more cash sooner with less risk.

22-7b Payback Period

The **payback period technique**, as the name suggests, measures how long it will take to recover the initial cash outlay of an investment. It deals with cash flows as opposed to accounting profits. The merits of a project are judged on whether the initial investment outlay can be recovered in less time than some maximum acceptable payback period. For example, an owner may not want to invest in any project that will require more than five years to recoup the original investment.

To illustrate the payback method, let's assume that a small business owner is considering an investment in equipment with an expected life of 10 years. The investment outlay will be $15,000, with the cost of the equipment depreciated on a straight-line basis, at $1,500 per year. If the owner makes the investment, the annual after-tax profits have been estimated to be as follows:

Years	After-Tax Profits
1–2	$1,000
3–6	2,000
7–10	2,500

To determine the after-tax cash flows from the investment, the owner merely adds back the depreciation of $1,500 each year to the profit. The reason for adding the depreciation to the profit is that it was deducted when the profits were calculated (as an accounting entry), even though it was not a cash outflow. The results, then, are as follows:

Years	After-Tax Cash Flows
1–2	$2,500
3–6	3,500
7–10	4,000

payback period technique
A capital budgeting technique that measures the amount of time it will take to recover the initial cash outlay of an investment.

By the end of the second year, the owner will have recovered $5,000 of the investment outlay ($2,500 per year). By the end of the fourth year, another $7,000, or $12,000 in total, will have been recouped. The additional $3,000 can be recovered in the fifth year, when $3,500 is expected. Thus, it will take 4.86 years $[4 \text{ years} + (\$3{,}000 \div \$3{,}500)]$ to recover the investment. Since the maximum acceptable payback is less than five years, the owner will accept the investment.

Many managers and owners of companies use the payback period technique in evaluating investment decisions. Although it uses cash flows rather than accounting profits, this technique has two significant weaknesses. First, it does not consider the time value of money (cash is preferred sooner rather than later). Second, it fails to consider the cash flows received after the payback period (more cash is preferred, rather than less).

22-7c Discounted Cash Flows

Managers can avoid the deficiencies of the accounting return on investment and payback period techniques by using discounted cash flow analysis. Discounted cash flow techniques take into consideration the fact that cash received today is more valuable than cash received one year from now (called the *time value of money*). For example, interest can be earned on cash that is available for immediate investment. This is not true for cash to be received at some future date. **Discounted cash flow (DCF) techniques** compare the present value of future cash flows with the investment outlay. Such an analysis may take either of two forms: net present value or internal rate of return.

discounted cash flow (DCF) techniques
Capital budgeting techniques that compare the present value of future cash flows with the cost of the initial investment.

net present value (NPV)
The present value of expected future cash flows less the initial investment outlay.

internal rate of return (IRR)
The rate of return a firm expects to earn on a project.

The **net present value (NPV)** method estimates the current value of the cash that will flow into the firm from the project in the future and deducts the amount of the initial outlay. To find the present value of expected future cash flows, we discount them back to the present at the firm's cost of capital, where the cost of capital is equal to the investors' required rate of return. If the net present value of the investment is positive (that is, if the present value of future cash flows discounted at the rate of return required to satisfy the firm's investors exceeds the initial outlay), the project is acceptable.

The **internal rate of return (IRR)** method estimates the rate of return that can be expected from a contemplated investment. To calculate the IRR, you must find the discount rate that gets the present value of all future cash inflows just equal to the cost of the project, which is also the rate that gives you a zero net present value. For the investment outlay to be attractive, the internal rate of return must exceed the firm's cost of capital—the rate of return required to satisfy the firm's investors.

Discounted cash flow techniques can generally be trusted to provide a more reliable basis for decisions than can the accounting return on investment or the payback period technique.

Describe the capital budgeting practices of small firms.

22-8 CAPITAL BUDGETING PRACTICES IN SMALL FIRMS

In the past, few small business owners relied on any type of quantitative analysis in making capital budgeting decisions. The decision to buy new equipment or expand facilities was based more on intuition and instinct than on economic analysis. If any quantitative analysis was used, it was usually the payback period technique, followed by the accounting return on investment technique. Rarely did small business owners use the discounted cash flow (DCF) methods.

More recently, an increasing number of small business owners are using some form of quantitative measure to assess a capital investment, but it is complemented by judgment based on their experience. It is also encouraging that a larger number of owners are attempting to forecast future cash flows as part of their analysis. Still, only a small number of owners rely on discounted cash flow techniques.

We could conclude that small business owners are still not very sophisticated about using theoretically sound financial methods. However, the cause of their limited use of DCF tools probably has more to do with the nature of small business itself than with the owners' unwillingness to learn. Several important reasons might explain the limited use of these financial techniques, including the following:

- For many owners of small firms, the business is an extension of their lives—that is, business events affect them personally. The same is true in reverse: What happens to the owner personally affects his or her decisions about the firm. The firm and its owner are inseparable. Consequently, nonfinancial variables may play a significant part in an owner's decisions. For example, the desire to be viewed as a respected part of the community may be more important to an owner than the present value of a business decision.
- The undercapitalization and liquidity problems of a small business can directly affect the decision-making process, and survival often becomes the top priority. Long-term planning, therefore, is not viewed by the owner as a high priority in the total scheme of things.
- The greater uncertainty of cash flows within small firms makes long-term forecasting and planning seem unappealing and even a waste of time. The owner simply has no confidence in his or her ability to predict cash flows beyond two or three years, so calculating the cash flows for the entire life of a project is viewed as a futile effort.
- The value of a closely held firm is less easily observed than that of a publicly held firm, whose securities are actively traded in the marketplace. Therefore, the owner of a small firm may consider the market-value rule of maximizing net present values irrelevant. Estimating the cost of capital is also much more difficult for a small company than for a large firm.
- The limited size of a small firm's projects may make net present value computations less feasible in a practical sense. The time and expense required to analyze a capital investment are generally the same whether the project is large or small, so it is relatively more costly for a small firm to conduct such a study.
- Financial management talent within a small firm is a scarce resource. The owner-manager frequently has a technical background, as opposed to a business or finance orientation, and his or her perspective is influenced greatly by that background.

These characteristics of a small business and its owner have a significant effect on the decision-making process within the firm. The result is often a short-term mindset, caused partly by necessity and partly by choice. However, the owner of a small firm should make every effort to use discounted cash flow techniques and to be certain that contemplated investments will, in fact, provide returns that exceed the firm's cost of capital.

22-1. **Describe the working capital cycle of a small business.**

- A firm's working capital cycle is the flow of resources through the company's accounts as part of its day-to-day operations.
- The only current liability included in the working capital cycle is accounts payable.
- The working capital cycle begins with the purchase or production of inventory and ends with the collection of accounts receivable.
- The cash conversion period is critical because it is the time period during which cash flow problems can arise.

22-2. **Identify the important issues in managing a firm's cash flow.**

- A firm's cash flows consist of cash flowing into a business (through sales revenue, borrowing, and so on) and cash flowing out of the business (through purchases, operating expenses, and so on).
- Calculating cash flows requires that a small business owner distinguish between sales revenue and cash receipts and between expenses and disbursements.
- To anticipate when cash will enter and leave a business, an owner *must* develop a cash budget.

22-3. **Explain the key issues in managing accounts receivable.**

- The most important factor in managing cash well is the ability to collect accounts receivable quickly.
- Granting credit to customers, although primarily a marketing decision, directly affects a firm's cash account.
- Days sales outstanding measures how many days, on average, a firm extends credit to its customers.
- Some small businesses speed up the cash flows from receivables by borrowing against them.
- The two types of accounts receivable financing are pledged accounts receivable and factoring.

22-4. **Discuss the key financial issues in managing inventory.**

- A concerted effort to manage inventory can trim excess inventory and free cash for other uses.
- Days in inventory represents the number of days, on average, that a company carries inventory.
- Improperly managed and uncontrolled stockpiling may greatly increase inventory carrying costs and place a heavy drain on the funds of a small business.

22-5. **Describe key issues in managing accounts payable.**

- Accounts payable, a primary source of financing for small firms, directly affect a firm's cash flow situation.
- Financial management of accounts payable hinges on paying at various times and renegotiating in some cases.
- Days in payables is a measure of how long a business takes to pay its suppliers.

22-6. **Calculate and interpret a company's cash conversion period.**

- The cash conversion period is the time span during which a firm's investment in accounts receivable and inventory must be financed.
- A cash conversion period equals days in inventory plus days sales outstanding minus days in payables.

22-7. **Discuss the techniques commonly used in making capital budgeting decisions.**

- Capital budgeting techniques include accounting return on investment, payback period, and discounted cash flows.
- The accounting return on investment technique compares the average annual after-tax profits a firm expects to receive with the average book value of the investment.
- This technique has two significant shortcomings: It is based on accounting profits rather than actual cash flows received, and it ignores the time value of money.
- The payback period technique measures how long it will take to recover the initial cash outlay of an investment.
- This technique also has two major weaknesses: It ignores the time value of money, and it doesn't consider cash flows received after the payback period.
- The discounted cash flow techniques—net present value and internal rate of return—compare the present value of future cash flows with the investment outlay.
- DCF techniques provide the best basis for decision making in capital budgeting analysis.

22-8. Describe the capital budgeting practices of small firms.

- Increasing numbers of small business owners are using some type of quantitative measure to assess a capital investment, along with judgment based on their experience.
- The short-term mindset of small firms may explain, to some degree, why they seldom use the conceptually richer techniques for evaluating long-term investments.
- Nonfinancial variables, attempts to just survive, uncertainty of cash flows, difficulty in estimating the cost of capital, and an owner's lack of a business background all affect the decision-making process in a small company.

Key Terms

You Make the Call

Situation 1

A small company specializing in the sale and installation of swimming pools was profitable but has devoted very little attention to the management of its working capital. It had, for example, never prepared or used a cash budget.

To be sure that money was available for payments as needed, the firm kept a minimum of $25,000 in a checking account. At times, this account grew larger; it totaled $43,000 on one occasion. The owner felt that this approach to cash management worked well for the small company because it eliminated all of the paperwork associated with cash budgeting. Moreover, it enabled the firm to pay its bills in a timely manner. (*Note:* In answering the questions for this situation, refer both to this chapter and to Chapter 10, where we describe cash budgets.)

Question 1 What are the advantages and weaknesses of the minimum cash balance practice?

Question 2 There is a saying, "If it ain't broke, don't fix it." In view of the firm's present success in paying bills promptly, should it be encouraged to use a cash budget? Be prepared to support your answer.

Situation 2

Ruston Manufacturing Company is a small firm selling entirely on a credit basis. It has experienced successful operations and earned modest profits.

Sales are made on the basis of net payment in 30 days. Collections from customers run approximately 70 percent in 30 days, 20 percent in 60 days, 7 percent in 90 days, and 3 percent remain uncollected.

The owner has considered the possibility of offering a cash discount for early payment. However, the practice seems costly and possibly unnecessary. As the owner puts it, "Why should I bribe customers to pay what they legally owe?"

Question 1 Is offering a cash discount the equivalent of a bribe?

Question 2 How would a cash discount policy relate to bad debts?

Question 3 What cash discount policy, if any, would you recommend?

Question 4 What other approaches might the owner use to improve cash flows from receivables?

Situation 3

Below are the financial statements of two general contractors. The two companies are primarily commercial builders, as opposed to residential builders. They typically bid for the opportunity to build such facilities as office buildings, hospitals, and university buildings. As the general contractor, they use subcontractors who undertake most of the actual work. (*Note:* While the financial information provided is real in this situation, the names of the companies have been changed to maintain confidentiality.)

Balance Sheets	BRC, Inc.		Arch Construction	
Assets				
Current assets				
Cash	$ 1,199,921	4.1%*	$ 2,826,328	10.2%*
Short-term Investment	14,704,132	50.4%	16,239,811	58.7%
Accounts receivable	12,460,468	42.7%	7,307,234	26.4%
Other current assets	21,482	0.1%	34,067	0.1%
Total current assets	$ 28,386,008	97.2%	$ 26,407,440	95.5%
Property and equipment	807,597	2.8%	1,252,408	4.5%
TOTAL ASSETS	$ 29,193,600	100.0%	$ 27,659,848	100.0%
Debt (Liabilities) and Equity				
Current liabilities				
Short-term notes	$ 72,322	0.2%*	$ 79,564	0.3%*
Accounts payable	19,975,233	68.4%	14,898,131	53.9%
Accrued liabilities	899,472	3.1%	2,068,695	7.5%
Total current liabilities	$ 20,947,027	71.8%	$ 17,046,390	61.7%
Long-term debt	1,862,265	6.4%	1,782,700	6.4%
Total debt	$ 22,809,292	78.1%	$ 18,829,090	68.1%
Stockholders' equity				
Common stock	$ 4,254	0.0%	$ 4,254	0.0%
Paid in capital	768,281	2.6%	768,281	2.8%
Retained earnings	5,611,773	19.2%	8,058,223	29.1%
Total stockholders' equity	$ 6,384,308	21.9%	8,830,758	31.9%
TOTAL DEBT AND EQUITY	$ 29,193,600	100.0%	$ 27,659,848	100.0%

Income Statements	BRC, Inc.		Arch Construction	
Construction revenues	$ 90,070,000	100.0%*	$ 72,822,725	100.0%*
Cost of goods sold	(86,889,570)	(96.5)%	(68,090,781)	(93.5)%
Gross profits	$ 3,180,430	3.5%	$ 4,731,944	6.5%
Interest income	941,631	1.0%	1,308,801	1.8%
Total revenues	$ 4,122,061	4.6%	$6,040,745	8.3%
Operating expenses	1,665,711	1.8%	2,033,400	2.8%
Interest expense	226,367	0.3%	172,158	0.2%
Other expense	79,630	0.1%	123,737	0.2
Total expenses	$ (1,971,708)	(2.2)%	$ (2,329,295)	(3.2%)
Net profits	$ 2,150,353	2.4%	$ 3,711,450	5.1%

* All percentages have been rounded.

Question 1 Based on the information in the balance sheets, what do you notice about the nature of the general contracting business in terms of working capital? How are the two companies alike, and how do they differ?

Question 2 Have a general contractor explain to you what the financial statements say about this type of business.

Question 3 Compute the cash conversion period for each company, and interpret your findings.

Case 22

Pearson Air Conditioning & Service (p. 690)

This case looks at the financial performance of a small air conditioning and heating services company, with emphasis on its working capital policies.

Alternative Cases for Chapter 22

Case 10, Harper & Reiman, LLC, p. 662
Video Case 10, B2B CFO [website only]

Endnotes

1. The illustration in this section will remind you of the Lemonade Kids example in Chapter 10.
2. Michael Beller, "Go with the Flow," *MyBusiness*, May–June, 2013, p. 29, http://www.nfib.com/article/go-with-the-flow-62772, accessed March 12, 2015.
3. "2014 Working Capital Survey," http://www.relconsultancy.com, accessed March 17, 2015.
4. "Take Control of Your Working Capital," http://www.relconsultancy.com, accessed March 20, 2015.
5. Lena Basha, "Handle the Headaches," *MyBusiness*, June–July 2007, pp. 26–29, http://www.mybusinessmag.com/fullstory.php3?sid=1589, accessed March 26, 2015.
6. *Ibid.*
7. Personal interview with Johnny Stites, December 15, 2014.
8. Simona Covel and Kelly K. Spors, "To Help Collect the Bills, Firms Try the Soft Touch," *The Wall Street Journal*, January 27, 2009, p. B6.
9. "Buried Treasures: Unlocking Cash from Your Accounts Receivable," http://www.relconsultancy.com, accessed March 25, 2015.
10. "The Cure for Inventory Hoarding," http://www.relconsultancy.com, accessed March 15, 2015.
11. We use cost of goods sold in these equations as a reasonable approximation in order to simplify the presentation. To be more accurate, the equations should use the amount of purchases a company has made from suppliers, where purchases would be as follows:

$$\text{Purchases} = \text{Cost of goods sold} + \text{Change in inventory for the time period}$$

CHAPTER 23

Managing Risk

After studying this chapter, you should be able to. . .

23-1. Define *business risk*, and explain its two dimensions.

23-2. Identify the basic types of pure risk.

23-3. Describe the steps in the risk management process, and explain how risk management can be used in small companies.

23-4. Explain the basic principles used in evaluating an insurance program.

23-5. Identify the common types of business insurance coverage.

It can happen before you know it. One day, you have plenty of funds in your bank account; the next day, the money is gone. And the culprit isn't a client you've lost, a bad economy, or even a disgruntled employee. It's a hacker who has found a way to sneak into your online bank account, view sensitive financial data, and steal from your business. This scenario has become a cruel reality for some small business owners, and it presents a risk for anyone who conducts business or keeps financial records online.

Like most business owners, Bob Gray, owner of Vickery, Ohio–based Homestead Interior Doors, had virus protection for the firm's computers as well as a minimal firewall, but it wasn't enough to keep hackers from swiping $100,000 from his online business bank account late last year.

In the SPOTLIGHT
Homestead Interior Doors
www.door.cc

"I noticed a $50,000 transfer was posted on my account that didn't look right," he says. "I didn't remember doing anything like that. Then, right before my eyes, another $50,000 transfer popped up."

Gray eventually recovered half of the money, but it took several agonizing months of working with his bank and lawyers to sort things out. "There were times that I was convinced I was going to lose my business over this," says Gray, whose cash flows and incoming customer payments were frozen after the attack. "I was lucky because it could have been worse. I could have been wiped out completely."

Though he's more cautious now, Gray says, "These hackers are learning new stuff every day; they're staying one step ahead of the protections and will keep trying to figure out how to get into your computer if they think they can get money out of you. You've got to be vigilant. Nobody takes it seriously until it happens to them—but they need to because they could wake up one morning and have no money and no business."

Source: Emily McMackin, "Click Here to Destroy Your Business," *MyBusiness*, January–February 2010, pp. 32–34.

We live in a world of uncertainty, so understanding risk is vitally important in almost all dimensions of life. Risk must certainly be considered in making any business decisions. As sixth-century Greek poet and statesman Solon wrote,

> *There is risk in everything that one does, and no one knows where he will make his land-fall when his enterprise is at its beginning. One man, trying to act effectively, fails to foresee something and falls into great and grim ruination, but to another man, one who is acting ineffectively, a god gives good fortune in everything and escape from his folly.*[1]

Solon's insight reminds us that little is new in the world—including the need to acknowledge and compensate as best we can for the risks we encounter.

Risk means different things to different people. For a student, it might be represented by the possibility of failing an exam. For a retired person, risk could be the likelihood of not being able to live comfortably on limited income. For an entrepreneur, it takes the form of the possibility that a new venture will fail.

Benjamin Franklin once said, "In this world, nothing can be said to be certain, except death and taxes." Small business owners might extend this adage to include business risks. Chapter 1 noted the moderate risk-taking propensities of entrepreneurs and their desire to exert some control over the perilous situations in which they find themselves by minimizing business risks as much as possible. This chapter outlines how this can be done.

business risk
The possibility of losses associated with the assets and earnings potential of a firm.

market risk
The uncertainty associated with an investment decision.

pure risk
The uncertainty associated with a situation where only loss or no loss can occur.

23-1 WHAT IS BUSINESS RISK?

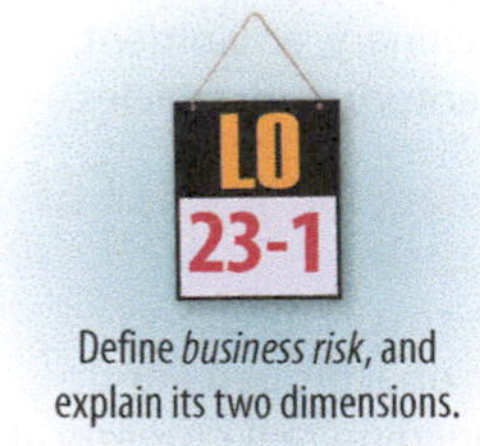

Define *business risk*, and explain its two dimensions.

Simply stated, *risk* is the "possibility of suffering harm or loss."[2] **Business risk**, then, is the possibility of losses associated with the assets and earnings potential of a firm. Here, the term *assets* includes not only inventory and equipment, but also such factors as a firm's employees, its customers, and its reputation.

The nature of business risk can be observed from two perspectives: market risk and pure risk. **Market risk** is the uncertainty associated with an investment decision. An entrepreneur who invests in a new business hopes for a gain but realizes that the eventual outcome may be a loss. Only after identifying the investment opportunity, developing strategies, and committing resources will she or he learn the final result.

Pure risk describes a situation where only loss or no loss can occur—there is no potential gain. Owning property, for instance, creates the possibility of loss due to fire or severe weather. The only outcomes are loss or no loss. As a general rule, only pure risk is insurable. That is, insurance is not intended to protect investors from market risks, where the chances of both gain and loss exist.

© SERGEY NIVENS/SHUTTERSTOCK.COM

Identify the basic types of pure risk.

23-2 BASIC TYPES OF PURE RISK

The pure risks that any business faces can be categorized as property, liability, and personnel. Let's take a look at these types of pure risk, which are related to the physical, legal, and human aspects of a business.

23-2a Property Risks

In the course of establishing a business, an owner acquires the property that will be necessary to provide the products and services of the company. If this property is damaged or destroyed, the business sustains a loss. In addition, the temporary loss of use of the property can add to the negative financial impact on the business. Several characteristics of business property and the risks associated with it are worthy of attention.

There are two general types of property—real property and personal property. **Real property** consists of land and anything physically attached to land, such as buildings. Some business owners purchase land and buildings, while others choose to lease necessary real property. It is important to note, however, that some leases make the lessee responsible for any damage or loss to the leased premises. **Personal property** can be defined simply as any property other than real property. Personal property includes machinery, equipment (such as computers), furniture, fixtures, inventory, and vehicles. While the location of real property is fixed, personal property can be moved from place to place. Among the risks to the personal property of the small firm are the security threats to its computers posed by hackers and spyware.

Property can be valued in several ways. The **replacement value of property** is the cost of replacing personal property and rebuilding real property at today's prices. For example, a building that was constructed 10 years ago at a cost of $1,000,000 may have a current replacement value of $1,400,000 because of the rising costs of materials and labor. The **actual cash value (ACV)** of property is very different from its replacement value, as this insurance term refers to the depreciated value of property. Assuming a rate of depreciation of 3 percent per year for the same 10-year-old building, we would find the building to have an estimated actual cash value of $980,000 (that is, $\$1,400,000 - [0.03 \times 10 \times \$1,400,000]$). By common practice, most commercial property insurance policies provide replacement value coverage as opposed to actual cash value coverage.

Property insurance also takes into account two primary features: perils (the cause) and losses (the effect).

real property
Land and anything physically attached to the land, such as buildings.

personal property
Any property other than real property, including machinery, equipment, inventory, and vehicles.

replacement value of property
The cost of replacing personal property and rebuilding real property at today's prices.

actual cash value (ACV)
An insurance term that refers to the depreciated value of property.

peril
A cause of loss, either through natural events or through the actions of people.

direct loss
A loss in which physical damage to property reduces its value to the property owner.

PERILS

A **peril** is defined as a cause of loss. Some perils are naturally occurring events, such as windstorms, floods, earthquakes, and lightning. The location of a property may increase the likelihood of its loss from certain perils—for example, coastal properties are more susceptible to wind damage and flooding, and properties near fault lines are more prone to damage from earthquakes.

Not all perils, however, are natural events; some are related to the actions of people. Perils such as theft and vandalism involve criminal acts performed by people against business owners. The rapid growth of e-commerce has led to new forms of dishonest acts, such as hacking, denial of access, and improper use of confidential information.

LOSSES

Usually, when you think of property loss, you envision a **direct loss**, in which physical damage to property reduces its value to the property owner. Direct loss of property as a result of a windstorm, fire, or explosion is obvious to everyone and has the potential to significantly hinder any business.

A less obvious type of property loss is an **indirect loss**, which arises from an inability to carry on normal operations due to a direct loss. For example, if a delivery truck is damaged in an accident, the resulting loss of its use can impair the ability of a business to get its products to customers. The indirect loss component of this event may cause a reduction in revenue or an increase in expenses (from having to outsource the delivery function), either of which will have an adverse impact on business income.

Business income can also be reduced by events or conditions that are not related to direct losses. For example, a strike by UPS employees several years ago created serious logistical problems for many of its business customers, which were unable to receive deliveries from suppliers or distribute products to customers. The financial impact of such a labor action may be just as real to a business as physical damage to property, but the insurance protection available for indirect losses applies only when *direct* damage events trigger the loss of use. This issue is discussed in more detail later in the chapter.

23-2b Liability Risks

A growing business risk today is the legal liability that may arise from various business activities. A society creates laws to govern interactions among its members. Individual rights and freedoms are protected by these laws. If a business or any of its agents violates these protected rights, the business can be held accountable for any resulting loss or damage to the affected party. Legal liability may arise from statutory liability, contractual liability, or tort liability.

STATUTORY LIABILITY

Some laws impose a statutory obligation on a business. For example, each state has enacted **workers' compensation legislation** that in most cases requires employers to provide certain benefits to employees when they are injured in a work-related incident, without regard to fault. While the benefits differ slightly from state to state, most workers' compensation statutes require employers to provide the following benefits to employees injured at work: coverage of medical expenses, compensation for lost wages, payment of rehabilitation expenses, and death benefits for employees' families.

This statutory liability is potentially significant for any business. The attacks on the World Trade Center provided a stark example of the magnitude of this liability, especially for companies whose employees worked in a concentrated area. Marsh, Inc., one of the leading insurance brokers in the world, lost over 300 employees in the 9/11 disaster, creating an enormous financial obligation on the part of the employer to the families of the victims. Most businesses protect themselves from this type of financial loss through the purchase of workers' compensation insurance. Some large employers choose to self-insure (that is, they set aside part of their earnings to offset any potential future losses), but most purchase extra insurance protection to guard against catastrophic events such as the 9/11 tragedy.

CONTRACTUAL LIABILITY

Businesses often enter into contracts with other parties. These contracts could involve, for example, a lease of premises, a sales agreement with a customer, or an arrangement with an outsourcing firm or a construction company. One common denominator among most of these contracts is the inclusion of some sort of indemnification clause. As businesses sign contracts containing indemnification clauses, they need to be well aware of the potential legal liabilities they may be assuming by virtue of the language

indirect loss
A loss arising from an inability to carry on normal operations due to a direct loss of property.

workers' compensation legislation
Laws that obligate an employer to pay employees for injury or illness related to employment, regardless of fault.

used. Simply put, an **indemnification clause** requires one party (the indemnitor) to assume the financial consequences of another party's legal liabilities (the indemnitee). In other words, the indemnitor agrees to pay on behalf of the indemnitee the legal liabilities of the indemnitee.

The idea behind the contractual transfer of liability is to shift the responsibility to the party with the most control over the risk exposure. Consider, for example, a general contractor who signs an agreement to construct a new building on a piece of land for an owner. Should someone be injured during the building process, it is highly unlikely that the injury would be a result of the negligence of the property owner. In all likelihood, the negligent party—the party causing or contributing to the accident—would be the general contractor or perhaps a subcontractor hired by the general contractor. Therefore, it is quite common and most appropriate for the general contractor to agree to indemnify the owner for any liability arising from the construction work.

In many cases, insurance covers the potential legal liabilities that a business may assume as a result of an indemnification clause in a contract. But good communication between a business owner and his or her insurance agent or broker is essential. In a review of contracts that contain indemnification clauses, the insurance agent or broker should be able to point out the main limitations or shortcomings of an insurance policy as they pertain to the firm's assuming the legal liabilities of another party.

indemnification clause
A contractual clause that requires one party to assume the financial consequences of another party's legal liabilities.

torts
Wrongful acts or omissions for which an injured party can take legal action against the wrongdoer for monetary damages.

reasonable (prudent person) standard
The typical standard of care, based on what a reasonable or prudent person would have done under similar circumstances.

compensatory damages
Economic or noneconomic damages intended to make the claimant whole by compensating the claimant for any injuries or loss arising from the negligent action.

economic damages
Compensatory damages that relate to economic loss, such as medical expenses and loss of income.

noneconomic damages
Compensatory damages for such losses as pain and suffering, mental anguish, and loss of physical abilities.

TORT LIABILITY

Civil wrongs include breach of contract and torts. **Torts** are wrongful acts or omissions for which an injured party can take legal action against the wrongdoer to seek monetary damages. Tort actions commonly include an allegation of negligence, but four elements must be present for someone to be found guilty of a negligent act:

1. *Existence of a legal duty between the parties.* For example, a restaurant owner has a legal duty to provide patrons with food and drink that are fit for consumption. Likewise, an employee making a delivery for an employer has a duty to operate a vehicle safely on public roads.
2. *Failure to provide the appropriate standard of care.* The standard of care normally used is the **reasonable (prudent person) standard**, based on what a reasonable or prudent person would do under similar circumstances. This standard of care may be elevated, however, if a "professional" is involved. In professional liability actions, the standard of care is determined by the established standards of the profession. For example, a negligence action against a CPA would use the standards of the accounting profession as the benchmark. Expert witnesses are often used to help establish the standard and determine what clients can reasonably expect.
3. *Presence of injury or damages.* Negligence may exist, but if no injury or damage is sustained by the claimant, tort liability does not exist. The two types of damages that may be awarded in a tort action are compensatory damages and punitive damages.

   Compensatory damages are intended to make the claimant whole—that is, to compensate the claimant for any injuries or loss arising from the negligent action. Compensatory damages can be economic or noneconomic in nature. **Economic damages** relate to economic loss, such as medical expenses, loss of income, or the cost of property replacement/restoration. Economic damages are relatively easy to quantify. **Noneconomic damages** cover such losses as pain and suffering, mental anguish, and loss of physical abilities. In comparison to economic damages, noneconomic damages are difficult to express in financial terms. Civil courts usually have a hard time setting these awards, but many of today's substantial awards include a large amount for noneconomic damages.

Punitive damages are a form of punishment that goes beyond any compensatory damages. Punitive damages have a dual purpose. First, they punish wrongdoers in instances where there is gross negligence or a callous disregard for the interests of others. Second, they are intended to have a deterrent effect, sending a message to society that such conduct will not be tolerated. In fact, punitive damages are sometimes referred to as *exemplary damages*. In other words, one of their purposes is to make an "example" out of the defendant. Whether or not an insurance policy will pay for the punitive damages awarded against a business is determined by the state in which the lawsuit is filed. As a matter of public policy, some states allow insurance companies to pay for punitive damages, while other states do not.

4. *Evidence that the negligent act is the proximate cause of the loss.* Generally speaking, **proximate cause** is defined as a negligent act that clearly produces an accident; without such *cause*, the accident would not have occurred. In other words, there must be proof that the negligence actually caused the damages sustained. There may be negligence and there may be damages, but if no link can be established between the two, there is no tort liability.

Tort liability can arise from a number of business activities. Some of the more significant sources of tort liability follow:

- *Premises liability.* People may sustain injuries while on a business's premises. Retailers have significant premises liability exposure because they have many customers entering stores to purchase goods. Some other businesses, however, have little in the way of premises liability exposure. A consulting firm or a Web-design company would not typically have clients visit its business location; therefore, its premises liability exposure would be minimal.
- *Operations liability.* People may also sustain injuries as a result of a company's operations that take place away from its premises. Contractors have significant operations liability exposure because they are performing work at various job sites, and such work could easily result in injury to another person. At the same time, some businesses (such as retailers) have little in the way of operations liability exposure; their exposure is limited to their store's premises.
- *Professional liability.* Any business providing professional services to the public is potentially subject to professional liability claims. Recognizing this exposure is important, since separate liability insurance is necessary to properly protect a business from professional liability claims. Businesses that have a professional liability exposure include accounting firms, architecture and engineering firms, dental offices, and doctors' offices.
- *Employers' liability.* As previously mentioned, employers have a statutory obligation to pay certain benefits to employees injured in the course of employment. In exchange for these benefits, employees are then prohibited from suing their employer in most circumstances. At the same time, it is possible that an employer may be sued by an altogether different party as a result of an injury to an employee. Perhaps the employee's injury in the workplace was caused by a faulty piece of equipment manufactured by another firm; the employee may sue the manufacturer of that faulty product. The manufacturer may then take action against the employer, alleging that the employer failed to maintain the equipment, which consequently caused injury to the employee.

punitive damages
A form of punishment beyond compensatory damages that intends to punish wrongdoers for gross negligence or callous disregard and to have a deterrent effect.

proximate cause
A negligent act that is the clear cause of damages sustained.

- *Automobile liability*. A business that uses vehicles for various purposes has automobile liability exposure. Even a company that does not own or lease vehicles has potential liability if employees use their personal vehicles for business purposes.
- *Product liability*. The products manufactured or sold by a business can be a source of legal liability. For example, someone who was injured while using a product may claim that the product was defective. She or he may allege that there was a manufacturing defect, a design defect, or a marketing defect. A **manufacturing defect** exists when something actually goes wrong during the manufacturing process and the product is not made according to the manufacturer's specifications. A **design defect** exists when the product is made in accordance with the manufacturer's specifications but the product is still unreasonably dangerous as designed. For example, a rotating blade inside a piece of equipment may not be properly covered by a shield. Finally, a **marketing defect** exists when the manufacturer has failed to convey to the user of the product a fair indication of the hazards associated with the product or adequate instructions on how to use the product safely.
- *Completed operations liability*. The completed operations or completed work of a business can be a source of legal liability. Consider, for example, a general contractor who has constructed a new building for another party. Someone standing on a balcony of the new building leans against a rail that gives way, thus causing the person to fall and sustain bodily injury. Generally, this would result in a lawsuit against the general contractor.
- *Employment practices liability*. An increasing concern among businesses today is the threat of lawsuits arising from employment-related issues and practices. Current employees, prior employees, and even job applicants may take legal action against employers and claim damages arising from discrimination, sexual harassment, or wrongful termination. Discrimination claims include discrimination based on age, disability, race/color, religion, gender, and sexual orientation.

manufacturing defect
A defect resulting from a problem that occurs during the manufacturing process, causing the product to subsequently not be made according to specification.

design defect
A defect resulting from a dangerous design, even though the product was made according to specifications.

marketing defect
A defect resulting from failure to convey to the user that hazards are associated with a product or to provide adequate instructions on safe product use.

personnel risks
Risks that directly affect individual employees but may have an indirect impact on a business as well.

23-2c Personnel Risks

Personnel risks are risks that directly affect individual employees but may have an indirect impact on a business as well. The primary risks in this category include premature death, poor health, and insufficient retirement income.

PREMATURE DEATH

The risk associated with death is not if, but when. While we all expect to die, there is a risk that we may die early in life. This risk poses a potential financial problem for both the family of the person and his or her employer. Individuals deal with this risk by maintaining a healthy lifestyle and purchasing life insurance to protect family members who rely on their income.

Employers can be quite adversely impacted by the untimely death of an employee if that employee cannot be easily replaced. And what if a partner or owner of the business dies? Normally, such an event triggers a buyout of the interest of the deceased owner. Life insurance is often used to fund these buyout provisions.

POOR HEALTH

A more likely occurrence than death of an employee is poor health. The severity of poor health varies, ranging from a mild disorder to a more serious, disabling illness.

And as with premature death, the consequences of this event may affect an employer as well as the employee's family members.

The financial consequences of poor health have two dimensions. First are medical expenses, which can range from the cost of a doctor's visit to catastrophic expenses related to surgeries and hospitalization. Second are the consequences of the inability to work. Disability most often is a temporary condition, but it can be lengthy or even permanent. A worker's permanent disability can have the same financial impact on her or his family as death.

© PAUL VASARHELYI/SHUTTERSTOCK.COM

Employers often provide some form of health insurance as a benefit of employment. In some instances, the cost of the health insurance is shared by the employer and the employee; in others, the bulk of the cost is absorbed by the employer. In addition to the health insurance costs, not having the services of the employee for some time period may add to the adverse financial impact on the business.

INSUFFICIENT RETIREMENT INCOME

The final category of personnel risk involves the possibility of outliving one's wealth. The goal in dealing with this risk is to defer income and accumulate sufficient wealth to provide a satisfactory level of income during the nonworking years.

There are three primary sources of retirement income: Social Security, employer-funded retirement programs, and personal savings. Social Security provides a retirement income benefit, although for most retirees this benefit is not sufficient to meet expected consumption during retirement. To supplement this income, most workers have a retirement program associated with their employment. In the past, these programs were primarily funded by employers as a form of deferred compensation. While employer-funded pension plans still exist, it is more common today to encounter employee-funded retirement plans, where the employee can elect to defer current income for retirement. Usually, these plans are partially funded by employers as an incentive for employees to participate. Finally, individual savings can be used to accumulate wealth for retirement. All of these sources should be carefully considered in the retirement income planning process.

23-3 RISK MANAGEMENT

Describe the steps in the risk management process, and explain how risk management can be used in small companies.

Risk management consists of all efforts to preserve the assets and earning power of a business. Since risk management has grown out of insurance management, the two terms are often used interchangeably. However, risk management has a much broader meaning, covering both insurable and uninsurable risks and including noninsurance approaches to reducing all types of risk. It is concerned with finding the best possible way to reduce the cost of dealing with risk. Insurance is only one of several approaches to minimizing the pure risks a firm is sure to encounter. A full discussion of all of the forms of liability protection goes beyond the scope of this text. Experts and specific sources of information on protecting a small business should be consulted when making these decisions.

risk management
Ways of coping with risk that are designed to preserve the assets and earning power of a firm.

23-3a The Process of Risk Management

Five steps are required to develop and implement a risk management program.

Step 1: Identify and understand risks. To reduce the chance of overlooking important risks, a business should adopt a systematic approach to identifying risks. A business owner's insurance agent or broker can prove very helpful in this process. Useful identification methods also include insurance policy checklists, questionnaires, analysis of financial statements, and careful analysis of a firm's operations, customers, and facilities. Exhibit 23.1 depicts just a few of the risks that a small company may encounter.

"I'm disappointed; if anyone should have seen the red flags, it's you."

Step 2: Evaluate the potential severity of risks. Once the various risks have been identified, they must be evaluated in terms of the potential size of each loss and the probability that it will occur. At a minimum, risks should be classified into three groups: critical (losses that could result in bankruptcy), extremely important (losses that would require investment of additional capital to continue operations), and moderately important (losses that could be covered with current income or existing assets).

Step 3: Select methods to manage risk. The two approaches used in dealing with risk are risk control and risk financing, both of which will be discussed later in this chapter.

EXHIBIT 23.1 Risks on the Road to Success

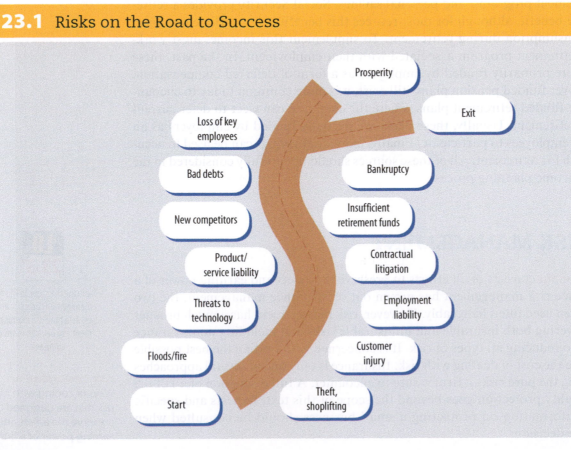

Prosperity
Exit
Loss of key employees
Bad debts
Bankruptcy
New competitors
Insufficient retirement funds
Product/service liability
Contractual litigation
Threats to technology
Employment liability
Floods/fire
Customer injury
Start
Theft, shoplifting

Step 4: Implement the decision. Once the decision has been made to use a particular technique or techniques to manage a firm's risks, this decision must be followed by action, such as purchasing insurance and setting aside dedicated funds to cope with any risks that have been retained. Failure to act—or even simple procrastination—could be fatal.

Step 5: Review and evaluate. Review and evaluation of the chosen risk management technique are essential because conditions change—new risks arise, and old ones disappear. Also, reviewing earlier decisions to use specific methods may identify mistakes made previously.

23-3b Risk Management in the Small Business

Regardless of the nature or size of a business, risk management is a serious issue. Too often, small businesses pay insufficient attention to analyzing potential risk. "Small companies often spend more time planning their company picnics than for an event that could put them out of business," says Katherine Heaviside, president of Epoch 5, a public relations firm that specializes in crisis communication.[3]

Risk management in a small business differs from that in a large firm. In a large firm, the responsibility of managing risk is frequently assigned to a specialized staff manager. It is more difficult for a small company to cope with risk management since its risk manager is usually the owner, who already has so many roles to perform. For this reason, the small business owner needs to rely on his or her insurance agent for advice. Furthermore, risk management is not something that requires immediate attention—until something happens. A prudent small business owner will take the time to identify the different types of risks faced by the firm and find ways to cope with them, through either risk control or risk financing.

RISK CONTROL

Risk control involves minimizing loss through prevention, avoidance, and/or reduction. **Loss prevention**, as the name implies, focuses on preventing losses from ever happening. For example, a business with a machine shop or manufacturing process may require all employees to wear safety glasses so as to prevent foreign particles from injuring their eyes. **Loss avoidance** is achieved by choosing not to engage in a particular hazardous activity. For instance, the liability exposure associated with operating a large truck on an interstate highway for the purposes of delivering a company's products to the marketplace is quite severe. An accident caused by a large truck on the highway can result in serious bodily injury and/or property damage. To avoid this liability exposure, a business may choose to hire a common carrier to deliver its products to the marketplace. This eliminates the exposure altogether. **Loss reduction** addresses the potential frequency, severity, or unpredictability of loss, thereby lessening the impact of the loss on the business. Crisis planning is a form of loss reduction in that it provides a template to follow in the case of a catastrophic loss. Installing automatic sprinkler systems in a building is another good example of a loss reduction strategy. If a fire occurs in a building with an automatic sprinkler system, the sprinklers will be activated, minimizing the amount of fire damage to the building.

In more recent times, social media have become useful tools for risk reduction, particularly when customer service or public relations issues arise. For example, Twitter was helpful to Innovative Beverage Group Holdings, Inc., when its website crashed after a surge in traffic following a Fox News segment about the company. The firm quickly tweeted that it was working diligently to fix the problem and monitored consumer comments about the crash in order to respond promptly about what it was doing

risk control
Minimizing potential losses by preventing, avoiding, and/or reducing risk.

loss prevention
Keeping a loss from happening.

loss avoidance
Choosing not to engage in hazardous activities.

loss reduction
Lessening the frequency, severity, or unpredictability of potential losses.

Living the Dream

USING TECHNOLOGY

Ten Security Tips for Small Businesses

© MAKSIM KABAKOU/SHUTTERSTOCK.COM

Broadband and information technology are powerful tools for small businesses that want to reach new markets and increase sales and productivity. However, cybersecurity threats are very real, and businesses must implement the best tools and tactics to protect themselves, their customers, and their data.

Here are 10 key cybersecurity tips offered by the U.S. Federal Communications Commission for protecting your small business:

1. Establish basic security practices and policies for employees, and train them well. Require the use of strong passwords, and establish appropriate Internet use guidelines that detail penalties for violating the company's cybersecurity policies.
2. Be sure that you regularly update your security software, browser, and operating system. They are the best defenses against viruses, malware, and other online threats.
3. Provide firewall security for your Internet connection.
4. Create a mobile device action plan. Require employees to password-protect their devices, encrypt their data, and install security apps to prevent criminals from stealing information while the phone is being used on public networks.
5. Backup data automatically, if possible, or at least weekly, and store the copies either offsite or in the cloud.
6. Control physical access to your computers, and create user accounts for each employee.
7. If you have a Wi-Fi network for your workplace, make sure that it is secure, encrypted, and hidden.
8. Employ best practices on payment cards. Work with banks or processors to ensure that the most trusted and validated tools and anti-fraud services are being used.
9. Limit employee access to data and information, and limit their authority to install software.
10. Require employees to use unique passwords and to change those passwords every three months. Consider implementing multifactor authentication, which requires additional information beyond a password to gain entry.

The FCC's Cybersecurity Hub at www.fcc.gov/cyberforsmallbiz has additional information, including links to free and low-cost security tools. You can also create a free, custom small business cybersecurity planning guide at www.fcc.gov/cyberplanner.

Source: Adapted from FCC, "Ten Cybersecurity Tips for Small Businesses, http://www.dhs.gov/sites/default/files/publications/FCC%20Small%20Biz%20Tip%20Sheet_0.pdf, accessed May 9, 2015.

to fix the problem. Peter Bianchi, Innovative's CEO, explained, "Twitter gave us an up-to-the-minute ability to take what would normally be a crisis situation and make it just another event. You can't do that with a 1-800-number."[4]

On the other hand, social media can create problems for a business and need to be monitored closely. Disgruntled customers and former employees can use social media to hurt a company's reputation. And although they can be valuable tools, social media do little good without regular use to garner followers and thus gain user trust.

RISK FINANCING

Risk financing focuses on making funds available for losses that cannot be eliminated by risk control. It involves transferring the risk or retaining the risk. **Risk transfer** is accomplished largely through buying insurance but can also be achieved by making other contractual arrangements that transfer the risk to others. As described earlier, indemnification clauses provide a means by which risk can be transferred from one party to another.

Risk retention entails financing all or part of a loss from a company's cash flows. Assuming that a firm's balance sheet is strong enough, the owner may choose to carry a high deductible applicable to property losses (perhaps a $25,000 deductible instead of a $5,000 deductible). For example, in the event of fire damage to a company's building, the business owner would pay up to $25,000 out of his or her pocket. The higher the deductible, the lower the insurance premium paid to the property insurance carrier. As another example, a business owner may choose to have a high deductible for a liability-type insurance claim. Again, in exchange for the higher deductible, the business owner is given a discounted liability insurance premium. Another form of risk retention is **self-insurance**, which is usually appropriate only for larger companies. Under self-insurance programs, a part of the organization's earnings is earmarked for a contingency fund against possible future losses.

Some small businesses have successfully relied on **partially self-funded programs** to provide medical coverage for employees. Partially self-funded programs allow the business to self-fund a portion of the health insurance benefits for its employees. For most small businesses, this self-funded portion is limited to between $30,000 and $100,000 per employee, depending on the number of employees and the firm's financial strength. This limitation per employee is more commonly referred to as a **specific stop loss limit.** After the specific stop loss limit has been met during the plan year, the health insurance company takes over the claim and pays the remaining portion.

An employer with 345 employees compared the costs of a traditional health insurance plan (also referred to as a fully insured medical plan) and a partially self-funded program. The fully insured plan would have cost the organization approximately $3,893,000 in premiums for a 12-month period. The partially self-funded medical plan had cost the employer a total of only $3,063,000 the previous year. So it appeared to be in the employer's best interest to maintain a partially self-funded program in anticipation of again saving approximately $830,000. Clearly, some risks are associated with a partially self-funded plan, since the employer never knows ahead of time how many employees might actually reach their specific spot loss limit. For this reason, these plans also have what is called an **aggregate stop loss limit**, which provides a cap on expenses for the year in case a number of employees reach the specific stop loss limit.

Partially self-funded programs are suitable for businesses that have a net worth of at least $2 million and 80 or more employees. Partially self-funded plans also offer more flexibility and cost advantages under the Affordable Care Act as compared to fully insured plans.

risk financing
Making funds available to cover losses that cannot be eliminated by risk control.

risk transfer
Buying insurance or making contractual arrangements that transfer risk to others.

risk retention
Financing loss intentionally, through a firm's cash flows.

self-insurance
Coverage that designates part of a firm's earnings as a cushion against possible future losses.

partially self-funded program
Program that designate part of firm's earnings to fund a portion of employee medical coverage.

specific stop loss limit
A firm's per-employee limit on self-funding for medical claims.

aggregate stop loss limit
A comprehensive limit on annual expenses should a number of employees reach the specific stop loss limit.

23-4 BASIC PRINCIPLES OF A SOUND INSURANCE PROGRAM

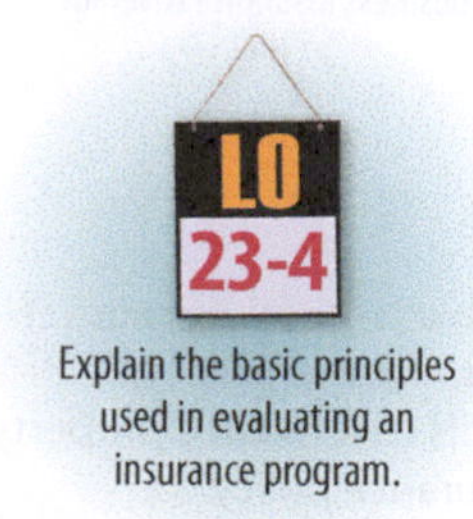

Explain the basic principles used in evaluating an insurance program.

What kinds of risks can be covered by insurance? What types of coverage should be purchased? How much coverage is adequate? Unfortunately, there are no clear-cut answers to these questions. A small business owner should become as knowledgeable as possible about the types of insurance that are available and then work with a reputable insurance agent in evaluating risks and designing proper protection plans. Three basic principles should be followed in evaluating an insurance program:

1. *Consider the various insurance policies that may be appropriate for your business.* "Bread-and-butter" type policies that are needed by almost all small businesses include property insurance for buildings and personal property, commercial general liability insurance, automobile insurance, workers' compensation insurance, and crime insurance. (Each of these policies is more fully described later in the chapter.) At the same time, there will very likely be other insurance policies needed by business owners depending on their particular industry (e.g., retail, construction, financial, etc.). A construction business, for example, may need an inland marine policy uniquely designed to cover its equipment (bulldozers, forklifts, etc.), which may be located at a job site.
2. *Secure insurance coverage for all major potential losses.* Small businesses must avoid incurring major uninsured losses that have the capacity to threaten the very existence of the business. For example, the total destruction of a building in a significant fire or windstorm event would be exceedingly difficult to overcome. For this reason, a business owner should make certain that insurance covers the *full replacement value* of the firm's buildings and personal property. Equally devastating might be a $1 million liability judgment against the business as a result of an automobile accident or someone being injured by the firm's products. It is imperative for the longevity of the business that these major potential loss exposures be properly insured.
3. *Consider the feasibility and affordability of insuring smaller potential losses.* Smaller potential losses do not pose the same threat as major potential losses do, so an owner will need to weigh the feasibility and affordability of absorbing those smaller losses. Of course, what determines whether a potential loss is "small" or "large" varies, depending on the strength of a company's financial position. As an example, claims that arise from employee lawsuits alleging wrongful termination, sexual harassment, or discrimination in the workplace range from $50,000 to $150,000, with insurance premiums ranging from $2,500 to $7,500. Only the owner can decide if the potential loss would be best handled through self-insurance or through payment of annual premiums. In this case, there is no single right answer.

Identify the common types of business insurance coverage.

23-5 COMMON TYPES OF BUSINESS INSURANCE

In this section, we examine the basic insurance policies used by many small companies. These policies fall under one of two categories: property and casualty insurance, or life and health insurance.

23-5a Property and Casualty Insurance

named-peril approach Identifying the specific perils covered in a property insurance policy.

Property and casualty insurance includes property insurance, commercial general liability insurance, automobile insurance, workers' compensation insurance, and crime insurance, as well as some miscellaneous policies.

PROPERTY INSURANCE

© DENPHUMI/SHUTTERSTOCK.COM

A property insurance policy is used by a business owner to insure buildings and personal property owned by the business, as well as buildings not owned by the business but which the business owner, as the lessee, has a responsibility to insure. As previously mentioned, property can be insured for either its replacement value or its actual cash value.

When purchasing property insurance, a business owner must also determine which "perils" will be covered by the policy. With the **named-peril approach**, the specific perils covered by the policy are identified. Covered perils generally include damage caused by fire, smoke, lightning, explosion, windstorm, hail, aircraft, vehicles, rioting, vandalism, sprinkler leakage, sinkhole collapse, and volcanic activity. With this approach, any damage caused by a peril not named in the policy is simply not covered. Examples of claims not covered by the named-peril approach include damage caused by frozen pipes within the building, falling objects, the weight of snow, and theft.

In contrast to the named-peril approach, a business owner can use the **all-risk approach**, which provides the broadest protection available. With the all-risk approach, all direct damage to property is covered except damage caused by perils specifically excluded. In other words, if it's not excluded, it's covered. Exclusions typically include damage caused by flood, earthquake, fungus or mold, normal wear and tear, and loss caused by the dishonest acts of employees.

all-risk approach
Stating in a property insurance policy that all direct damages are covered except those caused by perils specifically excluded.

coinsurance clause
A provision in a property insurance policy that requires the owner to have insurance for at least 80 percent of what it would cost to rebuild the building or replace the personal property.

An important provision in the property insurance policy is the **coinsurance clause**, which requires a business owner to insure the company's building and personal property for at least 80 percent of what it would cost to replace the building and the personal property. If, at the time of a claim, the building and personal property are insured for less than 80 percent of their replacement cost, then the business owner is assessed a penalty by the insurance company and, in essence, becomes a co-insurer.

As an example, assume that the replacement cost of a building is $1 million. The owner is therefore required to carry insurance equal to $800,000 (0.80 × $1,000,000) in order to avoid a co-insurance penalty. If the business owner insures the property for only $600,000, he or she then becomes a co-insurer, even in the case of a partial claim. Because the actual insurance is only 75 percent ($600,000 ÷ $800,000) of what it should have been, the insured is penalized 25 percent in the event of a claim. So, should the building experience partial fire and smoke damage in the amount of $100,000, the insurance company will pay only $75,000, even though the amount of insurance on the policy clearly exceeds the amount of the claim. The remaining $25,000 must be paid by the owner in his or her role as co-insurer. Therefore, it is important for a business owner to insure a building and personal property for an amount that exceeds at least 80 percent of its replacement value. When determining the replacement value of personal property for businesses that are leasing building space, an owner should include the value of all leasehold improvements in the limit of personal property insurance. Of course, in the event of a catastrophic loss, the owner would be better served by insuring the building and personal property for 100 percent of what it would cost to replace. For these reasons, the limits of property insurance should be carefully considered by all business owners.

Employee Fraud
Monitoring for employee fraud needs to be a constant focus for a small business owner. But there are two circumstances when an owner is particularly vulnerable, the first of which you may find surprising: when the firm is experiencing success, and when there is a personal distraction, such as a death in the family.

One type of optional coverage that can be added to a property insurance policy is **business interruption insurance**. As previously noted, the financial loss associated with a property loss is not limited to direct damage to the property. There may be an indirect loss associated with the "loss of use" of the damaged property. Business interruption insurance provides coverage for loss of income following the interruption of business operations. Without such income, it would be difficult for a business to continue paying for ongoing expenses, such as payroll expenses. This coverage also provides reimbursement for income that would have been earned by the business had no damage occurred. In addition, business interruption insurance may cover "extra expenses" incurred following an insured loss. For example, following major fire damage to a building, an owner may have to secure a temporary location elsewhere in order to continue business operations and avoid losing customers. Business interruption insurance is a critical element of coverage for a business owner's survival following a significant property loss event. Unfortunately, many owners fail to appreciate the importance of this coverage.

COMMERCIAL GENERAL LIABILITY INSURANCE

A **commercial general liability (CGL) insurance** policy is the cornerstone liability policy for small businesses. A CGL policy protects against premises liability, operations liability, product liability, and completed operations liability. Simply put, we live in a litigious society, and small businesses are easy targets for liability lawsuits. A CGL policy provides frontline protection against claims arising from any accident that results either in bodily injury or in property damage and is not otherwise excluded by the policy. It does not cover automobile liability, professional liability, or employer liability, all of which require a separate policy for adequate protection.

A CGL policy also provides for both medical payments coverage and protection against personal and advertising injury liability. The medical expenses of someone who is injured on the company's premises or as a result of its operations are reimbursed through medical payments coverage. The unique feature of this coverage is that it does not require any fault on the part of the business. This "no-fault" coverage is intended to build goodwill and prevent someone from then suing the business for negligence. Personal and advertising injury liability protection covers lawsuits alleging intentional torts, such as libel or slander (injury to a person's reputation within the community), false arrest, or malicious prosecution.

AUTOMOBILE INSURANCE

An **automobile insurance** policy is designed to provide liability protection as well as physical damage coverage as a result of such insured perils as collision, theft, vandalism, hail, and flood. The risk of physical damage to vehicles is much less than the risk of a large liability lawsuit following an at-fault accident. Small business owners may choose to self-insure against the lesser exposure from physical damage but should *not* self-insure when it comes to liability exposure.

WORKERS' COMPENSATION INSURANCE

Workers' compensation insurance provides benefits to employees injured at work, in compliance with states' statutes. Generally speaking, these benefits include coverage for medical expenses, loss of wages, and rehabilitation expenses, as well as death benefits for employees' families. Employers' liability insurance offers additional protection for the business owner against various types of liability lawsuits that may arise following an injury to or the death of an employee.

business interruption insurance
Coverage that reimburses a business for the loss of anticipated income following the interruption of business operations.

commercial general liability (CGL) insurance
Coverage for general liability loss exposure, including premises liability, operations liability, product liability, completed operations liability, and personal and advertising injury liability.

automobile insurance
Coverage designed to provide liability and physical damage protection for a vehicle.

workers' compensation insurance
Coverage that provides benefits to employees injured at work.

CRIME INSURANCE

© ISTOCKPHOTO.COM/MIKKEL WILLIAM

While there are different types of crime insurance coverage that the small business owner may want to consider, first and foremost is coverage against employee dishonesty. Small businesses are generally very trusting of their employees and would not knowingly have someone working within the organization if they thought that person was dishonest. Unfortunately, not every employee is honest. The weak financial controls often found in a small business offer a perfect opportunity for a dishonest employee to embezzle large sums of money. The potential for loss can easily be covered by a **crime insurance** policy at a nominal cost. Premiums vary according to the size of the small business, running from a few hundred dollars up to $2,000 for a $500,000 policy. Because it is possible for an embezzlement scheme to continue for a number of years, an insurance limit should be selected that is high enough to cover a multi-year loss.

Another element of crime insurance that should not be overlooked is **funds transfer fraud** coverage. Cyber criminals have become increasingly innovative in finding ways to steal money, including the electronic wire transfer of funds out of a business's bank account. Thieves have created new viruses that are sent to businesses in the form of an e-mail attachment. If the attachment is opened, the virus will extract important bank account numbers and passwords, thereby enabling the thieves to successfully transfer money out of a bank account. This is a growing risk for business owners and needs to be part of every business owner's crime insurance policy.

BUSINESS OWNERS' AND PACKAGE POLICIES

Property insurance and commercial general liability insurance can generally be obtained together under a single insurance policy, called a **business owner's policy (BOP)**. However, construction businesses, manufacturers, financial institutions, and any other businesses with annual revenues in excess of $10 million will frequently not qualify for a BOP. The advantages of a BOP at any one location include (1) a lower premium than would otherwise be required to purchase all coverages separately, (2) the automatic inclusion of business interruption insurance, and (3) automatic replacement value protection, as opposed to actual cash value protection.

For businesses that do not qualify for a BOP, property insurance and commercial general liability insurance can be combined together in a **package policy**. The advantages of a package policy include (1) a lower premium than would otherwise be required to purchase all coverages separately, (2) the ease of adding other coverages more economically, (3) the inclusion of business interruption insurance, and (4) the inclusion of crime insurance.

MISCELLANEOUS POLICIES

A variety of miscellaneous insurance policies can also be utilized by small businesses. These include employment practices liability policies, umbrella liability policies, inland marine policies, professional liability policies, and cyber liability policies. As mentioned earlier, *employment practices liability policies* are designed to protect the business owner against employment-related lawsuits arising from discrimination, sexual harassment, or wrongful termination. *Umbrella liability policies* provide supplemental layers of liability protection. Such policies may provide an additional $1,000,000 (or more) of liability insurance in excess of the liability limits provided by automobile insurance, a CGL policy, and employers' liability insurance. Umbrella liability policies can be of extreme importance to small businesses in the event of a significant accident that severely injures or kills someone, resulting in a multimillion-dollar lawsuit.

crime insurance
Coverage primarily against employee dishonesty.

funds transfer fraud
The criminal transfer of funds from a bank account.

business owner's policy (BOP)
A business version of a homeowner's policy, designed to meet the property and general liability insurance needs of some small business owners.

package policy
A policy for small businesses that do not qualify for a BOP that combines property insurance, commercial general liability insurance, business interruption insurance, and crime insurance.

Living the Dream

ENTREPRENEURIAL EXPERIENCES

Sweet Dreams Can End Quickly

When a Collin Street Bakery accounting clerk in Corsicana, Texas, reported irregularities in the company's computerized accounting system, the bakery never expected that its own corporate controller, Sandy Jenkins, had embezzled over $16 million from the company. During the five years that Jenkins was employed at Collin Street Bakery, he wrote over 800 phony checks to creditors and manipulated the accounting system to show that checks had been voided.

With these checks, Jenkins funded a lavish lifestyle, which included owning 43 luxury vehicles, maintaining a vacation home in Santa Fe, and owning a multimillion-dollar watch and jewelry collection. Both Jenkins and his wife would frequently travel on private planes for vacations and incurred over $11 million in charges on American Express credit cards, all of which was at the expense of the bakery.

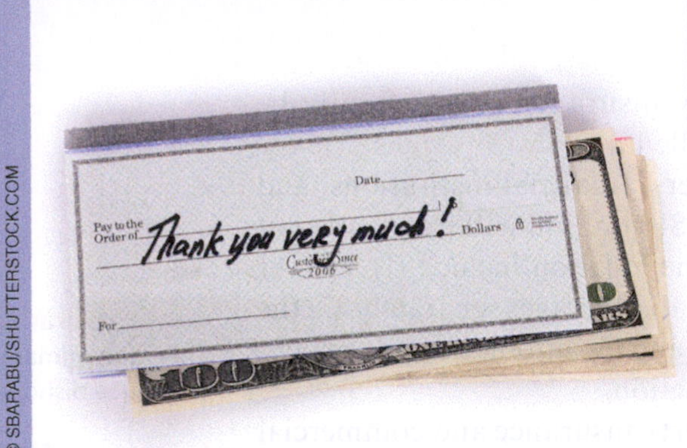

© SBARABU/SHUTTERSTOCK.COM

Jenkins scheme came to light when an accounting clerk asked him about the discrepancies. She became suspicious when his explanation was that it was simply an error and not to worry about it. The clerk then looked further into the check register report and noticed 16 cleared checks that were not reflected in the accounting system. She reported it to the vice president of finance.

Eventually, Jenkins was accused of fraud and terminated from the company. He pleaded guilty and, as of early 2015, is awaiting trial.

If Collin Street Bakery had purchased employee dishonesty insurance, it would not have incurred the entire $16 million loss from Jenkins's dishonest actions. Even more regrettable, this story is played out in small businesses every day.

Sources: "FBI Searches Home of Former Collin Street Bakery Official," KBTX, July 26, 2013, http://www.kbtx.com/home/headlines/FBI-Searches-Home-Of-Former-Collin-Street-Bakery-Official-217096701.html, accessed April 8, 2015; and "Grand Jury Indicts Wife of Former Executive at Collin Street Bakery on Felony Conspiracy," Federal Bureau of Investigation, March 12, 2014, http://www.fbi.gov/dallas/press-releases/2014/grand-jury-indicts-wife-of-former-executive-at-collin-street-bakery-on-felony-conspiracy-money-laundering-and-false-statement-charges, accessed April 8, 2015.

Inland marine policies are unique policies designed to insure personal property against the risk of physical damage when such property is located *away* from a firm's premises. For example, contracting equipment being used at a job site (bulldozers, forklifts, cranes) and manufactured products being transported by a truck to a customer's warehouse can be insured under an inland marine policy. *Professional liability policies* are used to protect professionals against lawsuits arising from errors made while providing their services. Professionals that need such coverage include physicians, dentists, accountants, architects, engineers, attorneys, insurance agents, and real estate agents.

Cyber liability policies are available to protect businesses against the broad range of loss exposures arising from their use of the Internet and their holding of confidential information. Coverage may include the following:

- Liability protection against lawsuits arising from the loss or unauthorized disclosure of confidential data that are in the care and custody of a business

- Crisis management expenses incurred by a firm following a network security breach, including the cost of notifying affected individuals
- Liability protection for claims arising from a computer virus that originates from a company's network

23-5b Life and Health Insurance

Three types of insurance provide coverage for employees within a business: health insurance, key-person life insurance, and disability insurance. (Workers' compensation insurance was discussed earlier as a type of property and casualty insurance.)

HEALTH INSURANCE

Also commonly referred to as medical insurance, *health insurance* is one of the most valuable benefits that a small business can offer its employees. Furthermore, it is required under the Affordable Care Act for employers with more than 50 employees. Group health insurance policies offer coverage for medical care at hospitals, doctors' offices, and rehabilitation facilities. The Affordable Care Act also requires these policies to cover outpatient services, prescription drugs, and preventive care.

Coverage is often offered to employees only through a specific group of health care providers, or "network." Types of health insurance plans that fall into this category include **health maintenance organizations (HMOs)** and **preferred provider organizations (PPOs)**. An HMO is a managed-care network that provides health insurance that is generally less expensive than a PPO, but it limits employees' choices of medical care providers more than a PPO does. However, with a PPO, employees still must stay within a network of providers or face higher out-of-pocket expenses in the event of a claim.

Out-of-pocket expenses that employees must pay themselves, regardless of the type of health insurance plan provided by the employer, generally include the following:

- A co-pay at the doctor's office for each office visit, usually between $20 and $40
- A co-pay at the pharmacy for each prescription drug purchased, usually between $10 and $100
- A deductible at the hospital for each hospital admission, usually between $1,000 and $6,000
- A percentage of the total cost of the health care provided by a hospital, usually between 20 and 30 percent, up to a maximum out-of-pocket cost to the employee of between $3,000 and $6,000. The Affordable Care Act may generally limit this expense.

KEY-PERSON LIFE INSURANCE

By carrying **key-person life insurance**, a small business can protect itself against the death of key personnel. Such insurance may be written on an individual or group basis. It is purchased by a firm, with the firm as the sole beneficiary.

Most small business advisors suggest term insurance for key-person life insurance policies, primarily because of lower premiums. How much key-person life insurance to buy is more difficult to decide. Face values of such policies usually begin around $500,000 and may go as high as several million dollars.

DISABILITY INSURANCE

One risk that small businesses often do not consider is loss due to the disability of a partner or other key employees of the company. Statistics, however, show that the odds of a person becoming disabled are much higher than most people think.

health maintenance organizations (HMO)
A managed-care network providing health insurance that is less expensive than that of a PPO but more limiting in choices of medical care providers.

preferred provider organizations (PPO)
A managed-care network providing health insurance that is more expensive than that of an HMO but offers a broader choice of medical providers.

key-person life insurance
Coverage that provides benefits to a firm upon the death of key personnel.

The most common type of **disability insurance** provides for the payment of a portion (typically two-thirds) of the disabled person's normal monthly income for a period of time after the disability occurs. However, it protects only the disabled person and not the business. Alternatively, partners can purchase **disability buyout insurance**. This type of disability insurance protects both partners by guaranteeing that the healthy partner will have enough cash to buy out the disabled partner without draining capital from the business.

Also available is disability insurance that replaces lost revenue because of the disability of a key employee. For example, if a firm's top salesperson, who brings in $25,000 a month, becomes disabled, this coverage will provide the company up to 125 percent of replacement income for a year or more. This gives the business time to recruit and train someone else.

Another type of disability insurance is designed to cover fixed overhead expenses, such as rent, utilities, employee salaries, and general office expenses, while an owner or other key employee recuperates. This type of insurance is especially well suited for a sole proprietorship, since the firm would have no income if the owner were unable to work.

disability insurance
Coverage that provides benefits upon the disability of a firm's partner or other key employees.

disability buyout insurance
Coverage that guarantees a healthy partner enough cash to buy out a partner who becomes disabled.

There is no question that risk is a part of life, but how you manage it will affect the success of your small business. That's why an understanding of business risks, the basic principles of a sound insurance program, and the various types of business insurance is so important. It can help you deal with many of the uncertainties that you will surely encounter.

23-1. Define *business risk*, and explain its two dimensions.

- Business risk is the possibility of losses associated with the assets and earnings potential of a firm.
- Business risks can be classified into two broad categories: market risk and pure risk.
- Market risk is the uncertainty associated with an investment decision.
- Pure risk exists in a situation where only loss or no loss can occur—there is no potential gain.
- In general, only pure risk is insurable.

23-2. Identify the basic types of pure risk.

- Pure risks that any business faces fall into three groups: property risks, liability risks, and personnel risks.
- Property risks involve potential damage to or loss of real property (e.g., land and buildings) and personal property (e.g., equipment).
- Liability risks arise from statutory liability, contractual liability, or tort liability.
- Personnel risks, such as premature death, poor health, and insufficient retirement income, directly affect individuals but may indirectly impact the business as well.

23-3. Describe the steps in the risk management process, and explain how risk management can be used in small companies.

- Risk management is concerned with protecting the assets and the earning power of a business against loss.
- The risk management process involves identifying and understanding risks, evaluating the potential severity of risks, selecting methods to manage risk, implementing the decision, and reviewing and evaluating the chosen risk management technique.

- The two ways to manage business risks are risk control and risk financing.
- Risk control is designed to minimize loss through prevention, avoidance, and/or reduction of risk.
- Risk financing—making funds available for losses that cannot be eliminated by risk control—involves transferring the risk to another party or retaining the risk within the firm.

23-4. Explain the basic principles used in evaluating an insurance program.

- Three basic principles should be followed in evaluating an insurance program: (1) Consider the various policies appropriate for your business, (2) secure coverage for all major potential losses, and (3) consider the feasibility and affordability of insuring smaller potential losses.
- Basic coverage needed by almost all small businesses includes property insurance, commercial general liability insurance, automobile liability insurance, workers' compensation insurance, and crime insurance.
- Property insurance must cover the full replacement value of a firm's buildings and personal property.
- A small business owner must determine what distinguishes a "smaller" potential loss from a "major" potential loss and then decide if it makes sense to insure against smaller potential losses.

23-5. Identify the common types of business insurance coverage.

- Basic insurance policies used by many small companies fall under one of two categories: property and casualty insurance, or life and health insurance.
- A property insurance policy is used to insure both buildings and personal property owned or leased by the business.
- A decision must be made by the business owner as to whether to insure the firm's property using a named-peril approach or an all-risk approach.
- Business interruption insurance, which reimburses a firm for the loss of anticipated income following the interruption of operations, should be given careful consideration as an optional coverage that can be added to the property insurance policy.
- A commercial general liability insurance policy is the cornerstone liability policy for small businesses and protects against premises liability, operations liability, product liability, completed operations liability, and personal and advertising injury liability.
- An automobile insurance policy is designed to provide liability protection for the business owner arising from the use of vehicles for business purposes as well as physical damage coverage on owned vehicles.
- Workers' compensation insurance provides employee benefits in compliance with states' statutes.
- A small business owner must accept the fact that he or she is vulnerable to the possibility of employee dishonesty and purchase the appropriate crime insurance coverage.
- A small business owner should consider the advantages of purchasing either a business owner's policy or a package policy as a way to consolidate coverage at less cost and with broader protection.
- Employment practices liability policies, umbrella liability policies, inland marine policies, professional liability policies, and cyber liability policies are also available to small business owners.
- The three types of life and health insurance that provide protection for employees within a business are health insurance, key-person life insurance, and disability insurance.

Key Terms

actual cash value (ACV) p. 626
aggregate stop loss limit p. 635
all-risk approach p. 637
automobile insurance p. 638
business interruption insurance p. 638
business owner's policy (BOP) p. 639
business risk p. 625
coinsurance clause p. 637
commercial general liability (CGL) insurance p. 638
compensatory damages p. 628
crime insurance p. 639
design defect p. 630
direct loss p. 626
disability buyout insurance p. 642
disability insurance p. 642
economic damages p. 628
funds transfer fraud p. 639
health maintenance organization (HMO) p. 641
indemnification clause p. 628
indirect loss p. 627
key-person life insurance p. 641
loss avoidance p. 633
loss prevention p. 633

loss reduction p. 633
manufacturing defect p. 630
market risk p. 625
marketing defect p. 630
named-peril approach p. 636
noneconomic damages p. 628
package policy p. 639
partially self-funded program p. 635
peril p. 626
personal property p. 626
personnel risks p. 630
preferred provider organization (PPO) p. 641
proximate cause p. 629
punitive damages p. 629
pure risk p. 625
real property p. 626
reasonable (prudent person) standard p. 628
replacement value of property p. 626
risk control p. 633
risk financing p. 635
risk management p. 631
risk retention p. 635
risk transfer p. 635
self-insurance p. 635
specific stop loss limit p. 635
torts p. 628
workers' compensation insurance p. 638
workers' compensation legislation p. 627

You Make the Call

Situation 1

The Amigo Company manufactures motorized wheelchairs in its Bridgeport, Michigan, plant, under the supervision of Alden Thieme. Alden is the brother of the firm's founder, Allen Thieme. The company has 100 employees and does $10 million in sales a year. Like many other firms, Amigo is faced with increased liability insurance costs. Although Alden is contemplating dropping all coverage, he realizes that the users of the firm's product are individuals who have already suffered physical and emotional pain. Therefore, if an accident occurred and resulted in a liability suit, a jury might be strongly tempted to favor the plaintiff. In fact, the company is currently facing litigation. A woman in an Amigo wheelchair was killed by a car on the street. Because the driver of the car had no insurance, Amigo was sued.

Question 1 Do you agree that the type of customer to whom the Amigo Company sells should influence Thieme's decision regarding insurance?
Question 2 In what way, if any, should the outcome of the current litigation affect Thieme's decision about renewing the company's insurance coverage?
Question 3 What options does Amigo have if it drops all insurance coverage? What is your recommendation?

Situation 2

Pansy Ellen Essman is a 48-year-old grandmother who is chairperson of a company that does $5 million in sales each year. Her company, Pansy Ellen Products, Inc., based in Atlanta, Georgia, grew out of a product idea that Essman had as she was bathing her squealing, squirming granddaughter in the bathroom tub. Her idea was to produce a sponge pillow that would cradle a child in the tub, thus freeing the caretaker's hands to clean the baby. From this initial product, the company expanded its product line to include nursery lamps, baby food organizers, strollers, and hook-on baby seats. Essman has seemingly managed her product mix risk well. However, she is concerned that other sources of business risk may have been ignored or slighted.

Question 1 What types of business risk do you think Essman might have overlooked? Be specific.
Question 2 Would risk retention be a good strategy for this company? Why or why not?
Question 3 What kinds of insurance coverage should this type of company carry?

Situation 3

H. Abbe International, owned by Herb Abbe, is a travel agency and freight forwarder located in downtown Minneapolis. When the building that housed the firm's offices suffered damage as a result of arson, the firm was forced to relocate its two computers and 11 employees. Moving into the offices of a client, Abbe worked from this temporary location for a month before returning to his regular offices. The disruption cost him about $70,000 in lost business and moving expenses. In addition, he had to lay off four employees.

Question 1 What are the major types of risk faced by a firm such as H. Abbe International? What kind of insurance will cover these risks?
Question 2 What kind of insurance would have helped Abbe cope with the loss resulting from arson? In purchasing this kind of insurance, what questions must be answered about the amount and terms?
Question 3 Would you have recommended that Abbe purchase insurance that would have covered the losses in this case?

Video Case 23

Jack's Restaurant (p. 693)

Jack, a successful restaurant owner whose upscale establishment offers signature dishes, is selling his business to two of his employees. He wishes to retain the intellectual property rights of his frozen food items as he enters into retirement and suggests that a noncompete agreement be drawn before the sale is final. The new buyers disagree, and the deal is in jeopardy unless an amicable agreement is reached.

Alternative Case for Chapter 23

Video Case 15, Graeter's Ice Cream, p. 677

Endnotes

1. Translated by Arthur W. H. Adkins from the Greek text of Solon's poem "Prosperity, Justice and the Hazards of Life," in M. L. West (ed.), *Iambi et Elegi Gracci ante Alexandrum Canttati*, Vol. 2 (Oxford: Clarendon Press, 1972).
2. http://www.thefreedictionary.com/risk, accessed March 30, 2015.
3. Daniel Tynan, "In Case of Emergency," *Entrepreneur*, Vol. 3, No. 4 (April 2003), p. 60.
4. Sarah E. Needleman, "Entrepreneurs 'Tweet' Their Way through Crises," *The Wall Street Journal*, September 15, 2009, p. B5.

CASE 1

DashLocker

New York Businessman Trades Banking for Laundry StartUp

In 2010, corporate businessman Robert Hennessy traded his job as a research analyst at a New York hedge fund to start his own company, a high-tech laundry service on Manhattan's Upper East Side. Hennessy, who grew up in Atlanta and moved to New York in 2008, pursued banking for just two short years before starting his own company. What inspired the career change? Hennessy simply saw a need in the market and felt called to respond:

> *It always baffled me that dry cleaners had the same hours as most hard-working New Yorkers and were closed on Sunday. Not many of us without laundry [service] in our apartments have three hours to spend washing our clothes.*

The strength of the business idea that Hennessy identified lies in the inelasticity of demand for dry-cleaning services. As he explains, "You're going to breathe, you're going to get dirty, you're going to need to clean those clothes."

What initially began as a simple coin-operated laundromat grew into a business currently known as DashLocker, a round-the-clock dry-cleaning and wash-and-fold service. DashLocker operates as a kiosk system that enables customers to lock and unlock laundry bins with a credit card at any time of day. This allows them to drop off and retrieve laundry after traditional work hours have ended.

By simply registering a credit card online, customers are granted immediate access to the lockers. This type of access allows the storefront to be unstaffed throughout the day, minimizing operating expenses. The locker technology takes photographic inventory of the laundry so that no clothes are lost. Within 24 hours of drop-off, customers receive an e-mail or a text informing them that their laundry is ready for pick up.

The technology is powered by San Francisco–based laundry startup, Laundry Locker. Hennessy spent a year petitioning the company to allow him to license the software. His perseverance paid off. In the first month of operation, the store generated almost $6,000 in sales and served over 100 customers. Within three months, monthly sales grew to $13,500. Since then, Hennessy has opened other locations.

The company targets "tech-savvy 20- to 40-year-olds with discretionary income." Prices for DashLocker services are at the upper end of dry-cleaning rates. Wash-and-fold services are priced at $1.25/pound, and dry-cleaning services are priced at $6 for pants and $2.25 for pressed shirts.

The business maintains strong growth potential, as lockers have the potential to be installed just about anywhere. Currently being considered are apartment buildings, gyms, and parking garages. Hennessy has also expanded services to include shoe shining and delivery.

DashLocker is committed to a social mission. It seeks to employ green, earth-friendly technology in its operations. The company's GreenEarth dry-cleaning machines use liquid silicone rather than perchloroethylene (perc). Hennessy describes liquid silicone as "liquefied sand that when broken down, deteriorates into sand, water, and carbon dioxide—natural elements whose exposure doesn't put anyone at risk." DashLocker not only seeks to transform the Manhattan laundry landscape but to shrink its carbon footprint globally.

Sources: Based on Katherine Duncan. "A Fresh Spin on Clean Clothes." *Entrepreneur*. January 2013: p. 70; Nate Hindman, "DashLocker Formed As Banker Turned Entrepreneur Tries to Shake Up Dry-Cleaning World," *Huffington Post*, June 15, 2012, www.huffingtonpost.com/2012/06/15/dashlocker-dry-cleaning_n_1599767.html, accessed March 17, 2013; Matt Petronzio, "3 Ways to Simplify Your Offline Errands," *Mashable*. July 5, 2012, www.mashable.com/2012/07/05/tech-city-errands, accessed March 17, 2013; Alessia Pirolo, "The Latest in Laundry," *The Wall Street Journal*, July 23, 2012, http://online.wsj.com/article/SB100008723963904435709045775432235120305 02.html, accessed March 17, 2013; and Jason Shefiell, "New York Businessman's Start-Up Lets Customers Drop Off and Pick Up Laundry and Dry Cleaning at Conveniently-Placed Lockers," *NY Daily News*, January 17, 2013, www.nydailynews.com/life-style/real-estate/bizman-hopes-clean-laundry-start-article-1.1240764, accessed March 17, 2013.

Questions

1. How did Hennessy's background prepare him for starting a business? What entrepreneurial qualities does he embody?
2. What were Hennessy's entrepreneurial motivations for founding DashLocker?
3. What type of entrepreneurial opportunity did Hennessy identify, and how did he capitalize on those opportunities?
4. Describe DashLocker's growth potential.
5. Describe DashLocker's competitive advantage.
6. What impact does DashLocker have on society?
7. What do you think about DashLocker's social mission? What else could the company do to reduce its carbon footprint? Should businesses be concerned with social entrepreneurship?
8. Visit DashLocker's website at www.dashlocker.com and explore the process of signing up for its services. What recommendations would you give to Hennessy to make the process easier?

PortionPac Chemicals

Integrity and Stakeholder Relationships

VIDEO CASE 2

PortionPac® Chemicals was founded on social and environmental principles. Since 1964, sustainability led the business, their products, their relationships, and their success. Decades before it became a buzzword, PortionPac's founders, Syd Weisberg and Marvin Klein, believed in the value of sustainability and what it meant for the environment, the industry, and the people who lived and worked in both. Built on a foundation of environmental stewardship and social responsibility, PortionPac continues to strive toward creating the world's most sustainable solutions for clean buildings.

For PortionPac, being a leader in sustainability means considering the impact of everything they do, across all operations. Sustainable thinking permeates the entire company. This orientation shows up in the company's solutions, its facility, and its founding principles. PortionPac has always seen sustainability as an opportunity: a way to differentiate itself from the competition and a chance to do their part. This has never been viewed as a hindrance or an expense—it's just the way business is done. With premeasured packaging, safer product systems, and ongoing education, PortionPac's sustainable solutions help improve people's health, the environment, and the customers' bottom line.

PortionPac believes strongly in the critical work and tremendous effort of housekeepers, janitors, and food service professionals. The firm's goal is to make effective cleaning products that offer maximum safety for their employees to produce and for their clients to use. The company also holds itself accountable to the end-user and recognizes its role in health and safety.

In the early years, PortionPac had opportunities to enter lucrative markets where toxic cleaning products were commonplace. But rather than make standard dangerous germicides, the firm's founders opted for safer alternatives. In doing so, they demonstrated that less toxic options could actually be more effective at cleaning and disinfecting. It took years, but convincing the industry to make the switch became one of the company's founding principles and underscored the owners' commitment to worker safety.

PortionPac's commitment to the health and well-being of customers goes beyond manufacturing safer products—at the heart of the company's mission is education. PortionPac was the first chemical company in the cleaning industry to emphasize educational materials for the proper use of cleaning products as the most effective method to guarantee worker safety, boost productivity, and reduce error. By using international symbols and color-coding, simple to understand audiovisual materials, and interactive programming to teach customers and staff how to clean better, more safely, and with fewer chemicals, they've achieved this goal.

You won't find a separate "green" division within PortionPac because the entire company is committed to creating the world's most sustainable solutions for clean buildings. Its goal has always been to reduce the company's environmental footprint by decreasing the energy used in the production and distribution of its products, minimizing the adverse effect of its cleaning detergents on the environment, and avoiding the use of improper cleaning procedures that can turn out to be ineffective or even unsafe.

Caring about the environment and putting people first sounds like a pretty good way to do business, and PortionPac demonstrates every day that it's also great for a company's financial success. While growing the firm's operations, its owners have always considered the "triple bottom line" of social, environmental, and economic balance while growing operations. They made the conscientious decision before starting the company to continually improve environmental standards and the human condition—all while remaining profitable. That's why the company is recognized today as a leader in sustainability.

As more and more companies look for green products and consider the "3 P's" of people, the planet, and profit, it's clear—whether by regulation or recognition—that sustainability considerations are no longer just a smart way of looking at the world: It's becoming a practical way to run a profitable business. PortionPac helps organizations find sustainable solutions for their janitorial and sanitation needs. With over 40 years of experience connecting sustainability, accountability, and cleaning, they know the best solutions continually evolve, adapt, and improve. Because every company is different, they collaborate with clients one-on-one to create custom programs that work for them.

View the video and answer the questions that follow.

Questions

1. Based on what you have learned about PortionPac, what do you think the owners would claim to be the most important features of doing business with integrity? Do you agree? Why or why not?
2. Who are the most important stakeholders for PortionPac? What is the order of emphasis on the interests for these stakeholders—from most important and influential to least important and influential—on the company's decision-making processes? In your opinion, does this represent a wise ordering of stakeholder interests?
3. PortionPac is very concerned about the environment. Is the company's environmental focus good for the company? Why or why not?
4. Would you want to work for a company that operates according to the goals discussed in the case? What would be the pros and cons of working there?

Source: Compiled from interviews and information provided by PortionPac. www.portionpaccorp.com. © 2012, Cengage Learning.

The Kollection: From Music Hobby to Startup and Beyond

CASE 3

Brian Lovin is founder of The Kollection, a blog/website dedicated to emerging musicians and fans who want to know about the newest music available. He explains below, in his own words, how the site got started as a labor of love, with hopes of filling a gap in the marketplace. It wasn't long before The Kollection evolved into a popular online venue for music lovers around the world and a revenue-generating enterprise. Lovin's reflections about the business and his experiences with it provide instructive insights into a number of topics that are relevant to most startups. These topics include recognizing an opportunity, launching the business, dealing with growing pains from enterprise expansion, choosing a strategic direction, and adjusting business models in response to changing conditions.

It was June of 2010, during the year between my senior year of high school and freshman year of college. I was on vacation in Martha's Vineyard, without much in the way of entertainment. Back then, my music tastes largely originated from albums I had previously bought or heard online through services like Pandora. I had heard of music blogs, like Pitchfork, but had never really considered them to be anything worth following.

Around that time, mashups, a type of music combining two or more melodically similar songs into one new hybrid track, were becoming amazingly popular. I remembered how my high school friends always seemed to find the coolest mashups on the web. While relaxing in Martha's Vineyard that summer, I too found myself browsing online for mashups and other music and inadvertently stumbled upon blogs targeted to the college demographic. What immediately struck me about these blogs was their 90's-era visual design, their lack of organization, and their snail-paced downloads. It seemed painfully obvious that these blogs were set up and run by high school and college kids who had stumbled into the world of blogging and were struggling to find their way.

After checking out the blogs that were out there, I knew that I could do better. I was very confident of this because I had three years of web design and development experience under my belt from building blogs and websites for clients. I had learned how to drive traffic, improve search results, write content, etc. Leaning on this expertise, I pulled up a domain name I had bought the previous year, thekollection.com, installed a quick blog, and began my search for new music online. I ended up finding some songs from lesser-known artists who had put their work online for free. I uploaded those songs to The Kollection, and began sharing them with my friends.

Those first few weeks were pretty slow. I was working hard to find sources of new music that would allow me to post at least one new song each day. Every time I posted a track, a trickle of visitors—just one or two at first—would stop by the site to listen and download. But word spread rather quickly and soon the trickle of hits was growing into a torrent of activity. By August of that year, The Kollection saw 2,800 visits. In September, 85,000 visitors stopped by to find new music. In October, the site had more than 200,000 hits. This rapid growth didn't continue forever, but by 2011 the site was tracking over 30,000 visits per day and nearly 1 million per month.

What had started out as a hobby and a personal project quickly became much more than that. Soon I was worried about being able to pay for our servers (only $200 per month at the time, but enough to be of concern for a college freshman). So in October of 2010, as traffic on the site was growing so fast, I printed my first line of Kollection tee shirts. The design was simple, and quite unremarkable—in fact, it was my first time ever designing for print, so I had to learn quite a lot—but that first batch of shirts sold faster than I had expected.

At that point I was confident that apparel would be a feasible option to make money on the site. We were still growing and gaining a lot of attention, and quickly. Artists begged to be on the site, fans praised the music selection, and people were sharing music across the web. It wasn't unusual for us to give a previously unknown artist tens of thousands of plays and downloads within a day.

In January of 2011, fans began to approach me and ask to write for the site. They saw The Kollection as a fun and worthwhile way to get a taste of the music industry. As a result of the interest, my team of authors grew quickly, peaking at around 15, but finally settling comfortably at around 6 writers in 2012 and into 2013. The team truly made The Kollection possible in 2011 and 2012—they helped me publish thousands of posts to the site in just a few years and upload several new songs per day. We were able to see from our tracking that fans visiting The Kollection were listening to and downloading millions of songs a month. We were revved up and running on a full tank of gas, and it didn't seem like things could possibly slow down.

But slow down they did. As 2011 turned into 2012, more and more college students and high schoolers were learning how easy it was to set up a blog and start sharing music for free online. Blogs began to pop up by the dozens, if not more, within a few months' time. Each of these tried hard to bring a unique essence to the game, but for a music blog with such a simple process, there really isn't much room to expand horizontally. In late 2011 I started to notice that more and more music blogs were consistently posting the same songs as every other site. This meant that the music blogging niche that I was in had become an easily replicable commodity that anybody could copy with very little effort.

So it was time to think more carefully about how to differentiate the site. Through 2011 we were able to make The Kollection stand out from the crowd with our emphasis on minimal design, structured organization, searchability, and speed. We always focused on making it as easy as possible for fans to quickly listen to and download new music. But as 2012 was approaching, other contenders had made headway with their website designs, and it became harder to separate them from The Kollection.

After giving it a lot of thought, I decided to take The Kollection in a few directions, which in hindsight probably caused me to spread the business too thin. First, I hired a company to develop an iOS and Android app so that fans could stream our music from their phones. Second, we spent over $4,000 on a run of tee shirts to expand our line of merchandise. Third, I redesigned and rebuilt the site with a functionality that allowed users to build their own playlists directly on the site, using songs we had posted.

Considered separately, these three avenues all performed very well. Our apps saw more than 30,000 downloads within two months, with fans listening to more than 1 million songs on their phones. Our apparel sold well, too, often with as much as several hundred dollars of merchandise being purchased a day. In fact, we broke even and started to make a profit on apparel within one month. The site redesign was also successful—pageviews continued to stay strong, and fans loved having the ability to build their own customized playlists with their favorite music.

But in early 2012, a few things came crashing down on The Kollection. You see, up until that point we had been using Soundcloud to upload and host all of our audio files. This allowed us to power mobile apps and make the most of the site redesign, while tracking the number of plays and downloads across the network. But, almost without warning, the plug was pulled on all of this due to a handful of copyright complaints. The Kollection has always focused on sharing music available for free from the artists themselves, but occasionally a song would slip through the cracks, one that really should not have been uploaded. As a result, in the first quarter of 2012 we lost our Soundcloud account, and because of that, our mobile apps no longer functioned and the playlist builder on the website could not operate.

We had spent thousands of dollars building The Kollection around Soundcloud, so this was a major disruption to the venture as a whole. We saw traffic stall, and fans became frustrated as a result of the loss of our differentiating features.

But we pushed on. My authors and I revived our core focus of sharing new music with fans around the world. We found failsafe ways to share music (legally) without worrying about copyright issues. We stripped the site down to its core features, removing the ability to build playlists, and we pulled our app from the app stores.

2012 also brought with it a host of new problems for The Kollection. Though services like Pandora had been around for a long time, that year the public's attention seemed to shift quickly toward online radio. Pandora, Spotify, Rdio, and other such services gained enormous traction in the music-discovery market, making it easier for friends to share with one another the music that they came across on the web. The Kollection and other blogs like it had the distinct advantage of being the first to share new music (for example, we could post a new song within minutes of its release), but as soon as these songs found their way into the libraries of big players like Spotify and Rdio, we lost the competitive advantage of having this new music.

Throughout 2012 our month-to-month costs remained relatively stable, but our income fluctuated wildly. We were running banner ads on a pay-per-click basis, earning us anywhere from $300 to $1,000 per month. But at the same time, merchandise sales slowed as inventory dwindled, and I had a hard time making a decision about the best way to move forward with the venture. On the one hand, I was in college and my time was limited, so I knew it was important to focus on one business model and revenue stream. While clothing ultimately made more money, it required a lot more work to design new lines, pack and ship every order, and support customers around the world who had problems with their orders. On the other hand, ads were a passive way to make money and didn't *require any extra day-to-day effort. The downside of this option, however, is that the ads didn't generate as much profit as the merchandise, and earning $300 to $1,000 per month was just barely enough to maintain our server costs.*

Ultimately, the biggest decision I had to make as the owner was to determine how much time and effort I was willing to invest in the website. It had grown to such a size that I couldn't run it on my own and had to have the help of my team of authors to make it work. At the same time, though, we weren't generating enough revenue to pay them as employees. So, I still needed to decide how to divide my time and effort between school and the venture, and I knew that it was unrealistic to expect The Kollection to continue growing without a new vision and drastic changes that would sufficiently differentiate the site from the competition.

The best road forward for The Kollection is not obvious to me at this point. Some things are non-negotiable. For example, we still want the site to drive a lot of traffic and remain a respected source in the music blog niche. Also, we definitely want to continue to promote new artists and their music and do this very well, pushing up pageviews and ad sales, but finding an ad platform that will allow us to make significant revenue from the traffic we generate has not been easy. Merchandise sales from The Kollection have been very helpful in the past, but they require a lot of time and attention, and I won't really have much extra bandwidth to give to this as long as I am a college student with a part-time job. This leaves me with some difficult decisions to make, but I am ready for the challenge and look forward to my future as an entrepreneur—no matter what direction it takes.

Source: Story as told by Brian Lovin, founder and owner of The Kollection, March 26, 2013.

Questions

1. How did Lovin come to recognize the opportunity for his young venture? Of the three types of startups mentioned in Chapter 3, which one does The Kollection fit into? What was the source of this opportunity?
2. Complete a SWOT analysis for The Kollection. What does it say about the strengths that the startup can build on or the weaknesses that it must be particularly careful to protect itself against? Does this analysis reveal any promising future opportunities for Lovin and his venture? By your analysis, what threats put the enterprise most at risk?
3. What broad-based strategy is Lovin following at The Kollection? Is this the only and best way to position the company? Why or why not?
4. Conduct a feasibility analysis on the company, being sure to consider its market potential, industry attractiveness, and leadership. According to your assessment, how much promise does the venture offer?
5. What recommendations would you make to Lovin as he thinks about the company and its future?

VIDEO CASE 4

Two Men and a Truck®/ International, Inc.

Exceeding Customers' Expectations

Background

In 2007, TWO MEN AND A TRUCK®/INTERNATIONAL, Inc., was recognized on *Entrepreneur* magazine's list of Top 500 (it was ranked at number 171), named as one of America's top global franchises, listed on *Franchise Business Review*'s "Franchise 50," and selected as one of the top 25 franchises for Hispanics by the National Minority Franchising Initiative. According to the company's website (www.twomenandatruck.com), it is the first and largest local moving franchise system in the United States and offers a full range of home and business moving services.

History

TWO MEN AND A TRUCK started in the early 1980s as a way for two brothers to make extra money while they were in high school. Now, over 20 years later, the company has grown to more than 200 locations worldwide.

Brothers Brig Sorber and Jon Sorber started moving people in the Lansing, Michigan, area using an old pickup truck. They had their mom, Mary Ellen Sheets, develop a logo to put in a weekly community newspaper. That stick men logo still rests on every truck, sign, and advertisement for the company. After the brothers left for college, Sheets continued to field calls for moving services while she also worked a full-time data-processing job with the state of Michigan. In 1985, she decided to make things official by purchasing a 14-foot truck for $350 and hiring a pair of movers. That $350 is the only capital Sheets has ever invested in the company. Her experience with data analysis, combined with her commitment to customer service, earned her a spot on a 1988 graduate business panel at Michigan State University. When a fellow panelist suggested she franchise her little company, Sheets decided to consult with an attorney.

In 1989, Sheets awarded the first location outside of Michigan to her daughter, Melanie Bergeron. The office was in Atlanta, Georgia. When the company reached 39 franchises, Sheets asked Bergeron to assume the role of company president while she pursued a seat in the Michigan State Senate. Bergeron is now chair of the board. TWO MEN AND A TRUCK's long track record of aggressive growth continues under Bergeron's progressive leadership and keen business strategies. Her accomplishments have been showcased on the cover of *Franchising World* magazine and in numerous other publications, including *Franchise Times.* Brig and Jon Sorber returned to their Lansing roots in the mid-1990s to team up with their mom and older sister. Brig is now the president and chief executive officer, while Jon serves as executive vice president. The first truck that Sheets bought in 1985 has now multiplied into a fleet of more than 1,200 trucks.

Customers benefit from having trained, uniformed movers who are insured and bonded to handle any home move and business moving tasks. The company has come a long way—and logged a lot of miles—since Sheets sketched the first "stick men." TWO MEN AND A TRUCK continues to pave the way for future growth and innovation, while remaining focused on exceeding customers' expectations.

The firm now has more than 200 locations operating worldwide, including 32 U.S. states, Canada, and Ireland. In 2010 alone, with 1,300 trucks currently on the road, the system completed 317,841 moves. The company reached the milestone of 2,000,000 moves in 2005.

Franchising

Franchise territories are based on population, generally between 250,000 and 420,000 people per marketing area. The initial franchise fee is $45,000, or $85,000 if the franchisee has previously operated in the area. Total startup costs (including facility, trucks, equipment, and other expenses) range from $158,000 to $460,910. Franchisees pay a royalty of 6 percent of gross revenue, plus 1 percent for advertising.

TWO MEN AND A TRUCK has always focused on training its employees with the latest techniques and the best equipment available—and on treating everyone as they would want their grandmother treated, otherwise known as THE GRANDMA RULE®. Before a new franchisee can open a location, he or she must attend a two-week training course in Lansing, Michigan, conducted by home office staff at STICK MEN UNIVERSITY®. There, franchisees are taught by subject-matter experts about the computer systems, how to market their new business, and how to hire, manage, and lead their teams. (Throughout the year, STICK MEN UNIVERSITY offers online classes that cover everything from marketing tactics to leadership to making accurate estimates. Several instructor-led courses are also available online.)

Franchisees also work in a two-story home built inside the TWO MEN AND A TRUCK headquarters. During this portion of the training, students are taught how to maneuver, wrap, pack, and load items such as a grand piano, a china cabinet filled with breakables, glass tables, a washer and dryer, and a flat-screen television. Students are expected to be able to recognize obstacles and empty the house as quickly and efficiently as possible. A truck box, built to scale, is also located in the training facility. Students must be able to fully pack the back of the truck with the items from the home.

Many other tools are available to franchisees, including detailed monthly reports, newsletters, extranet, a system-wide annual meeting, a toll-free support line, a tradeshow booth, a complete line of TWO MEN AND A TRUCK branded clothing and professional marketing materials, and a system-wide purchasing system.

Before answering the following questions, reread Chapter 4 and watch the TWO MEN AND A TRUCK video for this chapter.

Source: Compiled from interviews and information provided by TWO MEN AND A TRUCK. www.twomenandatruck.com.

View the video and answer the questions that follow.

Questions

1. Limiting sales territories is one of the common restrictions that franchise contracts impose on franchisees. Do an Internet search for TWO MEN AND A TRUCK franchises in your immediate area. How many are there? Does this number reflect the company's population requirements?
2. Which moving companies compete with TWO MEN AND A TRUCK in your area? Are there differences in their rates of success? How could you measure those differences? Are there differences in their advertising? In their rates for items such as boxes and packing supplies? Which companies have an advantage, and why?
3. Suppose that after owning a TWO MEN AND A TRUCK franchise for five years, you decided to go out on your own with a new moving company called Four Movers. What kinds of legal issues would you face?

CASE 5 Iaccarino & Son

Tough Decisions for a Family

He labeled it "a typical immigrant story." Francis X. Iaccarino ("Fran" to his friends) was talking about his grandfather Raffaele. Raffaele emigrated from Italy to the United States, searching for better opportunities for his children. He had been a boat builder in Italy and expected to find the same kind of work in his new country. After being processed through Ellis Island, however, he was sent inland to Worcester, Massachusetts, because some of his relatives had already located there.

Ralph, as he became known in Worcester, found that his boat-building skills could be transferred to woodworking, so he began taking on whatever projects he could find. After a while, he rented a garage and established his own woodworking business. Ralph changed with the times, building refrigerator cases when electric refrigeration became widespread. There was a homebuilding explosion after World War II, and Ralph's company evolved into residential woodworking, specializing in moulding for doors and cabinets.

As an Italian immigrant with limited fluency in English, Ralph was taken advantage of by building contractors. He passed his business along to his sons and returned to Italy for the final years of his life. Ralph's boys, Carl and Joseph, were home after their war service and ready to take on responsibility for the company. Initially, they were frustrated by how erratic the workload was. They both had families to feed and wanted a more stable income. Carl noticed that the glass company across the street from his location was always busy. The owner told him the key was to have commercial rather than residential customers. So Carl and Joseph shifted their focus and went the commercial route.

During the 1960s, Carl ran the factory, while Joseph was in charge of the office. When Joseph was diagnosed with multiple sclerosis, he had to reduce his involvement in the firm. Their sister came in to help out. Even though they were second-generation Americans, the Iaccarinos still faced discrimination in the private sector. They began concentrating on public contracts. They found that having a union manage their employees gave them an advantage in government contracting. The union set the pay rates, making everything transparent in the public sector.

The 1970s saw an increase in disagreements among family members. Eventually, Carl bought Joseph's 50 percent stake in the company. As sole owner, Carl named his company Iaccarino & Son, in the expectation of persuading Fran to join the firm. But first, Carl had to get the business back on track. A recession hit just after he bought his brother's shares. Carl was able to stay afloat and slowly grew the business through the 1980s. Then, in 1991, another recession hit . . . a housing bust.

At the time, Fran was managing his own picture framing business. He felt the pull of the family legacy and felt he needed to help his father. So he sold his company and joined Iaccarino & Son, overseeing accounting and estimating the costs of completing contracts. Going into the recession, the firm had revenues in the range of $10 million. Fran's baptism in the business involved cutbacks and downsizing. By 1994, although the company was profitable, revenues were down to $4.5 million.

Fran completed his MBA degree in 1992. When he joined Iaccarino & Son, he saw the company as a case study, much as his professors had taught him. Fran wanted to focus on growth, on replacing old technology, on finding new markets. By the end of the decade, the company was again reaching the $10 million mark, with higher profits. But Fran did not detect what was going on behind the scenes. Long-time employees were intimidated by Fran's presence and felt threatened. Wherever possible, they actively worked to reverse the changes that Fran had made. And Fran's father, Carl, was worried by Fran's growth strategy and was unwilling to back him on key issues. Fran had made a big mistake when he agreed to join Iaccarino & Son—he failed to negotiate an ownership position. And he found his father would not let go of the power.

By 2001, Fran had had enough. He told his father that he was leaving the business unless Carl agreed to bring in outside consultants to reorganize the company. Carl agreed. The consultants implemented many of the changes Fran had previously attempted. They also instituted stronger analytical tools. Fran was optimistic about the company's future. In 2007, he drafted a plan for aggressive expansion, intending to double the size of the firm. Then came the Great Recession in 2008. But Iaccarino & Son did not feel it immediately. Its type of contracting made it a lagging indicator of economic trends. But it was hit hard in 2010 and 2011. There was a dwindling backlog of projects by 2012. The company lost three projects in one day and could not shrink fast enough to absorb the shock.

Iaccarino & Son reached its highest level of sales, over $15 million, in 2011. The next year, it filed for

Chapter 7 bankruptcy. The company had lost bargaining strength in the recession, cutting profit margins to obtain contracts. And a major hospital project had proved especially costly. Bills came due, and there was not enough left over to acquire inventory. The 83-year-old company had nearly 50 employees at the time the decision to close was made.

Entrepreneurs are told, "Fail early; fail often." Fran was not used to failing, and the closure certainly did not come early. Nevertheless, he came away with the sense that he had learned lessons. He felt he knew far more than when he started about how to deal with banks and with bonding companies. He concluded that business is all about relationships. His experience taught him that the relationships he had established with customers and vendors helped not only in growing a business, but also in failing in one. To his surprise, he found when it was over that he still had great relationships with many of the firms he had traded with.

And Fran has not lost the entrepreneurial spirit. He is planning his next venture. He is looking at options where barriers to entry are low. For now, he wants something small, but with serious profit potential.

Questions

1. If you were in Fran's shoes when he was running his own company, what factors might have attracted you to close your business and join Iaccarino & Son? What factors might have discouraged you from entering the family business?
2. Why do you think Carl wanted to retain ownership and decision-making authority over Iaccarino & Son after bringing Fran into the company?
3. When the recession hit in 2008, what advice would you have given Carl and Fran to increase the chances of survival for Iaccarino & Son?

Sources: Personal interview with Francis X. Iaccarino, January 2, 2015; personal correspondence with Francis X. Iaccarino, May 20, 2015; Obituary for Carl Iaccarino, http://www.legacy.com/obituaries/telegram/obituary.aspx?pid=172336478; and Matt Pilon, "83-Year-Old Boylston Millwork Firm Bankrupt," http://www.wbjournal.com/article/20121212/NEWS01/121219972/83-year-old-boylston-millwork-firm-bankrupt, accessed May 24, 2015.

Hyper Wear, Inc.

Writing an Executive Summary for a Business Plan

Hyper Wear was founded in 2008 to participate in the functional fitness market, along with such recognized brands as CrossFit and Zumba. The company first designed a men's weight vest called a Hyper Vest®, followed by the SandBell® and SteelBell®, which were designed to be used as free weights. In 2011, the firm raised money from outside investors and hired Denver Fredenburg as its CEO. By 2012, sales were approximately $1 million, and the firm needed more money to fund its growth. Fredenburg has written a business plan to be used in raising the needed money. The Hyper Wear, Inc., Executive Summary is presented on the text's website.

Questions

1. Is Hyper Wear's executive summary more of a synopsis or a narrative?
2. If you were an investor, would the executive summary spark your interest in the opportunity? In other words, would you continue reading the business plan for more details?
3. What do you like about this executive summary? What do you dislike?
4. Would you suggest that Fredenburg make any changes or additions to the executive summary? If so, what do you suggest?

ReadyMade Magazine

Focus and Segmentation

ReadyMade markets itself as a magazine catering to GenNesters, the group of consumers ages 25 to 35 who are just settling down after college. These young consumers are buying their first houses and taking on domestic and decorating roles for the first time. They are interested in being stylish, while at the same time maintaining their own unique personalities.

But the magazine appeals to a wide variety of readers other than just GenNesters. *ReadyMade* has subscribers in all age groups—from teens looking to update their rooms to retirees looking for projects to enliven their homes. This diversity offers a unique challenge to *ReadyMade* as it tries to promote itself to advertisers who need to know what sort of people will be reached through advertisements appearing in the publication.

ReadyMade is named after the term that Marcel Duchamp coined in 1915 for a series of sculptures that playfully rethought the relationship between people and mass-produced objects, everyday items, and art. *ReadyMade* magazine is about people who make things and the culture of making, so it consists mostly of do-it-yourself projects and both short and long articles. Subscribers are invited to submit projects, recipes, and story ideas relating to the culture of making, inventive practices and people, of-the-moment cultural trends and products, and food trends.

Before answering the questions below, reread Chapter 7 and watch the *ReadyMade* video for this chapter.

View the video and answer the questions that follow.

Questions

1. How does *ReadyMade* communicate the demographics of its reader base to advertisers who want to see specific statistics about *ReadyMade*'s target market?
2. What sort of segmentation does *ReadyMade* use when it markets to businesses and investors?
3. What ideas do you have that would help *ReadyMade* reach out to new subscribers without alienating its loyal base?

Source: From Lamb/Hair/McDaniel, *Essentials of Marketing*, 7e.

CASE 8

Couchsurfing International

A Story of Startup, Growth, and Transformation

In ancient civilizations, it was a common practice to open one's home to travelers who needed a place to sleep. This prompted the sharing of news, stories, and information. Couchsurfing International, a travel-oriented social networking site based in San Francisco, is dedicated to reviving the ancient practice and the social exchange that goes along with it.

Chapter One: The Founders

THE CONCEPTIONIST After graduating from college in 1997 with a degree in computer science, Casey Fenton decided to see some of the world before settling down. When he came across a relatively inexpensive flight from Boston to Reykjavik, Iceland, he decided to buy it but had no idea where he would stay or what he should see while there. He knew that he did not want to be a garden-variety tourist, staying in a hotel and traveling to the typical sights. Rather, he wanted to immerse himself in the Icelandic way of life—this, he believed, was what traveling should be all about.

To zero in on definite travel plans, Fenton called and e-mailed almost 2,000 students from the University of Iceland, asking if they had a couch or spare room that he could stay in for a night or two. He received more than 50 offers for possible accommodations not only in Reykjavik, where the university is situated, but also in other towns located nearby. Using these leads, he made connections, set up specific travel plans, and left for his Icelandic adventure.

The trip ended up being a truly unforgettable experience. The locals showed him things he could never have found on his own, and he built great friendships along the way. Fenton decided that he wanted to help others see the world as he was able to, through the eyes of native hosts. On the flight home, he came up with the idea that would become the foundation of "The Couchsurfing Project." Fenton spent the next couple of years programming and setting up the website for Couchsurfing.org. He also took a position with a startup called Fuxito Worldwide, but he continued working on the code that would lead to the eventual launch of his slowly blossoming website project.

THE ENTREPRENEUR Daniel Hoffer had three well-defined passions that developed at a young age: a love for traveling, helping others, and computer programming. An avid traveler since he was a boy, he gained a sense of purpose and perspective from learning about different cultures. With this confidence and direction, he figured out how to use his computer science skills to fulfill his desire to help others. The first online community that Hoffer launched grew into what would become a nonprofit educational program in Massachusetts and an online bulletin board that allowed physically disabled patients to connect with high school students.

Prior to getting his MBA from Columbia Business School and working for numerous computer technology companies, Hoffer studied philosophy at Harvard University. Apparently, his studies weren't enough to keep him busy, because he remained actively engaged in the computer science world during that time and helped launch multiple startups. One of these companies, founded in 1999 as a venture-backed operation, was an international soccer website called Fuxito Worldwide. Although this endeavor was only one of hundreds of projects with which Hoffer would become involved, Fuxito was the venture that would lead Hoffer to his true calling.

THE VISIONARY Sebastian Le Tuan was born to help cultivate a world of cultural acceptance through travel. A native of France, Le Tuan eventually followed his heart and his love for technology to Silicon Valley in California. But while he was still a teenager, he spent time with a host family in Catalan, Spain, which helped him to understand that experiencing cultures on a personal level is paramount to releasing judgment and embracing differences. Though he had an undergraduate degree in cognitive science from the University of California at Berkley, Le Tuan managed to harness his passion for software development, as well, through various research initiatives. He worked for several companies as a software designer, with a focus on user experience. Eventually, he landed a position at a Web-based company called Fuxito Worldwide, where he would come to find his broad span of interests and experience perfectly matched for an innovative endeavor that was just waiting to come together.

Chapter Two: Birth of a Business

Fenton, Hoffer, and Le Tuan brought their own unique backgrounds, interests, and talents when they joined Fuxito Worldwide and ended up making important contributions to the venture. Though they worked on different aspects of the company, the three formed a close friendship based on a shared love for innovation, exploration, and serving those in need. They realized that their diverse specialties, together with a unified purpose and vision, could help them develop a website that would revolutionize the way people travel. Thus began The Couchsurfing Project.

THE PATH TO 501(C)(3) STATUS After spending a number of years forming their ideas into a concrete plan, Fenton, Hoffer, and Le Tuan all agreed steadfastly on many aspects of their startup concept, the most important of which was that it would be launched as a nonprofit organization. In March 2003, the three co-founders filed in New Hampshire to incorporate Couchsurfing as a 501(c) (3), but it was not added to the official list of registered charities in the state until November 14, 2007. (See Chapter 8 for more information about 501(c)(3) status.) Why the delay? By taking their time to register the organization as a nonprofit with the state attorney general (which is required by law in the state of New Hampshire), Couchsurfing sidestepped certain recordkeeping and reporting responsibilities. This move led the Department of Justice in New Hampshire to investigate the organization at the end of 2007. With the pressure to comply growing, the company eventually sent the required documents for 2003 to 2006 to the attorney general, and the organization was officially added to the registered charities list.

WEBSITE LAUNCH After filing for 501(c)(3) status in 2003, the three co-founders finally launched a beta version of the website. Because he had been so involved with the development of the basic idea and the coding that was needed, Fenton naturally accepted the role of executive director. Hoffer had experience managing small startup companies, so he gravitated toward strategic development–related responsibilities. LeTuan had a solid grasp of the connection between human experience and both technology and cultural acceptance, so he headed the development of the website's overall purpose and mission. This provided the budding venture with a vision that could support and sustain the dedication and commitment of its members. A year after its beta testing was initiated, the website went public, and the founders were confident that users would come to discover and appreciate the power of relationship-based, reduced-cost travel.

Chapter Three: Riding the Wave of a ".org"

The founders fully believed that their venture would touch the lives of millions of people, but in the year following the website's launch, only 6,000 members joined the community. The founders continued to follow the same strategy for the next year, which saw membership jump to nearly 50,000. And with the continued growth came other new opportunities—that is, until 2006 rolled around.

In June 2006, the venture hit a serious snag: As a result of numerous technical errors within Couchsurfing's databases, the profiles of all of its members were lost. Because so much information had vanished and the future of the venture seemed to be so in doubt, Fenton sent out an e-mail to the masses, reporting, "It is with a heavy heart that I face the truth of this situation. Couchsurfing as we knew it doesn't exist anymore."

Immediately upon sending out this message, Fenton started receiving a great deal of criticism. But at the same time, many members were very supportive, which inspired the Couchsurfing team to design a new website (called CS2.0) within a couple of weeks after the technical failures. The team also created a new slogan for the venture, "Participate in Creating a Better World, One Couch at a Time," which fit the new culture of the rehabilitated enterprise. With the continued support of past and current members, in addition to the international media attention that the new website received, Couchsurfing's membership exploded from around 50,000 to over 3.5 million individuals by the beginning of 2012. During this period, nearly 5.5 million travel-related connections were formed using this one-of-a-kind community website.

Chapter Four: What to Do When Growing Too Fast

Up to this point, the only revenues that Couchsurfing had received were from donations and its identification verification service (highly recommended, but not required), which could be used to confirm that a member was who he or she claimed to be. Fenton and Hoffer were strongly committed to providing an online source of help to travelers looking for free places to stay and to offering that service without the advertisements and expenses that other travel websites featured. But with the explosion of growth Couchsurfing had experienced, the management team needed to decide if remaining a nonprofit was best for the future of the company. To complicate matters further, Couchsurfing applied to receive 501(c)(3) status in November of 2007, only to see its application be formally rejected by the IRS in early 2011. From this setback, Hoffer came to realize that the nonprofit structure can blunt organizational innovation and flexibility as a result of increased regulatory oversight and various auditing requirements stipulated by law.

In their search for guidance, they sought the advice of four people who were members of the venture's board of directors: Tony Espinoza, Matt Cohler, Jonathan Teo, and Todor Tashev. These seasoned executives brought a wealth of experience to discussions about the company and its future. Espinoza had worked at Apple and had served as vice president and general manager for MTV Networks, vice president and co-founder of When.com, vice president of AOL, and CEO of SuperSecret.com. Cohler was one of the founding members of LinkedIn, where he served as vice president and general manager. He was also one of the first five employees hired at Facebook and is currently a general partner at Benchmark, a venture capital firm. Teo was a member of the strategy team at Google and a principal at Benchmark, where he helped initiate the original investments in companies like Twitter and Instagram. Tashev had worked as a venture capital analyst for JP Morgan and later became a partner at investment firm Omidyar Network, where he directed consumer Internet and mobile initiatives.

These board members suggested using a new organizational form specifically designed to use the power of business to solve a social or environmental problem. As a B Corporation (or benefit corporation), performance and accountability standards are demanding, sustainability must be a primary thrust, and transparency is forced through B Impact Reports that have to be filed. But the team quickly realized that converting to this form would allow them to accept investments, and be nimble and flexible while remaining true to their original and continuing social mission. Responding to this advice, the team decided to change its status officially to a B corporation in late 2011.

This new organizational form brought new opportunities, but also greater challenges. On the opportunity side, it led to $15 million in investments to fuel the expansion of the company so that it could keep up with escalating market interest. This funding was led by investment heavyweights like Benchmark, General Catalyst Partners, Menlo Ventures, and Omidyar Network. It also allowed the firm to begin to earn profits from its nearly 3.5 million users, but the founders maintained that Couchsurfing would continue to offer its services free of charge to its users. They added, however, that the change would also allow them to explore "alternative revenue streams."

While the change in status at Couchsurfing opened the door to greater opportunity, it also presented its share of risk. Change can erode confidence and will almost always generate at least some resistance. It certainly created significant backlash for Couchsurfing. About 3,000 members of the company's online community actually formed a group under the title "We are against CS becoming a for-profit corporation." This group voiced their reactions, which were varied and included statements such as "The structure of CS belongs to the community," "Members are no longer part of a true community, they are customers/consumers of a service sold by Couchsurfing International Inc.," and "The worst part is that the assets of a non-profit should not be allowed to change into a for-profit." These reactions indicate that the struggles at Couchsurfing International—following its conversion from a nonprofit organization to a for-profit entity that continues to provide benefits to society—are probably far from over.

Questions

1. How would you describe the founding team of Fenton, Hoffer, and Le Tuan? Is it a balanced team? What does each member bring to the business? Can you see gaps in their skill sets and capabilities that should be adjusted for in some way?
2. What is the form of organization that Fenton, Hoffer, and Le Tuan first chose for Couchsurfing International? Assess the advantages and disadvantages of the major organizational forms mentioned in Chapter 8. Which of these would have been best for the company when it was founded? Why?
3. Identify and describe the organizational form to which the team most recently transitioned the firm. Was it a good decision to make this change? In your opinion, how well was the transition handled? In what ways might it have been managed better?
4. Assess the fit of the board of directors with Couchsurfing based on the profiles of those members mentioned in the case (the company has additional directors). What are the strengths and weaknesses of these board members, including potential gaps in their knowledge? Do you see any ways in which their advice to the entrepreneurial team may not have been in the best interests of the company?

Sources: Case contributed by Garad Soderman; www.opencouchsurfing.org/tag/legal, accessed April 5, 2013; Nicole Perlroth, "Non-Profit Couchsurfing Raises Millions in Funding," *Forbes*, August 24, 2011, www.forbes.com/sites/nicoleperlroth/2011/08/24/non-profit-couchsurfing-raises-millions-in-funding, accessed April 4, 2013; Bobbie Johnson, "After Going For-Profit, Couchsurfing Faces Revolt," http://gigaom.com/2011/09/01/after-going-for-profit-couchsurfing-faces-user-revolt, accessed April 3, 2013; and Michael del Castillo, "Global Traveler Raises $15 Million to Put Strangers in Your Living Room," *Upstart Business Journal*, August 22, 2012, http://upstart.bizjournals.com/money/loot/2012/08/22/couchsurfing-raises-15m-for-mobile-apps.html?page=all, accessed April 4, 2013.

Cookies-N-Cream

A Moveable Location

Cookies-N-Cream is an independent brand that sells its products from a truck that provides a moveable location and low overhead. Based in Brooklyn, New York, the company's owners, Scrills, P Loc and DJ Jon Blak, are preparing a second truck, which they're renovating and planning to move into Los Angeles sometime in the next year.

The Cookies-N-Cream brand is one that encompasses two creative outlets—clothing and designer toys—neither of which are cookies or cream. In an era of "me-too" clothing brands and toys, the owners set out to create a culture brand that draws on different influences—New York City lifestyle/culture, art, street couture, designer toys, high fashion, music, and pop/underground culture, just to name a few—all with a distinct personality and attitude of their own. Designer toys refer to toys and other collectibles created in limited quantities by artists and designers, and collected mostly by adults. Some of the toys/art pieces include the Puma SneakerHead, Hapiko, Dumny, and Shoot sculptures.

Based on their belief in being "true to yourself," the owners called their brand Cookies-N-Cream and built a grassroots company that's authentic and fun. With their attention to detail and focus on creating "playful luxury" products, they've developed a cult following that enjoys the experience that is Cookies-N-Cream. The owners represent the independent and avant-garde attitude that embodies their roots and today's youth.

View the video and answer the questions that follow.

Questions

1. What are some location advantages that Cookies-N-Cream has that a brick-and-mortar retailer doesn't have? Are there any drawbacks to a mobile vendor's choice of location?
2. Discuss site costs, retailing and office equipment, and other financial considerations of a mobile vendor such as Cookies-N-Cream.
3. What legal considerations affect Cookies-N-Cream's choice of location? How do those compare with the legal considerations of brick-and-mortar and home-based businesses?

Source: Compiled from interviews and information provided by Cookies-N-Cream. http://www.bakedinny.com.

Harper & Reiman, LLC

Understanding a Firm's Financial Statements

Harper & Reiman, LLC, is a consulting firm that caters to nonprofit organizations. The company is headquartered in Dallas, Texas, and has recently expanded to include an office in Amarillo, Texas, Harper's home town.

The business was founded in 2000 by Brett Harper and Anna Reiman, who met in an entrepreneurship class in college and discovered that they shared a passion for serving and developing the nonprofit sphere. Following graduation, they both were employed by J.P. Morgan. They frequently worked together on common assignments. On a number of occasions, they worked with nonprofit organizations whose innovative processes allowed them to "do more with less." The not-for-profits simply were not able to throw a lot of cash at problems, as many large business organizations do, and had to think and act like entrepreneurs if they were to achieve their missions. Harper and Reiman soon came to believe that for-profit businesses could learn from the really good nonprofits.

After eight years at JP Morgan, Harper and Reiman decided to start their own consulting firm, Harper & Reiman, LLC. At first, they limited their work to financial advisory services, knowing that many nonprofits needed help in managing their financial operations. The company developed financial management software that centers on liquidity analytics and enables nonprofits to shorten cash conversion cycles and strengthen liquidity. They gradually expanded into other services, including sustainable business solutions, infrastructure consulting, risk management, and innovation services.

The company has experienced significant growth, with sales approaching $29 million in 2013—far beyond anything the owners could have imagined. For one thing, the company distinguished itself in the industry by designing a payment system that allows nonprofits to make payments for Harper & Reiman services in seasons when donations are the highest. However, it also required Harper & Reiman to diversify its client base so that receivables are consistently being collected. Essentially, the company has applied the advice it gives to clients to itself.

While the majority of consulting clients are located near the two regional offices, the firm's software has been sold nationwide on a limited basis. Wanting to enter new geographical markets, Harper and Reiman are considering a marketing strategy to increase the firm's national visibility. However, before beginning a major expansion, they want to evaluate the firm's financial health.

Harper & Reiman, LLC

Balance Sheets for years ending 2012 and 2013

	2012	2013	Changes
Assets			
Current assets:			
Cash	$ 15,500	$ 218,500	$ 203,000
Accounts receivable	3,989,000	4,428,000	439,000
Inventory	4,155,000	4,678,000	523,000
Prepaid expenses and deposits	138,500	144,000	5,500
Other current assets	105,500	105,500	—
Total current assets	$ 8,403,500	$ 9,574,000	$1,170,500
Fixed assets:			
Gross fixed assets	$ 7,541,000	$ 8,519,000	$ 978,000
Accumulated depreciation	(3,822,500)	(4,377,000)	(554,500)
Net fixed assets	3,718,500	4,142,000	423,500

	2012	2013	Changes
Other assets	11,500	1,000	(10,500)
TOTAL ASSETS	$ 12,133,500	$ 13,717,000	$ 1,583,500
Debt (Liabilities) and Equity			
Current liabilities:			
Notes payable to bank	$ 1,100,000	$ 1,192,000	$ 92,000
Accounts payable	1,931,000	2,238,500	307,500
Accrued expenses	920,500	884,000	(36,500)
Total current liabilities	$ 3,951,500	$ 4,314,500	$ 363,000
Long-term debt	3,614,000	4,257,000	643,000
Total debt	$ 7,565,500	$ 8,571,500	$ 1,006,000
Stockholders' equity:			
Common stock	$ 356,000	$ 391,500	$ 35,500
Additional paid-in capital	498,000	649,000	151,000
Retained earnings	3,714,000	4,105,000	391,000
Total stockholders' equity	$ 4,568,000	$ 5,145,500	$ 577,500
TOTAL DEBT AND EQUITY	$ 12,133,500	$ 13,717,000	$ 1,583,500

Income Statements for Years Ending 2012 and 2013

	2012	2013
Net sales	$ 27,069,000	$ 28,911,500
Cost of goods sold	(18,880,500)	(20,524,500)
Gross profits	$ 8,188,500	$ 8,387,000
Selling and general and administrative expenses	(6,805,500)	(6,953,000)
Operating profits	$ 1,383,000	$ 1,434,000
Interest expense	(481,500)	(535,500)
Interest income	5,500	10,000
Profits before tax	$ 907,000	$ 908,500
Income taxes	(385,000)	(377,000)
Net profits	$ 522,000	$ 531,500

Statement of Retained Earnings for years ending 2012 and 2013

	2012	2013
Beginning retained earnings	$ 3,298,000	$ 3,714,000
Net profits	522,000	531,500
Dividends	(106,000)	(140,500)
Ending retained earnings	$ 3,714,000	$ 4,105,000

(Continued)

Statement of Cash Flows for years ending 2012 and 2013

	2012	2013
Operating activities:		
Net profits	$ 522,000	$ 531,500
Depreciation	564,500	554,500
Profits before depreciation	$ 1,086,500	$ 1,086,000
Increase in accounts receivable	$ (464,000)	$ (439,000)
Payments for inventory:		
Increase in inventory	(572,000)	(523,000)
Increase in accounts payable	68,500	307,500
Total payment for inventory	(503,500)	(215,500)
Increase in prepaid expenses	(19,000)	(5,500)
Increase (decrease) in accrued expenses	87,500	(36,500)
Cash flows from operations	$ 187,500	$ 389,500
Investing activities:		
Increase in gross fixed assets	$ (861,500)	$ (978,000)
Decrease (increase) in other assets	—	10,500
Cash flows from investing activities	$ (861,500)	$ (967,500)
Financing activities:		
Increase in notes payable	$ 625,000	$ 92,000
Increase (decrease) in long-term debt	(112,500)	643,000
Issued common stock	77,500	186,500
Cash dividends paid	(81,000)	(140,500)
Cash flows from financing activities	$ 509,000	$ 781,000
Net change in cash	$ (165,000)	$ 203,000
Beginning cash	180,500	15,500
Ending cash	$ 15,500	$ 218,500
Industry norms:		
Current ratio	2.2	
Return on assets	12.6%	
Operating profit margin	6.3%	
Total asset turnover	2.00	
Debt ratio	40.0%	
Return on common equity	15.0%	

Question

1. Harper and Reiman are interested in examining four specific issues: liquidity, profitability, the risk occurring from debt financing, and the rate of return the business is providing to them as owners. They also want to have a good sense of the sources and uses of cash flows in the business. Given the firm's recent financial results, as shown above, evaluate the company's financial situation as it relates to the owners' concerns. What advice would you give to Harper and Reiman?

Source: This case was prepared by Lauren Houser, April 2013.

Ashley Palmer Clothing, Inc.

Financial Forecasting

Ashley Palmer Clothing, Inc., produces dresses for women. The firm was launched in June 2009 by Ashley Jantz and Amanda Palmer, both graduates of Boston College. Ashley Palmer designs apparel for the modern woman's shape rather than using the traditional standard sizing.

History of Sizing Clothing

In 1939, the National Bureau of Home Economics of the U.S. Department of Agriculture was charged with standardizing sizing for women's clothing. Over a two-year period, some 15,000 women were given full-body measurements. This system created the sizing system that is still in use today.

Studies have found that the average body proportions of American women when the sizing charts were created are different from the body proportions of today's women. Specifically, American women in 1939 were markedly more slender and shorter. The result is that it is difficult for some women to find clothing that fits well. In the September 2009 issue of *Fashionista Magazine*, Jantz, who stands six feet tall, said:

> *[W]e were tired of not finding the clothes that were the right fit so we decided it would be a good venture to create products for today's women based on bust measurement, cup size and torso length.*

The Opportunity

For Jantz and Palmer, this problem represented an opportunity. After considerable research, they decided to start a business that produced fitted clothing for today's young women. They recruited a young up-and-coming fashion designer, Joy Lee, who had experience in apparel design for several major women's clothing brands. Seven months after starting the business, they offered their first dresses for sale online.

Then, in early 2010, the firm began supplying clothes to two well-known high-end retailers. Within a year after becoming a supplier to these exclusive retail outlets, the company's production orders had more than doubled. In order to keep up, the firm added five more team members in October 2010.

Sales continued to increase over the next three years, reaching \$4.7 million in 2013. During this same time, the number of employees grew from 7 to 16. The company also moved into a 4,000-square-foot facility and added additional sewing equipment and presses.

Planning for Growth

In August 2013, Ashley Palmer ventured into creating professional attire for young women. The products received rave reviews. Within three months, the retail outlets had sold over 90 percent of their inventories, quickly placing orders for more products.

The founders, while excited about the prospect of sales growth, began to worry. Based on their estimates, the company would most probably experience a 50 percent growth rate, compared to the 25 percent they had experienced over the past two years. They knew that if they were to avoid cash flow problems from the anticipated growth, they needed to anticipate the asset requirements and additional financing that would be required to sustain their business.

The owners believed they would need to purchase state-of-the-art industrial sewing machines, cutting tables, and pressing machines at a cost of \$280,000. The new equipment would be depreciated over 14 years, using straight-line depreciation. Jantz also thought that the following assumptions were appropriate:

1. Cash, accounts receivable, and inventory would follow their same relationships to sales as in the past two years; that is, each asset would maintain the average asset-to-sales percentages experienced in 2012 and 2013.
2. Both cost of goods sold and marketing expenses are variable and would approximate the same percentage of sales as in 2012 and 2013.
3. General and administrative costs are fixed in nature but should increase to \$130,000 in the next year.
4. The interest rates on the already outstanding debt would be renegotiated, which would reduce the interest on this debt to \$45,000.
5. The firm's tax rate should be about 40 percent.

To meet the firm's financing needs, Palmer has negotiated a line of credit (short-term debt) with Amway Bank for up to $100,000. The bank has also agreed to loan the firm $150,000 for purchasing new equipment; this is to be repaid over five years. The principal on the latter loan is to be repaid in $30,000 annual payments, with interest payments being made on the remaining balance of the note. Both notes will carry a 5 percent interest rate. The short-term notes payable and long-term debt owed in 2013 will be reduced by $50,000 and $30,000, respectively. Accounts payable and other current liabilities should increase proportionally with sales increases.

Finally, Jantz and Palmer are willing to provide more of their own money in the form of equity up to a total of $100,000 in equity if needed. They will also lower the amount of dividends they have been paying themselves (about 40 percent of earnings over the past two years). They both have decided to limit their dividends individually to $15,000, or a total of $30,000.

Ashley Palmer Clothing, Inc.
Income Statements for the Years Ending December 31, 2011, 2012, and 2013

	2011		2012		2013	
Sales	$3,000,000	100.0%	$3,760,000	100.0%	$4,700,000	100.0%
Cost of goods sold	(2,400,000)	80.0%	(3,045,600)	81.0%	(3,877,500)	82.5%
Gross profits	$ 600,000	20.0%	$ 714,400	19.0%	$ 822,500	17.5%
Marketing expenses	(215,000)	7.2%	(250,000)	6.6%	(275,000)	5.9%
General & administrative expenses	(90,000)	3.0%	(100,000)	2.7%	(110,000)	2.3%
Depreciation expense	(25,000)	0.8%	(25,000)	0.7%	(25,000)	0.5%
Operating profits	$ 270,000	9.0%	$ 339,400	9.0%	$ 412,500	8.8%
Interest expense	(66,000)	2.2%	(66,000)	1.8%	(66,000)	1.4%
Profits before taxes	$ 204,000	6.8%	$ 273,400	7.3%	$ 346,500	7.4%
Taxes @ 40%	(81,600)	2.7%	(109,360)	2.9%	(138,600)	2.9%
Net profits	$ 122,400	4.1%	$ 164,040	4.4%	$ 207,900	4.4%
Dividends paid	$ (48,960)		$ (65,616)		$ (83,160)	
Addition to retained earnings	$ 73,440		$ 98,424		$ 124,740	

Ashley Palmer Clothing, Inc.
Balance Sheets for the Years Ending December 31, 2011, 2012, and 2013

	2011	2012	2013
Assets			
Cash	$ 48,000	$ 95,424	$ 60,000
Accounts receivable	150,000	175,000	246,816
Inventory	335,000	390,000	511,500
Total current assets	$ 533,000	$ 660,424	$ 818,316
Plant & equipment	$ 560,000	$ 560,000	$ 560,000
Accumulated depreciation	(125,000)	(150,000)	(175,000)
Net plant & equipment	$ 435,000	$ 410,000	$ 385,000
TOTAL ASSETS	$ 968,000	$1,070,424	$1,203,316

Balance Sheets for the Years Ending December 31, 2011, 2012, and 2013 (continued)

	2011	2012	2013
Debt (Liabilities) and Equity			
Accounts payable	$ 128,000	$ 153,000	$ 135,000
Short-term notes payable	250,000	275,000	275,000
Other current liabilities	46,000	50,000	51,152
Total current liabilities	$ 424,000	$ 478,000	$ 461,152
Long-term debt	300,000	250,000	275,000
Total debt	$ 724,000	$ 728,000	$ 736,152
Owner's capital	$ 155,560	$ 155,560	$ 155,560
Retained earnings	88,440	186,864	311,604
Total equity	$ 244,000	$ 342,424	$ 467,164
TOTAL DEBT AND EQUITY	$ 968,000	$1,070,424	$1,203,316

Source: Written by Thomas Totoe, April 2013.

Questions

1. Given the assumptions that Jantz and Palmer have made, prepare a pro forma income statement and balance sheet for 2014. Assume that the line of credit provided by the bank will be needed for the full year.
2. Using the financial ratios presented in Chapter 10, compare Ashley Palmer's ratios over time, including the pro forma ratios for 2014. If the bank requires a current ratio of at least 1.5 and a debt ratio not to exceed 55 percent, can the owners expect to be able to honor these covenants?
3. Prepare a statement of cash flows for 2013 and the 2014 projections. What did you learn from these statements?

Moonworks

From Gutters to Home Remodeling

Not only is financing a startup business a challenge, but sometimes remaining fiscally fit for survival is itself a difficult hurdle to overcome. The first three years of starting a business can be the toughest, but how does a company that has been operating for several years continue to find sources of financing? Economic conditions, products, and customer bases can change, sometimes leaving a once-sustainable company in jeopardy of not meeting the day-to-day expenses of operation.

Managing cash flows invariably takes more than just matching payables with receivables, covering payroll, and paying taxes and insurance. As business conditions change, so can the money coming into a company. Even after startup loans have been retired, a line of credit or loan from a good funding provider is essential to keep a business moving forward.

Moonworks, a Rhode Island–based remodeling business founded as Moon Associates in 1993, enjoyed a modest rise to financial success by selling a product called GutterHelmet. Backed by the financial resources of BankRI, president and CEO Jim Moon turned GutterHelmet into a household name in New England by marketing it with help from local celebrities. Between 1993 and 2005, Moon Associates grew to $14 million in revenue by selling the product throughout New England, New York, and southwest Florida, while working out of a 10,000-square-foot building the company owns in Woonsocket, Rhode Island. During that time, the company installed more gutters in the New England states and New York than all other gutter companies combined.

As business boomed, Moon assembled a top-notch management team and started offering other products like garage organizing systems and hurricane shutters, but GutterHelmet remained the company's largest cash generator. To set the stage for future growth, the company's management began implementing industry-leading business systems.

The tide started to change in 2006. The market for gutter protection and remodeling showed signs of weakening in a slowing housing market, and the competition started putting a dent in GutterHelmet. There was no seasonal uptick in fall orders, and Moon Associates began exploring other means of generating operating cash, including the sale of their Florida operation. About the same time, Andersen Company's full-service window replacement division, Renewal by Andersen, had entered the Rhode Island home improvement market and was seeking a partner. After months of negotiation, Moon Associates struck a deal to be the sole southern New England partner, and Renewal by Andersen of Rhode Island soon debuted. With this partnership, Moon Associates was positioned to serve its existing customer base with Andersen's stylish, energy-efficient windows.

Yet the partnership didn't provide Moon Associates with the necessary boost. In 2007, GutterHelmet sales dropped 50 percent, to $6 million. Despite efforts to advertise on the Internet, new business leads were hard to generate. Renewal by Andersen of Rhode Island endured the normal financial hardships of starting up, and Moon Associates' bottom line went in the red after total company revenues plummeted 30 percent. Moon Associates needed something more than a new product line or division to return the company to profitability.

New England winters can be hard, and the winter of 2007/2008 was even tougher for Moon Associates. For the first time, the company's management team had to figure out how to turn around a negative bottom line at a time when business in general was changing. Moon went back to the drawing board to look for top-level talent. Local celebrities weren't the answer, so he recruited industry veteran Paul Thibeault, formerly Home Depot's Home Services northeast manager, to inject muscle into the company's sales force. But building sales would take time, and the company needed new capital to move forward. Moon Associates called on an old friend, the company's long-term financial partner, BankRI. Banker Matt Weiner and BankRI believed in Moon Associates' business plan and increased the company's credit line to keep Moon Associates on track.

The capital enabled Moon Associates' management team to play a hunch that Renewal by Andersen of Rhode Island could make a dent in the Cape Cod, Massachusetts, market. Further, the company diversified its product line to include general exterior home replacement products like roofing and siding, as well as insulation and hot water heaters. Moon Associates changed its name to Moonworks and shifted its focus to being a leading regional home improvement company and began to emphasize repeat customer business instead of new customer generation.

By the end of 2008, the company had emerged from the red and had a solid black bottom line. Revenues had grown 39 percent, and cash flows were positive. Moonworks was named the "Best of the Best, Smaller Market," an award that goes to the best-performing Renewal by Andersen dealer in the country.

Moonworks continued to grow over the next two years, again receiving top recognition from Renewal by Andersen, while expanding its window-remodeling territory into Hartford and northern Connecticut. In 2010, the company posted revenues of $12.7 million, more than twice that in 2007. A crowning achievement was the company's receipt of the "Big 50 Award," *Remodeling Magazine's* annual award recognizing exceptional performance in the remodeling and replacement contracting industry.

View the video and answer the questions that follow.

Questions

1. Describe what a line of credit involves, and explain the legal obligation of a bank to provide capital with a line of credit.
2. On what three priorities might BankRI representative Matt Weiner have based the decision to extend Moon Associates' line of credit or offer additional financing? What are the "five C's of credit"?
3. Even as the remodeling market weakened and taking on extra financing became risky, what are some things that Moon Associates' president and CEO Jim Moon did to sustain the company's long-term profitability?
4. Could Moon Associates have obtained the needed capital to not only keep the company running but expand its Renewal by Andersen line through a mortgage loan? If so, how long could such a loan be financed?

CASE 13

Network Collie

In June 2010, William Casey had just finished his last day at a national conference for IT and software companies. He was attending on behalf of his current employer but was also there to promote Network Collie, a data management company he had started a little more than two years earlier with three college friends. Launching the new company had been hard work but also exciting for Casey and his three co-founders: Dallena Nguyen, Cody Rose, and John Dalton. Today was no different. Throughout the conference, they had received positive feedback from potential customers about their new service. However, Casey was still questioning whether Network Collie would be a long-term success. He definitely had a passion to be an entrepreneur and believed that Network Collie had potential for success. However, the team was having difficulty closing larger sales orders, and he questioned the commitment from the founding team, including his own. He knew that these two areas needed to be addressed and a firm direction for the company needed to be established before he would begin to feel comfortable with the company's future.

After dinner, the team began to share stories about conversations they had had with potential customers during the conference. The discussion quickly turned to how they should move forward. They talked about continuing down the same path, but everyone agreed that something different needed to happen if they were going to achieve success. Their conversation focused on the long-term prospects and the potential value of Network Collie, as well as the individual needs and circumstances of the founders. Each of the founders had different ideas about how to move forward, but the final choices were to (1) quit their jobs and commit to Network Collie on a full-time basis, (2) hire someone to run the company, (3) try to sell the company, or (4) walk away.

The team debated the pros and cons of each idea. They still believed their service was the best among their competition. At the same time, all of them were concerned about the risk of leaving their current jobs. Another concern was that the first two options would require the company to obtain capital from outside investors, which was something they had never attempted before. Casey knew that the time for a decision about the future of Network Collie was now. He just wasn't sure which choice was the right choice.

Background

If ever there was a fast-rising and potentially sustainable growth market, social networking certainly was in 2009. Its foreseeable future is truly exciting based on long-term projections. As shown in Exhibit C13.1, the social network

EXHIBIT C13.1 U.S. Social Network Users and Penetration, 2009–2013

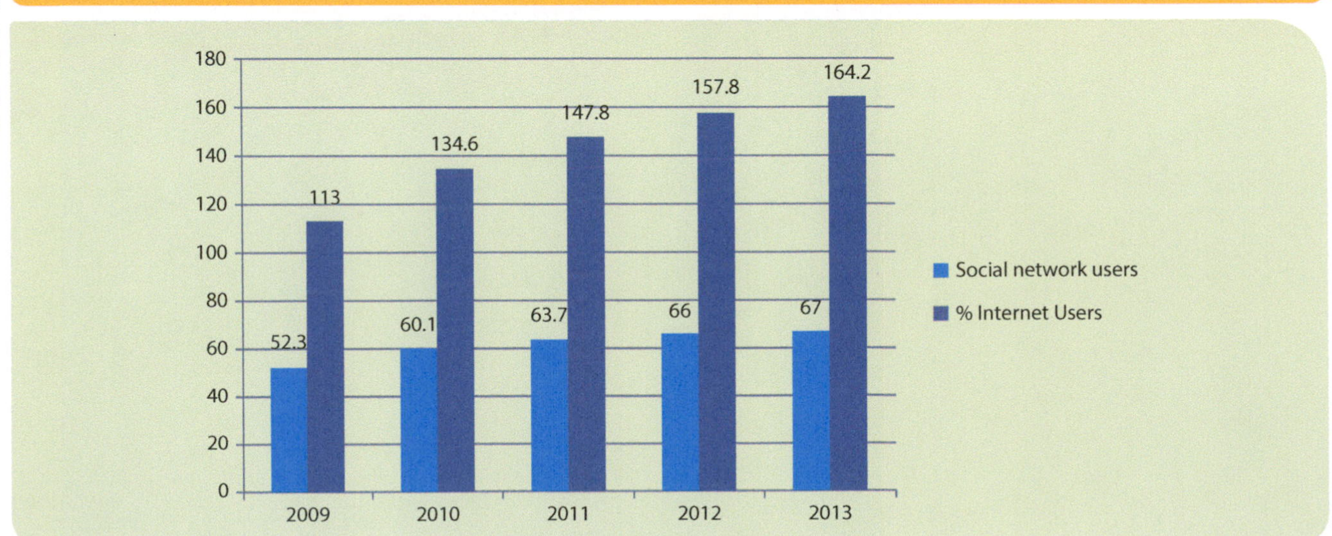

phenomenon was projected to grow to over 164 million users and to comprise over 67 percent of the online population by 2013.

When Network Collie was started, social networking was beginning to find a solid niche in the business world for connecting with customers and promoting products and services. Thus, the challenge of tracking information across a vast array of sites and capturing the data in a useful format for business utilization had the potential to open a whole new area of business information management. Participating in this new industry and developing a sustainable business model that allowed businesses to monitor and utilize the potential marketing benefits seemed like a logical path to follow.

In spring 2009, in an effort to refine the service's value proposition and their ability to communicate the firm's potential value as an investment opportunity, the Network Collie team entered and won a business plan competition at the local university. They were then recognized at an awards banquet where potential investors were also in attendance. At the dinner, Rose had a conversation with a local entrepreneur who was very impressed with the Network Collie concept. During their conversation, the entrepreneur commented that Rose and his team could easily develop the software application, prove its viability, and sell it to someone for around $1 million. Their work was beginning to pay off, and the future looked amazingly bright. They had never thought that it would be so easy to build and grow the idea into such a valuable enterprise so quickly.

Opportunities to Exit

Within a week of winning the business plan competition, Casey was contacted by representatives from two separate companies who expressed an interest in acquiring Network Collie: GNS, Inc., and Groovy ID.

GNS, INC. GNS, Inc., was a local business that offered rural outsourcing options to larger U.S.-based firms. The recent economic downturn had been tough on GNS, and it was looking for opportunities to broaden its existing lines of business and potential revenue streams. Mark Farrell, the firm's CEO, was interested in finding a way to bring Network Collie into the GNS product line, possibly through an acquisition. Following their initial meeting, Farrell began to make inquiries with his board members and significant investors to gauge their willingness to pursue Network Collie as a potential partner or acquisition. The Network Collie team was hopeful that GNS could help Network Collie get to market and capture a broader customer base more quickly.

Casey and Rose attended a lunch meeting with Farrell in May 2009, hoping that the terms of a potential deal would be discussed. After that meeting, it became clear that Farrell was also interested in bringing Casey on board as a full-time employee at GNS. This added another layer of uncertainty and anxiety for Casey and the rest of the team. Casey now had to consider leaving his current employer to work for a different company across town. It also raised concerns that GNS might attempt to include more value in Casey's employment offer, which would not benefit the rest of the team. Casey decided to have a separate meeting with Farrell to discuss his possible employment with GNS in the hopes that he could keep it a separate issue from the acquisition.

On July 1, 2009, Farrell delivered an official offer from GNS. While the team was hoping for a cash offer, GNS presented a royalty model that would pay the Network Collie founders 12 percent of gross proceeds for existing sales leads and 7 percent of gross proceeds for those generated by GNS. The founders would also be entitled to 12 percent of the proceeds from any sale of the intellectual property behind the Network Collie application.

Approximately two weeks later, Farrell presented a spreadsheet showing the potential royalty payments to the Network Collie founders. He had increased the percentages in his original offer from 12 percent to 15 percent and from 7 percent to 10 percent, respectively. Based on these increased royalty percentages and the projections in the company's business plan, the royalty payments could reach $2.8 million by 2013, as shown in Exhibit C13.2. Farrell also stressed that under the proposed royalty model, GNS would assume responsibility for further marketing and development of the Network Collie application, limiting the risk of the Network Collie founders moving forward.

EXHIBIT **C13.2** Projected Royalty Payments in GNS Offer

Royalties from:	2009	2010	2011	2012	2013
Existing sales leads	$11,340	$16,200	$ 17,820	$ 17,820	$ 17,820
GNS-generated sales leads	6,480	79,920	532,440	1,384,776	2,787,480
Total royalty payments	$17,820	$96,120	$550,260	$1,402,596	$2,805,300
Average royalty per founder	$ 4,455	$24,030	$137,565	$ 350,649	$ 701,325

GROOVY ID Groovy ID, the second firm expressing an interest in Network Collie, provided a service for consumers to organize, track, and analyze their social networks. Groovy ID had approached the Network Collie team earlier, expressing an interest in providing their research service as a bundled feature included in its paid accounts. Casey thought the most likely arrangement would be a fixed pricing schedule for each contact researched by Network Collie over the next 6–12 months. However, the Groovy ID representatives introduced the idea of acquiring Network Collie. This was a surprise to Casey and the rest of the team.

It was almost two months later before Casey heard from Groovy ID again. Its management team was struggling with the integration of another technology and an investor relationship that had turned sour. Casey had a handful of conversations regarding the integration of Network Collie's service into Groovy ID's paid accounts. In one of those conversations, the Groovy ID team brought up the possibility of acquiring Network Collie again, but this time they seemed more serious.

Several conversations about a potential acquisition moved quickly. Eventually, Groovy ID made an offer splitting the total compensation paid to Network Collie into three distinct pieces, based on Network Collie's intellectual property, potential revenue from existing sales leads, and Casey's joining Groovy ID (primarily to integrate the Network Collie service into the acquiring company). This again created the potential for Casey's interest in any potential transaction to differ from the rest of the Network Collie team. Casey decided he would negotiate his employment once they reached an agreement on the other two pieces of the potential deal.

Groovy ID was willing to make cash payment for the intellectual property. Its team would need to conduct due diligence, but it mentioned a price range of $150,000–$250,000. The potential revenue issue was more difficult for the two sides to agree upon. Groovy ID's senior management was intent on maintaining as much cash as possible, given that it was still in the early stages of development and could experience a lack of cash flow in the next 6 to 18 months without further investment. As a result, Groovy ID's offer did not include upfront or subsequent cash payments for the potential revenue. Instead, Groovy ID would credit the Network Collie founders with additional equity in Groovy ID based on the revenue generated from the existing sales leads.

Casey learned during the negotiations that Groovy ID was motivated to close the deal in the next four to six weeks. It was in the process of finishing a patent application and wanted to include Network Collie's intellectual property in the application before the deadline. Given their desire to close the deal quickly, the team responded to the initial offer by asking for $350,000 for the intellectual property, an additional $150,000 upfront for the potential revenue, plus a potential equity position depending on the success of Network Collie's existing sales leads. However, Casey received no response to the counteroffer from Groovy ID's management.

Waiting for a Better Deal

While Casey and the rest of the team were excited to have two companies interested in purchasing Network Collie, they were disappointed in how each offer was structured. With respect to the GNS royalty model, they did not feel comfortable exiting the company without a guaranteed payment and giving up control of the product development and marketing efforts that would determine the long-term value of the royalties. While the potential for annual payments in excess of $1 million was tempting, the team believed it could find another deal that would include a cash component or an equity position in an attractive acquirer. Because the Groovy ID offer would provide some cash and an equity position in a new, emerging company that could be more attractive in the future, the team was more interested in that offer. However, the cash component of Groovy ID's offer was still well below the team's target price of at least $750,000.

Casey and the other founders ultimately decided to turn down both offers because they would be giving up the company for too little and assuming too much risk. Casey and Rose still felt strongly that they should be able to secure close to $1 million or more for selling the company. They also were confident that Network Collie's application and existing sales leads would deliver significant success in the future. In fact, they estimated that the company had the potential to achieve almost $28 million in annual sales by 2013 (see Exhibit C13.3).

Progress Slows

Casey was beginning to get frustrated with the lack of progress Network Collie was making. During the past six months, he and the rest of the team continued to have the same experience over and over again with potential customers. Everyone acknowledged the growing use of social networking and seemed interested in the data Network Collie could provide. However, the sales consultants the team hired were not delivering substantial leads and orders. Overall, the potential revenue in the company's sales pipeline was not materializing as quickly as Casey wanted, with only $30,000 in orders to that point.

Even though Casey and the rest of the team believed in the potential of Network Collie, the lack of progress over the past six months had begun to wear on the four co-founders. Each of them was busy with a full-time job and a personal life, and finding time to focus on Network Collie was becoming more difficult. Regardless of how much business was coming in, a significant amount of time was required to update and maintain the software application

EXHIBIT

C13.3 Network Collie Pro Forma Income Statements

	2009	2010	2011	2012	2013
Revenues	$ 140,400	$ 907,200	$5,443,200	$13,996,800	$27,993,600
Operating expenses:					
Travel	$ 25,000	$ 51,500	$ 106,090	$ 163,909	$ 225,102
Marketing expenses	750,000	772,500	795,675	800,000	800,000
Office rent	9,750	9,270	9,548	9,835	10,130
Office utilities	2,400	2,472	2,546	2,623	2,701
Internet and server costs	1,200	3,708	3,819	3,934	4,052
Computers	12,000				
Technology improvements	10,000	10,300	10,609	10,927	11,255
Total operating expenses	$ 810,350	$ 849,750	$ 928,287	$ 991,228	$ 1,053,240
General & administrative expenses:					
Salaries	$ 280,000	$ 394,400	$ 869,664	$ 1,585,844	$ 2,702,994
Benefits	60,000	89,654	119,531	149,643	180,006
Furniture	5,000	5,000	5,000	5,000	5,000
Office improvements	3,000	8,240	8,487	8,742	9,004
Office supplies	6,000				
Total G&A expenses	$ 354,000	$ 497,294	$1,002,682	$ 1,749,229	$ 2,897,004
Earnings before depreciation and amortization (EBITDA)	$ (1,023,950)	$ (439,844)	$3,512,231	$11,256,343	$24,043,356
Depreciation expenses:					
Depreciation on computers	$ 2,400	$ 1,920	$ 2,458	$ 1,003	$ 486
Depreciation on furniture	715	612	900	485	286
Total depreciation expenses	$ 3,115	$ 2,532	$ 3,358	$ 1,488	$ 772
Total expenses	$ 1,167,465	$ 1,349,576	$1,934,327	$ 2,741,945	$ 3,951,016
Earnings before taxes	$ (1,027,065)	$ (442,376)	$3,508,873	$11,254,855	$24,042,584
Income tax	0	0	1,228,106	3,939,200	8,414,904
Net income	$ (1,027,065)	$ (442,376)	$2,280,767	$ 7,315,655	$15,627,680

and website for all of the changes taking place on each of the social networks. This became more of a problem in 2010 as a number of the social networks, including Facebook and Twitter, were making changes to their sites that required significant changes to the Network Collie application. The team was also receiving requests from some of its customers to perform research on certain smaller, niche social networks. The team felt it needed to meet these requests in order to develop a reputation for customer service and to keep existing customers coming back for more.

DECISION TIME It was time for Casey and the rest of the Network Collie team to make a decision. Where was the company headed, and did they want to commit 100 percent to the business? Were the team members ready to leave their jobs? Could they find investors? They had worked so hard over the past two years and believed they had created a valuable service, but the question remained whether it would translate into actual sales and the scalable company they were seeking. The team also began to question whether they should relent on their $1 million price tag and emphasis on an upfront cash payment, and instead actively shop the company. After talking through all of the different options a number of times, the team sat in silence for a few moments. Casey knew it was time to make a decision. He just hoped it was the right one.

Source: The case, as presented here, has been adapted from the original case, written by Professor Jim Litton in the College of Business Administration at Abilene Christian University. This case is based on an actual company; however, the names and places have been altered for confidentiality, per the entrepreneur's request.

Questions

1. Given the early stage of the business, should the Network Collie management team even be considering an exit at this time? Why or why not?
2. If a company acquires Network Collie, what are they buying? What are they not buying?
3. What criteria should the Network Collie management team use in making a decision on what they should do?
4. In your opinion, is Network Collie really worth $1 million?
5. What do you see as the advantages and disadvantages of the two offers the Network Collie founders have received?
6. What would you advise the Network Collie team to do?

Numi Tea

Cultivating Customer Relationships

Numi Tea was started in 1999 by brother and sister team Ahmed and Reem Rahim. Keeping it in the family is important at Numi. Reem's artwork adorns every box of tea. The Rahims' childhood friend, Hammad Atassi, is director of food service. Every member of the Tea'm, as they call it, is committed to the company's core values of sustainability, creativity, and quality organics. This extends to their corporate customers and their producers, as well. Like their teas, every relationship is carefully cultivated and maintained.

In recent years, demand for organic and ethically produced products has exploded. At the same time, economic influences have driven affluent and natural foods consumers to large discounters, grocery chains, warehouse clubs, and online shops. "In the positioning of our brand, we wanted to target a certain type of customer base, from natural health food stores to fine dining and hotels to universities and coffee shops," says Ahmed, Numi's CEO. "But what I've been most surprised about in our growth is the mass market consumer."

According to Jennifer Mullin, vice president of marketing for Numi, the average Numi consumer is college educated, female, and buys two to three boxes of tea per month—usually green tea. She also buys organic products whenever possible. Until Mullin joined the team, Numi had assumed its customers fit the same profile as its young staff. Mullin's findings proved that the company needed to focus additional energy on reaching older customers and moms, as well as its target college market.

To reach younger consumers, Numi boosts product awareness on college campuses, where people are more inclined to be interested in issues of sustainability, fair trade, and organics. The big hurdle with these potential customers is price. Because Numi teas are a premium product, they have a higher price point than conventionally produced teas. Numi prices range from $15.99 for 1.6 ounces and up, depending on the tea variety and size of package. Because college students have limited cash, Numi determined that it could access college customers best by getting university food service departments to serve tea as part of prepaid meal plans. The strategy has been a success. Not only do these food service contracts represent huge accounts for Numi, but they also encourage trial by students. Sampling is Numi's most successful marketing activity for attracting new users, and now students can drink Numi teas essentially for free.

For many organics consumers, the most compelling reason for drinking Numi tea is its health benefits. But while Numi is organic, the company rarely advertises this aspect of its business. Some analysts think that if *organic* and *natural* become mere marketing buzzwords, a lack of trust may arise among consumers, as some products will inevitably fail to live up to marketers' claims. With this in mind, Numi believes it is best to educate consumers about its products. "We have an in-house PR team that works with editors of women's magazines to educate consumers on tea and make sure they understand the healthy properties of tea," says Mullin. The team always follows up by samplings at Whole Foods stores or at events targeted toward environmentally conscious customers.

Numi has been fortunate to be the tea of choice in high-end restaurants, hotel chains, and cruise lines. The food service industry in total makes up about 40 percent of their business. Along with that comes added pressure to deliver on price, quality, and customer service. While the company clearly leads in quality, it is hard for any small business to compete with giant food service companies on price.

An important part of Numi Tea is its story. To tell that story, the management team needs to forge very hands-on, personal relationships with restaurant food and beverage managers, giving them a natural competitive advantage. A regular teabag may be cheaper, but there's not much else to say about it. When Atassi can conduct a private cupping (tea tasting) for the kitchen staff and explain all the different exotic teas, as well as talk about the farms and farmers that grow the tea all over the world and the company's commitment to sustainability, it's pretty much a slam dunk before the tea is even steeped. Turnover is notoriously high in the food service industry, so there's always a chance that a new chef or buyer will go another direction. Luckily for Numi, this hasn't been the case. Due in part to excellent customer relationships, it is more common for the company to keep the old client *and* follow the chef or buyer to his or her new restaurant.

Numi's success in the food service industry has driven retail business. While there are countless testimonials about customers' experiencing Numi tea at a friend's house for the first time, a surprising number of Numi converts come from restaurants. As the requests from consumers wanting to know where to get Numi in their local area have rolled in, the company has expanded to reach retail customers. Once available only at natural food stores and cafes, Numi teas can now be found in such stores as Target, large grocery store chains, and even some warehouse club stores. While good for the consumer, this poses a potential threat to the Rahims' carefully maintained fine-dining customer relationships. A problem could arise if the same premium tea served at a restaurant is also available at the local Target. So far the two channels have co-existed peacefully.

As the company grows, one of the biggest challenges to its marketing model will be to maintain the family feel on a global scale. Jennifer Mullin and her team have begun tailoring e-mail communications to newsletter subscribers to inform them about local events and are hoping to add some regional sales and marketing teams in the near future. They've also added Numi fan sites on Facebook and Twitter. The sites are monitored by a staffer to address any questions or concerns about the products. Most importantly, no matter how busy they may get, founders Ahmed and Reem will always be there, lending a personal touch through their art, personal stories, and experiences. While Numi is still fairly new, the company is expanding rapidly in the United States and enjoying success overseas, as well. Whatever the marketing and PR teams do to promote the tea products—store samplings, environmental events, or partnerships with like-minded companies—they always keep an eye on the demographic and psychographic profiles of their consumers.

View the video and answer the questions that follow.

Questions

1. Do you consider Numi's relationships with its producers as important to its marketing as the relationships with its customers?
2. How does Numi use technology to enhance its customer relationships? Can you suggest other ways in which the management team can use technology to reach consumers of Numi teas?
3. What methods would you suggest that Numi use to collect customer data?

Source: From *BOONE/KURTZ, Contemporary Marketing, 14e.* 2010 Cengage Learning.

Graeter's Ice Cream

Product Innovation and Long-Term Success

VIDEO CASE 15

Graeter's Ice Cream has been a Cincinnati tradition for generations. Since the days before refrigeration, the family-owned business, with its Fresh Pot process of making frosty treats, has been a popular choice among Ohioans. Since generating a loyal following in 1870, soon after the company's forefathers began selling fresh ice cream made two gallons at a time from an open-air street market, Graeter's has become synonymous with ice cream.

Ice cream was a novelty when Louis Charles Graeter and his wife, Regina, began making ice cream daily in the back room of a storefront on East McMillan Street. The couple sold their ice cream along with chocolate confections out front and lived upstairs. Since there were no mechanized freezers at the time, ice cream was a rare treat, and the Graeters had to make small batches using rock salt and ice.

As commercial refrigeration became widespread, Graeter's Ice Cream was able to produce and store more products while still servicing consumers from the McMillan street building. The business, however, took a blow when "Charlie" was killed in 1919 in a streetcar accident. In the 1920s, Regina realized that the company could reach more customers by expanding to other locations. She took a gamble and opened a satellite store across town—what would become the first of several neighborhood stores to open as the company positioned itself as a maker of quality ice cream available just about anywhere in town.

Following Regina's death in 1955, sons Wilmer and Paul took over the business, before ushering in a third generation of family leadership with Wilmer's four children. Over the next 30 years, the face of the ice cream business changed. As more ice cream makers entered the market and grocery stores became a viable outlet, selling ice cream entered a new realm. Most competitors built business on volume, and quality suffered, despite lower prices. Graeter's, meanwhile, stayed the course and continued with its time-consuming Fresh Pot process of spinning the recipe along a chilled container. Although Graeter's followed the trend and offered its ice cream in grocery stores, its retail outlets remained to offer consumers a distinctive buying experience.

Over the years, Graeter's developed a line of candy and bakery goods, but ice cream has been the company's staple, enabling the small business to gain a national reputation. In recent years, the company has appeared on the Food Network, Fine Living Channel, Travel Channel, and History Channel. A crowning achievement occurred when Oprah Winfrey gave her personal endorsement to Graeter's, calling it the best ice cream she'd ever tasted. Mail-order sales substantially increased.

Growth has come in leaps and bounds for Graeter's. With an aggressive marketing effort and a strong alliance with the Kroger chain, the company more than doubled its number of grocery store outlets in 2009. Today, the ice cream, now available in 22 flavors, can be found at 1,700 supermarkets and grocery stores, as well as company-owned retail stores in Ohio, Missouri, Kentucky, and nearby states. Graeter's also expanded its distribution network to include restaurants and country clubs, and it operates an online store that offers overnight shipping in 48 states, including California, its largest market. Also, the company has diversified its portfolio by offering a line of ice cream cakes and pies, travel packs, and sundaes, in addition to baked goods and candies.

But the company is committed to further expansion. Graeter's recently boosted its production capacity from one factory to three, aiming for distribution to even more supermarkets and grocery stores throughout the country. Additional retail stores as far away as Los Angeles and New York are planned.

While competition continues to stiffen, Graeter's remains one of the priciest ice creams on the market, even without the shipping costs associated with online ordering. At the retail level, the ice cream is considered a premium product and commands a higher price than other brands. With Kroger as its largest distribution partner, the company has been able to build strong brand loyalty, as evidenced by a recent trial in the Denver area. Graeter's marketed 12 flavors in 30 King Sooper stores in Denver with hopes of selling two or three gallons per store per week. Within a few weeks, stores were selling an average of five gallons.

The company continues to focus on making its product available at the country's largest food stores, but its leaders are cognizant that new products, including established brands in a new market, have a high failure rate. Challenges ahead are the company's ability to establish relationships with new consumers and build brand awareness.

View the video and answer the questions that follow.

Questions

1. What distinguishes Graeter's Ice Cream from other ice cream makers and makes its products desirable to consumers?
2. While its ice cream was a success from the start, what innovations has the company made to sustain its competitive advantage?
3. Cite examples of Graeter's Ice Cream's supply chain management. Explain how the company uses direct channel and indirect channel distribution.

Source: Compiled from interviews and information provided by Graeter's. http://www.graeters.com. Written by Tim Blackwell, Freelance Reporter.

Dynamic Network Services, Inc.

Finding the Right Price

The Story

The Dynamic Network Services (Dyn) story is not unlike those of many tech startups. The difference is that Dyn started during the dot-com boom, survived the bust, thrived after the dust settled, and surges ahead today. Deeply rooted as an Internet infrastructure company, it began with a focus on the domain name system (DNS) and continues to expand by offering a wider range of infrastructure services.

Since 1998, Dyn has served 4,000,000 homes, small businesses, and enterprise users with a suite of DNS, e-mail, domain registration, and virtual servers. It provides customers—from the hobbyist to the *Fortune* 500 enterprise—with reliable and scalable IT services at competitive and predictable prices, through easy-to-use and secure interfaces. Individuals and companies partner with Dyn to manage their website traffic, e-mail delivery, and uptime, and to harden their internal and external network connectivity.

It has built a rock-solid Global IP Anycast network using only top-level providers and equipment and has provided it at an affordable price. "Uptime is the bottom line" for them and for companies like 37 signals, Zappos, HomeAway, Twitter, Audience-Science, and more who depend on Dyn to keep their Web presence and e-mail delivery at peak performance for their users.

Like many of its Web 2.0 customers looking to monetize, Dyn Inc. has been there, done that. It started as a free service based out of a college apartment—a couple of guys with a big idea. That service, then operating as DynDNS.org, was a dynamic DNS service for a home user to host a website on a home computer or remote access back to a PC. Over time, as the user base grew and became more demanding, Dyn turned to a donation-based service in an effort to stay afloat and add complementary services. Later, Dyn transitioned to a recurring revenue software-as-a-service (SaaS) model with a suite of IT services aimed at the home/SMB market.

Fast-forward to 2005, and its story of maturation continues. Dyn initiated a customer audit and mining exercise of the over 2,000,000 active DynDNS.com users at the time. From this, the company realized that many high-profile corporations were using its consumer-grade service. This revelation, coupled with the simple fact that the premium, externally managed DNS industry lacked options, encouraged Dyn to unveil a new brand, the Dynect Platform. Dynect was introduced to the outsourced DNS market in the fall of 2007.

Today

Today, Dyn Inc. has served over 14,000,000 home/SMB users on the DynDNS.com brand and has over 1,000 corporate/enterprise customers on its globally deployed Dynect Platform. The company has moved beyond offering DNS exclusively and now offers e-mail delivery services through its SendLabs brand. The days of simple word-of-mouth growth are long gone, and Dyn has become a much more proactive player.

Not only does it provide services to consumers and corporations, it also provides services to the government. All federal government agencies that have the .gov designation were given until December 2009 to deploy DNS Security Extensions (DNSSEC) for their domains. DNSSEC adds a layer of security to DNS so that computers can verify that they have been directed to the proper server, preventing the most dangerous types of DNS attacks and cyber-hacking. Implementing DNSSEC is especially critical for high-risk government sites because they are often targeted by cyberattackers and are expected by users to be safe.

DNS is the backbone of the Internet's infrastructure. Without it, websites won't work, period. Once hackers have control over a DNS server, they have free reign to mislead and redirect Web users to unsafe territory. Due to the increase of companies reporting attacks of this nature, it has now become more critical than ever to implement this additional layer of security at the DNS level. Government and other critical industries such as banking, online retail, healthcare, and education are also prime candidates for DNSSEC, as they may be a larger target for potential attackers.

Pricing and Credit Decisions

Because technology changes rapidly from day to day, Dyn experiences shorter product cycles than do companies that deal with tangible products. In a noncommoditized scenario, the company finds it easier to be flexible with pricing. As a result, each customer requires different pricing strategies. Outliers—those who are not the average customer—can be more demanding of services, but are not more costly to the company because Dyn's costs are fixed. Customers, however, are willing to pay a different rate when traffic and consistency are different. When demand goes up, prices go up.

The company does expense analyses to determine pricing. In the beginning, pricing structure was evaluated monthly, but now that Dyn is more established, forecasting is done quarterly or semi-annually, depending on client needs. Its invoice structure is annual—one year in advance—so the greatest risk to Dyn is credit card fraud.

Before answering the questions below, reread Chapter 16, and watch the Dyn Inc. video for this chapter.

Questions

1. Explain the importance of fixed and variable costs to Dyn's pricing decisions.
2. Basing your answer on the discussion of prestige pricing in Chapter 16 and on the Dyn Inc. video, how does the concept of elasticity of demand relate to Dyn's pricing structure? Or does it?
3. Do you think Dyn would benefit from offering credit to its customers?

Source: Compiled from interviews and information provided by Dyn Inc. http://dyn.com.

HubSpot, Inc.

Transforming the Marketing Model

Brian Halligan and Dharmesh Shah, the founders of HubSpot®, met at MIT in 2004. The company is based in Cambridge, Massachusetts, directly across from the campus where it was first envisioned. Both Halligan and Shah were interested in the transformative impact of the Internet on small businesses and were early students of Web 2.0 concepts. After two years of discussions and early work, in June of 2006 the company was officially founded and funded.

The most interesting aspect of the Internet's impact on business from HubSpot's perspective is how it has changed the nature of shopping and subsequently the shape of every vendor's sales funnel. Ten years ago, if a company was interested in buying a new product or service, it started by attending trade shows, reading industry journals, and going to seminars to learn more. Early in the process, it would engage directly with key vendors' salespeople who would provide product information.

Today, that same process looks very different. The potential customer starts by googling relevant keywords. The prospect spends time on each vendor's site, subscribing to the most interesting vendor blogs, perhaps joining an industry discussion forum, and so on. Relatively late in the decision cycle, the prospect engages the vendor's salespeople directly. That first vendor conversation today is much different from the one a decade ago because the prospect often knows as much about the vendor's product as the sales rep does and the prospect is already much more "qualified."

The Internet has tended to make every marketplace more efficient. Just as eBay makes the niche market for Pez dispensers, WWI shovels, and 1975 World Series ticket stubs more efficient, the Internet as a whole is making niche markets for intellectual property law, system dynamics consulting, and food brokerage more efficient. It used to be that the size of a firm's sales force was the key to finding the most new customers, but that is not necessarily the case today. The good news for small businesses is that on the Internet, no one can tell if you are a sole proprietorship or a large consultancy.

The Internet disproportionately favors small businesses since it enables them to position their niche products so that they are available to everyone who is shopping for them, regardless of the prospective customer's location. HubSpot Inbound Marketing Software helps over 4,000 customers to generate traffic and leads through their websites, and to convert more of those leads into customers. Its vision has been to provide a killer marketing application and provide great advice to small businesses, enabling those companies to leverage the disruptive effects of the Internet and "get found" by more prospects.

Most small businesses have a website that behaves like their old paper-based brochures, but just sits online. It is rarely updated, is not given significant visibility by search engines, has low traffic levels, does not encourage return visits, does not enable/track conversions, etc. What HubSpot does is transform that relatively static website into a modern marketing machine that produces the right leads and helps convert a higher percentage of them into qualified opportunities.

HubSpot focuses on tools to help the small business owner create, optimize, and promote content; capture, manage, and nurture leads to win more customers; and learn to make smart marketing investments that get results. Some of the tools it provides include social media, blogging, search engine optimization, and content management.

View the video and answer the questions that follow.

Questions

1. How has the salesperson's role changed because of Internet marketing? Consider differences in prospecting and presentation.
2. Do you agree with HubSpot that a prospect is more "qualified" to make purchasing decisions when it uses information found on the Internet?
3. How might the salesperson's compensation be different or the same with Internet sales versus traditional sales methods?
4. Should a new small business rely solely on Internet promotion? What other methods should it use?

Source: Compiled from interviews and information provided by HubSpot, Inc. www.hubspot.com.

Auntie Anne's Pretzels in China

The news was something to celebrate. It was 2007, and Wen-Szu Lin and his partner, Joseph Sze, had just learned that they had been approved to be the first franchisees to take Auntie Anne's Pretzels into China. This promised to be the opportunity of a lifetime! With more than 1.3 billion potential customers and a fast-expanding economy, how could they miss?

Lin was very well prepared for this foray into entrepreneurship. After all, he had been born in neighboring Taiwan and lived there until the age of seven, so he was fluent in Mandarin Chinese. He also had completed an MBA in entrepreneurial management from the prestigious Wharton School of Business. Sze, who also had a Wharton MBA and was similarly prepared, shared Lin's assessment of the opportunity and his excitement for the chance to introduce Auntie Anne's to the Chinese market. With franchise agreement in hand, and after a great deal of planning and preparation, they opened their first store around the time of the Beijing Olympics in 2008. But it didn't take long for the new small business owners to realize that they might have bitten off more than they could comfortably chew.

Every Auntie Anne's pretzel sold around the world is made from the same secret recipe, and the expansion into China would use it as well. Lin's plan was very simple: Import the pretzel mix, along with other key ingredients, and start making pretzels fast enough to satisfy the fast-growing appetites of Chinese consumers. It seemed to be a foolproof strategy—that is, until the Chinese government decided to get involved. A key delivery of pretzel mix passed through customs quickly and without a hitch, but this probably makes sense, since that office cares mostly about collecting required taxes. But serious problems surfaced just after that, when the China Entry-Exit Inspection and Quarantine Bureau (CIQ), which is the agency that is responsible for determining whether imported food products are safe to eat, announced that it had tested the shipment and had to declare it unfit for human consumption.

When he got word of the decision, Lin immediately recognized that it had the power to ruin the new venture before it could get out of the starting block. How can you make Auntie Anne's pretzels if you can't use the exact mix of ingredients in the company's formula? But the CIQ office in China was warning Lin and his partner that they might have to dump about 5,000 bags (equal to an entire 40-foot shipping container) of the franchisor's proprietary mix down the drain. The agent assigned to their case, Mr. Zeng, delivered the ultimatum, contingent on his department's test of a second sample of the mix.

The loss would be devastating, effectively shutting down their operations—but even the challenge of disposal would take some work. They would have to open each bag of mix and pour it into a drain large enough to handle the load, being certain to wash it down slowly and with enough care to avoid clogs. Lin and his partner knew the drill all too well. The CIQ had already forced them to dispose of more than 1,300 pounds of caramel for having "dangerously high" levels of the preservative sorbic acid (five times the allowable limit), contrary to U.S. test results showing that the shipment was very safe.

So here they were . . . again! The situation would have been humorous if it had not been so tragic for the business. The official report claimed that the pretzel mix contained dangerous levels of a kind of bacteria that is found only in dairy products. What made these findings so interesting is that the mix contained no dairy products, only common ingredients such as flour, salt, and sugar. Challenging the report led nowhere; in fact, Mr. Zeng made it very clear that he would condemn the shipment outright if Lin continued his protests. The company's entire future was staked on its ability to get a second sample to pass tests performed by a CIQ lab that provided results that apparently were less than accurate or honest.

At one point, Lin was called to the CIQ headquarters to figure out what to do with a condemned shipment. What he found there was revealing, to say the least, and it gave him an up-close sense of how government offices can work in other countries. When he showed up to meet with the company's assigned inspector, he noticed that Mr. Zeng was focused intently on the computer screen in front of him, squinting as if he were trying to read fine print. Lin reports being "thoroughly impressed by his concentration, unexpected for a government employee." Mr. Zeng realized that he was waiting by the door and responded, "Please wait a few minutes as I finish up my work." Wanting to start this crucial relationship off on the right foot, Lin cheerfully indicated that he would. While he waited, Lin looked around the office and sized up the operation. What he noticed there was very eye-opening.

> *The shelves and table were filled with packaged food items, from wine bottles to canned foods to candies. They must receive many samples, I thought. . . . Empty cookie and chocolate candy wrappers littered each inspector's desk, all from the same company called Crai, an Italian firm that wanted to launch a group of restaurants and grocery stores in China at that time. A good friend of mine who headed up Crai's importing had been complaining to me about the lengthy process at CIQ for months. Specifically, she mentioned several items that had been rejected and "destroyed" by CIQ: cookies and chocolate candies. What a coincidence, I thought, as I looked at the crumb-covered desks. I sure hope that these customs agents did not hurt their stomachs during the "destruction" process.*

When he turned his attention back to Mr. Zeng, he found him still hard at work with his razor-sharp focus on the computer monitor unbroken. But by then it was clear that he was using one hand to type and the other to move the mouse wildly. The action he used was so frenzied that Lin couldn't help but wonder what in the world the inspector was doing. He concluded that Mr. Zeng must have been working with some kind of advanced Excel spreadsheet model or perhaps proprietary customs software. But it was neither, and that became obvious from what he heard next.

> *Faint sounds crackled and exploded from his computer. I leaned in and listened carefully. Shhuuuu . . . boom! Boom. Boom. Crack, pop, pop, pop. Boom!!! That was not music. It was the sounds of guns and bombs going off! I realized. Mr. Zeng continued wriggling the mouse, clicking on its buttons while his left hand tapped the space bar and several letter keys with lightning speed. I envied his focus. I could see his screen reflected in the window behind him. His computer monitor was full of monsters trying to kill each other. Warcraft! Well, a Chinese version of it. Mr. Zeng was not working tirelessly to clear as many customs forms as possible before the Olympics—he was playing computer games.*

And Mr. Zeng was really getting into it, with beads of sweat forming on his forehead after about five minutes of intense action. About ten minutes after that, the beads had gathered into streams that were starting to roll down the side of his face.

This was serious commitment, but Mr. Zeng was not alone in his extracurricular engagement. Based on the reflections in the window, Lin could see the computer monitors of other inspectors, too, and realized that very little work was actually being done in that office. Lin described the scene as follows:

> *One inspector preferred red blouses to green ones, and seemed like an adept shopper from the many windows she had opened to compare similar products across several websites. The next inspector had true, raw talent as well as commendable organization skills. He had ten small Instant Messenger windows placed evenly and symmetrically from the top left of his screen to bottom right. Conversations flowed smoothly and quickly across all ten. I could type nearly 100 words per minute, but I was no match for this inspector. I silently applauded his talent in keeping up with so many screens, and making it seem effortless.*

From these observations and the interactions Lin had during his visit with Mr. Zeng later that day, it seemed clear that the agency's work and the reports its employees were handing down were not very trustworthy.

As time went on and the hassles from CIQ mounted, Lin's frustrations continued to build. The inspection process was hardly serious or accurate, and yet it was destroying his new company, one rejected shipment at a time. And to add insult to injury, the Chinese government routinely gives wide berth to domestic producers, allowing them to get away with all manner of unsafe practices. At one point, Lin purchased a product from a local vendor that caused half of his employees to lose their sight, and no one seemed to care—it was simply par for the course in China. (These workers later recovered their eyesight, thanks to changes in health care practices that were just being made.) But when it came to his imported supplies, suddenly health concerns were paramount. It seemed to be a rigged system.

Lin eventually managed to save the pretzel mix from destruction, but only after he called in favors "from friends and friends of friends"—anyone who might have pull with the Chinese government. He finally received word that a second sample of the mix passed all tests—but this was nothing short of miraculous, since Lin had never provided one to the CIQ or to Mr. Zeng! This made the whole affair even more bizarre.

Perhaps Lin and his partner's situation could only be explained by something they learned from a conversation with the wife of the U.S. Ambassador. She revealed that their hassles with customs probably had nothing to do with the safety of the shipments. In the wake of a scandal that exposed melamine-tainted milk products in China, many countries—the United States included—put a hold on food and agricultural products from China. So Mr. Zeng's regulatory decisions may have been political tit for tat and nothing more, but this is scant comfort for the entrepreneur whose business fails as a result of political gamesmanship.

Lin has concluded that he and his business partner were always at a disadvantage when it came to doing business in China. "You really need to have that prior experience and those prior relationships," he says. "When we showed up, we didn't really have any prior relationships." This, among other shortcomings, led ultimately to the closing of the partners' Auntie Anne's Pretzel stores in 2012, and they have each moved on to greener pastures of opportunity. But their experiences abroad illustrate the stark differences that can exist between doing business in the United States and operating in other countries. These naturally ramp up the potential complications for small business owners who willingly accept the adventure of global expansion, with its inherent hazards and potential rewards.

Questions

1. What were the primary motivations that led Lin and his partner to start a new business in China? Given their experiences there, do you think they should have considered launching in another country instead? Where? Why?
2. Of the global strategies mentioned in Chapter 18, which option did Lin and Sze choose for their move into China? Did they choose the right strategy for them and their enterprise?
3. What do you think Lin and his partner did right when they attempted to start their business? What do you think they did wrong? What recommendations would you have for them?
4. Given the details of this case and other key facts that you know about China, assess the opportunities for U.S. small companies that may want to do business there. What features of the country should be particularly attractive to entrepreneurs who are seeking to expand internationally by going into China?
5. What challenges to doing business in China did Lin and Sze experience? List any issues that may present distinct problems for other U.S. small companies that may want to do business there.

Sources: Based on Kevin Hardy, "The Problem with China," *QSR* (October 2012), http://www.qsrmagazine.com/exclusives/problem-china, accessed April 8, 2013; Knowledge@Wharton, "Food for Thought: Why Auntie Anne's Pretzels Failed in China," (March 6, 2013), http://knowledge.wharton.upenn.edu/article.cfm?articleid=3203, accessed April 8, 2013; Frank Langfitt, "Auntie Anne's Pretzels in Beijing: Why the Chinese Didn't Bite," NPR Books, (February 11, 2013), http://www.npr.org/books/authors/171079606/wen-szu-lin, accessed April 8, 2013; Wen-Szu Lin, *The China Twist* (BC Publishing, 2012).

Andrew Mason and the Rise and Fall of Groupon

After four and a half intense and wonderful years as CEO of Groupon, I've decided that I'd like to spend more time with my family. Just kidding—I was fired today.

With these words, predictably flippant in their tone, Andrew Mason stepped down from his position at the helm of Groupon, the deal-of-the-day company that sells coupons for deeply discounted goods and services to customers who must get others to buy them, too, before they all can use them. Mason will always enjoy the distinction of having founded what became the "Fastest Growing Company Ever," to quote *Forbes* magazine. But Isaac Newton could have directed his words as aptly to Groupon as he did to gravity: What goes up apparently must come down.

So how did things go so horribly wrong? It may have been Mason's playful behavior that established the culture at the company that seemed to serve it so well for so long. He clearly had a reputation for being something of a goofball, often coming off more like a big kid than the leader of a major new firm with a multi-billion-dollar market value. These antics might have been seen as cheap entertainment while the company was growing, but when sales began to decline and the firm's stock price retreated, Mason's offbeat style and the company's fun-focused atmosphere suddenly became less than amusing.

It also didn't help that Mason had no significant business experience prior to starting Groupon. The music-major-turned-software-developer stumbled upon the idea for the company and became its CEO almost by default. And it showed. With his often-rumpled appearance and strong leaning toward all things wacky, he seemed more intent on promoting the company's comical vibe than on actually making the business work. Mason fashioned Groupon into a lively place to work, where the dress code and vacation policy were loose, and comedians wrote ad copy and served in customer support roles. But this was just the tip of the iceberg. Making the fun last at Groupon was very serious business.

And then there were the problems with the company's business model. Consumers didn't like the forward planning required to take advantage of its offers—that is, the need to buy a deal in advance, print it out, redeem it in time, and so on. Participating vendors also had complaints. If a deal ended up being a smash hit with subscribers, the merchant could very well be flooded with more customer demand than it could handle. And because the deals featured steep discounts in order to get new customers to bite, they could be expensive to offer. Many vendors quickly noticed that they were getting a lot of bargain hunters coming through their doors but few continuing customers, so as a result, they started to cool to the idea of signing up for more offers.

The extraordinary pace of change at the company was also creating serious headaches for Mason. The tempo of innovation was so fast and so furious that management struggled to keep up, which generated its share of conflict. One observer described the situation this way: "The size and complexity of Groupon grew so quickly that it outpaced the rate of maturity of the organizational culture—much like a gangly, pimply teenager [who] grows to 6 feet tall."

Finally, there were concerns about Mason's struggle to relate to some of the employees. Many respected his grasp of Web technology and keen product development prowess but recognized that he wasn't much of a people person and often failed to appreciate employees in roles that were vital to the company and its success, most notably sales. For example, there were at least five layers of bureaucracy between Mason and the company's sales staff, causing a disconnect between the two and leading some to believe that he probably would have preferred to have had fewer salespeople and the headaches that naturally go along with them.

Despite the problems, the firm did have something going for it; at least Google thought so. The online-search giant reportedly made an offer to buy the business for about $6 billion in November 2010. The two sides negotiated for weeks, but Mason, figuring the deal wasn't sweet enough, decided to walk away. It was at this point that observers seriously began to question his business judgment and his ability to lead such a large enterprise. But Mason stood by his decision:

> *Life is not about money. . . . The reason that we made a decision to be an independent company is we quite simply wanted control of our destiny. We wanted the ability to make big bets and take smart risks and go after what we saw as a big opportunity.*

The shortsightedness of Mason's decision is now very apparent, but life offers very few "do-overs."

Mason's rejection of Google's offer was only the beginning of his slide at Groupon. The chorus of questions about his ability to lead such a large and growing business were about to grow much louder. In June 2011, Groupon filed for an IPO (an initial public offering, allowing shares of the company to be sold to the general public) and raised $700 million in the process. But this focused an intense spotlight on the firm and how it was being managed. Suddenly Mason's "incessant jokiness" was no laughing matter for government regulators and investors. His college-kid-like demeanor raised doubts about his suitability to lead a publicly traded firm. One business writer recounts an episode that occurred during a series of presentations given to raise interest in the IPO that certainly lifted more than a few eyebrows:

> *Between meetings with bankers, Mason, a self-professed video game junkie, played a game called Whale Trail on his iPhone. In the game, the player navigates a cheerful flying whale named Willow through a psychedelic sky while trying to gobble rainbow-colored bubbles and avoid black clouds that do the bidding of the evil Baron Von Barry.*

Mason explained his behavior by saying that the game was great "for just tuning out," adding with a laugh that iTunes had just listed it as "one of the best games for four- to six-year-olds." That's not exactly what investors want to see in the CEO who is running their business.

In the wake of the IPO, Groupon's financial difficulties escalated. After the company posted a new loss of $67 million, the firm's stock took a tumble, from a peak of around $31 to a low of $2.63 in November 2012. It eventually settled at $5 per share, but by that point, the company had lost around 75 percent of its IPO value. And as a telling sign of investor sentiment, the price bounced up by nearly 12 percent when the news of Mason's firing was finally announced.

Before being forced out as CEO, Mason was already moving the company away from the daily-deal business and toward the creation of what he was calling an "operating system for local commerce." This software platform would allow customers to turn to Groupon as a source of information to guide their search for products, services, and the lowest prices for both. Merchants could use the system to advertise their offerings, as well as using it as a touchpoint for the sales they made and as a hook for pulling customers back for more business. It was an ambitious project, leading some investors to further question Mason's wisdom and business acumen—even *after* his departure from the firm. They came to think of Groupon as a public company that was in desperate search of a business that just might pull it out of its sticky situation. Also, there was a concern that existing competitors would challenge the company on its planned path for recovery. These included powerhouses like OpenTable (which dominates online restaurant reservations), customer loyalty program providers (such as American Express, Visa, Citibank, and Amazon), Google and PayPal (with recently expanded offerings for local merchants), and Square (with its suite of software that reduces the transaction costs and hassles for small businesses). Finding a competitive opening in such a crowded marketplace would not be easy.

While the Groupon story did not have a happy ending for Mason, it provides important lessons about entrepreneurial leadership. As one writer put it,

> *Andrew Mason has his own kind of panache. Not the epic, Steve Jobs panache. Or the eclectic, Barry Diller panache. Or even the oafish, Steve Ballmer panache. But as CEO of one of the fastest-growing startups in history, he had the small-scale, misfit quirkiness of an indie movie. Panache-ette.*

Without a doubt, the story is unique. But to be fair, Mason's distinctive leadership style and the company culture that it engendered may have been both Groupon's greatest advantage and the very anchor that eventually pulled it nearly under. The playful and giddy style that Mason personified spawned the company's meteoric rise to greatness, but did not endear it to the Wall Street players who laid a heavy hand to the rudder of this publicly traded company. That's the way the game is played, and some entrepreneurs are simply not suited to be a part of it. Perhaps Andrew Mason was one of them.

Questions

1. How would you describe the leadership skills of Andrew Mason? How would you rate his leadership style? In what ways does he fit the profile of the typical business founder? In what ways is he different?
2. Assess the organizational culture at Groupon. What are its strengths and its weaknesses? What changes would you make to the culture to improve the performance of the company?

3. Do you think that it was because of Mason that Groupon was unable to transition smoothly through its growth and development stages, or can you identify other possible causes?
4. What kind of leader do you think would be best suited to run Groupon? Create a profile of its ideal leader. Then create a profile of the ideal leader of a technology startup, and compare the two. What would you recommend as a plan for developing leaders of startups into leaders who are well equipped to manage large but still-entrepreneurial firms?
5. In your opinion, what are some of the other problems at Groupon?

Sources: David Streitfeld, "Groupon Dismisses Chief After a Dismal Quarter," *The New York Times*, March 1, 2013, p. B1; John Kotter, "Andrew Mason's Departure Reflected His Leadership Style," http://www.forbes.com/sites/johnkotter/2013/03/02/andrew-masons-departure-reflected-his-leadership-style, accessed March 23, 2013; Lauren Etter and Douglas MacMillan, "The Education of Groupon CEO Andrew Mason," www.businessweek.com/articles/2012-07-12/the-education-of-groupon-ceo-andrew-mason, accessed March 23, 2013; Kevin Kelleher, "The Defenestration of Andrew Mason," http://pandodaily.com/2013/02/28/the-defenestration-of-andrew-mason, accessed March 26, 2013; Eric Jackson, "Source of Groupon Problems: Managing People," www.forbes.com/sites/ericjackson/2012/08/14/source-of-groupon-problems-managing-people, accessed March 24, 2013; Joan Lappin, "Don't Cry for Groupon's Andrew Mason," http://www.forbes.com/sites/joanlappin/2013/03/05/dont-cry-for-groupons-andrew-mason, accessed March 23, 2013; Herb Greenberg, "Worst CEO in 2012," www.cnbc.com/id/100320782, accessed March 26, 2013; and "Hey Groupon, Can You Spare Some Culture Change?" http://chicagobrander.com/tag/groupon-culture, accessed March 25, 2013.

CASE 20

Jason Fried and Hiring Practices at 37signals

Intentional Selection

It takes excellent people to build a great company.

Since launching Chicago-based Web applications company 37signals in 1999, Jason Fried, its co-founder and president, has developed a careful and deliberate approach to finding and managing people for his company. Why is he so intentional in his hiring? This is how Fried answers that question:

> *Hiring people is like making friends. Pick good ones, and they'll enrich your life. Make bad choices, and they'll bring you down. Who you work with is even more important than who you hang out with, because you spend a lot more time with your workmates than with your friends.*

The company has a deliberately small staff of 20, and it works hard to keep them happy. After 11 years in business, only two people have left to pursue opportunities elsewhere—and one of those returned after working at another company for seven years.

Fried's hiring method has served 37signals well, but it is unusual in some ways. For example, he hires late (only "after it hurts") and never before a new employee is needed. He won't even hire "the perfect catch" if he doesn't have "the perfect job" open for that person. Invent a position to keep a talented person from getting away? Never! And Fried won't hire for a job he has never performed himself. In his mind, there is no way to find the right person for a job if you don't understand the position on a deep level.

Fried's approach to evaluating job candidates is also a little out of the ordinary. Résumés are ignored ("they're full of exaggerations, half-truths, embellishments—even outright lies"). Cover letters are given extra weight, because they reveal who wants the specific job being offered (and not just any job), and they also show who can write well. ("When in doubt, always hire the better writer," Fried suggests.) And during interviews, Fried listens carefully for signs of self-initiative. He reasons that candidates who ask, "How do I do that?" or "How can I find out this or that?" often are not used to figuring things out for themselves and thus would be a drain on others. On the other hand, Fried likes it when a candidate asks, "Why?" He interprets this as "a sign of deep interest in a subject" and "a healthy dose of curiosity." Details can make a huge difference.

Even if all indications are positive, Fried still chooses to go slow. "We . . . try to test-drive people before hiring them full time. We give designers a one-week design project to see how they approach the problem," paying them $1,500 for their time. Fried sometimes extends the project into a month-long contract "to see how we feel about the person and how the person feels about us." The point is to avoid hiring mistakes that would be bad for the company and unfair to the candidate.

As the economy continues to struggle, many small businesses are finding that they have to hire very carefully—as Fried is doing—or even get by with fewer workers. Some are turning to flexible management practices, like cross-training employees, hiring temporary workers on an as-needed basis, or forming outsourcing partnerships to adjust to fluctuations in market demand. But one way or another, the small business show must go on—and that means having the right people on board when you need them.

Questions

1. Do you think Fried's hiring methods are reasonable? Will they lead to good hires for his growing company? What are the best features of his approach (if you believe there are any)?
2. Do you think it is a good idea for Fried to take a pass on "perfect" candidates because he doesn't have an attractive job open for them at the moment? Is it smart for Fried to let talented candidates get away by refusing to create more suitable positions to keep them?
3. If Fried were to use the behavioral interview format, what kinds of questions might be especially helpful, given what you know of the types of people he prefers to hire?
4. What recommendations would you have for Fried regarding his hiring practices?

Sources: Based on Jason Fried, "The Importance of Hiring Late," BigThink.com, http://bigthink.com/users/jasonfried, accessed April 11, 2013; Jason Fried, "Never Read Another Resume," *Inc.*, Vol. 32, No. 5 (June 2010), pp. 36–37; Jason Fried and David Heinemeier Hansson, *Rework* (New York: Crown Publishing, 2010); Sarah E. Needleman, "Entrepreneurs Prefer to Keep Staffs Lean," *The Wall Street Journal*, March 2, 2010, p. B5; Heesun Wee, "Slow Crawl to Prosperity as Small Business Hiring Dives," CNBC.com, April 4, 2013, http://www.cnbc.com/id/100613971, accessed April 11, 2013; and "37signals: Our Story," http://37signals.com/about, accessed April 10, 2013.

River Pools & Spas

Managing Operations in a Challenging Economy

In 2001, 23-year-old Jason Hughes was working part-time on a construction crew for Jim Spiess, owner of Prestige Builders of Lancaster, Virginia. Impressed with Hughes's work ethic and capacity to learn, Spiess asked him to consider taking a full-time position with his firm. Hughes had been building homes every summer since his teens. But he told Speiss that what he really wanted to do was to start his own swimming pool construction company, and that he would do exactly that if he had the financial backing. This sparked Spiess's interest, and he asked Hughes to put some numbers together. What quickly followed was River Pools & Spas' first business plan.

The plan was just enough to give Spiess and Hughes the necessary enthusiasm and vision to start what today has become one of the premier pool and spa companies in the Maryland/Virginia area. During their first year, they installed a handful of pools, and 2002 was a year of solid growth, during which they installed about 40 pools. Despite record rainfall in 2003 and 2004, River Pools still grew in leaps and bounds, and by the end of 2004 the business model changed focus. They decided to move away from installing vinyl-liner above-ground and inground pools. Although they would still offer above-ground pools and spas, there was now an understanding within the company that, based on industry surveys, customers wanted a pool with low maintenance, longevity and exceptional warranties, and aesthetic appeal.

The only pool with these qualities is fiberglass/composite, and so the change was made. The renewed focus brought about more record years from 2005 throughout 2007. Such growth put River Pools & Spas in the top 5 percent of all inground pool companies in the country. It has also established the most popular and informative educational blog and video library in the swimming pool industry, showing the owners' commitment to excellence. Both of the owners are very family-oriented and believe they owe their success to moral values, great employees, dedicated customers, quality, service, and integrity.

Beating the Odds and the Economy

In 2005, River Pools & Spas had over 75 inground pool installations, 20 full-time employees, and a beautiful new 10,000-square-foot showroom/warehouse in Tappahannock, Virginia. Despite being a down-year for many companies, 2006 continued to show great promise for the future of the company, with another 80 inground pools being installed in the area. The following year was River Pools & Spas' greatest accomplishment to date. In an industry that had started to decline in most states due to the slow housing market, River Pools & Spas continued to demonstrate strong growth. Its final results in 2007 were 88 fiberglass pool installations.

Spiess and Hughes had a good system until the economy crashed. They were making plenty of money but had far too many employees and started to lose ground. They're now down to six employees: a bookkeeper, an office manager, two production managers—one of whom doubles as the service manager—and two installation crews.

They had been renting space at a retail location at \$8,000 per month, so they bought their own building and closed up the retail space, which was break-even at best. Their current office is a big metal building with a warehouse and five offices, and an empty showroom. After the brick-and-mortar plan was deemed too expensive, they moved everything to the Web, and this became their new storefront. They now have the world-leading website for fiberglass pools and get requests from Utah to Costa Rica.

Such growth has put River Pools & Spas in the top 5 percent of all inground pool companies in the country. One might assume that this growth has hurt quality, but that is clearly not the case when every potential customer receives a reference list with every inground pool customer (over 550) the company has ever installed a pool for, including the homeowner's name, address, and telephone number.

Source: Compiled from interviews and information provided by River Pools & Spas. http://www.riverpoolsandspas.com.

View the video and answer the questions that follow.

Questions

1. Review the history of the operations of River Pools & Spas, from start to success to scaling back. How was the company affected by scaling back? What changes made it more competitive?
2. Describe how River Pools & Spas' customer focus affects the business. What can the owners do to ensure that the quality of their products and services remains high?
3. Does this company use a synchronous management approach?

CASE 22

Pearson Air Conditioning & Service

Managing a Firm's Working Capital

Bob and Scott Pearson, father and son, are the owners of Pearson Air Conditioning & Service, based in Dallas, Texas. Bob serves as president, and Scott as general manager. The firm sells General Electric, Carrier, and York air-conditioning and heating systems to both commercial and residential customers and services these and other types of systems. Although the business has operated successfully since the Pearsons purchased it in 2002, it continues to experience working capital problems.

Pearson's Financial Performance

The firm has been profitable under the Pearsons' ownership. In fact, profits for 2011 were the highest for any year to date. Exhibit C22.1 shows the income statement for the year ending December 31, 2011.

The balance sheet as of December 31, 2011, is presented in Exhibit C22.2. Note that the firm's total debt now exceeds the owners' equity. However, $10,737 of the firm's liabilities was a long-term note payable to a stockholder. This note was issued at the time the Pearsons purchased the business, with payments going to the former owner.

Pearson's Cash Balance

Pearson Air Conditioning & Service currently has a cash balance in excess of $28,000. The owners have a policy of maintaining a minimum cash balance of $15,000, which allows them to "sleep well at night." Recently, Bob has thought that they would still be able to "breathe comfortably" as long as they kept a minimum balance of $10,000.

Pearson's Accounts Receivable

The accounts receivable at the end of 2011 were $56,753, but at times during the year, receivables could be twice this amount. These accounts receivable were not aged, so the firm had no specific knowledge of the number of overdue accounts. However, the firm had never experienced any significant loss from bad debts. The accounts receivable were thought, therefore, to be good accounts of a relatively recent nature.

Customers were given 30 days from the date of the invoice to pay the net amount. No cash discounts were offered. If payment was not received during the first 30 days, a second statement was mailed to the customer and monthly carrying charges of 1/10 of 1 percent were added.

On small residential jobs, the firm tried to collect from customers when the work was completed. When a service representative finished repairing an air-conditioning system, for example, he or she presented a bill to the customer and attempted to obtain payment at that time. However, this was not always possible. On major items, such as unit changeouts—which often ran as high as $2,500—billing was almost always necessary.

On new construction projects, the firm sometimes received partial payments prior to completion, which helped to minimize the amount tied up in receivables.

EXHIBIT **C22.1** Pearson Air Conditioning & Service Income Statement for the Year Ending December 31, 2011

Sales revenue	$727,679
Cost of goods sold	466,562
Gross profit	$261,117
Selling, general, and administrative expenses (including interest expense)	189,031
Profits before tax	$ 72,086
Income tax	17,546
Net profits	$ 54,540

Source: William J. Petty. © 2011, Cengage Learning.

EXHIBIT **C22.2** Pearson Air Conditioning & Service Balance Sheet December 31, 2011

Assets	
Current assets:	
Cash	$ 28,789
Accounts receivable	56,753
Inventory	89,562
Prepaid expenses	4,415
Total current assets	$ 179,519
Loans to stockholders	41,832
Autos, trucks, and equipment, at cost, less accumulated depreciation of $36,841	24,985
Other assets	16,500
Total assets	$ 262,836
Debt (Liabilities) and Equity	
Current debt:	
Current maturities of long-term notes payable*	$ 26,403
Accounts payable	38,585
Accrued payroll taxes	2,173
Income tax payable	13,818
Other accrued expenses	4,001
Total current debt	$ 84,980
Long-term notes payable*	51,231
Total stockholders' equity	126,625
Total debt and equity	$ 262,836

*Current and long-term portions of notes payable:

	Current	Long-Term	Total
• 10% note payable, secured by pickup, due in monthly installments of $200, including interest	$ 1,827	$ 1,367	$ 3,194
• 10% note payable, secured by equipment, due in monthly installments of $180, including interest	584	0	584
• 6% note payable, secured by inventory and equipment, due in monthly installments of $678, including interest	6,392	39,127	45,519
• 9% note payable to stockholder	0	10,737	10,737
• 12% note payable to bank in 30 days	17,600	0	17,600
	$26,403	$51,231	$77,634

Pearson's Inventory

Inventory accounted for a substantial portion of the firm's working capital. It consisted of the various heating and air-conditioning units, parts, and supplies used in the business.

The Pearsons had no guidelines or industry standards to use in evaluating their overall inventory levels. They believed that there *might* be some excessive inventory, but, in the absence of a standard, this was basically an opinion. When pressed to estimate the amount that might be eliminated by careful control, Scott pegged it at 15 percent.

The firm used an annual physical inventory that coincided with the end of its fiscal year. Since the inventory level was known for only one time in the year, the income statement could be prepared only on an annual basis. There was no way of knowing how much of the inventory had been used at other points and, thus, no way to calculate profits. As a result, the Pearsons lacked quarterly or monthly income statements to assist them in managing the business.

Scott and Bob had been considering changing from a physical inventory to a perpetual inventory system, which would enable them to know the inventory levels of all items at all times. An inventory total could easily be computed for use in preparing statements. Shifting to a perpetual inventory system would require that they purchase new computer software. However, the cost of such a system would not constitute a major barrier. A greater expense would be involved in the maintenance of the system—entering all incoming materials and all withdrawals. The Pearsons estimated that this task would require the work of one person on a less than full-time (possibly half-time) basis.

Pearson's Note Payable to the Bank

Bank borrowing was the most costly form of credit. The firm paid the going rate, slightly above prime, and owed $17,600 on a 90-day renewable note. Usually, some of the principal was paid when the note was renewed. The total borrowing could probably be increased if necessary. There was no obvious pressure from the bank to reduce borrowing to zero. The amount borrowed during the year typically ranged from $10,000 to $25,000.

The Pearsons had never explored the limits the bank might impose on borrowing, and there was no clearly specified line of credit. When additional funds were required, Scott simply dropped by the bank, spoke with a bank officer (who also happened to be a friend), and signed a note for the appropriate amount.

Pearson's Accounts Payable

A significant amount of Pearson's working capital came from its trade accounts payable. Although accounts payable at the end of 2011 were $38,585, payables varied over time and might be double this amount at another point in the year. Pearson obtained from various dealers such supplies as expansion valves, copper tubing, sheet metal, electrical wire, and electrical conduit. Some suppliers offered a discount for cash (2/10, net 30), but Bob felt that establishing credit was more important than saving a few dollars by taking a cash discount. By giving up the cash discount, the firm obtained the use of the money for 30 days. Although the Pearsons could stretch the payment dates to 45 or even 60 days before being "put on C.O.D.," they found it unpleasant to delay payment more than 45 days because suppliers would begin calling and applying pressure for payment.

Their major suppliers (Carrier, General Electric, and York) used different terms of payment. Some large products could be obtained from Carrier on an arrangement known as "floor planning," meaning that the manufacturer would ship the products without requiring immediate payment. The Pearsons made payment only when the product was sold. If still unsold after 90 days, the product had to be returned or paid for. (It was shipped back on a company truck, so no expense was incurred in returning unsold items.) On items that were not floor-planned but were purchased from Carrier, Pearson paid the net amount by the 10th of the month or was charged 18 percent interest on late payments.

Shipments from General Electric required payment at the bank soon after receipt of the products. If cash was not available at the time, further borrowing from the bank became necessary. Purchases from York required net payment without discount within 30 days. However, if payment was not made within 30 days, interest at 18 percent per annum was added.

Can Good Profits Become Better?

Although Pearson Air Conditioning & Service had earned a good profit in 2011, the Pearsons wondered whether they were realizing the *greatest possible* profit. The slowdown in the construction industry during 2011 was currently affecting their business. They wanted to be sure they were meeting the challenging times as prudently as possible.

Questions

1. Evaluate the overall performance and financial structure of Pearson Air Conditioning & Service.
2. What are the strengths and weaknesses in this firm's management of accounts receivable and inventory?
3. Should the firm reduce or expand the amount of its bank borrowing?
4. Evaluate Pearson's management of accounts payable.
5. Calculate Pearson's cash conversion period. Interpret your computation.
6. How could Pearson Air Conditioning & Service improve its working capital situation?

Source: Personal communication with Scott Pearson, president, Pearson Construction and Pearson Air Conditioning & Service, July 2012.

Jack's Restaurant

Intellectual Property Rights

Jack, a successful restaurant owner whose upscale establishment offers signature dishes, is selling his business to two of his employees—Sophia, his sous chef, and Hal, the maître d'. Jack's Place is a trendy neighborhood restaurant and bar that has a loyal customer base built from a frozen food line created by Jack and Sophia over the years from the restaurant's fresh menu.

Sophia and Hal are eager to purchase the restaurant and operate it under the same name, featuring the same dishes, frozen food line, and level of service that Jack's Place customers have come to expect. Sophia is a longtime employee who helped develop some of the signature dishes that made Jack's Place a popular destination in the neighborhood. A favorite dish is her Scaloppine al Marsala, which is based on a Sicilian family recipe.

As contract negotiations begin, Jack tells Sophia and Hal that he wishes to retain the intellectual property rights to the frozen food items as he enters into retirement. While he has no plans to open another restaurant, Jack believes that at some point he may want to market those dishes during his retirement for some residual income. Therefore, he suggests that a confidentiality agreement be drawn before the sale is final.

Sophia and Hal, who wish to continue operating Jack's Place under its existing business plan, feel that if Jack keeps the rights to the frozen food items the future success of the restaurant could be compromised. If Jack's Place can't offer the same food items that have enabled the business to succeed in years past, then the restaurant could lose its customer base. And if Jack would use the recipes—including Sophia's Scaloppine al Marsala—to open another restaurant, then Jack's Place would surely fail.

Ten years ago, when Sophia began working for Jack, the restaurant didn't offer the frozen food line. Over the years, she worked closely with Jack to develop the dishes, offering her own blends of spices and herbs. Therefore, she believes that she shares some intellectual property rights to the recipes. Jack, however, contends that Sophia doesn't have any rights because, as an employer, he paid her to help develop that product line. The recipes, Jack says, are his trade secrets.

While Jack insists that he isn't going to open another restaurant, Sophia and Hal believe they need protection if they agree to let Jack retain the rights to the recipes. On the advice of his brother-in-law, who is a lawyer, Hal suggests that a noncompete agreement be drawn up to protect the new buyers against competition from their former employer. The agreement would prohibit Jack from opening a restaurant within a 10-mile radius for five years. Should Jack default on the agreement, then Hal and Sophia would have grounds for legal action.

Jack contends that signing a noncompete agreement would be foolish on his part, because he doesn't know what the next five years will bring. Sophia and Hal believe it would be equally crazy on their part to buy the restaurant without its frozen food line and allow Jack to have the signature dishes and possibly to compete against them.

The seller and buyers are at an impasse. The deal is in jeopardy unless an amicable agreement is reached.

View the video and answer the questions that follow.

Questions

1. Do Sophia and Hal have valid grounds for asking Jack to sign a noncompete agreement?
2. Assume Jack signs the noncompete agreement. Two years later, he opens a restaurant five miles away. If Hal then sues for breach of the noncompete, what arguments might Jack raise?
3. Are Hal and Sophia's demands reasonable? Do you think the recipes constitute trade secrets?
4. What compromise might be met that would be legal, ethical, and fair? Can you think of a business solution that would help Jack, Hal, and Sophia resolve their differences?

Source: Based on Business Law Digital Video Library, Real World Legal series, video #77. Written by Tim Blackwell, Freelance Reporter.

Index

A

B

C

D

E

F

G

H

I

J

K

L

M

N

O

Q

R

S

T

U

V

W

Z